PIECES OF

THE

PERSONALITY

PUZZLE

READINGS IN THEORY AND RESEARCH
THIRD EDITION

David C. Funder
University of California, Riverside

Daniel J. Ozer
University of California, Riverside

W · W · NORTON & COMPANY

NEW YORK · LONDON

PIECES OF

THE

PERSONALITY

PUZZLE

READINGS IN THEORY AND RESEARCH
THIRD EDITION

W. W. Norton & Company has been independent since its founding in 1923, when William Warder Norton and Mary D. Herter Norton first published lectures delivered at the People's Institute, the adult education division of New York City's Cooper Union. The Nortons soon expanded their program beyond the Institute, publishing books by celebrated academics from America and abroad. By mid-century, the two major pillars of Norton's publishing program—trade books and college texts—were firmly established. In the 1950s, the Norton family transferred control of the company to its employees, and today—with a staff of four hundred and a comparable number of trade, college, and professional titles published each year—W. W. Norton & Company stands as the largest and oldest publishing house owned wholly by its employees.

Manufacturing by Quebecor World—Fairfield Division.
Book design by Joan Greenfield.
Production manager: Ben Reynolds.

Library of Congress Cataloging-in-Publication Data
Pieces of the personality puzzle : readings in theory and research / [edited by] David C. Funder,
Daniel J. Ozer.— 3rd ed.
    p. cm.
    Includes bibliographical references.
    ISBN 0–393–97997–0 (pbk.)
    1. Personality. I. Funder, David Charles. II. Ozer, Daniel J.

BF698.P525 2004
155.2—dc22

2003070245

W. W. Norton & Company, Inc., 500 Fifth Avenue, New York, N.Y. 10110
www.wwnorton.com

W. W. Norton & Company Ltd., Castle House,
75/76 Wells Street, London W1T 3QT

1 2 3 4 5 6 7 8 9 0

CONTENTS

Part III

Biological Approaches to Personality   119

Part IV

The Psychoanalytic Approach to Personality 231

Part V

Humanistic Approach to Personality 303

Part VI

Cross-Cultural Approaches to Personality 367

Part VII

Behavioral, Social Learning, and Cognitive Approaches to Personality 441

PREFACE

Theory and research in personality psychology address the ways in which people are different from one another, the relations between body and mind, how people think (consciously and unconsciously), what people want (consciously and unconsciously), and what people do. Personality is the broadest, most all-encompassing part of psychology.

This breadth of relevance is personality psychology's greatest attraction, but it also makes good work in this field difficult to do. Nearly all personality psychologists have therefore chosen to limit their approach in some way, by focusing on particular phenomena they deem of special interest, and more or less neglecting everything else. A group of psychologists who focus on the same basic phenomena could be said to be working within the same "paradigm," or following the same "basic approach."

The articles in this reader are organized by the basic approaches they follow. The first section presents articles that describe and discuss the research methods used by personality psychologists. The second section includes articles relevant to the trait approach, the approach that concentrates on the conceptualization and measurement of individual differences in personality. The third section presents articles that follow the biological approach, and attempt to connect the biology of the body and nervous system with the processes of emotion, thought, and behavior. The fourth section presents classic and modern research from the psychoanalytic approach, which considers (among other things) unconscious processes of the mind based, ultimately, on the writings of Sigmund Freud. The fifth section presents some examples from the humanistic approach, which focuses on experience, free will, and the meaning of life, and in recent years has branched into a "positive psychology" movement that tries to find and enhance the good things in life. Articles in the sixth section consider the constancy and variability of personality across different cultures. Articles in the seventh section trace the way the behavioristic approach developed into social learning theory and the modern social-cognitive approaches to personality, which in recent years has spurred a reexamination of that classic topic in psychology: the unconscious mind.

There is no substitute for reading original work in a field to appreciate its content and its style. But assembling a reader such as this does entail certain difficulties, and requires strategic choices. As the editors we chose, first of all, to be representative rather than exhaustive in our coverage of the domain of personality psychology. While we believe the most important areas of personality are represented by an exemplar or two in what follows, no topic is truly covered in depth. We hope readers who become seriously interested will use the reference sections that follow each article to guide their further reading.

A second choice was to search for articles most likely to be interesting to an audience that does *not* consist of professionally trained psychologists. At the same time, we tried to ensure that many of the most prominent personality psychologists of this century were represented. In some cases, this meant selecting a prominent psychologist's most accessible—rather than by some definition most "important"—writing.

A third decision—made reluctantly—was to excerpt nearly all of these articles. Most of the articles that follow are, in their original form, much longer. We tried to be judicious in our editing. We removed passages that would be uninformative to a non-professional reader, digressions, and treatments of issues beside the main point of each article. We have marked all changes to the original text; three asterisks centered on a blank line mark the omission of a complete paragraph or section, while three asterisks run into the text indicate that sentences within that paragraph have been omitted.

We probably should mention here one other thing that a reader might notice. Prior to about 1970, it was conventional to use the pronoun "he" to refer to both males and females. This practice is followed in some of the older selections in this volume, and we have left them intact. Current guidelines of the American Psychological Association (APA, 2001) require that "he or she" or similar inclusive constructions be used.

Most articles have footnotes. A few of these are by the original authors (we have indicated which these are) but we deleted most author footnotes. We added many footnotes of our own. These define bits of jargon, explain references to other research, and—when we couldn't help ourselves—provide editorial commentary.

Each section begins with an introduction that describes the articles to follow and lays out their sequence. Each article is preceded by a brief essay outlining what we see as its take-home message and some issues we believe readers should consider.

Finally, this volume contains a few surprises. Readers will find an excerpt from a nineteenth-century textbook in "physiognomy," a commentary from the *New York Times*, and a satire by Gloria Steinem. These were not written by psychologists, but we believe they are of interest and shed a unique kind of light on their topics.

Though it is divided into seven rather than six parts, the reader follows the same organization as Funder's (2004) textbook, *The Personality Puzzle* (3rd ed.), and some of the research referred to in that book will be found here. However, one does not need to use that text to use this reader; the two books are largely independent and this reader was designed to be useful in conjunction with almost any textbook—or even by itself. The reader includes representative writings in method, theory, and research—the three staples of any good personality course.

Changes in the Third Edition

Roughly a third of the articles are new to the Third Edition. In particular, research in the biological, cross-cultural, and cognitive approaches to personality is so active and changing so rapidly that we felt compelled to add new and up-to-date examples of research in those fields. We have also added other articles we thought illustrated important and interesting aspects of the various approaches to personality psychology, and removed some articles that appeared seldom to be assigned to students or that have simply become out-of-date. We also re-included a couple of articles from the First Edition that did not appear in the Second Edition, including Funder's article on "global traits" and Gloria Steinem's scathing and sarcastic attack on Freud's sexism. This latter piece we can truly say reappears by popular demand: for many readers of the First Edition it was their favorite article, and we are pleased to re-include it here.

ACKNOWLEDGMENTS

Many individuals assisted this project in a number of ways. For the First Edition, useful suggestions were provided by Jana Spain of Highpoint University, Susan Krauss Whitbourne of the University of Massachusetts (Amherst), Andrew J. Tomarken of Vanderbilt University, and Brian C. Hayden of Brown University. As we prepared the Second and Third Editions, we prowled many Web sites of courses around the world that used this book, trying to learn which chapters were really being assigned for students to read, and also received informal advice from many colleagues. We made adjustments accordingly in the Third Edition and thank the instructors who used this book for their explicit and implicit guidance.

For the First Edition, Liz Suhay of W. W. Norton assembled the manuscript and gathered copyright permissions, and April Lange, the editor, was an important source of organization and guidance. For the Second Edition, Mary Babcock copyedited and organized the manuscript, and Anne Hellman copyedited the Third. The original idea for a book of readings to accompany Funder's *Personality Puzzle* came from Don Fusting, a former Norton editor. We are grateful to all these individuals, and also to the authors who graciously and generously allowed us to edit and reproduce their work.

PIECES OF

THE

PERSONALITY

PUZZLE

READINGS IN THEORY AND RESEARCH
THIRD EDITION

PART I

Research Methods

How do you learn something that nobody has ever known before? This is the question of "research methods," the strategies and techniques that are used to obtain new knowledge. The knowledge of interest for personality psychology is knowledge about people, so for this field the question of research methods translates into a concern with the ways in which one can learn more about a person. These include techniques for measuring an individual's personality traits as well as his or her thoughts, motivations, emotions, and goals.

Personality psychologists have a long tradition of being particularly interested in and sophisticated about research methods. Over the years, they have developed new sources of data, invented innovative statistical techniques, and even provided some important advances in the philosophy of science. The selections in this section address some critical issues that arise when considering the methods one might use to learn more about people.

The opening selection, by Dan McAdams, asks, "What do we know when we know a person?" The article presents an introduction to and comparison of the various conceptual units—ranging from traits to the holistic meaning of life—that personality psychologists have used to describe and understand people.

The second selection, by Robert Rosenthal and Donald Rubin, concerns a particular statistic that is unavoidable by any reader of personality research—the correlation coefficient. Despite its ubiquity, this statistic is frequently misunderstood, and in particular, the effects it describes are often underestimated. For example, if someone tells you they have obtained a correlation between a trait and behavior equal to .32, is this big or little? For reasons Rosenthal and Rubin explain, the answer is "pretty big."

The third selection is one of the unquestioned, all-time classics of psychological methodology, and absolutely required reading for any psychologist. The article by Lee Cronbach and Paul Meehl concerns "construct validity," or the issue of how one determines whether a test of personality (or any other attribute) really measures what it is supposed to.

Personality psychology is now moving away from its former nearly exclusive reliance on self-report personality assessments, to include other methods such as online coding of videotaped behavior. In the final selection, Samuel Gosling and his colleagues demonstrate how a comparison between self-reports and observers' reports of behavior can illustrate not only the relative validity of each kind of data but also interesting psychological processes, such as self-enhancement, that produce discrepancies between different sources of data.

WHAT DO WE KNOW WHEN WE KNOW A PERSON?

Dan P. McAdams

Personality psychology is all about understanding individuals better. In this first selection, the personality psychologist Dan McAdams asks one of the fundamental questions about this enterprise, which is: when we learn about a person, what is it we learn? He begins by describing the kind of personality psychology that nonpsychologists (or psychologists when off duty) frequently practice: discussing an individual that one has just met. In such discussions, the individual is often considered at several different levels, ranging from surface descriptions of behavior to inferences about deeper motivations.

The challenge for professional personality psychologists, McAdams argues, is to become at least as sophisticated as amateur psychologists by taking into account aspects of individuals at multiple levels. In his own work, McAdams collects life stories and tries to understand individuals in holistic terms. He is a critic of the more dominant approach that characterizes individuals in terms of their personality traits. However, in this well-balanced article we see McAdams attempt to integrate the various levels of personality description into a complete portrait of what we know when we know a person.

From *Journal of Personality*, 63, 365–396, 1995.

One of the great social rituals in the lives of middle-class American families is "the drive home." The ritual comes in many different forms, but the idealized scene that I am now envisioning involves my wife and me leaving the dinner party sometime around midnight, getting into our car, and, finding nothing worth listening to on the radio, beginning our traditional post-party postmortem. Summoning up all of the personological wisdom and nuance I can muster at the moment, I may start off with something like, "He was really an ass." Or adopting the more "relational" mode that psychologists such as Gilligan (1982) insist comes more naturally to women than men, my wife may say something like, "I can't believe they stay married to each other." It's often easier to begin with the cheap shots. As the conversation develops, however, our attributions become more detailed and more interesting. We talk about people we liked as well as those we found offensive. There is often a single character who stands out from the party—the person we found most intriguing, perhaps; or the one who seemed most troubled; maybe the one we would like to get to know much better in the future. In the scene I am imagining, let us call that person "Lynn" and let us consider what my wife and I might say about her as we drive home in the dark.

I sat next to Lynn at dinner. For the first 15 minutes, she dominated the conversation at our end of the table with her account of her recent trip to Mexico where she was doing research for an article to appear in a national magazine. Most of the people at the party knew that Lynn is a freelance writer whose projects have taken her around the world, and they asked her many questions about her work and her travels. Early on, I felt awkward and intimidated in Lynn's presence. I have never been to Mexico; I was not familiar with her articles; I felt I couldn't keep up with the fast tempo of her account, how she moved quickly from one exotic tale to another. Add to this the fact that she is a strikingly attractive woman, about 40 years old with jet black hair, dark eyes, a seemingly flawless complexion, clothing both flamboyant and taste-ful, and one might be able to sympathize with my initial feeling that she was, in a sense, "just too much."

My wife formed a similar first impression ear-lier in the evening when she engaged Lynn in a lengthy conversation on the patio. But she ended up feeling much more positive about Lynn as they shared stories of their childhoods. My wife men-tioned that she was born in Tokyo during the time her parents were Lutheran missionaries in Japan. Lynn remarked that she had great admiration for missionaries "because they really believe in some-thing." Then she remarked: "I've never really believed in anything very strongly, nothing to get real passionate about. Neither did my parents, except for believing in us kids. They probably be-lieved in us kids too much." My wife immediately warmed up to Lynn for this disarmingly intimate comment. It was not clear exactly what she meant, but Lynn seemed more vulnerable now, and more mysterious.

I eventually warmed up to Lynn, too. As she

and I talked about politics and our jobs, she seemed less brash and domineering than before. She seemed genuinely interested in my work as a personality psychologist who, among other things, collects people's life stories. She had been a psy-chology major in college. And lately she had been reading a great many popular psychology books on such things as Jungian archetypes, the "child within," and "addictions to love." As a serious re-searcher and theorist, I must confess that I have something of a visceral prejudice against many of these self-help, "New Age" books. Still, I resisted the urge to scoff at her reading list and ended up enjoying our conversation very much. I did no-tice, though, that Lynn filled her wine glass about twice as often as I did mine. She never made eye contact with her husband, who was sitting di-rectly across the table from her, and twice she said something sarcastic in response to a story he was telling.

Over the course of the evening, my wife and I learned many other things about Lynn. On our drive home we noted the following:

1. Lynn was married once before and has two children by her first husband.
2. The children, now teenagers, currently live with her first husband rather than with her; she didn't say how often she sees them.
3. Lynn doesn't seem to like President Clinton and is very critical of his excessively "lib-eral" policies; but she admires his wife, Hillary, who arguably is more liberal in her views; we couldn't pin a label of conserva-tive or liberal to Lynn because she seemed to contradict herself on political topics.
4. Lynn hates jogging and rarely exercises; she claims to eat a lot of "junk food"; she ate very little food at dinner.
5. Lynn says she is an atheist.
6. Over the course of the evening, Lynn's ele-gant demeanor and refined speech style seemed to give way to a certain crudeness; shortly before we left, my wife heard her telling an off-color joke, and I noticed that she seemed to lapse into a street-smart Chi-

cago dialect that one often associates with growing up in the toughest neighborhoods.

As we compared our notes on Lynn during the drive home, my wife and I realized that we learned a great deal about Lynn during the evening, and that we were eager to learn more. But what is it that we thought we now knew about her? And what would we need to know to know her better? In our social ritual, my wife and I were enjoying the rather playful exercise of trying to make sense of persons. In the professional enterprise of personality psychology, however, making sense of persons is or should be the very raison d'être of the discipline. From the time of Allport (1937) and Murray (1938), through the anxious days of the "situationist" critique (Bowers, 1973; Mischel, 1968), and up to the present, upbeat period wherein we celebrate traits[1] (John, 1990; Wiggins, 1996) while we offer a sparkling array of new methods and models for personality inquiry (see, for example, McAdams, 1994a; Ozer & Reise, 1994; Revelle, 1995), making sense of persons was and is fundamentally what personality psychologists are supposed to do, in the lab, in the office, even on the drive home. But how should we do it?

Making Sense of Persons

* * *

Since the time of Allport, Cattell, and Murray, personality psychologists have offered a number of different schemes for describing persons. For example, McClelland (1951) proposed that an adequate account of personality requires assessments of stylistic traits (e.g., extraversion, friendliness), cognitive schemes (e.g., personal constructs, val-

ues, frames), and dynamic motives (e.g., the need for achievement, power motivation). In the wake of Mischel's (1968) critique of personality dispositions, many personality psychologists eschewed broadband constructs such as traits and motives in favor of more domain-specific variables, like "encoding strategies," "self-regulatory systems and plans," and other "cognitive social learning person variables" (Mischel, 1973). By contrast, the 1980s and 1990s have witnessed a strong comeback for the concept of the broad, dispositional trait, culminating in what many have argued is a consensus around the five-factor model of personality traits (Digman, 1990; Goldberg, 1993; McCrae & Costa, 1996). Personality psychologists such as A. H. Buss (1989) have essentially proclaimed that personality *is traits* and only traits. Others are less sanguine, however, about the ability of the Big Five trait taxonomy in particular and the concept of trait in general to provide all or even most of the right stuff for personality inquiry (Block, 1995; Briggs, 1989; Emmons, 1993; McAdams, 1992, 1994b; Pervin, 1994).

Despite the current popularity of the trait concept, I submit that I will never be able to render Lynn "knowable" by relying solely on a description of her personality traits. At the same time, a description that failed to consider traits would be equally inadequate. Trait descriptions are essential both for social rituals like the post-party postmortem and for adequate personological inquiry. A person cannot be known without knowing traits. But knowing traits is not enough. Persons should be described on at least *three separate* and, at best, *loosely related levels* of functioning. The three may be viewed as levels of comprehending *individuality* amidst otherness—how the person is similar to and different from *some* (but not all) other persons. Each level offers categories and frameworks for organizing *individual differences* among persons. Dispositional traits comprise the first level in this scheme—the level that deals primarily with what I have called (McAdams, 1992, 1994b) a "psychology of the stranger."

---

[1]The reference here is to the "person-situation debate" that dominated personality psychology from 1968 to 1988. The debate was about whether the most important causes of behavior were properties of people or of the situations they find themselves in. The "situationist" viewpoint was that situations were more important. As McAdams notes, the eventual resolution of this controversy reaffirmed the importance—but not all-importance—of stable individual differences in personality (traits) as important determinants of behavior.

The Power of Traits

Dispositional traits are those relatively nonconditional, relatively decontextualized, generally linear, and implicitly comparative dimensions of personality that go by such titles as "extraversion," "dominance," and "neuroticism." One of the first things both I and my wife noticed about Lynn was her social dominance. She talked loudly and fast; she held people's attention when she described her adventures; she effectively controlled the conversation in the large group. Along with her striking appearance, social dominance appeared early on as one of her salient characteristics. Other behavioral signs also suggested an elevated rating on the trait of neuroticism, though these might also indicate the situationally specific anxiety she may have been experiencing in her relationship with the man who accompanied her to the party. According to contemporary norms for dinner parties of this kind, she seemed to drink a bit too much. Her moods shifted rather dramatically over the course of the evening. While she remained socially dominant, she seemed to become more and more nervous as the night wore on. The interjection of her off-color joke and the street dialect stretched slightly the bounds of propriety one expects on such occasions, though not to an alarming extent. In a summary way, then, one might describe Lynn, as she became known during the dinner party, as socially dominant, extraverted, entertaining, dramatic, moody, slightly anxious, intelligent, and introspective. These adjectives describe part of her dispositional signature.

How useful are these trait descriptions? Given that my wife's and my observations were limited to one behavioral setting (the party), we do not have enough systematic data to say how accurate our descriptions are. However, if further systematic observation were to bear out this initial description— say, Lynn were observed in many settings; say, peers rated her on trait dimensions; say, she completed standard trait questionnaires such as the Personality Research Form (Jackson, 1974) or the NEO Personality Inventory (Costa & McCrae, 1985)—then trait descriptions like these, wherein the individual

is rated on a series of linear and noncontingent behavior dimensions, prove very useful indeed.

* * *

The Problem with Traits

It is easy to criticize the concept of trait. Trait formulations proposed by Allport (1937), Cattell (1957), Guilford (1959), Eysenck (1967), Jackson (1974), Tellegen (1982), Hogan (1986), and advocates of the Big Five have been called superficial, reductionistic, atheoretical, and even imperialistic. Traits are mere labels, it is said again and again. Traits don't explain anything. Traits lack precision. Traits disregard the environment. Traits apply only to score distributions in groups, not to the individual person (e.g., Lamiell, 1987). I believe that there is some validity in some of these traditional claims but that traits nonetheless provide invaluable information about persons. I believe that many critics expect too much of traits. Yet, those trait enthusiasts (e.g., A. H. Buss, 1989; Digman, 1990; Goldberg, 1993) who equate personality with traits in general, and with the Big Five in particular, are also claiming too much.

Goldberg (1981) contended that the English language includes five clusters of trait-related terms—the Big Five—because personality characteristics encoded in these terms have proved especially salient in human interpersonal perception, especially when it comes to the perennial and evolutionary crucial task of sizing up a stranger. I think Goldberg was more right than many trait enthusiasts would like him to be. Reliable and valid trait ratings provide an excellent "first read" on a person by offering estimates of a person's relative standing on a delimited series of general and linear dimensions of proven social significance. This is indeed crucial information in the evaluation of strangers and others about whom we know very little. It is the kind of information that strangers quickly glean from one another as they size one another up and anticipate future interactions. It did not take long for me to conclude that Lynn was high on certain aspects of Extraversion and moderately high on Neuroticism. What makes trait information like this so valuable is that it is comparative and relatively nonconditional. A highly extraverted person is generally more extraverted than most other people (comparative) and tends to be extraverted in a wide variety of settings (nonconditional), although by no means in all.

Consider, furthermore, the phenomenology of traditional trait assessment in personality psychology. In rating one's own or another's traits on a typical paper-and-pencil measure, the rater/subject must adopt an observational stance in which the target of the rating becomes an object of comparison on a series of linear and only vaguely conditional dimensions (McAdams, 1994c). Thus, if I were to rate Lynn, or if Lynn were to rate herself, on the Extraversion-keyed personality item "I am not a cheerful optimist" (from the NEO), I (or Lynn) would be judging the extent of Lynn's own "cheerful optimism" in comparison to the cheerful optimism of people I (or she) know or have heard about, or perhaps even an assumed average level of cheerful optimism of the rest of humankind. Ratings like these must have a social referent if they are to be meaningful. The end result of my (or her) ratings is a determination of the extent to which Lynn is seen as more or less extraverted across a wide variety of situations, conditions, and contexts, and compared to other people in general. There is, therefore, no place in trait assessment for what Thorne (1989) calls the conditional patterns of personality (see also Wright & Mischel, 1987). Here are some examples of conditional patterns: "My dominance shows when my competence is threatened; I fall apart when people try to comfort me; I talk most when I am nervous" (Thorne, 1989, p. 149). But to make traits into conditional statements is to rob them of their power as nonconditional indicators of general trends.

The two most valuable features of trait description—its comparative and nonconditional qualities—double as its two greatest limitations as well.[2] As persons come to know one another better,

they seek and obtain information that is both non-comparative and highly conditional, contingent, and contextualized. They move beyond the mindset of comparing individuals on linear dimensions. In a sense, they move beyond traits to construct a more detailed and nuanced portrait of personality, so that the stranger can become more fully known. New information is then integrated with the trait profile to give a fuller picture. My wife and I began to move beyond traits on the drive home. As a first read, Lynn seemed socially dominant (Extraversion) and mildly neurotic (Neuroticism). I would also give her a high rating on Openness to Experience; I would say that Agreeableness was probably medium; I would say that Conscientiousness was low to medium, though I do not feel that I received much trait-relevant information on Conscientiousness. Beyond these traits, however, Lynn professed a confusing set of political beliefs: She claimed to be rather conservative but was a big fan of Hillary Clinton; she scorned government for meddling in citizens' private affairs and said she paid too much in taxes to support wasteful social programs, while at the same time she claimed to be a pacifist and to have great compassion for poor people and those who could not obtain health insurance. Beyond traits, Lynn claimed to be an atheist but expressed great admiration for missionaries. Beyond traits, Lynn appeared to be having problems in intimate relationships; she wished she could believe in something; she enjoyed her work as a freelance writer; she was a good listener one on one but not in the large group; she expressed strong interest in New Age psychology; she seemed to think her parents invested too much faith in her and in her siblings. To know Lynn well, to know her more fully than one would know a stranger, one must be privy to information that does not fit trait categories, information that is exquisitely conditional and contextualized.

Going beyond Traits: Time, Place, and Role

There is a vast and largely unmapped domain in personality wherein reside such constructs as mo-

---

[2]This observation provides an example of Funder's First Law, which states that great strengths are often great weaknesses and, surprisingly often, the opposite is also true (Funder, 2004).

tives (McClelland, 1961), values (Rokeach, 1973), defense mechanisms (Cramer, 1991), coping styles (Lazarus, 1991), developmental issues and concerns (Erikson, 1963; Havighurst, 1972), personal strivings (Emmons, 1986), personal projects (Little, 1989), current concerns (Klinger, 1977), life tasks (Cantor & Kihlstrom, 1987), attachment styles (Hazan & Shaver, 1990), conditional patterns (Thorne, 1989), core conflictual relationship themes (Luborsky & Crits-Christoph, 1991), patterns of self-with-other, domain-specific skills and talents (Gardner, 1993), strategies and tactics (D. M. Buss, 1991), and many more personality variables that are both linked to behavior (Cantor, 1990) and important for the full description of the person (McAdams, 1994a). This assorted collection of constructs makes up a second level of personality, to which I give the generic and doubtlessly inadequate label of *personal concerns*. Compared with dispositional traits, personal concerns are typically couched in motivational, developmental, or strategic terms. They speak to what people want, often during particular periods in their lives or within particular domains of action, and what life methods people use (strategies, plans, defenses, and so on) in order to get what they want or avoid getting what they don't want over time, in particular places, and/or with respect to particular roles.

What primarily differentiates, then, personal concerns from dispositional traits is the contextualization of the former within time, place, and/or role. Time is perhaps the most ubiquitous context. In their studies of the "intimacy life task" among young adults, Cantor, Acker, and Cook-Flanagan (1992) focus on "those tasks that individuals see as personally important and time consuming at particular times in their lives" (p. 644). In their studies of generativity across the adult life span, McAdams, de St. Aubin, and Logan (1993) focus on a cluster of concern, belief, commitment, and action oriented toward providing for the well-being of the next generation, a cluster that appears to peak in salience around middle age. Intimacy and generativity must be contextualized in the temporal life span if they are to be properly understood. By contrast, the traits of Extraversion and Agreeableness are easily defined and understood outside of time. They are not linked to developmental stages, phases, or seasons.

The temporal context also distinguishes traits on the one hand from motives and goals on the other. Motives, goals, strivings, and plans are defined in terms of future ends. A person high in power motivation wants, desires, strives for power—having impact on others is the desired end state, the temporal goal (Winter, 1973). To have a strong motive, goal, striving, or plan is to orient oneself in a particular way in time. The same cannot be readily assumed with traits. Extraversion is not naturally conceived in goal-directed terms. It is not necessary for the viability of the concept of extraversion that an extraverted person strive to obtain a particular goal in time, although of course such a person may do so. Extraverted people simply *are* extraverted; whether they try to be or not is irrelevant. The case is even clearer for neuroticism, for the commonsense assumption here is that highly neurotic people do not strive to be neurotic over time. They simply are neurotic. While dispositional traits may have motivational properties (Allport, 1937; McCrae & Costa, 1996), traits do not exist in time in the same way that motives, strivings, goals, and plans are temporally contextualized. To put it another way, I cannot understand Lynn's life in time when I merely consider her dispositional traits. Developmental and motivational constructs, by contrast, begin to provide me with the temporal context, the life embedded in and evolving over time.

Contextualization of behavior in place was a major theme of the situationist critique in the 1970s (Frederiksen, 1972; Magnusson, 1971). The situationists argued that behavior is by and large local rather than general, subject to the norms and expectations of a given social place or space. Attempts to formulate taxonomies of situations have frequently involved delineating the physical and interpersonal features of certain kinds of prototypical behavioral settings and social environments, like "church," "football game," "classroom," and "party" (Cantor, Mischel, & Schwartz, 1982; Krahe, 1992; Moos, 1973). Certain domain-specific skills, competencies, attitudes, and schemas are examples of personality variables contextualized in place. For example, Lynn is both a very good listener in one-on-one conversations, especially when the topic concerns psychology, and an extremely effective storyteller in large groups, especially when she is talking about travel. When she is angry with her husband in a social setting, she drinks too much. The latter is an example of a conditional pattern (Thorne, 1989) or perhaps a very simple personal script. Some varieties of personal scripts and conditional patterns are contextualized in place and space: "When I am at home, I am unable to relax"; "When the weather is hot, I think about how miserable I was as a child, growing up in St. Louis"; "If I am lost in Chicago, I never ask for directions." To know a person well, it is not necessary to have information about all of the different personal scripts and conditional patterns that prevail in all of the different behavioral settings he or she will encounter. Instead, the personologist should seek information on the most salient settings and environments that make up the ecology of a person's life and investigate the most influential, most common, or most problematic personal scripts and conditional patterns that appear within that ecology (Demorest & Alexander, 1992).

Another major context in personality is social role. Certain strivings, tasks, strategies, defense mechanisms, competencies, values, interests, and styles may be role-specific. For example, Lynn may employ the defense mechanism of rationalization to cope with her anxiety about the setbacks she has experienced in her role as a mother. In her role as a writer, she may excel in expressing herself in a laconic, Hemingway-like style (role competence, skill) and she may strive to win certain journalistic awards or to make more money than her husband (motivation, striving). In the role of student/learner, she is fascinated with New Age psychology (interests). In the role of daughter, she manifests an insecure attachment style, especially with her mother, and this style seems to carry over to her relationships with men (role of lover/spouse) but not with women (role of friend). Ogilvie (Ogilvie & Ashmore, 1991) has developed a new approach to personality assessment that matches personality descriptors with significant persons in one's life, resulting in an organization of self-with-other constructs. It would appear that some of the more significant self-with-other constellations in a person's life are those associated with important social roles. Like social places, not all social roles are equally important in a person's life. Among the most salient in the lives of many American men and women are the roles of spouse/lover, son/daughter, parent, sibling, worker/provider, and citizen.

* * *

There is no compelling reason to believe that the language of nonconditional and decontextualized dispositions should work well to describe constructs that are situated in time, place, and role. Consistent with this supposition, Kaiser and Ozer (under review) found that personal goals, or what they term "motivational units," do not map onto the five-factor structure demonstrated for traits. Instead, their study suggests that the structure of personal goals may be more appropriately conceptualized in terms of various content domains (e.g., work, social). It seems reasonable, therefore, to begin with the assumption that an adequate description of a person should bring together contrasting and complementary attributional schemes, integrating dispositional insights with those obtained from personal concerns. To know Lynn well is to be able to describe her in ways that go significantly beyond the language of traits. This is not to suggest that Levels I and II are or must be completely unrelated to each other, that Lynn's extraversion, for example, has nothing to do with her personal career strivings. In personality psychology, linkages between constructs at these different levels should and will be investigated in research. But the linkages, if they indeed exist, should be established empirically rather than assumed by theorists to be true.

What Is Missing?

As we move from Level I to Level II, we move from the psychology of the stranger to a more detailed and nuanced description of a flesh-and-blood, in-the-world person, striving to do things over time, situated in place and role, expressing herself or himself in and through strategies, tactics, plans, and goals. In Lynn's case, we begin our very provisional sketch with nonconditional attributions suggesting a high level of extraversion and moderately high neuroticism and we move to more contingent statements suggesting that she seems insecurely attached to her parents and her husband, strives for power and recognition in her career, wants desperately to believe in something but as yet has not found it in religion or in spirituality, holds strong but seemingly contradictory beliefs about politics and public service, employs the defense of rationalization to cope with the frustration she feels in her role as mother, has interests that tend toward books and ideas rather than physical health and fitness, loves to travel, is a good listener one on one but not in groups, is a skilled writer, is a good storyteller, tells stories that are rambling and dramatic. If we were to continue a relationship with Lynn, we would learn more and more about her. We would find that some of our initial suppositions were naive, or even plain wrong. We would obtain much more information on her traits, enabling us to obtain a clearer and more accurate dispositional signature. We would learn more about the contextualized constructs of her personality, about how she functions in time, place, and role. Filling in more and more information in Levels I and II, we might get to know Lynn very well.

But I submit that, as Westerners living in this modern age, we would not know Lynn "well enough" until we moved beyond dispositional traits and personal concerns to a third level of personality. Relatedly, should Lynn think of herself only in Level I and Level II terms, then she, too, as a Western, middle-class adult living in the last years of the 20th century, would not know herself "well enough" to comprehend her own identity. The problem of identity is the problem of overall unity and purpose in human lives (McAdams, 1985). It is a problem that has come to preoccupy men and women in Western democracies during the past 200 years (Baumeister, 1986; Langbaum, 1982). It

is not generally a problem for children, though there are some exceptions. It is probably not as salient a problem for many non-Western societies that put less of a premium on individualism and articulating the autonomous adult self, although it is a problem in many of these societies. It is not equally problematic for all contemporary American adults. Nonetheless, identity is likely to be a problem for Lynn, for virtually all people attending that dinner party or reading this article, and for most contemporary Americans and Western Europeans who at one time or another in their adult lives have found the question "Who am I?" to be worth asking, pondering, and worth working on.

Modern and postmodern democratic societies do not explicitly tell adults who they should be. At the same time, however, these societies insist that an adult should be someone who both fits in and is unique (Bellah, Madsen, Sullivan, Swidler, & Tipton, 1985). The self should be defined so that it is both separate and connected, individuated and integrated at the same time. These kinds of selves do not exist in prepackaged, readily assimilated form. They are not passed down from one generation to the next, as they were perhaps in simpler times. Rather, selves must be made or discovered as people become what they are to become in time. The selves that we make before we reach late adolescence and adulthood are, among other things, "lists" of characteristics to be found in Levels I and II of personality. My 8-year-old daughter, Amanda, sees herself as relatively shy (low Extraversion) and very caring and warm (high Agreeableness); she knows she is a good ice skater (domain-specific skill); she loves amusement parks (interests); and she has strong feelings of love and resentment toward her older sister (ambivalent attachment style, though she wouldn't call it that). I hazard to guess that these are a few items in a long list of things, including many that are not in the realm of personality proper ("I live in a white house"; "I go to Central School"), that make up Amanda's self-concept. A list of attributes from Levels I and II is not, however, an identity. Then again, Amanda is too young to have an identity because she is probably not able to experience unity and purpose as problematic in her life. Therefore, one can know Amanda very well by sticking to Levels I and II.

But not so for Lynn. As a contemporary adult, Lynn most likely can understand and appreciate, more or less, the problem of unity and purpose in her life. While the question of "Who am I?" may seem silly or obvious to Amanda, Lynn is likely to see the question as potentially problematic, challenging, interesting, ego-involving, and so on. For reasons that are no doubt physiological and cognitive, as well as social and cultural, it is in late adolescence and young adulthood that many contemporary Westerners come to believe that the self must or should be constructed and told in a manner that integrates the disparate roles they play, incorporates their many different values and skills, and organizes into a meaningful temporal pattern their reconstructed past, perceived present, and anticipated future (Breger, 1974; Erikson, 1959; McAdams, 1985). The challenge of identity demands that the Western adult construct a telling of the self that synthesizes synchronic and diachronic elements in such a way as to suggest that (*a*) despite its many facets the self is coherent and unified and (*b*) despite the many changes that attend the passage of time, the self of the past led up to or set the stage for the self of the present, which in turn will lead up to or set the stage for the self of the future (McAdams, 1990, 1993).

What form does such a construction take? A growing number of theorists believe that the only conceivable form for a unified and purposeful telling of a life is the story (Bruner, 1990; Charme, 1984; Cohler, 1982, 1994; Hermans & Kempen, 1993; Howard, 1991; Kotre, 1984; Linde, 1990; MacIntyre, 1984; Polkinghorne, 1988). In my own theoretical and empirical work, I have argued that identity is itself an internalized and evolving life story, or personal myth (McAdams, 1984, 1985, 1990, 1993, 1996). Contemporary adults create identity in their lives to the extent that the self can be told in a coherent, followable, and vivifying narrative that integrates the person into society in a productive and generative way and provides the person with a purposeful self-history that explains how the self of yesterday became the self of today

and will become the anticipated self of tomorrow. Level III in personality, therefore, is the level of identity as a life story. Without exploring this third level, the personologist can never understand how and to what extent the person is able to find unity, purpose, and meaning in life. Thus what is missing so far from our consideration of Lynn is her very identity.

Misunderstandings About Level III

Lynn's identity is an inner story, a narration of the self that she continues to author and revise over time to make sense, for herself and others, of her own life in time. It is a story, or perhaps a collection of related stories, that Lynn continues to fashion to specify who she is and how she fits into the adult world. Incorporating beginning, middle, and anticipated ending, Lynn's story tells how she came to be, where she has been and where she may be going, and who she will become (Hankiss, 1981). Lynn continues to create and revise the story across her adult years as she and her changing social world negotiate niches, places, opportunities, and positions within which she can live, and live meaningfully.

What is Lynn's story about? The dinner party provided my wife and me with ample material to begin talking about Lynn's personality from the perspectives of Levels I and II. But life-story information is typically more difficult to obtain in a casual social setting. Even after strangers have sized each other up on dispositional traits and even after they have begun to learn a little bit about each others' goals, plans, defenses, strategies, and domain-specific skills, they typically have little to say about the other person's identity. By contrast, when people have been involved in long-term intensive relationships with each other, they may know a great deal about each others' stories, about how the friend or lover (or psychotherapy client) makes sense of his or her own life in narrative terms. They have shared many stories with each other; they have observed each other's behavior in many different situations; they have come to see how the other person sees life, indeed, how the other sees his or her own life organized with purpose in time.

Without that kind of intimate relationship with Lynn, my wife and I could say little of substance about how Lynn creates identity in her life. We left the party with but a few promising hints or leads as to what her story might be about. For example, we were both struck by her enigmatic comment about passionate belief. Why did she suggest that her parents believed too strongly in her and in her siblings? Shouldn't parents believe in their children? Has she disappointed her parents in a deep way, such that their initial belief in their children was proven untenable? Does her inability to believe passionately in things extend to her own children as well? It is perhaps odd that her ex-husband has custody of their children; how is this related to the narrative she has developed about her family and her beliefs? And what might one make of that last incident at the party, when Lynn seemed to lapse into a different mode of talking, indicative perhaps of a different persona, a different public self, maybe a different "character" or "imago" (McAdams, 1984) in her life story? One can imagine many different kinds of stories that Lynn might create to make sense of her own life—adventure stories that incorporate her exotic travels and her considerable success; tragic stories that tell of failed love and lost children; stories in which the protagonist searches far and wide for something to believe in; stories in which early disappointments lead to cynicism, hard-heartedness, despair, or maybe even hope. We do not know Lynn well enough yet to know what kinds of stories she has been working on. Until we can talk with some authority both to her and about her in the narrative language of Level III, we cannot say that we know her well at all. On the drive home, my wife and I know Lynn a little better than we might know a stranger. Our desire to know her much better than we know her now is, in large part, our desire to know her story. And were we to get to know her better and come to feel a bond of intimacy with her, we would want her to know our stories, too (McAdams, 1989).

*   *   *

References

Allport, G. W. (1937). *Personality: A psychological interpretation.* New York: Holt, Rinehart & Winston.

Baumeister, R. F. (1986). *Identity: Cultural change and the struggle for self.* New York: Oxford University Press.

Bellah, R. N., Madsen, R., Sullivan, W. M., Swidler, A., & Tipton, S. M. (1985). *Habits of the heart.* Berkeley: University of California Press.

Block, J. (1995). A contrarian view of the five-factor approach to personality description. *Psychological Bulletin.*

Bowers, K. S. (1973). Situationism in psychology: An analysis and critique. *Psychological Review, 80,* 307–336.

Breger, L. (1974). *From instinct to identity: The development of personality.* Englewood Cliffs, NJ: Prentice-Hall.

Briggs, S. R. (1989). The optimal level of measurement for personality constructs. In D. M. Buss & N. Cantor (Eds.), *Personality psychology: Recent trends and emerging directions* (pp. 246–260). New York: Springer-Verlag.

Bruner, J. S. (1990). *Acts of meaning.* Cambridge, MA: Harvard University Press.

Buss, A. H. (1989). Personality as traits. *American Psychologist, 44,* 1378–1388.

Buss, D. M. (1991). Evolutionary personality psychology. In M. R. Rosenzweig & L. W. Porter (Eds.), *Annual review of psychology* (Vol. 42, pp. 459–491). Palo Alto, CA: Annual Reviews.

Cantor, N. (1990). From thought to behavior: "Having" and "doing" in the study of personality and cognition. *American Psychologist, 45,* 735–750.

Cantor, N., Acker, M., & Cook-Flanagan, C. (1992). Conflict and preoccupation in the intimacy life task. *Journal of Personality and Social Psychology, 63,* 644–655.

Cantor, N., & Kihlstrom, J. F. (1987). *Personality and social intelligence.* Englewood Cliffs, NJ: Prentice-Hall.

Cantor, N., Mischel, W., & Schwartz, J. C. (1982). A prototype analysis of psychological situations. *Cognitive Psychology, 14,* 45–77.

Cattell, R. B. (1957). *Personality and motivation structure and measurement.* New York: Harcourt, Brace & World.

Charme, S. T. (1984). *Meaning and myth in the study of lives: A Sartrean perspective.* Philadelphia: University of Pennsylvania Press.

Cohler, B. J. (1982). Personal narrative and the life course. In P. Baltes & O. G. Brim, Jr. (Eds.), *Life span development and behavior* (Vol. 4, pp. 205–241). New York: Academic Press.

Cohler, B. J. (1994, June). *Studying older lives: Reciprocal acts of telling and listening.* Paper presented at annual meeting of the Society for Personology, Ann Arbor.

Costa, P. T., Jr., & McCrae, R. R. (1985). *The NEO Personality Inventory.* Odessa, FL: Psychological Assessment Resources.

Cramer, P. (1991). *The development of defense mechanisms.* New York: Springer-Verlag.

Demorest, A. P., & Alexander, I. E. (1992). Affective scripts as organizers of personal experience. *Journal of Personality, 60,* 645–663.

Digman, J. M. (1990). Personality structure: Emergence of the five-factor model. In M. R. Rosenzweig & L. W. Porter (Eds.), *Annual review of psychology* (Vol. 41, pp. 417–440). Palo Alto, CA: Annual Reviews.

Emmons, R. A. (1986). Personal strivings: An approach to personality and subjective well-being. *Journal of Personality and Social Psychology, 51,* 1058–1068.

Emmons, R. A. (1993). Current status of the motive concept. In K. H. Craik, R. Hogan, & R. N. Wolfe (Eds.), *Fifty years of personality psychology* (pp. 187–196). New York: Plenum.

Erikson, E. H. (1959). Identity and the life cycle: Selected papers. *Psychological Issues, 1*(1), 5–165.

Erikson, E. H. (1963). *Childhood and society* (2nd ed.). New York: Norton.

Eysenck, H. J. (1967). *The biological basis of personality.* Springfield, IL: Thomas.

Frederiksen, N. (1972). Toward a taxonomy of situations. *American Psychologist, 27,* 114–123.

Gardner, H. (1993). *Creating minds.* New York: Basic Books.

Gilligan, C. (1982). *In a different voice.* Cambridge, MA: Harvard University Press.

Goldberg, L. R. (1981). Language and individual differences: The search for universals in personality lexicons. In L. Wheeler (Ed.), *Review of personality and social psychology* (Vol. 2, pp. 141–166). Beverly Hills: Sage.

Goldberg, L. R. (1993). The structure of phenotypic personality traits. *American Psychologist, 48,* 26–34.

Guilford, J. P. (1959). *Personality.* New York: McGraw-Hill.

Hankiss, A. (1981). On the mythological rearranging of one's life history. In D. Bertaux (Ed.), *Biography and society: The life history approach in the social sciences* (pp. 203–209). Beverly Hills: Sage.

Havighurst, R. J. (1972). *Developmental tasks and education* (3rd ed.). New York: McKay.

Hazan, C., & Shaver, P. (1990). Love and work: An attachment-theoretical perspective. *Journal of Personality and Social Psychology, 59,* 270–280.

Hermans, H. J. M., & Kempen, H. J. G. (1993). *The dialogical self.* New York: Academic Press.

Hogan, R. (1986). *Hogan Personality Inventory manual.* Minneapolis: National Computer Systems.

Howard, G. S. (1991). Culture tales: A narrative approach to thinking, cross-cultural psychology, and psychotherapy. *American Psychologist, 46,* 187–197.

Jackson, D. N. (1974). *The Personality Research Form.* Port Huron, MI: Research Psychologists Press.

John, O. P. (1990). The "Big Five" factor taxonomy: Dimensions of personality in the natural language and in questionnaires. In L. Pervin (Ed.), *Handbook of personality theory and research* (pp. 66–100). New York: Guilford.

Kaiser, R. T., & Ozer, D. J. (under review). The structure of personal goals and their relation to personality traits. Manuscript under editorial review.

Klinger, E. (1977). *Meaning and void.* Minneapolis: University of Minnesota Press.

Kotre, J. (1984). *Outliving the self: Generativity and the interpretation of lives.* Baltimore: Johns Hopkins University Press.

Krahe, B. (1992). *Personality and social psychology: Toward a synthesis.* London: Sage.

Lamiell, J. T. (1987). *The psychology of personality: An epistemological inquiry.* New York: Columbia University Press.

Langbaum, R. (1982). *The mysteries of identity: A theme in modern literature.* Chicago: University of Chicago Press.

Lazarus, R. J. (1991). *Emotion and adaptation.* New York: Oxford University Press.

Linde, C. (1990). *Life stories: The creation of coherence* (Monograph No. IRL90-0001). Palo Alto, CA: Institute for Research on Learning.

Little, B. R. (1989). Personal projects analysis: Trivial pursuits, magnificent obsessions, and the search for coherence. In D. M. Buss & N. Cantor (Eds.), *Personality psychology: Recent trends and emerging directions* (pp. 15–31). New York: Springer-Verlag.

Loevinger, J. (1976). *Ego development.* San Francisco: Jossey-Bass.

Luborsky, L., & Crits-Christoph, P. (1991). *Understanding transference: The core conflictual relationship theme method.* New York: Basic Books.

MacIntyre, A. (1984). *After virtue.* Notre Dame: University of Notre Dame Press.

Magnusson, D. (1971). An analysis of situational dimensions. *Perceptual and Motor Skills, 32,* 851–867.

McAdams, D. P. (1984). Love, power, and images of the self. In C. Z. Malatesta & C. E. Izard (Eds.), *Emotion in adult development* (pp. 159–174). Beverly Hills: Sage.

McAdams, D. P. (1985). *Power, intimacy, and the life story: Personological inquiries into identity.* New York: Guilford.

McAdams, D. P. (1989). *Intimacy: The need to be close.* New York: Doubleday.

McAdams, D. P. (1990). Unity and purpose in human lives: The emergence of identity as a life story. In A. I. Rabin, R. A. Zucker, R. A. Emmons, & S. Frank (Eds.), *Studying persons and lives* (pp. 148–200). New York: Springer.

McAdams, D. P. (1992). The five-factor model in personality: A critical appraisal. *Journal of Personality, 60,* 329–361.

McAdams, D. P. (1993). *The stories we live by: Personal myths and the making of the self.* New York: Morrow.

McAdams, D. P. (1994a). *The person: An introduction to personality psychology* (2nd ed.). Fort Worth: Harcourt Brace.

McAdams, D. P. (1994b). A psychology of the stranger. *Psychological Inquiry, 5,* 145–148.

McAdams, D. P. (1994c). Can personality change? Levels of stability and growth in personality across the life span. In T. F. Heatherton & J. L. Weinberger (Eds.), *Can personality change?* (pp. 299–314). Washington, DC: American Psychological Association.

McAdams, D. P. (1996). Narrating the self in adulthood. In J. Birren, G. Kenyon, J. E. Ruth, J. J. F. Schroots, & T. Svensson (Eds.), *Aging and biography: Explorations in adult development.* New York: Springer.

McAdams, D. P., de St. Aubin, E., & Logan, R. L. (1993). Generativity among young, midlife, and older adults. *Psychology and Aging, 8,* 221–230.

McClelland, D. C. (1951). *Personality.* New York: Holt, Rinehart & Winston.

McClelland, D. C. (1961). *The achieving society.* New York: D. Van Nostrand.

McCrae, R. R., & Costa, P. T., Jr. (1996). Toward a new generation of personality theories: Theoretical contexts for the five-factor model. In J. S. Wiggins (Ed.), *The five-factor model of personality.* New York: Guilford.

Mischel, W. (1968). *Personality and assessment.* New York: Wiley.

Mischel, W. (1973). Toward a cognitive social-learning reconceptualization of personality. *Psychological Review, 80,* 252–283.

Moos, R. H. (1973). Conceptualization of human environments. *American Psychologist, 28,* 652–665.

Murray, H. A. (1938). *Explorations in personality*. New York: Oxford University Press.

Ogilvie, D. M., & Ashmore, R. D. (1991). Self-with-other representation as units of analysis in self-concept research. In R. A. Curtis (Ed.), *The relational self: Theoretical convergences in psychoanalysis and social psychology* (pp. 282–314). New York: Guilford.

Ozer, D. J., & Reise, S. P. (1994). Personality assessment. In L. W. Porter & M. R. Rosenzweig (Eds.), *Annual review of psychology* (Vol. 45, pp. 357–388). Palo Alto, CA: Annual Reviews.

Pervin, L. (1994). A critical analysis of current trait theory. *Psychological Inquiry, 5*, 103–113.

Polkinghorne, D. (1988). *Narrative knowing and the human sciences*. Albany, NY: SUNY Press.

Revelle, W. (1995). Personality processes. In L. W. Porter & M. R. Rosenzweig (Eds.), *Annual review of psychology* (Vol. 46, pp. 295–328). Palo Alto, CA: Annual Reviews.

Rokeach, M. (1973). *The nature of human values*. New York: Free Press.

Tellegen, A. (1982). *Brief manual for the Differential Personality Questionnaire*. Unpublished manuscript, University of Minnesota.

Thorne, A. (1989). Conditional patterns, transference, and the coherence of personality across time. In D. M. Buss & N. Cantor (Eds.), *Personality psychology: Recent trends and emerging directions* (pp. 149–159). New York: Springer.

Wiggins, J. S. (Ed.). (1996). *The five-factor model of personality*. New York: Guilford.

Winter, D. G. (1973). *The power motive*. New York: Free Press.

Wright, J. C., & Mischel, W. (1987). A conditional approach to dispositional constructs: The local predictability of social behavior. *Journal of Personality and Social Psychology, 53*, 1159–1177.

A Simple, General-Purpose Display of Magnitude of Experimental Effect

Robert Rosenthal and Donald B. Rubin

The most widely used statistic in personality psychology, the correlation coefficient, has been the source of considerable, needless confusion. An r of 1 (or −1) means that two variables are perfectly correlated, and an r of 0 means they are not correlated at all. But how should we interpret the r's in between, as most are?

Confusion has been engendered by a commonly taught practice of squaring correlations to yield the "percentage of variance explained" by the relationship. While this phrase sounds rather close to what one would want to know, it causes people to interpret correlations of .32, for example, as "explaining only 10% of the variance" (because .32 squared is about .10), which leaves 90% "unexplained." This does not make it sound like much has been accomplished.

In the next selection, psychologist Robert Rosenthal and statistician Donald Rubin team up to explain why this common calculation is misleading. In particular, they believe it causes strong effects, such as those indexed by correlations between .30 and .40, to seem smaller than they are. They introduce a simple technique of their own invention for illustrating the real size and importance of correlations. The "binomial effect size display" (BESD) allows correlation coefficients to be interpreted in terms of the percentage of correct classification or effective treatment they represent.

The basic calculation is even simpler than this article may make it sound. Look at Table 1.1 and assume an r of 0. This would yield an entry of 50 in each of the four cells. To see what a correlation of .32 looks like, divide 32 by 2, which gives you 16. Add the 16 to 50 and put this 66 in the upper-left and lower-right cells. Now subtract 16 from 50 and put 34 in the lower-left and upper-right cells. The rows and columns still each add up to 100, but now show what r = .32 looks like. It's easy! And it shows that a correlation between a treatment and an outcome, or between a predictor and a criterion, of a size of .32 would give you the right result almost twice as often as the wrong result.

The BESD is particularly important for personality psychology because most of the strongest relations between traits or between traits and behaviors are

found to yield correlations between about .30 and .40. Rosenthal and Rubin
show us that this means the prediction of one trait from another, or of a behavior
on the basis of a trait, is usually more than twice as likely to be right as it is to
be wrong.

From *Journal of Educational Psychology*, 74, 166–169, 1982.

* * *

Traditionally, behavioral researchers have concentrated on reporting significance levels of experimental effects. Recent years, however, have shown a welcome increase in emphasis on reporting the magnitude of experimental effects obtained (Cohen, 1977; Fleiss, 1969; Friedman, 1968; Glass, 1976; Hays, 1973; Rosenthal, 1978; Rosenthal & Rubin, 1978; Smith & Glass, 1977).

Despite the growing awareness of the importance of estimating sizes of effects along with estimating the more conventional levels of significance, there is a problem in interpreting various effect size estimators such as the Pearson r. For example, we found experienced behavioral researchers and experienced statisticians quite surprised when we showed them that the Pearson r of .32 associated with a coefficient of determination (r^2) of only .10 was the correlational equivalent of increasing a success rate from 34% to 66% by means of an experimental treatment procedure; for example, these values could mean that a death rate under the control condition is 66% but is only 34% under the experimental condition. We believe (Rosenthal & Rubin, 1979) that there may be a widespread tendency to underestimate the importance of the effects of behavioral (and biomedical) interventions (Mayo, 1978; Rimland, 1979) simply because they are often associated with what are thought to be low values of r^2.

The purpose of the present article is to introduce an intuitively appealing general purpose effect size display whose interpretation is perfectly transparent: the binomial effect size display (BESD). In no sense do we claim to have resolved the differences and controversies surrounding the use of various effect size estimators (e.g., Appelbaum & Cramer, 1974). Our display is useful because it is (a) easily understood by researchers, students, and lay persons; (b) applicable in a wide variety of contexts; and (c) conveniently computed.

The question addressed by BESD is: What is the effect on the success rate (e.g., survival rate, cure rate, improvement rate, selection rate, etc.) of the institution of a certain treatment procedure? It displays the change in success rate (e.g., survival rate, cure rate, improvement rate, selection rate, etc.) attributable to a certain treatment procedure. An example shows the appeal of our procedure.

In their meta-analysis of psychotherapy outcome studies, Smith and Glass (1977) summarized the results of some 400 studies. An eminent critic stated that the results of their analysis sounded the "death knell" for psychotherapy because of the modest size of the effect (Rimland, 1979). This modest effect size was calculated to be equivalent to an r of .32 accounting for "only 10% of the variance" (p. 192).

Table 1 is the BESD corresponding to an r of .32 or an r^2 of .10. The table shows clearly that it is absurd to label as "modest indeed" (Rimland, 1979, p. 192) an effect size equivalent to increasing the success rate from 34% to 66% (e.g., reducing a death rate from 66% to 34%).

Table 2 shows systematically the increase in success rates associated with various values of r^2 and r. Even so small an r as .20, accounting for only 4% of the variance, is associated with an increase in success rate from 40% to 60%, such as a reduction in death rate from 60% to 40%. The last column of Table 2 shows that the difference

TABLE 1

THE BINOMIAL EFFECT SIZE DISPLAY: AN EXAMPLE "ACCOUNTING FOR ONLY 10% OF THE VARIANCE"

Condition	Alive	Dead	Σ
Treatment	66	34	100
Control	34	66	100
Σ	100	100	200

TABLE 2

BINOMIAL EFFECT SIZE DISPLAYS: CORRESPONDING TO VARIOUS VALUES OF r^2 AND r

r^2	r	Success rate increased From	To	Difference in success rates
.01	.10	.45	.55	.10
.04	.20	.40	.60	.20
.09	.30	.35	.65	.30
.16	.40	.30	.70	.40
.25	.50	.25	.75	.50
.36	.60	.20	.80	.60
.49	.70	.15	.85	.70
.64	.80	.10	.90	.80
.81	.90	.05	.95	.90
1.00	1.00	.00	1.00	1.00

TABLE 3

COMPUTATION OF r FROM COMMON TEST STATISTICS

Test statistic	$r^{[a]}$ given by
t	$\sqrt{\dfrac{t^2}{t^2 + df}}$
$F^{[b]}$	$\sqrt{\dfrac{F}{F + df\,(error)}}$
$\chi^{2,[c]}$	$\sqrt{\dfrac{\chi^2}{N}}$

[a] The sign of r should be positive if the experimental group is superior to the control group and negative if the control group is superior to the experimental group.
[b] Used only when df for numerator = 1 as in the comparison of two group means or any other contrast.
[c] Used only when df for $\chi^2 = 1$.

in success rates is identical to r. Consequently the experimental success rate in the BESD is computed as $.50 + r/2$, whereas the control group success rate is computed as $.50 - r/2$. Cohen (1965) and Friedman (1968) have useful discussions of computing the r associated with a variety of test statistics, and Table 3 gives the three most frequently used equivalences.

We propose that the reporting of effect sizes can be made more intuitive and more informative by using the BESD. It is our belief that the use of the BESD to display the increase in success rate due to treatment will more clearly convey the real world importance of treatment effects than do the commonly used descriptions of effect size based on the proportion of variance accounted for. The BESD is most appropriate when the variances within the two conditions are similar, as they are assumed to be whenever we compute the usual t test.

It might appear that the BESD can be employed only when the outcome variable is dichotomous and the mean outcome in one group is the same amount above .5 as the mean outcome in the other group is below .5. Actually, the BESD is often a realistic representation of the size of treatment effect when the variances of the outcome variable are approximately the same in the two approximately equal sized groups, as is commonly the case in educational and psychological studies.

* * *

References

Appelbaum, M. I., & Cramer, E. M. (1974). The only game in town. *Contemporary Psychology*, 19, 406–407.

Cohen, J. (1965). Some statistical issues in psychological research. In B. B. Wolman (Ed.), *Handbook of clinical psychology*. New York: McGraw-Hill.

Cohen, J. (1977). *Statistical power analysis for the behavioral sciences* (Rev. ed.). New York: Academic Press.

Fleiss, J. L. (1969). Estimating the magnitude of experimental effects. *Psychological Bulletin*, 72, 273–276.

Friedman, H. (1968). Magnitude of experimental effect and a table for its rapid estimation. *Psychological Bulletin*, 70, 245–251.

Glass, G. V. (1976, April). *Primary, secondary, and meta-analysis of research*. Paper presented at the meeting of the American Educational Research Association, San Francisco.

Hays, W. L. (1973). *Statistics for the social sciences* (2nd ed.). New York: Holt, Rinehart & Winston.

Mayo, R. J. (1978). Statistical considerations in analyzing the results of a collection of experiments. *The Behavioral and Brain Sciences, 3*, 400–401.

Rimland, B. (1979). Death knell for psychotherapy? *American Psychologist, 34*, 192.

Rosenthal, R. (1978). Combining results of independent studies. *Psychological Bulletin, 85*, 185–193.

Rosenthal, R., & Rubin, D. B. (1978). Interpersonal expectancy effects: The first 345 studies. *The Behavioral and Brain Sciences, 3*, 377–386.

Rosenthal, R., & Rubin, D. B. (1979). A note on percent variance explained as a measure of the importance of effects. *Journal of Applied Social Psychology, 9*, 395–396.

Smith, M. L., & Glass, G. V. (1977). Meta-analysis of psychotherapy outcome studies. *American Psychologist, 32*, 752–760.

CONSTRUCT VALIDITY IN PSYCHOLOGICAL TESTS

Lee J. Cronbach and Paul E. Meehl

Lee Cronbach and Paul Meehl are two of the most prominent methodologists in the history of psychology. In the following classic selection, they team up to address the knotty question of "construct validity," which is, how do you know whether a test—such as a personality test—really measures what it is supposed to measure? As is mentioned in the opening paragraphs, the article was occasioned by concerns in the mid-1950s over the proper way to establish the validity of a test. This issue generated political heat both within and outside the American Psychological Association, the professional organization of many psychologists, because the tests that people take often have consequences. They are used for selection in education and employment, for example. Thus, the degree to which a test is valid is more than an academic issue. Its resolution has real consequences for real people.

This article is a fairly difficult piece, but worth some effort. Psychologists who have been doing research for years can reread this article and learn something important that escaped them on previous readings. The essential points to glean from this article are that no single study or one source of data will ever sufficiently explain any important aspect of personality, and that psychological theory plays an essential role in developing an understanding of what any measure of personality really means. Multiple methods must always be employed, and the validation of a test will emerge only gradually from an examination of how different methods produce results that are sometimes the same and sometimes different. The present excerpt concludes with the important observation that the aim of construct validation is not to conclude that a test "is valid," but rather to assess its degree of validity for various purposes.

From *Psychological Bulletin, 52,* 281–302, 1955.

Validation of psychological tests has not yet been adequately conceptualized, as the APA Committee on Psychological Tests learned when it undertook (1950–54) to specify what qualities should be investigated before a test is published. In order to make coherent recommendations the Committee found it necessary to distinguish four types of validity, established by different types of research and requiring different interpretation. The chief innovation in the Committee's report was the term *construct validity*. This idea was first formulated by a subcommittee (Meehl and R. C. Challman) studying how proposed recommendations would apply to projective techniques, and later modified and clarified by the entire Committee (Bordin, Challman, Conrad, Humphreys, Super, and the present writers). The statements agreed upon by the Committee (and by committees of two other associations) were published in the *Technical Recommendations* (American Psychological Association, 1954). The present interpretation of construct validity is not "official" and deals with some areas where the Committee would probably not be unanimous. The present writers are solely responsible for this attempt to explain the concept and elaborate its implications.

Identification of construct validity was not an isolated development. Writers on validity during the preceding decade had shown a great deal of dissatisfaction with conventional notions of validity, and introduced new terms and ideas, but the resulting aggregation of types of validity seems only to have stirred the muddy waters. Portions of the distinctions we shall discuss are implicit in Jenkins's (1946) paper, Gulliksen (1950), Goodenough's (1950) distinction between tests as "signs" and "samples," Cronbach's (1949) separation of "logical" and "empirical" validity, Guilford's (1946) "factorial validity," and Mosier's (1947, 1951) papers on "face validity" and "validity generalization." Helen Peak (1953) comes close to an explicit statement of construct validity as we shall present it.

Four Types of Validation

The categories into which the *Recommendations* divide validity studies are: predictive validity, concurrent validity, content validity, and construct validity. The first two of these may be considered together as *criterion-oriented* validation procedures.

The pattern of a criterion-oriented study is familiar. The investigator is primarily interested in some criterion which he wishes to predict. He administers the test, obtains an independent criterion measure on the same subjects, and computes a correlation. If the criterion is obtained some time after the test is given, he is studying *predictive validity*. If the test score and criterion score are determined at essentially the same time, he is studying *concurrent validity*. Concurrent validity is studied when one test is proposed as a substitute for another (for example, when a multiple-choice form of spelling test is substituted for taking dictation), or a test is shown to correlate with some contemporary criterion (e.g., psychiatric diagnosis).

Content validity is established by showing that the test items are a sample of a universe in which the investigator is interested. Content validity is ordinarily to be established deductively, by defining a universe of items and sampling systematically within this universe to establish the test.

Construct validation is involved whenever a test is to be interpreted as a measure of some attribute or quality which is not "operationally defined." The problem faced by the investigator is, "What constructs account for variance in test performance?" Construct validity calls for no new scientific approach. Much current research on tests of personality (Child, 1954) is construct validation, usually without the benefit of a clear formulation of this process.

Construct validity is not to be identified solely by particular investigative procedures, but by the orientation of the investigator. Criterion-oriented validity, as Bechtoldt emphasizes (1951, p. 1245), "involves the *acceptance* of a set of operations as an adequate definition of whatever is to be measured." When an investigator believes that no criterion available in him is fully valid, he perforce becomes interested in construct validity because this is the only way to avoid the "infinite frustration" of relating every criterion to some more ultimate standard (Gaylord, unpublished manuscript). In content validation, *acceptance* of the universe of content as defining the variable to be measured is essential. Construct validity must be investigated whenever no criterion or universe of content is accepted as entirely adequate to define the quality to be measured. Determining what psychological constructs account for test performance is desirable for almost any test. Thus, although the MMPI was originally established on the basis of empirical discrimination between patient groups and so-called normals (concurrent validity), continuing research has tried to provide a basis for describing the personality associated with each score pattern. Such interpretations permit the clinician to predict performance with respect to criteria which have not yet been employed in empirical validation studies (cf. Meehl, 1954, pp. 49–50, 110–111).

> We can distinguish among the four types of validity by noting that each involves a different emphasis on the criterion. In predictive or concurrent validity, the criterion behavior is of concern to the tester, and he may have no concern whatsoever with the type of behavior exhibited in the test. (An employer does not care if a worker can manipulate blocks, but the score on the block test may predict something he cares about.) Content validity is studied when the tester *is* concerned with the type of behavior involved in the test performance. Indeed, if the test is a work sample, the behavior represented in the test may be an end in itself. Construct validity is ordinarily studied when the tester has no definite criterion measure of the quality with which he is concerned, and must use indirect measures. Here the trait or quality underlying the test is of central importance, rather than either the test behavior or the scores on the criteria (APA, 1954, p. 14).

Construct validation is important at times for every sort of psychological test: aptitude, achievement, interests, and so on. Thurstone's statement is interesting in this connection:

> In the field of intelligence tests, it used to be common to define validity as the correlation between a test score and some outside criterion. We have reached a stage of sophistication where the test-criterion correlation is too coarse. It is obsolete. If we attempted to ascertain the validity of a test for the second space-factor, for example, we would have to get judges [to] make reliable judgments about people as to this factor. Ordinarily their [the available judges'] ratings would be of no value as a criterion. Consequently, validity studies in the cognitive functions now depend on criteria of internal consistency ... (Thurstone, 1952, p. 3).

Construct validity would be involved in answering such questions as: To what extent is this test of intelligence culture-free? Does this test of "interpretation of data" measure reading ability, quantitative reasoning, or response sets? How does a person with A in Strong Accountant, and B in Strong CPA, differ from a person who has these scores reversed?

Example of construct validation procedure. Suppose measure X correlates .50 with Y, the amount of palmar sweating induced when we tell a student that he has failed a Psychology I exam. Predictive validity of X for Y is adequately described by the coefficient, and a statement of the experimental and sampling conditions. If someone were to ask, "Isn't there perhaps another way to interpret this correlation?" or "What other kinds of evidence can you bring to support your interpretation?" we would hardly understand what he was asking because no interpretation has been made. These questions become relevant when the correlation is advanced as evidence that "test X measures anxiety proneness." Alternative interpretations are possible; e.g., perhaps the test measures "academic aspiration," in which case we will expect different results if we induce palmar sweating by economic threat. It is then reasonable to inquire about other *kinds* of evidence.

Add these facts from further studies: Test X correlates .45 with fraternity brothers' ratings on "tenseness." Test X correlates .55 with amount of intellectual inefficiency induced by painful electric shock, and .68 with the Taylor Anxiety scale. Mean X score decreases among four diagnosed groups in this order: anxiety state, reactive depression, "normal," and psychopathic personality. And palmar sweat under threat of failure in Psychology I correlates .60 with threat of failure in mathematics. Negative results eliminate competing explanations of the X score; thus, findings of negligible correlations between X and social class, vocational aim, and value-orientation make it fairly safe to reject the suggestion that X measures "academic aspiration." We can have substantial confidence that X does measure anxiety proneness if the current theory of anxiety can embrace the variates which yield positive correlations, and does not predict correlations where we found none.

* * *

The Relation of Constructs to "Criteria"

CRITICAL VIEW OF THE CRITERION IMPLIED An unquestionable criterion may be found in a practical operation, or may be established as a consequence of an operational definition. Typically, however, the psychologist is unwilling to use the directly operational approach because he is interested in building theory about a generalized construct. A theorist trying to relate behavior to "hunger" almost certainly invests that term with meanings other than the operation "elapsed-time-since-feeding." If he is concerned with hunger as a tissue need, he will not accept time lapse as *equivalent* to his construct because it fails to consider, among other things, energy expenditure of the animal.

In some situations the criterion is no more valid than the test. Suppose, for example, that we want to know if counting the dots on Bender-Gestalt figure five indicates "compulsive rigidity," and take psychiatric ratings on this trait as a criterion. Even a conventional report on the resulting correlation will say something about the extent and intensity of the psychiatrist's contacts and should describe his qualifications (e.g., diplomate status? analyzed?).

Why report these facts? Because data are needed to indicate whether the criterion is any good. "Compulsive rigidity" is not really intended to mean "social stimulus value to psychiatrists." The implied trait involves a range of behavior-dispositions which may be very imperfectly sampled by the psychiatrist. Suppose dot-counting does not occur in a particular patient and yet we find that the psychiatrist has rated him as "rigid." When questioned the psychiatrist tells us that the patient was a rather easy, free-wheeling sort: however, the patient *did* lean over to straighten out a skewed desk blotter, and this, viewed against certain other facts, tipped the scale in favor of a "rigid" rating. On the face of it, counting Bender dots may be just as good (or poor) a sample of the compulsive-rigidity domain as straightening desk blotters is.

Suppose, to extend our example, we have four tests on the "predictor" side, over against the psychiatrist's "criterion," and find generally positive correlations among the five variables. Surely it is artificial and arbitrary to impose the "test-should-predict-criterion" pattern on such data. The psychiatrist samples verbal content, expressive pattern, voice, posture, etc. The psychologist samples verbal content, perception, expressive pattern, etc. Our proper conclusion is that, from this evidence, the four tests and the psychiatrist all assess some common factor.

The asymmetry between the "test" and the so-designated "criterion" arises only because the terminology of predictive validity has become a commonplace in test analysis. In this study where a construct is the central concern, any distinction between the merit of the test and criterion variables would be justified only if it had already been shown that the psychiatrist's theory and operations were excellent measures of the attribute.

Inadequacy of Validation in Terms of Specific Criteria

The proposal to validate constructual interpretations of tests runs counter to suggestions of some others. Spiker and McCandless (1954) favor an operational approach. Validation is replaced by compiling statements as to how strongly the test predicts other observed variables of interest. To avoid requiring that each new variable be investigated completely by itself, they allow two variables to collapse into one whenever the properties of the operationally defined measures are the same: "If a new test is demonstrated to predict the scores on an older, well-established test, then an evaluation of the predictive power of the older test may be used for the new one." But accurate inferences are possible only if the two tests correlate so highly that there is negligible reliable variance in either test, independent of the other. Where the correspondence is less close, one must either retain all the separate variables operationally defined or embark on construct validation.

The practical user of tests must rely on constructs of some generality to make predictions about new situations. Test *X* could be used to predict palmar sweating in the face of failure without invoking any construct, but a counselor is more likely to be asked to forecast behavior in diverse or even unique situations for which the correlation of test *X* is unknown. Significant predictions rely on knowledge accumulated around the generalized construct of anxiety. The "Technical Recommendations" state:

> It is ordinarily necessary to evaluate construct validity by integrating evidence from many different sources. The problem of construct validation becomes especially acute in the clinical field since for many of the constructs dealt with it is not a question of finding an imperfect criterion but of finding any criterion at all. The psychologist interested in construct validity for clinical devices is concerned with making an estimate of a hypothetical internal process, factor, system, structure, or state and cannot expect to find a clear unitary behavioral criterion. An attempt to identify any one criterion measure or any composite as *the* criterion aimed at is, however, usually unwarranted (APA, 1954, pp. 14–15).

This appears to conflict with arguments for specific criteria prominent at places in the testing literature. Thus Anastasi (1950) makes many statements of the latter character: "It is only as a measure of a specifically defined criterion that a test can be objectively validated at all . . . To claim that a test measures anything over and above its crite-

rion is pure speculation" (p. 67). Yet elsewhere this article supports construct validation. Tests can be profitably interpreted if we "know the relationships between the tested behavior . . . and other behavior samples, none of these behavior samples necessarily occupying the preeminent position of a criterion" (p. 75). Factor analysis with several partial criteria might be used to study whether a test measures a postulated "general learning ability." If the data demonstrate specificity of ability instead, such specificity is "useful in its own right in advancing our knowledge of behavior; it should not be construed as a weakness of the tests" (p. 75).

We depart from Anastasi at two points. She writes, "The validity of a psychological test should not be confused with an analysis of the factors which determine the behavior under consideration." We, however, regard such analysis as a most important type of validation. Second, she refers to "the will-o'-the-wisp of psychological processes which are distinct from performance" (Anastasi, 1950, p. 77). While we agree that psychological processes are elusive, we are sympathetic to attempts to formulate and clarify constructs which are evidenced by performance but distinct from it. Surely an inductive inference based on a pattern of correlations cannot be dismissed as "pure speculation."

SPECIFIC CRITERIA USED TEMPORARILY: THE "BOOTSTRAPS" EFFECT Even when a test is constructed on the basis of a specific criterion, it may ultimately be judged to have greater construct validity than the criterion. We start with a vague concept which we associate with certain observations. We then discover empirically that these observations covary with some other observation which possesses greater reliability or is more intimately correlated with relevant experimental changes than is the original measure, or both. For example, the notion of temperature arises because some objects feel hotter to the touch than others. The expansion of a mercury column does not have face validity as an index of hotness. But it turns out that (a) there is a statistical relation between expansion and sensed temperature; (b) observers employ the mercury method with good interobserver agreement; (c) the regularity of observed relations is increased by using the thermometer (e.g., melting points of samples of the same material vary little on the thermometer; we obtain nearly linear relations between mercury measures and pressure of a gas). Finally, (d) a theoretical structure involving unobservable microevents—the kinetic theory—is worked out which explains the relation of mercury expansion to heat. This whole process of conceptual enrichment begins with what in retrospect we see as an extremely fallible "criterion"—the human temperature sense. That original criterion has now been relegated to a peripheral position. We have lifted ourselves by our bootstraps, but in a legitimate and fruitful way.

Similarly, the Binet scale was first valued because children's scores tended to agree with judgments by schoolteachers. If it had not shown this agreement, it would have been discarded along with reaction time and the other measures of ability previously tried. Teacher judgments once constituted the criterion against which the individual intelligence test was validated. But if today a child's IQ is 135 and three of his teachers complain about how stupid he is, we do not conclude that the test has failed. Quite to the contrary, if no error in test procedure can be argued, we treat the test score as a valid statement about an important quality, and define our task as that of finding out what other variables—personality, study skills, etc.—modify achievement or distort teacher judgment.

Experimentation to Investigate Construct Validity

VALIDATION PROCEDURES We can use many methods in construct validation. Attention should particularly be drawn to Macfarlane's survey of these methods as they apply to projective devices (Macfarlane, 1942).

Group differences. If our understanding of a construct leads us to expect two groups to differ on the test, this expectation may be tested directly. Thus Thurstone and Chave validated the Scale for Measuring Attitude Toward the Church by showing score differences between church members and nonchurchgoers. Churchgoing is not *the* criterion of attitude, for the purpose of the test is to measure something other than the crude sociological fact of church attendance; on the other hand, failure to find a difference would have seriously challenged the test.

Only coarse correspondence between test and group designation is expected. Too great a correspondence between the two would indicate that the test is to some degree invalid, because members of the groups are expected to overlap on the test. Intelligence test items are selected initially on the basis of a correspondence to age, but an item that correlates .95 with age in an elementary school sample would surely be suspect.

Correlation matrices and factor analysis. If two tests are presumed to measure the same construct, a correlation between them is predicted. (An exception is noted where some second attribute has positive loading in the first test and negative loading in the second test; then a low correlation is expected. This is a testable interpretation provided an external measure of either the first or the second variable exists.) If the obtained correlation departs from the expectation, however, there is no way to know whether the fault lies in test A, test B, or the formulation of the construct. A matrix of intercorrelations often points out profitable ways of dividing the construct into more meaningful parts, factor analysis being a useful computational method in such studies.

Guilford (1948) has discussed the place of factor analysis in construct validation. His statements may be extracted as follows:

"The personnel psychologist wishes to know 'why his tests are valid.' He can place tests and practical criteria in a matrix and factor it to identify 'real dimensions of human personality.' A factorial description is exact and stable; it is economical in explanation; it leads to the creation of pure tests which can be combined to predict complex behaviors." It is clear that factors here function as constructs. Eysenck (1950) in his "criterion analysis," goes further than Guilford and shows that factoring can be used explicitly to test hypotheses about constructs.

Factors may or may not be weighted with surplus meaning. Certainly when they are regarded as "real dimensions" a great deal of surplus meaning is implied, and the interpreter must shoulder a substantial burden of proof. The alternative view is to regard factors as defining a working reference frame, located in a convenient manner in the "space" defined by all behaviors of a given type. Which set of factors from a given matrix is "most useful" will depend partly on predilections, but in essence the best construct is the one around which we can build the greatest number of inferences, in the most direct fashion.

Studies of internal structure. For many constructs, evidence of homogeneity within the test is relevant in judging validity. If a trait such as *dominance* is hypothesized, and the items inquire about behaviors subsumed under this label, then the hypothesis appears to require that these items be generally intercorrelated. Even low correlations, if consistent, would support the argument that people may be fruitfully described in terms of a generalized tendency to dominate or not dominate. The general quality would have power to predict behavior in a variety of situations represented by the specific items. Item-test correlations and certain reliability formulas describe internal consistency.

It is unwise to list uninterpreted data of this sort under the heading "validity" in test manuals, as some authors have done. High internal consistency may *lower* validity. Only if the underlying theory of the trait being measured calls for high item intercorrelations do the correlations support construct validity. Negative item-test correlations may support construct validity, provided that the items with negative correlations are believed irrelevant to the postulated construct and serve as suppressor variables (Horst, 1941, pp. 431–436; Meehl, 1945).

Study of distinctive subgroups of items within a test may set an upper limit to construct validity by showing that irrelevant elements influence scores. Thus a study of the PMA space tests shows that variance can be partially accounted for by a response set, tendency to mark many figures as similar (Cronbach, 1950). An internal factor analysis of the PEA Interpretation of Data Test shows that in addition to measuring reasoning skills, the test score is strongly influenced by a tendency to say "probably true" rather than "certainly true," regardless of item content (Damrin, 1952). On the other hand, a study of item groupings in the DAT Mechanical Comprehension Test permitted rejection of the hypothesis that knowledge about specific topics such as gears made a substantial contribution to scores (Cronbach, 1951).

Studies of change over occasions. The stability of test scores ("retest reliability," Cattell's "N-technique") may be relevant to construct validation. Whether a high degree of stability is encouraging or discouraging for the proposed interpretation depends upon the theory defining the construct.

More powerful than the retest after uncontrolled intervening experiences is the retest with experimental intervention. If a transient influence swings test scores over a wide range, there are definite limits on the extent to which a test result can be interpreted as reflecting the typical behavior of the individual. These are examples of experiments which have indicated upper limits to test validity: studies of differences associated with the examiner in projective testing, of change of score under alternative directions ("tell the truth" vs. "make yourself look good to an employer"), and of coachability of mental tests. We may recall Gulliksen's (1950) distinction: When the coaching is of a sort that improves the pupil's intellectual functioning in school, the test which is affected by the coaching has validity as a measure of intellectual functioning; if the coaching improves test taking but not school performance, the test which responds to the coaching has poor validity as a measure of this construct.

Sometimes, where differences between individuals are difficult to assess by any means other than the test, the experimenter validates by determining whether the test can detect induced intraindividual differences. One might hypothesize that the Zeigarnik effect is a measure of ego involvement, i.e., that with ego involvement there is more recall of incomplete tasks. To support such an interpretation, the investigator will try to induce ego involvement on some task by appropriate directions and compare subjects' recall with their recall for tasks where there was a contrary induction. Sometimes the intervention is drastic. Porteus (1950) finds that brain-operated patients show disruption of performance on his maze, but do not show impaired performance on conventional verbal tests and argues therefrom that his test is a better measure of planfulness.

Studies of process. One of the best ways of determining informally what accounts for variability on a test is the observation of the person's process of performance. If it is supposed, for example, that a test measures mathematical competence, and yet observation of students' errors shows that erroneous reading of the question is common, the implications of a low score are altered. Lucas (1953) in this way showed that the Navy Relative Movement Test, an aptitude test, actually involved two different abilities: spatial visualization and mathematical reasoning.

Mathematical analysis of scoring procedures may provide important negative evidence on construct validity. A recent analysis of "empathy" tests is perhaps worth citing (Cronbach, 1955). "Empathy" has been operationally defined in many studies by the ability of a judge to predict what responses will be given on some questionnaire by a subject he has observed briefly. A mathematical argument has shown, however, that the scores depend on several attributes of the judge which enter into his perception of *any* individual, and that they therefore cannot be interpreted as evidence of his ability to interpret cues offered by particular others, or his intuition.

THE NUMERICAL ESTIMATE OF CONSTRUCT VALIDITY   There is an understandable tendency to seek a "construct validity coefficient." A numerical statement of the degree of construct validity would be a statement of the proportion of the test score variance that is attributable to the construct variable. This numerical estimate can sometimes be arrived at by a factor analysis, but since present methods of factor analysis are based on linear relations, more general methods will ultimately be needed to deal with many quantitative problems of construct validation.

Rarely will it be possible to estimate definite "construct saturations," because no factor corresponding closely to the construct will be available. One can only hope to set upper and lower bounds to the "loading." If "creativity" is defined as something independent of knowledge, then a correlation of .40 between a presumed test of creativity and a test of arithmetic knowledge would indicate that at least 16 per cent of the reliable test variance is irrelevant to creativity as defined. Laboratory performance on problems such as Maier's "hat-rack" would scarcely be an ideal measure of creativity, but it would be somewhat relevant. If its correlation with the test is .60, this permits a tentative estimate of 36 per cent as a lower bound. (The estimate is tentative because the test might overlap with the irrelevant portion of the laboratory measure.) The saturation seems to lie between 36 and 84 per cent; a cumulation of studies would provide better limits.

It should be particularly noted that rejecting the null hypothesis does not finish the job of construct validation (Kelly, 1954, p. 284). The problem is not to conclude that the test "is valid" for measuring the construct variable. The task is to state as definitely as possible the degree of validity the test is presumed to have.

* * *

References

American Psychological Association (1954). Technical recommendations for psychological tests and diagnostic techniques. *Psychological Bulletin Supplement, 51, Part 2,* 1–38.

Anastasi, A. (1950). The concept of validity in the interpretation of test scores. *Educational and Psychological Measurement, 10,* 67–78.

Bechtoldt, H. P. (1951). Selection. In S. S. Stevens (Ed.), *Handbook of experimental psychology* (pp. 1237–1267). New York: Wiley.

Child, I. L. (1954). Personality. *Annual Review of Psychology, 5,* 149–171.

Cronbach, L. J. (1949). *Essentials of psychological testing.* New York: Harper.

Cronbach, L. J. (1950). Further evidence on response sets and test design. *Educational and Psychological Measurement, 10,* 3–31.

Cronbach, L. J. (1951). Coefficient alpha and the internal structure of tests. *Psychometrika, 16,* 297–335.

Cronbach, L. J. (1955). Processes affecting scores on "understanding of others" and "assumed similarity." *Psychology Bulletin, 52,* 177–193.

Damrin, Dora E. (1952). A comparative study of information derived from a diagnostic problem-solving test by logical and factorial methods of scoring. Unpublished doctor's dissertation, University of Illinois.

Eysenck, H. J. (1950). Criterion analysis—an application of the hypothetico-deductive method in factor analysis. *Psychology Review, 57,* 38–53.

Gaylord, R. H. Conceptual consistency and criterion equivalence: a dual approach to criterion analysis. Unpublished manuscript (PRB Research Note No. 17). Copies obtainable from ASTIA-DSC, AD-21 440.

Goodenough, F. L. (1950). *Mental testing.* New York: Rinehart.

Guilford, J. P. (1946). New standards for test evaluation. *Educational and Psychological Measurement, 6,* 427–439.

Guilford, J. P. (1948). Factor analysis in a test-development program. *Psychology Review, 55,* 79–94.

Gulliksen, H. (1950). Intrinsic validity. *American Psychologist, 5,* 511–517.

Horst, P. (1941). The prediction of personal adjustment. *Social Science Research Council Bulletin,* No. 48.

Jenkins, J. G. (1946). Validity for what? *Journal of Consulting Psychology, 10,* 93–98.

Kelly, E. L. (1954). Theory and techniques of assessment. *Annual Review of Psychology, 5,* 281–311.

Lucas, C. M. (1953). Analysis of the relative movement test by a method of individual interviews. *Bureau Naval Personnel Res. Rep.,* Contract Nonr-694 (00), NR 151-13, Educational Testing Service, March 1953.

Macfarlane, J. W. (1942). Problems of validation inherent in projective methods. *American Journal of Orthopsychiatry, 12,* 405–410.

Meehl, P. E. (1945). A simple algebraic development of Horat's suppressor variables. *American Journal of Psychology, 58,* 550–554.

Meehl, P. E. (1954). *Clinical vs. statistical prediction.* Minneapolis: University of Minnesota Press.

Mosier, C. I. (1947). A critical examination of the concepts of face validity. *Educational and Psychological Measurement, 7,* 191–205.

Mosier, C. I. (1951). Problems and designs of cross-validation. *Educational and Psychological Measurement, 11,* 5–12.

Peak, H. (1953). Problems of objective observation. In L. Festinger and D. Katz (Eds.), *Research methods in the behavioral sciences* (pp. 243–300). New York: Dryden Press.

Porteus, S. D. (1950). *The Porteus maze test and intelligence.* Palo Alto: Pacific Books.

Spiker, C. C., & McCandless, B. R. (1954). The concept of intelligence and the philosophy of science. *Psychology Review, 61,* 255–267.

Thurstone, L. L. (1952). The criterion problem in personality research. *Psychometric Laboratory Report,* No. 78. Chicago: University of Chicago.

Do People Know How They Behave? Self-Reported Act Frequencies Compared with On-line Codings by Observers

Samuel D. Gosling, Oliver P. John, Kenneth H. Craik, and Richard W. Robins

Self-reports of personality and behavior are by far the most commonly used method of personality assessment. As we saw in the earlier selection by McAdams, however, other methods are available as well. One particularly interesting possibility is to observe directly the behavior of research participants and record on videotape what they do. The use of such a method immediately raises interesting questions, such as, What is the relationship between behavior as recorded on-line and behavior as reported by the person being observed?

This selection reports data that address this question directly, comparing self-reports of behavior with counts of these same behaviors as recorded off of videotaped interactions. As the data quickly reveal, such a comparison raises issues that go beyond a mere methodological comparison of self-reports and observers' ratings. Some of the discrepancies illustrate interesting psychological processes such as self-enhancement (striving to appear in a more favorable light than is objectively justifiable) and personality traits such as narcissism (the disposition to habitually practice self-enhancement).

Which illustrates a still broader point: Discrepancies between sources of data about personality often are more than merely errors to be explained away. They can be clues to interesting and important psychological processes that deserve research attention.

From *Journal of Personality and Social Psychology*, 74, 1397–1349, 1998.

"You interrupted my mother at least three times this morning" exclaims Roger. "That's not true," responds Julia, "I only interrupted her *once!*" And so the discussion continues. Disagreements about who did and did not do what are commonplace in social interactions. When such disagreements arise, whom should we believe? Perhaps Julia was distorting the truth to paint a favorable picture of herself. Alternatively, Roger may remember that Julia interrupted his mother, when really the conversation was interrupted by a telephone call; or perhaps Julia was so caught up with what she was trying to say that she did not notice that Roger's mother had not finished speaking. When caught in such situations, many of us, convinced that we are right, wish that somehow past events had been recorded on videotape so that we could triumphantly rewind the tape and reveal the veracity of our own reports. Unfortunately, in everyday life, no such video is available.

In the present study, however, we compared individuals' reports of their behavior with observer codings of their behavior from videotapes. Specifically, participants interacted in a 40-min group-discussion task and then reported how frequently they had performed a set of acts. Observers later coded (from videotapes) the frequency with which each participant had performed each act. Thus, this design allowed us to compare retrospective act frequency reports by the self with on-line act frequency codings by observers.[1] Specifically, we examined whether individuals can accurately report how they behaved in a specific situation, and when and why their reports are discrepant from observer codings of their behavior. Understanding the processes that lead to accurate judgments about act performances is fundamental to the study of social perception.

∗   ∗   ∗

The present research examined the following questions. First, to what extent do people agree about how often an act occurred? For example, do Julia's self-reports of her behavior agree with Roger's reports of her behavior, and will Roger agree with other observers about Julia's behavior? Second, what makes an act easy to judge? That is, are there some attributes or properties intrinsic to a given act that influence the degree to which both self and observer agree about its occurrence? Third, do people accurately report what they did in a particular situation? For example, did Julia really interrupt Roger's mother only once? Fourth, are

self-reports of specific acts biased by a motive to self-enhance, and are some individuals more likely to self-enhance than others? For example, does Julia tend to exaggerate her desirable behaviors?

The present research builds on recent investigations of the determinants of agreement and accuracy in personality judgments. For example, John and Robins (1993, 1994) and Kenny (1994) found observer–observer agreement in trait judgments to be consistently higher than self–observer agreement. Furthermore, Funder and Colvin (1988) and John and Robins (1993) found trait properties, such as observability, social desirability, and location within the five-factor model (FFM) of personality structure (John, 1990), to be related to observer–observer and self–observer agreement in trait judgments. Finally, John and Robins (1994) found that self-judgments at the trait level are influenced by self-enhancement bias, which in turn is associated with individual variations in narcissism. Ozer and Buss (1991) have begun to address issues of this kind at the level of act frequency reports. They showed, for example, that agreement between retrospective observer and self act frequency reports is higher for acts associated with Extraversion but lower for acts associated with Agreeableness.

The present study extends this line of inquiry by examining determinants of agreement and accuracy using on-line act reports by observers and retrospective act reports by the self. On-line observer reports warrant study because in aggregated form they represent an important criterion for act occurrence. Retrospective self-reports warrant study because the self is an ever-present monitor of act occurrence and because the self enjoys a distinctive and, in certain respects, privileged vantage point for interpreting the nature of acts as they are performed. At the same time, however, self-reports are vulnerable to self-enhancement and other biases. Below we formulate hypotheses based on self-concept theory and previous research in the act and trait domains.

---

[1] By *on-line codings*, we mean that observers coded and recorded acts as they occurred rather than relying on memory.—Authors

How Well Do People Agree About How Often an Act Occurred?

Two types of agreement can be distinguished: agreement between observers (observer–observer agreement) and agreement between observers and the targets' own self-reports of their behavior (self–observer agreement). Bem (1967, 1972) and other cognitive-informational self-theorists have argued that individuals perceive their own behavior in much the same way as external observers do: the way individuals perceive themselves should, therefore, correspond closely with the way they are perceived by others. This view suggests that self and observer reports of act frequencies should show substantial convergence, especially when the reports concern an interaction situation that is brief and clearly delimited.

In contrast, studies of global trait judgments (Funder & Colvin, 1997; John & Robins, 1993; Kenny, 1994) and evaluations of task performance (John & Robins, 1994) have shown that the self is a unique judge: Self-judgments tend to agree less with observer judgments than observers agree with each other. On the basis of this research, we predicted that self–observer agreement on act frequency reports would be lower than observer–observer agreement (Hypothesis 1).

Do Acts Differ in How Much Individuals Agree About Act Frequencies?

What makes an act easy to judge? To address this question, Ozer and Buss (1991) asked spouses to report how frequently they had performed a set of acts over the previous 3 months. Agreement between spouses varied across acts and depended on a number of properties of the acts. For example, spouses showed relatively high levels of agreement about acts related to Extraversion (e.g., "I danced in front of a crowd") but relatively little agreement about acts related to Agreeableness (e.g., "I let someone cut into the parking space I was waiting for"). The Ozer and Buss study provides insights

into act properties that might moderate interjudge agreement. Several studies have identified properties of traits that influence agreement, including the observability of trait-relevant behaviors, the social desirability of the trait, and the Big Five content domain of the trait judged. If acts are indeed the building blocks of personality, then the properties affecting agreement about traits may also affect agreement about acts, and findings for acts should therefore parallel those for traits.

Thus, drawing on trait research, we made the following predictions about acts. First, we predicted higher observer–observer and self–observer agreement for acts that are easily observed (Funder & Dobroth, 1987; John & Robins, 1993; Kenrick & Stringfield, 1980; Ozer & Buss, 1991) (Hypothesis 2a). Some acts refer to psychological events or processes within the mind of the actor that may not be directly observable (e.g., "I appeared cooperative in order to get my way"), whereas other acts are more easily observed from an external vantage point (e.g., "I sat at the head of the table"). Highly observable acts will be more salient to observers (who focus on visible behaviors) than to the self-perceiver, for whom internal experiences (e.g., intentions and motives) are also available (Funder, 1980). Whereas observable behavior is, in principle, available to both observer and self, less observable aspects of an act (such as intentions) are available primarily to the self and are potentially more salient than observable aspects of the act (Robins & John, 1997b; White & Younger, 1988). Thus, it seems unlikely that all acts can be coded with high reliability by even the most conscientious observers.

Second, we predicted higher agreement for acts that occur frequently (Funder & Colvin, 1991; Ozer & Buss, 1991) (Hypothesis 2b). If an act has a low base rate of occurrence, then observers are more likely to miss it over the course of an interaction. Moreover, on psychometric grounds, low base-rate acts will have less variance across targets, which will tend to reduce correlations between observers. Both observability and base rate involve informational factors that might limit agreement about act performances.

We also expected motivational factors to play a role. In particular, we predicted that agreement would be related to the social desirability of the act (Hypothesis 2c). However, trait research provides conflicting evidence about whether this relation will be linear or curvilinear. That is, Funder and Colvin (1988) and Hayes and Dunning (1997) found a positive linear relation, with higher agreement for more desirable traits. In contrast, the two studies reported by John and Robins (1993) showed a curvilinear relation, with higher agreement for evaluatively neutral traits and lower agreement for evaluatively extreme traits (either highly undesirable or highly desirable). The present study will examine the effects of desirability and evaluativeness on agreement in the act domain.

Fourth, extrapolating from earlier findings, we predicted higher agreement for acts related to Extraversion (Funder & Colvin, 1988; John & Robins, 1993; Kenny, 1994; Norman & Goldberg, 1966; Ozer & Buss, 1991) and lower agreement for acts related to Agreeableness (John & Robins, 1993) (Hypothesis 2d).

How Accurate Are Self-Reports of Act Frequency?

The accuracy of self-perception has been a long-standing concern in psychology (see Robins & John, 1997a, for a review). Many theorists are less than sanguine about the ability of people to perceive their behavior objectively. Hogan (1996), for example, spoke of the "inevitability of human self-deception" (p. 165), and Thorne (1989) observed that "due to self-deception, selective inattention, repression, or whatever one wishes to call lack of self-enlightenment, self-views may be less accurate than outsiders' views" (p. 157).

Assessing the accuracy of self-reports requires a criterion—a measure of "reality" against which self-perceptions can be compared. Given the absence of a single objective standard for evaluating the accuracy of global personality traits, the social consensus (i.e., aggregated trait ratings by others) has often been used as an accuracy criterion (e.g.,

Funder, 1995; Hofstee, 1994; Norman & Goldberg, 1966; Robins & John, 1997a). For example, much research on the accuracy of self-reports has compared self-ratings with judgments provided by peers (John & Robins, 1994; Kolar, Funder, & Colvin, 1996). However, some researchers have been skeptical of reports by such informants and have instead emphasized the need for direct behavioral observation (e.g., Kenny, 1994, p. 136). Hence, the present research focused on observer codings of act frequencies from videotapes in a specific interaction task. These codings provide a more objective measure of the behavioral reality in the task and can therefore serve as a criterion to evaluate accuracy and bias in self-reports of behavior in this task (Funder, 1995; Kenny, 1994; Robins & John, 1997b). We expected self-reported act frequencies to reflect, at least in part, the observed "reality" of participants' behavioral conduct. Thus, we predicted that the self-reports would show levels of accuracy similar to those found in trait research (Hypothesis 3). However, we did not expect the accuracy correlations to be uniformly high, so we also examined the properties of acts that might explain why accuracy is higher for some behaviors than for others.

Are Self-Reports of Act Frequency Biased?

Do individuals overreport socially desirable acts to enhance their self-views? Most self-concept theorists assume that people are motivated to maintain and enhance their feelings of self-worth (e.g., Allport, 1937; Greenwald, 1980; James, 1890; Rogers, 1959; Tesser, 1988). According to Taylor and Brown (1988, 1994) and others, most individuals have "positive illusions" about themselves, presumably stemming from the basic motive toward self-enhancement. Several studies have examined positive illusions by comparing self-reports to observer ratings of global personality traits, such as friendly and outgoing (Campbell & Fehr, 1990; Colvin, Block, & Funder, 1995; Lewinsohn, Mischel, Chaplin, & Barton, 1980). This research on trait ratings shows that, on average, individuals perceive themselves somewhat more positively than they are perceived by others. If these positive illusions extend to perceptions of specific behaviors, then we would also expect individuals to show a self-enhancement bias in their act reports.

* * *

Illusory self-enhancement is sometimes described as if it is present in all normal, psychologically healthy individuals: Taylor (1989) concluded that "normal human thought is marked not by accuracy but by positive self-enhancing illusions" (p. 7); Paulhus and Reid (1991) emphasized that "the healthy person is prone to self-deceptive positivity" (p. 307); and Greenwald and Pratkanis (1984) believed that self-enhancing biases pervade the "self-knowledge of the average normal adult of (at least) North American culture" (p. 139). However, John and Robins (1994) found self-enhancement bias in only 60% of their participants who evaluated their performance in a group discussion task more positively than did a group of independent observers. This finding raises the question of whether some individuals are particularly prone to positive illusions. As noted by John and Robins, the most theoretically relevant construct is narcissism. The *Diagnostic and Statistical Manual of Mental Disorders* (4th ed.; *DSM-IV*) criteria for the narcissistic personality include a grandiose sense of self-importance, a tendency to exaggerate accomplishments and talents, and an expectation to be recognized as "extraordinary" even without appropriate accomplishments (American Psychiatric Association, 1994). Research suggests that narcissistic individuals respond to threats to their self-worth by perceiving themselves more positively than is justified (Gabriel, Critelli, & Ee, 1994; John & Robins, 1994) and by denigrating others (Morf & Rhodewalt, 1993). Narcissists may be particularly prone to positively distorted self-evaluations because their inflated sense of self-importance is easily threatened. Thus, we predicted that narcissistic individuals will show more self-enhancement bias than non-narcissistic individuals in their act frequency self-reports (Hypothesis 4).

Method

PARTICIPANTS Ninety Masters of Business Administration (MBA) students (41 women, 49 men) volunteered to participate in a personality and managerial assessment program. Because of technical problems, the videotapes of 2 participants were unusable; thus, the final N was 88. Their median age was 29 years, and on average they had more than 3 years of postcollege work experience. We collected data from two samples: 54 participants (26 women) in Sample 1 and 36 participants (15 women) in Sample 2.

GROUP DISCUSSION TASK The group discussion task we used is a standardized exercise commonly used to assess managerial performance (e.g., Howard & Bray, 1988; Thornton & Byham, 1982). The task simulates a committee meeting in a large organization. Participants were randomly assigned to mixed-sex groups, with 6 members in each. Participants were told that the purpose of the meeting was to allocate a fixed amount of money to 6 candidates for a merit bonus. Each participant was assigned the role of supervisor of one candidate and was instructed to present a case for that candidate at the meeting; participants were seated at a round table and no leader was assigned. Participants received a realistic written summary of the employment backgrounds of all candidates, including salary, biographical information, and appraisals of prior job performance, and were given 10 min to review this information. They were instructed to start the meeting by each giving a 3- to 5-min presentation on the relative merits of their candidate. The groups had 40 min to reach consensus on how to allocate the merit bonuses. Instructions emphasized two goals: (a) obtain a large bonus for the candidate they represented and (b) help the group achieve a fair overall allocation of the bonus money. Thus, effective performance required behaviors that promoted the achievement of both goals. To permit subsequent coding of act frequencies, the task was videotaped with cameras mounted unobtrusively on the walls and focused on each participant's face and upper body.

SELECTION OF ACTS   We studied a total of 34 acts (20 acts in Sample 1 and 14 acts in Sample 2). * * * We selected 20 acts * * * that seemed likely to occur in our task (e.g., "Target issued orders that got the group organized"). In Sample 2, five psychologists familiar with the group discussion task generated a second set of 14 acts that refer to easily observable behaviors and occur often in this task (e.g., "Target outlined a set of criteria for determining how to allocate the money").

SELF-REPORTS OF ACT FREQUENCY   Immediately after completing the task, participants reported how frequently they had performed each act during the group discussion. The acts were worded in the first person (e.g., "I persuaded the others to accept my opinion on the issue"). * * * We used a 4-point scale referring to the actual frequency of acts performed (0 = *not at all*, 1 = *once*, 2 = *two or three times*, 3 = *more than three times*).

VIDEO-BASED OBSERVER CODINGS OF ACT FREQUENCY   In Sample 1, four observers viewed the videotaped behavior of each participant and coded the frequencies of each of the 20 acts. In Sample 2, a second set of four observers coded the additional 14 acts for each participant. Both sets of observers were students at the same university but unacquainted with the videotaped participants. Acts were worded in the third person (e.g., "Target persuaded the others to accept his/her opinion on the issue"). Before viewing the videotapes, the observers watched four practice videotapes (which were not used in this research) to familiarize themselves with typical behavioral repertoires and the way the acts were manifested in the task.
　　* * * The four observers coded participants' act frequencies with reasonable reliability; across the 34 acts, the average coefficient alpha reliability of the composited ratings was .69 ($SD = .29$).[2]

INDEPENDENT VARIABLES: PROPERTIES OF ACTS   For each of the 34 acts, we measured four properties hypothesized to influence interjudge agreement and accuracy and bias in self-reported act frequencies.

Observability. Two facets of observability were rated by eight judges who were familiar with the group discussion task: *Noticeability* was defined by how well the act stands out from the stream of behavior ($\alpha = .89$), and *high inferential content* was the degree of inference about internal thoughts and motivations required for an observer to be sure that the act has occurred ($\alpha = .96$).[3] * * * We standardized both variables, reverse scored high inferential content, and combined the two ratings into one overall measure of observability. The most observable act was "Target reminded the group of their time limit"; the least observable act was "Target took the opposite point of view just to be contrary."

Social desirability. Using a 9-point scale (Hampson, Goldberg, & John, 1987), the judges also rated how socially desirable it was to perform each act in the group discussion. The mean ratings were used as an index of each act's desirability ($\alpha = .94$). The most desirable act was "Target settled the dispute among other members of the group"; the least desirable act was "Target yelled at someone." Evaluativeness was measured by folding the 9-point scale such that 1 and 9 were recoded as 4, 2 and 8 were recoded as 3, and so on.

Base rate. The base rate of an act was the number of times the act was performed by any participant, on

---

[2]"Reliability" in this context refers to the statistical stability of the averaged observers' ratings. This number is higher to the degree that (a) the different observers agree in their ratings and (b) there is a large number of observers. With four observers being averaged here, a

composite reliability of .69 is good but not excellent. Other reliabilities reported later (e.g., of act properties) were higher, as you will see.

[3]The Greek letter α is a conventional label for the reliability (stability) of a personality scale. A scale is more reliable to the degree that (a) its items correlate with each other and (b) it has more items. Reliability in this sense is a necessary but not sufficient condition for validity.

the basis of the observer codings. This index was computed separately for each observer and then composited; the mean alpha (averaged across the two sets of observers) was .83. The act with the highest base rate was "Target expressed her/his agreement with a point being made by another member of the group"; the act with the lowest base rate was "Target monopolized the conversation." * * *

Big Five personality domain. Acts in the group discussion task tend to be overt behaviors that are either interpersonal (e.g., negotiation and persuasion) or task-oriented (setting goals and organizing group activities; Bass, 1954). In terms of the Big Five personality domains, the interpersonal domains of Extraversion and Agreeableness and the task-focused domain of Conscientiousness were most relevant. In contrast, the other two Big Five domains (Neuroticism, Openness to Experience) refer primarily to an individual's covert experiences. Three expert judges rated the prototypicality of each act for each of the Big Five domains, with low ratings indicating the act was unrelated to that Big Five domain and high ratings indicating the act was highly related to either high or low pole. For example, the Extraversion rating for each act ranged from 0 (*act is unrelated to Extraversion or Introversion*) to 4 (*act is extremely prototypical of Extraversion or Introversion*). The alpha reliabilities of their composite judgments were high for Extraversion (.81), Agreeableness (.86), and Conscientiousness (.88) and somewhat lower for Neuroticism (.67) and Openness to Experience (.62). There were no prototypical examples of the Neuroticism and Openness to Experience domains. All acts had their highest mean prototypicality values on Extraversion, Agreeableness, or Conscientiousness, and therefore only these three Big Five domains will be examined in our analyses. "Target laughed out loud" was the most prototypical act for the Extraversion domain, "Target took the opposite point of view just to be contrary" for (low) Agreeableness, and "Target reminded the group of their time limit" for Conscientiousness. We used these continuous prototypicality ratings in our correlational analyses. * * *

NARCISSISM   We used the 33-item version of the Narcissistic Personality Inventory (NPI; $\alpha = 70$; Raskin & Terry, 1988) to assess participants' level of narcissism. The NPI is the best validated self-report measure of overt narcissism for nonclinical populations (Raskin & Terry, 1988; see also Hendin & Cheek, 1997) and has been shown to predict psychologists' ratings of narcissism (e.g., John & Robins, 1994).

DEPENDENT VARIABLES

Interjudge agreement: Observer–observer and self–observer agreement. To assess how much the observers agreed about the frequency of each act, we computed the correlation (across participants) between each pair of observers' video-based codings. We then averaged the resulting six pairwise observer–observer correlations. This index reflects the average observer–observer agreement for each act.

To assess how much self and observer agreed about the frequency of each act, we computed the correlation (across participants) between the self-reports and video-based codings by each of the four observers. We then averaged the resulting four dyadic self–observer correlations. This index reflects the average agreement between self and a single observer and is therefore directly comparable to the dyadic observer–observer agreement index.

Accuracy and bias in self-reported acts. To assess accuracy and bias, we used the aggregated video-based observer codings as a behavior-based criterion measure of act frequency. Accuracy was defined by the correlation (computed across participants) between self-reports of act frequency and the observer criterion for act frequency. Bias was defined by the discrepancy between each participant's self-report and the observer criterion; positive values indicate that participants overreported how frequently they performed the act, and negative values indicate they underreported how frequently they performed the act. Bias can be computed both at the aggregate level (i.e., do individuals, on average, overreport or underreport some acts more than others?) and at the level of the individual person (i.e., do some persons overreport or underreport an act more than others?). Both accuracy and bias were computed separately for each act.

The dependent variables were computed separately for the acts in each sample. However, because the findings were similar in both samples, analyses across acts used the whole set of 34 acts.

Results and Discussion

DO OBSERVERS AGREE MORE WITH EACH OTHER THAN THEY DO WITH THE SELF? We first tested Hypothesis 1, which predicts that observer–observer agreement would be higher than self–observer agreement. Across the 34 acts, observer–observer agreement ($M = .40$, $SD = .25$) was significantly higher than self–observer agreement ($M = .19$, $SD = .19$), as shown by a t-test for paired samples, $t(33) = 5.2$, $p < .001$, one-tailed.[4] This effect held for 83% of the acts. In short, two observers generally agreed more about an act's frequency than did the self and an observer. * * *

We also found that acts eliciting high levels of observer–observer agreement also tended to elicit high self–observer agreement; the correlation between the two agreement indices across the 34 acts was .65, closely replicating the .64 value reported by John and Robins (1993) for trait ratings. In other words, when two observers agree about an act (or a trait), self and observer are also likely to agree.

WHAT MAKES AN ACT EASY TO JUDGE? EFFECTS OF OBSERVABILITY, SOCIAL DESIRABILITY, BASE RATE, AND BIG FIVE DOMAIN The level of agreement varied substantially across acts, ranging from −.08 to .88 for observer–observer agreement, and

[4]M is the mean and SD is the standard deviation. The p-level reported implies that a difference of the size found would occur less than 1 time in 1,000 if there really is no difference between the two kinds of agreement.

from −.12 to .62 for self–observer agreement. Why are some acts judged more consensually than others? To address this question, we correlated the act properties with observer–observer and self–observer agreement across the 34 acts. These across-act correlation coefficients are given in Table 1. As predicted by Hypotheses 2a, 2b, and 2c, observability, social desirability, and base rate of the acts were all positively and substantially correlated with both observer–observer and self–observer agreement. The observability effect is consistent with Ozer and Buss's (1991) research on acts, as well as with Funder and Dobroth's (1987) and John and Robins's (1993) research on traits. The positive linear relation between social desirability and agreement is consistent with Funder and Dobroth (1987) and Hayes and Dunning (1997). However, we did not find the evaluativeness effect reported by John and Robins, who

TABLE 1		

CORRELATIONS BETWEEN ACT PROPERTIES AND INTERJUDGE AGREEMENT ON ACT FREQUENCY REPORTS (COMPUTED ACROSS THE 34 ACTS)

Act properties	Observer–observer agreement	Self–observer agreement
Observability	.38*	.34*
Base rate	.44*	.35*
Desirability	.52*	.46*
Evaluativeness	−.14	−.06
Prototypicality for Big Five domain		
Extraversion	.08	.32*
Agreeableness	−.27†	−.51*
Conscientiousness	.20	.38*

Note. Numbers in this table are correlations computed across the 34 acts. For example, the correlation of .38 between observability and observer–observer agreement indicates that more observable acts tended to elicit higher levels of agreement than less observable acts. Similarly, the correlation of −.51 between Agreeableness and self–observer agreement indicates that acts from the Agreeableness domain (i.e., prototypical examples of either Agreeableness or Disagreeableness) tended to elicit lower levels of self–observer agreement than acts unrelated to Agreeableness.
†$p < .10$ (marginally significant). *$p < .05$.

	TABLE 2	

THE 12 MOST RELIABLY CODED ACTS ($\alpha > .80$) RANKED BY THEIR SELF-OBSERVER VALIDITY

Act	Big Five domain	Self-observer validity
Told joke to lighten tense moment	E	.72
Made humorous remark	E	.60
Took charge of things at the meeting	E	.57
Laughed out loud	E	.52
Outlined set of steps thought group should follow	C	.45
Pointed out the distinction between a merit bonus and salary increase	C	.45
Reminded group of time limit	C	.41
Said was willing to lower the money recommending for our candidate	A	.32
Expressed agreement with another group member	A	.31
Pointed out possible effects on employee morale	A	.08
Interrupted someone else	A	.07
Suggested they give some money to every candidate	A	.03
M		.40
SD		.26

Note. The act descriptions have been slightly abbreviated. All acts are desirable (i.e., rated above 6 on the 9-point social desirability scale) except "Interrupted someone else," which was undesirable (mean desirability = 2.8), and "Laughed out loud," which was relatively neutral (mean desirability = 5.6). E = Extraversion; A = Agreeableness; C = Conscientiousness.

found that both extremely negative and extremely positive traits elicit lower levels of agreement. In summary, acts that were observable, desirable, and occurred relatively frequently were judged with relatively more agreement than acts that were difficult to observe, undesirable, and relatively infrequent.

Table 2 also shows the correlation between Big Five content domain and interjudge agreement. These correlations are generally consistent with Hypothesis 2d. Self–observer agreement correlated positively with act prototypically for both Extraversion and Conscientiousness and negatively with prototypicality for Agreeableness, indicating that self–observer agreement was higher for acts from the Extraversion and Conscientiousness domains and lower for acts from the Agreeableness domain. The same pattern was found for observer–observer agreement, but the correlations did not reach conventional levels of significance. These findings are generally consistent with previous research in both the act and trait domains. However, there were two differences. First, we did not find the Extraversion

effect for observer–observer agreement found in several previous studies (e.g., John & Robins, 1993; Kenny, 1994). Second, we found a Conscientiousness effect for self–observer agreement that has not been found in previous research.

* * *

HOW ACCURATE ARE SELF-REPORTS OF ACT FREQUENCY? To examine accuracy, we correlated the self-reported act frequencies with the aggregated observer codings. Across all 34 acts, the mean correlation was .24 ($SD = .26$). However, this value underestimates the accuracy of the self-reports because for some acts the video-based observer codings were not highly reliable. Thus, as a fairer test, we considered only those 12 acts that observers coded with high reliability (i.e., those with an alpha above .80). Consistent with Hypothesis 3, the self-reports showed a significant level of accuracy, with a mean correlation of .40 ($SD = .26$; see Table 2).

However, the accuracy correlations varied considerably even within this subset of highly reliable acts, ranging from a high of .72 to a low of .03. Table 2 presents the Big Five classifications of these 12 acts. The 4 acts with the highest accuracy correlations (mean $r = .61$) were all from the Extraversion domain, whereas the 5 acts with the lowest accuracy correlations (mean $r = .16$) were all from the Agreeableness domain; the 3 Conscientiousness acts fell in between, with a mean r of .44.

* * *

INDIVIDUAL DIFFERENCES IN SELF-ENHANCEMENT BIAS * * * Now we turn to the question of whether certain kinds of individuals give biased reports of their behavior. To establish the existence of such individual differences, we examined for each desirable act the percentage of individuals whose self-reported act frequencies were greater than, less than, and the same as the observer codings. Averaging the percentages across the 15 desirable acts, 57% of the participants overreported (i.e., showed self-enhancement bias), 24% underreported (i.e., self-diminishment bias), and 19% were exactly accurate. That is, 43% of the participants failed to show the general self-enhancement effect (Taylor & Brown, 1988). Clearly, then, individuals show substantial differences in self-perception bias, suggesting that the self-enhancement tendency should not be treated as a general law of social behavior (John & Robins, 1994).

To test the prediction that narcissism will predict these individual differences in self-enhancement, we computed a self-enhancement index based on the degree to which participants overreported their desirable acts plus the degree to which they underreported their undesirable acts. Consistent with Hypothesis 4, the NPI correlated .27 ($p < .05$) with this self-enhancement index. Analyses of individual acts revealed that narcissists were particularly inclined to overreport desirable acts such as "I took charge of things at the meeting" and "I made an argument that changed another person's mind." The tendency for narcissistic individuals to exaggerate the frequency with which they performed desirable acts provides further support for the link between narcissism and positive illusions about the self (John & Robins, 1994).

General Discussion

This research addressed a fundamental question about self-perception: Do people know how they acted in a particular situation? We compared individuals' reports of how frequently they performed a set of acts with observer codings of their behavior from videotapes. We found that for some acts there is a clear consensus about how often the act occurred whereas for other acts individuals simply do not agree. We explored several factors that might account for these differences and found that individuals tend to agree about acts that are observable, desirable, frequently occurring, and are from the Extraversion and Conscientiousness (rather than the Agreeableness) domains. We also examined how accurately people report on their behavior and whether their reports are positively biased. We found that individuals' recollections of their behavior showed some correspondence with codings of their behavior, but the degree of correspondence varied systematically across acts. Finally, we found a general tendency toward self-enhancement bias in the act self-reports, but the degree of bias depended on both the individual act and the individual person. Specifically, self-enhancement was greatest for acts that were highly desirable and difficult to observe and for persons who were particularly narcissistic.

What can these findings tell us about the disagreement between Julia and Roger regarding how many times she had interrupted his mother that morning? First, we can expect less agreement between self and other, Julia and Roger, than between Roger and another observer. Second, however, for both Julia and Roger, the amount of agreement will depend on the specific act being monitored; we would expect relatively low agreement because "interrupting another person" is an undesirable and disagreeable act. Third, given that act self-reports are susceptible to self-enhancement bias, we would expect Julia to underestimate how often she had in fact interrupted Roger's mother, especially if she has narcissistic tendencies. In short, our analysis suggests that their disagreement may resist easy resolution.

We now move beyond the rather specific context of Julia and Roger's disagreement and turn to the wider implications of the findings. * * *

COMPARISON OF ACT AND TRAIT RESEARCH ON AGREEMENT AND ACCURACY

* * *

* * * There appear to be both similarities and differences between agreement on acts and agreement on traits. Clearly, an important avenue for future research concerns the psychological roots of these similarities and differences. Such research will need to take into account differences in the way act and trait judgments are made. One might expect judges to agree more about acts than about general personality traits because many acts are directly observable (Buss & Craik, 1980, 1983; Kenny, 1994), whereas traits represent summary impressions of multiple-act occurrences. Thus, trait inferences require first perceiving specific behaviors and then abstracting them into trait ascriptions. On the other hand, agreement may be higher for traits because trait inferences are typically based on a diverse set of relevant behavioral episodes. The broader observational base of traits means that observers are less likely to miss all of the many trait-relevant behaviors than they are to miss a specific performance of a single act. For example, it would be perfectly plausible for some judges to miss an instance of the specific act of "interrupting someone." It is less plausible that a judge will miss all disagreeable behaviors in the situation (including, among others, "interrupting someone," "loudly correcting someone's mistake," and "insisting on having the last word"). The present findings indicate higher observer–observer agreement for acts than for trait ratings by peers, thus suggesting that the greater observability of acts may outweigh the greater breadth of traits in determining agreement among observers.

In addition, act and trait reports may differ because they derive from two different forms of memory. Specific behaviors are encoded in episodic memory whereas representations of traits are encoded in semantic memory (Klein & Loftus, 1993). Consequently, judgments about acts require recall of specific behavioral instances (i.e., episodic memory) and are likely to proceed through a different cognitive process than judgments about traits, which require retrieval of abstract, generalized information about a person (i.e., semantic memory). One implication of this distinction is that self-perception bias may occur either at the initial stage of encoding behavior into episodic memory or at the stage when memories of specific acts are generalized into semantic knowledge as trait representations (e.g., by selectively attending to desirable episodic memories). The present findings imply the former—that act perceptions themselves are biased. Thus, self-judgments about traits may be biased just because self-judgments about acts are biased. Clearly, however, our findings do not exclude the possibility that bias also exists when semantic knowledge about the self is formed. In summary, understanding the processes by which perceptions of act occurrences are translated into trait judgments will help elucidate the factors that cause accuracy and bias in personality impressions.

* * *

IMPLICATIONS FOR ACT-BASED TRAIT ASSESSMENT The present study has some implications for the feasibility and practice of act-based personality assessment using both on-line and retrospective act frequency reports. Our findings for on-line act reports showed levels of interobserver agreement that were reasonably high for the majority of acts, and, indeed, slightly higher than that obtained for trait ratings. These results support the feasibility of this fundamental mode of act-based trait assessment. Furthermore, Borkenau and Ostendorf (1987) studied a situation similar to that used in this research and found substantial accuracy for retrospective observer act reports. Finally, it is important to keep in mind that our findings focus on reports of single acts and do not benefit from aggregation across acts. Thus, reliability and validity of both on-line observer and retrospective self-reports would be substantially higher for the multiple-act indices advocated by the AFA (Cheek, 1982).

However, the present findings suggest some limitations of retrospective self-reports as surrogates for on-line codings of act frequency. Although we found some degree of correspondence between self-reports and aggregated on-line act reports by observers, the more salient finding was the great variability in self–observer agreement across acts. For some acts, self-reports appear to correspond with the on-line observer codings (i.e., Extraversion) but for other acts self-reports do not (i.e., Agreeableness). Furthermore, our results indicate that the operation of self-enhancement bias, previously found for trait ratings, cannot be avoided at the act report level. Finally, unlike observer reports, self-reports of acts have the intrinsic limitation that aggregation across "multiple selves" is not possible (Hofstee, 1994).

* * *

The present findings suggest that some practical challenges remain to be overcome to fully implement the AFA and realize its envisioned theoretical potential. For example, valid retrospective self-reports are difficult to obtain for acts related to Agreeableness, results consistent with those reported by Ozer and Buss (1991). These findings for acts parallel those for trait ratings, thus indicating that the problem may reside not with act monitoring per se but rather with the distinctiveness of self–other perspectives in this behavioral domain. Thus, the implications of these findings pertain not just to AFA assessment methods but more generally to method effects in construct validation (e.g., Ozer, 1989). In particular, researchers should specify what kinds of method effects should be expected given the conceptual definition of the particular trait construct in question.

* * *

In conclusion, a greater understanding of when and why individuals can accurately report what they and others did in a situation should be the goal of further psychological research. Not only can such research inform studies that use observer and self-report methods, but it can also illuminate the processes that underlie disagreements in such domains as romantic relationships, conflict resolution, and negotiation.

References

Allport, G. W. (1937). *Personality: A psychological interpretation.* New York: Holt.

American Psychiatric Association. (1994). *Diagnostic and statistical manual of mental disorders* (4th ed.). Washington, DC: Author.

Bass, B. (1954). The leaderless group discussion. *Psychological Bulletin, 51,* 465–492.

Bem, D. J. (1967). Self-perception: An alternative interpretation of cognitive dissonance phenomena. *Psychological Review, 74,* 183–200.

Bem, D. J. (1972). Self-perception theory. In L. Berkowitz (Ed.), *Advances in experimental social psychology* (Vol. 6, pp. 1–62). New York: Academic Press.

Borkenau, P., & Ostendorf, F. (1987). Retrospective estimates of act frequencies: How accurately do they reflect reality? *Journal of Personality and Social Psychology, 52,* 626–638.

Botwin, M. D., & Buss, D. M. (1989). Structure of act-report data: Is the five-factor model of personality recaptured? *Journal of Personality and Social Psychology, 56,* 988–1001.

Buss, D. M., & Craik, K. H. (1980). The frequency concept of disposition: Dominance and prototypically dominant acts. *Journal of Personality, 48,* 379–392.

Buss, D. M., & Craik, K. H. (1983). The act frequency approach to personality. *Psychological Review, 90,* 105–126.

Campbell, J. D., & Fehr, B. (1990). Self-esteem and perceptions of conveyed impressions: Is negative affectivity associated with greater realism? *Journal of Personality and Social Psychology, 58,* 122–133.

Cheek, J. M. (1982). Aggregation, moderator variables, and the validity of personality tests: A peer rating study. *Journal of Personality and Social Psychology, 43,* 1254–1269.

Colvin, C. R., Block, J., & Funder, D. C. (1995). Overly positive self-evaluations and personality: Negative implications for mental health. *Journal of Personality and Social Psychology, 68,* 1152–1162.

Funder, D. C. (1980). On seeing ourselves as others see us: Self–other agreement and discrepancy in personality ratings. *Journal of Personality, 48,* 473–493.

Funder, D. C. (1995). On the accuracy of personality judgment: A realistic approach. *Psychological Review, 102,* 652–670.

Funder, D. C., & Colvin, C. R. (1988). Friends and strangers: Acquaintanceship, agreement, and the accuracy of personality judgment. *Journal of Personality and Social Psychology, 55,* 149–158.

Funder, D. C., & Colvin, C. R. (1991). Explorations in behavioral consistency: Properties of persons, situations, and behaviors. *Journal of Personality and Social Psychology, 60,* 773–794.

Funder, D. C., & Colvin, C. R. (1997). Congruence of self and others' judgments of personality. In R. Hogan, J. A. Johnson, & S. R. Briggs (Eds.), *Handbook of personality psychology* (pp. 617–647). New York: Academic Press.

Funder, D. C., & Dobroth, K. M. (1987). Differences between traits: Properties associated with interjudge agreement. *Journal of Personality and Social Psychology, 52,* 409–418.

Gabriel, M. T., Critelli, J. W., & Ee, J. S. (1994). Narcissistic illusions in self-evaluations of intelligence and attractiveness. *Journal of Personality, 62,* 143–155.

Greenwald, A. G. (1980). The totalitarian ego: Fabrication and revision of personal history. *American Psychologist, 35,* 603–618.

Greenwald, A. G., & Pratkanis, A. R. (1984). The self. In R. S. Wyer & T. K. Srull (Eds.), *Handbook of social cognition* (Vol. 3, pp. 129–178). Hillsdale, NJ: Erlbraum.

Hampson, S. E., Goldberg, L. R., & John, O. P. (1987). Category-breadth and social-desirability values for 573 personality terms. *European Journal of Personality, 1,* 241– 258.

Hayes, A. F., & Dunning, D. (1997). Construal processes and trait ambiguity: Implications for self–peer agreement in personality judgment. *Journal of Personality and Social Psychology, 72,* 664–677.

Hendin, H. M., & Cheek, J. M. (1997). Assessing hypersensitive narcissism: A reexamination of Murray's Narcissism scale. *Journal of Research in Personality, 31,* 588–599.

Hofstee, W. K. B. (1994). Who should own the definition of personality? *European Journal of Personality, 8,* 149–162.

Hogan, R. (1996). A socioanalytic perspective on the five-factor model. In J. S. Wiggins (Ed.), *The five-factor model of personality: Theoretical perspectives* (pp. 163–179). New York: Guilford Press.

Howard, A., & Bray, D. W. (1988). *Managerial lives in transition: Advancing age and changing times.* New York: Guilford Press.

James, W. (1890). *The principles of psychology.* Cambridge, MA: Harvard University.

John, O. P. (1990). The "Big Five" factor taxonomy: Dimensions of personality in the natural language and in questionnaires. In L. A. Pervin (Ed.), *Handbook of personality: Theory and research* (pp. 66–100). New York: Guilford Press.

John, O. P., & Robins, R. W. (1993). Determinants of interjudge agreement on personality traits: The Big Five domains, observability, evaluativeness, and the unique perspective of the self. *Journal of Personality, 61,* 521–551.

John, O. P., & Robins, R. W. (1994). Accuracy and bias in self-perception: Individual differences in self-enhancement and the role of narcissism. *Journal of Personality and Social Psychology, 66,* 206–219.

Kenny, D. A. (1994). *Interpersonal perception: A social relations analysis.* New York: Guilford Press.

Kenrick, D. T., & Stringfield, D. O. (1980). Personality traits and the eye of the beholder: Crossing some traditional philosophical boundaries in the search for consistency in all of the people. *Psychological Review, 87,* 88–104.

Klein, S. B., & Loftus, J. (1993). The mental representation of trait and autobiographical knowledge about the self. In T. K. Srull & R. S. Wyer, Jr. (Eds.), *Advances in social cognition* (Vol. 5, pp. 1–49). Hillsdale, NJ: Erlbaum.

Kolar, D. W., Funder, D. C., & Colvin, C. R. (1996). Comparing the accuracy of personality judgments by the self and knowledgeable others. *Journal of Personality, 64,* 311–337.

Lewinsohn, P. M., Mischel, W., Chaplin, W., & Barton, R. (1980). Social competence and depression: The role of illusory self-perceptions. *Journal of Abnormal Psychology, 89,* 203–212.

Morf, C. C., & Rhodewalt, F. (1993). Narcissism and self-evaluation maintenance: Explorations in object relations. *Personality and Social Psychology Bulletin, 19,* 668–676.

Norman, W. T., & Goldberg, L. R. (1966). Raters, ratees, and randomness in personality structure. *Journal of Personality and Social Psychology, 4,* 681–691.

Ozer, D. J. (1989). Construct validity in personality assessment. In D. M. Buss & N. Cantor (Eds.), *Personality psychology: Recent trends and emerging directions* (pp. 224–234). New York: Springer-Verlag.

Ozer, D. J., & Buss, D. M. (1991). Two views of behavior: Agreement and disagreement among marital partners. In D. J. Ozer, J. M. Healy, Jr., & A. J. Stewart (Eds.), *Perspectives in personality* (Vol. 3, pp. 91–106). London: Jessica Kingsley.

Paulhus, D. L., & Reid, D. B. (1991). Enhancement and denial in socially desirable responding. *Journal of Personality and Social Psychology, 60,* 307–317.

Raskin, R., & Terry, H. (1988). A principal-components analysis of the Narcissistic Personality Inventory and some further evidence of its construct validity. *Journal of Personality and Social Psychology, 54,* 890–902.

Robins, R. W., & John, O. P. (1997a). The quest for self-insight: Theory and research on accuracy and bias in self-perception. In R. Hogan, J. Johnson, & S. Briggs (Eds.), *Handbook of personality psychology* (pp. 649–679). New York: Academic Press.

Robins, R. W., & John, O. P. (1997b). Self-perception, visual perspective, and narcissism: Is seeing believing? *Psychological Science, 8,* 37–42.

Rogers, C. R. (1959). A theory of therapy, personality, and interpersonal relations, developed in the client-centered framework. In S. Koch (Ed.), *Psychology: A study of a science* (Vol. 3, pp. 185–256). New York: McGraw-Hill.

Taylor, S. E. (1989). *Positive illusions: Creative self-deception and the healthy mind.* New York: Basic Books.

Taylor, S. E., & Brown, J. (1988). Illusion and well-being: A social psychological perspective on mental health. *Psychological Bulletin, 103,* 193–210.

Taylor, S. E., & Brown, J. (1994). Positive illusions and well-being revisited: Separating fact from fiction. *Psychological Bulletin, 116,* 21–27.

Tesser, A. (1988). Toward a self-evaluation maintenance model of social behavior. In L. Berkowitz (Ed.), *Advances in experimental social psychology* (Vol. 21, pp. 181–227). New York: Academic Press.

Thorne, A. (1989). Conditional patterns, transference, and the coherence of personality across time. In D. M. Buss & N. Cantor (Eds.), *Personality psychology: Recent trends and emerging directions* (pp. 149–159). New York: Springer-Verlag.

Thornton, G. C., & Byham, W. C. (1982). *Assessment centers and managerial performance.* San Diego, CA: Academic Press.

White, P. A., & Younger, D. (1988). Differences in the ascription of transient internal states to self and other. *Journal of Experimental Social Psychology, 24,* 292–309.

PART II

The Trait Approach to Personality

People are not all the same. They think differently, feel differently, and act differently. This raises an important question: What is the best way to describe enduring psychological differences among persons? The purpose of the trait approach to personality psychology is to attempt to answer this question. The ordinary language of personality—found in any dictionary—consists of terms like "sociable" and "anxious" and "dominant." The goal of many researchers who follow the trait approach is to transform this everyday language into a scientifically valid technology for describing individual differences in personality that can be used for predicting a person's behavior and, more importantly, for understanding what he or she does and feels.

This section begins with a brief essay about introversion, written by a self-described introvert, which illustrates how a trait can be important for how one affects others, for how one views oneself, and how it can even lead one to feel sorely misunderstood. The second selection is a study that illustrates a classic and highly useful way to study personality: to measure personality in a sample of participants and then measure their behavior, and see how the two relate. In this case, the behavior under investigation is hand-shaking, which indeed turns out to have implications for personality and also for the impression one makes on others.

The third selection begins our consideration of theoretical issues in the study of personality. Gordon Allport, the person widely recognized as the founder of modern personality psychology, describes what he thinks a personality trait is and why traits are important. The fourth selection is an excerpt from a book by Walter Mischel that was widely read as a frontal assault on the very existence of personality. Although Allport anticipated many of Mischel's criticisms, the book had a widespread impact and inspired numerous rebuttals. One of the shortest of these rebuttals is the fifth selection, by Jack Block. This article briefly and elegantly describes the uncertain connection between behavior and personality and the reasons why variability in the first does not necessarily imply inconsistency in the second. The sixth selection, by Douglas Kenrick and David Funder, sums up the lessons learned from the controversy over the existence of personality, which include not just the conclusion that "traits exist," but concern the circumstances under which personality is most likely to be clearly seen.

The seventh selection, by Robert McCrae and Paul Costa Jr., argues that a wide swathe of the personality domain is encompassed by five broad traits (extraversion, openness, agreeableness, and conscientiousness), and they suggest that these traits describe the "basic tendencies" that underlie all of human personality. The eighth and final selection returns us to Allport's original question, "What is a trait of personality?" by describing the "neo-Allportian" approach favored by one of the editors of this volume. The answer is that a trait is a real psychological entity that has broad implications for behavior in a range of situations and also is intuitively understood as important by almost everybody. This is what Allport said; Funder argues it is still true.

CARING FOR YOUR INTROVERT

Jonathan Rauch

The first selection in this section is a not-quite-serious plea from an introvert for greater understanding of his kind. The personality trait the author describes is real, and the research evidence he alludes to really does exist. Introversion is the opposite or low end of the trait of Extraversion (spelled "extroversion" in the article), which is one of the basic, "Big Five" traits of personality, and the description in this article describes several of the characteristics of introverts.

Docs the personality pattern described in this article sound like anyone you know, such as a close friend, relative, or perhaps even yourself? More generally, note how this article contains an implicit argument for the acceptance of individual differences. Introverts, the author claims, are misunderstood and mistreated. Is the same true about other kinds of people?

From *The Atlantic Monthly*, March 2003.

Do you know someone who needs hours alone every day? Who loves quiet conversations about feelings or ideas, and can give a dynamite presentation to a big audience, but seems awkward in groups and maladroit at small talk? Who has to be dragged to parties and then needs the rest of the day to recuperate? Who growls or scowls or grunts or winces when accosted with pleasantries by people who are just trying to be nice?

If so, do you tell this person he is "too serious," or ask if he is okay? Regard him as aloof, arrogant, rude? Redouble your efforts to draw him out?

If you answered yes to these questions, chances are that you have an introvert on your hands—and that you aren't caring for him properly. Science has learned a good deal in recent years about the habits and requirements of introverts. It has even learned, by means of brain scans, that introverts process in-formation differently from other people (I am not making this up). If you are behind the curve on this important matter, be reassured that you are not alone. Introverts may be common, but they are also among the most misunderstood and aggrieved groups in America, possibly the world.

I know. My name is Jonathan, and I am an introvert.

Oh, for years I denied it. After all, I have good social skills. I am not morose or misanthropic. Usually. I am far from shy. I love long conversations that explore intimate thoughts or passionate interests. But at last I have self-identified and come out to my friends and colleagues. In doing so, I have found myself liberated from any number of damaging misconceptions and stereotypes. Now I am here to tell you what you need to know in order to respond sensitively and supportively to your own introverted family members, friends, and colleagues. Remember, someone you know, respect, and interact with every day is an introvert, and you are probably driving this person nuts. It pays to learn the warning signs.

WHAT IS INTROVERSION? In its modern sense, the concept goes back to the 1920s and the psychologist Carl Jung. Today it is a mainstay of personality tests, including the widely used Myers-Briggs Type Indicator. Introverts are not necessarily shy. Shy people are anxious or frightened or self-excoriating in social settings; introverts generally are not. Introverts are also not misanthropic, though some of us do go along with Sartre as far as to say "Hell is other people at breakfast." Rather, introverts are people who find other people tiring.

Extroverts are energized by people, and wilt or fade when alone. They often seem bored by themselves, in both senses of the expression. Leave an extrovert alone for two minutes and he will reach for his cell phone. In contrast, after an hour or two of being socially "on," we introverts need to turn off and recharge. My own formula is roughly two hours alone for every hour of socializing. This isn't antisocial. It isn't a sign of depression. It does not call for medication. For introverts, to be alone with our thoughts is as restorative as sleeping, as nourishing as eating. Our motto: "I'm okay, you're okay—in small doses."

* * *

ARE INTROVERTS MISUNDERSTOOD? Wildly. That, it appears, is our lot in life. "It is very difficult for an extrovert to understand an introvert," write the education experts Jill D. Burruss and Lisa Kaenzig. * * * Extroverts are easy for introverts to understand, because extroverts spend so much of their time working out who they are in voluble, and frequently inescapable, interaction with other people. They are as inscrutable as puppy dogs. But the street does not run both ways. Extroverts have little or no grasp of introversion. They assume that company, especially their own, is always welcome. They cannot imagine why someone would need to be alone; indeed, they often take umbrage at the suggestion. As often as I have tried to explain the

matter to extroverts, I have never sensed that any of them really understood. They listen for a moment and then go back to barking and yipping.

ARE INTROVERTS OPPRESSED? I would have to say so. For one thing, extroverts are overrepresented in politics, a profession in which only the garrulous are really comfortable. Look at George W. Bush. Look at Bill Clinton. They seem to come fully to life only around other people. To think of the few introverts who did rise to the top in politics—Calvin Coolidge, Richard Nixon—is merely to drive home the point. With the possible exception of Ronald Reagan, whose fabled aloofness and privateness were probably signs of a deep introverted streak (many actors, I've read, are introverts, and many introverts, when socializing, feel like actors), introverts are not considered "naturals" in politics.

Extroverts therefore dominate public life. This is a pity. If we introverts ran the world, it would no doubt be a calmer, saner, more peaceful sort of place. As Coolidge is supposed to have said, "Don't you know that four fifths of all our troubles in this life would disappear if we would just sit down and keep still?" (He is also supposed to have said, "If you don't say anything, you won't be called on to repeat it." The only thing a true introvert dislikes more than talking about himself is repeating himself.)

With their endless appetite for talk and attention, extroverts also dominate social life, so they tend to set expectations. In our extrovertist society, being outgoing is considered normal and therefore desirable, a mark of happiness, confidence, leadership. Extroverts are seen as bighearted, vibrant, warm, empathic. "People person" is a compliment. Introverts are described with words like "guarded," "loner," "reserved," "taciturn," "self-contained," "private"—narrow, ungenerous words, words that suggest emotional parsimony and smallness of personality. Female introverts, I suspect, must suffer especially. In certain circles, particularly in the Midwest, a man can still sometimes get away with being what they used to call a strong and silent type; introverted women, lacking that alternative, are even more likely than men to be perceived as timid, withdrawn, haughty.

ARE INTROVERTS ARROGANT? Hardly. I suppose this common misconception has to do with our being more intelligent, more reflective, more independent, more level-headed, more refined, and more sensitive than extroverts. Also, it is probably due to our lack of small talk, a lack that extroverts often mistake for disdain. We tend to think before talking, whereas extroverts tend to think *by* talking, which is why their meetings never last less than six hours. "Introverts," writes a perceptive fellow named Thomas P. Crouser, in an online review of a recent book called *Why Should Extroverts Make All the Money?* (I'm not making *that* up, either), "are driven to distraction by the semi-internal dialogue extroverts tend to conduct. Introverts don't outwardly complain, instead roll their eyes and silently curse the darkness." Just so.

The worst of it is that extroverts have no idea of the torment they put us through. Sometimes, as we gasp for air amid the fog of their 98-percent-content-free talk, we wonder if extroverts even bother to listen to themselves. Still, we endure stoically, because the etiquette books—written, no doubt, by extroverts—regard declining to banter as rude and gaps in conversation as awkward. We can only dream that someday, when our condition is more widely understood, when perhaps an Introverts' Rights movement has blossomed and borne fruit, it will not be impolite to say "I'm an introvert. You are a wonderful person and I like you. But now please shush."

HOW CAN I LET THE INTROVERT IN MY LIFE KNOW THAT I SUPPORT HIM AND RESPECT HIS CHOICE? First, recognize that it's not a choice. It's not a lifestyle. It's an *orientation*.

Second, when you see an introvert lost in thought, don't say "What's the matter?" or "Are you all right?"

Third, don't say anything else, either.

Handshaking, Gender, Personality, and First Impressions

William F. Chaplin, Jeffrey B. Phillips, Jonathan D. Brown, Nancy R. Clanton, and Jennifer L. Stein

One of the oldest and still most interesting approaches to personality is to examine its relations with "expressive" behaviors such as facial expression, tone of voice, and physical movements. In this selection, William Chaplin and his colleagues examine the relationships between personality and the way one shakes hands. This is an interesting choice of behavior, because many people think that they can tell a great deal about a person from his or her handshake, and the evidence in this paper suggests they are not completely wrong. The study also demonstrates that a firm handshake—traditionally well thought of—might be even more important for women than for men.

Many undergraduate students of personality find themselves in the position of needing to come up with a research project for a course or for their degree program. The present study provides a model for the kind of interesting, valuable, yet relatively simple study that might be possible for such a project. Indeed, four of the authors of this study (everyone except Chaplin) was an undergraduate student at the time this study was done. The basic design is simple: Measure a personality trait (e.g., with a self-report inventory), and measure a behavior, in a sample of participants. Then see how the two are related. There is an almost infinite number of possible studies like this that one could do, and nearly all of them would have the potential to yield interesting results.

From *Journal of Personality*, 79, 110–117, 2000.

Handshaking is a common greeting behavior and is often one of the first observations that individuals make of each other upon meeting. Thus, the handshake may be a basis for some of the initial impressions that an individual forms about another. Although handshakes are anecdotally believed to communicate information about a person's personality, little systematic research has been done on the relation between handshaking and personality. Indeed, the extent to which handshaking is sufficiently stable across time and consistent across situations to reflect stable individual differences is largely unknown. Handshaking has also historically been more common among men than it has been among women or between men and women. However, we know little about gender differences in handshaking characteristics or about how gender may be involved in relations between personality, initial impressions, and handshaking. The purpose of the present research is to assess the generalizability of some characteristics of handshaking behavior across time and gender; to test some hypotheses about the relations among handshaking dimensions, personality, and gender; and to evaluate the relation between handshaking dimensions and initial impressions formed about strangers.

Characteristics of Handshaking

Handshakes can differ in a variety of ways. There is an extensive literature on handshaking in books on etiquette (e.g., Post, 1934; Reid, 1955; Vanderbilt, 1957) that refer to a number of dimensions on which handshakes differ, such as limp versus firm, dry versus clammy, or warm versus cold. Accompanying features, such as eye contact and skin texture, are also mentioned. Within the scientific literature, the only serious mention of handshaking characteristics can be found in the classic work by Allport and Vernon (1933, p. 34) on expressive movements, in which the authors briefly discuss individual differences in the dimensions of strength, duration, vigor, and grip, as well as differences in how the hand is offered.

Handshaking has historically been viewed as a male activity. Although probably apocryphal, legends about handshaking imply that the custom originated to provide a signal between male combatants that they would be nonaggressive (Eichler, 1937). Regardless of the accuracy of these legends, books on etiquette have clearly emphasized a gender difference in handshaking (e.g., Vanderbilt, 1957), in which men are expected to shake hands more frequently than women (Post, 1934).

Handshaking and Personality

There is a widespread belief that an individual's handshake reveals much about that person's personality. Vanderbilt (1957) suggested the trait-like properties of a handshake and its relation to personality: "A handshake is as much a part of personality as the way we walk, and although we may modify and improve a poor handshake if someone calls our attention to it, it will still usually be just like us, assured or timid, warm or cool" (p. 185). The predictions about the relation between handshaking characteristics and personality traits made by experts on the etiquette of handshaking have a compelling face validity. However, there has been little systematic empirical study of the handshaking-personality relation. Thus, the validity of these conjectures is largely unknown. * * *

* * *

Regardless of any empirical support for a relation between handshaking and personality, it is generally believed that the handshake is an important component of the first impression that one forms of a person. This belief is evidenced in the large number of professional and business training seminars (e.g., Leadership Skills Inc., http://www.etiquette42day.com; Protocol School of Palm Beach, http://www.psopb.com; Polished Professionals, http://www.polishedprofessionals.com) that advertise proper handshaking as a component in their curriculum. However, empirical studies of the relation between handshaking characteristics and the initial impression or evaluation of a person are lacking.

In many circumstances a handshake provides an initial, standardized behavior sample from a person one is meeting for the first time. Moreover, nearly everyone will have an extensive set of handshake observations in their memory against which new handshakes can be compared and evaluated. Thus, it is reasonable to expect that a handshake might have an impact on the first impression one forms of an individual's personality. * * *

The Present Study

* * * We selected eight characteristics of handshaking that were frequently mentioned or implied by the existing literature. These characteristics were dryness, temperature, texture (to differentiate the

cold, clammy handshake from the warm, dry one; Vanderbilt, 1957), strength, vigor, completeness of grip, duration (to differentiate the firm handshake from the boneless, limp one; Reid, 1955), and eye contact.

* * * We selected nine personality dimensions to assess in our study. The view that good handshakes communicate sociability, friendliness, and dominance, whereas poor handshakes communicate social introversion, shyness, and neuroticism led us to select the Big Five Factors of Extraversion, Agreeableness, Neuroticism, and Openness to Experience as possible correlates of handshaking. We also included Conscientiousness to complete a broad representation of personality in our study. We supplemented the Big Five with an assessment of Shyness (Cheek & Buss, 1981), Emotional Expressiveness (Friedman, Prince, Riggio, & DiMatteo, 1980), and Positive and Negative Affect (Watson, Clark, & Tellegen, 1988).

One of the major goals of this study is to assess the consistency of an individual's handshake. Although Astroem et al. (1993) reported some reliability in the assessment of handshaking dimensions, his studies did not include a systematic assessment of handshakes across time or situations. Although the situation in the present study is limited to strangers participating in an experiment, we systematically assess the generalizability of handshakes across a 2 (times: greeting the participant and thanking the participant at the end of the experiment) x 2 (gender: male and female handshake coders) x 2 (individual coders within each gender) design. Thus each participant's handshake is rated a total of eight times during the entire study.

A second goal of the study is to describe any gender differences in the characteristics of handshakes. We expected that women's handshakes would be less strong, less vigorous, have a less complete grip, and be of shorter duration then men's handshakes. We expected the texture of men's handshakes to be rougher than women's but on the basis of the general literature about eye contact (e.g., Argyle & Dean, 1965), we expected women to have more eye contact than men. We did not

expect any gender differences on dryness or temperature.

A third goal of this study is to assess the relation between personality characteristics and handshaking characteristics. We intend to assess these relations in general, but on the basis of Astroem's (1994) finding that some of the relations between handshaking characteristics and personality differed for men and women, we will also consider the moderating effect of gender on these relations. In addition, because the handshake coders were aware of the participants' gender while evaluating the handshakes, we will also assess the relation between handshaking and personality after statistically controlling for gender. The purpose of this analysis is to assess the extent to which any handshake-personality relations might be a spurious function of the influence of gender on the coder's ratings of the handshakes and the relation between gender and some of the personality variables.

Our final goal is to assess the relation between a person's handshaking characteristics and the initial impression that person makes on others. * * * Because of the influence of general factors, such as evaluation, on ratings of strangers (e.g., Paunonen, 1991), we recognize that the ratings of the coders on the different personality dimensions may not be highly differentiated. We will thus consider combining the ratings on different dimensions into more general composites reflecting an overall positive or negative impression of the participant. We expect that handshakes that are stronger, longer lasting, warmer, drier, more vigorous, with a more complete grip and more eye contact will result in a more favorable impression. We will again consider the moderating and possible confounding role of gender in these evaluations.

Method

PARTICIPANTS

One hundred twelve (48 men and 64 women) college undergraduates were offered course credit to participate in this study.

RATERS

Four advanced psychology undergraduates (2 men and 2 women) served as experimenters and were trained as handshake coders in this study. The coders are the last four authors of this article. Thus, they were not blind to the general hypotheses about the relation between personality and handshaking characteristics. However, the focus of the coder's work until the study was completed was on developing agreement about the coding of the characteristics of the handshakes and on conducting the research. * * *

MEASURES

Handshake ratings. The raters assessed the eight handshake characteristics on 5-point rating scales as follows: completeness of grip (1 = *very incomplete*, 5 = *full*), temperature (1 = *cold*, 5 = *warm*), dryness (1 = *damp*, 5 = *dry*), strength (1 = *weak*, 5 = *strong*), duration (1 = *brief*, 5 = *long*), vigor (1 = *low*, 5 = *high*), texture (1 = *soft*, 5 = *rough*), eye contact (1 = *none*, 5 = *direct*).

Personality ratings. The handshake coders made global ratings on a 5-point scale of each participant's personality on eight dimensions. Five of the dimensions represented the Big Five (Extraversion, Agreeableness, Conscientiousness, Neuroticism, and Openness to Experience). One dimension concerned General Affect, ranging from 1 (*negative*) to 5 (*positive*). Another dimension concerned Shyness and a final dimension concerned Emotional Expressiveness, ranging from 1 (*not skilled*) to 5 (*skilled*).

Big Five Inventory-44 (BFI-44). The BFI-44 (Benet-Martínez & John, 1998) is a 44-item, self-report inventory designed to assess the Big Five Factors of personality. Eight items assess Extraversion, 9 items assess Agreeableness, 9 items assess Conscientiousness, 8 items assess Neuroticism, and 10 items assess Openness to Experience.

Positive and Negative Affect Scales (PANAS). The PANAS (Watson, Clark, & Tellegen, 1988) consists of 20 adjectives that are rated on a 5-point scale, ranging from 1 (*very slightly or not at all*) to 5 (*extremely*), concerning how a person feels. Various time frames can be used for the ratings. In this study, we asked participants to rate how they "generally feel." Ten of the items concern Positive Affect and 10 concern Negative Affect. The two scales are relatively independent.

Revised Cheek and Buss Shyness Scale (RCBS). The RCBS is a 13-item scale that assesses Shyness (Cheek & Briggs, 1990). It is a revision of the original 9-item Cheek and Buss Shyness Scale (Cheek & Buss, 1981).

Affective Communication Test (ACT). This is a 13-item scale developed by Friedman, Prince, Riggio, and DiMatteo (1980) to assess nonverbal Emotional Expressiveness.

RATER TRAINING

Before the study began the four raters received 1 month of training and practice in shaking hands and evaluating the handshakes. In the initial training sessions the raters practiced offering their hand in a neutral way to initiate a handshake. * * *

The next phase of training was understanding the eight handshaking dimensions included in the study and attaining agreement about those dimensions on handshakes that varied on the dimensions. Definitions of the dimensions were provided and extreme examples of each dimension were illustrated using a handshake. Individuals were then recruited to shake hands with the raters, with the instructions to try to shake hands in the same way with all four coders. Coders then rated the practice handshakes on all eight dimensions, and discrepancies in the ratings were discussed.

* * *

PROCEDURE

Participants were recruited from introductory psychology classes for a study entitled "Personality Questionnaires." They obtained one of three required experimental credits for participating. The participants were scheduled in groups of four and were initially asked to come to a room in which they waited until all 4 participants arrived. When the participants arrived, they were greeted by an experimenter and given a sheet of paper on which the following description of the experiment appeared:

> Explanation of the Personality Questionnaires
> Experiment
> (Separate Condition)
>
> One common method for assessing personality, attitudes, and beliefs is to ask people to describe their thoughts, behaviors, and feelings on questionnaires. Often a large number of questionnaires are administered together in a single packet. A possible problem with this method is that how a person answers questions on one questionnaire may be affected by their answers to other questionnaires. The purpose of this study is to try to find out if people tend to answer questionnaires differently depending upon whether the questionnaires are given together in the same packet or administered separately. You are participating in the condition where the questionnaires are administered separately.
>
> In this condition we will ask you to complete four brief personality questionnaires. Each questionnaire will be administered by a separate experimenter in a separate room. To emphasize the separateness, each experimenter will greet you as though you were coming to them for an individual experiment. So, they will introduce themselves, shake your hand, ask your name, and ask you to come into the room where you will be given one questionaire. This will happen four times during the experiment. * * *

The purpose of this description was to provide a cover story for why the participants would be administered four brief questionnaires by four separate experimenters and why so much handshaking would occur. The experimenter asked if the participants had any questions, reemphasizing that the participants should think of their experience as four separate experiments and that they would be formally greeted with and dismissed with handshakes and other formalities by the experimenters "to reinforce the participants' experience of separateness."

The participants then went to the experimental room, which consisted of a large central room and smaller rooms along its sides. Each of the four experimenters was standing next to one of the smaller rooms, and the participants were directed to the experimenter who matched the first letter on the list they had been given. Each experimenter greeted a participant by shaking his or her hand and then asked the participant to come into the smaller room, sit down at a desk, and complete one of the four personality questionnaires. During this time, the experimenters rated the participant's handshake on the eight dimensions and also rated their impressions of the participant's personality on the eight global rating scales. When a participant had finished completing the first questionnaire, he or she was thanked by the experimenter, who again shook the participant's hand and asked the participant to go back into the large room, have a seat, and wait for all the participants to finish. The experimenter then rated the second handshake on the eight handshake scales.

After all the participants finished the first questionnaire, they were sent to the second experimenter on the list. The process was repeated until each participant had shaken hands twice with all four experimenters and completed all four questionnaires. Different experimenters administered different questionnaires across the experimental sessions. * * *

Results

GENERALIZABILITY OF THE HANDSHAKE RATINGS

The eight ratings on each handshake dimension represent a 2 (time: 2 occasions) $\times$ 2 (gender: male or female coder) $\times$ 2 (individual coder: 2 of each gender) generalizability design. Table 1 presents the generalizability coefficients (coefficient alpha) for the eight scales across the eight ratings. The means and standard deviations for the eight ratings are also presented. As indicated in Table 1, the handshake ratings were generally consistent across time, gender, and individual coders.

TABLE 1

GENERALIZABILITY COEFFICIENTS, MEANS, AND
STANDARD DEVIATIONS FOR THE EIGHT HANDSHAKE
RATING DIMENSIONS

Dimension	M	SD	Coefficient alpha
Strength	3.10	1.40	.91
Grip	3.84	1.16	.88
Dryness	3.30	1.19	.87
Temperature	3.86	1.01	.83
Vigor	1.91	0.89	.81
Duration	2.21	0.88	.77
Eye contact	4.35	0.72	.77
Texture	2.30	0.78	.70

Note. N = 112. The values are computed across the eight ratings, 2 (time periods) × 2 (gender) × 2 (coders within each gender). Ratings were made on a 5-point scale. Dimensions are ordered by the size of coefficient alpha.

CORRELATIONS AMONG THE HANDSHAKING DIMENSIONS

Table 2 shows the correlations among the average of the eight ratings for the eight handshaking dimensions. As can be seen in Table 2, there are substantial correlations among some of the dimensions. In particular, the dimensions of duration, eye contact, completeness of grip, strength, and vigor are positively correlated. We created a composite variable by averaging the ratings of the five variables and will refer to this variable as the Firm Handshake Composite. Coefficient alpha for this composite is .88. The remainder of the analyses reported here will be based on this composite. * * *

GENDER DIFFERENCES IN HANDSHAKING

To assess gender differences in handshaking we considered the gender of the participant, the gender of the coder, and their interaction in a 2 × 2 mixed analysis of variance.[1] The two levels of coder ratings

were the average of the four ratings made by the two female coders and the average of the four ratings made by the two male coders on the Firm Handshake Composite. We found a main effect for participant gender, $F(1, 110) = 43.2$, $MSE = 0.95$, $r = .53$, and a main effect for coder gender, $F(1, 110) = 21.5$, $MSE = 0.26$, but no interaction.[2] Male participants had a higher score on the Firm Handshake Composite ($M = 3.50$, $SD = 0.67$) than female participants ($M = 2.60$, $SD = 0.70$).[3] Likewise, the male coders had a more positive impression of the handshakes they received ($M = 3.10$, $SD = 1.00$) than did the female coders ($M = 2.80$, $SD = 0.76$). However, the male and female coders still exhibited substantial agreement in their composite ratings. The correlation between the composite based on the female coders and the composite based on the male coders is .69.

HANDSHAKING AND PERSONALITY

Correlations between the personality scales and the handshaking dimensions. Table 3 presents the simple correlations between the personality scales and the Firm Handshake Composite. These correlations suggest that individuals whose handshakes are firmer (i.e., have a more complete grip, are stronger, more vigorous, longer in duration, and associated with more eye contact) are more extraverted and open to experience and are less neurotic and shy.

The effect of controlling for gender on the handshaking-personality relation. We also assessed whether the asso-

---

[1] A 2 × 2 analysis of variance is a commonly used statistical technique for assessing the significance of the effect of two variables, in this case gender of participant and

coder, and their interaction. The results described in this paragraph indicate that male participants had firmer handshakes than did female participants, and male coders made more positive ratings of handshakes than did female coders.

[2] F is the statistic from an analysis of variance that, along with the degrees of freedom (1 and 110 in this case), tells you the significance of the mean difference. MSE stands for mean squared error, a measure of the overall variability of the scores, and r is the same effect-size measure considered in Rosenthal and Rubin's chapter in Part I of this book.

[3] M stands for "mean" or average, and SD is the standard deviation.

TABLE 2

CORRELATIONS AMONG THE AGGREGATE HANDSHAKE RATINGS

Dimension	1	2	3	4	5	6	7	8
1. Duration	—							
2. Eye contact	.39	—						
3. Grip	.60	.57	—					
4. Strength	.84	.48	.80	—				
5. Vigor	.79	.32	.51	.76	—			
6. Texture	.35	.06	.32	.39	.22	—		
7. Temperature	.24	.26	.33	.37	.27	.22	—	
8. Dryness	−.18	.10	−.03	−.18	−.18	.32	.01	—

Note. $N = 112$. Correlations larger than .19 are significant at the .05 level, two-tailed test.

ciations between the Firm Handshake Composite and personality could be attributed to the mutual influence of gender on both variables. Thus, we calculated the partial correlations between the Firm Handshake Composite and personality after controlling for gender. Interestingly, the partial correlation between the Firm Handshake Composite and Extraversion is larger (.31 vs. .19) after gender was controlled for. This was also true for Emotional Expression (.31 vs. .16) and for Shyness (−.35 vs. −.29). The relation between Neuroticism and the Firm Handshake Composite was reduced after partialling out gender (−.12 vs. −.24). For Openness to Experience, the relation was essentially unchanged (.19 vs. .20).

The moderating effect of participant gender on the personality-handshaking relation. We also considered the possibility that the relation between personality and handshaking characteristics would be different for men and women. We evaluated the moderating effect of gender on the personality-handshaking relation by using hierarchical regression analysis to assess the contribution of the partialled product of Gender × Firm Handshake (with gender and firm handshake controlled) to predicting each of the nine personality variables.[4]

We found a significant moderating effect of gender on the relation between the Firm Handshake Composite and Openness to Experience (semi-partial correlation = .18), $t(108) = 2.18$, $p = .031$. A plot of the regression line for predicting Openness to Experience from the Firm Handshake Composite separately for men and women indicated that women who had a firmer handshake were more open to experience (regression coefficient = .32). For men, there was little relation between their handshake and how open they were (regression coefficient = −.06.

TABLE 3

CORRELATIONS BETWEEN THE FIRM HANDSHAKE COMPOSITE AND THE PERSONALITY SCALES

Personality Scale	Firm Handshake Composite
Shyness	−.29
Neuroticism	−.24
Openness	.20
Extraversion	.19
Emotional Expression	.16
Positive Affect	.14
Negative Affect	−.09
Conscientiousness	−.08
Agreeableness	−.06

Note. $N = 112$. Correlations larger than .19 are significant at the .05 level, two-tailed test. Dimensions are ordered by the magnitude of their correlation with the Firm Handshake Composite.

---

[4]Hierarchical regression analysis is a statistical technique that is designed to separate out the effects of interrelated variables. In this case it is being used to see whether the results depend on the gender of the handshaker (they do, to some extent).

Handshaking and First Impressions

In addition to rating the handshaking characteristics of the participants, the coders also rated each participant's personality on eight dimensions that corresponded to the personality scales the participant had completed. The coders exhibited a reasonable degree of consistency in their personality ratings across the 112 participants (coefficient alphas ranged from .37 to .65 * * *). Thus, we aggregated the ratings across the four coders. However, we found that the aggregate of the coders' personality ratings on the eight scales were substantially correlated (all correlations were positive and ranged from .21 to .92). As we expected, the coders, who did not know the participants, appear to have based their ratings on a general impression factor, such as evaluation. If a participant made a good impression, the participant tended to be rated higher on extraversion, conscientiousness, agreeableness, emotional stability, openness, emotional expression, outgoingness (the opposite of shyness), and positive affect. A poor impression tended to elicit lower evaluation on these dimensions. Thus, we elected to form a composite of the eight personality ratings (after reverse scoring the Shyness scale), which we named the First Impression Composite Coefficient alpha for this First Impression Composite across the eight personality scales was .92.

This composite is essentially uncorrelated with participant gender ($r = .05$). However, it was correlated with several of the self-report personality scales; specifically, Extraversion ($r = .35$), Emotional Expressiveness ($r = .37$) and Shyness ($r = -.36$). Interestingly, we also found that there was an interaction between gender and Openness for predicting the First Impression Composite. * * * To interpret this interaction we examined the relation between Openness and First Impression separately for men and women. For women, Openness is positively related to First Impression (regression coefficient = .26), $t(62) = 1.82$, $p = .07$, whereas for men Openness is negatively related to First Impression, although this relation is weaker (regression coefficient = −.22), $t(46) = −1.30$, $p = .20$. Thus, women who are more open make a more favorable

impression, whereas more open men make a slightly poorer impression. The correlation between the First Impression Composite and the Firm Handshake Composite is .56. This relation is consistent across the total sample and for male and female participants considered separately. It is also consistent across the male and female coders.

Discussion

Summary and Interpretation of the Results

We found that an individual's handshake is stable across time and consistent across gender. We also found that five of the eight handshaking characteristics that we studied covaried. These five characteristics (strength, vigor, duration, eye contact, and completeness of grip) represent what the literature on handshaking etiquette refers to as a firm handshake, and we focused our analyses on this composite. We found that men's and women's handshakes differ on most of the dimensions we studied and on the Firm Handshake Composite. Specifically, the male participants' handshakes were generally viewed as firmer.

A person's handshake is related to some aspects of his or her personality. Specifically, an individual with a firm handshake is more extraverted and open to experience and less neurotic and shy. We find these correlations persuasive, because the source of data for the handshakes (trained coders) is independent of the source of data for the personality variables (multi-item, self-report scales). We were concerned that the relation of gender to handshaking and to personality might be the basis for these results. However, when we partialed gender for these correlations,[5] the partial correlations between a firm handshake and extraversion, shyness, and emotional expressiveness were larger than the simple correlations. This suggests that those aspects of handshaking that are related to gender are not the basis for handshaking's relation to these personality variables. Indeed, for extraver-

---

[5] "Partialling" gender for these correlations means statistically removing the effect of gender.

sion, shyness, and emotional expressiveness, gender operates to suppress some of the handshaking variance that is unrelated to these characteristics.

Only the relation between neuroticism and handshaking can be partially explained by a mutual association with gender. Finally, we also found that the general relation between Openness and a firm handshake is complicated by a moderating effect of gender. Specifically, it was only for the women participants that Openness is related to a firm handshake; women who are more open to experience have a firmer handshake than women who are less open.

Regardless of the accuracy of the impressions formed about individuals on the basis of their handshake, the literature on handshaking etiquette and business protocol strongly suggests that a handshake has a substantial impact on how people evaluate others. We were somewhat disappointed, although perhaps not surprised, that our coders did not differentiate among the eight personality characteristics they rated. Instead these ratings seem to be influenced by the general first impression the coders formed of the participants, who were strangers to the coders. This general impression factor precluded us from exploring the accuracy of the coder's impressions at predicting the personality measures. Instead, we formed a First Impression Composite and restricted our analyses of the relation between handshaking and personality inferences to this composite. Consistent with the etiquette and business literature, we found a substantial relation between the features that characterize a firm handshake and the coder's first impression. We did not, however, find any substantial gender differences in the impressions formed by the coders and the handshake characteristics.

All of these interpretations must be made in light of the limitations of this study. We view the major limitation as the restricted situation in which we assessed the handshakes. Specifically, the handshaking occurred between strangers in a situation in which the interaction between the individuals was brief and somewhat formal. That is, the coders and participants greeted each other in a context in which there was no expectation that

their interaction was the beginning of a long association. Thus, the participants were unlikely to be invested in making a good impression and the handshakes and greetings were probably more perfunctory than would be the case in more committed interactions. We believe that the main result of this limitation is to attenuate the variance on some of the handshaking characteristics. Thus, any of our null results might be a function of the lack of variability in the handshakes. Despite this limitation, we did find a number of effects. Also, although our experimental situation was limited, it is not an uncommon situation in which handshaking occurs and in which impressions are formed.

IMPLICATIONS

* * *

We found that women who are more liberal, intellectual, and open to new experiences have a firmer handshake and make a more favorable impression than women who are less open and have a less firm handshake. For men, the relations among these variables are substantially weaker, but in the opposite direction: More open men have a slightly less firm handshake and make a somewhat poorer impression than less open men. The differential relation between openness and favorable impressions for men and women is, in this study, almost completely mediated or "explained" by the nature of the person's handshake. We emphasize that these findings were not expected and are in need of replication (Kerr, 1998). However, the size of the effects in this set of mediational analyses are, bluntly speaking, huge. Thus, we are cautiously optimistic about their replication.

We think that the implications of these analyses for self-promotion strategies used by women may be important. Women have historically been at a disadvantage relative to men when competing for jobs (Broverman, Vogel, Broverman, Clarkson, & Rosenkrantz, 1972). Glick, Zion, and Nelson (1998) argued that to remove this historical disadvantage women need to overcome the general impression that they are less competent or qualified. However, overcoming this impression has costs for women, because behaving assertively and confidently often results in a more negative impression for a woman relative to an assertive and confident man (e.g., Butler & Geis, 1990; Eagly, Makhijani, & Klonsky, 1992). Our results provide one instance in which women who exhibit a behavior (a firm handshake) that is more common for men and that is related to confidence and assertiveness are evaluated more positively than are women who exhibit a more typical feminine handshake. More important, the predicted favorable impression score for women who are 1 standard deviation above the mean on the firmness of their handshake is 3.61 (on a 5-point scale), whereas men who are 1 standard deviation above the mean on firmness are predicted to score 3.45 on impression. This result differs from the typical finding that women who exhibit confident behavior that is similar to the behavior of men often make a more negative impression than the men.

Of course, this finding is limited to situations in which a handshake is given and probably also to situations in which the focus is on the person's handshake, as in the present study. But this situation is similar to the real-world situations of business contacts, employment, and school interviews. In these situations, giving a firm handshake may provide an effective initial form of self-promotion for women that does not have the costs associated with other less subtle forms of assertive self-promotion.

Conclusion

It would be something of an overstatement to claim that a person's handshake provides a window to his or her soul. However, we did find that handshakes are stable and consistent across time and gender, at least within the limitations of this study. Also, handshaking characteristics are related to both objective personality measures and the impressions people form about each other. Given what we know about the potency of first impressions, it might be a good idea to heed the recommendations of experts on handshaking etiquette and try to make that first handshake a firm one.

References

Allport, G. W., & Vernon, P. E. (1933). *Studies in expressive movement.* New York: Macmillan.

Argyle, M., & Dean, J. (1965). Eye contact, distance, and affiliation. *Sociometry, 28,* 289–304.

Astroem, J. (1994). Introductory greeting behavior: A laboratory investigation of approaching and closing salutation phases. *Perceptual and Motor Skills, 79,* 863–897.

Astroem, J., Thorell, L., Holmlund, U., & d'Elia, G. (1993). Handshaking, personality, and psychopathology in psychiatric patients: A reliability and correlational study. *Perceptual and Motor Skills, 77,* 1171–1186.

Benet-Martínez, V., & John, O. P. (1998). *Los Cincos Grandes* across cultures and ethnic groups: Multitrait multimethod analyses of the Big Five in Spanish and English. *Journal of Personality and Social Psychology, 75,* 729–750.

Broverman, I. K., Vogel, R. S., Broverman, D. M., Clarkson, T. E., & Rosenkrantz, P. S. (1972). Sex-role stereotypes: A current appraisal. *Journal of Social Issues, 28,* 59–78.

Butler, D., & Geis, F. L. (1990). Nonverbal affect responses to male and female leaders: Implications for leadership evaluations. *Journal of Personality and Social Psychology, 58,* 48–59.

Cheek, J. M., & Briggs, S. R. (1990). Shyness as a personality trait. In W. R. Crozier (Ed.), *Shyness and embarrassment: Perspectives from social psychology* (pp. 315–337). Cambridge, England: Cambridge University Press.

Cheek, J. M., & Buss, A. H. (1981). Shyness and sociability. *Journal of Personality and Social Psychology, 41,* 330–339.

Eagly, A. H., Makhijani, M. G., & Klonsky, B. G. (1992). Gender and the evaluation of leaders: A meta-analysis. *Psychological Bulletin, 111,* 3–22.

Eichler, L. (1937). *The new book of etiquette.* Garden City, NY: Garden City Publishing.

Friedman, H. S., Prince, L. M., Riggio, R. E., & DiMatteo, M. R. (1980). Understanding and assessing nonverbal expressiveness: The Affective Communication Test. *Journal of Personality and Social Psychology, 39,* 333–351.

Glick, P., Zion, C., & Nelson, C. (1988). What mediates sex discrimination in hiring decisions? *Journal of Personality and Social Psychology, 55,* 178–186.

Kerr, N. L. (1998). HARKing: Hypothesizing after the results are known. *Personality and Social Psychology Review, 2,* 196–217.

Paunonen, S. V. (1991). On the accuracy of ratings of personality by strangers. *Journal of Personality and Social Psychology, 61,* 471–477.

Post, E. (1934). *Etiquette: The blue book of social usage.* New York: Funk & Wagnalls.

Reid, L. N. (1955). *Personality and etiquette.* Boston: Heath.

Vanderbilt, A. (1957). *Amy Vanderbilt's complete book of etiquette.* Garden City, NY: Doubleday.

Watson, D., Clark, L. A., & Tellegen, A. (1988). Development and validation of brief measures of positive and negative affect: The PANAS scales. *Journal of Personality and Social Psychology, 54,* 1063–1070.

WHAT IS A TRAIT OF PERSONALITY?

Gordon W. Allport

The next selection begins our consideration of personality theory, with a classic statement by the original and still perhaps most important trait theorist. What Sigmund Freud is to psychoanalysis, Gordon Allport is—almost—to trait psychology.

In this selection, Allport offers one of the earliest—and still one of the best—psychological definitions of a personality trait. This article was written for a conference held in 1929, when the modern field of personality psychology was just beginning to be formed. Allport's fundamental contribution, in efforts like this paper, was to take the study of normal variations in personality out of the exclusive hands of novelists, dramatists, theologians, and philosophers and to begin to transform it into a scientific discipline.

Especially considering how old this article is, it is remarkable to observe how many modern issues it anticipates, and how cogently it addresses them. These issues include the person-situation debate (see the upcoming selection by Mischel), the issue of whether a trait is a cause or just a summary of behavior (Allport says it is a cause), and the distinction between focusing on how traits are structured within a single individual (now called the "idiographic approach") and focusing on how traits distinguish between people (now called the "nomothetic approach"). Almost 70 years after it was written, this article still has much to say to the modern field of personality psychology.

From *Journal of Abnormal and Social Psychology*, 25, 368–372, 1931.

At the heart of all investigation of personality lies the puzzling problem of the nature of the unit or element which is the carrier of the distinctive behavior of a man. *Reflexes* and *habits* are too specific in reference, and connote constancy rather than consistency in behavior; *attitudes* are ill defined, and as employed by various writers refer to determining tendencies that range in inclusiveness from the *Aufgabe* to the *Weltan-schauung;*[1] *dispositions* and *tendencies* are even less definitive. But *traits*, although appropriated by all manner of writers for all manner of purposes, may still be salvaged, I think, and limited in their refer-

[1]With these German words, Allport is describing the range from the specific tasks an individual must perform (*Aufgabe*) to his or her entire view of the world (*Weltanschauung*).

ence to a certain definite conception of a generalized response-unit in which resides the distinctive quality of behavior that reflects personality. Foes as well as friends of the doctrine of traits will gain from a more consistent use of the term.

The doctrine itself has never been explicitly stated. It is my purpose with the aid of eight criteria to define *trait*, and to state the logic and some of the evidence for the admission of this concept to good standing in psychology.

1. A trait has more than nominal existence. A trait may be said to have the same kind of existence that a habit of a complex order has. Habits of a complex, or higher, order have long been accepted as household facts in psychology. There is no reason to believe that the mechanism which produces such habits (integration, *Gestaltung*, or whatever it may be) stops short of producing the more generalized habits which are here called traits of personality.

2. A trait is more generalized than a habit. Within a personality there are, of course, many independent habits; but there is also so much integration, organization, and coherence among habits that we have no choice but to recognize great systems of interdependent habits. If the habit of brushing one's teeth can be shown, statistically or genetically, to be unrelated to the habit of dominating a tradesman, there can be no question of a common trait involving both these habits; but if the habit of dominating a tradesman can be shown, statistically or genetically, to be related to the habit of bluffing one's way past guards, there is the presumption that a common trait of personality exists which includes these two habits. Traits may conceivably embrace anywhere from two habits to a legion of habits. In this way, there may be said to be major, widely extensified traits and minor, less generalized traits in a given personality.

3. A trait is dynamic, or at least determinative. It is not the stimulus that is the crucial determinant in behavior that expresses personality; it is the trait itself that is decisive. Once formed a trait seems to have the capacity of directing responses to stimuli into characteristic channels. This emphasis upon the dynamic nature of traits, ascribing to them a capacity for guiding the specific response, is variously recognized by many writers. The principle is nothing more than that which has been subscribed to in various connections by Woodworth, Prince, Sherrington, Coghill, Kurt Lewin, Troland, Lloyd Morgan, Thurstone, Bentley, Stern, and others.[2] From this general point of view traits might be called "derived drives" or "derived motives." Whatever they are called they may be regarded as playing a motivating role in each act, thus endowing the separate adjustments of the individual to specific stimuli with that *adverbial* quality that is the very essence of personality.

* * *

4. The existence of a trait may be established empirically or statistically. In order to know that a person has a *habit* it is necessary to have evidence of repeated reactions of a constant type. Similarly in order to know that an individual has a trait it is necessary to have evidence of repeated reactions which, though not necessarily constant in type, seem none the less to be consistently a function of the same underlying determinant. If this evidence is gathered casually by mere observation of the subject or through the reading of a casehistory or biography, it may be called empirical evidence.

More exactly, of course, the existence of a trait may be established with the aid of statistical techniques that determine the degree of coherence among the separate responses. Although this employment of statistical aid is highly desirable, it is not necessary to wait for such evidence before speaking of traits, any more than it would be necessary to refrain from speaking of the habit of biting fingernails until the exact frequency of the occurrence is known. Statistical methods are at present better suited to intellective than to conative

---

[2]This is an all-star list of important psychologists and scientists at the time this article was written. Of these, Kurt Lewin and Allport himself had the most lasting influence on personality psychology.

functions, and it is with the latter that we are chiefly concerned in our studies of personality.[3]

5. Traits are only relatively independent of each other. The investigator desires, of course, to discover what the fundamental traits of personality are, that is to say, what broad trends in behavior do exist independently of one another. Actually with the test methods and correlational procedures in use, completely independent variation is seldom found. In one study expansion correlated with extroversion to the extent of +.39, ascendance with conservatism, +.22, and humor with insight, +.83, and so on. This overlap may be due to several factors, the most obvious being the tendency of the organism to react in an integrated fashion, so that when concrete acts are observed or tested they reflect not only the trait under examination, but also simultaneously other traits; several traits may thus converge into a final common path. It seems safe, therefore, to predict that traits can never be completely isolated for study, since they never show more than a relative independence of one another.

In the instance just cited, it is doubtful whether humor and insight (provided their close relationship is verified in subsequent studies) represent distinct traits. In the future perhaps it may be possible to agree upon a certain magnitude of correlation below which it will be acceptable to speak of *separate* traits, and above which *one* trait only will be recognized. If one trait only is indicated it will presumably represent a broadly generalized disposition. For example, if humor and insight cannot be established as independent traits, it will be necessary to recognize a more inclusive trait, and name it perhaps "sense of proportion."

6. A trait of personality, psychologically considered, is not the same as moral quality. A trait of personality may or may not coincide with some well-defined, conventional, social concept. Extroversion, ascendance, social participation, and insight are free from preconceived moral significance, large because each is a word newly coined or adapted to fit a psychological discovery. It would be ideal if we could in this way find our traits first and then name them. But honesty, loyalty, neatness, and tact, though encrusted with social significance, *may* likewise represent true traits of personality. The danger is that in devising scales for their measurement we may be bound by the conventional meanings, and thus be led away from the precise integration as it exists in a given individual. Where possible it would be well for us to find our traits first, and then seek devaluated terms with which to characterize our discoveries.

7. Acts, and even habits, that are inconsistent with a trait are not proof of the non-existence of the trait. The objection most often considered fatal to the doctrine of traits has been illustrated as follows: "An individual may be habitually neat with respect to his person, and characteristically slovenly in his handwriting or the care of his desk."[4]

In the first place this observation fails to state that there are cases frequently met where a constant level of neatness is maintained in all of a person's acts, giving unmistakable empirical evidence that the trait of neatness is, in some people at least, thoroughly and permanently integrated. All people must not be expected to show the same degree of integration in respect to a given trait. *What is a major trait in one personality may be a minor trait, or even nonexistent in another personality.*[5]

---

[3]"Conative functions" here refer to motivation; at the time this was written, statistical methods of psychological measurement (psychometrics) had been used exclusively for the measurement of intellectual skills, not motivation or personality. Over the following decades, this situation changed and psychometrics became a foundation of modern personality psychology.

[4]This comment anticipates the "person-situation" debate that flared up in 1968, almost 40 years later, with the publication of a book by Walter Mischel (excerpted in the following selection). Interestingly, the inconsistency of neatness, almost exactly as Allport here describes it, *was* used as an argument against the doctrine of traits in an even later article by Mischel and Peake (1982).

[5]This comment—that not all traits apply to all people— was developed into an important article many years later by the psychologists Daryl Bem and Andrea Allen (1974).

In the second place, we must concede that there may be opposed integrations, i.e., contradictory traits, in a single personality. The same individual may have a trait *both* of neatness *and* of carelessness, of ascendance *and* submission, although frequently of unequal strength.

In the third place there are in every personality instances of acts that are unrelated to existent traits, the product of the stimulus and of the attitude of the moment. Even the characteristically neat person may become careless in his haste to catch a train.

But to say that not all of a person's acts reflect some higher integration is not to say that no such higher integrations exist.

8. A trait may be viewed either in the light of the personality which contains it, or in the light of its distribution in the population at large. Each trait has both its unique and its universal aspect. In its unique aspect, the trait takes its significance entirely from the role it plays in the personality as a whole. In its universal aspect, the trait is arbitrarily isolated for study, and a comparison is made between individuals in respect to it. From this second point of view traits merely extend the familiar field of the psychology of individual differences.

There may be relatively few traits, a few hundred perhaps, that are universal enough to be scaled in the population at large; whereas there may be in a single personality a thousand traits distinguishable to a discerning observer. For this reason, after a scientific schedule of universal traits is compiled, there will still be the field of *artistic* endeavor for psychologists in apprehending correctly the subtle and unique traits peculiar to one personality alone, and in discovering the *pattern* which obtains *between* these traits in the same personality.

CONSISTENCY AND SPECIFICITY IN BEHAVIOR

Walter Mischel

The "book that launched a thousand rebuttals" is Walter Mischel's (1968) Person-ality and Assessment. This book, widely perceived as an all-out frontal assault on the existence of personality traits and the viability of personality psychology, touched off the "person-situation debate," which lasted 20 years. Put briefly, the debate was over this issue: For determining what an individual does, which is more important, stable aspects of his or her personality, or the situation he or she happens to be in at the time? You have already seen that Allport's view, which is the traditional view of the trait approach, is that personality is an important de-terminant of behavior. Mischel's view is that people act very differently in different situations, to the point that characterizing them in terms of broad personality traits may be neither meaningful nor useful.

The next selection is drawn from one of the key chapters of Mischel's book. In it, Mischel argues that inconsistency in behavior is the rule rather than the excep-tion. He surveys, very briefly, a large number of studies that attempted to find strong relationships between what individuals did in one situation and what they did in another. In Mischel's view, such studies generally have failed. Specifically, Mischel assumes that if the relationship between behaviors in two different situa-tions yields a correlation coefficient of less than about .30, not enough of the vari-ance in behavior has been explained to make it useful to assume that both behaviors are affected by the same underlying personality trait. Of course, the se-lection by Rosenthal and Rubin in Part I provides a different—and more opti-mistic—interpretation of a correlation of about .30.

Although the field of personality and what Allport called the "doctrine of traits" ultimately survived the Mischelian onslaught, the book and this chapter re-main important landmarks in the recent history of personality psychology. First, the ideas presented in this chapter had a powerful effect on the viewpoint of many psychologists within and outside the field of personality, an effect that more than 35 years later has still not dissipated. To this day, a surprising number of psycholo-gists "don't believe in personality." Second and even more important, with the words you are about to read Mischel forced the field of personality into an agoniz-ing reappraisal of some of its most basic and cherished assumptions. Although these assumptions can be said to have survived, their close reexamination was on the whole potentially beneficial for our understanding of personality (see the selection by Kenrick and Funder later in this section).

From *Personality and Assessment* (New York: Wiley, 1968), pp. 13–39.

For more than 50 years personality psychologists have tried to measure traits and states in order to discover personality structure and dynamics. There has been an enormous effort to investigate the reliability and, more recently, the validity of the results. This chapter examines some of the evidence for the assumption of generalized personality traits and states. Empirically, the generality of a trait is established by the associations found among trait indicators. The evidence consists of obtained correlations between behaviors measured across similar situations. Data that demonstrate strong generality in the behavior of the same person across many situations are critical for trait and state personality theories; the construct of personality itself rests on the belief that individual behavioral consistencies exist widely and account for much of the variance in behavior. Most definitions of personality hinge on the assumption that an individual's behavior is consistent across many stimulus conditions (e.g., Sanford, 1963).

Data on the generality-specificity of behavior usually fall under the rubric of "reliability" and are separated from "validity" evidence. This distinction between reliability and validity is not very sharp. Both reliability and validity are established by demonstrating relations between responses to various stimulus conditions. The stimulus conditions are the particular measures and settings used to sample responses. *Reliability* concerns the congruence among responses measured under maximally *similar* stimulus conditions (Campbell, 1960; Campbell & Fiske, 1959). *Validity*, in contradistinction to reliability, requires convergence between responses to maximally *different*, independent stimulus conditions or measures.[1] The distinction between reliability and validity research depends chiefly on judgments about the degree of similarity among the stimuli used to evoke responses with the particular eliciting techniques or tests employed. For example, correlations among two similar tests, or of two forms of one test, or of the same test administered to the same person on different occasions, all are taken as reliability evidence; correlations among more dissimilar tests, on the other hand, are interpreted as validity data. This chapter is concerned mainly with reliability evidence and evaluates the behavioral consistencies obtained under relatively similar stimulus conditions. We shall look at several kinds of data, first examining the consistency of intellectual variables and then turning to measures of personality. Throughout this chapter some of the empirical evidence for the cross-situational generality of behavior will be reviewed in order to assess more concretely the appropriateness of the trait assumptions which have had such a marked impact on the field.

* * *

---

[1] Our reading of Cronbach and Meehl (see Part I) suggests that validity implies something much more than, and sometimes much different from, this simple characterization. Validity concerns the convergence between patterns of data that are theoretically predicted and those that are empirically obtained. The patterns are not necessarily simple consistency of the sort Mischel describes.

Personality Variables

* * *

Personality variables have been examined thoroughly to determine individual consistencies with respect to particular dimensions or dispositions. The following personality dimensions are representative of those attracting most theoretical and research interest during the last decade, and some of the evidence for their consistency is examined. It will become apparent rapidly that the generality of these dispositions usually is far less than that found for cognitive and intellectual variables.[2]

ATTITUDES TOWARD AUTHORITY AND PEERS The belief that an individual has generalized attitudes toward classes of persons pervades clinical, diagnostic, and research practice. This belief is reflected in the common assumption that problems of sibling rivalry repeat themselves in peer relations, and that attitudes toward parental figures are mirrored in reactions to diverse authority figures throughout life and toward the psychotherapist in particular. Psychologists of many theoretical orientations often agree that persons develop highly generalized attitudes toward authority. Freud, Piaget, and Rogers, among others, all posit that reactions toward authority originate in the family situation and manifest themselves as broadly generalized attitudes expressed in many contexts toward superiors in later social situations. As Piaget puts it:

> Day to day observation and psycho-analytic experience show that the first personal schemas are afterward generalised and applied to many people. According as the first inter-individual experiences of the child who is just learning to speak are connected with a father who is understanding or dominating, loving or cruel, etc., the child will tend (even throughout life if these relationships have influenced his whole youth) to assimilate all other individuals to this father schema. (Piaget, 1951, p. 207)

These assumptions have been subjected to a rare and extensive test by Burwen and Campbell (1957). Burwen and Campbell studied a large sample of Air Force personnel by means of interviews, TAT,[3] description of self and others, judgments of photos, and autobiographical inventories, as well as an attitude survey and sociometric questionnaire.[4] Through each of these techniques, where possible, attitudes were scored toward own father, symbolic authority (e.g., in responses to pictures of older persons on the TAT), immediate boss, immediate peers, and symbolic peers. The topics or attitude objects and the measures for scoring attitudes toward authority on each are summarized below:

Topic	Measures
Father	Interview; description of self and others; autobiographical inventory
Symbolic authority	Interview; TAT (scored globally); TAT (scored objectively); judgments of photos (of older persons); attitude survey
Boss	Interview; description of self and others; autobiographical inventory; sociometric questionnaire

Similar measures were used to score attitudes toward real and symbolic peers.

The interjudge reliability of all ratings on each instrument was adequately high, and scores were available on twenty variables. Their intercorrelations revealed, first of all, the major impact of stimulus similarity or "method variance": for

---

[2]In a section of this chapter that has been omitted, Mischel acknowledged that cognitive and intellectual variables, such as IQ and cognitive style, are relatively consistent over time and across situations.

[3]The TAT is the Thematic Apperception Test, in which a person looks at a picture (e.g., of a person working at a desk) and makes up a story about what is going on. This story can then be scored in various ways, most commonly as to the motivations that it reveals.

[4]A sociometric questionnaire is one in which members of a group are asked about their impressions of or feelings about one another.

TABLE 1

MEAN CORRELATIONS AMONG ATTITUDES MEASURED
BY DIFFERENT METHODS

Attitude toward		F	SA	B	P	SP
Father	F	.35	.12	.03	.06	.08
Symbolic authority	SA		.15	.08	.10	.06
Boss	B			.09	.13	.03
Peer	P				.22	.07
Symbolic peer	SP					.01

(Adapted from Burwen & Campbell, 1957, p . 26.)

three quarters of all the variables the highest correlations occurred between measures of different attitudes based on the *same* instrument. When these method-produced correlations were disregarded, there was little evidence for generality of attitudes either toward authority or toward peers. Attitudes toward father, symbolic authority, and boss were no more highly correlated with each other than they were with attitudes toward real or symbolic peers, and all correlations tended to be low.

Table 1 shows the average of transformed correlations between attitude topics, eliminating those based on the same instrument. Of the correlations between different measures of attitude toward a *single* type of authority figure, only among attitudes toward father and among attitudes toward peers are there any indications that independent methods tap a specific attitude focus at least to some extent. Even these associations among different measures of attitudes toward the same type of authority were very modest, being .35 for father and .22 for peers. Attitude toward *different* types of authority figures showed no consistency at all. For example, attitude toward one's father correlated .03 with attitude toward one's boss. The authors appropriately concluded that:

> Evidence for a generalized attitude toward authority which encompasses attitudes toward father, symbolic authority, and boss is totally negative, suggesting the need for reconsideration of the applicability of commonly held theory in this area. (Burwen & Campbell, 1957, p. 31)

MORAL BEHAVIOR Psychodynamic theory has emphasized the role of the "superego" as an internalized moral agency that has a critical role in the regulation of all forms of conduct and in the control of impulses. Theorizing regarding the superego has focused on the way in which authority figures and their values become "incorporated" during the course of socialization. It has been assumed that as a result of this process the child adopts parental standards and controls as his own. There is no doubt that in the course of development most children acquire the capacity to regulate, judge, and monitor their own behavior even in the absence of external constraints and authorities. An important theoretical issue, however, is the consistency of these self-regulated patterns of conduct and self-control.

In the extraordinarily extensive and sophisticated Character Education Inquiry, more than thirty years ago,[5] thousands of children were exposed to various situations in which they could cheat, lie, and steal in diverse settings, including the home, party games, and athletic contexts (Hartshorne & May, 1928; Hartshorne, May, & Shuttleworth, 1930).

Although moral conduct was relatively inconsistent, the children showed substantial consistency in their self-reported opinions and thoughts about moral issues elicited on paper-and-pencil tests ad-

---

[5]That is, more than 30 years before this book was published in 1968.

ministered in the classroom. High correlations also were found between various forms of these paper-and-pencil tests. However, if children took alternate equivalent forms of the same tests in diverse social settings—such as at home, in Sunday school, at club meetings, as well as in the classroom—the correlations of their scores among situations were reduced to about .40. The investigators concluded that children vary their opinions to "suit the situation" (Hartshorne, May, & Shuttleworth, 1930, p. 108) and do not have a generalized code of morals.

The specificity of responses, and their dependence on the exact particulars of the evoking situation, was keenly noted by Hartshorne and May (1928). For example:

> . . . even such slight changes in the situation as between crossing out A's and putting dots in squares are sufficient to alter the amount of deception both in individuals and in groups. (p. 382)

To illustrate further from their data, copying from an answer key on one test correlated .696 with copying from a key on another test, and cheating by adding on scores from a speed test correlated .440 with adding on scores on another speed test. However, copying from a key on one test correlated only .292 with adding on scores. Moreover, the average intercorrelations among four classroom tests was only .256 (Hartshorne & May, 1928, p. 383). The more the situation changed the lower the correlations became. The average correlation between four classroom tests and two out-of-classroom tests (contests and stealing) was .167. The lying test given in the classroom averaged .234 with the other classroom tests but only .061 with the two out-of-classroom deception tests (p. 384).

* * *

The observations that Hartshorne and May reported for the relative specificity of moral behavior accurately foreshadowed the findings that emerged from later research on other behavioral consistencies. Response specificity of the kind emphasized by Hartshorne and May is also reflected, for example, in the finding that questionnaires dealing with attitudes and hypothetical matters may correlate with other questionnaires but are less likely to relate to non-self-report behavior (Mischel, 1962). In one study, children were asked questions about whether or not they would postpone immediate smaller rewards for the sake of larger but delayed outcomes in hypothetical situations. Their answers in these hypothetical delay of reward situations were found to relate to other questionnaires dealing with trust and a variety of verbally expressed attitudes. What they said, however, was unrelated to their actual delay of reward choices in real situations (Mischel, 1962). Likewise, measures eliciting direct nonverbal behavior may relate to other behavioral indices in the same domain but not to questionnaires. Thus real behavioral choices between smaller but immediately available gratifications, as opposed to larger but delayed rewards, correlated significantly with such behavioral indices as resistance to temptation, but not with self reports on questionnaires (Mischel, 1962).

Moral guilt also has been studied utilizing projective test[6] responses. For example, in a study with teenage boys (Allinsmith, 1960) moral feelings were inferred from the subjects' projective story completions in response to descriptions of various kinds of immoral actions. The findings led Allinsmith to the view that a person with a truly generalized conscience is a statistical rarity. Johnson (1962) also found that moral judgments across situations tend to be highly specific and even discrepant.

Recent research on moral behavior has concentrated on three areas: moral judgment and verbal standards of right and wrong (e.g., Kohlberg, 1963); resistance to temptation in the absence of external constraint (e.g., Aronfreed & Reber, 1965; Grinder, 1962; MacKinnon, 1938; Mischel & Gilligan, 1964); and post-transgression indices of remorse and guilt (e.g., Allinsmith, 1960; Aronfreed,

---

[6]A projective test is one in which a subject is shown an ambiguous stimulus (e.g., an inkblot, a TAT picture) and asked for his or her interpretation. The subject's answer is assumed to be a "projection" of some aspect of his or her underlying psychology.

1961; Sears, Maccoby, & Levin, 1957; Whiting, 1959). These three areas of moral behavior turn out to be either completely independent or at best only minimally interrelated (Becker, 1964; Hoffman, 1963; Kohlberg, 1963). Within each area specificity also tends to be the rule. For example, an extensive survey of all types of reactions to transgression yielded no predictable relationships among specific types of reaction (Aronfreed, 1961). Similarly, Sears and his coworkers (1965, chapter 6) did not find consistent associations among various reactions to transgression. Thus the data on moral behavior provide no support for the widespread psychodynamic belief in a unitary intrapsychic moral agency like the superego, or for a unitary trait entity of conscience or honesty. Rather than acquiring a homogeneous conscience that determines uniformly all aspects of their self-control, people seem to develop subtler discriminations that depend on many considerations.

SEXUAL IDENTIFICATION, DEPENDENCY, AND AGGRESSION It is widely assumed in most dynamic and trait theories that people develop firm masculine or feminine identifications early in life. These stable identifications, in turn, are believed to exert pervasive effects on what the person does in many diverse situations (e.g., Kohlberg, 1966). There is, of course, no doubt that boys and girls rapidly learn about sex differences and soon recognize their own gender permanently. A much less obvious issue is the extent to which children develop highly consistent patterns of masculine or feminine "sex-typed" behavior. This question has received considerable research attention. The chief strategy has involved studying the associations among different indicators of masculine and feminine sex-typed behavior.

Dependency and aggression often serve conceptually as behavioral referents for sex typing, with boys expected to be more aggressive and girls more dependent. In dependency research, although Beller's (1955) correlations ranged from .48 to .83 for teacher ratings of five dependency components in nursery school children, it is likely that a "halo" effect spuriously inflated the teachers' ratings.[7] Mann (1959) obtained ratings of 55 two-minute observations of 41 nursery school children in free play on six kinds of dependency behavior. He found only 1 of 15 intercorrelations among components of dependency significant. Likewise, observations of nursery school children revealed that the frequencies of "affection seeking" and "approval seeking" were unrelated (Heathers, 1953).

Sears (1963) extensively studied the intercorrelations between five categories of dependency behavior in preschool girls and boys. The five categories were: *negative attention seeking*, e.g., attention getting by disruption or aggressive activity; *positive attention seeking*, as in seeking praise; nonaggressive *touching or holding*; *being near*, e.g., following a child or teacher; and *seeking reassurance*. The frequency of these behaviors was carefully and reliably scored by observing the children at nursery school with an extensive time-sampling procedure. Each child was observed in free play for a total of 7 to 10 hours. The intercorrelations among the five dependency categories for 21 boys and 19 girls are shown in Table 2. Note that only 1 of the 20 correlations reached statistical significance since for 20 degrees of freedom correlations of .423 and .537 would have been needed to reach significance at the .05 and .01 levels respectively.[8]

* * *

Some support for sex differences in the generality of particular patterns of sex-typed behaviors comes in the form of more (and stronger) intercorrelations for girls than boys on five observation measures of dependency (Sears, 1963), whereas the reverse holds for aggression, with more intercorrelations among aggression variables for boys than for girls (Lansky, Crandall, Kagan, & Baker, 1961; Sears, 1961). However, individuals discriminate sharply between situations. The specificity of ag-

---

[7] A "halo effect" occurs when a rater's global positive or negative evaluation of a target person affects all of her or his ratings.

[8] The .05 and .01 significance levels are conventional criteria by which findings are judged not to have occurred merely by chance.

TABLE 2

INTERCORRELATIONS AMONG DEPENDENCY MEASURES[a]

Measures		I	II	III	IV	V
Negative attention	I		.06	.10	.15	.37
Reassurance	II	.24		.25	.19	.26
Positive attention	III	.23	.11		.11	.03
Touching and holding	IV	.01	.11	.16		.71
Being near	V	.03	.12	.14	.13	

(Adapted from Sears, 1963, p. 35.)
[a]Girls above diagonal, boys below.

gressive behavior, for example, is documented in a study of highly aggressive boys by Bandura (1960). Parents who punished aggression in the home, but who simultaneously modeled aggressive behavior and encouraged it in their sons' peer relationships, produced boys who were nonaggressive at home but markedly aggressive at school.

RIGIDITY AND TOLERANCE FOR AMBIGUITY If individuals did develop strongly consistent character structures that channelized them in stable ways, it would be important to identify these syndromes. One of the most thoroughly studied personality patterns is the "authoritarian personality." Intolerance for ambiguity attracted considerable interest as a characteristic of the authoritarian personality (Adorno, Frenkel-Brunswik, Levinson, & Sanford, 1950), and a voluminous literature was devoted to elaborating its correlates.

Several behavioral signs have been used as the referents for intolerance for ambiguity. These signs include resistance to reversal of apparent fluctuating stimuli, early selection and adherence to one solution in perceptually ambiguous situations, seeking for certainty, rigid dichotomizing into fixed categories, premature closure, and the like. In one study, an extensive battery of tests to measure intolerance of ambiguity was designed and administered (Kenny & Ginsberg, 1958). Only 7 of the 66 correlations among intolerance of ambiguity measures reached significance and the relationship for 2 of these was opposite to the predicted direc-

tion. Moreover, the measures in the main failed to correlate with the usual questionnaire indices of authoritarianism submissiveness as elicited by a form of the California F scale.

Closely related to authoritarianism, "rigidity" is another personality dimension that has received much attention as a generalized trait (Chown, 1959; Cronbach, 1956). In one study (Applezweig, 1954), among 45 correlations between behaviors on six measures of rigidity (including arithmetic problems, Rorschach,[9] and F scale), 22 were negative, 21 were positive, and 2 were zero; only 3 of the 45 correlations were significant and 2 of these were negative. Likewise, Pervin's (1960) data on five noninventory performance measures of rigidity, including the water-jars problems, provide generally low associations and suggest that "individuals may be rigid in one area of personality functioning and not in another" and that "rigidity is not a general personality characteristic" (p. 394). The conclusion that rigidity is not a unitary trait is also supported by the modest intercorrelations between measures obtained by Wrightsman and Baumeister (1961) and by the specificity found earlier by Maher (1957).

* * *

Thus investigators frequently measure and describe a purportedly general dimension of behavior only to discover later that it has dubious

---

[9]The Rorschach is the famous projective test in which subjects are asked what they see in blots of ink.

consistency. As a result the popular dimensions of personality research often wax and wane almost like fashions. Research on the generality of the behavioral indices of personality dimensions has generated its own truisms. Over and over again the conclusions of these investigations, regardless of the specific content area, are virtually identical and predictable. The following paragraph, from Applezweig's (1954) own summary, is essentially interchangeable with those from a plethora of later researches on the generality of many different traits:

> The following conclusions appear to be justified:
> (a) There is no general factor of rigidity among a number of so-called measures of rigidity; the interrelationships of these measures appear to vary with the nature of the tests employed and the conditions of test administration as well as behavioral determinants within S's.[10]
> (b) Scores obtained by an individual on any so-called measure of rigidity appear to be a function not only of the individual, but also of the nature of the test and the conditions of test administration. (Applezweig, 1954, p. 228)

*   *   *

CONDITIONABILITY Classical learning formulations place great emphasis on conditioning as a basic process in learning. Consequently psychologists with an interest in both learning and individual differences have been especially interested in studying conditionability as a personality dimension. In spite of a great deal of research, however, there is no evidence for the existence of a general factor or trait of "conditionability" in either classical or operant conditioning paradigms.

Correlations among different measures and types of conditioning tend to be low or zero (e.g., Bunt & Barendregt, 1961; Campbell, 1938; Davidson, Payne, & Sloane, 1964; Eysenck, 1965; Franks, 1956; Lovibond, 1964; Moore & Marcuse, 1945; Patterson & Hinsey, 1964). Moore and Marcuse (1945) noted many years ago that "the concept of good or poor conditioners must always be with reference to a specific response." Reviewing the literature two decades later, Eysenck (1965) points out that correlations between conditionability measures depend on specific peripheral factors (sweat glands in the hand, pain sensitivity of the cornea). He also notes that even if these sources were eliminated correlations would still be affected by situational circumstances such as the sequence and massing of stimuli, the scheduling of reinforcement, the strength of CS and UCS,[11] temporal intervals, and so on.

The evidence that learning variables like conditionability are unitary traitlike entities is no more convincing than the data for the consistency of personality traits couched in any other theoretical language. Whenever individual differences are elicited, however, the failure to demonstrate impressive reliability does not preclude the existence of extensive correlations with other response measures (e.g., Franks, 1961).

MODERATOR VARIABLES Wallach (1962) and Kogan and Wallach (1964) have called attention to the fact that "moderator variables" may influence the correlations found in research on behavioral consistency. By moderator variables Wallach and Kogan mean interactions among several variables that influence the correlations obtained between any one of the variables and other data. For example, correlations between two response patterns may be found for males, but not for females, or may even be positive for one sex but negative for the other. Thus, if the correlations between two response patterns are examined for both sexes combined, the different relations that might be obtained if each sex were taken into account separately could become obscured. Similarly, relations between two measures might be positive for children with high IQ but negative for those with low IQ. In other words, there are complex interactions so that the

---

[10]The abbreviation S's refers to subjects (now usually called "participants").

[11]The abbreviation CS means conditioned stimulus; UCS means unconditioned stimulus. In learning experiments, the stimuli employed, of either type, may vary in intensity or strength.

relations between any two variables depend on several other variables.

By analyzing their data to illuminate higher-order interactions of this kind, these investigators have been able to demonstrate significant associations among various measures of risk taking, and between risk taking and other variables. The resulting associations of course apply only to some subjects under a few conditions. This strategy of searching for interactions holds some promise. Since the interactions are obtained post hoc rather than predicted, however, considerable interpretative caution must be observed. Otherwise the analysis of the same data for many interactions provides many additional chances to obtain seemingly statistically significant results that actually monopolize on chance. That is, more "significant" associations occur by chance when more correlations are computed.

TEMPORAL STABILITY So far, our discussion of consistency has focused on relationships among a person's behaviors across situations sampled more or less at the same time. Equally important, however, are data that examine how stable the individual's behavior remains in any one particular domain when he is reassessed at later times.

Results from the Fels Longitudinal Study give some typical examples of the stability of a person's behavior patterns over time (Kagan & Moss, 1962). The overall findings suggest some significant consistency between childhood and early adulthood ratings of achievement behavior, sex-typed activity, and spontaneity for both sexes. For certain other variables, like dependency, some consistency was found for one sex but not the other. Thus the rated dependency of girls at age six years to ten years correlated .30 with their adult dependence on family; the comparable correlation for boys was near zero. In the same longitudinal study of middle-class subjects the most highly significant positive associations were found between ratings of achievement and recognition strivings obtained at various periods of childhood and in early adulthood (Kagan & Moss, 1962; Moss & Kagan, 1961). Children who were rated as showing strong desires

for recognition also tended to be rated as more concerned with excellence and with the attainment of high self-imposed standards when they were interviewed as young adults. Some of the many correlations between achievement strivings in childhood and comparable adult preoccupation with attaining excellence were exceptionally high, in several instances reaching the .60 to .70 range.

Apart from ratings the motive or need to achieve ("n Ach") has also been studied most extensively by scoring the subject's achievement imagery in the stories he tells to selected TAT cards. For example, if the person creates stories in which the hero is studying hard for a profession and aspires and strives to improve himself and to advance in his career, the story receives high n Ach scores. This technique, developed thoroughly by McClelland and his associates (1953), has become the main index of the motive to achieve and to compete against standards of excellence. As a result considerable attention has been devoted to studying the stability of this need by comparing n Ach scores obtained from the same individuals at different times. Moss and Kagan (1961) reported a stability coefficient of .31 for their sample over a 10-year period from adolescence to adulthood. They also reported a 3-year stability coefficient of .32 for TAT achievement themes obtained at ages 8 and 11 (Kagan & Moss, 1959). However, the correlation between n Ach at age 8 and at age 14 was only .22; the correlation between n Ach at age 11 and at 14 years was a nonsignificant .16.

The stability of achievement motivation was also studied closely for shorter time intervals with other samples of people. Birney (1959) reported a coefficient of only .29 for n Ach on equivalent picture forms administered to college students within six months. He concluded that ". . . the n Ach measure is highly situational in character . . ." (p. 267). Similarly, a significant but modest coefficient of .26 was reported for a 9-week test-retest study with college students (Krumboltz & Farquhar, 1957). Higher correlations ranging from .36 to .61 have been found for shorter time intervals of 3 weeks to 5 weeks (Haber & Alpert, 1958; Morgan, 1953). Reviewing a great deal of information from many studies, Skolnick (1966a, b) reported extensive correlations between diverse adolescent and adult measures. Many correlations reached significance, especially for achievement and power imagery indices, although the associations tended to be extremely complicated and most often of modest magnitude.

Just as with consistency across situations, stability over time tends to be greatest for behaviors associated with intelligence and cognitive processes (e.g., Bloom, 1964; Gardner & Long, 1960; Kagan & Moss, 1962; Moss & Kagan, 1961). Most notably, extremely impressive stability over long time periods has been found for certain cognitive styles. Retest correlations on Witkin's rod-and-frame test (RFT), for example, were as high as .92 for time intervals of a few years (Witkin, Goodenough, & Karp, 1967). A time lapse of 14 years was the lengthiest interval sampled in their longitudinal study. Even after such a long period, the stability correlation for boys tested with the RFT at age 10 and retested at age 24 was .66. Data of this kind demonstrate genuine durability in aspects of cognitive and perceptual functioning.

A representative illustration of temporal stability comes from studies of behavior during interviews. Reasonable stability has been demonstrated for certain interaction patterns during interviews. These patterns were measured by an interaction chronograph devised to record selected temporal aspects of verbal and gestural behavior (e.g., Matarazzo, 1965; Saslow, Matarazzo, Phillips, & Matarazzo, 1957). In these studies the interviewer followed a standardized pattern of behavior, including systematic periods of "not responding," "interrupting," and other variations in style. The subject's corresponding behavior was scored on formal dimensions such as the frequency of his actions, their average duration, and the length of his silences. The results indicated that these interactions are highly stable across short time periods (such as 1-week retests) when the interviewer's behavior remains fixed. The same interactions, however, were readily and predictably modifiable by planned changes in the interviewer's behavior.

The trait-descriptive categories and personality labels with which individuals describe themselves on questionnaires and trait-rating scales seem to be especially long lasting. E. L. Kelly (1955) compared questionnaire trait self-descriptions obtained almost 20 years apart. During the years 1935–1938 several personality questionnaires were administered to 300 engaged couples, and most of them were retested with the same measures in 1954. The questionnaires included the Strong Vocational Interest Blank, the Allport-Vernon values test, and the Bernreuter personality questionnaire, among others. Self-reports of attitudes about marriage were highly unstable ($r < .10$), but the stability coefficients for self-descriptions of interests, of economic and political values, of self-confidence and sociability were high. The coefficients for these areas of self-reported traits ranged from about .45 to slightly over .60, indicating impressive stability, considering the long temporal delay between assessments.

As another example, the test-retest correlations on the California Psychological Inventory scales for high school students retested after 1 year, and for a sample of prisoners retested after a lapse of 7 to 21 days, were also high (Gough, 1957). In general, trait self-descriptions on many personality questionnaires show considerable stability (Byrne, 1966). Studies of the semantic differential also suggest that the meanings associated with semantic concepts may be fairly stable (Osgood, Suci, & Tannenbaum, 1957).

Research on the temporal stability of personal constructs evoked by Kelly's Role Construct Repertory Test (Reptest) also indicates considerable consistency in constructs over time (Bonarius, 1965). For example, a retest correlation of .79 was found for constructs after a 2-week interval (Landfield, Stern, & Fjeld, 1961). * * * Thus the trait categories people attribute to themselves and others may be relatively permanent, and may be more enduring than the behaviors to which they refer.

Implications

The data on cross-situational consistency and stability over time reviewed in this chapter merely provide representative examples from an enormous domain. The results indicate that correlations across situations tend to be highest for cognitive and intellectual functions. Moreover, behaviors sampled in closely similar situations generally yield the best correlations. Considerable stability over time has been demonstrated for some domains, and again particularly for ability and cognitive measures. Self-descriptions on trait dimensions also seem to be especially consistent even over very long periods of time.

As early as 1928 Hartshorne and May surprised psychologists by showing that the honesty or moral behavior of children is not strongly consistent across situations and measures. The Hartshorne and May data were cited extensively but did not influence psychological theorizing about the generality of traits. Similar evidence for behavioral specificity across situations has been reported over and over again for personality measures since the earliest correlational studies at the turn of the century. Considerable specificity has been found regularly even for syndromes like attitudes toward authority, or aggression and dependency, whose assumed generality has reached the status of a cliché in psychological writings.

The interpretation of all data on behavioral consistency is affected of course by the criteria selected. Consistency coefficients averaging between .30 and .40, of the kind obtained by Hartshorne and May, can be taken either as evidence for the relative specificity of the particular behaviors or as support for the presence of underlying generality. Indeed, the Hartshorne and May data have been reinterpreted as evidence for generality in children's moral behavior, at least across related situations (Burton, 1963). Similarly, McGuire (1968) reviewed data on the consistency of suggestibility, persuasibility, and conformity and concluded that each has the status of a generalized, although "weak," trait. McGuire noted the tenuousness of the evidence, since the data consisted mostly of low but positive correlations which often reached the .05 statistical confidence level, sometimes did not, and which never accounted for more than a trivial proportion of the variance.[12]

There is nothing magical about a correlation coefficient, and its interpretation depends on many considerations. The accuracy or reliability of measurement increases with the length of the test. Since no single item is a perfect measure, adding items increases the chance that the test will elicit a more accurate sample and yield a better estimate of the person's behavior. Second, a test may be reliable at one score level but unreliable at another. That is, the accuracy of the test is not necessarily uniform for different groups of people; a test that yields reliable achievement scores for 10-year-old children may be so difficult for 7-year-olds that they are reduced to guessing on almost all items. Moreover, different items within the same test do not necessarily yield uniformly reliable information (Cronbach, 1960). The interpretation of reliability coefficients is influenced by the relative homogeneity or heterogeneity in the tested behavior range of the sample of subjects. For example, if an ability test is given to a more or less uniformly bright group of college students, very slight errors in measurement could obscure actual individual differences. Any one set of observations provides merely a sample of behavior whose meaning may be confounded by numerous errors of measurement.

These and similar statistical considerations (Cronbach, 1960) caution us to interpret the meaning of particular coefficients with care. In spite of methodological reservations, however, it is evident that the behaviors which are often construed as stable personality trait indicators actually are highly specific and depend on the details of the evoking situations and the response mode employed to measure them.

---

[12]Mischel is here following the common practice of squaring a correlation to yield the percent of variance "explained" (see the selection by Rosenthal and Rubin in Part I). Thus a correlation of .30 is said to explain 9% of the variance (.30 squared being .09) and a correlation of .40 is said to explain 16% of the variance (.40 squared being .16). Mischel regards these percentages as "trivial." But recall that Rosenthal and Rubin (Part I) demonstrated that a correlation of .32 yields correct classification twice as often as incorrect classification.

* * *

It is important to distinguish clearly between "statistically significant" associations and equivalence. A correlation of .30 easily reaches statistical significance when the sample of subjects is sufficiently large, and suggests an association that is highly unlikely on the basis of chance. However, the same coefficient accounts for less than 10 percent of the relevant variance. Statistically significant relationships of this magnitude are sufficient to justify personality research on individual and group differences. It is equally plain that their value for making statements about an individual is severely limited. Even when statistically significant behavioral consistencies are found, and even when they replicate reliably, the relationships usually are not large enough to warrant individual assessment and treatment decisions except for certain screening and selection purposes.

It is very easy to misunderstand the meaning of the findings on behavioral consistency and specificity surveyed in this chapter. It would be a complete misinterpretation, for instance, to conclude that individual differences are unimportant.[13] To remind oneself of their pervasive role one need merely observe the differences among people's responses to almost any complex social stimulus under most supposedly uniform laboratory conditions. The real questions are not the existence of differences among individuals but rather their nature, their causes and consequences, and the utility of inferring them for particular purposes and by particular techniques.

Consistency coefficients of the kind reviewed in this chapter are only one of several types of data pertinent to an appropriate evaluation of the empirical status of the main trait and state approaches to personality. It would be premature therefore to attempt to draw conclusions at this point. Sophisticated dispositional personality theories increasingly have come to recognize that behavior tends to change with alterations in the situations in which it occurs. They note, however, that the same basic underlying disposition (or "genotype") may manifest itself behaviorally in diverse ways in different situations so that heterogeneous behaviors can be signs of the same underlying trait or state. According to this argument, the dependent person, for example, need not behave dependently in all situations; indeed his basic dependency may show itself in diverse and seemingly contradictory overt forms. Although fundamentally dependent, he may, for instance, try to appear aggressively independent under some circumstances, and even may become belligerent and hostile in other settings in efforts to deny his dependency. Similarly, and in accord with psychodynamic theorizing, seemingly diverse acts may be in the service of the same underlying motivational force. For example, a person's overtly liberal political behavior and his overt social conservativism, although apparently inconsistent, may actually both be understandable as expressions of a more fundamental motive, such as his desire to please and win approval and recognition. These arguments for basic consistencies that underlie surface diversity are theoretically defensible, but they ultimately depend, of course, on supporting empirical evidence.

* * *

References

Adorno, I. W., Frenkel-Brunswik, Else, Levinson, D. J., & Sanford, R. N. (1950). *The authoritarian personality*. New York: Harper.

Allinsmith, W. (1960). The learning of moral standards. In D. R. Miller & G. E. Swanson (Eds.), *Inner conflict and defense* (pp. 141–176). New York: Holt.

Applezweig, Dee G. (1954). Some determinants of behavioral rigidity. *Journal of Abnormal and Social Psychology, 49,* 224–228.

Aronfreed, J. (1961). The nature, variety, and social patterning of moral responses to transgression. *Journal of Abnormal and Social Psychology, 63,* 223–240.

Aronfreed, J. (1964). The origin of self-criticism. *Psychological Review, 71,* 193–218.

Aronfreed, J., & Reber, A. (1965). Internalized behavioral suppression and the timing of social punishment. *Journal of Personality and Social Psychology, 1,* 3–16.

Bandura, A. (1960). Relationship of family patterns to child behavior disorders. Progress Report, U.S.P.H. Research Grant M-1734, Stanford University.

---

[13]Despite this disclaimer, the book from which this excerpt is drawn *was* widely interpreted as arguing—even proving—that stable individual differences in personality are unimportant.

Becker, W. C. (1964). Consequences of different kinds of parental discipline. In M. L. Hoffman & Lois W. Hoffman (Eds.), *Review of child development research* (Vol. 1, pp. 169–208). New York: Russell Sage Foundation.

Beller, E. K. (1955). Dependency and independence in young children. *Journal of Genetic Psychology, 87*, 25–35.

Birney, R. C. (1959). The reliability of the achievement motive. *Journal of Abnormal and Social Psychology, 58*, 266–267.

Bloom, R. S. (1964). *Stability and change in human characteristics.* New York: Wiley.

Bonarius, J. C. J. (1965). Research in the personal construct theory of George A. Kelly: Role Construct Repertory Test and basic theory. In B. A. Maher (Ed.), *Progress in experimental personality research* (Vol. 2, pp. 1–46). New York: Academic Press.

Bunt, A. van de, & Barendregt, J. T. (1961). Inter-correlations of three measures of conditioning. In J. T. Barendregt (Ed.), *Research in psychodiagnostics.* The Hague: Mouton.

Burton, R. V. (1963). Generality of honesty reconsidered. *Psychological Review, 70*, 481–499.

Burwen, L. S., & Campbell, D. T. (1957). The generality of attitudes toward authority and nonauthority figures. *Journal of Abnormal and Social Psychology, 54*, 24–31.

Byrne, D. (1966). *An introduction to personality.* Englewood Cliffs, N. J.: Prentice-Hall.

Campbell, A. A. (1938). The interrelations of two measures of conditioning in man. *Journal of Experimental Psychology, 22*, 225–243.

Campbell, D. T. (1960). Recommendations for APA test standards regarding construct, trait, or discriminant validity. *American Psychologist, 15*, 546–553.

Campbell, D., & Fiske, D. (1959). Convergent and discriminant validation by the multitrait-multimethod matrix. *Psychological Bulletin, 56*, 81–105.

Chown, Sheila M. (1959). Rigidity—A flexible concept. *Psychological Bulletin, 56*, 195–223.

Cronbach, L. J. (1956). Assessment of individual differences. *Annual Review of Psychology, 7*, 173–196.

Cronbach, L. J. (1960). *Essentials of psychological testing* (2nd ed.) New York: Harper.

Davidson, P. O., Payne, R. W., & Sloane, R. B. (1964). Introversion, neuroticism, and conditioning. *Journal of Abnormal and Social Psychology, 68*, 136–148.

Eysenck, II. J. (1965). Extraversion and the acquisition of eyeblink and GSR conditioned responses. *Psychological Bulletin, 63*, 258–270.

Franks, C. M. (1956). Conditioning and personality: A study of normal and neurotic subjects. *Journal of Abnormal and Social Psychology, 52*, 143–150.

Franks, C. M. (1961). Conditioning and abnormal behaviour. In H. J. Eysenck (Ed.), *Handbook of abnormal psychology* (pp. 457–487). New York: Basic Books.

Gardner, R. W., & Long, R. I. (1960). The stability of cognitive controls. *Journal of Abnormal Social Psychology, 61*, 485–487.

Gough, H. G. (1957). *Manual for the California Psychological Inventory.* Palo Alto, Calif: Consulting Psychologists Press.

Grinder, R. E. (1962). Parental childrearing practices, conscience, and resistance to temptation of sixth-grade children. *Child Development, 33*, 803–820.

Haber, R. N., & Alpert, R. (1958). The role of situation and picture cues in projective measurement of the achievement motive. In J. W. Atkinson (Ed.), *Motives in fantasy, action, and society* (pp. 644–663). Princeton: Van Nostrand.

Hartshorne, H., & May, M. A. (1928). *Studies in the nature of character.* Vol. I., *Studies in deceit.* New York: Macmillan.

Hartshorne, H., May, M. A., & Shuttleworth, F. K. (1930). *Studies in the nature of character.* Vol. 3, *Studies in the organization of character.* New York: Macmillan.

Heathers, G. (1953). Emotional dependence and independence in a physical threat situation. *Child Development, 24*, 169–179.

Hoffman, M. L. (1963). Child rearing practices and moral development: Generalizations from empirical research. *Child Development, 34*, 295–318.

Johnson, R. C. (1962). A study of children's moral judgments. *Child Development, 33*, 327–354.

Kagan, J., & Moss, H. A. (1959). Stability and validity of achievement fantasy. *Journal of Abnormal and Social Psychology, 58*, 357–364.

Kagan, J., & Moss, H. A. (1962). *Birth to maturity: A study in psychological development.* New York: Wiley.

Kelly, E. L. (1955). Consistency of the adult personality. *American Psychologist, 10*, 659–681.

Kenny, D. T., & Ginsberg, Rose. (1958). The specificity of intolerance of ambiguity measures. *Journal of Abnormal and Social Psychology, 56*, 300–304.

Kogan, N., & Wallach, M. A. (1964). *Risk taking: A study in cognition and personality.* New York: Holt, Rinehart & Winston.

Kohlberg, L. (1963). The development of children's orientations toward a moral order: I. Sequence in the development of moral thought. *Vita Humana, 6*, 11–33.

Kohlberg, L. (1966). A cognitive-developmental analysis of children's sex-role concepts and attitudes. In Eleanor E. Maccoby (Ed.), *The development of sex differences* (pp. 25–55). Stanford: Stanford University Press.

Krumboltz, J. D., & Farquhar, W. W. (1957). Reliability and validity of the *n*-Achievement test. *Journal of Consulting Psychology, 21*, 226–228.

Landfield, A. W., Stern, M., & Fjeld, S. (1961). Social conceptual processes and change in students undergoing psychotherapy. *Psychological Reports, 8*, 63–68.

Lansky, L. M., Crandall, V. J., Kagan, J., & Baker, C. T. (1961). Sex differences in aggression and its correlates in middle-class adolescents. *Child Development, 32*, 45–58.

Lovibond, S. H. (1964). Personality and conditioning. In B. A. Maher (Ed.), *Progress in experimental personality research* (pp. 115–168). Vol. 1. New York: Academic Press.

MacKinnon, D. W. (1938). Violation of prohibitions. In H. A. Murray, *Explorations in personality* (pp. 491–501). New York: Oxford University Press.

Maher, B. A. (1957). Personality, problem solving, and the Einstellung effect. *Journal of Abnormal and Social Psychology, 54*, 70–74.

Mann, R. D. (1959). A review of the relationships between personality and performance in small groups. *Psychological Bulletin, 56*, 241–270.

Matarazzo, J. D. (1965). The interview. In B. B. Wolman (Ed.), *Handbook of clinical psychology* (pp. 403–450). New York: McGraw-Hill.

McClelland, D. C., Atkinson, J. W., Clark, R. A., & Lowell, E. I. (1953). *The achievement motive.* New York: Appleton-Century-Crofts.

McGuire, W. J. (1968). Personality and susceptibility to social influence. In E. F. Borgatta & W. W. Lambert (Eds.), *Handbook of personality theory and research* (pp. 1130–1187). Chicago: Rand McNally.

Mischel, W. (1962). Delay of gratification in choice situations. NIMH Progress Report, Stanford University.

Mischel, W., & Gilligan, C. (1964). Delay of gratification, motivation for the prohibited gratification, and responds to temptation. *Journal of Abnormal and Social Psychology, 69,* 411–417.

Moore, A. U., & Marcuse, F. I. (1945). Salivary, cardiac and motor indices of conditioning in two sows. *Journal of Comparative Psychology, 38,* 1–16.

Morgan, H. H. (1953). Measuring achievement motivation with "picture interpretations." *Journal of Consulting Psychology, 17,* 289–292.

Moss, H. A., & Kagan, J. (1961). Stability of achievement and recognition seeking behaviors from early childhood through adulthood. *Journal of Abnormal and Social Psychology, 62,* 504–518.

Osgood, C. E., Suci, G. J., & Tannenbaum, P. H. (1957). *The measurement of meaning.* Urbana: University of Illinois Press.

Patterson, G. R., & Hinsey, W. C. (1964). Investigations of some assumptions and characteristics of a procedure for instrumental conditioning in children. *Journal of Experimental Child Psychology, 1,* 111–122.

Pervin, L. A. (1960). Rigidity in neurosis and general personality functioning. *Journal of Abnormal and Social Psychology, 61,* 389–395.

Piaget, J. (1951). *Play, dreams, and imitation in childhood.* New York: Norton.

Sanford, N. (1963). Personality: Its place in psychology. In S. Koch (Ed.), *Psychology: A study of a science.* Vol. 5 (pp. 488–592). New York: McGraw-Hill.

Saslow, G., Matarazzo, J. D., Phillips, Jeanne S., & Matarazzo, Ruth C. (1957). Test-retest stability of interaction patterns during interviews conducted one week apart. *Journal of Abnormal and Social Psychology, 54,* 295–802.

Sears, R. R. (1961). Relation of early socialization experiences to aggression in middle childhood. *Journal of Abnormal and Social Psychology, 63,* 466–492.

Sears, R. R. (1963). Dependency motivation. In M. R. Jones (Ed.), *Nebraska symposium on motivation* (pp. 25–64). Lincoln: University of Nebraska Press.

Sears, R. R., Maccoby, Eleanor E., & Levin, H. (1957). *Patterns of child rearing.* Evanston, IL: Row, Peterson.

Sears, R. R., Rau, Lucy, & Alpert, R. (1965). *Identification and child rearing.* Stanford, CA: Stanford University Press.

Skolnick, Arlene. (1966a). Motivational imagery and behavior over twenty years. *Journal of Consulting Psychology, 30,* 463–478.

Skolnick, Arlene. (1966b). Stability and interrelations of thematic test imagery over 20 years. *Child Development, 37,* 389–396.

Wallach, M. A. (1962). Commentary: Active-analytical vs. passive-global cognitive functioning. In S. Messick & J. Ross (Eds.), *Measurement in personality and cognition* (pp. 199–215). New York: Wiley.

Whiting, J. W. M. (1959). Sorcery, sin, and the superego. A cross-cultural study of some mechanisms of social control. In M. R. Jones (Ed.), *Nebraska symposium on motivation* (pp. 174–195). Lincoln: University of Nebraska Press.

Witkin, H. A., Goodenough, D. R., & Karp, S. A. (1967). Stability of cognitive style from childhood to young adulthood. *Journal of Personality and Social Psychology, 7,* 291–300.

Wrightsman, L. S., Jr., & Baumeister, A. A. (1961). A comparison of actual and paper-and-pencil versions of the Water Jar Test of Rigidity. *Journal of Abnormal and Social Psychology, 63,* 191–198.

SOME REASONS FOR THE APPARENT INCONSISTENCY OF PERSONALITY

Jack Block

The next selection may have been the first, the briefest, and ultimately one of the most important of the rebuttals to Mischel's argument in the previous selection. This brief article sets forth several reasons why actions that seem inconsistent might in fact all be produced by a stable personality structure. If trivial behaviors are correlated with important ones, or if the context of behavior is not taken into account, or if the underlying dynamics of behavior are ignored, then behavior will appear inconsistent even though personality is not. This article appeared at about the same time as Mischel's book and does not mention it by name, but the several possible misunderstandings Block lists are ones that some observers believe to have been present in many of the demonstrations, reviewed by Mischel, that "behavior is inconsistent."

 However, the most important aspect of this article is not the way in which it rebuts Mischel but in its clear illustration of the complex and far-from-obvious processes by which personality affects what a person does.

From *Psychological Bulletin, 70*, 210–212, 1968.

The study of personality seeks regularities in behavior and this search is usually made operational by evaluations of the correlations among different, theoretically related behaviors. To date, the empirical evidence for personality consistency has not been inspiring. As a principle or aspiration of a science aimed at human understanding, the idea of continuity and coherence in personality functioning must be affirmed. Whereupon the question becomes: Why have psychologists, in their many research efforts, been unable to display the presumed harmonies in individual behavior?

The present note collects and lists some of the reasons for this state of affairs. The problem is viewed as arising both from deficiencies in the way psychologists operationalize their concepts and from deficiencies in the way they conceptualize their operations; and it is in these terms that our discussion will proceed. There are some psychometric reasons, as well, for the apparent inconsistency observed in behaviors, having to do with such matters as attenuation effects and the vexing influence of "method variance," but these statistical concerns have been dealt with elsewhere (Block, 1963, 1964; Humphreys, 1960); so the present argument can be entirely psychological.

To exemplify the several points to be made, the personality dimension of ego control will be used, although, of course, other personality constructs instead might have been employed. By ego control is meant something akin to excessive behavioral constraint or rigidity ("the overcontroller") at one end of the dimension and something like excessive behavioral reactivity or spontaneity ("the undercontroller") at the other end of the continuum. For further articulation of the ego-control concept, the reader may wish to consult other sources (e.g., Block, 1965; Block & Turula, 1963).

There is evidence for a common thread through a large variety of behaviors that can be accounted for by the concept of ego control. Undercontrollers in one situation are often undercontrollers in another context as well and the same is true of overcontrollers. But also, and often, an individual who is impulsive in one situation will appear constrained in another circumstance; such behavior apparently denies the usefulness of a generalizing personality variable. This last kind of datum, of apparent inconsistency, cannot be questioned or explained away by psychometric manipulation;[1] it is there and further instances can be multiplied at will. What can be questioned, however, is the implication immediately, frequently, and strongly drawn from such observations to the effect that a personality dimension—in the present instance, ego control—necessarily loses its cogency as a basis for conceptualizing behavior because of the inconsistencies observed. We can question this implication if, and only if, a higher form of lawfulness can be found in the behaviors pointed to as evidence for temperamental inconsistency. The apparent discordancies must be resolved within a framework provided by a theory, or, at least, a theory must have the promise of integrating these otherwise upsetting data.

There are at least four ways in which these su-

perficially embarrassing behavioral inconsistencies may come about:

1. *The behaviors being contrasted and correlated may not all be significant or salient for the individual.* Thus, it is psychologically uneconomical and as a rule not necessary to deliberate excessively before deciding whether to walk down the right aisle or the left aisle of a theater. The decision problem confronting the individual in this particular situation is essentially unimportant. Consequently, an individual may make his theater-lobby decision in a rather cavalier or "impulsive" way. Or he may give reign to a slight position preference which, because it is consistent, may suggest a "rigidity" or highly controlled patterning in his behavior. It is specious to contrast such peripheral behaviors of an individual with the way in which he copes with centrally involving situations such as friendship formation or aggression imposition, and yet, unwittingly, the comparison is often made. When correlation is sought between behaviors formulated in salient situations on the one hand and behaviors formulated in uninvolving situations on the other, then behavior will appear more whimsical than congruent. If we are to seek consistency, it must be sought among behaviors that are at comparable levels in the hierarchy of behaviors.

2. *Formulations of personality which are context blind or do not attempt to take environmental factors into account will encounter many behaviors that will appear inconsistent.* Thus, a generally spontaneous child may in certain circumstances behave in a highly constricted way. This vacillation and apparent inconsistency readily becomes understandable when it is realized that these certain circumstances are always *unfamiliar* ones for the child. Behavior often appears capricious because the nature of the stimulus situation in which the individual finds himself is not comprehended or attended to by the observer and his theory. Explicit theoretical conceptualization of environmental factors is a fruitful way of integrating and assimilating behaviors which from a context-blind viewpoint

---

[1]In other words, these inconsistencies are not just a matter of statistical imprecision or error.

appear inconsistent. It is still a way that is almost untried.[2]

3. *The behaviors being related may not be mediated by the same underlying variables.* Thus, in a basketball game two players may each demonstrate a wide variety of shots and sequencing of shots at the basket. The one player may have spent solitary, obsessive years before a hoop, planfully developing precisely the repertoire and combinations he is now manifesting. The second player, in the heat of athletic endeavor, may in spontaneous and impromptu fashion manifest a fully equivalent variety of basket-making attempts (and with no less accuracy if he is a good athlete). These phenotypically equivalent behaviors are in the first player mediated by controlled, deliberate development of a differentiated behavioral repertoire; in the second player, behavioral variety is mediated by his kinesthetic spontaneity. In a rather different situation, where prior cultivation of ability is not available as a resource, the first player may now appear rigid and behaviorally impoverished; the second player can continue to be spontaneous. These two individuals, behaviorally equivalent in the first situation, are quite different in the second situation; and this difference suggests an inconsistency of behavior. If the mediating variables underlying a given action are not analyzed or considered, behavior can appear paradoxical when closer assessment will reveal a lawful basis for the discrepancy.

4. *When an individual has reached certain personal limits, previous behavioral consistencies may break down.* Thus, an acutely paranoid individual will manifest both extremely overcontrolled behaviors and extremely undercontrolled behaviors more or less conjointly. Etiologically, this contrary behavioral state appears to come about when the preparanoid individual finds his former ability to consistently contain his excessive impulses is becoming exceeded in certain directions of expression, with a resultant absence of control in these special areas. The former, often quite striking coherence the preparanoid personality manifests has been disrupted because the *bounds* or *limits* within which the coherence can be maintained have been transcended. Such extremist behaviors are especially likely to be judged psychopathological. Indeed, one of the explanations why psychiatrists and clinical psychologists often argue against the existence of an internally consistent ego apparatus is that they in their practice so often encounter those relatively few individuals in whom personal limits have been reached and therefore personal consonance shattered. More generally, psychologists have not given the notion of bounds or limits sufficient attention and application. Relationships tend to be posited unequivocally, without recognizing the bounds within which the relationship can be expected to hold and beyond which the relationship fails and is replaced by other relationships.

The foregoing remarks and recognitions are not new but their implications are often neglected by the busy psychologist concerned more with the action of research than with contemplative conceptualization. But both are required. If we are to respond to our empirical disappointments in the pursuit of personality consistency, that response should comprehend the reasons for former failure rather than perpetuate and proliferate a fundamentally unpsychological approach to the understanding of personality.

References

Block, J. (1963). The equivalence of measures and the correction for attenuation. *Psychological Bulletin, 60*, 152–156.

Block, J. (1964). Recognizing attenuation effects in the strategy of research. *Psychological Bulletin, 62*, 214–216.

Block, J. (1965). *The challenge of response sets.* New York: Appleton-Century-Crofts.

Block, J., & Turula, E. (1963). Identification, ego control, and adjustment. *Child Development, 34*, 945–953.

Humphreys, L. G. (1960). Note on the multitrait-multimethod matrix. *Psychological Bulletin, 57*, 86–88.

---

[2]More than 3 decades later, the integration of situational context into our understanding of how personality affects behavior is still seldom even attempted. Part of the problem seems to be that we lack a vocabulary and technology for assessing the psychologically important aspects of situations that is comparable to our vocabulary and technology for assessing persons (see Bem & Funder, 1978).

Profiting from Controversy: Lessons from the Person-Situation Debate

Douglas T. Kenrick and David C. Funder

When Mischel proposed that personality traits are not important, this proposal immediately ran into the fact that nearly everybody thinks that they are. Personality traits are not only an important topic of psychological research, but obviously a major part of the way we think and talk about people in daily life. Mischel's response to this paradox was a further proposal, that our perceptions of personality traits in ourselves and each other are cognitive illusions. This position was bolstered by the development of research in social psychology describing many errors that people make in their judgments of each other. Indeed, the tendency to see personality traits as affecting behaviors that are really due to the situation became dubbed the "fundamental attribution error" (Ross, 1977).

The following article, by the social-personality psychologist Douglas Kenrick and one of the editors of this reader, was intended to sum up the person-situation debate by directly addressing this question: Are personality traits merely illusions? The article is structured by considering seven hypotheses that range from the most to the least pessimistic about the existence and importance of personality traits. Traits are not just illusions in the eye of the beholder, Kenrick and Funder conclude, nor is their appearance the mere by-product of processes—such as discussion among peers about what somebody is like—that may have nothing to do with the personality of the person who is being described. Rather, the accumulated evidence supports the conclusion that traits are real and have a major influence on what people do.

Kenrick and Funder conclude—contrary to the opinion of some—that the person-situation controversy was good for personality psychology. It forced the reconsideration of some of the basic premises of the field in the light of new evidence and illuminated a number of ways in which the influence of personality can and cannot be validly demonstrated. For example, personality judgments of traits that are visible (such as "talkative") are more likely to be accurate than judgments of traits that are hard to see (such as "tends to fantasize"), and judgments by people who know well the people they are judging are more likely to be valid than judgments by relative strangers. These points might seem obvious in retrospect but,

Kenrick and Funder point out, it took the field of personality a surprisingly long time to realize how important they are.

Notice that this article originally appeared in 1988, exactly 20 years after the publication of Mischel's influential book. The article attempted not just to sum up the lessons learned from the person-situation controversy, but to declare the war over. In the years since 1988, the field of personality largely has turned its attention to other issues.

From *American Psychologist, 43,* 23–34, 1988.

* * *

Whether we are acting as professional psychologists, as academic psychologists, or simply as lay psychologists engaging in everyday gossip, the assumption that people have "traits" (or enduring cross-situational consistencies in their behavior) provides a basis for many of our decisions. When a clinical or counseling psychologist uses a standard assessment battery, he or she assumes that there is some degree of traitlike consistency in pathological behavior to be measured. When an organizational psychologist designs a personnel selection procedure, he or she assumes that consistent individual differences between the applicants are there to be found. When an academic psychologist teaches a course in personality, he or she must either assume some consistency in behavior or else face a bit of existential absurdity for at least 3 hours a week. Likewise, a good portion of our courses on clinical and developmental psychology would be unimaginable unless we assumed some cross-situational consistency. Even in everyday lay psychology, our attempts to analyze the behaviors of our friends, relatives, and co-workers are riddled with assumptions about personality traits.

Despite the wide appeal of the trait assumption, personality psychologists have been entangled for some time in a debate about whether it might be based more on illusion than reality (e.g., Alker, 1972; Allport, 1966; Argyle & Little, 1972; Bem, 1972; Block, 1968, 1977; Bowers, 1973; Epstein, 1977, 1979, 1980; Fiske, 1974; Gormly & Edelberg, 1974; Hogan, DeSoto, & Solano, 1977; Hunt, 1965; Magnusson & Endler, 1977; Mischel, 1968, 1983; West, 1983). Murmurs of the current debate could be heard more than 40 years ago (Ichheisser, 1943), but the volume increased markedly after Mischel's (1968) critique, and things have not quieted down yet (Bem, 1983; Epstein, 1983; Funder, 1983; Kenrick, 1986; Mischel, 1983; Mischel & Peake, 1982, 1983). Of late, discussants have begun to express yearning to end what some see as an endless cycle of repeating the same arguments. Mischel and Peake (1982) and Bem (1983), for instance, both use the term *déjà vu* in the titles of recent contributions, suggesting that they feel as if they have been here before. Other commentators maintain that the debate has been a "pseudocontroversy" (Carlson, 1984; Endler, 1973) that never should have occurred in the first place.

However fatiguing it may now seem to some of its erstwhile protagonists, the debate over the alleged inconsistency of personality has been more than an exercise in sophistry. In the course of the nearly two decades since Mischel's (1968) critique, a number of provocative hypotheses have been put forward, along with a host of studies to evaluate them. Platt (1964) and Popper (1959), among others, maintained that science typically progresses through the accumulation of negative information—that is, by eliminating hypotheses that data suggest are no longer tenable. From this perspective, it may be worth taking a look back at the hypotheses suggested during the consistency controversy, this time in the improved light shed by two decades of research. In this light, the debate can be seen as an intellectually stimulating chapter in the history of the discipline, replete with useful lessons for professionals who include assessment in their repertoire.

The "Pure Trait" Model and Its Alternatives

Discussions of the "person versus situation" debate traditionally begin with the "pure trait" model (Alston, 1975; Argyle & Little, 1972; Mischel, 1968): that people show powerful, unmodulated consistencies in their behavior across time and diverse situations. This position has been attacked frequently over the years. However, it is really just a "straw man," and even traditional personality researchers find it unacceptable (see, e.g., Allport, 1931, 1966; Block, 1977; Hogan et al., 1977; Jackson, 1983; Wiggins, 1973; Zuroff, 1986). Complete invariance in behavior is associated more with severe psychopathology than with "normal" behavior.

If the consensus rejects the "pure trait" position, then what can replace it? Several alternative hypotheses have been advanced over the years. These hypotheses differ with regard to four issues, which can be arranged into a logical hierarchy:

1. Consensus versus solipsism. Are traits merely idiosyncratic constructs that reside solely inside the heads of individual observers, or can observers reach agreement in applying trait terms?

2. Discriminativeness versus generality. If observers can agree with one another in ascribing traits to targets, is it simply because they apply a nondiscriminative "one size fits all" approach?

3. Behavior versus labeling. If observers can agree with one another, and can also differentiate between who is low or high on a given trait, does this occur because they really observe behavior? Or do they merely provide their judgments based on superficial stereotypes, targets' self-presentations, or other socially assigned labels?

4. Internal versus external locus of causal explanation. If observers can agree with one another and can distinguish individual differences on the basis of *actual behavior* of the people they are observing, are the causes of these consistencies located within each person or within his or her situation and role?

Each of these issues depends on the resolution of those earlier in the list. For instance, if observers cannot agree with one another about who has which traits, there is no point in going on to debate whether traits have a behavioral basis. Ultimately, assumptions about traits must pass the tests of consensus, discriminativeness, behavioral foundation, and internality. We will discuss seven hypotheses that assume that traits fail one or more of these tests. In Table 1, we list the hypotheses in terms of the four hierarchical issues just discussed. As can be seen, the hypotheses can be arranged more or less in order of their pessimism regarding the existence of (consensually verifiable, discriminative, internal) traitlike consistencies.

We will consider each hypothesis in its purest form and, for the moment, disregard the various qualifications that have sometimes been attached to each. Placing each hypothesis in bold relief allows us to assess it most clearly, and philosophers of science tell us that we learn most when hypotheses are stated in such a way as to allow disproof (e.g., Platt, 1964; Popper, 1959). Moreover, each of these hypotheses has, at some time, actually been stated in its bold form. In 1968, for instance, one social psychologist argued that

> the prevalent view that the normal behavior of individuals tends toward consistency is misconceived [and the research evidence] . . . strongly suggests that consistency, either in thought or action, does not constitute the normal state of affairs. (Gergen, 1968, pp. 305–306)

In the same year, a behavioral psychologist stated that "I, for one, look forward to the day when personality theories are regarded as historical curiosities" (Farber, 1964, p. 37).

Such extreme pessimism was clearly unwarranted. The data available now, more than two

TABLE 1

HIERARCHY OF HYPOTHESES FROM THE PERSON-SITUATION CONTROVERSY, ARRANGED FROM MOST TO LEAST PESSIMISTIC

Critical assumptions	Hypotheses
Solipsism over consensus	1. Personality is in the eye of the beholder.
Consensus without discrimination	2. Agreement between raters is an artifact of the semantic structure of the language used to describe personality.
	3. Agreement is an artifact of base-rate accuracy (rater's tendency to make similar guesses about what people in general are like).
Discriminative consensus without behavioral referents	4. Differential agreement is an artifact of the shared use of invalid stereotypes.
	5. Observers are in cahoots with one another; that is, their agreement results from discussion rather than accurate observation.
Differential agreement about behavior without internal traits	6. Raters see targets only within a limited range of settings and mistake situational effects for traits.
	7. Compared with situational pressures, cross-situational consistencies in behavior are too weak to be important.

decades later, argue strongly against all seven of the hypotheses in Table 1. However, it would be a mistake to presume, as some personologists seem to do, that the issues raised by the "situationists" were merely diversions from the true path that can now be safely disregarded. We have learned, in the course of the debate, about a number of sources of distortion in trait judgments. These not only are of interest in their own right but are useful to personality assessment professionals, whose main goal may be to eliminate as much clutter from their path as possible.

HYPOTHESIS 1: PERSONALITY IS IN THE EYE OF THE BEHOLDER The first and most pessimistic hypothesis that must be considered is that our perceptions of personality traits in our friends, acquaintances, and selves might be largely or exclusively by-products of the limitations and flaws of human information processing. Although no personality researcher has ever advocated that personality exists solely in the head and not in the external world, social psychologists such as Gergen (1968) and behavioral analysts such as Farber (1964) have done so. Moreover, the issue lies in the logical path of any further inquiries into the origin of trait attributions.

Social psychologists have often emphasized how personality impressions can arise in the absence of supporting evidence in the real world:

Unwitting evidence provided by countless personality psychologists shows how objectively low or nonexistent covariations (between personality and behavior) can be parlayed into massive perceived covariations through a priori theories and assumptions. (Nisbett & Ross, 1980, p. 109)

The personality theorists' (and the layperson's) conviction that there are strong cross-situational consistencies in behavior may be seen as merely another instance of theory-driven covariation assessments operating in the face of contrary evidence. (Nisbett & Ross, 1980, p. 112)

Research relevant to the "eye of the beholder" hypothesis has mainly consisted of (a) demonstrations of various "errors" in the way that people process social information, or (b) claims that different judges rating the same personality rarely agree with each other or with the person being rated.

The demonstrations of error (for reviews, see Nisbett & Ross, 1980; Ross, 1977) establish that information given to subjects in laboratory settings is frequently distorted. People tend to jump to conclusions, biasing their judgments and their memories on the basis of their "implicit personality theories" (Schneider, 1973) or "scripts" (Abelson, 1976; Schank & Abelson, 1977). Studies of these attributional errors clearly demonstrate that people have biased expectations and that they routinely go beyond the information they are given.

However, for two reasons such studies do not establish that personality resides solely in the eye of the beholder. First, some of the errors are more a product of the unusual experimental situation than of a fundamentally biased cognitive process (cf. Block, Weiss, & Thorne, 1979; Trope, Bassok, & Alon, 1984). More important, the existence of judgmental biases does not necessarily imply the existence of mistakes. The expectations and biases demonstrated in laboratory tasks are, in principle, liable to lead to correct judgments in the real world (Funder, 1987). Many demonstrations of this principle can be found in the field of visual perception, where a useful rule of thumb underlies every "optical illusion" (Gregory, 1971). The "Ponzo" or "railroad lines" illusion, for example, produces errors in the lab but correct judgments when applied to three-dimensional reality. In the field of

social perception, even the "fundamental attribution error" will lead to correct judgments to the extent that real people actually are somewhat consistent in their behavior. In short, demonstrations of laboratory errors are not informative, one way or the other, as to whether the associated judgmental biases lead mostly to mistakes or correct judgments in real life (see also McArthur & Baron, 1983).

A different line of support for the "eye of the beholder" hypothesis has been the belief that people generally do not agree with each other in their judgments of the same personality. For example, Dornbusch, Hastorf, Richardson, Muzzy, and Vreeland (1965) found that the constructs children in a summer camp used to describe personality were more a function of the person doing the ratings than they were of the person being rated. Such studies do show that people have individually preferred constructs for thinking about others. But these judgmental idiosyncrasies must be interpreted in the light of frequent findings that (a) when raters and ratees get a chance to know one another, their ratings come to agree with each other more (Funder & Colvin, 1987; Norman & Goldberg, 1966), and (b) when common rating categories are imposed on raters, their judgments will show substantial agreement in orderings of individual targets (e.g., Amelang & Borkenau, 1986; Bem & Allen, 1974; Cheek, 1982; Funder, 1987; Funder & Dobroth, 1987; Kenrick & Braver, 1982; Koretzky, Kohn, & Jeger, 1978; McCrae, 1982; Mischel & Peake, 1982).

Table 2 demonstrates some fairly typical findings in the area. In each of these studies, adult targets rated their own personalities and were also rated by more than one person who knew them well (parents, spouses, housemates, or friends). Correlations represent agreement about the same person by different raters who filled out the scales independently. Studies on the left side of the table used single-item scales (Funder & Dobroth, 1987; Kenrick & Stringfield, 1980); Dantchik (1985) and Cheek (1982) used 5-item and 3-item scales, respectively; and the studies to the right used lengthier scales with better established psychometric

TABLE 2

INTERRATER CORRELATIONS FROM RECENT TRAIT STUDIES

Trait	Kenrick & Stringfield (1980)		Funder & Dobroth (1987)	Dantchik (1985)		Cheek (1982)		McCrae (1982)	Paunonen & Jackson (1985)	Mischel & Peake (1982)
		Obs[a]			Obs[a]	1/2/3[b]	Obs[a]			
	(n = 71)	(n = 34)	(n = 69)	(n = 92)	(n = 36)	(n = 81)	(n = 40)	(n = 139)	(n = 90)	(n = 63)
Intellectance	.17	.04	.36	.40	.52		.36	.50	.53	
Likability	.35	.52	.41	.14	.14	.22/.33/.39	.49	.47	.57	
Self-control	.26	.26	.25	.19	.47	.27/.40/.47	.64	.48	.67	.52
Sociability	.40	.55	.34	.46	.53	.43/.53/.59	.46	.53	.74	
Adjustment	.23	.43	.23	.38	.40	.22/.25/.27		.58	.48	
Dominance	.35	.41	.40	.58	.61			.52	.60	
M	.29	.37	.34	.37	.45	.29/.38/.44	.50	.51	.59	.52
	(.53)[c]	(.67)		(.51)	(.64)					

Note. The trait labels used here are based on Hogan's (1982) terminology, and we have used roughly equivalent scales from studies that did not use those exact terms (denoting the major "factors" usually found in trait rating studies).
[a] Data from subjects who rated their behaviors on a given dimension as publicly observable (Obs).
[b] Data based on 1, 2, and 3 judges, respectively.
[c] Figures in parentheses are corrected for attenuation.

properties. It is clear that the use of reliable rating scales leads to high agreement regarding a target's personality, but even single-item scales can produce consistently positive (and statistically significant) levels of agreement.[1] * * *

A consideration of this first hypothesis has taught us something about when the eyes of different beholders will behold different characteristics in the persons at whom they are looking. For instance, when rating strangers, observers will be quite happy to make attributions about what the strangers are like but will show little consensus (Funder & Colvin, 1987; Monson, Keel, Stephens, & Genung, 1982; Passini & Norman, 1966). So, although strangers' ratings provide an excellent domain for the study of bias (Fiske & Taylor, 1984), it

is probably futile to expect them to manifest much validity. However, when observers are well acquainted with the person they are judging, they nevertheless do manage to see something on which they can agree. The findings of consensus (such as those in Table 2) are sufficient to rule out the radical hypothesis that personality resides solely in the eye of the beholder.

* * *

HYPOTHESIS 2: AGREEMENT IS DUE TO SEMANTIC GENERALIZATION The first hypothesis, in its radical form, considered traits to be idiosyncratic constructions of the individual perceiver. The second hypothesis concedes that there is consensus in the use of trait terms but views that agreement as due simply to shared delusions based on common linguistic usage. According to the semantic generalization hypothesis, as soon as one judgment about another person is made, many other judgments follow based on nothing more than implicit expectations about which words "go together." Anyone judged as "friendly" may also be judged as "empathic," "altruistic," and "sincere" because the

---

[1]Most rating scales consist of a total score computed across the ratings of several or more individual items. The more the ratings of these different items within a scale tend to agree with each other, the more reliable the total scale is. More reliable scales tend to yield larger correlations with other variables. Single-item scales, by contrast, usually produce lower correlations.

concepts are semantically linked, even though the component behaviors themselves may not be so linked. For instance, "helping others in distress" and "contributing to charities" (behavioral components of "altruism") may not be correlated with "smiling a lot" and "talking to strangers" (behavioral components of "friendliness"), but judges who see evidence of "smiling a lot" might still infer "altruism," at least sometimes incorrectly. Shweder (1975) argued that shared preconceptions about "what goes with what" affected judgments so pervasively as to raise the question "How relevant is an individual differences theory of personality?" (See also D'Andrade, 1974.) Bourne (1977) went even further, suggesting that trait ratings might not reflect "anything more than raters' conceptual expectancies about which traits go together" (p. 863).

* * *

It is crucial to realize, as Block, Weiss, and Thorne (1979) pointed out, that semantic generalization cannot explain how different judges agree on attributing a *single* trait to a target person (as research such as that in Table 2 shows they do). To take a well-known example, the Passini and Norman (1966) study has been cited as evidence that trait ratings are based on "nothing more" than semantic similarity judgments. Indeed, Passini and Norman's data yielded a similar factor structure for ratings of friends and for ratings of strangers (who had been observed only briefly).[2] Because the strangers had very little time to observe one another, it is clear that an implicit personality theory guided their judgments. However, this issue of the relationships between trait words is completely orthogonal to the question of accuracy in application of any one of those words. Passini and Norman's subjects not only reached significant agreement about which trait applied to which person but they

also agreed more about friends' ratings than about strangers' (see also Funder & Colvin, 1987; Norman & Goldberg, 1966).

In light of such arguments, Shweder and D'Andrade (1979) seem to have reversed their earlier claim that semantic generalization negates the importance of judgments of individual differences. Although semantic structure might tell us to expect "friendly" to go with "altruistic" and not with "aggressive," it does not tell us whether we should apply the term more strongly to Walter or Seymour or Daryl. We must seek further for an adequate explanation of findings like those in Table 2.

HYPOTHESIS 3: AGREEMENT IS DUE TO BASE-RATE ACCURACY According to this hypothesis, interrater agreement is an artifact of the highly stable base rates that many traits have in the population at large. For example, the trait "needs to be with other people" characterizes most of us, whereas "has murderous tendencies" characterizes few. If one is trying to describe someone one does not know, therefore, one can achieve a certain degree of "accuracy" just by rating the first trait higher than the second. The base-rate hypothesis, like the semantic structure hypothesis, allows for consensus between observers but regards their judgments as indiscriminate. "Accuracy" of this sort might reflect knowledge about what people in general are like, what Cronbach (1955) called "stereotype accuracy," but does not necessarily reflect any knowledge specific to the person being described.

The base-rate accuracy problem helps us understand phenomena such as the "Barnum effect" (Ulrich, Stachnik, & Stainton, 1963), reflected in widespread acceptance of generalized descriptions such as, "You have a strong need for other people to like you and for them to admire you."[3] Ques-

---

[2]This reference to "factor structure" means that the different traits on which raters judged others tended to be correlated with each other in a similar manner whether the targets of judgment were close acquaintances or strangers. For example, people rated high on "talkativeness" also tend to be rated high on "friendliness," whether these people are well known to the rater or not.

[3]The "Barnum effect" was named for the circus promoter P. T. Barnum, who is said to have claimed "there's a sucker born every minute." In demonstrations of this effect a group of people are all given descriptions of their personalities that include phrases such as "you have a strong need for other people to like you." People often report that the descriptions are remarkably accurate, but in reality they were all given the same description!

tions of when and for whom base-rate accuracy becomes an issue are interesting ones. For example, a recent study by Miller, McFarland, and Turnbull (1985) found that Barnum statements are more likely to be accepted by subjects when the statements refer to attributes that are publicly observable and flattering. However, to argue that base-rate accuracy is a basis for doubting whether we "can . . . describe an individual's personality" (Bourne, 1977) takes things too far. The base-rate accuracy hypothesis, like the semantic similarity hypothesis, can explain how judges reach consensus but not how they distinguish *between* the targets they judge. To take a simple case, imagine that a group of sorority sisters rates one another on a dichotomous item (as either "friendly" or "unfriendly"). If "friendly" is chosen over "unfriendly" 9 out of 10 times, there could be a very high percentage of "agreement," in terms of overlapping judgments, even if there were absolutely no agreement about who the 10th, unfriendly person is. But if there is truly no agreement about individual targets, correlations calculated between judges will show no relationship at all. So base-rate accuracy cannot explain the results of inter-rater studies such as those in Table 2 either (cf. Funder, 1980a; Funder & Colvin, 1987; Funder & Dobroth, 1987).

Summarizing thus far, we may say that whatever role solipsism and glittering generality play as noise in personality assessment, a signal of consensus and discrimination comes through. Can that signal be explained without acceding to the existence of trait-like consistencies in behavior? The answer is still yes, and in at least three ways.

HYPOTHESIS 4: AGREEMENT IS DUE TO STEREOTYPES BASED ON OBVIOUS (BUT ERRONEOUS) CUES

None of the arguments considered so far can account for interjudge agreement about the differences between people. One hypothesis that does is this: Perhaps agreement about peers is due to shared (but incorrect) stereotypes based on one or another readily accessible (e.g., physical) cues. Many such stereotypes come to mind: physical types (athlete, fat person, dumb blonde), racial and

ethnic stereotypes, and so forth. Judges might share cultural stereotypes and so "agree" about burly, obese, or blond targets regardless of whether there were any corresponding consistencies in the targets' behavior.

Note that this hypothesis is very different from the sort of "stereotype accuracy" discussed under Hypothesis 3. That hypothesis referred to the possibility of indiscriminate responding based on raters' common preconceptions about what *everybody* is like. Hypothesis 4 refers to consensual agreement about traits that are *differentially* assigned to others. None of the first three hypotheses requires the observer to really "observe" anything distinctive about the person he or she is describing. This hypothesis, however, does require that the observer at least take a look at the target person—but assumes that the observer hardly looks much further than the end of his or her nose, just enough to assign the target person to a general category.

Such categorical stereotypes undoubtedly exist, but this does not mean we cannot become more accurate after getting to know someone beyond their "surface" categorization. Raters will try to make "reasonable" (i.e., stereotypic) guesses in the absence of real behavioral information. But as we mentioned earlier, their ratings increasingly converge as they actually observe the person's behavior (e.g., Funder & Colvin, 1987; Monson, Tanke, & Lund, 1980; Moskowitz & Schwarz, 1982; Norman & Goldberg, 1966; Passini & Norman, 1966).

The data that are most difficult for the stereotype hypothesis to explain are relationships between judgments and independent, objective behavioral measurements. For example, parents and teachers can provide general personality descriptions of children that not only agree with each other but also predict the children's "delay of gratification" behavior, measured in minutes and seconds, in a lab situation that none of the raters have ever seen (Bem & Funder, 1978; Funder, Block, & Block, 1983; Mischel, 1984). Other examples include Funder's studies of personality correlates of attributional style (1980b), attitude change (1982), and social acuity (Funder & Harris, 1986b);

Gormly and Edelberg's (1974) work on aggression; Moskowitz and Schwarz's (1982) work on dominance; and Alker and Owen's (1977) research on reactions to stressful events. This sort of predictive capability must arise from something beyond the use of invalid stereotypes.

Although the existence of stereotypes does not negate the existence of traits, it is useful to consider how stereotypes and personality traits interact. For example, physical attractiveness may actually lead one to become more friendly, via self-fulfilling prophecies (Goldman & Lewis, 1977; Snyder, Tanke, & Berscheid, 1977). Likewise, burly males really are more aggressive (Glueck & Glueck, 1956), probably because aggressiveness has a higher payoff for a muscular youth than it does for a skinny or flabby one.

In sum, although stereotypes may be informative about the genesis of some traits, and may account for judgments of strangers, the findings that observers agree more with one another after they have gotten to know the target and the correlations between ratings and independent assessments of behavior rule out the possibility that interrater agreement is due solely to the use of shared stereotypes based on superficial cues.

HYPOTHESIS 5: AGREEMENT IS DUE TO DISCUSSION BETWEEN OBSERVERS We just considered evidence that observers agree with each other better when they know the target person well. Is this because acquaintances have had more time to observe the relevant behaviors and hence are more truly accurate than strangers? Perhaps not. It could be argued that observers ignore the truly relevant nonverbal behaviors of a target person but are attentive to the target's verbalizations about himself or herself and come to regard the target as the target does for that reason (cf. Funder, 1980a; Funder & Colvin, 1987). Alternatively, observers might get together and discuss the target (McClelland, 1972), agree on his or her reputation, and then inform the target about how to regard himself or herself (as in the classical "looking glass self" formulations of C. H. Cooley, 1902).

The research cited earlier, showing how ratings of personality traits can predict behavior in unique settings, strongly suggests that such explicit "negotiation" is not all that underlies interjudge agreement. Moreover, several researchers have found that agreement between parents "back home" and peers at college is about as good as that among peers or among parents (Bem & Allen, 1974; Kenrick & Stringfield, 1980). Likewise, Koretzky et al. (1978) found respectable agreement between judges from different settings. In that study, the various settings were all within the same (mental) institution, but the Kenrick and Stringfield (1980) study was conducted in an isolated college town in Montana and used parents who often lived several hundred miles away from campus and were unlikely to have met the peers (whose home towns may have been hundreds of miles in the opposite direction), much less to have had intimate discussions with them about their children's traits.

Findings of higher agreement on traits that relate to observable behaviors (such as "friendliness" as opposed to "emotionality") are also relevant here. Kenrick and Stringfield (1980) found that "observable" traits are reported with better agreement than "unobservable" ones. * * * Related findings are reported by Amelang and Borkenau (1986), Cheek (1982), Funder and Colvin (1987), Funder and Dobroth (1987), and McCrae (1982) and in two unpublished studies, one by Dantchik (1985) and one by McCall, Linder, West, and Kenrick (1985). If judges simply manufacture a reputation for a subject, it seems that it would be just as easy to agree about terms relating to emotionality as it would be to agree about terms relating to extraversion. Higher agreement about publicly observable traits thus suggests that behavior is in fact being observed and accurately reported.

A tenacious adherent could still rescue this hypothesis by adding one more assumption. Perhaps we talk more about the so-called observable traits like extraversion than about "unobservable" traits. However, other findings further undermine the "discussion" hypothesis. Several studies have shown that when subjects' self-reports contradict their nonverbal behaviors, observers pay more attention to what is done than to what is said

(Amabile & Kabat, 1982; Bryan & Walbek, 1970). In the Amabile and Kabat study, subjects viewed a target who described herself as either "introverted" or "extraverted," and they also watched her behave in a way that was either consistent with, or inconsistent with, her self-description. Observers' subsequent judgments were much more strongly influenced by her actual behaviors than by the way she had described herself. It seems, then, that observers give more credence to trait-relevant behaviors than to self-descriptions.

Summarizing our arguments thus far, there is good evidence that trait ratings are more than solipsistic fantasies. Observers can agree in their trait ratings and can use them differently for different people. For those we know well, at least, trait ratings involve more than just stereotypes based on easily observable categories, and they are based more on behavioral observation than on unfounded gossip. Are we therefore now compelled to allow some veracity to the trait construct? Alas, the answer is still no, not necessarily.

HYPOTHESIS 6: AGREEMENT IS DUE TO SEEING OTHERS IN THE SAME SETTING

It is possible to allow for consensus and discrimination in the use of trait terms, and even to allow that observers are really and truly observing behavioral consistencies, without allowing that those behavioral consistencies stem from factors that are "internal" to the target person. As William James (1890), noted,

> Many a youth who is demure enough before his parents and teachers, swears and swaggers like a pirate among his "tough" young friends. We do not show ourselves to our children as to our club-companions, to our customers as to the laborers we employ, to our masters and employers as to our intimate friends. (p. 294)

Fellow club-companions may all agree that a particular merchant is consistently rather "wild," whereas his customers agree that he is quite "conventional." Because club-companions and customers live in "separate worlds," their different mutual delusions about the merchant's traits can be maintained. If behavior is mostly due to the situation, then the people who inhabit a given situation with a target will agree about that person's behavioral attributes, even if they are not actually general attributes of the individual's personality.

A good deal of the evidence we have already discussed poses difficulties for this hypothesis as a final explanation of rater agreement. Much of the research that uses trait ratings is based on studies of students who are rated by fellow fraternity members or college roommates (e.g., Bem & Allen, 1974; Cheek, 1982; Funder, 1980a; Funder & Dobroth, 1987; Kenrick & Stringfield, 1980). These individuals see each other across many settings, yet agree well. Recall also that studies such as those done by Bem and Allen (1974) and Kenrick and Stringfield (1980) found agreement across peer and parent groups—who see the targets in very different situations. In the Kenrick and Stringfield (1980) study, for instance, peers knew the target as a college student (and perhaps fellow beer drinker), whereas parents knew the target as a child (and perhaps a ranch hand). Restriction of range of environmental experience could even constrain correlations. For example, perhaps the college dorm is a setting that constrains one to be "friendly." If so, it will be a difficult and subtle task for raters who know two targets only in that setting to agree about which one is the more "dispositionally" friendly.

Finally, a good deal of the research just discussed shows how personality ratings made by parents, teachers, and friends often correlate well with behavior measured in settings that are very different from the contexts from which their judgments were derived. From observing their children at home, for example, parents can provide personality descriptions that predict behavior measured in a unique experimental setting (Bem & Funder, 1978)—even when a dozen or more years separate the personality judgments from the behavior (Mischel, 1984). Such predictability has to be based on the parents' detection of true "cross-situational consistency."

Although the "situational" hypothesis is often viewed as an alternative to the trait position, they need not be at odds with one another. Researchers have begun to uncover useful information about how persons and situations "interact" (e.g., Bem & Funder, 1978; Kenrick & Dantchik, 1983; Magnusson & Endler, 1977; Snyder & Ickes, 1985):

1. Traits influence behavior only in relevant situations (Allport, 1966; Bem & Funder, 1978). Anxiety, for example, shows up only in situations that the person finds threatening.

2. A person's traits can change a situation (Rausch, 1977). For instance, an aggressive child can bring out the hostility in a previously peaceful playground.

3. People with different traits will choose different settings (Snyder & Ickes, 1985). Highly sex-typed males, for example, seek out sexually stimulating situations; highly sex-typed females avoid them (Kenrick, Stringfield, Wagenhals, Dahl, & Ransdell, 1980).

4. Traits can change with chronic exposure to certain situations. For instance, Newcomb's students became less conservative during their Bennington college experience and stayed that way for decades (Newcomb, Koenig, Flacks, & Warwick, 1967).

5. Traits are more easily expressed in some situations than others. They have more influence when situations are low in constraint—for example, a picnic as opposed to a funeral (Monson et al., 1982; Price & Bouffard, 1974; Schutte, Kenrick, & Sadalla, 1985). Traits are also more likely to be influential in settings that are highly prototypical or exemplary (Schutte et al., 1985). For instance, the postinterview cocktail party for an academic job applicant is more difficult to categorize than the in-office interview or the office Christmas party and would probably allow for the operation of greater individual differences. Note that laboratory situations, where psychologists often look for evidence of individual differences, will constrain the operation of traits precisely because they are rigidly controlled, are imposed arbitrarily on subjects, and are usually not reactive to anything the subject does (Monson & Snyder, 1977; Wachtel, 1973).

The data we have discussed thus far require us to concede that some degree of consensus, discrimination, and internality exists in the trait domain. Is it time, therefore, to give the store back to the "trait" position? Even with the distance we have come, the answer is still no. It is possible to argue that although some true cross-situational consistencies in behavior may exist, they are too small to worry about.

HYPOTHESIS 7: THE RELATIONSHIPS BETWEEN TRAITS AND BEHAVIOR ARE "TOO SMALL" TO BE IMPORTANT

Just how small is "too small"? Mischel's (1968) review concluded that correlations between trait scores and behaviors and between different behaviors are seldom larger than about .30. This conclusion hit the field of personality with devastating force because of two separable assumptions: (a) The coefficient .30 is not simply an artifact of poorly developed research tools but is the true upper limit for the predictability of behavior from personality, and (b) this upper limit is a small upper limit. Acceptance of both of these assumptions was necessary for Mischel's critique to have had a major impact, and many initially did accept them.

Several personologists (e.g., Block, 1977; Hogan, DeSoto, & Solano, 1977) have challenged the first assumption, arguing that Mischel's review did not give a fair hearing to the better studies in the personality literature. More than the several studies cited in earlier sections of this article have used direct behavioral observations and found larger correlations with behavior (see also Block, Buss, Block, & Gjerde, 1981; Block, von der Lippe, & Block, 1973; McGowen & Gormly, 1976; Moskowitz, 1982). Epstein (1979, 1983) reported that such correlations can be especially high when aggregates of behavior[4] rather than single instances are used.

Indeed, in everyday life, what we usually wish

---

[4]An "aggregate" is an average of several variables or observations. Aggregates tend to be more reliable and therefore more predictable than single observations. For example, the average of your friendliness on 10 different occasions over the next 3 weeks would be easier to predict than how friendly you will be tomorrow at 3 P.M.

to predict on the basis of our personality judgments are not single acts, but aggregate trends: Will this person make an agreeable friend, a reliable employee, an affectionate spouse? Given such broad criteria, the Spearman-Brown formula shows how even "small" single-act correlations compound into extremely high predictive validities. For example, Mischel and Peake (1982) found that interitem correlations between behavior measures are relatively low (.14 to .21) for single, unaggregated observations but that coefficient alpha for their total behavioral aggregate is .74. That is, a similar aggregate of behaviors would correlate .74 with that one. Along the same lines, Epstein and O'Brien (1985) reanalyzed several classical studies in the field of personality. In all of these studies behavior was situation specific at the single-item level (in line with Mischel's point) but cross-situationally general at the level of behavioral aggregates. Protagonists on both sides of the controversy now seem ready to allow that the ".30 ceiling" applies only to behavior in unaggregated form (Epstein, 1983; Mischel, 1983).

Even if one were to allow that it is difficult to surpass correlations of .30 to .40 (e.g., in the case of unaggregated measures), it may be a mistake to assume that such correlations are "small." In fact, correlations in this range characterize the strength of some of the most interesting and important situational effects found by experimental social psychology (Funder & Ozer, 1983; Sarason, Smith, & Diener, 1975) and even some of Mischel's own work on situational determinants of delay of gratification behavior (Funder & Harris, 1986a). These observations echo Hogan et al.'s (1977) warning that a correlation of .30 does not necessarily mean that the "remaining 91% of the variance" can be assigned, by subtraction, to the situation.

Moreover, a correlation of .30 may not be as small as many psychologists seem to believe. Common practice, as exemplified in the above warning, is to square such a correlation and report that it "accounts for 9% of the variance." However, Ozer (1985) claimed that, contrary to common belief and practice, the unsquared correlation coefficient is directly interpretable as the percentage of the variance accounted for. For example, $r = .30$ ac-

counts for 30%, not 9%, of the relevant variance. Another way of clarifying the size of an effect in this range is Rosenthal and Rubin's (1979, 1982) binomial effect size display, which reveals that a predictor that correlates .30 with a dichotomous criterion will yield correct discriminations 65% of the time.[5] Abelson (1985) made the point in a vivid way with an application of the "percentage of variance" approach to batting performances in major league baseball players. Noting that most are in the .200s to .300s, he calculates that the percentage of variance explained in a single batting performance is less than 1%. Yet, with aggregation over seasons, these minuscule differences compound to result in discriminations important enough to determine hundreds of thousands of dollars in salary differentials. Thus, the .30 statistic that had such a devastating effect on the enterprise of personality assessment may have been badly misunderstood.

The hypothesis that personality coefficients are "too small" has been quite useful in elucidating some important limitations on what can be measured and how it should be measured. Minute and unaggregated behavioral indexes, no matter what their face validity, are not necessarily good criterion measures (Golding, 1978; West, 1983). They may be full of various sorts of error, lack temporal stability, or measure something other than what they seem to measure (Bem & Funder, 1978; Moskowitz & Schwarz, 1982; Romer & Revelle, 1984). Even if it is true, as Fiske (1979) pointed out, that judges can agree quite well about the occurrence of a given facial twitch, the twitch may be meaningless unless its context is understood (Block et al., 1979; Dahlstrom, 1972; Hogan, DeSoto, & Solano, 1977). These problems may account for the repeated finding that when objective behavioral measures are compared with observers' ratings, the results do not support the superiority of behavioral measures (e.g., Eaton & Enns, 1986; Moskowitz & Schwarz, 1982).

---

[5]See the selection by Rosenthal and Rubin in Part I, which is what is being referred to here.

What Have We Learned?

As with most controversies, the truth finally appears to lie not in the vivid black or white of either extreme, but somewhere in the less striking gray area. It would be a mistake, however, to claim that the interchange served only to bring out a number of "straw man" positions that no one ever took seriously anyway, that the repetitive cycle of argument and reply produced no more than fatigue and déjà vu, or that we are no closer to understanding personality traits than we were two decades ago. Radical versions of each of these hypotheses were suggested, not just for rhetorical purposes, and were passed uncritically onward to a generation of students in psychology courses. We were trained as experimental social psychologists during the heat of the debate, and the shade of gray we see now seemed much closer to a gloomy black back then. Indeed, for a time, and in some places, it was not unusual for the very idea of personality traits to be dismissed out of hand and even ridiculed.

On the other hand, one of us also underwent clinical training during that era and came across a viewpoint much closer to the "pure trait" position than is remotely tenable on the basis of the data available now. Ten years ago, there were, and probably still are (Mischel, 1983; Wade & Baker, 1977), clinical professionals overconfidently making grand predictions from minute samples of behavior of highly questionable reliability and validity. We can eliminate the radical forms of each of the seven critical hypotheses, but that does not imply that the so-called "pure trait" position has regained the day. Systematic sources of judgmental bias, systematic effects of situations, and systematic interactions between persons and situations must be explicitly dealt with before we can predict from trait measures.

So although there may be enough signal amidst the noise in this research area to make it worthwhile to turn on the radio, the device must still be carefully tuned. Instead of simply viewing each of the seven critical hypotheses as being resolved in favor of the trait position, it is better to view each as a clue about one ever-present source of noise to be tuned out. Kenny and La Voie (1984) showed how factors such as idiosyncratic rater bias (the problem of Hypothesis 1) can even, under the proper circumstances, be turned to statistical advantage in estimating a person's "true" trait score.

Other practical lessons have emerged from this controversy. The research now indicates quite clearly that anyone who seeks predictive validity from trait ratings will do better to use (a) raters who are thoroughly familiar with the person being rated; (b) multiple behavioral observations; (c) multiple observers; (d) dimensions that are publicly observable; and (e) behaviors that are relevant to the dimension in question.

On the other hand, one should *not* expect great accuracy when predicting (a) behavior in "powerful" and clearly normatively scripted situations from trait ratings and (b) a single behavioral instance from another single behavioral instance.

Those who would respond to this list by claiming that they "knew it all along" may or may not be guilty of hindsight bias (Fischoff, 1975). But they should at least acknowledge that many of us did not know these principles all along and needed the light generated by controversy to open our eyes. For instance, the apparently "obvious" insight that we should not rely on ratings made by strangers can help us understand why some of the data on clinical assessment (e.g., Goldberg & Werts, 1966; Golden, 1964; Soskin, 1959) have been so disappointing, and the awareness that traits will not show up in overpowering situations has led to a dramatic reassessment of failures to find "consistency" in brief laboratory observations. Likewise, if these issues and that of the unreliability of single behavioral instances were so obvious, one is left to wonder why the field responded so strongly to Mischel's (1968) critique. "Déjà vu" may be an accurate description of our current situation after all, because the term actually refers to the *illusion* that one has previously experienced something that is really new.

One side effect of the person-situation debate has been an intensification of the antagonism between personality and social psychology. Social psychologists have historically focused on situational determinants of behavior and were therefore quite willing to join with behavioral clinicians in the situationist attack on personality (Hogan & Emler, 1978; Kenrick & Dantchik, 1983). Personologists share a very different set of assumptions, and the two subdisciplines have sometimes seemed intent on defining each other out of existence (Kenrick, 1986). To continue such separation between the two fields would be a mistake. Many exciting developments are beginning to emerge at the interface of social and personality psychology. For instance, research that combines personality with biology suggests a vast array of questions about the connection between personality traits and social interaction (Kenrick, 1987; Kenrick & Trost, 1987; Sadalla, Kenrick, & Vershure, 1987). And research on the accuracy of interpersonal judgment draws equally on both personality and social psychology (Funder, 1987; Funder & Colvin, 1987; Funder & Dobroth, 1987).

Houts, Cook, and Shadish (1986) made a strong case that science best progresses through multiple and mutually critical attempts to understand the same problem. When camps with strongly opposing sets of biases manage to come to some level of agreement, we may be more confident of the validity of the conclusions that are agreed upon. Viewed in this light, the controversy stimulated by the situationist attack on personality may be seen more as a life-giving transfusion than as a needless bloodletting.

References

Abelson, R. P. (1976). A script theory of understanding, attitude, and behavior. In J. Carroll & J. Payne (Eds.), *Cognition and social behavior* (pp. 33–45). Hillsdale, NJ: Erlbaum.

Abelson, R. P. (1985). A variance explanation paradox: When a little is a lot. *Psychological Bulletin, 97,* 129–133.

Alker, H. A. (1972). Is personality situationally specific or intrapsychically consistent? *Journal of Personality, 40,* 1–16.

Alker, H. A., & Owen, D. W. (1977). Biographical, trait, and behavioral-sampling predictions of performance in a stressful life setting. *Journal of Personality and Social Psychology, 35,* 717–723.

Allport, G. W. (1931). What is a trait of personality? *Journal of Abnormal and Social Psychology, 25,* 368–372.

Allport, G. W. (1966). Traits revisited. *American Psychologist, 21,* 1–10.

Alston, W. P. (1975). Traits, consistency, and conceptual alterna-

tives for personality theory. *Journal for the Theory of Social Behavior, 5,* 17–48.

Amabile, T. M., & Kabat, L. G. (1982). When self-description contradicts behavior: Actions do speak louder than words. *Social Cognition, 1,* 311–335.

Amelang, M., & Borkenau, P. (1986). The trait concept: Current theoretical considerations, empirical facts, and implications for personality inventory construction. In A. Angleitner & J. S. Wiggins (Eds.), *Personality assessment via questionnaire* (pp. 7–24). Berlin: Springer-Verlag.

Argyle, M., & Little, B. R. (1972). Do personality traits apply to social behavior? *Journal for the Theory of Social Behavior, 2,* 1–35.

Bem, D. J. (1972). Constructing cross-situational consistencies in behavior: Some thoughts on Alker's critique of Mischel. *Journal of Personality, 40,* 17–26.

Bem, D. J. (1983). Further *déjà vu* in the search for cross situational consistency: A reply to Mischel and Peake. *Psychological Review, 90,* 390–393.

Bem, D. J., & Allen, A. (1974). On predicting some of the people some of the time: The search for cross-situational consistencies in behavior. *Psychological Review, 81,* 506–520.

Bem, D. J., & Funder, D. C. (1978). Predicting more of the people more of the time: Assessing the personality of situations. *Psychological Review, 85,* 485–501.

Block, J. (1968). Some reasons for the apparent inconsistency of personality. *Psychological Bulletin, 70,* 210–212.

Block, J. (1977). Advancing the science of personality: Paradigmatic shift or improving the quality of research? In D. Magnusson & N. S. Endler (Eds.), *Personality at the crossroads: Current issues in interactional psychology* (pp. 37–63). Hillsdale, NJ: Erlbaum.

Block, J., Buss, D. M., Block, J. M., & Gjerde, P. F. (1981). The cognitive style of breadth of categorization: The longitudinal consistency of personality correlates. *Journal of Personality and Social Psychology, 40,* 770–779.

Block, J., von der Lippe, A., & Block, J. H. (1973). Sex-role and socialization patterns: Some personality concomitants and environmental antecedents. *Journal of Consulting and Clinical Psychology, 41,* 321–341.

Block, J., Weiss, D. S., & Thorne, A. (1979). How relevant is a semantic similarity interpretation of personality ratings? *Journal of Personality and Social Psychology, 37,* 1055–1074.

Bourne, E. (1977). Can we describe an individual's personality? Agreement on stereotype versus individual attributes. *Journal of Personality and Social Psychology, 35,* 863–872.

Bowers, K. S. (1973). Situationism in psychology: An analysis and critique. *Psychological Review, 80,* 307–336.

Bryan, J., & Walbek, N. (1970). Impact of words and deeds concerning altruism upon children. *Child Development, 41,* 747–757.

Carlson, R. (1984). What's social about social psychology? Where's the person in personality research? *Journal of Personality and Social Psychology, 35,* 1055–1074.

Cheek, J. M. (1982). Aggregation, moderator variables, and the validity of personality tests: A peer-rating study. *Journal of Personality and Social Psychology, 43,* 1254–1269.

Cooley, C. H. (1902). *Human nature and the social order.* New York: Scribner's.

Cronbach, L. J. (1955). Processes affecting scores on "understanding of others" and "assumed similarity." *Psychological Bulletin, 52,* 177–193.

Dahlstrom, W. G. (1972). *Personality systematics and the problem of types.* Morristown, NJ: General Learning Press.

D'Andrade, R. G. (1974). Memory and the assessment of behavior. In H. M. Blalock (Ed.), *Measurement in the social sciences* (pp. 159–186). Chicago: Aldine-Atherton.

Dantchik, A. (1985). *Idiographic approaches to personality assessment.* Unpublished master's thesis, Arizona State University, Tempe.

Dornbusch, S. M., Hastorf, A. H., Richardson, S. A., Muzzy, R. E., & Vreeland, R. S. (1965). The perceiver and perceived: Their relative influence on categories of interpersonal perception. *Journal of Personality and Social Psychology, 1,* 434–440.

Eaton, W. D., & Enns, L. R. (1986). Sex differences in human activity level. *Psychological Bulletin, 100,* 19–28.

Endler, N. S. (1973). The person vs. situation: A pseudo issue? *Journal of Personality, 41,* 287–303.

Epstein, S. (1977). Traits are alive and well. In D. Magnusson & N. S. Endler (Eds.), *Personality at the crossroads: Current issues in interactional psychology* (pp. 83–98). Hillsdale, NJ: Erlbaum.

Epstein, S. (1979). The stability of behavior: I. On predicting most of the people much of the time. *Journal of Personality and Social Psychology, 37,* 1097–1126.

Epstein, S. (1980). The stability of behavior: II. Implications for psychological research. *American Psychologist, 35,* 790–806.

Epstein, S. (1983). The stability of confusion: A reply to Mischel and Peake. *Psychological Review, 90,* 390–393.

Epstein, S., & O'Brien, E. J. (1985). The person-situation debate in historical and current perspective. *Psychological Bulletin, 98,* 513–537.

Farber, I. E. (1964). A framework for the study of personality as a behavioral science. In P. Worchel & D. Bryne (Eds.), *Personality change* (pp. 3–37). New York: Wiley.

Fischoff, B. (1975). Hindsight does not equal foresight: The effect of outcome knowledge on judgment under uncertainty. *Journal of Experimental Psychology: Human Perception and Performance, 1,* 288–299.

Fiske, D. W. (1974). The limits for the conventional science of personality. *Journal of Personality, 42,* 1–11.

Fiske, D. W. (1979). Two worlds of psychological phenomena. *American Psychologist, 34,* 733–739.

Fiske, S., & Taylor, S. (1984). *Social cognition.* New York: Random House.

Funder, D. C. (1980a). On seeing ourselves as others see us: Self-other agreement and discrepancy in personality ratings. *Journal of Personality, 48,* 473–493.

Funder, D. C. (1980b). The "trait" of ascribing traits: Individual differences in the tendency to trait ascription. *Journal of Research in Personality, 14,* 376–385.

Funder, D. C. (1982). On assessing social psychological theories through the study of individual differences: Template matching and forced compliance. *Journal of Personality and Social Psychology, 43,* 100–110.

Funder, D. C. (1983). Three issues in predicting more of the people: A reply to Mischel and Peake. *Psychological Review, 90,* 283–289.

Funder, D. C. (1987). Errors and mistakes: Evaluating the accuracy of social judgment. *Psychological Bulletin, 101,* 75–90.

Funder, D. C., Block, J., & Block, J. H. (1983). Delay of gratification: Some longitudinal personality correlates. *Journal of Personality and Social Psychology, 44,* 1198–1213.

Funder, D. C., & Colvin, C. R. (1987). *Friends and strangers: Acquaintanceship, agreement, and the accuracy of personality judgment.* Manuscript submitted for publication.

Funder, D. C., & Dobroth, J. M. (1987). Differences between traits: Properties associated with interjudge agreement. *Journal of Personality and Social Psychology, 52,* 409–418.

Funder, D. C., & Harris, M. J. (1986a). Experimental effects and person effects in delay of gratification. *American Psychologist, 41,* 476–477.

Funder, D. C., & Harris, M. J. (1986b). On the several facets of personality assessment: The case of social acuity. *Journal of Personality, 54,* 528–550.

Funder, D. C., & Ozer, D. J. (1983). Behavior as a function of the situation. *Journal of Personality and Social Psychology, 44,* 107–112.

Gergen, K. J. (1968). Personal consistency and the presentation of self. In C. Gordon & K. J. Gergen (Eds.), *The self in social interaction* (pp. 299–308). New York: Wiley.

Glueck, S., & Glueck, E. (1956). *Physique and delinquency.* New York: Harper & Row.

Goldberg, L. R., & Werts, C. E. (1966). The reliability of clinician's judgments: A multitrait-multimethod approach. *Journal of Consulting Psychology, 30,* 199–206.

Golden, M. (1964). Some effects of combining psychological tests on clinical inferences. *Journal of Consulting Psychology, 28,* 440–446.

Golding, S. L. (1978). Toward a more adequate theory of personality: Psychological organizing principles. In H. London (Ed.), *Personality: A new look at metatheories* (pp. 69–96). New York: Wiley.

Goldman, W., & Lewis, P. (1977). Beautiful is good: Evidence that the physically attractive are more socially skilled. *Journal of Experimental Social Psychology, 13,* 125–130.

Gormly, J., & Edelberg, W. (1974). Validity in personality trait attributions. *American Psychologist, 29,* 189–193.

Gregory, R. L. (1971). Visual illusions. In R. C. Atkinson (Ed.), *Contemporary psychology* (pp. 167–177). San Francisco: W. H. Freeman.

Hogan, R. (1982). A socioanalytic theory of personality. In R. A. Dienstbier & M. M. Page (Eds.), *Nebraska symposium on motivation* (Vol. 30, pp. 55–89). Lincoln: University of Nebraska Press.

Hogan, R., DeSoto, C. B., and Solano, C. (1977). Traits, tests, and personality research. *American Psychologist, 32,* 255–264.

Hogan, R. T., & Emler, N. P. (1978). The biases in contemporary social psychology. *Social Research, 45,* 478–534.

Houts, A. C., Cook, T. D., & Shadish, W. R. (1986). The person-situation debate: A critical multiplist perspective. *Journal of Personality, 54,* 52–105.

Hunt, J. McV. (1965). Traditional personality theory in the light of recent evidence. *American Scientist, 53,* 80–96.

Ichheiser, G. (1943). Misinterpretations of personality in everyday life and the psychologist's frame of reference. *Character and Personality, 12,* 145–160.

Jackson, D. N. (1983). Some preconditions for valid person perception. In M. P. Zanna, E. T. Higgins, & C. P. Herman (Eds.), *Consistency in social behavior: The Ontario Symposium* (pp. 251–279). Hillsdale, NJ: Erlbaum.

James, W. (1890). *Principles of psychology* (Vol. 1). London: Macmillan.

Kenny, D. A., & La Voie, L. (1984). The social relations model. In

L. Berkowitz (Ed.), *Advances in experimental social psychology* (Vol. 18, pp. 141–182). Orlando, FL: Academic Press.

Kenrick, D. T. (1986). How strong is the case against contemporary social and personality psychology? A response to Carlson. *Journal of Personality and Social Psychology, 50,* 839–844.

Kenrick, D. T. (1987). Gender, genes, and the social environment. In P. C. Shaver & C. Hendrick (Eds.), *Review of personality and social psychology: Vol. 7. Sex and gender* (pp. 14–43). Beverly Hills, CA: Sage.

Kenrick, D. T., & Braver, S. L. (1982). Personality: Idiographic and nomothetic! A rejoinder. *Psychological Review, 89,* 182–186.

Kenrick, D. T., & Dantchik, A. (1983). Interactionism, idiographics, and the social psychological invasion of personality. *Journal of Personality, 51,* 286–307.

Kenrick, D. T., & Stringfield, D. O. (1980). Personality traits and the eye of the beholder: Crossing some traditional philosophical boundaries in the search for consistency in all of the people. *Psychological Review, 87,* 88–104.

Kenrick, D. T., Stringfield, D. O., Wagenhals, W. L., Dahl, R. H., & Ransdell, H. J. (1980). Sex differences, androgyny, and approach responses to erotica: A new variation on the old volunteer problem. *Journal of Personality and Social Psychology, 40,* 1039–1056.

Kenrick, D. T., & Trost, M. R. (1987). A biosocial theory of heterosexual relationships. In K. Kelley (Ed.), *Males, females, and sexuality: Theory and research* (pp. 59–100). Albany: State University of New York Press.

Koretzky, M. B., Kohn, M., & Jeger, A. M. (1978). Cross-situational consistency among problem adolescents: An application of the two-factor model. *Journal of Personality and Social Psychology, 36,* 1054–1059.

Magnusson, D., & Endler, N. S. (Eds.). (1977). *Personality at the crossroads: Current issues in interactional psychology.* Hillsdale, NJ: Erlbaum.

McArthur, L. Z., & Baron, R. M. (1983). Toward an ecological theory of social perception. *Psychological Review, 90,* 215–235.

McCall, M., Linder, D. E., West, S. G., & Kenrick, D. T. (1985). *Some cautions on the template-matching approach to assessing person/environment interactions.* Unpublished manuscript, Arizona State University, Tempe.

McClelland, D. C. (1972). Opinions reflect opinions: So what else is new? *Journal of Consulting and Clinical Psychology, 38,* 325–326.

McCrae, R. R. (1982). Consensual validation of personality traits: Evidence from self-reports and ratings. *Journal of Personality and Social Psychology, 43,* 293–303.

McGowen, J., & Gormly, J. (1976). Validation of personality traits: A multicriteria approach. *Journal of Personality and Social Psychology, 34,* 791–795.

Miller, D. T., McFarland, C., & Turnbull, W. (1985). *Pluralistic ignorance: Its causes and consequences.* Paper presented at the annual meeting of the Eastern Psychological Association, Boston.

Mischel, W. (1968). *Personality and assessment.* New York: Wiley.

Mischel, W. (1983). Alternatives in the pursuit of the predictability and consistency of persons: Stable data that yield unstable interpretations. *Journal of Personality, 51,* 578–604.

Mischel, W. (1984). Convergences and challenges in the search for consistency. *American Psychologist, 39,* 351–364.

Mischel, W., & Peake, P. K. (1982). Beyond *déjà vu* in the search for cross-situational consistency. *Psychological Review, 89,* 730–755.

Mischel, W., & Peake, P. K. (1983). Some facets of consistency: Replies to Epstein, Funder, and Bem. *Psychological Review, 90,* 394–402.

Monson, T. C., Keel, R., Stephens, D., & Genung, V. (1982). Trait attributions: Relative validity, covariation with behavior, and prospect of future interaction. *Journal of Personality and Social Psychology, 42,* 1014–1024.

Monson, T. C., Tanke, E. D., & Lund, J. (1980). Determinants of social perception in a naturalistic setting. *Journal of Research in Personality, 14,* 104–120.

Monson, T. C., & Snyder, M. (1977). Actors, observers, and the attribution process: Toward a reconceptualization. *Journal of Experimental Social Psychology, 13,* 89–111.

Moskowitz, D. S. (1982). Coherence and cross-situational generality in personality: A new analysis of old problems. *Journal of Personality and Social Psychology, 43,* 754–768.

Moskowitz, D. S., & Schwarz, J. C. (1982). Validity comparison of behavior counts and ratings by knowledgeable informants. *Journal of Personality and Social Psychology, 42,* 518–528.

Newcomb, T. M., Koenig, K. E., Flacks, R., & Warwick, D. P. (1967). *Persistence and change: Bennington College and its students after twenty-five years.* New York: Wiley.

Nisbett, R. E., & Ross, L. D. (1980). *Human inference: Strategies and shortcomings of social judgment.* New York: Prentice-Hall.

Norman, W. T., & Goldberg, L. R. (1966). Raters, ratees, and randomness in personality structure. *Journal of Personality and Social Psychology, 4,* 681–691.

Ozer, D. J. (1985). Correlation and the coefficient of determination. *Psychological Bulletin, 97,* 307–315.

Passini, F. T., & Norman, W. T. (1966). A universal conception of personality structure? *Journal of Personality and Social Psychology, 4,* 44–49.

Paunonen, S. V., & Jackson, D. N. (1985). Idiographic measurement strategies for personality and prediction: Some unredeemed promissory notes. *Psychological Review, 92,* 486–511.

Platt, J. R. (1964). Strong inference. *Science, 146,* 347–353.

Popper, K. (1959). *The logic of scientific discovery.* New York: Basic Books.

Price, R. H., & Bouffard, D. L. (1974). Behavioral appropriateness and situational constraint as dimensions of social behavior. *Journal of Personality and Social Psychology, 30,* 579–586.

Rausch, M. L. (1977). Paradox, levels, and junctures in person-situation systems. In D. Magnusson & N. S. Endler (Eds.), *Personality at the crossroads* (pp. 287–304). Hillsdale, NJ: Erlbaum.

Romer, D., & Revelle, W. (1984). Personality traits: Fact or fiction? A critique of the Shweder and D'Andrade systematic distortion hypothesis. *Journal of Personality and Social Psychology, 47,* 1028–1042.

Rosenthal, R., & Rubin, D. B. (1979). A note on percent variance explained as a measure of the importance of effects. *Journal of Applied Social Psychology, 9,* 385–396.

Rosenthal, R., & Rubin, D. B. (1982). A simple, general purpose display of magnitude of experimental effect. *Journal of Educational Psychology, 74,* 166–169.

Ross, L. (1977). The intuitive psychologist and his shortcomings: Distortions in the attribution process. In L. Berkowitz (Ed.), *Advances in experimental social psychology* (Vol. 10, pp. 174–221). New York: Academic Press.

Sadalla, E. K., Kenrick, D. T., & Vershure, B. (1987). Dominance and heterosexual attraction. *Journal of Personality and Social Psychology, 52,* 730–738.

Sarason, I. G., Smith, R. E., & Diener, E. (1975). Personality research: Components of variance attributable to the person and the situation. *Journal of Personality and Social Psychology, 32,* 199–204.

Schank, R. C., & Abelson, R. P. (1977). *Scripts, plans, goals, and understanding.* Hillsdale, NJ: Erlbaum.

Schneider, D. (1973). Implicit personality theory: A review. *Psychological Bulletin, 79,* 294–309.

Schutte, N. A., Kenrick, D. T., & Sadalla, E. K. (1985). The search for predictable settings: Situational prototypes, constraint, and behavioral variation. *Journal of Personality and Social Psychology, 49,* 121–128.

Shweder, R. A. (1975). How relevant is an individual-difference theory of personality? *Journal of Personality, 43,* 455–485.

Shweder, R. A., & D'Andrade, R. G. (1979). Accurate reflection or systematic distortion: A reply to Block, Weiss, and Thorne. *Journal of Personality and Social Psychology, 37,* 1075–1084.

Snyder, M., & Ickes, W. (1985). Personality and social behavior. In G. Lindzey & E. Aronson (Eds.), *Handbook of social psychology* (3rd ed., Vol. 2, pp. 883–948). Reading, MA: Addison-Wesley.

Snyder, M., Tanke, E. D., & Berscheid, E. (1977). Social perception and interpersonal behavior: On the self-fulfilling nature of social stereotypes. *Journal of Personality and Social Psychology, 35,* 656–666.

Soskin, W. F. (1959). Influence of four types of data on diagnostic conceptualization in psychological testing. *Journal of Abnormal and Social Psychology, 58,* 69–78.

Trope, Y., Bassok, M., & Alon, E. (1984). The questions lay interviewers ask. *Journal of Personality, 52,* 90–106.

Ulrich, R. E., Stachnik, T. J., & Stainton, N. R. (1963). Student acceptance of generalized personality interpretations. *Psychological Reports, 13,* 831–834.

Wachtel, P. (1973). Psychodynamics, behavior therapy, and the implacable experimenter: An inquiry into the consistency of personality. *Journal of Abnormal Psychology, 82,* 324–334.

Wade, T. C., & Baker, T. B. (1977). Opinions and use of psychological tests: A survey of clinical psychologists. *American Psychologist, 32,* 874–882.

West, S. G. (1983). Personality and prediction: An introduction. *Journal of Personality, 51,* 275–285.

Wiggins, J. S. (1973). *Personality and prediction: Principles of personality assessment.* Reading, MA: Addison-Wesley.

Zuroff, D. C. (1986). Was Gordon Allport a trait theorist? *Journal of Personality and Social Psychology, 51,* 993–1000.

A Five-Factor Theory of Personality

Robert R. McCrae and Paul T. Costa Jr.

More than 60 years ago, Gordon Allport and one of his students counted the trait words in an unabridged dictionary and came up with 17,953 (Allport & Odbert, 1936)! Personality psychologists have not made up tests to measure all of these, but it is safe to estimate that at least a couple of thousand different personality traits have been investigated by one researcher or another. It is reasonable to wonder whether all these different traits are strictly necessary. Can we reduce the vast number of trait terms in the language and the research literature down to an essential few? If so, this would be an important accomplishment, for it would vastly simplify the task of personality assessment and go a long way toward making it possible to compare the research of different psychologists.

In recent years, the personality psychologists Robert McCrae and Paul Costa Jr. have argued that the "Big Five" traits of personality are the truly essential ones. They call these traits extraversion, neuroticism, openness to experience, agreeableness, and conscientiousness. Not everybody believes these traits are important (see Block, 1995, for one vigorous dissent), but many psychologists find the Big Five to be a useful—if not all-encompassing—common framework for the conceptualization of individual differences in personality. As Ozer and Reise (1994) stated, the Big Five can serve a useful purpose as the "latitude and longitude" along which the thousands of possible personality traits can be located.

In this article, McCrae and Costa present the latest wrinkle in their thinking about the Big Five, which is that these traits are useful not only for describing personality but also for explaining it. They present a theory of personality that presents the Big Five traits as the "basic tendencies" that underlie all of personality, and include a figure that shows how these tendencies interact with culture, situations, the self-concept, and behavior.

The research and theorizing relevant to the Big Five—pro and con—continue to be lively, and the final chapter on this topic has not yet been written. In the meantime, it is worth pondering two questions. First, how much of human personality can be encompassed by five basic traits—is anything important

*left out? And second, are these traits simply descriptions of personality, or are
they the actual causes?*

From *Handbook of Personality: Theory and Research* (2nd ed.), edited by L. A. Pervin and
O. P. John (New York: Guilford, 1999), pp. 139–153.

Empirical and Conceptual Bases of a New Theory

In a narrow sense, the Five-Factor Model (FFM) of personality is an empirical generalization about the covariation of personality traits. As Digman and Inouye (1986) put it, "If a large number of rating scales is used and if the scope of the scales is very broad, the domain of personality descriptors is almost completely accounted for by five robust factors" (p. 116). The five factors, frequently labeled Neuroticism (N), Extraversion (E), Openness (O), Agreeableness (A), and Conscientiousness (C), have been found not only in the peer rating scales in which they were originally discovered (Tupes & Christal, 1961/1992) but also in self-reports on trait descriptive adjectives (Saucier, 1997), in questionnaire measures of needs and motives (Costa & McCrae, 1988), in expert ratings on the California Q-Set (Lanning, 1994), and in personality disorder symptom clusters (Clark & Livesley, 1994). Much of what psychologists mean by the term *personality* is summarized by the FFM, and the model has been of great utility to the field by integrating and systematizing diverse conceptions and measures.

In a broader sense, the FFM refers to the entire body of research that it has inspired, amounting to a reinvigoration of trait psychology itself. Research associated with the FFM has included studies of diverse populations (McCrae, Costa, del Pilar, Rolland, & Parker, 1998), often followed over decades of the lifespan (Costa & McCrae, 1992c); employed multiple methods of assessment (Funder, Kolar, & Blackman, 1995); and even featured case studies (Costa & McCrae, 1998b; McCrae, 1993–94). * * * After decades of floundering, personality psychology has begun to make steady progress, accumulating a store of replicable findings about the origins, development, and functioning of personality traits (McCrae, 1992).

But neither the model itself nor the body of research findings with which it is associated constitutes a theory of personality. A theory organizes findings to tell a coherent story, to bring into focus those issues and phenomena that can and should be explained. * * * Five-Factor Theory (FFT; McCrae & Costa, 1996) represents an effort to construct such a theory that is consistent with current knowledge about personality. In this chapter we summarize and elaborate it.

* * *

ASSUMPTIONS ABOUT HUMAN NATURE The trait perspective, like every psychological theory, is based on a set of assumptions about what people are like and what a theory of personality ought to do. Most of these assumptions—for example, that explanations for behavior are to be sought in the circumstances of this life, not karma from a previous one—are implicit. FFT explicitly acknowledges four assumptions about human nature (cf. Hjelle & Siegler, 1976)—*knowability, rationality, variability,* and *proactivity*; all of these appear to be implicit in the standard enterprise of trait research.

Knowability is the assumption that personality is a proper object of scientific study. In contrast to some humanistic and existential theories that celebrate human freedom and the irreducible uniqueness of the individual, FFT assumes that there is much to be gained from the scientific study of personality in individuals and groups.

* * *

Rationality is the assumption that, despite errors and biases (e.g., Robins & John, 1997), people are in general capable of understanding themselves and others (Funder, 1995). In this respect, psychology is an unusual science. Physicians would not ask their patients to estimate their own white blood cell count, because patients could not be expected to possess such information. But trait psychologists routinely—and properly—ask people how sociable or competitive or irritable they are and interpret the answers (suitably aggregated and normed) as meaning what they say. Psychologists are able to do this because with respect to personality traits, laypersons are extraordinarily sophisticated judges who employ a trait language evolved over centuries to express important social judgments (cf. Saucier & Goldberg, 1996).

*   *   *

Variability asserts that people differ from each other in psychologically significant ways—an obvious premise for differential psychology. Note, however, that this position sets trait theories apart from all those views of human nature, philosophical and psychological, that seek a single answer to what human nature is really like. Are people basically selfish or altruistic? Creative or conventional? Purposeful or lazy? Within FFT, those are all meaningless questions; *creative* and *conventional* define opposite poles of a dimension along which people vary.

Proactivity refers to the assumption that the locus of causation of human action is to be sought in the person. It goes without saying that people are not absolute masters of their destinies, and that (consistent with the premise of variability) people differ in the extent to which they control their lives. But trait theory holds that it is worthwhile to seek the origins of behavior in characteristics of the person. People are neither passive victims of their life circumstances nor empty organisms programmed by histories of reinforcements. Personality is actively involved in shaping people's lives.

*   *   *

A Universal Personality System

Personality traits are individual difference variables; to understand them and how they operate, it is necessary to describe personality itself, the dynamic psychological organization that coordinates experience and action. *   *   *

COMPONENTS OF THE PERSONALITY SYSTEM   The personality system [shown in Figure 1] consists of components that correspond to the definitions of FFT and dynamic processes that indicate how these components are interrelated—the basic postulates of FFT. The definitions would probably seem reasonable to personologists from many different theoretical backgrounds; the postulates distinguish FFT from most other theories of personality and reflect interpretations of empirical data.

The core components of the personality system, indicated in rectangles, are designated as *basic tendencies, characteristic adaptations*, and the *self-concept* (actually a subcomponent of characteristic adaptations, but one of sufficient interest to warrant its own box). The elliptical peripheral components, which represent the interfaces of personality with adjoining systems, are labeled *biological bases, external influences*, and the *objective biography*. Figure 1 can be interpreted cross-sectionally as a diagram of how personality operates at any given time; in that case the external influences constitute the situation, and the objective biography is a specific instance of behavior, the output of the system. Figure 1 can also be interpreted longitudinally to indicate personality development (in basic tendencies and characteristic adaptations) and the unfolding of the life course (objective biography).

It may be helpful to consider some of the substance of personality to flesh out the abstractions in Figure 1. Table 1 presents some examples. For each of the five factors, an illustrative trait is identified in the first column of the table. The intrapsychic and interpersonal adaptations that develop over time as expressions of these facet traits are illustrated in the second column, and the third column mentions an instance of behavior from an individual characterized by the high or low pole of the facet.

At present, FFT has relatively little to say about the peripheral components of the personality system. Biological bases certainly include genes and brain structures, but the precise mechanisms—developmental, neuroanatomical, or psychophysiological—are not yet specified. Similarly, FFT does not detail types of external influences or aspects of

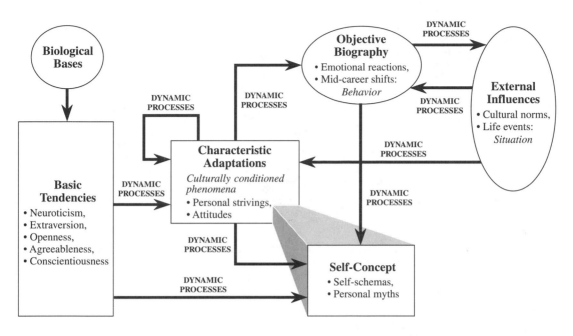

Figure 1. A representation of the five-factor theory personality system. Core components are in rectangles; interfacing components are in ellipses. Adapted from McCrae and Costa (1996).

the objective biography. Like most theories of personality, FFT presumes that "situation" and "behavior" are more or less self-evident.

What FFT does focus attention on is the distinction between basic tendencies (abstract psychological potentials) and characteristic adaptations (their concrete manifestations). Somewhat similar distinctions have been made by others—for example, in the familiar contrast of genotypic and phenotypic traits (Wiggins, 1973/1997) and in McAdams's (1996) distinction between Level 1 and Level 2 personality variables. FFT, however, insists on a distinction that other theories usually make only in passing, and it assigns traits exclusively to the category of basic tendencies. In FFT, traits are not patterns of behavior (Buss & Craik, 1983), nor are they the plans, skills, and desires that lead to patterns of behavior (Johnson, 1997). They are directly accessible neither to public observation nor to private introspection. Instead, they are deeper psychological entities that can only be *inferred* from behavior and experience. Self-reports of personality traits are based on such inferences, just as observer ratings are.

Although it smacks of obfuscation, there are good reasons to uncouple personality traits from the more observable components of personality. Characteristic adaptations—habits, attitudes, skills, roles, relationships—are influenced both by basic tendencies and by external influences. They are *characteristic* because they reflect the enduring psychological core of the individual, and they are *adaptations* because they help the individual fit into the ever-changing social environment. Characteristic adaptations and their configurations inevitably vary tremendously across cultures, families, and portions of the lifespan. *But personality traits do not:* The same five factors are found in all cultures studied so far (McCrae & Costa, 1997); parent–child relations have little lasting effect on personality traits (Rowe, 1994; see also Fraley, 1998, on the precipitous drop in the continuity of attachment); and traits are generally stable across the adult lifespan (McCrae & Costa, 1990). These

TABLE 1

SOME EXAMPLES OF FFT PERSONALITY SYSTEM COMPONENTS

Basic tendencies	Characteristic adaptations	Objective biography
Neuroticism N3: Depression (a tendency to experience dysphoric effect—sadness, hopelessness, guilt)	Low self-esteem, irrational perfectionistic beliefs, pessimistic attitudes	"Betty" (very high N3) feels guilty about her low-prestige job (Bruehl, 1994).
Extraversion E2: Gregariousness (a preference for companionship and social stimulation)	Social skills, numerous friendships, enterprising vocational interests, participation in sports, club memberships	J.-J. Rousseau (very low E2) leaves Paris for the countryside (McCrae, 1996).
Openness to Experience O4: Actions (a need for variety, novelty, and change)	Interest in travel, many different hobbies, knowledge of foreign cuisine, diverse vocational interests, friends who share tastes	Diane Ackerman (high O4) cruises the Antarctic (McCrae, 1993–1994).
Agreeableness A4: Compliance (a willingness to defer to others during interpersonal conflict)	Forgiving attitudes, belief in cooperation, inoffensive language, reputation as a pushover	Case 3 (very low A4) throws things at her husband during a fight (Costa & McCrae, 1992b).
Conscientiousness C4: Achievement Striving (strong sense of purpose and high aspiration levels)	Leadership skills, long-term plans, organized support network, technical expertise	Richard Nixon (very high C4) runs for President (Costa & McCrae, 2000).

well-replicated empirical generalizations make sense only if personality traits are insulated from the direct effects of the environment. Human nature is proactive because personality traits are endogenous basic tendencies (McCrae, Costa, Ostendorf, et al., 1998).

OPERATION OF THE SYSTEM   The welter of arrows in Figure 1 indicate some of the most important paths by which personality components interact. The plural *processes* is used because many quite distinct processes may be involved in each pathway. For example, the arrow from objective biography to self-concept implies that we learn who we are in part from observing what we do. But interpreting what we have done may involve social comparison, selective attention, defensive denial, implicit learning, or any number of other cognitive-affective processes. * * *

One implication is that personality theories that posit a small handful of key dynamic processes (repression, learning, self-actualization, getting ahead and getting along) are unlikely to prove adequate. Another is that psychologists who prefer to study processes instead of traits—"doing" instead of "having" (Cantor, 1990)—face the challenging prospect of identifying the most important of these many processes to study. There is as yet nothing like an adequate taxonomy of processes, and although evolutionary theory points to certain adaptive functions for which mechanisms must presumably have evolved, the evolutionary significance of much of human behavior is not clear (Buss, Haselton, Shackelford, Bleske, & Wakefield, 1998). FFT acknowledges the issue of multiple dynamic processes and specifies important categories of processes that share a common function in the organization of the personality system. It does not, however, detail the specifics. A complete theory of personality will ultimately include subtheories that elaborate on such specific topics (cf. Mayer, 1998).

Table 2 lists the 16 postulates originally proposed to specify how the personality system operates (McCrae & Costa, 1996). They are intended to be empirically testable, and in fact most of them are based on a body of empirical literature. Although it may generate novel predictions, FFT was designed primarily to make understandable what was already known.

The most radical of these postulates is 1b, *Origin*, which flatly declares that traits are endogenous basic tendencies. This postulate is based chiefly on results from studies of behavior genetics, which consistently point to a large role played by genetic factors and little or no role for common environmental factors (Riemann, Angleitner, & Strelau, 1997). Future research may well force some modification of this postulate; culture (McCrae, Yik, Trapnell, Bond, & Paulhus, 1998) or birth order (Sulloway, 1996) may be shown to affect trait levels. But as stated, Postulate 1b parsimoniously summarizes most of what is now known and offers a clear alternative to most older theories of personality, which emphasize the importance of culture and early life experience in forming personality. Today, even clinicians have begun to recognize that the standard environmental theories of personality are inadequate (Bowman, 1997).

Postulates 1b and 1d recently inspired a novel twin study (Jang, McCrae, Angleitner, Riemann, & Livesley, 1998). FFT clearly implies that N, E, O, A, and C are heritable, a claim long since supported in the cases of N and E, and more recently with respect to O, A, and C (Loehlin, McCrae, Costa, & John, 1998; Riemann, Angleitner, & Strelau, 1997). But are the specific facet traits that define the five factors also specifically heritable; or are they better interpreted as characteristic adaptations, the environmentally molded forms in which the heritable factors are manifested? One could easily suppose that people inherit only a global tendency to be Open to Experience and become open to Aesthetics, or to Ideas, or to Values as a result of individual learning experiences. But behavior genetic analyses of specific facet scores (from which the variance accounted for by the five factors had been partialled) showed that in almost all cases, specific variance was significantly heritable. It appears that the genetic blueprint for personality includes detailed specifications of dozens, perhaps hundreds, of traits.

Postulate 1c is also ripe for minor revision. At the time it was proposed, there was little convincing evidence of systematic personality change after age 30. Newer analyses, especially cross-cultural analyses (McCrae, Costa, Lima, et al., 1999), suggest that cross-sectional decreases in N, E, and O and increases in A and C continue at a very modest pace throughout adulthood. Strikingly similar results from cross-cultural studies of adult age differences in personality do, however, strongly support the basic idea that change in the level of personality traits is part of an intrinsic, endogenous maturational process that belongs in the category of basic tendencies.

* * *

Postulate 2a states the obvious claim that traits affect the way one adapts to the world. A recent example is found in analyses of the need for closure (Kruglanski & Webster, 1996). This tendency to "seize" the first credible answer and to "freeze" on one's initial decisions was shown to be strongly inversely related to Openness to Experience. It is easy to imagine the paths by which such habits of thought might develop:

> Lacking a need for change and uncertainty, closed people come to prefer a simple, structured, familiar world. Through experience they discover that tradition, conventionality, and stereotypes offer tried-and-true answers that they can adopt without much thought. They begin to think of themselves as conservative, down-to-earth people, and they seek out like-minded friends and spouses who will not challenge their beliefs. Thus, basic tendencies of closedness develop into preferences, ideologies, self-construals, and social roles; these characteristic adaptations habitualize, legitimize, and socially support a way of thinking that expresses a high need for closure. (Costa & McCrae, 1998a, p. 117)

TABLE 2

Five-Factor Theory Postulates

1. Basic tendencies
    1a. *Individuality.* All adults can be characterized by their differential standing on a series of personality traits that influence patterns of thoughts, feelings, and actions.
    1b. *Origin.* Personality traits are endogenous basic tendencies.
    1c. *Development.* Traits develop through childhood and reach mature form in adulthood; thereafter they are stable in cognitively intact individuals.
    1d. *Structure.* Traits are organized hierarchically from narrow and specific to broad and general dispositions; Neuroticism, Extraversion, Openness to Experience, Agreeableness, and Conscientiousness constitute the highest level of the hierarchy.

2. Characteristic adaptations
    2a. *Adaptation.* Over time, individuals react to their environments by evolving patterns of thoughts, feelings, and behaviors that are consistent with their personality traits and earlier adaptations.
    2b. *Maladjustment.* At any one time, adaptations may not be optimal with respect to cultural values or personal goals.
    2c. *Plasticity.* Characteristic adaptations change over time in response to biological maturation, changes in the environment, or deliberate interventions.

3. Objective biography
    3a. *Multiple determination.* Action and experience at any given moment are complex functions of all those characteristic adaptations that are evoked by the situation.
    3b. *Life course.* Individuals have plans, schedules, and goals that allow action to be organized over long time intervals in ways that are consistent with their personality traits.

4. Self-concept
    4a. *Self-schema.* Individuals maintain a cognitive–affective view of themselves that is accessible to consciousness.
    4b. *Selective perception.* Information is selectively represented in the self-concept in ways that (i) are consistent with personality traits; and (ii) give a sense of coherence to the individual.

5. External influences
    5a. *Interaction.* The social and physical environment interacts with personality dispositions to shape characteristic adaptations and with characteristic adaptations to regulate the flow of behavior.
    5b. *Apperception.* Individuals attend to and construe the environment in ways that are consistent with their personality traits.
    5c. *Reciprocity.* Individuals selectively influence the environment to which they respond.

6. Dynamic processes
    6a. *Universal dynamics.* The ongoing functioning of the individual in creating adaptations and expressing them in thoughts, feelings, and behaviors is regulated in part by universal cognitive, affective, and volitional mechanisms.
    6b. *Differential dynamics.* Some dynamic processes are differentially affected by basic tendencies of the individual, including personality traits.

Note. Adapted from McCrae & Costa (1996).

According to FFT, the personality system represented in Figure 1 is a universal of human nature. All people have basic tendencies, characteristic adaptations, and a self-concept, and they are related to biology and to society in the same basic ways. FFT adopts this system as a framework for explaining the operation of personality; it does not explain why the system exists. Various hypotheses might be offered, most probably based on Darwinian evolution (Buss, 1991); rudimentary forms of this system might be seen in animals (Gosling & John, in press). More formally, the FFT personality system includes the two features that characterize many dynamic systems: a distinctive core that is preserved, and mechanisms for adapting to a changing environment. Species that did not reproduce or adapt to their environments are now extinct; personality traits that did not endure over time and transcend situational influences would never have been recognized in lay lexicons or psychological theories.

Individual Differences in Personality

Consider as a thought experiment the possibility of a utopian community—call it Walden Three—based on the findings of trait psychology. Because individual differences can lead to misunderstanding and conflict (McCrae, 1996), its founders decide to people their society with clones from a single individual; to ensure happiness, they choose an adjusted extravert (Costa & McCrae, 1980). We will let medical ethicists and social philosophers debate the wisdom of this plan and turn our attention to the consequences for personality psychology.

In one respect nothing will have changed. The personality system is universal, and the denizens of Walden Three would still have needs, plans, skills, habits, relationships; they would still interact with the world in ways that external observers would recognize as reflecting their sociability and emotional stability—they would be happy people.

But personality psychologists who attempted to study them by the usual methods would reach startling conclusions. Except for error of measurement, everyone would score the same on every personality scale, and with no variance there could be no covariance. Traits would appear to have no longitudinal stability, no heritability, no five-factor structure. Indigenous psychologists might conclude that traits were a myth, and if asked, residents of Walden Three would probably attribute their behavior solely to situational causes ("Why did you go to that party?" "I was invited!").

What this thought experiment demonstrates is the curious relation of trait psychology to individual differences. On the one hand, it might be argued that personality psychology is not about individual differences; it is about how basic tendencies of a certain class affect thoughts, feelings, and actions. Employers seek conscientious employees not because they differ from lazy and careless employees, but because they work hard and well (Barrick & Mount, 1991). On the other hand, it is only the existence of individual differences in personality that reveals that hard work and carefulness are in part the result of heritable and enduring dispositions. Variation in personality traits across individuals is the ultimate natural experiment that illuminates the workings of personality.

* * *

Five-Factor Theory and the Individual

Although it is doubtless true that every person is in some respects like no other person (Kluckhohn & Murray, 1953), FFT (like most personality theories) has nothing to say about this aspect of the person. It is, from a scientific perspective, error variance. This most emphatically does not mean that personality is irrelevant to understanding the individual.

In the typical application in clinical or personnel psychology, the individual case is understood by inferring personality traits from one set of indicators and using the resulting personality profile to interpret a life history or predict future adjustment. This is not circular reasoning, because if valid personality measures are used, the traits identified carry surplus meaning that allows the interpreter to go beyond the information given (McCrae & Costa, 1995b). If respondents tell us that they are cheerful and high-spirited, we detect Extraversion and can guess with better-than-chance accuracy that they will be interested in managerial and sales positions. However, it would be much harder to predict their current occupation: Just as the theory of evolution is better at explaining how existing species function than it is at predicting which species will evolve, so personality profiles are more useful in understanding a life than in making specific predictions about what a person will do. This is not a limitation of FFT; it is an intrinsic feature of complex and chaotic systems.

Postulate 3a, *Multiple determination*, points out that there is rarely a one-to-one correspondence between characteristic adaptations and behaviors; the same is of course equally true for the traits that underlie characteristic adaptations. Consequently, interpreting individual behaviors even when the personality profile is well known is a somewhat speculative art. Consider the case of Horatio, Lord Nelson (Costa & McCrae, 1998b; Southey, 1813/1922). In the course of his campaigns against Napoleon's France, he spent many months defending the woefully corrupt court of Naples against a democratic insurrection that had been encouraged by the French. Why would so heroic a figure take on so shabby a task?

We know from a lifetime of instances that Nelson was a paragon of dutifulness, and we might suspect that he was simply following orders—certainly he would have rationalized his conduct as devotion to the war against France. But we also know that Nelson was fiercely independent in his views of what constituted his duty: "I always act as I feel right, without regard to custom" (Southey, 1813/1922, p. 94). He might equally well have supported the insurrection and won its allegiance to the English cause.

We should also consider another trait Nelson possessed: He was excessively low in modesty. Great as his naval achievements were, he never failed to remind people of them. His sympathies were thus with the aristocracy, and he was flattered by the court of Naples, which ultimately named him Duke Di Bronte.

Together, diligence (C), independence (O), and vanity (low A) go far to explain this episode of behavior.

To be sure, there are other factors, including Nelson's relationship to the English ambassador's wife, Lady Hamilton (Simpson, 1983). That notorious affair itself reflects Nelson's independence and vanity, but seems strikingly incongruent with his dutifulness. At the level of the individual, the operations of personality traits are complex and often inconsistent (a phenomenon Mischel and Shoda, 1995, have recently tried to explain).

THE SUBJECTIVE EXPERIENCE OF PERSONALITY A number of writers (e.g., Hogan, 1996) have suggested that the FFM does not accurately represent personality as it is subjectively experienced by the individual. Daniel Levinson dismissed the whole enterprise of trait psychology as a concern for trivial and peripheral aspects of the person (Rubin, 1981). McAdams (1996) has referred to it as the "psychology of the stranger," because standing on the five factors is the sort of thing one would want to know about a stranger to whom one has just been introduced. Ozer (1996) claims that traits are personality as seen from the standpoint of the other, not the self.

We believe this last position represents a slight confusion. Individuals, who have access to private thoughts, feelings, and desires, and who generally have a more extensive knowledge of their own history of behavior, have a quite different perspective on their own traits than do external observers. What they nonetheless share with others is the need to infer the nature of their own traits and to express their inference in the comparative language of traits. We have no direct intuition of our trait profile; we can only guess at it from its manifestations in our actions and experience. (One possible reason for the increasing stability of personality as assessed by self-reports from age 20 to age 30—see Siegler et al., 1990—is that we continue to learn about ourselves in this time period.)

The fact that traits must be inferred does not, however, mean that they are or seem foreign. When adults were asked to give 20 different answers to the question "Who am I?," about a quarter of the responses were personality traits, and many others combined trait and role characteristics (e.g., "a loving mother"). Traits seem to form an important component of the spontaneous self-concept (McCrae & Costa, 1988); even children use trait terms to describe themselves (Donahue, 1994).

Sheldon, Ryan, Rawsthorne, and Ilardi (1997) brought a humanistic perspective to this issue by assessing sense of authenticity in individuals as they occupied different social roles. They also asked for context-specific self-reports of personality (e.g., how extraverted respondents were as students and as romantic partners). They found that individuals who described themselves most consistently across roles also claimed the highest feelings of authenticity. They concluded that "more often than not, one's true self and one's trait self are one and the same" (p. 1392).

Conclusion

* * *

Historically, personality psychology has been characterized by elaborate and ambitious theories with only the most tenuous links to empirical findings, and theorists have often been considered profound to the extent that their visions of human nature departed from commonsense. Freud's glorification of the taboo, Jung's obscure mysticism, Skinner's denial of that most basic experience of having a mind—such esoteric ideas set personality theorists apart from normal human beings and suggested they were privy to secret knowledge. By contrast, FFT is closely tied to the empirical findings it summarizes, and its vision of human nature, at least at the phenotypic level, is not far removed from folk psychology. If that makes it a rather pro-

saic Grand Theory, so be it. What matters is how far it takes us in understanding that endlessly fascinating phenomenon, personality.

References

Barrick, M. R., & Mount, M. K. (1991). The Big Five personality dimensions and job performance: A meta-analysis. *Personnel Psychology, 44,* 1–26.

Bowman, M. (1997). *Individual differences in posttraumatic response: Problems with the adversity–distress connection.* Mahwah, NJ: Erlbaum.

Bruehl, S. (1994). A case of borderline personality disorder. In P. T. Costa, Jr., & T. A. Widiger (Eds.), *Personality disorders and the five-factor model of personality* (pp. 189–197). Washington, DC: American Psychological Association.

Buss, D. M. (1991). Evolutionary personality psychology. *Annual Review of Psychology, 42,* 459–491.

Buss, D. M., & Craik, K. H. (1983). The act frequency approach to personality. *Psychological Review, 90,* 105–126.

Buss, D. M., Haselton, M. G., Shackelford, T. K., Bleske, A. L. & Wakefield, J. C. (1998). Adaptations, exaptations, and spandrels. *American Psychologist, 53,* 533–548.

Cantor, N. (1990). From thought to behavior: "Having" and "doing" in the study of personality and cognition. *American Psychologist, 45,* 735–750.

Clark, L. A., & Livesley, W. J. (1994). Two approaches to identifying dimensions of personality disorder: Convergence on the five-factor model. In P. T. Costa Jr. & T. A. Widiger (Eds.), *Personality disorders and the five-factor model of personality* (pp. 261–278). Washington, DC: American Psychological Association.

Costa, P. T., Jr., & McCrae, R. R. (1980). Influence of extraversion and neuroticism on subjective well-being: Happy and unhappy people. *Journal of Personality and Social Psychology, 38,* 668–678.

Costa, P. T., Jr., & McCrae, R. R. (1988). From catalog to classification: Murray's needs and the five-factor model. *Journal of Personality and Social Psychology, 55,* 258–265.

Costa, P. T., Jr., & McCrae, R. R. (1992a). *Revised NEO Personality Inventory (NEO-PI-R) and NEO Five-Factor Inventory (NEO-FFI) professional manual.* Odessa, FL: Psychological Assessment Resources.

Costa, P. T., Jr., & McCrae, R. R. (1992b). Trait psychology comes of age. In T. B. Sonderegger (Ed.), *Nebraska Symposium on Motivation: Psychology and aging* (pp. 169–204). Lincoln: University of Nebraska Press.

Costa, P. T., & McCrae, R. R. (1998a). Trait theories of personality. In D. F. Barone, M. Hersen, & V. B. V. Hasselt (Eds.), *Advanced personality* (pp. 103–121). New York: Plenum Press.

Costa, P. T., Jr., & McCrae, R. R. (1998b). Six approaches to the explication of facet-level traits: Examples from conscientiousness. *European Journal of Personality, 12,* 117–134.

Costa, P. T., Jr., & McCrae, R. R. (2000). Theories of personality and psychopathology: Approaches derived from philosophy and psychology. In H. I. Kaplan & B. J. Saddock (Eds.), Kaplan & Saddock's *Comprehensive textbook of psychiatry* (7th ed.) Philadelphia: Lippincott, Williams & Wilkins.

Digman, J. M., & Inouye, J. (1986). Further specification of the five robust factors of personality. *Journal of Personality and Social Psychology, 50*, 116–123.

Donahue, E. M. (1994). Do children use the Big Five, too? Content and structural form in personality description. *Journal of Personality, 62*, 45–66.

Fraley, R. C. (1998). *Attachment continuity from infancy to adulthood: Meta-analysis and dynamic modeling of developmental mechanisms.* Unpublished manuscript, University of California, Davis.

Funder, D. C. (1995). On the accuracy of personality judgment: A realistic approach. *Psychological Review, 102*, 652–670.

Funder, D. C., Kolar, D. C., & Blackman, M. C. (1995). Agreement among judges of personality: Interpersonal relations, similarity, and acquaintanceship. *Journal of Personality and Social Psychology, 69*, 656–672.

Gosling, S. D., & John, O. P. (in press). Personality dimensions in non-human animals: A cross-species review. *Current Directions in Psychological Science.*

Hjelle, L. A., & Siegler, D. J. (1976). *Personality: Theories, basic assumptions, research and applications.* New York: McGraw-Hill.

Hogan, R. (1996). A socioanalytic perspective on the five-factor model. In J. S. Wiggins (Ed.), *The five-factor model of personality: Theoretical perspectives* (pp. 163–179). New York: Guilford Press.

Jang, K. L., McCrae, R. R., Angleitner, A., Riemann, R., & Livesley, W. J. (1998). Heritability of facet-level traits in a cross-cultural twin study: Support for a hierarchical model of personality. *Journal of Personality and Social Psychology, 74*, 1556–1565.

Johnson, J. A. (1997). Units of analysis for the description and explanation of personality. In R. Hogan, J. A. Johnson, & S. R. Briggs (Eds.), *Handbook of personality psychology* (pp. 73–93). New York: Academic Press.

Kluckhohn, C., & Murray, H. A. (1953). Personality formation: The determinants. In C. Kluckhohn, H. A. Murray, & D. M. Schneider (Eds.), *Personality in nature, society, and culture* (pp. 53–67). New York: Knopf.

Kruglanski, A. W., & Webster, D. M. (1996). Motivated closing of the mind: "Seizing" and "freezing." *Psychological Review, 103*, 263–283.

Lanning, K. (1994). Dimensionality of observer ratings on the California Adult Q-Set. *Journal of Personality and Social Psychology, 67*, 151–160.

Loehlin, J. C., McCrae, R. R., Costa, P. T., Jr., & John, O. P. (1998). Heritabilities of common and measure-specific components of the Big Five personality factors. *Journal of Research in Personality, 32*, 431–453.

Mayer, J. D. (1998). A systems framework for the field of personality. *Psychological Inquiry, 9*, 118–144.

McAdams, D. P. (1996). Personality, modernity, and the storied self: A contemporary framework for studying persons. *Psychological Inquiry, 7*, 295–321.

McCrae, R. R. (1992). The five-factor model: Issues and applications [Special issue]. *Journal of Personality, 60*(2).

McCrae, R. R. (1993–1994). Openness to Experience as a basic dimension of personality. *Imagination, Cognition and Personality, 13*, 39–55.

McCrae, R. R. (1996). Social consequences of experiential openness. *Psychological Bulletin, 120*, 323–337.

McCrae, R. R., & Costa, P. T., Jr. (1988). Age, personality, and the spontaneous self-concept. *Journal of Gerontology: Social Sciences, 43*, S177–S185.

McCrae, R. R., & Costa, P. T., Jr. (1990). *Personality in adulthood.* New York: Guilford Press.

McCrae, R. R., & Costa, P. T., Jr. (1995b). Trait explanations in personality psychology. *European Journal of Personality, 9*, 231–252.

McCrae, R. R., & Costa, P. T., Jr. (1996). Toward a new generation of personality theories: Theoretical contexts for the five-factor model. In J. S. Wiggins (Ed.), *The five-factor model of personality: Theoretical perspectives* (pp. 51–87), New York: Guilford Press.

McCrae, R. R., & Costa, P. T., Jr. (1997). Personality trait structure as a human universal. *American Psychologist, 52*, 509–516.

McCrae, R. R., Costa, P. T., Jr., del Pilar, G. H., Rolland, J. P., & Parker, W. D. (1998). Cross-cultural assessment of the five-factor model: The Revised NEO Personality Inventory. *Journal of Cross-Cultural Psychology, 29*, 171–188.

McCrae, R. R., Costa, P. T., Jr., Lima, M. P., Simóes, A., Ostendorf, F., Angleitner, A., Marusic, I., Bratko, D., Caprara, G. V., Barbaranelli, C., Chae, J. H., & Piedmont, R. L. (1999). Age differences in personality across the adult lifespan: Parallels in five cultures. *Development Psychology 35*, 466–477.

McCrae, R. R., Costa, P. T., Jr., Ostendorf, F., Angleitner, A., Hrebickova, M., Avia, M. D., Sanz, J., Sánchez-Bernardos, M. L., Kusdil, M. E., Wood-field, R., Saunders, P. R., & Smith, P. B. (1998). *Nature over nurture: Temperament, personality, and lifespan development.* Unpublished manuscript. Gerontology Research Center.

McCrae, R. R., Yik, M. S. M., Trapnell, P. D., Bond, M. H., & Paulhus, D. L. (1998). Interpreting personality profiles across cultures: Bilingual, acculturation, and peer rating studies of Chinese undergraduates. *Journal of Personality and Social Psychology 74*, 1041–1058.

Mischel, W., & Shoda, Y. (1995). A cognitive–affective system theory of personality: Reconceptualizing situations, dispositions, dynamics, and invariance in personality structure. *Psychological Review, 102*, 246–268.

Ozer, D. J. (1996). The units we should employ. *Psychological Inquiry, 7*, 360–363.

Riemann, R., Angleitner, A., & Strelau, J. (1997). Genetic and environmental influences on personality: A study of twins reared together using the self-and-peer report NEO-FFI scales. *Journal of Personality, 65*, 449–475.

Robins, R. W., & John, O. P. (1997). Effects of visual perspective and narcissism on self-perceptions: Is seeing believing? *Psychological Science, 8*, 37–42.

Rowe, D. C. (1994). *The limits of family influence: Genes, experience, and behavior.* New York: Guilford Press.

Rubin, Z. (1981). Does personality really change after 20? *Psychology Today, 15*, 18–27.

Saucier, G. (1997). Effects of variable selection on the factor structure of person descriptors. *Journal of Personality and Social Psychology, 73*, 1296–1312.

Saucier, G., & Goldberg, L. R. (1996). The language of personality: Lexical perspectives on the five-factor model. In J. S. Wiggins (Ed.), *The five-factor model of personality: Theoretical perspectives* (pp. 21–50). New York: Guilford Press.

Sheldon, K. M., Ryan, R. M., Rawsthorne, L. J., & Ilardi, B.

(1997). Trait self and true self: Cross-role variation in the Big-Five personality traits and its relations with psychological authenticity and subjective well-being. *Journal of Personality and Social Psychology, 73,* 1380–1393.

Siegler, I. C., Zonderman, A. B., Barefoot, J. C., Williams, R. B., Jr., Costa, P. T., Jr., & McCrae, R. R. (1990). Predicting personality in adulthood from college MMPI scores: Implications for follow-up studies in psychosomatic medicine. *Psychosomatic Medicine, 52,* 644–652.

Simpson, C. (1983). *Emma: The life of Lady Hamilton.* London: The Bodley Head.

Southey, R. (1922). *Life of Nelson.* New York: Dutton. (Original work published 1813)

Sulloway, F. J. (1996). *Born to rebel: Birth order, family dynamics, and creative lives.* New York: Pantheon Books.

Tupes, E. C., & Christal, R. E. (1992). Recurrent personality factors based on trait ratings. *Journal of Personality, 60,* 225–251. (Original work published 1961)

Wiggins, J. S. (1997). In defense of traits. In R. Hogan, J. A. Johnson, & S. R. Briggs (Eds.), *Handbook of personality psychology* (pp. 97–115). San Diego: Academic Press. (Original work presented 1973)

Global Traits: A Neo-Allportian Approach to Personality

David C. Funder

Allport's question "What is a trait of personality?" remains the key theoretical question for the field. In the final selection in this section, one of your editors presents an updated, "neo-Allportian" answer. The article argues that the most fruitful way to begin the investigation is to try to understand "global" traits, traits that have wide implications for behavior in a variety of situations, that are intuitively viewed as important even by non-psychologists, and that in most cases have widely used labels in the English language (and other languages). The most important assertion in this article is that traits are real; they are not arbitrary ideas or artificial constructions. This is a controversial point of view within personality psychology, but the author of this article believes that the best path for any scientific investigation is to begin with the assumption that the object of its study actually exists. This is also the most fundamentally "Allportian" of Funder's assertions; Allport said almost exactly the same thing more than 50 years earlier. This means either (a) Funder's position is incredibly old-fashioned or (b) truths remain true across time.

From *Psychological Science, 2,* 31–39, 1992.

But let us not join the camp of skeptics who say an individual's personality is "a mere construct tied together with a name"—that there is nothing outer and objectively structured to be assessed. No scientist, I think, could survive for long if he heeded this siren song of doubt, for it leads to shipwreck. (Allport, 1958, p. 246)

One of the most widely used concepts of intuitive psychology is the global personality trait. Almost everyone is accustomed to thinking about and describing the people one knows using terms like "conscientious," "sociable," and "aggressive."

Traits like these are *global* because each refers not just to one or a few specific behaviors, but to *patterns* of behavior presumed to transcend time and specific situations. Historically, the global trait used to be an important part of formal psychological theory as well. Gordon Allport (1931, 1937) wrote extensively about traits more than a half century ago, and for a time many research programs either developed general trait theories (Cattell, 1946), or investigated in detail specific traits (Witkin et al., 1954).

In recent years, however, theorizing about dispositional constructs such as global traits has been at a relative standstill. As Buss and Craik (1983) pointed out, "the field of personality appears to have set its theoretical gears into neutral" (p. 105). One cause of this inactivity may have been the field's two decades of immersion in a distracting debate over whether significant individual differences in social behavior exist at all (Mischel, 1968). Although, in the end, the existence of important individual regularities was reaffirmed (Kenrick & Funder, 1988), a lingering effect of the controversy seems to be an image of traits—most especially global ones—as old-fashioned, rather quaint ideas not relevant for modern research in personality. Indeed, when global traits do appear in the literature nowadays, it is usually to play the role of straw man. The recent literature has seen a plethora of "reconceptualizations" of personality each of which begins, typically, by announcing its intention to replace global traits.

Modern reconceptualizations differ from global traits in at least three ways. First and most obviously, many constructs of the new personality psychology go out of their way *not* to be global. The range of life contexts to which they are relevant is specified narrowly and specifically, and this narrowness is touted as an important virtue. For instance, the recently promulgated "social intelligence" view of personality "guides one away from generalized assessments . . . towards more particular conclusions about the individual's profile of expertise in the life-task domains of central concern at that point in time" (Cantor & Kihlstrom, 1987, p. 241).

Second, and just as importantly, many modern personality variables are relatively *esoteric*—they are deliberately nonintuitive or even counterintuitive. For instance, in the place of trait terms found in ordinary language, one prominent investigator has offered person variables such as "self-regulatory systems," "encoding strategies," and the like (Mischel, 1973).

Third, some modern reconceptualizations go so far as to eschew an explanatory role for personality variables altogether. For instance, the act frequency approach treats personality dispositions as little more than frequency counts of "topographi-

cally" (i.e., superficially) similar acts (Buss & Craik, 1983).

The intent of these reconceptualizations is laudable. Each is designed to correct one or more of the problems of overgenerality, vagueness, and even philosophical confusion to which trait psychology has sometimes been prone. The present article, however, is motivated by a belief that the movement away from global traits, however fashionable it may be, entails several dangers that are not usually acknowledged.

Briefly, the dangers are these. First, when we use dispositional terms that are framed *narrowly*, we discard any possibility of generating statements about individual differences that have real explanatory power. Second, when we use dispositional terms that are *esoteric*, we fail to make contact with traits as used in everyday social discourse, lose any basis for understanding and evaluating lay trait judgments, and discard the vast lore of common sense and wisdom that they embody. And third, when we are content to define traits as *frequencies* of superficially similar behaviors, we run the risk of being fundamentally deceived when, as often happens, the causes of behavior turn out to be complex. Each of these points will be expanded later in this article.

What follows is a brief outline of a modern, *neo-Allportian* theory of global traits, presented in the form of 17 assertions. The term "neo-Allportian" is meant to emphasize that this approach to personality is fundamentally based on the seminal writings of Gordon Allport (especially Allport, 1937), but also to acknowledge that his basic theory was published more than a half-century ago and so is ripe for updating and reinvigoration (Zuroff, 1986). As it turns out, Allport's basic ideas look remarkably sound even with 53 years of hindsight, and yield a large number of implications for conceptualization and research in modern personality psychology.

Definitional Assertions

TRAITS ARE REAL   This assertion is the most fundamental of Allport's assumptions, one he believed was essential for subsequent research to be meaningful. He held this position in the face of objections that it was philosophically naive and arguments (still heard today) that traits should be regarded not as entities that have objective reality, but merely as hypothetical constructs (Carr & Kingsbury, 1938). Allport believed that this idea made about as much sense as astronomers regarding stars as hypothetical constructs rather than astronomical objects. He failed to see how any science, including personality psychology, could proceed without assuming its subject of study to be real.

More specifically, Allport (1931, 1966) said traits are "neurodynamic structures" (1966, p. 3) that have "more than nominal existence" (1966, p. 1). If it is obvious that all behavior originates in the neurons of the brain, and that does seem obvious, then it follows that stable individual differences in behavior—to the extent they exist—must similarly be based on stable individual differences in neural organization.

Unfortunately, a method to assess the neural basis of personality is not yet in sight. The presence of a trait can only be *inferred* on the basis of overt behavior. For all practical purposes, therefore, a global trait must refer to two things at the same time: (a) a complex pattern of behavior from which the trait is inferred, and (b) the psychological structures and processes that are the source of the pattern. When we call someone "friendly" or "aggressive" or "generous," we are saying something both about how the person behaves (or would behave) in certain kinds of situations *and* about the functioning of his or her mind. The next assertion follows as a consequence.

TRAITS ARE MORE THAN JUST SUMMARIES A viewpoint prominently expressed in recent years is that "dispositions" (a.k.a. traits) should be considered as no more than summaries of behavioral frequencies, or "act trends" (Buss & Craik, 1983). An individual's generosity then becomes the frequency, over a specified unit of time, of his or her superficially generous acts.

This definition deliberately abdicates any ex-

planatory role. Dispositions are treated as circular constructs in which a generous act implies generosity, and the attribution of generosity is used to predict future generous acts *solely* "on actuarial grounds" (Buss & Craik, 1983, p. 106).

However, the appearance of behavior can be misleading (Block, 1988). As Allport pointed out:

> A bearer of gifts may not be, in spite of all appearances, a truly generous person: he may be trying to buy favor. . . . Pseudo-traits, then, are errors of inference, misjudgments that come from fixing attention solely upon appearances. The best way to avoid such errors is to find the genotype that underlies the conduct in question. What is the individual trying to do when he brings his gifts? (Allport, 1937, p. 326)

THE MEANING OF A BEHAVIOR DEPENDS ON TWO KINDS OF CONTEXT A single behavior, considered out of context, is frequently ambiguous. Depending on the intention with which the act was performed, there may be multiple possible and plausible alternatives for the traits that might be relevant. This is not to deny that there are interpretational defaults. The act of gift-giving might be interpreted as generous, all other things being equal. All other things are seldom equal, however, so the gift-giving might also reflect insecurity, Machiavellianism, or even anger, depending on the situational circumstances, the gift-giver's behavior in other situations, and what together they imply about the gift-giver's inner state and motives.

Two kinds of context help disambiguate an act. The first is the immediate situation. The giving of a gift becomes more interpretable if one knows whether it was given to a subordinate who performed a job well, or to a superior considering the promotion of the gift-giver. The usefulness of this kind of situational information has been discussed in detail by attribution theorists within social psychology (Heider, 1958; Kelley, 1967), but has been taken into account less often by personality psychologists.

The other kind of context is just as important, but is mentioned even more rarely. Acts become less ambiguous to the extent they fit into a pattern of the individual's other acts. A consistent pattern of generous behavior provides a more plausible context in which to infer that generosity is the trait underlying the gift-giving than does a consistent pattern of mean, nasty, and sneaky behavior. (Indeed, an act that seems inconsistent with the actor's past patterns of behavior is commonly called suspicious.) A pattern of sneaky behavior might lead to an attribution of Machiavellianism that would explain, in turn, why the person gave a lavish gift to his worst enemy.

Developmental Assertions

TRAITS ARE LEARNED Global traits are manifest by patterns of perception and action in the social world; therefore, they must be a product of how one has learned to interact with that world. The process of learning that produces a trait almost certainly involves an interaction between one's experience (in one's particular social environment) and one's genetic endowment (Scarr & McCartney, 1983). Thus, two people with identical environments, or two people with identical genes, could and often do have very different traits.

Because traits are learned, they are not necessarily immutable. Anything learned can in principle be unlearned. Global trait theory is not necessarily pessimistic about possibilities for either personal or social change.

However, traits are relatively stable. Presumably, the difficulty in unlearning a trait (the amount of retraining or new experience required) will be proportional to the amount and salience of the experience through which it was learned in the first place. Genetic predispositions, and perhaps even species-specific characteristics, may also make some traits easier to learn and harder to unlearn than others (Buss, 1984). But the present analysis asserts that because all traits are, in the final analysis, learned, all traits can, in theory if not always in practice, be unlearned.

THE PROCESS OF LEARNING A TRAIT IS COMPLEX Such learning is far more than a simple matter of reward and punishment or S and R. That simple kind of learning can produce, at most, the narrow

patterns of behavior that Allport (1931) called "habits." Traits are the result of complex patterns of experience and of higher-order inductions the person makes from that experience. Kelly (1955) believed that *any* pattern of experience could lead a person to any of at least a large number of behavioral outcomes (just as any pattern of data can always lead a scientist to more than one interpretation). Kelly believed that the ability to choose between these alternative outcomes provided a basis for free will. The comedian Bill Cosby has described his childhood neighborhood as a place where adolescents were all on the verge of deciding whether to be killers or priests. The point is that similar patterns of past experience do not necessarily produce similar outcomes.

When *fully* analyzed, every person's pattern of behavior will be every bit as complex as the unique pattern of endowment and experience that produced it. Again, in Allport's (1937, p. 295) words: "Strictly speaking, no two persons ever have precisely the same trait. . . . What else could be expected in the view of the unique hereditary endowment, the different developmental history, and the never-repeated external influences that determine each personality?"

But there are commonalities among people that are useful for characterizing individual differences. A trait like sociability is relevant to behavior in a set of situations regarded as functionally equivalent by people in general: specifically, situations with other people in them. Hence, it is *generally* meaningful to rank-order people on their overall sociability. Allport acknowledged this point as well: "The case for the ultimate individuality of every trait is indeed invincible, but . . . for all their ultimate differences, normal persons within a given culture-area tend to develop a limited number of roughly comparable modes of adjustment" (1937, pp. 297–298).

Still, the list of social situations that are functionally equivalent for people in general is unlikely to fully capture the situations that are regarded as functionally equivalent by any *single* individual. To capture general trends or gists, and to detect things that are true of people in general, one always loses the details of each individual case. This trade-off between nomothetic and idiographic analyses can be and often has been lamented, but it is inevitable.

Functional Assertions

A BEHAVIOR MAY BE AFFECTED BY SEVERAL TRAITS AT ONCE

> The chief danger in the concept of trait is that, through habitual and careless use, it may come to stand for an assembly of separate and self-active faculties, thought to govern behavior all by themselves, without interference. We must cast out this lazy interpretation of the concept. . . . The basic principle of behavior is its continuous flow, each successive act representing a convergent mobilization of all energy available at the moment. (Allport, 1937, pp. 312–313)

The fact that every behavior is the product of multiple traits implies that disentangling the relationship between a given trait and a given behavior is extremely difficult. It also implies that the ability of any particular trait to predict behavior by itself is limited. Ahadi and Diener (1989) showed that if a behavior is totally caused by only four traits whose influence combines additively, the maximum correlation between any one trait and behavior that could be expected is .45. If different traits combine multiplicatively, which seems plausible, the ceiling is even lower.

A third implication is that modern research on traits should conduct a renewed examination of the way traits combine in the determination of behavior. Investigators should more often look beyond the traditional research question of how single traits affect single behaviors, to how multiple traits interact within persons (Carlson, 1971).

TRAITS ARE SITUATIONAL EQUIVALENCE CLASSES
In a trenchant phrase, Allport wrote that traits have the capacity "to render many stimuli functionally equivalent" (1937, p. 295). The tendency to view different situations as similar causes a person to respond to them in a like manner, and the patterns of behavior that result are the overt manifestations of traits.

The template-matching technique (Bem & Funder, 1978) provides one empirical approach to the study of situational equivalence classes. The technique looks for empirical ties between behavior in real-life situations that subjects' acquaintances have viewed and interpreted, and laboratory situations in which subjects' behavior is measured directly. To the extent higher-order similarity or functional equivalence exists, correlations will be found. The experimental situations are then interpreted, or in Bem and Funder's words, the subjects' "personalities assessed," based on the equivalence classes thus established.

For instance, in one of Bem and Funder's first studies (1978), the parents of nursery school children provided judgments of the degree to which their children were cooperative with adults. These ratings of cooperativeness turned out to correlate highly with minutes and seconds of delay time measured directly in our delay-of-gratification experiment. We inferred that our experimental situation must have been in some way functionally equivalent to the situations at home from which the parents had judged cooperativeness. Our final conclusion was that delay time in our experiment was a symptom of such cooperativeness as much as it was of self control or anything like it. The equivalence class to which the delay experiment seemed to belong consisted of other cooperation situations, not necessarily other self-control situations.

ACCESS TO ONE'S OWN TRAITS IS INDIRECT
The interpretation of a trait as a subjective, situational-equivalence class offers an idea about phenomenology—about what it feels like to have a trait, to the person who has it. It doesn't feel like anything, directly. Rather, the only subjective manifestation of a trait *within* a person will be his or her tendency to react and feel similarly across the situations to which the trait is relevant. As Allport wrote, "For some the world is a hostile place where men are evil and dangerous: for others it is a stage for fun and frolic. It may appear as a place to do one's duty grimly; or a pasture for cultivating friendship and love" (1961, p. 266).

Certainly a friendly person (ordinarily) does

nothing like say to him- or herself, "I am a friendly person; therefore, I shall be friendly now." Rather, he or she responds in a natural way to the situation as he or she perceives it. Similarly, a bigoted person does not decide, "I'm going to act bigoted now." Rather, his or her bigoted behavior is the result of his or her perception of a targeted group as threatening, inferior, or both (Geis, 1978).

But on reflection one can indeed begin to come to opinions about one's own traits (Bem, 1972; Thorne, 1989). One might realize that one is always happy when there are other people around, or always feels threatened, and therefore conclude that one must be "sociable" or "shy," respectively. But again, this can only happen retrospectively, and probably under unusual circumstances. Psychotherapy might be one of these: when "on the couch," one is encouraged to relate past experiences, and the client and therapist together come up with interpretations. Whether called that or not, these interpretations often involve the discovery of the client's situational equivalence classes, or traits. Certain profound life experiences might also stimulate conscious introspection.

In rare cases, explicit, volitional self-direction toward a trait-relevant behavior might take place. For example, one might say to oneself (before going to an obligatory party attended by people one detests), "now, I'm going to be *friendly* tonight," or, before asking one's boss for a raise, self-instruct "be *assertive*." As a matter of interesting psychological fact, however, in such circumstances the resulting behavior is *not* authentically a product of the trait from which it might superficially appear to emanate. The other people at the party, or the boss, probably would interpret the behavior very differently if they knew about the individual's more general behavior patterns and certainly would interpret it differently if they knew about the self-instruction.

TRAITS INFLUENCE PERCEPTIONS OF SITUATIONS THROUGH DYNAMIC MECHANISMS
Different situations may be rendered functionally equivalent through at least three kinds of mechanism. One kind is *motivational*. A person who is hungry

arranges situations along a continuum defined by the degree to which food is offered. A person who is dispositionally fearful sees situations in terms of potential threat. A person with a high degree of sociability approaches most situations where other people are present in a positive frame of mind. Another way to say this is that one's perception of the world is partially structured by one's goals (Cantor & Kihlstrom, 1987).

A second kind of mechanism concerns *capacities* and *tendencies*. A person with great physical strength will respond to the world in terms of situational equivalence classes that are different than those experienced by one who is weak. Situations containing physical obstacles may appear interesting and challenging rather than discouraging. Similarly, a person with a tendency to overcontrol motivational impulses will behave differently across a variety of motivationally involving situations than a person whose tendency is towards undercontrol. The overcontroller will restrain his or her impulses, whereas the undercontroller will tend to express them (Funder & Block, 1989).

A third kind of mechanism is *learning*. Perhaps one has been rewarded consistently in athletic settings. Then one will approach most new athletic-like settings with an expectation of reward, with direct consequences for behavior. (This learning experience might itself be a function of one's physical prowess, an example of how these mechanisms can interact.) Perhaps one has been consistently punished for risk-taking. Such an individual is likely to perceive situations involving risk as threatening, and behave across them in a consistently cautious manner.

An important direction for future research is to specify further the dynamic mechanisms through which global traits influence behavior. Several modern approaches bypass trait concepts on the way to examining goals, perceptions, or abilities. Instead, or at least additionally, it might be helpful to ascertain how people with different traits perceive and categorize situations. In turn, it might be useful to explore how these perceptions and categorizations can be explained through motivational mechanisms, abilities and capacities, and learning.

Assessment Assertions

SELF-REPORT IS A LIMITED TOOL FOR PERSONAL-
ITY ASSESSMENT   Because people are not directly
aware of the operation of their own traits, their self-
reports cannot always be taken at face value. Such
reports might be wrong because of errors in
retrospective behavioral analysis—including failures of memory and failures of insight. Both kinds
of failure are very common. Self-reports are also
subject to self-presentation effects, the desire to
portray oneself in the most favorable possible light.

This is one point where the present analysis
diverges from previous and traditional presentations of trait theory. Self-reports have been and
continue to be the most widely used tool for trait
measurement (see McClelland, 1984, and Block &
Block, 1980, for notable exceptions). This is unfortunate because, according to the present analysis, the person is in a relatively poor position to
observe and report accurately his or her own traits,
except under exceptional circumstances. Indeed,
certain important traits may be almost invisible to
the persons who have them. Imagine a chronic re-
pressor asked to rate him- or herself on the item,
"tends to deny one's own shortcomings."

This analysis helps account for one of the best
known findings of attribution research. Observers
of a person's behavior are more likely to report that
it was influenced by traits than is the person him-
or herself. Traditional accounts of this finding have
assumed this is because the observers are, simply,
wrong (Jones & Nisbett, 1972). The present analysis views the actor-observer effect as a natural
result of the person being in a relatively poor position to observe his or her own traits. A more objective, external point of view is necessary. This leads
to the next assertion.

THE SINGLE BEST METHOD OF TRAIT ASSESSMENT
IS PEER REPORT   As was discussed above, traits
are manifest by complex patterns of behavior the
precise nature of which have by and large gone un-
specified, as personality psychologists focused their
attention elsewhere. However, our intuitions daily
utilize complex *implicit* models of how traits are

manifest in behavior. Making explicit these implicit
understandings is an important but almost un-
touched area for further research. In the meantime,
such intuitions are there to be used.

The intuitions available are those of the person being assessed, and those of the people who
know him or her in daily life. Self-judgments of
personality are easy to gather, and research suggests
that by and large they agree well with judgments by
peers (Funder & Colvin, in press). Nonetheless,
self-reports are also suspect for a number of reasons, as was discussed earlier.

The impressions a person makes on those
around him or her may provide a more reliable
guide for how he or she can be accurately characterized. Peers' judgments have the advantage of being based on large numbers of behaviors viewed in
realistic daily contexts, and on the filtering of these
behavioral observations through an intuitive system capable of adjusting for both immediate situational and long-term individual contexts (Funder,
1987). Moreover, as Hogan and Hogan (1991) have
observed, "personality has its social impact in
terms of the qualities that are ascribed to individuals by their friends, neighbors, employers, and colleagues" (p. 12). For social traits at least, it is hard
to imagine a higher court of evidential appeal that
could over-rule peers' judgments, *assuming the
peers have had ample opportunity to observe the target's behavior in daily life.* If everyone you meet decides you are sociable, for instance, then you *are*
(Allport & Allport, 1921).

This assertion implies that an important direction for future research is to find out more
about how judges of personality perform (Neisser,
1980). A better understanding of the cues that are
used by everyday acquaintances in judging personality, and the circumstances under which those
cues are accurate, will lead to progress regarding
two important issues: (a) how personality is manifest in behavior, and (b) how personality can most
accurately be judged. My own current research focuses on these topics (Funder, 1987, 1989).

Epistemological Assertions

For Purposes of Explanation, the Most Important Traits Are Global (but for Purposes of Prediction, the Narrower the Better) It appears to have become fashionable in the personality literature to eschew generality by constructing individual difference variables that are as narrow as possible. Cantor and Kihlstrom (1987) espouse a theory of "social intelligence" that regards the attribute as central to personality but *not* a general individual difference. Rather, it is viewed as a collection of relatively discrete, independent, and narrow social capacities, each relevant to performance only within a specific domain of life. A related viewpoint is that of Sternberg and Smith (1985), who suggest that different kinds of social skill are relevant only to extremely narrow classes of behavior, and that as a general construct "social skill" has little or no validity (but see Funder & Harris, 1986).

The use of narrow constructs may well increase correlations when predicting single behaviors, just as at the same time (and equivalently) it decreases the range of behaviors that can be predicted (Fishbein & Ajzen, 1974). But beyond whatever predictive advantages narrowly construed variables may have, they are often presented as if they were somehow *conceptually* superior as well. They are not. Indeed, explaining behavior in terms of a narrow trait relevant to it and little else represents an extreme case of the circularity problem sometimes (unfairly) ascribed to trait psychology in general. If "social skill at parties" is a trait detected by measuring social skill at parties, and is then seen as a *predictor* or even *cause* of social skill at parties, it is obvious that psychological understanding is not getting anywhere.

Global traits, by contrast, have real explanatory power. The recognition of a pattern of behavior is a *bona fide* explanation of each of the behaviors that comprise it.[1] Indeed, the more global a trait is, the more explanatory power it has. Connections between apparently distal phenomena are the most revealing of the deep structure of nature. For instance, if a general trait of social skill exists (see Funder & Harris, 1986), then to explain each of various, diverse behavioral outcomes with that trait is not circular at all. Instead, such an explanation relates a specific behavioral observation to a complex and general pattern of behavior. Such movement from the specific to the general is what explanation is all about.

This is not to say the explanatory task is then finished—it never is. These general patterns called traits should be the targets of further explanatory effort. One might want to investigate the developmental history of a trait, or its dynamic mechanisms, or its relationships with other traits, or the way it derives from even more general personality variables. But traits remain important stopping points in the explanatory regress. To *any* explanation, one can always ask "why?" (as every 4-year-old knows). Still, between each "why" is a legitimate step towards understanding.

The Source of Trait Constructs Should Be Life and Clinical Experience, as Filtered by Insightful Observers It has often been argued that personality constructs should be formulated independently of, or even in explicit avoidance of, the constructs used by ordinary intuition. Indeed, this is one point upon which investigators as diverse as R.B. Cattell and Walter Mischel have found common ground. Often, mechanical procedures (e.g., factor analysis, behavioral analysis) have been touted as ways to construct personality variables uncontaminated by erroneous preconceptions. The results can be quite esoteric, having ranged from

---

[1] A reviewer of this paper expressed concern that it fails to distinguish sufficiently "between trait words as descriptions of regularities in others' behavior, and trait words as explanations of those regularities." My position is that the identification of a regularity in a person's behavior *is* an explanation of the specific instances that comprise the regularity, albeit an incomplete explanation (i.e., the next question will always be, What is the source of the regularity?). Thus, rather than confounding the two meanings of trait, the present analysis does not regard them as truly distinct.—Author

Cattell's (1946) favored variables of "alexia," "praxernia," and the like, to Mischel's (1973) cognitive social-learning variables of "subjective expected values," "encoding strategies," and so forth.

However, the theory of global traits asserts that trait constructs *should* be intuitively meaningful, for three reasons. First, intuitively discernible traits are likely to have greater social utility. Many global traits describe directly the kinds of relationships people have or the impacts they have on each other. More esoteric variables, by and large, do not.

Second, psychology's direct empirical knowledge of human social behavior incorporates only a small number of behaviors, and those only under certain specific and usually artificial circumstances. Restricting the derivation of individual difference variables to the small number of behaviors that have been measured in the laboratory (or the even smaller number that have been measured in field settings) adds precision to their meaning, to be sure, but inevitably fails to incorporate the broader patterns of behaviors and contexts that make up daily life. Our intuitions, by contrast, leapfrog ahead of painstaking research. The range of behaviors and contexts immediately brought to mind by a trait like "sociable" goes far beyond anything research could directly address in the foreseeable future. Of course, our intuitions are unlikely to be completely accurate, so traits as we think of them informally and as they actually exist in nature may not be identical. However, to be useful in daily life our intuitions must provide at least roughly accurate organizations of behavior, and provide a logical starting point for research (Clark, 1987). Corrections and refinements can come later, but to begin analysis of individual differences by eschewing intuitive insight seems a little like beginning a race before the starting line.

Third, the omission of intuitively meaningful concepts from personality psychology makes study of the *accuracy* of human judgments of personality almost meaningless. People make global trait judgments of each other all the time, and the accuracy of such judgments is obviously important (Funder, 1987). However, unless one wishes to finesse the issue by studying only agreement between *perceptions* of personality (Kenny & Albright, 1987), research on accuracy requires a psychology of personality assessment to which informal, intuitive judgments can be compared. Gibson (1979) has persuasively argued that the study of perception cannot proceed without knowledge about the stimulus array and, ultimately, the reality that confronts the perceiver. This point applies equally to person perception. A theory of personality will be helpful in understanding judgments of people for the same reason that a theory of the physics of light is helpful in understanding judgments of color.

Empirical Assertions

GLOBAL TRAITS INTERACT WITH SITUATIONS IN SEVERAL WAYS   Every global trait is situation specific, in the sense that it is relevant to behavior in some (perhaps many), but not all, life situations. Sociability is relevant only to behavior in situations with other people present, aggressiveness when there is the potential for interpersonal confrontation, friendliness when positive interaction is possible, and so forth. Our intuitions handle this sort of situational delimitation routinely and easily.

The delimitation of the situational relevance of a trait is sometimes called a "person-situation interaction." The empirical and conceptual development of this idea is an important achievement of the past two decades of personality research, and a valuable byproduct of the consistency controversy (Kenrick & Funder, 1988). The kind of interaction just described has been called the ANOVA or "passive" form (Buss, 1977). All that is meant is that different traits are relevant to the prediction of behavior in different situations. A child whose cooperativeness leads her to delay gratification in a situation with an adult present may be the first to quit if left alone (Bem & Funder, 1978).

At least two other, more active kinds of interaction are also important. The first is situation selection. Personality traits affect how people choose what situations to enter (Synder & Ickes, 1985). A party might contain strong, general pressures to socialize, pressures that affect the behavior of nearly everyone who attends. But sociable people are more likely to have chosen to go to the party in the first place. Thus, the trait of sociability influences behavior in part by affecting the situational influences to which the individual is exposed.

Traits can also magnify their influence on behavior through another kind of interaction. Most situations are changed to some extent by the behavior of the people in it. The presence of a sociable person can cause a situation to become more sociability-inducing. An aggressive child can turn a previously peaceful playground into a scene of general mayhem.

However, certain situations are *not* freely chosen, being imposed arbitrarily, and some situations will *not* change, no matter what the people in them may do. By short-circuiting the two kinds of person-situation interactions just discussed, such situations limit severely the influence traits can have on behavior. A prototypic example is the psychological experiment. Experiments assign subjects to conditions randomly, and the experimenter works from a set script. The subject's personality then cannot influence which situation he or she is exposed to, nor can his or her actions change the nature of the situation into which he or she is thrust (Wachtel, 1973).

But even in experiments like this, the influence of global traits is frequently detected; many examples could be cited. Consider the delay-of-gratification experiment already discussed (Bem & Funder, 1978). Nearly all the children who happened to be enrolled in a certain nursery school class entered this situation, and the experimenter worked from a set script that did not vary as a function of what the child did. Even so, the children's delay-of-gratification behavior had many and meaningful ties to their global personality traits, as assessed by their parents.

EVIDENCE CONCERNING PERSONALITY CORRELATES OF BEHAVIOR SUPPORTS THE EXISTENCE OF GLOBAL TRAITS Findings such as those summarized in the preceding paragraph have been obtained again and again. Numerous studies report correlations between behavior in arbitrarily imposed, implacable situations, and personality traits judged

on the basis of behavior observed in real life. These correlations constitute powerful evidence of the important influence of personality traits on behavior, even under circumstances where one would expect their influence to be weakened.

Most of this evidence has accumulated since 1937, and so was not available to Allport, but has been summarized many times in the course of the person-situation debate. Reviews can be found in articles by Funder (1987), Kenrick and Funder (1988), and many others.

EVIDENCE CONCERNING INTERJUDGE AGREEMENT SUPPORTS THE EXISTENCE OF GLOBAL TRAITS Another form of evidence for the existence of global traits is the good agreement that can be obtained between judgments of traits rendered by peers who know the subject in diverse life situations, and between such judgments and the subject's own self-judgments. Allport regarded evidence of this sort as especially persuasive:

> What is most noteworthy in reserach on personality is that different observers should agree as well as they do in judging any one person. This fact alone proves that there must be something really there, something objective in the nature of the individual himself that compels observers, in spite of their own prejudices, to view him in essentially the same way. (Allport, 1937, p. 288)

Fifty-three years later, the evidence is even stronger. Acquaintances who are well-acquainted with the people they judge can provide personality ratings that agree with ratings provided by other acquaintances as well as by the targets themselves (see Funder & Colvin, in press, for a review). This issue being settled, more recent work has focused on the circumstances that make interjudge agreement higher and lower, including level of acquaintanceship and the nature of the specific trait being judged (Funder, 1989).

EVIDENCE CONCERNING THE STABILITY OF PERSONALITY ACROSS THE LIFE SPAN SUPPORTS THE EXISTENCE OF GLOBAL TRAITS Allport lacked access to well-designed longitudinal studies that examined the stability of personality over time. Today, a vast body of research convincingly demonstrates that general traits of personality can be highly stable across many years. Data showing how behaviors can be predicted from measures of traits taken years before, or "post-dicted" by measures taken years later, have been reported by Funder, Block, and Block (1983), Funder and Block (1989), and Shedler and Block (1990). Similar findings from other longitudinal studies have been reported by Block (1971), Caspi (1987), McCrae and Costa (1984), and others.

Directions for Research

As a fruitful theory should, the theory of global traits raises a host of unanswered questions that deserve to be the focus of future research. They include matters of definition, origin, function, and implication.

Definition. How many global traits are there? Allport (1937, p. 305) reported finding 17,953 terms in an unabridged dictionary. Fortunately, these can be partially subsumed by more *general* constructs. Personality psychology seems to be achieving a consensus that most trait lists boil down to about five overarching terms (Digman, 1990). This does not mean there are "only" five traits, but rather that five broad concepts can serve as convenient, if very general, summaries of a wide range of the trait domain. They are Surgency (extraversion), Neuroticism, Openness (or culture), Agreeableness, and Conscientiousness.

Global traits may also be partially reducible to more narrow constructs. Perhaps friendliness is a blend of social potency and positive affect, for instance. The reduction of global traits into more specific (and possibly more factorially pure) constructs is a worthwhile direction for research. But the position taken here is that the appropriate level of analysis at which investigation should *begin*, and which more specific investigations should always remember to *inform*, is the level of intuitively accessible, global traits.

Origin. Developmental psychology has been dominated in recent years by studies of cognitive development, with the term "cognitive" sometimes construed rather narrowly. The theory of global traits draws renewed attention to the importance of investigations, especially longitudinal investigations, into the genetic and environmental origins of personality traits.

Function. The dynamic mechanisms through which global traits influence behavior remain poorly understood. As Allport hinted, they seem to involve the way individuals perceive situations and group them into equivalence classes. But the exact learning, motivational, and perceptual mechanisms involved, the way that different traits interact within individuals, and the circumstances under which a person can become consciously aware of his or her own traits are all issues needing further empirical examination.

Implication. Given that a person has a given level of a global trait, what kinds of behaviorial predictions can be made accurately, into what kinds of situations? This *deductive* question will require further and more detailed examination of person-situation interactions. And, given that a person has performed a certain pattern of behavior across a certain set of situations, what can we conclude about his or her global traits? This *inductive* question will require close attention to the behavioral cues that laypersons use in their intuitive judgments of personality, and an empirical examination of the validity of these cues. Progress toward answering this question will help to provide a valid basis by which human social judgment can be evaluated and, therefore, improved (Funder, 1987).

In the current literature, these issues receive much less attention than they deserve. A neo-Allportian perspective may lead not only to a renewed examination of these central issues, but to progress in the study of personality's historic mission of integrating the various subfields of psychology into an understanding of whole, functioning individuals.

References

Ahadi, S., & Diener, E. (1989). Multiple determinants and effect size. *Journal of Personality and Social Psychology, 56,* 398–406.

Allport, F. H., & Allport, G. W. (1921). Personality traits: Their classification and measurement. *Journal of Abnormal and Social Psychology, 16,* 6–40.

Allport, G. W. (1931). What is a trait of personality? *Journal of Abnormal and Social Psychology, 25,* 368–372.

Allport, G. W. (1937). *Personality: A psychological interpretation.* New York: Henry Holt & Co.

Allport, G. W. (1958). What units shall we employ? In G. Lindzey (Ed.), *Assessment of human motives* (pp. 239–260). New York: Rinehart.

Allport, G. W. (1961). *Pattern and growth in personality.* New York: Henry Holt.

Allport, G. W. (1966). Traits revisited. *American Psychologist, 21,* 1–10.

Bem, D. J. (1972). Self-perception theory. In L. Berkowitz (Ed.), *Advances in experimental social psychology* (Vol. 6). New York: Academic Press.

Bem, D. J., & Funder, D. C. (1978). Predicting more of the people more of the time: Assessing the personality of situations. *Psychological Review, 85,* 485–501.

Block, J. (1971). *Lives through time.* Berkeley, CA: Bancroft Books.

Block, J. (1988). Critique of the act frequency approach to personality. *Journal of Personality and Social Psychology, 56,* 234–245.

Block, J. H., & Block, J. (1980). The role of ego-control and ego-resiliency in the organization of behavior. In W. A. Collins (Ed.), *Minnesota symposium on child psychology* (Vol. 13). Hillsdale, NJ: Erlbaum.

Buss, A. R. (1977). The trait-situation controversy and the concept of interaction. *Personality and Social Psychology Bulletin, 3,* 196–201.

Buss, D. M. (1984). Evolutionary biology and personality psychology: Toward a conception of human nature and individual differences. *American Psychologist, 39,* 1135–1147.

Buss, D. M., & Craik, K. H. (1983). The act frequency approach to personality. *Psychological Review, 90,* 105–126.

Cantor, N., & Kihlstrom, J. F. (1987). *Personality and social intelligence.* Englewood Cliffs, NJ: Prentice-Hall.

Carlson, R. (1971). Where is the person in personality research? *Psychological Bulletin, 75,* 203–219.

Carr, H. A., & Kingsbury, F. A. (1938). The concept of trait. *Psychological Review, 45,* 497–524.

Caspi, A. (1987). Personality in the life course. *Journal of Personality and Social Psychology, 6,* 1203–1213.

Cattell, R. B. (1946). *Description and measurement of personality.* Yonkers, NY: World Book.

Clark, A. (1987). From folk psychology to naive psychology. *Cognitive Psychology, 11,* 139–154.

Digman, J. M. (1990). Personality structure: Emergence of the five-factor model. In M. R. Rosenzweig & L. W. Porter (Eds.), *Annual Review of Psychology* (pp. 417–440). Palo Alto, CA: Annual Reviews.

Fishbein, M., & Ajzen, I. (1974). Attitudes toward objects as predictors of single and multiple behavioral criteria. *Psychological Review, 81,* 59–74.

Funder, D. C. (1987). Errors and mistakes: Evaluating the accuracy of social judgment. *Psychological Bulletin, 101,* 75–90.

Funder, D. C. (1989). Accuracy in personality judgment and the dancing bear. In D. M. Buss & N. Cantor (Eds.), *Personality psychology: Recent trends and emerging directions* (pp. 210–223). New York: Springer-Verlag.

Funder, D. C., & Block, J. (1989). The role of ego-control, ego-resiliency, and IQ in delay of gratification in adolescence. *Journal of Personality and Social Psychology, 57,* 1041–1050.

Funder, D. C., Block, J. H., & Block, J. (1983). Delay of gratification: Some longitudinal personality correlates. *Journal of Personality and Social Psychology, 44,* 1198–1213.

Funder, D. C., & Colvin, C. R. (1997). Congruence of self and others' judgments of personality. In R. Hogan, J. Johnson, & S. Briggs (Eds.), *Handbook of personality psychology.* Orlando, FL: Academic Press.

Funder, D. C., & Harris, M. J. (1986). On the several facets of personality assessment: The case of social acuity. *Journal of Personality, 54,* 528–550.

Geis, F. L. (1978). The psychological situation and personality traits in behavior. In H. London (Ed.), *Personality: A new look at metatheories.* Washington, DC: Hemisphere Publishing.

Gibson, J. J. (1979). *The ecological approach to visual perception.* New York: Harper & Row.

Heider, F. (1958). *The psychology of interpersonal relations.* New York: Wiley.

Hogan, R., & Hogan, J. (1991). Personality and status. In D. G. Gilbert & J. J. Conley (Eds.), *Personality, social skills, and psychopathology: An individual differences approach* (pp. 137–154). New York: Plenum.

Jones, E. E., & Nisbett, R. E. (1972). The actor and the observer: Divergent perceptions of the cause of behavior. In E. E. Jones, D. Kanouse, H. H. Kelley, R. E. Nisbett, S. Valins, & B. Weiner (Eds.), *Attribution: Perceiving the causes of behavior.* Morristown, NJ: General Learning Press.

Kelley, H. H. (1967). Attribution theory in social psychology. In D. Levin (Ed.), *Nebraska symposium on motivation* (pp. 192–241). Lincoln: University of Nebraska Press.

Kelly, G. A. (1955). *The psychology of personal constructs* (Vols. 1 and 2). New York: Norton.

Kenny, D. A., & Albright, L. (1987). Accuracy in interpersonal perception: A social relations analysis. *Psychological Bulletin, 102,* 390–402.

Kenrick, D. T., & Funder, D. C. (1988). Profiting from controversy: Lessons from the person-situation debate. *American Psychologist, 43,* 23–34.

McClelland, D. C. (1984). *Motives, personality and society.* New York: Praeger.

McCrae, R. R., & Costa, P. C., Jr. (1984). *Emerging lives, enduring dispositions.* Boston: Little, Brown.

Mischel, W. (1968). *Personality and assessment.* New York: Wiley.

Mischel, W. (1973). Toward a cognitive social learning reconceptualization of personality. *Psychological Review, 80,* 252–283.

Neisser, U. (1980). On "social knowing." *Personality and Social Psychology Bulletin, 6,* 601–605.

Scarr, S., & McCartney, K. (1983). How people make their own environments: A theory of genotype –> environment effects. *Child Development, 54,* 424–435.

Shedler, J., & Block, J. (1990). Adolescent drug use and psychological health. *American Psychologist, 45,* 612–630.

Snyder, M., & Ickes, W. (1985). Personality and social behavior. In G. Lindzey & E. Aronson (Eds.), *The handbook of social psychology* (3rd ed., pp. 883–948). New York: Random House.

Sternberg, R. J., & Smith, C. (1985). Social intelligence and decoding skills in nonverbal communication. *Social Cognition, 3,* 168–192.

Thorne, A. (1989). Conditional patterns, transference, and the coherence of personality across time. In D. Buss & N. Cantor (Eds.), *Personality: Recent trends and emerging directions.* New York: Springer-Verlag.

Wachtel, P. (1973). Psychodynamics, behavior therapy, and the implacable experimenter: An inquiry into the consistency of personality. *Journal of Abnormal Psychology, 82,* 324–334.

Witkin, H. A., Lewis, H. B., Hertzman, M., Machover, K., Meissner, P., & Wapner, S. (1954). *Personality through perception.* New York: Harper.

Zuroff, D. C. (1986). Was Gordon Allport a trait theorist? *Journal of Personality and Social Psychology, 51,* 993–1000.

PART III

Biological Approaches to Personality

*The field of biology has made remarkable progress over the past century, and par-
ticularly in the past few decades. It was only natural, therefore, for personality psychologists to begin to use biology to help them understand the roots of important
human behaviors. A biological psychology of personality has developed that is
based upon four different areas of biology and that therefore comprises four rather
different approaches.*

*One approach relates the anatomy of the brain to personality. Perhaps the old-
est field of biological psychology, work in this area began by cataloging the ways in
which accidental brain damage affected behavior, and has proceeded in recent
years to the use of sophisticated techniques such as fMRI (functional magnetic resonance imaging). A second approach, very active today, relates the physiology of
the nervous system to personality. This approach can be traced back to the ancient
Greeks, who proposed that "humors" or bodily fluids influenced personality. Modern research addresses the complex interactions still being discovered between neurotransmitters, hormones, and behavior. A third approach, called "behavioral
genetics," studies the way individual differences in personality are inherited from
one's parents and shared among family members. Finally, a fourth approach applies Darwin's theory of evolution—the foundation of modern biology—to understand the behavioral propensities of the human species.*

*The readings in this section sample from all of these approaches. The section
begins with a chapter, more than a century old, that describes the ancient humoral
theory of personality and proposes a "modern"—as of the mid-nineteenth-
century—modification. The next selection, by James Dabbs and his colleagues,
describes research on the association between a "humor" of modern interest—
testosterone—and aggressive or, as they call it, "rambunctious" behavior by members of college fraternities. Research on testosterone can be traced back to ancient
humoral theories of personality. The next selection, by William Kelley and his*

colleagues at Dartmouth, could be said to have its ultimate roots in phrenology. Their paper describes very recent research using fMRI technology to ascertain the precise location in the brain of the "self"(!). The next article, by Shelley Taylor and her colleagues, addresses the complex pattern of the nervous system's response to threat called the "fight or flight" response. Arraying a large amount of physiological and behavioral research in animals and humans, she argues that this response is fundamentally different in women, where it may take on the pattern she calls "tend and befriend."

Behavioral genetics is introduced in the next selection, by Peter Borkenau and his colleagues working on the large and impressive German Observational Study of Adult Twins (GOSAT). Their research, based on direct behavioral observations of a large number of monozygotic and dizygotic twins, challenges the widely advertised finding of behavioral genetics that the shared family environment has only a small influence on personality development. Just as importantly, their article illustrates the state of the art for research in this rapidly developing field.

The next three articles address the application of evolutionary theory to personality psychology. David Buss and his co-workers describe research that measures gender differences in jealousy through self-report and physiological indicators, and provide an evolution-based account of their results. Martie Haselton explores some of the implications of "error management theory" (EMT), including the idea that some biases in thinking may have more advantages than disadvantages. These might include the bias of some males to think that females are more sexually interested in them than they really are. The evolutionary approach to psychology comes under fire in the next selection, by Alice Eagly and Wendy Wood, which argues that sex differences in behavior are better viewed as stemming from social structure than biological mechanisms.

The final selection, by Daryl Bem, illustrates what may be the wave of the future for biological approaches to personality. Bem introduces a theory of sexual orientation that explains this important personality characteristic as a result of a complex interplay between predisposing biological factors, basic biological mechanisms, and a child's and adolescent's social interactions in a sexually polarized society. Other theories of sexual development are likely to appear in the future to compete with Bem's. Even more importantly, we may begin to see other complete theories of complex phenomena such as violence, extraversion, and jealousy, theories that move step-by-step from genes to temperament to early experience to interaction with society.

The Temperaments

Samuel R. Wells

Modern biological psychology attempts to connect physical form and function with psychological outcomes by studying the anatomy of the brain and nervous system, and substances in the body such as neurotransmitters and hormones, to determine their effect upon behavior and personality.

The attempt to connect the physical with the mental has a very long history. The ancient physicians Hippocrates and Galen believed that the balance of four "humors," or fluids, in the body produced four distinct personality types. As recently as 100 years ago, it was widely believed that the structure of the brain could be determined by feeling bumps in the head, and in this way "phrenology" could be used to assess an individual's personality.

The first selection in the biological section is an excerpt from a book published more than a century ago by Samuel R. Wells. Not much is known about Wells today except that he was the editor of something called The Phrenological Journal and Life Illustrated. *In this book, Wells summarized the ancient humoral theory of personality and then replaced it with one of his own. Wells seems to have been what would today be called a biological reductionist; he believed that all aspects of human character and personality reside and can be seen in the physical form. The book provides detailed guidance on how to assess personality from appearance.*

The excerpted chapter begins with a brief summary of the theory he attributes to Hippocrates, then quickly moves on to his own modification. It is interesting to see that more than 2,000 years after Hippocrates, and just over 100 years ago, this ancient theory was still taken seriously enough to be the jumping-off place for what was portrayed as state-of-the-art knowledge.

Perhaps this book marks the last gasp of the ancient humoral and phrenological approach. The research of the twentieth century, based upon dramatic breakthroughs in the study of physiology, genetics, and evolution, quickly began to look very different.

And maybe it doesn't. Recent research in health psychology relates some of the ancient types to disease-proneness. The "choleric" person, described not much differently today than by the ancient Greeks, seems at exceptional risk for heart attack (Booth-Kewley & Friedman, 1987)!

Still, and perhaps needless to say, the specific biological factors and psychological characteristics do not in fact relate to each other in the manner described by Wells. Please do not read this selection to learn how to do personality assessment by looking at the individual's face. Instead, read it for historical background, its style of argument, and the richness of its description of psychological types. Wells may have been wrong in his biology, but he provides a description of some types of people that seem recognizable.

From *New Physiognomy, or, Signs of Character, as Manifested Through Temperament and External Forms, and Especially in 'the Human Face Divine,'* by S. R. Wells (New York: Samuel R. Wells, 1873), pp. 94–109.

Made him of well-attempered clay,
As such high destiny befitted,
And bade him rule.

—MARVEL

The first condition to be noted in the study of character through its physical manifestations, is temperament; which may be defined as "a particular state of the constitution, depending upon the relative proportion of its different masses, and the relative energy of its different functions."

In their last analysis, the temperaments are as numerous as the individuals of the human race, no two persons being found with precisely the same physical constitution. Tracing them back, however, we find them all to result from the almost infinite combinations of a few simple elements.

The Ancient Doctrine

Hippocrates, "the father of medicine," describes four temperamental conditions depending, according to his theory, upon what he called the four primary components of the human body—the blood, the phlegm, the yellow bile, and the black bile. The preponderance of one or the other of these components in a person produces his peculiar constitution or temperament. Bodies in which blood superabounds have, he says, the sanguine temperament; if phlegm be in excess, the phlegmatic temperament; if yellow bile be most fully developed, the choleric temperament is produced;

and if the black bile (*atrabilis*) be most abundant, the melancholic or atrabilious temperament. These four temperaments are thus described by Paulus Ægineta, an ancient physician, who adopts the theory and follows the classification of Hippocrates:

1. The sanguine or hot and moist temperament is more fleshy than is proper, hairy, and hot to the touch. Persons having this temperament in excess are liable to putrid disorders.

2. The phlegmatic or cold and moist temperament is gross, fat, and lax. The skin is soft and white; the hair tawny and not abundant; the limbs and muscles weak; the veins invisible, and the character timid, spiritless, and inactive.

3. The choleric or warm and dry temperament is known by abundant dark hair; large and prominent veins and arteries, dark skin, and a firm, well-articulated, and muscular body.

4. The melancholic or cold and dry temperament is known by hard, slender, and white bodies; fine muscles, small joints, and little hair. As to disposition, persons of this temperament are spiritless, timid, and desponding.

*   *   *

The New Classification

The human body is composed of three grand classes or systems of organs, each of which has its special function in the general economy. We denominate them—

Figure 1 Hon. Wm. Maule Panmure, M.P.

Figure 2 Thomas Moore.

Figure 3 D. C. McCallum.

Figure 4 McDonald Clarke.

1. The Motive or Mechanical System;
2. The Vital or Nutritive System; and
3. The Mental or Nervous System.

On this natural anatomical basis rests the most simple and satisfactory doctrine of the temperaments, of which there are primarily three, corresponding with the three systems of organs just named. We call them—

1. The Motive Temperament;
2. The Vital Temperament; and,
3. The Mental Temperament.

Each of these temperaments is determined by the predominance of the class of organs from which it takes its name. The first is marked by a superior development of the osseous and muscular systems, forming the locomotive apparatus; in the second the vital organs, the principal seat of which is in the trunk, give the tone to the organization; while in the third the brain and nervous system exert the controlling power.

I. THE MOTIVE TEMPERAMENT   The bony framework of the human body determines its general configuration, which is modified in its details by the muscular fibers and cellular tissues which overlay it. In the motive temperament, the bones are proportionally large and generally long rather than broad, and the outlines of the form manifest a tendency to angularity. The figure is commonly tall and striking if not elegant; the face oblong, the cheekbones rather high; the front teeth large; the neck rather long; the shoulders broad and definite; the chest moderate in size and fullness; the abdomen proportional; and the limbs long and tapering. The muscles are well developed and correspond in form with the bones. The complexion and eyes are generally but not always dark, and the hair dark, strong, and abundant. The features are strongly marked, and their expression striking. Firmness of texture characterizes all the organs, imparting great strength and endurance.

This temperament gives great bodily strength, ease of action, love of physical exercise, energy, and capacity for work. Those in whom it predom-

Figure 5   James Monroe.

inates generally possess strongly marked characters, and are in a high degree capable of receiving and combining rapidly many and varied impressions. They are the acknowledged leaders and rulers in the sphere in which they move; and are often carried away, bearing others with them, by the torrent of their own imagination and passions. This is the temperament for rare talents—especially of the executive kind—great works, great errors, great faults, and great crimes. It is sometimes, though not necessarily, characterized by an objectionable degree of coarseness and harshness of feelings, manifested by a corresponding coarseness of fiber in the bodily organs, bushy hair and beard, and a harsh expression of countenance.

The motive temperament is emphatically the American temperament, as it was that of the ancient Romans, though with us it is modified by a larger proportion of the mental temperament than with them. An aquiline or a Roman nose, great ambition, and an insatiable love of power and conquest go with it.

Men of this temperament often pursue their ends with a stern and reckless disregard of their own and others' physical welfare. Nothing can turn

Figure 6 Silas Wright.

the joints. This will be particularly observable in the wrists and ankles.

The third modification of this temperament is that which presents proportionally shorter bones, and, except around the pelvis, smaller and more rounded muscles, affording less strongly marked reliefs and more of that rounded plumpness essential to the highest style of female beauty. In this characteristic, it approaches the vital temperament, to which this modification is allied.

In accordance with the law of homogeneousness, we find, on examining this temperament more closely, that it is characterized in details, as well as in general form, by length. The face is oblong, the head high, the nose long and prominent, and all the features correspond. This structure indicates great power and activity in some particular direction, but lack of breadth or comprehensiveness.

* * *

II. The Vital Temperament As this temperament depends upon the preponderance of the vital or nutritive organs, which occupy the great cavities of the trunk, it is necessarily marked by a breadth and thickness of body proportionally greater, and a stature and size of limbs proportionally less than the motive temperament. Its most striking physical characteristic is *rotundity*. The face inclines to roundness; the nostrils are wide; the neck rather short; the shoulders broad and rounded; the chest full; the abdomen well developed; the arms and legs plump but tapering, and terminating in hands and feet relatively small. The complexion is generally florid; the countenance smiling; the eyes light; the nose broad, and the hair soft, light, and silky.

In a woman of this temperament (which seems to be peculiarly the temperament of woman), the shoulders are softly rounded, and owe any breadth they may possess rather to the expanded chest, with which they are connected, than to the bony or muscular size of the shoulders themselves; the bust is full and rounded; the waist, though sufficiently marked, is, as it were, encroached upon by the plumpness of the contiguous parts; the haunches are greatly expanded; the limbs tapering; the feet

them aside from their purpose; and they attain success by means of energy and perseverance rather than by forethought or deep scheming. They are men of the field rather than of the closet—men with whom to think and to feel is to act. As speakers, they make use of strong expressions, emphasize many words, and generally hit the nail with a heavy blow.

In its typical form, the motive temperament is less proper to woman than to man, but there are several modifications of it which give much elegance and beauty to the female figure.

The first is that in which the bones, except those of the pelvis, are proportionally small, which gives the figure additional delicacy and grace. This conformation, while it adds to the beauty of the female figure, detracts from the strength and consequently the beauty of the masculine form. The Diana of Grecian sculpture furnishes a fine example of the motive temperament thus modified.

The second modification is that in which the ligaments and the articulations which they form are proportionally small, which corrects the tendency to angularity which is characteristic of this temperament, and tends to round the contour of and hands small, but plump; the complexion, depending on nutrition, has the rose and the lily so exquisitely blended that we are surprised that it should defy the usual operations of the elements; and there is a profusion of soft, and fine flaxen or auburn hair. The whole figure is plump, soft and voluptuous. This temperament is not so common among American women as could be desired.

Persons of this temperament have greater vigor, but less density and toughness of fiber than those in whom the motive predominates. They love fresh air and exercise, and must be always doing something to work off their constantly accumulating stock of vitality; but they generally love play better than hard work.

Mentally, they are characterized by activity, ardor, impulsiveness, enthusiasm, versatility, and sometimes by fickleness. They are distinguished by elasticity rather than firmness, and possess more diligence than persistence, and more brilliancy than depth. They are frequently violent and passionate, but are as easily calmed as excited; are generally cheerful, amiable, and genial; always fond of good living, and more apt than others to become addicted to the excessive use of stimulants. Their motto is *dum vivimus, vivamus*—let us live while we live. There is great enjoyment to them in the mere sense of being alive—in the consciousness of animal existence. The English furnish some of the best examples of the vital temperament. Our illustration gives a good idea of it so far as its outlines are concerned.

* * *

III. THE MENTAL TEMPERAMENT The mental temperament, depending upon the brain and nervous system, is characterized by a slight frame; a head relatively large, an oval or a pyriform face; a high, pale forehead; delicate and finely chiseled features; bright and expressive eyes; slender neck; and only a moderate development of the chest. The whole figure is delicate and graceful, rather than striking or elegant. The hair is soft, fine, and not abundant or very dark; the skin soft and delicate in texture; the voice somewhat high-keyed, but flexible and varied in its intonations; and

Figure 7   Prof. Tholuck.

the expression animated and full of intelligence.

Women in whom this temperament predominates, though often very beautiful, lack the rounded outlines, the full bosom, and the expanded pelvis, which betoken the highest degree of adaptation to the distinctive offices of the sex.

The mental temperament indicates great sensitiveness, refined feelings; excellent taste; great love of the beautiful in nature and art; vividness of conception; and intensity of emotion. The thoughts are quick, the senses acute, the imagination lively and brilliant, and the moral sentiments active and influential.

This is the literary, the artistic, and especially the poetic temperament.

There is at the present day, in this country especially, an excessive and morbid development of this temperament which is most inimical to health, happiness, and longevity. It prevails particularly among women (to whom even in its normal predominance it is less proper than the preceding), and answers to the nervous temperament of the old classification. It is characterized by the smallness and emaciation of the muscles, the quickness and intensity of the sensations, the suddenness and fickleness of the determinations, and a morbid impressibility. It is caused by sedentary habits, lack of bodily exercise, a premature or disproportionate development of the brain, the immoderate use of tea and coffee, late hours, and other hurtful indulgences.

The three primary temperaments, combining with each other in different proportions and being modified by various causes, form sub-temperaments innumerable, presenting differences and resemblances depending upon the relative proportion of the primitive elements. The simplest combination of which the three temperaments already described are susceptible, gives us six sub-temperaments, which we designate as—

1. The Motive-Vital Temperament;
2. The Motive-Mental Temperament;
3. The Vital-Motive Temperament;
4. The Vital-Mental Temperament;
5. The Mental-Motive Temperament; and,
6. The Mental-Vital Temperament.

The names of these compound temperaments sufficiently indicate their character. The motive-vital and the vital-motive differ but slightly, the name placed first in either case indicating the element which exists in the larger proportion. The same remark applies to the motive-mental and the mental-motive, and to the vital-mental and mental-vital.

Perfection of constitution, it is evident, must consist in a proper balance of temperaments.

Where any one of them exists in great excess, the result must necessarily be a departure from symmetry and harmony, both of form and character. Whatever, therefore, has a tendency to promote this disproportionate development should be carefully avoided.

Each person is born with a particular temperament in which there is an inherent tendency to maintain and increase itself, since it gives rise to habits which exercise and develop it; but this tendency may be greatly modified, if not counteracted entirely, by external circumstances—by education, occupation, superinduced habits, climate, and so forth; and more especially by direct and special training instituted for that purpose.

It will be seen by the foregoing statements, which we have aimed to make as clear and explicit as the nature of the subject will admit, that a thorough practical knowledge of the temperaments alone will enable one to form a very correct general estimate of individual character. The character, as a whole, which we have attributed to the motive temperament, is never found in connection with either of the others; and the same remark applies equally to the vital and the mental. The difficulty (which is not insurmountable, however) lies in estimating correctly the relative proportion of the different elements in each individual temperament so as to give to each its due degree of influence on the character. Study, observation, and practice will enable the persevering student to do this, in time, with great exactness.

Testosterone Differences Among College Fraternities: Well-Behaved vs. Rambunctious

James M. Dabbs Jr., Marian F. Hargrove, and Colleen Heusel

Of all the substances in the body that might affect behavior, the male sex hormone testosterone probably has received the most attention. Although both males and females have testosterone in their bodies, males have much more and, it is commonly observed, are more aggressive. These observations have led directly to the hypothesis that testosterone might be a cause of aggressive or "rambunctious" behavior.

This hypothesis is tested in the next selection, by the personality psychologist James Dabbs Jr. and several of his collaborators. Dabbs has spent much of his career in pursuit of the relationship between testosterone, behavior, and personality. His usual technique is to have subjects spit in a cup and to measure the testosterone level in their saliva. He then gathers some measure of his subjects' personality or behavior and correlates the two measurements.

For the research reported in the next selection, Dabbs and his colleagues addressed a phenomenon that is familiar to any college student: some fraternities are always getting themselves into trouble by their habitually rambunctious behavior, while others are more sedate. Dabbs speculated that such an average difference in behavior between groups might be explained, in part, by average differences in testosterone level of the groups' members. So he sent assistants to both kinds of fraternities at two universities, convinced their members to donate some of their saliva, and obtained ratings of the fraternities' behavior. The results showed that fraternities with higher average testosterone levels tended to be the more rambunctious ones.

Of course, these are correlational data. That means the direction of causality cannot be assumed to be one-way. Perhaps testosterone causes rambunctious behavior, but perhaps, too, living in a house full of rambunctious "brothers" tends to raise one's testosterone level. Probably both happen. High-testosterone students are drawn to certain fraternities, and certain environments (such as fraternity houses) make testosterone levels higher.

Finally, notice how the research on the behavioral correlates of testosterone is squarely in the tradition of theorizing about bodily "humors" and temperament, such as exemplified in the previous selection by Wells. Here, the humor is testosterone and the behavior is aggressiveness. The technology is modern and the data much better, but the basic idea—substances in the body explain why people behave as they do—is ancient.

From *Personality and Individual Differences, 20,* 157–161, 1996.

Introduction

The character of groups arises from their circumstances and history. It also arises from the nature of the people who belong to the groups. People are social and biological creatures, and among the qualities that affect their behavior in groups is the hormone testosterone.

Testosterone in animals is related to aggression, dominance, and sexual activity (Archer, 1988; Lesher, 1978). In people it is related to dominance (Gladue, Boechler, & McCaul, 1989), aggression (Archer, 1991), libido (Booth & Dabbs, 1993; Morris, Udry, Kahn-Dawood, & Dawood, 1987; Sherwin, Gelfand, & Brender, 1985), sensation seeking (Daitzman & Zuckerman, 1980), drug abuse (Dabbs & Morris, 1990), low educational achievement (Dabbs, 1992; Kirkpatrick, Campbell, Wharry, & Robinson, 1993), and marital discord and divorce (Booth & Dabbs, 1993). The picture is one of excess and delinquency, although Dabbs and Ruback (1988) found high testosterone college students engaging and likeable.

Testosterone can be regarded as a characteristic of groups as well as of individuals. Mean testosterone levels differ across occupations (Dabbs, 1992; Dabbs, de La Rue, & Williams, 1990a; Schindler, 1979). Because people affiliate with others similar to themselves (Buss, 1985), we might expect them to have testosterone levels like those of their friends and associates. When individuals join together into groups, their shared conversations and social activities should intensify their preexist-

ing characteristics. Testosterone is important in the lives of young men, and it is plausibly related to the kind of groups to which they belong. Relationships between testosterone and group behavior could be studied in friendship groups, civic clubs, or college fraternities.

The present study dealt with college fraternities. Fraternities are allowed a large latitude of behavior on most campuses, and there is room for individual members to shape the overall tone of the fraternity. The present study was initiated by Hargrove's (1991) observation that *Ss*[1] from a fraternity known for good behavior and high grades appeared somewhat low in testosterone, although she had no comparative data from other fraternities. Hargrove hypothesized that, consistent with findings about other occupations including the ministry (Dabbs et al., 1990a), low testosterone fraternities would be more intellectually oriented and socially responsible than high testosterone fraternities. Based on this hypothesis and the studies cited above, we expected higher testosterone groups to be wilder and more rambunctious and lower testosterone groups to be more docile and well-behaved. The present study addresses two specific questions: Do fraternities differ among themselves in mean testosterone level? If they do, what best describes the behavior associated with these differences?

---

[1]Following the format of the journal in which this article originally appeared, *Ss* stands for subjects, or research participants.

Method

We examined five fraternities at the one university and seven fraternities at another. At the first university there were 26 fraternities, and interfraternity council members helped us identify those most similar to and those most different from the one studied by Hargrove (1991). This resulted in two sets of fraternities, containing two and three fraternities each. We labeled the first set, which included Hargrove's original fraternity, "responsible," and we labeled the second set "rambunctious." At the second university there were 31 fraternities. We were unable to group these clearly, but a university official helped us identify a diverse set of seven that represented a range of popularity, social skill, academic achievement, and university rule violations.

A female researcher visited each fraternity in the hour before noon on a weekday. She contacted a fraternity officer and offered $75 for a set of saliva samples from approx. 20 members. The officer recruited Ss, each of whom chewed a stick of sugar-free gum and deposited 3 ml saliva into a 20-ml polyethylene vial. The samples were stored frozen until assayed. While Ss collected saliva samples, the officer completed a questionnaire that asked about the fraternity's current grade point average; its number of parties and community service projects during the past year; and its number of academic awards, sports awards, interfraternity council awards, and national fraternity awards during the past two years.

Photographs of Ss and the researcher's notes provided other information. At the first university three judges, blind as to testosterone scores, examined the photographs of all members of the five fraternities appearing in the university yearbook. Each judge scored each picture as smiling or not, with a smile defined as "an apparent smile with teeth showing." The task was not difficult, and all judges agreed on 99% of the photographs. Each fraternity was assigned a score representing the proportion of its members the judges agreed were smiling. At the second university, the yearbook did not contain individual student photographs, and smiling was scored differently. Two judges counted smiles in fraternity group pictures that appeared in the yearbook, and two judges visited the fraternity houses and counted smiles in composite membership photographs hanging there. There was 100% agreement between the judges. Each fraternity was assigned a mean score combining the proportion smiling in the yearbook and the proportion smiling in the house photograph. All smile proportion scores, including the separate yearbook and house scores at the second university, were transformed from proportions to arcsin values prior to any statistical treatment.

Salivary testosterone levels were determined using an in-house radioimmunoassay procedure with ^{125}I-testosterone tracer and charcoal separation (Dabbs, 1990). Testosterone concentrations in saliva and serum are highly correlated, and the day-to-day reliability of salivary testosterone measurements is about $r = 0.64$ (Dabbs, 1990), approximately the same as the reliability of serum measurements (Gutai, Dai, La Porte, & Kuller, 1988). * * *

Results

UNIVERSITY ONE We analyzed testosterone scores from the first university using a two factor (Fraternity and Set) analysis of variance, with 98 Ss in five Fraternities nested in two Sets. Mean testosterone level was significantly higher in the rambunctious than the responsible set (14.3 vs 12.3 ng/dL), $F(1, 93) = 6.59$, $P < 0.05$. Differences in testosterone among fraternities within the sets was not significant, $F < 1.0$.

Questionnaire responses and yearbook smile scores were analyzed using t-tests, with the fraternities treated as five Ss in two groups. Rambunctious fraternities had more parties (33.0 vs 10.5 each), $t(3) = 3.68$, $P < 0.05$, lower grade point averages (2.5 vs 2.9), $t(3) = 5.03$, $P < 0.05$, fewer academic awards (0.0 vs 2.5), $t(3) = 6.71$, $P < 0.01$, fewer community service projects (0.3 vs 3.0), $t(3) = 6.20$, $P < 0.01$, and fewer members smiling in yearbook photographs (34 vs 62%), $t(3) = 3.61$, $P < 0.05$, than responsible fraternities.[2]

The researcher's notes indicated the fraternities differed in other ways. Fraternities in the rambunctious set more often ignored letters of inquiry or failed to return telephone calls. When the researcher arrived at their houses, all they needed to comply was an offer of money. One fraternity officer listened to her request and translated it for his brothers: "Hey guys, want to spit for a keg?" Two of the three houses were decorated in spartan fashion, with furniture in disrepair, as with a sofa supported by three legs and a brick. The third house, according to the housemother, was "only standing because it was constructed of steel and concrete." (Note: As of the time of publication, two of the three rambunctious fraternities had been banned from campus for misbehavior.)

Fraternities in the responsible set were more deliberate and considerate. One postponed participating to discuss the researcher's request at a chapter meeting, and the other telephoned her advisor long distance to make sure the request was legitimate. The responsible fraternities were polite when she visited. They invited her to have a seat and offered her something to eat or drink. Rambunctious fraternities were slower to respond to her arrival, letting her stand unattended, unfed, and apparently unwanted.

UNIVERSITY TWO At the second university we had no clear basis for clustering fraternities into sets, and we analyzed the data using one-way analysis of variance, which 142 Ss nested in seven fraternities. The fraternities differed significantly among themselves in testosterone, $F(6, 135) = 2.64$, $P < 0.05$. Their mean scores, ordered from low to high, were 10.3, 10.5, 11.2, 11.5, 11.6, 12.1 and 14.0 ng/dL. In comparisons among specific fraternities, Neuman–Keuls tests indicated that the highest fraternity was significantly different from the two lowest fraternities.

Contrary to the difference between two sets of fraternities at the first university, questionnaires completed by fraternity officers did not differentiate significantly among the seven fraternities at the second university. However, as at the first university, more smiling was associated with lower levels of testosterone. The correlation between proportion of members smiling and mean testosterone level across the seven fraternities was $r = -0.78$, 5 d.f.,[3] $P < 0.05$. The proportion smiling ranged from 55% in the fraternity with the lowest testosterone level to 35% in the fraternity with the highest level.

The researcher's notes revealed behavioral differences between fraternities that the Neuman–Keuls tests found significantly different in testosterone, the highest one and the two lowest ones. The highest fraternity was rough to a degree beyond rambunctiousness. The notes, stated, "I felt as if I'd been thrown to the lions. Very good looking, pumped up. No manners. They'd walk around without shirts, belch. 'Macho meatheads' is very fitting." The two lowest fraternities shared a common friendliness, though they differed in social skill. The notes on one of the two stated, "They talked a lot about computers and calculus. Very mild-mannered. They were nice, and we all sat around and talked while waiting for more people. Not great socially or good looking. Discussed their difficulty finding girls." The notes on the other stated, "These guys were nice and cooperative. Their house was well kept, and everyone was neatly dressed (preppy). One guy went upstairs and recruited other members of the fraternity to come spit."

[2]The t's and F's reported in this article are derived from t-tests and the analysis of variance, respectively, both of which yield p-values, which are estimates of the probability that between-group differences of the magnitude found would appear, by chance, if no such differences existed.

[3]The abbreviation "d.f." represents degrees of freedom, which is related to N or the number of participants.

Discussion

At both universities there were significant mean differences in testosterone among fraternities. At both universities there was less smiling in higher testosterone fraternities. At the first university, fraternities with higher testosterone levels were lower in academic achievement and community service and less friendly, as revealed by questionnaire measures and reactions to the researcher. Although they smiled less they had more parties, reminiscent of Barratt's (1993) description of impulsive aggressive individuals, high in gregariousness but low in warmth. At the second university, members of the highest testosterone fraternity were boisterous and macho, and members of the lowest testosterone fraternities were attentive and helpful. Testosterone was not related to academic achievement or community service at the second university.

Inconsistencies between the universities in the relationship of testosterone to academic achievement and community service present a puzzle. We spent more time identifying extreme fraternities at the first university, which may account for our finding of differences in socially responsible behavior there. However, we did examine a diverse set of fraternities at the second university, and we think that different cultures at the two universities may have led to different correlates of testosterone. The second university placed more emphasis on engineering and less on service and altruistic activities. To obtain descriptions of the two universities, we examined *The Insider's Guide to Colleges* (Yale Daily News, 1991). According to this source, the second university had half as many students as the first. It accepted fewer applicants (69 vs 79%), and its students had higher mean SAT scores (1190 vs 1080). It had fewer degree-granting programs (4 vs 12), and its academic pressure was more intense. It was located near the heart of a city, and more of its students came from urban backgrounds.

At the larger and more heterogenous first university, there was more room for students of varied abilities and more time for students to express values of community, altruism, and responsibility.

The university was in a small town in a rural setting. The community depended upon help from students to get things done, while the urban community around the other university was relatively independent of student participation.

We would expect the more diverse academic and civic activities at the first university to allow more room for the play of individual differences. Low testosterone *S*s were friendly at both universities, but only at the first was their friendliness translated into what we called more socially responsible behavior. We suspect that university differences moderated the positive effects of low testosterone, analogous to the way in which social control forces can moderate violent and antisocial aspects of high testosterone (Dabbs & Morris, 1990; Udry, 1990). We think that while high testosterone fraternities are rambunctious, low-testosterone fraternities are not necessarily responsible. "Well-behaved vs rambunctious" may be better than "responsible vs rambunctious" to describe the underlying dimension that characterized the differences between fraternities.

We have several caveats regarding the present findings. There was undoubtedly some error in the information provided by fraternity officers. We cannot know that testosterone caused the behavioural differences we found, although we are unaware of studies showing causation in the opposite direction, in which behavioral differences like those we observed cause differences in testosterone. And finally, smiles may be something other than a measure of friendliness. There is literature on the enjoyment reflected in smiles (Ekman, Davidson, & Friesen, 1990) and on emotional feeling vs social context as determinants of smiles (Hess, Banse, & Kappas, 1995), but there is little information on whether people who smile are more friendly in other ways. People smile for many reasons, including a desire to ingratiate themselves to others (DePaulo, 1992). In the present findings we have taken smiling to indicate friendliness, and we suggest that friendliness provides a link between smiling and low testosterone. Consistent with this notion about friendliness, Hargrove (1991) found low testosterone *Ss* more generous than high testosterone *Ss* in judging their peers. At the other end of the friendliness continuum, there is considerable evidence linking high testosterone to hostile and antisocial behavior (Booth & Dabbs, 1993; Dabbs, Carr, Frady, & Riad, 1995; Dabbs & Morris, 1990) and thus, one might expect, to lower levels of smiling.

It is somewhat surprising to find differences in testosterone among fraternities, given the paucity of other testosterone findings with college students. Questionnaire studies have seldom found personality measures related to testosterone (Dabbs, Hopper, & Jurkovic, 1990b), though Harris and Rushton (1993) found testosterone in college students related to high aggression and low pro-social behavior, when they treated aggression and pro-social behavior as latent variables defined by several indicators. The present findings suggest mean testosterone level can be regarded as a significant characteristic of a fraternity. It is possible that testosterone has more effect in groups than in individuals, as small individual tendencies accumulate into large group tendencies. Observing groups rather than individuals may be a way of making more visible the effects of testosterone.

Findings with fraternities may extend beyond the college campus. Many groups are central to modern life, and groups can have distinct and lasting natures. An acquaintance explained to one of the present authors when she moved to a new city, "Marian, this town is just like any other. The Rotarians own it, the Kiwanians raise money for it, and the Lions just enjoy it." These stereotypes fitted with her own knowledge of stuffy Rotary balls and luncheons where Lions threw rolls at their speakers. Fraternity members are like young Rotarians, Kiwanians, or Lions in training, waiting to take their place in the grown-up clubs when they leave the university. The hormones of individuals may shape the culture of groups.

References

Archer, J. (1988). *The behavioral biology of aggression.* Cambridge: Cambridge University Press.

Archer, J. (1991). The influence of testosterone on human aggression. *British Journal of Psychology, 82,* 1–28.

Barratt, E. S. (1993). Defining impulsive aggression. Unpublished manuscript, University of Texas Medical Branch at Galveston.

Booth, A., & Dabbs, J. M., Jr. (1993). Testosterone and men's marriages. *Social Forces, 72,* 463–477.

Buss, D. M. (1985). Human mate selection. *American Scientist, 73,* 47–51.

Dabbs, J. M., Jr. (1990). Salivary testosterone measurements: Reliability across hours, days, and weeks. *Physiology and Behavior, 48,* 83–86.

Dabbs, J. M., Jr. (1992). Testosterone and occupational achievement. *Social Forces, 70,* 813–824.

Dabbs, J. M., Jr. Carr, T. S., Frady, R. L., & Riad, J. K. (1995). Testosterone, crime, and misbehavior among 692 male prison inmates. *Personality and Individual Differences, 18,* 627–633.

Dabbs, J. M., Jr., de La Rue, D., & Williams, P. M. (1990a). Testosterone and occupational choice: Actors, ministers, and other men. *Journal of Personality and Social Psychology, 59,* 1261–1265.

Dabbs, J. M., Jr., Hopper, C. H., & Jurkovic, G. J. (1990b). Testosterone and personality among college students and military veterans. *Personality and Individual Differences, 11,* 1263–1269.

Dabbs, J. M., Jr., & Morris, R. (1990). Testosterone, social class, and antisocial behavior in a sample of 4,462 men. *Psychological Science, 1,* 209–211.

Dabbs, J. M., Jr., & Ruback, R. B. (1988). Saliva testosterone and personality of male college students. *Bulletin of the Psychonomic Society, 26,* 244–247.

Daitzman, R., & Zuckerman, M. (1980). Disinhibitory sensation seeking, personality and gonadal hormones. *Personality and Individual Differences, 1,* 103–110.

DePaulo, B. M. (1992). Nonverbal behavior and self-presentation. *Psychological Bulletin, 111,* 203–243.

Ekman, P., Davidson, R., & Friesen, W. V. (1990). Emotional expression and brain physiology II: The Duchenne smile. *Journal of Personality and Social Psychology, 58,* 342–353.

Gladue, B. A., Boechler, M., & McCaul, K. D. (1989). Hormonal response to competition in human males. *Aggressive Behavior, 15,* 409–422.

Gutai, J. P., Dai, W. S., LaPorte, R. E., & Kuller, L. H. (1988). The reliability of sex hormone measurements in men for epidemiologic research. Unpublished manuscript, University of Pittsburgh.

Hargrove, M. F. (1991). An investigation of personality correlates of testosterone using peer perceptions. Unpublished Master's Thesis, Georgia State University.

Harris, J. A., & Rushton, J. P. (1993). Salivary testosterone and aggression and altruism. Unpublished manuscript, University of Western Ontario.

Hess, U., Banse, R., & Kappas, A. (1995). Implicit audience and solitary smiling revisited. *Journal of Personality and Social Psychology, 69,* 280–288.

Kirkpatrick, S. W., Campbell, P. S., Wharry, R. E., & Robinson, S. L. (1993). Saliva testosterone in children with and without learning disabilities. *Physiology and Behavior, 53,* 583–586.

Lesher, A. I. (1978). *An introduction to behavioral endocrinology.* New York: Oxford.

Morris, N. M., Udry, J. R., Kahn-Dawood, F., & Dawood, M. Y. (1987). Marital sex frequency and midcycle female testosterone. *Archives of Sexual Behavior, 16,* 27–37.

Schindler, G. L. (1979). Testosterone concentration, personality patterns, and occupational choice in women. *Dissertation Abstracts International, 40,* 1411A (University Microfilms No. 79–19, 403).

Sherwin, B. B., Gelfand, M. M., & Brender, W. (1985). Androgen enhances sexual motivation in females: A prospective, crossover study of sex steroid administration in the surgical menopause. *Psychosomatic Medicine, 47,* 339–351.

Udry, J. R. (1990). Biosocial models of adolescent behavior problems. *Social Biology, 37,* 1–10.

Yale Daily News (1991). *The insider's guide to the colleges, 1991* (17th ed.). New Haven: Yale Daily News.

Finding the Self? An Event-Related fMRI Study

William M. Kelley, C. Neil Macrae, Carrie L. Wyland, Selin Caglar, Sara Inati, and Todd F. Heatherton

One of the earliest approaches to trying to understand brain functioning, besides the humoural approach, was "phrenology," which sought to find the physical locations of various psychological functions, such as movement and feeling, and even psychological traits, such as creativity and prudence. Phrenology fell from favor in part because it was often practiced by charlatans who claimed to be able to diagnose one's personality and even predict the future by feeling the bumps on one's head, and also because the technology of the day prevented gathering any real evidence about where psychological functioning was occurring in living brains.

This latter situation is rapidly changing. Newly developed techniques, such as fMRI (functional magnetic resonance imaging), are allowing subjects to begin to observe where the brain is most active as it performs various kinds of cognitive tasks and holds different kinds of thoughts. The present article, by a group of investigators at Dartmouth College, reports one of the most ambitious questions of this modern "phrenology": the attempt to find the self in the brain. The research sought to find the physical location of processes relevant to the "self-reference effect," which is that information thought of in relation to the self tends to be remembered longer than information thought of in other ways. The study concludes that, just maybe, the self is located in the medial prefrontal cortex!

From *Journal of Cognitive Neuroscience, 14*, 785–794, 2002.

Introduction

An impressive human talent is the ability to reflect on past experiences and to project the self into imagined futures. Indeed, it is this introspective ability that has prompted a host of noted thinkers to raise some vexing questions about the nature and status of the self (James, 1890). In experimental psychology, the debate has centered on two main issues. Is the self a unique cognitive structure? Does self-referential processing have some privileged status in the brain, or is it functionally equivalent to semantic processing about other classes of stimuli, such as cars, politicians, and Caribbean islands (Klein & Kihlstrom,

1986; Klein & Loftus, 1988; Maki & McCaul, 1985; Bower & Gilligan, 1979; Markus, 1977; Rogers, Kuiper, & Kirker, 1977)? Put simply, is self-referential processing special in any way?

Early research on this topic was revealing as it demonstrated a memorial advantage for information that was processed in a self-referential manner. Rogers et al. (1977), for instance, showed that trait adjectives that were processed with reference to the self (e.g., "Does the word 'honest' describe you?") were better recalled than comparable items that were processed only for their general meaning (e.g., "Does the word 'honest' mean the same as 'trustworthy'?"). This finding was important as it extended the seminal work of Craik and Tulving (1975) on depth of processing, which had previously shown that words processed for their semantic meaning were remembered better on a subsequent memory test than words processed for their structural features (e.g., "Is the word 'dependable' in lowercase letters?"). The message that has emerged from subsequent studies that have investigated the relationship between self and memory function is a consistent one—self-reference permits superior memory relative to other semantic encoding tasks (see Symons & Johnson, 1997). But why exactly does this self-reference effect occur?

Two putative explanations have been offered for the self-reference effect in memory. One account suggests that the self is a unique cognitive structure that possesses extraordinary or additional mnemonic abilities, hence the enhanced memorability of material that is processed in a self-referential manner (e.g., Maki & McCaul, 1985; Rogers et al., 1977). As Rogers et al. have suggested, the self functions as a "superordinate schema" (p. 686) that serves to facilitate the encoding and retrieval of information. However, other researchers take a different view. The basis of their argument is that there is nothing special about the self per se (i.e., no distinct structure or neural process devoted to self-referential processing). Rather, the memory enhancement afforded to self-reference can be interpreted as an extension of the basic depth-of-processing effect (e.g., Greenwald &

Banaji, 1989; Klein & Kihlstrom, 1986). That is, the wealth of knowledge we have about ourselves in memory simply encourages more elaborative encoding (and representation) of material that is processed in relation to the self (Klein & Loftus, 1988). In turn, this elaborative processing supports the enhanced memorability of self-relevant information.

Despite the clarity of these competing viewpoints, how self-referential processing boosts memory performance remains open to debate. A problematic feature of these candidate theoretical accounts is that they are difficult to evaluate competitively using purely behavioral measures. As such, researchers have recently turned to neuroimaging techniques in an attempt to inform current understanding of self-referential processing and its impact on memory function (e.g., Craik et al., 1999). Building on this work, the present investigation used event-related functional magnetic resonance imaging (fMRI) to investigate whether there is indeed anything special about self-referential processing. To address this question, participants were imaged while making various judgments about trait adjectives (see also Craik et al., 1999). Each trait word was presented concurrently with a "cue" that instructed participants as to which type of judgment they were required to make (Figure 1).

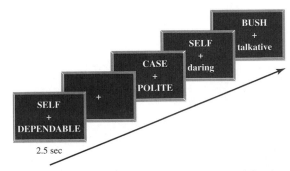

Figure 1. Examples of the self, other, case, and fixation trial types. Trials were randomly intermixed, and one trial was presented every 2.5 sec. For each of the three judgment trial types, the "cue" (presented above the central fixation) indicated which type of judgment to make for the trait adjective (presented below the fixation).

Participants judged each trait adjective in one of three ways: self ("Does the adjective describe you?"), other ("Does the adjective describe current U.S. President George Bush?"), and case ("Is the adjective presented in uppercase letters?").

These judgments were expected to produce varying levels of subsequent memory performance (self > other > case). Critically, however, they also permitted a direct test of the competing explanations for the self-reference effect. Functional imaging studies have previously identified multiple regions within the left frontal cortex that show greater activation for elaborative semantic encoding of words than for nonsemantic, surface-based encoding of words (Wagner et al., 1998; Gabrieli et al., 1996; Demb et al., 1995; Kapur et al., 1994; for review, see Buckner, Kelley, & Petersen, 1999). If the self-reference effect results from an extension of ordinary memory processes, then one might expect to observe greater activation for self-relevant judgments than for other- and case-based judgments in those same left frontal regions known to be sensitive to semantic encoding. Alternatively, if the self-reference effect results from properties of a unique cognitive self, then one might expect self-referential processing to selectively engage brain regions that are distinct from those involved in general semantic processing. We investigated these possibilities in the following experiment.

Results

BEHAVIORAL RESULTS   Table 1 shows behavioral performance measures for each trial type. An analysis of variance (ANOVA) showed that response latencies for encoding trials were slowest for other judgments (M = 1881 msec)[1] and fastest for case judgments (M = 1607 msec) [$F(2, 40)$ = 44.03, $p < .0001$]. Post hoc statistical tests revealed that response latencies were significantly faster for case judgments than for self judgments [$F(1, 20)$ =

---

[1]M is the mean; msec stands for milleseconds.

TABLE 1

BEHAVIORAL PERFORMANCE DURING ENCODING AND RECOGNITION TASKS

Task	Encoding Reaction Time (msec)	Hits–False Alarms	Recognition Reaction Time (msec)
Self	1812 (27)	0.49 (0.02)	1137 (31)
Other	1881 (24)	0.36 (0.03)	1188 (23)
Case	1607 (34)	0.17 (0.03)	1152 (24)

Standard errors are given in parentheses.

80.10, $p < .0001$] and other judgments [$F(1, 20)$ = 47.61, $p < .0001$].[2] The difference in response latencies between other and self judgments was also significant [$F(1, 20)$ = 7.12, $p < .05$].

Accurate performance on the yes/no recognition memory test was used as an indication that successful encoding had occurred. Recognition memory performance was determined by calculating corrected recognition scores (proportion of hits–false alarms). An ANOVA revealed a significant main effect of trial type [$F(1, 40)$ = 80.88, $p < .0001$]. Post hoc statistical tests revealed significant differences in subsequent memory between self and other adjectives [$F(1, 20)$ = 45.75, $p < .0001$], self and case adjectives [$F(1, 20)$ = 145.44, $p < .0001$], and other and case adjectives [$F(1, 40)$ = 42.77, $p < .0001$]. Response latencies during the recognition memory test did not differ across trial types [$F(3, 60)$ = 1.66, ns].

fMRI RESULTS   Figure 2 shows statistical activation maps for all encoding trials relative to base-

---

[2]The analysis of variance is a widely used technique for testing the significance of differences between means. It yields an F statistic that is evaluated in conjuction with the degrees of freedom in the experimental design, which are given in parentheses following the F and generally depend upon the number of participants in the study and/or the number of experimental conditions. Taken together, the F and the degrees of freedom yield a p value, which is interpreted as the probability of the "null hypothesis" that the real difference in means is 0.

Figure 2. Whole-brain statistical activation maps show general task-related activity in relation to baseline averaged across all 21 participants. * * * Colored pixels exceeded the statistical threshold and are superimposed on corresponding anatomy images. The left side of the image corresponds to the left side of the brain. Increases in activation were observed in (A) the posterior visual cortex ex-

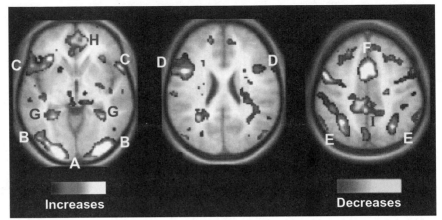

tending into (B) the extrastriate visual cortex, (C) the inferior frontal cortex, (D) the dorsal frontal cortex, (E) the lateral parietal cortex, and (F) the anterior cingulate. Decreases in activation were noted in (G) the medial temporal cortex, (H) the medial prefrontal cortex, and (I) the posterior cingulate.

Figure 3. Statistical activation maps comparing self and other trials to case trials demonstrate greater activity during semantic encoding trials (self and other) than nonsemantic encoding trials (case) in (A) the left inferior frontal cortex and (B) the anterior cingulate. Displayed at the left are axial sections through the activation foci averaged across participants. The left side of the image corresponds to the left side of the brain. Time courses (right panel) were computed for each condition within a 3-D region surrounding the peak voxel identified from the combined statistical map (shown in Figure 2). * * * Bars indicate standard error of the mean (*SEM*).

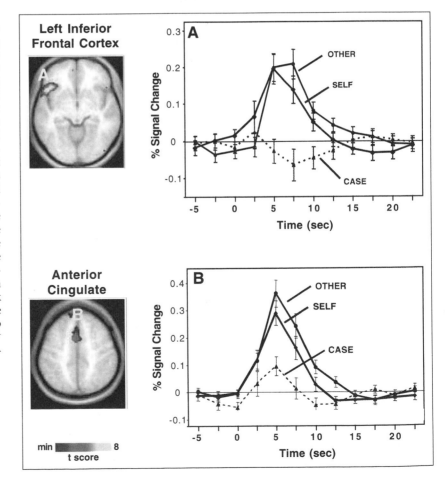

Figure 4. Statistical activation maps directly comparing self and other trials demonstrate greater activity during self encoding trials in (A) the MPFC and (B) the posterior cingulate. Displayed at the left are axial and sagittal sections through the activation foci averaged across participants. The left side of the image corresponds to the left side of the brain. Time courses (right panel) were computed for each condition within a 3-D region surrounding the peak voxel identified from the combined statistical map (shown in Figure 2). * * * Bars indicate standard error of the mean (*SEM*). Activity in the MPFC (A) was uniquely sensitive to self encoding trials, whereas activity in the posterior cingulate (B) was comparable across self and case encoding trials.

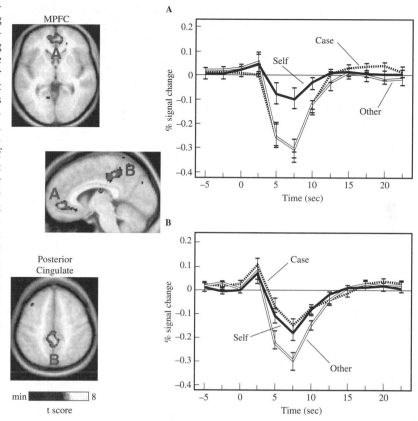

line. A network of brain regions was commonly activated, including bilateral regions of the striate and extrastriate visual cortex, the parietal cortex, the dorsal frontal cortex, the inferior frontal cortex, the motor cortex, and the cerebellum. Activations were also observed medially in the anterior cingulate gyrus the left thalamus, and the left caudate nucleus. * * * While a number of brain regions revealed significant increases in activation for encoding trials relative to baseline, other brain regions exhibited decreases in activation. Brain regions that exhibited significant decreased activity included the medial prefrontal cortex (MPFC), the posterior cingulate (near precuneus), and bilateral regions in the lateral frontal, parietal, and medial temporal cortex.

Figure 3 shows significant activations that were observed when relevance trials (self and other) were directly compared to case judgment trials. This contrast can be conceptualized as a traditional levels-of-processing contrast that compares deep, or semantic-based processing, to shallow, or surface-based processing. Areas showing greater activity for relevance judgments than for case judgments include the left inferior frontal cortex and the anterior cingulate. The time courses for each region are shown in Figure 3 (right panel). In both brain regions, the temporal profile of activity reveals clear differences between semantic judgments (self and other trials), which yielded robust positive hemodynamic responses, and nonsemantic judgments (case trials), which produced a much weaker response. The time courses for self and other trial types did not differ from each other in these two regions.

To identify brain regions that showed different patterns of activation across the two types of semantic judgments, self-judgment trials were directly compared to other judgment trials. Figure 4 shows significant activations that were observed in this direct comparison. Self judgments, when compared directly to other judgments, revealed greater activation in the MPFC and the posterior cingulate.

It should be noted that both of these regions exhibited decreased activity when all encoding trials were contrasted with baseline (see Figure 2). The "apparent" positive activation of these regions in the direct comparison results from the difference between two decreases relative to baseline (with other trials exhibiting a greater decrease from baseline relative to self trials). This can be seen clearly by examining the time courses for each region (Figure 4, right panel).

It is also important to note that the pattern of activation across the three trial types differs between the two brain regions. The hemodynamic response observed in the MPFC exhibits selectivity for self judgments. In this region, both other and case judgments produced robust decreases in activity relative to baseline that did not differ from each other. Self judgments yielded a much weaker decrease in the MPFC. By contrast, the activation pattern observed in the posterior cingulate was not uniquely sensitive to self-referential processing. In this region, other judgments elicited the greatest decrease; self and case judgments produced weaker decreases of comparable magnitudes.

Discussion

Consistent with levels-of-processing predictions (Craik & Tulving, 1975), trait adjectives judged in a semantic fashion (self and other) were later remembered better than adjectives judged only for surface-based features (case). More importantly, however, adjectives judged for self-relevance were remembered better than adjectives judged for relevance to a familiar other (President Bush). This finding is consistent with a number of behavioral studies that have demonstrated a self-reference superiority effect in memory (see Symons & Johnson, 1997).

Behavioral differences in subsequent memory

for the three different trial types were accompanied by differences in neural activation during encoding judgments as indexed by blood oxygen level-dependent (BOLD) contrast fMRI. The activation pattern suggests a hierarchy of neural involvement. A number of brain regions were commonly activated across all three trial types, including activations in the occipital and parietal lobes, the motor cortex, the thalamus, and the cerebellum. These activations likely reflect brain regions involved in general aspects of task performance that were common to all three trial types (e.g., viewing words and generating a motor response).

Other brain regions exhibited greater specificity. The left inferior frontal cortex and the anterior cingulate were selectively active during semantic judgments. The greater activation of the left inferior frontal cortex is consistent with a number of previous imaging studies that report left inferior frontal activation during tasks that encourage meaning-based encoding of verbal materials (for review, see Buckner et al., 1999). One interpretation of these findings is that left frontal activation may subserve the levels-of-processing effect observed by psychologists. To the degree that a task encourages elaborative semantic encoding, left frontal regions are activated, and those items are later remembered well. In the present study, both self-relevant and other-relevant judgments encouraged semantic-based processing of trait adjectives and, as a result, produced greater left frontal activation and better subsequent memory than did case judgments. However, self judgments produced even greater subsequent memory than did other judgments. If the self-reference effect is to be thought of as an ordinary extension of the levels-of-processing effect, left frontal activity might be expected to mediate the effect. In the present study, however, self judgments did not result in any additional activation of left frontal regions. If left frontal activity is viewed as a surrogate for ordinary semantic processing, then these results argue against the notion that the self-reference effect is driven by ordinary memory processes.

It should be noted that behavioral studies suggest that subsequent memory performance for words judged in reference to another person may depend on how well known the other is to the participant. For instance, when judgments are made with reference to intimate others (e.g., a parent, spouse, or best friend), the self-reference effect is reduced (Keenan & Baillet, 1980; Bower & Gilligan, 1979). When the other is a familiar public figure, as was the case in the current study, the self-reference effect is noticeably stronger (Conway & Dewhurst, 1995; Keenan & Baillet, 1980; Bower & Gilligan, 1979). Future research is needed to examine the role that familiarity may play in the neural effects reported herein.

So, is there anything special about the self? The current results suggest that a region of the MPFC is selectively engaged during self-referential judgments. This finding is consistent with previous imaging studies of self-referential mental activity. * * *

In summary, the present results contribute to a debate that has interested cognitive and social psychologists for decades—is their something special about self-referential processing? If the self-reference effect in memory is accomplished by the additional engagement of "ordinary" brain regions involved in semantic processing, then self judgments would be expected to produce greater left inferior frontal activity than other judgments. However, left inferior frontal involvement did "not" differ during self and other judgments. Instead, the difference between self and other judgments was the additional recruitment of the MPFC, presumably reflecting access to knowledge unique to one's self. Accordingly, the current results are consistent with the idea that self-referential processing is unique in terms of its functional representation in the human brain, a notion that has received emerging support from recent functional imaging studies (Gusnard et al., 2001; Craik et al., 1999). Finally, the present results offer a potential neural substrate (MPFC) for the self-reference effect in memory, a possibility that awaits further empirical investigation.

Methods

PARTICIPANTS Twenty-four participants between the ages of 18 and 30 (13 men, 11 women, mean age = 20 years) were recruited from the local Dartmouth community. All participants were strongly right-handed as measured by the Edinburgh handedness inventory (Raczkowski, Kalat, & Nebes, 1974). Participants reported no significant abnormal neurological history and all had normal or corrected-to-normal visual acuity. * * * Of the 24 participants, 2 were removed from subsequent analysis due to technical difficulties with fMRI data reconstruction. A third participant was removed as a result of excessive movement during imaging. Results reported here reflect data analyzed from the remaining 21 participants (12 men, 9 women, mean age = 20 years).

* * *

BEHAVIORAL TASKS Participants were imaged during two functional runs while making judgments about trait adjectives. Judgments were one of three types: self ("Does this adjective describe you?"), other ("Does this adjective describe current U.S. President George Bush?"), and case ("Is this adjective printed in uppercase letters?"). Participants indicated their responses via a left- or right-handed key press. Each trial lasted 2500 msec and consisted of a four-letter "cue" word (either "self," "Bush," or "case") presented for 2000 msec above a central fixation and a unique trait adjective (e.g., "POLITE") presented for 2000 msec below a central fixation (Figure 1). The central fixation remained on the screen throughout the duration of each trial. * * * Prior to the first functional run, participants were given practice trials to familiarize them with the tasks. Practice continued until participants indicated they were comfortable with the tasks.

A total of 270 unique adjectives were selected from a pool of normalized personality trait adjectives (Anderson, 1968). Lists were counterbalanced for word length, number of syllables, and valence (half of the words in each list were positive traits, the remaining half were negative traits). Across participants, lists were rotated through conditions such that trait adjectives that appeared in the self-judgment trials for one participant appeared in a different condition (other or case) for other participants. During each of the two functional runs, 15 self trials, 15 other trials, 15 case trials, and 30 fixation trials were pseudorandomly intermixed such that each trial type followed every other trial type equally often. * * *

Following the two encoding runs, participants were given a "surprise" recognition memory test. Participants viewed the 90 trait adjectives that were previously presented during the encoding scans along with 90 novel trait adjectives that had not been presented during the encoding scans. Words were presented sequentially in the center of the computer screen for 2000 msec. A fixation point (500 msec) preceded each word. For each word, participants indicated (via left- and right-handed key presses) whether the word was old or new.

DATA ANALYSIS fMRI data were analyzed using Statistical Parametric Mapping software (SPM99, Wellcome Department of Cognitive Neurology, London, UK) (Friston et al., 1995). For each functional run, data were preprocessed to remove sources of noise and artifact. Functional data were corrected for differences in acquisition time between slices for each whole-brain volume, realigned within and across runs to correct for head movement, and coregistered with each participant's anatomical data. * * *

* * *

References

Anderson, N. H. (1968). Likableness ratings of 555 personality-trait words. *Journal of Personality and Social Psychology, 9,* 272–279.

Bower, G. H., & Gilligan, S.-G. (1979). Remembering information related to one's self. *Journal of Research in Personality, 13,* 420–432.

Buckner, R. L., Kelley, W. M., & Petersen, S. E. (1999). Frontal cortex contributes to human memory formation [Review]. *Nature Neuroscience, 2,* 311–314.

Conway, M. A., & Dewhurst, S. A. (1995). The self and recollective experience. *Applied Cognitive Psychology, 9,* 1–19.

Craik, F. I. M., Moroz, T. M., Moscovitch, M., Stuss, D. T., Winocur, G., Tulving, E., & Kapur, S. (1999). In search of the self: A positron emission tomography study. *Psychological Science, 10,* 26–34.

Craik, F. I. M., & Tulving, E. (1975). Depth of processing and the retention of words in episodic memory. *Journal of Experimental Psychology: General, 104,* 268–294.

Demb, J. B., Desmond, J. E., Wagner, A. D., Vaidya, C. J., Glover, G. H., & Gabrieli, J. D. E. (1995). Semantic encoding and retrieval in the left inferior prefrontal cortex: A functional MRI study of task difficulty and process specificity. *Journal of Neuroscience, 15,* 5870–5878.

Friston, K. J., Holmes, A. P., Worsley, K. J., Poline, J.-P., Frith, C. D., & Frackowiak, R. S. J. (1995). Statistical parametric maps in functional imaging: A general linear approach. *Human Brain Mapping, 2,* 189–210.

Gabrieli, J. D. E., Desmond, J. E., Demb, J. B., Wagner, A. D., Stone, M. V., Vaidya, C. J., & Glover, G. H. (1996). Functional magnetic resonance imaging of semantic memory processes in the frontal lobes. *Psychological Science, 7,* 278–283.

Greenwald, A. G., & Banaji, M. R. (1989). The self as a memory system: Powerful, but ordinary. *Journal of Personality and Social Psychology, 57,* 41–54.

Gusnard, D. A., Akbudak, E., Shulman, G. L., & Raichle, M. E. (2001). Medial prefrontal cortex and self-referential mental activity: Relation to a default mode of brain function. *Proceedings of the National Academy of Sciences, U.S.A., 98,* 4259–4264.

Gusnard, D. A., & Raichle, M. E. (2001). Searching for a baseline: Functional imaging and the resting human brain. *Nature Reviews Neuroscience, 10,* 685–694.

James, W. (1890). *Principles of psychology* (vol. 1). New York: Henry-Holt and Co.

Kapur, S., Craik, F. I. M., Tulving, E., Wilson, A. A., Houle, S., & Brown, G. M. (1994). Neuroanatomical correlates of encoding in episodic memory: Levels of processing effects. *Proceedings of the National Academy of Sciences, U.S.A., 91,* 2008–2011.

Keenan, J. M., & Baillet, S. D. (1980). Memory for personally and socially significant events. In R. S. Nickerson (Ed.), *Attention and performance* (vol. 8, pp. 651–669). Hillsdale, NJ: Erlbaum.

Klein, S. B., & Kihlstrom, J. F. (1986). Elaboration, organization, and the self-reference effect in memory. *Journal of Experimental Psychology: General, 115,* 26–38.

Klein, S. B., & Loftus, J. (1988). The nature of self-referent encoding: The contributions of elaborative and organizational processes. *Journal of Personality and Social Psychology, 55,* 5–11.

Maki, R. H., & McCaul, K. D. (1985). The effects of self-reference versus other reference on the recall of traits and nouns. *Bulletin of the Psychonomic Society, 23,* 169–172.

Markus, H. (1977). Self-schemata and processing information about the self. *Journal of Personality and Social Psychology, 35,* 63–78.

Raczkowski, D., Kalat, J. W., & Nebes, R. (1974). Reliability and validity of some handedness questionnaire items. *Neuropsychologia, 12,* 43–47.

Rogers, T. B., Kuiper, N. A., & Kirker, W. S. (1977). Self-reference and the encoding of personal information. *Journal of Personality and Social Psychology, 35,* 677–688.

Symons, C. S., & Johnson, B. T. (1997). The self-reference effect in memory: A meta-analysis. *Psychological Bulletin, 121,* 371–394.

Wagner, A. D., Schacter, D. L., Rotte, M., Koutstaal, W., Maril, A., Dale, A. M., Rosen, B. R., & Buckner, R. L. (1998). Building memories: Remembering and forgetting verbal experiences as predicted by brain activity. *Science, 281,* 1188–1191.

Biobehavioral Responses to Stress in Females: Tend-and-Befriend, Not Fight-or-Flight

Shelley E. Taylor, Laura Cousino Klein, Brian P. Lewis, Tara L. Gruenewald, Regan A. R. Gurung, and John A. Updegraff

One of the best-known and most widely studied physiological phenomena associated with behavior is the cascade of hormonal secretion and interaction that is produced by stress and threat, a pattern called the "fight or flight" response. This is the response that, for example, is associated with the familiar acceleration of heartbeat, rising of blood pressure, and tensing of muscles that goes along with fear and anger. The assumption has been that these reactions prepare the body either for fighting a foe, if possible, or running away, if necessary. In this article, Shelley Taylor and her colleagues make a radical proposal. Observing that almost all the research that has documented this response, in both animals and humans, has examined males rather than females, they propose that females have a characteristically different pattern of response to threat, one they call "tend and befriend." Rather than flying or fighting, they propose, women respond to stress and threat by staying in place, seeking to protect themselves and those close to them, especially children (the "tend" response), and seek allies and groups, especially of other females, for protection and support (the "befriend" response).

Taylor et al. assemble an impressive and even amazing amount of physiological and behavioral data, from animals and from humans, in support of their thesis. In the course of reading this article, you will learn a great deal about the hormonal regulation of behavior and the way that animal research can be combined with research on humans to yield important insights. You may be dazzled, or perhaps confused, by the mass of unfamiliar, difficult terminology and complex descriptions of intricate physiological systems. That's fine. This article conveys important lessons that much is already known about physiological functions relevant to behavior, and that even more—much more—remains to be learned.

Another important aspect of this article is that it is psychological, *in the best sense of the word. Some research on the biology of behavior seems to have much to say about biology but rather little to say about behavior. One could never level that complaint about this article. Taylor and her colleagues are on the trail of a radical and important hypothesis that may go to the heart of the most important behavioral and psychological differences between men and women.*

From *Psychological Review, 107*, 411–429, 2000.

Survival depends on the ability to mount a successful response to threat. The human stress response has been characterized as fight-or-flight (Cannon, 1932) and has been represented as an essential mechanism in the survival process. We propose that human female responses to stress (as well as those of some animal species) are not well characterized by fight-or-flight, as research has implicitly assumed, but rather are more typically characterized by a pattern we term "tend-and-befriend." Specifically, we suggest that, by virtue of differential parental investment, female stress responses have selectively evolved to maximize the survival of self and offspring. We suggest that females respond to stress by nurturing offspring, exhibiting behaviors that protect them from harm and reduce neuroendocrine responses that may compromise offspring health (the tending pattern), and by befriending, namely, affiliating with social groups to reduce risk. We hypothesize and consider evidence from humans and other species to suggest that females create, maintain, and utilize these social groups, especially relations with other females, to manage stressful conditions. We suggest that female responses to stress may build on attachment–caregiving processes that downregulate sympathetic and hypothalamic-pituitary-adrenocortical (HPA) responses to stress. In support of this biobehavioral theory, we consider a large animal and human literature on neuroendocrine responses to stress, suggesting that the tend-and-befriend pattern may be oxytocin mediated and moderated by sex hormones and endogenous opioid peptide mechanisms.

Background

The fight-or-flight response is generally regarded as the prototypic human response to stress. First described by Walter Cannon in 1932, the fight-or-flight response is characterized physiologically by sympathetic nervous system activation that innervates the adrenal medulla, producing a hormonal cascade that results in the secretion of catecholamines, especially norepinephrine and epinephrine, into the bloodstream. In addition to its physiological concomitants, fight-or-flight has been adopted as a metaphor for human behavioral responses to stress, and whether a human (or an animal) fights or flees in response to sympathetic arousal is thought to depend on the nature of the stressor. If the organism sizes up a threat or predator and determines that it has a realistic chance of overcoming the predator, then attack is likely. In circumstances in which the threat is perceived to be more formidable, flight is more probable.

A coordinated biobehavioral stress response is believed to be at the core of reactions to threats of all kinds, including attacks by predators; assaults by members of the same species; dangerous conditions such as fire, earthquake, tornado, or flooding; and other threatening events. As such, an appropriate and modulated stress response is at the core of survival. Through principles of natural selection, an organism whose response to stress was successful would likely pass that response on to subsequent generations, and the fight-or-flight response is thought to be such an evolved response.

A little-known fact about the fight-or-flight response is that the preponderance of research exploring its parameters has been conducted on males, especially on male rats. Until recently, the gender distribution in the human literature was inequitable as well. Prior to 1995, women constituted about 17% of participants in laboratory studies of physiological and neuroendocrine responses to stress. In the past 5 years, the gender balance has been somewhat redressed. We identified 200 studies of physiological and neuroendocrine responses to an acute experimental stressor conducted between 1985 and the present, utilizing 14,548 participants, 66% of whom were male, and 34% of whom were female. Despite movement toward parity, the inclusion of women in human stress studies remains heavily dependent on the specific topic under investigation. For example, women are overrepresented in studies of affiliative responses to stress, and men are overrepresented in studies of neuroendocrine responses to physical and mental challenges (Gruenewald, Taylor, Klein, & Seeman, 1999).

Why have stress studies been so heavily based on data from males? The justification for this bias is similar to the rationale for the exclusion, until recently, of females from many clinical trials of drugs, from research on treatments for major chronic diseases, and from animal research on illness vulnerabilities. The rationale has been that, because females have greater cyclical variation in neuroendocrine responses (due to the reproductive cycle), their data present a confusing and often uninterpretable pattern of results. The fight-or-flight response may also be affected by female cycling, and, as a result, evidence concerning a fight-or-flight response in females has been inconsistent. However, what if the equivocal nature of the female data is not due solely to neuroendocrine variation but also to the fact that the female stress response is not exclusively, nor even predominantly, fight-or-flight?

Theoretical Model

An empirical gap such as the identified gender bias in stress studies provides a striking opportunity to build theory. From a metatheoretical perspective, we reasoned that a viable theoretical framework for understanding female responses to stress may be derived by making a few conservative evolutionary assumptions and then building parallel and mutually constraining biological and behavioral models.

We propose, first, that successful responses to stress have been passed on to subsequent generations through principles of natural selection: Those without successful responses to threat are disproportionately unlikely to reach an age when reproduction is possible. An additional assumption is that, because females have typically borne a greater role in the care of young offspring, responses to threat that were successfully passed on would have been those that protected offspring as well as the self. The female of the species makes a greater investment initially in pregnancy and nursing and typically plays the primary role in activities designed to bring the offspring to maturity. High maternal investment should lead to selection for female stress responses that do not jeopardize the health of the mother and her offspring and that maximize the likelihood that they will survive. "Tending," that is, quieting and caring for offspring and blending into the environment, may be effective for addressing a broad array of threats. In contrast, fight responses on the part of females may put themselves and their offspring in jeopardy, and flight behavior on the part of females may be compromised by pregnancy or the need to care for immature offspring. Thus, alternative behavioral responses are likely to have evolved in females.

The protection of self and offspring is a complex and difficult task in many threatening circumstances, and those who made effective use of the social group would have been more successful against many threats than those who did not. This assumption leads to the prediction that females may selectively affiliate in response to stress, which maximizes the likelihood that multiple group members will protect both them and their offspring. Accordingly, we suggest that the female stress response of tending to offspring and affiliating with a social group is facilitated by the process of "befriending," which is the creation of networks of associations that provide resources and protection for the female and her offspring under conditions of stress.

We propose that the biobehavorial mechanism underlying the tend-and-befriend pattern is the attachment–caregiving system, a stress-related system that has been previously explored largely for its role in maternal bonding and child development. In certain respects, the female tending response under stressful conditions may represent the counterpart of the infant attachment mechanism that appears to be so critical for the development of normal biological regulatory systems in offspring (Hofer, 1995). Numerous investigations have explored the effects of the mother–infant bond on infants' emotional, social, and biological development, but less literature has explored the counterpart maternal mechanism, that is, what evokes tending behavior in the mother. We attempt to redress that balance here. In addition, we suggest that the befriending pattern may have piggybacked onto the attachment–caregiving system and thus may be at least partially regulated by the same biobehavioral systems that regulate tending. From this analysis, it follows that neuroendocrine mechanisms would have evolved to regulate these responses to stress, much as sympathetic activation is thought to provide the physiological basis for the fight-or-flight response. We propose that the neurobiological underpinnings of the attachment–caregiving system (e.g., Panksepp, 1998) provide a foundation for this stress regulatory system. Specifically, oxytocin and endogenous opioid mechanisms may be at the core of the tend-and-befriend response.

In essence, then, we are proposing the existence of an endogenous stress regulatory system that has heretofore been largely ignored in the biological and behavioral literatures on stress, especially in humans. Accordingly, the empirical evaluation of the viability of this theoretical position requires us to address several questions: Is there neuroendocrine and behavioral evidence for our contention that fight-or-flight is less characteristic of female than male responses to stress? Is there a neuroendocrinological basis for and behavioral evidence for tending under stress in females,

that is, nurturing and caring for offspring under conditions of threat? Is there evidence of differential affiliation by females under stress and a neuroendocrine mechanism that may underlie it?

To evaluate these hypotheses, we draw on several sources of scientific evidence. We begin with evidence for gender divergences in biological and behavioral responses to stress and examine substantial neuroendocrine data from animal studies that may account for these divergences. We use the animal literature not to draw direct connections to human behavior but because animal studies enable researchers to test neuroendocrine mechanisms directly, whereas such evidence is typically more indirect in human studies. We then consider whether there are neuroendocrine and behavioral parallels in the literature on human and nonhuman primate responses to stress. Clearly, there are risks in combining evidence from multiple sources that include behavioral studies with humans and nonhuman primates and neuroendocrine research from animal studies. However, any effort to understand stress responses that ignores one or more of these lines of evidence is potentially risky because a comprehensive biobehavioral account of stress response requires integration across multiple sources of evidence. We suggest appropriate caveats in generalizing from one line of work to another when they are warranted.

Females and the Fight-or-Flight Response

The basic neuroendocrine core of stress responses does not seem to vary substantially between human males and females. Both sexes experience a cascade of hormonal responses to threat that appears to begin with the rapid release of oxytocin, vasopressin, corticotropin-releasing factor (CRF), and possibly other hormones produced in the paraventricular nucleus of the hypothalamus. Direct neural activation of the adrenal medulla triggers release of the catecholamines, norepinephrine and epinephrine, and concomitant sympathetic responses, as noted. Hypothalamic release of CRF and other hormones stimulate the release of adrenocorticotropin hormone (ACTH) from the anterior pituitary, which, in turn, stimulates the adrenal cortex to release corticosteroids, especially cortisol or corticosterone, depending on the species (Jezova, Skulteryova, Tokarev, Bakos, & Vigas, 1995; Sapolsky, 1992b). As such, both males and females are mobilized to meet the short-term demands presented by stress.

As already noted, however, a stress response geared toward aggressing or fleeing may be somewhat adaptive for males but it may not address the different challenges faced by females, especially those challenges that arise from maternal investment in offspring. The demands of pregnancy, nursing, and infant care render females extremely vulnerable to external threats. Should a threat present itself during this time, a mother's attack on a predator or flight could render offspring fatally unprotected. Instead, behaviors that involve getting offspring out of the way, retrieving them from threatening circumstances, calming them down and quieting them, protecting them from further threat, and anticipating protective measures against stressors that are imminent may increase the likelihood of survival of offspring. Given the adaptiveness of such behaviors for females, neuroendocrine mechanisms may have evolved to facilitate these behaviors and inhibit behavioral tendencies to fight or flee.

NEUROENDOCRINE PERSPECTIVE ON FIGHT Consistent with the above analysis, neuroendocrine differences between the sexes suggest that females are unlikely to show a physical "fight" response to threat. Females largely lack androgens, which, in many species, act to develop the male brain for aggression either pre- or postnatally and then activate aggressive behavior in specific threatening contexts (such as responses to territorial establishment and defense). In humans, gonadal hormones appear to influence the development of both rough-and-tumble play and tendencies toward aggression, both of which show moderate to large sex differences (Collaer & Hines, 1995).

Although the exact role of testosterone in male attack behaviors remains controversial, testos-terone has been associated with hostility and aggressive behavior in both human (e.g., Bergman & Brismar, 1994; Olweus, Mattson, Schalling, & Low, 1980) and animal studies (Lumia, Thorner, & McGinnis, 1994). In humans, testosterone has been shown to increase with acute stress, including high-intensity exercise (e.g., Cumming, Brunsting, Strich, Ries, & Rebar, 1986; Mathur, Toriola, & Dada, 1986; Wheeler et al., 1994) and psychological stress (although the effects vary by the nature of the stressor and by individual differences; Christensen, Knussmann, & Couwenbergs, 1985; Hellhammer, Hubert, & Schurmeyer, 1985; Williams et al., 1982). Girdler, Jamner, and Shapiro (1997) found that, in men, testosterone increased significantly with acute stress and testosterone reactivity to acute stressors was significantly associated with level of hostility. Although human male aggression is generally regarded as being under greater cortical control than is true for lower order animals, a small but consistently positive relation between self-reported hostility and testosterone has been found in meta-analyses of aggression, as has a consistent relationship between testosterone levels and assessments of aggression made by others (Archer, 1990). Studies of captive human male populations, including incarcerated felons and psychiatric patients, also show positive relations between testosterone and ratings of aggressive behavior (Benton, 1992). Thus, testosterone may be a link by which sympathetic arousal is channeled into hostility and interpersonal attack behavior among males.

* * *

Human female aggressive responses are not organized by testosterone or androgens either pre- or postnatally, and the typical low levels of those hormones in juvenile and adult females means that predominantly male hormones are unlikely to be the organizing factors that evoke a female fight response as they do in males. The presence of either another male or another female does not typically act as an evocative stimulus for human female attack behavior, and human females do not engage in rough-and-tumble play at the levels observed in males (Maccoby & Jacklin, 1974). In human males, there appears to be a link between sympathetic reactivity and hostility, whereas hostility in females is not reliably linked to sympathetic arousal, suggesting that it is not a necessary component of a fight-or-flight response (Girdler et al., 1997).

Female aggression is well documented. Our argument is not that female aggression fails to occur but that it is not mediated by the sympathetic arousal–testosterone links that appear to be implicated in fight responses for men. Extensive reviews of the human aggression literature suggest that males may not be inherently more aggressive than females, but that the patterns of aggression between males and females differ (see Bjorkqvist & Niemela, 1992, for a review). Males are more likely to use physical aggression in struggles for power within a hierarchy or to defend territory against external enemies. Females reliably show less physical aggression than males but they display as much or more indirect aggression (Holmstrom, 1992), that is, aggression in the form of gossip, rumor-spreading, and enlisting the cooperation of a third party in undermining an acquaintance. However, human females still show lower levels of verbal aggression than males, although this sex difference is smaller than that for physical aggression (Eagly & Steffen, 1986). Overall, female aggressive responses appear to be tied less to sympathetic arousal than male aggression and are instead more cerebral in nature. For example, female aggressive behavior may be more moderated by social norms and learning and by cultural, situational, and individual differences (Bjorkqvist & Niemela, 1992; Eagly & Steffen, 1986).

The physical fight response is the most robust area of aggression that shows higher levels for males than females, and these differences are found in rodents, primates, and humans (Archer, 1990; Eagly & Steffen, 1986; Hyde, 1984). When female attack behavior is observed, it appears to be confined to particular circumstances. For example, female adult rats are aggressive toward intruder (i.e., unfamiliar) males and females, primarily when they are pregnant or nursing, behaviors that fall off rapidly as pups mature (Adams, 1992). In addition, maternal attack behavior toward potential predators that threaten offspring has been well documented (Adams, 1992; Brain, Haug, & Parmigiani,

1992; Sandnabba, 1992). In summary, female physical aggression appears to be confined to situations requiring defense, rather than to the broader array of threats that is found in males.

NEUROENDOCRINE PERSPECTIVE ON FLIGHT Although flight may appear to be the more probable first line of defense of females to stressful events or threatening circumstances, this response, too, may not be dominant in the hierarchy of stress responses of females. Females who are pregnant, nursing, or otherwise responsible for offspring may be unable to flee without jeopardizing the health and safety of their offspring. Although flight behavior among females is well documented in species whose offspring have the capability to flee within hours after birth (e.g., ungulates such as deer or antelope), in species whose offspring remain immature for long periods of time, flight by the female can require abandonment of offspring. Females of most species spend a substantial proportion of their fertile lives either pregnant, nursing, or raising young children, and until recently, this was largely true of human females as well. Given the very central role that these activities play in the perpetuation of the species, stress responses that enabled the female to protect simultaneously herself and her offspring are likely to have resulted in more surviving offspring.

If flight behavior in response to stress is indeed inhibited in females, may there be a neuroendocrine basis for this inhibition? McCarthy (1995) alluded to such a mechanism in her animal studies of the behavioral effects of oxytocin and its modulation by estrogen. In particular, she argued that animals in the natural environment face a constant barrage of stress and a continuous stress response can have deleterious physiological effects. Consequently, reactions that control stress responses have physiological advantages. Oxytocin release may be such a reaction. Oxytocin is a posterior pituitary hormone that is released to a broad array of stressors by both males and females. It is associated with parasympathetic (vagal) functioning, suggesting a counterregulatory role in fear responses to stress (Dreifuss, Dubois-Dauphin, Widmer, &

Raggenbass, 1992; Sawchenko & Swanson, 1982; Swanson & Sawchenko, 1980). In experimental studies of the effects of exogenously administered oxytocin with rodents, oxytocin has been found to enhance sedation and relaxation, reduce fearfulness, and decrease sympathetic activity, patterns of responses that are antithetical to the fight-or-flight response (Uvnas-Moberg, 1997). These effects appear to be substantially more pronounced in female rats than in males for several reasons. First, oxytocin release in response to stress appears to be greater in females than in males (Jezova, Jurankova, Mosnarova, Kriska, & Skultetyova, 1996). Second, androgens have been shown to inhibit oxytocin release under conditions of stress (Jezova et al., 1996). Third, the effects of oxytocin are strongly modulated by estrogen (McCarthy, 1995).

The estrogen-enhanced anxiolytic properties of oxytocin (e.g., Windle, Shanks, Lightman, & Ingram, 1997) may explain the consistent sex differences found in stress-related behavior among rats. For example, in response to acute stress, female laboratory rats show fewer behavioral indications of fear (e.g., freezing) than males (e.g., Klein, Popke, & Grunberg, 1998), slower withdrawal latencies to heat and mechanical stimuli, a longer tail-flick response (Uvnas-Moberg, 1997), higher ambulation scores in open-field tests, faster time to emerge from familiar into novel territory, and a greater amount of exploration of novel territory (Gray's studies, as cited in Gray & Lalljee, 1974). The exogenous administration of oxytocin in rats results in decreased blood pressure (effects that last longer in females), decreased pain sensitivity, and decreased corticosteroid levels, among other findings also suggestive of a reduced stress response (Uvnas-Moberg, 1997). Oxytocin is also known to promote maternal and other forms of affiliative behavior, which, McCarthy (1995) argued, may be functional under stress, representing more adaptive responses than extreme fear. Although McCarthy's oxytocin-based argument did not address flight behavior per se, its emphasis on fear reduction for moderating the typical behavioral responses to fear suggests that oxytocin may be implicated in the processes by which fear in the rat is reduced, flight is avoided, and maternal and other forms of affiliative behavior are increased under conditions of threat (see McCarthy, 1995). These effects may be conditional on the development of a maternal bond between mother and infant: Among mother–infant pairs where attachment bonds have been formed, abandonment of infants under stress is rarely, if ever, found (Keverne, Nevison, & Martel, 1999; Mendoza & Mason, 1999).

Whether and exactly how McCarthy's argument can be applied to the human situation remains to be seen. For example, although female rats show fewer behavioral signs of anxiety than males, that pattern may be reversed in nonhuman primates and humans, although the data are ambiguous (Gray's studies, as cited in Gray & Lalljee, 1974). Nonetheless, as we describe below, oxytocin in human females has been found to have similar effects on anxiety, affiliation, and maternal behavior (e.g., Uvnas-Moberg, 1997), and estrogen is associated with reduced anxiety in human females (Gray, 1971). In humans, oxytocin inhibits the release of glucocorticoids, also suggesting an anxiolytic effect (Chiodera et al., 1991). Consequently, the role of oxytocin in the inhibition of flight responses merits continued cross-species investigations.

In summary, we suggest that the flight response to stress may be inhibited in females and that such inhibition favors the survival of the female and her offspring under conditions of stress. The neuroendocrine underpinnings of this response may be oxytocin mediated.

Tending Under Stress

TENDING As we previously stated, the basic neuroendocrine core of stress responses does not seem to vary substantially between human males and females. In both sexes, threat triggers sympathetic-adrenal-medullary (SAM) and hypothalamic-pituitary-adrenal (HPA) activation, as well as the release of other neuroendocrine responses that operate to prepare the organism to respond to the stressor. How would a female responding to stress with sympathetic arousal nonetheless quiet and calm down offspring? We propose that the biobehavioral mechanism for the tending process builds on the attachment–caregiving system. We explore the hypothesis that the neuroendocrine mechanisms that may act to modulate sympathetic arousal and HPA activation also act to encourage tending to offspring under conditions of threat.

Attachment was originally conceived as a stress-related biobehavioral system that is the mainstay of maternal bonding and of child socialization (Bowlby, 1988). This largely innate caregiving system is thought to be especially activated in response to threat and to signs of offspring distress (such as "distress vocalization"). The caregiving system has been heavily explored through animal studies, with parallels in human developmental investigations. A paradigm researchers frequently adopt for empirical investigations of mother–infant attachment–caregiving processes involves separation, and under these circumstances, in a number of species, both mothers and offspring show distress at separation. For example, in a study of squirrel monkeys (*Saimiri sciureus*), a 30- to 60-min separation of mother and infant led to signs of distress and increased plasma cortisol in both mothers and infants (Coe, Mendoza, Smotherman, & Levine, 1978); however, on being reunited, the stress responses of both mother and infant declined (Mendoza, Coe, Smotherman, Kaplan, & Levine, 1980). Meaney and colleagues (e.g. Francis, Diorio, Liu, & Meaney, 1999; Liu et al., in press; Liu et al., 1997) explicitly link tending responses to stress and demonstrate consequent effects on the development of stress regulatory systems. In one of Meaney and colleagues' paradigms, infant rats are removed from the nest, handled by a human experimenter, and then returned to the nest. The immediate response of the mother is intense licking and grooming and arched-back nursing, which provides the pup with immediate stimulation that nurtures and soothes it. Over the long-term, this maternal behavior results in better regulation of somatic growth and neural development, especially enhancing hippocampal synaptic development and consequent spatial learning and memory in offspring. In certain respects, the female tending response under stressful conditions may represent the counterpart of the infant attachment and separation distress signaling system (Hofer, 1995). Although considerable research has explored the effects of the mother–infant bond on infants' development, less literature has explored the counterpart mechanism in the mother. We attempt here to outline elements of that response.

Oxytocin and endogenous opioid mechanisms may be at the core of the tending response (Panksepp, Nelson, & Bekkedal, 1999). Evidence from a broad array of animal studies involving rats, prairie voles, monkeys, and sheep show that central administration of oxytocin reduces anxiety and has mildly sedative properties in both males and females (e.g., Carter, Williams, Witt, & Insel, 1992; Drago, Pederson, Caldwell, & Prange, 1986; Fahrbach, Morrell, & Pfaff, 1985; McCarthy, Chung, Ogawa, Kow, & Pfaff, 1991; McCarthy, McDonald, Brooks, & Goldman, 1996; Uvnas-Moberg, 1997; Witt, Carter, & Walton, 1990). As noted, this response appears to be stronger in females than in males, and oxytocin may play two roles with regard to the female stress response. It may serve both to calm the female who is physiologically aroused by a stressor and also to promote affiliative behaviors, including maternal behavior toward offspring. For example, studies of ewes (*Ovis*) have found that intracerebroventricular administration of oxytocin stimulates maternal behavior (Kendrick, Keverne, & Baldwin, 1987; see also Kendrick et al., 1997). The resulting grooming and touching that occurs in mother–infant contact may help quiet infants. These effects appear to be bidirectional, inasmuch as oxytocin enhances affiliative and affectionate contact, which, in turn, enhances the flow of oxytocin (Uvnas-Moberg, 1999)[1] * * *

---

[1]Relevant to this point is a study of gender differences in responsivity to touch in humans in response to the stress of hospitalization (Whitcher & Fisher, 1979). Results revealed that, under stress, touch produced more favorable affective, behavioral, and physiological (especially cardiovascular) effects in females than was true for males, and touch was actually experienced as aversive by males.

* * *

The estrogen-enhanced oxytocin responses documented in rats and now explored in humans appear to be very strong. McCarthy (1995), for example, referred to the effects of estrogen on oxytocin as among the strongest known effects of estrogen. Uvnas-Moberg (1997) found that, in rats, oxytocin-induced calming may last for several weeks, suggesting that it is not continuously maintained by oxytocin flow but, instead, is maintained by secondary changes induced by the peptide. Moreover, these effects are not easily blocked by oxytocin antagonists. The surprisingly robust, long duration of these oxytocin-mediated effects suggests that they may be exerted at the level of the genome (Uvnas-Moberg, 1997). Thus, the oxytocin effect in females is potent, long-lasting, and maintained by secondary changes, suggesting centrality and importance, at least in animal studies.

Although studies with humans are less able to provide evidence of underlying mechanisms, mother–infant attachment processes have been found to have much the same benefits on human infants, and, as has been true in animal studies, oxytocin and endogenous opioid mechanisms are thought to be at their core. Some of the human evidence on the behavioral concomitants of oxytocin has involved studies of nursing mothers, because oxytocin levels are known to be high at this time. As in animal studies, nursing is soothing to both mothers and infants. Blass (1997) reported that consuming milk significantly reduced crying in human infants, and sucking on a nipple is known to have a physiologically calming effect in infants and can also reduce crying (Field & Goldson, 1984). Lower levels of sympathetic arousal have also been found in lactating versus nonlactating women (Wiesenfeld, Malatesta, Whitman, Grannose, & Vile, 1985). Women who are breastfeeding are calmer and more social than matched-age women who are not breastfeeding or pregnant, as determined by personality inventories (Uvnas-Moberg, 1996); moreover, the levels of oxytocin in these breastfeeding women correlated strongly with the level of calm reported, and oxytocin pulsatility was significantly correlated with self-reported sociability (Uvnas-Moberg, 1996). Similar findings are reported by Adler, Cook, Davidson, West, and Bancroft (1986). Altemus, Deuster, Galliven, Carter, and Gold (1995) found that lactating women showed suppressed HPA responses to stress, which is consistent with the animal literature showing reduced HPA activity in response to oxytocin (see also Chiodera et al., 1991; Lightman & Young, 1989). Dunn and Richards (1977) also reported higher levels of maternal behavior among lactating versus nonlactating mothers.

Until recently, it was difficult to examine the relation of oxytocin to human social behavior except during lactation, in part because of ethical issues involved with manipulating oxytocin levels and in part because there were no commercially available assays to measure oxytocin at the levels suspected to be implicated in stress responses. Emerging evidence suggests that oxytocin is associated with relaxation and interpersonal outcomes in nonlactating women as well. For example, in a sample of nulliparous women, Turner, Altermus, Enos, Cooper, and McGuinness (1999) found that oxytocin levels increased in response to relaxation massage and decreased in response to sad emotions. * * * In an experimental study with older women, Taylor, Klein, Greendale, and Seeman (1999) found that higher levels of oxytocin were associated with reduced cortisol responses to stress and with faster HPA recovery following an acute stress laboratory challenge.

As is true in animal studies, human studies show that nurturing behaviors under conditions of stress benefit both mother and offspring. Field and colleagues have shown that touching an infant and carrying an infant close to the mother's chest can soothe and calm the infant (Field, Malphurs, Carraway, & Pelaez-Nogueras, 1996; Field, Schanberg, Davalos, & Malphurs, 1996). High levels of physical affection and warmth between mother and child during stressful circumstances have been tied to normal HPA activation profiles in response to stress in offspring (e.g., Chorpita & Barlow, 1998; Flinn & England, 1997; Hertsgaard, Gunnar, Erickson, & Nachmias, 1995). In humans (as well as in nonhuman primates), these processes appear to be mediated by mother–infant attachment, with securely attached offspring less likely to show elevated cortisol in response to challenging circumstances (e.g., Gunnar, Brodersen, Krueger, & Rigatuso, 1996; Gunnar, Brodersen, Nachmias, Buss, & Rigatuso, 1996; Nachmias, Gunnar, Mangelsdorf, Parritz, & Buss, 1996).

Nurturing behavior under stressful conditions may not only quiet and soothe offspring but it may also have discernible effects on health-related outcomes, directly affecting the likelihood that offspring will survive and mature properly. For example, in humans, inadequate physical maternal care has been tied to growth retardation, social withdrawal, and poor interpersonal relatedness, among other complications (e.g., Harlow, 1986; Shaffer & Campbell, 1994). Premature human infants given a pacifier or massage grow better, become calmer, and become more tolerant to pain (Bernbaum, Pereira, Watkins, & Peckham, 1983; Field & Goldson, 1984; Scafidi, Field, & Schanberg, 1993; Uvnas-Moberg, Marchini, & Winberg, 1993). In experimental investigations with humans, touch and massage have been found to increase immune system function, decrease pain, reduce subjective reports of stress, and maintain normal growth in infants (Field, 1995, 1996; Ironson et al., 1996; Scafidi & Field, 1996).

If mothers in particular exhibit nurturing behavior under conditions of stress, it should also be possible to see behavioral evidence for this prediction in parenting behaviors. Such evidence is provided by Repetti's (Repetti, 1989, 1997) studies of the effects of stressful workdays on parenting behavior. Repetti gave questionnaires to both fathers and mothers about their workdays and their behaviors at home on those days and to children regarding their experiences with their parents on those days. She found that fathers who had experienced an interpersonally conflictual day at work were more likely to be interpersonally conflictual in the home after work. Fathers who had highly stressful workdays, but not involving interpersonal conflict, were more likely to withdraw from their families (Repetti, 1989). A very different pattern

was found for mothers. Specifically, women were more nurturant and caring toward their children on their stressful work days. In particular, on days when women reported that their stress levels at work had been the highest, their children reported that their mothers had shown them more love and nurturance (Repetti, 1997). A second study replicated these differences in mothers' and fathers' responses to offspring under stress (Repetti, 2000).

The underpinnings of the tending response appear to be oxytocin based initially, at least in rodent and animal species and possibly also in human females; prolactin, endogenous opioids, and social learning may be more important for sustaining the tending response, once the behavior pattern has developed (Panksepp, 1998). The extent to which the tending response is hormonally regulated over the long term is unclear, however. Rat studies show that tending responses under stress (e.g., pup retrieval) lose their complete dependence on hormonal regulation relatively quickly and are thought to be socially maintained instead in response to distress vocalizations (DeVries & Villalba, 1999). Tending responses in human females also appear to depend, in part, on characteristics of human infant cries, and such qualities as pitch and tone convey often quite subtle information to mothers about the urgency and nature of the infants' needs (Bates, Freeland, & Lounsbury, 1979; Crowe & Zeskind, 1992; Zeskind, 1980, 1987; Zeskind & Collins, 1987; Zeskind, Sale, Maio, Huntington, & Weiseman, 1985). The human female not only brings the possibility of social evocation by offspring to stressful situations but a large neocortex as well, and so tending behavior in human females may be oxytocin based, socially mediated, mediated by higher-order brain functions, or some combination of these three processes.

In summary, whereas male responses to stress may be tied to sympathetic arousal and to a fight-or-flight pattern that is, at least in part, organized and activated by androgens, female stress responses do not show these androgen links and, instead, may be tied, at least in part, to the release of oxytocin and its biobehavioral links to caregiving behavior. Oxytocin is believed not only to underlie attachment processes between mothers and offspring but it may also be implicated in other close social bonds. We extend this analysis in the next section by arguing that female responses to stress are also characterized by affiliation with social groups because group living provides special benefits for females.

Befriending Among Females

Group living is generally regarded as an evolutionary adaptation among many species that benefits both males and females (Caporeal, 1997). Groups provide more eyes for the detection of predators, and most predators are reluctant to attack potential prey if they believe there are others who may come to that prey's rescue (Janson, 1992; Rubenstein, 1978). Moreover, groups can create confusion in a predator. If a predator charges a large group, the group may disband in many directions, which may confuse the predator long enough to reduce the likelihood that any one member of the group can be taken down. Group life, then, is fundamental to primate existence, making it an important evolutionary strategy by which primates have survived (Caporeal, 1997; Dunbar, 1996). As we have noted, female stress responses have likely evolved in ways that not only protect the female herself but also protect her offspring. As such, group life is likely to have been an especially important adaptation for females and offspring, because of the limitations of fight-or-flight as a female response to stress. Like human males, human females once required successful defense against external predators, such as tigers, leopards, hyenas, packs of hunting dogs, and other primates. In addition, human females have much to fear from human males, including rape, assault, homicide, and abuse of offspring. The pairing of human females with human males may be, in part, an evolutionary adaptation that protects females and offspring against random assault by males. However, under some conditions, human females also have reason to fear their own male partners. In North

America, estimates of the percentage of women who have been assaulted by their partners range from 20% to 50% (Bray, 1994; Goodman, Koss, Fitzgerald, Russo, & Keita, 1993; Koss et al., 1994; Malamuth, 1998; Straus & Gelles, 1986), and statistical analyses of assault and homicide data reveal that human females are most likely to be assaulted or killed by their own partners (see Daly & Wilson, 1988; Daly, Wilson, & Weghorst, 1982). There is no reason to believe that this is a particularly modern phenomenon. Thus, evolved mechanisms of female survival likely protected against a broad array of threats, including those from males of her own species.

If the above reasoning is true, one would predict a strong tendency among females to affiliate under conditions of stress. There is animal data consistent with this analysis. Crowding has been found to stress male rodents but to calm female rodents, as assessed by corticosteroid levels (specifically, spatial crowding is problematic for males, whereas the number of other animals present is positively related to calming in females; Brown, 1995; Brown & Grunberg, 1995). McClintock (personal communication, May 6, 1998) has reported that female rats housed together in five-female groupings live 40% longer than females housed in isolation. Research on prairie voles (*Microtus ochrogaster*), a preferred species for studying behavioral concomitants of oxytocin, has found that, under conditions of stress, female prairie voles show selective preference for their same-sex cage companions (DeVries & Carter, unpublished raw data, as cited in Carter, 1998).

HUMAN EVIDENCE FOR AFFILIATION UNDER STRESS Research on human males and females shows that, under conditions of stress, the desire to affiliate with others is substantially more marked among females than among males. In fact, it is one of the most robust gender differences in adult human behavior, other than those directly tied to pregnancy and lactation, and it is the primary gender difference in adult human behavioral responses to stress (Belle, 1987; Luckow, Reifman, & McIntosh, 1998). * * * Indeed, so reliable is this effect that, following the early studies on affiliation in response to stress by Schachter (1959), most subsequent research on affiliation under stress used only female participants.

Nonetheless, some research has compared males' and females' responses to stress. Bull et al. (1972) found that exposure to noise stress led to decreased liking among male participants but greater liking by females toward familiar others. Bell and Barnard (1977) found that males prefer less social interaction in response to heat or noise stress, whereas females preferred closer interpersonal distance. Affiliation under stress, however, is not random (Bull et al., 1972; Kenrick & Johnson, 1979; Schachter, 1959). Women's affiliative tendencies under stress are heavily to affiliate with other women (Schachter, 1959). When given a choice to affiliate with an unfamiliar male versus alone prior to a stressful experience, women choose to wait alone (Lewis & Linder, 2000). In summary, then, women are more likely than men to choose to affiliate in response to a laboratory challenge, but affiliation appears to be selectively with similar others, especially with other women.

Across the entire life cycle, females are more likely to mobilize social support, especially from other females, in times of stress. They seek it out more, they receive more support, and they are more satisfied with the support they receive. Adolescent girls report more informal sources of support than do boys, and they are more likely to turn to their same-sex peers for support than are boys (e.g., Copeland & Hess, 1995; see Belle, 1987, for a review). Female college students report more available helpers and report receiving more support than do males (e.g., Ptacek, Smith, & Zanas, 1992; see Belle, 1987, for a review). Adult women maintain more same-sex close relationships than do men, they mobilize more social support in times of stress than do men, they rely less heavily than do men on their spouses for social support, they turn to female friends more often, they report more benefits from contact with their female friends and relatives (although they are also more vulnerable to network events as a cause of psychological dis-

tress), and they provide more frequent and more effective social support to others than do men (Belle, 1987; McDonald & Korabik, 1991; Ogus, Greenglass, & Burke, 1990). Although females give help to both males and females in their support networks, they are more likely to seek help and social support from other female relatives and female friends than from males (Belle, 1987; Wethington, McLeod, & Kessler, 1987).

Women are also more engaged in their social networks than are men. They are significantly better at reporting most types of social network events than men, such as major illnesses of children, and they are more likely to report being involved if there is a crisis event in the network (Wethington et al., 1987). In an extensive study of social networks, Veroff, Kulka, and Douvan (1981) reported that women were 30% more likely than men to have provided some type of support in response to network stressors, including economic and work-related difficulties, interpersonal problems, death, and negative health events. So consistent and strong are these findings that theorists have argued for basic gender differences in orientation toward others, with women maintaining a collectivist orientation (Markus & Kitayama, 1991) or connectedness (Clancy & Dollingér, 1993; Kashima, Yamaguchi, Choi, Gelfand, & Yuki, 1995; Niedenthal & Beike, 1997) and males, a more individualistic orientation (Cross & Madson, 1997). These findings appear to have some cross-cultural generalizability: In their study of six cultures, Whiting and Whiting (1975) found that women and girls seek more help from others and give more help to others than men and boys do. Edwards (1993) found similar sex differences across 12 cultures.

* * *

The preceding analysis is not intended to suggest that males are not benefitted by social group living or that they do not form social groups in response to external threats or stress. However, anthropological accounts, as well as survey literature, suggest that the functions of the groups that men and women form and turn to under stress are somewhat different. In a broad array of cultures, men have been observed to form groups for purposes of defense, aggression, and war (Tiger, 1970). They tend toward larger social groups than is true of women (Baumeister & Sommer, 1997), and these groups are often organized around well-defined purposes or tasks. Although men orient toward and invest in a large number of social relationships, many of these relationships emphasize hierarchies of status and power rather than intimate bonding (Baumeister & Sommer, 1997; Spain, 1992). Female groupings tend to be smaller, often consisting of dyads or a few women, and although some such groups are focused around tasks (such as food preparation, sewing, or collective child care), these groups often have the establishment and maintenance of socioemotional bonds at their core, a characteristic less true of male groupings (Cross & Madson, 1997). Women in women's social groups show more affiliative behaviors, including smiling, disclosure, attention to others, and ingratiation (Baumeister & Sommer, 1997; Pearson, 1981), and they interact at closer physical distances than do men's groups (Patterson & Schaeffer, 1977).

A NEUROENDOCRINE PERSPECTIVE ON AFFILIATION UNDER STRESS Studies of affiliative behaviors in animal studies suggest a mechanism whereby enhanced social activity of females may occur under conditions of stress. In particular, they suggest that oxytocin reduces stress and enhances affiliation. For example, social contact is enhanced and aggression diminished following central oxytocin treatment in estrogen-treated female prairie voles (Witt et al., 1990), and the exogenous administration of oxytocin in rats causes an increase in social contact and in grooming (Argiolas & Gessa, 1991; Carter, DeVries, & Getz, 1995; Witt, Winslow, & Insel, 1992). With reference to humans, Carter (1998) suggested that oxytocin may be at the core of many forms of social attachment, including not only mother–infant attachments but also adult pair bonds and friendships (Drago et al., 1986; Fahrbach et al., 1985; Panksepp, 1998). Keverne et al. (1999) suggested that female-to-female bonding may have piggybacked onto maternal–infant bonding attachment processes. Consistent with Keverne

et al.'s (1999) hypothesis, research has reported that animals prefer to spend time with animals in whose presence they have experienced high brain oxytocin and endogenous opioid activities in the past (Panksepp, 1998), suggesting that friendships may be mediated by the same neurochemical systems that mediate maternal urges. As is true of the maternal–infant caregiving system, contact with a friend or a supportive other person during stressful events down-regulates sympathetic and neuroendocrine responses to stress and facilitates recovery from the physiological effects of acute stress (Christenfeld et al., 1997; Fontana, Diegnan, Villeneuve, & Lepore, 1999; Gerin, Milner, Chawla, & Pickering, 1995; Gerin, Pieper, Levy, & Pickering, 1992; Glynn, Christenfeld, & Gerin, 1999; Kamarck, Manuck, & Jennings, 1990; Kirschbaum et al., 1995; Kors, Linden, & Gerin, 1997; Lepore, Allen, & Evans, 1993; Roy, Steptoe, & Kirschbaum, 1998; Sheffield & Carroll, 1994; Thorsteinsson, James, & Gregg, 1998). Both men and women experience these stress-regulatory benefits of social support, but women disproportionately seek such contact, and the stress-reducing benefits are more consistent when the support provider is female rather than male (e.g., Gerin et al, 1995).

The enhanced desire for social contact that females demonstrate under conditions of stress, relative to males, may also be modulated by endogenous opioid mechanisms. Endogenous opioid peptides are released during stress and are believed to influence social interaction (Benton, 1988; Jalowiec, Calcagnetti, & Fanselow, 1989). Animal studies suggest that higher levels of endogenous opioids are associated with higher levels of social interaction and maternal behavior. For example, Martel et al. (1993) found that administration of naloxone (an opioid antagonist) in female rhesus monkeys reduced both maternal behavior as well as social grooming of other females. Further support for this hypothesis and for its possible differential relevance for females is provided by an experimental investigation of the effects of opioids on affiliative behavior in humans. Jamner, Alberts, Leigh, and Klein (1998) found that administration of naltrexone (a long-acting opioid antagonist) increased the amount of time women spent alone, reduced the amount of time that they spent with friends, and reduced the pleasantness of women's social interactions, as compared with men. In addition, women who were given naltrexone initiated fewer social interactions than when they received a placebo. Thus, endogenous opioids appear to play a role in regulating social interactions, especially for women. Endogenous opioids also moderate the release of other peptides in the limbic system (e.g., oxytocin, vasopressin), as well as other "stress-related" neurohormones, such as norepinephrine (Keverne et al., 1999), and cortisol (Klein, Alberts, et al., 1998), which may contribute to the sex differences observed in social behavior under conditions of stress.

ADVANTAGES OF AFFILIATION UNDER STRESS

What are the advantages of social affiliation under stress, and why do females seek to do it more? Why does female affiliation under stress appear to be at least somewhat selectively with other females? We reasoned that an examination of evidence from humans' closest relatives, namely Old World nonhuman primates, may provide some insights into the patterns and functions of female affiliative responses to stress.

Female–female networks of associations are common in nonhuman primate societies. Among many Old World primates, female coalitions and networks are formed early and are in place when they are needed (Dunbar, 1996; Wallen & Tannenbaum, 1997). For example, in Gelada baboons (*Theropithecus gelada*), a mother and her two daughters, or a sister, mother, and daughter may form an alliance to provide support against threat. These long-term commitments are solidified through grooming behavior, which may take up as much as 10% to 20% of an animal's time (Dunbar, 1996). Intrasexual aggression within these matrilineal groupings is reported to be low among females (although high among males), whereas the reverse is true of affiliative behavior, with females exhibiting more affiliative behaviors than males. These findings appear to be similar across several species of monkeys and other primates (Burbank,

1987; Glazer, 1992; Keverne et al., 1999). Although these bonds and their functions appear to be stronger when kin relationships are involved (Silk, 2000), unrelated females in several primate species form similar bonds. Wallen and Tannenbaum (1997) found that rhesus monkeys establish social bonds with female peers, which provide security and promote the maintenance of a matrilineal social system. Squirrel monkeys typically associate with females of roughly the same age and spend considerable time in close association (Baldwin, 1985; Mason & Epple, 1969). In captive situations, female squirrel monkeys show signs of distress in response to being separated from their cagemates. In an experimental investigation, when female squirrel monkeys were introduced to a novel environment, they showed more distress when alone than when they experienced the new environment in the company of their same-sex cagemates (Hennessy, Mendoza, & Kaplan, 1982). These adverse reactions were stronger for lactating mothers with infants than for nonlactating females (Jordan, Hennessy, Gonzalez, & Levine, 1985).

The so-called harem structure that characterizes the breeding patterns of many primates also suggests what some of the protective functions of female groups may be (Wrangham, 1980). The harem structure typically consists of a dominant male and several females and their offspring. Primatologists have tended to emphasize the benefits that the harem structure has for males, enabling them to have all their eggs in one basket, so to speak, and have somewhat overlooked the functions that the harem may afford to females and offspring. Evidence suggests that the female harem may provide protection for females. With reference to the Gelada baboons, Dunbar (1996) noted that daughters mature into a harem grouping of females to join their mothers, older sisters, aunts, and female cousins in a "coalition of great intensity and loyalty . . . these alliances are formed at birth, the product of being born to a particular mother" (p. 20). Mother–daughter, sister–sister, and female friend grooming are all widely documented and are described by Dunbar as "the cement that holds alliances together" (p. 20). Although males rarely groom each other, adult females will often groom their close female relations and friends in this fashion. Grooming does not occur at random but rather takes place within the context of clearly defined social relationships, most of which involve matrilineal relatives or special friends (see also De Waal, 1996; Wrangham, 1980).

Grooming can be an indication of status as well as a form of hygiene and an expression of friendship. The frequency with which a female is groomed by others predicts how likely it is that those others will come to her aid if she is attacked by members of another harem, the male in her own harem, or an outside predator (Dunbar, 1996; Wrangham, 1980). In his studies of rhesus monkeys, S. Datta (cited in Dunbar, 1996, p. 25) noted that whether a particular female is attacked may depend on such factors as whether that female's mother or other females with whom that female has formed alliances are nearby. The probability of attack is reduced if the targeted female is of high status or if her mother is of high status, because there is greater potential to enlist the support of other females to drive off a potential attacker. Grooming behavior appears to be enhanced by oxytocin and may be moderated by endogenous opioid mechanisms. For example, among monkeys, naxolone has been found to reduce mother's grooming behavior toward their infants and toward other group members (Martel et al., 1993).

These female groups may also provide protection for females from their own males. On the one hand, the harem itself may be protected by a dominant male who attempts to keep the females in line, in particular, preventing them from breeding with other males. On the other hand, if he is overly aggressive or threatening to a particular female, the chances that her female relatives will come to her aid and threaten the male as a group is very high. Dunbar (1996) described an example of this protection:

> The harem male's attempts to ride herd on his females when they stray too far from him often backfire. The luckless victim's grooming partners invariably come to her aid. Standing shoulder-to-shoulder, they outface the male with outraged

threats and furious barks of their own. The male will usually back off, and walk huffily away, endeavoring to maintain an air of ruffled dignity. However, occasionally, the male will persist, feeling, perhaps, unusually sensitive about his honor and security. This only leads to more of the group's females racing in to support their embattled sisters. The male invariably ends up being chased 'round the mountainside by his irate females in an impressive display of sisterly solidarity. (pp. 20–21)

Similar accounts are found in De Waal (1996).

Female bonded groups also appear to be important for the control of resources related to food (Silk, 2000; Wrangham, 1980). Wrangham (1980) suggested that female bonded groups may have evolved, in part, because of the competition that exists for high-quality food patches under conditions of limited feeding sites. Cooperative relationships among females may provide for the sharing of information about food sites and also help supplant others from preferred food patches (Silk, 2000; Wrangham, 1980). Matrilocal primate groupings also provide opportunities for the exchange of caretaking responsibilities under some circumstances (Wrangham, 1980), and examples of one female taking care of the offspring of another female appear commonly throughout the primate literature (e.g., De Waal, 1996).

Studies of primates suggest that these groups of females and their offspring may also constitute a critical mechanism by which juvenile females gain experience in the tending of infants, enabling them to observe the behaviors of other mothers. For example, studies with rhesus macaque monkeys have reported that females who have not yet given birth frequently help care for younger siblings (Keverne et al., 1999). Research data from monkeys that have been deprived of maternal or social contact during the first 8 months of their lives reveal significant adverse effects on subsequent maternal care, including infanticide and abuse. Social contact and opportunities to provide maternal care subsequently improves maternal care, but that care does not approach that of feral mothers (e.g., Ruppenthal, Harlow, Eisele, Harlow, & Suomi, 1974). When mothers and infants are given opportunities to form bonds with each other, abandonment of infants is rarely observed (Keverne et al., 1999; Mendoza & Mason, 1999), but in captive-reared animals and other circumstances when mother–infant bonds have not formed, mothering behavior can be inadequate. Researchers believe this maternal behavior is mediated, in part, by endogenous opioid mechanisms. Related findings appear in studies of human affiliative behavior (Jamner et al., 1998).

Although oxytocin and endogenous opioid mechanisms may be important in affiliative and maternal behavior in primates and humans, the important role of higher brain functioning must also be noted. As Keverne et al. (1999) pointed out, the development of a large neocortex in primates has allowed affiliative behavior and maternal caregiving to take place without the hormonal regulation prompted by pregnancy and parturition that elicits similar behaviors in rats. Freeing behavior from exclusive neuroendocrine control enables females to engage in affiliation and infant caregiving through learning by modeling other females. These points suggest an important socialization role for these all-female social groupings. Indeed, Keverne et al. (1999) argued that, through such learning, females provide social stability and group cohesion, with their affiliative processes helping to maintain the continuity of the group over successive generations.

Two caveats regarding the research on female networks in primate groups are warranted. First, there are more than 130 different primate species, and there is substantial variability in the specifics of female networks. For example, female associations are based on kin in some primate social groupings but on nonkin dominance hierarchies in others. In most primate species, networks of females are responsible for rearing offspring, but in titi monkeys (*Callicebus*), fathers are responsible for the rearing of offspring, and titi females actually show aversion to being left alone with their offspring (Mendoza & Mason, 1999). Although it would be unwise to draw direct links from primate behavior to humans, it would be foolish to claim that there is nothing to be learned from primate behavior merely because there is variability among primate species. Thus, although these primate ex-

amples should be interpreted with caution, they provide illustrations of the befriending patterns common to many primates, including human females.

Second, the preceding analysis runs the risk of romanticizing the networks that females create. It must be noted that these networks are by no means stress-free, particularly nonkin female networks (e.g., Silk, 2000). Studies of primates reveal how females who are more dominant in a hierarchy may harass less dominant females, a behavior that can have many adverse effects, including the suppression of fertility (Abbott, Saltzman, Schultz-Darken, & Smith, 1999; Shively, Laber-Laird, & Anton, 1997). A more extreme response has been reported by Fossey (1983) in gorillas and by Goodall (1986) in chimpanzees. The researchers found that, in both species, dominant females, together with their oldest female offspring occasionally cannibalized the young of less dominant females. In humans, interpersonal strain, conflict, and the potential for misunderstanding and mistreatment are common in social groups, and all-female groups are no exception. The networks that women help create and may become enmeshed in are themselves sources of stress, and women report that interpersonal stressors are the most common and stressful types of stressors they experience (Davis, Matthews, & Twamley, 1999). Nonetheless, on the whole, these female networks may confer more benefits than harm.

Conclusions, Implications, and Limitations

We propose a theory of female responses to stress characterized by a pattern termed "tend-and-befriend." Specifically, we propose that women's responses to stress are characterized by patterns that involve caring for offspring under stressful circumstances, joining social groups to reduce vulnerability, and contributing to the development of social groupings, especially those involving female networks, for the exchange of resources and responsibilities. We maintain that aspects of these responses, both maternal and affiliative, may have built on the biobehavioral attachment—caregiving system that depends, in part, on oxytocin, estrogen, and endogenous opioid mechanisms, among other neuroendocrine underpinnings. We suggest that these patterns may have evolved according to principles of natural selection and by virtue of differential parental investment. We propose this theory as a biobehavioral alternative to the fight-or-flight response (Cannon, 1932), which has dominated stress research of the past 5 decades and has been disproportionately based on studies of males.

To evaluate our theory, we examined several empirical literatures that provide convergent support. A neuroendocrine literature on stress hormones and their relation to behavior derived largely from studies with male rats and, to a lesser extent, on nonhuman primates, suggests that the fight-or-flight response may be heavily tied to androgenic pre- or postnatal organization of an aggressive response to threat that is activated, in part, by testosterone. A substantial neuroendocrine literature from animal studies with females suggests, in contrast, that sympathetic and HPA responses may be downregulated by oxytocin under stressful circumstances and that oxytocin, coupled with endogenous opioid mechanisms and other sex-linked hormones, may foster maternal and affiliative behavior in response to stress. The neuroendocrine model links to a literature on humans, suggesting that oxytocin and endogenous opioid mechanisms may have similar maternal and affiliative concomitants. Finally, literatures on both human and nonhuman primates point to differential maternal and affiliative activities among females, compared with males and provides evidence of a substantial female preference to affiliate under stress. The tend-and-befriend pattern may be maintained not only by sex-linked neuroendocrine responses to stress but by social and cultural roles as well.

* * *

Social and Political Implications

* * *

An analysis that posits biological bases for gender differences in behavior raises important political concerns. Many women feel, with some justification, that such models can be used to justify patterns of discrimination and social oppression. To head off any such effort, we emphatically point out that our analysis makes no prescriptive assumptions about the social roles that women occupy. Our analysis should not be construed to imply that women should be mothers, will be good mothers, or will be better parents than men by virtue of these mechanisms. Similarly, this analysis should not be construed as evidence that women are naturally more social than men or that they should shoulder disproportionate responsibility for the ties and activities that create and maintain the social fabric.

Other political concerns, however, may be based on false assumptions about what biological underpinnings signify. Biological analyses of human behavior are sometimes misconstrued by social scientists as implying inflexibility or inevitability in human behavior or as reductionist efforts that posit behavioral uniformity. These perceptions constitute unwarranted concerns about biological bases of behavior. Biology is not so much destiny as it is a central tendency, but a central tendency that influences and interacts with social, cultural, cognitive, and emotional factors, resulting in substantial behavioral flexibility (Crawford & Anderson, 1989; Tooby & Cosmides, 1992). The last few decades of biological research have shown that, just as biology affects behavior, so behavior affects biology, in ways ranging from genetic expression to acute responses to stressful circumstances. Rather than viewing social roles and biology as alternative accounts of human behavior, a more productive theoretical and empirical strategy will be to recognize how biology and social roles are inextricably interwoven to account for the remarkable flexibility of human behavior.

* * *

References

Abbott, D. H., Saltzman, W., Schultz-Darken, N. J., & Smith, T. E. (1999). Specific neuroendocrine mechanisms not involving generalized stress mediate social regulation of female reproduction in cooperatively breeding marmoset monkeys.

In C. S. Carter, I. I. Lederhendler, & B. Kirkpatrick (Eds.), *The integrative neurobiology of affiliation* (pp. 199–220). Cambridge, MA: MIT Press.

Adams, D. (1992). Biology does not make men more aggressive than women. In K. Bjorkqvist & P. Niemela (Eds.), *Of mice and women: Aspects of female aggression* (pp. 17–26). San Diego, CA: Academic Press.

Adler, E. M., Cook, A., Davidson, D., West, C., & Bancroft, J. (1986). Hormones, mood and sexuality in lactating women. *British Journal of Psychiatry, 148*, 74–79.

Altemus, M. P., Deuster, A., Galliven, E., Carter, C. S., & Gold, P. W. (1995). Suppression of hypothalamic-pituitary-adrenal axis response to stress in lactating women. *Journal of Clinical Endocrinology and Metabolism, 80*, 2954–2959.

Archer, J. (1990). The influence of testosterone on human aggression. *British Journal of Psychology, 82*, 1–28.

Argiolas, A., & Gessa, G. L. (1991). Central functions of oxytocin. *Neuroscience and Biobehavioral Reviews, 15*, 217–231.

Baldwin, J. D. (1985). The behavior of squirrel monkeys (*Saimiri*) in natural environments. In L. A. Rosenblum & C. L. Coe (Eds.), *Handbook of squirrel monkey research* (pp. 35–53). New York: Plenum.

Bates, J. E., Freeland, C. A. B., & Lounsbury, M. L. (1979). Measurement of infant difficulties. *Child Development, 50*, 794–802.

Baumeister, R. F., & Sommer, K. L. (1997). What do men want? Gender differences and two spheres of belongingness: Comment on Cross and Madson (1997). *Psychological Bulletin, 122*, 38–44.

Bell, P. A., & Barnard, S. W. (1977, May). *Sex differences in the effects of heat and noise stress on personal space permeability.* Paper presented at the annual meetings of the Rocky Mountain Psychological Society, Albuquerque, NM.

Belle, D. (1987). Gender differences in the social moderators of stress. In R. C. Barnett, L. Biener, & G. K. Baruch (Eds.), *Gender and stress* (pp. 257–277). New York: Free Press.

Benton, D. (1988). The role of opiate mechanisms in social relationships. In M. Lader (Ed.), *The psychopharmacology of addiction.* (British Association for Psychopharmacology Monograph, 10, pp. 115–140). London: Oxford University Press.

Benton, D. (1992). Hormones and human aggression. In K. Bjorkqvist & P. Niemela (Eds.), *Of mice and women: Aspects of female aggression* (pp. 37–50). San Diego, CA: Academic Press.

Bergman, B., & Brismar, B. (1994). Hormone levels and personality traits in abusive and suicidal male alcoholics. *Alcoholism: Clinical and Experimental Research, 18*, 311–316.

Bernbaum, J. C., Pereira, G., Watkins, J., & Peckham, G. (1983). Nonnutritive sucking during gavage feeding enhances growth and maturation in premature infants. *Pediatrics, 71*, 41–45.

Bjorkqvist, K., & Niemela, P. (1992). New trends in the study of female aggression. In K. Bjorkqvist & P. Niemela (Eds.), *Of mice and women: Aspects of female aggression* (pp. 3–16). San Diego, CA: Academic Press.

Blass, E. M. (1997). Infant formula quiets crying human newborns. *Journal of Developmental and Behavioral Pediatrics, 18*, 162–165.

Brain, P. F., Haug, M., & Parmigiani, S. (1992). The aggressive female rodent: Redressing a "scientific" bias. In K. Bjorkqvist & P. Niemela (Eds.), *Of mice and women: Aspects of female aggression* (pp. 27–36). San Diego, CA: Academic Press.

Bray, R. L. (1994, September/October). Remember the children. *Ms. Magazine, 5*, 38–43.

Brown, K. J. (1995). *Effects of housing conditions on stress responses, feeding, and drinking in male and female rats.* Unpublished master's thesis, Uniformed Services University of the Health Sciences, Bethesda, MD.

Brown, K. J., & Grunberg, N. E. (1995). Effects of housing on male and female rats: Crowding stresses males but calms females. *Physiology and Behavior, 58*, 1085–1089.

Bull, A. J., Burbage, S. E., Crandall, J. E., Fletcher, C. I., Lloyd, J. T., Ravenberg, R. L., & Rockett, S. L., (1972). Effects of noise and intolerance of ambiguity upon attraction for similar and dissimilar others. *Journal of Social Psychology, 88*, 151–152.

Burbank, V. K. (1987). Female aggression in cross-cultural perspective. *Behavior Science Research, 21*, 70–100.

Cannon, W. B. (1932). *The wisdom of the body.* New York: Norton.

Caporeal, L. R. (1997). The evolution of truly social cognition: The core configuration model. *Personality and Social Psychology Review, I,* 276–298.

Carter, C. S. (1998). Neuroendocrine perspectives on social attachment and love. *Psychoneuroendocrinology, 23*, 779–818.

Carter, C. S., DeVries, A. C., & Getz, L. L. (1995). Physiological substrates of mammalian monogamy: The prairie vole model. *Neuroscience and Biobehavioral Reviews, 19*, 303–314.

Carter, C. S., Williams, J. R., Witt, D. M., & Inset, T. R. (1992). Oxytocin and social bonding. In C. A. Pedersen, G. F. Jirikowski, J. D. Caldwell, & T. R. Insel (Eds.), Oxytocin in maternal sexual and social behaviors. *Annals of the New York Academy of Science, 652*, 204–211.

Chiodera, P., Salvarani, C., Bacchi-Modena, A., Spailanzani, R., Cigarini, C., Alboni, A., Gardini, E., & Coiro, V. (1991). Relationship between plasma profiles of oxytocin and adrenocorticotropic hormone during sucking or breast stimulation in women. *Hormone Research, 35*, 119–123.

Chorpita, B. F., & Barlow, D. H. (1998). The development of anxiety: The role of control in the early environment. *Psychological Bulletin, 124*, 3–21.

Christenfeld, N., Gerin, W., Lindon, W., Sanders, M., Mathur, J., Deich, J. D., & Pickering, T. G. (1997). Social support effects on cardiovascular reactivity: Is a stranger as effective as a friend? *Psychosomatic Medicine, 59*, 388–398.

Christensen, K., Knussman, R., & Couwenbergs, C. (1985). Sex hormones and stress in the human male. *Hormones and Behavior, 19*, 426–440.

Clancy, S. M., & Dollinger, S. J. (1993). Photographic description of the self: Gender and age differences in social connectedness. *Sex Roles, 29*, 477–495.

Coe, C. L., Mendoza, S. P., Smotherman, W. P., & Levine, S. (1978). Mother–infant attachment in the squirrel monkey: Adrenal response to separation. *Behavior and Biology, 22*, 256–263.

Collaer, M. L., & Hines, M. (1995). Human behavioral sex differences: A role for gonadal hormones during early development? *Psychological Bulletin, 118*, 55–107.

Copeland, E. P., & Hess, R. S. (1995). Differences in young adolescents' coping strategies based on gender and ethnicity. *Journal of Early Adolescence, 15*, 203–219.

Crawford, C. B., & Anderson, J. L. (1989). Sociobiology: An environmentalist discipline? *American Psychologist, 44*, 1449–1459.

Cross, S. E., & Madson, L. (1997). Models of the self: Self-construals and gender. *Psychological Bulletin, 122,* 5–37.

Crowe, J. J. P., & Zeskind, P. S. (1992). Psychophysiological and perceptual responses to infant cries varying in pitch: Comparison of adults with low and high scores on the child abuse potential inventory. *Child Abuse and Neglect, 16,* 19–29.

Cumming, D. C., Brunsting, L. A., Strich, G., Ries, A. L., & Rebar, R. W. (1986). Reproductive hormone increases in response to acute exercise in men. *Medical Science in Sports and Exercise, 18,* 369–373.

Daly, M., & Wilson, M. (1988). *Homicide.* New York: Aldine de Gruyter.

Daly, M., Wilson, M., & Weghorst, S. J. (1982). Male sexual jealousy. *Ethology and Sociobiology, 3,* 11–27.

Davis, M. C., Matthews, K. A., & Twamley, E. W. (1999). Is life more difficult on Mars or Venus? A meta-analytic review of sex differences in major and minor life events. *Annals of Behavioral Medicine, 21,* 83–97.

DeVries, G. J., & Villalba, C. (1999). Brain sexual dimorphism and sex differences in parental and other social behaviors. In C. S. Carter, I. I. Lederhendler, & B. Kirkpatrick (Eds.), *The integrative neurobiology of affiliation* (pp. 155–168). Cambridge, MA: MIT Press.

De Waal, F. (1996). *Good natured: The origins of right and wrong in humans and other animals.* Cambridge, MA: Harvard University Press.

Drago, F., Pederson, C. A., Caldwell, J. D., & Prange, A. J., Jr. (1986). Oxytocin potently enhances novelty-induced grooming behavior in the rat. *Brain Research, 368,* 287–295.

Dreifuss, J. J., Dubois-Dauphin, M., Widmer, H., & Raggenbass, M. (1992). Electrophysiology of oxytocin actions on central neurons. *Annals of the New York Academy of Science, 652,* 46–57.

Dunbar, R. (1996). *Grooming, gossip, and the evolution of language.* Cambridge, MA: Harvard University Press.

Dunn, J. B., & Richards, M. P. (1977). Observations on the developing relationship between mother and baby in the neonatal period. In H. R. Scaefer (Ed.), *Studies in mother–infant interaction* (pp. 427–455). New York: Academic Press.

Eagly, A. H., & Steffen, V. J. (1986). Gender and aggressive behavior: A meta-analytic review of the social psychological literature. *Psychological Bulletin, 100,* 309–330.

Edwards, C. P. (1993). Behavioral sex differences in children of diverse cultures: The case of nurturance to infants. In M. E. Pereira & L. A. Fairbanks (Eds.), *Juvenile primates: Life history, development, and behavior* (pp. 327–338). New York: Oxford University Press.

Fahrbach, S. E., Morrell, J. I., & Pfaff, D. W. (1985). Possible role for endogenous oxytocin in estrogen-facilitated maternal behavior in rats. *Neuroendocrinology, 40,* 526–532.

Field, T. M. (1995). Massage therapy for infants and children. *Journal of Developmental & Behavioral Pediatrics, 16,* 105–111.

Field, T. M. (1996), Touch therapies for pain management and stress reduction. In R. J. Resnick & H. R. Ronald (Eds.), *Health psychology through the life span: Practice and research opportunities* (pp. 313–321). Washington, DC: American Psychological Association.

Field, T., & Goldson, E. (1984). Pacifying effects of nonnutritive sucking on term and preterm neonates during heelstick procedures. *Pediatrics, 74,* 1012–1015.

Field, T. M., Malphurs, J., Carraway, K., & Pelaez-Nogueras, M. (1996). Carrying position influences infant behavior. *Early Child Development & Care, 121,* 49–54.

Field, T. M., Schanberg, S., Davalos, M., & Malphurs, J. (1996). Massage with oil has more positive effects on normal infants. *Pre- & Peri-Natal Psychology Journal, 11,* 75–80.

Flinn, M. V., & England, B. G. (1997). Social economics of childhood gluticosteroid stress responses and health. *American Journal of Physical Anthropology, 102,* 33–53.

Fontana, A. M., Diegnan, T., Villeneuve, A., & Lepore, S. J. (1999). Nonevaluative social support reduces cardiovascular reactivity in young women during acutely stressful performance situations. *Journal of Behavioral Medicine, 22,* 75–91.

Fossey, D. (1983). *Gorillas in the mist.* Boston: Houghton Mifflin.

Francis, D., Diorio, J., Liu, D., & Meaney, M. J. (1999, November). Nongenomic transmission across generations of maternal behavior and stress responses in the rat. *Science, 286,* 1155–1158.

Gerin, W., Milner, D., Chawla, S., & Pickering, T. G. (1995). Social support as a moderator of cardiovascular reactivity: A test of the direct effects and buffering hypothesis. *Psychosomatic Medicine, 57,* 16–22.

Gerin, W., Pieper, C., Levy, R., & Pickering, T. G. (1992). Social support in social interaction: A moderator of cardiovascular reactivity. *Psychosomatic Medicine, 54,* 324–336.

Girdler, S. S., Jamner, L. D., & Shapiro, D. (1997). Hostility, testosterone, and vascular reactivity to stress: Effects of sex. *International Journal of Behavioral Medicine, 4,* 242–263.

Glazer, I. M. (1992). Interfemale aggression and resource scarcity in a cross-cultural perspective. In K. Bjorkqvist & P. Niemela (Eds.), *Of mice and women: Aspects of female aggression* (pp. 163–172). San Diego, CA: Academic Press.

Glynn, L. M., Christenfeld, N., & Gerin, W. (1999). Gender, social support, and cardiovascular responses to stress. *Psychosomatic Medicine, 61,* 234–242.

Goodall, J. (1986). *The chimpanzees of Gombe: Patterns of behavior.* Cambridge, MA: Belknap Press of Harvard University Press.

Goodman, L. A., Koss, M. P., Fitzgerald, L. F., Russo, N. F., & Keita, G. P. (1993). Male violence against women: Current research and future directions. *American Psychologist, 48,* 1054–1058.

Gray, J. A. (1971). Sex differences in emotional behaviour in mammals including Man: Endocrine bases. *Acta Psychologica, 35,* 29–46.

Gray, J. A., & Lalljee, B. (1974). Sex differences in emotional behaviour in the rat: Correlation between open-field defecation and active avoidance. *Animal Behaviour, 22,* 856–861.

Gruenewald, T. L., Taylor, S. E., Klein, L. C., & Seeman, T. E. (1999). Gender disparities in acute stress research [Abstract]. *Proceedings of the Society of Behavioral Medicine's 20th Annual Meeting: Annals of Behavioral Medicine, 21*(Suppl.), S141.

Gunnar, M. R., Brodersen, L., Krueger, K., & Rigatuso, J. (1996). Dampening of adrenocortical responses during infancy: Normative changes and individual differences. *Child Development, 67,* 877–889.

Gunnar, M. R., Brodersen, L., Nachmias, M., Buss, K., & Rigatuso, J. (1996). Stress reactivity and attachment security. *Developmental Psychology, 29,* 191–204.

Harlow, C. M. (Ed.) (1986). *Learning to love: The selected papers of H. F. Harlow.* New York: Praeger.

Hellhammer, D. H., Hubert, W., & Schurmeyer, T. (1985). Changes in saliva testosterone after psychological stimulation in men. *Psychoneuroendocrinology, 10,* 77–81.

Hennessy, M. B., Mendoza, S. P., & Kaplan, J. N. (1982). Behavior and plasma cortisol following brief peer separation in juvenile squirrel monkeys. *American Journal of Primatology, 3,* 143–151.

Hertsgaard, L. G., Gunnar, M. R., Erickson, M. R., & Nachmias, M. (1995). Adrenocortical responses to the strange situation in infants with disorganized/disoriented attachment relationships. *Child Development, 66,* 1100–1106.

Hofer, M. A. (1995). Hidden regulators: Implications for a new understanding of attachment, separation, and loss. In S. Goldberg, R. Muir, & J. Kerr (Eds.), *Attachment theory: Social, developmental, and clinical perspectives* (pp. 203–230). Hillsdale, NJ: Analytic Press.

Holmstrom, R. (1992). Female aggression among the great apes: A psychoanalytic perspective. In K. Bjorkqvist & P. Niemela (Eds.), *Of mice and women: Aspects of female aggression* (pp. 295–306). San Diego, CA: Academic Press.

Hyde, J. S. (1984). How large are gender differences in aggression? A developmental meta-analysis. *Developmental Psychology, 20,* 722–736.

Ironson, G., Field, T., Scafidi, F., Hashimoto, M., Kumar, M., Kumar, A., Price, A., Goncalves, A., Burman, I., Tetenman, C., Patarca, R., & Fletcher, M. A. (1996). Massage therapy is associated with enhancement of the immune system's cytotoxic capacity. *International Journal of Neuroscience, 84,* 205–217.

Jalowiec, J. E., Calcagnetti, D. J., & Fanselow, M. S. (1989). Suppression of juvenile social behavior requires antagonism of central opioid systems. *Pharmacology Biochemistry and Behavior, 33,* 697–700.

Jamner, L. D., Alberts, J., Leigh, H., & Klein, L. C. (1998, March). *Affiliative need and endogenous opioids.* Paper presented at the annual meetings of the Society of Behavioral Medicine, New Orleans, LA.

Janson, C. H. (1992). Evolutionary ecology of primate structure. In E. A. Smith & B. Winterhalder (Eds.), *Evolutionary ecology and human behavior* (pp. 95–130). New York: Aldine.

Jezova, D., Jurankova, E., Mosnarova, A., Kriska, M., & Skultetyova, I. (1996). Neuroendocrine response during stress with relation to gender differences. *Acta Neurobiologae Experimentalis, 56,* 779–785.

Jezova, D., Skultetyova, I., Tokarev, D. I., Bakos, P., & Vigas, M. (1995). Vasopressin and oxytocin in stress. In G. P. Chrousos, R. McCarty, K. Pacak, G. Cizza, E. Sternberg, P. W. Gold, & R. Kvetnansky (Eds.), *Stress: Basic mechanisms and clinical implications* (Vol. 771, pp. 192–203). New York, NY: Annals of the New York Academy of Sciences.

Jordan, T. C., Hennessy, M. B., Gonzalez, C. A., & Levine, S. (1985). Social and environmental factors influencing mother–infant separation-reunion in squirrel monkeys. *Physiology and Behavior, 34,* 489–493.

Kamarck, T. W., Manuck, S. B., & Jennings, J. R. (1990). Social support reduces cardiovascular reactivity to psychological challenge: A laboratory model. *Psychosomatic Medicine, 52,* 42–58.

Kashima, Y., Yamaguchi, S. K., Choi, S., Gelfand, M. J., & Yuki, M. (1995). Culture, gender, and self: A perspective from the individualism-collectivism research. *Journal of Personality and Social Psychology, 69,* 925–937.

Kendrick, K. M., Da Costa, A. P., Broad, K. D., Ohkura, S., Guevara, R., Levy, F., & Keverne, E. B. (1997). Neural control of maternal behavior and olfactory recognition of offspring. *Brain Research Bulletin, 44,* 383–395.

Kendrick, K. M., Keverne, E. B., & Baldwin, B. A. (1987). Intracerebroventricular oxytocin stimulates maternal behaviour in the sheep. *Neuroendocrinology, 46,* 56–61.

Kenrick, D. T., & Johnson, G. A. (1979). Interpersonal attraction in aversive environments: A problem for the classical conditioning paradigm? *Journal of Personality and Social Psychology, 37,* 572–579.

Keverne, E. B., Nevison, C. M., & Martel, F. L. (1999). Early learning and the social bond. In C. S. Carter, I. I. Lederhendler, & B. Kirkpatrick (Eds.), *The integrative neurobiology of affiliation* (pp. 263–274). Cambridge, MA: MIT Press.

Kirschbaum, C., Klauer, T., Filipp, S., & Hellhammer, D. H. (1995). Sex-specific effects of social support on cortisol and subjective responses to acute psychological stress. *Psychosomatic Medicine, 57,* 23–31.

Klein, L. C., Alberts, J., Jamner, J. D., Leigh, H., Levine, L. J., & Orenstein, M. D. (1998). Naltrexone administration increases salivary cortisol units in women but not men. *Psychophysiology, 35,* S49.

Klein, L. C., Popke, E. J., & Grunberg, N. E. (1998). Sex differences in effects of opioid blockade on stress-induced freezing behavior. *Pharmacology Biochemistry and Behavior, 61,* 413–417.

Kors, D., Linden, W., & Gerin, W. (1997). Evaluation interferes with social support: Effects on cardiovascular stress reactivity. *Journal of Social and Clinical Psychology, 16,* 1–23.

Koss, M. P., Goodman, L. A., Browne, A., Fitzgerald, L. F., Keita, L. F., & Russo, N. F. (1994). *No safe haven: Male violence against women at home, at work, and in the community.* Washington, DC: American Psychological Association.

Lepore, S. J., Allen, K. A. M., & Evans, G. W. (1993). Social support lowers cardiovascular reactivity to an acute stress. *Psychosomatic Medicine, 55,* 518–524.

Lewis, B. P., & Linder, D. E. (2000). *Fear and affiliation: Replication and extension of Schachter.* Manuscript in preparation.

Lightman, S. L., & Young, W. S., III. (1989). Lactation inhibits stress-mediated secretion of corticosterone and oxytocin and hypothalamic accumulation of corticotropin-releasing factor and enkephalin messenger ribonucleic acids. *Endocrinology, 124,* 2358–2364.

Liu, D., Diorio, J., Day, J. C., Francis, D. D., Mar, A., & Meaney, M. J. (in press). Maternal care, hippocampal synaptogenesis and cognitive development in the rat. *Science.*

Liu, D., Diorio, J., Tannenbaum, B., Caldji, C., Francis, D., Freedman, A., Sharma, S., Pearson, D., Plotsky, P. M., & Meaney, M. J. (1997, September 12). Maternal care, hippocampal glucocorticoid receptors, and hypothalamic-pituitary-adrenal responses to stress. *Science, 277,* 1659–1662.

Luckow, A., Reifman, A., & McIntosh, D. N. (1998, August). *Gender differences in coping: A meta-analysis.* Poster session presented at the 106th Annual Convention of the American Psychological Association, San Francisco, CA.

Lumia, A. R., Thorner, K. M., & McGinnis, M. Y. (1994). Effects of chronically high doses of anabolic androgenic steroid, testosterone, on intermale aggression and sexual behavior in male rats. *Physiology and Behavior, 55,* 331–335.

Maccoby, E. E., & Jacklin, C. H. (1974). *The psychology of sex differences*. Stanford, CA: Stanford University Press.

Malamuth, N. M. (1998). An evolutionary-based model integrating research on the characteristics of sexually coercive men. In J. G. Adair, D. Belanger, & K. L. Dion (Eds.), *Advances in psychological science* (Vol. 1, pp. 151–184). New York: Psychology Press.

Markus, H. R., & Kitayama, S. (1991). Culture and the self: Implications for cognition, emotion, and motivation. *Psychological Review, 98*, 224–253.

Martel, F. L., Nevison, C. M., Rayment, F. D., Simpson, M. J. A., & Keverne, E. B. (1993). Opioid receptor blockade reduces maternal affect and social grooming in rhesus monkeys. *Psychoneuroimmunology, 18*, 307–321.

Mason, W. A., & Epple, G. (1969). Social organization in experimental groups of *Saimiri* and *Callicebus*. *Proceedings of the Second International Congress of Primatology, 1*, 59–65.

Mathur, D. N., Toriola, A. L., & Dada, O. A. (1986). Serum cortisol and testosterone levels in conditioned male distance runners and non-athletes after maximal exercise. *Journal of Sports Medicine and Physical Fitness, 26*, 245–250.

McCarthy, M. M. (1995). Estrogen modulation of oxytocin and its relation to behavior. In R. Ivell & J. Russell (Eds.), *Oxytocin: Cellular and molecular approaches in medicine and research* (pp. 235–242). New York: Plenum Press.

McCarthy, M. M., Chung, S. K., Ogawa, S., Kow, L., & Pfaff, D. W. (1991). Behavioral effects of oxytocin: Is there a unifying principle? In S. Jard & J. Ramison (Eds.), *Vasopressin* (pp. 195–212). Montrouge, France: John Libbey Eurotext.

McCarthy, M. M., McDonald, C. H., Brooks, P. J., & Goldman, D. (1996). An anxiolytic action of oxytocin is enhanced by estrogen in the mouse. *Physiology and Behavior, 60*, 1209–1215.

McDonald, L. M., & Korabik, K. (1991). Sources of stress and ways of coping among male and female managers. *Journal of Social Behavior and Personality, 6*, 185–198.

Mendoza, S. P., Coe, C. L., Smotherman, W. P., Kaplan, J., & Levine, S. (1980). Functional consequences of attachment: A comparison of two species. In R. W. Bell & W. P. Smotherman (Eds.), *Maternal ifluences and early behavior* (pp. 235–252). New York: Spectrum.

Mendoza, S. P., & Mason, W. A. (1999). Attachment relationships in New World primates. In C. S. Carter, I. I. Lederhendler, & B. Kirkpatrick (Eds.), *The integrative neurobiology of affiliation* (pp. 93–100). Cambridge, MA: MIT Press.

Nachmias, M., Gunnar, M. R., Mangelsdorf, S., Parritz, R. H., & Buss, K. (1996). Behavioral inhibition and stress reactivity: The moderating role of attachment security. *Child Development, 67*, 508–522.

Niedenthal, P. M., & Beike, D. R. (1997). Interrelated and isolated self-concepts. *Personality and Social Psychology Review, 1*, 106–128.

Ogus, E. D., Greenglass, E. R., & Burke, R. J. (1990). Gender-role differences, work stress and depersonalization. *Journal of Social Behavior and Personality, 5*, 387–398.

Olweus, D., Mattson, A., Schalling, D., & Low, H. (1980). Testosterone, aggression, physical, and personality dimensions in normal adolescent males. *Psychosomatic Medicine, 42*, 352–269.

Panksepp, J. (1998). *Affective neuroscience*. London: Oxford University Press.

Panksepp, J., Nelson, E., & Bekkedal, M. (1999). Brain systems for the mediation of social separation distress and social-reward: Evolutionary antecedents and neuropeptide intermediaries. In C. S. Carter, I. I. Lederhendler, & B. Kirkpatrick (Eds.), *The integrative neurobiology of affiliation* (pp. 221–244). Cambridge, MA: MIT Press.

Patterson, M. L., & Schaeffer, R. E. (1977). Effects of size and sex composition on interaction distance, participation, and satisfaction in small groups. *Small Group Behavior, 8*, 433–442.

Pearson, J. C. (1981). The effects of setting and gender on self-disclosure. *Group and Organization Studies, 6*, 334–340.

Ptacek, J. T., Smith, R. E., & Zanas, J. (1992). Gender, appraisal, and coping: A longitudinal analysis. *Journal of Personality, 60*, 747–770.

Repetti, R. L. (1989). Effects of daily workload on subsequent behavior during marital interactions: The role of social withdrawal and spouse support. *Journal of Personality and Social Psychology, 57*, 651–659.

Repetti, R. L. (1997, April). *The effects of daily job stress on parent behavior with preadolescents*. Paper presented at the biennial meeting of the Society for Research in Child Development, Washington, DC.

Repetti, R. L. (2000). *The differential impact of chronic job stress on mothers' and fathers' behavior with children*. Manuscript in preparation.

Roy, M. P., Steptoe, A., & Kirschbaum, C. (1998). Life events and social support as moderators of individual differences in cardiovascular and cortisol reactivity. *Journal of Personality and Social Psychology, 75*, 1273–1281.

Rubenstein, D. E. (1978). On predation, competition, and the advantages of group living. In P. P. G. Bateson & P. H. Klopfer (Eds.), *Perspectives in ethnology* (Vol. 3, pp. 205–231). New York: Plenum Press.

Ruppenthal, G. C. Harlow, M. K., Eisele, C. D., Harlow, H. F., & Suomi, S. F. (1974). Development of peer interactions of monkeys reared in a nuclear family environment. *Child Development, 45*, 670–682.

Sandnabba, N. K. (1992). Aggressive behavior in female mice as a correlated characteristic in selection for aggressiveness in male mice. In K. Bjorkqvist & P. Niemela (Eds.), *Of mice and women: Aspects of female aggression* (pp. 367–381). San Diego, CA: Academic Press.

Sapolsky, R. M. (1992b). *Stress, the aging brain, and the mechanisms of neuron death*. Cambridge, MA: MIT Press.

Sawchenko, P. E., & Swanson, L. W. (1982). Immunohistochemical identification of neurons in the paraventricular nucleus of the hypothalamus that project to the medulla or to the spinal cord in the rat. *Journal of Comparative Neurology, 205*, 260–272.

Scafidi, F., & Field, T. (1996). Massage therapy improves behavior in neonates born to HIV-positive mothers. *Journal of Pediatric Psychology, 21*, 889–897.

Scafidi, F. A., Field, T., & Schanberg, C. M. (1993). Factors that predict which preterm infants benefit most from massage therapy. *Journal of Developmental and Behavioral Pediatrics, 14*, 176–180.

Schachter, S. (1959). *The psychology of affiliation*. Stanford, CA: Stanford University Press.

Shaffer, D., & Campbell, M. (1994). Reactive attachment disorder of infancy or early childhood. In A. Frances, H. A. Pincus, & H. B. First (Eds.), *Diagnostic and statistical manual of men-*

tal disorders: DSM–IV (4th ed., pp. 116–118). Washington, DC: American Psychiatric Association.

Sheffield, D., & Carroll, D. (1994). Social support and cardiovascular reactions to active laboratory stressors. *Psychology and Health, 9,* 305–316.

Shively, C. A., Laber-Laird, K., & Anton, R. F. (1997). Behavior and physiology of social stress and depression in female Cynomolgus monkeys. *Biolological Psychiatry, 41,* 871–882.

Silk, J. B. (2000). Ties that bond: The role of kinship in primate societies. In L. Stone (Ed.), *New directions in anthropological kinship.* Boulder, CO: Rowman and Littlefield.

Spain, D. (1992). The spatial foundations of men's friendships and men's power. *Men's friendships, 246,* 59–73.

Straus, M. A., & Gelles, R. J. (1986). Societal change and change in family violence from 1975 to 1985 as revealed by two national surveys. *Journal of Marriage and the Family, 48,* 465–479.

Swanson, L. W., & Sawchenko, P. E. (1980). Paraventricular nucleus: A site for the integration of neuroendocrine and autonomic mechanisms. *Neuroendocrinology, 31,* 410–417.

Taylor, S. E., Klein, L. C., Greendale, G., & Seeman, T. E. (1999). *Oxytocin and HPA responses to acute stress in women with or without HRT.* Manuscript in preparation.

Thorsteinsson, E. B., James, J. E., & Gregg, M. E. (1998). Effects of video-relayed social support on hemodynamic reactivity and salivary cortisol during laboratory-based behavioral challenge. *Health Psychology, 17,* 436–444.

Tiger, L. (1970). *Men in groups.* New York: Vintage Books.

Tooby, J., & Cosmides, L. (1992). Psychological foundations of culture. In J. Barkow, L. Cosmides, & J. Tooby (Eds.), *The adapted mind* (pp. 19–136). New York: Oxford University Press.

Turner, R. A., Altemus, M., Enos, T., Cooper, B., & McGuinness, T. (1999). Preliminary research on plasma oxytocin in healthy, normal cycling women investigating emotion and interpersonal distress. *Psychiatry, 62,* 97–113.

Uvnas-Moberg, K. (1996). Neuroendocrinology of the mother–child interaction. *Trends in Endocrinology and Metabolism, 7,* 126–131.

Uvnas-Moberg, K. (1997). Oxytocin linked antistress effects—the relaxation and growth response. *Acta Psychologica Scandinavica, 640* (Suppl.), 38–42.

Uvnas-Moberg, K. (1999). Physiological and endocrine effects of social contact. In C. S. Carter, I. I. Lederhendler, & B. Kirkpatrick (Eds.), *The integrative neurobiology of affiliation* (pp. 245–262). Cambridge, MA: MIT Press.

Uvnas-Moberg, K., Marchini, G., & Winberg, J. (1993). Plasma cholecystokinin concentrations after breast feeding in healthy four-day-old infants. *Archives of Diseases in Childhood, 68,* 46–48.

Veroff, J., Kulka, R., & Douvan, E. (1981). *Mental health in America: Patterns of help-seeking from 1957 to 1976.* New York: Basic Books.

Wallen, K., & Tannenbaum, P. L. (1997). Hormonal modulation of sexual behavior and affiliation in rhesus monkeys. *Annals of the New York Academic of Science, 807,* 185–202.

Wethington, E., McLeod, J. D., & Kessler, R. C. (1987). The importance of life events for explaining sex differences in psychological distress. In R. C. Barnett, L. Biener, & G. K. Baruch (Eds.), *Gender and stress* (pp. 144–156). New York: Free Press.

Wheeler, G., Cumming, D., Burnham, R., Maclean, I., Sloley, B. D., Bhambhani, Y., & Steadward, R. D. (1994). Testosterone, cortisol and catecholamine responses to exercise stress and autonomic dysreflexia in elite quadiplegic athletes. *Paraplegia, 32,* 292–299.

Whiting, B., & Whiting, J. (1975). *Children of six cultures.* Cambridge, MA: Harvard University Press.

Wiesenfeld, A. R., Malatesta, C. Z., Whitman, P. B., Grannose, C., & Vile, R. (1985). Psychophysiological response of breast- and bottle-feeding mothers to their infants' signals. *Psychophysiology, 22,* 79–86.

Williams, R. B., Lane, J. D., Kuhn, C. M., Melosh, W., White, A. D., & Schanberg, S. M. (1982, October 29). Type A behavior and elevated physiological and neuroendocrine responses to cognitive tasks. *Science, 218,* 483–485.

Windle, R. J., Shanks, N., Lightman, S. L., & Ingram, C. D. (1997). Central oxytocin administration reduces stress-induced corticosterone release and anxiety behavior in rats. *Endocrinology, 138,* 2829–2834.

Witt, D. M., Carter, C. S., & Walton, D. (1990). Central and peripheral effects of oxytocin administration in prairie voles (*Microtus ochrogaster*). *Pharmacology Biochemistry and Behavior, 37,* 63–69.

Witt, D. M., Winslow, J. T., & Insel, T. R. (1992). Enhanced social interactions in rats following chronic, centrally infused oxytocin. *Pharmacology Biochemistry and Behavior, 43,* 855–886.

Wrangham, R. W. (1980). An ecological model of female-bonded primate groups. *Behaviour, 75,* 262–300.

Zeskind, P. S. (1980). Adult responses to cries of low and high risk infants. *Infant Behavior and Development, 3,* 167–177.

Zeskind, P. S. (1987). Adult heart rate responses to infant cry sounds. *British Journal of Developmental Psychology, 5,* 73–79.

Zeskind, P. S., & Collins, V. (1987). The pitch of infant crying and caregiver responses in a natural setting. *Infant Behavior and Development, 10,* 501–504.

Zeskind, P. S., Sale, J., Maio, M. L., Huntington, L., & Weiseman, J. (1985). Adult perceptions of pain and hunger cries: A synchrony of arousal. *Child Development, 14,* 549–554.

Genetic and Environmental Influences on Observed Personality: Evidence from the German Observational Study of Adult Twins

Peter Borkenau, Rainer Riemann, Alois Angleitner, and Frank M. Spinath

Behavioral genetics is a field of research that seeks the bases of individual differences in personality and ability by estimating the degree to which they can be accounted for by variation in genes, as opposed to variation in the environment. The usual method for doing this is the twin study. While analytic methods are complex, the basic idea is simple: If monozygotic (MZ, genetically identical) twins resemble each other on a trait more closely than do dizygotic twins (DZ, who share only 50% of their variable genes), then variation in the trait can be attributed, to some degree, to variation in genes. The past three decades of research have established conclusively that many attributes of personality and ability, and maybe all of them, are in fact influenced to some degree by genes.

Beyond this fact, one of the best-known and most controversial conclusions to emerge so far from research on behavioral genetics is that very little if any variation in personality can be attributed to the "shared family environment," usually interpreted as the aspects of the childhood environment that are the same for all children in a family. This would include variables such as family income, neighborhood, father presence in the home, and so on. A large number of behavioral genetic studies have found that siblings raised together actually resemble each other to a surprisingly small degree, and various more complex analyses have shared the conclusion that, for all intents and purposes, the family doesn't matter (e.g., Harris, 1995).

The present article notes that almost all of the research leading to this conclusion has been based upon self-report measures of personality, such as standard personality inventories. Despite what the term might seem to imply, "behavioral genetics" research has rarely included direct measures of behavior. The purpose of the ambitious German Observational Study of Adult Twins (GOSAT) is to remedy this deficiency. The study brings together a large number of MZ and DZ twins and observes their behavior in a variety of experimental situations, ranging from simply introducing oneself to "rigging a high and stable paper tower." Behaviors are rated from videotapes of these situations and combined into observationally based personality estimates, which can then be put through the usual behavioral genetic analyses.

The conclusion of this study is important and, given the pre-existing literature, surprising. It turns out that behaviorally based estimates of personality appear to be influenced much more by the shared family environment than have been previously obtained self-report-based estimates. This conclusion has two implications. First, it implies that behavioral geneticists were a bit too quick to conclude that the shared family environment is not an important influence on the development of personality. Second, it points out the danger of basing sweeping conclusions on limited methods. Multimethod studies are not only highly desirable, as the authors state near the end of this article, they are probably necessary before we can have much confidence in the conclusions from research.

From *Journal of Personality and Social Psychology, 80,* 655–668, 2001.

Numerous behavior-genetic studies suggest that individual differences in adult personality are almost exclusively accounted for by genetic and nonshared environmental influences. In a meta-analysis[1] of behavior-genetic studies on personality, Loehlin (1992) concluded that additive effects of genes accounted for 22–46% of the phenotypic variance, that nonshared environment accounted for another 44–55%, and that shared environmental influences were weak, accounting for 0–11% of individual differences in personality. More recently, Plomin, DeFries, McClearn, and Rutter (1997) suggested that genes accounted for about 40% of the variance in personality, that nonshared environment accounted for the other 60%, and that there were no effects of the shared environment.

Whereas it is now generally accepted that genes have a substantial influence on individual differ-

ences in personality, it is still a puzzle why almost all environmental influences on personality seem to be of the nonshared variety. *Shared environment* is defined as environmental factors that contribute to twin and sibling similarity, whereas *nonshared environment* is defined as environmental factors that do not contribute to sibling similarity. * * *

Lack of importance of the shared environment is inferred from three findings. First, the correlations between adoptive siblings and those between adoptees and their adoptive parents tend to be small, usually about .05[2] (Loehlin, Willerman, & Horn, 1987; Plomin, Corley, Caspi, Fulker, & DeFries, 1998; Scarr, Webber, Weinberg, & Wittig, 1981). Second, twins reared together are not systematically more similar in personality than are twins reared apart (Loehlin, 1992). Finally, the correlations between monozygotic (MZ) twins tend to be twice or even more than twice as high as are the correlations between dizygotic (DZ) twins

---

[1]A meta-analysis is a technique for reviewing large research literatures that yields quantitative estimates of the effects of variables, based on many participants in a large number of studies.

[2]For background on how to interpret a correlation coefficient, see the selection by Rosenthal and Rubin in Part I.

(Loehlin, 1989, 1992; Plomin, DeFries, McClearn, & Rutter, 1997), which suggests genetic and non-shared environmental but no shared environmental influence.

Psychology has reacted to these findings in several ways. Some authors (Rowe, 1994; Harris, 1995, 1998) have suggested theories of peer socialization to explain why children in the same family are so different from one another. Other authors have set out to demonstrate that there are shared environmental influences on at least some traits, such as religious orthodoxy (Beer, Arnold, & Loehlin, 1998). Finally, theorists have suggested that the importance of the shared environment may be systematically underestimated in adoption studies, because of range restriction (Stoolmiller, 1999), as well as in studies that rely on self-reports or ratings by knowledgeable informants, because of contrast effects (Miles & Carey, 1997; Rose, 1995; Saudino & Eaton, 1991). The present article focuses on the latter hypothesis.

* * *

Peer Report Studies on Adult Twins

Peer reports by at least two independent judges per target allow one to separate reliable target variance from perceiver effects and thus overcome a drawback of self-reports. Despite that advantage, however, there are only two peer-report studies on adult personality in twins (Heath et al., 1992; Riemann, Angleitner, & Strelau, 1997). In the study by Heath et al. (1992), 460 pairs of MZ and 366 pairs of same-gender DZ twins described their own and their twin's extraversion and neuroticism. Genes accounted for 63% of the reliable variance in Neuroticism and for 73% of the reliable variance in Extraversion, the remaining variance being accounted for by nonshared environment. Riemann, Angleitner, and Strelau (1997) administered the German self-report version (Borkenau & Ostendorf, 1993) of Costa and McCrae's (1992) NEO Five-Factor Inventory (NEO-FFI) to 660 pairs of MZ and 200 pairs of same-gender DZ twins and collected additional peer reports by two acquaintances per twin, using the peer report version of the NEO-

FFI. In their analyses, the broad-sense heritabilities of the true scores ranged from 57% to 81% for the five trait domains measured by the NEO-FFI, the remaining variance being accounted for by nonshared environment. Thus, these two peer report studies suggest that genes account for about two thirds and nonshared environment accounts for the other third of the reliable variance in peer reports of adult personality. This is quite different from the 40% genetic and 60% nonshared environmental variance that are usually estimated from self-report studies (Plomin, DeFries, et al., 1997).

Contrast Effects

However, self-reports and peer reports share the problem that they may be subject to contrast effects. Two kinds of contrast effects have to be distinguished in behavior-genetic research on personality.

1. Relatives in general and twins in particular may mutually influence each other in ways that make their actual personalities different from one another. An example might be different roles taken by twins or siblings to emphasize their unique identities.

2. Apart from the relatives' actual behavioral similarity, contrast effects may affect the similarity of their personality descriptions, because they may be compared (and may compare themselves) with each other instead of with the population mean. This kind of rater bias would inflate the differences within and reduce the differences between pairs, resulting in lower correlations between relatives. Such a process is quite plausible, as persons tend to compare the targets of personality descriptions with particular other persons who come to their minds (Schwarz, 1999), and for twins, a particularly accessible other person may be their cotwin. Consider, for example, the questionnaire item "Do you enjoy going to parties?" that is a marker of Extraversion. Twins may endorse this item if they enjoy parties more than their cotwin does, and they may deny it if the cotwin enjoys parties more. This would reduce the correlations between cotwins and result in underestimates of the importance of

the shared environment, no matter whether it operated in MZ and DZ twins alike or whether the effect was stronger in DZ twins.

Both kinds of contrast effects may yield negative correlations between relatives, a phenomenon that is inconsistent with the standard behavior-genetic models that imply positive (or at least zero) correlations between all kinds of relatives. But even for DZ twins who share half their genes in addition to their family environment, negative correlations have repeatedly been found (Heath et al., 1992), particularly if young twins were described by their parents (Neale & Stevenson, 1989; Spinath & Angleitner, 1998). Such negative correlations indicate one or the other sort of contrast effect.

Whereas negative correlations between relatives clearly indicate contrast effects, positive correlations are no proof of the lack of contrast effects. This is because contrast effects may attenuate the usually positive correlations between relatives without turning them negative. If contrast effects affect the actual behavior of relatives only, the influence of shared environment will actually be reduced and the parameter estimates will not be biased. However, if rater bias is involved, the importance of the shared environment may be underestimated. This makes it desirable to use personality measures in twin research that may not be subject to that kind of rater bias. That requires observational studies. * * *

Observational Twin and Adoption Studies

We identified about a dozen observational studies on twins and adoptees and reviewed them in another article (Borkenau, Riemann, Spinath, & Angleitner, 2000). In none of these studies were the observed target persons adults. Generally, lack of shared environmental influence is not as clearly suggested by these observational studies as it is by studies that rely on self-reports and ratings by knowledgeable informants. However, most of the observational studies used small samples, and in many of these studies, short-term external influ-

ences shared by cotwins or adoptees may have contributed to the similarity of their behavior.

Miles and Carey (1997) published a meta-analysis on genetic and environmental influences on human aggression and concluded that shared environmental effects seemed to be stronger for observational than for rating measures. However, their meta-analysis included only two observational studies on aggression in children. Moreover, they did not find the behavioral measures of aggression convincing, arguing that "perhaps one or both of the studies capitalized on state-specific, reciprocal influences of twin or adoptive dyads when they were tested at the same time" (p. 213).

Thus, the answer to the question of whether there is shared environmental influence on children's behavior is still open. However, even if observational studies on children conveyed a clear message, any straightforward inference from these studies to adult personality would be questionable: Behavior-genetic evidence suggests that genetic and environmental influences on human behavior change across the life span and that shared environmental influence decreases with age (McCartney, Harris, & Bernieri, 1990; Plomin, DeFries, et al., 1997). Thus, observational behavior-genetic studies on adult personality are highly desirable. This was the prime reason that we started the German Observational Study of Adult Twins (GOSAT).

Method

A comprehensive description of the procedure and the data that were collected in GOSAT has been published elsewhere (Spinath et al., 1999). Therefore, we describe only those measures here for which results are reported below.

PARTICIPANTS Three hundred pairs of adult twins (168 MZ and 132 DZ) who had been recruited from all over Germany by reports in German media participated in GOSAT. They were invited for a 1-day testing session that took place at the University of Bielefeld in Germany. * * *

Women (234 pairs) participated more frequently than men did (66 pairs), with gender not significantly associated with zygosity, $\chi^2(1, N = 300) = 2.00$, $p = .16$.[3] The twins' age varied between 18 and 70 years, with a mean of 34.28 ($SD = 12.99$) and a median of 30.5 years. An analysis of variance (ANOVA) showed that neither gender nor zygosity nor their interaction was significantly related to the participants' age, all Fs ≤ 1.[4]

* * *

MEASURES

Self-reports and peer reports. Most of the GOSAT twin pairs had previously participated in the peer rating study reported by Reimann et al. (1997), in which they had been administered, among others, the German version of Costa and McCrae's (1992) NEO-FFI. The NEO-FFI measures the personality domains Neuroticism, Extraversion, Openness to Experience, Agreeableness, and Conscientiousness with 12 items each. Moreover, each twin had been described by two acquaintances who differed between cotwins, using the peer-report version of the NEO-FFI, in which the items are worded in the third person instead of the first person singular. A few twin pairs had not participated in the peer rating study, but for most of these pairs, self-reports and peer reports could be collected in GOSAT.

Videotaped behavior sequences. A main goal of GOSAT was to obtain reliable and valid personality measures of twins that could not be subject to rater bias. We achieved this by (a) videotaping the twins

in 15 settings in which they had to complete different tasks, (b) presenting these videotapes to judges who never met the twins they described, and (c) never letting a judge of 1 twin observe the cotwin as well.

Because it was desirable to collect personality descriptions by strangers that were highly informative of the targets' actual personality, we wanted to have the twins complete tasks in which personality differences were likely to become observable. * * * Specifically, our tasks included the following (with average duration in parentheses):

1. Introduce oneself (1.25 min).
2. Arrange three photographs in a meaningful order and tell an interesting story that the three pictures might illustrate (4.50 min).
3. Tell dramatic stories about three cards from Murray's (1943) Thematic Apperception Test (6.00 min).
4. Tell a joke to an experimental confederate (1.50 min).
5. Persuade an "obstinate neighbor" (actually a confederate) on the phone to reduce the volume of her stereo after 11 PM (2.25 min).
6. Refuse a request for help by "a friend" (actually a confederate) who says that she has just had a car accident (2.00 min).
7. Introduce oneself to a stranger (an experimental confederate) and tell her about one's hobbies after the confederate has introduced herself (12.00 min).
8. Recall objects that one has just seen in a waiting room (3.00 min).
9. Solve a complex logical problem as fast as possible. Another "participant" (actually the confederate) received the same problem and ostensibly "solved" it at an enormous speed (4.50 min).
10. Introduce the stranger from Setting 4 to the experimenter (2.50 min).
11. Invent a "definition" for a neologism and provide arguments for why that definition would be appropriate (6.25 min).

---

[3] The "chi-square" test is a statistical technique for estimating the probability that the distribution of outcomes across categories can be attributed solely to chance. The "1" refers to the degrees of freedom in the test. N is the number of participants, and p is the probability of this result as a chance outcome.

[4] SD means "standard deviation." The F statistic, derived from an analysis of variance, when combined with the degrees of freedom in the design, yields an estimate of the probability that observed mean differences occurred solely by chance. F's less than 1 are very small and are generally interpreted as reflecting chance variation.

12. Rig up a high and stable paper tower within 5 min, using scissors, paper, and glue only (5.25 min).

13. Read 14 newspaper headlines and their subtitles aloud (3.00 min).

14. Describe multiple uses of a brick, using pantomime only (2.75 min).

15. Sing a song of one's choice (1.00 min).

Approximately 60 min of videotapes per participant, or about 600 hrs of videotapes altogether, were collected this way.

Video-based personality ratings. Numerous judges provided trait ratings of the twins, relying solely on these videotapes. To increase the reliability of the trait ratings, each twin was observed in each setting by four independent judges. Moreover, the behavior in different settings was rated by different panels of four judges to secure independence of ratings for different settings. Finally, different panels of judges were employed for twins from the same pair to prevent contrast effects in twin perception. Thus, 4 (parallel judgments) × 15 (number of settings) × 2 (cotwins) = 120 judges were employed, each of them providing ratings of 300 persons. All judges were students either of the University of Bielefeld or of the University of Halle and were paid for their participation.

The judges provided by a computer their ratings on bipolar 5-point ratings scales. Each of Goldberg's (1990) Big Five factors (i.e., Extraversion, Agreeableness, Conscientiousness, Emotional Stability, and Intellect) was represented by 4 scales, and 4 additional scales were included to measure Openness to Experience (McCrae & Costa, 1987). * * * Moreover, ratings of the targets' attractiveness and likeability were included, mainly to control for the higher expected similarity of MZ twins in physical attractiveness. * * *

The judges' work stations were equipped with a video recorder, a video monitor, and a computer. The judges were instructed to watch a video sequence for 1 twin and then provide the trait ratings for that twin using the computer keyboard, then restart the video recorder to watch 1 twin from another pair, and so forth, until they had provided ratings of 300 persons, 1 twin of each pair. The computer had been programmed (a) to present the adjective scales in a random order that differed between video sequences and (b) to store the judges' responses. * * *

Ratings by experimenters and confederates. The twins were also described by the experimenter and the confederate, using the peer-rating version of the NEO-FFI. The (always female) confederate was involved in six observational settings (Setting 4– Setting 9), and she provided her descriptions when she had interacted with the target for about 1 hr. The experimenter described the target at the end of the observation day after about 6 hrs of interaction and observation. Whereas the experimenter saw both cotwins of a pair (although 1 much longer than the other), the confederate met only 1 twin sibling.

* * *

Results

* * *

BEHAVIOR-GENETIC ANALYSES OF THE VIDEO-BASED PERSONALITY RATINGS

Twin correlations. * * * Table 1 reports the inter-rater reliabilities and the ICCs between MZ and DZ twins separately for the 7 odd settings, the 8 even settings, and all 15 settings.[5] * * * The inter-rater reliabilities predict the ICC of the averaged rating by 28 (odd settings), 32 (even settings), or 60 (all settings) judges with averaged ratings by the same number of hypothetical judges who observed the same targets. This is a useful standard of com-

[5]ICC means "intraclass correlation," which is a type of correlation coefficient calculated when assessing covariation of twin pairs. Although the formula for its computation is different, it can be interpreted in the same way as the standard *r* correlation discussed by Rosenthal and Rubin in Part I.

TABLE 1

RELIABILITIES (r_k) AND TWIN CORRELATIONS FOR THE RESIDUALIZED VIDEO-BASED RATINGS AVERAGED ACROSS ODD SETTINGS, ACROSS EVEN SETTINGS, AND ACROSS ALL SETTINGS

Adjective and domain	Odd settings			Even settings			All settings		
	r_{28}	MZ	DZ	r_{32}	MZ	DZ	r_{60}	MZ	DZ
Frank	.89	.54	.24	.89	.49	.26	.94	.55	.30
Active	.86	.50	.18	.87	.47	.25	.93	.55	.25
Talkative	.90	.51	.20	.92	.55	.23	.95	.61	.25
Gregarious	.90	.54	.20	.92	.59	.24	.95	.61	.25
Extraversion	.92	.55	.21	.93	.55	.25	.96	.59	.23
Assertive	.89	.60	.35	.87	.51	.33	.93	.62	.40
Calm	.84	.49	.33	.82	.40	.31	.90	.54	.39
Self-confident	.88	.57	.36	.86	.51	.31	.93	.59	.37
Even-tempered	.75	.29	.19	.80	.35	.38	.87	.42	.34
Emotional Stability	.90	.59	.37	.88	.51	.33	.94	.61	.38
Kind	.86	.52	.39	.86	.54	.32	.92	.62	.38
Polite	.84	.48	.32	.83	.47	.24	.91	.57	.31
Agreeable	.83	.58	.33	.82	.50	.32	.90	.63	.39
Pleasant	.73	.32	.29	.80	.47	.31	.85	.49	.35
Agreeableness	.89	.54	.38	.88	.55	.32	.93	.61	.38
Thorough	.80	.44	.38	.82	.47	.34	.89	.53	.38
Neat	.79	.45	.19	.79	.36	.32	.88	.48	.32
Conscientious	.81	.45	.34	.84	.48	.33	.90	.51	.37
Systematic	.77	.44	.20	.78	.31	.41	.87	.49	.40
Conscientiousness	.86	.51	.31	.86	.44	.39	.92	.52	.39
Inventive	.83	.44	.29	.85	.56	.45	.91	.59	.42
Imaginative	.81	.43	.29	.84	.46	.38	.90	.53	.40
Original	.84	.40	.23	.84	.49	.23	.91	.52	.26
Creative	.81	.43	.25	.83	.51	.40	.90	.56	.39
Openness to Experience	.87	.47	.28	.88	.54	.40	.93	.56	.38
Refined	.85	.48	.41	.85	.46	.36	.91	.55	.44
Intelligent	.89	.63	.38	.89	.59	.52	.94	.66	.52
Sophisticated	.84	.56	.38	.85	.56	.46	.91	.62	.50
Flexible	.80	.42	.34	.79	.38	.27	.88	.56	.34
Intellect	.91	.62	.43	.90	.57	.50	.95	.64	.51
Median single adjectives	.84	.48	.31	.84	.49	.32	.91	.56	.38
Median domain scores	.90	.55	.32	.88	.55	.36	.94	.60	.38

Note. Domain names are in italics. MZ = monozygotic; DZ = dizygotic.

parison for the correlations between cotwins who were observed by different panels of judges: The differences between the reliability coefficients and the MZ correlations estimate the contribution of the nonshared environment apart from error of measurement. As the reliabilities of the video-based personality ratings were about .35 higher than the MZ correlations, nonshared environmental influence turned out to be substantial even when measurement error was controlled.

Another notable feature in Table 1 is that although the MZ correlations were higher than the DZ correlations, suggesting genetic influence, the DZ correlations exceeded half the MZ correlations for all personality domains except Extraversion, thus suggesting shared environmental influence.

* * *

Thus, there was strong evidence for genetic influence on the twins' personality as assessed by the video-based personality ratings.

The support for shared environmental influence on the video-based personality ratings was weaker, because although the estimates of c^2 from the video-based personality ratings had a mean of .23 and a median of .29, in only 5 of the 30 (16.7%) relevant comparisons the ACE model fit significantly better than the AE model did.

* * *

ESTIMATES FROM SELF-REPORTS AND PEER REPORTS Whereas the estimates of genetic contributions were by and large consistent with previous findings (Plomin, DeFries, et al., 1997), the partitioning of environmental influences between the shared and the nonshared variety was different. These different estimates might reflect differences between the methods of personality assessment (e.g., methods allowing or not allowing for contrast effects) or differences between samples: Twins who have the time and who are willing to travel large distances to spend an entire day at a university under extensive observation may differ from twins who merely complete self-report or peer report instruments at home. Thus, a within-sample comparison was desirable. We therefore analyzed the MZ and DZ correlations for the NEO-FFI self-report and peer report data that had been collected for the GOSAT twin sample. Complete self-reports were available for 277 (159 MZ and 118 DZ) of the 300 GOSAT pairs, and complete peer reports were available for 278 (159 MZ and 119 DZ) of these pairs. These data overlap with those that were published by Riemann et al. (1997) for a larger sample.

Twin correlations and univariate models. * * * Table 2 reports the twin ICCs for MZ and DZ twins and the tests of univariate models for the self-report and averaged peer report data. Table 2 does not suggest that the GOSAT sample differs system-atically from previous twin samples. Rather, the finding of approximately 40% genetic and 60% nonshared environmental influence is consistent with the results of previous studies. A significant c^2 parameter was obtained for self-reported Extraversion but did not replicate for peer-reported Extraversion. Thus, the significant c^2 for self-reported Extraversion may be a chance finding. For Openness to Experience, substantial shared environmental influence was found according to self-reports as well as peer reports. We come back to that point in the Discussion.

* * *

Discussion

The main finding of the present study is that video-based personality ratings yield estimates of shared environmental influence of about .15 higher than suggested by self-reports and peer reports; the main source of these higher c^2 estimates is the relatively high DZ correlations. At the level of the trait domains, the median twin correlations were .60 (MZ) and .38 (DZ) for the video-based personality ratings, .45 (MZ) and .26 (DZ) for the twins' self-reports, and .42 (MZ) and .13 (DZ) for the averaged peer reports. If these correlations are corrected for lack of interrater reliability (which is not possible for self-reports for obvious reasons), they become, approximately, .64 (MZ) and .44 (DZ) for video-based ratings and .72 (MZ) and .21 (DZ) for peer ratings. These findings support the assumption of a contrast effect in descriptions of DZ twins by parents and peers (Health et al., 1992; Neale & Stevenson, 1989; Saudino & Eaton, 1991; Spinath & Angleitner, 1998), whereas they do not point to a contrast effect in descriptions of MZ twins or in self-reports of twins in general. This is consistent with findings by Saudino and Eaton (1991), who also reported a contrast effect in ratings of DZ but not of MZ twins.

* * *

DIFFERENCES BETWEEN PERSONALITY DOMAINS Generally, the video-based personality ratings suggest more shared environmental influence than do

TABLE 2

RESULTS FROM THE UNIVARIATE MODEL FIT ANALYSES OF SELF- AND AVERAGED PEER RATINGS ON THE NEO FIVE FACTOR INVENTORY (NEO-FFI) IN THE GOSAT SAMPLE

| NEO-FFI scale | Twin correlations | | Parameter estimates | | | Fit of the ACE model | | Comparisons | |
	MZ	DZ	a^2	c^2	e^2	χ^2	p ($df = 3$)	AE vs. ACE	CE vs. ACE
Self-reports									
Extraversion	.45	.41	.06	.38	.56	1.67	.64	*	
Agreeableness	.42	.04	.36	.00	.64	16.38	.00		**
Conscientiousness	.50	.24	.48	.00	.52	0.30	.96		**
Neuroticism	.40	.26	.27	.12	.61	1.78	.62		
Openness to Experience	.60	.38	.44	.16	.41	7.12	.07		**
Averaged peer reports									
Extraversion	.42	.13	.41	.00	.59	1.94	.58		**
Agreeableness	.37	.11	.35	.00	.65	1.25	.74		*
Conscientiousness	.45	.20	.44	.00	.56	3.04	.39		*
Neuroticism	.38	.02	.33	.00	.67	4.18	.24		**
Openness to Experience	.47	.28	.40	.07	.52	1.93	.59		*

Note. For chi-squares, $N = 277$ for self-reports and 278 for averaged peer reports. Asterisks in the two right-most columns indicate that the full model fit significantly better than the reduced model did. ACE is a model that combines the additive effects of genes (A), the effects of the shared environment (C), and the effects of the nonshared environment (E). *a*, *c*, and *e* are parameter estimates of the additive effects of genes, the effects of the shared environment, and the effects of the nonshared environment, respectively. GOSAT = German Observational Study of Adult Twins; MZ = monozygotic; DZ = dizygotic.
*$p < .05$. **$p < .01$.

the self-reports and peer reports. But there are also differences between personality domains. Thus, we did not find any shared environmental influence on Extraversion. This is consistent with the results of Loehlins's (1989, 1992) meta-analyses, which identified Extraversion as the domain that was least influenced by the shared environment. Moreover, the lack of shared environmental influence on Extraversion in our study shows that there is no general bias that inflated the DZ-twin correlations.

The trait domain that was most strongly influenced by shared environment was Intellect, which raises the issue of whether substantial shared environmental influence on Intellect is also found if it is measured by intelligence tests. In his model-fitting meta-analysis of studies on family resemblance in IQ, Loehlin (1989) concluded that environments shared by twins account for 39% of

their individual differences in IQ. Admittedly, there is some consensus now that this estimate relies largely on studies of intelligence in children and should not be generalized to adults, as the importance of shared environment for IQ tends to decrease with age (McCartney et al., 1990; Plomin, Fulker, Corley, & DeFries, 1997; Wilson, 1983). Thus, it is useful to look at the intelligence test data that were collected for the GOSAT sample.

In a behavior-genetic analysis of these data that is reported in detail by Neubauer et al. (2000), no shared environmental influence on Raven's APM was found. It is important to note, however, that the APM was less strongly related to the video-based ratings of Intellect than was the LPS. Thus, the behavior-genetic findings for the LPS are of greater interest here. Shared environment accounted for 24% of the variance in the LPS scores

(Neubauer et al., 2000), thus supporting the assumption that the video-based ratings of Intellect reflect actual shared environmental influence on this trait.

LIMITATIONS OF THE TWIN DESIGN It is widely known that the twin design has several limitations, as it relies on three assumptions that can only be tested with additional data: (a) the equal environments assumption, (b) the assumption of random mating, and (c) the assumption that there are no interactive effects of genes. If the equal environments assumption does not hold, environmental effects are misinterpreted as genetic effects, resulting in underestimates of the importance of the shared environment. Similarly, interactive effects of genes are detected by twin studies only if they overrule all possible effects of the shared environment and result in MZ correlations that exceed twice the DZ correlations. Otherwise, interactive effects of genes result in overestimates of additive genetic influence and underestimates of shared environmental influence. Consequently, our estimates of shared environment would be too low if there were unequal environments for MZ and DZ twins or interactive effects of genes.

Assortative mating has opposite effects, in that it increases the DZ but not the MZ correlation and thus inflates the estimates of shared environmental influence (Jensen, 1978). Assortative mating for personality traits like Extraversion, Agreeableness, Conscientiousness, and Emotional Stability is low, but it is substantial for intelligence and social attitudes (Beer et al., 1998; Buss 1985) that may be related to Openness to Experience. * * *

NEED OF AWARENESS OF MEASUREMENT ISSUES A more general conclusion from our study is that behavior-genetic research needs a widened awareness of assessment issues. * * * Genetic research has its roots mainly in biology and in medicine, where measurement issues cause less problems than in psychology. However, when it comes to the genetics of personality, where the data are self-reports and observer ratings, awareness of psychometric principles and of social–psychological evidence on

person perception are indispensable, and multimethod studies that incorporate such considerations become highly desirable.

References

Beer, J. M., Arnold, R. D., & Loehlin, J. C. (1998). Genetic and environmental influences on MMPI factor scales: Joint model fitting to twin and adoption data. *Journal of Personality and Social Psychology, 74*, 818–827.

Borkenau, P., & Ostendorf, F. (1993). *NEO-Fuenf-Faktoren-Inventar (NEO-FFI) nach Costa und McCrae* [NEO Five-Factor Inventory by Costa & McCrae]. Goettingen, Germany: Hogrefe.

Borkenau, P., Riemann, R., Spinath, F. M., & Angleitner, A. (2000). Behavior-genetics of personality: The case of observational studies. In I. Mervielde (Series Ed.) & S. E. Hampson (Vol. Ed.), *Advances in personality psychology* (Vol. 1, pp. 107–137). Philadelphia: Taylor & Francis.

Buss, D. M. (1985). Human mate selection. *American Scientist, 73*, 47–51.

Costa, P. T., & McCrae, R. R. (1992). *Revised NEO Personality Inventory (NEO-PI-R) and NEO Five-Factor Inventory (NEO-FFI) professional manual.* Odessa, FL: Psychological Assessment Resources.

Goldberg, L. R. (1990). An alternative "description of personality": The big-five factor structure. *Journal of Personality and Social Psychology, 59*, 1216–1229.

Harris, J. R. (1995). Where is the child's environment? A group socialization theory of development. *Psychological Review, 102*, 458–489.

Harris, J. R. (1998). *The nurture assumption: Why children turn out the way they do.* New York: The Free Press.

Heath, A. C., Neale, M. C., Kessler, R. C., Eaves, L. J., & Kendler, K. S. (1992). Evidence for genetic influences on personality from self-reports and informant ratings. *Journal of Personality and Social Psychology, 63*, 85–96.

Jensen, A. R. (1978). Genetic and behavioral effects of nonrandom mating. In R. T. Osborne, C. E. Noble, & N. Weyl (Eds.), *Human variation: The biopsychology of age, race, and sex* (pp. 51–105). New York: Academic Press.

Loehlin, J. C. (1989). Partitioning environmental and genetic contributions to behavioral development. *American Psychologists, 44*, 1285–1292.

Loehlin, J. C. (1992). *Genes and environment in personality development.* Newbury Park, CA: Sage.

Loehlin, J. C. Willerman, L., & Horn, J. M. (1987). Personality resemblance in adoptive families: A 10-year-following-up. *Journal of Personality and Social Psychology, 53*, 961–969.

McCartney, K., Harris, M. J., & Bernieri, F. (1990). Growing up and growing apart: A developmental meta-analysis of twin studies. *Psychological Bulletin, 107*, 226–237.

McCrae, R. R., & Costa, P. T. (1987). Validation of the five factor model of personality across instruments and observers. *Journal of Personality and Social Psychology, 52*, 81–90.

Miles, D. R., & Carey, G. (1997). Genetic and environmental architecture of human aggression. *Journal of Personality and Social Psychology, 72*, 207–217.

Neale, M. C., & Stevenson, J. (1989). Rater bias in the EASI temperament scales: A twin study. *Journal of Personality and Social Psychology, 56,* 446–455.

Neubauer, A. C., Spinath, F. M., Riemann, R., Borkenau, P., Angleitner, A. (2000). Genetic and environmental influences on two measures of speed of information processing and their relation to psychometric intelligence. *Intelligence, 26,* 267–289.

Plomin, R., Corley, R., Caspi, A., Fulker, D. W., & DeFries, J. C. (1998). Adoption results for self-reported personality: Evidence for nonadditive effects? *Journal of Personality and Social Psychology, 75,* 211–218.

Plomin, R., DeFries, J. C., McClearn, G. E., & Rutter, M. (1997). *Behavioral genetics.* New York: Freeman.

Plomin, R., Fulker, D. W., Corley, R., & DeFries, J. C. (1997). Nature, nurture, and cognitive development from 1 to 16 years: A parent–offspring adoption study. *Psychological Science, 8,* 442–447.

Riemann, R., Angleitner, A., & Strelau, J. (1997). Genetic and environmental influences on personality: A study of twins reared together using the self- and peer report NEO-FFI scales. *Journal of Personality, 65,* 449–475.

Rose, R. (1995). Genes and human behavior. *Annual Review of Psychology, 46,* 625–654.

Rowe, D. C. (1994). *The limits of family influence: Genes, experience, and behavior.* New York: Guilford Press.

Saudino, K. J., & Eaton, W. O. (1991). Infant temperament and genetics: An objective twin study of motor activity level. *Child Development, 62,* 1167–1174.

Scarr, S., Webber, P. L., Weinberg, R. A., & Wittig, M. A. (1981). Personality resemblance among adolescents and their parents in biologically related and adoptive families. *Journal of Personality and Social Psychology, 40,* 885–898.

Schwarz, N. (1999). Self-reports: How the questions shape the answers. *American Psychologist, 54,* 93–105.

Spinath, F. M., & Angleitner, A. (1998). Contrast effects in Buss and Plomin's EAS questionnaire: A behavioral genetic study on early developing personality traits assessed through parental ratings. *Personality and Individual Differences, 25,* 947–963.

Stoolmiller, M. (1999). Implications of the restricted range of family environments for estimates of heritability and non-shared environment in behavior-genetic adoption studies. *Psychological Bulletin, 125,* 392–409.

Wilson, R. S. (1983). The Louisville Twin Study: Developmental synchronies in behavior. *Child Development, 54,* 298–316.

Sex Differences in Jealousy: Evolution, Physiology, and Psychology

David M. Buss, Randy J. Larsen, Drew Westen, and Jennifer Semmelroth

The essence of Darwin's theory of evolution is that those traits that are associated with successful reproduction will be increasingly represented in succeeding generations. For this reason, the obvious place to look for an evolutionarily based influence on behavior is in the area of sex. It is unsurprising, therefore, that as the evolutionary biology of personality has grown into an active research area in its own right, sex has come in for special attention.

The following article is a collaboration of several personality psychologists led by David Buss, one of the leaders in the application of evolutionary theory to personality. It derives hypotheses about the different approaches to mating that evolutionary theory would expect to be manifest by women and by men. In a nutshell, evolutionary considerations would lead one to expect men to be particularly worried that "their" children might have been fathered by other men, and therefore to be prone to sexual jealousy. Women, however, are not doubtful about their maternity but rather about the possibility that their mates might not continue to provide resources and protection for their children. They would, therefore, be more prone to emotional jealousy.

The next step taken by Buss and his co-workers is to test this hypothesis in a sample of undergraduates, presenting each with scenarios designed to trigger emotional and sexual jealousy. Not only are the expected sex differences found, but physiological indices of emotional arousal, such as heart rate, yield results that are consistent with the feelings that the subjects report.

The final paragraphs of this article acknowledge that these findings might be the result of cultural conditioning, not a process biologically built in through evolution. Nonetheless, Buss et al. point out that their results were predicted *by their evolutionary theorizing, not merely explained after they were obtained. This fact does not prove their theory, but does give it added plausibility.*

From *Psychological Science, 3,* 251–255, 1992.

In species with internal female fertilization and gestation, features of reproductive biology characteristic of all 4,000 species of mammals, including humans, males face an adaptive problem not confronted by females—uncertainty in their paternity of offspring. Maternity probability in mammals rarely or never deviates from 100%. Compromises in paternity probability come at substantial reproductive cost to the male—the loss of mating effort expended, including time, energy, risk, nuptial gifts, and mating opportunity costs. A cuckolded male also loses the female's parental effort, which becomes channeled to a competitor's gametes. The adaptive problem of paternity uncertainty is exacerbated in species in which males engage in some postzygotic parental investment (Trivers, 1972). Males risk investing resources in putative offspring that are genetically unrelated.

These multiple and severe reproductive costs should have imposed strong selection pressure on males to defend against cuckoldry. Indeed, the literature is replete with examples of evolved anti-cuckoldry mechanisms in lions (Bertram, 1975), bluebirds (Power, 1975), doves (Erickson & Zenone, 1976), numerous insect species (Thornhill & Alcock, 1983), and nonhuman primates (Hrdy, 1979). Since humans arguably show more paternal investment than any other of the 200 species of primates (Alexander & Noonan, 1979), this selection pressure should have operated especially intensely on human males. Symons (1979); Daly, Wilson, and Weghorst (1982); and Wilson and Daly (1992) have hypothesized that male sexual jealousy evolved as a solution to this adaptive problem (but see Hupka, 1991, for an alternative view). Men who were indifferent to sexual contact between their mates and other men presumably experienced lower paternity certainty, greater investment in competitors' gametes, and lower reproductive success than did men who were motivated to attend to cues of infidelity and to act on those cues to increase paternity probability.

Although females do not risk maternity uncertainty, in species with biparental care they do risk the potential loss of time, resources, and commitment from a male if he deserts or channels investment to alternative mates (Buss, 1988; Thornhill & Alcock, 1983; Trivers, 1972). The redirection of a mate's investment to another female and her offspring is reproductively costly for a female, especially in environments where offspring suffer in survival and reproductive currencies without investment from both parents.

In human evolutionary history, there were likely to have been at least two situations in which a woman risked losing a man's investment. First, in a monogamous marriage, a woman risked having her mate invest in an alternative woman with whom he was having an affair (partial loss of investment) or risked his departure for an alternative woman (large or total loss of investment). Second, in polygynous marriages, a woman was at risk of having her mate invest to a larger degree in other wives and their offspring at the expense of his investment in her and her offspring. Following Buss (1988) and Mellon (1981), we hypothesize that cues to the development of a deep emotional attachment have been reliable leading indicators to women of potential reduction or loss of their mate's investment.

Jealousy is defined as an emotional "state that is aroused by a perceived threat to a valued relationship or position and motivates behavior aimed at countering the threat. Jealousy is 'sexual' if the valued relationship is sexual" (Daly et al., 1982, p. 11; see also Salovey, 1991; White & Mullen, 1989). It is reasonable to hypothesize that jealousy involves physiological reactions (autonomic arousal) to perceived threat and motivated action to reduce the threat, although this hypothesis has not been examined. Following Symons (1979) and Daly et al. (1982), our central hypothesis is that the events that activate jealousy physiologically and psychologically differ for men and women because of the different adaptive problems they have faced over human evolutionary history in mating contexts. Both sexes are hypothesized to be distressed over both sexual and emotional infidelity, and previous findings bear this out (Buss, 1989). However, these two kinds of infidelity should be weighted differently by men and women. Despite the importance of these hypothesized sex differences, no systematic scientific work has been directed toward verifying or falsifying their existence (but for suggestive data, see Francis, 1977; Teismann & Mosher, 1978; White & Mullen, 1989).

Study 1: Subjective Distress Over a Partner's External Involvement

This study was designed to test the hypothesis that men and women differ in which form of infidelity—sexual versus emotional—triggers more upset and subjective distress, following the adaptive logic just described.

METHOD After reporting age and sex, subjects ($N = 202$ undergraduate students) were presented with the following dilemma:

> Please think of a serious committed romantic relationship that you have had in the past, that you currently have, or that you would like to have. Imagine that you discover that the person with whom you've been seriously involved became interested in someone else. What would distress or upset you more (*please circle only one*):
>
> (A) Imagining your partner forming a deep emotional attachment to that person.
>
> (B) Imagining your partner enjoying passionate sexual intercourse with that other person.
>
> Subjects completed additional questions, and then encountered the next dilemma, with the same instructional set, but followed by a different, but parallel, choice:
>
> (A) Imagining your partner trying different sexual positions with that other person.
>
> (B) Imagining your partner falling in love with that other person.

RESULTS Shown in Figure 1 are the percentages of men and women reporting more distress in response to sexual infidelity than emotional infidelity. The first empirical probe, contrasting distress over a partner's sexual involvement with distress over a partner's deep emotional attachment, yielded a large and highly significant sex dif-

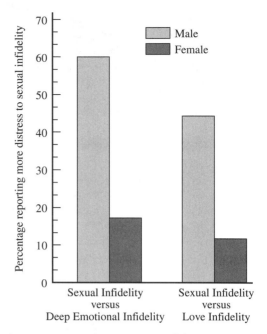

Figure 1 Reported comparisons of distress in response to imagining a partner's sexual or emotional infidelity. The panel shows the percentage of subjects reporting more distress to the sexual infidelity scenario than to the emotional infidelity (left) and the love infidelity (right) scenarios.

ference ($\chi^2 = 47.56$, $df = 3$, $p < .001$).[1] Fully 60% of the male sample reported greater distress over their partner's potential sexual infidelity; in contrast, only 17% of the female sample chose that option, with 83% reporting that they would experience greater distress over a partner's emotional attachment to a rival.

This pattern was replicated with the contrast between sex and love. The magnitude of the sex difference was large, with 32% more men than women reporting greater distress over a partner's sexual involvement with someone else, and the majority of women reporting greater distress over a partner's falling in love with a rival ($\chi^2 = 59.20$, $df = 3$, $p < .001$).

---

[1]This "chi-square" statistic is a test for the randomness of arrangement of outcomes into categories, *df* refers to the degrees of freedom in the design, and the *p* is the "significance," or probability that a χ^2 this large would have been produced by chance if the population value were 0.

Study 2: Physiological Responses to a Partner's External Involvement

Given the strong confirmation of jealousy sex linkage from Study 1, we sought next to test the hypotheses using physiological measures. Our central measures of autonomic arousal were electrodermal activity (EDA), assessed via skin conductance, and pulse rate (PR). Electrodermal activity and pulse rate are indicators of autonomic nervous system activation (Levenson, 1988). Because distress is an unpleasant subjective state, we also included a measure of muscle activity in the brow region of the face—electromyographic (EMG) activity of the *corrugator supercilii* muscle. This muscle is responsible for the furrowing of the brow often seen in facial displays of unpleasant emotion or affect (Fridlund, Ekman, & Oster, 1987). Subjects were asked to image two scenarios in which a partner became involved with someone else—one sexual intercourse scenario and one emotional attachment scenario. Physiological responses were recorded during the imagery trials.

SUBJECTS Subjects were 55 undergraduate students, 32 males and 23 females, each completing a 2-hr laboratory session.

PHYSIOLOGICAL MEASURES Physiological activity was monitored on the running strip chart of a Grass Model 7D polygraph and digitized on a laboratory computer at a 10-Hz rate, following principles recommended in Cacioppo and Tassinary (1990).

Electrodermal activity. Standard Beckman Ag/AgCl surface electrodes, filled with a .05 molar NaCl solution in a Unibase paste, were placed over the middle segments of the first and third fingers of the right hand. A Wheatstone bridge applied a 0.5-V voltage to one electrode.

Pulse rate. A photoplethysmograph was attached to the subject's right thumb to monitor the pulse wave. The signal from this pulse transducer was fed into a Grass Model 7P4 cardiotachometer to detect the rising slope of each pulse wave, with the internal circuitry of the Schmitt trigger individually adjusted for each subject to output PR in beats per minute.

Electromyographic activity. Bipolar EMG recordings were obtained over the *corrugator supercilii* muscle. The EMG signal was relayed to a wideband AC-preamplifier (Grass Model 7P3), where it was band-pass filtered, full-wave rectified, and integrated with a time constant of 0.2 s.[2]

PROCEDURE After electrode attachment, the subject was made comfortable in a reclining chair and asked to relax. After a 5-min waiting period, the experiment began. The subject was alone in the room during the imagery session, with an intercom on for verbal communication. The instructions for the imagery task were written on a form which the subject was requested to read and follow.

Each subject was instructed to engage in three separate images. The first image was designed to be emotionally neutral: "Imagine a time when you were walking to class, feeling neither good nor bad, just neutral." The subject was instructed to press a button when he or she had the image clearly in mind, and to sustain the image until the experimenter said to stop. The button triggered the computer to begin collecting physiological data for 20 s, after which the experimenter instructed the subject to "stop and relax."

The next two images were infidelity images, one sexual and one emotional. The order of presentation of these two images was counterbalanced. The instructions for sexual jealousy imagery were as follows: "Please think of a serious romantic relationship that you have had in the past, that you currently have, or that you would like to have. Now imagine that the person with whom you're seriously involved becomes interested in someone else. *Imagine you find out that your partner is having sex-*

---

[2]The preceding paragraphs are a detailed technical description of state-of-the-art techniques for measuring autonomic arousal, for the use of researchers who might want to replicate these results.

ual intercourse with this other person. Try to feel the feelings you would have if this happened to you."

The instructions for emotional infidelity imagery were identical to the above, except the italicized sentence was replaced with "*Imagine that your partner is falling in love and forming an emotional attachment to that person.*" Physiological data were collected for 20 s following the subject's button press indicating that he or she had achieved the image. Subjects were told to "stop and relax" for 30 s between imagery trials.

RESULTS

Physiological scores. The following scores were obtained: (a) the amplitude of the largest EDA response occurring during each 20-s trial; (b) PR in beats per minute averaged over each 20-s trial; and (c) amplitude of EMG activity over the *corrugator supercilii* averaged over each 20-s trial. Difference scores were computed between the neutral imagery trial and the jealousy induction trials. Within-sex *t* tests revealed no effects for order of presentation of the sexual jealousy image, so data were collapsed over this factor.

Jealousy induction effects. Table 1 shows the mean scores for the physiological measures for men and women in each of the two imagery conditions. Differences in physiological responses to the two jealousy images were examined using paired-comparison *t* tests for each sex separately for EDA, PR, and EMG. The men showed significant increases in EDA during the sexual imagery compared with the emotional imagery ($t = 2.00$, $df = 29$, $p < .05$).[3] Women showed significantly greater EDA to the emotional infidelity image than to the sexual infidelity image ($t = 2.42$, $df = 19$, $p < .05$). A similar pattern was observed with PR. Men showed a substantial increase in PR to both images, but significantly more so in response to the

---

[3]The *t* statistic here indicates that given the number of subjects (related to *df*) in this sample, the data obtained would have occurred less than 5% of the time if there were no sex differences.

TABLE 1			
MEANS AND STANDARD DEVIATIONS ON PHYSIOLOGICAL MEASURES DURING TWO IMAGERY CONDITIONS			
Measure	Imagery type	Mean	SD
Males			
EDA	Sexual	1.30	3.64
	Emotional	−0.11	0.76
Pulse rate	Sexual	4.76	7.80
	Emotional	3.00	5.24
Brow EMG	Sexual	6.75	32.96
	Emotional	1.16	6.60
Females			
EDA	Sexual	−0.07	0.49
	Emotional	0.21	0.78
Pulse rate	Sexual	2.25	4.68
	Emotional	2.57	4.37
Brow EMG	Sexual	3.03	8.38
	Emotional	8.12	25.60

Note. Measures are expressed as changes from the neutral image condition. EDA is in microsiemen units, pulse rate is in beats per minute, and EMG is in microvolt units.

sexual infidelity image ($t = 2.29$, $df = 31$, $p < .05$). Women showed elevated PR to both images, but not differentially so. The results of the *corrugator* EMG were similar, although less strong. Men showed greater brow contraction to the sexual infidelity image, and women showed the opposite pattern, although results with this nonautonomic measure did not reach significance ($t = 1.12$, $df = 30$, $p < .14$, for males; $t = −1.24$, $df = 22$, $p < .12$, for females). The elevated EMG contractions for both jealousy induction trials in both sexes support the hypothesis that the effect experienced is negative.

*   *   *

Discussion

The results of the empirical studies support the hypothesized sex linkages in the activators of jealousy. Study 1 found large sex differences in reports of the subjective distress individuals would experience upon exposure to a partner's sexual infidelity versus emotional infidelity. Study 2 found a sex linkage in autonomic arousal to imagined sexual infidelity versus emotional infidelity; the results were particularly strong for the EDA and PR. * * *

These studies are limited in ways that call for additional research. First, they pertain to a single age group and culture. Future studies could explore the degree to which these sex differences transcend different cultures and age groups. Two clear evolutionary psychological predictions are (a) that male sexual jealousy and female commitment jealousy will be greater in cultures where males invest heavily in children, and (b) that male sexual jealousy will diminish as the age of the male's mate increases because her reproductive value decreases. Second, future studies could test the alternative hypotheses that the current findings reflect (a) domain-specific psychological adaptations to cuckoldry versus potential investment loss or (b) a more domain-general mechanism such that any thoughts of sex are more interesting, arousing, and perhaps disturbing to men whereas any thoughts of love are more interesting, arousing, and perhaps disturbing to women, and hence that such responses are not specific to jealousy or infidelity. Third, emotional and sexual infidelity are clearly correlated, albeit imperfectly, and a sizable percentage of men in Study 1 reported greater distress to a partner's emotional infidelity. Emotional infidelity may signal sexual infidelity and vice versa, and hence both sexes should become distressed at both forms (see Buss, 1989). Future research could profitably explore in greater detail the correlation of these forms of infidelity as well as the sources of within-sex variation.

Within the constraints of the current studies, we can conclude that the sex differences found here generalize across both psychological and physiological methods—demonstrating an empirical robustness in the observed effect. The degree to which these sex-linked elicitors correspond to the hypothesized sex-linked adaptive problems lends support to the evolutionary psychological framework from which they were derived. Alternative theoretical frameworks, including those that invoke culture, social construction, deconstruction,

arbitrary parental socialization, and structural powerlessness, undoubtedly could be molded post hoc to fit the findings—something perhaps true of any set of findings. None but the Symons (1979) and Daly et al. (1982) evolutionary psychological frameworks, however, generated the sex-differentiated predictions in advance and on the basis of sound evolutionary reasoning. The recent finding that male sexual jealousy is the leading cause of spouse battering and homicide across cultures worldwide (Daly & Wilson, 1988a, 1988b) offers suggestive evidence that these sex differences have large social import and may be species-wide.

References

Alexander, R. D., & Noonan, K. M. (1979). Concealment of ovulation, parental care, and human social evolution. In N. Chagnon & W. Irons (Eds.), *Evolutionary biology and human social behavior* (pp. 436–453). North Scituate, MA: Duxbury.

Bertram, B. C. R. (1975). Social factors influencing reproduction in wild lions. *Journal of Zoology, 177,* 463–482.

Buss, D. M. (1988). From vigilance to violence: Tactics of mate retention. *Ethology and Sociobiology, 9,* 291–317.

Buss, D. M. (1989). Conflict between the sexes: Strategic interference and the evocation of anger and upset. *Journal of Personality and Social Psychology, 56,* 735–747.

Cacioppo, J. T., & Tassinary, L. G. (Eds.). (1990). *Principles of psychophysiology: Physical, social, and inferential elements.* Cambridge, England: Cambridge University Press.

Daly, M., & Wilson, M. (1988a). Evolutionary social psychology and family violence. *Science, 242,* 519–524.

Daly, M., & Wilson, M. (1988b). *Homicide.* Hawthorne, NY: Aldine.

Daly, M., Wilson, M., & Weghorst, S. J. (1982). Male sexual jealousy. *Ethology and Sociobiology, 3,* 11–27.

Erickson, C. J., & Zenone, P. G. (1976). Courtship differences in male ring doves: Avoidance of cuckoldry? *Science, 192,* 1353–1354.

Francis, J. L. (1977). Toward the management of heterosexual jealousy. *Journal of Marriage and Family Counseling, 10,* 61–69.

Fridlund, A., Ekman, P., & Oster, J. (1987). Facial expressions of emotion. In A. Siegman & S. Feldstein (Eds.), *Nonverbal behavior and communication* (pp. 143–224). Hillsdale, NJ: Erlbaum.

Hrdy, S. B. G. (1979). Infanticide among animals: A review, classification, and examination of the implications for the reproductive strategies of females. *Ethology and Sociobiology, 1,* 14–40.

Hupka, R. B. (1991). The motive for the arousal of romantic jealousy: Its cultural origin. In P. Salovey (Ed.), *The psychology of jealousy and envy* (pp. 252–270). New York: Guilford Press.

Levenson, R. W. (1988). Emotion and the autonomic nervous system: A prospectus for research on autonomic specificity.

In H. Wagner (Ed.), *Social psychophysiology: Theory and clinical applications* (pp. 17–42). London: Wiley.

Mellon, L. W. (1981). *The evolution of love*. San Francisco: W. H. Freeman.

Power, H. W. (1975). Mountain bluebirds: Experimental evidence against altruism. *Science, 189*, 142–143.

Salovey, P. (Ed.). (1991). *The psychology of jealousy and envy*. New York: Guilford Press.

Symons, D. (1979). *The evolution of human sexuality*. New York: Oxford University Press.

Teismann, M. W., & Mosher, D. L. (1978). Jealous conflict in dating couples. *Psychological Reports, 42*, 1211–1216.

Thornhill, R., & Alcock, J. (1983). *The evolution of insect mating systems*. Cambridge, MA: Harvard University Press.

Trivers, R. (1972). Parental investment and sexual selection. In B. Campbell (Ed.), *Sexual selection and the descent of man, 1871–1971* (pp. 136–179). Chicago: Aldine.

White, G. L., & Mullen, P. E. (1989). *Jealousy: Theory, research, and clinical strategies*. New York: Guilford Press.

Wilson, M., & Daly, M. (1992). The man who mistook his wife for a chattel. In J. Barkow, L. Cosmides, & J. Tooby (Eds.), *The adapted mind: Evolutionary psychology and the generation of culture*. New York: Oxford University Press.

THE SEXUAL OVERPERCEPTION BIAS: EVIDENCE OF A SYSTEMATIC BIAS IN MEN FROM A SURVEY OF NATURALLY OCCURRING EVENTS

Martie G. Haselton

One of the most important developments in psychology in the past decade or so has been increasing attention to the implications of evolutionary theory. While the theory of evolution has long been a key part of biology at all levels, Darwin is a relative latecomer to psychology. The implication for psychology is that behavioral patterns that have promoted survival and reproduction in the past ought to be most prevalent in our species today, whereas patterns that harm survival and reproduction should tend to be selected out. This principle raises important questions about the frequent finding in psychology that people are cognitively "biased" in various ways. If the human mind is biased, how did the species ever survive to this point?

In the present article, the evolutionary psychologist Martie Haselton offers an answer, called "error management theory" (EMT). The premise of the theory is that some errors are more costly than others. For example, if a fire alarm is oversensitive, it will buzz too often and annoy the homeowner. But if it is undersensitive, the house may burn down and kill the homeowner. Clearly, it is preferable to have an oversensitive alarm compared to an undersensitive one (and they do seem to be designed that way). In the same way, Haselton suggests, various human cognitive biases may have benefits that outweigh their costs, at least for some individuals.

One of these might be the bias in males she calls the "sexual overperception bias." This is the name for the tendency of males to think that females are more sexually interested (in them) than they really are. According to EMT, this may be an adaptive bias, because it prevents males from foregoing mating opportunities even while it sets them up for repeated rejection. Anecdotes on this phenomenon abound, and we would bet the reader has a few of his or her own. In any case, Haselton both documents the existence of this bias and some of the variables that influence its frequency. For example, people with high "mate value" appear to be more prone to be misperceived than others.

The way one relates to the opposite sex is surely an important part of one's personality. Haselton's article proposes that to some degree differences between men and women in the way they relate to each other can be explained by evolution and by EMT, and that variation within sex can to some degree be accounted for in the same way.

From *Journal of Research in Personality, 37,* 34–47, 2003.

Mammalian males and females faced different selection pressures during their evolution. According to Trivers theory of parental investment (Trivers, 1972), the sex with a greater obligatory investment in reproduction, typically the female, should evolve to be choosy in selecting a mate. The sex with lower obligatory investment, typically the male, should evolve to be less choosy and to be highly competitive for access to members of the high investing sex.

The logic of parental investment theory suggests that for males the fitness costs of missed sexual opportunities will often be greater than the costs of some lost time or effort wasted on unsuccessful courtship (Alcock, 1993). Within a given population, males who miss reproductive opportunities with some regularity will be out-reproduced by males who do not. This is not true for most females. The reproductive variance among females, including human females, is typically far more constrained because of limits imposed by the time and energetic costs of gestation and offspring care (Trivers, 1972). At any point in time, females may receive low to non-existent marginal reproductive benefits of additional mating opportunities because of current pregnancy, lactational amenorrhea, or because they have ready access to another fertile mate (Symons, 1979). Although courtship effort is costly for males, in the currency of differential reproduction these costs will often pale in comparison to the costs of missed mating opportunities.

According to error management theory (EMT; Haselton & Buss, 2000), asymmetries in the recurrent costs of errors in inference can lead to the evolution of biases, even when these biases result in greater rates of inferential error. This principle applies in artifact engineering (Green & Swets, 1966) when, for example, fire alarms are designed with highly sensitive triggers that reduce the likelihood of missed fires. The principle also applies to the design of the body and its immune system, which often overresponds to disease threats (Nesse & Williams, 1998). EMT proposes that the same principle should apply to psychological design. In signal detection contexts in which there is an asymmetry in the reproductive costs of errors, all else equal, a bias should evolve toward making the less costly error (Haselton & Buss, 2000). If males face greater costs of missing sexual opportunities than of pursuing disinterested females, they should be selected to err on the side of pursuit, even if this causes them to make more errors overall.

Experimental evidence suggests that human males may indeed possess this bias. In laboratory experiments (e.g., Abbey, 1982; Saal, Johnson, & Weber, 1989), photographic and video stimuli experiments (e.g., Abbey & Melby, 1986; Shotland & Craig, 1988), and minimal experiments using written scenarios or brief descriptions of dating cues (Haselton & Buss, 2000), researchers have compared men's perceptions of women's sexual intent with women's perceptions of women's sexual intent. Men's estimates of women's sexual intent are consistently higher than are women's. This pattern holds when men's perceptions are compared to women's perceptions of their own sexual intent and when compared to women's perceptions of third-party women's intent (Haselton & Buss, 2000). When women's interpretations of men's behavior have been examined, there has been little evidence of bias (Abbey, 1982; Haselton & Buss, 2000).

A lingering question is whether this mistaken inference in men occurs regularly in the world outside of the laboratory. Evidence from the sole naturalistic survey, conducted by Abbey (1987), provides a provisional answer. In the study, women and men indicated whether a member of the opposite sex had ever misconstrued their friendly behavior as sexual interest. Significantly more women (72%) than men (60%) reported that a member of the opposite sex had overestimated their sexual interest (Abbey, 1987). Although this study suggested that sexual overperceptions occurred in the natural world and were experienced by more women than men, it remains unclear whether men *systematically* overperceived women's sexual intent. There are two potential alternative explanations for Abbey's finding.

First, based upon evidence that women may be superior to men in decoding non-verbal signals (Hall, 1978), one might infer that a greater number of overperceptions by men simply reflects a greater rate of decoding error in general. Second, based on emerging evidence that women's initial communications of sexual interest are more ambiguous than are men's (Grammer, Kruck, Juette, & Fink, 2000), one might conclude that men make a greater number of erroneous inferences because women's sexual signals are more difficult to decode. In sum, the evidence from Abbey's survey is consistent with several different interpretations.

The current study sought to address the ambiguity of Abbey's results by asking men and women about sexual *overperception* experiences (false alarms) and sexual *underperception* experiences (misses). If men have a false alarm bias, women should report more experiences in which a man overestimated her sexual intent than in which a man underestimated it. Alternatively, if there is no difference in reports of the types of misperceptions women have experienced, the sex difference documented in Abbey's survey (1987) could be a result of poorer mind-reading ability in men than in women or greater ambiguity in women's sexual behavior. A second goal of this study was to examine whether women possess a bias in interpreting men's sexual communications.

A third goal of this study was to obtain several pieces of additional information not obtained in prior studies. Whereas the past study assessed the overall number of sexual overperceptions men and women had ever experienced (Abbey, 1987)—arguably a very heavy burden on memory—this study collected information on the frequency of overperception and underperception experiences within the delimited time period of one year. In addition, this study assessed several potential predictors of the frequency of sexual misperceptions that were not tested previously. These include relationship experience, attractiveness as a mate ("mate value"), and sociosexuality (Simpson & Gangestad, 1991).

Haselton and Buss (2000) proposed that men possess a false alarm bias designed to err on the side of overperceiving women's sexual intent but that women possess no such bias in interpreting men's actions. Consistent with this hypothesis, the following predictions were advanced:

1. The percentage of women who report having at least one past experience in which a man overperceived their sexual intent will be larger than the percentage who report an experience in which a man underperceived their sexual intent.
2. Women will report more instances within the last year in which their sexual intent was overperceived by a man than in which it was underperceived.
3. Differences between men's sexual overperception and underperception experiences should be non-existent or markedly smaller than the differences between women's experiences.

Method

Participants

Participants were undergraduate students recruited from an introductory psychology course at a large university in Texas. They received partial credit for a course research requirement. The sample consisted of 114 heterosexual men and 102 heterosexual women. The average age of the men was 19.17 ($SD = .92$) and of the women was 19.18 ($SD = 2.45$).

Procedure

In groups of 5–15 same-sex individuals, participants completed questionnaire packets that included a biographical information survey followed by the sexual misperception questionnaire. Participants were assured that their responses would be completely confidential and that any identifying information, such as their name or social security number (which appeared on their consent forms), would be stored separately from their questionnaires. After collecting the consent forms, the researcher distributed large unmarked envelopes along with the questionnaire packet and instructed participants to place their completed questionnaire in the envelope, seal it, and drop it into a box containing other completed questionnaires. The researcher explained that the envelopes would not be opened until the study was completed. The attending researcher was always a member of the same sex as the participants.

Instruments

Biographical and personality information. The biographical information form included a series of questions designed to assess participants' mate value. Each item was stated in the following form: "Compared with other women [men] you know who are about your age, *how desirable do men [women] find you as a long-term mate or marriage partner?*" The italicized portion of this question differed across items to assess various aspects of mate value. In addition to desirability as a long-term mate, these items asked (a) "how desirable do men [women] find you a short-term mate or casual sex partner?" (b) "how attractive is your body to men [women]?" (c) "how attractive is your face to men [women]?" (d) what is your present financial status?" (e) "what is your estimated future financial status?" (f) "how high are you in social status at the present time?" (g) "what is your esti-

mated future social status?" and (h) "how sexy would men [women] say you are?" These items were averaged to form a composite score ($\alpha = .85$). To assess participants' experience in long-term relationships, a variable that could be related to men's and women's ability to accurately convey their intentions to members of the opposite sex, the participants were asked how many "serious romantic relationships" they had had in the past. The sociosexuality inventory (SOI; Simpson & Gangestad, 1991), a measure of attitudes and behaviors concerning causal sex, was also included in the biographical questionnaire. A composite score was computed according to the guidelines outlined by Simpson and Gangestad (1991). One item on the SOI asked how often participants sexually fantasized about individuals other than their current relationship partner. Because only about half of the participants were currently involved in relationships, inclusion of this item dramatically reduced the number of participants for whom SOI scores could be computed. For this reason, the item was dropped from the composite score.

Sexual misperception questionnaire. The following instructions appeared at the top of the questionnaire:

> Has your behavior ever been misinterpreted by a member of the opposite sex? Please respond to the following items with a YES or NO response as indicated. If you did experience the event in question, please indicate approximately how many times this event happened to you in the last year. If the event has not occurred in the last year, please write in a zero in the blank.

The items included in this instrument were based on Abbey's (1987) sexual misperception study. Abbey used a single misperception item that read as follows:

> Have you ever been friendly to someone of the opposite sex only to discover that she/he had misperceived your friendliness as a sexual come-on; you were just trying to be nice but she/he assumed you were sexually attracted to him/her. (Abbey, 1987, p. 176).

To prevent potential confusion, this item was broken down into the following two items in the questionnaire.

1. Have you ever been friendly to someone of the opposite sex only to discover that he [she] had misperceived your friendliness as a sexual come-on?
2. Have you ever been in a situation with a member of the opposite sex in which you were just trying to be nice but he [she] assumed you were sexually attracted to him [her]?

To examine sexual underperception experiences ("misses"), the following reversed items were included in the study:

1. Have you ever attempted to sexually "come-on" to someone of the opposite sex only to discover that he [she] had misperceived your sexual interest as friendliness?
2. Have you ever been in a situation with a member of the opposite sex in which you were sexually attracted to him [her] but he [she] assumed you were just trying to be nice?

Results

SEX DIFFERENCES IN MISINTERPRETATION EXPERIENCES

Factorial ANOVAs were conducted with sex of subject as a between-subjects factor and type of misperception (false alarm vs. miss) as a within-subjects factor. * * * The two versions of each item were combined to produce composite indices. The categorical response data were combined in the following way: if the participant responded with a *Yes* to either question, his or her response was recorded as a *Yes*, if he or she responded with a *No* to both items the response was recorded as a *No*. The frequency data were averaged across the two versions of the item. There were four resulting dependent measures: (a) combined sexual overperception experiences (Yes vs. No), (b) combined sexual underperception experiences (Yes vs. No),

(c) average number of sexual overperception experiences within the last year, and (d) average number of sexual underperception experiences within the last year.

For the categorical response data, there was a significant interaction of sex and type of misperception error ($F(1, 208) = 16.28, p < .001$; see Figure 1).[1] Simple effects tests showed that more women reported experiencing sexual overperceptions than sexual underperceptions ($F(1, 208) = 34.05, p < .001$). There was not a significant difference between the number of men who experienced these two types of misperception errors ($F(1, 208) = .13, p > .05$). These results confirm predictions 1 and 3.

The identical pattern of results was obtained for the frequency data. There was a significant interaction of sex and type of error ($F(1, 208) = 15.81, p < .001$; see Figure 2). Simple effects tests showed that women reported being victims of more sexual overperception errors than sexual underperception errors ($F(1, 208) = 45.68, p < .001$). The difference between these experiences for men was not significant ($F(1, 208) = 2.08, p > .05$). These results confirm predictions 2 and 3.

In summary, the experiences women and men reported are consistent with the hypothesis that men possess a sexual overperception bias, but women do not. More women experienced at least one event in which a member of the opposite sex overestimated their sexual intent than in which a member of the opposite sex underestimated it. The same pattern was not observed for men. Roughly equal numbers of men reported being victims of each type of misperception. The same effects were observed when men and women were asked how many separate misperception errors they experienced in the last year. Women reported being victims of quantitatively more sexual overperception experiences than underperception experiences,

---

[1]The *F* statistic from the analysis of variance, in conjunction with the degrees of freedom in the design (given within parentheses), yields an estimate of the probability that the difference in means could have been produced by chance alone.

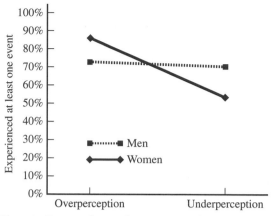

Figure 1. Percent of respondents reporting that a member of the opposite sex misperceived their sexual intent. Overperception: participant's friendly behavior was construed as evidence of sexual interest. Underperception: participant was sexually interested in perceiver, but his or her sexual intent was construed as mere friendliness.

whereas there was no difference between these experiences for men.

PREDICTORS OF SEXUAL MISPERCEPTIONS

Dependent variables. Two misperception variables were constructed for the regression analysis. The first was computed by adding the number of sexual overperception experiences to the number of underperception experiences to produce an index of the overall number of errors experienced within the last year. The second was computed by dividing the number of overperceptions by the total number of misperceptions. This produced an estimate of false alarm bias—the proportion of misinterpretations that were false alarms as opposed to misses. If all of the misperceptions a participant experienced were false alarms, his or her score would be 1. If all of the misperceptions were misses, his or her score would be 0.

Age and relationship experience (number of long-term relationships) were entered first into a hierarchical regression analysis along with the first focal predictor, mate value. Sociosexuality was entered at the next step. Two participants had extreme SOI scores falling within 4 and 5 standard deviations above the mean. To prevent undue in-

fluence of these scores, they were converted to scores two standard deviations above the mean. Sex, with males coded −1 and females coded +1, was entered last to see if sex predicted above and beyond within-sex individual differences. The interactions of sex and each predictor were also tested in the regression models. None were significant ($ps > .05$), therefore none of these interaction terms were included in the final regression analysis.

Predictors of overall error rates. * * * Mate value was a significant or marginally significant predictor of misperceptions. The relationship was positive, suggesting that individuals higher in mate value experienced more misperceptions by members of the opposite sex. SOI was also positively associated with misperceptions. This relationship suggests that individuals oriented toward short-term sexual relationships experienced more misperceptions than did long-term oriented individuals. Sex did not predict the overall number of misperception experiences.

Predictors of false alarm bias. Mate value was a significant positive predictor of false alarm rates. This suggests that the relationship of mate value and number of misperceptions (see above) may be

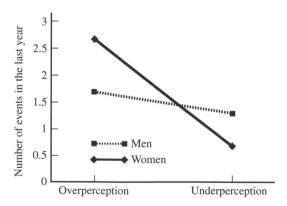

Figure 2. Number of misperceptions of sexual intent by members of the opposite sex within the last year. Overperception: participant's friendly behavior was construed as evidence of sexual interest. Underperception: participant was sexually interested in perceiver, but his or her sexual intent was construed as mere friendliness.

driven by the tendency of high mate value individuals to elicit false alarm errors by members of the opposite sex. SOI was not a significant predictor in the analysis ($ps > .10$). Sex predicted false alarm rates above and beyond all of the individual difference variables ($p < .001$).

Discussion

SEX AS A PREDICTOR OF SEXUAL OVERPERCEPTION EXPERIENCES

The results of this study complement results observed in laboratory and experimental designs (e.g., Abbey, 1982; Haselton & Buss, 2000). Women reported more experiences in which men overperceived their sexual interest than in which men underperceived it. In contrast, men's reports of women's overperception and underperception errors did not differ. Sex predicted false alarm rates even after controlling for potentially relevant individual differences, such as relationship experience, mate value, and sociosexuality. Whereas sex predicted false alarm rates, it did not predict the overall number of errors experienced. These results make a new contribution to the literature by showing that (1) evidence of an overperception bias in men is not limited to potentially artificial experiments, (2) in reports of naturally occurring misperceptions there is evidence of a bias in men but not in women, as predicted by the EMT account, and (3) the prior finding that women have experienced more sexual overperceptions than men (Abbey, 1987) cannot be attributed solely to greater ambiguity in women's signaling behavior or to better mind-reading ability in women as compared to men.

WITHIN-SEX INDIVIDUAL DIFFERENCES IN MISPERCEPTION EXPERIENCES

In this study several individual differences in susceptibility to misperception were documented. First, the sociosexual orientation of the target was related to the overall number of misperceptions experienced, perhaps indicating that short-term sex-

ual strategists frequently put themselves "out on the market," leading to a greater number of opportunities for others to misinterpret their true intentions. Second, mate value was linked to the rate of false alarms. There are several possible interpretations of this effect. One explanation is consistent with the logic of EMT. It is possible that men and women are biased toward overperceiving the sexual interest of high mate value individuals because missing their potential interest was more costly over selective history than was overestimating their interest.

A second possibility is that high mate value individuals are simply "hit on" more often than those lower in mate value. This increased rate of positive behaviors by others could produce a higher rate of false-positive errors as perceived by the targets. However, in order for this possibility to account for the results, the targets of misperceptions would have to infer that the display of interest by the actor was caused by the actor's belief that the target was sexually interested in him or her. Displays of interest are likely to be contingent upon inferred reciprocal interest to some degree, but many clearly are not. When groups of young men or women boisterously admire an attractive passerby, they are clearly not inferring that the passerby noticed them and found them attractive. Likewise, admiring glances or comments at singles bars do not require their target's notice or interest. In sum, it remains unclear whether the higher base rate of positive behaviors can account for this finding, but it is a possibility that should be borne in mind for future study.

METHODOLOGICAL LIMITATIONS

* * *

There are several weaknesses of the current study that are related to its naturalistic character. These weaknesses largely reflect the familiar trade-off between internal and external validity that researchers face when selecting between controlled experiments and more naturalistic designs. The results in the current study, although subject to some potential methodological problems, nicely complement the results in more controlled laboratory interactions. Strong convergent results obtained using differing methods are unlikely to be attributable to problems that are unshared by those methods. Thus, the laboratory and naturalistic survey methods are cross-validating and mutually supporting of their common conclusions.

WHY DO MEN OVERPERCEIVE WOMEN'S SEXUAL INTENT?

The collective evidence from experiments and surveys of naturally occurring events suggests that men possess a false-positive bias in interpreting women's sexual interest. This evidence alone, of course, is not sufficient to unambiguously support the EMT explanation. Alternative models include the general oversexualization hypothesis (Abbey, 1982, 1991), the media hypothesis (e.g., Abbey, 1991), and the default model hypothesis (Shotland & Craig, 1988; see Haselton & Buss, 2000 for a summary and evaluation of these models). Some effects predicted by the EMT model, but not directly derivable from alternative models, have been tested and supported (Haselton & Buss, 2000). For example, Haselton and Buss (2000) showed that men do not overperceive their sister's sexual interest in a third-party man.

Further testable predictions from the error management perspective include the following: (1) men's bias should be elicited primarily by women of reproductive age (not preadolescent or postmenopausal women); (2) men's bias should emerge even in cultures not exposed to Western media—as long as there is sufficient ambiguity in the meaning of women's sexual communications, it should be possible to document a false-positive bias in men; (3) similarly, within cultures, it should be possible to document men's bias across different demographic groups, including among men varying in age, ethnicity, and education levels.

IMPLICATIONS OF THE SEXUAL OVERPERCEPTION BIAS

Recently 13 employees of the Safeway supermarket chain, 12 of them women, filed grievances over the supermarket's "service-with-smile" policy (Curtis, 1998). The employees reported that customers, nearly all of whom were men, misconstrued their obligatory friendliness as sexual interest. One employee reported that the unwanted sexual attention and harassment was so extreme that she was forced to hide in the back room to avoid customers who repeatedly "hit on" her and followed her to her car. As this incident suggests, sexual overperception by men can lead to sexual harassment and sexual aggression (Abbey, 1991; Abbey, McAuslan, & Ross, 1998; Bondurant & Donat, 1999, but also see Malamuth & Brown, 1994).

An additional implication of men's bias not noted by prior researchers is a problem it presents for men themselves. Buss and Haselton (Buss, 1994; Haselton, 1999) hypothesize that women can benefit from leading some men to believe that they are slightly more sexually interested than they actually are. A man who is motivated to pursue sex with a woman, and who believes she is interested in him, might be more inclined to do her favors, protect her from harm, or might simply give her flattering attention that can increase on-lookers' perceptions of her mate value. Co-evolutionary models suggest that because manipulation is costly, the exploited party (in this case the man) should not tolerate it for long (Krebs & Dawkins, 1984). However, Wiley (1994) has shown that deception can remain evolutionarily stable when the costs of inferential errors differ reliably over time. Senders can continue to successfully deceive receivers because the benefits of a bias to a receiver (e.g., avoiding a "miss") off-set the costs of moderate levels of deceivability (Wiley, 1994). In sum, the sexual overperception bias not only leads men to genuinely misperceive women's sexual interest, but it can also set the stage for deceptive manipulation of men by women.

CONCLUSION

Although there is now a reasonably large experimental literature documenting the sexual overperception effect in United States undergraduates, further research on this topic remains important.

This research will help to adjudicate between competing explanations for the purpose of further theoretical development. There are also significant practical implications of this research. Knowledge of the causes and contexts in which sexual miscommunication occurs will aid our understanding of conflict between the sexes, not only by enhancing our understanding of the causes of sexual victimization, as many researchers have persuasively argued, but also by enhancing our understanding of the dynamics of communication when conflicts of interest exist.

References

Abbey, A. (1982). Sex differences in attributions for friendly behavior: Do males misperceive females' friendliness? *Journal of Personality and Social Psychology, 42,* 830–838.

Abbey, A. (1987). Misperceptions of friendly behavior as sexual interest: A survey of naturally occurring instances. *Psychology of Women Quarterly, 11,* 173–194.

Abbey, A. (1991). Misperception as an antecedent of acquaintance rape: A consequence of ambiguity in communication between men and women. In A. Parrot & L. Bechhofer (Eds.). *Acquaintance rape: The hidden crime* (pp. 96–111). New York: Wiley & Sons.

Abbey, A., McAuslan, P., & Ross, L. T. (1998). Sexual assault perpetration by college men: The role of misperception of sexual intent and sexual beliefs and experiences. *Journal of Social and Clinical Psychology, 17,* 167–195.

Abbey, A., & Melby, C. (1986). The effects of nonverbal cues on gender differences in perceptions of sexual intent. *Sex Roles, 15,* 283–289.

Alcock, J. (1993). *Animal behavior: An evolutionary approach* (5th ed.). Sunderland, MA: Basic.

Bondurant, B., & Donat, P. L. (1999). Perceptions of women's sexual interest and acquaintance rape: The role of sexual overperception and affective attitudes. *Psychology of Women Quarterly, 23,* 691–705.

Buss, D. M. (1994). *The evolution of desire: Strategies of human mating.* New York: Basic Books.

Curtis, K. (1998). *Safeway clerks object to smile rule.* Associated Press.

Grammer, K., Kruck, K., Juette, A., & Fink, B. (2000). Nonverbal behavior as courtship signals: The role of control and choice in selecting partners. *Evolution & Human Behavior, 21,* 371–390.

Green, D. M., & Swets, J. A. (1966). *Signal detection and psychophysics,* New York: Wiley.

Hall, J. (1978). Gender effects in decoding non-verbal cues. *Psychological Bulletin, 4,* 845–857.

Haselton, M. G. (1999, June). Sex, lies, and strategic interference: The psychology of deception between the sexes. Human Behavior and Evolution Society Conference, Salt Lake City, Utah.

Haselton, M. G., & Buss, D. M. (2000). Error management theory: A new perspective on biases in cross-sex mind reading. *Journal of Personality and Social Psychology, 78,* 81–91.

Krebs, J. R., & Dawkins, R. (1984). Animal signals: Mind-reading and manipulation. In J. R. Krebs & N. B. Davies (Eds.), *Behavioral ecology: An evolutionary approach* (2nd ed., pp. 380–402). Oxford: Blackwell.

Malamuth, N. M., & Brown, L. M. (1994). Sexually aggressive men's perceptions of women's communications: Testing three explanations. *Journal of Personality and Social Psychology, 67,* 699–712.

Nesse, R. M., & Williams, G. C. (1998). Evolution and the origins of disease. *Scientific American, 11,* 86–93.

Saal, F. E., Johnson, C. B., & Weber, N. (1989). Friendly or sexy? It may depend on whom you ask. *Psychology of Women Quarterly, 13,* 263–276.

Shotland, R. L., & Craig, J. M. (1988). Can men and women differentiate between friendly and sexually interested behavior? *Social Psychology Quarterly, 51,* 66–73.

Simpson, J. A., & Gangestad, S. W. (1991). Individual differences in sociosexuality: Evidence for convergent and discriminant validity. *Journal of Personality & Social Psychology, 60,* 870–883.

Symons, D. (1979). *The evolution of human sexuality.* New York: Oxford.

Trivers, R. L. (1972). Parental investment and sexual selection. In B. Campbell (Ed.), *Sexual selection and the descent of man: 1871–1971* (pp. 136–179). Chicago: Aldine.

Wiley, H. R. (1994). Errors, exaggeration, and deception in animal communication. In L. A. Real (Ed.), *Behavioral mechanisms in evolutionary ecology* (pp. 157–189). Chicago: University of Chicago.

The Origins of Sex Differences in Human Behavior: Evolved Dispositions Versus Social Roles

Alice H. Eagly and Wendy Wood

The increasing fame and popularity of evolutionary explanations of behavior such as seen in the previous two selections have been accompanied by an increasing amount of criticism. Not all critics offer alternative explanations of their own, however. Alice Eagly and Wendy Wood, to their credit, do have an explanation of widespread sex differences in behavior that is different from the evolutionary account. Their alternative, which they call "social structural theory," is that it is the structure of society rather than biological evolution that determines differences between what men and women desire and view as important. So the next selection offers both a critique of some evolutionary reasoning and an alternative framework for understanding some important data.

Although Eagly and Wood believe that evolutionary theorizing about personality is mostly wrong, to some degree the evolutionary and structural approaches address different data, rather than necessarily being incompatible. Evolutionary theorists such as Buss and Haselton explain the components of sex differences that seem to be universal across cultures, whereas social structural theory addresses the components that vary. Thus, in the data that are reinterpreted in this article, Buss (who gathered the data) focused on how the direction of the sex difference was the same in all cultures, whereas Eagly and Wood address how the degree of difference differs across cultures. Both components are clearly important and perhaps deserve to be examined together in an integrated approach.

Eagly and Wood's article can be read as an argument for social change. If, as they maintain, sex differences in behavior are a function of social structure, then if society can be changed, behavioral change will soon follow. The evolutionary account of these differences can be taken to imply that things will not be so simple, because any changes in social structure will interact with and perhaps in some cases be resisted by innate biological preferences, propensities, and mechanisms.

From *American Psychologist*, 54, 408–423, 1999.

As more research psychologists have become willing to acknowledge that some aspects of social behavior, personality, and abilities differ between women and men (e.g., Eagly, 1995; Halpern, 1997), their attention has begun to focus on the causes of these differences. Debates about causes center, at least in part, on determining what can be considered the basic or ultimate causes of sex differences. Theories of sex differences that address causes at this level are termed in this article *origin theories* (Archer, 1996). In such theories, causation flows from a basic cause to sex-differentiated behavior, and biological, psychological, and social processes mediate the relation between the basic cause and behavior. In this article, we consider two types of origin theories: One of these implicates evolved psychological dispositions, and the other implicates social structure. Evolutionary psychology, as illustrated in the work of Buss (1995a), Kenrick and Keefe (1992), and Tooby and Cosmides (1992), thus represents the first type of origin theory, and social psychological theories that emphasize social structure represent the second type of origin theory (e.g., Eagly, 1987; Eagly, Wood, & Diekman, in press; Lorenzi-Cioldi, 1998; Ridgeway, 1991; West & Zimmerman, 1987; Wiley, 1995).

In the origin theory proposed by evolutionary psychologists, the critical causal arrow points from evolutionary adaptations to psychological sex differences. Because women and men possess sex-specific evolved mechanisms, they differ psychologically and tend to occupy different social roles. In contrast, in the social structural origin theory, the critical causal arrow points from social structure to psychological sex differences. Because men and women tend to occupy different social roles, they become psychologically different in ways that adjust them to these roles.

One important feature is shared by these two origin theories: Both offer a functional analysis of behavior that emphasizes adjustment to environ-mental conditions. However, the two schools of thought differ radically in their analysis of the nature and timing of the adjustments that are most important to sex-differentiated behavior. Evolutionary psychologists believe that females and males faced different pressures in primeval environments and that the sexes' differing reproductive status was the key feature of ancestral life that framed sex-typed adaptive problems. The resolutions of these problems produced sex-specific evolved mechanisms that humans carry with them as a species and that are held to be the root cause of sex-differentiated behavior. Although evolutionary psychologists readily acknowledge the abstract principle that environmental conditions can influence the development and expression of evolved dispositions, they have given limited attention to variation of sex differences in response to individual, situational, and cultural conditions (e.g., Archer, 1996; Buss, 1995b; Buss & Kenrick, 1998). For example, Buss (1998, p. 421) emphasized "universal or near-universal sex differences" in preferences for long-term mates.

Social structuralists maintain that the situations faced by women and men are quite variable across societies and historical periods as social organization changes in response to technological, ecological, and other transformations. From a social structural perspective, a society's division of labor between the sexes is the engine of sex-differentiated behavior, because it summarizes the social constraints under which men and women carry out their lives. Sex differences are viewed as accommodations to the differing restrictions and opportunities that a society maintains for its men and women, and sex-differentiated behavior is held to be contingent on a range of individual, situational, and cultural conditions (see Deaux & LaFrance, 1998). Despite this emphasis on the social environment, social structuralists typically acknowledge the importance of some genetically mediated sex differences. Physical differences between the sexes, particularly men's greater size and strength and women's childbearing and lactation, are very important because they interact with shared cultural beliefs, social organization, and the

Author's note. Thanks are extended to David Buss for making available for reanalysis data from his 37 cultures study (Buss, 1989b; Buss et al., 1990).

demands of the economy to influence the role assignments that constitute the sexual division of labor within a society and produce psychological sex differences (Eagly, 1987; Wood & Eagly, 1999).

These thumbnail sketches of these two origin theories should make it clear that this debate about the origins of sex differences cannot be reduced to a simple nature-versus-nurture dichotomy. Both evolutionary psychology and social structural theory are interactionist in the sense that they take both biological and environmental factors into account, but they treat these factors quite differently. Evolutionary psychology views sex-specific evolved dispositions as psychological tendencies that were built in through genetically mediated adaptation to primeval conditions; the theory treats contemporary environmental factors as cues that interact with adaptations to yield sex-typed responses. Social structural theory views sex-differentiated tendencies as built in through accommodation to the contemporaneous sexual division of labor; in this approach, physical differences between the sexes serve as one influence on role assignment.

* * *

To illustrate the contrasting approaches of evolutionary psychology and social structural theory, we first present and discuss each theory. Then we examine their predictions concerning the criteria men and women use in selecting mates. This domain of behavior has been central to evolutionary theorizing about human sex differences (e.g., Buss & Schmitt, 1993; Kenrick & Keefe, 1992), and the cross-cultural findings available in this area provide an opportunity to examine empirically some of the predictions of evolutionary and social structural analyses.

Evolutionary Psychology as an Origin Theory of Sex Differences

From the perspective of evolutionary psychology, human sex differences reflect adaptations to the pressures of the differing physical and social environments that impinged on females and males during primeval times (Buss, 1995a; Tooby & Cosmides, 1992). Evolutionary psychologists thus label the environment that produced a species' evolved tendencies as its environment of evolutionary adaptedness (EEA; Cosmides, Tooby, & Barkow, 1992; Symons, 1979, 1992; Tooby & Cosmides, 1990b). They loosely identify the Pleistocene era as the human EEA and generally assume that it was populated by hunter–gatherer groups. To the extent that males and females faced different adaptive problems as they evolved, the two sexes developed different strategies to ensure their survival and to maximize their reproductive success. The resolutions to these problems produced evolved psychological mechanisms that are specific to each problem domain and that differ between women and men.

Although humans' evolved mechanisms developed in response to the types of problems consistently encountered by their ancestors and thus are presumed to be universal attributes of humans, environmental input affects how these mechanisms develop in individuals and how they are expressed in behavior (e.g., Buss & Kenrick, 1998). Because culture influences developmental experiences and patterns current situational input, culture is in principle important to the expression of adaptive mechanisms (Tooby & Cosmides, 1992). However, evolutionary psychologists have devoted relatively little attention to the interaction between such broader attributes of the social and cultural environment and the evolved mechanisms that may underlie sex differences. The contextual factors that have interested them generally relate directly to these hypothesized mechanisms. For example, Buss and Schmitt (1993) maintained that the characteristics that people seek in mates depend, not only on their sex, but also on whether they are engaging in short-term or long-term mating. Because of a relative neglect of broader social context, evolutionary psychologists have generated little understanding of how variation in sex-differentiated behavior arises from developmental factors and features of social structure and culture (for an exception, see Draper & Harpending, 1982).

The aspect of evolutionary theory that has been applied most extensively to sex differences is the theory of sexual selection initially proposed by

Darwin (1871) and further developed by Trivers (1972). In the evolutionary psychologists' rendition of these views, sex-typed features of human behavior evolved through male competition and female choice of mates. Because women constituted the sex that devoted greater effort to parental investment, they were a limited reproductive resource for men, who were the less investing sex. Women were restricted in the number of children they could propagate during their life span because of their investment through gestating, bearing, and nursing their children; men did not have these restrictions. Men therefore competed for access to women, and women chose their mates from among the available men. As the more investing sex, women were selected for their wisdom in choosing mates who could provide resources to support their parenting efforts. Women's preferences for such men, in turn, produced sexual selection pressures on men to satisfy these criteria.

Proponents of sexual selection theory argue that sex differences in parental investment favored different strategies for reproductive success for men and women and consequently established different adaptive mechanisms governing mating behavior (Buss, 1996; Kenrick, Trost, & Sheets, 1996). It was to men's advantage in terms of fitness outcomes to "devote a larger proportion of their total mating effort to short-term mating than do women" (Buss & Schmitt, 1993, p. 205)—that is, to be relatively promiscuous. Women, in contrast, benefited from devoting a smaller proportion of their effort to short-term mating and a larger proportion to long-term mating. Also, because of women's concealed fertilization, men were unable to determine easily which children could proffer the fitness gains that follow from genetic relatedness. Men ostensibly adapted to this problem of paternity uncertainty by exerting sexual control over women and developing sexual jealousy and a motive to control women's sexuality (Daly & Wilson, 1998).

According to evolutionary psychologists (e.g., Buss, 1995b; Buss & Kenrick, 1998), sex differences in numerous psychological dispositions arose from differing fitness-related goals of women and men

that followed from their contrasting sexual strategies. Because men competed with other men for sexual access to women, men's evolved dispositions favor violence, competition, and risk taking. Women in turn developed a proclivity to nurture and a preference for long-term mates who could support a family. As a result, men strived to acquire more resources than other men in order to attract women, and women developed preferences for successful, ambitious men who could provide resources.

Critical to some of evolutionary psychologists' claims about sex differences is the assumption that ancestral humans living in the EEA had a hunter–gatherer socioeconomic system (e.g., Buss, 1995b; Cosmides et al., 1992; DeKay & Buss, 1992). The idea of a division of labor in which men hunted while women gathered suggests sex-differentiated pressures linked to survival and reproduction. Such an ancestral division of labor might have favored men who were psychologically specialized for hunting and women who were specialized for gathering. For example, cognitive abilities could have been affected, with men acquiring the superior spatial skills that followed from ancestral hunting, and women acquiring the superior spatial location memory that followed from ancestral gathering (e.g., Geary, 1995; Silverman & Phillips, 1998).

Various mediating processes are implied in evolutionary psychology models of behavioral sex differences. The first and most important involves some means of retaining effective adaptations in human design and perpetuating them over time. Thus, sex-differentiated psychological mechanisms and developmental programs, like other adaptations, are "genetic, hereditary, or inherited in the sense that . . . their structured design has its characteristic form because of the information in our DNA" (Tooby & Cosmides, 1990a, p. 37; see also Buss, Haselton, Shackelford, Bleske, & Wakefield, 1998; Crawford, 1998). Some evolutionary accounts also emphasize that genetic factors trigger biochemical processes that mediate psychological sex differences, especially by means of sex differences in hormone production (e.g., Daly & Wilson,

1983; Geary, 1995, 1996). In addition, sex-typed evolved mechanisms are translated into behavioral sex differences by various cognitive and affective processes. Establishing these links requires theoretical understanding and empirical documentation of the range of processes by which the genetic factors implicated in innate dispositions might affect human behavior (e.g., Collear & Hines, 1995).

Buss and Kenrick (1998) described evolutionary psychology's approach to understanding sex differences as a "metatheory" and summarized it as follows: "Men and women differ in domains where they faced different adaptive problems over human evolutionary history" (p. 994). These theorists thus derive sex differences from heritable adaptations built into the human species. Because these differences are assumed to follow from evolutionary adaptations, they are predicted to occur as central tendencies of male versus female behavior. Human behavior would thus be characterized by a deep structure of sex-differentiated dispositions, producing similar, albeit not identical, behavioral sex differences in all human societies.

CRITIQUE OF THE EVOLUTIONARY ORIGIN THEORY

A number of questions can be raised about evolutionary psychology's account of the origins of sex differences. One consideration is that evolutionary analyses have generally identified adaptations by relying on "informal arguments as to whether a presumed function is served with sufficient precision, economy, efficiency, etc. to rule out pure chance as an adequate explanation" (Williams, 1966, p. 10). Explanations that reflect this approach consist of an analysis of the functional relations served by a particular psychological mechanism, along with the construction of a convincing story about how the adaptation might have made an efficient contribution to genetic survival or to some other goal contributing to reproduction in the EEA. These explanations serve as hypotheses that require additional validation and thus can be useful for initiating scientific research.

In developing these analyses of the possible functions of behaviors, evolutionary scientists face special challenges in distinguishing adaptations from other possible products of evolution—for example, features that were random or that had utility for one function but were subsequently coopted to fulfill a new function (see Buss et al., 1998; Gould, 1991; Williams, 1966). Moreover, the products of evolution must be distinguished from the products of cultural change. Behaviors that provide effective solutions to problems of reproduction and survival can arise from inventive trial-and-error among individuals who are genetically indistinguishable from other members of their living groups; such beneficial behaviors are then imitated and transmitted culturally.

An understanding of humans' primeval environment might help validate evolutionary hypotheses because adaptations evolved as solutions to past environmental challenges. Various bodies of science have some relevance, including observational studies of other primates, the fossil record, and ethnographic studies. However, models of human nature constructed from the behavior of nonhuman primates do not yield a uniform picture that reflects key features of sex differences in modern human societies (see Fedigan, 1986: Strier, 1994; Travis & Yeager, 1991). Similarly ambiguous concerning sex differences are the models of early human social conditions that paleontologists and paleoanthropologists have developed from fossil evidence. Anthropologists continue to debate fundamental points—for example, whether hunting of dangerous prey might have emerged during the period that is usually identified as the human EEA (e.g., Potts, 1984; Rose & Marshall, 1996). As a consequence, assumptions that certain traits were adaptive and consequently are under genetic control cannot be firmly supported from analyzing attributes of the EEA. Moreover, early human societies likely took a wide variety of forms during the period when the species was evolving toward its modern anatomical form (Foley, 1996). Variability in social organization is consistent with observations of more contemporary hunter–gatherer societies, which show great diversity in their social organization (Kelly, 1995). For example, studies of power relations between the sexes across diverse cultures show variability in the extent to which men control women's sexuality (Whyte, 1978), although evolutionary psychologists have assumed that this control is a defining feature of male–female relations. Therefore, because the EEA likely encompassed a variety of conditions, tracing humans' evolution requires understanding of the timing, social organization, and ecological circumstances of multiple periods of adaptation (Foley, 1996). The ambiguity and complexity of the relevant scientific findings leave room for evolutionary psychologists to inadvertently transport relatively modern social conditions to humans' remote past by inappropriately assuming that the distinctive characteristics of contemporary relations between the sexes were also typical of the EEA.

Given the difficulty of knowing the functions of behaviors and the attributes of the EEA, other types of scientific evidence become especially important to validating the claims of evolutionary psychologists. The most convincing evidence that a behavioral pattern reflects an adaptation would be that individuals who possessed the adaptation enjoyed a higher rate of survival and reproduction than individuals who did not possess it. However, such evidence is difficult, if not impossible, to produce. Because humans' evolved mechanisms emerged in relation to past selection pressures, present reproductive advantage does not necessarily reflect past advantage, and evolutionary psychologists have warned against relying on measures of current reproductive success to validate hypothesized adaptations (Buss, 1995a; Tooby & Cosmides, 1992). In the absence of evidence pertaining to reproductive success, scientists might document the genetic inheritance of postulated mechanisms and the processes by which genetic factors result in sex differences in behavior. However, for the psychological dispositions considered in this article, such evidence has not been produced. Instead, the scientific case for these sex-differentiated evolved dispositions rests on tests of evolutionary psychologists' predictions concerning the behavior of men and women in contemporary societies (e.g., Buss & Schmitt, 1993; Kenrick & Keefe, 1992). We evaluate some of these predictions in this article.

Social Structural Theory as an Origin Theory of Sex Differences

A respected tradition in the social sciences locates the origins of sex differences, not in evolved psychological dispositions that are built into the human psyche, but in the contrasting social positions of women and men. In contemporary American society, as in many world societies, women have less power and status than men and control fewer resources. This feature of social structure is often labeled gender hierarchy, or in feminist writing it may be called patriarchy. In addition, as the division of labor is realized in the United States and many other nations, women perform more domestic work than men and spend fewer hours in paid employment (Shelton, 1992). Although most women in the United States are employed in the paid workforce, they have lower wages than men, are concentrated in different occupations, and are thinly represented at the highest levels of organizational hierarchies (Jacobs, 1989; Reskin & Padavic, 1994; Tomaskovic-Devey, 1995). From a social structural perspective, the underlying cause of sex-differentiated behavior is this concentration of men and women in differing roles.

The determinants of the distribution of men and women into social roles are many and include the biological endowment of women and men. The sex-differentiated physical attributes that influence role occupancy include men's greater size and strength, which gives them priority in jobs demanding certain types of strenuous activity, especially activities involving upper body strength. These physical attributes of men are less important in societies in which few occupational roles require these attributes, such as postindustrial societies. Also important in relation to role distributions are women's childbearing and in many societies their activity of suckling infants for long periods of time; these obligations give them priority in roles involving the care of very young children and cause conflict with roles requiring extended absence from home and uninterrupted activity. These reproductive activities of women are less important in societies with low birthrates, less reliance on lactation for feeding infants, and greater reliance on nonmaternal care of young children.

In general, physical sex differences, in interaction with social and ecological conditions, influence the roles held by men and women because certain activities are more efficiently accomplished by one sex. The benefits of this greater efficiency can be realized when women and men are allied in cooperative relationships and establish a division of labor. The particular character of the activities that each sex performs then determines its placement in the social structure (see Wood & Eagly, 1999). As historians and anthropologists have argued (e.g., Ehrenberg, 1989; Harris, 1993; Lerner, 1986; Sanday, 1981), men typically specialized in activities (e.g., warfare, herding) that yielded greater status, wealth, and power, especially as societies became more complex. Thus, when sex differences in status emerged, they tended to favor men.

The differing distributions of men and women into social roles form the basis for a social structural metatheory of sex differences, just as evolutionary theory provides a metatheory. The major portion of this social structural theory follows from the typical features of the roles of men and women. Thus, the first metatheoretical principle derives from the greater power and status that tends to be associated with male-dominated roles and can be succinctly stated as follows: Men's accommodation to roles with greater power and status produces more dominant behavior, and women's accommodation to roles with lesser power and status produces more subordinate behavior (Ridgeway & Diekema, 1992). Dominant behavior is controlling, assertive, relatively directive and autocratic, and may involve sexual control. Subordinate behavior is more compliant to social influence, less overtly aggressive, more cooperative and conciliatory, and may involve a lack of sexual autonomy.

The second metatheoretical principle follows from the differing balance of activities associated with the typical roles of each sex. Women and men seek to accommodate sex-typical roles by acquiring the specific skills and resources linked to successful role performance and by adapting their social behavior to role requirements. A variety of sex-specific skills and beliefs arise from the typical family and economic roles of men and women, which in many societies can be described as resource provider and homemaker. Women and men seek to accommodate to these roles by acquiring role-related skills, for example, women learning domestic skills such as cooking and men learning skills that are marketable in the paid economy. The psychological attributes and social behaviors associated with these roles have been characterized in terms of the distinction between communal and agentic characteristics (Bakan, 1966; Eagly, 1987). Thus, women's accommodation to the domestic role and to female-dominated occupations favors a pattern of interpersonally facilitative and friendly behaviors that can be termed communal. In particular, the assignment of the majority of child rearing to women encourages nurturant behaviors that facilitate care for children and other individuals. The importance of close relationships to women's nurturing role favors the acquisition of superior interpersonal skills and the ability to communicate nonverbally. In contrast, men's accommodation to the employment role, especially to male-dominated occupations, favors a pattern of assertive and independent behaviors that can be termed agentic (Eagly & Steffen, 1984). This argument is not to deny that paid occupations show wide variation in the extent to which they favor more masculine or feminine qualities. In support of the idea that sex-differentiated behaviors are shaped by paid occupations are demonstrations that to the extent that occupations are male dominated, they are thought to require agentic personal qualities. In contrast, to the extent that occupations are female dominated, they are thought to require communal personal qualities (Cejka & Eagly, 1999; Glick, 1991).

In social structural theories, differential role occupancy affects behavior through a variety of mediating processes. In social role theory (Eagly, 1987; Eagly et al., in press), an important mediating process is the formation of gender roles by which people of each sex are expected to have characteristics that equip them for the tasks that they typically carry out. These expectations encompass the preferred or desirable attributes of men and women as well as their typical attributes. Gender roles are emergents from the productive work of the sexes; the characteristics that are required to perform sex-typical tasks become stereotypic of women or men. To the extent that women more than men occupy roles that demand communal behaviors, domestic behaviors, or subordinate behaviors for successful role performance, such tendencies become stereotypic of women and are incorporated into a female gender role. To the extent that men more than women occupy roles that demand agentic behaviors, resource acquisition behaviors, or dominant behaviors for successful role performance, such tendencies become stereotypic of men and are incorporated into a male gender role. Gender roles facilitate the activities typically carried out by people of each sex. For example, the expectation that women be other-oriented and compassionate facilitates their nurturing activities within the family as well as their work in many female-dominated occupations (e.g., teacher, nurse, social worker).

People communicate gender-stereotypic expectations in social interaction and can directly induce the targets of these expectations to engage in behavior that confirms them (e.g., Skrypnek & Snyder, 1982; Wood & Karten, 1986). Such effects of gender roles are congruent with theory and research on the behavioral confirmation of stereotypes and other expectancies (see Olson, Roese, & Zanna, 1996). Gender-stereotypic expectations can also affect behavior by becoming internalized as part of individuals' self-concepts and personalities (Feingold, 1994). Under such circumstances, gender roles affect behavior through self-regulatory processes (Wood, Christensen, Hebl, & Rothgerber, 1997). The individual psychology that underlies these processes is assumed to be the maximization of utilities. People perceive these utilities from the rewards and costs that emerge in social interaction, which takes place within the constraints of organizational and societal arrangements.

* * *

In summary, in social structural accounts, women and men are differently distributed into social roles, and these differing role assignments can be broadly described in terms of a sexual division of labor and a gender hierarchy. This division of labor and the patriarchal hierarchy that sometimes accompanies it provide the engine of sex-differentiated behavior because they trigger social and psychological processes by which men and women seek somewhat different experiences to maximize their outcomes within the constraints that societies establish for people of their sex. Sex differences in behavior thus reflect contemporaneous social conditions.

* * *

Sex Differences in Mate Selection Criteria Predicted From Evolutionary Psychology and Social Structural Theory

One reasonable area for comparing the predictive power of the evolutionary and the social structural origin theories of sex differences is human mating behavior, especially the criteria that people use for selecting mates. Evolutionary predictions have been articulated especially clearly for mating activities, and these behaviors can also be used to test a social structural perspective. Furthermore, empirical findings concerning mate selection preferences have been well-established for many years in the literature on the sociology of the family (e.g., Coombs & Kenkel, 1966). Powers's (1971) summary of 30 years of research concluded that at least in the United States, women generally prefer mates with good earning potential, whereas men prefer mates who are physically attractive and possess good domestic skills. Furthermore, women typically prefer a mate who is older than them, whereas men prefer a mate who is younger. Feingold's (1990, 1991, 1992a) meta-analyses of studies drawn from various research paradigms established that the sex differences in valuing potential mates' earning potential and physical attractiveness are robust, despite sex similarity on most criteria for selecting mates. Subsequent research based on a national probability sample of single adults provided further confirmation of the sex differences in age preferences as well as in valuing earning potential and physical attractiveness (Sprecher, Sullivan, & Hatfield, 1994).

Evolutionary psychologists have adopted mate preferences as signature findings of their analysis. Women's valuing of mates' resources and men's valuing of mates' youth and physical attractiveness are thought to arise from the different parental investment of the sexes that was outlined in Trivers's (1972) sexual selection theory. It is commonly argued that women, as the more investing sex, seek mates with attributes that can support their parenting efforts. However, human mate selection does not follow a strict version of Trivers's males-compete-and-females-choose model, because among humans, selection is a product of the behavior of both sexes, a process Darwin (1871) called "dual selection." In Buss's (1989a) account, male choice derives from women's time-limited reproductive capacity and the tendency for men to seek mates with attributes that suggest such capacity. In Kenrick and Keefe's (1992) account, men and women are both selective about potential mates and both invest heavily in offspring but with different kinds of resources. In particular, "males invest relatively more indirect resources (food, money, protection, and security), and females invest relatively more direct physiological resources (contributing their own bodily nutrients to the fetus and nursing child)" (Kenrick & Keefe, 1992, p. 78). As a result, women prefer mates who can provide indirect resources, and men prefer healthy mates with reproductive potential.

In contrast, from a social structural perspective, the psychology of mate selection reflects people's effort to maximize their utilities with respect to mating choices in an environment in which these utilities are constrained by societal gender roles as well as by the more specific expectations associated with marital roles. Consistent with these ideas, Becker's (1976) economic analysis of mating decisions characterized marriage as occurring between utility-maximizing men and women who can reach an equilibrium with a variety of types of exchanges, including, for example, an exchange be-

tween men's wages and women's household production and other attributes such as education and beauty. This cost–benefit analysis of mating appears even on occasion in the writings of evolutionary scientists. For example, Tattersall (1998) maintained that behavioral regularities, such as sex differences in mate selection criteria, are as likely to be due to rational economic decisions as to inherited predispositions, and Hrdy (1997) wrote that "a woman's preference for a wealthy man can be explained by the simple reality that . . . males monopolize ownership of productive resources" (p. 29).

The outcomes that are perceived to follow from mating decisions depend on marital and family arrangements. To the extent that women and men occupy marital and family roles that entail different responsibilities and obligations, they should select mates according to criteria that reflect these divergent responsibilities and obligations. Consider, for example, the family system based on a male provider and a female domestic worker. This system became especially pronounced in industrial economies and is still prevalent in many world societies. To the extent that societies have this division of labor, women maximize their outcomes by seeking a mate who is likely to be successful in the economic, wage-earning role. In turn, men maximize their outcomes by seeking a mate who is likely to be successful in the domestic role.

The sex differences in the preferred age of mates also can be understood as part of the general tendency of men and women to seek partners likely to provide a good fit to their society's sexual division of labor and marital roles. Specifically, the marital system based on a male breadwinner and a female homemaker favors the age gap in marriage. Marriageable women who are younger than their potential mates tend to have lesser wages, social status, and education and knowledge than women who are the same age as potential mates. With the combination of a younger, less experienced woman and an older, more experienced man, it would be easier to establish the power differential favoring men that is normative for marital roles defined by a male breadwinner and a female domestic worker (Lips, 1991; Steil, 1997). Moreover, compared with somewhat older women, young women lack independent resources and therefore are more likely to perceive that their utilities are maximized in the domestic worker role. In complementary fashion, older men are more likely to have acquired the economic resources that make them good candidates for the provider role. The older man and younger woman thus fit more easily than same-age partners into the culturally expected pattern of breadwinner and homemaker.

CROSS-CULTURAL EVIDENCE FOR SEX DIFFERENCES IN MATE PREFERENCES Evolutionary psychologists' predictions that women select for resources and older age and men for attractiveness and younger age have been examined cross-culturally. Buss's (1989a; Buss et al., 1990) impressive study in 37 cultures of the characteristics that people desire in mates suggested that consistent with evolutionary psychology, these sex differences in mate preferences emerged cross-culturally. Similarly, Kenrick and Keefe (1992) examined the preferred ages of mates in five countries and across various time periods in the 20th century and concluded that all provided evidence of sex differences in these preferences. Specifically, for dating and marriage, women preferred older men and men preferred younger women, although men's preferences were moderated by their age, with teenage boys preferring girls of similar age.

On the basis of these investigations, evolutionary accounts have emphasized the cross-cultural commonality in women's preference for resources and older age and men's preference for attractiveness and younger age. According to Buss (1989a) and Tooby and Cosmides (1989), uniformity across diverse cultures and social circumstances suggests powerful sex-differentiated evolved mechanisms that reflect an innate, universal human nature. Kenrick and Keefe (1992) also argued that "invariance across cultures is evidence that supports a species-specific, rather than a culture-specific, explanation" (p. 76).

Despite evidence for cross-cultural commonality in sex differences in mate selection criteria, these investigations also yielded evidence for cul-

tural variation. For example, Kenrick and Keefe (1992) found that the preference for younger wives was evident among Philippine men of all ages, but only among older men (i.e., age 30 or over) in the United States. However, the simple existence of uniformity or variability does not provide a definitive test of either the evolutionary or the social structural origin theory. Although evolutionary psychologists emphasize uniformity and social structural theorists emphasize variability, both perspectives have some power to explain both of these cross-cultural patterns. To account for uniformity, social structuralists can point to similarities in the sexual division of labor in the studied societies and can argue that these similarities produce these relatively invariant sex differences. As Buss (1989a) noted, his 37 cultures, which were drawn from 33 nations, were biased toward urbanized cash-economy cultures, with 54% from Europe and North America. Furthermore, respondents selected from each society tended to be young, comparatively well-educated, and of relatively high socioeconomic status. To the extent that these societies similarly defined the roles of women and men and that the respondents were similarly placed in these societies' social structures, commonality in the sex differences that follow from social structure should characterize these societies.

To account for cross-cultural variability, both evolutionary and social structural origin theories recognize that developmental processes and social factors that are unique to each society direct behavior in ways that can yield variability in sex differences across cultures. Beyond this insight that some evidence of cross-cultural variability would not surprise theorists in either camp, the particular pattern of cross-cultural variation provides an informative test of the mechanisms underlying sex differences. Specifically, the social structural argument that a society's sexual division of labor and associated gender hierarchy are responsible for sex differences in social behavior yields predictions concerning cross-cultural variability in mate preferences.

In the nations included in Buss et al.'s (1990) cross-cultural sample, whose economies ranged from agrarian to postindustrial, some cultures were still strongly marked by this division of labor between the provider and domestic worker, whereas other cultures had departed from it. In advanced economies like the United States, women have entered the paid labor force and spend a smaller proportion of their time in domestic labor (Haas, 1995; Shelton, 1992). Although the tendency for men to increase their hours of domestic work is much more modest, the lives of men and women become more similar with greater gender equality. Therefore, people of both sexes should lessen their emphasis on choosing mates whose value is defined by their fit to the division between domestic work and wage labor. Even in postindustrial economies such as the United States, however, the sex-typed division of labor remains in modified form, with men devoting longer hours than women to wage labor and women devoting longer hours to domestic work (e.g., Ferree, 1991; Presser, 1994; Shelton, 1992). Therefore, the social structural prediction is that the sex differences in mate selection criteria that follow from the male-female division of labor should be substantially weakened in societies characterized by greater gender equality, albeit they should still be present to the extent that complete equality has not been achieved.

REANALYSIS OF BUSS ET AL.'S (1990) 37 CULTURES DATA

To evaluate whether the division of labor within a society could explain the mate preferences of men and women, we reanalyzed Buss et al.'s (1990) 37 cultures data. Our efforts focused on men's tendencies to select wives for domestic skill and younger age and women's tendencies to select husbands for earning capacity and older age. To test the hypothesis that a higher level of gender equality lessens these sex differences, we represented societies' gender equality in terms of archival data available from the United Nations (United Nations Development Programme, 1995).

Buss et al. (1990) derived the data on criteria for selecting mates from questionnaire measures of preferences for a wide range of characteristics that might be desired in a mate: (a) One instrument obtained rankings of a set of 13 characteristics

according to "their desirability in someone you might marry" (p. 11); (b) the other instrument obtained ratings on a 4-point scale of each of 18 characteristics on "how important or desirable it would be in choosing a mate" (p. 11). Buss et al. represented each culture by the male and female respondents' mean ranking of each of the 13 male selection criteria and by their mean rating of each of the 18 criteria. A separate question inquired about preferences for a spouse's age. The data that we reanalyzed consisted of mean preferences for each culture.

Our reanalysis confirmed Buss et al.'s (1990) conclusion that women placed more value than men on a mate's wage-earning ability. Furthermore, consistent with the greater domestic responsibility of women than men in most cultures, men valued *good cook and housekeeper* more than women did, a sex difference that has received little attention from evolutionary psychologists. When the sex differences in the mean preference ratings were averaged across the cultures, this difference was of comparable magnitude to those obtained on the attributes most strongly emphasized by evolutionary psychologists. Specifically, in both the rating and ranking data, the criteria of *good earning capacity*, *good housekeeper and cook*, and *physically attractive* produced the largest sex differences. The appropriateness of focusing on the criteria pertaining to earning ability and domestic skill within Buss et al.'s data was also supported by the good agreement across the ranking and rating data sets for sex differences in the valuation of the qualities of financial prospect, $r(33) = .76$, $p < .001$, and domestic skill, $r(33) = .68$, $p < .001$, whereas the agreement in the valuation of physical attractiveness was poorer, $r(33) = .34$, $p < .05$.[1] In addition, as Buss et al. reported, the sex difference in the preferred age of mates was fully intact in the 37 cultures data.

---

[1] r is the correlation coefficient, the number in parentheses is the degrees of the freedom (in this case the number of participants minus 2), and p is the significance, or probability that an r this large would have been found by chance alone if the population value were in fact 0.

Additional evidence for the social structural predictions emerged when we evaluated the pattern of sex differences in preferences across societies. Consistent with the division of labor principle, a substantial relation emerged between the sex difference in valuing a spouse's domestic skills and the sex difference in valuing a spouse's capacity to provide a good income. Specifically, on the basis of the ranking measure, the sex differences in the good earning capacity criterion and the good housekeeper criterion were correlated across the cultures, $r(33) = .67$, $p < .001$. On the basis of the rating measure, the sex differences in the financial prospect criterion and the housekeeper–cook criterion were also correlated, $r(35) = .38$, $p < .05$. These positive correlations indicate that to the extent that women more than men reported seeking a mate who is a good breadwinner, men more than women reported seeking a mate who is a good homemaker. In addition, the sex difference in the preferred age of one's spouse bore a positive relation to the sex difference in preference for a good earner, $r(33) = .34$, $p < .05$ for the ranking data, and $r(35) = .32$, $p < .06$ for the rating data. Similarly, the sex difference in preferred age bore a positive relation to the sex difference in preference for a good housekeeper and cook, $r(33) = .58$, $p < .001$ for the ranking data, and $r(35) = .60$, $p < .001$ for the rating data. These relationships show that to the extent that the sex difference in the preferred age of spouses was large, women more than men preferred mates who were good providers and men more than women preferred mates who were good domestic workers. The division of labor provides the logic of all of these relationships: Women who serve in the domestic role are the complement of men who serve as breadwinners, and the combination of older husbands and younger wives facilitates this form of marriage.

Analysis of gender equality. To test our hypothesis that sex differences in mate preferences erode to the extent that women and men are similarly placed in the social structure, we sought cross-national indicators of gender equality. Among the many such indicators compiled by United Nations researchers, the most direct indicator of gender equality is the aggregate Gender Empowerment Measure, which represents the extent to which women participate equally with men in economic, political, and decision-making roles (United Nations Development Programme, 1995). This index increases as (a) women's percentage share of administrative and managerial jobs and professional and technical jobs increases, (b) women's percentage share of parliamentary seats rises, and (c) women's proportional share of earned income approaches parity with men's.

The Gender-Related Development Index is another useful indicator of societal-level gender equality provided by United Nations researchers. It increases with a society's basic capabilities to provide health (i.e., greater life expectancy), educational attainment and literacy, and wealth, but imposes a penalty for gender inequality in these capabilities (United Nations Development Programme, 1995). Whereas this measure reflects equality in basic access to health care, education and knowledge, and income, the Gender Empowerment Measure is a purer indicator of equal participation in economic and political life.

In the set of 37 cultures, the Gender Empowerment Measure and the Gender-Related Development Index were correlated, $r(33) = .74$, $p < .001$, and both of these indexes were moderately correlated with general indexes of human development and economic development. One limitation of the indexes of gender equality is that they are based on data from the early 1990s. Because Buss et al.'s (1990) data were collected in the mid-1980s, these indexes are from a slightly later time period, but the relative positions of the cultures should remain approximately the same.

To examine the relation between societal gender equality and mate preferences, we calculated the correlations of these indexes with the sex differences in valuing a mate as a breadwinner and as a domestic worker—the two criteria most relevant to the traditional division of labor. These correlations for the ranking and the rating data, which appear in Table 1, are generally supportive of the

TABLE 1

CORRELATIONS OF MEAN RANKINGS AND RATINGS OF MATE SELECTION CRITERIA WITH UNITED NATIONS INDEXES OF GENDER EQUALITY FOR BUSS ET AL.'S (1990) 37 CULTURES SAMPLE

	Ranked criteria		Rated criteria	
Mate selection criterion and rater	Gender Empowerment Measure ($n = 33$)	Gender-Related Development Index ($n = 34$)	Gender Empowermnt Measure ($n = 35$)	Gender-Related Devevlopment Index ($n = 36$)
Good earning capacity (financial prospect)				
Sex difference	−.43*	−.33†	−.29†	−.23
Women	−.29	−.18	−.49**	−.42**
Men	.24	.27	−.40*	−.36*
Good housekeeper (and cook)				
Sex difference	−.62***	−.54**	−.61***	−.54**
Women	.04	−.01	.11	−.07
Men	−.46**	−.42*	−.60***	−.61***
Physically attractive (good looks)				
Sex difference	.13	−.12	.20	.18
Women	.14	.34†	−.45**	−.25
Men	.20	.28	−.33†	−.14

Note. The criteria were described slightly differently in the ranking and the rating tasks: The ranking term is given first, with the rating term following in parentheses. Higher values on the gender equality indexes indicate greater equality. For the preferences of women or men, higher values of the mean rankings and ratings of mate selection criteria indicate greater desirability in a mate; therefore, a positive correlation indicates an increase in the desirability of a criterion as gender equality increased, and a negative correlation indicates a decrease. Sex differences in these preferences were calculated as female minus male means for good earning capacity and male minus female means for good housekeeper and physically attractive. A positive correlation thus indicates an increase in the sex difference as gender equality increased, and a negative correlation indicates a decrease in the sex difference.
†$p < .10.$ *$p < .05.$ **$p < .01.$ ***$p < .001.$

social structural predictions. As the Gender Empowerment Measure increased in value, the tendency decreased for women to place greater emphasis than men on a potential spouse's earning capacity, although the correlation with the rated criterion was relatively weak. Also, as the Gender Empowerment Measure increased, the tendency decreased for men to place greater emphasis than women on a potential spouse's domestic skills. As expected in terms of the Gender-Related Development Index's less direct representation of the similarity of the roles of women and men, its correlations with these sex differences were somewhat weaker.

The preference data for each sex reported in Table 1 provide insight into these sex-difference findings. For good housekeeper and cook, the correlations for both the rating data and the ranking data indicated that as gender equality increased, men decreased their interest in choosing mates for their skill as domestic workers, and women showed no change in this preference. In contrast, for good earning capacity, as gender equality increased, women decreased their emphasis on mates' earning potential in the rating data (although nonsignificantly in the ranking data). However, men's preferences for good earning capacity are more difficult to interpret because their relations to gender equality were inconsistent across the ranking and rating measures. Inconsistencies between the two measures may reflect that rankings are judgments of the relative importance of the criteria in relation to

| | TABLE 2 | |

CORRELATIONS OF MEAN PREFERRED AGE DIFFERENCE BETWEEN
SELF AND SPOUSE WITH UNITED NATIONS INDEXES OF GENDER
EQUALITY FOR BUSS ET AL.'S (1990) 37 CULTURES SAMPLE

Rater	Gender Empowerment Measure ($n = 35$)	Gender-Related Development Index ($n = 36$)
Sex difference	−.73***	−.70***
Women	−.64***	−.57***
Men	.70***	.70***

Note. Higher values on the gender equality indexes indicate greater equality. Positive ages indicate preference for an older spouse, and negative ages indicate preference for a younger spouse. Therefore, for the preferences of women, a negative correlation indicates a decrease in the tendency to prefer an older spouse as gender equality increased, whereas for the preferences of men, a positive correlation indicates a decrease in the tendency to prefer a younger spouse. Because the sex difference in preferred age was calculated as female minus male mean preferred spouse age in relation to self, a negative correlation indicates a decrease in the sex difference in preferred age as gender equality increased.

***$p < .001$.

the others in the list, whereas ratings are judgments of the absolute importance of the different criteria.

As shown in Table 2, examination of preferences for a spouse's age showed that as gender equality increased, women expressed less preference for older men, men expressed less preference for younger women, and consequently the sex difference in the preferred age of mates became smaller. These relations suggest that sex differences in age preferences reflect a sex-differentiated division of labor.

* * *

Preference for physical attractiveness. As also shown in Table 1, correlations between the sex difference in valuing potential mates' physical attractiveness and the United Nations indexes of gender equality were low and nonsignificant. These findings are not surprising, because this mate selection criterion does not mirror the division between wage labor and domestic labor in the manner that earning potential, domestic skill, and age do. Nevertheless, under some circumstances, physical attractiveness

may be part of what people exchange for partners' earning capacity and other attributes.

Assuming that attractiveness is sometimes exchanged for other gains, the social structural perspective offers possibilities for understanding its value. Research on the physical attractiveness stereotype has shown that attractiveness in both sexes conveys several kinds of meaning—especially social competence, including social skills, sociability, and popularity (Eagly, Ashmore, Makhijani, & Longo, 1991; Feingold, 1992b). Therefore, men's greater valuing of attractiveness might follow from the greater importance of this competence in women's family and occupational roles, including women's paid occupations in postindustrial societies (Cejka & Eagly, 1999; Lippa, 1998), and the consequent inclusion of this competence in the female gender role. If women's roles demand greater interpersonal competence in societies with greater and lesser gender equality, the tendency for men to place greater value on mates' attractiveness would not covary with indexes that assess equality.

Another possibility is that the value of attractiveness stems from its perceived association with the ability to provide sexual pleasure. This idea receives support from research showing that attractiveness conveys information about sexual warmth (Feingold, 1992b). If so, men might seek sexiness in a mate in all societies, in addition to attributes such as domestic skill, whose importance varies with the society's level of gender equality. Given that the female gender role often includes sexual restraint and lack of sexual autonomy, women may place less emphasis on sexiness in mates than men do.

It is less certain that physical attractiveness conveys information about women's fertility, as should be the case if men's preference for attractiveness in mates developed because attractiveness was a cue to fertility (Buss, 1989a; Jones, 1995; Singh, 1993). It seems reasonable that perceptions of attractiveness and potential fertility would covary even in contemporary data, but these relations have proven to be inconsistent (e.g., Cunningham, 1986; Tassinary & Hansen, 1998). Moreover, Singh's (1993) research on judgments of female figures that varied in weight and waist-to-hip ratio suggested three somewhat independent groupings of attributes: health, attractiveness, and sexiness; capacity and desire for children; and youth.

Although little is known about the relation between women's attractiveness and their actual fecundity, Kalick, Zebrowitz, Langlois, and Johnson (1998) found that facial attractiveness in early adulthood was unrelated to number of children produced or to health across the life span. Although the few participants in their sample who did not marry were less attractive than those who did marry, once the nonmarried were excluded, physical attractiveness was unrelated to the number of children produced by male or female participants. Kalick et al. (1998) concluded that "any relation between attractiveness and fecundity was due to mate-selection chances rather than biological fertility" (p. 10). Of course, as we noted in our critique of evolutionary psychology in this article, proponents of the theory do not predict that hypothesized evolved dispositions, such as men's preference for physically attractive partners, would necessarily be related to current reproductive success. Evolutionary psychologists argue instead that

actual fertility in modern societies may bear little relation to the factors indicative of reproductive success in the EEA.

In summary, several aspects of the findings from Buss et al.'s (1990) 37 cultures study are compatible with the social structural origin theory of sex differences. The idea that the extremity of the division between male providers and female homemakers is a major determinant of the criteria that people seek in mates fits with the observed covariation between men placing more emphasis than women on younger age and domestic skill and women placing more emphasis than men on older age and earning potential. The lessening of these sex differences with increasing gender equality, as represented by the United Nations indexes, is consistent with our claim that these sex differences are by-products of a social and family structure in which the man acts as a provider and the woman acts as a homemaker. More ambiguous are the sex differences in valuing mates' physical attractiveness. Without evidence that men's greater valuing of attractiveness follows from one or more specific mechanisms, the simple absence of a relation between gender equality and sex differences in valuing attractiveness in our reanalysis does not advance the claims of evolutionary psychology or the social structural theory. Convincing evidence for either interpretation has yet to be generated. However, with respect to the other sex differences emphasized by evolutionary psychologists, their cross-cultural patterning suggests that they arise from a particular economic and social system.

*   *   *

Conclusion

Considered at the level of a general metatheory of sex differences, social structural theories provide alternative explanations of the great majority of the general predictions about sex-differentiated social behavior that have been featured in evolutionary psychology. Because the central tendencies of sex differences (see Eagly, 1995; Halpern, 1997; Hyde, 1996) are readily encompassed by both of these perspectives, neither the evolutionary metatheory nor the social structural metatheory is convincingly substantiated by a mere noting of the differences established in the research literature. It is far too easy to make up sensible stories about how these differences might be products of sex-differentiated evolved tendencies or the differing placement of women and men in the social structure. This overlap in general main-effect predictions calls for more refined testing of the two theoretical perspectives, and each perspective is associated with numerous more detailed predictions and empirical tests.

Certainly there are many possibilities for distinguishing between the two approaches with appropriate research designs (see Jackson, 1992). Evolutionary psychologists have been especially resourceful in obtaining cross-cultural data intended to support their claims of invariance across cultures in sex-differentiated behavior. To be maximally informative about social structural factors, cross-cultural research should be systematically designed to represent cultures with differing forms of social organization and levels of gender equality. In addition, a variety of other research methods, including experiments and field studies, can yield tests of predictions that emerge from evolutionary and social structural perspectives.

Although this article contrasts social structural explanations of sex differences with those based on evolutionary psychology, social structural analyses may be generally compatible with some evolutionary perspectives, as we noted in the introductory section of this article. Our argument that sex differences in behavior emerge primarily from physical sex differences in conjunction with influences of the economy, social structure, ecology, and cultural beliefs is potentially reconcilable with theories of coevolution by genetic and cultural processes (Janicki & Krebs, 1998). Our position is also sympathetic to the interest that some evolutionary biologists and behavioral ecologists have shown in the maintenance of behavioral patterns from generation to generation through nongenetic, cultural processes (e.g., Sork, 1997). However, despite our acknowledgement of the importance of some evolved genetic influences on the behavior of women and men, an implicit assumption of our approach is that social change emerges, not from individuals' tendencies to maximize their inclusive fitness, but instead from their efforts to maximize their personal benefits and minimize their personal costs in their social and ecological settings.

One test of the evolutionary psychology and social structural origin theories of sex differences lies in the future—that is, in the emerging postindustrial societies in which the division between men's wage labor and women's domestic labor is breaking down. Notable is the increase in women's paid employment, education, and access to many formerly male-dominated occupations. Accompanying these changes is a marked attitudinal shift toward greater endorsement of equal opportunity for women in the workplace and role-sharing in the home (e.g., Simon & Landis, 1989; Spence & Hahn, 1997; Twenge, 1997). Nonetheless, occupational sex segregation is still prevalent with women concentrated in occupations that are thought to require feminine qualities and with men in occupations thought to require masculine qualities (Cejka & Eagly, 1999; Glick, 1991). Given that occupational distributions currently take this form and that the homemaker–provider division of labor remains weakly in place, social structuralists would not predict that sex differences in behavior should have already disappeared. Instead, to the extent that the traditional sexual division between wage labor and domestic labor disappears and women and men become similarly distributed into paid occupations, men and women should converge in their psychological attributes.

References

Archer, J. (1996). Sex differences in social behavior: Are the social role and evolutionary explanations compatible? *American Psychologist, 51*, 909–917.

Bakan, D. (1966). *The duality of human existence: An essay on psychology and religion.* Chicago: Rand McNally.

Becker, G. S. (1976). *The economic approach to human behavior.* Chicago: University of Chicago Press.

Buss, D. M. (1989a). Sex differences in human mate preferences: Evolutionary hypotheses tested in 37 cultures. *Behavioral and Brain Sciences, 12*, 1–14.

Buss, D. M. (1989b). Toward an evolutionary psychology of human mating. *Behavioral and Brain Sciences, 12*, 39–49.

Buss, D. M. (1995a). Evolutionary psychology: A new paradigm for psychological science. *Psychological Inquiry, 6*, 1–30.

Buss, D. M. (1995b). Psychological sex differences: Origins through sexual selection. *American Psychologist, 50*, 164–168.

Buss, D. M. (1996). The evolutionary psychology of human social strategies. In E. T. Higgins & A. W. Kruglanski (Eds.), *Social psychology: Handbook of basic principles* (pp. 3–38). New York: Guilford Press.

Buss, D. M. (1998). The psychology of human mate selection: Exploring the complexity of the strategic repertoire. In C. Crawford & D. L. Krebs (Eds.), *Handbook of evolutionary psychology: Ideas, issues, and applications* (pp. 405–429). Mahwah, NJ: Erlbaum.

Buss, D. M., et al. (1990). International preferences in selecting mates: A study of 37 cultures. *Journal of Cross-Cultural Psychology, 21*, 5–47.

Buss, D. M., Haselton. M. G., Shackelford, T. K., Bleske, A. L., & Wakefield, J. C. (1998). Adaptations, exaptations, and spandrels. *American Psychologist, 53*, 533–548.

Buss, D. M., & Kenrick, D. T. (1998). Evolutionary social psychology. In D. T. Gilbert, S. T. Fiske, & G. Lindzey (Eds.). *The handbook of social psychology* (4th ed., Vol. 2, pp. 982–1026). Boston: McGraw-Hill.

Buss, D. M., & Schmitt, D. P. (1993). Sexual strategies theory: An evolutionary perspective on human mating. *Psychological Review, 100*, 204–232.

Cejka, M. A., & Eagly, A. H. (1999). Gender-stereotypic images of occupations correspond to the sex segregation of employment. *Personality and Social Psychology Bulletin, 25*, 413–423.

Collear, M. L., & Hines, M. (1995). Human behavioral sex differences: A role for gonadal hormones during early development? *Psychological Bulletin, 118*, 55–107.

Coombs, R. H., & Kenkel, W. F. (1966). Sex differences in dating aspiration and satisfaction with computer-selected partners. *Journal of Marriage and the Family, 28*, 62–66.

Cosmides, L., Tooby, J., & Barkow, J. H. (1992). Introduction: Evolutionary psychology and conceptual integration. In J. H. Barkow, L. Cosmides, & J. Tooby (Eds.). *The adapted mind: Evolutionary psychology and the generation of culture* (pp. 3–15). New York: Oxford University Press.

Crawford, C. (1998). The theory of evolution in the study of human behavior: An introduction and overview. In C. Crawford & D. L. Krebs (Eds.), *Handbook of evolutionary psychology: Ideas, issues, and applications* (pp. 3–41). Mahwah, NJ: Erlbaum.

Cunningham, M. R. (1986). Measuring the physical in physical attractiveness: Quasi-experiments on the sociobiology of female facial beauty. *Journal of Personality and Social Psychology, 50*, 925–935.

Daly, M., & Wilson, M. (1983). *Sex, evolution, and behavior* (2nd ed.). Boston: Grant Press.

Daly, M., & Wilson, M. (1998). The evolutionary social psychology of family violence. In C. Crawford & D. L. Krebs (Eds.), *Handbook of evolutionary psychology: Ideas, issues, and applications* (pp. 431–456). Mahwah, NJ: Erlbaum.

Darwin, C. (1871). *The descent of man and selection in relation to sex.* London: Murray.

Deaux, K., & LaFrance, M. (1998). Gender. In D. T. Gilbert, S. T. Fiske, & G. Lindzey (Eds.), *The handbook of social psychology* (4th ed., Vol. 1, pp. 788–827). Boston: McGraw-Hill.

DeKay, W. T., & Buss. D. M. (1992). Human nature, individual differences, and the importance of context: Perspectives from evolutionary psychology. *Current Directions in Psychological Science, figure 1*, 184–189.

Draper, P., & Harpending, H. (1982). Father absence and reproductive strategy: An evolutionary perspective. *Journal of Anthropological Research, 38*, 255–273.

Eagly, A. H. (1987). *Sex differences in social behavior: A social-role interpretation.* Hillsdale, NJ: Erlbaum.

Eagly, A. H. (1995). The science and politics of comparing women and men. *American Psychologist, 50*, 145–158.

Eagly, A. H., Ashmore, R. D., Makhijani, M. G., & Longo, L. C. (1991). What is beautiful is good, but . . . : A meta-analytic review of research on the physical attractiveness stereotype. *Psychological Bulletin, 110*, 109–128.

Eagly, A. H., & Steffen, V. J. (1984). Gender stereotypes stem from the distribution of women and men into social roles. *Journal of Personality and Social Psychology, 46*, 735–754.

Eagly, A. H., Wood, W., & Diekman, A. (in press). Social role theory of sex differences and similarities: A current appraisal. In T. Eckes & H. M. Trautner (Eds.), *The developmental social psychology of gender.* Mahwah, NJ: Erlbaum.

Ehrenberg, M. (1989). *Women in prehistory.* London: British Museum Publications.

Fedigan, L. M. (1986). The changing role of women in models of human evolution. *Annual Review of Anthropology, 15*, 25–66.

Feingold, A. (1990). Gender differences in effects of physical attractiveness on romantic attraction: A comparison across five research paradigms. *Journal of Personality and Social Psychology, 59*, 981–993.

Feingold, A. (1991). Sex differences in the effects of similarity and physical attractiveness on opposite-sex attraction. *Basic and Applied Social Psychology, 12*, 357–367.

Feingold, A. (1992a). Gender differences in mate selection preferences: A test of the parental investment model. *Psychological Bulletin, 112*, 125–139.

Feingold, A. (1992b). Good-looking people are not what we think. *Psychological Bulletin, 111*, 304–341.

Feingold, A. (1994). Gender differences in personality: A meta-analysis. *Psychological Bulletin, 116*, 429–456.

Ferree, M. M. (1991). The gender division of labor in two-earner marriages: Dimensions of variability and change. *Journal of Family Issues, 12*, 158–180.

Foley, R. (1996). The adaptive legacy of human evolution: A search for the environment of evolutionary adaptedness. *Evolutionary Anthropology, 4*, 194–203.

Geary, D. C. (1995). Sexual selection and sex differences in spatial cognition. *Learning and Individual Differences, 7*, 289–301.

Geary, D. C. (1996). Sexual selection and sex differences in mathematical abilities. *Behavioral and Brain Sciences, 19*, 229–284.

Glick, P. (1991). Trait-based and sex-based discrimination in occupational prestige, occupational salary, and hiring. *Sex Roles, 25*, 351–378.

Gould, S. J. (1991). Exaptation: A crucial tool for an evolutionary psychology. *Journal of Social Issues, 47*, 43–65.

Haas, L. L. (1995). Household division of labor in industrial societies. In B. B. Ingoldsby & S. Smith (Eds.), *Families in multicultural perspective: Perspectives on marriage and the family* (pp. 268–296). New York: Guilford Press.

Halpern, D. F. (1997). Sex differences in intelligence: Implications for education. *American Psychologist, 52,* 1091– 1102.

Harris, M. (1993). The evolution of human gender hierarchies: A trial formulation. In B. D. Miller (Ed.), *Sex and gender hierarchies* (pp. 57–79). New York: Cambridge University Press.

Hrdy, S. B. (1997). Raising Darwin's consciousness: Female sexuality and the prehominid origins of patriarchy. *Human Nature, 8,* 1–49.

Hyde, J. S. (1996). Where are the gender differences? Where are the gender similarities? In D. M. Buss & N. M. Malamuth (Eds.), *Sex, power, conflict: Evolutionary and feminist perspectives.* New York: Oxford University Press.

Jackson, L. A. (1992). *Physical appearance and gender: Sociobiological and sociocultural perspectives.* Albany: State University of New York Press.

Jacobs, J. A. (1989). *Revolving doors: Sex segregation and women's careers.* Stanford, CA: Stanford University Press.

Janicki, M. G., & Krebs, D. L. (1998). Evolutionary approaches to culture. In C. Crawford & D. L. Krebs (Eds.), *Handbook of evolutionary psychology: Ideas, issues, and applications* (pp. 163–207), Mahwah, NJ: Erlbaum.

Jones, D. (1995). Sexual selection, physical attractiveness, and facial neoteny: Cross-cultural evidence and implications. *Current Anthropology, 36,* 723–748.

Kalick, S. M., Zebrowitz, L. A., Langlois, J. H., & Johnson, R. M. (1998). Does human facial attractiveness honestly advertise health? Longitudinal data on an evolutionary question. *Psychological Science, 9,* 8–13.

Kelly, R. L. (1995). *The foraging spectrum: Diversity in hunter–gatherer lifeways.* Washington, DC: Smithsonian Institution Press.

Kenrick, D. T., & Keefe, R. C. (1992). Age preferences in mates reflect sex differences in human reproductive strategies. *Behavioral and Brain Sciences, 15,* 75–91.

Kenrick, D. T., Trost, M. R., & Sheets, V. L. (1996). Power, harassment, and trophy mates: The feminist advantages of an evolutionary perspective. In D. M. Buss & N. M. Malamuth (Eds.), *Sex, power, and conflict: Evolutionary and feminist perspectives* (pp. 29–53). New York: Oxford University Press.

Lemer, G. (1986). *The creation of patriarchy.* New York: Oxford University Press.

Lippa, R. (1998). Gender-related individual differences and the structure of vocational interests: The importance of the "people-things" dimension. *Journal of Personality and Social Psychology, 74,* 996–1009.

Lips, H. M. (1991). *Women, men, and power.* Mountain View, CA: Mayfield.

Lorenzi-Cioldi, F. (1998). Group status and perceptions of homogeneity. In W. Stroebe & M. Hewstone (Eds.), *European review of social psychology* (Vol. 9, pp. 31–75). Chichester, England: Wiley.

Olson, J. M., Roese, N. J., & Zanna, M. P. (1996). Expectancies. In E. T. Higgins & A. W. Kruglanski (Eds.), *Social psychology: Handbook of basic principles* (pp. 211–238). New York: Guilford.

Potts, R. (1984). Home bases and early hominids. *American Scientist, 72,* 338–347.

Powers, E. A. (1971). Thirty years of research on ideal mate characteristics: What do we know? *International Journal of Sociology of the Family, 1,* 207–215.

Presser, H. B. (1994). Employment schedules among dual-earner spouses and the division of household labor by gender. *American Sociological Review, 59,* 348–364.

Reskin, B. F., & Padavic, I. (1994). *Women and men at work.* Thousand Oaks, CA: Pine Forge Press.

Ridgeway, C. L. (1991). The social construction of status value: Gender and other nominal characteristics. *Social Forces, 70,* 367–386.

Ridgeway, C. L., & Diekema, D. (1992). Are gender differences status differences? In C. L. Ridgeway (Ed.), *Gender, interaction, and inequality* (pp. 157–180). New York: Springer-Verlag.

Rose, L., & Marshall, F. (1996). Meat eating, hominid sociality, and home bases revisited. *Current Anthropology, 37,* 307– 338.

Sanday, P. R. (1981). *Female power and male dominance: On the origins of sexual inequality.* New York: Cambridge University Press.

Shelton, B. A. (1992). *Women, men and time: Gender differences in paid work, housework, and leisure.* New York: Greenwood Press.

Silverman, I., & Phillips, K. (1998). The evolutionary psychology of spatial sex differences. In C. Crawford & D. L. Krebs (Eds.), *Handbook of evolutionary psychology: Ideas, issues, and applications* (pp. 595–612). Mahwah, NJ: Erlbaum.

Simon, R. J., & Landis, J. M. (1989). The polls—A report: Women's and men's attitudes about a woman's place and role. *Public Opinion Quarterly, 53,* 265–276.

Singh, D. (1993). Adaptive significance of female physical attractiveness: Role of waist-to-hip ratio. *Journal of Personality and Social Psychology, 65,* 293–307.

Skrypnek, B. J., & Snyder, M. (1982). On the self-perpetuating nature of stereotypes about women and men. *Journal of Experimental Social Psychology, 18,* 277–291.

Sork, V. L. (1997). Quantitative genetics, feminism, and evolutionary theories of gender differences. In P. A. Gowaty (Ed.), *Feminism and evolutionary biology: Boundaries, intersections, and frontiers* (pp. 86–115). New York: Chapman & Hall.

Spence, J. T., & Hahn, E. D. (1997). The Attitudes Toward Women: Scale and attitude change in college students. *Psychology of Women Quarterly, 21,* 17–34.

Sprecher, S., Sullivan, Q., & Hatfield, E. (1994). Mate selection preferences: Gender differences examined in a national sample. *Journal of Personality and Social Psychology, 66,* 1074–1080.

Steil, J. M. (1997). *Marital equality: Its relationship to the well-being of husbands and wives.* Thousand Oaks, CA: Sage.

Strier, K. B. (1994). Myth of the typical primate. *Yearbook of Physical Anthropology, 37,* 233–271.

Symons, D. (1979). *The evolution of human sexuality.* New York: Oxford University Press.

Symons, D. (1992). On the use and misuse of Darwinism in the study of human behavior. In J. H. Barkow, L. Cosmides, & J. Tooby (Eds.), *The adapted mind: Evolutionary psychology and the generation of culture* (pp. 137–159). New York: Oxford University Press.

Tassinary, L. G., & Hansen, K. A. (1998). A critical test of the waist-to-hip-ratio hypothesis of female physical attractiveness. *Psychological Science, 9,* 150–155.

Tattersall, I. (1998). *Becoming human: Evolution and human uniqueness.* New York: Harcourt Brace.

Tomaskovic-Devey, D. (1995). Sex composition and gendered earnings inequality: A comparison of job and occupational models. In J. A. Jacobs (Ed.), *Gender inequality at work* (pp. 23–56). Thousand Oaks, CA: Sage.

Tooby, J., & Cosmides, L. (1989). The innate versus the manifest: How universal does universal have to be? *Behavioral and Brain Sciences, 12*, 36–37.

Tooby, J., & Cosmides, L. (1990a). On the universality of human nature and the uniqueness of the individual: The role of genetics and adaptation. *Journal of Personality, 58*, 17–67.

Tooby, J., & Cosmides, L. (1990b). The past explains the present: Emotional adaptations and the structure of ancestral environments. *Ethology and Sociobiology, 11*, 375–424.

Tooby, J., & Cosmides, L. (1992). The psychological foundations of culture. In J. H. Barkow, L. Cosmides, & J. Tooby (Eds.), *The adapted mind: Evolutionary psychology and the generation of culture* (pp. 19–136). New York: Oxford University Press.

Travis, C. B., & Yeager, C. P. (1991). Sexual selection, parental investment, and sexism. *Journal of Social Issues, 47*(3), 117–129.

Trivers, R. (1972). Parental investment and sexual selection. In B. Campbell (Ed.), *Sexual selection and the descent of man: 1871–1971* (pp. 136–179). Chicago: Aldine.

Twenge, J. M. (1997). Attitudes toward women, 1970–1995: A meta-analysis. *Psychology of Women Quarterly, 21*, 35–51.

United Nations Development Programme. (1995). *Human development report 1995*. New York: Oxford University Press.

West, C., & Zimmerman, D. H. (1987). Doing gender. *Gender & Society, 1*, 125–151.

Whyte, M. K. (1978). *The status of women in preindustrial societies*. Princeton, NJ: Princeton University Press.

Wiley, M. G. (1995). Sex category and gender in social psychology. In K. S. Cook, G. A. Fine, & J. S. House (Eds.). *Sociological perspectives on social psychology* (pp. 362–386). Boston: Allyn & Bacon.

Williams, G. C. (1966). *Adaptation and natural selection: A critique of some current evolutionary thought*. Princeton, NJ: Princeton University Press.

Wood, W., Christensen, P. N., Hebl, M. R., & Rothgerber, H. (1997). Conformity to sex-typed norms, affect, and the self-concept. *Journal of Personality and Social Psychology, 73*, 523–535.

Wood, W., & Eagly, A. H. (1999). *Social structure and the origins of sex differences in social behavior*. Manuscript in preparation.

Wood, W., & Karten, S. J. (1986). Sex differences in interaction style as a product of perceived sex differences in competence. *Journal of Personality and Social Psychology, 50*, 341–347.

Exotic Becomes Erotic: A Developmental Theory of Sexual Orientation

Daryl J. Bem

Despite the rapid and impressive gains made by biological approaches to personality in recent years, some observers have found the results disappointing, for a couple of reasons. First, biological approaches to psychological issues often have become reductionistic—treating the identification of a gene associated with a behavior as a complete explanation, for example, or even concluding that behavior and personality are "nothing but" by-products of a bioneurological system best explained in terms of anatomy and physiology. A second and related criticism of biological approaches is that they generally limit themselves to positing a biological cause on one hand, a psychological result on the other hand, and then showing that the two are connected. As we have seen, the biological cause might be testosterone, cortisol, one's DNA, or the evolutionary history of the species. And the behavioral result might be violence, overreaction to stress, one's degree of extraversion, or the murder of one's wife!

Although such demonstrations of connections between biology and behavior are interesting and useful, they typically leap over all the processes in between—the traditional domain of psychology. For example, what does it feel like to be a high-testosterone prison inmate, and how does that feeling affect your motivations? What is it, exactly, that develops in the DNA of two extraverted twins, and how does that interact with their early experiences to produce the people they eventually become? And what really goes on in the mind of a spouse considering infidelity? These are the kinds of questions many people—including psychologists—expect psychology to address. But, as we have seen, biological approaches to personality typically neither answer nor ask questions like these.

The real potential for a biological approach to psychology, therefore, is for it to be integrated with psychological and social factors in a way that leads all the way and step by step from genetically based predeterminants, on the one hand, to important behavioral outcomes on the other. Such integration is yet rare, but a superb example is provided by the final selection in this section. The well-known social and personality psychologist Daryl Bem tackles the issue of sexual orientation—what makes a person turn out to be heterosexual or homosexual.

Although this article contains a wide range of interesting commentary on many issues, the heart of the theory is portrayed in a simple fashion in Figure 1. Notice how the development of sexual orientation begins with genes, prenatal hormones, and other purely biological variables. These variables produce the basic personality styles, evident in early childhood, called "temperaments." These temperaments in turn lead to preferences and aversions to different kinds of activities. Since our gender-polarized society sees rough-and-tumble play as appropriate for boys but more sedate activities as appropriate for girls, the activity preferences of a given child quickly become identified as either appropriate or inappropriate to his or her gender. Depending on which kind of activities one prefers, one associates with either same-sex or opposite-sex peers, leading in turn to a viewing of the nonassociated sex as mysterious or, in Bem's term, "exotic." A basic biological mechanism then engages, which leads stimuli seen as exotic to become endowed with erotic appeal. Finally, one has eroticized either the opposite or same sex, and thus become either heterosexual or homosexual.

Bem's theory may be right or it may be wrong. Although he arrays an impressive amount of evidence in its favor, new theories as complex as this one have a small chance of being correct in their entirety. But the most important aspect of the theory is how it points the way for biological personality psychology in general. Unlike so many other biologically based explanations, Bem's is complete. Rather than leaping over the gap between biology and behavior, it explains how each link in a complex chain leads to an important attribute of the person.

From *Psychological Review, 103*, 320–335, 1996.

* * *

The question "What causes homosexuality?" is both politically suspect and scientifically misconceived. Politically suspect because it is so frequently motivated by an agenda of prevention and cure. Scientifically misconceived because it presumes that heterosexuality is so well understood, so obviously the "natural" evolutionary consequence of reproductive advantage, that only deviations from it are theoretically problematic. Freud himself did not so presume: "[Heterosexuality] is also a problem that needs elucidation and is not a self-evident fact based upon an attraction that is ultimately of a chemical nature" (1905/1962, pp. 11–12).

Accordingly, this article proposes a developmental theory of erotic/romantic attraction that provides the same basic account for both opposite-sex and same-sex desire—and for both men and women. In addition to finding such parsimony politically, scientifically, and aesthetically satisfying, I believe that it can also be sustained by the evidence.

The academic discourse on sexual orientation is currently dominated by the biological essentialists—who can point to a corpus of evidence linking sexual orientation to genes, prenatal hormones, and brain neuroanatomy—and the social constructionists—who can point to a corpus of historical and anthropological evidence showing that the very concept of sexual orientation is a culture-bound notion (De Cecco & Elia, 1993). The personality, clinical, and developmental theorists who once dominated the discourse on this topic have fallen conspicuously silent. Some have probably become closet converts to biology because they cannot point to a coherent corpus of evidence that supports an experience-based account of sexual orientation. This would be understandable; experience-based theories have not fared well empirically in recent years.

The most telling data come from an intensive, large-scale interview study conducted in the San Francisco Bay Area by the Kinsey Institute for Sex Research (Bell, Weinberg, & Hammersmith, 1981a). Using path analysis to test several developmental hypotheses,[1] the investigators compared approximately 1,000 gay men and lesbians with 500 heterosexual men and women. The study (hereinafter, the San Francisco study) yielded virtually no support for current experience-based accounts of sexual orientation. With respect to the classical psychoanalytic account, for example,

> our findings indicate that boys who grow up with dominant mothers and weak fathers have nearly the same chances of becoming homosexual as they would if they grew up in "ideal" family settings. Similarly, the idea that homosexuality reflects a failure to resolve boys' "Oedipal" feelings during childhood receives no support from our study. Our data indicate that the connection between boys' relationships with their mothers and whether they become homosexual or heterosexual is hardly worth mentioning. . . . [Similarly,] we found no evidence that prehomosexual girls are "Oedipal victors"—having apparently usurped their mothers' place in the fathers' affections. . . . [Finally,] respondents' identification with their opposite-sex parents while they were growing up appears to have had no significant impact on whether they turned out to be homosexual or heterosexual. (pp. 184, 189)

More generally, no family variables were strongly implicated in the development of sexual orientation for either men or women.[2]

The data also failed to support any of several possible accounts based on mechanisms of learning or conditioning, including the popular layperson's "seduction" theory of homosexuality. In particular, the kinds of sexual encounters that would presumably serve as the basis for such learning or conditioning typically occurred after, rather than before, the individual experienced the relevant sexual feelings. Gay men and lesbians, for example, had typically not participated in any "advanced" sexual activities with persons of the same sex until about 3 years after they had become aware of same-sex attractions. Moreover, they neither lacked opposite-sex sexual experiences during their childhood and adolescent years nor found them unpleasant.

And finally, there was no support for "labeling" theory, which suggests that individuals might adopt a homosexual orientation as a consequence of being labeled homosexual or sexually different by others as they were growing up. Although gay men and lesbians were, in fact, more likely to report that they had been so labeled, the path analysis revealed the differential labeling to be the result of an emerging homosexual orientation rather than a cause of or even a secondary contributor to it.

But before we all become geneticists, biopsychologists, or neuroanatomists, I believe it's worth another try. In particular, I believe that the theoretical and empirical building blocks for a coherent, experience-based developmental theory of sexual orientation are already scattered about in the literature. What follows, then, is an exercise in synthesis and construction—followed, in turn, by analysis and deconstruction.

Overview of the Theory

The theory proposed here claims to specify the causal antecedents of an individual's erotic or romantic attractions to opposite-sex and same-sex persons. In particular, Figure 1 displays the proposed temporal sequence of events that leads to sexual orientation for most men and women in a gender-polarizing culture like ours—a culture that emphasizes the differences between the sexes by pervasively organizing both the perceptions

---

[1]"Path analysis" is a statistical technique that evaluates numerous correlations in complex data sets to try to disentangle cause and effect.

[2]This is reminiscent of Plomin's conclusion, in the earlier selection, that shared family experience has a small impact on development.

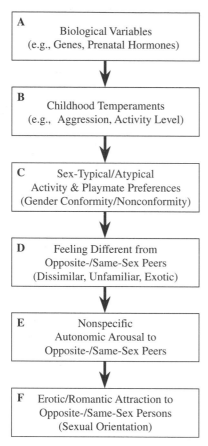

Figure 1 The temporal sequence of events leading to sexual orientation for most men and women in a gender-polarizing culture.

and realities of communal life around the male-female dichotomy (S. Bem, 1993). The sequence begins at the top of the figure with biological variables (labeled **A**) and ends at the bottom with erotic/romantic attraction (**F**).

A → B. Biological variables such as genes or prenatal hormones do not code for sexual orientation per se but for childhood temperaments, such as aggression or activity level.

B → C. A child's temperaments predispose him or her to enjoy some activities more than others. One child will enjoy rough-and-tumble play and competitive team sports (male-typical activities); another will prefer to socialize quietly or play

jacks or hopscotch (female-typical activities). Children will also prefer to play with peers who share their activity preferences; for example, the child who enjoys baseball or football will selectively seek out boys as playmates. Children who prefer sex-typical activities and same-sex playmates are referred to as gender conforming; children who prefer sex-atypical activities and opposite-sex playmates are referred to as gender nonconforming.

C → D. Gender-conforming children will feel different from opposite-sex peers, perceiving them as dissimilar, unfamiliar, and exotic. Similarly, gender-nonconforming children will feel different—even alienated—from same-sex peers, perceiving them as dissimilar, unfamiliar, and exotic.

D → E. These feelings of dissimilarity and unfamiliarity produce heightened autonomic arousal. For the male-typical child, it may be felt as antipathy or contempt in the presence of girls ("girls are yucky"); for the female-typical child, it may be felt as timidity or apprehension in the presence of boys. A particularly clear example is provided by the "sissy" boy who is taunted by male peers for his gender nonconformity and, as a result, is likely to experience the strong autonomic arousal of fear and anger in their presence. Although girls are punished less than boys for gender nonconformity, a "tomboy" girl who is ostracized by her female peers may feel similar, affectively toned arousal in their presence. The theory claims, however, that every child, conforming or nonconforming, experiences heightened, nonspecific autonomic arousal in the presence of peers from whom he or she feels different. In this modal case, the arousal will not necessarily be affectively toned or consciously felt.

E → F. Regardless of the specific source or affective tone of the childhood autonomic arousal, it is transformed in later years into erotic/romantic attraction. Steps **D → E** and **E → F** thus encompass specific psychological mechanisms that transform exotic into erotic (**D → F**). For brevity, the entire sequence outlined in Figure 1 will be referred to as the EBE (Exotic Becomes Erotic) theory of sexual orientation.

As noted above, Figure 1 does not describe an

TABLE 1				

PERCENTAGE OF RESPONDENTS REPORTING GENDER-NONCONFORMING PREFERENCES AND
BEHAVIORS DURING CHILDHOOD

	Men		Women	
Response	Gay ($n = 686$)	Heterosexual ($n = 337$)	Lesbian ($n = 293$)	Heterosexual ($n = 140$)
Had not enjoyed sex-typical activities	63	10	63	15
Had enjoyed sex-atypical activities	48	11	81	61
Atypical sex-typed (masculinity/femininity)	56	8	80	24
At least half of childhood friends were of the opposite sex	42	13	60	40

Note. Percentages have been calculated from the data given in Bell, Weinberg, and Hammersmith (1981b, pp. 74–75, 77). All chi-square comparisons between gay and heterosexual subgroups are significant at $p < .0001$.

inevitable, universal path to sexual orientation but the modal path followed by most men and women in a gender-polarizing culture like ours. Individual variations, alternative paths, and cultural influences on sexual orientation are discussed in the final sections of the article.

Evidence for the Theory

Evidence for EBE theory is organized into the following narrative sequence: Gender conformity or nonconformity in childhood is a causal antecedent of sexual orientation in adulthood ($C \rightarrow F$). This is so because gender conformity or nonconformity causes a child to perceive opposite or same sex peers as exotic ($C \rightarrow D$), and the exotic class of peers subsequently becomes erotically or romantically attractive to him or her ($D \rightarrow F$). This occurs because exotic peers produce heightened autonomic arousal ($D \rightarrow E$) which is subsequently transformed into erotic/romantic attraction ($E \rightarrow F$). This entire sequence of events can be initiated, among other ways, by biological factors that influence a child's temperaments ($A \rightarrow B$), which, in turn, influence his or her preferences for gender-conforming or gender-nonconforming activities and peers ($B \rightarrow C$).

GENDER CONFORMITY OR NONCONFORMITY IN CHILDHOOD IS A CAUSAL ANTECEDENT OF SEXUAL ORIENTATION ($C \rightarrow F$) In a review of sex-role socialization in 1980, Serbin asserted that "there is no evidence that highly sex-typed children are less likely to become homosexual than children showing less extreme sex-role conformity" (p. 85).

Well, there is now. In the San Francisco study, childhood gender conformity or nonconformity was not only the strongest but the only significant childhood predictor of later sexual orientation for both men and women (Bell et al., 1981a). As Table 1 shows, the effects were large and significant. For example, gay men were significantly more likely than heterosexual men to report that as children they had not enjoyed boys' activities (e.g., baseball and football), had enjoyed girls' activities (e.g., hopscotch, playing house, and jacks), and had been nonmasculine. These were the three variables that defined gender nonconformity in the study. Additionally, gay men were more likely than heterosexual men to have had girls as childhood friends. The corresponding comparisons between lesbian and heterosexual women were also large and significant. Moreover, the path analyses implied that gender conformity or nonconformity in childhood was a causal antecedent of later sexual orientation for both men and women—with the usual caveat that even path analysis cannot "prove" causality.

It is also clear from the table that relatively more women than men had enjoyed sex-atypical activities and had opposite-sex friends during childhood. (In fact, more heterosexual women than gay men had enjoyed boys' activities as children—61% versus 37%, respectively.) As I suggest later, this might account, in part, for differences between men and women in how their sexual orientations are distributed in our society.

The San Francisco study does not stand alone. A meta-analysis of 48 studies with sample sizes ranging from 34 to 8,751 confirmed that gay men and lesbians were more likely to recall gender-nonconforming behaviors and interests in childhood than were heterosexual men and women (Bailey & Zucker, 1995). The differences were large and significant for both men and women, ranging (in units of standard deviation) from 0.5 to 2.1 across studies, with means of 1.31 and 0.96 for men and women, respectively. As the authors noted, "these are among the largest effect sizes ever reported in the realm of sex-dimorphic behaviors" (p. 49).[3]

Prospective studies have come to the same conclusion. The largest of these involved a sample of 66 gender-nonconforming and 56 gender-conforming boys with a mean age of 7.1 years (Green, 1987). The researchers were able to assess about two thirds of each group in late adolescence or early adulthood, finding that about 75% of the previously gender-nonconforming boys were either bisexual or homosexual compared with only one (4%) of the gender-conforming boys. In six other prospective studies, 63% of gender-nonconforming boys whose sexual orientations could be ascertained in late adolescence or adulthood had homosexual orientations (Zucker, 1990). Unfortunately, there are no prospective studies of gender-nonconforming girls.

This body of data has led one researcher in the field to assert that the link between childhood gender nonconformity and an adult homosexual orientation "may be the most consistent, well-documented, and significant finding in the entire field of sexual-orientation research and perhaps in all of human psychology" (Hamer & Copeland, 1994, p. 166). That may be a bit hyperbolic—Hamer is a molecular geneticist, not a psychologist—but it is difficult to think of other individual differences (besides IQ or sex itself) that so reliably and so strongly predict socially significant outcomes across the life span, and for both sexes, too. Surely it must be true.

GENDER CONFORMITY AND NONCONFORMITY PRODUCE FEELINGS OF BEING DIFFERENT FROM OPPOSITE AND SAME-SEX PEERS, RESPECTIVELY (C → D) EBE theory proposes that gender-conforming children will come to feel different from their opposite-sex peers and gender-nonconforming children will come to feel different from their same-sex peers. To my knowledge, no researcher has ever asked children or adults whether they feel different from opposite-sex peers, probably because they expect the universal answer to be yes. The San Francisco researchers, however, did ask respondents whether they felt different from same-sex peers in childhood. They found that 71% of gay men and 70% of lesbian women recalled having felt different from same-sex children during the grade-school years, compared with 38% and 51% of heterosexual men and women, respectively ($p < .0005$ for both gay/heterosexual comparisons).

When asked in what way they felt different, gay men were most likely to say that they did not like sports; lesbians were most likely to say that they were more interested in sports or were more masculine than other girls. In contrast, the heterosexual men and women who had felt different from their same-sex peers in childhood typically cited differences unrelated to gender. Heterosexual men tended to cite such reasons as being poorer, more intelligent, or more introverted. Heterosexual women frequently cited differences in physical appearance.

---

[3]In other words, these differences are as large or larger than sex differences in general usually are.

Finally, the data showed that the gender-nonconforming child's sense of being different from same-sex peers is not a fleeting early experience but a protracted and sustained feeling throughout childhood and adolescence. For example, in the path model for men, gender nonconformity in childhood was also a significant predictor of feeling different for gender reasons during adolescence (which was, in turn, a significant predictor of a homosexual orientation). Similarly, the statistically significant difference between the lesbians and heterosexual women in feeling different from same-sex peers during childhood remained significant during adolescence. This is, I believe, why sexual orientation displays such strong temporal stability across the life course for most individuals.

EXOTIC BECOMES EROTIC (D → F) The heart of EBE theory is the proposition that individuals become erotically or romantically attracted to those who were dissimilar or unfamiliar to them in childhood. We have already seen some evidence for this in Table 1: Those who played more with girls in childhood, gay men and heterosexual women, preferred men as sexual/romantic partners in later years; those who played more with boys in childhood, lesbian women and heterosexual men, preferred women as sexual/romantic partners in later years. As we shall now see, however, the links between similarity and erotic/romantic attraction are complex.

Similarity and complementarity. One of the most widely accepted conclusions in social psychology, cited in virtually every textbook, is that similarity promotes interpersonal attraction and that complementarity ("opposites attract") does not.

For example, the vast majority of married couples in the United States are of the same race and religion, and most are significantly similar in age, socioeconomic class, educational level, intelligence, height, eye color, and even physical attractiveness (Feingold, 1988; Murstein, 1972; Rubin, 1973; Silverman, 1971). In one study, dating couples who were the most similar were the most likely to be together a year later (Hill, Rubin, & Peplau,

1976). In a longitudinal study of 135 married couples, spouses with similar personalities reported more closeness, friendliness, shared enjoyment in daily activities, marital satisfaction, and less marital conflict than less similar couples (Caspi & Herbener, 1990). In contrast, attempts to identify complementarities that promote or sustain intimate relationships have not been very successful (Levinger, Senn, & Jorgensen, 1970; Strong et al., 1988). Marital adjustment among couples married for up to 5 years was found to depend more on similarity than on complementarity (Meyer & Pepper, 1977).

But there is an obvious exception: sex. Most people choose members of the opposite sex to be their romantic and sexual partners. It is an indication of how unthinkingly heterosexuality is taken for granted that authors of articles and textbooks never seem to notice this quintessential complementarity and its challenge to the conclusion that similarity produces attraction. They certainly don't pause to ponder why we are not all gay or lesbian.

The key to resolving this apparent paradox is also a staple of textbooks: the distinction between liking and loving or between companionate and passionate love (Berscheid & Walster, 1974; Brehm, 1992). The correlation among dating or engaged couples between liking their partners and loving them is only .56 for men and .36 for women (Rubin, 1973). Both fiction and real life provide numerous examples of erotic attraction between two incompatible people who may not even like each other. Collectively, these observations suggest that similarity may promote friendship, compatibility, and companionate love, but it is dissimilarity that sparks erotic/romantic attraction and passionate love.

This is the resolution proposed by both Tripp (1975) and Bell (1982), the senior author of the San Francisco study:

> a necessary ingredient for romantic attachment is one's perception of the loved one as essentially different from oneself in terms of gender-related attributes. According to this view it would be argued that, among homosexuals and heterosexuals alike, persons perceived as essentially *different* from ourselves

become the chief candidates for our early romantic and, later, erotic investments. Only a superficial view of the matter would maintain that *heterogamy*, as it has been called, operates only among heterosexuals where anatomical differences make the principle, "opposites attract," most obvious. Among both groups we find romantic and sexual feelings aroused by others perceived to be different from ourselves, unfamiliar in manner, attitude, and interests, and whose differences offer the possibility of a relationship based upon psychological (not necessarily genital) complementarity. On the other side of the coin is the principle of *homogamy* in which perceived similarity and mutual identification and familiarity makes for friendship as opposed to the romantic . . . state. (Bell, 1982, p. 2)

But this account fails to resolve the paradox because it errs in the opposite direction, failing to account for the previously cited evidence that, except for sex itself, it is similarity and not complementarity that sustains the majority of successful heterosexual relationships. Similarly, for every gay or lesbian relationship that conforms to the "butch-femme" stereotype of the popular imagination, there appear to be many more in which the partners are strikingly similar to each other in both psychological and physical attributes—including sex. Bell's account resolves the paradox only if one is willing to accept the implausible implication that all those happy, similar partners must be devoid of erotic enthusiasm for each other.

Like the accounts of Tripp and Bell, EBE theory also proposes that dissimilarity promotes erotic/romantic attraction, but it locates the animating dissimilarity in childhood. Consider, for example, a gender-nonconforming boy whose emerging homoeroticism happens to crystallize around the muscular athlete or leather-jacketed motorcyclist. As he moves into adolescence and adulthood, he may deliberately begin to acquire the attributes and trappings of his eroticized hypermasculine ideal—working out at the gym, buying a leather jacket, getting a body tattoo, and so forth. This acquired "macho" image is not only self-satisfying but is also attractive to other gay men who have eroticized this same idealized image. Two such men will thus be erotically attracted to each other, and their striking similarities, including their shared eroticism, will have been produced by their shared childhood dissimilarities from highly masculine boys.

EBE theory thus proposes that once the dissimilarities of childhood have laid the groundwork for a sustained sexual orientation, the noncriterial attributes of one's preferred partners within the eroticized class can range from extremely similar to extremely dissimilar. More generally, the theory proposes that the protracted period of feeling different from same- or opposite-sex peers during childhood and adolescence produces a stable sexual orientation for most individuals but that within that orientation there can be wide ranging—and changing—idiosyncratic preferences for particular partners or kinds of partners.

Familiarity and unfamiliarity. Like similarity, familiarity is a major antecedent of liking. In fact, similarity probably promotes liking precisely because it increases familiarity: Social norms, situational circumstances, and mutual interests conspire to bring people together who are similar to one another, thereby increasing their mutual familiarity. When college roommates were systematically paired for similarity or dissimilarity in Newcomb's (1961) ambitious 2-year study of the acquaintance process, familiarity turned out to be a stronger facilitator of liking than similarity.

The "familiarity-breeds-liking" effect has been confirmed in so many contexts that it is now considered to be a general psychological principle. For example, rats repeatedly exposed to compositions by Mozart or Schönberg have shown an enhanced preference for the composer they heard, and humans repeatedly exposed to nonsense syllables, Chinese characters, or real people have come to prefer those they saw most often (Harrison, 1977).

But like childhood similarity, childhood familiarity does not produce erotic or romantic attraction; on the contrary, it appears to be antithetical to it. This was observed over a century ago by Westermarck (1891), who noted that two individuals who spent their childhood years together did not find each other sexually attractive even when there were strong social pressures favoring a bond between them. For example, he reported problematic sexual relations in arranged marriages in which the couple was betrothed in childhood and the girl was taken in by the future husband's family and treated like one of the siblings; similar findings have emerged from more recent studies of arranged marriages in Taiwan (cited in Bateson, 1978a).

A contemporary example is provided by children on Israeli kibbutzim, who are raised communally with age-mates in mixed-sex groups and exposed to one another constantly during their entire childhood. Sex play is not discouraged and is quite intensive during early childhood. After childhood, there is no formal or informal pressure or sanction against heterosexual activity within the peer group from educators, parents, or members of the peer group itself. Yet despite all this, there is a virtual absence of erotic attraction between peer group members in adolescence or adulthood (Bettelheim, 1969; Rabin, 1965; Shepher, 1971; Spiro, 1958; Talmon, 1964). A review of nearly 3,000 marriages contracted by second-generation adults in all Israeli kibbutzim revealed that there was not a single case of an intrapeer group marriage (Shepher, 1971).

*　*　*

The Sambian culture in New Guinea illustrates the phenomenon in a homosexual context. As described by Herdt in several publications (1981, 1984, 1987, 1990), Sambian males believe that boys cannot attain manhood without ingesting semen from older males. At age 7 years, Sambian boys are removed from the family household and initiated into secret male rituals, including ritualized homosexuality. For the next several years, they live in the men's clubhouse and regularly fellate older male adolescents. When they reach sexual maturity, they reverse roles and are fellated by younger initiates. During this entire time, they have no sexual contact with girls or women. And yet, when it comes time to marry and father children in their late teens or early twenties, all but a tiny minority of Sambian males become preferentially and exclusively heterosexual. Although Sambian boys enjoy their homosexual activities, the context of close familiarity in which it occurs either extinguishes or prevents the development of strongly charged homoerotic feelings.

During the years that a Sambian boy is participating in homosexual activities with his male peers, he is taught a misogynist ideology that portrays women as dangerous and exotic creatures—almost a different species. According to EBE theory, this should enhance their erotic attractiveness for him. More generally, EBE theory proposes that heterosexuality is the modal outcome across time and culture because virtually all human societies polarize the sexes to some extent, setting up a sex-based division of labor and power, emphasizing or exaggerating sex differences, and, in general, superimposing the male-female dichotomy on virtually every aspect of communal life. These gender-polarizing practices ensure that most boys and girls will grow up seeing the other sex as dissimilar, unfamiliar, and exotic—and, hence, erotic. Thus, the theory provides a culturally based alternative to the assumption that heterosexuality must necessarily be coded in the genes. I return to this point later.

Finally, the assertion that exotic becomes erotic should be amended to exotic—but not too exotic—becomes erotic (cf. Tripp, 1987). Thus, an erotic or romantic preference for partners of a different sex, race, or ethnicity is relatively common, but a preference for lying with the beasts in the field is not. This phenomenon appears to be a special case of the well-established motivational principle that there is an optimal, nonzero level of stimulus novelty and a correspondingly optimal nonzero level of internal arousal that an organism will seek to attain or maintain (Mook, 1987).

HOW DOES EXOTIC BECOME EROTIC? (D → E → F)

In Plato's *Symposium*, Aristophanes explains sexual attraction by recounting the early history of human beings. Originally, we were all eight-limbed creatures with two faces and two sets of genitals. Males had two sets of male genitals, females had two sets of female genitals, and androgynes had one set of each kind. As punishment for being overly ambitious, Zeus had all humans cut in half.

But because the two halves of each former individual clung to each other in such a desperate attempt to reunite, Zeus took pity on them and invented sexual intercourse so that they might at least reunite temporarily. Sexual attraction thus reflects an attempt to complete one's original self, and heterosexual attraction is what characterizes the descendents of the androgynes.

It is a durable myth. Both Bell (1982) and Tripp (1987) propose that we are erotically attracted to people who are different from us because we are embarked on a "quest for androgyny" (Bell); we seek to complete ourselves by "importing" gender-related attributes that we perceive ourselves as lacking (Tripp). As noted earlier, I do not believe this accurately characterizes the data; but even if it did, it would constitute only a description of them, not an explanation. There may not be much evidence for Aristophanes' historical account, but epistemologically at least, it is an explanation.

Because I prefer mechanism to metaphor, EBE theory is unabashedly reductionistic. As already discussed, it proposes that exotic becomes erotic because feelings of dissimilarity and unfamiliarity in childhood produce heightened nonspecific autonomic arousal (D → E) which is subsequently transformed into erotic/romantic attraction (E → F). To my knowledge, there is no direct evidence for the first step in this sequence beyond the well-documented observation that novelty and unfamiliarity produce heightened arousal (Mook, 1987); filling in this empirical gap in EBE theory must await future research. In contrast, there are at least three mechanisms that can potentially effect the second step, transforming generalized arousal into erotic/romantic attraction: the extrinsic arousal effect, the opponent process, and imprinting.[4]

The extrinsic arousal effect. In his 1st-century Roman handbook, *The Art of Love*, Ovid advised any man who was interested in sexual seduction to take the woman in whom he was interested to a gladia-

torial tournament, where she would more easily be aroused to passion. He did not say why this should be so, however, and it was not until 1887 that an elaboration appeared in the literature:

> Love can only be excited by strong and vivid emotion, and it is almost immaterial whether these emotions are agreeable or disagreeable. The Cid wooed the proud heart of Donna Ximene, whose father he had slain, by shooting one after another of her pet pigeons. (Horwicz, quoted in Finck, 1887, p. 240)

A contemporary explanation of this effect was introduced by Walster (1971; Berscheid & Walster, 1974), who suggested that it constituted a special case of Schachter and Singer's (1962) two-factor theory of emotion. That theory states that the physiological arousal of our autonomic nervous system provides the cues that we are feeling emotional but that the more subtle judgment of which emotion we are feeling often depends on our cognitive appraisal of the surrounding circumstances. According to Walster, then, the experience of passionate love or erotic/romantic attraction results from the conjunction of physiological arousal and the cognitive causal attribution (or misattribution) that the arousal has been elicited by the potential lover.

There is now extensive experimental evidence that an individual who has been physiologically aroused will show heightened sexual responsiveness to an appropriate target stimulus. In one set of studies, male participants were physiologically aroused by running in place, by hearing an audiotape of a comedy routine, or by hearing an audiotape of a grisly killing (White, Fishbein, & Rutstein, 1981). They then viewed a taped interview with a woman who was either physically attractive or physically unattractive. Finally, they rated the woman on several dimensions, including her attractiveness, her sexiness, and the degree to which they would be interested in dating her and kissing her. The results showed that no matter how the arousal had been elicited, participants were more erotically responsive to the attractive woman and less erotically responsive to the unattractive woman than were control participants who had not been aroused. In other words, the arousal in-

---

[4]Bem's discussion of "imprinting" and the "opponent process" are not included in this excerpt.

tensified both positive or negative reactions to the woman, depending on which was cognitively appropriate.

This extrinsic arousal effect (my term) is not limited to the individual's cognitive appraisal of his or her emotional state. In two studies, men or women watched a sequence of two videotapes. The first portrayed either an anxiety-inducing or non-anxiety-inducing scene; the second videotape portrayed a nude heterosexual couple engaging in sexual foreplay. Preexposure to the anxiety-inducing scene produced greater penile tumescence in men and greater vaginal blood volume increases in women in response to the erotic scene than did preexposure to the non-anxiety-inducing scene (Hoon, Wincze, & Hoon, 1977; Wolchik et al., 1980).

In addition to the misattribution explanation, several other explanations for the extrinsic arousal effect have been proposed, but experimental attempts to determine which explanation is the most valid have produced mixed results and the dispute is not yet settled (Allen, Kenrick, Linder, & McCall, 1989; Kenrick & Cialdini, 1977; McClanahan, Gold, Lenney, Ryckman, & Kulberg, 1990; White & Kight, 1984; Zillmann, 1983). For present purposes, however, it doesn't matter. It is sufficient to know that autonomic arousal, regardless of its source or affective tone, can subsequently be experienced cognitively, emotionally, and physiologically as erotic/romantic attraction. At that point, it *is* erotic/romantic attraction.

The pertinent question, then, is whether this effect can account for the link between autonomic arousal in childhood and erotic/romantic attraction later in life. In one respect, the experiments may actually underestimate the strength and reliability of the effect in real life. In the experiments, the arousal is deliberately elicited by a source extrinsic to the intended target, and there is disagreement over whether the effect even occurs when participants are aware of that fact (Allen et al., 1989; Cantor, Zillmann, & Bryant, 1975; McClanahan et al., 1990; White & Kight, 1984). But in the real-life scenario envisioned by EBE theory, the autonomic arousal is genuinely elicited by the class of individuals to which the erotic/romantic attraction develops. The exotic arousal and the erotic arousal are thus likely to be phenomenologically indistinguishable.

* * *

THE BIOLOGICAL CONNECTION: (A → F) VERSUS (A → B)

In recent years, researchers, the mass media, and segments of the lesbian/gay/bisexual community have rushed to embrace the thesis that a homosexual orientation is coded in the genes or determined by prenatal hormones and brain neuroanatomy. Even the authors of the San Francisco study, whose findings disconfirm most experience-based theories of sexual orientation, seem ready to concede the ball game to biology. In contrast, EBE theory proposes that biological factors influence sexual orientation only indirectly, by intervening earlier in the chain of events to determine a child's temperaments and subsequent activity preferences. Accordingly, my persuasive task in this section is to argue that any nonartifactual correlation between a biological factor and sexual orientation is more plausibly attributed to its influence in early childhood than to a direct link with sexual orientation.

Genes. Recent studies have provided some evidence for a correlation between an individual's genotype and his or her sexual orientation. For example, in a sample of 115 gay men who had male twins, 52% of monozygotic twin brothers were also gay compared with only 22% of dizygotic twin brothers and 11% of gay men's adoptive brothers (Bailey & Pillard, 1991). In a comparable sample of 115 lesbians, 48% of monozygotic twin sisters were also lesbian compared with only 16% of dizygotic twin sisters and 6% of lesbian women's adoptive sisters (Bailey, Pillard, Neale, & Agyei, 1993). A subsequent study of nearly 5,000 twins who had been systematically drawn from a twin registry confirmed the significant heritability of sexual orientation for men but not for women (Bailey & Martin, 1995). And finally, a pedigree and linkage analysis of 114 families of gay men and a DNA linkage analysis of 40 families in which there were two gay brothers suggested a correlation between a homosexual orientation and the inheritance of genetic markers on the X chromosome (Hamer & Copeland, 1994; Hamer, Hu, Magnuson, Hu, & Pattatucci, 1993).[5]

But these same studies have also provided evidence for the link proposed by EBE theory between an individual's genotype and his or her childhood gender nonconformity, even when sexual orientation is held constant. For example, in the 1991 twin study of gay men, childhood gender nonconformity was assessed by a composite of three scales that have been shown to discriminate between gay and heterosexual men: childhood aggressiveness, interest in sports, and effeminacy. Across twin pairs in which both brothers were gay ("concordant" pairs), the correlation on gender nonconformity for monozygotic twins was as high as the reliability of the scale would permit, .76 ($p < .0001$), compared with a correlation of only .43 for concordant dizygotic twins, implying significant heritability (Bailey & Pillard, 1991). In the family pedigree study of gay men, pairs of gay brothers who were concordant for the genetic markers on the X chromosome were also more similar on gender nonconformity than were genetically discordant pairs of gay brothers (Hamer & Copeland, 1994). Finally, childhood gender nonconformity was significantly heritable for both men and women in the large twin registry study, even though sexual orientation itself was not heritable for the women (Bailey & Martin, 1995).

These studies are thus consistent with the link specified by EBE theory between the genotype and gender nonconformity (A → C). The theory further specifies that this link is composed of two parts, a link between the genotype and childhood temperaments (A → B) and a link between those temperaments and gender nonconformity (B → C). This implies that the mediating temperaments should possess three characteristics: First, they should be plausibly related to those play activities that define gender conformity and nonconformity.

Second, because they manifest themselves in sex-typed preferences, they should show sex differences. And third, because they are hypothesized to derive from the genotype, they should have significant heritabilities.

One likely candidate is aggression and its benign cousin, rough-and-tumble play. As noted above, gay men score lower than heterosexual men on a measure of childhood aggression (Blanchard, McConkey, Roper, & Steiner, 1983), and parents of gender-nonconforming boys specifically rate them as having less interest in rough-and-tumble play than do parents of gender-conforming boys (Green, 1976). Second, the sex difference in aggression during childhood is about half a standard deviation, one of the largest psychological sex differences known (Hyde, 1984). Rough-and-tumble play in particular is more common in boys than in girls (DiPietro, 1981; Fry, 1990; Moller, Hymel, & Rubin, 1992). And third, individual differences in aggression have a large heritable component (Rushton, Fulker, Neale, Nias, & Eysenck, 1986).

Another likely candidate is activity level, considered to be one of the basic childhood temperaments (Buss & Plomin, 1975, 1984). Like aggression, differences in activity level would also seem to characterize the differences between male-typical and female-typical play activities in childhood, and gender-nonconforming boys and girls are lower and higher on activity level, respectively, than are control children of the same sex (Bates, Bentler, & Thompson, 1973, 1979; Zucker & Green, 1993). Second, the sex difference in activity level is as large as it is for aggression. A meta-analysis of 127 studies found boys to be about half a standard deviation more active than girls. Even before birth, boys in utero are about one-third of a standard deviation more active than girls (Eaton & Enns, 1986). And third, individual differences in activity level have a large heritable component (Plomin, 1986).

In sum, existing data are consistent with both a direct path between the genotype and sexual orientation and the EBE path which channels genetic influence through the child's temperaments and subsequent activity preferences. So why should one prefer the EBE account?

---

[5]This last finding is currently in dispute, and an independent attempt to replicate it has failed (Rice, Anderson, Risch, & Ebers, 1995).—Author

The missing theory for the direct path. The EBE account may be wrong, but I submit that a competing theoretical rationale for a direct path between the genotype and sexual orientation has not even been clearly articulated, let alone established. At first glance, the theoretical rationale would appear to be nothing less than the powerful and elegant theory of evolution. The belief that sexual orientation is coded in the genes would appear to be just the general case of the implicit assumption, mentioned in the introduction, that heterosexuality is the obvious, "natural" evolutionary consequence of reproductive advantage.

But if that is true, then a homosexual orientation is an evolutionary anomaly that requires further theoretical explication. How do lesbians and gay men manage to pass on their gene pool to successive generations? Several hypothetical scenarios have been offered (for a review, see Savin-Williams, 1987). One is that social institutions such as universal marriage can ensure that lesbians and gay men will have enough children to sustain a "homosexual" gene pool (Weinrich, 1987). Another is that the genes for homosexuality are linked to, or piggyback on, other genes that themselves carry reproductive advantage, such as genes for intelligence or dominance (Kirsch & Rodman, 1982; Weinrich, 1978). A third, based on kin selection, speculates that homosexual individuals may help nurture a sufficient number of their kin (e.g., nieces and nephews) to reproductive maturity to ensure that their genes get passed along to successive generations (Weinrich, 1978; Wilson, 1975, 1978).

Although these speculations have been faulted on theoretical, metatheoretical, and empirical grounds (Futuyma & Risch, 1983/84), a more basic problem with such arguments is their circularity. As Bleier has noted about similar accounts,

> this logic makes a *premise* of the genetic basis of behaviors, then cites a certain animal or human behavior, constructs a speculative story to explain how the behavior (*if* it were genetically based) could have served or could serve to maximize the reproductive success of the individual, and this *conjecture* then becomes evidence for the *premise* that the behavior was genetically determined. (1984, p. 17)

When one does attempt to deconstruct the evolutionary explanation for sexual orientation, homosexual *or* heterosexual, some problematic assumptions become explicit. For example, the belief that sexual orientation is coded in the genes embodies the unacknowledged assumption that knowledge of the distinction between male and female must also be hardwired into the human species, that sex is a natural category of human perception. After all, we cannot be erotically attracted to a class of persons unless and until we can discriminate exemplars from nonexemplars of that class.

Given what psychology has learned about human language and cognition in recent decades, the notion that humans have innate knowledge of the male-female distinction is not quite so inconceivable as it once was. An explicit version of this notion is embodied in the Jungian belief that an animus-anima archetype is part of our collective unconscious. It could also be argued that functional, if not cognitive, knowledge of the male-female distinction is embodied in innate responses to pheromones or other sensory cues, as it is for several other species.

As it happens, I find all these possibilities implausible, but that is not the point. Rather, it is that those who argue for the direct heritability of sexual orientation should be made cognizant of such assumptions and required to shoulder the burden of proof for them. More generally, any genetic argument, including a sociobiological one, must spell out the developmental pathway by which genotypes are transformed into phenotypes (Bronfenbrenner & Ceci, 1994). This is precisely what EBE theory attempts to do and what the competing claim for a direct path between genes and sexual orientation fails to do. It is not that an argument for a direct path has been made and found wanting, but that it has not yet been made.

I am certainly willing to concede that heterosexual behavior is reproductively advantageous, but it does not follow that it must therefore be sustained through genetic transmission. As noted earlier, EBE theory implies that heterosexuality is the modal outcome across time and culture because virtually every human society ensures that most boys and girls will grow up seeing the other sex as exotic and, hence, erotic.

The more general point is that as long as the environment supports or promotes a reproductively successful behavior sufficiently often, it will not necessarily get programmed into the genes. For example, it is presumably reproductively advantageous for ducks to mate with other ducks, but as long as most baby ducklings encounter other ducks before they encounter an ethologist, evolution can simply implant the imprinting process itself into the species rather than the specific content of what, reproductively speaking, needs to be imprinted. Analogously, because most cultures ensure that the two sexes will see each other as exotic, it would be sufficient for evolution to implant exotic-becomes-erotic processes into our species rather than heterosexuality per se. In fact, as noted earlier, an exotic-becomes-erotic mechanism is actually a component of sexual imprinting. If ducks, who are genetically free to mate with any moving object, have not perished from the earth, then neither shall we.

Prenatal hormones. One of the oldest hypotheses about sexual orientation is that gay men have too little testosterone and lesbians have too much. When the data failed to support this hypothesis (for reviews, see Gartrell, 1982, and Meyer-Bahlburg, 1984), attention turned from adult hormonal status to prenatal hormonal status. Reasoning from research on rats in which the experimental manipulation of prenatal androgen levels can "masculinize" or "feminize" the brain and produce sex-atypical mating postures and mounting responses, some researchers hypothesized that human males who are exposed prenatally to substantially lower than average amounts of testosterone and human females who are exposed to substantially higher than average amounts of testosterone will be predisposed toward a homosexual orientation in adult life (Ellis & Ames, 1987).

One body of data advanced in support of this hypothesis comes from interviews with women who have congenital adrenal hyperplasia (CAH), a chronic endocrine disorder that exposes them to abnormally high levels of androgen during the prenatal period, levels comparable to those received by normal male fetuses during gestation. Most of these women were born with virilized genitalia, which were surgically corrected soon after birth, and placed on cortisol medication to prevent further anatomical virilization. In three studies, CAH women have now reported more bisexual or homosexual responsiveness than control women (Dittmann et al., 1990a; Money, Schwartz, & Lewis, 1984; Zucker et al., 1992).

But a number of factors suggest that this link from prenatal hormones to sexual orientation is better explained by their effects on childhood temperaments and activity preferences. For example, both boys and girls who were exposed to high levels of androgenizing progestins during gestation have shown increased aggression later in childhood (Reinisch, 1981), and girls with CAH have shown stronger preferences for male-typical activities and male playmates in childhood than control girls (Berenbaum & Hines, 1992; Berenbaum & Snyder, 1995; Dittmann et al., 1990b; Money & Ehrhardt, 1972).

It is also possible that the correlation itself is artifactual, having nothing to do with prenatal hormonal exposure—let alone "masculinization" of the brain. The contemporaneous hormonal status of CAH girls could be producing some of these childhood effects. It is even conceivable that the cortisol medication could be increasing their activity level, thereby promoting their preference for male-typical activities (Quadagno, Briscoe, & Quadagno, 1977).

But from the perspective of EBE theory, the major reason for expecting CAH girls to be disproportionately homoerotic in adulthood is that they are overwhelmingly likely to feel different from other girls. Not only are they gender nonconforming in their play activities and peer preferences, as most lesbians are during the childhood years, but the salience of their CAH status itself aids and abets their perception of being different from other girls on gender-relevant dimensions. For example, they know about their virilized genitalia and they may be concerned that they will not be able to conceive and bear children when they grow up, one of the frequent complications of the CAH disorder. According to EBE theory, these are not girls who need masculinized brains to make them homoerotic.

A more critical test of the direct link between prenatal hormones and sexual orientation would seem to require a prenatal hormonal condition that is correlated with an adult homosexual orientation but uncorrelated with any of these childhood effects. Meyer-Bahlburg et al. (1995) have hypothesized that abnormally high levels of prenatal estrogens might produce such an outcome in women by masculinizing their brains.

Although the theoretical reasoning behind this hypothesis has been questioned (Byne & Parsons, 1993), Meyer-Bahlburg et al. (1995) cited some supporting evidence from women whose mothers had taken diethylstilbestrol (DES), a synthetic estrogen that was used to maintain high-risk pregnancies until it was banned in 1971. Three samples of such women have now been interviewed and rated on several Kinsey-like scales for heterosexual and homosexual responsiveness. According to the investigators, "more DES-exposed women than controls were rated as bisexual or homosexual . . ." (p. 12). Because DES does not produce any visible anomalies during childhood and evidence for childhood gender nonconformity among DES-exposed women was weak, this outcome would seem to favor the argument for a direct link between prenatal hormones and sexual orientation over the EBE account.

But the evidence for a bisexual or homosexual orientation among the DES-exposed women was also very weak. As Meyer-Bahlburg et al. (1995) themselves noted, "the majority of DES-exposed women in our study were exclusively or nearly exclusively heterosexual, in spite of their prenatal DES exposure" (p. 20). In fact, of 97 DES-exposed women interviewed, only 4 were rated as having a predominantly homosexual orientation, and not a single woman was rated as having an exclusively homosexual orientation. I think the jury is still out on the link between prenatal estrogens and sexual orientation.

* * *

Neuroanatomical correlates of sexual orientation. Even the general public now knows that there are neuroanatomical differences between the brains of gay men and those of heterosexual men and that some of these correspond to differences between the brains of women and men (Allen & Gorski, 1992; LeVay, 1991, 1993; Swaab & Hofman, 1990). Gay men also perform less well than heterosexual men on some cognitive, motor, and spatial tasks on which women perform less well than men (e.g., Gladue, Beatty, Larson, & Staton, 1990; McCormick & Witelson, 1991). (There are no comparable studies of lesbian women.)

But such differences are also consistent with the EBE account. Any biological factor that correlates with one or more of the intervening processes proposed by EBE theory could also emerge as a correlate of sexual orientation. For example, any neuroanatomical feature of the brain that correlates with childhood aggression or activity level could also emerge as a difference between gay men and heterosexual men, between women and men, and between heterosexual women and lesbians. Even if EBE theory turns out to be wrong, the more general point, that a mediating personality variable could account for observed correlations between biological variables and sexual orientation, still holds.

Like all well-bred scientists, biologically oriented researchers in the field of sexual orientation dutifully murmur the mandatory mantra that correlation is not cause. But the reductive temptation of biological causation is so seductive that the caveat cannot possibly compete with the excitement of discovering yet another link between the anatomy of our brains and the anatomy of our lovers' genitalia. Unfortunately, the caveat vanishes completely as word of the latest discovery moves from *Science* to *Newsweek*. The public can be forgiven for believing that research is but one government grant away from pinpointing the penis preference gene.

INDIVIDUAL VARIATIONS AND ALTERNATIVE PATHS

As noted earlier, Figure 1 is not intended to describe an inevitable, universal path to sexual orientation but only the modal path followed by most men and women in a gender-polarizing culture like ours. Individual variations can arise in several ways. First, different individuals might enter the EBE path at different points in the sequence. For example, a child might come to feel different from same-sex peers not because of a temperamentally induced preference for gender-nonconforming activities but because of an atypical lack of contact with same-sex peers, a physical disability, or an illness (e.g., the CAH girls). Similarly, I noted earlier that the nonmasculine lesbians in the San Francisco study were not significantly gender nonconforming in childhood. But they were more likely than heterosexual women to have mostly male friends in grade school, and, consistent with the subsequent steps in the EBE path, this was the strongest predictor for these women of homosexual involvements in adolescence and a homosexual orientation in adulthood.

In general, EBE theory predicts that the effect of any childhood variable on an individual's sexual orientation depends on whether it prompts him or her to feel more similar to or more different from same-sex or opposite-sex peers. For example, it has recently been reported that a gay man is likely to have more older brothers than a heterosexual man (Blanchard & Bogaert, 1996). This could come about, in part, if having gender-conforming older brothers especially enhances a gender-nonconforming boy's sense of being different from other boys.

Individual variations can also arise from differences in how individuals interpret the "exotic" arousal emerging from the childhood years, an interpretation that is inevitably guided by social norms and expectations. For example, girls might be more socially primed to interpret the arousal as romantic attraction whereas boys might be more primed to interpret it as sexual arousal. Certainly most individuals in our culture are primed to anticipate, recognize, and interpret opposite-sex arousal as erotic or romantic attraction and to ignore, repress, or differently interpret comparable same-sex arousal. In fact, the heightened visibility of gay men and lesbians in our society is now prompting individuals who experience same-sex arousal to recognize it, label it, and act on it at earlier ages than in previous years (Fox, 1995).

In some instances, the EBE process itself may be supplemented or even superseded by processes of conditioning or social learning, both positive and negative. Such processes could also produce shifts in an individual's sexual orientation over the life course. For example, the small number of bisexual respondents in the San Francisco study appeared to have added same-sex erotic attraction to an already established heterosexual orientation after adolescence. Similar findings were reported in a more extensive study of bisexual individuals (Weinberg, Williams, & Pryor, 1994), with some respondents adding heterosexual attraction to a previously established homosexual orientation. This same study also showed that different components of an individual's sexual orientation need not coincide; for example, some of the bisexual respondents were more erotically attracted to one sex but more romantically attracted to the other.

Negative conditioning also appears to be an operative mechanism in some cases of childhood sexual abuse or other upsetting childhood sexual experiences. For example, a reanalysis of the original Kinsey data revealed that a woman was more likely to engage in sexual activity with other women as an adult if she had been pressured or coerced into preadolescent sexual activity with an older male (Van Wyk & Geist, 1984).

Finally, some women who would otherwise be predicted by the EBE model to have a heterosexual orientation might choose for social or political reasons to center their lives around other women. This could lead them to avoid seeking out men for sexual or romantic relationships, to develop affectional and erotic ties to other women, and to self-identify as lesbians or bisexuals. In general, issues of sexual orientation *identity* are beyond the formal scope of EBE theory.

Deconstructing the Concept of Sexual Orientation

As noted in the introduction, the academic discourse on sexual orientation is currently dominated by the debate between the biological essentialists, who can point to the empirical links between biology and sexual orientation, and the social constructionists, who can point to the historical and anthropological evidence that the concept of sexual orientation is itself a culture-bound notion (De Cecco & Elia, 1993). I suggest that EBE theory can accommodate both kinds of evidence. I have already shown how the theory incorporates the biological evidence. To demonstrate how EBE theory also accommodates the cultural relativism of the social constructionists, it is necessary to deconstruct the theory itself, to explicitly identify its essentialist and culture-specific elements and to see what remains when the latter are stripped away.

There are three essentialist assumptions underlying the scenario outlined in Figure 1. First, it is assumed that childhood temperaments are partially coded in the genes and, second, that those temperaments can influence a child's preferences for male-typical or female-typical activities. Third, and most fundamentally, it is assumed that the psychological processes that transform exotic into erotic are universal properties of the human species. That's it. Everything else is cultural overlay, including the concept of sexual orientation itself.

* * *

References

Allen, J. B., Kenrick, D. T., Linder, D. E., & McCall, M. A. (1989). Arousal and attraction: A response-facilitation alternative to misattribution and negative-reinforcement models. *Journal of Personality and Social Psychology, 57*, 261–270.

Allen, L. S., & Gorski, R. A. (1992). Sexual orientation and the size of the anterior commissure in the human brain. *Proceedings of the National Academy of Sciences, 89*, 7199–7202.

Bailey, J. M., & Martin, N. G. (1995, September). *A twin registry study of sexual orientation.* Paper presented at the annual meeting of the International Academy of Sex Research, Provincetown, MA.

Bailey, J. M., & Pillard, R. C. (1991). A genetic study of male sexual orientation. *Archives of General Psychiatry, 48*, 1089–1096.

Bailey, J. M., Pillard, R. C., Neale, M. C., & Agyei, Y. (1993). Heritable factors influence sexual orientation in women. *Archives of General Psychiatry, 50*, 217–223.

Bailey, J. M., & Zucker, K. J. (1995). Childhood sex-typed behavior and sexual orientation: A conceptual analysis and quantitative review. *Developmental Psychology, 31*, 43–55.

Bates, J. E., Bentler, P. M., & Thompson, S. K. (1973). Measurement of deviant gender development in boys. *Child Development, 44*, 591–598.

Bates, J. E., Bentler, P. M., & Thompson, S. K. (1979). Gender-deviant boys compared with normal and clinical controls boys. *Journal of Abnormal Child Psychology, 7*, 243–259.

Bateson, P. P. G. (1978a). Early experience and sexual preferences. In J. B. Hutchison (Ed.), *Biological determinants of sexual behavior* (pp. 29–53). New York: Wiley.

Bell, A. P. (1982, November). Sexual preference: A postscript. *Siecus Report, 11*, 1–3.

Bell, A. P., Weinberg, M. S., & Hammersmith, S. K. (1981a). *Sexual preference: Its development in men and women.* Bloomington: Indiana University Press.

Bell, A. P., Weinberg, M. S., & Hammersmith, S. K. (1981b). *Sexual preference: Its development in men and women. Statistical appendix.* Bloomington: Indiana University Press.

Bem, S. L. (1993). *The lenses of gender: Transforming the debate on sexual inequality.* New Haven, CT: Yale University Press.

Berenbaum, S. A., & Hines, M. (1992). Early androgens are related to childhood sex-typed toy preferences. *Psychological Science, 3*, 203–206.

Berenbaum, S. A., & Snyder, E. (1995). Early hormonal influences on childhood sex-typed activity and playmate preferences: Implications for the development of sexual orientation. *Developmental Psychology, 31*, 31–42.

Berscheid, E., & Walster, E. (1974). A little bit about love. In T. Huston (Ed.), *Foundations of interpersonal attraction* (pp. 355–381). New York: Academic Press.

Bettelheim, B. (1969). *The children of the dream.* New York: Macmillan.

Blanchard, R., & Bogaert, A. F. (1996). Homosexuality in men and number of older brothers. *American Journal of Psychiatry, 153*, 27–31.

Blanchard, R., McConkey, J. G., Roper, V., & Steiner, B. W. (1983). Measuring physical aggressiveness in heterosexual, homosexual, and transsexual males. *Archives of Sexual Behavior, 12*, 511–524.

Bleier, R. (1984). *Science and gender: A critique of biology and its theories on women.* New York: Pergamon Press.

Brehm, S. S. (1992). *Intimate relationships* (2nd ed.). New York: McGraw-Hill.

Bronfenbrenner, U., & Ceci, S. J. (1994). Nature-nurture reconceptualized in developmental perspective: A bioecological model. *Psychological Review, 101*, 568–586.

Buss, A. H., & Plomin, R. (1975). *A temperament theory of personality development.* New York: Wiley.

Buss, A. H., & Plomin, R. (1984). *Temperament: Early developing personality traits.* Hillsdale, NJ: Erlbaum.

Byne, W., & Parsons, B. (1993). Human sexual orientation: The biologic theories reappraised. *Archives of General Psychiatry, 50*, 228–239.

Cantor, J. R., Zillmann, D., & Bryant, J. (1975). Enhancement of experienced sexual arousal in response to erotic stimuli through misattribution of unrelated residual excitation. *Journal of Personality and Social Psychology, 32*, 69–75.

Caspi, A., & Herbener, E. S. (1990). Continuity and change: Assortative marriage and the consistency of personality in adulthood. *Journal of Personality and Social Psychology, 58*, 250–258.

De Cecco, J. P., & Elia, J. P. (Eds.). (1993). *If you seduce a straight person, can you make them gay? Issues in biological essentialism versus social constructionism in gay and lesbian identities.* New York: Harrington Park Press.

DiPietro, J. A. (1981). Rough and tumble play: A function of gender. *Developmental Psychology, 17,* 50–58.

Dittmann, R. W., Kappes, M. H., Kappes, M. E., Borger, D., Meyer-Bahlburg, H. F. L., Stegner, H., Willig, R. H., & Wallis, H. (1990a). Congenital adrenal hyperplasia: II. Gender-related behavior and attitudes in female salt-wasting and simple-virilizing patients. *Psychoneuroendocrinology, 15,* 421–434.

Dittmann, R. W., Kappes, M. H., Kappes, M. E., Borger, D., Stegner, H., Willig, R. H., & Wallis, H. (1990b). Congenital adrenal hyperplasia: I. Gender-related behavior and attitudes in female patients and sisters. *Psychoneuroendocrinology, 15,* 410–420.

Eaton, W. O., & Enns, L. R. (1986). Sex differences in human motor activity level. *Psychological Bulletin, 100,* 19–28.

Ellis, L., & Ames, M. A. (1987). Neurohormonal functioning and sexual orientation: A theory of homosexuality-heterosexuality. *Psychological Bulletin, 101,* 233–258.

Feingold, A. (1988). Matching for attractiveness in romantic partners and same-sex friends: A meta-analysis and theoretical critique. *Psychological Bulletin, 104,* 226–235.

Finck, H. T. (1887). *Romantic love and personal beauty: Their development, causal relations, historic and national peculiarities.* London: Macmillan.

Fox, R. C. (1995). Bisexual identities. In A. R. D'Augelli & C. J. Patterson (Eds.), *Lesbian, gay and bisexual identities over the lifespan* (pp. 48–86). New York: Oxford University Press.

Freud, S. (1962). *Three essays on the theory of sexuality.* New York: Basic Books. (Original work published 1905.)

Fry, D. P. (1990). Play aggression among Zapotec children: Implications for the practice hypothesis. *Aggressive Behavior, 17,* 321–340.

Futuyma, D. J., & Risch, S. J. (1983/84). Sexual orientation, sociobiology, and evolution. *Journal of Homosexuality, 9,* 157–168.

Gartrell, N. K. (1982). Hormones and homosexuality. In W. Paul, J. D. Weinrich, J. C. Gonsiorek, & M. E. Hotvedt (Eds.), *Homosexuality: Social psychological and biological issues* (pp. 169–182). Beverly Hills, CA: Sage.

Gladue, B. A., Beatty, W. W., Larson, J., & Staton, R. D. (1990). Sexual orientation and spatial ability in men and women. *Psychobiology, 28,* 101–108.

Green, R. (1976). One-hundred ten feminine and masculine boys: Behavioral contrasts and demographic similarities. *Archives of Sexual Behavior, 5,* 425–426.

Green, R. (1987). *The "sissy boy syndrome" and the development of homosexuality.* New Haven, CT: Yale University Press.

Hamer, D., & Copeland, P. (1994). *The science of desire: The search for the gay gene and the biology of behavior.* New York: Simon & Schuster.

Hamer, D. H., Hu, S., Magnuson, V. L., Hu, N., & Patatucci, A. M. L. (1993). A linkage between DNA markers on the X chromosome and male sexual orientation. *Science, 261,* 321–327.

Harrison, A. A. (1977). Mere exposure. In L. Berkowitz (Ed.), *Advances in experimental social psychology* (Vol. 10, pp. 39–83). New York: Academic Press.

Herdt, G. (1981). *Guardians of the flutes: Idioms of masculinity.* New York: McGraw-Hill.

Herdt, G. (1987). *Sambia: Ritual and gender in New Guinea.* New York: Holt, Rinehart & Winston.

Herdt, G. (1990). Developmental discontinuities and sexual orientation across cultures. In D. P. McWhirter, S. A. Sanders, & J. M. Reinisch (Eds.), *Homosexuality/heterosexuality: Concepts of sexual orientation* (pp. 208–236). New York: Oxford University Press.

Herdt, G. (Ed.). (1984). *Ritualized homosexuality in Melanesia.* Berkeley: University of California Press.

Hill, C., Rubin, Z., & Peplau, L. A. (1976). Breakups before marriage: The end of 103 affairs. *Journal of Social Issues, 32,* 147–168.

Hoon, P. W., Wincze, J. P., & Hoon, E. F. (1977). A test of reciprocal inhibition: Are anxiety and sexual arousal in women mutually inhibitory? *Journal of Abnormal Psychology, 86,* 65–74.

Hyde, J. S. (1984). How large are gender differences in aggression? A developmental meta-analysis. *Developmental Psychology, 20,* 722–736.

Kenrick, D. T., & Cialdini, R. B. (1977). Romantic attraction: Misattribution versus reinforcement explanations. *Journal of Personality and Social Psychology, 35,* 381–391.

Kirsch, J. A. W., & Rodman, J. E. (1982). Selection and sexuality: The Darwinian view of homosexuality. In W. Paul, J. D. Weinrich, J. C. Gonsiorek, & M. E. Hotvedt (Eds.), *Homosexuality: Social psychological and biological issues* (pp. 183–195). Beverly Hills, CA: Sage.

LeVay, S. (1991). A difference in hypothalamic structure between heterosexual and homosexual men. *Science, 253,* 1034–1037.

LeVay, S. (1993). *The sexual brain.* Cambridge, MA: MIT Press.

Levinger, G., Senn, D. J., & Jorgensen, B. W. (1970). Progress toward permanence in courtship: A test of the Kerckhoff-Davis hypotheses. *Sociometry, 33,* 427–443.

McClanahan, K. K., Gold, J. A., Lenney, E., Ryckman, R. M., & Kulberg, G. E. (1990). Infatuation and attraction to a dissimilar other: Why is love blind? *Journal of Social Psychology, 130,* 433–445.

McCormick, C. M., & Witelson, S. F. (1991). A cognitive profile of homosexual men compared to heterosexual men and women. *Psychoneuroendocrinology, 16,* 459–473.

Meyer, J. P., & Pepper, S. (1977). Need compatibility and marital adjustment in young married couples. *Journal of Personality and Social Psychology, 35,* 331–342.

Meyer-Bahlburg, H. F. L. (1984). Psychoendocrine research on sexual orientation: Current status and future options. *Progress in Brain Research, 61,* 375–398.

Meyer-Bahlburg, H. F. L., Erhardt, A. A., Rosen, L. R., Gruen, R. S., Veridiano, N. P., Vann, F. H., & Neuwalder, H. F. (1995). Prenatal estrogens and the development of homosexual orientation. *Developmental Psychology, 31,* 12–21.

Moller, L. C., Hymel, S., & Rubin, K. H. (1992). Sex typing in play and popularity in middle childhood. *Sex Roles, 26,* 331–353.

Money, J., & Ehrhardt, A. A. (1972). *Man and woman, boy and girl: The differentiation and dimorphism of gender identity from conception to maturity.* Baltimore: Johns Hopkins Press.

Money, J., Schwartz, M., & Lewis, V. G. (1984). Adult erotosexual status and fetal hormonal masculinization and demasculinization: 46, XX congenital virilizing adrenal hyperplasia and 46, XY androgen-insensitivity syndrome compared. *Psychoneuroendocrinology, 9,* 405–414.

Mook, D. B. (1987). *Motivation: The organization of action.* New York: Norton.

Murstein, B. I. (1972). Physical attractiveness and marital choice. *Journal of Personality and Social Psychology, 22,* 8–12.

Newcomb, T. M. (1961). *The acquaintance process.* New York: Holt, Rinehart & Winston.

Pitz, G. F., & Ross, R. B. (1961). Imprinting as a function of arousal. *Journal of Comparative and Physiological Psychology, 54,* 602–604.

Plomin, R. (1986). *Development, genetics, and psychology.* Hillsdale, NJ: Erlbaum.

Quadagno, D. M., Briscoe, R., & Quadagno, J. S. (1977). Effect of perinatal gonadal hormones on selected nonsexual behavior patterns: A critical assessment of the nonhuman and human literature. *Psychological Bulletin, 84,* 62–80.

Rabin, I. A. (1965). *Growing up in a kibbutz.* New York: Springer.

Reinisch, J. M. (1981). Prenatal exposure to synthetic progestins increases potential for aggression in humans. *Science, 211,* 1171–1173.

Rice, G., Anderson, C., Risch, N., & Ebers, G. (1995, September). *Male homosexuality: Absence of linkage to micro satellite markers on the X-chromosome in a Canadian study.* Paper presented at the annual meeting of the International Academy of Sex Research, Provincetown, MA.

Rubin, Z. (1973). *Liking and loving.* New York: Holt, Rinehart & Winston.

Rushton, J. P., Fulker, D. W., Neale, M. C., Nias, D. K. B., & Eysenck, H. J. (1986). Altruism and aggression: The heritability of individual differences. *Journal of Personality and Social Psychology, 50,* 1192–1198.

Savin-Williams, R. C. (1987). An ethological perspective on homosexuality during adolescence. *Journal of Adolescent Research, 2,* 283–302.

Schachter, S., & Singer, J. E. (1962). Cognitive, social, and physiological determinants of emotional state. *Psychological Review, 69,* 379–399.

Serbin, L. A. (1980). Sex-role socialization: A field in transition. In B. B. Lahey & A. E. Kazdin (Eds.), *Advances in clinical child psychology* (Vol. 3, pp. 41–96). New York: Plenum.

Shepher, J. (1971). Mate selection among second generation kibbutz adolescents and adults: Incest avoidance and negative imprinting. *Archives of Sexual Behavior, 1,* 293–307.

Silverman, I. (1971). Physical attractiveness and courtship. *Archives of Sexual Behavior, 1,* 22–25.

Spiro, M. E. (1958). *Children of the kibbutz.* Cambridge, MA: Harvard University Press.

Strong, S. R., Hills, H. I., Kilmartin, C. T., DeVries, H., Lanier, K., Nelson, B. N., Strickland, D., & Meyer, C. W., III. (1988). The dynamic relations among interpersonal behaviors: A test of complementarity and anticomplementarity. *Journal of Personality and Social Psychology, 54,* 798–810.

Swaab, D. F., & Hofman, M. A. (1990). An enlarged suprachiasmatic nucleus in homosexual men. *Brain Research, 537,* 141–148.

Talmon, Y. (1964). Mate selection in collective settlements. *American Sociological Review, 29,* 481–508.

Tripp, C. A. (1975). *The homosexual matrix.* New York: McGraw-Hill.

Tripp, C. A. (1987). *The homosexual matrix* (2nd ed.). New York: New American Library.

Van Wyk, P. H., & Geist, C. S. (1984). Psychological development of heterosexual, bisexual, and homosexual behavior. *Archives of Sexual Behavior, 13,* 505–544.

Walster, E. (1971). Passionate love. In B. I. Murstein (Ed.), *Theories of attraction and love* (pp. 85–99). New York: Springer.

Weinberg, M. S., Williams, C. J., & Pryor, D. W. (1994). *Dual attraction: Understanding bisexuality.* New York: Oxford University Press.

Weinrich, J. D. (1978). Nonreproduction, homosexuality, transsexualism, and intelligence: I. A systematic literature search. *Journal of Homosexuality, 2,* 275–289.

Weinrich, J. D. (1987). A new sociobiological theory of homosexuality applicable to societies with universal marriage. *Ethology and Sociobiology, 8,* 37–47.

Westermarck, E. (1891). *The history of human marriage.* London: Macmillan.

White, G. L., Fishbein, S., & Rutstein, J. (1981). Passionate love and the misattribution of arousal. *Journal of Personality and Social Psychology, 41,* 56–62.

White, G. L., & Kight, T. D. (1984). Misattribution of arousal and attraction: Effects of salience of explanations for arousal. *Journal of Experimental Social Psychology, 20,* 55–64.

Wilson, E. O. (1975). *Sociobiology: The new synthesis.* Cambridge, MA: Harvard University Press.

Wilson, E. O. (1978). *On human nature.* Cambridge, MA: Harvard University Press.

Wolchik, S. A., Beggs, V. E., Wincze, J. P., Sakheim, D. K., Barlow, D. H., & Mavissakalian, M. (1980). The effect of emotional arousal on subsequent sexual arousal in men. *Journal of Abnormal Psychology, 89,* 595–598.

Zillmann, D. (1983). Transfer of excitation in emotional behavior. In J. T. Cacioppo & R. E. Petty (Eds.), *Social psychophysiology: A sourcebook.* New York: Guilford Press.

Zucker, K. J. (1990). Gender identity disorders in children: Clinical descriptions and natural history. In R. Blanchard & B. W. Steiner (Eds.), *Clinical management of gender identity disorders in children and adults* (pp. 1–23). Washington, DC: American Psychiatric Press.

Zucker, K. J., Bradley, S. J., Oliver, G., Hood, J. E., Blake, J., & Fleming, S. (1992, July). *Psychosexual assessment of women with congenital adrenal hyperplasia: Preliminary analyses.* Paper presented at the 18th Annual meeting of the International Academy of Sex Research, Prague, Czechoslovakia.

Zucker, K. J., & Green, R. (1993). Psychological and familial aspects of gender identity disorder. *Child and Adolescent Psychiatric Clinics of North America, 2,* 513–542.

PART IV

The Psychoanalytic Approach to Personality

About a century ago, the brilliant Viennese psychiatrist Sigmund Freud began to present his psychoanalytic theory of personality to the world. Freud continued to publish prolifically and to develop his theory right up to the time of his death, in 1939. The result of all this labor was not only a long-lasting and pervasive influence on the field of psychology, but also a fundamental influence on the way members of Western culture think about people. The "Freudian slip" is the commonplace idea most obviously identified with Freud, but his writings also continue to affect the way we talk about child-rearing, psychological conflict, sexuality, aggression, and emotion.

Freud's own contributions were impressive enough, but he also attracted a remarkable group of followers, several of whom eventually broke away from his influence. These include some of the major intellectual figures of the early twentieth century, including Carl Jung, Karen Horney, and Erik Erikson. Freud's theory continues to influence modern psychological research both directly and indirectly. The readings in this section sample from the writings of Freud himself, several other important figures in psychoanalysis, and other writers who have attempted to evaluate psychoanalysis on empirical or theoretical grounds.

The two lectures that begin this section concern the basic structure of the mind and the widely observed phenomenon of Freudian slips, or "parapraxes." The next three selections are from the writings of other major psychoanalysts. Carl Jung describes the nature of extraversion and introversion, Karen Horney explains the "distrust" between the sexes, and Erikson outlines the eight stages of psychological development that occur over an individual's entire life span.

The next paper, by Roy Baumeister, Karen Dale, and Kristin Sommer, is a recent survey of modern research particularly relevant to the psychoanalytic concept of the defense mechanism. It is followed by an experiment, by Brad Bushman, attempting to test the psychoanalytic idea of "catharsis," that expressing one's anger is better than attempting to hold it in. The final selection in this chapter is a scathing but also humorous critique of psychoanalytic theory, written by the feminist Gloria Steinem. Vehemently attacking psychoanalysis at perhaps its weakest point—its obvious sexism—Steinem describes how the theory might have looked if Freud were a woman, living in a matriarchy.

Perhaps no theory in psychology has been as admired, and as reviled, as psychoanalysis. As you will see in the following articles, there are good reasons for both kinds of reaction.

Lecture XXXI: The Dissection of the Psychical Personality

Sigmund Freud

In this first selection the founder of psychoanalysis, Sigmund Freud himself, describes the core of the theory. Freud describes how the mind is divided into three parts, the now-famous id, ego, and super-ego. These roughly map onto the animalistic part, the logical part, and the moral part of the mind.

One of your editors remembers years ago having seen a Donald Duck cartoon in which the unfortunate duck was tormented by an angel who rode on one shoulder and a devil who rode on the other. The angel was always scolding him, and the devil was always egging him on to do things he knew he shouldn't do. Donald himself, in the middle, was confused and prone to obey first one of his tormentors, then the other.

Disney's animators seem to have known their Freud. The situation described near the end of this selection is nearly identical. When Freud has the poor ego cry, "Life is not easy!" he is describing the torment of having to resolve the three-way conflict between what one believes one should do, what one wants to do, and what is really possible.

This selection was written late in Freud's career and originally published in 1933, six years before his death. Freud had 15 years earlier delivered a famous set of introductory lectures on psychoanalysis, and he hit upon the idea of writing a new set of lectures to update and expand upon the earlier ones. But by this time Freud, an old man, had undergone repeated surgeries for cancer of the palate and could not speak in public. So although this and several other articles were written in the form of lectures, they were never meant to be delivered. In Freud's own words (from his preface),

> If, therefore, I once more take my place in the lecture room during the remarks that follow, it is only by an artifice of the imagination; it may help me not to forget to bear the reader in mind as I enter more deeply into my subject. . . . [this lecture is] addressed to the multitude of educated people to whom we

may perhaps attribute a benevolent, even though cautious, interest in the characteristics and discoveries of the young science. (Freud, 1965/1933, p, 5).

From *New Introductory Lectures on Psycho-analysis*, by Sigmund Freud, in *The Standard Edition of the Complete Psychological Works of Sigmund Freud*, edited and translated by James Strachey (New York: Norton, 1966), pp. 51–71.

*   *   *

The situation in which we find ourselves at the beginning of our enquiry may be expected itself to point the way for us. We wish to make the ego the matter of our enquiry, our very own ego.[1] But is that possible? After all, the ego is in its very essence a subject; how can it be made into an object? Well, there is no doubt that it can be. The ego can take itself as an object, can treat itself like other objects, can observe itself, criticize itself, and do Heaven knows what with itself. In this, one part of the ego is setting itself over against the rest. So the ego can be split; it splits itself during a number of its functions—temporarily at least. Its parts can come together again afterwards. That is not exactly a novelty, though it may perhaps be putting an unusual emphasis on what is generally known. On the other hand, we are familiar with the notion that pathology, by making things larger and coarser, can draw our attention to normal conditions which would otherwise have escaped us. Where it points to a breach or a rent, there may normally be an articulation present. If we throw a crystal to the floor, it breaks; but not into haphazard pieces. It comes apart along its lines of cleavage into fragments whose boundaries, though they were invisible, were predetermined by the crystal's structure. Mental patients are split and broken structures of this same kind. Even we cannot withhold from them something of the reverential awe which peoples of the past felt for the insane. They have turned away from external reality, but for that very reason they know more about internal, psy-

chical reality and can reveal a number of things to us that would otherwise be inaccessible to us.

We describe one group of these patients as suffering from delusions of being observed. They complain to us that perpetually, and down to their most intimate actions, they are being molested by the observation of unknown powers—presumably persons—and that in hallucinations they hear these persons reporting the outcome of their observation: "now he's going to say this, now he's dressing to go out," and so on. Observation of this sort is not yet the same thing as persecution, but it is not far from it; it presupposes that people distrust them, and expect to catch them carrying out forbidden actions for which they would be punished. How would it be if these insane people were right, if in each of us there is present in his ego an agency like this which observes and threatens to punish, and which in them has merely become sharply divided from their ego and mistakenly displaced into external reality?

I cannot tell whether the same thing will happen to you as to me. Ever since, under the powerful impression of this clinical picture, I formed the idea that the separation of the observing agency from the rest of the ego might be a regular feature of the ego's structure, that idea has never left me, and I was driven to investigate the further characteristics and connections of the agency which was thus separated off. The next step is quickly taken. The content of the delusions of being observed already suggests that the observing is only a preparation for judging and punishing, and we accordingly guess that another function of this agency must be what we call our conscience. There is scarcely anything else in us that we so regularly separate from our ego and so easily set over against it as precisely our conscience. I feel an inclination to do some-

---

[1] "Ego" has also been translated as "the I." Freud is referring to the self as it experiences itself—a paradoxical but common situation that leads Freud to conclude that dividing up the self is not so odd as it might seem.

thing that I think will give me pleasure, but I abandon it on the ground that my conscience does not allow it. Or I have let myself be persuaded by too great an expectation of pleasure into doing something to which the voice of conscience has objected and after the deed my conscience punishes me with distressing reproaches and causes me to feel remorse for the deed. I might simply say that the special agency which I am beginning to distinguish in the ego is conscience. But it is more prudent to keep the agency as something independent and to suppose that conscience is one of its functions and that self-observation, which is an essential preliminary to the judging activity of conscience, is another of them. And since when we recognize that something has a separate existence we give it a name of its own, from this time forward I will describe this agency in the ego as the "*super-ego*."

*　*　*

Hardly have we familiarized ourselves with the idea of a super-ego like this which enjoys a certain degree of autonomy, follows its own intentions and is independent of the ego for its supply of energy, than a clinical picture forces itself on our notice which throws a striking light on the severity of this agency and indeed its cruelty, and on its changing relations to the ego. I am thinking of the condition of melancholia,[2] or, more precisely, of melancholic attacks, which you too will have heard plenty about, even if you are not psychiatrists. The most striking feature of this illness, of whose causation and mechanism we know much too little, is the way in which the super-ego—"conscience," you may call it, quietly—treats the ego. While a melancholic can, like other people, show a greater or lesser degree of severity to himself in his healthy periods, during a melancholic attack his super-ego becomes over-severe, abuses the poor ego, humiliates it and ill-treats it, threatens it with the direst punishments, reproaches it for actions in the remotest past which had been taken lightly at the time—as though it had spent the whole interval in

collecting accusations and had only been waiting for its present access of strength in order to bring them up and make a condemnatory judgement on their basis. The super-ego applies the strictest moral standard to the helpless ego which is at its mercy; in general it represents the claims of morality, and we realize all at once that our moral sense of guilt is the expression of the tension between the ego and the super-ego. It is a most remarkable experience to see morality, which is supposed to have been given us by God and thus deeply implanted in us, functioning [in these patients] as a periodic phenomenon. For after a certain number of months the whole moral fuss is over, the criticism of the super-ego is silent, the ego is rehabilitated and again enjoys all the rights of man till the next attack. In some forms of the disease, indeed, something of a contrary sort occurs in the intervals; the ego finds itself in a blissful state of intoxication, it celebrates a triumph, as though the super-ego had lost all its strength or had melted into the ego; and this liberated, manic ego permits itself a truly uninhibited satisfaction of all its appetites. Here are happenings rich in unsolved riddles!

No doubt you will expect me to give you more than a mere illustration when I inform you that we have found out all kinds of things about the formation of the super-ego—that is to say, about the origin of conscience. Following a well-known pronouncement of Kant's which couples the conscience within us with the starry Heavens, a pious man might well be tempted to honor these two things as the masterpieces of creation. The stars are indeed magnificent, but as regards conscience God has done an uneven and careless piece of work, for a large majority of men have brought along with them only a modest amount of it or scarcely enough to be worth mentioning. We are far from overlooking the portion of psychological truth that is contained in the assertion that conscience is of divine origin; but the thesis needs interpretation. Even if conscience is something "within us," yet it is not so from the first. In this it is a real contrast to sexual life, which is in fact there from the beginning of life and not only a later addition. But, as is well known, young children are amoral and possess

---

[2] "Modern terminology would probably speak of 'depression.' "—Translator

no internal inhibitions against their impulses striving for pleasure. The part which is later taken on by the super-ego is played to begin with by an external power, by parental authority. Parental influence governs the child by offering proofs of love and by threatening punishments which are signs to the child of loss of love and are bound to be feared on their own account. This realistic anxiety is the precursor of the later moral anxiety. So long as it is dominant there is no need to talk of a super-ego and of a conscience. It is only subsequently that the secondary situation develops (which we are all too ready to regard as the normal one), where the external restraint is internalized and the super-ego takes the place of the parental agency and observes, directs and threatens the ego in exactly the same way as earlier the parents did with the child.

The super-ego, which thus takes over the power, function and even the methods of the parental agency, is however not merely its successor but actually the legitimate heir of its body. It proceeds directly out of it, we shall learn presently by what process. First, however, we must dwell upon a discrepancy between the two. The super-ego seems to have made a one-sided choice and to have picked out only the parents' strictness and severity, their prohibiting and punitive function, whereas their loving care seems not to have been taken over and maintained. If the parents have really enforced their authority with severity we can easily understand the child's in turn developing a severe super-ego. But, contrary to our expectation, experience shows that the super-ego can acquire the same characteristic of relentless severity even if the upbringing had been mild and kindly and had so far as possible avoided threats and punishments. * * *

*   *   *

The basis of the process is what is called an 'identification'—that is to say, the assimilation of one ego to another one,[3] as a result of which the first ego behaves like the second in certain respects,

imitates it and in a sense takes it up into itself. Identification has been not unsuitably compared with the oral, cannibalistic incorporation of the other person. It is a very important form of attachment to someone else, probably the very first, and not the same thing as the choice of an object. The difference between the two can be expressed in some such way as this. If a boy identifies himself with his father, he wants to *be like* his father; if he makes him the object of his choice, he wants to *have* him, to possess him. In the first case his ego is altered on the model of his father; in the second case that is not necessary. Identification and object-choice are to a large extent independent of each other; it is however possible to identify oneself with someone whom, for instance, one has taken as a sexual object, and to alter one's ego on his model. It is said that the influencing of the ego by the sexual object occurs particularly often with women and is characteristic of femininity. I must already have spoken to you in my earlier lectures of what is by far the most instructive relation between identification and object-choice. It can be observed equally easily in children and adults, in normal as in sick people. If one has lost an object or has been obliged to give it up, one often compensates oneself by identifying oneself with it and by setting it up once more in one's ego, so that here object-choice regresses, as it were, to identification.

I myself am far from satisfied with these remarks on identification; but it will be enough if you can grant me that the installation of the super-ego can be described as a successful instance of identification with the parental agency. The fact that speaks decisively for this view is that this new creation of a superior agency within the ego is most intimately linked with the destiny of the Oedipus complex[4] so that the super-ego appears as the heir of that emotional attachment which is of such importance for childhood. With his abandon-

---

[3]"I.e., one ego coming to resemble another one."
—Translator

[4]The "Oedipus complex" is the result of a complex process in which, according to Freud, a young boy falls in love with his mother, fears his father's jealous retaliation, and as a defense against that fear comes to identify with his father.

ment of the Oedipus complex a child must, as we can see, renounce the intense object-cathexes[5] which he has deposited with his parents, and it is as a compensation for this loss of objects that there is such a strong intensification of the identifications with his parents which have probably long been present in his ego. Identifications of this kind as precipitates of object-cathexes that have been given up will be repeated often enough later in the child's life; but it is entirely in accordance with the emotional importance of this first instance of such a transformation that a special place in the ego should be found for its outcome. Close investigation has shown us, too, that the super-ego is stunted in its strength and growth if the surmounting of the Oedipus complex is only incompletely successful. In the course of development the super-ego also takes on the influences of those who have stepped into the place of parents—educators, teachers, people chosen as ideal models. Normally it departs more and more from the original parental figures; it becomes, so to say, more impersonal. Nor must it be forgotten that a child has a different estimate of its parents at different periods of its life. At the time at which the Oedipus complex gives place to the super-ego they are something quite magnificent; but later they lose much of this. Identifications then come about with these later parents as well, and indeed they regularly make important contributions to the formation of character; but in that case they only affect the ego, they no longer influence the super-ego, which has been determined by the earliest parental imagos.

* * *

* * * In face of the doubt whether the ego and super-ego are themselves unconscious or merely produce unconscious effects, we have, for good reasons, decided in favour of the former possibility. And it is indeed the case that large portions of the ego and super-ego can remain unconscious and are normally unconscious. That is to say, the individual knows nothing of their contents and it

requires an expenditure of effort to make them conscious. It is a fact that ego and conscious, repressed and unconscious do not coincide. We feel a need to make a fundamental revision of our attitude to the problem of conscious-unconscious. At first we are inclined greatly to reduce the value of the criterion of being conscious since it has shown itself so untrustworthy. But we should be doing it an injustice. As may be said of our life, it is not worth much, but it is all we have. Without the illumination thrown by the quality of consciousness, we should be lost in the obscurity of depth-psychology; but we must attempt to find our bearings afresh.

There is no need to discuss what is to be called conscious: it is removed from all doubt. The oldest and best meaning of the word "unconscious" is the descriptive one; we call a psychical process unconscious whose existence we are obliged to assume—for some such reason as that we infer it from its effects—but of which we know nothing. In that case we have the same relation to it as we have to a psychical process in another person, except that it is in fact one of our own. If we want to be still more correct, we shall modify our assertion by saying that we call a process unconscious if we are obliged to assume that it is being activated *at the moment*, though *at the moment* we know nothing about it. This qualification makes us reflect that the majority of conscious processes are conscious only for a short time; very soon they become *latent*, but can easily become conscious again. We might also say that they had become unconscious, if it were at all certain that in the condition of latency they are still something psychical. So far we should have learnt nothing new; nor should we have acquired the right to introduce the concept of an unconscious into psychology. [But] in order to explain a slip of the tongue, for instance, we find ourselves obliged to assume that the intention to make a particular remark was present in the subject. We infer it with certainty from the interference with his remark which has occurred; but the intention did not put itself through and was thus unconscious. If, when we subsequently put it before the speaker, he recognizes it as one familiar to him, then it was

---

[5]An "object-cathexis" is an investment of emotional energy in an important "object," usually a person.

only temporarily unconscious to him; but if he repudiates it as something foreign to him, then it was permanently unconscious. From this experience we retrospectively obtain the right also to pronounce as something unconscious what had been described as latent. A consideration of these dynamic relations permits us now to distinguish two kinds of unconscious—one which is easily, under frequently occurring circumstances, transformed into something conscious, and another with which this transformation is difficult and takes place only subject to a considerable expenditure of effort or possibly never at all. In order to escape the ambiguity as to whether we mean the one or the other unconscious, whether we are using the word in the descriptive or in the dynamic sense, we make use of a permissible and simple way out. We call the unconscious which is only latent, and thus easily becomes conscious, the "preconscious" and retain the term "unconscious" for the other. We now have three terms, "conscious," "preconscious," and "unconscious," with which we can get along in our description of mental phenomena. Once again: the preconscious is also unconscious in the purely descriptive sense, but we do not give it that name, except in talking loosely or when we have to make a defence of the existence in mental life of unconscious processes in general.

You will admit, I hope, that so far that is not too bad and allows of convenient handling. Yes, but unluckily the work of psychoanalysis has found itself compelled to use the word "unconscious" in yet another, third, sense, and this may, to be sure, have led to confusion. Under the new and powerful impression of there being an extensive and important field of mental life which is normally withdrawn from the ego's knowledge so that the processes occurring in it have to be regarded as unconscious in the truly dynamic sense, we have come to understand the term "unconscious" in a topographical or systematic sense as well; we have come to speak of a "system" of the preconscious and a "system" of the unconscious, of a conflict between the ego and the system Ucs. [unconscious], and have used the word more and more to denote a mental province rather than a quality of what is mental. The discov-

ery, actually an inconvenient one, that portions of the ego and super-ego as well are unconscious in the dynamic sense, operates at this point as a relief—it makes possible the removal of a complication. We perceive that we have no right to name the mental region that is foreign to the ego "the system Ucs.," since the characteristic of being unconscious is not restricted to it. Very well; we will no longer use the term "unconscious" in the systematic sense and we will give what we have hitherto so described a better name and one no longer open to misunderstanding. Following a verbal usage of Nietzsche's and taking up a suggestion by Georg Groddeck [1923],[6] we will in future call it the "id".[7] This impersonal pronoun seems particularly well suited for expressing the main characteristic of this province of the mind—the fact of its being alien to the ego. The super-ego, the ego and the id—these, then, are the three realms, regions, provinces, into which we divide an individual's mental apparatus, and with the mutual relations of which we shall be concerned in what follows.

* * *

You will not expect me to have much to tell you that is new about the id apart from its new name. It is the dark, inaccessible part of our personality; what little we know of it we have learnt from our study of the dream-work and of the construction of neurotic symptoms, and most of that is of a negative character and can be described only as a contrast to the ego. We approach the id with analogies: we call it a chaos, a cauldron full of seething excitations. We picture it as being open at its end to somatic influences, and as there taking up into itself instinctual needs which find their psychical expression in it, but we cannot say in what substratum. It is filled with energy reaching it from the instincts, but it has no organization, produces no collective will, but only a striving to bring about the satisfaction of the instinctual needs subject to the observance of the pleasure principle.

---

[6]"A German physician by whose unconventional ideas Freud was much attracted."—Translator

[7]"In German, Es, the ordinary word for 'it.' "—Translator

The logical laws of thought do not apply in the id, and this is true above all of the law of contradiction. Contrary impulses exist side by side, without cancelling each other out or diminishing each other: at the most they may converge to form compromises under the dominating economic pressure towards the discharge of energy. There is nothing in the id that could be compared with negation; and we perceive with surprise an exception to the philosophical theorem that space and time are necessary forms of our mental acts. There is nothing in the id that corresponds to the idea of time; there is no recognition of the passage of time, and—a thing that is most remarkable and awaits consideration in philosophical thought—no alteration in its mental processes is produced by the passage of time. Wishful impulses which have never passed beyond the id, but impressions, too, which have been sunk into the id by repression, are virtually immortal; after the passage of decades they behave as though they had just occurred. They can only be recognized as belonging to the past, can only lose their importance and be deprived of their cathexis of energy, when they have been made conscious by the work of analysis, and it is on this that the therapeutic effect of analytic treatment rests to no small extent.

Again and again I have had the impression that we have made too little theoretical use of this fact, established beyond any doubt, of the unalterability by time of the repressed. This seems to offer an approach to the most profound discoveries. Nor, unfortunately, have I myself made any progress here.

The id of course knows no judgements of value: no good and evil, no morality. The economic or, if you prefer, the quantitative factor, which is intimately linked to the pleasure principle, dominates all its processes. Instinctual cathexes seeking discharge—that, in our view, is all there is in the id.[8] It even seems that the energy of these instinctual impulses is in a state different from that in the other regions of the mind, far more mobile and capable of discharge; otherwise the displacements and condensations would not occur which are characteristic of the id and which so completely disregard the *quality* of what is cathected—what in the ego we should call an idea. We would give much to understand more about these things! You can see, incidentally, that we are in a position to attribute to the id characteristics other than that of its being unconscious, and you can recognize the possibility of portions of the ego and super-ego being unconscious without possessing the same primitive and irrational characteristics.

* * *

* * * We need scarcely look for a justification of the view that the ego is that portion of the id which was modified by the proximity and influence of the external world, which is adapted for the reception of stimuli and as a protective shield against stimuli, comparable to the cortical layer by which a small piece of living substance is surrounded. The relation to the external world has become the decisive factor for the ego; it has taken on the task of representing the external world to the id—fortunately for the id, which could not escape destruction if, in its blind efforts for the satisfaction of its instincts, it disregarded that supreme external power. In accomplishing this function, the ego must observe the external world, must lay down an accurate picture of it in the memory-traces of its perceptions, and by its exercise of the function of "reality-testing" must put aside whatever in this picture of the external world is an addition derived from internal sources of excitation. The ego controls the approaches to motility under the id's orders; but between a need and an action it has interposed a postponement in the form of the activity of thought, during which it makes use of the mnemic residues of experience. In that way it has dethroned the pleasure principle which dominates the course of events in the id without any restriction, and has replaced it by the reality principle, which promises more certainty and greater success.

* * *

* * * To adopt a popular mode of speaking, we might say that the ego stands for reason and

---

[8]In other words, the id seeks immediately to satisfy all "instinctual"—physical—desires.

good sense while the id stands for the untamed passions.

So far we have allowed ourselves to be impressed by the merits and capabilities of the ego; it is now time to consider the other side as well. The ego is after all only a portion of the id, a portion that has been expediently modified by the proximity of the external world with its threat of danger. From a dynamic point of view it is weak, it has borrowed its energies from the id, and we are not entirely without insight into the methods—we might call them dodges—by which it extracts further amounts of energy from the id. One such method, for instance, is by identifying itself with actual or abandoned objects. The object-cathexes spring from the instinctual demands of the id. The ego has in the first instance to take note of them. But by identifying itself with the object it recommends itself to the id in place of the object and seeks to divert the id's libido on to itself. * * * The ego must on the whole carry out the id's intentions, it fulfils its task by finding out the circumstances in which those intentions can best be achieved. The ego's relation to the id might be compared with that of a rider to his horse. The horse supplies the locomotive energy, while the rider has the privilege of deciding on the goal and of guiding the powerful animal's movement. But only too often there arises between the ego and the id the not precisely ideal situation of the rider being obliged to guide the horse along the path by which it itself wants to go.

* * *

We are warned by a proverb against serving two masters at the same time. The poor ego has things even worse: it serves three severe masters and does what it can to bring their claims and demands into harmony with one another. These claims are always divergent and often seem incompatible. No wonder that the ego so often fails in its task. Its three tyrannical masters are the external world, the super-ego and the id. When we follow the ego's efforts to satisfy them simultaneously—or rather, to obey them simultaneously—we cannot feel any regret at having personified this ego and having set it up as a separate organism. It feels hemmed in on three sides, threatened by three kinds of danger, to which, if it is hard pressed, it reacts by generating anxiety. Owing to its origin from the experiences of the perceptual system, it is earmarked for representing the demands of the external world, but it strives too to be a loyal servant of the id, to remain on good terms with it, to recommend itself to it as an object and to attract its libido to itself. In its attempts to mediate between the id and reality, it is often obliged to cloak the *Ucs.* commands of the id with its own *Pcs.* [preconscious] rationalizations, to conceal the id's conflicts with reality, to profess, with diplomatic disingenuousness, to be taking notice of reality even when the id has remained rigid and unyielding. On the other hand it is observed at every step it takes by the strict super-ego, which lays down definite standards for its conduct, without taking any account of its difficulties from the direction of the id and the external world, and which, if those standards are not obeyed, punishes it with tense feelings of inferiority and of guilt. Thus the ego, driven by the id, confined by the super-ego, repulsed by reality, struggles to master its economic task of bringing about harmony among the forces and influences working in and upon it; and we can understand how it is that so often we cannot suppress a cry: "Life is not easy!" If the ego is obliged to admit its weakness, it breaks out in anxiety—realistic anxiety regarding the external world, moral anxiety regarding the super-ego and neurotic anxiety regarding the strength of the passions in the id.

I should like to portray the structural relations of the mental personality, as I have described them to you, in the unassuming sketch which I now present you with:[9]

---

[9] The "perceptual conscious" (pcpt.-cs) is Freud's name for the system and processes that create our sense of consciousness and the immediate contents of our awareness.

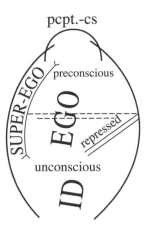

Figure 1 Freud's diagram of the structure of personality.

As you see here, the super-ego merges into the id; indeed, as heir to the Oedipus complex it has intimate relations with the id; it is more remote than the ego from the perceptual system. The id has intercourse with the external world only through the ego—at least, according to this diagram. It is certainly hard to say to-day how far the drawing is correct. In one respect it is undoubtedly not. The space occupied by the unconscious id ought to have been incomparably greater than that of the ego or the preconscious. I must ask you to correct it in your thoughts.

And here is another warning, to conclude these remarks, which have certainly been exacting and not, perhaps, very illuminating. In thinking of this division of the personality into an ego, a super-ego and an id, you will not, of course, have pictured sharp frontiers like the artificial ones drawn in political geography. We cannot do justice to the characteristics of the mind by linear outlines like those in a drawing or in primitive painting, but rather by areas of colour melting into one another as they are presented by modern artists. After making the separation we must allow what we have separated to merge together once more. You must not judge too harshly a first attempt at giving a pictorial representation of something so intangible as psychical processes. It is highly probable that the development of these divisions is subject to great variations in different individuals; it is possible that in the course of actual functioning they may change and go through a temporary phase of involution. Particularly in the case of what is phylogenetically the last and most delicate of these divisions—the differentiation between the ego and the super-ego—something of the sort seems to be true. There is no question but that the same thing results from psychical illness. It is easy to imagine, too, that certain mystical practices may succeed in upsetting the normal relations between the different regions of the mind, so that, for instance, perception may be able to grasp happenings in the depths of the ego and in the id which were otherwise inaccessible to it. It may safely be doubted, however, whether this road will lead us to the ultimate truths from which salvation is to be expected. Nevertheless it may be admitted that the therapeutic efforts of psycho-analysis have chosen a similar line of approach. Its intention is, indeed, to strengthen the ego, to make it more independent of the super-ego, to widen its field of perception and enlarge its organization, so that it can appropriate fresh portions of the id. Where id was, there ego shall be. It is a work of culture—not unlike the draining of the Zuider Zee.[10]

---

[10] The "Zuider Zee" was a landlocked arm of the North Sea in the Netherlands. Its draining was a major land-reclamation project completed in 1932, about the time this essay was written.

LECTURE III: PARAPRAXES

Sigmund Freud

The following selection comes from one of the original series of introductory lectures that Freud delivered in Vienna in 1916, about 15 years before writing the previous lecture. In this excerpt we see Freud doing his best to sell psychoanalysis to his audience, by answering their objections as he imagines them and illustrating his points with a large number of compelling examples.

Freud contributed many ideas that have entered everyday thought and speech. One of the most influential of those was his explanation of the phenomenon now popularly called the "Freudian slip." In the following selection, you can read in his own words what Freud thought about Freudian slips.

From *Introductory Lectures on Psycho-analysis*, by Sigmund Freud, in *The Standard Edition of the Complete Psychological Works of Sigmund Freud*, translated by James Strachey (New York: W. W. Norton, 1964), pp. 48–72.

Ladies and Gentlemen,—We arrived last time at the idea of considering parapraxes[1] not in relation to the intended function which they disturbed but on their own account; and we formed an impression that in particular cases they seemed to be betraying a sense of their own. We then reflected that if confirmation could be obtained on a wider scale that parapraxes have a sense, their sense would soon become more interesting than the investigation of the circumstances in which they come about.

Let us once more reach an agreement upon what is to be understood by the "sense" of a psychical process. We mean nothing other by it than the intention it serves and its position in a psychical continuity.[2] In most of our researches we can replace "sense" by "intention" or "purpose." Was it, then, merely a deceptive illusion or a poetic exaltation of parapraxes when we thought we recognized an intention in them?

We will take slips of the tongue as our examples. If we now look through a considerable number of observations of that kind, we shall find whole categories of cases in which the intention, the sense, of the slip is plainly visible. Above all there are those in which what was intended is replaced by its contrary. The President of the Lower

---

[1]Freud used the German word "*Fehlleistungen*," which means "faulty acts" or "faulty functions." According to his translator, James Strachey, the concept did not exist before Freud and so a new word—*parapraxis*, the plural of which is *parapraxes*—was invented for use in English translations of Freud's writing (Freud, 1920/1989).

[2]By "psychical continuity" Freud means the interrelated functions of the different parts of the mind.

House said in his opening speech: "I declare the sitting closed."[3] That is quite unambiguous. The sense and intention of his slip was that he wanted to close the sitting. * * * We need only take him at his word. Do not interrupt me at this point by objecting that that is impossible, that we know that he did not want to close the sitting but to open it, and that he himself, whom we have just recognized as the supreme court of appeal, could confirm the fact that he wanted to open it. You are forgetting that we have come to an agreement that we will begin by regarding parapraxes on their own account; their relation to the intention which they have disturbed is not to be discussed till later. Otherwise you will be guilty of a logical error by simply evading the problem that is under discussion—by what is called in English "begging the question."

In other cases the slip of the tongue merely adds a second sense to the one intended. The sentence then sounds like a contraction, abbreviation, or condensation of several sentences. Thus, when the energetic lady said: "He can eat and drink what I want,"[4] it was just as though she had said: "He can eat and drink what he wants; but what has *he* to do with wanting? *I* will want instead of him." A slip of the tongue often gives the impression of being an abbreviation of this sort. For instance, a professor of anatomy at the end of a lecture on the nasal cavities asked whether his audience had understood what he said and, after general assent, went on: "I can hardly believe that, since even in a city with millions of inhabitants, those who understand the nasal cavities can be counted *on one finger* . . . I beg your pardon, on the fingers of one hand." The abbreviated phrase has a sense too—namely, that there is only one person who understands them.

In contrast to these groups of cases, in which

the parapraxis itself brings its sense to light, there are others in which the parapraxis produces nothing that has any sense of its own, and which therefore sharply contradict our expectations. If someone twists a proper name about by a slip of the tongue or puts an abnormal series of sounds together, these very common events alone seem to give a negative reply to our question whether all parapraxes have some sort of sense. Closer examination of such instances, however, shows that these distortions are easily understood and that there is by no means so great a distinction between these more obscure cases and the earlier straightforward ones.

A man who was asked about the health of his horse replied: "Well, it *draut* [a meaningless word] . . . it *dauert* [will last] another month perhaps." When he was asked what he had really meant to say, he explained that he had thought it was a "*traurige* [sad]" story. The combination of "*dauert*" and "*traurig*" had produced "*draut*."

* * *

We seem now to have grasped the secret of a large number of slips of the tongue. If we bear this discovery in mind, we shall be able to understand other groups as well which have puzzled us hitherto. In cases of distortion of names, for instance, we cannot suppose that it is always a matter of competition between two similar but different names. It is not difficult, however, to guess the second intention. The distortion of a name occurs often enough apart from slips of the tongue; it seeks to give the name an offensive sound or to make it sound like something inferior, and it is a familiar practice (or malpractice) designed as an insult, which civilized people soon learn to abandon, but which they are *reluctant* to abandon. It is still often permitted as a "joke," though a pretty poor one. As a blatant and ugly example of this way of distorting names, I may mention that in these days [of the first World War] the name of the President of the French Republic, Poincaré, has been changed into "*Schweinskarré*."[5] It is therefore plausible to

---

[3]In his previous lecture, Freud had told of a politician who opened Parliament by saying, "Gentlemen, I take notice that a full quorum of members is present and herewith declare the sitting closed."

[4]The story referred to a woman who said, "My husband asked his doctor what diet he ought to follow; but the doctor told him he had no need to diet: he could eat and drink what I want."

---

[5]"The Viennese term for a pork chop."—Translator

suppose that the same insulting intention is present in these slips of the tongue and is trying to find expression in the distortion of a name. * * *

* * *

Well, it looks now as though we have solved the problem of parapraxes, and with very little trouble! They are not chance events but serious mental acts; they have a sense; they arise from the concurrent action—or perhaps rather, the mutually opposing action—of two different intentions. But now I see too that you are preparing to overwhelm me with a mass of questions and doubts which will have to be answered and dealt with before we can enjoy this first outcome of our work. I certainly have no desire to force hasty decisions upon you. Let us take them all in due order, one after the other, and give them cool consideration.

What is it you want to ask me? Do I think that this explanation applies to *all* parapraxes or only to a certain number? Can this same point of view be extended to the many other kinds of parapraxis, to misreading, slips of the pen, forgetting, bungled actions, mislaying, and so on? In view of the psychical nature of parapraxes, what significance remains for the factors of fatigue, excitement, absent-mindedness and interference with the attention? Further, it is clear that of the two competing purposes in a parapraxis one is always manifest, but the other not always. What do we do, then, in order to discover the latter? And, if we think we have discovered it, how do we prove that it is not merely a probable one but the only correct one? Is there anything else you want to ask? If not, I will go on myself. You will recall that we do not set much store by parapraxes themselves, and that all we want is to learn from studying them something that may be turned to account for psychoanalysis. I therefore put this question to you. What are these intentions or purposes which are able to disturb others in this way? And what are the relations between the disturbing purposes and the disturbed ones? Thus, no sooner is the problem solved than our work begins afresh.

First, then, is this the explanation of *all* cases of slips of the tongue? I am very much inclined to think so, and my reason is that every time one in-

vestigates an instance of a slip of the tongue an explanation of this kind is forthcoming. But it is also true that there is no way of proving that a slip of the tongue cannot occur without this mechanism. It may be so; but theoretically it is a matter of indifference to us, since the conclusions we want to draw for our introduction to psycho-analysis remain, even though—which is certainly not the case—our view holds good of only a minority of cases of slips of the tongue. The next question—whether we may extend our view to other sorts of parapraxis—I will answer in advance with a "yes." You will be able to convince yourselves of this when we come to examining instances of slips of the pen, bungled actions, and so on. * * *

A more detailed reply is called for by the question of what significance remains for the factors put forward by the authorities—disturbances of the circulation, fatigue, excitement, absent-mindedness and the theory of disturbed attention—if we accept the psychical mechanism of slips of the tongue which we have described. Observe that we are not denying these factors. It is in general not such a common thing for psycho-analysis to *deny* something asserted by other people; as a rule it merely adds something new—though no doubt it occasionally happens that this thing that has hitherto been overlooked and is now brought up as a fresh addition is in fact the essence of the matter. The influence on the production of slips of the tongue by physiological dispositions brought about by slight illness, disturbances of the circulation or states of exhaustion, must be recognized at once; daily and personal experience will convince you of it. But how little they explain! Above all, they are not necessary preconditions of parapraxes. Slips of the tongue are just as possible in perfect health and in a normal state. These somatic factors only serve therefore, to facilitate and favour the peculiar mental mechanism of slips of the tongue. I once used an analogy to describe this relation, and I will repeat it here since I can think of none better to take its place. Suppose that one dark night I went to a lonely spot and was there attacked by a rough who took away my watch and purse. Since I did not see the robber's face clearly, I laid my complaint at the nearest police station with the words: "Loneliness and darkness have just robbed me of my valuables." The police officer might then say to me: "In what you say you seem to be unjustifiably adopting an extreme mechanistic view. It would be better to represent the facts in this way: 'Under the shield of darkness and favoured by loneliness, an unknown thief robbed you of your valuables.' In your case the essential task seems to me to be that we should find the thief. Perhaps we shall then be able to recover the booty."

Such psycho-physiological factors as excitement, absent-mindedness and disturbances of attention will clearly help us very little towards an explanation. They are only empty phrases, screens behind which we must not let ourselves be prevented from having a look. The question is rather what it is that has been brought about here by the excitement, the particular distracting of attention. And again, we must recognize the importance of the influence of sounds, the similarity of words and the familiar associations aroused by words. These facilitate slips of the tongue by pointing to the paths they can take. But if I have a path open to me, does that fact automatically decide that I shall take it? I need a motive in addition before I resolve in favour of it and furthermore a force to propel me along the path. So these relations of sounds and words are also, like the somatic dispositions, only things that *favour* slips of the tongue and cannot provide the true explanation of them. Only consider: in an immense majority of cases my speech is not disturbed by the circumstance that the words I am using recall others with a similar sound, that they are intimately linked with their contraries or that familiar associations branch off from them. Perhaps we might still find a way out by following the philosopher Wundt, when he says that slips of the tongue arise if, as a result of physical exhaustion, the inclination to associate gains the upper hand over what the speaker otherwise intends to say. That would be most convincing if it were not contradicted by experience, which shows that in one set of cases the *somatic* factors favouring slips of the tongue are absent and in another set of cases the *associative* factors favouring them are equally absent.

I am particularly interested, however, in your next question: how does one discover the two mutually interfering purposes? You do not realize, probably, what a momentous question this is. One of the two, the purpose that is disturbed, is of course unmistakable: the person who makes the slip of the tongue knows it and admits to it. It is only the other, the disturbing purpose, that can give rise to doubt and hesitation. Now, we have already seen, and no doubt you have not forgotten, that in a number of cases this other purpose is equally evident. It is indicated by the *outcome* of the slip, if only we have the courage to grant that outcome a validity of its own. Take the President of the Lower House, whose slip of the tongue said the contrary of what he intended. It is clear that he wanted to open the sitting, but it is equally clear that he also wanted to close it. That is so obvious that it leaves us nothing to interpret. But in the other cases, in which the disturbing purpose only *distorts* the original one without itself achieving complete expression, how do we arrive at the disturbing purpose from the distortion?

In a first group of cases this is done quite simply and securely—in the same way, in fact, as with the *disturbed* purpose. We get the speaker to give us the information directly. After his slip of the tongue he at once produces the wording which he originally intended: "It *draut* . . . no, it *dauert* [will last] another month perhaps." [p. 257]. Well, in just the same way we get him to tell us the *disturbing* purpose. 'Why', we ask him, 'did you say "*draut*"?' He replies: 'I wanted to say "It's a *traurige* [sad] story".' * * * The speaker had to be asked why he had made the slip and what he could say about it. Otherwise he might perhaps have passed over his slip without wanting to explain it. But when he was asked he gave the explanation with the first thing that occurred to him. And now please observe that this small active step and its successful outcome are already a psycho-analysis and are a model for every psycho-analytic investigation which we shall embark upon later.

Am I too mistrustful, however, if I suspect that at the very moment at which psycho-analysis makes its appearance before your resistance to it simultaneously raises its head? Do you not feel inclined to object that the information given by the person of whom the question was asked—the person who made the slip of the tongue—is not completely conclusive? He was naturally anxious, you think, to fulfil the request to explain the slip, so he said the first thing that came into his head which seemed capable of providing such an explanation. But that is no proof that the slip did in fact take place in that way. It *may* have been so, but it may just as well have happened otherwise. And something else might have occurred to him which would have fitted in as well or perhaps even better.

It is strange how little respect you have at bottom for a psychical fact! Imagine that someone had undertaken the chemical analysis of a certain substance and had arrived at a particular weight for one component of it—so and so many milligrammes. Certain inferences could be drawn from this weight. Now do you suppose that it would ever occur to a chemist to criticize those inferences on the ground that the isolated substance might equally have had some other weight? Everyone will bow before the fact that this was the weight and none other and will confidently draw his further inferences from it. But when you are faced with the psychical fact that a particular thing occurred to the mind of the person questioned, you will not allow the fact's validity: something else might have occurred to him! You nourish the illusion of there being such a thing as psychical freedom, and you will not give it up. I am sorry to say I disagree with you categorically over this.

You will break off at that, but only to take up your resistance again at another point. You proceed: "It is the special technique of psycho-analysis, as we understand, to get people under analysis themselves to produce the solution of their problems. Now let us take another example—the one in which a speaker proposing the toast of honour on a ceremonial occasion called on his audience to hiccough [*aufzustossen*] to the health of the Chief. You say that the disturbing intention in this case was an insulting one: that was what was opposing the speaker's expression of respect. But this is pure interpretation on your part, based upon observations apart from the slip of the tongue. If in this instance you were to question the person responsible for the slip, he would not confirm your idea that he intended an insult; on the contrary, he would energetically repudiate it. Why, in view of this clear denial, do you not abandon your unprovable interpretation?"

Yes. You have lighted on a powerful argument this time. I can imagine the unknown proposer of the toast. He is probably a subordinate to the Chief of the Department who is being honoured—perhaps he himself is already an Assistant Lecturer, a young man with excellent prospects in life. I try to force him to admit that he may nevertheless have had a feeling that there was something in him opposing his toast in honour of the Chief. But this lands me in a nice mess. He gets impatient and suddenly breaks out: "Just you stop trying to cross-question me or I shall turn nasty. You're going to ruin my whole career with your suspicions. I simply said '*aufstossen* [hiccough to]' instead of '*anstossen* [drink to]' because I'd said '*auf*' twice before in the same sentence. That's what Meringer calls a perseveration and there's nothing more to be interpreted about it. D'you understand? *Basta!*"—H'm! That was a surprising reaction, a truly energetic denial. I see there's nothing more to be done with the young man. But I also reflect that he shows a strong personal interest in insisting on his parapraxis not having a sense. You may also feel that there was something wrong in his being quite so rude about a purely theoretical enquiry. But, you will think, when all is said and done he must know what he wanted to say and what he didn't.

But must he? Perhaps that may still be the question.

Now, however, you think you have me at your mercy. "So that's your technique," I hear you say. "When a person who has made a slip of the tongue says something about it that suits you, you pronounce him to be the final decisive authority on the subject. "He says so himself!" But when what he says doesn't suit your book, then all at once you say he's of no importance—there's no need to believe him."

That is quite true. But I can put a similar case

to you in which the same monstrous event occurs. When someone charged with an offence confesses his deed to the judge, the judge believes his confession; but if he denies it, the judge does not believe him. If it were otherwise, there would be no administration of justice, and in spite of occasional errors we must allow that the system works.

"Are you a judge, then? And is a person who has made a slip of the tongue brought up before you on a charge? So making a slip of the tongue is an offence, is it?"

Perhaps we need not reject the comparison. But I would ask you to observe what profound differences of opinion we have reached after a little investigation of what seemed such innocent problems concerning the parapraxes—differences which at the moment we see no possible way of smoothing over. I propose a provisional compromise on the basis of the analogy with the judge and the defendant. I suggest that you shall grant me that there can be no doubt of a parapraxis having a sense if the subject himself admits it. *I* will admit in return that we cannot arrive at a direct proof of the suspected sense if the subject refuses us information, and equally, of course, if he is not at hand to give us the information. Then, as in the case of the administration of justice, we are obliged to turn to circumstantial evidence, which may make a decision more probable in some instances and less so in others. In the law courts it may be necessary for practical purposes to find a defendant guilty on circumstantial evidence. We are under no such necessity; but neither are we obliged to disregard the circumstantial evidence. It would be a mistake to suppose that a science consists entirely of strictly proved theses, and it would be unjust to require this. Only a disposition with a passion for authority will raise such a demand, someone with a craving to replace his religious catechism by another, though it is a scientific one. Science has only a few apodeictic[6] propositions in its catechism: the rest are assertions promoted by it to some particular degree of probability. It is actually a sign of a scientific mode of thought to find satisfaction in these approximations to certainty and to be able to pursue constructive work further in spite of the absence of final confirmation.

But if the subject does not himself give us the explanation of the sense of a parapraxis, where are we to find the starting-points for our interpretation—the circumstantial evidence? In various directions. In the first place from analogies with phenomena apart from parapraxes: when, for instance, we assert that distorting a name when it occurs as a slip of the tongue has the same insulting sense as a deliberate twisting of a name. Further, from the psychical situation in which the parapraxis occurs, the character of the person who makes the parapraxis, and the impressions which he has received before the parapraxis and to which the parapraxis is perhaps a reaction. What happens as a rule is that the interpretation is carried out according to general principles: To begin with there is only a suspicion, a suggestion for an interpretation, and we then find a confirmation by examining the psychical situation. Sometimes we have to wait for subsequent events as well (which have, as it were, announced themselves by the parapraxis) before our suspicion is confirmed.

I cannot easily give you illustrations of this if I limit myself to the field of slips of the tongue, though even there some good instances are to be found. * * * The lady whose husband could eat and drink what *she* wanted is known to me as one of those energetic women who wear the breeches in their home. * * *

But I can give you a large selection of circumstantial evidence of this kind if I pass over to the wide field of the other parapraxes.

If anyone forgets a proper name which is familiar to him normally or if, in spite of all his efforts, he finds it difficult to keep it in mind, it is plausible to suppose that he has something against the person who bears the name so that he prefers not to think of him. Consider, for instance, what we learn in the following cases about the psychical situation in which the parapraxis occurred.

"A Herr Y. fell in love with a lady, but he met with no success, and shortly afterward she married

---

[6]Indisputable.

a Herr X. Thereafter, Herr Y., in spite of having known Herr X. for a long time and even having business dealings with him, forgot his name over and over again, so that several times he had to enquire what it was from other people when he wanted to correspond with Herr X." Herr Y. evidently wanted to know nothing of his more fortunate rival: "never thought of shall he be."

Or: A lady enquired from her doctor for news of a common acquaintance, but called her by her maiden name. She had forgotten her friend's married name. She admitted afterwards that she had been very unhappy about the marriage and disliked her friend's husband.

* * *

The forgetting of intentions can in general be traced to an opposing current of thought, which is unwilling to carry out the intention. But this view is not only held by us psycho-analysts; it is the general opinion, accepted by everyone in their daily lives and only denied when it comes to theory. A patron who gives his protégé the excuse of having forgotten his request fails to justify himself. The protégé immediately thinks: "It means nothing to him; it's true he promised, but he doesn't really want to do it." For that reason forgetting is banned in certain circumstances of ordinary life; the distinction between the popular and the psycho-analytic view of these parapraxes seems to have disappeared. Imagine the lady of the house receiving her guest with the words: "What? have you come today? I'd quite forgotten I invited you for today." Or imagine a young man confessing to his fiancée that he had forgotten to keep their last rendezvous. He will certainly not confess it; he will prefer to invent on the spur of the moment the most improbable obstacles which prevented his appearing at the time and afterwards made it impossible for him to let her know. We all know too that in military affairs the excuse of having forgotten something is of no help and is no protection against punishment, and we must all feel that that is justified. Here all at once everyone is united in thinking that a particular parapraxis has a sense and in knowing what that sense is. Why are they not consistent enough to extend this

knowledge to the other parapraxes and to admit them fully? There is of course an answer to this question too.

* * *

Cases of forgetting an intention are in general so clear that they are not of much use for our purpose of obtaining circumstantial evidence of the sense of a parapraxis from the psychical situation. Let us therefore turn to a particularly ambiguous and obscure kind of parapraxis—to losing and mislaying. You will no doubt find it incredible that we ourselves can play an intentional part in what is so often the painful accident of losing something. But there are plenty of observations like the following one. A young man lost a pencil of his of which he had been very fond. The day before, he had received a letter from his brother-in-law which ended with these words: "I have neither the inclination nor the time at present to encourage you in your frivolity and laziness." The pencil had actually been given to him by this brother-in-law. Without this coincidence we could not, of course, have asserted that a part was played in the loss by an intention to get rid of the thing. Similar cases are very common. We lose an object if we have quarreled with the person who gave it to us and do not want to be reminded of him; or if we no longer like the object itself and want to have an excuse for getting another and better one instead. The same intention directed against an object can also play a part, of course, in cases of dropping, breaking, or destroying things. Can we regard it as a matter of chance when a schoolchild immediately before his birthday loses, ruins or smashes some of his personal belongings, such as his satchel or his watch?

Nor will anyone who has sufficiently often experienced the torment of not being able to find something that he himself has put away feel inclined to believe that there is a purpose in mislaying things. Yet instances are far from rare in which the circumstances attendant on the mislaying point to an intention to get rid of the object temporarily or permanently.

Here is the best example, perhaps, of such an occasion. A youngish man told me the following story: "Some years ago there were misunderstandings between me and my wife. I found her too cold, and although I willingly recognized her excellent qualities we lived together without any tender feelings. One day, returning from a walk, she gave me a book which she had bought because she thought it would interest me. I thanked her for this mark of 'attention,' promised to read the book and put it on one side. After that I could never find it again. Months passed by, in which I occasionally remembered the lost book and made vain attempts to find it. About six months later my dear mother, who was not living with us, fell ill. My wife left home to nurse her mother-in-law. The patient's condition became serious and gave my wife an opportunity of showing the best side of herself. One evening I returned home full of enthusiasm and gratitude for what my wife had accomplished. I walked up to my desk, and without any definite intention but with a kind of somnambulistic certainty opened one of the drawers. On the very top I found the long-lost book I had mislaid." With the extinction of the motive the mislaying of the object ceased as well.

Ladies and Gentlemen, I could multiply this collection of examples indefinitely; but I will not do so here. You will in any case find a profusion of case material for the study of parapraxes in my *Psychopathology of Everyday Life* (first published in 1901). All these examples lead to the same result: they make it probable that parapraxes have a sense, and they show you how that sense is discovered or confirmed by the attendant circumstances. I will be briefer to-day, because we have adopted the limited aim of using the study of these phenomena as a help towards a preparation for psychoanalysis. There are only two groups of observations into which I need enter more fully here: accumulated and combined parapraxes and the confirmation of our interpretations by subsequent events.

Accumulated and combined parapraxes are without doubt the finest flower of their kind. If we had only been concerned to prove that parapraxes have a sense we should have confined ourselves to them from the first, for in their case the sense is unmistakable even to the dull-witted and forces itself on the most critical judgement. An accumula-

tion of these phenomena betrays an obstinacy that is scarcely ever a characteristic of chance events but fits in well with something intentional. Finally, the mutual interchangeability between different species of parapraxes demonstrates what it is in parapraxes that is important and characteristic: not their form or the method which they employ but the purpose which they serve and which can be achieved in the most various ways. For this reason I will give you an instance of repeated forgetting. Ernest Jones[7] tells us that once, for reasons unknown to him, he left a letter lying on his desk for several days. At last he decided to send it off, but he had it returned to him by the Dead Letter Office since he had forgotten to address it. After he had addressed it he took it to the post, but this time it had no stamp. And then at last he was obliged to admit his reluctance to sending the letter off at all.

In another case a bungled action is combined with an instance of mislaying. A lady travelled to Rome with her brother-in-law, who was a famous artist. The visitor was received with great honour by the German community in Rome, and among other presents he was given an antique gold medal. The lady was vexed that her brother-in-law did not appreciate the lovely object sufficiently. When she returned home (her place in Rome having been taken by her sister) she discovered while unpacking that she had brought the medal with her—how, she did not know. She at once sent a letter with the news to her brother-in-law, and announced that she would send the article she had walked off with back to Rome next day. But next day the medal had been so cleverly mislaid that it could not be found and sent off; and it was at this point, that the meaning of her "absent-mindedness" dawned on the lady: she wanted to keep the object for herself.

* * *

It would be agreeable to add further, similar examples. But I must proceed, and give you a glimpse of the cases in which our interpretation has to wait for the future for confirmation. The

---

[7]An English psychoanalyst.

governing condition of these cases, it will be realized, is that the present psychical situation is unknown to us or inaccessible to our enquiries. Our interpretation is consequently no more than a suspicion to which we ourselves do not attach too much importance. Later, however, something happens which shows us how well-justified our interpretation had been. I was once the guest of a young married couple and heard the young woman laughingly describe her latest experience. The day after her return from the honeymoon she had called for her unmarried sister to go shopping with her as she used to do, while her husband went to his business. Suddenly she noticed a gentleman on the other side of the street, and nudging her sister had cried: "Look, there goes Herr L." She had forgotten that this gentleman had been her husband for some weeks. I shuddered as I heard the story, but I did not dare to draw the inference. The little incident only occurred to my mind some years later when the marriage had come to a most unhappy end.

Maeder tells of a lady who, on the eve of her wedding had forgotten to try on her wedding-dress and, to her dressmaker's despair, only remembered it late in the evening. He connects this forgetfulness with the fact that she was soon divorced from her husband. I know a lady now divorced from her husband, who in managing her money affairs frequently signed documents in her maiden name, many years before she in fact resumed it.—I know of other women who have lost their wedding-rings during the honeymoon, and I know too that the history of their marriages has given a sense to the accident.—And now here is one more glaring example, but with a happier ending. The story is told of a famous German chemist that his marriage did not take place, because he forgot the hour of his wedding and went to the laboratory instead of to the church. He was wise enough to be satisfied with a single attempt and died at a great age unmarried.

The idea may possibly have occurred to you that in these examples parapraxes have taken the place of the omens or auguries of the ancients. And indeed some omens were nothing else than parapraxes, as, for instance, when someone stumbled or fell down. Others of them, it is true, had the character of objective happenings and not of subjective acts. But you would hardly believe how difficult it sometimes is to decide whether a particular event belongs to the one group or to the other. An act so often understands how to disguise itself as a passive experience.

All those of us who can look back on a comparatively long experience of life will probably admit that we should have spared ourselves many disappointments and painful surprises if we had found the courage and determination to interpret small parapraxes experienced in our human contacts as auguries and to make use of them as indications of intentions that were still concealed. As a rule we dare not do so; it would make us feel as though, after a detour through science, we were becoming superstitious again. Nor do all auguries come true, and you will understand from our theories that they do not all need to come true.

PSYCHOLOGICAL TYPES

Carl Jung

*One mark of Freud's stature in intellectual history is the number of his adher-
ents—and former adherents—who became major figures in their own right. Perhaps the best known of these is Carl Jung. Jung began his career in psychoanalysis
as Freud's anointed "crown prince." Freud intended that Jung succeed him as president of the International Psychoanalytic Association. The two carried on an intense correspondence for years and also traveled to the United States together in
1909.*

*When it came, the split between Freud and Jung was bitter. Jung felt that
Freud overemphasized the role of sexuality and underemphasized the constructive
role of the unconscious. But the conflict may have been deeper than that; Jung
chafed under Freud's dominating role as his intellectual father figure and felt a
need to achieve more independence. For his part, Freud regarded major departures
from his theory simply as error, and was particularly alarmed by a turn Jung took
in midlife toward a mystical view of the human psyche. Jung formulated ideas, still
famous today, about a "collective unconscious" full of mysterious images and ideas
shared by all members of the human race, and an "oceanic feeling" of being at one
with the universe. Such ideas were anathema to the atheistic and hardheaded
Freud.*

*In the following selection Jung explains one of the more down-to-earth of his
theoretical ideas, his conception of introversion and extraversion and four related
styles of thinking. These ideas have had an obvious and lasting influence. Recall,
for example, that extraversion is one of the Big Five factors of personality espoused
in the second section of this reader by Costa and McCrae. But Jung's conception is
somewhat different from the behavioral styles labeled as extraversion and introversion today. Jung's introvert is someone who in a fundamental way has turned into
himself or herself and away from the world; his extravert is wholly dependent on
others for his or her intellectual and emotional life.*

*A widely used personality test, the Myers-Briggs Type Indicator (Myers &
McCaulley, 1985), was designed to classify people as to their style of thinking, in
Jungian terms. You might be classified as dominated by sensation, thinking, feeling, or intuition. This test is often used for vocational guidance. For example,
the sensation style might be appropriate for an athlete, the thinking style for a*

lawyer, the feeling style for a poet, and the intuitive style for a clinical psychologist.

The following selection is an excerpt from a lecture Jung delivered in Territet, Switzerland, in 1923. By this time Jung had split thoroughly from Freud and was well known for his own work.

From *Psychological Types*, translated by R. Hull and H. Baynes (Princeton, NJ: Princeton University Press, 1971), pp. 510–523.

* * *

We shall discover, after a time, that in spite of the great variety of conscious motives and tendencies, certain groups of individuals can be distinguished who are characterized by a striking conformity of motivation. For example, we shall come upon individuals who in all their judgments, perceptions, feelings, affects, and actions feel external factors to be the predominant motivating force, or who at least give weight to them no matter whether causal or final motives are in question. I will give some examples of what I mean. St. Augustine: "I would not believe the Gospel if the authority of the Catholic Church did not compel it." A dutiful daughter: "I could not allow myself to think anything that would be displeasing to my father." One man finds a piece of modern music beautiful because everybody else pretends it is beautiful. Another marries in order to please his parents but very much against his own interests. There are people who contrive to make themselves ridiculous in order to amuse others; they even prefer to make butts of themselves rather than remain unnoticed. There are not a few who in everything they do or don't do have but one motive in mind: what will others think of them? "One need not be ashamed of a thing if nobody knows about it." There are some who can find happiness only when it excites the envy of others; some who make trouble for themselves in order to enjoy the sympathy of their friends.

Such examples could be multiplied indefinitely. They point to a psychological peculiarity that can be sharply distinguished from another attitude which, by contrast, is motivated chiefly by internal or subjective factors. A person of this type might say: "I know I could give my father the great-est pleasure if I did so and so, but I don't happen to think that way." Or: "I see that the weather has turned out bad, but in spite of it I shall carry out my plan." This type does not travel for pleasure but to execute a preconceived idea. Or: "My book is probably incomprehensible, but it is perfectly clear to me." Or, going to the other extreme: "Everybody thinks I could do something, but I know perfectly well I can do nothing." Such a man can be so ashamed of himself that he literally dares not meet people. There are some who feel happy only when they are quite sure nobody knows about it, and to them a thing is disagreeable just because it is pleasing to everyone else. They seek the good where no one would think of finding it. At every step the sanction of the subject must be obtained, and without it nothing can be undertaken or carried out. Such a person would have replied to St. Augustine: "I would believe the Gospel if the authority of the Catholic Church did *not* compel it." Always he has to prove that everything he does rests on his own decisions and convictions, and never because he is influenced by anyone, or desires to please or conciliate some person or opinion.

This attitude characterizes a group of individuals whose motivations are derived chiefly from the subject, from inner necessity. There is, finally, a third group, and here it is hard to say whether the motivation comes chiefly from within or without. This group is the most numerous and includes the less differentiated normal man, who is considered normal either because he allows himself no excesses or because he has no need of them. The normal man is, by definition, influenced as much from within as from without. He constitutes the extensive middle group, on one side of which are those whose motivations are determined mainly by the external object, and, on the other, those whose motivations are determined from within. I call the first group *extraverted*, and the second group *introverted*. The terms scarcely require elucidation as they explain themselves from what has already been said.

Although there are doubtless individuals whose type can be recognized at first glance, this is by no means always the case. As a rule, only careful observation and weighing of the evidence permit a sure classification. However simple and clear the fundamental principle of the two opposing attitudes may be, in actual reality they are complicated and hard to make out, because every individual is an exception to the rule. Hence one can never give a description of a type, no matter how complete, that would apply to more than one individual, despite the fact that in some ways it aptly characterizes thousands of others. Conformity is one side of a man, uniqueness is the other. Classification does not explain the individual psyche. Nevertheless, an understanding of psychological types opens the way to a better understanding of human psychology in general.

Type differentiation often begins very early, so early that in some cases one must speak of it as innate. The earliest sign of extraversion in a child is his quick adaptation to the environment, and the extraordinary attention he gives to objects and especially to the effect he has on them. Fear of objects is minimal; he lives and moves among them with confidence. His apprehension is quick but imprecise. He appears to develop more rapidly than the introverted child, since he is less reflective and usually without fear. He feels no barrier between himself and objects, and can therefore play with them freely and learn through them. He likes to carry his enterprises to the extreme and exposes himself to risks. Everything unknown is alluring.

To reverse the picture, one of the earliest signs of introversion in a child is a reflective, thoughtful manner, marked shyness and even fear of unknown objects. Very early there appears a tendency to assert himself over familiar objects, and attempts are made to master them. Everything unknown is regarded with mistrust; outside influ-ences are usually met with violent resistance. The child wants his own way, and under no circumstances will he submit to an alien rule he cannot understand. When he asks questions, it is not from curiosity or a desire to create a sensation, but because he wants names, meanings, explanations to give him subjective protection against the object. I have seen an introverted child who made his first attempts to walk only after he had learned the names of all the objects in the room he might touch. Thus very early in an introverted child the characteristic defensive attitude can be noted which the adult introvert displays towards the object; just as in an extraverted child one can very early observe a marked assurance and initiative, a happy trustfulness in his dealings with objects. This is indeed the basic feature of the extraverted attitude: psychic life is, as it were, enacted outside the individual in objects and objective relationships. In extreme cases there is even a sort of blindness for his own individuality. The introvert, on the contrary, always acts as though the object possessed a superior power over him against which he has to defend himself. His real world is the inner one.

Sad though it is, the two types are inclined to speak very badly of one another. This fact will immediately strike anyone who investigates the problem. And the reason is that the psychic values have a diametrically opposite localization for the two types. The introvert sees everything that is in any way valuable for him in the subject; the extravert sees it in the object. This dependence on the object seems to the introvert a mark of the greatest inferiority, while to the extravert the preoccupation with the subject seems nothing but infantile autoeroticism. So it is not surprising that the two types often come into conflict. This does not, however, prevent most men from marrying women of the opposite type. Such marriages are very valuable as psychological symbioses so long as the partners do not attempt a mutual "psychological" understanding. But this phase of understanding belongs to the normal development of every marriage provided the partners have the necessary leisure or the necessary urge to development—though even if both these *introverts*

are present real courage is needed to risk a rupture of the marital peace. In favourable circumstances this phase enters automatically into the lives of both types, for the reason that each type is an example of one-sided development. The one develops only external relations and neglects the inner; the other develops inwardly but remains outwardly at a standstill. In time the need arises for the individual to develop what has been neglected. The development takes the form of a differentiation of certain functions, to which I must now turn in view of their importance for the type problem.

The conscious psyche is an apparatus for adaptation and orientation, and consists of a number of different psychic functions. Among these we can distinguish four basic ones: *sensation, thinking, feeling, intuition*. Under sensation I include all perceptions by means of the sense organs; by thinking I mean the function of intellectual cognition and the forming of logical conclusions; feeling is a function of subjective valuation; intuition I take as perception by way of the unconscious, or perception of unconscious contents.

So far as my experience goes, these four basic functions seem to me sufficient to express and represent the various modes of conscious orientation. For complete orientation all four functions should contribute equally: thinking should facilitate cognition and judgment, feeling should tell us how and to what extent a thing is important or unimportant for us, sensation should convey concrete reality to us through seeing, hearing, tasting, etc., and intuition should enable us to divine the hidden possibilities in the background, since these too belong to the complete picture of a given situation.

In reality, however, these basic functions are seldom or never uniformly differentiated and equally at our disposal. As a rule one or the other function occupies the foreground, while the rest remain undifferentiated in the background. Thus there are many people who restrict themselves to the simple perception of concrete reality, without thinking about it or taking feeling values into account. They bother just as little about the possibilities hidden in a situation. I describe such people as *sensation types*. Others are exclusively oriented by

extroverts

what they think, and simply cannot adapt to a situation which they are unable to understand intellectually. I call such people *thinking types*. Others, again, are guided in everything entirely by feeling. They merely ask themselves whether a thing is pleasant or unpleasant, and orient themselves by their feeling impressions. These are the *feeling types*. Finally, the *intuitives* concern themselves neither with ideas nor with feeling reactions, nor yet with the reality of things, but surrender themselves wholly to the lure of possibilities, and abandon every situation in which no further possibilities can be scented.

Each of these types represents a different kind of one-sidedness, but one which is linked up with and complicated in a peculiar way by the introverted or extraverted attitude. It was because of this complication that I had to mention these function-types, and this brings us back to the question of the one-sidedness of the introverted and extraverted attitudes. This one-sidedness would lead to a complete loss of psychic balance if it were not compensated by an unconscious counterposition. Investigation of the unconscious has shown, for example, that alongside or behind the introvert's conscious attitude there is an unconscious extraverted attitude which automatically compensates his conscious one-sidedness.

* * *

The alteration of the conscious attitude is no light matter, because any habitual attitude is essentially a more or less conscious ideal, sanctified by custom and historical tradition, and founded on the bedrock of one's innate temperament. The conscious attitude is always in the nature of a *Weltanschauung*, if it is not explicitly a religion. It is this that makes the type problem so important. The opposition between the types is not merely an external conflict between men, it is the source of endless inner conflicts; the cause not only of external disputes and dislikes, but of nervous ills and psychic suffering. It is this fact, too, that obliges us physicians constantly to widen our medical horizon and to include within it not only general psychological standpoints but also questions concerning one's views of life and the world.

*   *   *

Recapitulating, I would like to stress that each of the two general attitudes, introversion and extraversion, manifests itself in a special way in an individual through the predominance of one of the four basic functions. Strictly speaking, there are no introverts and extraverts pure and simple, but only introverted and extraverted function-types, such as thinking types, sensation types, etc. There are thus at least eight clearly distinguishable types. Obviously one could increase this number at will if each of the functions were split into three subgroups, which would not be impossible empirically. One could, for example, easily divide thinking into its three well-known forms: intuitive and speculative, logical and mathematical, empirical and positivist, the last being mainly dependent on sense perception. Similar subgroups could be made of the other functions, as in the case of intuition, which has an intellectual as well as an emotional and sensory aspect. In this way a large number of types could be established, each new division becoming increasingly subtle.

For the sake of completeness, I must add that I do not regard the classification of types according to introversion and extraversion and the four basic functions as the only possible one. Any other psychological criterion could serve just as well as a classifier, although, in my view, no other possesses so great a practical significance.

The Distrust Between the Sexes

Karen Horney

*Like Jung, Karen Horney began her psychoanalytic career as a follower and de-
fender of Freud. But Horney was too much of an independent thinker to remain
anyone's disciple for long. First practicing in Germany and then in America for
most of her career, Horney invented a distinctly feminist form of psychoanalysis.
The combination of a psychoanalytic style of thinking with ideas of the sort that it
is difficult to imagine a male analyst propounding is well illustrated in the following selection.*

*The selection comes from a paper Horney delivered before the German
Women's Medical Association in 1930. Horney was ahead of her time, and
her gentle critique of and subtle revisions to conventional psychoanalytic theory
anticipated feminist objections that would be expressed over the following
decades.*

From *Feminine Psychology* (New York: Norton, 1967), pp. 104–116.

* * *

The relationship between men and women is
quite similar to that between children and
parents, in that we prefer to focus on the
positive aspects of these relationships. We prefer
to assume that love is the fundamentally given factor and that hostility is an accidental and avoidable occurrence. Although we are familiar with
slogans such as "the battle of the sexes" and "hostility between the sexes," we must admit that they
do not mean a great deal. They make us overfocus
on sexual relations between men and women,
which can very easily lead us to a too one-sided
view. Actually, from our recollection of numerous

case histories, we may conclude that love relationships are quite easily destroyed by overt or covert
hostility. On the other hand we are only too ready
to blame such difficulties on individual misfortune, on incompatibility of the partners, and on
social or economic causes.

The individual factors, which we find causing
poor relations between men and women, may be
the pertinent ones. However, because of the great
frequency, or better, the regular occurrence of disturbances in love relations, we have to ask ourselves whether the disturbances in the individual
cases might not arise from a common background;
whether there are common denominators for this
easily and frequently arising suspiciousness between the sexes?

* * *

I would like to start with something very commonplace—namely, that a good deal of this atmosphere of suspiciousness is understandable and even justifiable. It apparently has nothing to do with the individual partner, but rather with the intensity of the affects and with the difficulty of taming them.

We know or may dimly sense that these affects can lead to ecstasy, to being beside oneself, to surrendering oneself, which means a leap into the unlimited and the boundless. This is perhaps why real passion is so rare. For like a good businessman, we are loath to put all our eggs in one basket. We are inclined to be reserved and ever ready to retreat. Be that as it may, because of our instinct for self-preservation, we all have a natural fear of losing ourselves in another person. That is why what happens to love, happens to education and psychoanalysis; everybody thinks he knows all about them, but few do. One is inclined to overlook how little one gives of oneself, but one feels all the more this same deficiency in the partner, the feeling of "You never really loved me." A wife who harbors suicidal thoughts because her husband does not give her all his love, time, and interest will not notice how much of her own hostility, hidden vindictiveness, and aggression are expressed through her attitude. She will feel only despair because of her abundant "love," while at the same time she will feel most intensely and see most clearly the lack of love in her partner. * * *

Here we are not dealing with pathological phenomena at all. In pathological cases we merely see a distortion and exaggeration of a general and normal occurrence. Anybody, to a certain extent, will be inclined to overlook his own hostile impulses, but under pressure of his own guilty conscience, may project them onto the partner. This process must, of necessity, cause some overt or covert distrust of the partner's love, fidelity, sincerity, or kindness. This is the reason why I prefer to speak of distrust between the sexes and not of hatred; for in keeping with our own experience we are more familiar with the feeling of distrust.

A further, almost unavoidable, source of disappointment and distrust in our normal love life derives from the fact that the very intensity of our feelings of love stirs up all of our secret expectations and longings for happiness, which slumber deep inside us. All our unconscious wishes, contradictory in their nature and expanding boundlessly on all sides, are waiting here for their fulfillment. The partner is supposed to be strong, and at the same time helpless, to dominate us and be dominated by us, to be ascetic and to be sensuous. He should rape us and be tender, have time for us exclusively and also be intensely involved in creative work. As long as we assume that he could actually fulfill all these expectations, we invest him with the glitter of sexual overestimation. We take the magnitude of such overvaluation for the measure of our love, while in reality it merely expresses the magnitude of our expectations. The very nature of our claims makes their fulfillment impossible. Herein lies the origin of the disappointments with which we may cope in a more or less effective way. Under favorable circumstances we do not even have to become aware of the great number of our disappointments, just as we have not been aware of the extent of our secret expectations. Yet there remain traces of distrust in us, as in a child who discovers that his father cannot get him the stars from the sky after all.

Thus far, our reflections certainly have been neither new nor specifically analytical and have often been better formulated in the past. The analytical approach begins with the question: What special factors in human development lead to the discrepancy between expectations and fulfillment and what causes them to be of special significance in particular cases? Let us start with a general consideration. There is a basic difference between human and animal development—namely, the long period of the infant's helplessness and dependency. The paradise of childhood is most often an illusion with which adults like to deceive themselves. For the child, however, this paradise is inhabited by too many dangerous monsters. Unpleasant experiences with the opposite sex seem to be unavoidable. We need only recall the capacity that children possess, even in their very early years, for passionate and instinctive sexual desires similar to those of adults and yet different from them. Children are different in the aims of their drives, but above all, in the pristine integrity of their demands. They find it hard to express their desires directly, and where they do, they are not taken seriously. Their seriousness sometimes is looked upon as being cute, or it may be overlooked or rejected. In short, children will undergo painful and humiliating experiences of being rebuffed, being betrayed, and being told lies. They also may have to take second place to a parent or sibling, and they are threatened and intimidated when they seek, in playing with their own bodies, those pleasures that are denied them by adults. The child is relatively powerless in the face of all this. He is not able to ventilate his fury at all, or only to a minor degree, nor can he come to grips with the experience by means of intellectual comprehension. Thus, anger and aggression are pent up within him in the form of extravagant fantasies, which hardly reach the daylight of awareness, fantasies that are criminal when viewed from the standpoint of the adult, fantasies that range from taking by force and stealing, to those about killing, burning, cutting to pieces, and choking. Since the child is vaguely aware of these destructive forces within him, he feels, according to the talion law,[1] equally threatened by the adults. Here is the origin of those infantile anxieties of which no child remains entirely free. This already enables us to understand better the fear of love of which I have spoken before. Just here, in this most irrational of all areas, the old childhood fears of a threatening father or mother are reawakened, putting us instinctively on the defensive. In other words, the fear of love will always be mixed with the fear of what we might do to the other person, or what the other person might do to us. A lover in the Aru Islands, for example, will never make a gift of a lock of hair to his beloved, because should an argument arise, the beloved might burn it, thus causing the partner to get sick.

I would like to sketch briefly how childhood conflicts may affect the relationship to the opposite sex in later life. Let us take as an example a typical situation: The little girl who was badly hurt through some great disappointment by her father will transform her innate instinctual wish to receive from the man into a vindictive one of taking from him by force. Thus the foundation is laid for a direct line of development to a later attitude, according to which she will not only deny her maternal instincts, but will have only one drive, i.e., to harm the male, to exploit him, and to suck him dry. She has become a vampire. Let us assume that there is a similar transformation from the wish to receive to the wish to take away. Let us further assume that the latter wish was repressed due to anxiety from a guilty conscience; then we have here the fundamental constellation for the formation of a certain type of woman who is unable to relate to the male because she fears that every male will suspect her of wanting something from him. This really means that she is afraid that he might guess her repressed desires. Or by completely projecting onto him her repressed wishes, she will imagine that every male merely intends to exploit her, that he wants from her only sexual satisfaction, after which he will discard her. Or let us assume that a reaction formation of excessive modesty will mask the repressed drive for power. We then have the type of woman who shies away from demanding or accepting anything from her husband. Such a woman, however, due to the return of the repressed, will react with depression to the nonfulfillment of her unexpressed, and often unformulated, wishes. She thus unwittingly jumps from the frying pan into the fire, as does her partner, because a depression will hit him much harder than direct aggression. Quite often the repression of aggression against the male drains all her vital energy. The woman then feels helpless to meet life. She will shift the entire responsibility for her helplessness onto the man, robbing him of the very breath of life. Here you have the type of woman who, under the guise of being helpless and childlike, dominates her man.

These are examples that demonstrate how the fundamental attitude of women toward men can be disturbed by childhood conflicts. In an attempt

---

[1]The law of retaliative justice, sometimes called "an eye for an eye."

to simplify matters, I have stressed only one point, which, however, seems crucial to me—the disturbance in the development of motherhood.

I shall now proceed to trace certain traits of male psychology. I do not wish to follow individual lines of development, though it might be very instructive to observe analytically how, for instance, even men who consciously have a very positive relationship with women and hold them in high esteem as human beings, harbor deep within themselves a secret distrust of them; and how this distrust relates back to feelings toward their mothers, which they experienced in their formative years. I shall focus rather on certain typical attitudes of men toward women and how they have appeared during various eras of history and in different cultures, not only as regards sexual relationships with women, but also, and often more so, in nonsexual situations, such as in their general evaluation of women.

I shall select some random examples, starting with Adam and Eve.[2] Jewish culture, as recorded in the Old Testament, is outspokenly patriarchal. This fact reflects itself in their religion, which has no maternal goddesses; in their morals and customs, which allow the husband the right to dissolve the marital bond simply by dismissing his wife. Only by being aware of this background can we recognize the male bias in two incidents of Adam's and Eve's history. First of all, woman's capacity to give birth is partly denied and partly devaluated: Eve was made of Adam's rib and a curse was put on her to bear children in sorrow. In the second place, by interpreting her tempting Adam to eat of the tree of knowledge as a sexual temptation, woman appears as the sexual temptress, who plunges man into misery. I believe that these two elements, one born out of resentment, the other out of anxiety, have damaged the relationship between the sexes from the earliest times to the present. Let us follow this up briefly. Man's fear of woman is deeply rooted in sex, as is shown by the simple fact that it

is only the sexually attractive woman of whom he is afraid and who, although he strongly desires her, has to be kept in bondage. Old women, on the other hand, are held in high esteem, even by cultures in which the young woman is dreaded and therefore suppressed. In some primitive cultures the old woman may have the decisive voice in the affairs of the tribe; among Asian nations also she enjoys great power and prestige. On the other hand, in primitive tribes woman is surrounded by taboos during the entire period of her sexual maturity. Women of the Arunta tribe are able to magically influence the male genitals. If they sing to a blade of grass and then point it at a man or throw it at him, he becomes ill or loses his genitals altogether. Women lure him to his doom. In a certain East African tribe, husband and wife do not sleep together, because her breath might weaken him. If a woman of a South African tribe climbs over the leg of a sleeping man, he will be unable to run; hence the general rule of sexual abstinence two to five days prior to hunting, warfare, or fishing. Even greater is the fear of menstruation, pregnancy, and childbirth. Menstruating women are surrounded by extensive taboos—a man who touches a menstruating woman will die. There is one basic thought at the bottom of all this: Woman is a mysterious being who communicates with spirits and thus has magic powers that she can use to hurt the male. He must therefore protect himself against her powers by keeping her subjugated. Thus the Miri in Bengal do not permit their women to eat the flesh of the tiger, lest they become too strong. The Watawela of East Africa keep the art of making fire a secret from their women, lest women become their rulers. The Indians of California have ceremonies to keep their women in submission; a man is disguised as a devil to intimidate the women. The Arabs of Mecca exclude women from religious festivities to prevent familiarity between women and their overlords. We find similar customs during the Middle Ages—the Cult of the Virgin side by side with the burning of witches; the adoration of "pure" motherliness, completely divested of sexuality, next to the cruel destruction of the sexually seductive woman. Here again is the implication of

---

[2]The long paragraph that follows provides a good illustration of Horney's distinctly feminist style of psychoanalytic thinking.

underlying anxiety, for the witch is in communication with the devil. Nowadays, with our more humane forms of aggression, we burn women only figuratively, sometimes with undisguised hatred, sometimes with apparent friendliness. * * * In friendly and secret autos-da-fé, many nice things are said about women, but it is just unfortunate that in her God-given natural state, she is not the equal of the male. Moebius pointed out that the female brain weighs less than the male one, but the point need not be made in so crude a way. On the contrary, it can be stressed that woman is not at all inferior, only different, but that unfortunately she has fewer or none of those human or cultural qualities that man holds in such high esteem. She is said to be deeply rooted in the personal and emotional spheres, which is wonderful; but unfortunately, this makes her incapable of exercising justice and objectivity, therefore disqualifying her for positions in law and government and in the spiritual community. She is said to be at home only in the realm of eros. Spiritual matters are alien to her innermost being, and she is at odds with cultural trends. She therefore is, as Asians frankly state, a second-rate being. Woman may be industrious and useful but is, alas, incapable of productive and independent work. She is, indeed, prevented from real accomplishment by the deplorable, bloody tragedies of menstruation and childbirth. And so every man silently thanks his God, just as the pious Jew does in his prayers, that he was not created a woman.

Man's attitude toward motherhood is a large and complicated chapter. One is generally inclined to see no problem in this area. Even the misogynist is obviously willing to respect woman as a mother and to venerate her motherliness under certain conditions, as mentioned above regarding the Cult of the Virgin. In order to obtain a clearer picture, we have to distinguish between two attitudes: men's attitudes toward motherliness, as represented in its purest form in the Cult of the Virgin, and their attitude toward motherhood as such, as we encounter it in the symbolism of the ancient mother goddesses. Males will always be in favor of motherliness, as expressed in certain spiritual qualities of women, i.e., the nurturing, selfless, self-sacrificing mother; for she is the ideal embodiment of the woman who could fulfill all his expectations and longings. In the ancient mother goddesses, man did not venerate motherliness in the spiritual sense, but rather motherhood in its most elemental meaning. Mother goddesses are earthy goddesses, fertile like the soil. They bring forth new life and they nurture it. It was this life-creating power of woman, an elemental force, that filled man with admiration. And this is exactly the point where problems arise. For it is contrary to human nature to sustain appreciation without resentment toward capabilities that one does not possess. Thus, a man's minute share in creating new life became, for him, an immense incitement to create something new on his part.[3] He has created values of which he might well be proud. State, religion, art, and science are essentially his creations, and our entire culture bears the masculine imprint.

However, as happens elsewhere, so it does here; even the greatest satisfactions or achievements, if born out of sublimation,[4] cannot fully make up for something for which we are not endowed by nature. Thus there has remained an obvious residue of general resentment of men against women. This resentment expresses itself, also in our times, in men's distrustful defensive maneuvers against the threat of women's invasion of their domains; hence their tendency to devalue pregnancy and childbirth and to overemphasize male genitality. This attitude does not express itself in scientific theories alone, but is also of far-reaching consequence for the entire relationship between the sexes, and for sexual morality in general. Motherhood, especially illegitimate motherhood, is very insufficiently protected by law. * * * Conversely, there is ample opportunity for the fulfillment of the male's sexual needs. Emphasis on irresponsible

---

[3]Famously, Freud thought women suffered from "penis envy." In this passage, Horney seems to claim that men suffer from womb envy.

[4]"Sublimation" is the psychoanalytic mechanism by which a motivation to do one thing is turned to another purpose.

sexual indulgence, and devaluation of women to an object of purely physical needs, are further consequences of this masculine attitude.

* * *

I do not want to be misunderstood as having implied that all disaster results from male supremacy and that relations between the sexes would improve if women were given the ascendency. However, we must ask ourselves why there should have to be any power struggle at all between the sexes. At any given time, the more powerful side will create an ideology suitable to help maintain its position and to make this position acceptable to the weaker one. In this ideology the differentness of the weaker one will be interpreted as inferiority, and it will be proven that these differences are unchangeable, basic, or God's will.[5] It is the function of such an ideology to deny or conceal the existence of a struggle. Here is one of the answers to the question raised initially as to why we have so little awareness of the fact that there is a struggle between the sexes. It is in the interest of men to obscure this fact; and the emphasis they place on their ideologies has caused women, also, to adopt these theories. Our attempt at resolving these rationalizations and at examining these ideologies as to their fundamental driving forces, is merely a step on the road taken by Freud.

* * *

That many-faceted thing called love succeeds in building bridges from the loneliness on this shore to the loneliness on the other one. These bridges can be of great beauty, but they are rarely built for eternity and frequently they cannot toler-

ate too heavy a burden without collapsing. Here is the other answer to the question posed initially of why we see love between the sexes more distinctly than we see hate—because the union of the sexes offers us the greatest possibilities for happiness. We therefore are naturally inclined to overlook how powerful are the destructive forces that continually work to destroy our chances for happiness.

We might ask in conclusion, how can analytical insights contribute to diminish the distrust between the sexes? There is no uniform answer to this problem. The fear of the power of the affects and the difficulty in controlling them in a love relationship, the resulting conflict between surrender and self-preservation, between the I and the Thou, is an entirely comprehensible, unmitigatable, and as it were, normal phenomenon. The same thing applies in essence to our readiness for distrust, which stems from unresolved childhood conflicts. These childhood conflicts, however, can vary greatly in intensity, and will leave behind traces of variable depth. Analysis not only can help in individual cases to improve the relationship with the opposite sex, but it can also attempt to improve the psychological conditions of childhood and forestall excessive conflicts. This, of course, is our hope for the future. In the momentous struggle for power, analysis can fulfill an important function by uncovering the real motives of this struggle. This uncovering will not eliminate the motives, but it may help to create a better chance for fighting the struggle on its own ground instead of relegating it to peripheral issues.

---

[5]Some modern, feminist critiques of evolutionary personality theory (see Part III) are suspicious of its account of sex differences on exactly these grounds.

EIGHT STAGES OF MAN

Erik Erikson

The last of the classic neo-Freudians to be included in these readings, Erik Erikson, was not really a contemporary of Freud. His career took place across the years following Freud's death in 1939, until Erikson's own death in 1994. But Erikson became the major figure among the neo-Freudians who never broke with the master. He considered himself a loyal disciple to the end, as many passages in the following selection demonstrate.

Despite his loyalty, Erikson's theory goes into territory far outside anything Freud ever seriously considered. The theoretical development for which he is best known, described in this selection, goes beyond Freud in a specific way. Freud viewed psychosexual development as a process that occurred in infancy and early childhood, and was essentially finished shortly after the attainment of puberty. For many years developmental psychology followed the same basic presumption.

But Erikson changed all that. Of his "eight stages of man," four take place during and after the final stage of development from a traditional Freudian perspective. Erikson viewed psychological development as something that occurs throughout life, as challenges, opportunities, and obligations change. At the very last stage, one comes to terms with one's impending death and the meaning of one's life past. The outcome of this stage is crucial for the next generation. In one of his most thought-provoking comments, Erikson writes "healthy children will not fear life if their parents have integrity enough not to fear death." So the last stage of one's own development intersects with the earlier stages in one's children, and the cycle begins again.

The entire field of developmental psychology—not just the part within psychoanalysis—was changed in a profound way as Erikson's framework became widely influential. Without ever using the term, Erikson invented what is today called "life-span developmental psychology," a psychology that studies the way people develop every step of the way from the first day of their life to the last. Erikson's most lasting contribution is the reminder that development is not aimed at an end point, but is a continuing process.

From *Childhood and Society* (New York: Norton, 1950), pp. 219–234.

1. Trust vs. Basic Mistrust

The first demonstration of social trust in the baby is the ease of his feeding, the depth of his sleep, the relaxation of his bowels. The experience of a mutual regulation of his increasingly receptive capacities with the maternal techniques of provision gradually helps him to balance the discomfort caused by the immaturity of homeostasis with which he was born. In his gradually increasing waking hours he finds that more and more adventures of the senses arouse a feeling of familiarity, of having coincided with a feeling of inner goodness. Forms of comfort, and people associated with them, become as familiar as the gnawing discomfort of the bowels. The infant's first social achievement, then, is his willingness to let the mother out of sight without undue anxiety or rage, because she has become an inner certainty as well as an outer predictability. Such consistency, continuity, and sameness of experience provide a rudimentary sense of ego identity which depends, I think, on the recognition that there is an inner population of remembered and anticipated sensations and images which are firmly correlated with the outer population of familiar and predictable things and people. Smiling crowns this development.

The constant tasting and testing of the relationship between inside and outside meets its crucial test during the rages of the biting stage, when the teeth cause pain from within and when outer friends either prove of no avail or withdraw from the only action which promises relief: biting. I would assume that this experience of an urge turning upon the self has much to do with the masochistic tendency of finding cruel and cold comfort in hurting oneself whenever an object has eluded one's grasp.

Out of this, therefore, comes that primary sense of badness, that original sense of evil and malevolence which signifies the potential loss of all that is good because we could not help destroying it inside, thus driving it away outside. This feeling persists in a universal homesickness, a nostalgia for familiar images undamaged by change. Tribes dealing with one segment of nature develop a collective magic which seems to treat the Supernatural Providers of food and fortune as if they were angry and must be appeased by prayer and self-torture. Primitive religions, the most primitive layer in all religions, and the religious layer in each individual, abound with efforts at atonement which try to make up for vague deeds against a maternal matrix and try to restore faith in the goodness of one's strivings and in the kindness of the powers of the universe.

* * * The general state of trust implies not only that one has learned to rely on the sameness and continuity of the outer providers, but also that one may trust oneself and the capacity of one's own organs to cope with urges; and that one is able to consider oneself trustworthy enough so that the providers will not need to be on guard lest they be nipped.

In psychopathology the absence of basic trust can best be studied in infantile schizophrenia, while weakness of such trust is apparent in adult personalities of schizoid and depressive character. The reestablishment of a state of trust has been found to be the basic requirement for therapy in these cases. For no matter what conditions may have caused a psychotic break, the bizarreness and withdrawal in the behavior of many very sick individuals hides an attempt to reconquer social mutuality by a testing of the borderlines between senses and physical reality, between words and social meanings.

Psychoanalysis assumes the early process of differentiation between inside and outside to be the origin of the mechanisms of projection and introjection which remain some of our deepest and most dangerous defense mechanisms. In introjection we feel and act as if an outer goodness had become an inner certainty. In projection, we experience an inner harm as an outer one: we endow significant people with the evil which actually is in us. These two mechanisms, then, projection and introjection, are assumed to be modeled after whatever goes on in infants when they would like to externalize pain and internalize pleasure, an intent which must yield to the testimony of the maturing senses and ultimately of reason. These mechanisms are, more or less normally, reinstated in acute crises of love, trust, and faith in the adult. Where they persist, they mark the "psychotic character."

The firm establishment of enduring patterns for the solution of the nuclear conflict of basic trust versus basic mistrust in mere existence is the first task of the ego, and thus first of all a task for maternal care. But let it be said here that the amount of trust derived from earliest infantile experience does not seem to depend on absolute quantities of food or demonstrations of love, but rather on the quality of the maternal relationship. Mothers, I think, create a sense of trust in their children by that kind of administration which in its quality combines sensitive care of the baby's individual needs and a firm sense of personal trustworthiness within the trusted framework of their culture's life style. This forms the basis in the child for a sense of identity which will later combine a sense of being "all right," of being oneself, and of becoming what other people trust one will become. * * *

2. Autonomy vs. Shame and Doubt

Anal-muscular maturation sets the stage for experimentation with two simultaneous sets of social modalities: holding on and letting go. As is the case with all of these modalities, their basic conflicts can lead in the end to either hostile or benign expectations and attitudes. Thus, to hold can become a destructive and cruel retaining or restraining, and it can become a pattern of care: to have and to hold. To let go, too, can turn into an inimical letting loose of destructive forces, or it can become a relaxed "to let pass" and "to let be." Culturally speaking, these attitudes are neither good nor bad; their value depends on whether their hostile implications are turned against enemy, or fellow man— or the self.

The latter danger is the one best known to us. For if denied the gradual and well-guided experience of the autonomy of free choice (or if, indeed, weakened by an initial loss of trust) the child will turn against himself all his urge to discriminate and to manipulate. He will overmanipulate himself, he will develop a precocious conscience. Instead of taking possession of things in order to test them by purposeful repetition, he will become obsessed by his own repetitiveness. By such obsessiveness, of course, he then learns to repossess the environment and to gain power by stubborn and minute control, where he could not find large-scale mutual regulation. Such hollow victory is the infantile model for a compulsion neurosis. It is also the infantile source of later attempts in adult life to govern by the letter, rather than by the spirit.

Outer control at this stage, therefore, must be firmly reassuring. The infant must come to feel that the basic faith in existence, which is the lasting treasure saved from the rages of the oral stage, will not be jeopardized by this about-face of his, this sudden violent wish to have a choice, to appropriate demandingly, and to eliminate stubbornly. Firmness must protect him against the potential anarchy of his as yet untrained sense of discrimination, his inability to hold on and to let go with discretion. As his environment encourages him to "stand on his own feet," it must protect him against meaningless and arbitrary experiences of shame and of early doubt.

Shame is an emotion insufficiently studied, because in our civilization it is so early and easily absorbed by guilt. Shame supposes that one is completely exposed and conscious of being looked at: in one word, self-conscious. One is visible and not ready to be visible; which is why we dream of shame as a situation in which we are stared at in a condition of incomplete dress, in night attire, "with one's pants down." Shame is early expressed in an impulse to bury one's face, or to sink, right then and there, into the ground. But this, I think, is essentially rage turned against the self. He who is ashamed would like to force the world not to look at him, not to notice his exposure. He would like to destroy the eyes of the world. Instead he must wish for his own invisibility. This potentiality is abundantly used in the educational method of "shaming" used so exclusively by some primitive peoples; its destructiveness is balanced in some civilizations by devices for "saving face." Visual shame precedes auditory guilt, which is a sense of badness to be had all by oneself when nobody watches and when everything is quiet—except the voice of the superego. Such shaming exploits an increasing sense of being small, which can develop only as the child stands up and as his awareness permits him to note the relative measures of size and power. * * *

Doubt is the brother of shame. Where shame is dependent on the consciousness of being upright and exposed, doubt, so clinical observation leads me to believe, has much to do with a consciousness of having a front and a back—and especially a "behind." For this reverse area of the body, with its aggressive and libidinal focus in the sphincters and in the buttocks, cannot be seen by the child, and yet it can be dominated by the will of others. The "behind" is thus the individual's dark continent, an area of the body which can be magically dominated and effectively invaded by those who would attack one's power of autonomy and who would designate as evil those products of the bowels which were felt to be all right when they were being passed. This basic sense of doubt in whatever one has left behind forms a substratum for later and more verbal forms of compulsive doubting; this finds its adult expression in paranoiac fears concerning hidden persecutors and secret persecutions threatening from behind and from within the behind.

3. Initiative vs. Guilt

The ambulatory stage and that of infantile genitality add to the inventory of basic social modalities that of "making," first in the sense of "being on the make." There is no simpler, stronger word to match the social modalities previously enumerated. The word suggests pleasure in attack and conquest. In the boy, the emphasis remains on phallic-intrusive modes; in the girl it turns to modes of "catching" in more aggressive forms of snatching and "bitchy" possessiveness, or in the milder form of making oneself attractive and endearing.

The danger of this stage is a sense of guilt over the goals contemplated and the acts initiated in one's exuberant enjoyment of new locomotor and mental power: acts of aggressive manipulation and coercion which go far beyond the executive capacity of organism and mind and therefore call for an energetic halt on one's contemplated initiative. While autonomy concentrates on keeping potential rivals out, and is therefore more an expression of jealous rage most often directed against encroachments by younger siblings, initiative brings with it anticipatory rivalry with those who have been there first and may, therefore, occupy with their superior equipment the field toward which one's initiative is directed. Jealousy and rivalry, those often embittered and yet essentially futile attempts at demarcating a sphere of unquestioned privilege, now come to a climax in a final contest for a favored position with the mother; the inevitable failure leads to resignation, guilt, and anxiety. The child indulges in fantasies of being a giant and a tiger, but in his dreams he runs in terror for dear life. This, then, is the stage of the "castration complex," the fear of losing the (now energetically eroticized) genitals as a punishment for the fantasies attached to their excitements.

Infantile sexuality and incest taboo, castration complex and superego all unite here to bring about that specifically human crisis during which the child must turn from an exclusive, pregenital attachment to his parents to the slow process of becoming a parent, a carrier of tradition. Here the most fateful split and transformation in the emotional powerhouse occurs, a split between potential human glory and potential total destruction. For here the child becomes forever divided in himself. The instinct fragments which before had enhanced the growth of his infantile body and mind now become divided into an infantile set which perpetuates the exuberance of growth potentials, and a parental set which supports and increases self-observation, self-guidance, and self-punishment.

Naturally, the parental set is at first infantile in nature: the fact that human conscience remains partially infantile throughout life is the core of human tragedy. For the superego of the child can be primitive, cruel, and uncompromising, as may be observed in instances where children overcontrol and overconstrict themselves to the point of self-obliteration; where they develop an over-obedience more literal than the one the parent has wished to exact; or where they develop deep regressions and lasting resentments because the parents themselves do not seem to live up to the new conscience which they have installed in the child. One of the deepest conflicts in life is the hate for a parent who served as the model and the executor of the superego, but who (in some form) was found trying to get away with the very transgressions which the child can no longer tolerate in himself. The suspiciousness and evasiveness which is thus mixed in with the all-or-nothing quality of the superego, this organ of tradition, makes moral (in the sense of moralistic) man a great potential danger to his own ego—and to that of his fellow men.

The problem, again, is one of mutual regulation. Where the child, now so ready to overmanipulate himself, can gradually develop a sense of paternal responsibility, where he can gain some insight into the institutions, functions, and roles which will permit his responsible participation, he will find pleasurable accomplishment in wielding tools and weapons, in manipulating meaningful toys—and in caring for younger children.

* * *

4. Industry vs. Inferiority

Before the child, psychologically already a rudimentary parent, can become a biological parent, he must begin to be a worker and potential provider. With the oncoming latency period,[1] the normally advanced child forgets, or rather sublimates, the necessity to "make" people by direct attack or to become papa and mama in a hurry: he now learns to win recognition by producing things. He has mastered the ambulatory field and the organ modes. He has experienced a sense of finality regarding the fact that there is no workable future within the womb of his family, and thus becomes ready to apply himself to given skills and tasks, which go far beyond the mere playful expression of his organ modes or the pleasure in the function of his limbs. He develops industry—i.e., he adjusts himself to the inorganic laws of the tool world. He can become an eager and absorbed unit of a productive situation. To bring a productive situation to completion is an aim which gradually supersedes the whims and wishes of his autonomous organism. His ego boundaries include his tools and skills: the work principle teaches him the pleasure of work completion by steady attention and persevering diligence.

His danger, at this stage, lies in a sense of inadequacy and inferiority. If he despairs of his tools and skills or of his status among his tool partners, his ego boundaries suffer, and he abandons hope for the ability to identify early with others who apply themselves to the same general section of the tool world. To lose the hope of such "industrial" association leads back to the more isolated, less tool-conscious "anatomical" rivalry of the Oedipal time.[2] The child despairs of his equipment in the tool world and in anatomy, and considers himself doomed to mediocrity or mutilation. It is at this point that wider society becomes significant in its ways of admitting the child to an understanding of meaningful roles in its total economy. Many a child's development is disrupted when family life may not have prepared him for school life, or when school life may fail to sustain the promises of earlier stages.

5. Identity vs. Role Diffusion

With the establishment of a good relationship to the world of skills and tools, and with the advent of

---

[1]At the end of the phallic period, around age 7, Freud described children as entering a "latency period" until the beginning of puberty a few years later. During this period issues of sexual development are temporarily set aside while the child learns important skills for later life.

[2]Part of the story of the Oedipal crisis told by Freud consists of the young boy comparing the size of his genitals with that of his father's, and feeling thoroughly inferior as a result.

sexual maturity, childhood proper comes to an end. Youth begins. But in puberty and adolescence all samenesses and continuities relied on earlier are questioned again, because of a rapidity of body growth which equals that of early childhood and because of the entirely new addition of physical genital maturity. The growing and developing youths, faced with this physiological revolution within them, are now primarily concerned with what they appear to be in the eyes of others as compared with what they feel they are, and with the question of how to connect the roles and skills cultivated earlier with the occupational prototypes of the day. In their search for a new sense of continuity and sameness, adolescents have to re-fight many of the battles of earlier years, even though to do so they must artificially appoint perfectly well-meaning people to play the roles of enemies; and they are ever ready to install lasting idols and ideals as guardians of a final identity: here puberty rites "confirm" the inner design for life.

The integration now taking place in the form of ego identity is more than the sum of the childhood identifications. It is the accrued experience of the ego's ability to integrate these identifications with the vicissitudes of the libido, with the aptitudes developed out of endowment, and with the opportunities offered in social roles. The sense of ego identity, then, is the accrued confidence that the inner sameness and continuity are matched by the sameness and continuity of one's meaning for others, as evidenced in the tangible promise of a "career."

The danger of this stage is role diffusion. Where this is based on a strong previous doubt as to one's sexual identity, delinquent and outright psychotic incidents are not uncommon. If diagnosed and treated correctly, these incidents do not have the same fatal significance which they have at other ages. It is primarily the inability to settle on an occupational identity which disturbs young people. To keep themselves together they temporarily overidentify, to the point of apparent complete loss of identity, with the heroes of cliques and crowds. This initiates the stage of "falling in love,"

which is by no means entirely, or even primarily, a sexual matter—except where the mores demand it. To a considerable extent adolescent love is an attempt to arrive at a definition of one's identity by projecting one's diffused ego images on one another and by seeing them thus reflected and gradually clarified. This is why many a youth would rather converse, and settle matters of mutual identification, than embrace.

Puberty rites and confirmations help to integrate and to affirm the new identity. * * *

6. Intimacy vs. Isolation

It is only as young people emerge from their identity struggles that their egos can master the sixth stage, that of intimacy. What we have said about genitality now gradually comes into play. Body and ego must now be masters of the organ modes and of the nuclear conflicts, in order to be able to face the fear of ego loss in situations which call for self-abandon: in orgasms and sexual unions, in close friendships and in physical combat, in experiences of inspiration by teachers and of intuition from the recesses of the self. The avoidance of such experiences because of a fear of ego loss may lead to a deep sense of isolation and consequent self-absorption.

This, then, may be the place to complete our discussion of genitality.

For a basic orientation in the matter I shall quote what has come to me as Freud's shortest saying. It has often been claimed, and bad habits of conversation seem to sustain the claim, that psychoanalysis as a treatment attempts to convince the patient that before God and man he has only one obligation: to have good orgasms, with a fitting "object," and that regularly. This, of course, is not true. Freud was once asked what he thought a normal person should be able to do well. The questioner probably expected a complicated answer. But Freud, in the curt way of his old days, is reported to have said: "Lieben und arbeiten" (to love and to work). It pays to ponder on this simple formula; it gets deeper as you think about it. For when Freud said "love" he meant *genital* love, and genital *love*; when he said love *and* work, he meant a general work-productiveness which would not preoccupy the individual to the extent that he loses his right or capacity to be a genital and a loving being. Thus we may ponder, but we cannot improve on the formula which includes the doctor's prescription for human dignity—and for democratic living.

Genitality, then, consists in the unobstructed capacity to develop an orgastic potency so free of pregenital interferences that genital libido (not just the sex products discharged in Kinsey's "outlets"[3]) is expressed in heterosexual mutuality, with full sensitivity of both penis and vagina, and with a convulsion-like discharge of tension from the whole body. This is a rather concrete way of saying something about a process which we really do not understand. To put it more situationally: the total fact of finding, via the climactic turmoil of the orgasm, a supreme experience of the mutual regulation of two beings in some way breaks the point off the hostilities and potential rages caused by the oppositeness of male and female, of fact and fancy, of love and hate. Satisfactory sex relations thus make sex less obsessive, overcompensation less necessary, sadistic controls superfluous.

* * * The kind of mutuality in orgasm which psychoanalysis has in mind[4] is apparently easily obtained in classes and cultures which happen to make a leisurely institution of it. In more complex societies this mutuality is interfered with by so many factors of health, of tradition, of opportunity, and of temperament, that the proper formulation of sexual health would be rather this: A human being should be potentially able to accomplish mutuality of genital orgasm, but he should also be so constituted as to bear frustration in the matter without undue regression wherever considerations of reality and loyalty call for it.

* * * In order to be of lasting social significance, the utopia of genitality should include:

1. mutuality of orgasm
2. with a loved partner
3. of the other sex[5]
4. with whom one is able and willing to share a mutual trust
5. and with whom one is able and willing to regulate the cycles of
   a. work
   b. procreation
   c. recreation
6. so as to secure to the offspring, too, a satisfactory development.

It is apparent that such utopian accomplishment on a large scale cannot be an individual or, indeed, a therapeutic task. Nor is it a purely sexual matter by any means.

7. Generativity vs. Stagnation

The discussion of intimacy versus isolation has already included a further nuclear conflict which, therefore, requires only a short explicit formulation: I mean generativity versus stagnation. I apologize for creating a new and not even pleasant term. Yet neither creativity nor productivity nor any other fashionable term seems to me to convey what must be conveyed—namely, that the ability to lose oneself in the meeting of bodies and minds leads to a gradual expansion of ego interests and of libidinal cathexis over that which has been thus generated and accepted as a responsibility. Generativity is primarily the interest in establishing and guiding the next generation or whatever in a given case may become the absorbing object of a parental kind of responsibility. Where this enrichment fails, a regression from generativity to an obsessive need for pseudo intimacy, punctuated by moments of mutual repulsion, takes place, often with a pervading sense (and objective evidence) of individual stagnation and interpersonal impoverishment.

---

[3]The reference here is to Alfred Kinsey, one of the first modern sex researchers. Kinsey focused closely on the nature and meaning of literal sex acts and "outlets," a term and approach Erikson obviously found limited and even distasteful.

[4]As the ideal outcome of a sexual relationship.

[5]Although Erikson obviously here expresses a different view, current psychology generally does not regard homosexuality as a neurosis or psychological failure.

8. Ego Integrity vs. Despair

Only he who in some way has taken care of things and people and has adapted himself to the triumphs and disappointments adherent to being, by necessity, the originator of others and the generator of things and ideas—only he may gradually grow the fruit of these seven stages. I know no better word for it than ego integrity. Lacking a clear definition, I shall point to a few constituents of this state of mind. It is the ego's accrued assurance of its proclivity for order and meaning. It is a postnarcissistic love of the human ego—not of the self—as an experience which conveys some world order and spiritual sense, no matter how dearly paid for. It is the acceptance of one's one and only life cycle as something that had to be and that, by necessity, permitted of no substitutions; it thus means a new, a different love of one's parents. It is a comradeship with the ordering ways of distant times and different pursuits, as expressed in the simple products and sayings of such times and pursuits. Although aware of the relativity of all the various lifestyles which have given meaning to human striving, the possessor of integrity is ready to defend the dignity of his own life style against all physical and economic threats. For he knows that an individual life is the accidental coincidence of but one life cycle with but one segment of history; and that for him all human integrity stands or falls with the one style of integrity of which he partakes. The style of integrity developed by his culture or civilization thus becomes the "patrimony of his soul," the seal of his moral paternity of himself.[6] * * * Before this final solution, death loses its sting.

The lack or loss of this accrued ego integration is signified by fear of death: the one and only life cycle is not accepted as the ultimate of life. Despair expresses the feeling that the time is short, too short for the attempt to start another life and to try

out alternate roads to integrity. Disgust hides despair.

Each individual, to become a mature adult, must to a sufficient degree develop all the ego qualities mentioned, so that a wise Indian, a true gentleman, and a mature peasant share and recognize in one another the final stage of integrity. But each cultural entity, to develop the particular style of integrity suggested by its historical place, utilizes a particular combination of these conflicts, along with specific provocations and prohibitions of infantile sexuality. Infantile conflicts become creative only if sustained by the firm support of cultural institutions and of the special leader classes representing them. In order to approach or experience integrity, the individual must know how to be a follower of image bearers in religion and in politics, in the economic order and in technology, in aristocratic living and in the arts and sciences. Ego integrity, therefore, implies an emotional integration which permits participation by followership as well as acceptance of the responsibility of leadership.

Webster's dictionary is kind enough to help us complete this outline in a circular fashion. Trust (the first of our ego values) is here defined as "the assured reliance on another's integrity," the last of our values. I suspect that Webster had business in mind rather than babies, credit rather than faith. But the formulation stands. And it seems possible to further paraphrase the relation of adult integrity and infantile trust by saying that healthy children will not fear life if their parents have integrity enough not to fear death.

* * * In order to indicate the whole conceptual area which is awaiting systematic treatment, I shall conclude this chapter with a diagram.[7] In this, as in the diagram of pregenital zones and modes, the diagonal represents the sequence of enduring

---

[6]Erikson seemed to take this advice to heart. He never knew his father and in midlife abandoned his stepfather's name and took instead the name Erikson, as a way of claiming his own moral paternity of himself.

[7]The meaning of this diagram, reproduced in many textbooks, is not made entirely clear by Erikson. But Franz and White (1985) "fill in" the rows and columns associated with identity and intimacy, showing the heuristic power of Erikson's theory even as they seek to offer their own revision of it.

	1	2	3	4	5	6	7	8
Oral Sensory	Trust vs. Mistrust							
Muscular-Anal		Autonomy vs. Shame, Doubt						
Locomotor-Genital			Initiative vs. Guilt					
Latency				Industry vs. Inferiority				
Puberty and Adolescence					Identity vs. Role Diffusion			
Young Adulthood						Intimacy vs. Isolation		
Adulthood							Generativity vs. Stagnation	
Maturity								Integrity vs. Disgust, Despair

Figure 1

solutions, each of which is based on the integration of the earlier ones. At any given stage of the life cycle the solution of one more nuclear conflict adds a new ego quality, a new criterion of increasing strength. The criteria proposed in this chart are to be treated in analogy to the criteria for health and illness in general—i.e., by ascertaining whether or not there is "a pervading subjective sense of" the criterion in question, and whether or not "objec- tive evidence of the dominance of" the criterion can be established by indirect examination (by means of depth psychology). Above the diagonal there is space for a future elaboration of the precursors of each of these solutions, all of which begin with the beginning; below the diagonal there is space for the designation of the derivatives of these solutions in the maturing and the mature personality.

Freudian Defense Mechanisms and Empirical Findings in Modern Social Psychology: Reaction Formation, Projection, Displacement, Undoing, Isolation, Sublimation, and Denial

Roy F. Baumeister, Karen Dale, and Kristin L. Sommer

In the following selection, Roy Baumeister, Karen Dale, and Kristin Sommer manage to recruit a surprising amount of contemporary research to the task of evaluating Freudian ideas. They do this by making a crucial reinterpretation of the psychoanalytic idea of the defense mechanism. Freud originally said that defense mechanisms existed to protect the ego. Baumeister and colleagues interpret the purpose of these mechanisms as the defense of self-esteem. *This narrows the focus of the defense mechanisms because a psychoanalyst would surely believe that their purpose is to defend against* anxiety, *and a threat to self-esteem is just one among many things that might cause a person anxiety. However, this narrowing of focus makes a huge amount of literature suddenly relevant; nearly everything published on the self—thousands of studies—is pertinent to psychological defense.*

From *Journal of Personality*, 66, 1081–1124, 1998.

Nearly all adults hold preferred views of themselves. In most cases, these are favorable views of self—indeed, somewhat more favorable than the objective facts would entirely warrant, as nearly all writers on the self have observed. A recurrent problem of human functioning, therefore, is how to sustain these favorable views of self. Patterns of self-deception can help create these inflated self-perceptions (for reviews, see Baumeister, 1998; Gilovich, 1991; Taylor, 1989). Yet a particular crisis in self-perception may arise when an internal or external event occurs that clearly violates the preferred view of self. In such cases, it is necessary for the self to have some mechanism or process to defend itself against the threatening implications of this event. Such processes are commonly called *defense mechanisms* (e.g., Cramer, 1991; A. Freud, 1936).

Sigmund Freud proposed a set of defense mechanisms, in a body of work that has long been influential (e.g., S. Freud, 1915/1961a, 1923/1961c, 1926/1961d). His work focused on how the ego defended itself against internal events, specifically, impulses that were regarded by the ego as unacceptable. He emphasized sexual or aggressive desires that would violate the ego's internalized standards, such as if those desires were directed toward one's parents. In his view, the efforts by the self to avoid recognizing its own sexual and aggressive desires were systematically important in shaping the personality.

Modern personality and social psychology has not generally accepted the view that personality is heavily based on efforts to disguise one's sexual and aggressive impulses. Nonetheless, the need for defense mechanisms remains quite strong. A revisionist idea, proposed by Fenichel (1945), is that defense mechanisms are actually designed to protect self-esteem. This reformulation is far more in keeping with current work in social and personality psychology than Freud's original view was. One can search long and hard through today's research journals without finding much evidence about how human behavior reflects attempts to ward off sexual and violent feelings, but evidence about efforts to protect self-esteem is abundant.

Ultimately, the view that defense mechanisms are oriented toward protecting self-esteem may not contradict Freud's views so much as it merely changes his emphasis. Acknowledging that one possessed socially unacceptable impulses of sex or violence may have constituted a self-esteem threat for the Victorian middle-class adults he studied. Today's adults are presumably less afraid of having sexual or violent feelings, and indeed the absence of sexual interest may constitute an esteem threat to some modern citizens—in which case their defense mechanisms would ironically try to increase the self-perceived frequency or power of sexual impulses, contrary to the Freudian pattern.

Most researchers in personality and social psychology today would readily acknowledge that people defend their self-concepts against esteem threats. Yet relatively few researchers have made explicit efforts to relate their findings about defensive processes to the general theory of defense mechanisms. The purpose of the present article is to review research findings from personality and social

psychology that can be interpreted as reflecting the major defense mechanisms that Freud proposed. In a sense, then, this review will ask how Freud's list of insights stacks up against today's experimental work.

How much should one expect? Obviously, any accuracy at all would be impressive. Few researchers today would feel confident about having dozens of their theoretical hypotheses tested many decades into the future by empirical techniques that they today could not even imagine.

To anticipate the conclusion, we found substantial support for many (but not all) of the processes of defense Freud outlined. There are also some aspects to the causal process that Freud does not appear to have anticipated, as one would naturally expect. We shall describe a series of the major defense mechanisms and conclude that some of his ideas were correct, some require minor or major revision, and others have found little support. All in all, this amounts to a rather impressive positive testimony to Freud's seminal theorizing.

Plan and Task

* * *

We have chosen to emphasize defenses that are arguably most relevant to normal (as opposed to clinical) human functioning. The list is as follows: reaction formation, projection, displacement, * * * and denial.[1]

With each defense mechanism, we shall first ask whether research evidence shows that it actually occurs. The strength and generality of this evidence must also be considered. If the defense mechanism is supported in some sense, then we must ask what the cognitive, affective, and behavioral processes are. A related question is whether there is evidence of defensive motivation, as opposed to evidence of some merely cognitive error or bias. To qualify as a full-fledged defense, it must do more than merely make people feel better: It must actually ward off some threat to the self.

---

[1]The original article also addressed three other defense mechanisms: undoing, isolation, and sublimation.

Purely conscious maneuvers are not generally considered full-fledged defense mechanisms. Like self-deception generally, defense mechanisms must involve some motivated strategy that is not consciously recognized, resulting in a desirable conclusion or favorable view of self that is conscious.

Review of Findings

In this section, we shall examine * * * major defense mechanisms in turn. The review will try to ascertain how well each defense mechanism is supported in modern research in personality and social psychology and what theoretical adjustments may be required to make the theory fit modern findings.

* * *

REACTION FORMATION

Concept. The concept of reaction formation involves converting a socially unacceptable impulse into its opposite. To apply this notion to esteem protection, one may propose the following: People respond to the implication that they have some unacceptable trait by behaving in a way that would show them to have the opposite trait. Insinuations of hostility or intolerance might, for example, be countered with exaggerated efforts to prove oneself a peace-loving or tolerant person.

Evidence. The original ideas about reaction formation pertained to aggressive and sexual impulses, and these are still plausible places for finding defenses, provided that acknowledging those impulses or feelings would damage self-esteem. With sex, there are undoubtedly still cases in which people regard their own potential sexual responses as unacceptable.

One such finding was provided by Morokoff (1985), who exposed female subjects to erotic stimuli after assessing sex guilt. Women high in sex guilt would presumably regard erotica as unacceptable, and consistent with this attitude they reported lower levels of arousal in response to those stimuli. Physiological measures suggested, how-

ever, that these women actually had higher sexual arousal than other participants. The contradiction between the genital response and the self-report findings suggests that these women subjectively repudiated their physical sexual arousal and insisted that they were not aroused.

A comparable finding with male subjects was recently reported by Adams, Wright, and Lohr (1996). They assessed homophobia and then exposed participants to videotapes depicting homosexual intercourse. Homophobic men reported low levels of sexual arousal, but physiological measures indicated higher levels of sexual response than were found among other participants. Thus, again, the subjective response reported by these participants was the opposite of what their bodies actually indicated. This finding also fits the view that homophobia may itself be a reaction formation against homosexual tendencies, insofar as the men who were most aroused by homosexuality were the ones who expressed the most negative attitudes toward it.

Prejudice would provide the most relevant form of unacceptable aggressive impulse, because American society has widely endorsed strong norms condemning prejudice. If people are led to believe that they may hold unacceptably prejudiced beliefs (or even that others perceive them as being prejudiced), they may respond with exaggerated displays of not being prejudiced.

An early and convincing demonstration of reaction formation (although it was not called that) against prejudice was provided by Dutton and Lake (1973; see also Dutton, 1976). Nonprejudiced, egalitarian, White individuals were provided with false physiological feedback allegedly indicating that they held racist prejudices against Blacks. In one study, for example, they were shown slides of interracial couples, and the experimenter commented that the subject's skin response indicated severe intolerance of interracial romance, which was tantamount to racism. After the procedure was ostensibly completed, the participant left the building and was accosted by either a Black or a White panhandler. People who had been implicitly accused of racism gave significantly more money to the Black panhandler than people who had not been threatened in that way. Donations to the White panhandler were unaffected by the racism feedback. The implication was that people became generous toward the Black individual as a way of counteracting the insinuation that they were prejudiced against Blacks.

*   *   *

There is a related set of findings in which White subjects show preferential favorability toward Black stimulus persons without any threat. One might argue that White people often feel threatened by the possibility of seeming racist when interacting with Black people. Rogers and Prentice-Dunn (1981) found that White subjects playing the role of teacher administered fewer shocks to a Black than to a White confederate in the role of learner, although the effect was reversed if the learner had previously insulted them. Johnson, Whitestone, Jackson, and Gatto (1995) showed that White subjects as simulated jurors gave lighter sentences to Black than to White defendants, although this effect was reversed when a more severe sentence to the Black man could be defended on nonracial grounds. Shaffer and Case (1982) found that heterosexual simulated jurors gave lighter sentences to a homosexual defendant than to a heterosexual one, although this effect was found only among people who scored low in dogmatism.

Whether these effects constitute reaction formation is not entirely clear. Biernat, Manis, and Nelson (1991) provided evidence that people may use different standards when judging minority targets as opposed to judging members of the majority category. For example, a Black candidate for law school might be judged more favorably than a White candidate with identical credentials if the judges use more lenient criteria for Blacks. (Then again, the use of more lenient criteria might itself qualify as a reaction formation, insofar as it is a strategy to defend against one's own prejudice.)

*   *   *

Reaction formation may also be involved when self-appraisals paradoxically rise in response to negative feedback. McFarlin and Blascovich

(1981) showed that people with high self-esteem made more optimistic predictions for future performance following initial failure than following initial success. Baumeister, Heatherton, and Tice (1993) showed this confidence to be irrational and unwarranted, and also showed it to be sufficiently powerful to motivate costly monetary bets. These responses do appear defensive and irrational, for there is no obvious reason that confidence should be increased by an initial failure experience.

Last, some evidence suggests a loose pattern of increasing favorable self-ratings in response to receiving bad (instead of good) personality feedback. Baumeister and Jones (1978) found enhanced self-ratings in response to bad feedback that was seen by other people, although the increased favorability was found only on items unrelated to the content of the feedback, indicating a compensatory mechanism rather than a pure reaction formation. Baumeister (1982b) provided evidence that people with high self-esteem were mainly responsible for the effect. Greenberg and Pyszczynski (1985) showed that this inflation of self-ratings occurred even on private ratings, although again mainly in response to public feedback. They pointed out that public bad feedback constitutes a stronger threat than private feedback. *   *   *

Conclusion. Plenty of research findings conform to the broad pattern of reaction formation, defined loosely as a means of defending against esteem threat by exhibiting an exaggerated or extreme reaction in the opposite direction. Although the mechanism underlying reaction formation may not conform precisely to Freud's model, the human phenomena he characterized with that term do appear to be real. In particular, when people are publicly or implicitly accused of having socially undesirable sexual feelings, prejudiced attitudes, or failures of competence, some respond by asserting the opposite (and attempting to prove it) to an exceptionally high degree.

The consistency of these results across seemingly quite different spheres of esteem threat suggests that reaction formation deserves acceptance in social and personality psychology. Apparently it is one of the more prominent and common responses to esteem threat.

Still, the causal process underlying reaction formation remains to be elaborated. Many of the findings may be merely self-presentational strategies designed to correct another person's misperception rather than a genuinely intrapsychic defense mechanism. Moreover, if reaction formation can be firmly established as an intrapsychic response, it would be desirable to know how it operates. How, for example, does someone manage to feel sexually turned off when his or her body is exhibiting a strong positive arousal? How do people come to convince themselves that the money they give to a Black panhandler reflects a genuine attitude of racial tolerance rather than a response to the specific accusation of racism they recently received—especially when, as the researchers can show, those people would not have given nearly as much money to the same panhandler if they had not been accused of racism?

PROJECTION

Concept. Projection is a popular concept in everyday discourse as well as in psychological thought. In its simplest form, it refers to seeing one's own traits in other people. A more rigorous understanding involves perceiving others as having traits that one inaccurately believes oneself not to have. As a broad form of influence of self-concept on person perception, projection may be regarded as more a cognitive bias than a defense mechanism. Nonetheless, projection *can* be seen as defensive if perceiving the threatening trait in others helps the individual in some way to avoid recognizing it in himself or herself, and indeed this is how Freud (e.g., 1915/1961a) conceptualized projection. Thus, there are multiple ways of understanding projection, and they vary mainly along the dimension of how effectively the undesirable trait or motive is repudiated as part of the self.

Evidence. The simpler, more loosely defined version of projection is fairly well documented. The *false consensus effect*, first described by Ross, Greene, and House (1977), is probably the best-known form of this, insofar as it is a broad tendency to assume that others are similar to oneself. The false consensus effect is defined as overestimating the percentage of other people who share one's traits, opinions, preferences, or motivations. This effect has both cognitive and motivational influences (Krueger & Clement, 1994; Marks, Graham, & Hansen, 1992; Sherman, Presson, & Chassin, 1984); is found if anything more with positive, desirable traits than with bad traits (Davis, Conklin, Smith, & Luce 1996; Halpern & Goldschmitt, 1976; Lambert & Wedell, 1991; Paulhus & Reynolds, 1995); has been especially shown with competitiveness (Kelley & Stahelski, 1970a, 1970b) and jealousy (Pines & Aronson, 1983); and is linked to higher self-esteem and lower depression (Campbell, 1986; Crocker, Alloy, & Kayne, 1988). Some contrary patterns have been found, especially insofar as people wish to regard their good traits and abilities as unusual (Dunning & Cohen, 1992; Suls & Wan, 1987). In general, these findings show that people like to see themselves as similar to others, but the evidence does not show this to be a defense mechanism that helps people avoid recognizing their own bad traits.

It could be argued that the false consensus effect achieves a kind of defensive success insofar as it reduces the distinctiveness of one's bad traits. To be the only person who cheats on taxes or breaks the speed limit would imply that one is uniquely immoral, even evil—but if everyone else is likewise breaking those laws, one's own actions can hardly be condemned with great force. Consistent with this, Sherwood (1981) concluded that attributing one's undesirable traits to targets who are perceived favorably can reduce stress. This explanation could also fit Bramel's (1962, 1963) demonstration that males who were told they had homosexual tendencies were later more likely to interpret other males' behavior as having similar tendencies. Likewise, it may explain the findings of Agostinelli, Sherman, Presson, and Chassin (1992): Receiving bogus failure feedback on a problem-solving task made people (except depressed people) more likely to predict that others would fail too.

None of these findings links seeing the trait in others to denying it in oneself, and so they fall short of the more rigorous definition of projection. Given the failure to show that projective responses can function to conceal one's own bad traits, Holmes (1968, 1978, 1981) concluded that defensive projection should be regarded as a myth. In retrospect, it was never clear how seeing another person as dishonest (for example) would enable the individual to avoid recognizing his or her own dishonesty. The notion that projection would effectively mask one's own bad traits was perhaps incoherent.

Recognizing the implausibility in the classical concept of projection, Newman, Duff, and Baumeister (1997) proposed a new model of defensive projection. In this view, people try to suppress thoughts of their undesirable traits, and these efforts make those trait categories highly accessible—so that they are then used all the more often when forming impressions of others (see Wegner, 1994; Wegner & Erber, 1992). In a series of studies, Newman et al. showed that repressors (as defined by Weinberger, Schwartz, & Davidson, 1979) were more likely than others to deny having certain bad traits, even though their acquaintances said they did have those bad traits. Repressors were then also more likely to interpret the ambiguous behaviors of others as reflecting those bad traits. Thus, they both denied their own faults and overinterpreted other people as having those faults.

The view that suppressing thoughts about one's undesirable traits leads to projection was then tested experimentally by Newman et al. (1997). Participants were given bogus feedback based on a personality test, to the effect that they had both good and bad traits. They were then instructed to avoid thinking about one dimension on which they had received (bad) feedback. Next, they observed a videotape of a stimulus person and rated that person on all the dimensions on which they had received feedback. Participants rated the stimulus person about the same on all dimensions, except that they rated her higher on the trait for which they had received bad feedback and been instructed to suppress. They did not rate the stimulus

person higher on traits for which they had received bad feedback without trying to suppress it. Thus, projection results from trying to suppress thoughts about some bad trait in oneself.

Conclusion. Considerable evidence indicates that people's conceptions of themselves shape their perceptions of other people. The tendency to see others as having one's own traits has limitations and is found with good traits along with bad ones. The view that people defensively project specific bad traits of their own onto others as a means of denying that they have them is not well supported. The concept of projection thus needs to be revised in order to fit modern research findings.

The view of projection as a defense mechanism is best supported by the findings of Newman et al. (1997), but even these deviate from the classic psychodynamic theory of projection. Newman et al. found that efforts to suppress thoughts about a particular bad trait made this trait into a highly accessible category that thereafter shaped the perception of others. In this view, the projecting of the trait onto other people is a by-product of the defense, rather than being central to the defensive strategy. To put this another way: In the original Freudian view, seeing the bad trait in another person is the essential means of avoiding seeing it in oneself. In Newman et al.'s view, however, the defense is simply a matter of trying not to recognize one's bad trait, and the success of that effort is not related to whether a suitable target for projection presents himself or herself.

This mechanism could well account for the observations that might have led Freud to postulate the defense mechanism of projection in the first place. After all, the person does refuse at some level to accept some fault in himself or herself and does, as a result, end up seeing other people as having that same fault. The Freudian view implied the transfer of the schema from one's self-concept directly into the impression of the other person. It may, however, be more accurate to see the effect on impression formation as simply a consequence of heightened accessibility resulting from efforts at suppression.

DISPLACEMENT

Concept. Displacement refers to altering the target of an impulse. For example, an unacceptable violent impulse toward one's father might be transformed into a hostile attitude toward policemen or other authority figures. The targets of the actual aggression would be related by meaningful associations to the target of the original, inhibited impulse.

Evidence. Several studies have directly examined displacement of aggression. In a study by Hokanson, Burgess, and Cohen (1963), subjects were frustrated (or not) by the experimenter and then given an opportunity to aggress against the experimenter, the experimenter's assistant, a psychology student, or no one. The experiment yielded a marginal main effect for frustration, insofar as frustrated subjects were more aggressive than others, but the target made no difference. Measurements of systolic blood pressure did, however, suggest that tension levels among frustrated subjects dropped most when they aggressed against the experimenter, followed by the assistant, followed by the psychology major. Thus, the level of aggression remained the same whether it was aimed at the original target, at a relevant displaced target, or at an irrelevant target, but there was some physiological evidence suggesting that aggressing against the original target (or a closely linked one) was most satisfying.

The possibility of displaced aggression was also investigated by Fenigstein and Buss (1974). In this study, the instigator was not the experimenter, thereby removing alternative explanations based on the experimenter–subject relationship. Angered and nonangered subjects were given an opportunity to aggress either toward the instigator directly or toward a friend of his. As in the Hokanson et al. (1963) study, anger produced a main effect on aggression, but there were no differences in aggressive behavior as a function of target.

These findings can be interpreted in various ways. One might point to them as evidence for the high efficacy of displacement, given that people are equally aggressive toward other people as toward the person who has provoked them—suggesting, in other words, that the full amount of aggression can be displaced readily.

On the other hand, they could be interpreted as mere mood or arousal effects: People who are angry are more aggressive in general. Indeed, Miller (1948) showed similar effects with rats (e.g., attacking a dummy doll when the original enemy, another rat, is absent), and it is difficult to assert that rats have defense mechanisms. Meanwhile, there is ample evidence that arousal can carry over from one situation to another. Research by Zillman and his colleagues has shown *excitation transfer* effects, in which arousal from one situation can carry over into another and influence aggressive behavior. Riding a stationary bicycle boosts arousal while not being either especially pleasant or unpleasant, but people who ride a bicycle are then subsequently more aggressive in response to a provocation than people who have not just exercised (Zillman, Katcher, & Milavsky, 1972), and indeed highly aroused subjects will ignore mitigating circumstances when someone provokes them, unlike moderately aroused people who will tone down their aggressive responses when they learn of the same mitigating facts (Zillman, Bryant, Cantor, & Day, 1975). Arousal that is caused by watching exciting films can likewise increase aggressive responses to provocation, even though the arousal itself has no relation to the provocation (Cantor, Zillmann, & Einsiedel, 1978; Ramirez, Bryant, & Zillman, 1982; Zillman, 1971).

To complicate matters further, recent work has not confirmed displacement. Bushman and Baumeister (1998) studied aggressive responses to an ego threat as a function of narcissism. Narcissists became more aggressive toward someone who had insulted them, but neither narcissists nor nonnarcissists showed any increased aggression toward a third person. This study was specifically designed to examine displaced aggression and failed to find any sign of it.

Scapegoating has been regarded as one instance of displaced aggression. In this view, people may become angry or hostile toward one target but are required for whatever reasons to avoid aggressing, and so they redirect their aggression toward a safer target. A classic paper by Hovland and Sears (1940) showed that the frequency of lynchings in the American South was negatively correlated with cotton prices. When prices dropped, according to the scapegoat interpretation, farmers suffered material deprivation, frustration, and hostility, and they redirected their hostility toward relatively safe targets in the form of Black men accused of crimes. Hepworth and West (1988) reexamined those data with more modern statistical techniques and confirmed the relationship.

Such evidence of scapegoating does not, however, embody a pure instance of displacement. The original hostility may not have had a specific target; rather, the cotton farmers may have been generally distraught. Recent work by Esses and Zanna (1995) offered an alternative explanation in terms of mood-congruent stereotypes. They showed that bad moods induced by musical stimuli (hence having no esteem threat) caused negative stereotypes to become more accessible. This accessibility might explain the southern farmers' willingness to react violently to alleged misdeeds by Black citizens, without postulating that the violence was borrowed from another source or impulse.

In principle, unacceptable sexual or other impulses should also be amenable to displacement. Mann, Berkowitz, Sidman, Starr, and West (1974) exposed long-married couples to pornographic movies and found that this exposure led to an increased likelihood of marital intercourse on that same evening. This could be interpreted as displacement of sexual desire from the inaccessible movie star onto the socially acceptable target of one's mate. Unfortunately, however, this effect is likewise amenable to alternative explanations based simply on a generalized arousal response.

Conclusion. Despite the intuitive appeal of the concept of displacement, research has not provided much in the way of clear evidence for it. The handful of findings that do suggest displacement are susceptible to alternative explanations such as general tendencies for arousal or bad moods to facilitate aggression.

Some might contend that the arousal or mood effects should not be considered alternative explanations but rather can be subsumed under a looser conception of displacement. If Harry gets angry at his boss for criticizing him, and because of this anger Harry later gets into a fight with a stranger whom he normally might have ignored, should this qualify as displacement? It is, however, in no sense the same impulse that is displaced onto a new target. Whether he had inhibited his anger against his boss or expressed it might make no difference. Given that artificial mood or arousal inductions, even including the arousal from riding a bicycle, can produce the same readiness to respond aggressively to a new provocation, it seems misleading to speak of such an effect as displacement.

More to the point, there is no evidence that such arousal or mood effects serve a defensive function. Displacement would only qualify as a defense mechanism if the original, unacceptable impulse were prevented from causing some damage to self-esteem (or having some similar effect, such as stimulating anxiety). There is no evidence of any such effect.

The concept of displacement seems to be based on the now largely discredited catharsis model, according to which people have a well-defined quantity of aggressive impulses that require expression in one sphere or another. If aggression (or sexual desire, for that matter) cannot be expressed toward its original target, it must be redirected toward another, in this view. Meanwhile, of course, if it could be expressed toward the original target, there would be no displacement. Both effects seem highly implausible in light of what is now known about aggression. More likely, a person who is aggressive in one situation would be more, not less, aggressive in a subsequent one.

* * *

DENIAL

Concept. Freudian conceptions of denial embrace everything from a rare, almost psychotic refusal to perceive the physical facts of the immediate environment, to the common reluctance to accept the implications of some event (e.g., Laplanche & Pontalis, 1973). The distinction between denial and repression is sometimes blurred and difficult to articulate in a meaningful fashion (Cramer, 1991). For the present, it is sufficient to consider denial as the simple refusal to face certain facts. Insofar as these facts are highly upsetting or represent potential damage to self-esteem, denial can in principle be a very useful defense mechanism.

Denial can be understood very narrowly or quite broadly. Broad definitions encompass an assortment of other defenses. Cramer (1991) subsumes perceptual defenses, constructing personal fantasies, negation, minimizing, maximizing, ridicule, and reversal as forms of denial. Paulhus, Fridhandler, and Hayes (1997) suggested that previous theoretical works were sufficient to distinguish at least seven different kinds of denial. If such a broad view proves correct, it may be more appropriate to regard denial as a category of defense mechanisms than as a single defense.

Evidence. Personality and social psychologists have not provided much evidence that people systematically refuse to accept the physical reality of actual events, especially when confronted with palpable proof. (They are of course willing to be skeptical of rumors or other reports that lack credibility and that attest to disagreeable events.) On the other hand, there is abundant evidence that people will reject implications and interpretations that they find threatening.

Probably the most common form of denial involves dismissive responses to failure or other bad feedback. When people receive negative evaluations, they often reject the implications rather than incorporating them into their self-concepts. Making external attributions for failure, such as by pointing to bad luck or task difficulty, is one common and well-documented pattern of denying the implications of failure, because it insists that the failure does not reflect any lack of ability or of other good traits on the part of the self. Zuckerman (1979) reviewed 38 studies to confirm a general pattern that people make more external attributions for failure than for success.

A variation on the response of external attribution is to find faults or flaws in whatever method of evaluation led to one's bad feedback. Several studies have shown that students believe a test to be invalid or unfair when they perform poorly on it, whereas the same test will be regarded more favorably if their feedback is positive (Pyszczynski, Greenberg, & Holt, 1985; Schlenker, Weigold, & Hallam, 1990; Wyer & Frey, 1983; see also Kunda, 1990). Kernis, Cornell, Sun, Berry, and Harlow (1993) found this to be especially common among people with unstable high self-esteem, suggesting that it is an appealing mode of defense to people who especially need to shore up a fragile sense of personal superiority.

Another variation is to dismiss bad feedback as motivated by prejudice. Crocker, Voelkl, Testa, and Major (1991) measured self-esteem among African American subjects who had received negative feedback from a White evaluator. Self-esteem decreased in response to the criticism if the subject believed the evaluator to be unaware of his race. But if the subject thought the evaluator did know his race, then the evaluation had no effect on self-esteem. In the latter case, subjects attributed the bad evaluation to racist prejudice and therefore denied its validity, so it did not affect their self-esteem.

Researchers in health psychology have provided some findings that parallel the ones about threats to self-esteem. The notion that people use denial in response to health-related threats can be traced back at least to Kübler-Ross's (1969) listing of denial as one "stage" or type of response to learning that one's illness will be fatal. Recent work has demonstrated some mechanisms of denial with less extreme threats. Croyle and Hunt (1991) showed that people minimize risks, specifically reducing their level of personal concern over a threatening test result if a confederate made a minimizing comment ("It doesn't seem like a big deal to me"; p. 384). Ditto and Lopez (1992) showed that people selectively questioned the validity of a test when it produced an unfavorable result. Liberman and Chaiken (1992) showed that caffeine users tended to criticize (selectively) and dismiss evidence of a link between caffeine consumption and fibrocystic disease, whereas nonusers showed no such bias.

A quite different sphere in which to find evidence of denial is people's projections about their personal futures. Weinstein (1980) demonstrated that people tend to be unrealistically optimistic, and subsequent work has confirmed that pattern repeatedly (see Taylor & Brown, 1988, for a review). That is, on average people think they are less likely than the average person to suffer various misfortunes, such as career failure, debilitating illness, or accidental crippling. Perloff and Fetzer (1986) coined the term "the illusion of unique invulnerability" to refer to the average person's sense that bad things will not happen to him or her. By definition, the average person cannot be below average in the likelihood of experiencing such misfortunes, so the subjective perceptions must be based in some sense on a denial of the actual likelihood of such events.

The illusion of unique invulnerability does not remain an abstract or vague surmise. Burger and Burns (1988) linked it to sexual risk-taking, as in unprotected promiscuous sexual intercourse. It is well established that sexually transmitted diseases can be serious and even fatal and that they can be prevented by condom use, but people's sense of personal invulnerability leads them to neglect such precautions. In such cases, denying risks makes people take more extreme ones.

Potentially maladaptive consequences of denial were also shown by Carver and Scheier (1994). In a longitudinal study, they measured stress and coping responses before an exam, right after the exam, and later when grades were posted. Various forms of denial were evident at all times, but none was effective overall at reducing negative emotions. Dispositional denial, evident particularly among people who used denial prior to the exam, led to greater feelings of threat and harm. Carver et al. (1993) found that denial predicted greater distress among breast cancer patients. A review by Suls and Fletcher (1985) concluded that avoidance responses such as denial promote positive outcomes in the short run but are inferior to other coping strategies in the long run.

Although denial may undermine some potentially adaptive responses, it may be quite adaptive in other circumstances. We have already noted that denial of personal responsibility for failure tends to be associated with high self-esteem. Indeed, much of the impact of works by Alloy and Abramson (1979) and Taylor and Brown (1988) came from their conclusion that mental health and high self-esteem were associated with biased processing patterns that denied personal responsibility for bad outcomes while taking credit for good outcomes. Low self-esteem and depression were associated with the more even-handed approach of accepting responsibility equally for both positive and negative outcomes.

Such links are essentially correlational, but they could possibly mean that denial contributes (presumably as a successful defense mechanism) to mental health and high self-esteem. Recent work by Forgas (1994) suggests the opposite causal direction, however. Forgas induced sad and happy moods experimentally, by having people read passages with a strong affective tone, and then he investigated their attributions for relationship conflicts. Sad people blamed themselves more than happy people, who attributed conflict to the situation or to the partner. Apparently happy moods foster denial while sad moods undermine it. An optimal defense mechanism would presumably show the opposite pattern.

Janoff-Bulman (1992) suggested that denial may be especially adaptive following trauma, because it allows the reinterpretation process to proceed piecemeal. After suffering a serious personal trauma such as an accident or victimization, there is often little that the person can do, and so denial does not prevent adaptive responses. Meanwhile, the task of coping with the trauma involves restoring one's positive conceptions of self and world. In Janoff-Bulman's view, one starts by denying the trauma in general, and then the denial drops away piece by piece, allowing the person to begin the task of rebuilding those positive conceptions, as opposed to having to find some new interpretations all at once.

Although we have emphasized the more elaborate forms of denial, such as discrediting sources of criticism, there is some evidence for the more elementary forms as well. Lipp, Kolstoe, James, and Randall (1968) defined perceptual defense operationally in terms of the difference in minimal recognition time for nonthreatening pictures as opposed to threatening ones. The threatening ones in their study were pictures of people who were disabled. Subjects in the study included disabled and nondisabled people. The researchers found that disabled people showed greater perceptual defense: that is, they took relatively longer to recognize tachistoscopically presented slides of disabled people. The authors interpreted this as evidence of denial. To be sure, it was hardly a successful defense mechanism in this case, because all it accomplished was delaying the recognition by a fraction of a second. Still, it suggests that some people do have defenses that work to minimize the recognition of threatening stimuli.

Perceptual denial may be difficult, but memory may be far more amenable to denial. Crary (1966) showed that people protected their self-esteem by not remembering failures. Kulper and Derry (1982) showed that nondepressed people recalled favorable adjectives pertaining to self better than unfavorable ones. Mischel, Ebbesen, and Zeiss (1976) found that people recalled feedback about their good traits better than feedback about their faults and shortcomings. Whether these effects reflect biased encoding, biased recall, or both is unclear. Baumeister and Cairns (1992) showed that repressors tend to minimize the encoding of bad feedback, but it is plausible that additional biases operate on recall processes. In any case, the memory processes seem quite up to the task of selectively denying disagreeable information.

The heterogeneity of findings on denial suggests that a more differentiated conceptual framework may be useful. Baumeister and Newman (1994) reviewed the ways in which people try to alter and direct their cognitive processes, and in particular they distinguished between regulating the collection of evidence versus regulating the interpretive meaning assigned to the evidence. Most of what we have reviewed here pertains to the latter (interpretation) stage, such as denying the possible implications. More evidence is needed about whether (and how) people prevent disagreeable evidence from entering into the conscious decision process.

Conclusion. The concept of denial encompasses a variety of possible defenses, and it may eventually become desirable on theoretical grounds for the concept to be replaced by several more specific and particular mechanisms. This may be particularly desirable insofar as the various mechanisms are not all equally well documented. Still, for the present, it is fair to say that denial is a genuine and efficacious defense mechanism.

The most stringent definition of denial involves the failure of sensory perception to recognize physical stimuli associated with threat. Restricted to this definition, denial is not a common or successful defense mechanism. There is some evidence of perceptual defense, but it seems to involve slight delays rather than an effective misperception of threat. It is possible that such processes occur among the mentally ill, but researchers in personality and social psychology have found little evidence of perceptual denial in the normal population.

There is, however, ample evidence of other forms of denial. People dispute or minimize information that threatens their self-esteem, and they reject its implications. They discount bad feedback about their health. They dismiss various risks and dangers and sometimes act as if they were personally invulnerable. They selectively forget material that is disagreeable or esteem-threatening. Some patterns have been linked to high self-esteem, adjustment, and happiness, which is consistent with the view that denial can be an effective defense, although some questions remain about how denial actually operates and whether it actually functions to defend self-esteem.

General Discussion

* * *

REVISING DEFENSE MECHANISM THEORY The present review has identified several key challenges for the theory of the defense mechanisms. One concerns the extremity of the response. We noted for several defense mechanisms (* * * [e.g.], denial) that pure, severe forms of the defense had not been documented in the normal population whereas weaker versions were well supported. It is plausible that the extreme forms (e.g., being physically unable to see a person who represents a threat) would occur among the mentally ill.

* * *

Another key issue is whether defense mechanisms involve intrapsychic maneuvers or interpersonal, self-presentational strategies. Freud's theories pertained mainly to the former, but many research findings used explicitly interpersonal settings. In our view, it would be justified to speak of defense mechanisms in both cases, because the logic would be similar. For example, donating money to someone of a different race may counter the accusation of racism regardless of whether the origin of that accusation is internal or external. Furthermore, it is well established that there are important links between public self and private self, so that convincing others of one's good traits may be an important step toward convincing oneself (e.g., Baumeister, 1982a, 1986; Haight, 1980; Schlenker, 1980; Tice, 1992; Wicklund & Gollwitzer, 1982). In any case, further work would benefit from attending to evidence of any systematic differences between defense mechanisms that operate at the interpersonal level and those that operate intrapsychically.

Meanwhile, the change from an energy model to a cognitive model as the basic framework for defense mechanism theory appears to be underway. It is probably no accident that the * * * least well supported defense mechanism in our survey (displacement * * *) * * * [was] also the one most tied to a model based on instinctual energy—while the more cognitive defenses, such as denial, * * *

and projection, fared much better. Clearly, shifting the emphasis from unacceptable impulses to self-esteem threats has implications beyond the nature of the threat: Self-esteem threats are more easily rendered in cognitive terms, while the transformation of unacceptable impulses is inherently more closely tied to energy models. Modern theories about the self tend to be heavily cognitive and not at all energy-based, and defense mechanism theory may have to adjust similarly. Thus, the thrust of our review suggests that defense mechanism theory may need to shift its emphasis from impulse transformation to cognitive and behavioral rejection.

The nature of threat is perhaps the undesirable image of self rather than the impulse itself. The nature of defense is therefore to refute or otherwise reject an undesirable view of self. Such a characterization fits the defenses that fared best in this review (reaction formation, * * * denial). It also encompasses other defenses that were not necessarily on Freud's list. It is far beyond the scope of this article to suggest what further defense mechanisms might exist, but while doing this review we did certainly find plenty of evidence of various self-esteem maintenance strategies that did not correspond directly to our list of Freudian defense mechanisms. Future work may make a valuable contribution by listing, taxonomizing, and providing a conceptual framework for all these defenses.

CONCLUDING REMARKS It is impressive to consider how well modern findings in social psychology, mostly obtained in systematic laboratory experiments with well-adjusted American university students, have confirmed the wisdom of Freud's theories, which were mostly based on informal observations of mentally afflicted Europeans nearly a century ago. Not only were several of the defense mechanisms well supported, but in other cases the basic behavioral observations appear to have been sound and only the underlying causal process needs revision.

To be sure, social psychologists have not always given Freud full credit for his insights. Many of the findings covered in this literature review made no reference to defense mechanism theory or to Freud's work. The phenomena Freud described have in some cases been relabeled or rediscovered under the aegis of social cognition or other current theoretical frameworks. Some of these cases may be attributable to career pressures to come up with novel ideas, but others may reflect the fact that researchers working with new ideas and problems are led back to defensive patterns resembling what Freud discussed. The latter cases suggest the pervasive and fundamental importance of defense mechanisms, insofar as Freudian observations and modern socially psychological experimentation converge in producing evidence for the same phenomena.

Our review has suggested that some specific psychoanalytic concepts of defense should be tentatively discarded and some other views need serious revision. More generally, we have suggested that defense mechanism theory may need to downplay its original focus on impulse transformations and instead focus more directly on how possible images of self are protected and rejected. Regardless of these changes, our review provides a solid endorsement of the fundamental insight that human life in civilized society powerfully motivates people to cultivate a set of cognitive and behavioral strategies in order to defend their preferred views of self against threatening events.

References

Adams, H. E., Wright, L. W., & Lohr, B. A. (1996). Is homophobia associated with homosexual arousal? *Journal of Abnormal Psychology, 105,* 440–445.

Agostinelli, G., Sherman, S. J., Presson, C. C., & Chassin, L. (1992). Self-protection and self-enhancement biases in estimates of population prevalence. *Personality and Social Psychology Bulletin, 18,* 631–642.

Alloy, L. B., & Abramson, L. Y. (1979). Judgment of contingency in depressed and nondepressed students: Sadder but wiser? *Journal of Experimental Psychology: General, 108,* 441–485.

Baumeister, R. F. (1982a). A self-presentational view of social phenomena. *Psychological Bulletin, 91,* 3–26.

Baumeister, R. F. (1982b). Self-esteem, self-presentation, and future interaction: A dilemma of reputation. *Journal of Personality, 50,* 29–45.

Baumeister, R. F. (Ed.). (1986). *Public self and private self.* New York: Springer-Verlag.

Baumeister, R. F. (1998). The self. In D. T. Gilbert, S. T. Fiske, & G. Lindzey (Eds.), *Handbook of social psychology* (4th ed., pp. 680–740). New York: McGraw-Hill.

Baumeister, R. F., & Cairns, K. J. (1992). Repression and self-presentation: When audiences interfere with self-deceptive strategies. *Journal of Personality and Social Psychology, 62,* 851–862.

Baumeister, R. F., Heatherton, T. F., & Tice, D. M. (1993). When ego-threats lead to self-regulation failure: The negative consequences of high self-esteem. *Journal of Personality and Social Psychology, 64,* 141–156.

Baumeister, R. F., & Jones, E. E. (1978). When self-presentation is constrained by the target's knowledge: Consistency and compensation. *Journal of Personality and Social Psychology, 36,* 608–618.

Baumeister, R. F., & Newman, L. S. (1994). Self-regulation of cognitive inference and decision processes. *Personality and Social Psychology Bulletin, 20,* 3–19.

Biernat, M., Manis, M., & Nelson, T. E. (1991). Stereotypes and standards of judgment. *Journal of Personality and Social Psychology, 60,* 485–499.

Bramel, D. (1962). A dissonance theory approach to defensive projection. *Journal of Abnormal and Social Psychology, 64,* 121–129.

Bramel, D. (1963). Selection of a target for defensive projection. *Journal of Abnormal and Social Psychology, 66,* 318–324.

Burger, J. M., & Burns, L. (1988). The illusion of unique invulnerability and the use of effective contraception. *Personality and Social Psychology Bulletin, 14,* 264–270.

Bushman, B., & Baumeister, R. F. (1998). Threatened egotism, narcissism, self-esteem, and direct and displaced aggression: Does self-love or self-hate lead to violence? *Journal of Personality and Social Psychology, 75,* 219–229.

Campbell, J. D. (1986). Similarity and uniqueness: The effects of attribute type, relevance, and individual differences in self-esteem and depression. *Journal of Personality and Social Psychology, 50,* 281–294.

Cantor, J. R., Zillman, D., & Einsiedel, E. G. (1978). Female responses to provocation after exposure to aggressive and erotic films. *Communication Research, 5,* 395–411.

Carver, C. S., Pozo, C., Harris, S. D., Noriega, V., Scheier, M. F., Robinson, D. S., Ketcham, A. S., Moffat, F. L., Jr., & Clark, K. C. (1993). How coping mediates the effect of optimism on distress: A study of women with early stage breast cancer. *Journal of Personality and Social Psychology, 65,* 375–390.

Carver, C. S., & Scheier, M. F. (1994). Situational coping and coping dispositions in a stressful transaction. *Journal of Personality and Social Psychology, 66,* 184–195.

Cramer, P. (1991). *The development of defense mechanisms.* New York: Springer-Verlag.

Crary, W. G. (1966). Reactions to incongruent self-experiences. *Journal of Consulting Psychology, 30,* 246–252.

Crocker, J., Alloy, L. B., & Kayne, N. T. (1988). Attributional style, depression, and perceptions of consensus for events. *Journal of Personality and Social Psychology, 54,* 840–846.

Crocker, J., Voelkl, K., Testa, M., & Major, B. (1991). Social stigma: The affective consequences of attributional ambiguity. *Journal of Personality and Social Psychology, 60,* 218–228.

Croyle, R. T., & Hunt, J. R. (1991). Coping with health threat: Social influence processes in reactions to medical test results. *Journal of Personality and Social Psychology, 60,* 382–389.

Davis, M. H., Conklin, L., Smith, A., & Luce, C. (1996). Effects of perspective taking on the cognitive representation of persons: A merging of self and other. *Journal of Personality and Social Psychology, 70,* 713–726.

Ditto, P. H., & Lopez, D. F. (1992). Motivated skepticism: Use of differential decision criteria for preferred and nonpreferred conclusions. *Journal of Personality and Social Psychology, 63*, 568–584.

Dunning, D., & Cohen, G. L. (1992). Egocentric definitions of traits and abilities in social judgment. *Journal of Personality and Social Psychology, 63*, 341–355.

Dutton, D. G. (1976). Tokenism, reverse discrimination, and egalitarianism in interracial behavior. *Journal of Social Issues, 32*, 93–107.

Dutton, D. G., & Lake, R. A. (1973). Threat of own prejudice and reverse discrimination in interracial situations. *Journal of Personality and Social Psychology, 28*, 94–100.

Esses, V. M., & Zanna, M. P. (1995). Mood and the expression of ethnic stereotypes. *Journal of Personality and Social Psychology, 69*, 1052–1068.

Fenichel, O. (1945). *The psychoanalytic theory of neurosis.* New York: Norton.

Fenigstein, A., & Buss, A. H. (1974). Association and affect as determinants of displaced aggression. *Journal of Research in Personality, 7*, 306–313.

Forgas, P. (1994). Sad and guilty? Affective influences on the explanation of conflict in close relationships. *Journal of Personality and Social Psychology, 66*, 56–68.

Freud, A. (1936). *The ego and the mechanisms of defense.* New York: Hogarth Press.

Freud, S. (1961a). Instincts and their vicissitudes. In J. Strachey (Ed. and Trans.), *The standard edition of the complete works of Sigmund Freud* (Vol. 14, pp. 111–142). London: Hogarth Press. (Original work published in 1915.)

Freud, S. (1961c). The ego and the id. In J. Strachey (Ed. and Trans.), *The standard edition of the complete works of Sigmund Freud* (Vol. 19, pp. 12–66). London: Hogarth Press. (Original work published in 1923.)

Freud, S. (1961d). Inhibitions, symptoms, and anxiety. In J. Strachey (Ed. and Trans.), *The standard edition of the complete works of Sigmund Freud* (Vol. 20, pp. 77–178). London: Hogarth Press. (Original work published in 1926.)

Gilovich, T. (1991). *How we know what isn't so: The fallibility of human reason in everyday life.* New York: Free Press.

Greenberg, J., & Pyszczynski, J. (1985). Compensatory self-inflation: A response to the threat to self-regard of public failure. *Journal of Personality and Social Psychology, 49*, 273–280.

Haight, M. R. (1980). *A study of self-deception.* Atlantic Highlands, NJ: Humanities Press.

Halpern, J., & Goldschmitt, M. (1976). Attributive projection: Test of defensive hypotheses. *Perceptual and Motor Skills, 42*, 707–711.

Hepworth, J. T., & West, S. G. (1988). Lynchings and the economy: A time-series reanalysis of Hofland and Sears (1940). *Journal of Personality and Social Psychology, 55*, 239–247.

Hokanson, J. E., Burgess, M., & Cohen, M. F. (1963). Effects of displaced aggression on systolic blood pressure. *Journal of Abnormal and Social Psychology, 67*, 214–218.

Holmes, D. S. (1968). Dimensions of projection. *Psychological Bulletin, 69*, 248–268.

Holmes, D. S. (1978). Projection as a defense mechanism. *Psychological Bulletin, 85*, 677–688.

Holmes, D. S. (1981). Existence of classical projection and the stress-reducing function of attributive projection: A reply to Sherwood. *Psychological Bulletin, 90*, 460–466.

Hovland, C. I., & Sears, R. (1940). Minor studies of aggression: Correlation of lynchings with economic indices. *Journal of Psychology, 9*, 301–310.

Janoff-Bulman, R. (1992). *Shattered assumptions: Towards a new psychology of trauma.* New York: Free Press.

Johnson, J. D., Whitestone, E., Jackson, L. A., & Gatto, L. (1995). Justice is still not colorblind: Differential racial effects of exposure to inadmissible evidence. *Personality and Social Psychology Bulletin, 21*, 893–898.

Kelley, H. H., & Stahelski, A. J. (1970a). Errors in perception of intentions in a mixed motive game. *Journal of Experimental Social Psychology, 6*, 379–400.

Kelley, H. H., & Stahelski, A. J. (1970b). Social interaction basis of cooperators and competitors' beliefs about others. *Journal of Personality and Social Psychology, 16*, 66–91.

Kernis, M. H., Cornell, D. P., Sun, C-R., Berry, A., & Harlow, T. (1993). There's more to self-esteem whether it's high or low: The importance of stability of self-esteem. *Journal of Personality and Social Psychology, 65*, 1190–1204.

Krueger, J., & Clement, R. W. (1994). The truly false consensus effect: An ineradicable and egocentric bias in social perception. *Journal of Personality and Social Psychology, 67*, 596–610.

Kubler-Ross, E. (1969). *On death and dying.* New York: Macmillan.

Kuiper, N. A., & Derry, P. A. (1982). Depressed and nondepressed content self-reference in mild depression. *Journal of Personality, 50*, 67–79.

Kunda, Z. (1990). The case for motivated reasoning. *Psychological Bulletin, 108*, 480–498.

Lambert, A. J., & Weddell, D. H. (1991). The self and social judgment: Effects of affective reaction and "own position" on judgments of unambiguous and ambiguous information about others. *Journal of Personality and Social Psychology, 61*, 884–897.

Laplanche, J., & Pontalis, J.-B. (1973). *The language of psychoanalysis* (D. Nicholson-Smith, Trans.). New York: Norton.

Liberman, A., & Chaiken, S. (1992). Defensive processing of personally relevant health messages. *Personality and Social Psychology Bulletin, 18*, 669–679.

Lipp, L., Kolstoe, R., James, W., & Randall, H. (1968). Denial of disability and internal control of reinforcement: A study using a perceptual defense paradigm. *Journal of Consulting and Clinical Psychology, 32*, 72–75.

Mann, J., Berkowitz, L., Sidman, J., Starr, S., & West, S. (1974). Satiation of the transient stimulating effect of erotic films. *Journal of Personality and Social Psychology, 30*, 729–735.

Marks, G., Graham, J. W., & Hansen, W. B. (1992). Social projection and social conformity in adolescent alcohol use: A longitudinal analysis. *Personality and Social Psychology Bulletin, 18*, 96–107.

McFarlin, D. B., & Blascovich, J. (1981). Effects of self-esteem and performance feedback on future affective preferences and cognitive expectations. *Journal of Personality and Social Psychology, 40*, 521–531.

Miller, N. E. (1948). Theory and experiment relating psychoanalytic displacement to stimulus-response generalization. *Journal of Abnormal and Social Psychology, 43*, 155–178.

Mischel, W., Ebbesen, E. B., & Zeiss, A. R. (1976). Determinants of selective memory about the self. *Journal of Consulting and Clinical Psychology, 44*, 92–103.

Morokoff, P. J. (1985). Effects of sex guilt, repression, sexual "arousability," and sexual experience on female sexual arousal during erotica and fantasy. *Journal of Personality and Social Psychology, 49,* 177–187.

Newman, L. S., Duff, K., & Baumeister, R. F. (1997). A new look at defensive projection: Suppression, accessibility, and biased person perception. *Journal of Personality and Social Psychology, 72,* 980–1001.

Paulhus, D. L., Fridhandler, B., & Hayes, S. (1997). Psychological defense: Contemporary theory and research. In R. Hogan & J. Johnson (Eds.), *Handbook of personality psychology* (pp. 543–579). San Diego, CA: Academic Press.

Paulhus, D. L., & Reynolds, S. (1995). Enhancing target variance in personality impressions: Highlighting the person in person perception. *Journal of Personality and Social Psychology, 69,* 1233–1242.

Perloff, L. S., & Fetzer, B. K. (1986). Self-other judgments and perceived vulnerability to victimization. *Journal of Personality and Social Psychology, 50,* 502–510.

Pines, M., & Aronson, E. (1983). Antecedents, correlates, and consequences of sexual jealousy. *Journal of Personality, 51,* 108–135.

Pyszczynski, T., Greenberg, J., & Holt, K. (1985). Maintaining consistency between self-serving beliefs and available data: A bias in information processing. *Personality and Social Psychology Bulletin, 11,* 179–190.

Ramirez, J., Bryant, J., & Zillman, D. (1982). Effects of erotica on retaliatory behavior as a function of level of prior provocation. *Journal of Personality and Social Psychology, 43,* 971–978.

Rogers, R. W., & Prentice-Dunn, S. (1981). Deindividuation and anger-mediated interracial aggression: Unmasking regressive racism. *Journal of Personality and Social Psychology, 41,* 63–73.

Ross, L., Greene, D., & House, P. (1977). The "false consensus effect": An egocentric bias in social perception and attribution processes. *Journal of Experimental Social Psychology, 13,* 279–301.

Schlenker, B. R. (1980). *Impression management: The self-concept, social identity, and interpersonal relations.* Monterey, CA: Brooks/Cole.

Schlenker, B. R., Weigold, M. F., & Hallam, J. R. (1990). Self-serving attributions in social context: Effects of self-esteem and social pressure. *Journal of Personality and Social Psychology, 58,* 855–863.

Shaffer, D. R., & Case, T. (1982). On the decision to testify in one's own behalf: Effects of withheld evidence, defendant's sexual preferences, and juror dogmatism on juridic decisions. *Journal of Personality and Social Psychology, 42,* 335–346.

Sherman, S. J., Presson, C. C., & Chassin, L. (1984). Mechanisms underlying the false consensus effect: The special role of threats to the self. *Personality and Social Psychology Bulletin, 10,* 127–138.

Sherwood, G. G. (1981). Self-serving biases in person perception: A reexamination of projection as a mechanism of defense. *Psychological Bulletin, 90,* 445–459.

Suls, J., & Fletcher, B. (1985). The relative efficacy of avoidant and nonavoidant coping strategies: A meta-analysis. *Health Psychology, 4,* 249–288.

Suls, J., & Wan, C. K. (1987). In search of the false-uniqueness phenomenon: Fear and estimates of social consensus. *Journal of Personality and Social Psychology, 52,* 211–217.

Taylor, S. E. (1989). *Positive illusions: Creative self-deception and the healthy mind.* New York: Basic Books.

Taylor, S. E., & Brown, J. D. (1988). Illusion and well-being: A social psychological perspective on mental health. *Psychological Bulletin, 103,* 193–210.

Tice, D. M. (1992). Self-presentation and self-concept change: The looking glass self as magnifying glass. *Journal of Personality and Social Psychology, 63,* 435–451.

Wegner, D. M. (1994). Ironic processes of mental control. *Psychological Review, 101,* 34–52.

Wegner, D. M., & Erber, R. (1992). The hyperaccessibility of suppressed thoughts. *Journal of Personality and Social Psychology, 63,* 903–912.

Weinberger, D. A., Schwartz, G. E., & Davidson, R. J. (1979). Low-anxious, high-anxious, and repressive coping styles: Psychometric patterns and behavioral and physiological responses to stress. *Journal of Abnormal Psychology, 88,* 369–380.

Weinstein, N. D. (1980). Unrealistic optimism about future life events. *Journal of Personality and Social Psychology, 39,* 806–820.

Wicklund, R. A., & Gollwitzer, P. M. (1982). *Symbolic self-completion.* Hillsdale, NJ: Erlbaum.

Wyer, R. S., & Frey, D. (1983). The effects of feedback about self and others on the recall and judgments of feedback-relevant information. *Journal of Experimental Social Psychology, 19,* 540–559.

Zillmann, D. (1971). Excitation transfer in communication-mediated aggressive behavior. *Journal of Experimental Social Psychology, 7,* 419–434.

Zillmann, D., Bryant, J., Cantor, J. R., & Day, K. D. (1975). Irrelevance of mitigating circumstances in retaliatory behavior at high levels of excitation. *Journal of Research in Personality, 9,* 286–306.

Zillman, D., Katcher, A. H., & Milavsky, B. (1972). Excitation transfer from physical exercise to subsequent aggressive behavior. *Journal of Experimental Social Psychology, 8,* 247–259.

Zuckerman, M. (1979). Attribution of success and failure revisited; or, The motivational bias is alive and well in attribution theory. *Journal of Personality, 47,* 245–287.

Does Venting Anger Feed or Extinguish the Flame? Catharsis, Rumination, Distraction, Anger, and Aggressive Responding

Brad J. Bushman

One message from traditional psychoanalytic theory that many people "know" to be true is that it is good to express one's anger rather than hold it in. As this article notes, everything from Hollywood movies to public-service billboards to everyday advice to friends is often based on this principle. But is it true? The present article reports an experiment examining the effects hitting a punching bag has on anger and aggressive behavior. The author concludes that this kind of "catharsis" makes anger and aggression worse rather than better.

    Die-hard advocates of psychoanalysis would no doubt argue that the kind of catharsis Freud and other psychoanalysts have in mind can scarcely be captured in a study where college students think angry thoughts and hit punching bags. They would have a point. But then, what evidence does *support the idea that catharis is beneficial? One could argue that experiments like this one do not fully capture the real-life situations in which catharsis is important. However, even an advocate of psychoanalysis would have to be disturbed by the present results, which are in the* opposite *direction from what he or she would predict.*

From *Personality and Social Psychology Bulletin, 28*, 724–731, 2002.

The belief in the value of venting anger has become widespread in our culture. In movies, magazine articles, and even on billboards, people are encouraged to vent their anger and "blow off steam." For example, in the movie *Analyze This*, a psychiatrist (played by Billy Crystal) tells his New York gangster client (played by Robert De Niro), "You know what I do when I'm angry? I hit a pillow. Try that." The client promptly pulls out his gun, points it at the couch, and fires several bullets into the pillow. "Feel better?" asks the psychiatrist. "Yeah, I do," says the gunman. In a *Vogue* magazine article, female model Shalom concludes that boxing helps her release pent-up anger. She said,

I found myself looking forward to the chance to pound out the frustrations of the week against Carlos's (her trainer) mitts. Let's face it: A personal boxing trainer has advantages over a husband or lover. He won't look at you accusingly and say, "I don't know where this irritation is coming from." . . . Your boxing trainer knows it's in there. And he wants you to give it to him. ("Fighting Fit," 1993, p. 179)

In a *New York Times Magazine* article about hate crimes, Andrew Sullivan writes, "Some expression of prejudice serves a useful purpose. It lets off steam; it allows natural tensions to express themselves incrementally; it can siphon off conflict through words, rather than actions" (Sullivan, 1999, p. 113). A large billboard in Missouri states, "Hit a Pillow, Hit a Wall, But Don't Hit Your Kids!"

Catharsis Theory

The theory of catharsis is one popular and authoritative statement that venting one's anger will produce a positive improvement in one's psychological state. The word *catharsis* comes from the Greek word *katharsis*, which literally translated means a cleansing or purging. According to catharsis theory, acting aggressively or even viewing aggression is an effective way to purge angry and aggressive feelings.

Sigmund Freud believed that repressed negative emotions could build up inside an individual and cause psychological symptoms, such as hysteria (nervous outbursts). Breuer and Freud (1893–1895/1955) proposed that the treatment of hysteria required the discharge of the emotional state previously associated with trauma. They claimed that for interpersonal traumas, such as insults and threats to the ego, emotional expression could be obtained through direct aggression: "The reaction of an injured person to a trauma has really only . . . a 'cathartic' effect if it is expressed in an adequate reaction like revenge" (p. 5). Breuer and Freud believed that expressing anger was much better than bottling it up inside.

Freud's therapeutic ideas on emotional catharsis form the basis of the hydraulic model of anger. The hydraulic model suggests that frustrations lead to anger and that anger, in turn, builds up inside an individual, similar to hydraulic pressure inside a closed environment, until it is released in some way. If people do not let their anger out but try to keep it bottled up inside, it will eventually cause them to explode in an aggressive rage. The modern theories of catharsis are based on this model. Catharsis is seen as a way of relieving the pressure that the anger creates inside the psyche. The core idea is that it is better to let the anger out here and there in little bits as opposed to keeping it inside as it builds up to the point at which a more dangerous explosion results.

If venting really does get anger "out of your system," then venting should decrease aggression because people are less angry. Almost as soon as psychology researchers began conducting scientific tests of catharsis theory, the theory ran into trouble. In one of the first experiments on the topic (Hornberger, 1959), participants first received an insulting remark from a confederate. Next, half of the participants pounded nails for 10 minutes—an activity that resembles many of the "venting" techniques that people who believe in catharsis continue to recommend even today. The other half did not get a chance to vent their anger by pounding nails. After this, all participants had a chance to criticize the person who had insulted them. If catharsis theory is true, the act of pounding nails should reduce subsequent aggression. The results showed the opposite effect. The people who had hammered the nails were more (rather than less) hostile toward the confederate afterward than were the ones who did not get to pound any nails.

In 1973, Albert Bandura issued a statement calling for a moratorium on catharsis theory and the use of venting in therapy. Four years later, Geen and Quanty (1977) published their influential review of catharsis theory in *Advances in Experimental Social Psychology*. After reviewing the relevant data, they concluded that venting anger does not reduce aggression. If anything, they concluded, it makes people more aggressive afterward. More recent research has come to similar conclusions (e.g., Bushman, Baumeister, & Stack, 1999). Geen and Quanty also concluded that venting anger can reduce physiological arousal but people must express their anger directly against the provocateur. People also must believe that the provocateur will not retaliate. Venting against substitute targets does not reduce arousal.

Cognitive Neoassociation Theory

According to cognitive neoassociation theory (Berkowitz, 1993), aversive events (e.g., frustrations, provocations, hot temperatures) produce negative affect. Negative affect, in turn, automatically stimulates thoughts, memories, expressive motor reactions, and physiological responses associated with both fight and flight tendencies. The fight associations give rise to rudimentary feelings of anger, whereas the flight associations give rise to rudimentary feelings of fear.

Cognitive neoassociation theory posits that aggressive thoughts are linked together in memory, thereby forming an associative network. Once an aggressive thought is processed or stimulated, activation spreads out along the network links and primes or activates associated thoughts as well. Not only are associated aggressive thoughts linked together in memory, but thoughts are also linked along the same sort of associative lines to emotional reactions and action tendencies (Bower, 1981; Lang, 1979). Thus, the activation of aggressive thoughts can engender a complex of associations consisting of aggressive ideas, emotions related to violence, and the impetus for aggressive actions.

Cognitive neoassociation theory predicts that venting should increase rather than decrease angry feelings and aggressive behaviors. Venting involves behaving aggressively, often against "safe" inanimate objects. To vent, people punch pillows, wallop punching bags, beat on couches with foam baseball bats, throw dishes on the ground, kick trash cans, scream and swear into pillows, and so forth. In essence, venting is practicing how to behave aggressively. Such aggressive activity should prime aggressive thoughts, feelings, and behavioral tendencies, especially if the people think about the source of their anger while venting. Thus, venting should keep angry feelings active in memory and also should increase the likelihood of subsequent aggressive responses.

Rumination and Distraction

Most pop psychology and self-help books implicitly assume that people are ruminating about their provocateur while venting anger. Some authors, however, are more explicit. For example, John Lee (1993) gives the following advice to angry people in his popular book *Facing the Fire: Experiencing and Expressing Anger Appropriately*.

> Punch a pillow or a punching bag. Punch with all the frenzy you can. If you are angry at a particular person, imagine his or her face on the pillow or punching bag, and vent your rage physically and verbally. You will be doing violence to a pillow or punching bag so that you can stop doing violence to yourself by holding in poisonous anger (p. 96)

Some devices for venting anger make it easy for people to ruminate about their provocateur. For example, consider the following advertisement from a toy catalog:

> WHEN YOU NEED SOMETHING THAT WON'T HIT BACK. *Wham-It* stands 42″ tall and takes abuse from kids and adults alike. When you feel like you just have to strike out, *Wham-It* is always on call. New clear vinyl pocket lets you insert a photo or drawing.

Rumination is defined as "self-focused attention," or directing attention inward on the self, and particularly on one's negative mood (Lyubomirsky & Nolen-Hoeksema, 1995). Any process that serves to exacerbate a negative mood, such as rumination, should increase anger and aggression. In contrast, any process that distracts attention away from an angry mood should reduce anger and aggression. If provoked individuals are induced to think about how they feel, they will maintain, or exacerbate, their angry mood. If they are induced to think about something else, however, the anger will dissipate in time.

Previous research has shown that rumination increases angry feelings. In one study (Rusting &

Nolen-Hoeksema, 1998), college students were angered by reading a story about a professor who treated a student unfairly and were told to imagine themselves in a similar situation. Some students ruminated by writing about emotion-focused and self-focused topics (i.e., "Why do you think the way you do"), whereas others were distracted by writing about nonemotional, irrelevant topics (i.e., "the layout of the local post office"). Participants who ruminated for 20 minutes reported being angrier than did participants who were distracted. Another study found that aggression toward an insulting confederate was decreased by having people solve distracting math problems (Konecni, 1974). Solving the math problems presumably distracted people from the source of their anger. Two other studies found that rumination increased displaced aggression after a minor triggering event (Bushman, Pedersen, Vasquez, Bonacci, & Miller, 2001). In Study 1, provoked participants focused attention on or away from their negative mood and later engaged in displaced aggression against a competent or fumbling confederate. Provoked participants who ruminated engaged in more displaced aggression against the fumbling confederate than did participants who were distracted. Study 2 replicated the findings from Study 1 using different operational definitions and a substantially longer (8-hour) rumination period.

To date, no research has examined the effects of rumination and distraction in the effects of venting activities on anger and subsequent aggression. According to cognitive neoassociation theory, ruminating while venting should prime aggressive thoughts, feelings, and behavioral tendencies.

Overview

In the present study, 600 college students (300 men, 300 women) were first angered by another participant who criticized an essay they had written. In fact, there was no other participant. Next, participants were randomly assigned to rumination, distraction, or control groups. Participants in the rumination group hit a punching bag as long, as hard, and as many times as they wanted to. While

they hit the bag, they were told to think about the other participant who had criticized their essay. For a visual aid, they were shown a photo ID of a same-sex college student described as the "other participant" on a 15-inch computer monitor. Participants in the distraction group also hit a punching bag as long, as hard, and as many times as they wanted to. While they hit the bag, they were told to think about becoming physically fit. As a visual aid, they were shown a photo ID of a same-sex athlete from a health magazine on a 15-inch computer monitor. Participants in the control group did not hit the punching bag. Instead, they sat quietly for a couple minutes while the experimenter supposedly worked on the other participant's computer. No attempt was made to reduce the anger of participants in the control group. Anger was measured using a mood form. Aggression was measured by allowing participants to blast their provocateur with loud and long noises through a pair of headphones on a competitive reaction time task. Catharsis theory would predict the lowest levels of anger and aggression among participants in the rumination condition. Cognitive neoassociation theory would predict the exact opposite results.

Method

PARTICIPANTS

Participants were 602 undergraduate college students (300 men and 302 women) enrolled in introductory psychology courses. Students received extra course credit in exchange for their voluntary participation. The data from 2 women were discarded because they refused to hit the punching bag. The final sample consisted of 300 men and 300 women. There were 100 men and 100 women in each of the three experimental conditions (i.e., rumination, distraction, control).

PROCEDURE   Participants were tested individually, but each was led to believe that he or she would be interacting with another participant of the same sex. They were told that the researchers were studying first impressions.

After giving informed consent, each participant wrote a one-paragraph essay on abortion, either pro-choice or pro-life (whichever the participant supported). After finishing, the participant's essay was taken away to be shown to the other participant (who was in fact nonexistent) for evaluation. Meanwhile, the participant was permitted to evaluate the partner's essay, which expressed the opposite view on abortion (e.g., if the participant's essay was pro-choice, the partner's essay was pro-life).

A short time later, the experimenter brought the participant's own essay back with comments ostensibly made by the other participant. All participants received bad evaluations consisting of negative ratings on organization, originality, writing style, clarity of expression, persuasiveness of arguments, and overall quality. The ratings ranged from −10 to −8 on a 21-point scale ranging from −10 (*very bad*) to +10 (*very good*). There was also a handwritten comment stating "This is one of the worst essays I have read!" Previous research has shown that this procedure makes people quite angry (e.g., Bushman & Baumeister, 1998; Bushman, Baumeister, & Phillips, 2001; Bushman et al., 1999).

After reading the evaluation, the participants rated how much they wanted to perform each of 10 activities on a list. Included in this list of activities was "hitting a punching bag." Other activities included playing solitaire, reading a short story, watching a comedy, and playing a computer game. Ratings were made on a 10-point scale ranging from 1 (*not at all*) to 10 (*extremely*).

The punching bag manipulation came next. Two thirds of participants received the punching bag procedure. If the participant did not rank the punching bag activity first, the experimenter asked if the participant would be willing to hit the punching bag, explaining that ratings were needed for each activity on the list and that more ratings were needed for the punching bag activity. By requesting the participant to agree, we were able to ensure that the punching bag activity was the result of choice by all participants, including those who had not originally listed it as their top choice.

Participants who received the punching bag procedure were told that because physical appearance could influence their impression of their partner, a coin would be tossed to determine whether they would know what their partner looked like. On the basis of the coin toss, participants were assigned to rumination or distraction conditions. Participants in the rumination condition were told that they would know what their partner looked like. On a 15-inch computer monitor, participants were shown a photo ID of another Iowa State University student of the same sex. The experimenter actually rolled a die to determine which of six photo IDs to show. The names and identification numbers were removed from all IDs. The experimenter then gave the participant some boxing gloves and demonstrated how to hit the 70-pound punching bag. Participants were told that they should think about their partner while hitting the bag.

Participants in the distraction condition were told that they would not know what their partner looked like. Instead of thinking about their partner while hitting the bag, they were told to think about becoming physically fit. Instead of seeing a photo ID of their partner on the computer screen, they saw a photo of someone of the same sex exercising. The photos were taken from fitness magazines and the experimenter rolled a die to determine which photo to show.

Participants in both the rumination and distraction condition were told that their partner would not see them (due to the coin toss). The participant was left alone to hit the punching bag. They were told they could hit it as long and as many times as they wanted to. Because there was an intercom system in the participant's room, the experimenter was able to time how long the participant hit the bag and count the number of times the participant hit the bag. The experimenter also rated how hard the participant hit the bag on a 10-point scale ranging from 1 (*very soft*) to 10 (*very hard*). The experimenter also asked the participant how hard he or she hit the bag (using the same 10-point scale). Participants then indicated how much they enjoyed hitting the punching bag on a

10-point scale ranging from 1 (*not at all*) to 10 (*extremely*).

Participants in the control condition did not hit the punching bag. Instead, they sat quietly for 2 minutes. The justification for the delay was that the experimenter was fixing their partner's computer. No attempt was made to reduce participant's anger during the 2-minute delay. Instead, participants in the no punching bag group did nothing at all. This allowed a test of the hypothesis that angry people are better off doing nothing at all than engaging in cathartic activities.

Next, participants completed a mood form that measured anger and positive affect. The anger measure consisted of 15 adjectives (e.g., *angry, annoyed, furious*) from the hostility subscale of the revised Multiple Affect Adjective Checklist (Zuckerman & Lubin, 1985). The positive affect measure consisted of 10 adjectives (e.g., *alert, determined, enthusiastic*) from the positive affect subscale of the Positive and Negative Affect Schedule (Watson, Clarke, & Tellegen, 1988). Watson and his colleagues define positive affect as a state of "high energy, full concentration, and pleasurable engagement" (p. 1063). All adjectives were rated along a 5-point Likert-type scale, where 1 = *very slightly or not at all*, 2 = *a little*, 3 = *moderately*, 4 = *quite a bit*, and 5 = *extremely*. Participants were told to "indicate to what extent you feel this way right now, that is, at the present moment." The alpha coefficients for the measures of anger and positive affect were .88 and .89, respectively.

The next part of the procedure was presented as a competitive reaction time task, based on a paradigm developed by Taylor (1967). Previous studies have established the construct validity of this paradigm (e.g., Bernstein, Richardson, & Hammock, 1987; Giancola & Zeichner, 1995). The participant was told that he or she and the partner would have to press a button as fast as possible on each trial and whoever was slower would receive a blast of noise. The participant was permitted to set in advance the intensity of the noise that the other person would receive between 60 decibels (level 1) and 105 decibels (level 10) if the other lost. A nonaggressive no-noise setting (level 0) also was offered. In addition to deciding the intensity, the winner decided the duration of the loser's suffering because the duration of the noise depended on how long the winner held the button pressed down. In effect, each participant controlled a weapon that could be used to blast the other person if the participant won the competition to react faster.

The reaction time task consisted of 25 trials. After the initial (no provocation) trial, the remaining 24 trials were divided into three blocks with eight trials in each block. Within each block of trials, the other participant set random noise levels (ranging from 65 decibels to 100 decibels) and random noise durations (ranging from 0.25 seconds to 2.5 seconds). The participant heard noise on half of the trials within each block (randomly determined). An iMac computer controlled the events in the reaction time task and recorded the noise levels and noise durations the participant set for the other person. The white noise was delivered through a pair of Telephonics TDH-39P headphones.

Half of participants completed the mood form first, followed by the competitive reaction time task. The other half of the participants completed the competitive reaction time task first, followed by the mood checklist. A full oral debriefing (with probe for suspicion) followed. Because none of the participants expressed any suspicion, all 600 were included in the data analyses.

Results

PRELIMINARY ANALYSES

* * *

Punching Bag Preference. It was important to determine whether participants in the three groups differed in their desire to hit the punching bag after they had been angered. Because participants were randomly assigned to conditions, no differences were expected. We also tested for sex differences in punching bag preferences. Because aggressive activities are more socially acceptable among men than among women, punching bag preferences were expected to be higher among men.

Desire to hit the punching bag. Ratings of how much participants wanted to hit the punching bag were analyzed using a 3 (rumination, distraction, control) × 2 (men, women) analysis of variance. Men wanted to hit the punching bag more than did women, $M = 4.33$, $SD = 2.77$, and $M = 3.10$, $SD = 2.33$, $F(1, 588) = 33.87$, $p < .0001$, $d = 0.48$.[1] As expected, the effects involving experimental condition were nonsignificant ($ps > .05$).

* * *

Punching Bag Measures. It was important to test whether participants in the rumination group vented more than did participants in the distraction group.

How hard the punching bag was hit. The intraclass correlation between experimenter and participant ratings of how hard the bag was hit was .69[2] (Shrout & Fleiss, 1979). The same pattern of results also was found for the two ratings. Thus, the two ratings were averaged.

Overall, men hit the punching bag harder than did women, $M = 6.69$, $SD = 2.05$, and $M = 4.73$, $SD = 1.88$, $F(1, 396) = 99.14$, $p < .0001$, $d = 1.00$. No other effects were significant ($ps > .05$).

Number of times punching bag was hit. Participants who thought about becoming physically fit hit the punching bag more times than did participants who thought about the person who insulted them, $M = 127.5$, $SD = 63.5$, and $M = 112.2$, $SD = 57.5$, $F(1, 396) = 6.31$, $p < .05$, $d = 0.25$. In other words, participants in the rumination group vented less did participants in the distraction group. No other effects were significant ($ps > .05$).

---

[1] M stands for mean and the SD is the standard deviation. The F statistic from the anaysis of variance, in conjunction with the degrees of freedom of the experimental design (given in parentheses), yields an estimate of the probability that the mean differences could be due solely to chance. The d statistic is a measure of the strength of the effect.

[2] The "intraclass correlation" is a variant on the standard correlation coefficient discussed by Rosenthal and Rubin (Part I), but is interpreted in the same way.

Time spent hitting punching bag. No significant effects were found for time spent hitting the punching bag ($ps > .05$).

Enjoyed hitting the punching bag. Men enjoyed hitting the punching bag more than did women, $M = 6.11$, $SD = 2.53$, and $M = 4.96$, $SD = 2.51$, $F(1, 396) = 20.85$, $p < .0001$, $d = 0.46$. No other effects were significant ($ps > .05$).

PRIMARY ANALYSES

Positive Mood There was no significant effect for experimental condition on positive mood, $F(2, 594) = 0.24$, $p > .05$ (see Table 1). Regardless of the condition they were in, men were in a more positive mood than were women, $M = 31.51$, $SD = 7.85$, and $M = 28.12$, $SD = 7.40$, $F(1, 594) = 29.31$, $p < .0001$, $d = 0.44$.

Anger There was a main effect for experimental condition on anger, $F(2, 594) = 5.23$, $p < .01$ (see Table 1). Participants in the rumination group felt more angry than did participants in the distraction and control groups, $t(594) = 2.20$, $p < .05$, $d = 0.22$, and $t(594) = 3.15$, $p < .005$, $d = 0.31$. Participants in distraction and control groups did not differ in terms of how angry they felt, $t(594) = 0.95$, $p > .05$.

Aggressive Behavior The same pattern of results was found for the two measures of aggression—noise intensity and noise duration. Thus, the two measures were standardized and summed to form a more reliable measure of aggression. The same pattern of results also was obtained on Trial 1 and on the remaining 24 trials of the competitive reaction-time task. Thus, the responses on the 25 trials were standardized and summed.

There was a main effect for experimental condition on aggression, $F(2, 594) = 5.03$, $p < .01$ (see Table 1). Participants in the rumination group were more aggressive than participants in the control group, $t(594) = 3.17$, $p < .005$, $d = 0.30$. Participants in the distraction group were more aggressive than participants in the control group and were less aggressive than participants in the rumination group, although neither difference was

TABLE 1

ANGER AND AGGRESSION LEVELS FOR PARTICIPANTS IN THE CONTROL, DISTRACTION, AND RUMINATION GROUPS

Measure	Control		Distraction		Rumination	
Positive mood	29.61_a	(7.34)	29.71a	(7.86)	30.11_a	(8.23)
Anger	26.25_b	(10.98)	27.32_b	(10.88)	29.78_a	(11.56)
Aggression	-0.21_b	(1.27)	0.01_{ab}	(1.39)	0.21_a	(1.54)

Note. $n = 200$ in each group. Standard deviations are in parentheses. Subscripts refer to within-row comparisons. Means having the same subscript are not significantly different at the .05 significance level.

statistically significant, $ts(594) = 1.68$ and 1.49, $ps > .05$. Men were also more aggressive than were women, $M = 0.44$, $SD = 1.62$, and $M = -0.44$, $SD = 0.99$, $F(1, 594) = 66.52$, $p <.0001$, $d = 0.33$.

Discussion Does venting anger extinguish or feed the flame? The results from the present research show that venting to reduce anger is like using gasoline to put out a fire—it only feeds the flame. By fueling aggressive thoughts and feelings, venting also increases aggressive responding. People who walloped the punching bag while thinking about the person who had provoked them were the most angry and the most aggressive in the present experiment. Venting did not lead to a more positive mood either.

People in the distraction group were less angry than were people in the rumination group, but they were not less aggressive. Thus, performing an aggressive activity such as hitting a punching bag can increase aggression even if people are distracted while performing the activity.

In the present experiment, people were best off doing nothing at all than venting their anger. No attempt was made to reduce anger or aggressive impulses in the control group. Even so, anger and aggression levels were lowest in the control group. The results might have been more dramatic if participants in the control group actively sought to reduce their angry feelings.

Overall, the present results support cognitive neoassociation theory (Berkowitz, 1993) and directly contradict catharsis theory. Venting while ruminating about the source of provocation kept aggressive thoughts and angry feelings active in memory and only made people more angry and more aggressive. These results provide one more nail in the coffin containing catharsis theory.

MAGNITUDE OF OBSERVED EFFECTS   Although the effects obtained in the present study were small to moderate in size (see Cohen, 1988), they are in the opposite direction predicted by catharsis theory. In the present study, the distraction activity was an aggressive one—angered people hit a punching bag. Larger effects might have been obtained if distraction activity would have been a nonaggressive one, such as working a crossword puzzle. Similarly, larger effects might have been obtained if angered people would have engaged in a behavior incompatible with anger and aggression, such as watching a funny TV program or petting a puppy (e.g., Baron, 1976, 1983).

CAN THESE FINDINGS BE DUE TO AROUSAL?   One well-known finding in psychology is that arousal enhances whatever response is dominant (e.g., Cottrell & Wack, 1967; Criddle, 1971; Eysenck, 1975; Markovsky & Berger, 1983; Zajonc, Heingartner, & Herman, 1969; Zajonc & Sales, 1966). This finding is central to the drive theory of social facilitation (e.g., Geen & Bushman, 1987, 1989). Walloping a punching bag for a few minutes can certainly increase arousal levels. Because participants in the present study all were provoked, it seems likely that aggression would be a dominant response for them. Arousal cannot, however, explain the pattern of results obtained in the present study. If the results were due to arousal, people in the distraction group should have been more aggressive than people in the rumination group because they hit the punching bag a greater number of times. The results, however, were in the opposite direction.

IS INTENSE PHYSICAL ACTIVITY AN EFFECTIVE TECHNIQUE FOR MANAGING ANGER?

If used as a form of distraction, intense physical activity does not necessarily increase anger, even if the activity is aggressive in nature (e.g., hitting a punching bag). Physical activity should, however, increase anger if the person is provoked after engaging in the intense physical activity. According to excitation transfer theory, the arousal from the physical activity will be misattributed to the provocation and will therefore transfer to the provocation (e.g., Zillmann, 1979). Mislabeling the arousal from the physical activity as anger would therefore increase aggressive responding (e.g., Zillmann, Katcher, & Milavsky, 1972). In the present study, participants were provoked before engaging in an intense physical activity, so excitation transfer should not occur. Although it might be good for your heart, intense physical activity is probably not an effective technique for reducing anger and aggression.

CONCLUSION

Catharsis theory predicts that venting anger should get rid of it and should therefore reduce subsequent aggression. The present findings, as well as previous findings, directly contradict catharsis theory (e.g., Bushman et al., 1999; Geen & Quanty, 1977). For reducing anger and aggression, the worst possible advice to give people is to tell them to imagine their provocateur's face on a pillow or punching bag as they wallop it, yet this is precisely what many pop psychologists advise people to do. If followed, such advice will only make people angrier and more aggressive.

References

Bandura, A. (1973). *Aggression: A social learning theory analysis.* Englewood Cliffs, NJ: Prentice Hall.

Baron, R. A. (1976). The reduction of human aggression: A field study of the influence of incompatible reactions. *Journal of Applied Social Psychology, 6,* 260–274.

Baron, R. A. (1983). The control of human aggression: An optimistic perspective. *Journal of Social and Clinical Psychology, 1,* 97–119.

Berkowitz, L. (1993). *Aggression: Its causes, consequences, and control.* New York: McGraw-Hill.

Bernstein, S., Richardson, D., & Hammock, G. (1987). Convergent and discriminant validity of the Taylor and Buss measures of physical aggression. *Aggressive Behavior, 13,* 15–24.

Bower, G. (1981). Mood and memory. *American Psychologist, 36,* 129–148.

Breuer, J., & Freud, S. (1955). *Studies on hysteria* (Standard ed., Vol. II). London: Hogarth. (Original work published 1893–1895.)

Bushman, B. J., & Baumeister, R. F. (1998). Threatened egotism, narcissism, self-esteem, and direct and displaced aggression: Does self-love or self-hate lead to violence? *Journal of Personality and Social Psychology, 75,* 219–229.

Bushman, B. J., Baumeister, R. F., & Phillips, C. M. (2001). Do people aggress to improve their mood? Catharsis beliefs, affect regulation opportunity, and aggressive responding. *Journal of Personality and Social Psychology, 81,* 17–32.

Bushman, B. J., Baumeister, R. F., & Stack, A. D. (1999). Catharsis, aggression, and persuasive influence: Self-fulfilling or self-defeating prophecies? *Journal of Personality and Social Psychology, 76,* 367–376.

Bushman, B. J., Pedersen, W. C., Vasquez. E. A., Bonacci, A. M., & Miller, N. (2001). *Chewing on it can chew you up: Effects of rumination on displaced aggression triggered by a minor event.* Manuscript submitted for publication.

Cohen, J. (1988). *Statistical power analysis for the behavioral sciences* (2nd ed.). New York: Academic Press.

Cottrell, N. B., & Wack, D. L. (1967). Energizing effects of cognitive dissonance upon dominant and subordinate responses. *Journal of Personality and Social Psychology, 6,* 132–138.

Criddle, W. D. (1971). The physical presence of other individuals as a factor in social facilitation. *Psychonomic Science, 22,* 229–230.

Eysenck, M. W. (1975). Effects of noise, activation level, and response dominance on retrieval from semantic memory. *Journal of Experimental Psychology: Human Learning and Memory, I,* 143–148.

Fighting fit. (1993, July). *Vogue, 183,* 176–179.

Geen, R. G., & Bushman, B. J. (1987). Drive theory: The effects of socially engendered arousal. In B. Mullen & G. R. Goethals (Eds.), *Theories of group behavior* (pp. 89–109). New York: Springer-Verlag.

Geen, R. G., & Bushman, B. J. (1989). The arousing effects of social presence. In H. Wagner & A. Manstead (Eds.), *Handbook of psychophysiology* (pp. 261–281). New York: John Wiley.

Geen, R. G., & Quanty, M. B. (1977). The catharsis of aggression: An evaluation of a hypothesis. In L. Berkowitz (Ed.), *Advances in experimental social psychology* (Vol. 10. pp. 1–37). New York: Academic Press.

Giancola, P. R., & Zeichner, A. (1995). Construct validity of a competitive reaction-time aggression paradigm. *Aggressive Behavior, 21,* 199–204.

Hornberger, R. H. (1959). The differential reduction of aggressive responses as a function of interpolated activities. *American Psychologist, 14,* 354.

Konecni, V. J. (1974). Self-arousal, dissipation of anger, and aggression. *Personality and Social Psychology Bulletin, 1,* 192–194.

Lang, P. J. (1979). A bio-informational theory of emotional imagery. *Psychophysiology, 16,* 495–512.

Lee, J. (1993). *Facing the fire: Experiencing and expressing anger appropriately.* New York: Bantam.

Lyubomirsky, S., & Nolen-Hoeksema, S. (1995). Effects of self-focused rumination on negative thinking and interpersonal problem solving. *Journal of Personality and Social Psychology, 69,* 176–190.

Markovsky, B., & Berger, S. M. (1983). Crowd noise and mimicry. *Personality and Social Psychology Bulletin, 9,* 90–96.

Rusting, C. L., & Nolen-Hoeksema, S. (1998). Regulating responses to anger: Effects of rumination and distraction on angry mood. *Journal of Personality and Social Psychology, 74,* 790–803.

Shrout, P. E., & Fleiss, J. L. (1979). Intraclass correlations: Uses in assessing rater reliability. *Psychological Bulletin, 86,* 420–428.

Sullivan, A. (1999, September 27). What's so bad about hate? *New York Times Magazine,* pp. 50–57, 88, 104, 112–113.

Taylor, S. P. (1967). Aggressive behavior and physiological arousal as a function of provocation and the tendency to inhibit aggression. *Journal of Personality, 35,* 297–310.

Watson, D., Clarke, L. A., & Tellegen, A. (1988). Development and validation of brief measures of positive and negative affect: The PANAS scales. *Journal of Personality and Social Psychology, 54,* 1063–1070.

Zajonc, R. B., Heingartner, A., & Herman, E. M. (1969). Social enhancement and impairment of performance in the cockroach. *Journal of Personality and Social Psychology, 13,* 83–92.

Zajonc, R. B., & Sales, S. M. (1966). Social facilitation of dominant and subordinate responses. *Journal of Experimental Social Psychology, 2,* 160–168.

Zillmann, D. (1979). *Hostility and aggression.* Hillsdale, NJ: Lawrence Erlbaum.

Zillmann, D., Katcher, A. H., & Milavsky, B. (1972). Excitation transfer from physical exercise to subsequent aggressive behavior. *Journal of Experimental Social Psychology, 8,* 247–259.

Zuckerman, M., & Lubin, B. (1985). *Manual for the MAACL-R: The Multiple Affective Adjective Checklist Revised.* San Diego, CA: Educational and Industrial Testing Service.

Womb Envy, Testyria, and Breast Castration Anxiety: What If Freud Were Female?

Gloria Steinem

Over the century since its introduction, both psychoanalysis and Freud personally have been the subject of numerous criticisms. Freud has been pilloried for being a plagiarist, liar, and sexist. His theory has been denounced as immoral, dirty, unscientific, and politically incorrect. During his lifetime Freud complained about the criticism he received, but also seemed to revel in it somewhat (Gay, 1988). He expected his theory to upset people. In fact, Freud believed that because psychoanalysis exposes essential but uncomfortable truths, it should upset people.

It is astonishing to see how often modern critics attack psychoanalysis by attacking Freud himself. The underlying assumption seems to be that if Freud was a scoundrel, then his theory must be wrong. (It is tempting to wonder if this very unscientific style of argument is at all related to modern trends in political reporting, where the desperate race to uncover "scandal" in politicians' lives increasingly pushes out analysis of the policies they pursue.)

Other, more legitimate criticisms of Freud have some degree of merit. For example, there is no question that the empirical base of psychoanalytic theory would not be considered even marginally sufficient for a new theory today. Freud based his theory on introspection and his experience with patients; he reported very little that would today be considered "data." Modern research, such as seen in the preceding selection, only begins to rectify this shortcoming. But other kinds of information besides controlled research—such as the degree to which therapists and people in general have found the theory useful over the years—may also be relevant.

The most difficult charge from which to defend Freud and psychoanalysis is that of sexism. Unlike so many other areas of his thought, Freud's view of women seems to have been influenced by the conventional attitudes of his time. As a result, some of his ideas appear strange by contemporary standards. Freud thought women experienced "penis envy," and in general seemed to describe men as normal humans, and women as damaged men.

In the final selection in this section, the prominent feminist writer Gloria Steinem (writing in Ms. *magazine) attacks without mercy Freud's most vulnerable point. She invents a fictitious psychoanalyst named Dr. Phyllis Freud. The Madame Doctor expounds a famous theory that takes everything psychoanalysis says about women, and says it about men instead. Steinem appends footnotes to this paper documenting some astonishing statements about women uttered by psychoanalysts over the years. Steinem's article also demonstrates the continuing truth of an aspect of Freud's theory that he expected, and even seemed to relish, from the beginning—psychoanalysis makes people mad.*

Freud will perhaps always be a controversial figure, and psychoanalysis is a highly imperfect creation. It is a challenging task to balance what the theory has to offer with the things that are clearly wrong about it. Similarly, when reading pieces such as the one that follows, it is difficult to separate out serious criticisms from outspoken indignation. And it is worth pondering just what it is about psychoanalysis that makes it still worth attacking, again and again, more than half a century after its founder's death.*

From "Womb Envy, Testyria, and Breast Castration Anxiety: What If Freud Were Female?" by G. Steinem (1994). In *Ms.*, 49–56. Adapted with permission.

To sense the difference between *what is* and *what could be*, we may badly need the "Aha!" that comes from exchanging subject for object; the flash of recognition that starts with a smile. I've grown to have a lot of faith in this technique of reversal. It not only produces empathy, but it's a great detector of bias, in ourselves as well as in others. In fact, the deeper the bias, the more helpful it is to make a similar statement about the other gender—or a different race, class, sexuality, physical ability, whatever—and see how it sounds.

*   *   *

In pursuit of the reasons why Sigmund Freud is still with us, and, most important, how it feels to be on the wrong side of his ubiquitous presence, I propose that male human beings in general, as well as everyone in the psychological trade, male or female, imagine themselves on the receiving end of a profession—indeed, a popular culture—suffused with the work and worship of one of the most enduring, influential, and fiercely defended thinkers in Western civilization: Dr. Phyllis Freud.

You will come to know her here through the words of her biographer, a scholar who is a little defensive because of criticisms of Freud, but still starstruck, and very sure of being right—in other words, a typical Freudian. Every detail of Phyllis' biography springs from Sigmund's, with only first names, pronouns, and anything else related to gender changed in order to create a gender-reversed world.

As in so much of life, the fun is in the text, but the truth is in the footnotes. Read both.

It's important to understand that when little Phyllis was growing up in Vienna in the mid-1800s, women were considered superior because of their ability to give birth. This belief in female superiority was so easily mistaken for an immutable fact of life that conditions like *womb envy* had become endemic among males.[1]

---

*All footnotes are by the author (Gloria Steinem) and appeared in the original.

[1]Modern Freudians *still* won't give up on penis envy. In 1981, *Freud and Women*, by Lucy Freeman and Dr. Herbert S. Strean (Continuum), contained this typical de-

Indeed, the belief in women's natural right to dominate was the very foundation of matriarchal Western civilization. At the drop of a hat, wise women would explain that, while men might dabble in the arts, they could never become truly *great* painters, sculptors, musicians, poets, or anything else that demanded creativity, for they lacked the womb, which was the very source of creativity. Similarly, since men had only odd, castrated breasts that created no sustenance, they might become adequate family cooks, but certainly they could never become great chefs, vintners, herbalists, nutritionists, or anything else that required a flair for food, a knowledge of nutrition, or a natural instinct for gustatory nuance. And because childbirth caused women to use the health care system more than men did, making childbirth its natural focus,[2] there was little point in encouraging young men to become physicians, surgeons, researchers, or anything other than low-paid health care helpers.

Even designing their own clothes was left to men only at the risk of unfortunate results. When allowed to dress themselves, they could never get beyond the envy of wombs and female genitals that condemned them to an endless repetition of female sexual symbolism. Thus, the open button-to-neck "V" of men's jackets was a recapitulation of the "V" of female genitalia; the knot in men's ties replicated the clitoris while the long ends of the tie took the shape of labia; and men's bow ties were the clitoris *erecta* in all its glory. They were, to use Phyllis Freud's technical term, "representations."[3]

In addition, men's lack of firsthand experience with birth and nonbirth—with choosing between conception and contraception, existence and nonexistence, as women did so wisely for all their fertile years—also reduced any sense of justice and ethics they might develop.[4] This tended to disqualify them as philosophers, whose very purview was the question of existence versus nonexistence plus all the calibrations in between. Certainly, it also lessened men's ability to make life-and-death judgments, which explained—and perhaps still does—their absence from decision-making positions in the law, law enforcement, the military, or other such professions.

After life-giving wombs and sustenance-giving breasts, women's ability to menstruate was the most obvious proof of their superiority. Only women could bleed without injury or death; only they rose from the gore each month like a phoenix; only their bodies were in tune with the ululations of the universe and the timing of the tides. Without this innate lunar cycle, how could men have a sense of time, tides, space, seasons, the movement of the universe, or the ability to measure anything at all? How could men mistress that skills of measurement for mathematics, engineering, architecture, surveying—and many other fields? In Christian churches, how could males serve the Daughter of

---

fense: "Contemporary psychoanalysts . . . agree penis envy is a universal fantasy of little girls at the age of four, [but . . .] if a little girl's emotional needs are understood by a loving mother and protective father, the normal fantasies of penis envy that occur during her phallic stage of sexual development will be accepted, then suppressed . . . and she will be able to love a man not for the physical attribute which, as a little girl, she envied and unconsciously wished to possess, but out of her feelings for him as a total person. She will want him not as a possessor of the desired phallus, but as mate and father of her child. In Freud's words, her original wish for a penis has changed into the wish for a baby."—Author

[2]Actually, this is true—women do use the health care system about 30 percent more than men do—but you'd never know it from who's in charge. Logic is in the eye of the logician.—Author

[3]Here are Freeman and Strean: "In her unconscious envy of the penis, many a woman adorns herself with feathers, sequins, furs, glistening silver and gold ornaments that 'hang down'—what psychoanalysts call 'representations' of the penis." I rest my case.—Author

[4]At the age of 76, with all the wisdom of his career to guide him, Freud wrote: "We also regard women as weaker in their social interests and as having less capacity for sublimating their instincts than men." His assumption that women were incapable of reaching the highest stage of ethical development—which was, in masculinist thought, the subordination of the individual to an abstract principle—became the foundation of the field of ethics. For an antidote, see Carol Gilligan's *In a Different Voice* (Harvard University Press). —Author

the Goddess with no monthly evidence of Her death and resurrection? In Judaism, how could they honor the Matriarchal God without the symbol of Her sacrifices recorded in the Old Ovariment? Thus insensible to the movements of the planets and the turning of the universe, how could men become astronomers, naturalists, scientists—or much of anything at all?[5]

It was simply accepted for males to be homemakers, ornaments, devoted sons, and sexual companions (providing they were well trained, of course, for, though abortion was well accepted, it was painful and to be avoided, and a careless impregnation could be punished by imprisonment).[6]

Once Phyllis Freud got into brilliant theorizing that went far beyond her training as a nineteenth-century neurologist, however, her greatest impact was to come not from phrases like *womb envy* and *anatomy is destiny*. No, those truths were already part of the culture. It was her interest in and treatment of *testyria*, a disease marked by uncontrollable fits of emotion and mysterious physical symptoms so peculiar to males that most experts assumed the condition to be related to the testicles.

Though testyrical males were often thought to be perverse, pretending, or otherwise untreatable, some treatments had been devised. They ranged from simple water cures, bed rest, mild electric shock, or, for the well-to-do, trips to a spa, to circumcision, the removal of the testicles, cauterization of the penis, and other remedies that may seem draconisn now, but were sometimes successful in subduing testyrical fits, and, in any case, were a product of their times.[7] In Paris, Phyllis Freud had also been among the hundreds of women who assembled in lecture halls to see demonstrations of hypnosis—a new technique for treating these mysterious symptoms by reaching into the unconscious—on male testyrics brought in for the purpose.

In fact, that sight had coalesced in Freud's mind with a case of testyria she had heard about in Vienna. A neurologist colleague, Dr. Josephine Breuer, had discussed her progress in relieving testyrical symptoms by encouraging a patient to explore the memories of earlier painful experiences with which the symptoms seemed associated—first with the aid of hypnosis, later by just talking them out through free association. Actually, this method had been improvised and named the "talking cure" by the young patient in question, Bert Pappenheim.

When Freud began her practice in the study of her Vienna apartment, hypnosis and Pappenheim's "talking cure" combined in her courageous focus on testyria. The symptoms she saw included depression, hallucinations, and a whole array of ailments, from paralysis, incapacitating headaches, chronic vomiting and coughing, and difficulty in swallowing, to full-scale testyrical fits, imitative pregnancies, and self-injury that included "cou-

---

[5]As another antidote to antimenstruation bias, try this argument: Since in women's "difficult" days before the onset of the menstrual period, the female hormone is at its lowest ebb, women are in those few days the most like what men are like *all month long.*—Author

[6]Yes, abortion was punishable by imprisonment at that time, and yes, the other reversals are also true. Descriptions of the era's sexism have been used to make Sigmund's attitude toward women seem understandable, even enlightened. Ignoring the many advances of his day flattens the ground around him to make him look taller. Here are a few other realities: George Sand was born a half century before Freud, and was one of many women who managed to live a life more free and unconventional than Freud could imagine even for himself. U.S. suffragists had issued the Declaration of Sentiments at Seneca Falls eight years before Freud was born. Throughout his formative years, Austrian suffragists, socialists, and reformers were working on every area of women's social and political rights—as were their counterparts in other countries. And there was an active movement in Austria for homosexual rights at the turn of the century.—Author

---

[7]For from-the-horse's-mouth documents of the period on the sadistic treatment of female patients—from electrical shocks to clitoridectomy and other sex-related surgeries—see Jeffrey Moussaieff Masson's *A Dark Science: Women, Sexuality, and Psychiatry in the Nineteenth Century* (Farrar, Straus & Giroux). For this tradition as adapted in the Freudian era, see Phyllis Chesler's *Women and Madness* (Harcourt Brace Jovanovich). —Author

vade," or slitting the skin of the penis—an extreme form of womb and menstruation envy that was an imitation of female functions.[8]

Even as Freud worked first with hypnosis, then more and more with psychoanalysis (for she had honored Pappenheim's "talking cure" with that new and scientific name), she theorized about what might be the cause. Because testyria was particularly common among men in their teens and twenties, she surmised that homemaking, child-rearing, sexual service, sperm production, and other parts of men's natural sphere had not yet yielded their mature satisfactions. Since some young men were also indulging in the dangerous practice of masturbation, they were subject to severe neurosis and sexual dysfunction per se. Among older and more rebellious or intellectual men, there was also the problem of being too womb-envying to attract a mate. Finally, there were those husbands who were married to women who had no regard for their sexual satisfaction; who, for example, practiced coitus interruptus either as a form of contraception, or from simple disregard.[9]

Extreme gratitude from her patients was understandable. Not only was Phyllis Freud the rare woman who listened to men, but she took what they said seriously and made it the subject of her own brilliant theories, even of science. This advanced attitude joins other evidence in exposing the gratuitous hostility of masculinists who accuse Freud of androphobia.[10] As a young woman, Phyllis had even translated into German Harriet Taylor Mill's *The Emancipation of Men*, a tract on male equality that a less enlightened woman would never have read.[11] Later, she supported the idea that men could also become psychoanalysts—provided, of course, they subscribed to Freudian theory, just as any female analyst would do. (Certainly, Freud would not have approved of the current school of equality that demands "men's history" and other special treatment.)

I'm sure that if you read carefully each of Freud's case histories, you will see the true depth of her understanding for the opposite sex.[12]

Freud wisely screened all she heard from testyrical men through her understanding, well accepted to this day, that men are sexually passive, just as they are intellectually and ethically. The libido was intrinsically feminine, or, as she put it with her genius for laywoman's terms, "man possesses a weaker sexual instinct."

This was proved by man's mono-orgasmic nature. No serious authority disputed the fact that females, being multiorgasmic, were well adapted to pleasure, and thus were the natural sexual aggressors; in fact, "envelopment," the legal term for intercourse, was an expression of this active/passive understanding.[13] It was also acted out in micro-

---

[8]I couldn't resist *couvade*, a pregnancy-imitating ritual among men in tribal cultures where pregnancy and birth are worshiped. Women are made out to be the "naturally" masochistic ones in patriarchal cultures, but doesn't slitting the penis sound pretty masochistic to you?

In the case of Freud and his colleagues, however, the self-cutting and other mutilations they were seeing in their practices were probably what has now been traced to real events of sexual and other sadistic abuse in childhood: females (and males when they are similarly abused) repeat what was done to them, punishing the body that "attracted" or "deserved" such abuse, and anesthetizing themselves against pain, just as they were forced to do in the past.—Author

[9]Interesting—this one works both ways. Since "coitus interruptus" could be defined as an "interruptus" by whichever half of the pair has finished coitus—if you see what I mean—it needs no reversal.—Author

[10]O.K., maybe it's not perfect, but you try making up a word for man-hating. Also try figuring out why there isn't one.—Author

[11]Freud picked up a little extra money by translating John Stuart Mill's *The Emancipation of Women* while doing peacetime military service. What this mostly proves is that he was exposed to ideas of equality early—and rejected them. As he wrote to his wife, Martha: "Am I to think of my delicate sweet girl as a competitor?. . . the position of woman cannot be other than what it is: to be an adored sweetheart in youth, and a beloved wife in maturity."—Author

[12]You bet.—Author

[13]Try replacing "penetration" with "envelopment" and see what happens to your head.—Author

cosm in the act of conception itself. Think about it: the large ovum expends no energy, waits for the sperm to seek out its own destruction in typically masculine and masochistic fashion, and then simply envelops the infinitesimal sperm. As the sperm disappears into the ovum, it is literally eaten alive—much like the male spider eaten by his mate. Even the most quixotic male liberationist would have to agree that biology leaves no room for doubt about an intrinsic female dominance.[14]

What intrigued Freud was not these biological facts, however, but their psychological impact: for instance, the way males were rendered incurably narcissistic, anxious, and fragile by having their gentials so precariously perched and visibly exposed on the outside of their bodies. Men's womblessness and loss of all but vestigial breasts and useless nipples were the end of a long evolutionary journey toward the sole functions of sperm production, sperm carrying, and sperm delivery. Women were responsible for all the other processes of reproduction. Female behavior, health, and psychology governed gestation and birth. Since time immemorial, this disproportionate share in reproductive influence had unbalanced the sexes. (Freud realized the consequences for women as well, among them *breast castration anxiety*: a woman who looks at the flattened male chest with its odd extraneous nipples fears deep in her psyche that she will return to that breast castrated state.)

Finally, there was the physiological fact of the penis. It confirmed the initial bisexuality of all humans.[15] After all, life begins as female, in the womb as elsewhere[16] (the explanation for men's residual nipples). Penile tissue has its origin in, and thus has retained a comparable number of nerve endings as, the clitoris.[17] But somewhere along the evolutionary line, the penis acquired a double function: excretion of urine and sperm delivery. (Indeed, during boys' feminine, masturbatory, clitoral stage of development—before they had seen female genitals and realized that their penises were endangered and grotesque compared to the compact, well-protected clitoris—the penis had a third, albeit immature, function of masturbatory pleasure.)[18] All this results in an organ suffering from functional overload. The most obvious, painful, diurnal, nocturnal (indeed, even multidiurnal and multinocturnal) outcome for this residual clitoral tissue was clear: *men were forced to urinate through their clitorises.*

No doubt, this was the evolutionary cause for the grotesque enlargement and exposure of the penis, and for its resulting insensitivity due to lack of protection. Though the nerve endings in the female's clitoris remained exquisitely sensitive and close to the surface—carefully carried, as they were, in delicate mucous membranes, which were protected by the labia—the exposed penile versions of the same nerve endings had gradually become encased in a protective, deadening epidermis; a fact that deprived men of the intense, radiating, whole-body pleasure that only the clitoris could

---

[14]Let's face it. Biology can be used to prove anything. Phyllis descries fertilization in terms of female dominance. Sigmund's terms are better suited to rape: "The male sex cell is actively mobile and searches out the female one, and the latter, the ovum, is immobile and waits passively," he wrote in "Femininity." "This behavior of the elementary sexual organisms is indeed a model for the conduct of sexual individuals during intercourse. The male pursues the female for the purpose of sexual union, seizes hold of her, and penetrates into her." What feminism asks—and I hope science, too, will ask one day—is, why do we have to assume domination? How about cooperation?—Author

[15]Actually, S. F. did believe in bisexuality—especially in young children, for they hadn't yet figured out how precious the penis was.—Author

[16]True.—Author

[17]Also true. *Somebody* had equality in mind.—Author

[18]Here is Sigmund in "Some Psychological Consequences of the Anatomical Distinction Between the Sexes": There is "a momentous discovery which little girls are destined to make. They notice the penis of a brother or playmate, strikingly visible and of large proportions, at once recognize it as the superior counterpart of their own small and inconspicuous organ, and from that time forward fall a victim to envy for the penis. . . . She has seen it and knows that she is without it and wants to have it."—Author

provide. Men's lesser sex drive and diminished capacity for orgasm followed, as day follows night.

As Phyllis Freud proved in clinical studies that would become both widely accepted and tremendously influential, male sexuality became mature only when pleasure was transferred from the penis to the mature and appropriate area: the fingers and tongue. Freud reasoned brilliantly that since insemination and pregnancy could not accompany every orgasm experienced by multiorgasmic females, it must also be the case for males that sexual maturity would be measured by their ability to reach climax in a nonprocreative way. Immature *penile* orgasms had to be replaced by *lingual* and *digital* ones. In "Masculinity" as elsewhere, Phyllis Freud was very clear: "In the clitoral phase of boys, the penis is the leading erotogenic zone. But it is not, of course, going to remain so. . . . The penis should . . . hand over its sensitivity, and at the same time its importance, to the lingual/digital areas."[19]

---

[19]In "Femininity," Sigmund explained: "In the phallic phase of girls the clitoris is the leading erotogenic zone. But it is not, of course, going to remain so. . . . The clitoris should . . . hand over its sensitivity, and at the same time, its importance, to the vagina."

Should we excuse him as a man of his time? Here's the conclusion of Lisa Appignanesi and John Forrester in *Freud's Women* (HarperCollins): "It is almost inconceivable that Freud was not aware of the orthodox views of contemporary anatomists and physiologists, who had, from well before the early nineteenth century, demonstrated that the clitoris was the specific site of female sexual pleasure, and who, in the medical writing of his time, had asserted that the vagina had virtually no erotic functions at all. Nineteenth-century medical encyclopedia writers closed the file on the vagina in the same way Alfred Kinsey [did] in the mid-20th century, with a flourish of definitively and chillingly rank-pulling medical rhetoric: virtually the entire vagina could be operated on without the need of an anesthetic."

Still think the digital/lingual reversal is too outrageous? Maybe—but it allows men a lot more nerve endings than Freud allowed us.—Author

PART V

Humanistic Approach to Personality

The humanistic approaches to personality emphasize what is uniquely human about psychology's object of study. Studying people is not the same as studying rocks, trees, or animals, because people are fundamentally different. The unique aspects on which humanistic approaches focus are experience, awareness, free will, dignity, and the meaning of life. None of these mean much to rocks, trees, or animals, but they are all crucial to the human condition.

Our first selection, by the philosopher Jean-Paul Sartre, describes the existential philosophy that forms the bedrock of humanistic psychology. Existential analysis begins with the concrete and specific analysis of a single human being existing in a particular moment in time and space. It leads directly to concerns with phenomenology (the study of experience), free will, and the meaning of life. All of these existential issues are important for humanistic psychologists.

Sartre seems to view free will as a burden—it leaves one "forlorn," without external guidance about the right way to live—and happiness as irrelevant to a meaningful life. But the humanistic psychologists who borrowed so much from existential philosophy instead view free will as an opportunity, and happiness as the essential goal. In the second selection, Abraham Maslow presents his well-known theory of motivation, often referred to as the "hierarchy of needs." What is humanistic about this theory is that motivation begins rather than ends with the basic needs for survival and safety. After those are satisfied, Maslow proposes, uniquely human needs for understanding, beauty, and self-actualization become important for happiness.

The best known of the humanistic psychologists surely was Carl Rogers. In the third selection, Rogers argues that the "unconditional positive regard" that a humanistic psychotherapist gives his or her clients allows a clear, undistorted picture of his or her personality to emerge. He then draws on some experiences in the therapeutic context to illustrate his theory of personality dynamics, particularly what he regards as every individual's ability to reorganize his or her own personality. The next selection is by the modern humanistic psychologist Mihalyi Csikszentmihalyi. Csikszentmihalyi addresses the classic humanistic question: What is positive experience (the good life) and how does one attain it? He concludes that true happiness consists not of ecstasy but rather in choosing to enter a state of calm absorption he calls "flow."

In the past few years, humanistic psychology has revived under the new rubric of "positive psychology," which echoes Csikszentmihalyi's point that happiness is more a matter of how one thinks about events, than the events in one's life themselves. Lyubomirsky explains this point in detail, outlining the ways in which some people are able to maintain high levels of happiness regardless of their income level, living circumstances, and even physical health. In the final selection, Norem and Chang point out that an overly optimistic view on life can have disadvantages. The seemingly gloomy people they call "defensive pessimists" are good at avoiding certain kinds of disaster precisely because of their gift for anticipating every possible thing that can go wrong. On a more general level, Norem and Chang return us to Sartre's point that while happiness can be pleasant, it can also be misleading and dangerous.

THE HUMANISM OF EXISTENTIALISM

Jean-Paul Sartre

The philosophical basis of humanistic psychology is existentialism. And the leading exponent of existentialism has been Jean-Paul Sartre. Sartre was a French philosopher, dramatist, and novelist. He was a person of high principles. He was imprisoned by the Germans when they invaded France in 1940, and after his release he became active in the French Resistance. He was awarded the 1964 Nobel Prize in Literature but rejected it, saying that to accept such an award would compromise his integrity as a writer.

Existentialism is a philosophy that claims that "existence precedes essence." This means that first one exists—this is the only given—and then one must decide what such existence means. Since a person's existence occurs only a moment at a time, the experience of life in each moment is all-important. Any influence from the environment, the past, or the future can only affect one to the degree one is aware of it now. Sartre derives from these postulates an ethical code that emphasizes the freedom of oneself and others, and an accompanying, inescapable, total responsibility for everything one thinks and does.

We will see in later selections how humanistic psychologists integrate several key observations of existential philosophy into their theories. For now, note how Sartre argues that

- *the experience of each moment of existence is the basis for all else;*
- *each individual must interpret what reality is and what it means;*
- *people have complete freedom and total responsibility for their actions;*
- *there is no moral or ethical code beyond that which each individual must invent—with the one exception that it is essential to take responsibility for our own free choices, whatever they are; and*
- *it is in accepting freedom and taking responsibility—despite everything—that humans achieve dignity.*

From *Essays in Existentialism*, edited by W. Baskin (Secaucus, NJ: Citadel Press, 1965), pp. 31–62.

Wᴡhat is meant by the term *existentialism*? * * * It is the most austere of doctrines. It is intended strictly for specialists and philosophers. Yet it can be defined easily. * * * What [existentialists] have in common is that they think that existence precedes essence, or, if you prefer, that subjectivity must be the starting point.

* * *

Atheistic existentialism, which I represent, states that if God does not exist, there is at least one being in whom existence precedes essence, a being who exists before he can be defined by any concept, and that this being is man, or, as Heidegger[1] says, human reality. What is meant here by saying that existence precedes essence? It means that, first of all, man exists, turns up, appears on the scene, and, only afterwards, defines himself. If man, as the existentialist conceives him, is indefinable, it is because at first he is nothing. Only afterward will he be something, and he himself will have made what he will be. Thus, there is no human nature, since there is no God to conceive it. Not only is man what he conceives himself to be, but he is also only what he wills himself to be after this thrust toward existence.

Man is nothing else but what he makes of himself. Such is the first principle of existentialism. It is also what is called subjectivity. * * * [By this,] we mean that man first exists, that is, that man first of all is the being who hurls himself toward a future and who is conscious of imagining himself as being in the future. Man is at the start a plan which is aware of itself, rather than a patch of moss, a piece of garbage, or a cauliflower; nothing exists prior to this plan; there is nothing in heaven; man will be what he will have planned to be. Not what he will want to be. Because by the word "will" we generally mean a conscious decision, which is subsequent to what we have already made of ourselves. I may want to belong to a political party, write a book, get mar-

ried; but all that is only a manifestation of an earlier, more spontaneous choice that is called "will." But if existence really does precede essence, man is responsible for what he is. Thus, existentialism's first move is to make every man aware of what he is and to make the full responsibility of his existence rest on him. And when we say that a man is responsible for himself, we do not only mean that he is responsible for his own individuality, but that he is responsible for all men.

* * * When we say that man chooses his own self, we mean that every one of us does likewise; but we also mean by that that in making this choice he also chooses all men. In fact, in creating the man that we want to be, there is not a single one of our acts which does not at the same time create an image of man as we think he ought to be. To choose to be this or that is to affirm at the same time the value of what we choose, because we can never choose evil. We always choose the good, and nothing can be good for us without being good for all.

If, on the other hand, existence precedes essence, and if we grant that we exist and fashion our image at one and the same time, the image is valid for everybody and for our whole age. Thus, our responsibility is much greater than we might have supposed, because it involves all mankind. * * * If I want to marry, to have children; even if this marriage depends solely on my own circumstances or passion or wish, I am involving all humanity in monogamy and not merely myself. Therefore, I am responsible for myself and for everyone else. I am creating a certain image of man of my own choosing. In choosing myself, I choose man.

This helps us understand what the actual content is of such rather grandiloquent words as anguish, forlornness, despair.[2] As you will see, it's all quite simple.

First, what is meant by anguish? The existentialists say at once that man is anguish. What that means is this: the man who involves himself and who realizes that he is not only the person he

---

[1]A German existentialist philosopher whose thinking underlies much of the theory that Sartre espouses in this article.

[2]Gloomy-sounding words like these are a staple of existentialist philosophy.

chooses to be, but also a lawmaker who is, at the same time, choosing all mankind as well as himself, can not help escape the feeling of his total and deep responsibility. Of course, there are many people who are not anxious; but we claim that they are hiding their anxiety, that they are fleeing from it. Certainly, many people believe that when they do something, they themselves are the only ones involved, and when someone says to them, "What if everyone acted that way?" they shrug their shoulders and answer, "Everyone doesn't act that way." But really, one should always ask himself, "What would happen if everybody looked at things that way?" There is no escaping this disturbing thought except by a kind of double-dealing. A man who lies and makes excuses for himself by saying "Not everybody does that," is someone with an uneasy conscience, because the act of lying implies that a universal value is conferred upon the lie.

Anguish is evident even when it conceals itself. This is the anguish that Kierkegaard called the anguish of Abraham. You know the story: an angel has ordered Abraham to sacrifice his son; if it really were an angel who has come and said, "You are Abraham, you shall sacrifice your son," everything would be all right. But everyone might first wonder, "Is it really an angel, and am I really Abraham? What proof do I have?"

There was a madwoman who had hallucinations; someone used to speak to her on the telephone and give her orders. Her doctor asked her, "Who is it who talks to you?" She answered, "He says it's God." What proof did she really have that it was God? If an angel comes to me, what proof is there that it's an angel? And if I hear voices, what proof is there that they come from heaven and not from hell, or from the subconscious, or a pathological condition? What proves that they are addressed to me? What proof is there that I have been appointed to impose my choice and my conception of man on humanity? I'll never find any proof or sign to convince me of that. If a voice addresses me, it is always for me to decide that this is the angel's voice; if I consider that such an act is a good one, it is I who will choose to say that it is good rather than bad.

Now, I'm not being singled out as an Abraham, and yet at every moment I'm obliged to perform exemplary acts. For every man, everything happens as if all mankind had its eyes fixed on him and were guiding itself by what he does. And every man ought to say to himself, "Am I really the kind of man who has the right to act in such a way that humanity might guide itself by my actions?" And if he does not say that to himself, he is masking his anguish.

There is no question here of the kind of anguish which would lead to quietism, to inaction. It is a matter of a simple sort of anguish that anybody who has had responsibilities is familiar with. For example, when a military officer takes the responsibility for an attack and sends a certain number of men to death, he chooses to do so, and in the main he alone makes the choice. Doubtless, orders come from above, but they are too broad; he interprets them, and on this interpretation depend the lives of ten or fourteen or twenty men. In making a decision he can not help having a certain anguish. All leaders know this anguish. That doesn't keep them from acting; on the contrary, it is the very condition of their action. For it implies that they envisage a number of possibilities, and when they choose one, they realize that it has value only because it is chosen. We shall see that this kind of anguish, which is the kind that existentialism describes, is explained, in addition, by a direct responsibility to the other men whom it involves. It is not a curtain separating us from action, but is part of action itself.

When we speak of forlornness, a term Heidegger was fond of, we mean only that God does not exist and that we have to face all the consequences of this. The existentialist is strongly opposed to a certain kind of secular ethics which would like to abolish God with the least possible expense. About 1880, some French teachers tried to set up a secular ethics which went something like this: God is a useless and costly hypothesis; we are discarding it; but, meanwhile, in order for there to be an ethics, a society, a civilization, it is essential that certain values be taken seriously and that they be considered as having an *a priori* existence. It must be obligatory, *a priori*, to be honest, not to lie, not to beat your wife, to have children, etc., etc. So we're going to try a little device which will make it possible to show that values exist all the same, inscribed in a heaven of ideas, though otherwise God does not exist. In other words—and this, I believe, is the tendency of everything called reformism in France—nothing will be changed if God does not exist. We shall find ourselves with the same norms of honesty, progress, and humanism, and we shall have made of God an outdated hypothesis which will peacefully die off by itself.

The existentialist, on the contrary, thinks it very distressing that God does not exist, because all possibility of finding values in a heaven of ideas disappears along with Him; there can no longer be an *a priori* Good, since there is no infinite and perfect consciousness to think it. Nowhere is it written that the Good exists, that we must be honest, that we must not lie; because the fact is we are on a plane where there are only men. Dostoievsky[3] said, "If God didn't exist, everything would be possible." That is the very starting point of existentialism. Indeed, everything is permissible if God does not exist, and as a result man is forlorn, because neither within him nor without does he find anything to cling to. He can't start making excuses for himself.

If existence really does precede essence, there is no explaining things away by reference to a fixed and given human nature. In other words, there is no determinism, man is free, man is freedom. On the other hand, if God does not exist, we find no values or commands to turn to which legitimize our conduct. So, in the bright realm of values, we have no excuse behind us, nor justification before us. We are alone, with no excuses.

That is the idea I shall try to convey when I say that man is condemned to be free. Condemned, because he did not create himself, yet, in other respects is free; because, once thrown into the world, he is responsible for everything he does. The existentialist does not believe in the power of passion.

He will never agree that a sweeping passion is a ravaging torrent which fatally leads a man to certain acts and is therefore an excuse. He thinks that man is responsible for his passion.

The existentialist does not think that man is going to help himself by finding in the world some omen by which to orient himself. Because he thinks that man will interpret the omen to suit himself. Therefore, he thinks that man, with no support and no aid, is condemned every moment to invent man. * * *

To give you an example which will enable you to understand forlornness better, I shall cite the case of one of my students who came to see me under the following circumstances: his father was on bad terms with his mother, and, moreover, was inclined to be a collaborationist[4]; his older brother had been killed in the German offensive of 1940, and the young man, with somewhat immature but generous feelings, wanted to avenge him. His mother lived alone with him, very much upset by the half-treason of her husband and the death of her older son; the boy was her only consolation.

The boy was faced with the choice of leaving for England and joining the Free French Forces—that is, leaving his mother behind—or remaining with his mother and helping her to carry on. He was fully aware that the woman lived only for him and that his going-off—and perhaps his death—would plunge her into despair. He was also aware that every act that he did for his mother's sake was a sure thing, in the sense that it was helping her to carry on, whereas every effort he made toward going off and fighting was an uncertain move which might run aground and prove completely useless; for example, on his way to England he might, while passing through Spain, be detained indefinitely in a Spanish camp; he might reach England or Algiers and be stuck in an office at a desk job. As a result,

---

[3]Fyodor Dostoyevsky (the more common English spelling) was a 19th-century Russian novelist.

[4]A "collaborationist" was a resident of a country occupied by Germany in World War II who cooperated with the invaders. Germany conquered France, where Sartre lived, in 1940. Sartre was imprisoned by the Germans for a year, then freed. Upon his release, Sartre became active in the French Resistance, at great personal risk.

he was faced with two very different kinds of action: one, concrete, immediate, but concerning only one individual; the other concerned an incomparably vaster group, a national collectivity, but for that very reason was dubious, and might be interrupted en route. And, at the same time, he was wavering between two kinds of ethics. On the one hand, an ethics of sympathy, of personal devotion; on the other, a broader ethics, but one whose efficacy was more dubious. He had to choose between the two.

Who could help him choose? Christian doctrine? No. Christian doctrine says, "Be charitable, love your neighbor, take the more rugged path, etc., etc." But which is the more rugged path? Whom should he love as a brother? The fighting man or his mother? Which does the greater good, the vague act of fighting in a group, or the concrete one of helping a particular human being to go on living? Who can decide *a priori*? Nobody. No book of ethics can tell him. The Kantian ethics says, "Never treat any person as a means, but as an end." Very well, if I stay with mother, I'll treat her as an end and not as a means; but by virtue of this very fact, I'm running the risk of treating the people around me who are fighting, as means; and, conversely, if I go to join those who are fighting, I'll be treating them as an end, and, by doing that, I run the risk of treating my mother as a means.

If values are vague, and if they are always too broad for the concrete and specific case that we are considering, the only thing left for us is to trust our instincts. That's what this young man tried to do; and when I saw him, he said, "In the end, feeling is what counts. I ought to choose whichever pushes me in one direction. If I feel that I love my mother enough to sacrifice everything else for her—my desire for vengeance, for action, for adventure—then I'll stay with her. If, on the contrary, I feel that my love for my mother isn't enough, I'll leave."

But how is the value of a feeling determined? What gives his feeling for his mother value? Precisely the fact that he remained with her. I may say that I like so-and-so well enough to sacrifice a certain amount of money for him, but I may say so only if I've done it. I may say "I love my mother well enough to remain with her" if I have remained with her. The only way to determine the value of this affection is, precisely, to perform an act which confirms and defines it. But, since I require this affection to justify my act, I find myself caught in a vicious circle.

On the other hand, a mock feeling and a true feeling are almost indistinguishable; to decide that I love my mother and will remain with her, or to remain with her by putting on an act, amount somewhat to the same thing. In other words, the feeling is formed by the acts one performs; so, I can not refer to it in order to act upon it. Which means that I can neither seek within myself the true condition which will impel me to act, nor apply to a system of ethics for concepts which will permit me to act. You will say, "At least, he did go to a teacher for advice." But if you seek advice from a priest, for example, you have chosen this priest; you already knew, more or less, just about what advice he was going to give you. In other words, choosing your adviser is involving yourself. The proof of this is that if you are a Christian, you will say, "Consult a priest." But some priests are collaborating, some are just marking time, some are resisting. Which to choose? If the young man chooses a priest who is resisting or collaborating, he has already decided on the kind of advice he's going to get. Therefore, in coming to see me he knew the answer I was going to give him, and I had only one answer to give: "You're free, choose, that is, invent." No general ethics can show you what is to be done; there are no omens in the world. The Catholics will reply, "But there are." Granted—but, in any case, I myself choose the meaning they have.

When I was a prisoner,[5] I knew a rather remarkable young man who was a Jesuit. He had entered the Jesuit order in the following way: he had had a number of very bad breaks; in childhood, his father died, leaving him in poverty, and he was a scholarship student at a religious institution where he was constantly made to feel that he was being kept out of charity; then, he failed to get any of the

---

[5]That is, a prisoner of the Germans in 1940–1941.

honors and distinctions that children like; later on, at about eighteen, he bungled a love affair; finally, at twenty-two, he failed in military training, a childish enough matter, but it was the last straw.

This young fellow might well have felt that he had botched everything. It was a sign of something, but of what? He might have taken refuge in bitterness or despair. But he very wisely looked upon all this as a sign that he was not made for secular triumphs, and that only the triumphs of religion, holiness, and faith were open to him. He saw the hand of God in all this, and so he entered the order. Who can help seeing that he alone decided what the sign meant?

Some other interpretation might have been drawn from this series of setbacks; for example, that he might have done better to turn carpenter or revolutionist. Therefore, he is fully responsible for the interpretation. Forlornness implies that we ourselves choose our being. Forlornness and anguish go together.

As for despair, the term has a very simple meaning. It means that we shall confine ourselves to reckoning only with what depends upon our will, or on the ensemble of probabilities which make our action possible. When we want something, we always have to reckon with probabilities. I may be counting on the arrival of a friend. The friend is coming by rail or street-car; this supposes that the train will arrive on schedule, or that the street-car will not jump the track. I am left in the realm of possibility; but possibilities are to be reckoned with only to the point where my action comports with the ensemble of these possibilities, and no further. The moment the possibilities I am considering are not rigorously involved by my action, I ought to disengage myself from them, because no God, no scheme, can adapt the world and its possibilities to my will. When Descartes said, "Conquer yourself rather than the world," he meant essentially the same thing.

* * *

Things will be as man will have decided they are to be. Does that mean that I should abandon myself to quietism? No. First, I should involve myself; then, act on the old saw "Nothing ventured,

nothing gained." Nor does it mean that I shouldn't belong to a party, but rather that I shall have no illusions and shall do what I can. For example, suppose I ask myself, "Will socialization, as such, ever come about?" I know nothing about it. All I know is that I'm going to do everything in my power to bring it about. Beyond that, I can't count on anything. Quietism is the attitude of people who say, "Let others do what I can't do." The doctrine I am presenting is the very opposite of quietism, since it declares, "There is no reality except in action." Moreover, it goes further, since it adds, "Man is nothing else than his plan; he exists only to the extent that he fulfills himself; he is therefore nothing else than the ensemble of his acts, nothing else than his life."

According to this, we can understand why our doctrine horrifies certain people. Because often the only way they can bear their wretchedness is to think, "Circumstances have been against me. What I've been and done doesn't show my true worth. To be sure, I've had no great love, no great friendship, but that's because I haven't met a man or woman who was worthy. The books I've written haven't been very good because I haven't had the proper leisure. I haven't had children to devote myself to because I didn't find a man with whom I could have spent my life. So there remains within me, unused and quite viable, a host of propensities, inclinations, possibilities, that one wouldn't guess from the mere series of things I've done."

Now, for the existentialist there is really no love other than one which manifests itself in a person's being in love. There is no genius other than one which is expressed in works of art; the genius of Proust is the sum of Proust's works; the genius of Racine is his series of tragedies. Outside of that, there is nothing. Why say that Racine could have written another tragedy, when he didn't write it? A man is involved in life, leaves his impress on it, and outside of that there is nothing. To be sure, this may seem a harsh thought to someone whose life hasn't been a success. But, on the other hand, it prompts people to understand that reality alone is what counts, that dreams, expectations, and hopes warrant no more than to define a man as a disappointed dream, as miscarried hopes, as vain expectations. In other words, to define him negatively and not positively. However, when we say, "You are nothing else than your life," that does not imply that the artist will be judged solely on the basis of his works of art; a thousand other things will contribute toward summing him up. What we mean is that a man is nothing else than a series of undertakings, that he is the sum, the organization, the ensemble of the relationships which make up these undertakings.

When all is said and done, what we are accused of, at bottom, is not our pessimism, but an optimistic toughness. If people throw up to us our works of fiction[6] in which we write about people who are soft, weak, cowardly, and sometimes even downright bad, it's not because these people are soft, weak, cowardly, or bad; because if we were to say that they are that way because of heredity, the workings of environment, society, because of biological or psychological determinism, people would be reassured. They would say, "Well, that's what we're like, no one can do anything about it." But when the existentialist writes about a coward, he says that this coward is responsible for his cowardice. He's not like that because he has a cowardly heart or lung or brain; he's not like that on account of his physiological make-up; but he's like that because he has made himself a coward by his acts. There's no such thing as a cowardly constitution; there are nervous constitutions; there is poor blood, as the common people say, or there are strong constitutions. But the man whose blood is poor is not a coward on that account, for what makes cowardice is the act of renouncing or yielding. A constitution is not an act; the coward is defined on the basis of the acts he performs. People feel, in a vague sort of way, that this coward we're talking about is guilty of being a coward, and the thought frightens them. What people would like is that a coward or a hero be born that way.

*　*　*

[Existentialism] is the only [theory] which gives man dignity, the only one which does not reduce him to an object. The effect of all materialism is to treat every man, including the one philosophizing, as an object, that is, as an ensemble of determined reactions in no way distinguished from the ensemble of qualities and phenomena which constitute a table or a chair or a stone. We definitely wish to establish the human realm as an ensemble of values distinct from the material realm. But the subjectivity that we have thus arrived at, and which we have claimed to be truth, is not a strictly individual subjectivity, for we have demonstrated that one discovers in the *cogito*[7] not only himself, but others as well.

*　*　*

If it is impossible to find in every man some universal essence which would be human nature, yet there does exist a universal human condition. It's not by chance that today's thinkers speak more readily of man's condition than of his nature. By condition they mean, more or less definitely, the *a priori* limits which outline man's fundamental situation in the universe. Historical situations vary; a man may be born a slave in a pagan society or a feudal lord or a proletarian. What does not vary is the necessity for him to exist in the world, to be at work there, to be there in the midst of other people, and to be mortal there. The limits are neither subjective nor objective, or, rather, they have an objective and a subjective side. Objective because they are to be found everywhere and are recognizable everywhere; subjective because they are *lived* and are nothing if man does not live them, that is, freely determine his existence with reference to them. And though the configurations may differ, at least none of them are completely strange to me, because they all appear as attempts either to pass beyond these limits or recede from them or deny them or adapt to them. Consequently, every configuration, however individual it may be, has a universal value.

---

[6]Sartre wrote novels and plays about the human condition, including the novel *Nausea* (published in 1938) and the play *No Exit* (1944).

[7]The reference here is to *cogito ergo sum*, "I think, therefore I am." This is the famous existentialist pronouncement by the philosopher Descartes.

* * *

* * * One may choose anything if it is on the grounds of free involvement.

* * *

* * * Fundamentally [humanism means] this: man is constantly outside of himself; in projecting himself, in losing himself outside of himself, he makes for man's existing; and, on the other hand, it is by pursuing transcendent goals that he is able to exist; man, being this state of passing-beyond, and seizing upon things only as they bear upon this passing-beyond, is at the heart, at the center of this passing-beyond. There is no universe other than a human universe, the universe of human subjectivity. This connection between transcendency, as a constituent element of man—not in the sense that God is transcendent, but in the sense of passing beyond—and subjectivity, in the sense that man is not closed in on himself but is always present in a human universe, is what we call existentialist humanism. Humanism, because we remind man that there is no lawmaker other than himself, and that in his forlornness he will decide by himself; because we point out that man will fulfill himself as man, not in turning toward himself, but in seeking outside of himself a goal which is just this liberation, just this particular fulfillment.

* * *

A Theory of Human Motivation

Abraham H. Maslow

Maslow's best-known contribution to psychology is his proposal that human motivation is organized by a hierarchy of needs. Lower, physiological and safety needs must be satisfied before higher needs can emerge. These include the need for esteem, the need for self-actualization, the need to know and understand, and aesthetic needs. None of these latter needs are directly tied to survival; they become potent only after the survival needs are taken care of.

Maslow's theory, described in the following selection, is humanistic in two ways. First, he explicitly states that the study of human motivation does not need to be based on findings from research with animals. "It is no more necessary to study animals before one can study man than it is to study mathematics before one can study geology or psychology or biology." Second and more important, Maslow's higher needs are uniquely human. The needs to experience beauty, to understand the world, and to fulfill one's potential all stem from the quest for authentic existence at the core of existential philosophy and humanistic psychology.

Maslow's theory leads him to write a couple of prescriptions for human development. First, he observes that a child satisfied in basic needs early in life becomes relatively tolerant of deprivation in later life, and better able to focus on higher goals. Therefore, children should be raised to feel satisfied and safe. Second, "a man who is thwarted in any of his basic needs may fairly be envisaged as a sick man." Maslow concludes that a society that thwarts the basic needs of individuals is therefore itself sick. On the other hand, "the good or healthy society would then be defined as one that permitted man's highest purposes to emerge by satisfying all his basic needs."

From *Motivation and Personality*, 3d ed., by A. H. Maslow, revised by R. Frager, J. Fadiman, C. McReynolds, and R. Cox (New York: Harper & Row, 1954), pp. 80–106.

* * *

The Basic Needs

THE PHYSIOLOGICAL NEEDS The needs that are usually taken as the starting point for motivation theory are the so-called physiological drives. Two recent lines of research make it necessary to revise our customary notions about these needs: first, the development of the concept of homeostasis, and second, the finding that appetites (preferential choices among foods) are a fairly efficient indication of actual needs or lacks in the body.

Homeostasis refers to the body's automatic efforts to maintain a constant, normal state of the blood stream. * * *

* * * If the body lacks some chemical, the individual will tend (in an imperfect way) to develop a specific appetite or partial hunger for that food element.

Thus it seems impossible as well as useless to make any list of fundamental physiological needs, for they can come to almost any number one might wish, depending on the degree of specificity of description. We cannot identify all physiological needs as homeostatic. That sexual desire, sleepiness, sheer activity, and maternal behavior in animals are homeostatic has not yet been demonstrated. Furthermore, this list would not include the various sensory pleasures (tastes, smells, tickling, stroking), which are probably physiological and which may become the goals of motivated behavior.

These physiological drives or needs are to be considered unusual rather than typical because they are isolable, and because they are localizable somatically. That is to say, they are relatively independent of each other, of other motivations, and of the organism as a whole, and second, in many cases, it is possible to demonstrate a localized, underlying somatic base for the drive. This is true less generally than has been thought (exceptions are fatigue, sleepiness, maternal responses) but it is still true in the classic instances of hunger, sex, and thirst.

It should be pointed out again that any of the physiological needs and the consummatory behavior involved with them serve as channels for all sorts of other needs as well. That is to say, the person who thinks he is hungry may actually be seeking more for comfort, or dependence, than for vitamins or proteins. Conversely, it is possible to satisfy the hunger need in part by other activities such as drinking water or smoking cigarettes. In other words, relatively isolable as these physiological needs are, they are not completely so.

Undoubtedly these physiological needs are the most prepotent of all needs. What this means specifically is that in the human being who is missing everything in life in an extreme fashion, it is most likely that the major motivation would be the physiological needs rather than any others. A person who is lacking food, safety, love, and esteem would most probably hunger for food more strongly than for anything else.

If all the needs are unsatisfied, and the organism is then dominated by the physiological needs, all other needs may become simply nonexistent or be pushed into the background. It is then fair to characterize the whole organism by saying simply that it is hungry, for consciousness is almost completely preëmpted by hunger. All capacities are put into the service of hunger-satisfaction, and the organization of these capacities is almost entirely determined by the one purpose of satisfying hunger. The receptors and effectors, the intelligence, memory, habits, all may now be defined simply as hunger-gratifying tools. Capacities that are not useful for this purpose lie dormant, or are pushed into the background. The urge to write poetry, the desire to acquire an automobile, the interest in American history, the desire for a new pair of shoes are, in the extreme case, forgotten or become of secondary importance. For the man who is extremely and dangerously hungry, no other interests exist but food. He dreams food, he remembers food, he thinks about food, he emotes only about food, he perceives only food, and he wants only food. The more subtle determinants that ordinarily fuse with the physiological drives in organizing even feeding, drinking, or sexual behavior, may now be so completely overwhelmed as to allow us to speak at this time (but *only* at this time) of pure hunger drive and behavior, with the one unqualified aim of relief.

Another peculiar characteristic of the human organism when it is dominated by a certain need is that the whole philosophy of the future tends also to change. For our chronically and extremely hungry man, Utopia can be defined simply as a place where there is plenty of food. He tends to think that, if only he is guaranteed food for the rest of his life, he will be perfectly happy and will never want anything more. Life itself tends to be defined in terms of eating. Anything else will be defined as unimportant. Freedom, love, community feeling, respect, philosophy, may all be waved aside as fripperies that are useless, since they fail to fill the stomach. Such a man may fairly be said to live by bread alone.

It cannot possibly be denied that such things are true, but their *generality* can be denied. Emergency conditions are, almost by definition, rare in the normally functioning peaceful society. That this truism can be forgotten is attributable mainly to two reasons. First, rats have few motivations other than physiological ones, and since so much of the research upon motivation has been made with these animals, it is easy to carry the rat picture over to the human being. Second, it is too often not realized that culture itself is an adaptive tool, one of whose main functions is to make the physiological emergencies come less and less often. In most of the known societies, chronic extreme hunger of the emergency type is rare, rather than common. In any case, this is still true in the United States. The average American citizen is experiencing appetite rather than hunger when he says, "I am hungry." He is apt to experience sheer life-and-death hunger only by accident and then only a few times through his entire life.

Obviously a good way to obscure the higher motivations, and to get a lopsided view of human capacities and human nature, is to make the organism extremely and chronically hungry or thirsty. Anyone who attempts to make an emergency picture into a typical one, and who will measure all of man's goals and desires by his behavior during extreme physiological deprivation is certainly being blind to many things. It is quite true that man lives by bread alone—when there is no bread. But what happens to man's desires when there *is* plenty of bread and when his belly is chronically filled?

At once other (*and higher*) *needs emerge* and these, rather than physiological hungers, dominate the organism. And when these in turn are satisfied, again new (and still higher) needs emerge, and so on. This is what we mean by saying that the basic human needs are organized into a hierarchy of relative prepotency.

One main implication of this phrasing is that gratification becomes as important a concept as deprivation in motivation theory, for it releases the organism from the domination of a relatively more physiological need, permitting thereby the emergence of other more social goals. The physiological needs, along with their partial goals, when chronically gratified cease to exist as active determinants or organizers of behavior. They now exist only in a potential fashion in the sense that they may emerge again to dominate the organism if they are thwarted. But a want that is satisfied is no longer a want. The organism is dominated and its behavior organized only by unsatisfied needs. If hunger is satisfied, it becomes unimportant in the current dynamics of the individual.

This statement is somewhat qualified by a hypothesis to be discussed more fully later, namely, that it is precisely those individuals in whom a certain need has always been satisfied who are best equipped to tolerate deprivation of that need in the future, and that furthermore, those who have been deprived in the past will react differently to current satisfactions than the one who has never been deprived.

THE SAFETY NEEDS If the physiological needs are relatively well gratified, there then emerges a new set of needs, which we may categorize roughly as the safety needs. All that has been said of the physiological needs is equally true, although in less degree, of these desires. The organism may equally well be wholly dominated by them. They may serve as the almost exclusive organizers of behavior, recruiting all the capacities of the organism in their service, and we may then fairly describe the whole organism as a safety-seeking mechanism. Again we may say of the receptors, the effectors, of the intellect, and of the other capacities that they are primarily safety-seeking tools. Again, as in the hungry man, we find that the dominating goal is a strong determinant not only of his current world outlook and philosophy but also of his philosophy of the future. Practically everything looks less important than safety (even sometimes the physiological needs, which being satisfied are now underestimated). A man in this state, if it is extreme enough and chronic enough, may be characterized as living almost for safety alone.

Although in this chapter we are interested primarily in the needs of the adult, we can approach an understanding of his safety needs perhaps more efficiently by observation of infants and children, in whom these needs are much more simple and obvious. One reason for the clearer appearance of the threat or danger reaction in infants is that they do not inhibit this reaction at all, whereas adults in our society have been taught to inhibit it at all costs. Thus even when adults do feel their safety to be threatened, we may not be able to see this on the surface. Infants will react in a total fashion and as if they were endangered, if they are disturbed or dropped suddenly, startled by loud noises, flashing light, or other unusual sensory stimulation, by rough handling, by general loss of support in the mother's arms, or by inadequate support.

Another indication of the child's need for safety is his preference for some kind of undisrupted routine or rhythm. He seems to want a predictable, orderly world. For instance, injustice, unfairness, or inconsistency in the parents seems to make a child feel anxious and unsafe. This attitude may be not so much because of the injustice *per se* or any particular pains involved, but rather because this treatment threatens to make the world look unreliable, or unsafe, or unpredictable. Young children seem to thrive better under a system that has at least a skeletal outline of rigidity, in which there is a schedule of a kind, some sort of routine, something that can be counted upon, not only for the present but also far into the future. Child psychol-

ogists, teachers, and psychotherapists have found that permissiveness within limits, rather than unrestricted permissiveness is preferred as well as *needed* by children. Perhaps one could express this more accurately by saying that the child needs an organized world rather than an unorganized or unstructured one.

The central role of the parents and the normal family setup are indisputable. Quarreling, physical assault, separation, divorce, or death within the family may be particularly terrifying. Also parental outbursts of rage or threats of punishment directed to the child, calling him names, speaking to him harshly, handling him roughly, or actual physical punishment sometimes elicit such total panic and terror that we must assume more is involved than the physical pain alone. While it is true that in some children this terror may represent also a fear of loss of parental love, it can also occur in completely rejected children, who seem to cling to the hating parents more for sheer safety and protection than because of hope of love.

Confronting the average child with new, unfamiliar, strange, unmanageable stimuli or situations will too frequently elicit the danger or terror reaction, as for example, getting lost or even being separated from the parents for a short time, being confronted with new faces, new situations, or new tasks, the sight of strange, unfamiliar, or uncontrollable objects, illness, or death. Particularly at such times, the child's frantic clinging to his parents is eloquent testimony to their role as protectors (quite apart from their roles as food givers and love givers).

From these and similar observations, we may generalize and say that the average child in our society generally prefers a safe, orderly, predictable, organized world, which he can count on, and in which unexpected, unmanageable, or other dangerous things do not happen, and in which, in any case, he has all-powerful parents who protect and shield him from harm.

* * *

The healthy, normal, fortunate adult in our culture is largely satisfied in his safety needs. The peaceful, smoothly running, good society ordinarily makes its members feel safe enough from wild animals, extremes of temperature, criminal assault, murder, tyranny, etc. Therefore, in a very real sense, he no longer has any safety needs as active motivators. Just as a sated man no longer feels hungry, a safe man no longer feels endangered. If we wish to see these needs directly and clearly we must turn to neurotic or near-neurotic individuals, and to the economic and social underdogs. In between these extremes, we can perceive the expressions of safety needs only in such phenomena as, for instance, the common preference for a job with tenure and protection the desire for a savings account and for insurance of various kinds (medical, dental, unemployment, disability, old age).

Other broader aspects of the attempt to seek safety and stability in the world are seen in the very common preference for familiar rather than unfamiliar things, or for the known rather than the unknown. The tendency to have some religion or world philosophy that organizes the universe and the men in it into some sort of satisfactorily coherent, meaningful whole is also in part motivated by safety seeking. Here too we may list science and philosophy in general as partially motivated by the safety needs (we shall see later that there are also other motivations to scientific, philosophical, or religious endeavor).

Otherwise the need for safety is seen as an active and dominant mobilizer of the organism's resources only in emergencies, e.g., war, disease, natural catastrophes, crime waves, societal disorganization, neurosis, brain injury, chronically bad situations.

Some neurotic adults in our society are, in many ways, like the unsafe child in their desire for safety, although in the former it takes on a somewhat special appearance. Their reaction is often to unknown, psychological dangers in a world that is perceived to be hostile, overwhelming, and threatening. Such a person behaves as if a great catastrophe were almost always impending, i.e., he is usually responding as if to an emergency. His safety needs often find specific expression in a search for a protector, or a stronger person on whom he may depend, perhaps a fuehrer.

* * *

The neurosis in which the search for safety takes its clearest form is in the compulsive obsessive neurosis. Compulsive-obsessives try frantically to order and stabilize the world so that no unmanageable, unexpected, or unfamiliar dangers will ever appear. They hedge themselves about with all sorts of ceremonials, rules, and formulas so that every possible contingency may be provided for and so that no new contingencies may appear. They are much like the brain-injured cases, described by Goldstein,[1] who manage to maintain their equilibrium by avoiding everything unfamiliar and strange and by ordering their restricted world in such a neat, disciplined, orderly fashion that everything in the world can be counted on. They try to arrange the world so that anything unexpected (dangers) cannot possibly occur. If, through no fault of their own, something unexpected does occur, they go into a panic reaction as if this unexpected occurrence constituted a grave danger. What we can see only as a none-too-strong preference in the healthy person, e.g., preference for the familiar, becomes a life-and-death necessity in abnormal cases. The healthy taste for the novel and unknown is missing or at a minimum in the average neurotic.

THE BELONGINGNESS AND LOVE NEEDS If both the physiological and the safety needs are fairly well gratified, there will emerge the love and affection and belongingness needs, and the whole cycle already described will repeat itself with this new center. Now the person will feel keenly, as never before, the absence of friends, or a sweetheart, or a wife, or children. He will hunger for affectionate relations with people in general, namely, for a place in his group, and he will strive with great intensity to achieve this goal. He will want to attain such a place more than anything else in the world and may even forget that once, when he was hungry, he sneered at love as unreal or unnecessary or unimportant.

---

[1] Kurt Goldstein was a neurologist and psychiatrist who wrote on clinical psychology, human nature, and language.

In our society the thwarting of these needs is the most commonly found core in cases of maladjustment and more severe psychopathology. Love and affection, as well as their possible expression in sexuality, are generally looked upon with ambivalence and are customarily hedged about with many restrictions and inhibitions. Practically all theorists of psychopathology have stressed thwarting of the love needs as basic in the picture of maladjustment. * * *

One thing that must be stressed at this point is that love is not synonymous with sex. Sex may be studied as a purely physiological need. Ordinarily sexual behavior is multidetermined, that is to say, determined not only by sexual but also by other needs, chief among which are the love and affection needs. Also not to be overlooked is the fact that the love needs involve both giving *and* receiving love.

THE ESTEEM NEEDS   All people in our society (with a few pathological exceptions) have a need or desire for a stable, firmly based, usually high evaluation of themselves, for self-respect, or self-esteem, and for the esteem of others. These needs may therefore be classified into two subsidiary sets. These are, first, the desire for strength, for achievement, for adequacy, for mastery and competence, for confidence in the face of the world, and for independence and freedom.[2] Second, we have what we may call the desire for reputation or prestige (defining it as respect or esteem from other people), status, dominance, recognition, attention, importance, or appreciation. These needs have been relatively stressed by Alfred Adler and his followers, and have been relatively neglected by Freud. More and more today, however, there is appearing widespread appreciation of their central importance, among psychoanalysts as well as among clinical psychologists.

Satisfaction of the self-esteem need leads to feelings of self-confidence, worth, strength, capability, and adequacy, of being useful and necessary in the world. But thwarting of these needs produces feelings of inferiority, of weakness, and of helplessness. These feelings in turn give rise to either basic discouragement or else compensatory or neurotic trends. * * *

* * * We have been learning more and more of the dangers of basing self-esteem on the opinions of others rather than on real capacity, competence, and adequacy to the task. The most stable and therefore most healthy self-esteem is based on *deserved* respect from others rather than on external fame or celebrity and unwarranted adulation.

THE NEED FOR SELF-ACTUALIZATION   Even if all these needs are satisfied, we may still often (if not always) expect that a new discontent and restlessness will soon develop, unless the individual is doing what he is fitted for. A musician must make music, an artist must paint, a poet must write, if he is to be ultimately at peace with himself. What a man *can* be, he *must* be. This need we may call self-actualization.

* * * [This term] refers to a man's desire for self-fulfillment, namely, to the tendency for him to become actualized in what he is potentially. This tendency might be phrased as the desire to become more and more what one is, to become everything that one is capable of becoming.

The specific form that these needs will take will of course vary greatly from person to person. In one individual it may take the form of the desire to be an ideal mother, in another it may be expressed athletically, and in still another it may be expressed in painting pictures or in inventions.

The clear emergence of these needs usually rests upon prior satisfaction of the physiological, safety, love, and esteem needs.

* * *

[2]Whether or not this particular desire is universal we do not know. The crucial question, especially important today, is, Will men who are enslaved and dominated inevitably feel dissatisfied and rebellious? We may assume on the basis of commonly known clinical data that a man who has known true freedom (not paid for by giving up safety and security but rather built on the basis of adequate safety and security) will not willingly or easily allow his freedom to be taken away from him. But we do not know that this is true for the person born into slavery.—Author

THE DESIRES TO KNOW AND TO UNDERSTAND

The main reason we know little about the cognitive impulses, their dynamics, or their pathology, is that they are not important in the clinic, and certainly not in the clinic dominated by the medical-therapeutic tradition, i.e., getting rid of disease. The florid, exciting, and mysterious symptoms found in the classical neuroses are lacking here. Cognitive psychopathology is pale, subtle, and easily overlooked, or defined as normal. It does not cry for help. As a consequence we find nothing on the subject in the writings of the great inventors of psychotherapy and psychodynamics, Freud, Adler, Jung, etc. Nor has anyone yet made any systematic attempts at constructing cognitive psychotherapies.

* * *

* * * There are some reasonable grounds for postulating positive *per se* impulses to satisfy curiosity, to know, to explain, and to understand.

1. Something like human curiosity can easily be observed in the higher animals. The monkey will pick things apart, will poke his finger into holes, will explore in all sorts of situations where it is improbable that hunger, fear, sex, comfort status, etc., are involved. Harlow's experiments (1950) have amply demonstrated this in an acceptably experimental way.

2. The history of mankind supplies us with a satisfactory number of instances in which man looked for facts and created explanations in the face of the greatest danger, even to life itself. There have been innumerable humbler Galileos.

3. Studies of psychologically healthy people indicate that they are, as a defining characteristic, attracted to the mysterious, to the unknown, to the chaotic, unorganized, and unexplained. This seems to be a *per se* attractiveness; these areas are in themselves and of their own right interesting. The contrasting reaction to the well known is one of boredom.

4. It may be found valid to extrapolate from the psychopathological. The compulsive-obsessive neurotic (and neurotic in general), Goldstein's brain-injured soldiers, Maier's fixated rats (1939), all show (at the clinical level of observation) a compulsive and anxious clinging to the familiar and a dread of the unfamiliar, the anarchic, the unexpected, the undomesticated. On the other hand, there are some phenomena that may turn out to nullify this possibility. Among these are forced unconventionality, a chronic rebellion against any authority whatsoever, Bohemianism, the desire to shock and to startle, all of which may be found in certain neurotic individuals, as well as in those in the process of deacculturation.

* * *

5. Probably there are true psychopathological effects when the cognitive needs are frustrated. For the moment, though, we have no really sound data available. The following clinical impressions are pertinent.

6. I have seen a few cases in which it seemed clear to me that the pathology (boredom, loss of zest in life, self-dislike, general depression of the bodily functions, steady deterioration of the intellectual life, of tastes, etc.) were produced in intelligent people leading stupid lives in stupid jobs. I have at least one case in which the appropriate cognitive therapy (resuming part-time studies, getting a position that was more intellectually demanding, insight) removed the symptoms.

I have seen *many* women, intelligent, prosperous, and unoccupied, slowly develop these same symptoms of intellectual inanition. Those who followed my recommendation to immerse themselves in something worthy of them showed improvement or cure often enough to impress me with the reality of the cognitive needs. In those countries in which access to the news, to information, and to the facts [was] cut off, and in those where official theories were profoundly contradicted by obvious facts, at least some people responded with generalized cynicism, mistrust of *all* values, suspicion even of the obvious, a profound disruption of ordinary interpersonal relationships, hopelessness, loss of morale, etc. Others seem to have responded in the more passive direction with dullness, submission, loss of capacity, coarctation, and loss of initiative.

7. The needs to know and to understand are seen in late infancy and childhood, perhaps even more strongly than in adulthood. Furthermore this

seems to be a spontaneous product of maturation rather than of learning, however defined. Children do not have to be taught to be curious. But they *may* be taught, as by institutionalization, *not* to be curious.

8. Finally, the gratification of the cognitive impulses is subjectively satisfying and yields end-experience. Though this aspect of insight and understanding has been neglected in favor of achieved results, learning, etc., it nevertheless remains true that insight is usually a bright, happy, emotional spot in any person's life, perhaps even a high spot in the life span.

The overcoming of obstacles, the occurrence of pathology upon thwarting, the widespread occurrence (cross-species, cross-cultural), the never-dying (though weak) insistent pressure, the need of gratification of this need as a prerequisite for the fullest development of human potentialities, the spontaneous appearance in the early history of the individual, all these point to a basic cognitive need.

This postulation, however, is not enough. Even after we know, we are impelled to know more and more minutely and microscopically on the one hand, and on the other, more and more extensively in the direction of a world philosophy, theology, etc. The facts that we acquire, if they are isolated or atomistic, inevitably get theorized about, and either analyzed or organized or both. This process has been phrased by some as the search for meaning. We shall then postulate a desire to understand, to systematize, to organize, to analyze, to look for relations and meanings, to construct a system of values.

Once these desires are accepted for discussion, we see that they too form themselves into a small hierarchy in which the desire to know is prepotent over the desire to understand. All the characteristics of a hierarchy of prepotency that we have described above seem to hold for this one as well.

We must guard ourselves against the too easy tendency to separate these desires from the basic needs we have discussed above, i.e., to make a sharp dichotomy between cognitive and conative needs. The desire to know and to understand are themselves conative, i.e., having a striving character, and are as much personality needs as the basic needs we have already discussed. Furthermore, as we have seen, the two hierarchies are interrelated rather than sharply separated; and as we shall see below, they are synergic rather than antagonistic.

THE AESTHETIC NEEDS   We know even less about these than about the others, and yet the testimony of history, of the humanities, and of aestheticians forbids us to bypass this uncomfortable (to the scientist) area. I have attempted to study this phenomenon on a clinical-personological basis with selected individuals, and have at least convinced myself that in *some* individuals there is a truly basic aesthetic need. They get sick (in special ways) from ugliness, and are cured by beautiful surroundings; they *crave* actively, and their cravings can be satisfied *only* by beauty. It is seen almost universally in healthy children. Some evidence of such an impulse is found in every culture and in every age as far back as the cavemen.

Much overlapping with conative and cognitive needs makes it impossible to separate them sharply. The needs for order, for symmetry, for closure, for completion of the act, for system, and for structure may be indiscriminately assigned to *either* cognitive, conative, or aesthetic, or even to neurotic needs. * * * What, for instance, does it mean when a man feels a strong conscious impulse to straighten the crookedly hung picture on the wall?

Further Characteristics of the Basic Needs

THE DEGREE OF FIXITY OF THE HIERARCHY OF BASIC NEEDS   We have spoken so far as if this hierarchy were a fixed order, but actually it is not nearly so rigid as we may have implied. It is true that most of the people with whom we have worked have seemed to have these basic needs in about the order that has been indicated. However, there have been a number of exceptions.

1. There are some people in whom, for instance, self-esteem seems to be more important than love. This most common reversal in the hierarchy is usually due to the development of the notion that the person who is most likely to be loved is a strong or powerful person, one who inspires respect or fear, and who is self-confident or aggressive. Therefore such people who lack love and seek it may try hard to put on a front of aggressive, confident behavior. But essentially they seek high self-esteem and its behavior expressions more as a means to an end than for its own sake; they seek self-assertion for the sake of love rather than for self-esteem itself.

2. There are other apparently innately creative people in whom the drive to creativeness seems to be more important than any other counterdeterminant. Their creativeness might appear not as self-actualization released by basic satisfaction, but in spite of lack of basic satisfaction.

3. In certain people the level of aspiration may be permanently deadened or lowered. That is to say, the less prepotent goals may simply be lost, and may disappear forever, so that the person who has experienced life at a very low level, e.g., chronic unemployment, may continue to be satisfied for the rest of his life if only he can get enough food.

4. The so-called psychopathic personality is another example of permanent loss of the love needs. These are people who, according to the best data available, have been starved for love in the earliest months of their lives and have simply lost forever the desire and the ability to give and to receive affection (as animals lose sucking or pecking reflexes that are not exercised soon enough after birth).

5. Another cause of reversal of the hierarchy is that when a need has been satisfied for a long time, this need may be underevaluated. People who have never experienced chronic hunger are apt to underestimate its effects and to look upon food as a rather unimportant thing. If they are dominated by a higher need, this higher need will seem to be the most important of all. It then becomes possible, and indeed does actually happen, that they may, for the sake of this higher need, put themselves into the position of being deprived in a more basic need. We may expect that after a longtime deprivation of the more basic need there will be a tendency to reevaluate both needs so that the more prepotent need will actually become consciously prepotent for the individual who may have given it up lightly. Thus a man who has given up his job rather than lose his self-respect, and who then starves for six months or so, may be willing to take his job back even at the price of losing his self-respect.

6. Another partial explanation of *apparent* reversals is seen in the fact that we have been talking about the hierarchy of prepotency in terms of consciously felt wants or desires rather than of behavior. Looking at behavior itself may give us the wrong impression. What we have claimed is that the person will *want* the more basic of two needs when deprived in both. There is no necessary implication here that he will act upon his desires. Let us stress again that there are many determinants of behavior other than the needs and desires.

7. Perhaps more important than all these exceptions are the ones that involve ideals, high social standards, high values, and the like. With such values people become martyrs; they will give up everything for the sake of a particular ideal, or value. These people may be understood, at least in part, by reference to one basic concept (or hypothesis), which may be called increased frustration-tolerance through early gratification. People who have been satisfied in their basic needs throughout their lives, particularly in their earlier years, seem to develop exceptional power to withstand present or future thwarting of these needs simply because they have strong, healthy character structure as a result of basic satisfaction. They are the strong people who can easily weather disagreement or opposition, who can swim against the stream of public opinion, and who can stand up for the truth at great personal cost. It is just the ones who have loved and been well loved, and who have had many deep friendships who can hold out against hatred, rejection, or persecution.

I say all this in spite of the fact that a certain amount of sheer habituation is also involved in any full discussion of frustration tolerance. For instance, it is likely that those persons who have been accustomed to relative starvation for a long time are partially enabled thereby to withstand food deprivation. What sort of balance must be made between these two tendencies, of habituation on the one hand, and of past satisfaction breeding present frustration tolerance on the other hand, remains to be worked out by further research. Meanwhile we may assume that both are operative, side by side, since they do not contradict each other. In respect to this phenomenon of increased frustration tolerance, it seems probable that the most important gratifications come in the first two years of life. That is to say, people who have been made secure and strong in the earliest years, tend to remain secure and strong thereafter in the face of whatever threatens.

DEGREES OF RELATIVE SATISFACTION   So far, our theoretical discussion may have given the impression that these five sets of needs are somehow in such terms as the following: If one need is satisfied, then another emerges. This statement might give the false impression that a need must be satisfied 100 percent before the next need emerges. In actual fact, most members of our society who are normal are partially satisfied in all their basic needs and partially unsatisfied in all their basic needs at the same time. A more realistic description of the hierarchy would be in terms of decreasing percentages of satisfaction as we go up the hierarchy of prepotency. For instance, if I may assign arbitrary figures for the sake of illustration, it is as if the average citizen is satisfied perhaps 85 percent in his physiological needs, 70 percent in his safety needs, 50 percent in his love needs, 40 percent in his self-esteem needs, and 10 percent in his self-actualization needs.

As for the concept of emergence of a new need after satisfaction of the prepotent need, this emergence is not a sudden, saltatory phenomenon, but rather a gradual emergence by slow degrees from nothingness. For instance, if prepotent need A is satisfied only 10 percent, then need B may not be visible at all. However, as this need A becomes sat-isfied 25 percent, need B may emerge 5 percent; as need A becomes satisfied 75 percent, need B may emerge 50 percent, and so on.

* * *

ANIMAL AND HUMAN CENTERING   This theory starts with the human being rather than any lower and presumably simpler animal. Too many of the findings that have been made in animals have been proved to be true for animals but not for the human being. There is no reason whatsoever why we should start with animals in order to study human motivation. The logic or rather illogic behind this general fallacy of pseudosimplicity has been exposed often enough by philosophers and logicians as well as by scientists in each of the various fields. It is no more necessary to study animals before one can study man than it is to study mathematics *before* one can study geology or psychology or biology.

* * *

THE ROLE OF GRATIFIED NEEDS   It has been pointed out above several times that our needs usually emerge only when more prepotent needs have been gratified. Thus gratification has an important role in motivation theory. Apart from this, however, needs cease to play an active determining or organizing role as soon as they are gratified.

What this means is that, e.g., a basically satisfied person no longer has the needs for esteem, love, safety, etc. The only sense in which he might be said to have them is in the almost metaphysical sense that a sated man has hunger, or a filled bottle has emptiness. If we are interested in what *actually* motivates us, and not in what has, will, or might motivate us, then a satisfied need is not a motivator. It must be considered for all practical purposes simply not to exist, to have disappeared. This point should be emphasized because it has been either overlooked or contradicted in every theory of motivation I know. The perfectly healthy, normal, fortunate man has no sex needs or hunger needs, or needs for safety, or for love, or for prestige, or self-esteem, except in stray moments of quickly passing threat. * * *

It is such considerations as these that suggest the bold postulation that a man who is thwarted in any of his basic needs may fairly be envisaged simply as a sick man. This is a fair parallel to our designation as sick of the man who lacks vitamins or minerals. Who will say that a lack of love is less important than a lack of vitamins? Since we know the pathogenic effects of love starvation, who is to say that we are invoking value questions in an unscientific or illegitimate way, any more than the physician does who diagnoses and treats pellagra or scurvy? If I were permitted this usage, I should then say simply that a healthy man is primarily motivated by his needs to develop and actualize his fullest potentialities and capacities. If a man has any other basic needs in any active, chronic sense, he is simply an unhealthy man. He is as surely sick as if he had suddenly developed a strong salt hunger or calcium hunger. If we were to use the word *sick* in this way, we should then also have to face squarely the relations of man to his society. One clear implication of our definition would be that (1) since a man is to be called sick who is basically thwarted, and (2) since such basic thwarting is made possible ultimately only by forces outside the individual, then (3) sickness in the individual must come ultimately from a sickness in the society. The good or healthy society would then be defined as one that permitted man's highest purposes to emerge by satisfying all his basic needs.

* * *

References

Harlow, H. F. (1950). Learning motivated by a manipulation drive. *Journal of Experimental Psychology, 40,* 228–234.

Maier, N. R. F. (1939). *Studies of abnormal behavior in the rat.* New York: Harper.

SOME OBSERVATIONS ON THE ORGANIZATION OF PERSONALITY

Carl R. Rogers

This selection is an article by perhaps the best known of the classic humanistic psychologists, Carl Rogers. One of the most famous and important parts of Rogers's theory is that a therapist needs to give his or her client "unconditional positive regard." This frees the client to say whatever is on his or her mind, and eventually helps the client to develop unconditional self-regard. Unconditional self-regard, in turn, allows the client to see himself or herself without defenses or distortions and thereby to become a fully functioning person.

In this article, Rogers argues that the nonjudgmental attitude of the therapist allows a complete and undistorted picture of the client's personality to emerge. He draws on some clinical experiences to illustrate his point, and—perhaps not surprisingly—finds that what his clients say in therapy tends to support his theory of personality dynamics and self-organization.

After you read this article, you may wish to think back to the earlier selections by Freud and his critics, and to note that the free-wheeling use of clinical anecdotes in support of one's theoretical position is not a practice limited to psychoanalysis. Just as Freud repeatedly found "confirmation" for his theoretical ideas in his clinical cases—and was roundly criticized for the shortcomings of such evidence later— so too Rogers was able to interpret what his clients said in the light of his own preferred theory. However, Rogers has yet to receive the kind of criticism for his method that Freud receives continually, and it is interesting to ponder just why this may be.

From *American Psychologist*, 2, 358–368, 1947.

In various fields of science rapid strides have been made when direct observation of significant processes has become possible. In medicine, when circumstances have permitted the physician to peer directly into the stomach of his patient, understanding of digestive processes has increased and the influence of emotional tension upon all aspects of that process has been more accurately observed and understood. In our work with nondirective therapy we often feel that we are having a psychological opportunity comparable to this medical experience—an opportunity to observe directly a number of the effective processes of personality. Quite aside from any question regarding nondirective therapy as therapy, here is a precious vein of observational material of unusual value for the study of personality.

Characteristics of the Observational Material

There are several ways in which the raw clinical data to which we have had access is unique in its value for understanding personality. The fact that these verbal expressions of inner dynamics are preserved by electrical recording makes possible a detailed analysis of a sort not heretofore possible. Recording has given us a microscope by which we may examine at leisure, and in minute detail, almost every aspect of what was, in its occurence, a fleeting moment impossible of accurate observation.

Another scientifically fortunate characteristic of this material is the fact that the verbal productions of the client are biased to a minimal degree by the therapist. Material from client-centered interviews probably comes closer to being a "pure" expression of attitudes than has yet been achieved through other means. One can read through a complete recorded case or listen to it, without finding more than a half-dozen instances in which the therapist's views on any point are evident. One would find it impossible to form an estimate as to the therapist's views about personality dynamics. One could not determine his diagnostic views, his standards of behavior, his social class. The one value or standard held by the therapist which would exhibit itself in his tone of voice, responses, and activity, is a deep respect for the personality and attitudes of the client as a separate person. It is difficult to see how this would bias the content of the interview, except to permit deeper expression than the client would ordinarily allow himself. This almost complete lack of any distorting attitude is felt, and sometimes expressed by the client. One woman says:

> "It's almost impersonal. I like you—of course I don't know why I should like you or why I shouldn't like you. It's a peculiar thing. I've never had that re-

lationship with anybody before and I've often thought about it. . . . A lot of times I walk out with a feeling of elation that you think highly of me, and of course at the same time I have the feeling that 'Gee, he must think I'm an awful jerk' or something like that. But it doesn't really—those feelings aren't so deep that I can form an opinion one way or the other about you."

Here it would seem that even though she would like to discover some type of evaluational attitude, she is unable to do so. Published studies and research as yet unpublished bear out this point that counselor responses which are in any way evaluational or distorting as to content are at a minimum, thus enhancing the worth of such interviews for personality study.

The counselor attitude of warmth and understanding, well described by Snyder (1946) and Rogers (1946), also helps to maximize the freedom of expression by the individual. The client experiences sufficient interest in him as a person, and sufficient acceptance, to enable him to talk openly, not only about surface attitudes, but increasingly about intimate attitudes and feelings hidden even from himself. Hence in these recorded interviews we have material of very considerable depth so far as personality dynamics is concerned, along with a freedom from distortion.

Finally the very nature of the interviews and the techniques by which they are handled give us a rare opportunity to see to some extent through the eyes of another person—to perceive the world as it appears to him, to achieve at least partially, the internal frame of reference of another person. We see his behavior through his eyes, and also the psychological meaning which it had for him. We see also changes in personality and behavior, and the meanings which those changes have for the individual. We are admitted freely into the backstage of the person's living where we can observe from within some of the dramas of internal change, which are often far more compelling and moving than the drama which is presented on the stage viewed by the public. Only a novelist or a poet could do justice to the deep struggles which we are permitted to observe from within the client's own world of reality.

This rare opportunity to observe so directly and so clearly the inner dynamics of personality is a learning experience of the deepest sort for the clinician. Most of clinical psychology and psychiatry involves judgements *about* the individual, judgements which must, of necessity, be based on some framework brought to the situation by the clinician. To try continually to see and think *with* the individual, as in client-centered therapy, is a mind-stretching experience in which learning goes on apace because the clinician brings to the interview no pre-determined yardstick by which to judge the material.

I wish in this paper to try to bring you some of the clinical observations which we have made as we have repeatedly peered through these psychological windows into personality, and to raise with you some of the questions about the organization of personality which these observations have forced upon us. I shall not attempt to present these observations in logical order, but rather in the order in which they impressed themselves upon our notice. What I shall offer is not a series of research findings, but only the first step in that process of gradual approximation which we call science, a description of some observed phenomena which appear to be significant, and some highly tentative explanations of these phenomena.

The Relation of the Organized Perceptual Field to Behavior

One simple observation, which is repeated over and over again in each successful therapeutic case, seems to have rather deep theoretical implications. It is that as changes occur in the perception of self and in the perception of reality, changes occur in behavior. In therapy, these perceptual changes are more often concerned with the self than with the external world. Hence we find in therapy that as the perception of self alters, behavior alters. Perhaps an illustration will indicate the type of observation upon which this statement is based.

A young woman, a graduate student whom we shall call Miss Vib, came in for nine interviews. If we compare the first interview with the last, striking changes are evident. Perhaps some features of this change may be conveyed by taking from the first and last interviews all the major statements regarding self, and all the major statements regarding current behavior. In the first interview, for example, her perception of herself may be crudely indicated by taking all her own statements about herself, grouping those which seem similar, but otherwise doing a minimum of editing, and retaining so far as possible, her own words. We then come out with this as the conscious perception of self which was hers at the outset of counseling.

"I feel disorganized, muddled; I've lost all direction; my personal life has disintegrated.

"I sorta experience things from the forefront of my consciousness, but nothing sinks in very deep; things don't seem real to me; I feel nothing matters; I don't have any emotional response to situations; I'm worried about myself.

"I haven't been acting like myself; it doesn't seem like me; I'm a different person altogether from what I used to be in the past.

"I don't understand myself; I haven't known what was happening to me.

"I have withdrawn from everything, and feel all right only when I'm all alone and no one can expect me to do things.

"I don't care about my personal appearance.

"I don't know *anything* anymore.

"I feel guilty about the things I have left undone.

"I don't think I could ever assume responsibility for anything."

If we attempt to evaluate this picture of self from an external frame of reference various diagnostic labels may come to mind. Trying to perceive it solely from the client's frame of reference we observe that to the young woman herself she appears disorganized, and not herself. She is perplexed and almost unacquainted with what is going on in herself. She feels unable and unwilling to function in any responsible or social way. This is at least a sampling of the way she experiences or perceives her self.

Her behavior is entirely consistent with this

picture of self. If we abstract all her statements describing her behavior, in the same fashion as we abstracted her statements about self, the following pattern emerges—a pattern which in this case was corroborated by outside observation.

> "I couldn't get up nerve to come in before; I haven't availed myself of help.
>
> "Everything I should do or want to do, I don't do.
>
> "I haven't kept in touch with friends; I avoid making the effort to go with them; I stopped writing letters home; I don't answer letters or telephone calls; I avoid contacts that would be professionally helpful; I didn't go home though I said I would.
>
> "I failed to hand in my work in a course though I had it all done; I didn't even buy clothing that I needed; I haven't even kept my nails manicured.
>
> "I didn't listen to material we were studying; I waste hours reading the funny papers; I can spend the whole afternoon doing absolutely nothing."

The picture of behavior is very much in keeping with the picture of self, and is summed up in the statement that "Everything I should do or want to do, I don't do." The behavior goes on, in ways that seem to the individual beyond understanding and beyond control.

If we contrast this picture of self and behavior with the picture as it exists in the ninth interview, thirty-eight days later, we find both the perception of self and the ways of behaving deeply altered. Her statements about self are as follows:

> "I'm feeling much better; I'm taking more interest in myself.
>
> "I do have some individuality, some interests.
>
> "I seem to be getting a newer understanding of myself. I can look at myself a little better.
>
> "I realize I'm just one person, with so much ability, but I'm not worried about it; I can accept the fact that I'm not always right.
>
> "I feel more motivation, have more of a desire to go ahead.
>
> "I still occasionally regret the past, though I feel less unhappy about it; I still have a long ways to go; I don't know whether I can keep the picture of myself I'm beginning to evolve.
>
> "I can go on learning—in school or out.

> "I do feel more like a normal person now; I feel more I can handle my life myself; I think I'm at the point where I can go along on my own."

Outstanding in this perception of herself are three things—that she knows herself, that she can view with comfort her assets and liabilities, and finally that she has drive and control of that drive.

In this ninth interview the behavioral picture is again consistent with the perception of self. It may be abstracted in these terms.

> "I've been making plans about school and about a job; I've been working hard on a term paper; I've been going to the library to trace down a topic of special interest and finding it exciting.
>
> "I've cleaned out my closets; washed my clothes.
>
> "I finally wrote my parents; I'm going home for the holidays.
>
> "I'm getting out and mixing with people; I am reacting sensibly to a fellow who is interested in me—seeing both his good and bad points.
>
> "I will work toward my degree; I'll start looking for a job this week."

Her behavior, in contrast to the first interview, is now organized, forward-moving, effective, realistic and planful. It is in accord with the realistic and organized view she has achieved of her self.

It is this type of observation, in case after case, that leads us to say with some assurance that as perceptions of self and reality change, behavior changes. Likewise, in cases we might term failures, there appears to be no appreciable change in perceptual organization or in behavior.

What type of explanation might account for these concomitant changes in the perceptual field and the behavioral pattern? Let us examine some of the logical possibilities.

In the first place, it is possible that factors unrelated to therapy may have brought about the altered perception and behavior. There may have been physiological processes occurring which produced the change. There may have been alterations in the family relationships, or in the social forces, or in the educational picture or in some other area of cultural influence, which might account for the rather drastic shift in the concept of self and in the behavior.

There are difficulties in this type of explanation. Not only were there no known gross changes in the physical or cultural situation as far as Miss Vib was concerned, but the explanation gradually becomes inadequate when one tries to apply it to the many cases in which such change occurs. To postulate that some external factor brings the change and that only by chance does this period of change coincide with the period of therapy, becomes an untenable hypothesis.

Let us then look at another explanation, namely that the therapist exerted, during the nine hours of contact, a peculiarly potent cultural influence which brought about the change. Here again we are faced with several problems. It seems that nine hours scattered over five and one-half weeks is a very minute portion of time in which to bring about alteration of patterns which have been building for thirty years. We would have to postulate an influence so potent as to be classed as traumatic. This theory is particularly difficult to maintain when we find, on examining the recorded interviews, that not once in the nine hours did the therapist express any evaluation, positive or negative, of the client's initial or final perception of self, or her initial or final mode of behavior. There was not only no evaluation, but no standards expressed by which evaluation might be inferred.

There was, on the part of the therapist, evidence of warm interest in the individual, and thoroughgoing acceptance of the self and of the behavior as they existed initially, in the intermediate stages, and at the conclusion of therapy. It appears reasonable to say that the therapist established certain definite conditions of interpersonal relations, but since the very essence of this relationship is respect for the person as he is at that moment, the therapist can hardly be regarded as a cultural force making for change.

We find ourselves forced to a third type of explanation, a type of explanation which is not new to psychology, but which has had only partial acceptance. Briefly it may be put that the observed phenomena of change seem most adequately explained by the hypothesis that *given certain psychological conditions, the individual has the capacity to reorganize his field of perception, including the way he perceives himself, and that a concomitant or a resultant of this perceptual reorganization is an appropriate alteration of behavior.* This puts into formal and objective terminology a clinical hypothesis which experience forces upon the therapist using a client-centered approach. One is compelled through clinical observation to develop a high degree of respect for the ego-integrative forces residing within each individual. One comes to recognize that under proper conditions the self is a basic factor in the formation of personality and in the determination of behavior. Clinical experience would strongly suggest that the self is, to some extent, an architect of self, and the above hypothesis simply puts this observation into psychological terms.

In support of this hypothesis it is noted in some cases that one of the concomitants of success in therapy is the realization on the part of the client that the self has the capacity for reorganization. Thus a student says:

> "You know I spoke of the fact that a person's background retards one. Like the fact that my family life wasn't good for me, and my mother certainly didn't give me any of the kind of bringing up that I should have had. Well, I've been thinking that over. It's true up to a point. But when you get so that you can see the situation, then it's really up to you."

Following this statement of the relation of the self to experience many changes occurred in this young man's behavior. In this, as in other cases, it appears that when the person comes to see himself as the perceiving, organizing agent, then reorganization of perception and consequent change in patterns of reaction take place.

On the other side of the picture we have frequently observed that when the individual has been authoritatively told that he is governed by certain factors or conditions beyond his control, it makes therapy more difficult, and it is only when the individual discovers for himself that he can organize his perceptions that change is possible. In veterans who have been given their own psychiatric diagnosis, the effect is often that of making the individual feel that he is under an unalterable doom, that he is unable to control the organization of his life. When however the self sees itself as capable of reorganizing its own perceptual field, a marked change in basic confidence occurs. Miss Nam, a student, illustrates this phenomenon when she says, after having made progress in therapy:

> "I think I do feel better about the future, too, because it's as if I won't be acting in darkness. It's sort of, well, knowing somewhat why I act the way I do . . . and at least it isn't the feeling that you're simply out of your own control and the fates are driving you to act that way. If you realize it, I think you can do something more about it."

A veteran at the conclusion of counseling puts it more briefly and more positively: "My attitude toward myself is changed now to where I feel I *can* do something with my self and life." He has come to view himself as the instrument by which some reorganization can take place.

There is another clinical observation which may be cited in support of the general hypothesis that there is a close relationship between behavior and the way in which reality is viewed by the individual. It has been noted in many cases that behavior changes come about for the most part imperceptibly and almost automatically, once the perceptual reorganization has taken place. A young wife who has been reacting violently to her maid, and has been quite disorganized in her behavior as a result of this antipathy, says "After I . . . discovered it was nothing more than that she resembled my mother, she didn't bother me any more. Isn't that interesting? She's still the same." Here is a clear statement indicating that though the basic perceptions have not changed, they have been differently organized, have acquired a new meaning, and that behavior changes then occur. * * *

Thus we have observed that appropriate changes in behavior occur when the individual acquires a different view of his world of experience, including himself; that this changed perception does not need to be dependent upon a change in the "reality," but may be a product of internal reorganization; that in some instances the awareness of the capacity for reperceiving experience accompanies this process or reorganization; that the altered behavioral responses occur automatically and without conscious effort as soon as the perceptual reorganization has taken place, apparently as a result of this.

In view of these observations a second hypothesis may be stated, which is closely related to the first. It is that *behavior is not directly influenced or determined by organic or cultural factors, but primarily,* (and perhaps only,) *by the perception of these elements.* In other words the crucial element in the determination of behavior is the perceptual field of the individual. While this perceptual field is, to be sure, deeply influenced and largely shaped by cultural and physiological forces, it is nevertheless important that it appears to be only the field as it is *perceived,* which exercises a specific determining influence upon behavior. This is not a new idea in psychology, but its implications have not always been fully recognized.

It might mean, first of all, that if it is the perceptual field which determines behavior, then the primary object of study for psychologists would be the person and his world as *viewed by the person himself.* It could mean that the internal frame of reference of the person might well constitute the field of psychology. * * * It might mean that the laws which govern behavior would be discovered more deeply by turning our attention to the laws which govern perception.

Now if our speculations contain a measure of truth, if the *specific* determinant of behavior is the perceptual field, and if the self can reorganize that perceptual field, then what are the limits of this process? Is the reorganization of perception capricious, or does it follow certain laws? Are there limits to the degree of reorganization? If so, what are they? In this connection we have observed with some care the perception of one portion of the field of experience, the portion we call the self.

The Relation of the Perception of the Self to Adjustment

Initially we were oriented by the background of both lay and psychological thinking to regard the outcome of successful therapy as the solution of problems. If a person had a marital problem, a vocational problem, a problem of educational adjustment, the obvious purpose of counseling or therapy was to solve that problem. But as we observe and study the recorded accounts of the conclusion of therapy, it is clear that the most characteristic outcome is not necessarily solution of problems, but a freedom from tension, a different feeling about, and perception of, self. Perhaps something of this outcome may be conveyed by some illustrations.

Several statements taken from the final interview with a twenty year old young woman, Miss Mir, give indications of the characteristic attitude toward self, and the sense of freedom which appears to accompany it.

"I've always tried to be what the others thought I should be, but now I am wondering whether I shouldn't just see that I am what I am."

"Well, I've just noticed such a difference. I find that when I feel things, even when I feel hate, I don't care. I don't mind. I feel more free somehow. I don't feel guilty about things."

"You know it's suddenly as though a big cloud has been lifted off. I feel so much more content."

Note in these statements the willingness to perceive herself as she is, to accept herself "realistically," to perceive and accept her "bad" attitudes as well as "good" ones. This realism seems to be accompanied by a sense of freedom and contentment.

Miss Vib, whose attitudes were quoted earlier, wrote out her own feelings about counseling some six weeks after the interviews were over, and gave the statement to her counselor. She begins:

"The happiest outcome of therapy has been a new feeling about myself. As I think of it, it might be the only outcome. Certainly it is basic to all the changes in my behavior that have resulted." In discussing her experience in therapy she states, "I was coming to see myself as a whole. I began to realize that I am *one* person. This was an important insight to me. I saw that the former good academic achievement, job success, ease in social situations, and the present withdrawal, dejection, apathy and failure were all adaptive behavior, performed by *me*. This meant that I had to reorganize my feelings about myself, no longer holding to the unrealistic notion that the very good adjustment was the expression of the real 'me' and this neurotic behavior was not. I came to feel that I am the same person, sometimes functioning maturely, and sometimes assuming a neurotic role in the face of what I had conceived as insurmountable problems. The acceptance of myself as one person gave me strength in the process of reorganization. Now I had a substratum, a core of unity on which to work." As she continues her discussion there are such statements as "I am getting more happiness in being myself." "I approve of myself more, and I have so much less anxiety."

As in the previous example, the outstanding aspects appear to be the realization that all of her behavior "belonged" to her, that she could accept both the good and bad features about herself and that doing so gave her a release from anxiety and a feeling of solid happiness. In both instances there is only incidental reference to the serious "problems" which had been initially discussed.

Since Miss Mir is undoubtedly above average intelligence and Miss Vib is a person with some psychological training, it may appear that such results are found only with the sophisticated individual. To counteract this opinion a quotation may be given from a statement written by a veteran of limited ability and education who had just completed counseling, and was asked to write whatever reactions he had to the experience. He says:

"As for the consoleing I have had I can say this, It really makes a man strip his own mind bare, and when he does he knows then what he realy is and what he can do. Or at least thinks he knows himself party well. As for myself, I know that my ideas were a little too big for what I realy am, but now I realize one must try start out at his own level.

"Now after four visits, I have a much clearer picture of myself and my future. It makes me feel a little depressed and disappointed, but on the other hand, it has taken me out of the dark, the load seems a lot lighter now, that is I can see my way now, I know what I want to do, I know about what I can do, so now that I can see my goal, I will be able to work a whole lot easier, at my own level."

Although the expression is much simpler one notes again the same two elements—the acceptance of self as it is, and the feeling of easiness, of lightened burden, which accompanies it.

As we examine many individual case records and case recordings, it appears to be possible to bring together the findings in regard to successful therapy by stating another hypothesis in regard to that portion of the perceptual field which we call the self. It would appear that *when all of the ways in which the individual perceives himself—all perceptions of the qualities, abilities, impulses, and attitudes of the person, and all perceptions of himself in relation to others—are accepted into the organized conscious concept of the self, then this achievement is accompanied by feelings of comfort and freedom from tension which are experienced as psychological adjustment.*

This hypothesis would seem to account for the observed fact that the comfortable perception of self which is achieved is sometimes more positive than before, sometimes more negative. When the individual permits all his perceptions of himself to be organized into one pattern, the picture is sometimes more flattering than he has held in the past, sometimes less flattering. It is always more comfortable.

It may be pointed out also that this tentative hypothesis supplies an operational type of definition, based on the client's internal frame of reference, for such hitherto vague terms as "adjustment," "integration," and "acceptance of self." They are defined in terms of perception, in a way which it should be possible to prove or disprove. When all of the organic perceptual experiences—the experiencing of attitudes, impulses, abilities and disabilities, the experiencing of others and of "reality"—when all of these perceptions are freely assimilated into an organized and consistent system, available to consciousness, then psychological

adjustment or integration might be said to exist. The definition of adjustment is thus made an internal affair, rather than dependent upon an external "reality."

Something of what is meant by this acceptance and assimilation of perceptions about the self may be illustrated from the case of Miss Nam, a student. Like many other clients she gives evidence of having experienced attitudes and feelings which are defensively denied because they are not consistent with the concept or picture she holds of herself. The way in which they are first fully admitted into consciousness, and then organized into a unified system may be shown by excerpts from the recorded interviews. She has spoken of the difficulty she has had in bringing herself to write papers for her university courses.

> "I just thought of something else which perhaps hinders me, and that is that again it's two different feelings. When I have to sit down and do (a paper), though I have a lot of ideas, underneath I think I always have the feeling that I just can't do it. . . . I have this feeling of being terrifically confident that I can do something, without being willing to put the work into it. At other times I'm practically afraid of what I have to do. . . ."

Note that the conscious self has been organized as "having a lot of ideas," being "terrifically confident" but that "underneath," in other words not freely admitted into consciousness, has been the experience of feeling "I just can't do it." She continues:

> "I'm trying to work through this funny relationship between this terrific confidence and then this almost fear of doing anything . . . and I think the kind of feeling that I can really do things is part of an illusion I have about myself of being, in my imagination, sure that it will be something good and very good and all that, but whenever I get down to the actual task of getting started, it's a terrible feeling of—well, incapacity, that I won't get it done either the way I want to do it, or even not being sure how I want to do it."

Again the picture of herself which is present in consciousness is that of a person who is "very good," but this picture is entirely out of line with the actual organic experience in the situation.

Later in the same interview she expresses very well the fact that her perceptions are not all organized into one consistent conscious self.

> "I'm not sure about what kind of a person I am—well, I realize that all of these are a part of me, but I'm not quite sure of how to make all of these things fall in line."

In the next interview we have an excellent opportunity to observe the organization of both of these conflicting perceptions into one pattern, with the resultant sense of freedom from tension which has been described above.

> "It's very funny, even as I sit here I realize that I have more confidence in myself, in the sense that when I used to approach new situations I would have two very funny things operating at the same time. I had a fantasy that I could do anything, which was a fantasy which covered over all these other feelings that I really couldn't do it, or couldn't do it as well as I wanted to, and it's as if now those two things have merged together, and it is more real, that a situation isn't either testing myself or proving something to myself or anyone else. It's just in terms of doing it. And I think I have done away both with that fantasy and that fear. . . . So I think I can go ahead and approach things—well, just sensibly."

No longer is it necessary for this client to "cover over" her real experiences. Instead the picture of herself as very able, and the experienced feeling of complete inability, have now been brought together into one integrated pattern of self as a person with real, but imperfect abilities. Once the self is thus accepted the inner energies making for self-actualization are released and she attacks her life problems more efficiently.

Observing this type of material frequently in counseling experience would lead to a tentative hypothesis of maladjustment, which like the other hypothesis suggested, focuses on the perception of self. It might be proposed that the tensions called psychological maladjustment exist when the organized concept of self (conscious or available to conscious awareness) is not in accord with the perceptions actually experienced.

This discrepancy between the concept of self and the actual perceptions seems to be explicable only in terms of the fact that the self concept resists assimilating into itself any percept which is inconsistent with its present organization. The feeling that she may not have the ability to do a paper is inconsistent with Miss Nam's conscious picture of herself as a very able and confident person, and hence, though fleetingly perceived, is denied organization as a part of her self, until this comes about in therapy.

The Conditions of Change of Self Perception

If the way in which the self is perceived has as close and significant a relationship to behavior as has been suggested, then the manner in which this perception may be altered becomes a question of importance. If a reorganization of self-perceptions brings a change in behavior; if adjustment and maladjustment depend on the congruence between perceptions as experienced and the self as perceived, then the factors which permit a reorganization of the perception of self are significant.

Our observations of psychotherapeutic experience would seem to indicate that absence of any threat to the self-concept is an important item in the problem. Normally the self resists incorporating into itself those experiences which are inconsistent with the functioning of self. But a point overlooked by Lecky and others[1] is that when the self is free from any threat of attack or likelihood of attack, then it is possible for the self to consider these hitherto rejected perceptions, to make new differentiations, and to reintegrate the self in such a way as to include them.

An illustration from the case of Miss Vib may serve to clarify this point. In her statement written six weeks after the conclusion of counseling Miss Vib thus describes the way in which unacceptable

---

[1]That is, by Rogers's intellectual adversaries.

percepts become incorporated into the self. She writes:

"In the earlier interviews I kept saying such things as, 'I am not acting like myself', 'I never acted this way before.' What I meant was that this withdrawn, untidy, and apathetic person was not myself. Then I began to realize that I was the same person, seriously withdrawn, etc. now, as I had been before. That did not happen until after I had talked out my self-rejection, shame, despair, and doubt, in the accepting situation of the interview. The counselor was not startled or shocked. I was telling him all these things about myself which did not fit into my picture of a graduate student, a teacher, a sound person. He responded with complete acceptance and warm interest without heavy emotional overtones. Here was a sane, intelligent person wholeheartedly accepting this behavior that seemed so shameful to me. I can remember an organic feeling of relaxation. I did not have to keep up the struggle to cover up and hide this shameful person."

Note how clearly one can see here the whole range of denied perceptions of self, and the fact that they could be considered as a part of self only in a social situation which involved no threat to the self, in which another person, the counselor, becomes almost an alternate self and looks with understanding and acceptance upon these same perceptions. She continues:

"Retrospectively, it seems to me that what I felt as 'warm acceptance without emotional overtones' was what I needed to work through my difficulties. . . . The counselor's impersonality with interest allowed me to talk out my feelings. The clarification in the interview situation presented the attitude to me as a 'ding an sich' which I could look at, manipulate, and put in place. In organizing my attitudes, I was beginning to organize me."

Here the nature of the exploration of experience, of seeing it as experience and not as a threat to self, enables the client to reorganize her perceptions of self, which as she says was also "reorganizing me."

If we attempt to describe in more conventional psychological terms the nature of the process which culminates in an altered organization and integration of self in the process of ther-

apy it might run as follows. The individual is continually endeavoring to meet his needs by reacting to the field of experience as he perceives it, and to do that more efficiently by differentiating elements of the field and reintegrating them into new patterns. Reorganization of the field may involve the reorganization of the self as well as of other parts of the field. The self, however, resists reorganization and change. In everyday life individual adjustment by means of reorganization of the field exclusive of the self is more common and is less threatening to the individual. Consequently, the individual's first mode of adjustment is the reorganization of that part of the field which does not include the self.

Client-centered therapy is different from other life situations inasmuch as the therapist tends to remove from the individual's immediate world all those aspects of the field which the individual can reorganize except the self. The therapist, by reacting to the client's feelings and attitudes rather than to the objects of his feelings and attitudes, assists the client in bringing from background into focus his own self, making it easier than ever before for the client to perceive and react to the self. By offering only understanding and no trace of evaluation, the therapist removes himself as an object of attitudes, becoming only an alternate expression of the client's self. The therapist by providing a consistent atmosphere of permissiveness and understanding removes whatever threat existed to prevent all perceptions of the self from emerging into figure. Hence in this situation all the ways in which the self has been experienced can be viewed openly, and organized into a complex unity.

It is then this complete absence of any factor which would attack the concept of self, and second, the assistance in focusing upon the perception of self, which seems to permit a more differentiated view of self and finally the reorganization of self.

* * *

Implications

* * * We have discovered with some surprise that our clinical observations, and the tentative hypotheses which seem to grow out of them, raise disturbing questions which appear to cast doubt on the very foundations of many of our psychological endeavors, particularly in the fields of clinical psychology and personality study. To clarify what is meant, I should like to restate in more logical order the formulations I have given, and to leave with you certain questions and problems which each one seems to raise.

If we take first the tentative proposition that the specific determinant of behavior is the perceptual field of the individual, would this not lead, if regarded as a working hypothesis, to a radically different approach in clinical psychology and personality research? It would seem to mean that instead of elaborate case histories full of information about the person as an object, we would endeavor to develop ways of seeing his situation, his past, and himself, as these objects appear to him. We would try to see with him, rather than to evaluate him. It might mean the minimizing of the elaborate psychometric procedures by which we have endeavored to measure or value the individual from our own frame of reference. It might mean the minimizing or discarding of all the vast series of labels which we have painstakingly built up over the years. Paranoid, preschizophrenic, compulsive, constricted—terms such as these might become irrelevant because they are all based in thinking which takes an external frame of reference. They are not the ways in which the individual experiences himself. If we consistently studied each individual from the internal frame of reference of that individual, from within his own perceptual field, it seems probable that we should find generalizations which could be made, and principles which were operative, but we may be very sure that they would be of a different order from these externally based judgements *about* individuals.

Let us look at another of the suggested propositions. If we took seriously the hypothesis that integration and adjustment are internal conditions related to the degree of acceptance or nonacceptance of all perceptions, and the degree of organization of these perceptions into one consistent system, this would decidedly affect our clinical procedures. It would seem to imply the abandonment of the notion that adjustment is dependent upon the pleasantness or unpleasantness of the environment, and would demand concentration upon those processes which bring about selfintegration within the person. It would mean a minimizing or an abandoning of those clinical procedures which utilize the alteration of environmental forces as a method of treatment. It would rely instead upon the fact that the person who is internally unified has the greatest likelihood of meeting environmental problems constructively, either as an individual or in cooperation with others.

If we take the remaining proposition that the self, under proper conditions, is capable of reorganizing, to some extent, its own perceptual field, and of thus altering behavior, this too seems to raise disturbing questions. Following the path of this hypothesis would appear to mean a shift in emphasis in psychology from focusing upon the fixity of personality attributes and psychological abilities, to the alterability of these same characteristics. It would concentrate attention upon process rather than upon fixed status. Whereas psychology has, in personality study, been concerned primarily with the measurement of the fixed qualities of the individual, and with his past in order to explain his present, the hypothesis here suggested would seem to concern itself much more with the personal world of the present in order to understand the future, and in predicting that future would be concerned with the principles by which personality and behavior are altered, as well as the extent to which they remain fixed.

Thus we find that a clinical approach, client-centered therapy, has led us to try to adopt the client's perceptual field as the basis for genuine understanding. In trying to enter this internal world of perception, not by introspection, but by observation and direct inference, we find ourselves in a new vantage point for understanding personality dynamics, a vantage point which opens up some disturbing vistas. We find that behavior seems to be better understood as a reaction to this reality-as-perceived. We discover that the way in which the person sees himself, and the perceptions he dares not take as belonging to himself, seem to have an important relationship to the inner peace which constitutes adjustment. We discover within the person, under certain conditions, a capacity for the restructuring and the reorganization of self, and consequently the reorganization of behavior, which has profound social implications. We see these observations, and the theoretical formula-tions which they inspire, as a fruitful new ap-proach for study and research in various fields of psychology.

References

Rogers, Carl R. (1946). Significant aspects of client-centered therapy. *American Psychologist, 1,* 415–422.

Snyder, W. U. (1946). 'Warmth' in nondirective counseling. *Journal of Abnormal and Social Psychology, 41,* 491–495.

If We Are So Rich, Why Aren't We Happy?

Mihaly Csikszentmihalyi

What was classically called "humanistic psychology" has faded from view in recent years, but now a successor is stepping forward in its place. The "positive psychology movement" has become suddenly quite prominent and has taken up the humanistic mission of arguing that human nature is basically good and that the proper topic of psychology is human experience—especially positive human experience, also known as "the good life." The author of the next selection, Mihaly Csikszentmihalyi (pronounced chick-sent-me-high), directly addresses the questions, what is positive experience and how does one attain it?

Csikszentmihalyi argues that positive experience—happiness—is not a matter of material goods or entertainment but rather comes from matching one's capacities to one's activities. This produces a state he calls "flow," characterized by total focus, a loss of sense of time, and mildly pleasant emotion.

Notice how the modern humanist Csikszentmihalyi draws directly on the classic theorist Carl Rogers, when he refers to the way "human consciousness uses its self-organizing ability to achieve a positive internal state through its own efforts" (see footnote 1). This is just one indication that the positive psychology movement is the modern version of humanistic psychology.

From *American Psychologist,* 54, 821–827, 1999.

Psychology is the heir to those "sciences of man" envisioned by Enlightenment thinkers such as Gianbattista Vico, David Hume, and the Baron de Montesquieu. One of their fundamental conclusions was that the pursuit of happiness constituted the basis of both individual motivation and social well-being. This insight into the human condition was condensed by John Locke (1690/1975) in his famous statement, "That we call Good which is apt to cause or increase pleasure, or diminish pain" (p. 2), whereas evil is the reverse—it is what causes or increases pain and diminishes pleasure.

The generation of utilitarian philosophers that followed Locke, including David Hartley, Joseph Priestley, and Jeremy Bentham, construed a good society as that which allows the greatest happiness for the greatest number (Bentham, 1789/1970, pp.

64–65). This focus on pleasure or happiness as the touchstone of private and public life is by no means a brainchild of post-Reformation Europe. It was already present in the writings of the Greeks—for instance, Aristotle noted that although humankind values a great many things, such as health, fame, and possessions, because we think that they will make us happy, we value happiness for itself. Thus, happiness is the only intrinsic goal that people seek for its own sake, the bottom line of all desire. The idea that furthering the pursuit of happiness should be one of the responsibilities of a just government was of course enshrined later in the Declaration of Independence of the United States.

Despite this recognition on the part of the human sciences that happiness is the fundamental goal of life, there has been slow progress in understanding what happiness itself consists of. Perhaps because the heyday of utilitarian philosophy coincided with the start of the enormous forward strides in public health and in the manufacturing and distribution of goods, the majority of those who thought about such things assumed that increases in pleasure and happiness would come from increased affluence, from greater control over the material environment. The great selfconfidence of the Western technological nations, and especially of the United States, was in large part because of the belief that materialism—the prolongation of a healthy life, the acquisition of wealth, the ownership of consumer goods—would be the royal road to a happy life.

However, the virtual monopoly of materialism as the dominant ideology has come at the price of a trivialization that has robbed it of much of the truth it once contained. In current use, it amounts to little more than a thoughtless hedonism, a call to do one's thing regardless of consequences, a belief that whatever feels good at the moment must be worth doing.

This is a far cry from the original view of materialists, such as John Locke, who were aware of the futility of pursuing happiness without qualifications and who advocated the pursuit of happiness through prudence—making sure that people do not mistake imaginary happiness for real happiness.

What does it mean to pursue happiness through prudence? Locke must have derived his inspiration from the Greek philosopher Epicurus, who 2,300 years ago already saw clearly that to enjoy a happy life, one must develop self-discipline. The materialism of Epicurus was solidly based on the ability to defer gratification. He claimed that although all pain was evil, this did not mean one should always avoid pain—for instance, it made sense to put up with pain now if one was sure to avoid thereby a greater pain later. He wrote to his friend Menoeceus

> The beginning and the greatest good . . . is prudence. For this reason prudence is more valuable even than philosophy: from it derive all the other virtues. Prudence teaches us how impossible it is to live pleasantly without living wisely, virtuously, and justly . . . take thought, then, for these and kindred matters day and night. . . . You shall be disturbed neither waking nor sleeping, and you shall live as a god among men. (Epicurus of Samos, trans. 1998, p. 48)

This is not the image of epicureanism held by most people. The popular view holds that pleasure and material comforts should be grasped wherever they can, and that these alone will improve the quality of one's life. As the fruits of technology have ripened and the life span has lengthened, the hope that increased material rewards would bring about a better life seemed for a while justified.

Now, at the end of the second millennium, it is becoming clear that the solution is not that simple. Inhabitants of the wealthiest industrialized Western nations are living in a period of unprecedented riches, in conditions that previous generations would have considered luxuriously comfortable, in relative peace and security, and they are living on the average close to twice as long as their great-grandparents did. Yet, despite all these improvements in material conditions, it does not seem that people are so much more satisfied with their lives than they were before.

The Ambiguous Relationship Between Material and Subjective Well-being

The indirect evidence that those of us living in the United States today are not happier than our ancestors were comes from national statistics of social pathology—the figures that show the doubling and tripling of violent crimes, family breakdown, and psychosomatic complaints since at least the halfway mark of the century. If material well-being leads to happiness, why is it that neither capitalist nor socialist solutions seem to work? Why is it that the crew on the flagship of capitalist affluence is becoming increasingly addicted to drugs for falling asleep, for waking up, for staying slim, for escaping boredom and depression? Why are suicides and loneliness such a problem in Sweden, which has applied the best of socialist principles to provide material security to its people?

Direct evidence about the ambiguous relationship of material and subjective well-being comes from studies of happiness that psychologists and other social scientists have finally started to pursue, after a long delay in which research on happiness was considered too soft for scientists to undertake. It is true that these surveys are based on self-reports and on verbal scales that might have different meanings depending on the culture and the language in which they are written. Thus, the results of culturally and methodologically circumscribed studies need to be taken with more than the usual grain of salt. Nevertheless, at this point they represent the state of the art—an art that will inevitably become more precise with time.

Although cross-national comparisons show a reasonable correlation between the wealth of a country as measured by its gross national product and the self-reported happiness of its inhabitants (Inglehart, 1990), the relationship is far from perfect. The inhabitants of Germany and Japan, for instance, nations with more than twice the gross national product of Ireland, report much lower levels of happiness.

Comparisons within countries show an even weaker relationship between material and subjec-tive well-being. Diener, Horwitz, and Emmons (1985), in a study of some of the wealthiest individuals in the United States, found their levels of happiness to be barely above that of individuals with average incomes. After following a group of lottery winners, Brickman, Coates, and Janoff-Bulman (1978) concluded that despite their sudden increase in wealth, their happiness was no different from that of people struck by traumas, such as blindness or paraplegia. That having more money to spend does not necessarily bring about greater subjective well-being has also been documented on a national scale by David G. Myers (1993). His calculations show that although the adjusted value of after-tax personal income in the United States has more than doubled between 1960 and 1990, the percentage of people describing themselves as "very happy" has remained unchanged at 30% (Myers, 1993, pp. 41–42).

In the *American Psychologist*'s January 2000 special issue on positive psychology, David G. Myers (2000) and Ed Diener (2000) discuss in great detail the lack of relationship between material and subjective well-being, so I will not belabor the point here. Suffice it to say that in current longitudinal studies of a representative sample of almost 1,000 American adolescents conducted with the experience sampling method * * * , a consistently low negative relationship between material and subjective well-being has been found (Csikszentmihalyi & Schneider, in press). For instance, the reported happiness of teenagers (measured several times a day for a week in each of three years) shows a very significant inverse relationship to the social class of the community in which teens live, to their parents' level of education, and to their parents' occupational status. Children of the lowest socioeconomic strata generally report the highest happiness, and upper-middle-class children generally report the least happiness. Does this mean that more affluent children are in fact less happy, or does it mean that the norms of their social class prescribe that they should present themselves as less happy? At this point, we are unable to make this vital distinction.

Yet despite the evidence that the relationship

between material wealth and happiness is tenuous at best, most people still cling to the notion that their problems would be resolved if they only had more money. In a survey conducted at the University of Michigan, when people were asked what would improve the quality of their lives, the first and foremost answer was "more money" (Campbell, 1981).

Given these facts, it seems that one of the most important tasks psychologists face is to better understand the dynamics of happiness and to communicate these findings to the public at large. If the main justification of psychology is to help reduce psychic distress and support psychic well-being, then psychologists should try to prevent the disillusionment that comes when people find out that they have wasted their lives struggling to reach goals that cannot satisfy them. Psychologists should be able to provide alternatives that in the long run will lead to a more rewarding life.

Why Material Rewards Do Not Necessarily Make People Happy

To answer this question, I'll start by reflecting on why material rewards, which people regard so highly, do not necessarily provide the happiness expected from them. The first reason is the well-documented escalation of expectations. If people strive for a certain level of affluence thinking that it will make them happy, they find that on reaching it, they become very quickly habituated, and at that point they start hankering for the next level of income, property, or good health. In a 1987 poll conducted by the *Chicago Tribune*, people who earned less than $30,000 a year said that $50,000 would fulfill their dreams, whereas those with yearly incomes of over $100,000 said they would need $250,000 to be satisfied ("Pay Nags," 1987; "Rich Think Big," 1987; see also Myers, 1993, p. 57). Several studies have confirmed that goals keep getting pushed upward as soon as a lower level is reached. It is not the objective size of the reward but its difference from one's "adaptation level" that provides subjective value (e.g., Davis, 1959; Michalos, 1985; Parducci, 1995).

The second reason is related to the first. When resources are unevenly distributed, people evaluate their possessions not in terms of what they need to live in comfort, but in comparison with those who have the most. Thus, the relatively affluent feel poor in comparison with the very rich and are unhappy as a result. This phenomenon of "relative deprivation" (Martin, 1981; Williams, 1975) seems to be fairly universal and well-entrenched. In the United States, the disparity in incomes between the top percentage and the rest is getting wider; this does not bode well for the future happiness of the population.

The third reason is that even though being rich and famous might be rewarding, nobody has ever claimed that material rewards alone are sufficient to make us happy. Other conditions—such as a satisfying family life, having intimate friends, having time to reflect and pursue diverse interests—have been shown to be related to happiness (Myers, 1993; Myers & Diener, 1995; Veenhoven, 1988). There is no intrinsic reason why these two sets of rewards—the material and the socioemotional—should be mutually exclusive. In practice, however, it is very difficult to reconcile their conflicting demands. As many psychologists from William James (1890) to Herbert A. Simon (1969) have remarked, time is the ultimate scarce resource, and the allocation of time (or more precisely, of attention over time) presents difficult choices that eventually determine the content and quality of our lives. This is why professional and business persons find it so difficult to balance the demands of work and family, and why they so rarely feel that they have not shortchanged one of these vital aspects of their lives.

Material advantages do not readily translate into social and emotional benefits. In fact, to the extent that most of one's psychic energy becomes invested in material goals, it is typical for sensitivity to other rewards to atrophy. Friendship, art, literature, natural beauty, religion, and philosophy become less and less interesting. The Swedish economist Stephen Linder was the first to point out that as income and therefore the value of one's time increases, it becomes less and less "rational" to spend it on anything besides making money—or on spending it conspicuously (Linder, 1970). The opportunity costs of playing with one's child, reading poetry, or attending a family reunion become too high, and so one stops doing such irrational things. Eventually a person who only responds to material rewards becomes blind to any other kind and loses the ability to derive happiness from other sources (see also Benedikt, 1999; Scitovsky, 1975). As is true of addiction in general, material rewards at first enrich the quality of life. Because of this, we tend to conclude that more must be better. But life is rarely linear; in most cases, what is good in small quantities becomes commonplace and then harmful in larger doses.

Dependence on material goals is so difficult to avoid in part because our culture has progressively eliminated every alternative that in previous times used to give meaning and purpose to individual lives. Although hard comparative data are lacking, many historians (e.g., Polanyi, 1957) have claimed that past cultures provided a greater variety of attractive models for successful lives. A person could be valued and admired because he or she was a saint, a bon vivant, a wise person, a good craftsman, a brave patriot, or an upright citizen. Nowadays the logic of reducing everything to quantifiable measures has made the dollar the common metric by which to evaluate every aspect of human action. The worth of a person and of a person's accomplishments are determined by the price they fetch in the marketplace. It is useless to claim that a painting is good art unless it gets high bids at Sotheby's, nor can we claim that someone is wise unless he or she can charge five figures for a consultation. Given the hegemony of material rewards in our culture's restricted repertoire, it is not surprising that so many people feel that their only hope for a happy life is to amass all the earthly goods they can lay hands on.

To recapitulate, there are several reasons for the lack of a direct relationship between material well-being and happiness. Two of them are sociocultural: (a) The growing disparity in wealth makes even the reasonably affluent feel poor. (b) This relative deprivation is exacerbated by a cultural factor,

namely, the lack of alternative values and a wide range of successful lifestyles that could compensate for a single, zero-sum hierarchy based on dollars and cents. Two of the reasons are more psychological: (a) When we evaluate success, our minds use a strategy of escalating expectations, so that few people are ever satisfied for long with what they possess or what they have achieved. (b) As more psychic energy is invested in material goals, less of it is left to pursue other goals that are also necessary for a life in which one aspires to happiness.

None of this is intended to suggest that the material rewards of wealth, health, comfort, and fame detract from happiness. Rather, after a certain minimum threshold—which is not stable but varies with the distribution of resources in the given society—they seem to be irrelevant. Of course, most people will still go on from cradle to grave believing that if they could only have had more money, or good looks, or lucky breaks, they would have achieved that elusive state.

Psychological Approaches to Happiness

If people are wrong about the relation between material conditions and how happy they are, then what *does* matter? The alternative to the materialist approach has always been something that used to be called a "spiritual" and nowadays we may call a "psychological" solution. This approach is based on the premise that if happiness is a mental state, people should be able to control it through cognitive means. Of course, it is also possible to control the mind pharmacologically. Every culture has developed drugs ranging from peyote to heroin to alcohol in an effort to improve the quality of experience by direct chemical means. In my opinion, however, chemically induced well-being lacks a vital ingredient of happiness: the knowledge that one is responsible for having achieved it. Happiness is not something that happens to people but something that they make happen.

In some cultures, drugs ingested in a ritual, ceremonial context appear to have lasting beneficial effects, but in such cases the benefits most likely result primarily from performing the ritual, rather than from the chemicals per se. Thus, in discussing psychological approaches to happiness, I focus exclusively on processes in which human consciousness uses its self-organizing ability to achieve a positive internal state through its own efforts[1] with minimal reliance on external manipulation of the nervous system.

There have been many very different ways to program the mind to increase happiness or at least to avoid being unhappy. Some religions have done it by promising an eternal life of happiness follows our earthly existence. Others, on realizing that most unhappiness is the result of frustrated goals and thwarted desires, teach people to give up desires altogether and thus avoid disappointment. Still others, such as Yoga and Zen, have developed complex techniques for controlling the stream of thoughts and feelings, thereby providing the means for shutting out negative content from consciousness. Some of the most radical and sophisticated disciplines for self-control of the mind were those developed in India, culminating in the Buddhist teachings 25 centuries ago. Regardless of its truth content, faith in a supernatural order seems to enhance subjective well-being: Surveys generally show a low but consistent correlation between religiosity and happiness (Csikszentmihalyi & Patton, 1997; Myers, 1993).

Contemporary psychology has developed several solutions that share some of the premises of these ancient traditions but differ drastically in content and detail. What is common to them is the assumption that cognitive techniques, attributions, attitudes, and perceptual styles can change the effects of material conditions on consciousness, help restructure an individual's goals, and consequently improve the quality of experience. Maslow's (1968, 1971) *self-actualization*, Block and Block's (1980) *ego-resiliency*, Diener's (1984, 2000) *positive emotionality*, Antonovsky's (1979) *salutogenic approach*, Seeman's (1996) *personality integration*,

Deci and Ryan's (1985; Ryan & Deci, 2000) *autonomy*, Scheier and Carver's (1985) *dispositional optimism*, and Seligman's (1991) *learned optimism* are only a few of the theoretical concepts developed recently, many with their own preventive and therapeutic implications.

THE EXPERIENCE OF FLOW My own addition to this list is the concept of the *autotelic experience*, or *flow*, and of the autotelic personality. The concept describes a particular kind of experience that is so engrossing and enjoyable that it becomes autotelic, that is, worth doing for its own sake even though it may have no consequence outside itself. Creative activities, music, sports, games, and religious rituals are typical sources for this kind of experience. Autotelic persons are those who have such flow experiences relatively often, regardless of what they are doing.

Of course, we never do anything purely for its own sake. Our motives are always a mixture of intrinsic and extrinsic considerations. For instance, composers may write music because they hope to sell it and pay the bills, because they want to become famous, because their self-image depends on writing songs—all of these being extrinsic motives. But if the composers are motivated only by these extrinsic rewards, they are missing an essential ingredient. In addition to these rewards, they could also enjoy writing music for its own sake—in which case, the activity would become autotelic. My studies (e.g., Csikszentmihalyi, 1975, 1996, 1997) have suggested that happiness depends on whether a person is able to derive flow from whatever he or she does.

A brief selection from one of the more than 10,000 interviews collected from around the world might provide a sense of what the flow experience is like. Asked how it felt when writing music was going well, a composer responded.

> You are in an ecstatic state to such a point that you feel as though you almost don't exist. I have experienced this time and time again. My hand seems devoid of myself, and I have nothing to do with what is happening. I just sit there watching in a state of awe and wonderment. And the music just flows out by itself. (Csikszentmihalyi, 1975, p. 44)

---

[1]This "self-organizing" ability is a classic concern of humanistic psychologists such as Maslow and Rogers.

This response is quite typical of most descriptions of how people feel when they are thoroughly involved in something that is enjoyable and meaningful to the person. First of all, the experience is described as "ecstatic": in other words, as being somehow separate from the routines of everyday life. This sense of having stepped into a different reality can be induced by environmental cues, such as walking into a sport event, a religious ceremony, or a musical performance, or the feeling can be produced internally, by focusing attention on a set of stimuli with their own rules, such as the composition of music.

Next, the composer claims that "you feel as though you almost don't exist." This dimension of the experience refers to involvement in the activity being so demanding that no surplus attention is left to monitor any stimuli irrelevant to the task at hand. Thus, chess players might stand up after a game and realize that they have splitting headaches and must run to the bathroom, whereas for many hours during the game they had excluded all information about their bodily states from consciousness.

The composer also refers to the felt spontaneity of the experience: "My hand seems devoid of myself . . . I have nothing to do with what is happening." Of course, this sense of effortless performance is only possible because the skills and techniques have been learned and practiced so well that they have become automatic. This brings up one of the paradoxes of flow: One has to be in control of the activity to experience it, yet one should not try to consciously control what one is doing.

As the composer stated, when the conditions are right, action "just flows out by itself." It is because so many respondents used the analogy of spontaneous, effortless flow to describe how it felt when what they were doing was going well that I used the term *flow* to describe the autotelic experience. Here is what a well-known lyricist, a former poet laureate of the United States, said about his writing:

> You lose your sense of time, you're completely enraptured, you are completely caught up in what you're doing, and you are sort of swayed by the possibilities you see in this work. If that becomes too

powerful, then you get up, because the excitement is too great. . . . The idea is to be so, so saturated with it that there's no future or past, it's just an extended present in which you are . . . making meaning. And dismantling meaning, and remaking it. (Csikszentmihalyi, 1996, p. 121)

This kind of intense experience is not limited to creative endeavors. It is reported by teenagers who love studying, by workers who like their jobs, by drivers who enjoy driving. Here is what one woman said about her sources of deepest enjoyment:

> [It happens when] I am working with my daughter, when she's discovered something new. A new cookie recipe that she has accomplished, that she has made herself, an artistic work that she's done and she is proud of. Her reading is something that she is really into, and we read together. She reads to me and I read to her, and that's a time when I sort of lose touch with the rest of the world. I am totally absorbed in what I am doing. (Allison & Duncan, 1988, p. 129)

This kind of experience has a number of common characteristics. First, people report knowing very clearly what they have to do moment by moment, either because the activity requires it (as when the score of a musical composition specifies what notes to play next), or because the person sets clear goals every step of the way (as when a rock climber decides which hold to try for next). Second, they are able to get immediate feedback on what they are doing. Again, this might be because the activity provides information about the performance (as when one is playing tennis and after each shot one knows whether the ball went where it was supposed to go), or it might be because the person has an internalized standard that makes it possible to know whether one's actions meet the standard (as when a poet reads the last word or the last sentence written and judges it to be right or in need of revision).

Another universal condition for the flow experience is that the person feels his or her abilities to act match the opportunities for action. If the challenges are too great for the person's skill, anxiety is likely to ensue; if the skills are greater than the challenges, one feels bored. When challenges are in balance with skills, one becomes lost in the activity and flow is likely to result (Csikszentmihalyi, 1975, 1997).

Even this greatly compressed summary of the flow experience should make it clear that it has little to do with the widespread cultural trope of "going with the flow." To go with the flow means to abandon oneself to a situation that feels good, natural, and spontaneous. The flow experience that I have been studying is something that requires skills, concentration, and perseverance. However, the evidence suggests that it is the second form of flow that leads to subjective well-being.

The relationship between flow and happiness is not entirely self-evident. Strictly speaking, during the experience people are not necessarily happy because they are too involved in the task to have the luxury to reflect on their subjective states. Being happy would be a distraction, an interruption of the flow. But afterward, when the experience is over, people report having been in as positive a state as it is possible to feel. Autotelic persons, those who are often in flow, tend also to report more positive states overall and to feel that their lives are more purposeful and meaningful (Adlai-Gail, 1994; Hektner, 1996).

The phenomenon of flow helps explain the contradictory and confusing causes of what we usually call happiness. It explains why it is possible to achieve states of subjective well-being by so many different routes: either by achieving wealth and power or by relinquishing them; by cherishing either solitude or close relationships; through ambition or through its opposite, contentment; through the pursuit of objective science or through religious practice. *People are happy not because of what they do, but because of how they do it.* If they can experience flow working on the assembly line, chances are they will be happy, whereas if they don't have flow while lounging at a luxury resort, they are not going to be happy. The same is true of the various psychological techniques for achieving positive mental health: If the process of becoming resilient or self-efficacious is felt to be boring or an external imposition, the technique is unlikely to

lead to happiness, even if it is mastered to the letter. You have to enjoy mental health to benefit from it.

MAKING FLOW POSSIBLE The prerequisite for happiness is the ability to get fully involved in life. If the material conditions are abundant, so much the better, but lack of wealth or health need not prevent one from finding flow in whatever circumstances one finds at hand. In fact, our studies suggest that children from the most affluent families find it more difficult to be in flow—compared with less well-to-do teenagers, they tend to be more bored, less involved, less enthusiastic, less excited.

At the same time, it would be a mistake to think that each person should be left to find enjoyment wherever he or she can find it or to give up efforts for improving collective conditions. There is so much that could be done to introduce more flow in schools, in family life, in the planning of communities, in jobs, in the way we commute to work and eat our meals—in short, in almost every aspect of life. This is especially important with respect to young people. Our research suggests, for instance, that more affluent teenagers experience flow less often because, although they dispose of more material possessions, they spend less time with their parents, and they do fewer interesting things with them (Hunter, 1998). Creating conditions that make flow experiences possible is one aspect of that "pursuit of happiness" for which the social and political community should be responsible.

Nevertheless, flow alone does not guarantee a happy life. It is also necessary to find flow in activities that are complex, namely, activities that provide a potential for growth over an entire life span, allow for the emergence of new opportunities for action, and stimulate the development of new skills. A person who never learns to enjoy the company of others and who finds few opportunities within a meaningful social context is unlikely to achieve inner harmony (Csikszentmihalyi, 1993; Csikszentmihalyi & Rathunde, 1998; Inghilleri, 1999), but when flow comes from active physical, mental, or emotional involvement—from work, sports, hobbies, meditation, and interpersonal relationships—then the chances for a complex life that leads to happiness improve.

The Limits of Flow

There is at least one more important issue left to consider. In reviewing the history of materialism, I have discussed John Locke's warnings about the necessity of pursuing happiness with prudence and about the importance of distinguishing real from imaginary happiness. Are similar caveats applicable to flow? Indeed, flow is necessary to happiness, but it is not sufficient. This is because people can experience flow in activities that are enjoyable at the moment but will detract from enjoyment in the long run. For instance, when a person finds few meaningful opportunities for action in the environment, he or she will often resort to finding flow in activities that are destructive, addictive, or at the very least wasteful (Csikszentmihalyi & Larson, 1978; Sato, 1988). Juvenile crime is rarely a direct consequence of deprivation but rather is caused by boredom or the frustration teenagers experience when other opportunities for flow are blocked. Vandalism, gang fights, promiscuous sex, and experimenting with psychotropic drugs might provide flow at first, but such experiences are rarely enjoyable for long.

Another limitation of flow as a path to happiness is that a person might learn to enjoy an activity so much that everything else pales by comparison, and he or she then becomes dependent on a very narrow range of opportunities for action while neglecting to develop skills that would open up a much broader arena for enjoyment later. A chess master who can enjoy only the game and a workaholic who feels alive only while on the job are in danger of stunting their full development as persons and thus of forfeiting future opportunities for happiness.

In one respect, the negative impact on the social environment of an addiction to flow is less severe than that of an addiction to material rewards. Material rewards are zero–sum: To be rich means that others must be poor; to be famous means that others must be anonymous; to be powerful means that others must be helpless. If everyone strives for such self-limiting rewards, most people will necessarily remain frustrated, resulting in personal unhappiness and social instability. By contrast, the rewards of flow are open-ended and inexhaustible: If I get my joy from cooking Mediterranean food, or from surfing, or from coaching Little League, this will not decrease anyone else's happiness.

Unfortunately, too many institutions have a vested interest in making people believe that buying the right car, the right soft drink, the right watch, the right education will vastly improve their chances of being happy, even if doing so will mortgage their lives. In fact, societies are usually structured so that the majority is led to believe that their well-being depends on being passive and contented. Whether the leadership is in the hands of a priesthood, of a warrior caste, of merchants, or of financiers, their interest is to have the rest of the population depend on whatever rewards they have to offer—be it eternal life, security, or material comfort. But if one puts one's faith in being a passive consumer—of products, ideas, or mind-altering drugs—one is likely to be disappointed. However, materialist propaganda is clever and convincing. It is not so easy, especially for young people, to tell what is truly in their interest from what will only harm them in the long run. This is why John Locke cautioned people not to mistake imaginary happiness for real happiness and why 25 centuries ago Plato wrote that the most urgent task for educators is to teach young people to find pleasure in the right things. Now this task falls partly on our shoulders. The job description for psychologists should encompass discovering what promotes happiness, and the calling of psychologists should include bringing this knowledge to public awareness.

References

Adlai-Gail, W. (1994). *Exploring the autotelic personality.* Unpublished doctoral dissertation, University of Chicago.

Allison, M. T., & Duncan. M. C. (1988). Women, work, and flow. In M. Csikszentmihalyi & I. Csikszentmihalyi (Eds.). *Optimal experience: Psychological studies of flow in consciousness* (pp. 118–137). New York: Cambridge University Press.

Antonovsky, A. (1979). *Health, stress, and coping*. San Francisco: Jossey-Bass.

Benedikt, M. (1999). *Values*. Austin: The University of Texas Press.

Bentham, J. (1970). *An introduction to the principles of morals and legislation*. Darien, CT: Hafner. (Original work published 1789)

Block, J. H., & Block, J. (1980). The role of ego-control and ego-resiliency in the organization of behavior. In W. A. Collins (Ed.). *The Minnesota Symposium on Child Psychology* (Vol. 13, pp. 39–101). Hillsdale, NJ: Erlbaum.

Brickman, P., Coates, D., & Janoff-Bulman, R. (1978). Lottery winners and accident victims: Is happiness relative? *Journal of Personality and Social Psychology, 36*, 917–927.

Campbell, A. (1981). *The sense of well-being in America*. New York: McGraw-Hill.

Csikszentmihalyi, M. (1975). *Beyond boredom and anxiety*. San Francisco: Jossey-Bass.

Csikszentmihalyi, M. (1993). *The evolving self*. New York: HarperCollins.

Csikszentmihalyi, M. (1996). *Creativity: Flow and the psychology of discovery and invention*. New York: HarperCollins.

Csikszentmihalyi, M. (1997). *Finding flow*. New York: Basic Books.

Csikszentmihalyi, M., & Larson, R. (1978). Intrinsic rewards in school crime. *Crime and Delinquency, 24*, 322–335.

Csikszentmihalyi, M., & Patton, J. D. (1997). *Le bonheur, l'experience optimale et les valeurs spirituelles: Une etude empirique aupres d'adolescents* [Happiness, the optimal experience, and spiritual values: An empirical study of adolescents]. *Revue Quebecoise de Psychologie, 18*, 167–190.

Csikszentmihalyi, M., & Rathunde, K. (1998). The development of the person: An experiential perspective on the ontogenesis of psychological complexity: In R. M. Lerner (Ed.). *Handbook of child psychology* (5th ed., Vol. 1). New York: Wiley.

Csikszentmihalyi, M., & Schneider, B. (in press). *Becoming adult: How teenagers prepare for work*. New York: Basic Books.

Davis, J. A. (1959). A formal interpretation of the theory of relative deprivation. *Sociometry, 22*, 289–296.

Deci, E., & Ryan, M. (1985). *Intrinsic motivation and self-determination in human behavior*. New York: Plenum.

Diener, E. (1984). Subjective well-being. *Psychological Bulletin, 95*, 542–575.

Diener, E. (2000). Subjective well-being: The science of happiness, and a proposal for a national index. *American Psychologist, 55*, 34–43.

Diener, E., Horwitz, J., & Emmons, R. A. (1985). Happiness of the very wealthy. *Social Indicators, 16*, 263–274.

Epicurus of Samos, (1998). Achieving the happy life. *Free Inquiry, 18*, 47–48.

Hektner, J. (1996). *Exploring optimal personality development: A longitudinal study of adolescents*. Unpublished doctoral dissertation, University of Chicago.

Hunter, J. (1998). The importance of engagement: A preliminary analysis. *North American Montessori Teacher's Association Journal, 23*, 58–75.

Inghilleri, P. (1999). *From subjective experience to cultural evolution*. New York: Cambridge-University Press.

Inglehart, R. (1990). *Culture shift in advanced industrial society*. Princeton, NJ: Princeton University Press.

James, W. (1890). *Principles of psychology* (Vol. 1). New York: Holt.

Linder, S. (1970). *The harried leisure class*. New York: Columbia University Press.

Locke, J. (1975). *Essay concerning human understanding*. Oxford, England: Clarendon Press. (Original work published 1690.)

Martin, J. (1981). Relative deprivation: A theory of distributive injustice for an era of shrinking resources. *Research in Organizational Behavior, 3*, 53–107.

Maslow, A. (1968). *Towards a psychology of being*. New York: Van Nostrand.

Maslow, A. (1971). *The farthest reaches of human nature*. New York: Viking.

Michalos, A. C. (1985). Multiple discrepancy theory (MDT). *Social Indicators Research, 16*, 347–413.

Myers, D. G. (1993). *The pursuit of happiness*. New York: Avon.

Myers, D. G. (2000). The funds, friends, and faith of happy people. *American Psychologist, 55*, 56–67.

Myers, D. G., & Diener, E. (1995). Who is happy? *Psychological Science, 6*, 10–19.

Parducci, A. (1995). *Happiness, pleasure, and judgment*. Mahwah, NJ: Erlbaum.

Pay nags at workers' job views. (1987, October 18). *Chicago Tribune*, 10B.

Polanyi, K. (1957). *The great transformation*. Boston: Beacon Press.

Rich think big about living well. (1987, September 24). *Chicago Tribune*, 3.

Ryan, R. M., & Deci, E. L. (2000). Self-determination theory and the facilitation of intrinsic motivation, social development, and well-being. *American Psychologist, 55*, 68–78.

Sato, I. (1988). Bozozoku: Flow in Japanese motorcycle gangs. In M. Csikszentmihalyi & I. Csikszentmihalyi (Eds.), *Optimal experience* (pp. 92–117). New York: Cambridge University Press.

Scheier, M. F., & Carver, C. S. (1985). Optimism, coping, and health: Assessment and implications of generalized outcome expectancies. *Health Psychology, 4*, 210–247.

Scitovsky, T. (1975). *The joyless economy*. New York: Random House.

Seeman, T. E. (1996). Social ties and health: The benefits of social integration. *Annals of Epidemiology, 6*, 442–451.

Seligman, M. E. P. (1991). *Learned optimism*. New York: Random House.

Simon, H. A. (1969). *Sciences of the artificial*. Boston: MIT Press.

Voenhoven, R. (1988). The utility of happiness. *Social Indicators Research, 20*, 333–354.

Williams, R. M., Jr. (1975). Relative deprivation. In L. A. Coser (Ed.). *The idea of social structure: Papers in honor of Robert K. Merton* (pp. 355–378). New York: Harcourt Brace Jovanovich.

Why Are Some People Happier Than Others? The Role of Cognitive and Motivational Processes in Well-Being

Sonja Lyubomirsky

The humanistic emphasis on subjective experience and positive psychology's emphasis on what is good about people have converged to produce a rapidly developing area of research on human happiness. In this selection, one of the major researchers in this area, Sonja Lyubomirsky, summarizes what is known about the bases of happiness. The article emphasizes the point that "objective" circumstances such as wealth and even health have a surprisingly small influence on happiness. Happiness is one area where consistent individual differences are much stronger than most people expect them to be. Some people, it appears, just know how to be happy almost regardless of external circumstances—others, sadly, are less fortunate.

As Gordon Allport noted, "For some the world is a hostile place where men are evil and dangerous: for others it is a stage for fun and frolic" (1961, p. 266). His point was that the same environment can be experienced differently by people depending upon their personalities. That is the message of the present paper as well. Lyubomirsky emphasizes how one's construal or interpretation of a situation can be as or more important than the objective nature of the situation itself in determining whether one will be happy. This is a classic existential observation. Research on happiness has yet to address one further issue, which is, as Lyubomirsky herself notes, "how to enhance happiness without forfeiting goodness or truth." At the beginning of this section, Jean-Paul Sartre argued that there are more important things in life than being happy. Was he right?

From *American Psychologist, 56,* 239–249, 2001.

The capacity of some people to be remarkably happy, even in the face of adverse circumstances or hard times, is striking. We can all identify individuals who appear to have a talent for happiness, to see the world around them through rose-colored glasses, to make out the silver lining even in misfortune, to live in the present, and to find joy in the little things from day to day (Freedman, 1978; Myers & Diener, 1995; Ryff, Singer, Love, & Essex, 1998; Taylor & Brown, 1988). Similarly, we are all familiar with people who, even in the best of times, seem chronically unhappy, peering at the world through gray-colored spectacles (M. W. Eysenck, 1990), always complaining, accentuating the negative, dwelling on the down side of both the trivial and the sublime (Lyubomirsky, Kasri, & Zehm, 2000), and generally deriving little pleasure from life (Myers & Diener, 1995). Thus, anecdotal evidence and everyday experience alike suggest that one of the most salient and significant dimensions of human experience and emotional life is happiness.

The question of why some people are happier than others is important for both theoretical and practical reasons, and the pursuit of its answer should be a central goal of a positive psychology (Seligman & Csikszentmihalyi, 2000). Indeed, the dawn of the new millennium finds increasing research evidence supporting Aristotle's (trans. 1974) two millennia-old argument that happiness is the whole aim and end of human existence. Although sources of personal happiness may vary (Lyubomirsky, 2000; Lyubomirsky & Lepper, 1999), in almost every culture examined by researchers, people rank the pursuit of happiness as one of their most cherished goals in life (Diener & Oishi, 2000; Diener, Suh, Smith, & Shao, 1995; Freedman, 1978; Triandis, Bontempo, Leung, & Hui, 1990; for an exception, see Lyubomirsky, 2000). Furthermore, happiness appears to have a number of positive by-products, which may benefit not only individuals, but families, communities, and societies (see Myers, 1992; Veenhoven, 1988, for reviews).

How much is currently known about the sources of individual differences in adult happiness—that is, why some people succeed at attaining and maintaining happiness and cheer, whereas others continuously languish in unhappiness and gloom? Fortunately, a great deal of research has addressed this question. However, because it is presently neither methodologically feasible nor ethical to manipulate an individual's chronic levels of happiness and unhappiness, all of this research has necessarily been correlational, examining the associations between happiness and a host of diverse proximal and distal factors. Much of the work has focused on the objective determinants of happiness in Western cultures—that is, the extent to which well-being is related to aspects of our environments, both imposed (e.g., native culture) and relatively controllable (e.g., income, marriage), as well as to aspects of persons not under our control (e.g., gender, age). According to this objectivist or bottom-up tradition, happy people are simply those with the most advantages—for example, a comfortable income, robust health, a supportive marriage, and lack of tragedy or trauma in their lives (see Argyle, 1999; Diener, Suh, Lucas, & Smith, 1999; M. W. Eysenck, 1990; Myers, 1992, for reviews). However, as an increasing number of authors have observed, the general conclusion from almost a century of research on the determinants of well-being is that objective circumstances, demographic variables, and life events are correlated with happiness less strongly than intuition and everyday experience tell us they ought to be (cf. Diener et al., 1999; Lyubomirsky & Ross, 1999). By several estimates, all of these variables put together account for no more than 8% to 15% of the variance in happiness (e.g., Andrews & Withey, 1976; Argyle, 1999; Diener, 1984; Diener et al., 1999).

Several studies have emerged as sine qua non examples of the failure of objective variables to predict happiness. For example, in their oft-cited classic survey, Brickman and his colleagues offered dramatic testimony that even such extreme and unexpected life events as winning hundreds of thousands of dollars or losing the ability to walk exert surprisingly weak effects on people's current happiness and no effects at all on their predictions for their well-being in the future (Brickman, Coates, & Janoff-Bulman, 1978; see also, Silver, 1982). Other examples include findings of remarkably small associations between happiness and wealth, such as Myers's (2000) observation that as Americans' personal income has nearly tripled in the last half century, their happiness levels have remained the same, and Diener and colleagues' finding that the wealthiest Americans—those earning more than $10 million annually—report levels of personal happiness only trivially greater than their less affluent peers (Diener, Horwitz, & Emmons, 1985).

A Construal Approach to Happiness

Do such findings of surprisingly small correlations suggest that objective circumstances and life events play only a trivial role in determining people's happiness? To answer this question, we must consider whether any life circumstances or events are truly objective. As many psychologists and philosophers have noted, people do not experience events or situations passively. Rather, all life events are "cognitively processed" (Scarr, 1988, p. 240)—that is, construed and framed, evaluated and interpreted, contemplated and remembered (Bruner, 1986; Ross, 1990)—so that each individual may essentially live in a separate subjective social world. To be sure, objective factors exert a tremendous impact on people's happiness, but they do so, I propose, through the operation of multiple cognitive and motivational processes. That is, the reason that such variables as wealth and health have such counterintuitively small effects on people's happiness is that a diverse set of psychological processes moderates the impact of events, life circumstances, and demographic factors on well-being. Thus, a construal theory of happiness suggests that to understand why some people are happier than others, we must understand the cognitive and motivational processes that serve to maintain or enhance both enduring happiness and transient mood.

An important implication of an approach to understanding happiness centered on cognitive and motivational processes is that any psychological process that has hedonic consequences—that is, positive or negative consequences for happiness and self-regard—is potentially relevant to elucidating individual differences in enduring happiness. Indeed, many familiar cognitive and judgmental processes that psychologists have been exploring over the past several decades happen to have hedonic consequences and, as such, may be linked to transient and enduring differences in happiness or well-being. Thus, my approach has been to explore hedonically relevant psychological processes, such as social comparison, dissonance reduction, self-reflection, self-evaluation, and person perception, in chronically happy and unhappy individuals. In support of a construal framework, self-rated happy and unhappy people have been shown to differ systematically and in a manner consistent with and supportive of their differing states and temperaments (Lyubomirsky et al., 2000; Lyubomirsky & Ross, 1997, 1999; Lyubomirsky & Tucker, 1998, 2000). That is, my colleagues and I have found that happy individuals construe naturally occurring life events, as well as situations constructed in the laboratory, in ways that seem to maintain and even promote their happiness and positive self-views, whereas unhappy individuals construe experiences in ways that seem to reinforce their unhappiness and negative self-views. Supporting a top-down perspective on well-being, my research shows that happy individuals experience and react to events and circumstances in relatively more positive and more adaptive ways (cf. Diener, 1984).

Notably, a construal framework is foreshadowed in previous theoretical and empirical work. Indeed, most theoretical perspectives on happiness, as well as a number of relevant theoretical models in related areas, attempt to explain how various cognitive and motivational processes account for differences in enduring and transient well-being (cf. DeNeve, 1999). For example, theories that single out aspiration levels, goals, social comparisons, and coping responses, among others (see Diener et al., 1999, for a review), all share a common concern with subjective psychological processes. These processes, I suggest, moderate the impact of the environment on well-being by forging reactive person–environment effects and, to some extent, evocative and proactive ones (Atkinson, Atkinson, Smith, Bem, & Nolen-Hoeksema, 1996; Plomin, DeFries, & Loehlin, 1977; Scarr, 1988; Scarr & McCartney, 1983). That is, people construe and respond to similar circumstances in different ways (e.g., positively reappraising their failure to complete graduate school or making inspiring comparisons with friends after meeting a potential Mr. Right). People evoke distinct responses from others (e.g., attracting social support from family members or promotions from bosses). And people select and construct different social worlds through their own acts (e.g., using humor to revive a stagnant relationship or choosing to pursue a career in a low-paying but intrinsically motivating field).

*   *   *

Research Evidence: Comparing Happy and Unhappy People

The findings of a wealth of prior studies—those specifically focused on predicting well-being as an outcome variable and those focused on related constructs—are consistent with a construal approach to understanding individual differences in happiness. My research seeks to test predictions from a construal theory directly by investigating hedonically relevant processes in people who show exceptionally high or low levels of happiness. Accordingly, the paradigms typically involve comparing the responses of happy and unhappy participants to a variety of experimental manipulations. Such quasi-experimental designs allow for the testing of both main effects (e.g., unhappy people are more sensitive to performance feedback than happy ones) and interactions (e.g., this effect is more pronounced under unfavorable feedback conditions). Accumulating evidence from my laboratory supports the notion that happy and unhappy individuals differ in the particular cognitive, judgmental, and motivational strategies they use. Moreover, these cognitive and motivational processes appear to operate largely automatically and without awareness.

MEASUREMENT OF SUBJECTIVE HAPPINESS Unlike measures of subjective well-being, which include evaluations of overall life quality and ratings of positive and negative emotions, the measure of happiness used in our research involves a global, subjective assessment of whether one is a happy or an unhappy person. Hence, this measure reflects a broader and more molar category of well-being, tapping into more global psychological phenom-

ena (Lyubomirsky & Lepper, 1999; cf. Diener, 1994). Indeed, a judgment of the extent to which one is a happy person (or an unhappy one) is likely not equivalent to a simple sum of one's recent levels of affect and one's satisfaction with life. In our studies, participants are selected on the basis of their responses to the four-item Subjective Happiness Scale (SHS; Lyubomirsky & Lepper, 1999). Two items ask respondents to characterize themselves using both absolute ratings and ratings relative to peers, whereas the other two items offer brief descriptions of happy and unhappy individuals and ask respondents the extent to which each characterization describes them. Responses to the four items are then combined and averaged to provide a single continuous composite score, ranging from 1 to 7. Depending on the study, those scoring above the median or in the top quartile of the distribution are classified as "happy" and those scoring below the median or in the bottom quartile are classified as "unhappy." Furthermore, to ensure that our unhappy participants are not, in fact, depressed, mildly to moderately dysphoric individuals are routinely excluded from participation.

SOCIAL COMPARISON In several studies, we have found that self-rated happy individuals appear to be less sensitive to social comparison information—especially unfavorable information—than are unhappy ones. Our research paints a portrait of unhappy individuals who are deflated rather than delighted about their peers' accomplishments and triumphs and are relieved rather than disappointed or sympathetic in the face of their colleagues' and acquaintances' failures and undoings. For example, in one experiment, students solved anagrams in the presence of a confederate who performed the task at a much faster or much slower pace (Lyubomirsky & Ross, 1997, Study 1). In another experiment, students received positive or negative feedback on a novel teaching task, and then heard a peer receive even more positive or even more negative feedback than they themselves did (Lyubomirsky & Ross, 1997, Study 2). In both studies, although the moods, self-confidence, and evaluations of personal abilities of both happy and unhappy individuals were bolstered by information about inferior peer performance, happy individuals were relatively less influenced by the superior performance of a peer. Indeed, one striking finding was that unhappy students reported feeling happier and more self-confident when they had received a *poor* evaluation (but heard their peer receive an even worse one) than when they had received an *excellent* evaluation (but heard their peer receive an even better one). Happy students, by contrast, did not show this pattern of sensitive responding to comparisons with peers.

Conceptually replicating these findings, two subsequent studies revealed that happy participants are also less influenced than unhappy ones by the relative performance of a competing group or team, as well as by their individual rank (Lyubomirsky & Tucker, 2000). For example, in one study, students working in teams of four competed against one other team in their performance on a novel word-generation task. After learning that their team had lost, unhappy students reported that they personally performed less well than did happy students, predicted that they would perform less well in the future on a similar task, and showed greater decreases in positive affect. The pattern of results suggested that unhappy people held themselves culpable for their team's losses, but failed to commend themselves for their team's victories.

Empirical evidence and anecdotal experience suggest that social comparison is an active, dynamic, and flexible process (see Wood, 1989), which may be used in the service of boosting or diminishing one's mood and self-regard. Thus, it is not surprising that chronically happy and unhappy people would differ in how they distort or manipulate social comparison information, how they use such information, and how they respond to it. The two groups may perceive, interpret, and weigh social comparison information differently, or they may draw from it enormous versus trivial implications. For example, happy people may view their abilities as relatively more malleable than fixed (see Dweck, 1999; Dweck & Leggett, 1988), so that a peer's exceptional performance constitutes not a threat but an incentive and an indication of their own prospects for future success. Our research suggests that happy individuals appear to be more inclined than unhappy ones to use social comparison information sparingly and to use it selectively to protect their well-being and self-esteem. For example, in the studies from our laboratory, happy students gave weight to relevant social comparison information only when it served to soften the implications of a poor evaluation, not when it threatened to undermine the value of a positive one. By contrast, unhappy students appeared to monitor information about peer performance carefully and conscientiously, exerting effort to bolster their well-being and self-esteem by actively (albeit unsuccessfully) pursuing favorable ways to compare themselves with others. Notably, in all the research from my laboratory, the pattern of results sometimes highlights a strategy used by happy individuals (but not unhappy ones), sometimes highlights a process shown solely by unhappy individuals, and sometimes brings into relief the two groups on a continuum (i.e., one group manifesting a process more than the other).

POSTDECISIONAL RATIONALIZATION Another illustration of unhappy individuals' relatively broader sensitivity to information carrying hedonic stakes has been observed in the context of situations involving choice or the restriction of alternatives, or both. One set of studies from our laboratory, for example, examined post-decisional rationalization and regret in college students, who selected among different foods, and in high school students, who made more consequential college choices. In one study, high school seniors evaluated colleges after applying for admission and then later after making their selections (Lyubomirsky & Ross, 1999, Study 1). In another study, undergraduates rated the attractiveness of desserts before and after learning which particular one they would receive (Lyubomirsky & Ross, 1999, Study 2). Our findings from both studies suggested that self-rated happy and unhappy individuals responded differently —and in a manner supportive of their affective temperaments—in reducing dissonance in the aftermath of decision making. Whether in choosing fancy desserts or selecting among prospective colleges, happy students tended to be satisfied with *all* of their options—even those they did not ultimately choose or receive—and to reduce dissonance only in the face of real ego threat (e.g., by sharply devaluing desirable colleges that rejected them). By contrast, unhappy students generally reduced dissonance by deciding that what they chose or received was mediocre but that the options they were denied were even worse.

EVENT CONSTRUAL Chronically happy and unhappy individuals have also been found to differ in the ways in which they respond to life events and daily situations, large and small. For example, three studies supported the notion that happy and unhappy individuals interpret, remember, and indeed experience both real and hypothetical life events in a way that serves to reinforce their respective affective dispositions (Lyubomirsky & Tucker, 1998). For example, students nominated by their peers as "very happy" reported experiencing similar types of positive and negative life events as did peer-nominated unhappy students. However, several weeks later, happy students tended to recall and think about both types of events more favorably and adaptively—for example, by drawing humor or didactic value from adversity or by emphasizing recent improvement in their lives. In another study, all of the participants interacted with a female peer in the laboratory, then watched a series of videotapes depicting a stranger in three different situations. Happy individuals liked the person they met and recalled her in more favorable terms, more than did unhappy ones. The same pattern of results, albeit weaker, was found for liking the videotaped stranger. In sum, these findings suggest that happy people perceive, evaluate, and think about the same events in more positive ways than do unhappy ones. When such perceptions and experiences are repeated over a lifetime, happy and unhappy people may be able to preserve (or even promote) their happiness and unhappiness, respectively.

SELF-REFLECTION Notwithstanding research evidence suggesting that happy individuals are relatively better equipped to manage life's stresses, downturns, and uplifts, they sometimes seem markedly less outwardly concerned with hedonic management than their unhappy peers. Recent research in our laboratory has focused on testing the hypothesis that happy individuals are less inclined than unhappy ones to self-reflect and dwell about themselves, their outcomes, and their moods. For example, several studies have demonstrated that unhappy individuals are relatively more likely to dwell on negative or ambiguous events, such as difficult decisions or unfavorable social comparisons (Lyubomirsky et al., 2000; Lyubomirsky & Ross, 1999). Unfortunately, such extensive dwelling or rumination may drain cognitive resources and thus bring to bear a variety of negative consequences, which could further reinforce unhappiness. For example, four experiments revealed that, after being outperformed by a fellow student or after trying to solve impossible anagrams, unhappy individuals spent significantly longer reading a passage from the Graduate Record Examination and completing a memory test, and showed poorer reading comprehension (Kim & Lyubomirsky, 1997; Lyubomirsky et al., 2000). These findings demonstrate some of the maladaptive by-products of self-reflection. That is, in addition to thwarting successful coping with life's problems (cf. Lyubomirsky & Tucker, 1998), this cognitive and motivational process may actually compound those very problems, qualifying it as a poor recipe for happiness.

HAPPINESS VERSUS RELATED INDIVIDUAL DIFFERENCE VARIABLES A question that remains to be addressed is whether these documented effects reflect the role of chronic happiness per se rather than that of self-esteem, optimism, extraversion, sensitivity to reward, or other individual difference constructs that intuition and prior research alike suggest should be related to happiness (see Lyubomirsky & Lepper, 2000, for a review). To address this issue, we have systematically tested (a) whether group differences in responses to hedonically relevant outcomes could be accounted for by controlling for differences in two factors traditionally associated with happiness, that is, optimism and self-esteem, and (b) whether these two factors would prove as potent as happiness when used as grouping variables. We are encouraged by our findings that, in every study examined so far, the differences found between happy and unhappy individuals have proven to be largely independent of optimism and self-esteem (Lyubomirsky et al., 2000; Lyubomirsky & Ross, 1997, 1999; Lyubomirsky & Tucker, 2000).

Although the extent to which other relevant individual difference variables might have independent predictive power in our studies is not yet known, it is worth speculating about the role of such factors as extraversion and neuroticism. Extraverts, like happy individuals, appear to be more sensitive to reward and thus may be inclined toward pleasant, positive emotions, whereas neurotics, like unhappy individuals, appear to be more sensitive to punishment, and thus may experience more frequent unpleasant, negative emotions (Gray, 1990; see also Diener et al., 1999). However, in none of the studies from my laboratory has the positivity of participants' emotional state provided a satisfactory account of the results. That is, group differences in our participants' responses and construals remain significant even after statistically controlling for current mood. Furthermore, in a recently completed study (Tucker, 2000), differences found between happy and unhappy students in their appreciation of both the trivial and the sublime (e.g., the experience of "finding a penny on the sidewalk," "the birth of your own child," or "looking at the stars") remained after covarying out a measure of a construct presumably closely linked with extraversion—behavioral activation sensitivity (Gray, 1990). Whether such related constructs may serve as necessary or sufficient conditions for happiness remains a topic for future research, as does the nature of the mechanisms that underlie the relationships in question (e.g., see Lyubomirsky & Lepper, 2000).

Future Research Directions

A common thread running through the research described above is that happy and unhappy individuals appear to experience—indeed, to reside in—different subjective worlds. Thus, promising research directions in pursuit of the sources of happiness lie in investigating additional cognitive and motivational processes that support the differing worlds of enduring happiness versus chronic unhappiness. Indeed, an array of psychological processes, which have previously been shown to have positive, negative, or mixed hedonic stakes, can potentially be tested for their role in sustaining or enhancing chronic well-being. Thus, further research drawing on prior theoretical work may prove fruitful in advancing our understanding of the causes of happiness, which is critical to a comprehensive scientific study of optimal human functioning (Seligman & Csikszentmihalyi, 2000).

As a case in point, prospect theory (Kahneman & Tversky, 1979) makes a number of predictions about which types of preferences, decisions, and framings of events have positive versus negative hedonic implications. For example, on the basis of an analysis of mental accounting, hedonic experiences should be optimized if people prefer to integrate losses (e.g., receive two rejection letters from an editor on the very same day), but to segregate gains (e.g., earn two bonuses on two separate days); Tversky & Kahneman, 1981; for empirical evidence, see Linville & Fischer, 1990; cf. Showers, 2000). Another example drawn from prospect theory is that people should feel more pain when construing a problem or an unfavorable event (e.g., a rejection letter or a breakdown of the family car) as a loss rather than a cost (Tversky & Kahneman, 1981). Because happy and unhappy people show cognitive, judgmental processes and strategies that seem to maintain or even boost their relative happiness and unhappiness, a construal approach applied to prospect theory predicts that happy people will choose to combine negative events and separate positive ones and to construe a rejection or a setback as the cost of doing business. Similar analyses can be developed on the basis of a variety of other theories, ranging from dissonance (Aronson, 1969; Festinger, 1957; cf. Lyubomirsky & Ross, 1999) and reactance (Brehm & Brehm, 1981; Wicklund, 1974) to self-affirmation (Steele, 1988) and time perspective (Zimbardo & Boyd, 1999). The distinctions between maximizing and satisficing (Simon, 1976; cf. Schwartz, Ward, & Monterosso, 2000), independent versus interdependent self-construals (Markus & Kitayama, 1991), and incremental versus entity theories of intelligence (Dweck, 1999; Dweck & Leggett, 1988) may also serve as valuable points of departure for investigating differences between chronically happy and unhappy people. For example, a construal perspective predicts that happy individuals will be relatively less inclined to strive to maximize all of their options or to experience reactance and regret, yet more prone to focus on the present or to believe that their intelligence can be increased.

Future research also promises to address additional questions raised by the construal approach to happiness. First, is the principal force underlying the documented differences between happy and unhappy individuals cognitive or motivational? Or, might these processes be linked in such a way that their unique contributions cannot be disentangled? One objective for future investigators would be to identify and measure the primary hedonically relevant motivations underlying happiness and unhappiness and to specify the links between these motivations and specific cognitive processes. Although almost everyone professes a desire to be happy (e.g., Diener et al., 1995), not all people share the goals and motivations compatible with happiness. That is, some individuals are principally motivated to perceive the world in positive ways—to appreciate themselves, to like other people, and to value the world at large, to be satisfied with what they have rather than focusing on what they do not have (cf. Taylor & Brown, 1988). In contrast, the primary motivation of other individuals is to perceive themselves, other people, and the world around them in a realistic manner (i.e., to see things as they really are), to seek to understand

themselves and their universe, and to maintain a consistent and accurate self-image (cf. Swann, 1983). As my findings suggest, these two sets of motivational processes are likely to be associated with greater chronic happiness and unhappiness, respectively. Such individual differences in hedonically related motivational concerns may have practical implications as well. For example, a vexing possibility is that the motivational processes underlying unhappiness may serve as a barrier to happiness-increasing interventions. That is, chronically unhappy individuals may not desire to reframe unexpected, negative life events in positive and optimistic ways or to avoid making comparisons with peers or to cope with traumatic outcomes through forgiveness and faith. These individuals may forego being happy in order to be "right." Thus, hedonic motivation should be an important focus of researchers concerned with happiness and well-being.

A second question for further research is to what extent can a construal approach to happiness be applied and generalized to other cultures or invoked to account for cultural variations in well-being? For example, cultural norms encouraging or deterring such practices as social comparison or self-reflection may moderate the effects of these psychological processes on the happiness of cultural members. Also, motives to pursue happiness or to focus on the positive aspects of experience may be reinforced or restrained in certain cultures (e.g., Lyubomirsky, 2000).

Finally, the question of causal direction remains an important topic of investigation for the future. That is, do the aforementioned cognitive and motivational processes directly increase happiness, or does happiness promote their use, or, alternatively, does a third factor possibly play a role in the relationship between hedonic functioning and construal processes? There is reason to believe, both from research experience and anecdotal evidence, that the influence is bidirectional (e.g., Ekman & Davidson, 1994; Fiske & Taylor, 1991; Forgas, 1995; Wegner & Pennebaker, 1993)—indeed, that the pathway may be cyclical and self-perpetuating. That is, one's level of happiness may promote particular construals of the world, which, in turn, increase or maintain one's happiness, and so on. Future research could shed light on the nature of this process and the mechanisms that underlie it by using experimental designs in which participants' cognitive and motivational strategies are manipulated or retrained.

Prescriptive Implications and Challenges for Future Interventions

The pursuit of happiness has long been an American cultural obsession. From philosophers and policymakers to poets, novelists, and self-help gurus, the secret to happiness has remained a subject of tremendous interest. Philosophers, from Aristotle and Epicurus to Mill and James, have offered widely divergent prescriptions for the happy life. Likewise, during the last several decades, authors of U.S. popular psychology have claimed that one can gain happiness via a myriad of ways—through the power of positive thinking, by finding one's inner child, by becoming one's own best friend, by not sweating the small stuff, or by not loving too little or too much. In light of both academic and popular interest, it is important to consider the implications of an approach to happiness centered on underlying cognitive and motivational processes for practical prescriptions for reinforcing or enhancing well-being. Because almost no well-controlled research exists in this area, such implications must necessarily be speculative.

An important question to consider is whether the cognitive and motivational processes associated with relatively greater happiness can be nurtured, acquired, or directly taught. Indeed, would it be wise or even prudent to attempt to increase individual levels of well-being? Hence, one ostensibly daunting challenge to happiness-enhancing interventions deserves mention. Accumulating evidence for a genetic predisposition to happiness (e.g., Braungart, Plomin, DeFries, & Fulker, 1992; Tellegen et al., 1988), combined with findings for its high cross-temporal stability (e.g., Costa, McCrae, & Zonderman, 1987; Headey & Wearing, 1989)

and relations to personality (see Diener & Lucas, 1999, for a review), suggest to some researchers that "trying to be happier is as futile as trying to be taller" (Lykken & Tellegen, 1996, p. 189). However, rather than discouraging further research, results indicating that people's happiness may be constrained to a set range can alternatively be interpreted as providing impetus to investigations of how to elevate each individual toward the high point of that range. Furthermore, even heritability coefficients as high as 50% to 80%, as Lykken and Tellegen (1996) have found, do not rule out the possibility that the mean level of happiness for a specific population can be raised. Finally, because it is unlikely that genes have a direct influence on happiness, it may be possible to intervene at the level of at least a subset of the intermediate processes, such as potentially malleable aspects of cognition (e.g., encouraging people to distract themselves after a disappointing performance; Lyubomirsky et al., 2000) and behavior (e.g., cultivating the conditions that promote "flow"; Csikszentmihalyi, 1990). Indeed, one direction for positive psychology might be to test systematically which processes are mutable in the majority of people and which are not (cf. Seligman, 1994).

Although happiness-enhancing research is still in its infancy, a few researchers have had preliminary success, albeit limited and short term, at such endeavors (e.g., Fordyce, 1977; Lichter, Haye, & Kammann, 1980; Sheldon, Kasser, Smith, & Share, in press; cf. Gloaguen, Cottraux, Cucherat, & Blackburn, 1998; Shatté, Gillham, & Reivich, in press). As an illustration, in one study, undergraduates partook in a semester-long intervention designed to modify their construals of their personal goals (e.g., to perceive greater meaningfulness within their goals, as well as a more optimal balance among them) and to provide strategies for their goal attainment (Sheldon et al., in press). The researchers succeeded in helping a portion of the participants to attain their goals and enhance their psychological well-being. Thus, I am optimistic that future research—prospective and longitudinal studies, in particular—will yield yet more successful interventions. One challenge to such investigations will be to identify effective and enduring ways to retrain people's cognitive and motivational strategies. Another will be to determine how to maintain successful gains and, perhaps, even to initiate an upward spiral (Sheldon & Houser-Marko, 2001). Finally, a third challenge will be to address the question of how to enhance happiness without forfeiting goodness or truth (cf. Schwartz, 2000).

Concluding Remark

There are multiple perspectives of ourselves, our circumstances, and the world at large—some more positive and affirming, others relatively hopeless and dark. A construal theory of happiness suggests that these alternative perspectives and constructions of reality have different hedonic consequences and, as such, are associated with different levels of enduring happiness and well-being. As Abraham Lincoln wisely said, "Most people are about as happy as they make up their minds to be" (Barton, 1976).

References

Andrews, F. M., & Withey, S. B. (1976). *Social indicators of well-being: America's perception of life quality.* New York: Plenum Press.

Argyle, M. (1999). Causes and correlates of happiness. In D. Kahneman, E. Diener, & N. Schwarz (Eds.), *Well-being: The foundations of hedonic psychology* (pp. 353–373). New York: Russell Sage Foundation.

Aristotle. (1974). *The Nichomacean ethics* (J. A. K. Thomson, Trans.) Harmondsworth, NY: Penguin.

Aronson, E. (1969). A theory of cognitive dissonance: A current perspective. *Advances in Experimental Social Psychology, 2,* 21–34.

Atkinson, R. L., Atkinson, R. C., Smith, E. E., Bem, D. J., & Nolen-Hoeksema, S. (1996). *Hilgard's introduction to psychology* (12th ed.). Fort Worth, TX: Harcourt Brace.

Barton, W. E. (1976). *Abraham Lincoln and his books: With selections from the writings of Lincoln and a bibliography of books in print relating to Abraham Lincoln.* Folcroft, PA: Folcroft Library Editions.

Braungart, J. M., Plomin, R., DeFries, J. C., & Fulker, D. W. (1992). Genetic influence on tester-rated infant temperament as assessed by Bayley's Infant Behavior Record: Nonadoptive and adoptive siblings and twins. *Developmental Psychology, 28,* 40–47.

Brehm, J. W., & Brehm, S. S. (1981). *Psychological reactance: A theory of freedom and control.* New York: Academic Press.

Brickman, P., Coates, D., & Janoff-Bulman, R. (1978). Lottery winners and accident victims: Is happiness relative? *Journal of Personality and Social Psychology, 36,* 917–927.

Bruner, J. (1986). *Actual minds, possible worlds.* Cambridge, MA: Harvard University Press.

Costa, P. T., McCrae, R. R., & Zonderman, A. B. (1987). Environmental and dispositional influences on well-being: Longitudinal follow-up of an American national sample. *British Journal of Psychology, 78,* 299–306.

Csikszentmihalyi, M. (1990). *Flow: The psychology of optimal experience.* New York: Harper & Row.

DeNeve, K. M. (1999). Happy as an extraverted clam? The role of personality for subjective well-being. *Current Directions in Psychological Science, 8,* 141–144.

Diener, E. (1984). Subjective well-being. *Psychological Bulletin, 95,* 542–575.

Diener, E. (1994). Assessing subjective well-being. Progress and opportunities. *Social Indicators Research, 31,* 103–157.

Diener, E. Horwitz, J., & Emmons, R. A. (1985). Happiness of the very wealthy. *Social Indicators Research, 16,* 263–274.

Diener, E., & Lucas, R. E. (1999). Personality and subjective well-being. In D. Kahneman, E. Diener, & N. Schwartz (Eds.), *Well-being: The foundations of hedonic psychology* (pp. 213–229). New York: Russell Sage.

Diener, E., & Oishi, S. (2000). Money and happiness: Income and subjective well-being across nations. In E. Diener & E. M. Sub (Eds.), *Culture and subjective well-being* (pp. 185–218). Cambridge, MA: MIT Press.

Diener, E., Suh, E. M., Lucas, R. E., & Smith, H. L. (1999). Subjective well-being: Three decades of progress. *Psychological Bulletin, 125,* 276–302.

Diener, E., Suh, E. K., Smith, H., & Shao, L. (1995). National differences in reported well-being: Why do they occur? *Social Indicators Research, 34,* 7–32.

Dweck, C. S. (1999). *Self-theories: Their role in motivation, personality, and development.* Philadelphia, PA: Psychology Press.

Dweck, C. S., & Leggett, E. (1988). A social–cognitive approach to motivation and personality. *Psychological Review, 95,* 256–273.

Ekman, P., & Davidson, R. J. (1994). *The nature of emotion: Fundamental questions.* Oxford, England: Oxford University Press.

Eysenck, M. W. (1990). *Happiness: Facts and myths.* East Sussex, England: Erlbaum.

Festinger, L. (1957). *A theory of cognitive dissonance.* Stanford, CA: Stanford University Press.

Fiske, S. T., & Taylor, S. E. (1991). *Social cognition* (2nd ed.). New York: McGraw-Hill.

Fordyce, M. W. (1977). Development of a program to increase personal happiness. *Journal of Counseling Psychology, 24,* 511–521.

Forgas, J. P. (1995): Mood and judgment: The affect infusion model (AIM). *Psychological Bulletin, 117,* 39–66.

Freedman, J. (1978). *Happy people: What happiness is, who has it, and why.* New York: Harcourt Brace Jovanovich.

Gloaguen, V., Cottraux, J., Cucherat, M., & Blackburn, I. (1998). A meta-analysis of the effects of cognitive therapy in depressed patients. *Journal of Affective Disorders, 49,* 59–72.

Gray, J. A. (1990). Brain systems that mediate both emotion and cognition. *Cognition and Emotion, 4,* 269–288.

Headey, B., & Wearing, A. (1989). Personality, life events, and subjective well-being: Toward a dynamic equilibrium model. *Journal of Personality and Social Psychology, 57,* 731–739.

Kahneman, D., & Tversky, A. (1979). Prospect theory: An analysis of decision under risk. *Econometrica, 47,* 263–291.

Kim, D. D., & Lyubomirsky, S. (1997). *Effects of unfavorable social comparisons on cognitive interference in happy and unhappy people.* Unpublished honors thesis, Department of Psychology, University of California, Riverside.

Lichter, S., Haye, K., & Kammann, R. (1980). Increasing happiness through cognitive training. *New Zealand Psychologist, 9,* 57–64.

Linville, P. W., & Fischer, G. W. (1990). Preferences for separating or combining events. *Journal of Personality and Social Psychology, 59,* 1–18.

Lykken, D., & Tellegen, A. (1996). Happiness is a stochastic phenomenon. *Psychological Science, 7,* 186–189.

Lyubomirsky, S. (2000). *Cultural differences in the pursuit of happiness: The case of the United States vs. Russia.* Unpublished manuscript, Department of Psychology, University of California, Riverside.

Lyubomirsky, S., Kasri, F., & Zehm, K. (2000). *Hedonic casualties of self-reflection.* Unpublished manuscript, Department of Psychology, University of California, Riverside.

Lyubomirsky, S., & Lepper, H. S. (1999). A measure of subjective happiness: Preliminary reliability and construct validation. *Social Indicators Research, 46,* 137–155.

Lyubomirsky, S., & Lepper, H. S. (2000). *What are the differences between happiness and self-esteem?* Manuscript submitted for publication.

Lyubomirsky, S., & Ross, L. (1997). Hedonic consequences of social comparison: A contrast of happy and unhappy people. *Journal of Personality and Social Psychology, 73,* 1141–1157.

Lyubomirsky, S., & Ross, L. (1999). Changes in attractiveness of elected, rejected, and precluded alternatives: A comparison of happy and unhappy individuals. *Journal of Personality and Social Psychology, 76,* 988–1007.

Lyubomirsky, S., & Tucker, K. L. (1998). Implications of individual differences in subjective happiness for perceiving, interpreting, and thinking about life events. *Motivation and Emotion, 22,* 155–186.

Lyubomirsky, S., & Tucker, K. L. (2000). *Social comparison processes among happy and unhappy people: Affective and cognitive responses to hedonically conflicting feedback.* Manuscript submitted for publication.

Lyubomirsky, S., Tucker, K. L., Caldwell, N. D., & Berg, K. (1999). Why ruminators are poor problem solvers: Clues from the phenomenology of dysphoric rumination. *Journal of Personality and Social Psychology, 77,* 1041–1060.

Markus, H. R., & Kitayama, S. (1991). Culture and the self: Implications for cognition, emotion, and motivation. *Psychological Review, 98,* 224–253.

Myers, D. G. (1992). *The pursuit of happiness.* New York: William Morrow.

Myers, D. G. (2000). The funds, friends, and faith of happy people. *American Psychologist, 55,* 56–67.

Myers, D. G. & Diener, E. (1995). Who is happy? *Psychological Science, 6,* 10–19.

Plomin, R., DeFries, J. C., & Loehlin, J. C. (1977). Genotype–environment interaction and correlation in the analysis of human behavior. *Psychological Bulletin, 84,* 309–322.

Ross, L. (1990). Recognizing the role of construal processes. In I. Rock (Ed.), *The legacy of Solomon Asch: Essays in cognition and social psychology* (pp. 77–96). Hillsdale, NJ: Erlbaum.

Ryff, C. D., Singer, B., Love, G. D., & Essex, M. J. (1998). Resilience in adulthood and later life: Defining features and dynamic processes. In J. Lomranz (Ed.), *Handbook of aging and mental health: An integrative approach* (pp. 69–96). New York: Plenum Press.

Scarr, S. (1988). How genotypes and environments combine: Development and individual differences. In N. Bolger, A. Caspi, G. Downey, & M. Moorehouse (Eds.), *Persons in context: Developmental processes* (pp. 217–244). New York: Cambridge University Press.

Scarr, S., & McCartney, K. (1983). How people make their own environments: A theory of genotype–environment effects. *Child Development, 54,* 424–435.

Schwartz, B. (2000). Pitfalls on the road to a positive psychology of hope. In J. E. Gillham & J. Templeton (Eds.), *The science of optimism and hope: Research essays in honor of Martin E. P. Seligman* (pp. 399–412). Radner, PA: Templeton Foundation Press.

Schwartz, B., Ward, A., & Monterosso, J. (2000). Satisficing versus maximizing: Happiness is a matter of choice. Manuscript in preparation, Department of Psychology, Swarthmore College.

Seligman, M. E. P. (1994). *What you can change and what you can't.* New York: Knopf.

Seligman, M. E. P., & Csikszentmihalyi, M. (2000). Positive psychology: An introduction. *American Psychologist, 55,* 5–14.

Shatté, A. J., Gillham, J. E., & Reivich, K. J. (in press). Promoting hope in children and adolescents. In J. E. Gillham & J. Templeton (Eds.), *The science of optimism and hope: Research essays in honor of Martin E. P. Seligman.* Radner, PA: Templeton Foundation Press.

Sheldon, K. M., Kasser, T., Smith, K., & Share, T. (in press). Personal goals and psychological growth: Testing an intervention to enhance goal-attainment and personality integration. *Journal of Personality.*

Sheldon, K. M., & Houser-Marko, A. (2001). Self-concordance, goal-attainment, and the pursuit of happiness: Can there be an upward spiral? *Journal of Personality and Social Psychology, 80,* 152–165.

Showers, C. J. (2000). Self-organization in emotional contexts. In J. P. Forgas (Ed.), *Feeling and thinking: The role of affect in social cognition* (pp. 283–307). New York: Cambridge University Press.

Silver, R. L. (1982). *Coping with an undesirable life event: A study of early reactions to physical disability.* Unpublished doctoral dissertation, Northwestern University, Evanston, IL.

Simon, H. A. (1976). *Administrative behavior: A study of decision-making processes in administrative organization* (3rd ed). New York: Free Press.

Steele, C. M. (1988). The psychology of self-affirmation: Sustaining the integrity of the self. *Advances in Experimental Social Psychology, 21,* 261–302.

Swann, Jr., W. B. (1983). Self-verification: Bringing social reality into harmony with the self. In J. Suls, & A. G. Greenwald (Eds.), *Social psychology perspectives* (Vol. 2, pp. 33–66). Hillsdale, NJ: Erlbaum.

Taylor, S. E., & Brown, J. D. (1988). Illusion and well-being: A social psychological perspective on mental health. *Psychological Bulletin, 103*, 193–210.

Tellegen, A., Lykken, D. T., Bouchard, T. J., Wilcox, K. J., Segal, N. L., & Rich, S. (1988). Personality similarity in twins reared apart and together. *Journal of Personality and Social Psychology, 54*, 1031–1039.

Triandis, H. C., Bontempo, R., Leung, K., & Hui, C. H. (1990). A method for determining cultural, demographic, and personal constructs. *Journal of Cross-Cultural Psychology, 21*, 302–318.

Tucker, K. L. (2000). *The role of the behavioral activation system in event construal: An examination of appreciation in happy and unhappy individuals.* Unpublished doctoral dissertation, University of California, Riverside.

Tversky, A., & Kahneman, D. (1981). The framing of decisions and the psychology of choice. *Science, 211*, 453–458.

Veenhoven, R. (1988). The utility of happiness. *Social Indicators Research, 20*, 333–354.

Wegner, D. M., & Pennebaker, J. W. (1993). *Handbook of mental control.* Englewood Cliffs, NJ: Prentice Hall.

Wicklund, R. A. (1974). *Freedom and reactance.* Potomac, MD: Erlbaum.

Wheeler, L., & Miyake, K. (1992). Social comparison in everyday life. *Journal of Personality and Social Psychology, 62*, 760–773.

Wood, J. V. (1989). Theory and research concerning social comparisons of personal attributes. *Psychological Bulletin, 106*, 231–248.

Zimbardo, P. G., & Boyd, J. N. (1999). Putting time in perspective: A valid, reliable individual-differences metric. *Journal of Personality and Social Psychology, 77*, 1271–1288.

THE POSITIVE PSYCHOLOGY
OF NEGATIVE THINKING

Julie K. Norem and Edward C. Chang

The previous selection by Lyubomirsky summarized research on the factors that promote happiness. The present article, by Julie Norem and Edward Chang, seeks to remind us that "feeling good is not always the highest priority." While most research in humanistic psychology tends to regard unhappiness as an unfortunate side effect of a maladaptive cognitive style, Norem and Chang propose that for at least one kind of person, the "defensive pessimist," unhappiness is actually neces-sary, or at least often helpful. Their research suggests that "strategic optimists" gen-erally feel good about themselves and the future, and indeed need to feel this way in order to perform well. Defensive pessimists, on the other hand, use pessimistic "worst case scenarios" in order to control their anxiety, and when they are pre-vented from doing this, their performance gets worse. As Norem and Chang ob-serve, this finding implies that " 'one size fits all' prescriptions for optimism and positive thinking do not, in fact fit some people very well."

Norem and Chang also have a larger lesson to teach. They point out that while American culture strongly values optimism, especially in leaders, unrealistic optimism has heavy costs. History provides many examples of proposals for fiscal policies, spaceflight launches, and even wars whose opponents were derided as pes-simists. Then the pessimists turned out to be right.

Norem and Chang's result is not completely pessimistic. True, they argue that there is an often-unseen downside to optimism. Then again, as the title of their ar-ticle reveals, they also see an upside to pessimism!

From *Journal of Clinical Psychology, 58,* 993–1001, 2002.

There is substantial evidence that optimism, in its many forms, is related to better out-comes (e.g., coping, satisfaction, well-being) measured in a variety of ways across a variety of contexts. This evidence makes it extremely tempt-ing to conclude that optimism is always to be desired over pessimism, and further, that as re-searchers, educators, policy consultants, therapists, and parents we should do everything we can to promote optimism—a conclusion, not coinciden-tally, supported by much of American popular cul-ture. This strong positivity zeitgeist means that it is especially important that we clarify for ourselves, and for those who might be consumers of our work, the ways in which our theories and research present a picture that is more complicated—and more useful—than "optimism is good" and "pessimism is bad."

The purpose of this article is to review some of those complications. Our aim is to be illustrative, not comprehensive, and many of our points are quite simple. Nevertheless, our experience is that complexities are easily obscured in both lay and professional discourse, and that it is thus useful to make them explicit. We will draw heavily on defensive pessimism research, both because we know it well and because its counterintuitive results clearly exemplify several of the points we hope to make. In summary, those points are:

1. Optimism and pessimism, as well as positive thinking and negative thinking, are umbrella terms that cover several concepts, the differences among which need to be kept clear.
2. The costs and benefits that accrue to one form of optimism or pessimism are not automatically associated with other kinds.
3. There are potential benefits *and* costs to *both* optimism and pessimism or positive and negative thinking (as they are variously defined); but several factors often combine in ways that lead to overemphasis on the merits of optimism and under-emphasis of its potential costs.
4. Those costs and benefits may be highly sensitive to context (broadly and variously defined); thus, our research designs, interpretations of results, advocacy, interventions and teaching need to be sensitive to costs, benefits, and context.
5. Positive psychology is not synonymous with positive thinking and optimism.

A quick sampling of the kinds of optimism and pessimism found in the literature makes clear that there is a daunting array of constructs. Norem and Chang (2001) list several, including disposi-

tional optimism and pessimism (Scheier & Carver, 1985), optimistic and pessimistic attributional or explanatory styles (Peterson & Seligman, 1987), naive optimism (Epstein & Meier, 1989), optimistic biases or illusions (Taylor & Brown, 1988), neurotic and rational pessimism (Kelman, 1945), unrealistic optimism (Weinstein & Klein, 1996), unrealistic pessimism (Dolinski, Gromski, & Zawisza, 1987), realistic pessimism (Fresc, 1992), and defensive pessimism and strategic optimism (Norem & Cantor, 1986).

Distinctions among these constructs are more than semantic because different constructs have different associated consequences and implications. In some research, for example, pessimism, but not optimism, has been associated with particular outcomes (Dember, Martin, Hummer, & Howe, 1989; Raikkoenen, Matthews, Flory, Owens, & Gump, 1999). Defensive pessimism is linked to more positive outcomes than dispositional pessimism, and both naïve and unrealistic optimism are linked to more negative outcomes than dispositional optimism.

Different types of optimism and pessimism also vary in both the extent to which and the circumstances under which they are potentially changeable. At one extreme, Seligman and colleagues have argued that attributional style is learned (e.g., Seligman, 1991), and that maladaptive attributional patterns can be readily changed in therapeutic and educational contexts. In contrast, there is little theoretical reason to suspect, and no empirical evidence to suggest, that dispositional optimism and pessimism are malleable. Taylor (1989) argued that optimistic illusions are adaptive in part because they are responsive to experience and feedback from the environment; nevertheless, to the extent that these illusions are maintained by unconscious processes, there is reason to suspect that they might be relatively resistant to change (Norem, 1998). Defensive pessimism, theoretically at least, is among the more malleable types of pessimism; yet as we will see later, it is far from clear that individuals necessarily benefit from being "cured" of their defensive pessimism (Norem, 2001b).

One of the explicit goals of positive psychology (Seligman & Csikszentmihalyi, 2000) is to apply psychological knowledge to the betterment of individuals and society. In applied contexts, we need to think carefully about what we might realistically endeavor to change in order to improve client, student, or employee outcomes, and when change might have unintended consequences. One of the biggest gaps in optimism and pessimism research—and one which is central to questions of change—concerns the intrapsychic context of optimism and pessimism. For example, optimism is correlated positively with extraversion, self-confidence, self-esteem, repression, self-deception, and positive affect, and negatively with anxiety, neuroticism, self-consciousness, and a host of other variables. Though we are becoming more sophisticated about isolating the statistical effects of single variables, we need to remember that in real life, characteristics are integrated within an individual's personality, and their effects do not occur in a vacuum.

As an example, Davidson and Prkachin (1997), in one of the few published attempts to disentangle the effects of dispositional optimism and unrealistic optimism, showed in two different studies that dispositional optimism and unrealistic optimism *interacted* to predict coronary heart disease (CHD)-related outcomes. In the first study, optimism alone was unrelated to exercise over time while unrealistic optimism was related to decreased exercise over time. Those participants who were high on both optimism and unrealistic optimism showed the largest *decreases* in exercise over time while those who were high in optimism and low in unrealistic optimism showed the greatest increases. A similar pattern was found in a second study, when the outcome variable was knowledge of CHD prevention after classroom instruction. In both studies, unrealistic optimism and dispositional optimism were positively correlated with each other. This study makes clear that (a) the distinctions among different kinds of optimism and pessimism are consequential, (b) all optimism is not equally beneficial, (c) we know very little about

interactions among different types of optimism and pessimism or how changing one kind of optimism (or pessimism or negative thinking) will change another.

Rethinking Affect as an Outcome

Particular life outcomes also do not occur in a vacuum. Not surprisingly, in a cultural context that highly values individualism, the vast majority of research on optimism and pessimism focuses on individual outcomes, and especially on outcomes related to positive affect and satisfaction. The most ubiquitous findings across optimism and pessimism research are those relating optimism of many sorts to more positive affect. Somewhat surprisingly perhaps, research on more objective outcomes such as task performance reveal much less reliable links across optimism constructs (Affleck, Tenne, & Apter, 2001; Norem, 2002b).

Affect is conceptually tricky as an outcome variable, however. For example, several recent lines of research converge to suggest that predispositions to experience positive and negative affect are genetically influenced and have distinct biological substrates (Ball & Zuckerman, 1990; Gray, 1987; Zuckerman, 2001). This does not mean, of course, that those tendencies cannot be changed through experience or influenced by environment, nor does it imply that variation in affect within individuals is not influenced by positive or negative thinking. It does suggest, however, that when one compares affective and other outcomes across individuals, it is important to remember that outcomes need to be evaluated relative to where people start. Finding a definitive starting point in the relationship between affect and expectations is difficult.

If one person begins with a stronger predisposition to experience negative affect, or a weaker tendency to feel positive affect, we have to consider both the extent to which mood influences initial expectations in a particular situation and variations in mood from individual to individual. Moreover, patterns of covariance of optimism/pessimism and mood across individuals do not necessarily mimic covariance *within* individuals.

Defensive Pessimism: Using Negative Thinking

These abstract points are clearly instantiated in research on defensive pessimism (for a review, see Norem, 2001a). Defensive pessimism refers to a strategy anxious individuals may use to pursue important goals: These individuals set unrealistically low expectations and then devote considerable energy to mentally playing through or reflecting on all the possible outcomes they can imagine for a given situation.

Research has typically contrasted defensive pessimism with strategic optimism. The latter refers to a strategy whereby individuals set optimistic expectations for their own performance and actively avoid extensive reflection. In addition to avoiding reflection prior to a task, strategic optimists typically employ the kinds of self-serving optimistic illusions Taylor and Brown (1988) describe.

Generally, research has shown that defensive pessimists perform as well as strategic optimists, and that both groups show performance decrements and increased anxiety when prevented from using their preferred strategies (Cantor & Norem, 1989; Cantor, Norem, Niedenthal, & Langston, 1987; Norem & Cantor, 1986; Norem & Illingworth, 1993; Spencer & Norem, 1996). For example, Norem and Illingworth (1993) found that, on both an arithmetic task in a laboratory experiment and when pursuing their personal goals in "real life," defensive pessimists did best when they thought through possible negative outcomes. Strategic optimists, in contrast, did best when they avoided reflecting on possible negative outcomes and significantly worse when they did reflect. Similarly, Spencer and Norem (1996) found that defensive pessimists performed best on a dart-throwing task when they engaged in coping imagery (imagining what could go wrong) and significantly worse when they engaged in relax-

ation imagery. The opposite pattern was obtained for strategic optimists.

Across a variety of settings, participants, and tasks, this research shows that when defensive pessimists and strategic optimists are left alone to use their strategies, they do equivalently well. Both groups also are vulnerable to disruptions that interfere with their strategies, but what disrupts one group's performance facilitates the other group's performance.

Beyond performance outcomes, however, this same research also has shown that strategic optimists tend to be more satisfied and in a better mood than defensive pessimists. From those results, one might conclude that strategic optimism is clearly better than defensive pessimism, even if defensive pessimists often perform well. After all, performing well and being really happy about it is obviously better than performing well but feeling less satisfied. It is very tempting, then, to think that people using defensive pessimism need to be calmed down and reassured, and that the best thing is to help them become more optimistic and thus more satisfied.

That conclusion, however, ignores the crucial point that people who use defensive pessimism are typically high in anxiety. That aspect of intrapsychic context is fundamental to understanding the strategy. Further research shows that it is possible to cheer up defensive pessimists—to put them in a positive mood—just as it is possible to put strategic optimists in a negative mood. Surprisingly, however, positive mood *impairs* the performance of defensive pessimists and does not lead to greater satisfaction. Negative mood typically impairs the performance of strategic optimists (Norem & Illingworth, in press; Sanna, 1996, 1998).

In other words, despite considerable evidence that dispositional pessimism can have debilitating motivational effects, *defensive* pessimism has a different and positive function: It helps anxious people manage their anxiety so that it does not interfere with their performance. Its meaning and consequences are only seen when considered in conjunction with the problem that anxiety poses for individuals motivated to pursue performance goals. Defensive pessimists perform better when they are allowed to maintain their low expectations and to reflect on negative possibilities before a task; their performance is impaired (and they feel *more* anxious) if that reflective process is disrupted by positive thinking and optimistic expectations or curtailed by positive mood.

Comparing defensive pessimists to strategic optimists is informative, but it is at least as illuminating to compare defensive pessimists to other people who are anxious but do not use defensive pessimism. In a longitudinal study, Norem (2002a) found that defensive pessimists show significant increases in self-esteem and satisfaction over time, perform better academically, form more supportive friendship networks, and make more progress on their personal goals than equally anxious students who do not use defensive pessimism. Anxious people who use defensive pessimism, in other words, do better than anxious people who do not. This research converges with that contrasting strategic optimism and defensive pessimism to suggest quite strongly that taking away their defensive pessimism is not the way to help anxious individuals.

Defensive pessimism research makes clear that "one size fits all" prescriptions for optimism and positive thinking do not, in fact, fit some people very well. From this perspective, the negative affect—specifically, the anxiety—experienced by the defensive pessimists is not so much an outcome of their negative approach, but part of the problem their approach is designed to tackle. The pessimism and focus on negative possible outcomes that make up defensive pessimism as a strategy function as a "do-it-yourself" (and quite effective) cognitive therapy for anxious individuals; imposing positive thinking disables them.

More generally, one important life outcome that we risk ignoring if we focus exclusively on the positive is the ability to tolerate negative affect and negative self-views while we work toward positive change. Defensive pessimists work through their anxiety on their way toward their goals rather than focusing on increasing their immediate happiness or satisfaction: They remind us that feeling good is not always the highest priority.

The Costs of Optimism?

Somewhat less obviously, research contrasting defensive pessimists with strategic optimists also illustrates that the strategic optimists are susceptible to derailment of their positive approach. Reflecting about possible outcomes impairs their performance. This is less a general indictment of their strategy—after all, they usually do quite well—than a hint about some of the potential costs of optimistic strategies and the vulnerabilities of those who use them. Situations or contexts that require review of alternative possible outcomes (e.g., "trouble-shooting" to diagnose potential problems) or involve negative outcomes that need to be acknowledged so that they can be prepared for may not mesh well with strategic optimism.

Aging may very well be one of those contexts. Some research suggests that the costs and benefits of optimism and pessimism may vary across the life span. Robinson Whelen, Kim, MacCallum, and Kiecolt Glaser (1997) found little evidence for the "power of positive thinking" in predicting anxiety, stress, depression, and self-appraised health among an older-aged group of caregivers and noncaregivers. Isaacowitz and Seligman (2001) reported that among the elderly, a realistically pessimistic perspective is associated with *better* adaptation to negative life events, in contrast to the typical findings with younger samples.

Optimism and positive thinking can derail us is if they lead us to ignore or discount important cues and warnings. Given the self-serving function of optimistic biases, strategic optimists should be motivated to preserve their positive self-images and positive outlooks, and thus potentially resistant to negative feedback that might be informative. Indeed, in one study, Norem (2001a) found that strategic optimists remembered feedback about a social performance as significantly more positive than it actually was, and also thought they had less need to improve their performance than observers perceived they did.

In many everyday life contexts, the mild positive biases reinforced by optimistic attributional styles may be so motivating of effective action that they compensate for the potential problems that could result from avoidance or distortion of negative feedback. If, for example, a strategic optimist perceives that a neighbor has a more positive impression of him than is the case, the optimist's likely response would be reciprocation: We tend to like those whom we think like us. If the optimist likes this neighbor (whom he believes likes him) and then behaves in a consistently friendly way to that neighbor, the neighbor is relatively likely to reciprocate in turn. Even if the neighbor's actual evaluation of the optimist never becomes quite as positive as the optimist's perception (or as the optimist's self-evaluation), it may well be positive enough to form the foundation for a mutually beneficial friendship.

Nevertheless, we know relatively little about when and how an inflated or self-deceptive sense of self-regard traverses the terrain between positive motivation and less adaptive, or even destructive, egotism. Bushman and Baumeister (1998), for example, showed how threatened egotism can lead to aggression and violence against others.

Considering Bushman and Baumeister's (1998) findings highlights once again that the majority of research on optimism and positive thinking has considered their consequences for individual achievement and satisfaction. There is a relative dearth of research that considers not just the outcomes of individuals but the influence of individual optimism on the outcomes of other people. Americans generally respond well to others' optimism, and we certainly expect it of our leaders (Chemers, Watson, & May, 2000). Much is made, for example, of the self-confidence, optimism, personal accomplishments, and resilience of American business leaders. When business practices fail, we are likely to attribute the soft landings (aided by "golden parachutes") of executives and their often spectacular comebacks to their positive attitudes. Much less often, however, do we tally up the costs to employees (and sometimes investors and clients) when overly optimistic expansions and acquisitions

lead to bankruptcy and layoffs. Indeed, throughout society we could point to delays and overruns as a result of overly optimistic projections, and disasters that might have been avoided or curtailed if we were willing to consider the negative. Nevertheless, just as in ancient times, we remain unreceptive to modern Cassandras—no matter how many times we are reminded that the original Cassandra was right. In these contexts, much as with the self-serving attributions of optimistic individuals, optimism gets the credit when things go well, but avoids blame when things go badly.

The costs and benefits of prototypically American, individualistic optimism also may vary across cultures. Chang (1996) found that Asian Americans were significantly more pessimistic than Caucasian Americans, but not significantly less optimistic. In addition, while pessimism was negatively associated with problem-solving and expressing emotion coping strategies for Caucasian Americans, it was *positively* associated with use of these coping strategies for Asian Americans. It seems likely that relationships between self-enhancement and other outcomes might vary in cultures that are less focused on individual achievement and satisfaction than American culture.

Positive Psychology and Negative Thinking

None of this is to suggest that the benefits of positive thinking and optimism are not both real and substantial in many cases. We just want to suggest that the kinds of research and arguments we have reviewed emphasize that positive psychology needs to include more than positive thinking and optimism. It should reflect the diversity of ways in which people achieve a diverse array of positive outcomes, including interpersonal and social outcomes. In studying how people achieve positive outcomes, we need to look beyond positive affect and personal satisfaction. We also need to look beyond what people have achieved at a given point in time to what they are working on achieving over time and what they accomplish relative to where they start.

The problem with any general zeitgeist is the extent to which it may blind us to the questions we are neglecting to ask and the answers we do not want to see. The challenge for positive psychology as it works to better the human condition is to remember that there is no one human condition. We live under many conditions, across our own life span, across different situations, in interactions with different people in our lives, and across a multitude of economic, social, environmental, and political circumstances. As we study how people make positive progress in their lives, we need to take care not to let the power of any one pathway keep us from seeing the alternative routes individuals devise toward their goals. Humans excel at adaptation to varied circumstances using varied means; it will take all of our collective insight to understand our own resourcefulness.

References

Affleck, G., Tennen, H., & Apter. A. (2001). Optimism, pessimism, and daily life with chronic illness. In E. C. Chang (Ed.), *Optimism and pessimism: Implications for theory, research, and practice* (pp. 147–168). Washington, DC: American Psychological Association.

Ball, S. A., & Zuckerman, M. (1990). Sensation seeking, Eysenck's personality dimensions, and reinforcement sensitivity in concept formation. *Personality and Individual Differences, 11,* 343–353.

Bushman, B. J., & Baumeister, R. F. (1998). Threatened egotism, narcissism, self-esteem, and direct and displaced aggression: Does self-love or self-hate lead to violence? *Journal of Personality and Social Psychology, 75,* 219–229.

Cantor, N., & Norem, J. K. (1989). Defensive pessimism and stress and coping. *Social Cognition, 7,* 92–112.

Cantor, N., Norem, J. K., Niedenthal, P. M., & Langston, C. A. (1987). Life tasks, self-concept ideals, and cognitive strategies in a life transition. *Journal of Personality and Social Psychology, 53,* 1178–1191.

Chang, E. C. (1996). Evidence for the cultural specificity of pessimism in Asians vs. Caucasians: A test of a general negativity hypothesis. *Personality and Individual Differences, 21,* 819–822.

Chemers, M. M., Watson, C. B., & May, S. T. (2000). Dispositional affect and leadership effectiveness: A comparison of self-esteem, optimism, and efficacy. *Personality and Social Psychology Bulletin, 26,* 267–277.

Davidson, K., & Prkachin, K. (1997). Optimism and unrealistic optimism have an interacting impact on health-promoting behavior and knowledge changes. *Personality and Social Psychology Bulletin, 23,* 617–625.

Dember, W. N., Martin, S. H., Hummer, M. K., & Howe, S. R. (1989). The measurement of optimism and pessimism. *Current Psychology: Research and Reviews, 8,* 102–119.

Dolinski, D., Gromski, W., & Zawisza, E. (1987). Unrealistic pessimism. *Journal of Social Psychology, 127,* 511–516.

Epstein, S., & Meier, P. (1989). Constructive thinking: A broad coping variable with specific components. *Journal of Personality and Social Psychology, 57,* 332–350.

Frese, M. (1992). A plea for realistic pessimism: On objective reality, coping with stress, and psychological dysfunction. In L. Montada (Ed.), *Life crises and experiences of loss in adulthood* (pp. 81–94). Hillsdale, NJ: Erlbaum.

Gray, J. A. (1987). The neuropsychology of emotion and personality. In S. M. Stahl, S. D. Iverson, & E. C. Goodman (Eds.), *Cognitive neurochemistry* (pp. 171–190). Oxford, England: Oxford University Press.

Isaacowitz, D. M., & Seligman, M. E. P. (2001). Is pessimism a risk factor for depressive mood among community-dwelling older adults? *Behaviour Research and Therapy, 39,* 255–272.

Kelman, H. (1945). Neurotic pessimism. *Psychoanalytic Review, 32,* 419–448.

Norem, J. K. (1986). Defensive pessimism: Harnessing anxiety as motivation. *Journal of Personality and Social Psychology, 51,* 1208–1217.

Norem, J. K. (2001a). Defensive pessimism, optimism, and pessimism. In E. C. Chang (Ed.), *Optimism and pessimism: Implications for theory, research, and practice* (pp. 77–100). Washington, DC: American Psychological Association.

Norem, J. K. (2001b). The power of negative thinking. New York: Basic Books.

Norem, J. K. (2002a). Defensive pessimism and personal growth: From negative thinking to positive outcomes. Unpublished manuscript, Wellesley College, Wellesley, MA.

Norem, J. K. (2002b). Pessimism: Accentuating the positive possibilities. In E. C. Chang & L. Sanna (Eds.), *Personality, strategy, and adjustment: Beyond virtue and vice.* Washington, DC: American Psychological Association.

Norem, J. K., & Cantor, N. (1986). Anticipatory and post hoc cushioning strategies: Optimism and defensive pessimism in "risky" situations. *Cognitive Therapy, and Research, 10,* 347–362.

Norem, J. K., & Chang, E. C. (2001). A very full glass: Adding complexity to our thinking about the implications and applications of optimism and pessimism research. In E. C. Chang (Ed.), *Optimism and pessimism: Implications for theory, research, and practice* (pp. 347–367). Washington, DC: American Psychological Association.

Norem, J. K., & Illingworth, K. S. S. (1993). Strategy-dependent effects of reflecting on self and tasks: Some implications of optimism and defensive pessimism. *Journal of Personality and Social Psychology, 65,* 822–835.

Norem, J. K., & Illingworth, K. S. S. (in press). Mood and performance among strategic optimists and defensive pessimists. *Journal of Research in Personality.*

Peterson, C., & Seligman, M. E. (1987). Explanatory style and illness. *Journal of Personality, 55,* 237–265.

Raikkoenen, K., Matthews, K. A., Flory, J. D., Owens, J. F., & Gump, B. B. (1999). Effects of optimism, pessimism, and trait anxiety on ambulatory blood pressure and mood during everyday life. *Journal of Personality and Social Psychology, 76,* 104–113.

Robinson Whelen, S., Kim, C., MacCallum, R. C., & Kiecolt Glaser, J. K. (1997). Distinguishing optimism from pessimism in older adults: Is it more important to be optimistic or not to be pessimistic? *Journal of Personality and Social Psychology, 73,* 1345–1353.

Sanna, L. J. (1996). Defensive pessimism, optimism, and stimulating alternatives: Some ups and downs of prefactual and counterfactual thinking. *Journal of Personality and Social Psychology, 71,* 1020–1036.

Sanna, L. J. (1998). Defensive pessimism and optimism: The bittersweet influence of mood on performance and prefactual and counterfactual thinking. *Cognition and Emotion, 12,* 635–665.

Scheier, M. F., & Carver, C. S. (1985). Optimism, coping, and health: Assessment and implications of generalized outcome expectancies. *Health Psychology, 4,* 219–247.

Seligman, M. E. P. (1991). *Learned optimism.* New York: Knopf.

Seligman, M. E. P., & Csikszentmihalyi, M. (2000). Positive psychology: An introduction. *American Psychologist, 55,* 5–14.

Spencer, S. M., & Norem, J. K. (1996). Reflection and distraction: Defensive pessimism, strategic optimism, and performance. *Personality and Social Psychology Bulletin, 22,* 354–365.

Taylor, S. E. (1989). *Positive illusions: Creative self-deception and the healthy mind.* New York: Basic Books.

Taylor, S. E. & Brown, J. D. (1988). Illusion and well-being: A social psychological perspective on mental health. *Psychological Bulletin, 103,* 193–210.

Weinstein, N. D., & Klein, W. M. (1996). Unrealistic optimism: Present and future. *Journal of Social and Clinical Psychology, 15,* 1–8.

Zuckerman, M. (2001). Optimism and pessimism: Biological foundations. In E. C. Chang (Ed.), *Optimism and pessimism: Implications for theory, research, and practice* (pp. 169–188). Washington, DC: American Psychological Association.

PART VI

Cross-Cultural Approaches to Personality

Migrations and technological advances have caused many cultures around the world to become both increasingly diverse and increasingly interconnected. This is perhaps nowhere more true than in America, where subcultures of European, African, Latin, and Asian origin coexist within the same borders. But elsewhere in the world as well cultural diversity is becoming more the rule than the exception.

It is only natural, therefore, that psychologists have turned some of their attention to the way that psychological processes and personality might vary among cultures. After a long period of slow but steady progress, research activity on these topics has dramatically accelerated in the past few years. The articles in this section sample from some of this recent work.

The section begins not with a research article but a commentary that was first published in the New York Times. In an example of cultural misunderstanding that received wide publicity a few years ago, a Danish mother visiting New York was arrested for leaving her baby parked in her carriage outside a restaurant. In this commentary, a fellow countrywoman comes to her defense and attempts to explain some of the—apparently surprisingly profound—cultural differences between New York City and Copenhagen.

The next article is a classic summary of key research by one of the first prominent researchers in cross-cultural psychology, Harry Triandis. Triandis organizes his survey around several fundamental dimensions of cultural variation, which include the difference between what are called "collectivist" and "individualist" cultures. This is the dimension of variation that has received the most attention, by far, in subsequent research. The basic idea is that people in Eastern or Asian cultures, such as Japan, see themselves as an integral part of an overall "collective" comprising many different individuals and groups. People in Western cultures, especially America, are more prone to see themselves as "individuals," separate and apart.

In the next selection, Hazel Markus and Shinobu Kitayama argue that this cultural difference is so profound that some American psychologists are literally afraid to think about it. Collectivist cultures promote fundamentally different values, they argue, including a much greater emphasis on interpersonal relations and mutual support, and a lesser emphasis on individual achievement, competition, and dominance. The next article, by Batja Mesquita, examines collectivism and individualism in association with emotional experience. She reports theory and evidence suggesting that for people in collectivist cultures, emotion is much more of a group experience than the isolated and solitary feelings more characteristic of a person in an individualistic culture. This paper is followed by another in a similar vein, by Eunkook Suh. Suh proposes that Western and individualistic cultures expect people to be consistent from one situation to the next, and even value such consistency as a sign of mental health. Collectivist cultures, in contrast, see the self as an ever-changing part of the larger social context and so observe and value this kind of consistency much less.

The final paper in this section is one that attempts to reach compromise between the tendencies to see people as psychologically the same the world over, and as so fundamentally different that they cannot even be compared across cultures. Verónica Benet-Martínez and Oliver John take a conception of the basic traits of personality—the "Big Five"—that originated in the United States, and seek to test its applicability in the more collectivist culture of Spain. The end result is a technique for assessing personality that allows common dimensions to be measured in different cultures while at the same time acknowledging and tapping into personality constructs that might be specific to a single cultural context. In that way, they argue, it might be possible to matar dos pájaros de un tiro ("kill two birds with one stone"). In the end, this is the challenge for cross-cultural investigations of personality: to reconcile the essential and universal aspects of human nature with the wide diversity of its expression across cultures.

The Danes Call It Fresh Air

Elisabeth Kallick Dyssegaard

On a chilly evening in the spring of 1997, several residents of New York City were horrified to see an unattended baby carriage, complete with a sleeping baby, parked on the sidewalk outside of a restaurant. They dialed 911 and the police promptly picked up the baby and took her to a temporary foster home for protection. When the baby's mother came out of the restaurant, realized her baby was gone, and went to the police herself, she was arrested.

In the media uproar and controversy that followed, at least one writer—the author of the present selection, which was published in the New York Times *shortly after this incident—came to the mother's defense. The mother was from Denmark, it turned out, and according to the author of the present article, in Denmark it is normal to park babies outside, even (or even especially?) when it is cold. The Danish mother had run afoul of cultural differences.*

The United States and Denmark are not usually held up as exemplars of cultural variation—they are both "Western" and individualistic, and indeed many Americans (including one of the editors of this volume) are of Danish descent. This episode reveals that the cultural similarity may be superficial. It would never occur to a New York mother to park her baby outside. It would never occur to a Danish mother, apparently, that this could be a problem. Cultural differences have a way of appearing suddenly, when they are least expected, where things are most taken for granted.

From *New York Times*, Op-Ed, 17 May 1997.

Last January I was home in Denmark with my American husband. As we walked through the wintry streets of Copenhagen with our 1-month-old son, we saw baby carriages, with babies in them, parked on the city's sidewalks. Inside the local cafes, mothers chatted with their friends.

My husband was shocked.

But we live in New York. New York, where I wouldn't leave a chained and padlocked empty baby carriage for one minute where I couldn't see it. New York, where we once parked two baby carriages outside a restaurant—without babies, of course—and in minutes had the neighborhood's homeless population checking them out as possible modes of transporting their belongings. We politely told them we were using the strollers and they, just as politely but with obvious regret, left.

But in Denmark, people park their empty

baby carriages unattended outside apartment buildings, supermarkets, and cafes. No one takes them. No one needs to take them. There are no street people; by American standards, there are no poor people.

Often, Danish parents also leave their babies outside. For one thing, Danish baby carriages are enormous. Babies ride high above the world on horse-carriage-size wheels. It's hard to get such a carriage into a cafe. (It would be impossible to get one into a New York apartment.) Besides, Danish cafes are very smoky places. Our baby would come home from our cafe visits smelling a lot like an ashtray, because, now that I'm a reasonably para-noid New Yorker, I brought him inside.

But there's a different health consideration as well. In Denmark, people have an almost religious conviction that fresh air, preferably cold air, is good for children. All Danish babies nap outside, even in freezing weather—tucked warmly under their plump goose-down comforters. In New York, play-grounds empty out when it's cold. In Denmark all children own a sort of polar survival suit that they wear from October to April, and they go out every day, even in winter.

In Norway, where the weather is even worse, my sister was told when she enrolled her 8-month-old son in day care that he would need a rain suit—the kind fishermen wear on the North Sea.

Though he wasn't yet walking, he was expected to crawl around in the playground every day; rain was no excuse.

So when I heard about the Danish mother ar-rested for leaving her 14-month-old daughter out-side a restaurant in the East Village, I at first laughed in disbelief at this gross cultural misun-derstanding. Perhaps she was being naive about the dangers of New York—and we may not know all the details of her situation—but in Denmark her behavior would have been considered perfectly normal. The woman's critics pointed out that it was "chilly" outside. But by Danish standards it was no doubt balmy.

Then I thought of the baby, who was taken by the police and temporarily placed in foster care. At 14 months, babies already know a lot about the pa-rameters of their safe little world. At its center are their parents. How horribly frightening to be sepa-rated from your mother and placed with complete strangers speaking a foreign language.

Maybe the people who called 911 to "save" the Danish baby really thought they were doing a good deed. Maybe the police thought they were teach-ing the mother a valuable lesson by jailing her. What they were really doing was punishing a par-ent. As is all too often the case, the well-being of the child was lost in this high-minded finger-wagging.

THE SELF AND SOCIAL BEHAVIOR IN DIFFERING CULTURAL CONTEXTS

Harry C. Triandis

In Part V, Jean-Paul Sartre argued that each individual's view of reality is distinct, but that there also is a universal human condition. This idea implies that the ultimate goal of cultural psychology should be to reconcile cultural variety with common humanity.

Few psychologists have achieved this goal so well as Harry Triandis. Born in Greece, for the past several decades Triandis has had a steady influence on the development of cross-cultural psychology from his base at the University of Illinois. In his research Triandis has consistently tried to describe the ways in which different cultures are both the same and different, and to formulate a set of dimensions along which all cultures can be characterized.

In the following selection, an excerpt from one of his major theoretical papers, Triandis proposes that cultures vary along three dimensions that are psychologically important. Some cultures are collectivist while others are relatively individualist; this is the dimension that is discussed in detail in the next selection by Markus and Kitayama. In addition, cultures vary in the degree to which they do or do not tolerate deviations from social norms (a dimension called looseness vs. tightness) and in their complexity. Triandis describes the relations between these variables and the development of the self. For example, North American culture is individualist, loose, and complex, which may produce a uniquely American kind of personality. He also describes how these dimensions are related to aspects of the environment, child-rearing patterns, and social behavior.

Notice how Triandis manages to avoid the trap of being painted into one or another extreme corner on the question of whether human nature is universal or variable. He consistently expresses the view that cultures all have aspects they share with each other (called "etics") and aspects that are locally unique (called "emics"). Second, he never implies—as do other writers such as Markus and Kitayama—that some positions on the dimensions of cultural variation are better than others. It is neither good nor bad to be collectivist, individualist, tight, loose, complex or simple. It is always a matter of trade-offs; the disadvantages of one position are compensated for by advantages of the other. For example, members of collectivist cultures gain in group support what they lose in individual freedom; the reverse could be said about members of individualistic cultures.

In the end, what Triandis describes could be called a "Big Three" for cultures. The traits of collectivism-individualism, tightness-looseness, and complexity are a group of psychologically relevant attributes that, Triandis demonstrates, can provide a sort of personality profile for an entire culture.

From "The Self and Social Behavior in Differing Cultural Contexts," by H. C. Triandis. In *Psychological Review, 96,* 506–520. Copyright © 1989 by the American Psychological Association. Adapted with permission.

The study of the self has a long tradition in psychology (e.g., Allport, 1943, 1955; Baumeister, 1987; Gordon & Gergen, 1968; James, 1890/1950; Murphy, 1947; Schlenker, 1985; Smith, 1980; Ziller, 1973), anthropology (e.g., Shweder & LeVine, 1984), and sociology (e.g., Cooley, 1902; Mead, 1934; Rosenberg, 1979). There is a recognition in most of these discussions that the self is shaped, in part, through interaction with groups. However, although there is evidence about variations of the self across cultures (Marsella, DeVos, & Hsu, 1985; Shweder & LeVine, 1984), the specification of the way the self determines aspects of social behavior in different cultures is undeveloped.

This article will examine first, aspects of the self; second, dimensions of variation of cultural contexts that have direct relevance to the way the self is defined; and third, the link between culture and self.

Definitions

THE SELF   For purposes of this article, the self consists of all statements made by a person, overtly or covertly, that include the words "I," "me," "mine," and "myself" (Cooley, 1902). This broad definition indicates that all aspects of social motivation are linked to the self. Attitudes (e.g., *I* like X), beliefs (e.g., *I* think that X results in Y), intentions (e.g., *I* plan to do X), norms (e.g., in *my* group, people should act this way), roles (e.g., in *my* family, fathers act this way), and values (e.g., *I*

think equality is very important) are aspects of the self.

The statements that people make that constitute the self have implications for the way people sample information (sampling information that is self-relevant more frequently than information that is not self-relevant), the way they process information (sampling more quickly information that is self-relevant than information that is not self-relevant), and the way they assess information (assessing more positively information that supports their current self-structure than information that challenges their self-structure). Thus, for instance, a self-instruction such as "I must do X" is more likely to be evaluated positively, and therefore accepted, if it maintains the current self-structure than if it changes this structure. This has implications for behavior because such self-instructions are among the several processes that lead to behavior (Triandis, 1977, 1980).

In other words, the self is an active agent that promotes differential sampling, processing, and evaluation of information from the environment, and thus leads to differences in social behavior. Empirical evidence about the link of measures of the self to behavior is too abundant to review here. A sample will suffice: People whose self-concept was manipulated so that they thought of themselves (a) as "charitable" gave more to charity (Kraut, 1973), (b) as "neat and tidy" threw less garbage on the floor (Miller, Brickman, & Bolen, 1975), and (c) as "honest" were more likely to return a pencil (Shotland & Berger, 1970). Self-definition results in behaviors consistent with that definition (Wicklund & Gollwitzer, 1982). People who defined themselves as doers of a particular behavior were more likely to do that behavior (Greenwald, Carnot, Beach, & Young, 1987). Identity salience leads to behaviors consistent with that identity (Stryker & Serpe, 1982). Self-monitoring (Snyder, 1974) has been linked to numerous behaviors (e.g., Snyder, 1987; Snyder, Simpson, & Gangestad, 1986). The more an attitude (an aspect of the self) is accessible to memory, the more likely it is to determine behavior (Fazio & Williams, 1986). Those with high self-esteem were found to be more likely to behave independently of group norms (Ziller, 1973).

* * *

To the extent such aspects are *shared* by people who speak a common language and who are able to interact because they live in adjacent locations during the same historical period, we can refer to all of these elements as a cultural group's *subjective culture* (Triandis, 1972). This implies that people who speak different languages (e.g., English and Chinese) or live in nonadjacent locations (e.g., England and Australia) or who have lived in different time periods (e.g., 19th and 20th centuries) may have different subjective cultures.

Some aspects of the self may be universal. "I am hungry" may well be an element with much the same meaning worldwide and across time. Other elements are extremely culture-specific. For instance, they depend on the particular mythology-religion-worldview and language of a culture. "My soul will be reincarnated" is culture-specific. Some elements of the self imply action. For example, "I should be a high achiever" implies specific actions under conditions in which standards of excellence are present. Other elements do not imply action (e.g., I am tall).

* * *

One major distinction among aspects of the self is between the private, public, and collective self (Baumeister, 1986b; Greenwald & Pratkanis, 1984). Thus, we have the following: *the private self*—cognitions that involve traits, states, or behaviors of the person (e.g., "I am introverted," "I am honest," "I will buy X"); *the public self*—cognitions concerning the *generalized other*'s view of the self, such as "People think I am introverted" or "People think I will buy X"; and *the collective self*—cognitions concerning a view of the self that is found in some collective (e.g., family, coworkers, tribe, scientific society); for instance, "My family thinks I am introverted" or "My coworkers believe I travel too much."

The argument of this article is that people sample these three kinds of selves with different probabilities, in different cultures, and that has specific consequences for social behavior.

The private self is an assessment of the self by the self. The public self corresponds to an assessment of the self by the generalized other. The collective self corresponds to an assessment of the self by a specific reference group. Tajfel's (1978) notion of a *social identity*, "that part of the individual's self-concept which derives from his (or her) knowledge of his (her) membership in a social group (or groups) together with the values and emotional significance attached to that membership," (p. 63) is part of the collective self. Tajfel's theory is that people choose ingroups that maximize their positive social identity. However, that notion reflects an individualistic emphasis, because in many collectivist cultures people do not have a choice of ingroups. For instance, even though the Indian constitution has banned castes, caste is still an important aspect of social identity in that culture. Historical factors shape different identities (Baumeister, 1986a).

The notion of sampling has two elements: a *universe* of units to be sampled and a *probability* of choice of a unit from that universe. The universe can be more or less complex. By complexity is meant that the number of distinguishable elements might be few versus many, the differentiation within the elements may be small or large, and the integration of the elements may be small or large. The number of nonoverlapping elements (e.g., I am bold; I am sensitive) is clearly relevant to complexity. The differentiation of the elements refers to the number of distinctions made within the element. For example, in the case of the social class element, a person may have a simple conception with little differentiation (e.g., people who are unemployed versus working versus leading the society) or a complex conception with much differentiation (e.g., rich, with new money, well educated versus rich with new money, poorly educated). *Integration* refers to the extent a change in one element changes few versus many elements. Self-structures in which changes in one element result in changes in many elements are more complex than self-structures in which such changes result in changes of only a few elements (Rokeach, 1960).

In families in which children are urged to be themselves, in which "finding yourself" is valued, or in which self-actualization is emphasized, the private self is likely to be complex. In cultures in which families emphasize "what other people will think about you," the public self is likely to be complex. In cultures in which specific groups are emphasized during socialization (e.g., "remember you are a member of this family," ". . . you are a Christian"), the collective self is likely to be complex, and the norms, roles, and values of that group acquire especially great emotional significance.

* * *

One of many methods that are available to study the self requires writing 20 sentence completions that begin with "I am . . ." (Kuhn & McPartland, 1954). The answers can be content-analyzed to determine whether they correspond to the private, public, or collective self. If a social group is part of the answer (e.g., I am a son = family; I am a student = educational institution; I am Roman Catholic = religion), one can classify the response as part of the collective self. If the generalized other is mentioned (e.g., I am liked by most people), it is part of the public self. If there is no reference to an entity outside the person (e.g., I am bold), it can be considered a part of the private self. Experience with this scoring method shows that coders can reach interrater reliabilities in the .9+ range. The percentage of the collective responses varies from 0 to 100, with sample means in Asian cultures in the 20% to 52% range and in European and North American samples between 15% and 19%. Public-

self responses are relatively rare, so sample means of private-self responses (with student samples) are commonly in the 81% to 85% range. In addition to such content analyses, one can examine the availability (how frequently a particular group, e.g., the family, is mentioned) and the accessibility (when is a particular group mentioned for the first time in the rank-order) of responses (Higgins & King, 1981).

This method is useful because it provides an operational definition of the three kinds of selves under discussion. Also, salience is reflected directly in the measure of accessibility, and the complexity of particular self is suggested by the availability measure.

Although this method has many advantages, a multimethod strategy for the study of the self is highly recommended, because every method has some limitations and convergence across methods increases the validity of our measurements. Furthermore, when methods are used in different cultures in which people have different expectations about what can be observed, asked, or analyzed, there is an interaction between culture and method. But when methods converge similarly in different cultures and when the antecedents and consequences of the self-construct in each culture are similar, one can have greater confidence that the construct has similar or equivalent meanings across cultures.

Other methods that can tap aspects of the self have included interviews (e.g., Lobel, 1984), Q-sorts of potentially self-descriptive attributes (e.g., Block, 1986), the Multistage Social Identity Inquirer (Zavalloni, 1975; Zavalloni & Louis-Guerin, 1984), and reaction times when responding to whether a specific attribute is self-descriptive (Rogers, 1981).

* * *

I have defined the self as one element of subjective culture (when it is shared by members of a culture) and distinguished the private, public, and collective selves, and indicated that the complexity of these selves will depend on cultural variables. The more complex a particular self, the more probable it is that it will be sampled. Sampling of a particular self will increase the probability that behaviors implicated in this aspect of the self will occur, when situations favor such occurrence. For example, data suggest that people from East Asia sample their collective self more frequently than do Europeans or North Americans. This means that elements of their reference groups, such as group norms or group goals, will be more salient among Asians than among Europeans or North Americans. In the next section I will describe cultural variation along certain theoretical dimensions that are useful for organizing the information about the sampling of different selves, and hence can account for differences in social behavior across cultures.

CULTURAL PATTERNS There is evidence of different selves across cultures (Marsella et al., 1985). However, the evidence has not been linked systematically to particular dimensions of cultural variation. This section will define three of these dimensions.

Cultural complexity. A major difference across cultures is in cultural complexity. Consider the contrast between the human bands that existed on earth up to about 15,000 years ago and the life of a major metropolitan city today. According to archaeological evidence, the bands rarely included more than 30 individuals. The number of relationships among 30 individuals is relatively small; the number of relationships in a major metropolitan area is potentially almost infinite. The number of potential relationships is one measure of cultural complexity. Students of this construct have used many others. One can get reliable rank orders by using information about whether cultures have writing and records, fixity of residence, agriculture, urban settlements, technical specialization, land transport other than walking, money, high population densities, many levels of political integration, and many levels of social stratification. Cultures that have all of these attributes (e.g., the Romans, the Chinese of the 5th century B.C., modern industrial cultures) are quite complex. As one or more of the aforementioned attributes are missing, the cultures are more simple, the simplest including the

contemporary food gathering cultures (e.g., the nomads of the Kalahari desert).

Additional measures of complexity can be obtained by examining various domains of culture. Culture includes language, technology, economic, political, and educational systems, religious and aesthetic patterns, social structures, and so on. One can analyze each of these domains by considering the number of distinct elements that can be identified in it. For example, (a) language can be examined by noting the number of terms that are available (e.g., 600 camel-related terms in Arabic; many terms about automobiles in English), (b) economics by noting the number of occupations (the U.S. Employment and Training Administration's *Dictionary of Occupational Titles* contains more than 250,000), and (c) religion by noting the number of different functions (e.g., 6,000 priests in one temple in Orissa, India, each having a different function).

One of the consequences of increased complexity is that individuals have more and more potential ingroups toward whom they may or may not be loyal. As the number of potential ingroups increases, the loyalty of individuals to any one ingroup decreases. Individuals have the option of giving priority to their personal goals rather than to the goals of an ingroup. Also, the greater the affluence of a society, the more financial independence can be turned into social and emotional independence, with the individual giving priority to personal rather than ingroup goals. Thus, as societies become more complex and affluent, they also can become more individualistic. However, there are some moderator variables that modify this simple picture, that will be discussed later, after I examine more closely the dimension of individualism-collectivism.

Individualism-collectivism. Individualists give priority to personal goals over the goals of collectives; collectivists either make no distinctions between personal and collective goals, or if they do make such distinctions, they subordinate their personal goals to the collective goals (Triandis, Bontempo, Villareal, Asai, & Lucca, 1988). Closely related to this dimension, in the work of Hofstede (1980), is *power distance* (the tendency to see a large difference between those with power and those without power). Collectivists tend to be high in power distance.

Although the terms *individualism* and *collectivism* should be used to characterize cultures and societies, the terms *idiocentric* and *allocentric* should be used to characterize individuals. Triandis, Leung, Villareal, and Clack (1985) have shown that within culture (Illinois) there are individuals who differ on this dimension, and the idiocentrics report that they are concerned with achievement, but are lonely, whereas the allocentrics report low alienation and receiving much social support. These findings were replicated in Puerto Rico (Triandis et al., 1988). The distinction of terms at the cultural and individual levels of analysis is useful because it is convenient when discussing the behavior of allocentrics in individualist cultures and idiocentrics in collectivist cultures (e.g., Bontempo, Lobel, & Triandis, 1989).

In addition to subordinating personal to collective goals, collectivists tend to be concerned about the results of their actions on members of their ingroups, tend to share resources with ingroup members, feel interdependent with ingroup members, and feel involved in the lives of ingroup members (Hui & Triandis, 1986). They emphasize the integrity of ingroups over time and deemphasize their independence from ingroups (Triandis et al., 1986).

Shweder's data (see Shweder & LeVine, 1984) suggest that collectivists perceive ingroup norms as universally valid (a form of ethnocentrism). A considerable literature suggests that collectivists automatically obey ingroup authorities and are willing to fight and die to maintain the integrity of the ingroup, whereas they distrust and are unwilling to cooperate with members of outgroups (Triandis, 1972). However, the definition of the ingroup keeps shifting with the situation. Common fate, common outside threat, and proximity (which is often linked to common fate) appear to be important determinants of the ingroup/outgroup boundary. Although the family is usually the most important ingroup, tribe, coworkers, coreligionists, and members of the same political or social collective or the same aesthetic or scientific persuasion can also function as important ingroups. When the state is under threat, it becomes the ingroup.

Ingroups can also be defined on the basis of similarity (in demographic attributes, activities, preferences, or institutions) and do influence social behavior to a greater extent when they are stable and impermeable (difficult to gain membership or difficult to leave). Social behavior is a function of ingroup norms to a greater extent in collectivist than individualist cultures (Davidson, Jaccard, Triandis, Morales, and Diaz-Guerrero, 1976).

In collectivist cultures, ingroups influence a wide range of social situations (e.g., during the cultural revolution in China, the state had what was perceived as "legitimate influence" on every collective). In some cases, the influence is extreme (e.g., the Rev. Jones's People's Temple influenced 911 members of that collective to commit suicide in 1978).

* * *

As discussed earlier, over the course of cultural evolution there has been a shift toward individualism. Content analyses of social behaviors recorded in written texts (Adamopoulos & Bontempo, 1986) across historical periods show a shift from communal to exchange relationships. Behaviors related to trading are characteristic of individualistic cultures, and contracts emancipated individuals from the bonds of tribalism (Pearson, 1977).

The distribution of collectivism-individualism, according to Hofstede's (1980) data, contrasts most of the Latin American, Asian, and African cultures with most of the North American and Northern and Western European cultures. However, many cultures are close to the middle of the dimension, and other variables are also relevant. Urban samples tend to be individualistic, and traditional-rural samples tend toward collectivism within the same culture (e.g., Greece in the work of Doumanis, 1983; Georgas, 1989; and Katakis, 1984). Within the United States one can find a good deal of range on this variable, with Hispanic samples much more collectivist than samples of Northern and Western European backgrounds (G. Marin & Triandis, 1985).

The major antecedents of individualism appear to be cultural complexity and affluence. The more complex the culture, the greater the number of ingroups that one may have, so that a person has the option of joining ingroups or even forming new ingroups. Affluence means that the individual can be independent of ingroups. If the ingroup makes excessive demands, the individual can leave it. Mobility is also important. As individuals move (migration, changes in social class) they join new ingroups, and they have the opportunity to join ingroups whose goals they find compatible with their own. Furthermore, the more costly it is in a particular ecology for an ingroup to reject ingroup members who behave according to their own goals rather than according to ingroup goals, the more likely are people to act in accordance with their personal goals, and thus the more individualistic is the culture. Such costs are high when the ecology is thinly populated. One can scarcely afford to reject a neighbor if one has only one neighbor. Conversely, densely populated ecologies are characterized by collectivism, not only because those who behave inappropriately can be excluded, but also because it is necessary to regulate behavior more strictly to overcome problems of crowding.

As rewards from ingroup membership increase, the more likely it is that a person will use ingroup goals as guides for behavior. Thus, when ingroups provide many rewards (e.g., emotional security, status, income, information, services, willingness to spend time with the person) they tend to increase the person's commitment to the ingroup and to the culture's collectivism.

The size of ingroups tends to be different in the two kinds of cultures. In collectivist cultures, ingroups tend to be small (e.g., family), whereas in individualist cultures they can be large (e.g., people who agree with me on important attitudes).

Child-rearing patterns are different in collectivist and individualist cultures. The primary concern of parents in collectivist cultures is obedience, reliability, and proper behavior. The primary con-

cern of parents in individualistic cultures is self-reliance, independence, and creativity. Thus, we find that in simple, agricultural societies, socialization is severe and conformity is demanded and obtained (Berry, 1967, 1979). Similarly, in working-class families in industrial societies, the socialization pattern leads to conformity (Kohn, 1969, 1987). In more individualist cultures such as food gatherers (Berry, 1979) and very individualistic cultures such as the United States, the child-rearing pattern emphasizes self-reliance and independence; children are allowed a good deal of autonomy and are encouraged to explore their environment. Similarly, creativity and self-actualization are more important traits and are emphasized in child-rearing in the professional social classes (Kohn, 1987).

It is clear that conformity is functional in simple, agricultural cultures (if one is to make an irrigation system, each person should do part of the job in a well-coordinated plan) and in working-class jobs (the boss does not want subordinates who do their own thing). Conversely, it is dysfunctional in hunting cultures, in which one must be ingenious, and in professional jobs, in which one must be creative. The greater the cultural complexity, the more is conformity to one ingroup dysfunctional, inasmuch as one cannot take advantage of new opportunities available in other parts of the society.

The smaller the family size, the more the child is allowed to do his or her own thing. In large families, rules must be imposed, otherwise chaos will occur. As societies become more affluent (individualistic), they also reduce the size of the family, which increases the opportunity to raise children to be individualists. Autonomy in childrearing also leads to individualism. Exposure to other cultures (e.g., through travel or because of societal heterogeneity) also increases individualism, inasmuch as the child becomes aware of different norms and has to choose his or her own standards of behavior.

* * *

Tight versus loose cultures. In collectivist cultures, ingroups demand that individuals conform to ingroup norms, role definitions, and values. When a society is relatively homogeneous, the norms and values of ingroups are similar. But heterogeneous societies have groups with dissimilar norms. If an ingroup member deviates from ingroup norms, ingroup members may have to make the painful decision of excluding that individual from the ingroup. Because rejection of ingroup members is emotionally draining, cultures develop tolerance for deviation from group norms. As a result, homogeneous cultures are often rigid in requiring that ingroup members behave according to the ingroup norms. Such cultures are *tight*. Heterogeneous cultures and cultures in marginal positions between two major cultural patterns are flexible in dealing with ingroup members who deviate from ingroup norms. For example, Japan is considered tight, and it is relatively homogeneous. Thailand is considered loose, and it is in a marginal position between the major cultures of India and China; people are pulled in different directions by sometimes contrasting norms, and hence they must be more flexible in imposing their norms. In short, tight cultures (Pelto, 1968) have clear norms that are reliably imposed. Little deviation from normative behavior is tolerated, and severe sanctions are administered to those who deviate. *Loose* cultures either have unclear norms about most social situations or tolerate deviance from the norms. For example, it is widely reported in the press that Japanese children who return to Japan after a period of residence in the West, are criticized most severely by teachers because their behavior is not "proper." Japan is a tight culture in which deviations that would be considered trivial in the West (such as bringing Western food rather than Japanese food for lunch) are noted and criticized. In loose cultures, deviations from "proper" behavior are tolerated, and in many cases there are no standards of "proper" behavior. Theocracies[1] are prototypical of tight cultures, but some contemporary relatively homogeneous cultures (e.g., the Greeks, the Japanese) are also relatively tight. In a heterogeneous culture, such as the United States, it is more difficult for people to agree on specific norms, and

even more difficult to impose severe sanctions. Geographic mobility allows people to leave the offended communities in ways that are not available in more stable cultures. Urban environments are more loose than rural environments, in which norms are clearer and sanctions can be imposed more easily. Prototypical of loose cultures are the Lapps and the Thais. In very tight cultures, according to Pelto, one finds corporate control of property, corporate ownership of stored food and production power, religious figures as leaders, hereditary recruitment into priesthood, and high levels of taxation.

* * *

The intolerance of inappropriate behavior characteristic of tight cultures does not extend to all situations. In fact, tight cultures are quite tolerant of foreigners (they do not know better), and of drunk, and mentally ill persons. They may even have rituals in which inappropriate behavior is expected. For example, in a tight culture such as Japan one finds the office beer party as a ritual institution, where one is expected to get drunk and to tell the boss what one "really" thinks of him (it is rarely her). Similarly, in loose cultures, there are specific situations in which deviance is not tolerated. For example, in Orissa (India), a son who cuts his hair the day after his father dies is bound to be severely criticized, although the culture is generally loose.

* * *

Culture and Self

Culture is to society what memory is to the person. It specifies designs for living that have proven effective in the past, ways of dealing with social situations, and ways to think about the self and social behavior that have been reinforced in the past. It includes systems of symbols that facilitate interaction (Geertz, 1973), rules of the game of life that have been shown to "work" in the past. When a person is socialized in a given culture, the person can use custom as a substitute for thought, and save time.

The three dimensions of cultural variation just

---

[1]Nations run by religious rule.

described reflect variations in culture that have emerged because of different ecologies, such as ways of surviving. Specifically, in cultures that survive through hunting or food gathering, in which people are more likely to survive if they work alone or in small groups because game is dispersed, individualism emerges as a good design for living. In agricultural cultures, in which cooperation in the building of irrigation systems and food storage and distribution facilities is reinforced, collectivist designs for living emerge. In complex, industrial cultures, in which loosely linked ingroups produce the thousands of parts of modern machines (e.g., a 747 airplane), individuals often find themselves in situations in which they have to choose ingroups or even form their own ingroups (e.g., new corporation). Again, individualistic designs for living become more functional. In homogeneous cultures, one can insist on tight norm enforcement; in heterogeneous, or fast changing, or marginal (e.g., confluence of two major cultural traditions) cultures, the imposition of tight norms is difficult because it is unclear whose norms are to be used. A loose culture is more likely in such ecologies.

Over time, cultures become more complex, as new differentiations prove effective. However, once complexity reaches very high levels, moves toward simplification emerge as reactions to too much complexity. For example, in art styles, the pendulum has been swinging between the "less is more" view of Oriental art and the "more is better" view of the rococo period in Europe. Similarly, excessive individualism may create a reaction toward collectivism, and excessive collectivism, a reaction toward individualism; or tightness may result from too much looseness, and looseness from too much tightness. Thus, culture is dynamic, ever changing.

* * *

The three dimensions of cultural variation described earlier are systematically linked to different kinds of self. In this section I provide hypotheses linking culture and self.

INDIVIDUALISM-COLLECTIVISM Child-rearing patterns in individualistic cultures tend to emphasize self-reliance, independence, finding yourself, and self-actualization. As discussed earlier, such child-rearing increases the complexity of the private self, and because there are more elements of the private self to be sampled, more are sampled. Thus, the probability that the private rather than the other selves will be sampled increases with individualism. Conversely, in collectivist cultures, child-rearing emphasizes the importance of the collective; the collective self is more complex and more likely to be sampled.

* * *

Such patterns are usually associated with rewards for conformity to ingroup goals, which leads to internalization of the ingroup goals. Thus, people do what is expected of them, even if that is not enjoyable. Bontempo et al. (1989) randomly assigned subjects from a collectivist (Brazil) and an individualist (U.S.) culture to two conditions of questionnaire administration: public and private. The questionnaire contained questions about how the subject was likely to act when the ingroup expected a behavior that was costly to the individual (e.g., visit a friend in the hospital, when this was time consuming). Both of the questions How should the person act? and How enjoyable would it be to act? were measured. It was found that Brazilians gave the same answers under both the anonymous and public conditions. Under both conditions they indicated that they would do what was expected of them. The U.S. sample indicated they would do what was expected of them in the public but not in the private condition. The U.S. group's private answers indicated that the subjects thought that doing the costly behaviors was unlikely, and certainly not enjoyable. Under the very same conditions the Brazilians indicated that they thought the costly prosocial behaviors were likely and enjoyable. In short, the Brazilians had internalized[2] the ingroup norms so that conformity to the ingroup appeared enjoyable to them.

* * *

Observations indicate that the extent to which an ingroup makes demands on individuals in few

---

[2]Made a part of themselves.

or in many areas shows considerable variance. For example, in the United States, states make very few demands (e.g., pay your income tax), whereas in China during the cultural revolution, the Communist Party made demands in many areas (artistic expression, family life, political behavior, civic action, education, athletics, work groups, even location, such as where to live). It seems plausible that the more areas of one's life that are affected by an ingroup, the more likely the individual is to sample the collective self.

* * *

TIGHT-LOOSE CULTURES Homogeneous, relatively isolated cultures tend to be tight, and they will sample the collective self more than will heterogeneous, centrally located cultures. The more homogeneous the culture, the more the norms will be clear and deviation from normative behavior can be punished. Cultural heterogeneity increases the confusion regarding what is correct and proper behavior. Also, cultural marginality[3] tends to result in norm and role conflict and pressures individuals toward adopting different norms. Because rejection of the ingroup members who have adopted norms of a different culture can be costly, individuals moderate their need to make their ingroup members conform to their ideas of proper behavior. So, the culture becomes loose (i.e., tolerant of deviations from norms).

The looser the culture, the more the individual can choose what self to sample. If several kinds of collective self are available, one may choose to avoid norm and role conflict by rejecting all of them and developing individual conceptions of proper behavior. Thus, sampling of the private self is more likely in loose cultures and sampling of the collective self is more likely in tight cultures. Also, tight cultures tend to socialize their children by emphasizing the expectations of the generalized other. Hence, the public self will be complex and will be more likely to be sampled. In other words,

tight cultures tend to sample the public and collective self, whereas loose cultures tend to sample the private self.

When the culture is both collectivist and tight, then the public self is extremely likely to be sampled. That means people act "properly," as that is defined by society, and are extremely anxious [about not acting] correctly. Their private self does not matter. As a result, the private and public selves are often different. Doi (1986) discussed this point extensively, comparing the Japanese public self (*tatemae*) with the private self (*honne*). He suggested that in the United States there is virtue in keeping public and private consistent (not being a hypocrite). In Japan, proper action matters. What you feel about such action is irrelevant. Thus, the Japanese do not like to state their personal opinions, but rather seek consensus.

Consistently with Doi's (1986) arguments is Iwao's (1988) research. She presented scenarios to Japanese and Americans and asked them to judge various actions that could be appropriate responses to these situations. For example, one scenario (daughter brings home person from another race) included as a possible response "thought that he would never allow them to marry but told them he was in favor of their marriage." This response was endorsed as the *best* by 44% of the Japanese sample but by only 2% of the Americans; it was the *worst* in the opinion of 48% of the Americans and 7% of the Japanese.

Although the private self may be complex, this does not mean that it will be communicated to others if one can avoid such communication. In fact, in tight cultures people avoid disclosing much of the self, because by disclosing they may reveal some aspect of the self that others might criticize. In other words, they may be aware of the demands of the generalized other and avoid being vulnerable to criticism by presenting little of this complex self to others. Barlund (1975) reported studies of the self-disclosure to same-sex friend, opposite-sex friend, mother, father, stranger, and untrusted acquaintance in Japan and in the United States. The pattern of self-disclosure was the same—that is, more to same-sex friend, and progressively less to

---

[3]Not being part of the mainstream of a culture and feeling that one or one's group is at the "margins."

opposite-sex friend, mother, father, stranger, and least to the untrusted acquaintance. However, the amount disclosed in each relationship was about 50% more in the United States than in Japan.

CULTURAL COMPLEXITY The more complex the culture, the more confused is likely to be the individual's identity. Dragonas (1983) sampled the self-concepts of 11- and 12-year-olds in Greek small villages (simple), traditional cities (medium), and large cities (complex) cultures. She found that the more complex the culture, the more confusing was the identity. Similarly, Katakis (1976, 1978, 1984) found that the children of farmers and fishermen, when asked what they would be when they are old, unhesitatingly said "farmer" or "fisherman," whereas in the large cities the responses frequently were of the "I will find myself" variety. Given the large number of ingroups that are available in a complex environment and following the logic presented here, individuals may well opt for sampling their private self and neglect the public or collective selves.

CONTENT OF SELF IN DIFFERENT CULTURES The specific content of the self in particular cultures will reflect the language and availability of mythological constructs of that culture. Myths often provide ideal types that are incorporated in the self forged in a given culture (Roland, 1984a). For example, peace of mind and being free of worries have been emphasized as aspects of the self in India (Roland, 1984b) and reflect Indian values that are early recognizable in Hinduism and Buddhism (which emerged in India). Mythological, culture-specific constructs become incorporated in the self (Sinha, 1982, 1987). Roland (1984b) claimed that the private self is more "organized around 'we', 'our' and 'us' . . ." (p. 178) in India than in the West. But particular life events may be linked to more than one kind of self. For example, Sinha (1987b) found that the important goals of Indian managers are their own good health and the good health of their family (i.e., have both private and collective self-elements).

Sinha (personal communication, November

1985) believes the public self is different in collectivist and individualist cultures. In individualistic cultures it is assumed that the generalized other will value autonomy, independence, and self-reliance, and thus individuals will attempt to act in ways that will impress others (i.e., indicate that they have these attributes). To be distinct and different are highly valued, and people find innumerable ways to show themselves to others as different (in dress, possessions, speech patterns). By contrast, in collectivist cultures, conformity to the other in public settings is valued. Thus, in a restaurant, everyone orders the same food (in traditional restaurants, only the visible leader gets a menu and orders for all). The small inconvenience of eating nonoptimal food is more than compensated by the sense of solidarity that such actions generate. In collectivist cultures, being "nice" to ingroup others is a high value, so that one expects in most situations extreme politeness and a display of harmony (Triandis, Marin, Lisansky, & Betancourt, 1984). Thus, in collectivist cultures, the public self is an extension of the collective self. One must make a good impression by means of prosocial behaviors toward ingroup members, acquaintances, and others who may become ingroup members. At the same time, one can be quite rude to outgroup members, and there is no concern about displaying hostility, exploitation, or avoidance of outgroup members.

* * *

The collective self in collectivist cultures includes elements such as "I am philotimos" (traditional Greece, meaning "I must act as is expected of me by my family and friends"; see Triandis, 1972), "I must sacrifice myself for my ingroup," "I feel good when I display affection toward my ingroup," and "I must maintain harmony with my ingroup even when that is very disagreeable." The person is less self-contained in collectivist than in individualistic cultures (Roland, 1984b, p. 176).

Identity is defined on the basis of different elements in individualistic and collectivist cultures. Individualistic cultures tend to emphasize elements of identity that reflect possessions—what do I own, what experiences have I had, what are my accomplishments (for scientists, what is my list of publications). In collectivist cultures, identity is defined more in terms of relationships—I am the mother of X, I am a member of family Y, and I am a resident of Z. Furthermore, the qualities that are most important in forming an identity can be quite different. In Europe and North America, being logical, rational, balanced, and fair are important attributes; in Africa, personal style, ways of moving, the unique spontaneous self, sincere self-expression, unpredictability, and emotional expression are most valued. The contrast between classical music (e.g., Bach or Mozart) and jazz reflects this difference musically.

Consequences of Sampling the Private and Collective Self

In the previous section I examined the relationship between the three dimensions of cultural variation and the probabilities of differential sampling of the private, public, and collective selves. In this section I review some of the empirical literature that is relevant to the theoretical ideas just presented.

An important consequence of sampling the collective self is that many of the elements of the collective become salient. Norms, roles, and values (i.e., proper ways of acting as defined by the collective) become the "obviously" correct ways to act. Behavioral intentions reflect such processes. Thus, the status of the other person in the social interaction—for example, is the other an ingroup or an outgroup member—becomes quite salient. Consequently, in collectivist cultures, individuals pay more attention to ingroups and outgroups and moderate their behavior accordingly, than is the case in individualistic cultures (Triandis, 1972).

* * *

Who is placed in the ingroup is culture specific. For example, ratings of the "intimacy" of relationships on a 9-point scale suggest that in Japan there is more intimacy with acquaintances, coworkers, colleagues, best friends, and close friends than in the United States (Gudykunst & Nishida, 1986).

Atsumi (1980) argued that understanding Japanese social behavior requires distinguishing relationships with benefactors, true friends,

coworkers, acquaintances, and outsiders (strangers). The determinants of social behavior shift depending on this classification. Behavior toward benefactors requires that the person go out of his way to benefit them. Behavior toward true friends is largely determined by the extent the behavior is enjoyable in itself, and the presence of these friends makes it enjoyable. Behavior toward coworkers is determined by both norms and cost/benefit considerations. Finally, behavior toward outsiders is totally determined by cost/benefit ratios.

* * *

The behavioral intentions of persons in collectivist cultures appear to be determined by cognitions that are related to the survival and benefit of their collective. In individualist cultures, the concerns are personal. An example comes from a study of smoking. A collectivist sample (Hispanics in the U.S.) showed significantly more concern than an individualist sample (non-Hispanics) about smoking affecting the health of others, giving a bad example to children, harming children, and bothering others with the bad smell of cigarettes, bad breath, and bad smell on clothes and belongings, whereas the individualist sample was more concerned about the physiological symptoms they might experience during withdrawal from cigarette smoking (G. V. Marin, Marin, Otero-Sabogal, Sabogal, & Perez-Stable, 1987).

The emphasis on harmony within the ingroup, found more strongly in collectivist than in individualist cultures, results in the more positive evaluation of group-serving partners (Bond, Chiu, & Wan, 1984), the choice of conflict resolution techniques that minimize animosity (Leung, 1985, 1987), the greater giving of social support (Triandis et al., 1985), and the greater support of ingroup goals (Nadler, 1986). The emphasis on harmony may be, in part, the explanation of the lower heart-attack rates among unacculturated than among acculturated Japanese-Americans (Marmot & Syme, 1976). Clearly, a society in which confrontation is common is more likely to increase the blood pressure of those in such situations, and hence the probability of heart attacks; avoiding conflict and saving face must be linked to lower probabilities that blood pressure will become elevated. The probability of receiving social support in collectivist cultures may be another factor reducing the levels of stress produced by unpleasant life events and hence the probabilities of heart attacks (Triandis et al., 1988).

Although ideal ingroup relationships are expected to be smoother, more intimate, and easier in collectivist cultures, outgroup relationships can be quite difficult. Because the ideal social behaviors often cannot be attained, one finds many splits of the ingroup in collectivist cultures. Avoidance relationships are frequent and, in some cases, required by norms (e.g., mother-in-law avoidance in some cultures). Fights over property are common and result in redefinitions of the ingroup. However, once the ingroup is defined, relationships tend to be very supportive and intimate within the ingroup, whereas there is little trust and often hostility toward outgroup members. Gabrenya and Barba (1987) found that collectivists are not as effective in meeting strangers as are individualists. Triandis (1967) found unusually poor communication among members of the same corporation who were not ingroup members (close friends) in a collectivist culture. Bureaucracies in collectivist cultures function especially badly because people hoard information (Kaiser, 1984). Manipulation and exploitation of outgroups is common (Pandey, 1986) in collectivist cultures. When competing with outgroups, collectivists are more competitive than individualists (Espinoza & Garza, 1985) even under conditions when competitiveness is counterproductive.

In individualistic cultures, people exchange compliments more frequently than in collectivist cultures (Barlund & Araki, 1985). They meet people easily and are able to cooperate with them even if they do not know them well (Gabrenya & Barba, 1987). Because individualists have more of a choice concerning ingroup memberships, they stay in those groups with whom they can have relatively good relationships and leave groups with whom they disagree too frequently (Verma, 1985).

Competition tends to be interpersonal in individualistic and intergroup in collectivist cultures

(Hsu, 1983; Triandis et al., 1988). Conflict is frequently found in family relationships in individualistic cultures and between families in collectivist cultures (Katakis, 1978).

There is a substantial literature (e.g., Berman, Murphy-Berman, & Singh, 1985; Berman, Murphy-Berman, Singh, & Kumar, 1984; Hui, 1984; G. Marin, 1985; Triandis et al., 1985) indicating that individualists are more likely to use equity, and collectivists to use equality or need, as the norms for the distribution of resources (Yang, 1981). This is consistent with the emphasis on trading discussed earlier. By contrast, the emphasis on communal relationships (Mills & Clark, 1982) found in collectivist cultures leads to emphases on equality and need. The parallel with gender differences, where men emphasize exchange and women emphasize communal relationships (i.e., equity and need; Major & Adams, 1983; Brockner & Adsit, 1986), respectively, is quite striking. * * *

* * *

Conclusions

Aspects of the self (private, public, and collective) are differentially sampled in different cultures, depending on the complexity, level of individualism, and looseness of the culture. The more complex, individualistic, and loose the culture, the more likely it is that people will sample the private self and the less likely it is that they will sample the collective self. When people sample the collective self, they are more likely to be influenced by the norms, role definitions, and values of the particular collective, than when they do not sample the collective self. When they are so influenced by a collective, they are likely to behave in ways considered appropriate by members of that collective. The more they sample the private self, the more their behavior can be accounted for by exchange theory and can be described as an exchange relationship. The more they sample the collective self, the less their behavior can be accounted for by exchange theory; it can be described as a communal relationship. However, social behavior is more likely to be communal when the target of that behavior is an ingroup member than when the target is an outgroup member. Ingroups are defined by common goals, common fate, the presence of an external threat, and/or the need to distribute resources to all ingroup members for the optimal survival of the ingroup. Outgroups consist of people with whom one is in competition or whom one does not trust. The ingroup-outgroup distinction determines social behavior more strongly in collectivist than in individualist cultures. When the culture is both collectivist and tight, the public self is particularly likely to be sampled. In short, a major determinant of social behavior is the kind of self that operates in the particular culture.

References

Adamopoulos, J., & Bontempo, R. N. (1986). Diachronic universals in interpersonal structures. *Journal of Cross-Cultural Psychology, 17,* 169–189.

Allport, G. W. (1943). The ego in contemporary psychology. *Psychological Review, 50,* 451–478.

Allport, G. W. (1955). *Becoming.* New Haven, CT: Yale University Press.

Atsumi, R. (1980). Patterns of personal relationships: A key to understanding Japanese thought and behavior. *Social Analysis, 6,* 63–78.

Barlund, D. C. (1975). *Public and private self in Japan and the United States.* Tokyo: Simul Press.

Barlund, D. C., & Araki, S. (1985). Intercultural encounters: The management of compliments by Japanese and Americans. *Journal of Cross-Cultural Psychology, 16,* 9–26.

Baumeister, R. F. (1986a). *Identity: Cultural change and the struggle for self.* New York: Oxford University Press.

Baumeister, R. F. (1986b). *Public self and private self.* New York: Springer.

Baumeister, R. F. (1987). How the self became a problem: A psychological review of historical research. *Journal of Personality and Social Psychology, 52,* 163–176.

Berman, J. J., Murphy-Berman, V., & Singh, P. (1985). Cross-cultural similarities and differences in perceptions of fairness. *Journal of Cross-Cultural Psychology, 16,* 55–67.

Berman, J. J., Murphy-Berman, V., Singh, P., & Kumar, P. (1984, September). *Cross-cultural similarities and differences in perceptions of fairness.* Paper presented at the International Congress of Psychology, in Acapulco, Mexico.

Berry, J. W. (1967). Independence and conformity in subsistence level societies. *Journal of Personality and Social Psychology, 7,* 415–418.

Berry, J. W. (1979). A cultural ecology of social behavior. In L. Berkowitz (Ed.), *Advances in experimental social psychology* (Vol. 12, pp. 177–207). New York: Academic Press.

Block, J. (1986, March). *Longitudinal studies of personality.* Colloquium given at the University of Illinois, Psychology Department.

Bond, M. H., Chiu, C., & Wan, K. (1984). When modesty fails: The social impact of group effacing attributions following success or failure. *European Journal of Social Psychology, 16,* 111–127.

Bontempo, R., Lobel, S. A., & Triandis, H. C. (1989). *Compliance and value internalization among Brazilian and U.S. students.* Manuscript submitted for publication.

Brockner, J., & Adsit, L. (1986). The moderating impact of sex on the equity satisfaction relationship: A field study. *Journal of Applied Psychology, 71,* 585–590.

Cooley, C. H. (1902). *Human nature and the social order.* New York: Scribner.

Davidson, A. R., Jaccard, J. J., Triandis, H. C., Morales, M. L., & Diaz-Guerrero, R. (1976). Cross-cultural model testing: Toward a solution of the etic-emic dilemma. *International Journal of Psychology, 11,* 1–13.

Doumanis, M. (1983). *Mothering in Greece: From collectivism to individualism.* New York: Academic Press.

Doi, T. (1986). *The anatomy of conformity: The individual versus society.* Tokyo: Kodansha.

Dragonas, T. (1983). *The self-concept of preadolescents in the Hellenic context.* Unpublished doctoral dissertation, University of Ashton, Birmingham, England.

Espinoza, J. A., & Garza, R. T. (1985). Social group salience and interethnic cooperation. *Journal of Experimental Social Psychology, 231,* 380–392.

Fazio, R. H., & Williams, C. J. (1986). Attitude accessibility as a moderator of the attitude-perception and attitude-behavior relations: An investigation of the 1984 presidential election. *Journal of Personality and Social Psychology, 51,* 505–514.

Gabrenya, W. K., & Barba, L. (1987, March). *Cultural differences in social interaction during group problem solving.* Paper presented at the meetings of the Southeastern Psychological Association, Atlanta.

Geertz, C. (1973). *The interpretation of cultures.* New York: Basic Books.

Georgas, J. (1989). Changing family values in Greece: From collectivist to individualist. *Journal of Cross-Cultural Psychology, 20,* 80–91.

Gordon, C., & Gergen, K. J. (Eds.). (1968). *The self in social interaction.* New York: Wiley.

Greenwald, A. G., Carnot, C. G., Beach, R., & Young, B. (1987). Increasing voting behavior by asking people if they expect to vote. *Journal of Applied Psychology, 71,* 315–318.

Greenwald, A. G., & Pratkanis, A. R. (1984). The self. In R. S. Wyer & T. K. Srull (Eds.), *Handbook of social cognition* (Vol. 3, pp. 129–178). Hillsdale, NJ: Erlbaum.

Gudykunst, W. B., & Nishida, T. (1986). The influence of cultural variability on perceptions of communication behavior associated with relationship terms. *Human Communication Research, 13,* 147–166.

Higgins, E. T., & King, G. (1981). Accessibility of social constructs: Information-processing consequences of individual and contextual variability. In N. Cantor & J. F. Kihlstrom (Eds.), *Personality, cognition and social interaction* (pp. 69–121). Hillsdale, NJ: Erlbaum.

Hofstede, G. (1980). *Culture's consequences.* Beverly Hills, CA: Sage.

Hsu, F. L. K. (1983). *Rugged individualism reconsidered.* Knoxville: University of Tennessee Press.

Hui, C. H. (1984). *Individualism-collectivism: Theory, measure-*

ment and its relationship to reward allocation. Unpublished doctoral dissertation, Department of Psychology, University of Illinois at Champaign-Urbana.

Hui, C. H., & Triandis, H. C. (1986). Individualism-collectivism: A study of cross-cultural researchers. *Journal of Cross-Cultural Psychology, 17,* 225–248.

Iwao, S. (1988, August). *Social psychology's models of man: Isn't it time for East to meet West?* Invited address to the International Congress of Scientific Psychology, Sydney, Australia.

James, W. (1950). *The principles of psychology.* New York: Dover. (Original work published 1890.)

Katakis, C. D. (1976). An exploratory multilevel attempt to investigate interpersonal and intrapersonal patterns of 20 Athenian families. *Mental Health and Society, 3,* 1–9.

Katakis, C. D. (1978). On the transaction of social change processes and the perception of self in relation to others. *Mental Health and Society, 5,* 275–283.

Katakis, C. D. (1984). Oi tris tautotites tis Ellinikis oikogenoias [The three identities of the Greek family]. Athens, Greece: Kedros.

Kohn, M. L. (1969). *Class and conformity.* Homewood, IL: Dorsey.

Kohn, M. L. (1987). Cross-national research as an analytic strategy. *American Sociological Review, 52,* 713–731.

Kraut, R. E. (1973). Effects of social labeling on giving to charity. *Journal of Experimental Social Psychology, 9,* 551–562.

Kuhn, M. H., & McPartland, T. (1954). An empirical investigation of self-attitudes. *American Sociological Review, 19,* 68–76.

Leung, K. (1985). *Cross-cultural study of procedural fairness and disputing behavior.* Unpublished doctoral dissertation, Department of Psychology, University of Illinois, Champaign-Urbana.

Leung, K. (1987). Some determinants of reactions to procedural models for conflict resolution: A cross-national study. *Journal of Personality and Social Psychology, 53,* 898–908.

Lobel, S. A. (1984). *Effects of sojourn to the United States. A SYMLOG content analysis of in-depth interviews.* Unpublished doctoral dissertation, Harvard University.

Major, B., & Adams, J. B. (1983). Role of gender, interpersonal orientation, and self-presentation in distributive justice behavior. *Journal of Personality and Social Psychology, 45,* 598–608.

Marin, G. (1985). Validez transcultural del principio de equidad: El colectivismo-individualismo como una variable moderatora [Transcultural validity of the principle of equity: Collectivism–individualism as a moderating variable]. *Revista Interamericana de Psichologia Occupational, 4,* 7–20.

Marin, G., & Triandis, H. C. (1985). Allocentrism as an important characteristic of the behavior of Latin Americans and Hispanics. In R. Diaz-Guerrero (Ed.), *Cross-cultural and national studies in social psychology* (69–80). Amsterdam, The Netherlands: North Holland.

Marin, G. V., Marin, G., Otero-Sabogal, R., Sabogal, F., & Perez-Stable, E. (1987). *Cultural differences in attitudes toward smoking: Developing messages using the theory of reasoned action* (Tech. Rep.). (Available from Box 0320, 400 Parnassus Ave., San Francisco, CA 94117.)

Marmot, M. G., & Syme, S. L. (1976). Acculturation and coronary heart disease in Japanese Americans. *American Journal of Epidemiology, 104,* 225–247.

Marsella, A. J., DeVos, G., & Hsu, F. L. K. (1985). *Culture and self.* New York: Tavistock.

Mead, G. H. (1934). *Mind, self, and society.* Chicago: University of Chicago Press.

Miller, R. L., Brickman, P., & Bolen, D. (1975). Attribution versus persuasion as a means of modifying behavior. *Journal of Personality and Social Psychology, 31,* 430–441.

Mills, J., & Clark, E. S. (1982). Exchange and communal relationships. In L. Wheeler (Ed.), *Review of personality and social psychology* (Vol. 3, pp. 121–144). Beverly Hills, CA: Sage.

Murphy, G. (1947). *Personality.* New York: Harper.

Nadler, A. (1986). Help seeking as a cultural phenomenon: Differences between city and kibbutz dwellers. *Journal of Personality and Social Psychology, 51,* 976–982.

Pandey, J. (1986). Sociocultural perspectives on ingratiation. *Progress in Experimental Personality Research, 14,* 205–229.

Pearson, H. W. (Ed.). (1977). *The livelihood of man: Karl Polanyi.* New York: Academic Press.

Pelto, P. J. (1968, April). The difference between "tight" and "loose" societies. *Transaction,* 37–40.

Rogers, T. B. (1981). A model of the self as an aspect of the human information processing system. In N. Cantor & J. F. Kihlstrom (Eds.), *Personality, cognition and social interaction* (pp. 193–214). Hillsdale, NJ: Erlbaum.

Rokeach, M. (1960). *The open and closed mind.* New York: Basic Books.

Roland, A. (1984a). Psychoanalysis in civilization perspective. *Psychoanalytic Review, 7,* 569–590.

Roland, A. (1984b). The self in India and America: Toward a psychoanalysis of social and cultural contexts. In V. Kovolis (Ed.), *Designs of selfhood* (pp. 123–130). New Jersey: Associated University Press.

Rosenberg, M. (1979). *Conceiving the self.* New York: Basic Books.

Schlenker, B. R. (1985). Introduction. In B. R. Schlenker (Ed.). *Foundations of the self in social life* (pp. 1–28). New York: McGraw-Hill.

Shotland, R. L., & Berger, W. G. (1970). Behavioral validation of several values from the Rokeach value scale as an index of honesty. *Journal of Applied Psychology, 54,* 433–435.

Shweder, R. A., & LeVine, R. A. (1984). *Cultural theory: Essays on mind, self and emotion.* New York: Cambridge University Press.

Sinha, J. B. P. (1982). The Hindu (Indian) identity. *Dynamische Psychiatrie, 15,* 148–160.

Sinha, J. B. P. (1987). *Work cultures in Indian Organizations* (ICSSR Report). New Delhi, India: Concept Publications House.

Smith, M. B. (1980). Attitudes, values and selfhood. In H. E. Howe & M. M. Page (Eds.), *Nebraska Symposium on Motivation, 1979* (pp. 305–358). Lincoln: University of Nebraska Press.

Snyder, M. (1974). Self-monitoring and expressive behavior. *Journal of Personality and Social Psychology, 30,* 526–537.

Snyder, M. (1987). *Public appearances as private realities: The psychology of self-monitoring.* New York: Freeman.

Snyder, M., Simpson, J. A., & Gangestad, S. (1986). Personality and sexual relations. *Journal of Personality and Social Psychology, 51,* 181–190.

Stryker, S., & Serpe, R. T. (1982). Commitment, identity salience, and role behavior: Theory and research example. In

W. Ickes & E. S. Knowles (Eds.), *Personality, roles and social behavior* (pp. 199–218). New York: Springer.

Tajfel, H. (1978). *Differentiation between social groups.* London: Academic Press.

Triandis, H. C. (1967). Interpersonal relations in international organizations. *Journal of Organizational Behavior and Human Performance, 2,* 26–55.

Triandis, H. C. (1972). *The analysis of subjective culture.* New York: Wiley.

Triandis, H. C. (1977). *Interpersonal behavior.* Monterey, CA: Brooks/Cole.

Triandis, H. C. (1980). Values, attitudes, and interpersonal behavior. In H. Howe & M. Page (Eds.), *Nebraska Symposium on Motivation,* 1979 (pp. 195–260). Lincoln: University of Nebraska Press.

Triandis, H. C., Bontempo, R., Betancourt, H., Bond, M., Leung, K., Brenes, A., Georgas, J., Hui, C. H., Marin, G., Setiadi, B., Sinha, J. B. P., Verma, J., Spangenberg, J., Touzard, H., & de Montmollin, G. (1986). The measurement of etic aspects of individualism and collectivism across cultures. *Australian Journal of Psychology* (Special issue on cross-cultural psychology), *38,* 257–267.

Triandis, H. C., Bontempo, R., Villareal, M. J., Asai, M., & Lucca, N. (1988). Individualism and collectivism: Cross-cultural perspectives on self-ingroup relationships. *Journal of Personality and Social Psychology, 54,* 323–338.

Triandis, H. C., Leung, K., Villareal, M. J., & Clack, F. L. (1985). Allocentric versus idiocentric tendencies: Convergent and discriminant validation. *Journal of Research in Personality, 19,* 395–415.

Triandis, H. C., Marin, G., Lisansky, J., & Betancourt, H. (1984). *Simpatia* as a cultural script of Hispanics. *Journal of Personality and Social Psychology, 47,* 1363–1375.

United States Employment and Training Administration. *Dictionary of occupational titles.* Washington, DC: Government Printing Office.

Verma, J. (1985). The ingroup and its relevance to individual behaviour: A study of collectivism and individualism. *Psychologia, 28,* 173–181.

Wicklund, R. A., & Gollwitzer, P. M. (1982). *Symbolic self-completion.* Hillsdale, NJ: Erlbaum.

Yang, K. S. (1981). Social orientation and individual modernity among Chinese students in Taiwan. *Journal of Social Psychology, 113,* 159–170.

Zavalloni, M. (1975). Social identity and the recoding of reality. *International Journal of Psychology, 10,* 197–217.

Zavalloni, M., & Louis-Guerin, C. (1984). *Identité sociale et conscience: Introduction á l'égo-écologie* [Social identity and conscience: Introduction to the ego ecology]. Montréal, Canada: Les presses de l'université de Montreal.

Ziller, R. C. (1973). *The social self.* New York: Pergamon.

A Collective Fear of the Collective: Implications for Selves and Theories of Selves

Hazel Rose Markus and Shinobu Kitayama

Personality psychology generally assumes—in fact, it takes for granted—that human beings are individuals who can be meaningfully characterized, one at a time, using personality traits. This assumption, "that people are independent, bounded, autonomous entities," is precisely what the authors of the next selection bring into question. The well-known American social psychologist Hazel Markus and her Japanese colleague Shinobu Kitayama describe the idea of the autonomous individual as a notion that is peculiar to Western, Euro-American culture. Japanese and other Asian cultures, they claim, have a very different view of what a person is all about.

Cultures outside Europe and North America emphasize the interdependence of the person with the larger culture, which Markus and Kitayama call "the collective." Habitual Western modes of thought as well as political ideology combine to see people as essentially separate from each other and emphasize independence, autonomy, and individual differences. However, this seemingly obvious idea may be a cultural artifact. In the East, individuals are seen as part of a greater whole, and it is not so important for one person to compete with or dominate another.

Perhaps because they are arguing against what they see as the conventional wisdom, Markus and Kitayama somewhat romanticize the Eastern view of the self. For example, they write that Asian child-rearing "places a continual emphasis on understanding and relating to others," and that the collective view is characterized by caring, responsibility, and love. But of course there is a tradeoff of advantages and disadvantages between the Eastern and Western way of life. For example, in collectivist cultures one's spouse is commonly chosen by others on the basis of a negotiation between families. Perhaps as a result of cultural conditioning, most Europeans and Americans would rather choose their own spouses! As Markus and Kitayama point out, individual rights of all sorts are not given a high priority in collectivist cultures.

Two aspects of the following article are of particular value. First, the article urges us to reexamine an assumption about human psychology held so deeply that few people in our culture are probably even aware of holding it. Second, Markus and Kitayama present, in Figure 1, a comprehensive model of the relationship between a culture's collective reality, social processes, individual reality, habitual psychological tendencies, and action. This model has the potential to be useful for the analysis of psychological differences among cultures on many different dimensions, not just collectivism vs. individualism.

From "A Collective Fear of the Collective: Implications for Selves and Theories of Selves," by H. R. Markus and S. Kitayama. In *Personality and Social Psychology Bulletin, 20,* 568–579. Copyright © 1994 by the Society for Personality and Social Psychology, Inc. Reprinted by permission of Sage Publications.

Our cultural nightmare is that the individual throb of growth will be sucked dry in slavish social conformity. All life long, our central struggle is to defend the individual from the collective.

—Plath, 1980, p. 216

Selves, as well as theories of selves, that have been constructed within a European-American cultural frame show the influence of one powerful notion—the idea that people are independent, bounded, autonomous entities who must strive to remain unshackled by their ties to various groups and collectives (Bellah, Madsen, Sullivan, Swidler, & Tipton, 1985; Farr, 1991; Sampson, 1985; Shweder & Bourne, 1984). This culturally shared idea of the self is a pervasive, taken-for-granted assumption that is held in place by language, by the mundane rituals and social practices of daily life, by the law, the media, the foundational texts like the Declaration of Independence and the Bill of Rights, and by virtually all social institutions. The individualist ideal as sketched in its extreme form in the opening quotation might not be explicitly endorsed by many Americans and Europeans. Some version of this view is, however, the basis of social science's persistent belief in the person as a rational, self-interested actor, and it occasions a desire not to be defined by others and a deep-seated wariness, in some instances even a fear, of the influence of the generalized other, of the social, and of the collective.

* * *

Recent analyses of the self in cultures other than the European-American (e.g., Daniels, 1984; Derné, 1992; Markus & Kitayama, 1991; Triandis, 1990; White & Kirkpatrick, 1985) reveal some very different perspectives on the relation between the self and the collective. Japanese culture, for example, emphasizes the *inter*dependence of the individual with the collective rather than independence from it. The analysis of non–European-American views of self has two notable benefits. First, such an analysis can illuminate some central characteristics of these non-Western cultures themselves. Second, and more important for our purposes, it can help uncover some aspects of European-American social behavior that are not well captured in the current social psychological theories.

Culture and Self

INDEPENDENCE OF SELF FROM THE COLLECTIVE—A CULTURAL FRAME The model that underlies virtually all current social science views the self as an entity that (a) comprises a unique, bounded configuration of internal attributes (e.g., preferences, traits, abilities, motives, values, and rights) and (b) behaves primarily as a consequence of these internal attributes. It is the individual level of reality—the thoughts and feelings of the single individual—that is highlighted and privileged in the explanation and analysis of behavior; the collective level of reality recedes and remains secondary. The major normative task is to maintain the independence of the individual as a self-contained entity or, more specifically, to be true to one's own internal structures of preferences, rights, convictions, and goals and, further, to be confident and to be efficacious. According to this *independent* view of the self, there is an enduring concern with expressing one's internal attributes both in public and in private. Other people are crucial in maintaining this construal of the self, but they are primarily crucial for their role in evaluating and appraising the self or as standards of comparison (see Markus & Kitayama, 1991; Triandis, 1990, for a discussion of the independent or individualist self). Others do not, however, *participate* in the individual's own subjectivity.

* * *

INTERDEPENDENCE OF THE SELF AND THE COLLECTIVE—AN ALTERNATIVE FRAME The pervasive influence of the individualist ideal in many aspects of European-American social behavior has appeared in high relief as we have carried out a set of studies on the self and its functioning in a variety of Asian countries, including Japan, Thailand, and Korea (Kitayama & Markus, 1993; Kitayama, Markus, & Kurokawa, 1991; Markus & Kitayama, 1991, 1992). What has become apparent is that the European-American view of the self and its relation to the collective is only *one* view. There are other, equally powerful but strikingly different, collective notions about the self and its relation to the collective.

From one such alternative view, the self is viewed not as an independent entity separate from the collective but instead as a priori fundamentally interdependent with others. Individuals do not stand in opposition to the confines and constraints of the external collective, nor do they voluntarily choose to become parts of this external collective. Instead, the self *is* inherently social—an integral part of the collective. This interdependent view grants primacy to the *relationship* between self and others. The self derives only from the individual's relationships with specific others in the collective. There is no self without the collective; the self is a part that becomes whole only in interaction with others (e.g., Kondo, 1990; Kumagai & Kumagai, 1985; Lebra, 1992). It is defined and experienced as inherently connected with others. In contrast to the European-American orientation, there is an abiding fear of being on one's own, of being separated or disconnected from the collective. A desire for independence is cast as unnatural and immature.

The major normative task of such a self is not to maintain the independence of the individual as a self-contained entity but instead to maintain *inter*dependence with others. Rather than as an independent decision maker, the self is cast as "a single thread in a richly textured fabric of relationships" (Kondo, 1990, p. 33). This view of the self and of the collective requires adjusting and fitting to important relationships, occupying one's proper place in the group, engaging in collectively appropriate actions, and promoting the goals of others. One's thoughts, feelings, and actions are made meaningful only in reference to the thoughts, feelings, and actions of others in the relationship, and consequently others are crucially important in the very definition of the self. (For more detailed descriptions of the interdependent self, see Hsu, 1953; Kondo, 1990; Markus & Kitayama, 1991.)

Interdependence in this sense is theoretically distinct from social identity (e.g., Tajfel & Turner, 1985; Turner & Oakes, 1989), which refers to social categorizations that define a person as a member of particular social categories (e.g., American, male, Protestant, engineer). Social identity, in the framework of Turner and colleagues, is always defined in counterpoint to personal identity, which is all the ways a person is *different* from his or her ingroups. The key feature of interdependence is not distinctiveness or uniqueness but a heightened awareness of the other, and of the nature of one's relation to the other, and an expectation of some mutuality in this regard across all behavioral domains, even those that can be designated as private or personal.

DIFFERENCES IN THE ENCULTURATION OF THE "BASIC" TASKS Although both European-American and Asian cultural groups recognize that independence from others and interdependence with others are essential human tendencies or tasks, these two tasks are weighted and organized quite differently in the two groups. The notion of the autonomous individual in continuous tension with the external collective is "natural" only from a particular cultural perspective. From an alternative perspective, such an arrangement appears somewhat unnatural and contrived. In Japan, for example, the culture in its dominant ideology, patterns of social customs, practices, and institutions emphasizes and foregrounds not independence from others but interdependence with others. Interdependence is the first goal to be taken care of; it is crafted and nurtured in the social episodes and scripted actions of everyday social life, so that it becomes spontaneous, automatic, and taken for granted. Although independence is also essential for social functioning, it remains a tacit and less culturally elaborated pursuit. It is left to the intentions and initiatives of each individual member, and so its pursuit is relatively optional and is the focus of personal and unofficial discourse because it is not strongly constrained or widely supported by socially sanctioned cultural practices.

THE CULTURAL SHAPING OF PSYCHOLOGICAL PROCESSES

In Figure 1, we have illustrated how the "reality" of independence is created and maintained in selves, as well as in theories of selves. According to this view, a cultural group's way of self-understanding is simultaneously related to a set of macrolevel phenomena, such as cultural views of personhood and their supporting collective practices, and to a set of microlevel phenomena, like individual lives and their constituent cognitive, emotional, and motivational processes.

Collective reality. Under the heading "collective reality" we have included cultural values and their related ecological, historical, economic, and sociopolitical factors. For example, the United States is a nation with a rich tradition of moral imperatives, but the most well elaborated is the need to protect the "natural rights" of each individual. This core cultural ideal is rooted most directly in the Declaration of Independence and the Bill of Rights, which protect certain inalienable rights, including life, liberty, and the pursuit of happiness. This high-lighting of individuals and their rights is objectified and reified in a variety of democratic political institutions and free-market capitalism. In Japan, as throughout Asia, the prevalent ideological and moral discourses are not tied to individual rights but to the inevitability of a strict hierarchical order and to the achievement of virtue through cultivation of the individual into a "social man" (Yu, 1992). This core cultural ideal is anchored in the works of Confucius and Mencius and finds expression in an array of economic, political, and social institutions.

Sociopsychological products and processes—transmitting the core ideas. The cultural ideals and moral imperatives of a given cultural group are given life by a diverse set of customs, norms, scripts, practices, and institutions that carry out the transformation of the collective reality into the largely personal or psychological reality. These sociopsychological products and processes objectify and make "real" the core ideas of the society (Bourdieu, 1972; D'Andrade, 1984; Durkheim, 1898/1953; Farr & Moscovici, 1984; Geertz, 1973; Oyserman & Markus, in press). For example, in the United States, the idea of human rights (including liberty from the thrall of the collective) as inherent and God-given gains its force from a large array of legal statutes protecting individual rights. In this way the individual gains superiority to the collective.

Child-rearing practices in the United States, rooted in Freudian theory and filtered through Dr. Spock and most recently the self-esteem movement, also work to develop the constituent elements of the self and to reinforce the importance of having a distinct self that the individual can feel good about. A recent study (Chao, 1993), for example, found that 64% of European-American mothers, in comparison with 8% of Chinese mothers, stressed building children's "sense of themselves" as an important goal of child-rearing. Many American mothers take every opportunity to praise

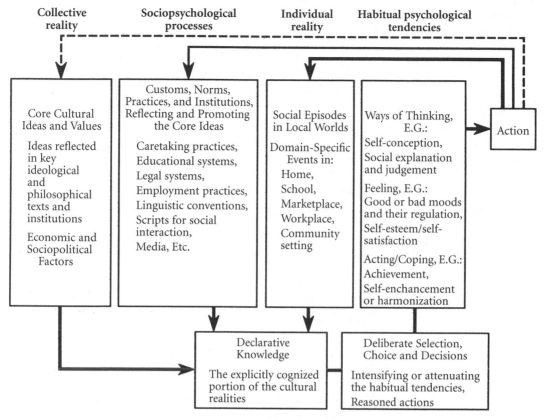

Figure 1 Cultural shaping of psychological reality

children and to help them realize the ways in which they are positively unique or different from their peers. Training in autonomy and the development of the appreciation of being alone also comes early. Day-old children sleep alone in their cribs, often in separate rooms from their parents (Shweder, Jensen, & Goldstein, 1995). On the playground, children are taught to stand up for themselves and fight back if necessary (Kashiwagi, 1989).

Another important quality of personhood, from the independent perspective, is the capacity to make one's own choice. In much of Western culture, but especially in North America, there are numerous examples of everyday scripts that presuppose the actor's right to make a choice. It is common for American hosts to instruct their guests, "Help yourself." With this suggestion, the host invites the guest to affirm the self by express-

ing some of those preferences that are thought to constitute the "real self." American children, then, are socialized to have distinct preferences. Long before the child is old enough to answer, caretakers pose questions like "Do you want the red cup or the blue cup?" With such questions, mothers signal to children that the capacity for independent choice is an important and desirable attribute. And the availability of choice gives rise to the need for preferences by which to make choices.

The practices of the media further create and foster the objectivity of the autonomous, independent self. Advertising in the United States makes appeals to nonconformity, originality, and uniqueness. A hard-sell approach is common in which the product is presented as the best or the leader of its kind, and purchasing it is claimed to reveal that the consumer has the "right" preferences or attitudes (Mueller, 1987; Zandpour, Chang, & Catalano, 1992). For example, Chanel recently marketed, in both the United States and Europe, a men's cologne with the strikingly unsubtle name of *Egoïste* and the slogan "For the man who walks on the right side of the fine line between arrogance and awareness of self-worth."

Perhaps the most powerful practice of all for the purpose of creating a shared concern with independence is that of advancing, promoting, and compensating people according to their "merit." This practice places a lifelong emphasis on inner attributes, capacities, and abilities as the "real" measure of the self and encourages people to define and develop these attributes.

In many Asian cultures, there is an equally diverse and powerful set of sociopsychological processes in each of these corresponding domains, but these practices are rooted in a view of the self as an interdependent entity. For example, in place of (or, to a certain extent, in addition to) the emphasis on human rights, there exist dense systems of rules and norms that highlight the duties of each individual to the pertinent collective, whether it is the company, school, or nation. Moreover, there are many fewer statutes protecting individual rights, and the Japanese resort to court suits to secure their rights far less readily than European-Americans (Hideo, 1988).

In the course of interpersonal interaction, the Japanese are encouraged to try to read the partner's mind and to satisfy what is taken as the partner's expectations or desires. A Japanese mother does not ask for a child's preference but instead tries to determine what is best for the child and to arrange it. Rather than asking a guest to make a choice, Japanese hosts do their best to prepare and offer what they infer to be the best possible meal for the guest, saying, for example, "Here's a turkey sandwich for you. I thought you said you like turkey better than beef last time we met."

Child rearing in many Asian cultures places a continual emphasis on understanding and relating to others, first to the mother and then to a wide range of others. The rules of interdependence are explicitly modeled, and the goal is to maintain harmonious relationships (Hsu, 1953). Interdependence can be found in all domains. In stark opposition to American practices and Freudian wisdom, cosleeping and cobathing are common in Japanese families. The emphasis is not on developing a good, private sense of self but on tuning in to and being sensitive to others. Punishing or reprimanding Japanese children often involves not the withholding of rights and privileges but a threat to the relationship. Mothers will say, "I don't like children like you" or "People will laugh at you" (Okimoto & Rohlen, 1988).

With respect to media practices, Japanese advertising often uses soft-sell appeals that focus on harmony or connection with nature or with others (Mueller, 1987). In classified ads, employers explicitly seek individuals with good interpersonal relations, as opposed to self-starters or innovators (Caproni, Rafaeli, & Carlile, 1993). A focus on relationships is also evident in all types of business practices. Japan stands out from all countries in the West because of its emphasis on durable and pervasive ties between government and industry, between banks and businesses, and among corporations. Okimoto and Rohlen (1988) contend that the emphasis on organizational networks and human relationships is so strong that Japanese capitalism can be labeled *relational capitalism*. In the pursuit of long-term relationships and mutual trust, Japanese corporations operate quite differently, often, for example, forgoing the maximization of short-term profits with the hope of gaining a long-term market share. And in contrast to the European-American emphasis on merit for promotion and compensation, wages and advancement in the majority of Japanese companies and institutions are tied to seniority in the system. In addition, employment in large corporations is typically permanent, and there is little lateral entry from the outside—all publicly scripted collective practices that foster and promote a view of the self as inherently relational and interdependent.

Beyond the caretaking, legal, business, and media practices we have alluded to are a host of others, including educational and linguistic practices, and all the scripts and institutions that structure everyday social interactions. An important element in understanding which practices will become socially established is how the practices reflect and carry the group's underlying cultural values. Americans, for example, will be particularly susceptible to ideas and practices that directly follow from individualism (Sperber, 1985). Other practices—welfare and universal health care programs are good examples—will have a more difficult time taking hold in the United States.

Local worlds—living the core ideas. The third segment of Figure 1 represents the specific settings, circumstances, and situations of everyday life that make up an individual's immediate social environment and in which particular customs, norms, and practices become lived experience. The local worlds—home, school, the workplace, the community center, the church, the restaurant, bar, or café, the marketplace—and the specific activities or episodes they support—helping a child with homework, shopping for a gift, drinking with friends, discussing politics, playing baseball, working with others to meet a deadline—demand specific, culturally appropriate responses if a person is to become a valued member of the family, school, workplace, or community.

It is within the demands and expectations of these domain-specific, recurrent social episodes that people, often quite unknowingly, live out the core cultural values. So Americans are likely to create and live within settings that elicit and promote the sense that one is a positively unique individual who is separate and independent from others. For example, in many American schools, each child in the class has the opportunity to be a "star" or a "Very Special Person" for a week during the school year. Likewise, Japanese will create and live with situations that promote the sense of self as interdependent with others. In Japanese schools, children routinely produce group pictures or story boards, and no child leaves to go to the playground or lunch until all members of the group are ready to leave.

Habitual psychological tendencies reflecting the core ideas. As a result of efforts to respond or adjust to the set of specific episodes that constitute the individual's life space, episodes that have themselves been shaped by norms, practices, and institutions supporting the cultural group's core ideas, a set of habitual psychological tendencies is likely to develop. The final segment of Figure 1 represents the individual's "authentic" subjective experience—particular, proceduralized ways of thinking, feeling, striving, knowing, understanding, deciding, managing, adjusting, adapting, which are, in some large part, structured, reinforced, and maintained by the constraints and affordances of the particular social episodes of the individual's local worlds. In this way, people who live within a society whose daily practices and formal institutions all promote independence will come not just to believe that they are, but to experience themselves as, autonomous, bounded selves who are distinct from other members of the collective. This will be evident in many ways of thinking, feeling, and acting, but it is particularly evident when people are asked to characterize themselves.

For example, by the time they are young adults, many Americans will seek an optimal distinctiveness from others (Brewer, 1990) and will "naturally" experience an ambivalence about their collective nature and a deep concern with being categorically perceived or socially determined. The journalist Barbara Ehrenreich (1992) describes an interchange with an acquaintance who has just rediscovered her own ethnic and religious heritage and now feels in contact with her 2000-year ancestral traditions. The acquaintance asks about Ehrenreich's ethnic background. The first word to come out of Ehrenreich's mouth in answer to the question is "None." She is surprised at how natural and right her answer seems, yet slightly embarrassed. She reflects and decides that her response when asked the nature of her ethnicity was quite correct. Her identity, she claims, comes from the realization that "we are the kind of people that whatever our distant ancestors' religions—we do not believe, we do not carry on traditions, we do not do things just because someone has done them before." Her ethnicity, she contends, is rooted not in a given group but in the ideas "Think for yourself" and

"Try new things." In conclusion, Ehrenreich tells of asking her own children whether they ever had any stirring of "ethnic or religious identity." "None," they all conclude, and she reports, "My chest swelled with pride as would my mother's to know that the race of 'None' marches on."

A tendency to define one's "real" self as distinct from one's social groups and obligations is characteristic of both younger and older cohorts of Americans as well. In a series of studies with young children, Hart and his colleagues (Hart, 1988; Hart & Edelstein, 1992) asked American children to imagine a "person machine" that makes the original person disappear but at the same time manufactures other people, copies of the original, which receive some but not all of the original person's characteristics. The respondent's task is to judge which new manufactured person—the one with the same physical attributes (looks like you), the one with the same social attributes (has the same friends and family), or the one with the same psychological attributes (same thoughts and feelings)—will be most like the original person. By ninth grade, Hart et al. (Hart, Fegley, Hung Chan, Mulvey, & Fischer, 1993) finds that most respondents believe it is the copy with the original's psychological characteristics that is the most similar to the original.

These findings are consistent with those of several other studies of cultural variation in self-categorization (Cousins, 1989; Triandis, 1990) and suggest that, for American students, it is the internal features of the self—the traits, attributes, and attitudes—that are privileged and regarded as critical to self-definition. From this perspective, the significant aspects of the self are those that are the inside, the private property—one's characteristic ways of behaving, one's habitual thoughts, feelings, and beliefs (e.g., think for yourself, try new things)—the elements that do not explicitly reference others or the social world. Such internal attributes are also mentioned by the Japanese, but they appear to be understood as relatively situation specific and therefore elusive and unreliable (Cousins, 1989) as defining features of self. For the Japanese, the critical features are those attributes—social roles, duties, obligations—that connect one to the larger world of social relationships. (For other detailed examples of the cultural shaping of judgment, self, and emotion, see Kitayama & Markus, 1993, 1995; Markus & Kitayama, 1994.) In a study examining response time for self-description,[1] Kitayama et al. (1991) find that Japanese respondents are decidedly slower to characterize themselves than American respondents and that this is particularly true for positive attributes.

The top level of Figure 1 indicates feedback loops from each individual's action. The most immediate and frequent feedback occurs at the micro level. Most obviously, what an individual does influences the very nature of the situation in which he or she has acted. There are, however, people who at times contribute, through their actions, not just to the micro level but also to the more macro level. The bottom level of Figure 1 represents a more cognitive influence. Some portion of the social realities—both macro and micro—can be represented cognitively. This cognized portion of culture is shaded in each segment of the figure. The articulated, declarative knowledge of cultural values, practices, and conventions may be recruited in modulating social action, either facilitating or inhibiting the automatized psychological tendencies. Importantly, however, psychological tendencies can develop independently of this second, articulated route of cultural influence. In this way, cultural values and beliefs can cause differences in psychological processes even when these beliefs (e.g., a fear of influence by the collective) are not cognitively encoded and overtly articulated. Of course, the values and beliefs often are encoded cognitively, but this current analysis implies that cognitive representations need not be central in the cultural shaping of psychological processes. Instead, we suggest that psychological processes and behavior can be best

---

[1]In such a study personality adjectives are presented on a screen, and subjects must respond "me" or "not me" by pressing a key. The time taken to respond is measured in milliseconds. A slower response implies that a particular attribute is a less central aspect of the self-concept.

understood as an important, but only partial, element of the dynamic cultural and historical process that involves the systematic (though by no means error-free or "faxlike") transmission of cultural imperatives to shape and define the nature of the specific, immediate life space—the microlevel reality—for each individual.

Implications of a Collective Fear of the Collective for Psychological Theorizing

Using Asian cultures, particularly Japan, as a point of reference and standard, we have sketched how the European-American fear of the collective may arise and how it is naturalized, enacted, and embodied so that people rarely see or feel the collective nature or source of their behavior and instead experience themselves as separate and self-contained entities. A large set of mutually reinforcing everyday rituals, social practices, and institutions work together to elaborate and objectify the culture's view of what the self is and what it should be. Independence and autonomy are thus the "natural" mode of being—in Geertz's (1975) terms, they become "experience near" phenomena. The subjective authenticity or "naturalness" of this mode, however, is a function of the degree of fit between habitual psychological tendencies and the cultural and social systems that are grounded in these cultural imperatives.

Theorists of European-American behavior have also been extremely influenced by the prevailing ideology of individualism. They have often viewed the self as in tension, or even as in opposition, to the "ruck of society" (Plath, 1980) or the "thrall of society" (Hewitt, 1989). The source of all important behavior is typically "found" in the unique configuration of internal attributes—thoughts, feelings, motives, abilities—that form the bounded, autonomous whole. As a consequence, the ways in which the self is, in fact, quite interdependent with the collective have been underanalyzed and undertheorized. It is our view that there are a number of important reasons for theo-

rists to go beyond theories that are directly shaped by the cultural ideal of individualism and to consider a broader view of the self.

First, and most obviously, although current descriptions of the largely independent and autonomous self could be argued to be reasonably adequate for European-American selves, a growing body of evidence suggests that they are simply not valid for many other cultural groups (see extended discussions of this point in Markus & Kitayama, 1991; Triandis, 1990; Triandis, Bontempo, & Villareal, 1988). Second, although the cultural ideal of independence is very influential in the nature and functioning of the European-American self, it does not determine it completely. For example, with respect to the bounded or fixed nature of the self, there are a variety of studies that reveal the self as decidedly malleable and its content and functioning as dependent on the social context. Typically these studies are not integrated with the literature that suggests stability of the self (e.g., Fazio, Effrein, & Falender, 1981; James, 1993; Jones & Pittman, 1982; Markus & Kunda, 1986; McGuire & McGuire, 1982; Schlenker, 1980).

Third, at least in the United States, the analysis of the selves of those groups in society that are somewhat marginalized—women, members of nondominant ethnic groups, the poor, the unschooled, and the elderly—reveals a more obvious interdependence between the self and the collective. For example, women describe themselves in relational terms (Gilligan, 1982; Jordan, Kaplan, Miller, Stivey, & Surrey, 1991), and they do not reveal the "typical" preference for being positively unique or different from others (Josephs, Markus, & Tafarodi, 1992). Other studies reveal that those groups that are in the minority with respect to language, skin color, or religion are decidedly more likely to define themselves in collective terms (Allen, Dawson, & Brown, 1989; Bowman, 1987; Husain, 1992). Further, Americans with less schooling are more likely to describe themselves in terms of habitual actions and roles, and less likely to characterize themselves in terms of psychological attributes, than those with more schooling (Markus, Herzog, Holmberg, & Dielman, 1992). And those with low self-esteem show a marked tendency to describe themselves as similar to others (Josephs et al., 1992). These findings suggest that those with power and privilege are those most likely to internalize the prevailing European-American cultural frame to achieve Ehrenreich's "ethnicity of none" and to "naturally" experience themselves as autonomous individuals.

Fourth, a number of recent studies show many Americans to be extremely concerned about others and the public good (Bellah et al., 1985; Bellah, Madsen, Sullivan, Swidler, & Tipton, 1991; Hewitt, 1989; Withnow, 1992) and to characterize themselves in interdependent terms. For example, a recent representative sample of 1,500 adults, aged 30 or over, found that although Americans indeed characterized themselves in terms of trait attributes and not social roles or obligations, the most frequently used attributes were *caring, responsible, loved*—all terms that imply some concern with a connection to the collective (Markus et al., 1992). Even if, as we have suggested, this connection is clearly voluntary and done on one's own terms, the prevailing model of the self could be modified.

And finally, increasingly throughout social psychology, there are indications that the individualist model of the self is too narrow and fails to take account of some important aspects of psychological reality. For example, within social psychology specifically, there is a great deal of evidence that people are exquisitely sensitive to others and to social pressure. People conform, obey, diffuse responsibility in a group, allow themselves to be easily persuaded about all manner of things, and become powerfully committed to others on the basis of minimal action (Myers, 1993). Despite the powerful cultural sanctions against allowing the collective to influence one's thoughts and actions, most people are still much less self-reliant, self-contained, or self-sufficient than the ideology of individualism suggests they should be. It appears in these cases that the European-American model of self is somewhat at odds with observed individual behavior and that it might be reformulated to reflect the substantial interdependence that characterizes even Western individualists.

Alternative Views of the Self and the Collective

In trying to formulate the collective sources of the self among Europeans or Americans, models of the self and the collective "Asian style" may be particularly informative.[2] If we assume, as does Shweder (1991), that every group can be considered an expert on some features of human experience and that different cultural groups "light up" different aspects of this experience, then Asian cultures may be an important source of conceptual resources in the form of concepts, frameworks, theories, or methods that can be employed to "see" interdependence. Even though interdependence American style will doubtlessly look quite different from interdependence Japanese style, an analysis of divergent cultural groups may further any theorist's understanding of the possibilities, potential, and consequences, both positive and negative, for socialness, for engagement, for interdependence, and for the ties that bind.

* * *

We have argued here that the cultural frame of individualism has put a very strong stamp on how social psychologists view the individual and his or her relation to the collective. Although this individualist view has provided a powerful framework for the analysis of social behavior, it has also, necessarily, constrained theories, methods, and domi-

---

[2]Some of the most important work suggesting the need for alternative models of the self comes from feminist theorists who have argued in the last 15 years that relations have a power and significance in women's lives that has gone unrecognized (Belenky, Clinchy, Goldberger, & Tarule, 1986; Gilligan, 1982; Jordan et al., 1991). The development of a psychology of women has shown that the "Lone Ranger" model of the self simply does not fit many women's experience because women's sense of self seems to involve connection and engagement with relationships and collective. In this work, being dependent does not invariably mean being helpless, powerless, or without control. It often means being interdependent—having a sense that one is able to have an effect on others and is willing to be responsive to others and become engaged with them (Jordan, 1991).—Author

nant interpretations of social behavior. Because individualism is not just a matter of belief or value but also one of everyday practice, including scientific practice, it is not easy for theorists to view social behavior from another cultural frame, and it is probably harder still to reflect a different frame in empirical work. But the comparative approach that is characteristic of the developing cultural psychology (e.g., Cole, 1990; Stigler, Shweder, & Herdt, 1990) may eventually open new and productive possibilities for the understanding and analysis of behavior.

For example, just as social influence, from the perspective of an interdependent cultural frame, can be seen as the mutual negotiation of social reality, helping can be seen as a result of obligation, duty, or morality, rather than as voluntary or intentional (e.g., Miller, Bersoff, & Harwood, 1990). Similarly, emotion can be viewed as an enacted interpersonal process (Rosaldo, 1984) or as an interpersonal atmosphere, as it is characterized in some non-Western theories (White, 1990). Further, cognition can be seen as an internalized aspect of communication (Zajonc, 1992), and the early idea of the social and interactive nature of the mind (e.g., Asch, 1952; Bruner, 1990; Vygotsky, 1978) can be taken much more seriously than it has been. In general, viewing the self and social behavior from alternative perspectives may enable theorists to see and elaborate at least one important and powerful universal that might otherwise be quite invisible— the ways in which psychological functioning (in this case, the nature of the self), as well as theories about psychological functioning (here, theories of the nature of the self), are in many ways culture specific and conditioned by particular, but tacit and taken-for-granted, meaning systems, values, and ideals.

References

Allen, R. L., Dawson, M. C., & Brown, R. E. (1989). A schema based approach to modeling an African American racial belief system. *American Political Science Review, 83,* 421–442.

Asch, S. E. (1952). *Social psychology.* Englewood Cliffs, NJ: Prentice-Hall.

Belenky, M. F., Clinchy, B. M., Goldberger, N. R., & Tarule, J. M. (1986). *Women's ways of knowing: The development of self, voice, and mind.* New York: Basic Books.

Bellah, R. N., Madsen, R., Sullivan, W. M., Swidler, A., & Tipton, S. M. (1985). *Habits of the heart: Individualism and commitment in American life.* Berkeley: University of California Press.

Bellah, R. N., Madsen, R., Sullivan, W. M., Swidler, A., & Tipton, S. M. (1991). *The good society.* New York: Knopf.

Bourdieu, P. (1972). *Outline of a theory of practice.* Cambridge: Cambridge University Press.

Bowman, P. J. (1987). Post-industrial displacement and family role strains: Challenges to the Black family. In P. Voydanoff & L. C. Majka (Eds.), *Families and economic distress.* Newbury Park, CA: Sage.

Brewer, M. B. (1990, August). *The social self: On being the same and different at the same time.* Presidential address to the Society for Personality and Social Psychology presented at the annual meeting of the American Psychological Association, Boston.

Bruner, J. (1990). *Acts of meaning.* Cambridge, MA: Harvard University Press.

Caproni, P., Rafaeli, A., & Carlile, P. (1993, July). *The social construction of organized work: The role of newspaper employment advertising.* Paper presented at the European Group on Organization Studies conference, Paris, France.

Chao, R. K. (1993). *East and West: Concepts of the self reflected in mothers' reports of their child-rearing.* Unpublished manuscript, University of California, Los Angeles.

Cole, M. (1990). Cultural psychology: A once and future discipline? In J. J. Berman (Ed.), *Nebraska Symposium on Motivation, 1989* (Vol. 37, pp. 279–336). Lincoln: University of Nebraska Press.

Cousins, S. (1989). Culture and selfhood in Japan and the U.S. *Journal of Personality and Social Psychology, 56,* 124–131.

D'Andrade, R. (1984). Cultural meaning systems. In R. A. Shweder & R. A. LeVine (Eds.), *Cultural theories: Essays on mind, self, and emotion* (pp. 88–119). New York: Cambridge University Press.

Daniels, E. V. (1984). *Fluid signs; Being a person the Tamil way.* Berkeley: University of California Press.

Derné, S. (1992). Beyond institutional and impulsive conceptions of self: Family structure and the socially anchored real self. *Ethos, 20,* 259–288.

Durkheim, E. (1953). Individual representations and collective representations. In E. Durkheim (Ed.), *Sociology and philosophy* (D. F. Pocok, Trans.) (pp. 1–38). New York: Free Press. (Original work published 1898.)

Ehrenreich, B. (1992, March). The race of none. *Sunday New York Times Magazine,* pp. 5–6.

Farr, R. M. (1991). Individualism as a collective representation. In V. Aebischer, J. P. Deconchy, & M. Lipiansky (Eds.), *Idéologies et représentations sociales* (pp. 129–143). Cousset (Fribourg), Switzerland: Delval.

Farr, R. M., & Moscovici, S. (Eds.). (1984). *Social representations.* Cambridge: Cambridge University Press.

Fazio, R. H., Effrein, E. A., & Falender, Y. J. (1981). Self-perceptions following social interactions. *Journal of Personality and Social Psychology, 41,* 232–242.

Geertz, C. (1973). *The interpretation of cultures.* New York: Basic Books.

Geertz, C. (1975). On the nature of anthropological understanding. *American Scientist, 63,* 47–53.

Gilligan, C. (1982). *In a different voice: Psychological theory and women's development.* Cambridge, MA: Harvard University Press.

Hart, D. (1988). The adolescent self-concept in social context. In D. Lapsley & F. Power (Eds.), *Self, ego, and identity: Integrative approaches* (pp. 71–90). New York: Springer-Verlag.

Hart, D., & Edelstein, W. (1992). Self understanding development in cultural context. In T. M. Brinthaupt & R. P. Lipka (Eds.), *The self: Definitional and methodological issues.* Albany: State University of New York Press.

Hart, D., Fegley, S., Hung Chan, Y., Mulvey, D., & Fischer, L. (1993). *Judgment about personal identity in childhood and adolescence.* Unpublished manuscript.

Hewitt, J. P. (1989). *Dilemmas of the American self.* Philadelphia: Temple University Press.

Hideo, T. (1988). The role of law and lawyers in Japanese society. In D. I. Okimoto & T. P. Rohlen (Eds.), *Inside the Japanese system: Readings on contemporary society and political economy* (pp. 194–196). Stanford, CA: Stanford University Press.

Hsu, F. L. K. (1953). *Americans and Chinese: Two ways of life.* New York: H. Schuman.

Husain, M. G. (1992, July). *Ethnic uprising and identity.* Paper presented at the 11th Congress of the International Association for Cross-Cultural Psychology, Liege, Belgium.

James, K. (1993). Conceptualizing self with in-group stereotypes: Context and esteem precursors. *Personality and Social Psychology Bulletin, 19,* 117–121.

Jones, E. E., & Pittman, T. S. (1982). Towards a general theory of strategic self-preservation. In J. Suls (Ed.), *Psychological perspectives on the self* (Vol. 1, pp. 231–262). Hillsdale, NJ: Lawrence Erlbaum.

Jordan, J. V. (1991). Empathy and self boundaries. In J. V. Jordan, A. G. Kaplan, J. B. Miller, I. P. Stivey, & J. L. Surrey (Eds.), *Women's growth in connection* (pp. 67–80). New York: Guilford.

Jordan, J. V., Kaplan, A. G., Miller, J. B., Stivey, I. P., & Surrey, J. L. (Eds.). (1991). *Women's growth in connection.* New York: Guilford.

Josephs, R. A., Markus, H., & Tafarodi, R. W. (1992). Gender differences in the source of self-esteem. *Journal of Personality and Social Psychology, 63,* 391–402.

Kashiwagi, K. (1989, July). *Development of self-regulation in Japanese children.* Paper presented at the tenth annual meeting of the International Society for the Study of Behavioral Development, Jyväskylä, Finland.

Kitayama, S., & Markus, H. (1993). Construal of the self as a cultural frame: Implications for internationalizing psychology. In J. D'Arms, R. G. Hastie, S. E. Hoelscher, & H. K. Jacobson (Eds.), *Becoming more international and global: Challenges for American higher education.* Manuscript submitted for publication.

Kitayama, S., & Markus, H. (1995). A cultural perspective on self-conscious emotions. In J. P. Tangney & K. W. Fisher (Eds.), *Shame, guilt, embarrassment and pride: Empirical studies of self-conscious emotions.* New York: Guilford.

Kitayama, S., Markus, H., & Kurokawa, M. (1991, October). *Culture, self, and emotion: The structure and frequency of emotional experience.* Paper presented at the biannual meeting of the Society for Psychological Anthropology, Chicago.

Kondo, D. (1990). *Crafting selves: Power, gender, and discourses of identity in a Japanese work place.* Chicago: University of Chicago Press.

Kumagai, H. A., & Kumagai, A. K. (1985). The hidden "I" in *amae:* "Passive love" and Japanese social perception. *Ethos, 14,* 305–321.

Lebra, T. S. (1976). *Japanese patterns of behavior.* Honolulu: University of Hawaii Press.

Lebra, T. S. (1992, June). *Culture, self, and communication.* Paper presented at the University of Michigan, Ann Arbor.

Markus, H., Herzog, A. R., Holmberg, D. E., & Dielman, L. (1992). *Constructing the self across the life span.* Unpublished manuscript, University of Michigan, Ann Arbor.

Markus, H., & Kitayama, S. (1991). Culture and the self: Implications for cognition, emotion, and motivation. *Psychological Review, 98,* 224–253.

Markus, H., & Kitayama, S. (1992). The what, why and how of cultural psychology: A review of R. Shweder's *Thinking through cultures. Psychological Inquiry, 3,* 357–364.

Markus, H., & Kitayama, S. (1994). The cultural construction of self and emotion: Implications for social behavior. In S. Kitayama & H. R. Markus (Eds.), *Emotion and culture: Empirical studies of mutual influence* (pp. 89–130). Washington, DC: American Psychological Association.

Markus, H., & Kunda, Z. (1986). Stability and malleability in the self-concept in the perception of others. *Journal of Personality and Social Psychology, 51,* 1–9.

McGuire, W. J., & McGuire, C. V. (1982). Significant others in self space: Sex differences and developmental trends in social self. In J. Suls (Ed.), *Psychological perspectives on the self* (Vol. 1, pp. 71–96). Hillsdale, NJ: Lawrence Erlbaum.

Miller, J. G., Bersoff, D. M., & Harwood, R. L. (1990). Perceptions of social responsibilities in India and in the United States: Moral imperatives or personal decisions? *Journal of Personality and Social Psychology, 58,* 33–46.

Mueller, B. (1987, June/July). Reflections of culture: An analysis of Japanese and American advertising appeals. *Journal of Advertising Research,* pp. 51–59.

Myers, D. (1993). *Social psychology* (4th ed.). New York: McGraw-Hill.

Okimoto, D. I., & Rohlen, T. P. (Eds.). (1988). *Inside the Japanese system: Readings on contemporary society and political economy.* Stanford, CA: Stanford University Press.

Oyserman, D., & Markus, H. R. (in press). Self as social representation. In S. Moscovici and U. Flick (Eds.), *Psychology of the social.* Berlin: Rowohlt Taschenbuch Verlag Gmbh.

Plath, D. W. (1980). *Long engagements: Maturity in modern Japan.* Stanford, CA: Stanford University Press.

Rosaldo, M. (1984). Toward an anthropology of self and feeling. In R. A. Shweder & R. A. LeVine (Eds.), *Culture theory: Essays on mind, self, and emotion* (pp. 137–157). Cambridge: Cambridge University Press.

Sampson, E. E. (1985). The decentralization of identity: Toward a revised concept of personal and social order. *American Psychologist, 40,* 1203–1211.

Schlenker, B. R. (1980). *Impression management.* Pacific Grove, CA: Brooks/Cole.

Shweder, R. A. (1991). *Thinking through cultures: Expeditions in cultural psychology.* Cambridge, MA: Harvard University Press.

Shweder, R. A., & Bourne, E. (1984). Does the concept of the person vary cross-culturally? In R. A. Shweder & R. A. LeVine (Eds.), *Culture theory: Essays on mind, self, and emotion* (pp. 158–199). Cambridge: Cambridge University Press.

Shweder, R. A., Jensen, L. A., & Goldstein, W. M. (1995). Who sleeps by whom revisted: A method for extracting the moral goods implicit in practice. In J. Goodnow, P. Miller, & F. Kessel (Eds.), *Cultural practices as contexts for development.* San Francisco: Jossey-Bass.

Sperber, D. (1985). Anthropology and psychology: Towards an epidemiology of representations. *MAN, 20,* 73–89.

Stigler, J. W., Shweder, R. A., & Herdt, G. (Eds.). (1990). *Cultural psychology: Essays on comparative human development.* London: Cambridge University Press.

Tajfel, H., & Turner, J. C. (1985). The social identity theory of intergroup behavior. In S. Worchel & W. G. Austin (Eds.), *Psychology of intergroup relations* (pp. 7–24). Chicago: Nelson-Hall.

Triandis, H. C. (1990). Cross-cultural studies of individualism and collectivism. In J. J. Berman (Ed.), *Nebraska Symposium on Motivation, 1989* (Vol. 37, pp. 41–143).

Triandis, H. C., Bontempo, R., & Villareal, M. (1988). Individualism and collectivism: Cross-cultural perspectives on self-ingroup relationships. *Journal of Personality and Social Psychology, 54,* 323–338.

Turner, J. C., & Oakes, P. J. (1989). Self-categorization theory and social influence. In P. B. Paulus (Ed.), *The psychology of group influence* (2nd ed.). Hillsdale, NJ: Lawrence Erlbaum.

Vygotsky, L. S. (1978). *Mind in society: The development of higher psychological processes* (M. Cole, V. John-Steiner, S. Scribner, & E. Souberman, Eds.). Cambridge, MA: Harvard University Press.

White, G. M. (1990). Moral discourse and the rhetoric of emotion. In C. Lutz & L. Abu-Lughod (Eds.), *Language and the politics of emotion.* Cambridge: Cambridge University Press.

White, G. M., & Kirkpatrick, J. (Eds.). (1985). *Person, self, and experience: Exploring Pacific ethnopsychologies.* Berkeley and Los Angeles: University of California Press.

Withnow, R. (1992). *Acts of compassion.* Princeton, NJ: Princeton University Press.

Yu, A. B. (1992, July). *The self and life goals of traditional Chinese: A philosophical and cultural analysis.* Paper presented at the 11th Congress of the International Association for Cross-Cultural Psychology, Liege, Belgium.

Zajonc, R. B. (1992, April). *Cognition, communication, consciousness: A social psychological perspective.* Invited address at the 20th Katz-Newcomb Lecture at the University of Michigan, Ann Arbor.

Zandpour, F., Chang, C., & Catalano, J. (1992, January/February). Stories, symbols, and straight talk: A comparative analysis of French, Taiwanese, and U.S. TV commercials. *Journal of Advertising Research,* pp. 25–38.

EMOTIONS IN COLLECTIVIST AND INDIVIDUALIST CONTEXTS

Batja Mesquita

The previous selections by Triandis and by Markus and Kitayama agreed that a critical dimension of cultural difference is that between collectivism and individualism. The present article, by Batja Mesquita, explores the complex question of how people might experience emotion differently within these two kinds of culture. This is a particularly interesting topic for cultural investigation, because many psychologists over the years have conducted research based on the assumption that emotions are "culturally universal," or experienced the same in all cultures. Mesquita expresses doubt about this assumption, because she believes that emotions are a critical aspect of the self, and the self has different boundaries and relations with other people in collectivist vs. individualist cultures. Her study, conducted in the Netherlands, compares individualist Dutch participants with participants living in the Netherlands but originally from and culturally identified with the collectivist cultures of Surinam and Turkey.

Emotion is a difficult topic to research because its most important aspect—the experience of emotion—occurs out of view. This study provides a good example not only of the theories and methods employed in the study of cultural differences, but also a model of some of the techniques that can be used to study emotion.

From *Journal of Personality and Social Psychology, 80,* 68–74, 2001.

Cross-cultural endeavors in psychology have focused on the universality of emotional phenomena (e.g., Ekman, 1973; Scherer & Wallbott, 1994), revealing a number of pancultural features of emotions. The psychological focus on universality has precluded the search for cultural variations in emotion. Ethnographic studies (e.g., Lutz, 1988) have clearly illustrated such differences, but methodological limitations do not allow for firm conclusions on the nature and the extent of cultural variation in emotion, either. The goal of the present study is, therefore, to determine whether within the context of similar emotional situations there are interpretable and predictable differences in emotional phenomena.

I studied differences in emotions by comparing individualist with collectivist cultures. Individualism and collectivism are best represented as systems of meanings, practices, and social institutions in the context of which the nature of emotion should be expected to vary. *Collectivism* is a set of meanings and practices that emphasize the relatedness of a person to his or her in-group and, more generally, to the world. Similarly, *individualism* is a set of meanings and practices that underline the individual as bounded, unique, and independent (Markus & Kitayama, 1991; Shweder & Levine, 1984; Triandis, 1995). Even though collectivism and individualism may characterize cultural groups, not all individuals in a given context engage in the same ideas and practices, nor do they engage in them in identical ways (Markus, Mulally, & Kitayama, 1997). However, across people within an individualist or collectivist context, emotions are patterned in some discernable ways.

In this study, it is assumed that cultural instantiations of emotion can be predicted from the meanings and practices within which they occur. Emotions in collectivist cultures are expected to stress and reproduce the self in relation to others or the self in relation to the world, whereas emotions in individualist cultures are assumed to underline and amplify a bounded, subjective self. Collectivism and individualism are not conceived of as independent variables in the traditional sense of the word. They are not causal determinants of emotions but rather characterizations of the syndromes of which emotions are a part.

Emotions: Social or Individual Events

In an open interview study preceding the current one (Mesquita, in press), self-reported emotions in collectivist contexts appeared to be quite different from those in individualist contexts. As an illustration, one may consider the following self-reports.

A respondent from a collectivist context (Turkish) said the following in an interview:

> I was admitted to Turkey's most competitive university. . . . It was the second time that I participated in the national competition, because after the first time I quit university. . . . I ended in the highest percentile.

My [extended] family did not want me to compete a second time, as this would lower the chances of their own children to get into good programs. There was resentment [about me participating], and so my honor was challenged. . . . I was forced to be competitive with the children of my relatives. . . . [That I won the competition] was important to my mom. It was my mother's pride that she could use my success against lots of people. They asked her if they could see my university ID and without me knowing it, my mom had taken it to show them. My parents had invited all their relatives and neighbors over to their house to celebrate this success. My relatives asked me questions to humiliate me: "Are you going to finish this time?" They kissed me, and wished me well, but I knew that they privately thought: "Damn it, you won again". . . . After I won [the competition], many families were prepared to offer me their daughters to marry. Of course, my self-esteem increased.

A respondent from an individualist context (Dutch) said the following in an interview:

> I gave my final presentation for my masters in civil engineering. . . . You feel like you have really done it. Yes [you wonder] how you have actually managed to do it. . . . I felt like enormously relieved. . . . Not really excited, but more like "It is finally over!" . . . I had set myself this deadline and it made me feel really good that I made it this time. . . . Afterwards I went out with some friends and relatives, seven people. We did not really talk about my presentation. Yes, sure, they are friends of mine, so they know that this is important for me. . . . They had come to listen to my presentation, of course, and so they did tell me that I did a good job. They also said "You are done now, it is over," that kind of things. . . . Other than that we just talked about other stuff. . . . For a few months, when I would run into people, I would tell them. It gave me a good feeling. Each time it dawns on you a little more that you are really done with it.

Both accounts, the collectivist and the individualist, are about good feelings in response to a significant personal accomplishment in the context of higher education. However, in the collectivist context, the meaning of the event (a) is constituted by its impact on the various relationships the respondent has, including a relationship with others in general, as expressed by the respondent's honor;

(b) is represented as obvious, as when the respondent reported that his honor is challenged and that he is forced to succeed; and (c) is relevant to other people who are emotionally involved in it. By contrast, in the individualist context, the emotion appears to be (a) described entirely in terms of its relevance to the respondent's own standards and goals, (b) focused on the subjective feelings of the respondent rather than on any social or objective consequence, and (c) of importance to the respondent alone. The described differences in emotions appear to reflect some of the core characteristics of collectivist and individualist cultures generally.

A Componential Model of Emotions

Specific predictions in the present study are based on a componential model of emotions (e.g., Frijda, 1986; Lazarus, 1991). This study focuses on the cultural similarities and variations in concerns, appraisal, action readiness, social sharing, and belief changes. Emotions develop when an event is appraised as being relevant to one's *concerns*—goals, motives, values, and expectations about oneself or others and about the world in which one lives. *Appraisal* processes have been conceived of as a series of evaluations with respect to a set of appraisal dimensions such as pleasantness–unpleasantness, controllability, and the attribution of agency (i.e., responsibility; Ellsworth, 1994; Scherer, 1997). Emotions also involve changes in *action readiness* changes in the relational goals of the individual (Frijda, 1986). *Social sharing of emotions* occurs when emotions are shared with others who were not necessarily involved in the emotional event to begin with (Rimé, Mesquita, Philippot, & Boca, 1991). *Belief changes* are thought to develop if appraisals of particular emotion-eliciting events generalize to beliefs about event classes or actors. In belief changes, the cognitive level of the appraisal is thus lifted from a particular act or event to the actor or class of events by which the appraisal gains predictive force (Semin & Fiedler, 1988). In componential models of emotion, components are conceived of as the constituents of emotion: The emotional experience per se is captured by its various components.

TABLE 1

KEY DIFFERENCES BETWEEN INDIVIDUALIST AND COLLECTIVIST EMOTIONS

Components of emotion	Collectivist emotions	Individualist emotions
Concerns	One's own social worth and the worth of the in-group	Focus on personal concerns only
Appraisal	Attention to the impact of other people's behavior on relative social positions (intentionality)	Less focus on the impact on relative social positions
Source of appraisal	The meaning of situations appears as given (obvious)	Awareness of the subjectivity of emotional appraisals
Action readiness	Focus on relationships and therefore more action readiness	Focus on bounded self and therefore less action readiness
Nature of shared emotions	Social sharing involves ensuring that others share in the concern and behave accordingly	Social sharing involves the sharing of information
Emotions as meanings	Emotions signal change of reality: changes of beliefs about self, others, and the relationship between self and others	Emotions signal internal, subjective feelings: few implications for beliefs

Specific Predictions on the Nature of Individualist and Collectivist Emotions

Emotions in collectivist contexts have been characterized as relational and contextualized phenomena, whereas emotions in individualist contexts are intrapersonal and subjective (Lutz, 1988). The current study takes these ideas one step beyond a general characterization by making predictions for each component separately (Table 1).

CONCERNS Because collectivist groups stress the relatedness between people, a major concern for those living in collectivist cultures is that they be perceived as qualifying for relationships with others, as illustrated by the Turkish respondent's concern for honor. Changes in social worth as well as in the respect of family and in-group (e.g., the Turkish mother's pride in her son's success) are thus expected to be associated with emotions to a larger extent in collectivist contexts than in individualist cultures.

APPRAISAL In collectivist cultures, the social worth of different people is perceived as interconnected. The Turkish man related in his interview that his social worth and that of his nuclear family correspond negatively with that of his relatives. In a collectivist context, a person who is made to lose respect will assume that the offender's motive was to gain it and thus will appraise the act as intentional. In individualist cultures, by contrast, the respect of different people appears to be unconnected and is less likely to be perceived as intentional.

THE PERCEIVED SOURCE OF APPRAISAL Because emotions in collectivist cultures tend to be about situations of shared concern, there must be consensual validation of what these situations mean. Hence, the meaning of emotional situations is perceived as obvious in collectivist cultures—that is, these situations are considered to be sources of information about the outside world to a larger extent than in individualist cultures, where emotions

are considered as subjective phenomena without much obviousness.

ACTION READINESS I predict that action readiness will gain force from the relational orientation of collectivist cultures. Although even an individualist self does, on occasion, seek to change its relationship with the environment, I expect the relational character of emotions in collectivist cultures to increase the outward orientation that is reflected by many action tendencies.

SOCIAL SHARING In collectivist cultures, the social sharing of emotions is expected to consist of letting other people in on what regards them. The parents of the Turkish respondent who won the competition organized a party to show off the success of their son and, therefore, their own success. In contrast, the individualist practice of social sharing has been found to consist of a mere exchange of information (Rimé et al., 1991), thus underlining the distinction between the individual and the sharing partner.

BELIEF CHANGES Whereas collectivist cultures appear to treat emotions as pieces of information that feed into the beliefs one has about the world, individualist cultures less readily consider emotions as pertinent to beliefs. Emotions in the collectivist groups result more often in belief changes than do emotions in the individualist culture.

Method

SAMPLING

The particular cultures included in this study were an indigenous Dutch group in the Netherlands, classified by previous research as individualist, and African Surinamese and Turkish groups in the Netherlands that had been characterized as collectivist cultures (e.g., Eppink, 1982; Hofstede, 1980). The interest was in getting samples that could reasonably be expected to have more between- than within-group variation in value orientation. Respondents were classified as Dutch, Surinamese, or

Turkish if they met at least two out of four criteria: (a) Most of their friends were from the same culture, (b) their partner or spouse was from the same culture, (c) they spoke the language of their own group, and (d) they had lived in their country of origin for more than half of their lives.

Respondents were approached by same-culture interviewers who explained the aims and procedures of the study concerned. The interviewers were asked to select (a) the same number of men and women, (b) respondents 18 years old or older, and (c) people from different age groups.

Participants were 86 Dutch, 88 Surinamese, and 83 Turkish individuals. Cultural differences were found for neither gender nor age. About half of the respondents in each group were women; the average age in all three groups was around 35 years. Self-reported education (four levels) differed across cultures, $\chi^2(6, N = 259) = 42.8, p < .01$, with the highest level of education in the Dutch group and the lowest in the Turkish.

SELECTION OF EMOTIONAL SITUATIONS: THE BASIS OF COMPARISON

I developed well-defined standards of comparison that were maximally comparable in meaning and, in addition, relevant in all three cultures. Unlike most previous cross-cultural studies that started with emotion words (Russell, 1991), this study started from common emotion-eliciting situations. One reason is that corresponding emotion words in different languages are often only partial translations of each other (Wierzbicka, 1992).

Two pilot studies were designed to find event types that were cross-culturally equivalent in both meaning and relevance (Mesquita, in press). In the first study, respondents from all three cultures generated emotion words. Out of the most frequent emotion words in each language obtained from this process, five classes of emotion words were selected—anger, sadness, shame, happiness, and pride. In the second study, different samples of respondents from all three cultures reported events that had led them to feel one of the emotions selected from the first study. The reported events were coded. The level of representation of the event categories was chosen to be as close to the experience of the participants as possible with out containing situation-specific or culture-specific details.

Six of these event categories were used in the current study on the basis of their relevance to each of the three cultures; success, positive attention, offense by a nonintimate other, offense by an intimate other, immoral behavior by an intimate other, and immoral behavior by the self. Participants in all three cultures recognized the stimulus events and were able to report instances from their own past that fit each event type.

QUESTIONNAIRES

Each questionnaire started with one of the six stimulus events.[1] Participants were asked to report an instance from the past that fit one of the six stimulus events and, subsequently, to answer questions pertaining to that situation. Questions were designed to fit the situation at hand, with the implication that only a selection of all the possible questions per component were asked and that the precise contents of the questionnaires differed by stimulus situation.

Four questions (rated on a 3-point scale ranging from 1 = no to 3 = yes) on a subset of concerns were designed to test cultural differences in the change in social worth: respect, prestige, family respect and in-group.

Appraisal scales (rated on a 5-point scale rang-

[1] For success, the questionnaire read "You had success because of some accomplishment or achievement; for example, passing an exam, etc." For positive attention, it began with "Other people complimented you on something or showed their admiration (You and the other people were together)." For the offense-by-nonintimate situation, the questionnaire read "An acquaintance, a neighbor or a colleague for example, offended you, did not take you seriously, or was inconsiderate of you," and for the offense-by-intimate situation, it read "Your partner, an intimate friend, or a close relative offended you, did not take you seriously, or was inconsiderate of you." For intimate immoral behavior, the questionnaire read "Your partner, an intimate friend, or a close relative treated you unfairly or improperly," and for self immoral behavior, it read "You treated your partner, an intimate friend or a close relative unfairly or improperly."

ing from 1 = *not at all* and 5 = *totally*) that the literature considers to be basic (e.g., Frijda, Kuipers, & Terschure, 1989; Scherer, 1997) served as a check on the similarity of meaning of the stimulus events. Dimensions for the positive events were as follows, with instantiations of the general dimensions for the situation type in parentheses: inexpected (expectedness), pleasant (pleasantness), fair (fairness), self responsible (agency), and self-esteem increased (self-esteem); for the offense situation and the intimate immoral situation, dimensions were inexpected (expectedness), unpleasant (pleasantness), other responsible (agency), self-esteem decreased (self-esteem), and avoidable (avoidability); for the situation of self immoral behavior, dimensions were unpleasant (pleasantness), self responsible (agency), self-esteem, avoidability, and immorality.

A second set of appraisal questions tested for cultural differences in the connectedness of respect. In the three situations in which another person inflicted harm, the intentionality of harm was measured by three questions (e.g., "Did the other person act in order to profit?").

Source of appraisal. Three questions (rated on a 3-point scale ranging from 1 = *no* to 3 = *yes*) referred to the obviousness of meaning and implications, asking whether another person would find the situation as pleasant or unpleasant as the respondent did, would think and feel in a similar way, and would react similarly to the way the respondent had. A considerable number of the respondents, mainly Dutch and, to a lesser extent, also Surinamese, indicated that they did not assume the existence of a general, obvious norm of interpretation or reaction. A post hoc fourth answer category of *I don't know* was added to the scale. The four answer categories were treated as an ordinal scale, ranging from 1 (*don't know*) to 4 (*yes*).

Action readiness questions were selected from the scale used by Frijida et al. (1989) on the basis of their relevance to the stimulus situation at hand. Where necessary, the items were adapted to a unipolar format (0 = *not at all*, 4 = *totally*). A few

items were added because of their apparent relevance to one or more of these groups particularly. Principal component analyses of the action readiness items yielded three to five factors for each event type, explaining 57–65% of the variance. To reduce the number of different dependent variables in the analyses, factor scores for each event type were added to form composite scores for the level of action readiness.

Social sharing of emotions. All questions on social sharing pertained to the first time the emotional experience was shared with someone else. Participants indicated to what extent the emotional event was of concern to the sharing partner. Respondents also checked on two different lists the precise behaviors of themselves and of the sharing partners. Both checklists were classified post hoc as points on ordinal scales representing the degree of commitment involved. Participants were assigned to the highest category in which they scored.

The participants' own sharing behaviors were classified as the degree of commitment solicited, on a 3-point scale ranging from 1 (*providing information*) to 3 (*actively involving behaviors*). Partners' behaviors were classified as the degree of commitment given, on a scale ranging from 1 (*listening*) to 4 (*taking an active role*) for positive situations and from 1 (*listening*) to 5 (*taking an active role*) for other situations.

Belief changes. In the positive situations, a five-item scale measuring increased self-confidence was created (α = .81).[2] For the situations that involved harm inflicted by another person, a six-item scale measuring decreased respect for others was created (α = .88), and in the situation of self immoral behavior, a six-item scale of decreased self-respect was created (α = .80; ratings for all scales ranged from 1 = *no* to 3 = *yes*).

---

[2] α or "alpha" is a conventional measure of the reliability of a measurement scale. In this case, the alpha of .81 means that the five items on the scale all tended to be answered the same way by individual participants.

PROCEDURES All interviews were based on written questionnaires in the language of the respondents. The questionnaires were administered in the context of an individual interview. Respondents reported an example of the stimulus situation, after which the respondent answered the questionnaire pertaining to that situation. The whole procedure was repeated for the second stimulus event. At the end of the questionnaires, respondents were asked to answer some demographic questions.

The interviewers were all women from the same cultural background as the respondents. The interviewers were not informed about the specific hypotheses of the study until after they had finished work. By implication, the respondents' debriefing did not contain any information about the specific hypotheses, either.

Each respondent answered the questions for two unrelated event types. This means that about one third of the total sample in each culture (about 25–30 respondents) answered the questions for each stimulus event. The questionnaires were presented in three fixed combinations, starting with stimulus events that were supposedly easy to share: success and offense by an intimate other, positive attention and self immoral behavior, offense by a nonintimate other, and intimate-other immoral behavior.

Results

COMPARABILITY OF STIMULUS EVENTS To ensure that respondents across cultures understood the stimulus events in reasonably similar terms, these events were "anchored" through their basic appraisals. Following other research (e.g., Frijda et al., 1989), I established the "presence" of these appraisals as a cultural mean greater than 2 on a scale ranging from 0 (not at all) to 4 (totally). With only two exceptions, all appraisal dimensions were present in all six events, which points to cross-cultural similarity in the meaning of the stimulus situations.

GENERAL ANALYTIC STRATEGY Hypotheses on concerns, appraisals, obviousness, social sharing, and belief changes were tested for three different combinations of stimulus situations: the positive situations (success and positive attention), the offense situations (offense by nonintimate other and offense by intimate other), and the immoral situations (intimate immoral and self immoral). The coupling of situations was chosen to guarantee that (a) within each analysis the data were independent and (b) the items of coupled situations had maximal overlap.

When the Culture × Situation interaction reached significance for a particular component, the culture effects were analyzed for each situation separately. Out of the 20 analyses performed, only two Culture × Situation interactions reached significance. Culture × Situation effects were found for belief changes in both the offense situations, $F(1, 168) = 5.6$, $p < .05$, and the immoral situations, $F(1, 176) = 9.3$, $p < .01$).[3]

All hypotheses on cultural differences in emotions were tested by contrasting the individualist Dutch culture with the two collectivist cultures, the Surinamese and the Turkish. All analyses controlled for the level of education. Multivariate analyses of covariance (MANCOVAs) with culture (individualist and collectivist) as a between-subjects factor were performed for respect concerns, relatedness of respect appraisals, obviousness, and action readiness. Means in these MANCOVAs were adjusted for education. * * * Furthermore, planned contrasts between individualist and collectivist scores, adjusted for level of education, were performed for social sharing and belief changes, as these components were measured by unrelated items and a single scale, respectively.

Cultural differences in concerns. Relational concerns were expected to have more relevance to the collec-

---

[3]This paragraph and several paragraphs that follow report results from a statistical technique called the "analysis of variance." This analysis yields an F statistic that, combined with the degrees of freedom in the experimental design (noted within parentheses), gives an estimate of the probability (p) that the observed differences between means could have occurred solely by chance.

tivist groups, in which emotions are perceived to be about relationships with other people, than to the individualist group, which supposedly lacks such a relational perspective. Indeed, main effects for culture were found for the positive situations, $F(4, 154) = 17.1$, $p < .001$, the offense situations, $F(4, 160) = 8.7$, $p = .001$, and the immoral situations, $F(4, 164) = 3.8$, $p = .01$. * * *

Differences in appraisal. In situations of harm by another person, appraisals of the connectedness of respect were expected to be more intense in collectivist than in individualist cultures. In the offense situation, appraisals of connectedness of respect were indeed more relevant in the collectivist than in the individualist cultures, $F(3, 161) = 4.2$, $p = .01$. * * *

Differences in obviousness. Cultural differences in the perceived source of appraisal were predicted, such that in the collectivist cultures, emotions would be appraised as more obvious—and thus more shared by others—than in the individualist cultures. As expected, significant main effects for culture were found with respect to positive, $F(3, 157) = 6.4$, $p < .001$, and offense situations, $F(3, 161) = 7.7$, $p < .001$. * * * Contrary to our predictions, the culture main effect did not reach significance in immoral situations, $F(2, 166) = 0.0$, $p > .10$.

Cultural differences in action readiness. Contrasts were carried out over the summed factor scores for each event type. As predicted, after controlling for education, main effects for culture were significant for all stimulus situations, such that the collectivist groups were higher on action readiness than was the individualist group, success: $F(1, 144) = 30.6$, $p < .001$; positive attention: $F(1, 146) = 24.4$, $p < .001$; offense by nonintimate: $F(1, 130) = 21.0$, $p < .001$; offense by intimate: $F(1, 146) = 5.9$, $p < .05$; intimate immoral behavior: $F(1, 152) = 5.6$, $p < .05$; self immoral behavior: $F(1, 158) = 34.7$, $p < .001$.

Cultural differences in social sharing. Because of the more permeable self–other boundaries in the col-

lectivist than in the individualist groups, a more involved kind of social sharing was expected in the collectivist cultures. Using planned contrasts, main effects for culture were found for each of the three variables of social sharing in the positive, offense, and immoral situations: the perceived concern of the sharing partner—positive situations: $F(1, 248) = 4.9$, $p < .05$; offense situations: $F(1, 330) = 7.5$, $p < .01$; immoral situations: $F(1, 254) = 4.0$, $p < .05$; the solicitation of commitment—positive situations: $F(1, 296) = 7.8$, $p < .01$; offense situations: $F(1, 254) = 4.9$, $p < .05$; immoral situations: $F(1, 256) = 26.3$, $p < .001$; and the degree of commitment on the part of the sharing partner—positive situations: $F(1, 318) = 4.2$, $p < .05$; offense situations: $F(1, 258) = 10.7$, $p < .001$; immoral situations: $F(1, 256) = 14.8$, $p < .001$.

Cultural differences in belief changes. Respondents in the collectivist cultures, in which emotions seem to inform people about reality, were expected to form more belief changes as a result of their emotions than were respondents in individualist cultures, who perceive emotions as strictly subjective. Indeed, planned contrasts suggested that respondents in the collectivist groups formed belief changes more readily than respondents in the individualist Dutch group did, although in two situations, the differences in belief changes were only marginally significant, positive situations: $F(1, 322) = 169.1$, $p < .001$; offense by nonintimate: $F(1, 170) = 143.0$, $p < .001$; offense by intimate: $F(1, 158) = 3.7$, $p < .1$; intimate immoral behavior: $F(1, 166) = 46.9$, $p < .001$; self immoral behavior: $F(1, 170) = 3.0$, $p < .1$.

Discussion

COLLECTIVIST AND INDIVIDUALIST EMOTIONS

Cultural differences between collectivist and individualist cultures were found in each of the emotion components studied, in ways consistent with the respective cultural syndromes in which they occurred. Because emotions were conceived of in this study in terms of the total of their constituent elements, one can conclude that emotional experience differs fundamentally between individualist and collectivist cultures.

As predicted, collectivist emotions emerged as relational phenomena, embedded in relationships with others and perceived to reflect the state of those relationships. Individualist emotions, on the other hand, refer much less to the social environment. Results on the relational concerns and connectedness of respect appraisals are good illustrations of this point.

The results also illustrate how boundaries between subjectivity and social reality are more permeable in collectivist than in individualist groups. Emotions in collectivist cultures tend to have an objective reality to the individual that emotions in the individualist group lack. In contrast to the participants from the individualist context, respondents in the collectivist cultures indicated that another person encountering a similar event would be affected by the event in similar ways as they had been. Whereas in the individualist culture, a clear distinction was made between subjectivity and objectivity, allowing for interindividual differences in response, the collectivist cultures seem to endorse the principle of a subjective reality.

Consistently, respondents in the collectivist cultures who reported a higher readiness for belief changes than did respondents from the individualist culture also appeared to assume that they experienced the social reality. Respondents in the individualist culture, on the other hand, did not as readily form belief changes and can thus be said to adhere to the boundaries between subjective evaluation and objective reality.

Finally, differences in the self–other boundaries appear to be reflected as well, predominantly in action readiness and social sharing. Whereas emotions in the collectivist cultures tend to embody the connectedness between individuals and their social environment, emotions in individualist cultures appear to underline the disparity of self and others.

As compared with emotions in individualist cultures, emotions in collectivist cultures (a) were more grounded in assessments of social worth and

of shifts in relative social worth, (b) were to a large extent taken to reflect reality rather than the inner world of the individual, and (c) belong to the self–other relationship rather than being confined to the subjectivity of the self.

Emotions are thus shaped in a fashion analogous to the ideas and practices of the cultures in which they occur. In turn, emotions are likely to reinforce and sustain the cultural themes that are significant in collectivist and individualist cultures, respectively. Emotions themselves can be seen as cultural practices that promote important cultural ideas.

The current study calls for a qualification of the idea that individualist cultures have more "self-focused" emotions, whereas collectivist cultures have more "other-focused" emotions (Markus & Kitayama, 1991). Rather than certain emotions such as anger and pride being invariably self-focused and other emotions such as the Japanese *amae* being other-focused, it seems that similar emotions such as anger may be instantiated in self-focused or other-focused ways. Other-focused emotions would focus on social worth, reflect reality, and belong to the self–other relationship.

* * *

FOCUS ON CULTURAL DIFFERENCES Unlike the psychological tradition of looking for universality in emotions, this study has focused on the cross-cultural differences in emotions and, moreover, has found them. The search for cultural differences in emotions is fundamentally different from the search for universality in that it requires (a) a theory of the principles of cultural variation in emotions, (b) systematic predictions based on that theory, and (c) items or tasks that are capable of registering those aspects of variation. Without those theoretically based efforts to discover cultural differences in emotions, the psychology of cultural variation will remain limited to the accidental finding of differences that are unexplained and, therefore, unappealing.

In this study, predictions on cultural differences were made on the basis of different characterizations of the meanings and practices constituting individualism and collectivism. The divergent meanings and practices thus helped to conceptualize and articulate differences in the various components of emotions. Hypotheses derived this way were generally confirmed. This study has suggested some of the ways in which individualist and collectivist syndromes may shape emotions. Its focus was to describe the variability of emotional phenomena in a theory-driven manner. Future research is needed to clarify how precisely cultural syndromes and emotions constitute each other.

References

Ellsworth, P. (1994). Sense, culture and sensibility. In S. Kitayama & M. R. Markus (Eds.), *Emotion and culture. Empirical studies of mutual influence* (pp. 23–50). Washington, DC: American Psychological Association.

Ekman, P. (1973). Cross-cultural studies of facial expression. In P. Ekman (Ed.), *Darwin and facial expression* (pp. 169–222). New York: Academic Press.

Eppink, A. (1982). Onze ik-psychologie en de wij-cultuur van migranten [Our me-psychology and the we-culture of migrants]. *De psycholoog, 17*, 10–17.

Frijda, N. H. (1986). *The emotions.* Cambridge: Cambrigde University Press.

Frijda, N. H., Kuipers, P., & Terschure, E. (1989). Relations between emotion, appraisal, and emotional action readiness. *Journal of Personality and Social Psychology, 57*, 212–228.

Hofstede, G. (1980). *Culture's consequences: International differences in work-related values.* Beverly Hills, CA: Sage.

Lazarus, R. (1991). *Emotion and adaptation.* New York: Oxford University Press.

Lutz, C. (1988). *Unnatural emotions: Everyday sentiments on a Micronesian atoll and their challenge to western theory.* Chicago: University of Chicago Press.

Markus, H. R., & Kitayama, S. (1991). Culture and the self: Implications for cognition, emotion, and motivation. *Psychological Review, 98*, 224–253.

Markus, H. R., Mullally, P. R., & Kitayama, S. (1997). Selfways: Diversity in modes of cultural participation. In U. Neisser & D. Jopling (Eds.), *The conceptual self in context* (pp. 13–16). New York: Cambridge University Press.

Mesquita, B. (in press). *Cultural variations in emotions. A comparative study of Dutch, Surinamese and Turkish people in the Netherlands.* Oxford University Press.

Mesquita, B., & Frijda, N. H. (1992). Cultural variations in emotions: A review. *Psychological Bulletin, 112*, 179–204.

Rimé, B., Mesquita, B., Philippot, P., & Boca, S. (1991). Beyond the emotional event: Six studies on the social sharing of emotion. *Cognition and Emotion, 5*, 435–465.

Russell, J. A. (1991). Cultural variations in emotions: A review. *Psychological Bulletin, 112*, 179–204.

Scherer, K. R. (1997). Patterns of emotion-antecedent appraisal across cultures. *Cognition and Emotion, 11*, 113–150.

Scherer, K. R., & Wallbott, H. G. (1994). Evidence for universality and cultural variation of differential emotion response patterning. *Journal of Personality and Social Psychology, 66*, 310–328.

Semin, G. R., & Fiedler, K. (1988). The cognitive functions of linguistic categories describing persons: Social cognition and language. *Journal of Personality and Social Psychology, 54*, 558–568.

Shweder, R. A., & Levine, M. A. (Eds.). (1984). *Culture theory: Essays on mind, self, and emotion.* Cambridge, MA: Cambridge University Press.

Triandis, H. C. (1995). *Individualism and collectivism.* Boulder, CO: Westview Press.

Wierzbicka, A. (1992). Talking about emotions: Semantics, culture, and cognition. *Cognition and Emotion, 6*, 285–319.

Culture, Identity Consistency, and Subjective Well-Being

Eunkook M. Suh

Personality psychology is the study of the individual, and the very concept of the "individual" would seem to imply consistency across the contexts of life. You are the same person you were yesterday and will be tomorrow; if not, then what are you? As self-evident as this idea may seem to the inhabitant of a Western culture who is likely to be reading this book, Eunkook Suh expresses doubt that it is quite so obvious in East Asian cultures, such as Korea. The reason is the collectivism-individualism dimension that dominates so much current cultural research. In collectivist cultures, Suh argues, the "self" appears to be more intertwined with other people, context-dependent, and malleable, whereas in individualist cultures the self is more independent and consistent. Furthermore, Suh observes, people in Western culture tend to believe that it is good to be consistent, whereas in East Asian cultures this value does not seem to apply.

The present study examines these issues by comparing American and Korean female college students. It is not clear why this investigation is limited to women. Do you think this makes a difference?

From *Journal of Personality and Social Psychology, 83*, 1378–1391, 2002.

One basic premise of social psychology is that individuals strive to resolve inconsistent psychological experiences (Abelson et al., 1968). In addition to being a major fabric of social psychology theory, the importance of consistency is also deeply ingrained in classical theories of mental health. According to prominent personality psychologists, developing and maintaining a consistent identity is a key foundation of psychological well-being (e.g., Jourard, 1965; Lecky, 1945; Maslow, 1954; Rogers, 1951). As Erikson (1968) encapsulated, for instance, possessing a sense of "invigorating sameness" (p. 19) has been long regarded as one of the staple conditions of mental health in mainstream psychology.

This theoretical position fits well with the North American cultural spirit, which heralds the supreme autonomy of the individual self. The self, not the context, is believed to be the primary anchor of behavior. Within this highly self-centered cultural scheme, it comes quite naturally that the self, the principal source of personal meaning and guidance, needs to be highly organized and consistent. A strong possibility exists, however, that the link between identity consistency and well-being could be more tenuous in East Asian cultures, where situational forces strongly dictate the experiences and expressions of the self (Markus, Mullally, & Kitayama, 1997).

Interpersonal harmony is the keynote in East Asian thinking (Moore, 1967; Rosenberger, 1992). It is a theme deriving from Confucian philosophy, which teaches that truly meaningful existence is conceivable only in relation to others (Bond & Hwang, 1986). For the purpose of fostering this ever-important harmony, social situations in these cultures call for a self-system that is relatively malleable and highly context sensitive (Cousins, 1989; Kitayama & Markus, 1999). In fact, extreme forms of self-consistency in such cultures, Markus and Kitayama (1994) argued, could be perceived as a "lack of flexibility, rigidity, or even immaturity" (p. 576).

Theories of psychological well-being are shaped by cultural beliefs concerning the fundamental nature of the person (Christopher, 1999; Kitayama & Markus, 2000; Suh, 2000). The long-standing belief in psychology that maintaining a consistent, unified self-identity is crucial to mental health might be another prime example of such synthesis between theory and culture. This classic assumption in psychology—that identity consistency is a prerequisite of mental health—is revisited in this cross-cultural research.

Identity Consistency and Psychological Well-Being

The idea that various negative experiences, such as anxiety, tension, and confusion, stem from a lack of consistency among self-concepts was widely shared among early personality theorists (e.g., Lecky, 1945). To achieve this crucial sense of psychological unity, they claimed that the self-view needs to be coherently organized (inner congruence) and also consistently maintained across situations (cross-situational consistency). For instance, regarding the importance of congruence, Maslow (1954) argued that inner conflicts need to be "merged and coalesced to form unities" (p. 233)

for the person to self-actualize. Similarly, Rogers (1951) suggested that a person reaches the most fully functioning psychological state after resolving incongruent internal experiences. The consistency of self-view across situations was also emphasized. Jourard (1965) contended that a person who has a healthy personality seeks behavioral guidance primarily from his or her inner beliefs and values rather than from external sources (e.g., norms, expectations). Accordingly, Jourard believed that the self-view of a mature person is highly consistent across social contexts.

A more contemporary line of research that again underscores the importance of identity consistency comes from the works of Swann and his colleagues (Swann, 1983; Swann & Read, 1981). According to their self-verification theory, people actively try to verify, validate, and sustain their existing self-views in social contexts. One way people achieve this goal is by selectively seeking out and interacting with those who see them as they view themselves. Swann and colleagues found, for instance, that people prefer to interact with partners who provide feedback that is congruent with their existing self-views rather than merely positive (Swann, de la Ronde, & Hixon, 1994). Another strategy people adopt to maintain their existing self-view is to behave in ways that elicit self-verifying reactions from others. When people think that others hold inaccurate impressions of them (even in an overly positive direction), for example, they deliberately behave in ways to correct the misconceptions (Swann & Read, 1981).

The self-verification research offers empirical support for the idea that each person actively negotiates with reality to maintain a consistent self-view. A number of recent studies extend this notion and demonstrate that the degree of identity consistency is predictive of psychological adjustment. Donahue, Robins, Roberts, and John (1993), for instance, found that people who view themselves highly inconsistently across social roles (high *self-concept differentiation*) were more depressed and more neurotic than others (see also Roberts & Donahue, 1994). Similarly, Sheldon, Ryan, Rawsthorne, and Ilardi (1997) found that consistency of self-view across roles was significantly associated with psychological thriving.

In sum, recent studies offer empirical support for the influential belief in psychology proposed by Lecky (1945), Rogers (1951), and other major personality psychologists. They demonstrate that individuals indeed dedicate themselves to establishing and sustaining a self-view that is consistent across different social contexts. Furthermore, the degree of identity consistency appears to be positively associated with levels of psychological adjustment. Although this is a powerful idea, virtually all of the theories and research findings that constitute the current knowledge on this topic come from North American participants. This is a critical blind spot of the literature, leaving open the question of whether identity consistency is a universally essential condition of psychological well-being.

Culture and Self-Consistency

"Persistent need for consistency and stability," according to Markus et al. (1997, p. 24), is one of the key characterizations of the European American self. Although consistency is strongly emphasized in North America, in East Asian cultures, the belief that behavior should be consistent with internal thoughts is less salient. A study by Iwao (1988, cited in Triandis, 1989) exemplifies this cultural difference. In the study, Japanese and Americans were presented with a scenario in which a daughter brings home a man whom she wishes to marry. Even though her father privately believes he will "never allow them to marry," he behaves as if he is in favor of the marriage. Although the majority of Americans disapproved of the father's inconsistent behavior, 44% of the Japanese respondents thought the father handled the situation "appropriately." Such greater tolerance for inconsistencies has been documented in various other psychological domains. For instance, East Asians are less disturbed by cognitively dissonant situations (Heine & Lehman, 1997), are less likely to believe that behavior should align with private attitudes (Kashima, Siegal, Tanaka, & Kashima, 1992), and are less critical of incongruent acts displayed

between private and public situations (Fu, Lee, Cameron, & Xu, 2001) than are North Americans.

Why are East Asians less preoccupied with the notion of self-consistency than are Westerners? Most notably, beliefs about the self, the social context, and the relation between the two differ considerably between the two cultures. In the West, the self is typically characterized as an autonomous, distinct, and self-sufficient entity (Fiske, Kitayama, Markus, & Nisbett, 1998; Lillard, 1998; Markus & Kitayama, 1991; Triandis, 1989). At the core of this inherently independent self are internal attributes, which are believed to be unique, self-diagnostic, and, most relevant to our discussion, highly stable. It is more imperative in Western cultures to cultivate and express these stable, self-defining inner attributes than to tailor the self to fit social mandates and expectations (Markus et al., 1997; Morling, Kitayama, & Miyamoto, 2002).

In contrast, one can realize the fundamental sense of East Asian selfhood by enriching the feeling of connectedness with significant others (Ho, 1993; King & Bond, 1985; Miller, 1997). The self is viewed preeminently as a social product. Because each self-defining relationship calls for unique sets of behaviors and expectations, self-experience is constantly referenced to the thoughts and feelings of others. A tree is often used as a metaphor for illustrating this highly malleable and context-dependent East Asian self (Rosenberger, 1992). The tree's seasonal change of appearance (e.g., color, shape) does not threaten the essence of the tree. Similarly, a person being somewhat different in interactions with people of different age, gender, or social status is understood as quite natural. In fact, the ability to spontaneously detect and align the self to the subtle expectations of different social situations is considered a critical social skill in East Asian cultures (*nunchi* in Korea, S. G. Choi, 2000; *kejime* in Japan, Bachnik, 1992).

This East Asian metatheory of selfhood also seems congruent with the culture's general cognitive outlook, which accepts change and contradictions as natural aspects of reality (Nisbett, Peng, Choi, & Norenzayan, 2001). Such a dialectic mode of thinking, according to Peng and Nisbett (1999), sharply contrasts with the traditional Western epistemological habit, which polarizes contradictions and inconsistencies. This cultural difference further suggests that East Asians and westerners might construe inconsistencies of the self in a somewhat different manner. East Asians might be more inclined to see the different selves across situations as inevitable manifestations of a complex selfhood, whereas westerners might view them essentially as contradictions.

Present Research

This research reexamines the long-standing belief that having a consistent identity is crucial for psychological well-being, from a culturally informed perspective. Before I investigate this issue at a cultural level, however, a better understanding of identity consistency is required. Study 1 addresses the question of what identity consistency, as an individual-differences variable, actually measures.

Study 2, by comparing U.S. and Korean college students, addresses three interrelated questions at a cross-cultural level. First, is the self-view of North Americans significantly more consistent across contexts than that of East Asians? Second, how crucial is the level of identity consistency to the subjective well-being of the members of the two cultures? Finally, are consistent people viewed more positively in one culture than in another?

One point that needs clarification is that there are at least three relevant but distinct dimensions of identity consistency: the cross-situational consistency of the self-view across social settings, the internal consistency (congruence) of various self-components, and the temporal consistency (stability) of the self-view. The present research focuses on the first type of consistency (i.e., the overall consistency of the self-view across multiple social situations) for two reasons. First, this dimension of consistency has been of most theoretical interest for both early and modern personality psychologists (e.g., Bem & Allen, 1974; Jourard, 1965; Lecky, 1945; Mischel & Peake, 1982). In addition, this cross-situational dimension of consistency is most likely to be affected by cultural factors that are of particular interest to social psychology (e.g., social norms, lay beliefs about selfhood).

Study 1: Who Is Self-Consistent?

Existing research offers only a broad sketch about the dispositional characteristics of a consistent person. For instance, Donahue et al. (1993) found that individuals who view themselves more consistently than others tend to be highly Conscientious, Agreeable, and low in Neuroticism. Sheldon et al. (1997) reported that people who have inconsistent self-views tend to be more depressed and have lower self-esteem than others. In this study, a number of more specific cognitive and motivational characteristics that are conceptually relevant to identity consistency are examined.

*   *   *

Method

PARTICIPANTS

Two samples enrolled in introductory psychology courses at a large U.S. university completed the questionnaire. Sample 1 consisted of 150 participants (119 women), and Sample 2 included 219 participants (158 women). The average ages of Sample 1 and Sample 2, respectively, were 20.7 and 18.9. All participants received extra course credit for their participation. All findings reported in Study 1 are based on the aggregated responses from the two samples ($N = 366$; 3 incomplete reports),[1] except for those related to the Social Awareness Inventory (SAI; Sheldon, 1996). Because the SAI was not administered to Sample 1, results pertaining to this measure are based only on Sample 2 data.

MEASURES *Identity consistency.* To obtain an index of the participant's identity consistency (IC) level, I first asked each person to rate how accurately 25 personality traits described his or her "general self" on a scale ranging from 1 (*not at all*

---

[1]The N is the number of participants.

like myself) to 7 (very much like myself). After completing a number of filler measures, the participants rated themselves again on these same 25 personality traits. In this second round, each personality trait was randomly paired with a specific interaction partner. For instance, one item read, "When I interact with <u>my parents</u>, I am talkative." The participant rated how accurately each of the 100 situation-specific statements (25 traits × 4 interaction partners) described them. The 25 adjectives consisted of positive (e.g., *cheerful*), neutral (e.g., *serious*), and negative (e.g., *cynical*) personality characteristics that were compiled in reference to the Big Five traits (Goldberg, 1993). In a pilot study, undergraduate students indicated that the three most significant people with whom they interact frequently are parents, a romantic partner, and a same-gender friend. In addition to these three, a stranger was included as a fourth interaction condition to increase the variability of the social situations. I obtained a personal index of IC by calculating the overall consistency of the five situation-specific self-views (detailed description follows in the Results section).

Subjective well-being. In addition to the trait ratings, participants completed measures of subjective well-being (SWB; Diener, Suh, Lucas, & Smith, 1999). The five-item Satisfaction With Life Scale (Diener, Emmons, Larsen, & Griffin, 1985) was used as a measure of global life satisfaction. Participants also indicated how frequently they had experienced four positive (joy, pride, love, affection) and four negative emotions (sadness, shame, anger, fear) during the previous month on a 7-point scale (Diener, Smith, & Fujita, 1995). The sums of the four positive and four negative emotion ratings were used, respectively, as the positive affect and negative affect scores.

Predictors of consistency: Self-monitoring. The 25-item Self-Monitoring Scale (Snyder, 1974) measures the degree to which people use social cues to monitor and control their behavior in public situations. Factor analyses suggest that the scale includes three factors (Briggs et al., 1980): Acting (e.g., "I would probably make a good actor"), Other-Directedness (e.g., "I guess I put on a show to impress or entertain people"), and Extraversion (e.g., "At a party I let others keep the jokes and stories going"; reverse scored). The alpha of the full scale was .57. Coefficient alphas for the three subscales were as follows: Acting = .60, Other-Directedness = .52 and Extraversion = .49.

Self-concept clarity. Campbell et al.'s (1996) Self-Concept Clarity Scale measures the extent to which self-beliefs are clearly and confidently defined. The measure consists of 12 items (e.g., "In general, I have a clear sense of who I am and what I am"), and the alpha for this measure was .81.

Self-awareness. A person may habitually attend to either the internal experience or the external appearance of the self from either his or her own or the other's psychological perspective. Crossing the two binary dimensions of self-content (e.g., experience vs. appearance) and perspective (self vs. other's) leads to four distinct self-awareness styles. The Social Awareness Inventory, developed by Sheldon (1996), measures the four self-awareness dimensions: Attending to self-experience from self-perspective (e.g., scrutinizing one's mood), self-experience from the other's perspective (SEOP; e.g., seeking insight from a therapist), self-appearance from self-perspective (e.g., studying oneself in front of the mirror), and self-appearance from the other's perspective (SAOP; e.g., reading a friend's reaction to one's new hairstyle). The coefficient alpha for the four self-awareness subscales ranged from .73 to .78.[2]

Assertiveness. Eight items tapping the social assertiveness facet of Extraversion (NEO–PI–R; Costa & McCrae, 1992) were included. A sample

---

[2]Coefficient alpha is a measure of the internal reliability of a self-report scale; in the present instance the results imply that the various items on each scale tended to be answered by individual participants in the same way.

item read, "I am dominant, forceful, and assertive." The coefficient alpha of these eight social assertiveness items was .79.

Results

IDENTITY CONSISTENCY

For each individual, I obtained an overall measure of IC by adopting a method originally developed by Block (1961) and included in Donahue et al.'s (1993) study. In the present study, each person made 125 ratings of his or her personality. After converting each person's 125 ratings into a 25 × 5 matrix (25 traits in five different contexts, including the general self), I factor analyzed each personal matrix. If a person views himself or herself consistently across all social contexts (e.g., impulsive in all situations), the first principal-components factor obtained from this within-subject factor analysis accounts for a large percentage of the person's self-view variance across the situations. Conversely, when a person views himself or herself very differently across situations (e.g., impulsive when with X but not when with Y), the first factor only accounts for a small amount of the variance in the self-rating matrix. On the basis of this statistical logic, the percentage of variance accounted for by the first factor was used as a personal index of IC. * * *

As an example, the self-ratings of 2 pilot study participants are presented in Figures 1 ("Leonard") and 2 ("Zelig"). Figure 1 reveals that Leonard's self-view was highly consistent across the five contexts (plus when he was alone). Each of the six poles stemming from the center of the diagram represents a specific interpersonal context (e.g., w/A = with Person A), each marked by a 7-point scale (1 = *not at all like myself*, 7 = *very much like myself*). Each of the 25 concentric lines surrounding the center represents a trait. For instance, the bold line in Figure 1 reflects Leonard's self-ratings for *affectionate* across the five settings (plus alone). As we can see, Leonard's self-rating of this trait was relatively consistent across the situations (his rat-

ings were mostly 7s). Leonard's IC score was 87.4%, and his five self-views, on average, correlated .87 with each other.

In contrast, Zelig's self-view varied considerably across contexts (Figure 2). For instance, Zelig's rating on *affectionate* (bold line) was high in some contexts (i.e., 7), but low (1 or 2) in others. As the heavy intersections among the trait lines suggest, Zelig's self-view changed quite significantly across interpersonal settings. Specifically, Zelig's IC score was 26.6%, and the average correlation of his five self-view profiles was only .16. Unlike Leonard, Zelig's self-profile in one situation was hardly predictable from another.

In total, 366 within subject matrices were factor analyzed in Study 1. Significant individual differences emerged in the overall level of IC. The percentage of variance accounted for by the first principal-components factor ranged from 22.6% (least consistent person) to 95.0% (most consistent person). The sample yielded a mean IC score of 58.4% (SD = 15.1).[3]

Correlates of Identity Consistency

The correlations between IC and the major variables are presented in the left column of Table 1.[4] The first notable finding is that IC was not significantly related to the overall self-monitoring score. Even though high self-monitors are known to behave quite inconsistently across social situations (Gangestad & Snyder, 2000), the finding suggests that self-monitoring does not predict the consistency of self-view. The null relation between IC and self-monitoring emerged in large part because two Self-Monitoring subscales were correlated with IC in opposite directions. The Extraversion factor re-

---

[3] SD is the standard deviation.

[4] The correlations in the table are r's, and their interpretation is discussed in the article by Rosenthal and Rubin in Part I. The p levels are statistical estimates of the probability that the r's in the whole population are 0 (the null hypothesis), given the fact that the reported r's were obtained in this sample.

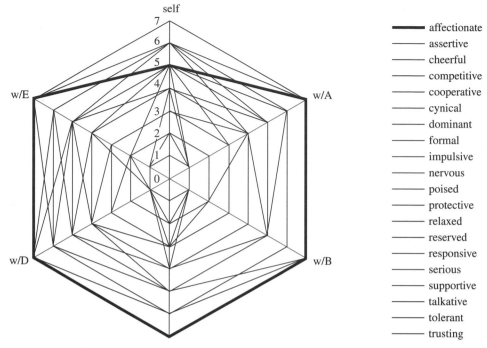

Figure 1   Personality ratings of Leonard (identity consistency = 87.4%).
w/A = with Person A, w/B = with Person B, and so on.

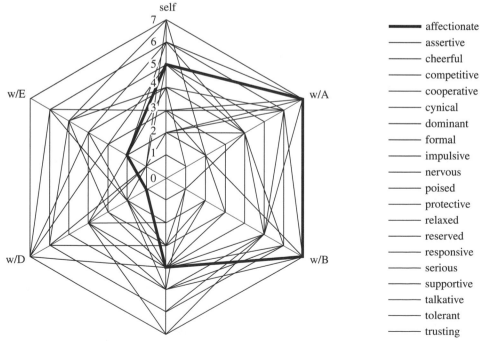

Figure 2   Personality ratings of Zelig (identity consistency = 26.6%).
w/A = with Person A, w/B = with Person B, and so on.

TABLE 1

CORRELATIONS FOR PREDICTING IDENTITY CONSISTENCY

Measure	Correlation with IC
Self-clarity	.37**
Assertiveness	.23**
SM: total score	−.08
SM: Acting	.03
SM: Other-Directedness	−.21**
SM: Extraversion	.27**
Self-perspective: experience	.01
Self-perspective: appearance	−.16*
Other's perspective: experience	−.42**
Other's perspective: appearance	−.26**

Note. IC = identity consistency; SM = self-monitoring.
*$p < .05$. **$p < .01$.

lated positively with IC ($r = .27$, $p < .001$), whereas the Other-Directedness factor correlated negatively with IC ($r = −.21$, $p < .001$). Ironically, people with highly consistent identity were similar to high self-monitors in one dimension but resembled low self-monitors in another. Like high self-monitors, they were proactive and outgoing people in social situations (Extraverted), yet, like low self-monitors, they were not that interested in how they might be perceived by others (low Other-Directedness).

Outcomes from the SAI measure reinforce the impression that highly self-consistent people are relatively less concerned about others' views. Significant negative associations were found between IC and the two other-grounded self-awareness tendencies ($r = −.26$, $p < .001$, with SAOP; $r = −.42$, $p < .001$, with SEOP). In short, a key dispositional feature of individuals who have a stable self-view is that they pay chronically less attention to how the self might be seen by other people. Also, as predicted, IC was significantly related with social assertiveness and with the degree of self-clarity.

* * *

IDENTITY CONSISTENCY AND SWB Across individuals, those who viewed themselves more consistently across situations were significantly more likely ($p < .001$) to experience higher life satisfac-

tion ($r = .29$), more positive affect ($r = .25$), and less negative affect ($r = −.38$). In support of past theory and research, Americans who were more consistent enjoyed higher levels of SWB.

Summary and Discussion

Study 1 makes a contribution to the literature by offering new insights about the psychological dispositions of highly self-consistent people. According to the findings, a person who maintains a consistent identity (a) is not necessarily a high self-monitor, (b) has a clear sense of self-knowledge, (c) tends to be assertive and extraverted in social interactions, and (d) pays relatively less attention to how others might think of his or her inner thoughts and feelings.

* * *

Study 2: Cross-Cultural Examination

Study 2 examines the relation between IC and SWB in the United States and in South Korea. Three key predictions were made. Compared with the U.S. sample, the Korean respondents were expected (a) to have a more flexible self-view across social contexts, (b) to experience SWB that is less dependent on IC level, and (c) to receive less positive social feedback from others for being self-consistent. I examined this last prediction by analyzing informant reports provided by family members and friends of the participants.

If consistency is less predictive of SWB in East Asian cultures, what might matter more? One significant predictor of SWB among those who have a strong relational self-view is perceived social appraisal—the degree to which one believes his or her life is approved by significant others (Suh & Diener, 2002; Suh et al., 1998). If so, in Korea, is social appraisal more important than IC in predicting SWB?

Pilot Study

Prior to the cross-cultural comparison, it was necessary to obtain a culturally representative pool of personality traits and social roles. In a pilot study, 50 American and 38 Korean college students were asked to provide the five most self-defining social roles and the 10 most self-descriptive personality traits. Both groups offered similar responses to the role nomination (friend and daughter or son were mentioned most frequently). One unique Korean response (mentioned by 24% of the respondents) was the status of being a few years younger (*hoobae*) or older (*sunbae*) than a fellow student. These social roles are salient in East Asian cultures, in which seniority plays a vital role in shaping the content and tone of social interactions.

Unlike the social role, the trait responses differed quite substantially. The 10 most frequently nominated self-descriptors in the U.S. sample were *friendly, optimistic, caring, intelligent, outgoing, trustworthy, honest, hardworking, fun-loving,* and *responsible.* The Koreans most often mentioned *optimistic, cheerful, social, hasty, passive, two-faced, calm, determined, positive,* and *conscientious.* Some English speakers might find it rather puzzling that many Koreans described themselves as two-faced. The very fact that the Koreans mentioned this term spontaneously in this open-ended questionnaire implies that the notion of inconsistency carries a less negative connotation in East Asian cultures than in North America. The traits and social roles nominated by the two cultural groups were used as inputs for constructing the questionnaire in Study 2.

Method

PARTICIPANTS

Eighty-four college students (43 women) in the United States and 123 undergraduates in Korea (72 women) participated in this study. The mean ages of the U.S. and Korean samples, respectively, were 18.4 and 20.4. Respondents in both countries received course credit for their participation.

In addition to self-reports, participants were asked to provide two informant reports, one from a family member, and another from a friend. In Korea, participants arranged the two sets of informant reports in exchange for a book certificate. American participants received additional experiment credit for providing informant data. Both the participants and the informants clearly understood that the contents of the informant report, mailed directly to the laboratory, would be confidential. Seventy-nine Korean participants (64% of the sample) and 57 U.S. participants (68%) had informant reports returned from both a friend and a family member. Individuals who provided informant reports showed no systematic mean differences from those who did not among the major variables.

MEASURES

SWB. The participants' SWB was assessed by the same measures described in Study 1. The alpha coefficients of the Satisfaction With Life Scale (Diener et al., 1985) for the Korean and U.S. samples were, respectively, .83 and .84. Individuals also reported how frequently they had experienced various pleasant and unpleasant emotions in the recent past. The alpha coefficients for the pleasant affect scale for the Korean and U.S. samples were, respectively, .82 and .80. The alpha of the negative affect scale was also equally high for both groups (Korea, .88; United States, .86).

Perceived social appraisal. Using a 7-point scale (1 = *strongly disagree,* 7 = *strongly agree*), respondents rated the degree to which they thought others approved their lives. The first item read, "People around me approve of the way I have lived my life." The other item was "My family is satisfied with my life." The two items were combined to obtain the perceived social appraisal score.

Identity consistency. To obtain a measure of IC across social roles, I constructed the role–trait matrix described earlier in Study 1. The five interaction partners included in the current role–trait matrix were close friend, parents, professor/teaching assistant, someone younger (5 years or less), and a stranger. Four of the five social roles were based on the results of the pilot study. An interaction involving a stranger was added to increase the range of interpersonal situations.

In selecting the 20 personality traits, I considered two points. First, the findings from the pilot study were given special attention. Second, overt personality traits (e.g., *talkative*), which are more likely to vary across social roles, were given priority over purely experiential traits (e.g., *optimistic*). Twelve of the final 20 traits were compiled from the pilot study (6 traits from each country); the 8 additional traits were sampled from Wiggins's (1979) circumplex of interpersonal traits to ensure comprehensiveness. The final list of 20 traits included in the questionnaire is as follows: *emotional, modest, cold, friendly, cooperative, talkative, impatient, impulsive, open-minded, outgoing, introverted, dominant, business-like, calculative, honest, two-faced, cheerful, kind, rational,* and *cranky.*

As in Study 1, participants were asked to rate how accurately the 20 personality traits describe them on a scale ranging from 1 (*not at all descriptive*) to 7 (*very much descriptive*). After describing their general self-view, the participants rated how accurately each of the 20 traits described them across the five different interpersonal contexts. An example item reads, "When I interact with my *parents,* I am *impatient.*" The 100 role–trait combinations were presented in random order.

The questionnaire was initially constructed in English. It was translated into Korean by the author who is bilingual. After the initial translation, two Korean graduate students studying in the United States provided feedback concerning translation equivalence. The English and the revised Korean draft were compared once again in Korea by two professors who were fluent in both lang-uages. The high measurement reliability observed in both cultures suggests that the translation was satisfactory.

Informant reports. Two informants (one family member, one friend) provided additional information about each participant. Of most interest was the informant's impression of the target person on the dimensions of social skill and likability. The underlying idea was that the Korean and the U.S. informants might differ in how favorably they thought of highly consistent versus inconsistent individuals. As a measure of social skill, informants evaluated how well the target person deals with social situations on a scale ranging from 1 (*very poorly*) to 4 (*very well*). Also, informants rated how likable they thought the target person was on a scale ranging from 1 (*not at all*) to 5 (*very likable*). Informants clearly understood that their responses would be confidential.

Results

The means and standard deviations of major variables are summarized in Table 2. Consistent with previous research (Diener, Suh, Smith, & Shao, 1995), the Korean sample reported lower life satisfaction, less positive affect, and more unpleasant affect than the U.S. participants ($p < .001$). The Koreans' perceived social appraisal score was significantly lower than the American mean ($p < .001$).

CULTURAL DIFFERENCE IN IDENTITY CONSISTENCY

The first key question was whether the self-view is more consistent in the United States than in Korea. This issue was examined both at the idiographic and at the nomothetic level. The idiographic analysis was based on the IC measure. As described in Study 1, the IC index reflects the extent to which each person's ordering of the least to the most self-descriptive trait is maintained across the five different social contexts (plus the general self). As anticipated, the Americans viewed themselves more consistently across social situations than did the Koreans. The mean IC score of the Korean re-

TABLE 2

MEANS AND STANDARD DEVIATIONS OF MAJOR VARIABLES

Variable	Korea		United States	
	M	*SD*	*M*	*SD*
SWLS	17.1	4.9	24.4	6.5
Pleasant emotions	15.7	3.1	18.7	3.5
Unpleasant emotions	13.5	2.9	11.1	2.6
IC (%)	52.8	11.6	64.0	13.1

Note. SWLS = Satisfaction With Life Scale; IC = identity consistency.

TABLE 3

MEAN CORRELATION BETWEEN GENERAL SELF-VIEW AND SITUATION-DEPENDENT SELF-VIEWS

| | General Self | | | |
| | Korea | | United States | |
Context	M	SD	M	SD
With parents	.32	.29	.58	.28
With a close friend	.35	.34	.66	.24
With a professor/teaching assistant	.29	.31	.54	.24
With a stranger	.29	.31	.52	.26
With a younger person	.37	.30	.58	.24
M	.32		.58	

spondents (52.8%) was significantly lower ($p < .001$) than the U.S. average (64.0%).

Another idiographic measure of IC is the within-subject correlation between the general self and each of the five situation-specific self-views. Table 3 summarizes the mean of the 121 within-subject correlations in Korea and the mean of the 84 within-subject correlations obtained from the U.S. sample. Compared with the United States, the correlations between the general self and the various context-dependent selves were consistently lower in Korea. For instance, on average, the general self and the with-parents self correlated .32 in Korea, whereas the average size of this correlation was .58 in the United States. * * * All 5 correlation means were significantly smaller in the Korean sample ($p < .001$). Thus, it was more difficult to predict the profiles of social selves from the general self in Korea than in the United States.

TABLE 4

RANKING OF SELF-DESCRIPTIVENESS OF TRAITS WITHIN CONTEXT: UNITED STATES

| | Context | | | | | | | |
Trait	Self	Friend	Parent	Professor	Stranger	Younger person	M	SD
Honest	1	2	4	6	8	4	4.2	2.6
Kind	2	5	1	4	1	2	2.5	1.6
Rational	3	10	5	2	2	9	5.2	3.5
Cooperative	4	6	6	1	5	7	4.8	2.1
Friendly	5	1	2	5	3	1	2.8	1.8
Open-minded	6	7	7	3	6	6	5.8	1.5
Talkative	7	3	3	12	12	8	7.5	4.0
Emotional	8	9	9	16	20	12	12.3	4.8
Cheerful	9	8	10	9	7	3	7.7	2.5
Outgoing	10	4	8	13	11	5	8.5	3.5
Modest	11	12	12	8	4	11	9.7	3.1
Impatient	12	15	11	14	15	14	13.5	1.6
Businesslike	13	17	16	7	9	16	13.0	4.1
Calculative	14	14	13	10	13	15	13.2	1.7
Dominant	15	13	17	18	14	10	14.5	2.9
Impulsive	16	11	14	15	16	13	14.2	1.9
Introverted	17	18	18	11	10	18	15.3	3.8
Cranky	18	16	15	19	19	17	17.3	1.6
Cold	19	20	20	20	18	20	19.5	0.8
Two-faced	20	19	19	17	17	19	18.5	1.2
Total								2.6
Spearman's correlation with self		.85	.94	.80	.73	.85	.83	

Note. 1 = most self-descriptive trait within context; 20 = least self-descriptive trait within context.

TABLE 5

RANKING OF SELF-DESCRIPTIVENESS OF TRAITS WITHIN CONTEXT: KOREA

Trait	Self	Friend	Parent	Professor	Stranger	Younger person	M	SD
Emotional	1	9	7	16	16	11	10.0	5.7
Cheerful	2	1	4	9	13	5	5.7	4.5
Kind	3	6	6	3	2	1	3.5	2.1
Cooperative	4	3	2	1	6	2	3.0	1.8
Friendly	5	2	1	7	14	4	5.5	4.7
Honest	6	7	3	5	5	3	4.8	1.6
Impatient	7	14	15	14	15	18	13.8	3.7
Impulsive	8	11	12	18	17	17	13.8	4.1
Outgoing	9	4	5	11	12	7	8.0	3.2
Rational	10	12	10	6	3	8	8.2	3.3
Modest	11	10	11	2	1	9	7.3	4.6
Open-minded	12	5	9	10	11	6	8.8	2.8
Introverted	13	20	16	4	4	12	11.5	6.4
Two-faced	14	17	14	13	10	15	13.8	2.3
Cranky	15	15	13	20	20	20	17.2	3.2
Talkative	16	8	8	17	19	10	13.0	4.9
Calculative	17	16	20	15	9	19	16.0	3.9
Dominant	18	13	18	19	18	14	16.7	2.5
Cold	19	18	17	12	8	13	14.5	4.2
Businesslike	20	19	19	8	7	16	14.8	5.8
Total								3.8
Spearman's correlation with self		.72	.80	.36	.08	.62	.52	

Note. 1 = most self-descriptive trait within context; 20 = least self-descriptive trait within context.

Nomothetic ratings also suggested that the self-view is significantly more consistent in the United States than in Korea. The American and Korean rankings of each trait (based on self-descriptiveness ratings) within each interpersonal context are summarized in Tables 4 and 5, respectively. Within each column, higher rankings indicate that the trait is more descriptive of the self in that particular context. For instance, American respondents reported that among the 20 traits, *honest* (Rank 1) is most self-descriptive, and *two-faced* (Rank 20) is least self-descriptive of their general self (second column, Table 4). Across contexts, *honest* was rated as the second most self-descriptive trait when Americans interact with friends, the fourth most self-descriptive trait when they are with their parents, and so forth (first row, Table 4). The trait *honest* across the six different contexts

was, on average, ranked as 4.2, with a standard deviation of 2.6. According to the standard deviation of each trait ranks, *cold* was ranked most consistently ($SD = 0.8$), whereas *emotional* was ranked least consistently ($SD = 4.8$). Among the five context-dependent selves, the with-parent self-profile was most similar to the general self (Spearman's $r = .94$), whereas the with-stranger self was least similar (Spearman's $r = .73$).

The rankings in Table 5 once again illustrate the highly context-dependent nature of the Korean self-view. For instance, although *emotional* was ranked as the most self-descriptive trait of the general self, it emerged as one of the least self-descriptive traits (Rank 16) in the with-professor or with-stranger contexts. The standard deviation of each trait ranking across contexts is summarized in the far right column of Table 5. According to these standard deviations, 15 out of the 20 trait rankings in Korea varied more across contexts than in the United States. The mean standard deviation of the total 20 rankings in Korea (3.8) was significantly larger ($p < .01$) than that of the U.S. (2.6), implying once again that the self-view shifts to a greater degree across situations in the former culture. Although the general self-profile correlated .80 with the with-parent self, it was weakly correlated with the with-professor (.36) and the with-stranger (.08) selves. The East Asian's self-view seems to take notably different forms, depending on whether the person interacts with an in-group or an out-group member.

In sum, the current study offers powerful evidence in support of the idea that the self-view is more consistent in cultures in which the autonomous, independent aspects of the self are prioritized over the relational, interdependent aspects of the self (Campbell et al., 1996; Cousins, 1989; Ip & Bond, 1995; Kanagawa, Cross, & Markus, 2001). The relatively unobtrusive nature of the current IC index (derived through a series of statistical analyses) weakens methodological threats, such as strong intrusion of cultural norms or values on the self-responses. Both the idiographic and the nomothetic data support the conclusion that the self-view changes quite drastically—especially between formal and informal situations—in East Asian cultures.

CONSISTENCY AND SWB The second major question was whether maintaining a consistent identity is more important to the SWB of Americans than of Koreans. Overall, IC was associated with higher SWB in both cultures. Individuals who viewed themselves more similarly across roles were more likely to be satisfied with their life and experienced more pleasant emotions. As anticipated, however, IC was a more effective predictor of SWB in the United States than in Korea.

The correlations between IC and the three SWB components were all significant in the United States ($r = .49$, $p < .001$, with life satisfaction; $r = .31$, $p < .01$, with positive affect; and $r = -.50$, $p < .001$, with negative affect). In Korea,

IC also correlated significantly with life satisfaction ($r = .22$, $p < .05$) and negative affect ($r = -.23$, $p < .05$). However, the size of these Korean correlations was significantly smaller than those of the U.S. sample ($p < .05$). Also, in contrast to the U.S. finding, the correlation between IC and positive affect in Korea was not significant ($r = .17$, ns).

The relative importance of IC and social appraisal in the prediction of SWB in each culture was examined by a regression analysis. Table 6 summarizes the standardized coefficients of IC and social appraisal in the prediction of SWB. A somewhat contrasting pattern emerged from the two cultures. Life satisfaction in Korea was predicted more effectively by social appraisal than by IC, whereas the reverse was true in the United States. For predictions of positive affect, only the beta of social appraisal was significant in Korea, whereas only IC reached significance in the United States. Finally, IC was clearly a more effective predictor of negative affect than was social appraisal in the United States, whereas this difference was attenuated in the Korean sample.

EVALUATIONS BY INFORMANTS Is there a cultural difference in how other people evaluate consistent versus inconsistent individuals? To examine this possibility, the informant's ratings of the target person's social skill and likability were correlated with the target person's IC level. Five Korean participants and 1 U.S. participant who each provided

TABLE 6

PREDICTING SUBJECTIVE WELL-BEING BY IDENTITY CONSISTENCY AND SOCIAL APPRAISAL (STANDARDIZED REGRESSION COEFFICIENT)

	Korea		United States	
Variable	IC	SA	IC	SA
Life satisfaction	.19*	.42***	.44***	.25*
Positive affect	.16	.21*	.27*	.19
Negative affect	−.22*	−.16	−.50***	−.02

Note. IC = identity consistency; SA = social appraisal.
*$p < .05$. ***$p < .001$.

only one informant report were also included in the analyses. For the rest of the sample, the mean of the two informant reports was used in the analyses (Korea, $n = 87$; United States, $n = 60$).

An intriguing pattern of cultural difference emerged. In the United States, the social skill ($r = .37$, $p < .01$) and general likability ($r = .33$, $p < .05$) ratings provided by the informants correlated significantly with the target person's IC level. In other words, there was a significant tendency among American informants to evaluate consistent people more favorably than less consistent people. In contrast, however, the Korean informants showed no preference between consistent and less consistent individuals. In Korea, neither the social skill ($r = .12$) nor the likability ($r = -.02$) ratings of the informants were correlated with the target person's IC level. In short, a link seems to exist between IC and social reward in individualist but not in collectivist cultures. This finding has implications for understanding the motive behind self-consistent behaviors, an issue that is addressed in the General Discussion.

Finally, cultural difference emerged in the correlations between the general self-view and the two informant reports. The mean convergence between the general self-view and the informant reports of friends (Korea, $r = .34$; United States, $r = .60$) and family members (Korea, $r = .33$; United States, $r = .63$) was consistently lower in Korea than in the United States ($p < .05$). Furthermore, when evaluating the target person's personality, the pair of Korean informants (friend and family member) agreed less with each other (on average, $r = .47$) than did the American informant pairs (on average, $r = .62$). Why is the agreement between the self and informant and between the two informants lower in Korea? Although the current study was not designed to specifically answer this question, past research documents that, all other things being equal, informant reports yield higher consensus when the target person's personality is expressed consistently across contexts (e.g., Bem & Allen, 1974; Colvin, 1993). Whether the consistency of the target's personality expression is directly linked with the cultural difference

in informant agreement deserves further examination.

Summary and Discussion

As anticipated, Koreans, compared with American respondents, construed themselves significantly more flexibly across situations, and the degree of consistency was less predictive of their SWB. Also, consistent individuals in the United States were rated highly by others on the dimensions of social skill and likability. Such a pattern was absent in the Korean data. Before I discuss the larger theoretical implications of these findings, two points warrant comment.

First, even though the East Asian self-view appears to be more malleable across situations, whether similar cultural difference exists in other dimensions of IC remains to be studied. For instance, when Campbell et al. (1996) examined how Japanese and Canadians responded to an item tapping the continuity of the self over time (i.e., "When I think about the kind of person I have been in the past, I'm not sure what I was really like," reverse scored), they found no cultural difference. As Campbell et al. correctly pointed out, the high situational variability observed among East Asians does not necessarily imply "a past self that lacks continuity with the present self" (p. 150). In a similar vein, one should not make quick cultural assumptions about the internal congruence dimension of identity from the current findings. Conceptual and methodological distinctions are required in studies of the temporal, cross-situational, and internal consistency of self-identity.

The interesting cultural difference found in the informant data raises a question. Why and on what basis do other people make such positive evaluations about consistent people? One possibility, namely that consistent individuals may simply have a good and nice personality, was not supported. Even when the informants' perception of highly positive traits (e.g., kind, friendly, honest) was controlled, they continued to think that more consistent people are more likable ($r = .26$, $p < .05$)

and more socially skilled ($r = .36$, $p < .01$). A more plausible scenario is suggested by Study 1. Highly consistent individuals, according to this study, are self-confident in social interactions, have clear opinions about themselves, and, most important, are less influenced by other people's thoughts. Such personality configuration seems to match more with the idealized picture of North American than East Asian selfhood (Markus & Kitayama, 1991). Because consistent people possess many of the personality trademarks cherished in Western cultures, they might convey a social image that appeals more to North Americans than to Koreans. Although this is the favored interpretation, more research is needed to clarify precisely why people like consistent persons more in the United States than in Korea and whether the cultural members are consciously aware of this link between consistency and social reward.

General Discussion

The concept of consistency is the backbone of many influential personality and social psychology theories (Triandis, 1999). Given its prominent position, it is rather surprising how little has been asked about the universal significance and applicability of this concept. This research hopes to shed light on how cultural factors come into the picture of consistency. The current findings have direct theoretical implications on SWB, the motive of self-consistency, and the study of personality across cultures.

Consistency and Well-Being

Many of the influential Western perspectives on well-being start with an implicit assumption that the needs of self-enhancement and self-consistency are fundamental and more or less universal (Suh, 2000). This assumption is strongly challenged by recent cross-cultural findings. Heine et al. (1999) contended, for instance, that the tendency to possess, to enhance, and to express positive self-views is in large part a feature of contemporary North American culture. Diener and Diener (1995) and

Kwan, Bond, and Singelis (1997) offered additional empirical support.

Compared with the self-esteem literature, very little is known about the cross-cultural validity of the IC and well-being link. According to the current findings, the gist of the classic idea—consistency predicts higher mental health—seems to be valid. However, it seems incorrect to assume that IC is a universally essential component of psychological well-being. It is vital to have a constant self-view and act accordingly in highly individualistic cultures, in which the person, more so than the situation, is expected to orchestrate his or her psychological behavior. In a sense, social context in individualist cultures is a canvas on which the values, desires, and interests of the relatively self-sufficient self are freely expressed.

The mental approach is somewhat different in East Asian cultures, in which others are deeply involved in the experience of being. The highest goal during the constant interactions with self-defining others is the fostering of long-term respect and harmony. When everyday attention is framed in terms of harmony, each individual becomes highly vigilant to social cues and, more often than in the West, feels the need to adjust the self to the social situation (cf. Morling et al., 2002). When these contrasting cultural priorities are considered, it makes sense that the psychological benefits associated with IC emerge more clearly in the West than in the East.

The larger implication of this study is that the experience of well-being results from a collaborative project between the individual and the culture (Kitayama & Markus, 2000). Well-being is not a vague, amorphous state but rather entails specific and concrete psychological experiences. The concrete experiences that the person feels most rewarding and meaningful, as Kitayama and Markus elaborately pointed out, are perpetually shaped by cultural ideals and practices. Current findings imply that IC, even though long considered as an indispensable element of mental health, might be one of those specific experiences that is more valued in one culture than in another.

* * *

Revisiting Consistency

One key question arising from this research is why members of some cultures seem less disturbed by inconsistent experiences than do those of others. More specifically, why is the correlation between IC and negative affect significantly weaker ($p < .05$) in Korea ($-.23$) than in the United States ($-.50$)? Although more systematic future research is required, I can think of at least two possibilities, one at the level of perception, and the other at the level of attribution. The first possibility is that the Eastern mind may have a higher threshold for dissonance. Cognitive habits or implicit world views that are prevalent in East Asian cultures, such as the dialectic mode of thinking (Nisbett et al., 2001) or the principles of yin and yang (Kitayama & Markus, 1999), have more generous assumptions about inconsistencies. Chronic exposure to such ideas may desensitize the Eastern mind from perceiving inconsistencies as unnatural, disturbing, or surprising (I. Choi & Nisbett, 2000).

Another possible reason is that cultural members may make different attributions about their inconsistent behaviors. In other words, East Asians may not differ from westerners so much in how they perceive inconsistencies but more in terms of how they interpret them. The uncomfortable feeling of dissonance arises when the sense of personal responsibility for the action is high (Cooper & Fazio, 1984). Compared with the United States, however, East Asian cultures are very "tight" (Triandis, 1995). A hallmark of a tight culture is that situation-specific norms are strictly imposed and personal deviations from norms are severely criticized. Also, many verbal and behavioral exchanges that take place during social interactions tend to be highly formal, ritualized, and driven by implicitly shared social scripts (S. G. Choi, 2000). The strong presence of such external factors may allow East Asians to feel somewhat less accountable for the inconsistencies they display across social contexts. In short, another possible reason why the distress associated with inconsistency is dampened in East Asian cultures might be because the cause of the inconsistency is chronically attributed to factors outside of the self. These two scenarios offer some directions for uncovering the mechanisms responsible for the cultural difference reported in this article.

Another key question prompted by this research concerns the psychological motive underlying self-consistency. The prevailing explanations in social psychology have been highly intrapsychic and cognitive ones. According to the most influential theory on this issue, cognitive dissonance theory (Festinger, 1957), people's efforts toward consistency stem from a basic, inner cognitive need. The rewards of achieving consistency also have been described most often in terms of internal psychological reasons, such as enhanced predictability or controllability of the world view (Lecky, 1945; Swann, Stein-Seroussi, & Giesler, 1992). However, if the efforts to be self-consistent emerge essentially from a basic need that serves to structure mental life, it is unclear why cultural members vary so much in their quest for self-consistency (Cialdini, Wosinska, Barrett, Butner, & Gornik-Durose, 1999; Heine & Lehman, 1997). The widely accepted cognitive explanations are certainly valid; nevertheless, they seem to severely underestimate the role of social and cultural factors in explaining why people try to be self-consistent.

The current informant data raise the possibility that social rewards also play a role in stimulating self-consistent thoughts and behavior. In the United States but not in Korea, consistent individuals were more likely to glean social praise from other people. It might not be a coincidence that the overall mean level of IC was higher in the former than in the latter culture. In addition to pure cognitive needs, the finding implies that positive social reinforcements may also fuel people's desire to be (or at least to appear) self-consistent. This possibility, even though discussed at times in the self-presentation literature (Tedeschi & Rosenfeld, 1981), warrants more serious attention in understanding why people try to be consistent.

The Self-Consistent Personality

From a personality standpoint, why do self-consistent individuals enjoy high SWB? In Study 1, the single most important predictor of IC was the tendency not to be overly conscious of how the inner self might be construed by others (low SEOP). The personal thoughts and feelings of consistent individuals, compared with inconsistent individuals, seem to be less constrained by other people's approvals, criticisms, and opinions. The idea implied here, that a certain degree of transcendence from external social input is psychologically beneficial, is also supported by studies on self-esteem. Well-adjusted people, for instance, have a sense of self-worth that requires less affirmation from external sources (Crocker & Wolfe, 2001) and fluctuates less in reaction to external feedback (Butler, Hokanson, & Flynn, 1994). In short, consistent people seem to have a more confident and self-sufficient version of self-view than others, which might play a key role in enhancing their SWB. Also, this strong sense of autonomy and self-sufficiency that characterizes consistent people might partly account for why their chances of being happy are higher in individualist than in collectivist cultures.

* * *

Conclusion

What is psychologically good, healthy, and worth emulating is constantly redefined by the forces of time and culture. One idea that has been very influential in mainstream psychology is that optimal psychological functioning requires the person to have a consistent self-identity across the different spheres of experience. The present findings suggest that this highly individualistic prescription might be less applicable to the SWB of cultural members who are inclined to think that the self is inherently social, multiple, and changing.

References

Abelson, R. P., Aronson, E., McGuire, W. J., Newcomb, T. M., Rosenberg, M. J., & Tannenbaum, P. H. (Eds.). (1968). *Theories of cognitive consistency: A sourcebook.* Chicago: Rand McNally.

Bachnik, J. M. (1992). Kejime: Defining a shifting self in multiple organizational modes. In N. R. Rosenberger (Ed.), *Japanese sense of self* (pp. 152–172). New York: Cambridge University Press.

Bem, D. J., & Allen, A. (1974). Predicting more of the people more of the time: The search for cross-situational consistencies in behavior. *Psychological Review, 81*, 506–520.

Block, J. (1961). Ego identity, role variability, and adjustment. *Journal of Consulting Psychology, 25*, 392–397.

Bond, M. H., & Hwang, K. (1986). The social psychology of Chinese people. In M. H. Bond (Ed.), *The psychology of the Chinese people* (pp. 213–266). Oxford, England: Oxford University Press.

Briggs, S. R., Cheek, J. M., & Buss, A. H. (1980). An analysis of the self-monitoring scale. *Journal of Personality and Social Psychology, 38*, 679–686.

Butler, A. C., Hokanson, J. E., & Flynn, H. A. (1994). A comparison of self-esteem liability and low self-esteem as vulnerability factors for depression. *Journal of Personality and Social Psychology, 66*, 166–177.

Campbell, J. D., Trapnell, P. D., Heine, S. J., Katz, I. M., Lavallee, L. F., & Lehman, D. R. (1996). Self-concept clarity: Measurement, personality correlates, and cultural boundaries. *Journal of Personality and Social Psychology, 70*, 141–156.

Choi, I., & Nisbett, R. E. (2000). Cultural psychology of surprise: Holistic theories and recognition of contradiction. *Journal of Personality and Social Psychology, 79*, 890–905.

Choi, S. G. (2000). *Hankookin shimleehak* [Korean's psychology]. Seoul, Korea: Jung-Ahng University Press.

Christopher, J. C. (1999). Situating psychological well-being: Exploring the cultural roots of its theory and research. *Journal of Counseling and Development, 77*, 141–152.

Cialdini, R. B., Wosinska, W., Barrett, D. W., Butner, J., & Gornik-Durose, M. (1999). Compliance with a request in two cultures: The differential influence of social proof and commitment/consistency on collectivists and individualists. *Personality and Social Psychology Bulletin, 25*, 1242–1253.

Colvin, C. R. (1993). Judgable people: Personality, behavior, and competing explanations. *Journal of Personality and Social Psychology, 64*, 861–873.

Cooper, J., & Fazio, R. H. (1984). A new look at dissonance theory. In L. Berkowitz (Ed.), *Advances in experimental social psychology* (Vol. 17, pp. 229–266). New York: Academic Press.

Costa, P. T. Jr., & McCrae, R. R. (1992). *Revised NEO Personality Inventory (NEO-PI-R) and NEO Five-Factor Inventory (NEO-FFI) professional manual.* Odessa, FL; Psychological Assessment Resources.

Cousins, S. D. (1989). Culture and self-perception in Japan and the United States. *Journal of Personality and Social Psychology, 56*, 124–131.

Crocker, J., & Wolfe, C. T. (2001). Contingencies of self-worth. *Psychological Review, 108*, 593–623.

Diener, E., & Diener, M. (1995). Cross-cultural correlates of life satisfaction and self-esteem. *Journal of Personality and Social Psychology, 68*, 653–663.

Diener, E., Emmons, R. A., Larsen, R. J., & Griffin, S. (1985). The Satisfaction With Life Scale. *Journal of Personality Assessment, 49*, 71–75.

Diener, E., Smith, H., & Fujita, F. (1995). The personality structure of affect. *Journal of Personality and Social Psychology, 69*, 130–141.

Diener, E., & Suh, E. M. (Eds.). (2000). *Culture and subjective well-being*. Cambridge, MA: MIT Press.

Diener, E., Suh, E. M., Lucas, R., & Smith, H. (1999). Subjective well-being: Three decades of progress. *Psychological Bulletin, 125*, 276–302.

Diener, E., Suh, E., Smith, H., & Shao, L. (1995). National differences in reported subjective well-being: Why do they occur? *Social Indicators Research, 34*, 7–32.

Donahue, E. M., Robins, R. W., Roberts, B. W., & John, O. P. (1993). The divided self: Concurrent and longitudinal effects of psychological adjustment and social roles on self-concept differentiation. *Journal of Personality and Social Psychology, 64*, 834–846.

Erikson, E. (1968). *Identity: Youth and crisis*. New York: Norton.

Festinger, L. (1957). *A theory of cognitive dissonance*. Evanston, IL: Row Peterson.

Fiske, A., P., Kitayama, S., Markus, H. R., & Nisbett, R. E. (1998). The cultural matrix of social psychology. In D. Gilbert, S. Fiske, & G. Lindzey (Eds.), *Handbook of social psychology* (4th ed., pp. 915–981). New York: McGraw-Hill.

Fu, G., Lee, K., Cameron, C. A., & Xu, F. (2001). Chinese and Canadian adults' categorization and evaluation of lie and truth-telling about pro-social and antisocial behaviors. *Journal of Cross-Cultural Psychology, 32*, 720–727.

Gangestad, S. W., & Snyder, M. (2000). Self-monitoring: Appraisal and reappraisal. *Psychological Bulletin, 126*, 530–555.

Goldberg, L. R. (1993). The structure of phenotypic personality traits. *American Psychologist, 48*, 26–34.

Heine, S. J., & Lehman, D. R. (1997). Culture, dissonance, and self-affirmation. *Personality and Social Psychology Bulletin, 23*, 389–400.

Heine, S. J., Lehman, D. R., Markus, H. R., & Kitayama, S. (1999). Is there a universal need for positive self-regard? *Psychological Review, 106*, 766–794.

Ho, D. F. (1993). Relational orientation in Asian social psychology. In U. Kim & J. W. Berry (Eds.), *Indigenous psychologies: Research and experience in cultural context* (pp. 240–259). Newbury Park, CA: Sage.

Ip, G. W. M., & Bond, M. H. (1995). Culture, values, and the spontaneous self-concept. *Asian Journal of Psychology, 1*, 29–35.

Jourard, S. M. (1965). *Personal adjustment: An approach through the study of healthy personality*. New York: Macmillan.

Kanagawa, C., Cross, S. E., & Markus, H. R. (2001). "Who am I?": The cultural psychology of the conceptual self. *Personality and Social Psychology Bulletin, 27*, 90–103.

Kashima, Y., Siegal, M., Tanaka, K., & Kashima, E. S. (1992). Do people believe behaviors are consistent with attitudes? Towards a cross-cultural psychology of attribution processes. *British Journal of Social Psychology, 31*, 111–124.

King, A. Y. C., & Bond, M. H. (1985). The Confucian paradigm of man: A sociological view. In W. S. Tseng & D. Y. H. Wu (Eds.), *Chinese culture and mental health* (pp. 29–46). New York: Academic Press.

Kitayama, S., & Markus, H. R. (1999). Yin and yang of the Japanese self: The cultural psychology of coherence. In D. Cervone & Y. Shoda (Eds.). *The coherence of personality: Social cognitive bases of personality consistency, variability, and organization* (pp. 242–302). New York: Guilford Press.

Kitayama, S., & Markus, H. R. (2000). The pursuit of happiness and the realization of sympathy: Cultural patterns of self, so-cial relations, and well-being. In E. Diener & E. M. Suh (Eds.), *Culture and subjective well-being* (pp. 113–161). Cambridge, MA: MIT Press.

Kwan, V. S. Y., Bond, M. H., & Singelis, T. M. (1997). Pancultural explanations for life satisfaction: Adding relationship harmony to self-esteem. *Journal of Personality and Social Psychology, 73*, 1038–1051.

Lecky, P. (1945). *Self-consistency: A theory of personality*. New York: Island.

Lillard, A. (1998). Ethnopsychologies: Cultural variations in theories of mind. *Psychological Bulletin, 123*, 3–32.

Markus, H. R., & Kitayama, S. (1991). Culture and self: Implications for cognition, emotion, and motivation. *Psychological Review, 98*, 224–253.

Markus, H. R., & Kitayama, S. (1994). A collective fear of the collective: Implications for selves and theories of selves. *Personality and Social Psychology Bulletin, 20*, 568–579.

Markus, H. R., Mullally, P. R., & Kitayama, S. (1997). Selfways: Diversity in modes of cultural participation. In U. Neisser & D. Jopling (Eds.), *The conceptual self in context: Culture, experience, self-understanding* (pp. 13–60). New York: Cambridge University Press.

Maslow, A. H. (1954). *Motivation and personality*. New York: Harper & Brothers.

Miller, M. (1997). Views of Japanese selfhood: Japanese and Western perspectives. In D. Allen (Ed.), *Culture and self: Philosophical and religious perspectives, East and West* (pp. 145–162). Boulder, CO: Westview.

Mischel, W., & Peake, P. K. (1982). Beyond déjà vu in the search for cross-situational consistency. *Psychological Review, 89*, 730–755.

Moore, C. A. (1967). (Ed.). *The Chinese mind: Essentials of Chinese philosophy and culture*. Honolulu: University of Hawaii Press.

Morling, B., Kitayama, S., & Miyamoto, Y. (2002). Cultural practices emphasize influence in the United States and adjustment in Japan. *Personality and Social Psychology Bulletin, 28*, 311–323.

Nisbett, R. E., Peng, K., Choi, L., & Norenzayan, A. (2001). Culture and systems of thought: Holistic versus analytic cognition. *Psychological Review, 108*, 291–310.

Peng, K., & Nisbett, R. E. (1999). Culture, dialectics, and reasoning about contradiction. *American Psychologist, 54*, 741–754.

Roberts, B. W., & Donahue, E. M. (1994). One personality, multiple selves: Integrating personality and social roles. *Journal of Personality, 62*, 199–218.

Rogers, C. R. (1951). *Client-centered therapy*. Boston: Houghton Mifflin.

Rosenberger, N. R. (Ed.). (1992). *Japanese sense of self*. New York: Cambridge University Press.

Sheldon, K. M. (1996). The Social Awareness Inventory: Development and applications. *Personality and Social Psychology Bulletin, 22*, 620–634.

Sheldon, K. M., Ryan, R. M., Rawsthorne, L. J., & Ilardi, B. (1997). Trait self and true self: Cross-role variation in the Big-Five personality traits and its relations with psychological authenticity and subjective well-being. *Journal of Personality and Social Psychology, 73*, 1380–1393.

Snyder, M. (1974). Self-monitoring of expressive behavior. *Journal of Personality and Social Psychology, 30*, 526–537.

Suh, E. M. (2000). Self, the hyphen between culture and subjective well-being. In E. Diener & E. M. Suh (Eds.), *Culture and subjective well-being* (pp. 63–86). Cambridge, MA: MIT Press.

Suh, E. M., & Diener, E. (2002). *Self-review, social appraisal, and life satisfaction judgments.* Manuscript in preparation, University of California, Irvine.

Suh, E., Diener, E., Oishi, S., & Triandis, H. C. (1998). The shifting basis of life satisfaction judgments across cultures: Emotions versus norms. *Journal of Personality and Social Psychology, 74*, 482–493.

Swann, W. B. Jr. (1983). Self-verification: Bringing social reality into harmony with the self. In J. Suls & A. G. Greenwald (Eds.), *Psychological perspectives on self* (Vol. 2, pp. 33–66).

Swann, W. B. Jr., de la Ronde, C., & Hixon, G. (1994). Authenticity and positivity strivings in marriage and courtship. *Journal of Personality and Social Psychology, 66*, 857–869.

Swann, W. B. Jr., & Read, S. J. (1981). Self-verification processes: How we sustain our self-conceptions. *Journal of Experimental Social Psychology, 17*, 351–373.

Swann, W. B. Jr., Stein-Seroussi, A., & Giesler, R. B. (1992). Why people self-verify. *Journal of Personality and Social Psychology, 62*, 392–401.

Tedeschi, J. T., & Rosenfeld, P. (1981). Impression management theory and the forced compliance situation. In J. T. Tedeschi (Ed.), *Impression management theory and social psychology research* (pp. 147–180). New York: Academic Press.

Triandis, H. C. (1989). Self and social behavior in differing cultural contexts. *Psychological Review, 96*, 269–289.

Triandis, H. C. (1995). *Individualism and collectivism.* Boulder, CO: Westview Press.

Triandis, H. C. (1999). Cross-cultural psychology. *Asian Journal of Social Psychology, 2*, 127–143.

Wiggins, J. S. (1979). A psychological taxonomy of trait-descriptive terms: The interpersonal domain. *Journal of Personality and Social Psychology, 37*, 395–412.

Toward the Development of Quasi-Indigenous Personality Constructs: Measuring Los Cinco Grandes in Spain with Indigenous Castilian Markers

Verónica Benet-Martínez and Oliver P. John

As we have seen in the articles throughout this section, a persistent issue in cross-cultural psychology is whether psychological ideas used to understand people within one culture can be applied in other cultures. For example, articles in this section argue that emotional experience, behavioral consistency, and even the very nature of the self are profoundly different from one culture to another. However, other researchers have argued that aspects of personality such as emotional experience and personality structure are nearly universal. The arguments tend to become polarized. The present article, by Verónica Benet-Martínez and Oliver P. John, seeks both a theoretical conception and a set of methods that represent a reasonable compromise.

The cross-cultural section of this volume concludes with an article that aims to begin building what the authors call "quasi-indigenous" personality constructs and measures for their constructs. In this case, the culture in the spotlight is Spain. Historically, American researchers have attempted to find the key words for describing personality in English by exhaustively (and exhaustingly) surveying unabridged dictionaries. The present authors do the same thing, using an unabridged dictionary of Castilian Spanish. After a careful series of analyses, which includes a study to see how personality-descriptive words are used by Spanish participants to describe themselves, the authors conclude that the widely known English "Big Five" personality traits (extraversion, neuroticism, agreeableness, conscientiousness, and openness to experience) indeed appear relevant in a Spanish cultural context, although their meaning is a bit different, and that additional dimensions of humor, good nature, and unconventionality are also important.

There is an essential core to human nature that transcends culture, and there are important and profound differences in behavior and experience between cultures. The present investigation seeks to integrate the study of both these similarities and differences. Hopefully the future will see many further studies that attempt to do the same in a wide variety of different cultural contexts.

From *American Behavioral Scientist, 44*, 141–157, 2000.

Research in cultural and ethnic-minority psychology has identified a number of general value differences between Latin cultures (e.g., Spanish and Hispanic) and U.S. Anglo-American culture (Hofstede, 1983; Marín & Marín, 1991; Schwartz, 1994; Triandis, 1990; Triandis, Lisansky, Marín, & Betancourt, 1984). Compared to Anglo-Americans, Latin individuals are less individualistic and more collectivist; that is, they emphasize interdependence and the goals of the in-group; they value *simpatía*, which may be described as the need for interpersonal behaviors that promote smooth and harmonious relationships such as expressing positive emotions and avoiding interpersonal conflict; they have a more flexible time orientation (being more present than future oriented) and are less likely to delay gratification. Latin individuals also value familialism; that is, they show strong attachment to and identification with the family. Despite these similarities, Latin cultures also differ from each other in important ways. For example, individuals of Latin-American background (e.g., Hispanics who live in the United States) speak a variant of Spanish that is different from the Castilian spoken by Spaniards living in Spain, and they seem to show the cultural characteristics of collectivism, *simpatía*, present-time orientation, and familialism to a greater extent than Spaniards (Hofstede, 1983; Marín & Marín, 1991).

An interesting empirical question is whether and how all these Anglo-Latin cultural differences at the group level translate into differences in the basic organization (or structure) of personality characteristics at the individual level. One possibility, as Gergen, Gulerce, Lock, and Misra (1996) suggested, is that each culture creates a unique personality structure, thus making multiple, culturally specific personality psychologies necessary. Alternatively, as McCrae and Costa (1997) recently suggested, there may be a basic universal personality structure, namely, the structure of traits comprising the Big Five (or five-factor model), that is culturally invariant. Several recent studies have examined this issue in the context of Latin cultures (Benet-Martínez, 1999; Benet-Martínez & John, 1998; Benet-Martínez & Waller, 1997). Using an imposed-etic approach (i.e., relying on translated instruments), Benet-Martínez and John (1998) conducted three studies to evaluate the generalizability of a Spanish version of the Big Five Inventory (BFI) (John, Donahue, & Kentle, 1991) and to explore the generalizability of the Big Five factor structure in three different Latin samples: college students from Spain and college and working-class Hispanic bilingual individuals living in California. These three studies failed to show substantial Anglo-Latin and Hispanic-Spanish cultural differences in personality at the broad level represented by the Big Five dimensions. Specifically, the factor composition and psychometric properties (e.g., alphas, means, and standard deviations) for the Big Five scales were very similar across all the cultural groups compared.

Benet-Martínez and John's (1998) use of a translated instrument optimally served the main goal of their study: to assess the robustness of the Big Five Inventory (John et al., 1991) in the Spanish language. Their use of imported instruments in this study, however, did not directly address the question of whether the Big Five taxonomy truly represents the basic structure of the indigenous Spanish personality lexicon. In other words, it is not clear whether the results from Benet-Martínez and John's (1998) study prove that Big Five dimensions best represent the actual structure of the

Spanish personality lexicon or merely that American Big Five markers can be translated into Spanish and still retain their structure. This issue can only be addressed by taking an emic approach, that is, by identifying the basic dimensions of personality variation in Spanish from a pool of indigenous Spanish personality descriptors. With this goal in mind, Benet-Martínez (1999; Benet-Martínez & Waller, 1997) conducted a series of emic studies that examined the structure of self-reports on a set of 299 indigenous Spanish (Castilian) personality descriptors selected from an unabridged Spanish dictionary and representative of the entire Spanish personality lexicon. Compared to the typical set of personality descriptors used to identify Big Five taxonomies (e.g., Angleitner, Ostendorf, & John, 1990; Goldberg, 1990; Norman, 1967), the Spanish set of 299 indigenous descriptors was selected using a broader definition of personality. In addition to traditional trait descriptors, Benet-Martínez and Waller also included historically excluded personality terms such as highly evaluative and affective state descriptors (for a discussion of this approach, see Benet & Waller, 1995; Tellegen, 1993; Waller, 1999). Self-ratings on the Spanish (Castilian) descriptors by a large Spanish college sample (N = 894) yielded a seven-factor structure (named the Big Seven in this and other studies). Three of these seven factors were very similar to the Big Five dimensions of Conscientiousness, Agreeableness, and Openness. The other four dimensions represented (and were named) Pleasantness and Engagement (affect dimensions representing rotations of Extraversion and Neuroticism) and Positive and Negative Valence (esteem dimensions representing positive and negative self-evaluation).

Can the Big Five be recovered in Spanish? The imposed-etic and emic studies described so far suggest the following: (a) Imported Big Five measures (e.g., Big Five Inventory) replicate well in Spanish, (b) there is little evidence for Anglo-Latin cultural differences in Big Five mean levels (see Table 1 in Benet-Martínez & John, 1998), and (c) existing indigenous Spanish personality taxonomies map only partially into the Big Five

(common dimensions are Conscientiousness, Agreeableness, and Openness). Researchers interested in measuring basic personality characteristics in Spain are then faced with the following two choices: (a) use translated Anglo-American personality descriptors and measure the Big Five or (b) use indigenous Spanish terms but measure instead a culture-specific Big Seven structure (which includes three of the Big Five dimensions).

In trying to decide between the two aforementioned choices, researchers will invariably have to deal with a couple of important issues (which were introduced earlier): The first choice, use translated Anglo-American personality descriptors and measure the Big Five, is a straightforward and economical one, but it is limited in that particular culture-specific personality elements and local expressions and meanings associated to them may be lost (Church & Katigbak, 1988; Triandis & Marín, 1983). The second choice, use indigenous Spanish terms and measure instead a culture-specific structure, is free of the fundamental limitations stemming from the first choice but presents a different (and perhaps equally important) disadvantage: It makes standard (i.e., empirical) cross-cultural comparisons very hard.

In this article, we propose a new midlevel approach that represents a compromise between the prior two conflicting choices and allows researchers simultaneously to achieve two desirable goals: measure the Big Five and use indigenous personality expressions. We illustrate the development and evaluation of this approach in the context of measuring the Big Five in Spain with local Castilian personality expressions.

Method

Participants

A sample of 894 native residents of Spain, 709 women and 185 men, participated in this study. The mean age of the sample was 21.24 years (SD = 3.91)[1]. All participants were undergraduate

---

[1]SD is the standard deviation.

students attending day or evening courses at the Universidad Autónoma de Barcelona, a large public university in Spain. To obtain a representative sample of Spanish college students, participants were enlisted from a diverse range of majors: psychology (417), economics (142), veterinary medicine (68), law (121), and education (146).

INSTRUMENTS All participants completed a booklet containing a dictionary-based list of 299 Castilian personality descriptors (Benet-Martínez, 1999) and a Spanish-translated version of the Big Five Inventory (John et al., 1991). We next describe these questionnaires in greater detail.

Indigenous Spanish (Castilian) personality descriptor list. This instrument consisted of 299 personality adjectives (with defining phrases) selected from a widely used, unabridged Spanish dictionary: *Diccionario Manual e Ilustrado de la Real Academia de la Lengua Española* (Real Academia Española, 1989). Descriptors were culled using a stratified sampling method: Every fourth page of the 1,666-page lexicon was carefully inspected to identify personality-descriptive adjectives. Only the first trait term on a page was included in the list. When no trait descriptors were found on the selected page, the next fourth page was examined. A team of two expert judges (a Ph.D. in Spanish and the first author, both native speakers from Spain) independently generated descriptor lists from the stratified sample of dictionary pages. Following Tellegen and Waller's (1987) method for descriptor selection, the two judges considered an adjective to be personality relevant if (a) it could be used to distinguish the behavior, thoughts, or feelings of one human being from those of another and (b) it could be meaningfully inserted into one or both of the following sentences: "Tends to be X" or "Is often X." These were the only inclusion criteria applied. Unlike previous lexical personality studies, no exclusion criteria were applied to descriptors that were highly evaluative or referred to emotional states. The judges, however, avoided nondistinctive terms that can apply to all individuals such as terms referring to geographic origin, nationality,

profession, social role, relationships, or physical qualities (see Angleitner et al., 1990, for similar criteria).

A total of 299 indigenous personality descriptors were found to be representative. These terms were assembled (with a fixed randomized order) in a research questionnaire. For all items, item responses were measured on a 5-point scale ranging from 1 (*disagree strongly*) to 5 (*agree strongly*). To enhance the definitional clarity of the descriptors, each term was followed by a synonym or short dictionary definition.

The Spanish Big Five Inventory. The Big Five Inventory (BFI) (John et al., 1991) uses 44 short phrases to assess the most prototypical traits associated with the Big Five dimensions in English (John, 1990). The trait adjectives (e.g., *thorough*) that form the core of each of the 44 BFI items (e.g., "Does a thorough job") have been shown in previous studies to be univocal prototypical markers of the Big Five dimensions (John, 1989, 1990). A Spanish version of the BFI was developed using the back-translation methods of Brislin (1980). This procedure can be briefly described as follows: Using standard Spanish-English and English-Spanish dictionaries, the first author (who is bilingual) undertook the translation of the BFI items into Spanish. Using the same dictionaries, a second bilingual (Ph.D. in Spanish) independently translated the material back into English. The bilingual team then compared the back-translated version to the initial English version, discussed discrepancies between the translations, and generated further translations until arriving at a final set of Spanish BFI items on which both translators could agree. Responses on the Spanish BFI items were measured on a 5-point scale ranging from 1 (*disagree strongly*) to 5 (*agree strongly*).

PROCEDURE Questionnaires were group-administrated during instructional time at the university. Participation was voluntary and anonymous. In addition to standard demographic questions, participants also indicated the primary language(s) spoken at home. This information was deemed im-

TABLE 1

PSYCHOMETRIC PROPERTIES OF THE QUASI-INDIGENOUS AND IMPORTED (BIG FIVE INVENTORY) SPANISH BIG FIVE SCALES

Scale	Alpha		M		SD	
	Quasi-Indigenous	Imported	Quasi-Indigenous	Imported	Quasi-Indigenous	Imported
Extraversion	.88	.85	3.7	3.4	.8	.8
Agreeableness	.79	.66	3.9	3.8	.6	.5
Conscientiousness	.79	.77	3.7	3.5	.7	.7
Neuroticism	.82	.80	3.2	3.2	.8	.8
Openness	.73	.79	3.1	3.8	.7	.6
Mean	.80	.78	3.5	3.5	.7	.7

Note. N = 444 Spaniards (cross-validation sample). Quasi-indigenous scales defined by indigenous Spanish terms. Imported scales defined by imported (Spanish-translated Big Five Inventory) terms.

portant because most Barcelona residents speak Castilian and Catalán, the two official languages of Catalonia. Participants were instructed to provide self-rating on the two instruments "according to the way they usually feel, think, or behave."

Results

As stated earlier, the basic goal of the present study is to illustrate a midlevel approach that allows researchers to measure imported personality models such as the Big Five with indigenous personality expressions. With that goal in mind, in the next sections we (a) identify a reliable and manageable set of indigenous Spanish (Castilian) markers of the Big Five and (b) evaluate the Big Five scales defined by these indigenous Castilian descriptors in terms of their reliability, factorial robustness, and construct validity.

IDENTIFYING A SET OF SPANISH (CASTILIAN) BIG FIVE MARKERS   For each participant, five Big Five scale scores were computed from their responses to the Spanish-translated BFI. These imported scale scores were then used to select a set of Big Five markers from the 299 indigenous Castilian personality descriptors also rated by the participants. To ensure replicability of the findings, we used a split-sample cross-validation procedure: The derivation

sample included 450 participants randomly selected from the total sample of 894, and 444 remained for cross-validation. Using the derivation sample, we computed correlations between the imported Spanish BFI scale scores and each of the 299 indigenous Castilian descriptors. Next, we selected the 20 indigenous terms that had the strongest correlations with each BFI scale. It is important to note here that the absolute magnitude of these correlations was the only criteria to select indigenous descriptors; no effort was made to filter out synonyms (e.g., *disquieted* or *restless*) or terms denoting related dispositions (e.g., *likes to travel* or *international*). When a factor analysis was performed on these 100 indigenous Castilian markers, a clear five-factor structure emerged representing the familiar five factors. Using the factor loadings as a guide, we selected the best 12 indigenous markers for each factor.[2]

---

[2]Factor analysis is a statistical technique for examining the correlations among a large number of variables to seek the essential few that might be the most central. The technique usually yields an estimate of the number of important factors that can account for most of the variance in all of the variables, and the variables that best exemplify the factors are called "markers."

TABLE 2

INTERCORRELATIONS AMONG QUASI-INDIGENOUS SPANISH BIG FIVE SCALES AND AMONG IMPORTED (BIG FIVE INVENTORY) SCALES

Scales	E	A	C	N	O
Extraversion (E)	—	.17	.09	−.18	.33
Agreeableness (A)	.04	—	.17	−.23	.16
Conscientiousness (C)	.16	.30	—	−.20	.17
Neuroticism (N)	−.24	−.10	−.31	—	−.14
Openness (O)	.12	−.05	−.07	.05	—

Note. N = 444 Spaniards (cross-validation sample). Correlations among quasi-indigenous scales are below the diagonal, and correlations among imported (Big Five Inventory) scales are above the diagonal.

PSYCHOMETRIC PROPERTIES OF THE CASTILIAN BIG FIVE MARKERS IN THE CROSS-VALIDATION SAMPLE

How well did this set of 60 indigenous Castilian Big Five markers hold up to cross-validation? Using the remaining 444 participants as a cross-validation sample, we computed five scales, each defined by 12 indigenous Castilian items. The internal consistency (alpha) reliabilities, means, and standard deviations for these scales are shown in Table 1.[3] For comparison purposes, each column shows statistics for both the newly developed quasi-indigenous scales and the imported BFI scales. Why are these new scales labeled *quasi-indigenous*? Although each term in these scales is in some sense indigenous (i.e., Castilian), the scales themselves are not because they did not naturally emerge from the Castilian personality lexicon but, rather, were created from those Castilian descriptors that correlated most strongly with the imported Big Five scales.

As shown in Table 1, the alphas for the quasi-indigenous Big Five scales are very high and even somewhat higher (except for Openness) than those for the imported Big Five scales. Table 1 also shows

the means and standard deviations for the quasi-indigenous and imported scales. Paired *t* tests between the two sets of scales revealed significant differences suggesting higher scores for the quasi-indigenous Extraversion, Conscientiousness, and Agreeableness scales and higher scores for the imported Openness scale. These differences are hard to interpret without further replication, but one possibility is that the higher mean levels obtained for these quasi-indigenous scales reflect an overall higher endorsement (relative to the imported scales) by the Spanish participants of particular culture-specific personality aspects represented in the quasi-indigenous Castilian scales.

Table 2 reports the intercorrelations among the quasi-indigenous and imported Big Five scales.[4] These findings are important because there has been concern that some of the Big Five dimensions are highly intercorrelated (e.g., Block, 1995). The present results show that the new quasi-indigenous Big Five scales are fairly independent: The absolute mean of the intercorrelations was .14, and even the highest intercorrelation was only −.31. All in all, the results reported so far show that the new quasi-indigenous Castillian Big Five scales have psychometric characteristics that are fairly similar (with the exception perhaps of means and standard deviations) to those for the imported BFI scales.

EXPLORING THE STRUCTURE OF THE CASTILIAN BIG FIVE MARKERS

The dimensional structure of the self-reports on the 60 indigenous Spanish Big Five markers was assessed via factor analysis. As in the previous analyses, only the cross-validation sample was used. A plot of the first 10 eigenvalues showed a clear break after the fifth eigenvalue, supporting the expected five-factor structure. The varimax-rotated five-factor structure defined by the indigenous markers is shown in Table 3.[5] As can be seen in this table, the 60 indigenous Castil-

---

[3]The alpha numbers in these tables are measures of internal reliability of each of the scales. Their high values indicate that individual participants tended to answer the items on each scale in a consistent manner. *M* is the mean and *SD* the standard deviation.

[4]The numbers in Table 2 are standard correlation coefficients, of the sort discussed by Rosenthal and Rubin in Part I.

[5]The "varimax rotated five-factor structure" is the authors' best estimate of the essential variables at the heart

ian terms define a clear structure easily identified as the Big Five. Furthermore, supporting the robustness of the indigenous Castilian terms as univocal markers of the Big Five, each of the 60 indigenous markers loaded on the predicted dimension, and most of the cross-loadings were consistently low.

An examination of the content areas represented by the indigenous Castilian markers reveals that the basic personality elements of the Big Five are generally well represented in the quasi-indigenous Castilian scales: sociability and positive affect (e.g., *charming* and *cheerful*) versus social disengagement and low positive affect (e.g., *isolated* and *gloomy*) for Extraversion, kindness and good character (e.g., *kind* and *good natured*) versus quarrelsomeness (e.g., *vindictive* and *irascible*) for Agreeableness, self-control and reflectiveness (e.g., *orderly* and *reasonable*) versus unrestraint and carelessness (e.g., *impulsive* and *sloppy*) for Conscientiousness, negative affect (e.g., *anxious* and *guilty*) for Neuroticism, which in the present structure lacks terms denoting emotional stability or low negative affect (e.g., *calm* and *stable*); and creativity and open-mindedness (e.g., *inventive* and *worldly*) versus conventionality (e.g., *conventional*) for Openness.

Also obvious when looking at the areas represented by the indigenous Castilian markers is that certain personality elements are more strongly emphasized in these scales than in most widely used English Big Five measures. In Extraversion, for instance, the expression of positive affect in social settings plays a prominent role, as indicated by the large number of traits and states referring to amusement and humor (e.g., *funny*, *jocular*, and *side-splitting*). In Agreeableness, we see a wealth of terms denoting good nature and a straightforward, unpretentious interpersonal style (e.g., *good-natured*, *good-hearted*, *down-to-earth*, and *unpretentious*). Finally, Openness dimension is defined more broadly than the imported Openness in that it refers explicitly to interests, preferences, and attitudes that define having a progressive lifestyle: unconventional attitudes and tastes (e.g., *eccentric* and *outlandish*), enjoyment of travel (e.g., *international* and *likes to travel*), a wordly wise approach to life (e.g., *bohemian* and *worldly*), and interest in spiritual and philosophical issues (e.g., *philosophical* and *mystical*). Interestingly, an examination of the indigenous factors reported in Benet-Martínez's emic studies (1999; Benet-Martínez & Waller, 1997) reveals that these personality elements (expression of positive affect in social settings, good nature, and progressive lifestyle) are also prominent in emic factors.

In sum, the factor definitions based on indigenous markers indicate that most basic personality elements of the Big Five are generally well represented in Castilian and suggest that relative to the American-English Big Five, the following personality facets are particularly salient in Spain: humor and social emotional expressivity for Extraversion, good nature for Agreeableness, and unconventionality, worldliness, and spirituality for Openness.

OVERLAP BETWEEN THE QUASI-INDIGENOUS AND IMPORTED SCALES The differences in content representation reported in the previous section raise the question of how much overlap there is between the newly created quasi-indigenous Castilian Big Five marker scales and the imported scales. In other words, do people who score high (or low) on a particular imported Big Five scale also tend to score high (or low) on the same indigenous Big Five scale? To address this question, correlations between these two sets of scales were computed in the cross-validation sample; these multitrait, multimethod correlations are reported in Table 4.

---

of all the personality ratings. The "factor loadings" in Table 3 reflect the association of each rated variable with each broader factor. To see what each factor includes, look at the rating terms (English on the left, Spanish on the right) associated with each of the bold faced numbers. A positive number means the term is positively associated with the factor; a negative number means it is negatively (inversely) related to the factor. The factor labeled "E" (extraversion) was scored in the direction of introversion, because positive markers include *mustia* and *apagada* ("gloomy") and negative markers include *alegre* ("happy") and *sandunguera* ("charming").

TABLE 3

FIVE-FACTOR MODEL DEFINED BY INDIGENOUS CASTILIAN PERSONALITY TERMS IN THE CROSS-VALIDATION SAMPLE

Abbreviated English Translation	Varimax-Rotated Principal Factor					Original Spanish (Castilian) Terms
	E	A	C	N	O	
Gloomy	65	07	−08	06	−02	*Mustia, apagada*
Isolated	64	00	−06	04	05	*Aislada, sola*
Dull	62	20	−12	00	−15	*Amuermada, aburrida*
Asocial	61	01	−08	−04	05	*Asocial, poco social*
Somber	59	−02	−06	10	04	*Sombria, triste*
Shy	55	28	00	11	−11	*Cortada, tímida*
Lethargic	53	19	−09	00	−17	*Parada, pasmada*
Jocular	−57	08	−13	−07	03	*Jocosa, chistosa*
Side-splitting	−60	01	−08	−03	04	*Trinchante, que te parte de la risa*
Charming	−62	05	−01	00	05	*Sandunguera, con gracía y salero*
Cheerful	−63	20	10	−15	−07	*Alegre*
Funny	−64	11	−08	−07	05	*Cómica, divertida*
Good-natured	02	64	05	05	−07	*Bonachona, dócil*
Good-hearted	03	63	10	00	01	*Buenaza, buena persona*
Patient	16	57	24	−15	00	*Paciente, tolerante*
Down-to-earth	05	54	13	−05	−17	*Sencilla, poco afectada*
Unpretentious	07	51	19	−04	−02	*Llana, sencilla*
Kind	−21	43	18	−03	−05	*Amable*
Obliging	−15	39	18	05	−04	*Complaciente, servicial*
Vindictive	01	−38	00	00	−13	*Revanchista, vengativa*
Unyielding	−06	−39	04	−11	02	*Peleadora, discutidora*
Quarrelsome	14	−40	05	−08	−15	*Cuadrada, inflexible*
Tyrannical	−09	−43	04	−03	−10	*Tirana, dominante*
Irascible	02	−45	−14	19	−05	*Colérica, que se enfada fácilmente*
Reflective	22	14	56	−04	00	*Reflexiva, analítica*
Well-balanced	−04	28	54	−26	−15	*Equilibrada, estable*
Orderly	−03	09	50	−02	−10	*Ordenada*
Reasonable	04	17	49	−16	00	*Razonable, lógica*
Has balanced life	−06	08	47	−14	−03	*Repartible, que se sabe distribuir*
Sensible	05	13	44	−06	−03	*Cuerda, juiciosa*
Competent	−23	00	37	−11	11	*Diestra, hábil*
Lazy	16	12	−32	−07	−12	*Perezosa, vaga*
Unrestrained	02	−04	−39	03	04	*Immoderada, que hace excesos*
Sloppy	14	02	−40	00	−08	*Chapucera*
Fickle	03	−05	−45	07	06	*Volátil, incostante*
Impulsive	−16	−08	−49	07	−03	*Atolondrada, precipitada*
Easily disquieted	13	03	−18	67	−05	*Trastornable, fácil de inquietar*
Restless	03	00	−10	67	−05	*Agitable, intranquila*
Sensitive	14	11	−03	52	00	*Afectable, sensible*
Easy to startle	−17	−04	−06	41	−05	*Saltadiza, sobresaltable*
Afflicted	30	03	−04	40	−01	*Consumida, afligida*
Feels guilty	22	03	−00	39	−02	*Culpable, con remordimientos*
Confused	35	08	−33	36	04	*Confusa, desconcertada*
Worried	30	−03	09	34	01	*Preocupada*
Fearful	16	17	−18	33	−21	*Cagada, miedosa*
Indecisive	31	16	−29	32	−06	*Vacilante, indecisa*

Anxious	−05	−16	−07	**31**	00	*Ansiosa, nerviosa*
Imperturbable	09	06	22	**−45**	09	*Impávida, imperturbable*
Outlandish	00	−01	−23	−13	**48**	*Pintoresca, extravagante*
Likes to travel	−13	03	−08	−10	**46**	*Nómada, con alma viajera*
Creative	−25	03	22	−09	**45**	*Creativa, inventiva*
Mystical	23	01	01	14	**45**	*Ascética, mística*
Inventive	−26	−04	15	−11	**44**	*Inventora, ocurrente*
Eccentric	−02	−04	−22	−12	**43**	*Estrafalaria, excéntrica*
Romantic	20	06	06	20	**42**	*Platónica, idealista*
Bohemian	10	03	−11	01	**41**	*Bohemia*
Worldly	−24	04	06	−13	**37**	*Viajera, aventurera*
International	−14	03	13	−09	**34**	*Internacional*
Philosophical	19	07	05	17	**30**	*Existencialista, filosófica*
Conventional	23	21	16	06	**−38**	*Convencional, poco original*

Note. N = 444 Spaniards (cross-validation sample). All loadings multiplied by 100; loadings .30 or larger are set in bold. E = Extraversion; A = Agreeableness; C = Conscientiousness; N = Neuroticism; O = Openness.

The size of the convergence correlations on the diagonal (mean = .67) clearly contrasts with the average off-diagonal discriminant correlations (mean = .15), suggesting considerable convergent and discriminant validity across the two instruments.

* * *

Discussion

The main aim of the present study was to identify a manageable set of indigenous Spanish (Castilian) personality descriptors that would allow researchers to measure the Big Five using local, culturally relevant terms. Using a split-sample cross-validation procedure, 60 indigenous Castilian Big Five markers were identified based on their high correlations with Spanish BFI scales (John et al., 1991). These markers defined reliable, quasi-indigenous Big Five scales and a clear five-factor structure that univocally represented the Big Five. A distinctive quality of this quasi-indigenous Spanish Big Five structure was the salience of the following personality elements: humor and social/emotional engagement (in Extraversion), good nature (in Agreeableness), and unconventionality, worldliness, and spirituality (in Openness)—all three personality domains that also have high visibility in indigenous Spanish personality taxonomies (Benet-Martínez, 1999).

How should the specific salience of the earlier described personality elements in the quasi-indigenous five-factor structure be interpreted? One could view this salience as mainly an artifact of the overrepresentation that terms denoting humor, social/emotional engagement, good nature, unconventionality, worldliness, and spirituality may have in the Castilian personality lexicon. In addition, one could view the salience of these personality elements in the factor structure as a reflection of the cultural relevance these dispositions may have in the Spanish culture. Note that these

TABLE 4

CONVERGENT-DISCRIMINANT CORRELATIONS BETWEEN THE QUASI-INDIGENOUS AND IMPORTED (BIG FIVE INVENTORY) SPANISH BIG FIVE SCALES

Quasi-Indigenous Scales

Imported Scales	E	A	C	N	O
Extraversion (E)	**.77**	−.08	.04	−.22	.18
Agreeableness (A)	.18	**.65**	**.31**	−.13	.02
Conscientiousness (C)	.12	.09	**.70**	−.20	−.03
Neuroticism (N)	−.22	−.27	−.35	**.70**	−.05
Openness (O)	**.31**	.00	.18	−.14	**.54**

Note. N = 444 Spaniards (cross-validation sample). Correlations greater than .30 are in boldface. Correlations between corresponding dimensions (validity coefficients) are shown on the diagonal in italics.

two views are complementary because cultural differences in the psychological relevance of particular personality domains are likely to be related to differences in linguistic content representation (Goldberg, 1992). We would like to make a more specific argument and suggest that the ubiquity of terms denoting humor, social/emotional engagement, good nature, unconventionality, worldliness, and spirituality in the quasi-indigenous Spanish structure may have resulted from a mixture of methodological and substantive factors, which we outline next.

As explained in the Method section, the original pool of 299 indigenous Castilian terms from which the Big Five markers were selected was compiled using a stratified sampling method, a technique that combines pure random and purposive sampling (McCready, 1996). This sampling method led to a large set of Castilian personality descriptors that can be seen as (a) representative of the entire Spanish personality lexicon and therefore (b) reflective of the different linguistic representation that certain personality aspects may have in the Spanish lexicon—probably due to a mixture of biological, historical, and sociocultural factors (Osgood & Tzeng, 1990; Sanchez, 1996). From this list of 299 indigenous personality descriptors, Big Five markers were selected exclusively on the basis of correlation size; that is, no effort was made to ensure a particular content representation (e.g., representing all well-known facets within each Big Five dimension, filtering out terms denoting similar dispositions). Consequently, because only 12 markers per dimension were chosen and terms with similar meaning were accepted, each factor ended up being defined only in terms of two or three different content areas. What kinds of areas emerged? The two or three Spanish-defined personality domains with the highest cooccurrence with the behaviors and dispositions represented in the imported Big Five dimensions. What determined the number of markers for each area? The relative representation of these areas in the original set of 299 indigenous Castilian markers. A conclusion that derives from these arguments is, therefore, that the salience of humor, social/emotional

engagement, good nature, unconventionality, worldliness, and spirituality in the quasi-indigenous Big Five structure may in fact be reflective of both the particular salience these dispositions have in the personality processes of Spaniards and the particular weight these areas have in the Spanish personality lexicon.

Along with the content specificity found in some of the quasi-indigenous Castilian Big Five scales, we also found a great degree of overlap between the imported and quasi-indigenous scales. * * *. These results provide strong evidence for the construct validity of the newly developed quasi-indigenous Castilian Big Five scales. The 60 quasi-indigenous Castilian personality descriptors then offer a reliable and factorially valid way to measure the Big Five personality dimensions in Spanish. These descriptors can be used as an alternative to imported personality measures when the goal is to measure the Big Five domain with indigenous terms (rather than translations) and when one does not need to measure all the facets of the Big Five.

The construct validity of the quasi-indigenous scales speaks to the usefulness of this instrument to measure the Big Five but does not tell us much about its predictive validity. Future research needs to examine the power of the quasi-indigenous Castilian Big Five scales (relative to other existing Spanish personality instruments) to predict important personality-related life outcomes such as self-esteem, well-being, or relationship satisfaction. More importantly, however, future studies should carry on the ultimate test of these scales' unique value: assessing the relative power (compared to imported measures) of the quasi-indigenous Castilian Big Five scales to predict Spanish culture-specific dispositions, attitudes, and behaviors such as *simpatía*, familialism, emotional expressiveness, or flexible time orientation.

From a methodological perspective, the study reported here broadens traditional imposed-etic and emic cross-cultural methodology by introducing a new midlevel approach that allows researchers to identify quasi-indigenous constructs, that is, measuring imported models (i.e., the Big

Five) with stimuli that are sensitive to the particularities of a specific cultural and linguistic context. Or as we say in Spain, an approach that allows cross-cultural researchers to *matar dos pajaros de un tiro* (kill two birds with one stone).

References

Angleitner, A., Ostendorf, F., & John, O. P. (1990). Towards a taxonomy of personality descriptors in German: A psycholexical study. *European Journal of Personality, 4,* 89–118.

Benet, V., & Waller, N. G. (1995). The "Big Seven" model of personality description: Evidence for its cross-cultural generality in a Spanish sample. *Journal of Personality and Social Psychology, 69,* 701–718.

Benet-Martínez, V. (1999). Exploring indigenous Spanish personality constructs with a combined emic-etic approach. In J. C. Lasry, J. G. Adair, & K. L. Dion (Eds.), *Latest contributions to cross-cultural psychology* (pp. 151–175). Lisse, the Netherlands: Swets & Zeitlinge.

Benet-Martínez, V., & John, O. P. (1998). Los Cinco Grandes across cultures and ethnic groups: Multitrait method analyses of the Big Five in Spanish and English. *Journal of Personality and Social Psychology, 75,* 729–750.

Benet-Martínez, V., & Waller, N. G. (1997). Further evidence for the cross-cultural generality of the "Big Seven" model: Imported and indigenous Spanish personality constructs. *Journal of Personality, 65,* 567–598.

Block, J. (1995). A contrarian view of the five-factor approach to personality description. *Psychological Bulletin, 117,* 187–215.

Brislin, R. W. (1980). Translation and content analysis of oral and written materials. In H. Triandis & J. W. Berry (Eds.), *Handbook of cross-cultural psychology* (Vol. 2, pp. 389–444). Boston: Allyn & Bacon.

Church, A. T., & Katigbak, M. S. (1988). The emic strategy in identification and assessment of personality dimensions in a non-Western culture. *Journal of Cross-Cultural Psychology, 19,* 140–163.

Gergen, K. J., Gulerce, A., Lock, A., & Misra, G. (1996). Psychological science in cultural context. *American Psychologist, 51,* 496–503.

Goldberg, L. R. (1990). An alternative "description of personality": The Big-Five factor structure. *Journal of Personality and Social Psychology, 59,* 1216–1229.

Goldberg, L. R. (1992). The development of markers for the Big-Five factor structure. *Psychological Assessment, 4,* 26–42.

Hofstede, G. (1983). Dimensions of national cultures in fifty countries and three regions. In J. Deregowski, S. Dzuirawiec, & R. Annis (Eds.), *Explications in cross-cultural psychology* (pp. 335–355). Lisse, The Netherlands: Swets and Zeitlinger.

John, O. P. (1989). Towards a taxonomy of personality descriptors. In D. M. Buss & N. Cantor (Eds.), *Personality psychology: Recent trends and emerging directions* (pp. 261–271). New York/Berlin: Springer-Verlag.

John, O. P. (1990). The "Big Five" factor taxonomy: Dimensions of personality in the natural language and in questionnaires. In L. A. Pervin (Ed.), *Handbook of personality: Theory and research* (pp. 66–100). New York: Guilford.

John, O. P., Donahue, E. M., & Kentle, R. L. (1991). *The "Big Five" Inventory—Versions 4a and 54* (Technical Report). Berkeley: Institute of Personality and Social Research, University of California.

Marín, G., & Marín, B. (1991). *Research with Hispanic populations.* Newbury Park, CA: Sage.

McCrae, R. R., & Costa, P. T., Jr. (1997). Personality trait structure as a human universal. *American Psychologist, 52,* 509–516.

McCready, W. C. (1996). Applying sampling procedures. In W. C. McCready (Ed.), *The psychology research handbook: A guide for graduate students and research assistants* (pp. 98–110). Thousand Oaks, CA: Sage.

Norman, W. T. (1967). *2800 personality trait descriptors: Normative operating characteristics for a university population.* Ann Arbor: University of Michigan.

Osgood, C. E., & Tzeng, O. C. (1990). *Language, meaning, and culture: The selected papers of C. E. Osgood.* New York: Praeger.

Real Academia Española, (1989). *Diccionario manual e ilustrado de la Real Academia de la Lengua Española (Cuarta Edición Revisada)* [Manual and illustrated dictionary of the Royal Spanish Academy of Language, revised fourth edition]. Madrid, Spain: Espassa-Calpe.

Sanchez, R. (1996). Mapping the Spanish language along a multiethnic and multilingual border. *Aztlan, 21,* 49–104.

Schwartz, S. H. (1994). Beyond individualism/collectivism: New cultural dimensions of values. In U. Kim, H. C. Triandis, Ç. Kâgitçbasi, S. Choi, & G. Yoon (Eds.), *Individualism and collectivism: Theory, methods, and applications* (pp. 85–119). Thousand Oaks, CA: Sage.

Tellegen, A. (1993). Folk concepts and psychological concepts of personality and personality disorder. *Psychological Inquiry, 4,* 122–130.

Tellegen, A., & Waller, N. G. (1987, August). *Reexamining basic dimensions of natural language trait descriptors.* Paper presented at the annual meeting of the American Psychological Association, New York.

Triandis, H. C. (1990). Cross-cultural studies of individualism and collectivism. In J. J. Berman (Ed.), *Nebraska Symposium on Motivation* (pp. 41–133). Lincoln: University of Nebraska Press.

Triandis, H. C., Lisansky, J., Marín, G., & Betancourt, H. (1984). Simpatía as a cultural script of Hispanics. *Journal of Personality and Social Psychology, 47,* 1363–1375.

Triandis, H. C., & Marín, G. (1983). Etic plus emic versus pseudoetic: A test of a basic assumption of contemporary cross-cultural psychology. *Journal of Cross-Cultural Psychology, 14,* 489–500.

Waller, N. G. (1999). Evaluating the structure of personality. In C. R. Cloninger (Ed.), *Personality and psychopathology* (pp. 155–197). Washington, DC: American Psychiatric Press.

PART VII

Behavioral, Social Learning, and Cognitive Approaches to Personality

Behavioristic psychology treats behavior as something that is produced by the immediate environment and the individual's history of rewards and punishments. In its original version, behaviorism avoided assuming the existence of any "inner," mental states or traits at all. For a "functional analysis" of behavior, it was sufficient to connect visible rewards and punishments with visible behaviors.

This point of view has evolved in an interesting way over the years. The social learning and cognitive theorists added one critical assumption to behaviorism, that one's beliefs about, or "representations" of, the rewards and punishments in the environment are more important than what the environment actually contains. For example, if you believe a behavior will be rewarded you will probably do it, even if in fact the behavior will be punished. But of course your representation of a belief like this is a non-visible, internal state, which means that modern, cognitive approaches to personality have grown a long distance from their behaviorist roots. Recent research within the cognitive approach to personality has moved even further away, as it begins to examine a topic that would have made B. F. Skinner cringe: the unconscious mind.

The first selection in this section is by the key figure in modern behaviorism, and one of the most important social scientists of the century. In "Why Organisms Behave," Skinner introduces the idea of functional analysis, and dismisses neural causes, psychic causes, and everything else that "radical" behaviorists find irrelevant to a sufficient understanding of behavior. Instead, he proposes that the answer to why organisms behave is always to be found in the external variables—rewards and punishments—of which behavior is always a function, and expresses optimism that this approach will solve all of the basic issues of psychology.

This was and remains an influential position within psychology, but the field has moved slowly but surely away from Skinner's version of behaviorism. An important catalyst in this movement was the second selection, a classic article by Albert Bandura and his colleagues. This article is one of the most widely cited in the history of psychology. It presents a demonstration of how learning can occur without reinforcement—thus undermining a critical assumption of behaviorism—and implies some dangers of televised violence. The article also opened the door to the development of cognitive approaches to personality, with its direct—though unstated—implication that a cognitive representation of an event that was merely depicted on film can be enough to affect an individual's future behavior.

The next selection is an article Bandura wrote many years later, summing up the cognitive approach to personality he had developed. In this article, Bandura both displays some fundamentally behavioristic leanings and goes way beyond behaviorism by describing the operation of what he calls the "self system." Through a process Bandura calls "reciprocal determinism," an individual's self system develops as a result of experience but also determines future behavior and the future environment. Thus, the environment may determine the person, as behaviorists would maintain, but the person also determines the environment.

The fourth selection is by Walter Mischel, whose influential attack on trait psychology we read in Part II. Mischel presents his "cognitive-affective personality system" (CAPS) approach to personality, which is fundamentally based on a distinctively cognitive idea, that the person's beliefs about and representations of the environment can become more important than the environment itself (in this we see an echo of the phenomenological ideas of Mischel's teacher, George Kelly). Mischel also introduces his if . . . then *conception of behavioral coherence, in which a person is described not in terms of global personality traits, but through the patterns of behavioral change he or she exhibits from one situation to the next.*

The fifth selection is by one of Mischel's former students, Nancy Cantor, in collaboration with one of her own students. This article exemplifies the way cognitive research in personality attempts to reconcile behavioral coherence and change. It examines people with different goals for their dating relationships, and how in some cases they can change their situation, or at least their point of view, to achieve those goals almost no matter what the goals of their partner might be—the sort of self-determination anticipated by Bandura's conception of the self system.

The sixth selection represents the beginning of a radical new direction for cognitive research on personality by opening a window on the unconscious sectors of the mind. Anthony Greenwald and his colleagues describe the Implicit Associations Test (IAT), which seeks to measure aspects of the self-concept of which the person himself or herself might be unaware. To put this aim another way, it tries to measure what you know about yourself, but don't know you know. The following selection, by Jens Asendorpf and his colleagues, applies this technique to investigate the conscious and unconscious aspects of shyness, and shows that different aspects of shyness-related behavior are controlled by the conscious and unconscious facets of this trait.

The final selection in this section and this book brings together several strands of personality research. Stan Klein and his colleagues use the intensive study of a single case, a young woman they call "W.J.," to explore the neurological and psychological underpinnings of personal identity. In particular, they examine the degree to which a person's self-knowledge depends on memory. In the first selection in this book McAdams asks what we know when we know a person; in the last Klein asks what we must know to know ourselves.

Behaviorism has evolved a long way from classic behaviorism to social learning theory to cognitive theory. The most recent developments offer a promise for the reintegration of personality psychology. The modern cognitive theorists of personality are renewing their attention to individual differences, and describing patterns of thought, motivation, and behavior of the sort that have long been of interest to some trait theorists. This development opens the possibility for cognitive and trait theorists to begin again to take one another's work seriously, and develop a personality psychology that draws on the strengths of both approaches. Even more recent work addresses an issue that goes back to Freud: the nature and functioning of the unconscious mind. The potential is beginning to emerge, therefore, for the integration of trait, humanistic, cognitive, and even psychoanalytic approaches to personality into a single, unified discipline.

Why Organisms Behave

B. F. Skinner

The major historical figure in behaviorism, and one of the best-known social scientists of the twentieth century, is B. F. Skinner. Over a career that spanned more than 60 years (he died in 1990), Skinner argued strenuously and consistently that behavior was a scientific topic no different, in principle, from any other. That is, behavior is best studied through experimental methods, and the best way to demonstrate that you understand a behavior is to show that you can control it. Skinner always expressed annoyance with theories that located causes of behavior in the mind or even in the physical brain. He felt this practice merely postponed understanding, because the mind cannot be observed and the brain is poorly understood. Instead, Skinner argued, psychology should address the powerful causes of behavior that can be both seen and experimentally manipulated: the rewards and punishments in the environment of the "organism."

The first selection in this section, an excerpt from a basic text on behaviorism Skinner published at the height of his career in 1953, clearly sets forth the behaviorist manifesto. Skinner argues that locating causes of behavior in the stars, the physique, genetics, or even the nervous system offers nothing to psychological understanding. Each only misleads or—at best—distracts analysis away from the causes of behavior that ought to be the real business of psychologists.

Skinner's model for a science of psychology is "functional analysis." Such an analysis entails identifying—and, in many cases, controlling—the environmental causes of which behavior is a "function." Skinner further urges that these causes be conceptualized in concrete, physical terms. Rather than abstract social forces, for example, Skinner urges us to pay attention to the specific, immediate, concrete rewards and punishments in the social environment that affect what a person does. This focus on specifics, he believed, could enable people to design environments that would elicit behaviors leading to better outcomes for all.

From *Science and Human Behavior*, by B. F. Skinner (Upper Saddle River, NJ: Prentice-Hall, 1953), pp. 23–42.

We are concerned with the causes of human behavior. We want to know why men behave as they do. Any condition or event which can be shown to have an effect upon behavior must be taken into account. By discovering and analyzing these causes we can predict behavior; to the extent that we can manipulate them, we can control behavior.

There is a curious inconsistency in the zeal with which the doctrine of personal freedom has been defended,[1] because men have always been fascinated by the search for causes. The spontaneity of human behavior is apparently no more challenging than its "why and wherefore." So strong is the urge to explain behavior that men have been led to anticipate legitimate scientific inquiry and to construct highly implausible theories of causation. This practice is not unusual in the history of science. The study of any subject begins in the realm of superstition. The fanciful explanation precedes the valid. Astronomy began as astrology; chemistry as alchemy. The field of behavior has had, and still has, its astrologers and alchemists. A long history of prescientific explanation furnishes us with a fantastic array of causes which have no function other than to supply spurious answers to questions which must otherwise go unanswered in the early stages of a science.

Some Popular "Causes" of Behavior

Any conspicuous event which coincides with human behavior is likely to be seized upon as a cause. The position of the planets at the birth of the individual is an example. Usually astrologers do not try to predict specific actions from such causes, but when they tell us that a man will be impetuous, careless, or thoughtful, we must suppose that specific actions are assumed to be affected. Numerology finds a different set of causes—for example, in the numbers which compose the street address of the individual or in the number of letters in his name. Millions of people turn to these spurious causes every year in their desperate need to understand human behavior and to deal with it effectively.

The predictions of astrologers, numerologists, and the like are usually so vague that they cannot be confirmed or disproved properly. Failures are easily overlooked, while an occasional chance hit is dramatic enough to maintain the behavior of the devotee in considerable strength. * * *

Another common practice is to explain behavior in terms of the structure of the individual. The proportions of the body, the shape of the head, the color of the eyes, skin, or hair, the marks on the palms of the hands, and the features of the face have all been said to determine what a man will do.[2] The "jovial fat man," Cassius with his "lean and hungry look," and thousands of other characters or types thoroughly embedded in our language affect our practices in dealing with human behavior. A specific act may never be predicted from physique, but different types of personality imply predispositions to behave in different ways, so that specific acts are presumed to be affected. This practice resembles the mistake we all make when we expect someone who looks like an old acquaintance to behave like him also. When a "type" is once established, it survives in everyday use because the predictions which are made with it, like those of astrology, are vague, and occasional hits may be startling.

* * *

When we find, or think we have found, that conspicuous physical features explain part of a man's behavior, it is tempting to suppose that inconspicuous features explain other parts. This is implied in the assertion that a man shows certain behavior because he was "born that way." To object to this is not to argue that behavior is never determined by hereditary factors. Behavior requires a behaving organism which is the product of a genetic process. Gross differences in the behavior of different species show that the genetic constitution, whether observed in the body structure of the indi-

---

[1]For example, by the humanists in Part V.

[2]Recall the selection by Wells in Part III.

vidual or inferred from a genetic history, is important. But the doctrine of "being born that way" has little to do with demonstrated facts. It is usually an appeal to ignorance. "Heredity," as the layman uses the term, is a fictional explanation of the behavior attributed to it.

Even when it can be shown that some aspect of behavior is due to season of birth, gross body type, or genetic constitution, the fact is of limited use. It may help us in predicting behavior, but it is of little value in an experimental analysis or in practical control because such a condition cannot be manipulated after the individual has been conceived. The most that can be said is that the knowledge of the genetic factor may enable us to make better use of other causes. If we know that an individual has certain inherent limitations, we may use our techniques of control more intelligently, but we cannot alter the genetic factor.[3]

The practical deficiencies of programs involving causes of this sort may explain some of the vehemence with which they are commonly debated. Many people study human behavior because they want to do something about it—they want to make men happier, more efficient and productive, less aggressive, and so on. To these people, inherited determiners—as epitomized in various "racial types"—appear to be insurmountable barriers, since they leave no course of action but the slow and doubtful program of eugenics.[4] The evidence for genetic traits is therefore closely scrutinized, and any indication that it is weak or inconsistent is

received with enthusiasm. But the practical issue must not be allowed to interfere in determining the extent to which behavioral dispositions are inherited. The matter is not so crucial as is often supposed, for we shall see that there are other types of causes available for those who want quicker results.

Inner "Causes"

Every science has at some time or other looked for causes of action inside the things it has studied. Sometimes the practice has proved useful, sometimes it has not. There is nothing wrong with an inner explanation as such, but events which are located inside a system are likely to be difficult to observe. For this reason we are encouraged to assign properties to them without justification. Worse still, we can invent causes of this sort without fear of contradiction. The motion of a rolling stone was once attributed to its *vis viva*. The chemical properties of bodies were thought to be derived from the *principles* or *essences* of which they were composed. Combustion was explained by the *phlogiston* inside the combustible object. Wounds healed and bodies grew well because of a *vis medicatrix*. It has been especially tempting to attribute the behavior of a living organism to the behavior of an inner agent, as the following examples may suggest.

NEURAL CAUSES The layman uses the nervous system as a ready explanation of behavior. The English language contains hundreds of expressions which imply such a causal relationship. At the end of a long trial we read that the *nerves* of the accused are *on edge*, that the wife of the accused is on the verge of a *nervous breakdown*, and that his lawyer is generally thought to have lacked the *brains* needed to stand up to the prosecution. Obviously, no direct observations have been made of the nervous systems of any of these people. Their "brains" and "nerves" have been invented on the spur of the moment to lend substance to what might otherwise seem a superficial account of their behavior.

---

[3]It is unclear why Skinner here portrays the inability to alter the genotype as an important limitation. In terms of Skinner's own analysis alteration of the phenotype (overt behavior) should be a sufficient goal.

[4]Skinner is referring to writings early in the twentieth century that identified "national" or "racial" characters. For example, southern Europeans were held to be emotional and northern Europeans to be cold and analytical. Skinner expresses (well-taken) doubts that such descriptions are accurate, and further argues that even if they were accurate the only prescription they offer is to "improve" the human species through selective breeding (eugenics). Skinner calls such a eugenic strategy "doubtful," surely an understatement.

The sciences of neurology and physiology have not divested themselves entirely of a similar practice. Since techniques for observing the electrical and chemical processes in nervous tissue had not yet been developed, early information about the nervous system was limited to its gross anatomy. Neural processes could only be inferred from the behavior which was said to result from them. Such inferences were legitimate enough as scientific theories, but they could not justifiably be used to explain the very behavior upon which they were based. The hypotheses of the early physiologist may have been sounder than those of the layman, but until independent evidence could be obtained, they were no more satisfactory as explanations of behavior. Direct information about many of the chemical and electrical processes in the nervous system is now available. Statements about the nervous system are no longer necessarily inferential or fictional. But there is still a measure of circularity in much physiological explanation, even in the writings of specialists. In World War I a familiar disorder was called "shell shock." Disturbances in behavior were explained by arguing that violent explosions had damaged the structure of the nervous system, though no direct evidence of such damage was available. In World War II the same disorder was classified as "neuropsychiatric." The prefix seems to show a continuing unwillingness to abandon explanations in terms of hypothetical neural damage.[5]

Eventually a science of the nervous system based upon direct observation rather than inference will describe the neural states and events which immediately precede instances of behavior. We shall know the precise neurological conditions which immediately precede, say, the response, "No, thank you." These events in turn will be found to be preceded by other neurological events, and these in turn by others. This series will lead us back to events outside the nervous system and, eventually, outside the organism. * * * We do not have and may never have this sort of neurological information at the moment it is needed in order to predict a specific instance of behavior. It is even more unlikely that we shall be able to alter the nervous system directly in order to set up the antecedent conditions of a particular instance. The causes to be sought in the nervous system are, therefore, of limited usefulness in the prediction and control of specific behavior.

PSYCHIC INNER CAUSES An even more common practice is to explain behavior in terms of an inner agent which lacks physical dimensions and is called "mental" or "psychic." The purest form of the psychic explanation is seen in the animism of primitive peoples. From the immobility of the body after death it is inferred that a spirit responsible for movement has departed. The *enthusiastic* person is, as the etymology of the word implies, energized by a "god within." It is only a modest refinement to attribute every feature of the behavior of the physical organism to a corresponding feature of the "mind" or of some inner "personality." The inner man is regarded as driving the body very much as the man at the steering wheel drives a car. The inner man wills an action, the outer executes it. The inner loses his appetite, the outer stops eating. The inner man wants and the outer gets. The inner has the impulse which the outer obeys.

It is not the layman alone who resorts to these practices, for many reputable psychologists use a similar dualistic system of explanation. The inner man[6] is sometimes personified clearly, as when delinquent behavior is attributed to a "disordered personality," or he may be dealt with in fragments, as when behavior is attributed to mental processes, faculties, and traits. Since the inner man does not occupy space, he may be multiplied at will. It has been argued that a single physical organism is controlled by several psychic agents and that its behavior is the resultant of their several wills. The Freudian concepts of the ego, superego, and id are often used in this way. They are frequently regarded as nonsubstantial creatures, often in violent

---

[5]The current label for this syndrome, post-traumatic stress disorder, is more in line with Skinner's descriptive preference without attributing cause.

[6]Sometimes called the "homunculus."

conflict, whose defeats or victories lead to the adjusted or maladjusted behavior of the physical organism in which they reside.

Direct observation of the mind comparable with the observation of the nervous system has not proved feasible. It is true that many people believe that they observe their "mental states" just as the physiologist observes neural events, but another interpretation of what they observe is possible. Introspective psychology[7] no longer pretends to supply direct information about events which are the causal antecedents, rather than the mere accompaniments, of behavior. It defines its "subjective" events in ways which strip them of any usefulness in a causal analysis. The events appealed to in early mentalistic explanations of behavior have remained beyond the reach of observation. Freud insisted upon this by emphasizing the role of the unconscious—a frank recognition that important mental processes are not directly observable. The Freudian literature supplies many examples of behavior from which unconscious wishes, impulses, instincts, and emotions are inferred. Unconscious thought-processes have also been used to explain intellectual achievements. Though the mathematician may feel that he knows "how he thinks," he is often unable to give a coherent account of the mental processes leading to the solution of a specific problem. But any mental event which is unconscious is necessarily inferential, and the explanation is therefore not based upon independent observations of a valid cause.

The fictional nature of this form of inner cause is shown by the ease with which the mental process is discovered to have just the properties needed to account for the behavior. When a professor turns up in the wrong classroom or gives the wrong lecture, it is because his *mind* is, at least for the moment, *absent*. If he forgets to give a reading assignment, it is because it has slipped his *mind* (a hint from the class may re*mind* him of it). He begins to tell an old joke but pauses for a moment, and it is evident to everyone that he is trying to make up his *mind* whether or not he has already used the joke that term. His lectures grow more tedious with the years, and questions from the class confuse him more and more, because his *mind* is failing. What he says is often disorganized because his *ideas* are confused. He is occasionally unnecessarily emphatic because of the force of his *ideas*. When he repeats himself, it is because he has an *idée fixe*; and when he repeats what others have said, it is because he borrows his *ideas*. Upon occasion there is nothing in what he says because he lacks *ideas*. In all this it is obvious that the mind and the ideas, together with their special characteristics, are being invented on the spot to provide spurious explanations. A science of behavior can hope to gain very little from so cavalier a practice. Since mental or psychic events are asserted to lack the dimensions of physical science, we have an additional reason for rejecting them.

CONCEPTUAL INNER CAUSES   The commonest inner causes have no specific dimensions at all, either neurological or psychic. When we say that a man eats *because* he is hungry, smokes a great deal *because* he has the tobacco habit, fights *because* of the instinct of pugnacity, behaves brilliantly *because* of his intelligence, or plays the piano well *because* of his musical ability, we seem to be referring to causes. But on analysis these phrases prove to be merely redundant descriptions. A single set of facts is described by the two statements: "He eats" and "He is hungry." A single set of facts is described by the two statements: "He smokes a great deal" and "He has the smoking habit." A single set of facts is described by the two statements: "He plays well" and "He has musical ability." The practice of explaining one statement in terms of the other is dangerous because it suggests that we have found the cause and therefore need search no further. Moreover, such terms as "hunger," "habit," and "intelligence" convert what are essentially the properties of a process or relation into what appear to be things. Thus we are unprepared for the properties eventually to be discovered in the behavior itself and continue to look for something which may not exist.

---

[7]A kind of psychology, prominent in the field's early days, in which trained "introspectionists" tried to observe their own mental processes.

The Variables of Which Behavior Is a Function

The practice of looking inside the organism for an explanation of behavior has tended to obscure the variables which are immediately available for a scientific analysis. These variables lie outside the organism, in its immediate environment and in its environmental history. They have a physical status to which the usual techniques of science are adapted, and they make it possible to explain behavior as other subjects are explained in science. These independent variables are of many sorts and their relations to behavior are often subtle and complex, but we cannot hope to give an adequate account of behavior without analyzing them.

Consider the act of drinking a glass of water. This is not likely to be an important bit of behavior in anyone's life, but it supplies a convenient example. We may describe the topography of the behavior in such a way that a given instance may be identified quite accurately by any qualified observer. Suppose now we bring someone into a room and place a glass of water before him. Will he drink? There appear to be only two possibilities: either he will or he will not. But we speak of the *chances* that he will drink, and this notion may be refined for scientific use. What we want to evaluate is the *probability* that he will drink. This may range from virtual certainty that drinking will occur to virtual certainty that it will not. The very considerable problem of how to measure such a probability will be discussed later. For the moment, we are interested in how the probability may be increased or decreased.

Everyday experience suggests several possibilities, and laboratory and clinical observations have added others. It is decidedly not true that a horse may be led to water but cannot be made to drink. By arranging a history of severe deprivation we could be "absolutely sure" that drinking would occur. In the same way we may be sure that the glass of water in our experiment will be drunk. Although we are not likely to arrange them experimentally, deprivations of the necessary magnitude sometimes occur outside the laboratory. We may

obtain an effect similar to that of deprivation by speeding up the excretion of water. For example, we may induce sweating by raising the temperature of the room or by forcing heavy exercise, or we may increase the excretion of urine by mixing salt or urea in food taken prior to the experiment. It is also well known that loss of blood, as on a battlefield, sharply increases the probability of drinking. On the other hand, we may set the probability at virtually zero by inducing or forcing our subject to drink a large quantity of water before the experiment.

If we are to predict whether or not our subject will drink, we must know as much as possible about these variables. If we are to induce him to drink, we must be able to manipulate them. In both cases, moreover, either for accurate prediction or control, we must investigate the effect of each variable quantitatively with the methods and techniques of a laboratory science.

Other variables may, of course, affect the result. Our subject may be "afraid" that something has been added to the water as a practical joke or for experimental purposes. He may even "suspect" that the water has been poisoned. He may have grown up in a culture in which water is drunk only when no one is watching. He may refuse to drink simply to prove that we cannot predict or control his behavior. These possibilities do not disprove the relations between drinking and the variables listed in the preceding paragraphs; they simply remind us that other variables may have to be taken into account. We must know the history of our subject with respect to the behavior of drinking water, and if we cannot eliminate social factors from the situation, then we must know the history of his personal relations to people resembling the experimenter. Adequate prediction in any science requires information about all relevant variables, and the control of a subject matter for practical purposes makes the same demands.

Other types of "explanation" do not permit us to dispense with these requirements or to fulfill them in any easier way. It is of no help to be told that our subject will drink provided he was born under a particular sign of the zodiac which shows a preoccupation with water or provided he is the lean and thirsty type or was, in short, "born thirsty." Explanations in terms of inner states or agents, however, may require some further comment. To what extent is it helpful to be told, "He drinks because he is thirsty"? If to be thirsty means nothing more than to have a tendency to drink, this is mere redundancy. If it means that he drinks because of a state of thirst, an inner causal event is invoked. If this state is purely inferential—if no dimensions are assigned to it which would make direct observation possible—it cannot serve as an explanation. But if it has physiological or psychic properties, what role can it play in a science of behavior?

The physiologist may point out that several ways of raising the probability of drinking have a common effect: they increase the concentration of solutions in the body. Through some mechanism not yet well understood, this may bring about a corresponding change in the nervous system which in turn makes drinking more probable. In the same way, it may be argued that all these operations make the organism "feel thirsty" or "want a drink" and that such a psychic state also acts upon the nervous system in some unexplained way to induce drinking. In each case we have a causal chain consisting of three links: (1) an operation performed upon the organism from without—for example, water deprivation; (2) an inner condition—for example, physiological or psychic thirst; and (3) a kind of behavior—for example, drinking. Independent information about the second link would obviously permit us to predict the third without recourse to the first. It would be a preferred type of variable because it would be nonhistoric; the first link may lie in the past history of the organism, but the second is a current condition. Direct information about the second link is, however, seldom, if ever, available. Sometimes we infer the second link from the third: an animal is judged to be thirsty if it drinks. In that case, the explanation is spurious. Sometimes we infer the second link from the first: an animal is said to be thirsty if it has not drunk for a long time. In that case, we obviously cannot dispense with the prior history.

The second link is useless in the *control* of behavior unless we can manipulate it. At the moment, we have no way of directly altering neural processes at appropriate moments in the life of a behaving organism, nor has any way been discovered to alter a psychic process. We usually set up the second link through the first: we make an animal thirsty, in either the physiological or the psychic sense, by depriving it of water, feeding it salt, and so on. In that case, the second link obviously does not permit us to dispense with the first. Even if some new technical discovery were to enable us to set up or change the second link directly, we should still have to deal with those enormous areas in which human behavior is controlled through manipulation of the first link. A technique of operating upon the second link would increase our control of behavior, but the techniques which have already been developed would still remain to be analyzed.

The most objectionable practice is to follow the causal sequence back only as far as a hypothetical second link. This is a serious handicap both in a theoretical science and in the practical control of behavior. It is no help to be told that to get an organism to drink we are simply to "make it thirsty" unless we are also told how this is to be done. When we have obtained the necessary prescription for thirst, the whole proposal is more complex than it need be. Similarly, when an example of maladjusted behavior is explained by saying that the individual is "suffering from anxiety," we have still to be told the cause of the anxiety. But the external conditions which are then invoked could have been directly related to the maladjusted behavior. Again, when we are told that a man stole a loaf of bread because "he was hungry," we have still to learn of the external conditions responsible for the "hunger." These conditions would have sufficed to explain the theft.

The objection to inner states is not that they do not exist, but that they are not relevant in a functional analysis.[8] We cannot account for the be-

---

[8]This important clarification and qualification of Skinner's position has often been neglected by his critics over the years.

havior of any system while staying wholly inside it; eventually we must turn to forces operating upon the organism from without. Unless there is a weak spot in our causal chain so that the second link is not lawfully determined by the first, or the third by the second, then the first and third links must be lawfully related. If we must always go back beyond the second link for prediction and control, we may avoid many tiresome and exhausting digressions by examining the third link as a function of the first. Valid information about the second link may throw light upon this relationship but can in no way alter it.

A Functional Analysis

The external variables of which behavior is a function provide for what may be called a causal or functional analysis. We undertake to predict and control the behavior of the individual organism. This is our "dependent variable"—the effect for which we are to find the cause. Our "independent variables"—the causes of behavior—are the external conditions of which behavior is a function. Relations between the two—the "cause-and-effect relationships" in behavior—are the laws of a science. A synthesis of these laws expressed in quantitative terms yields a comprehensive picture of the organism as a behaving system.

This must be done within the bounds of a natural science. We cannot assume that behavior has any peculiar properties which require unique methods or special kinds of knowledge. It is often argued[9] that an act is not so important as the "intent" which lies behind it, or that it can be described only in terms of what it "means" to the behaving individual or to others whom it may affect. If statements of this sort are useful for scientific purposes, they must be based upon observable events, and we may confine ourselves to such

events exclusively in a functional analysis. Although such terms as "meaning" and "intent" appear to refer to properties of behavior, they usually conceal references to independent variables. This is also true of "aggressive," "friendly," "disorganized," "intelligent," and other terms which appear to describe properties of behavior but in reality refer to its controlling relations.

The independent variables must also be described in physical terms. An effort is often made to avoid the labor of analyzing a physical situation by guessing what it "means" to an organism or by distinguishing between the physical world and a psychological world of "experience." This practice also reflects a confusion between dependent and independent variables. The events affecting an organism must be capable of description in the language of physical science. It is sometimes argued that certain "social forces" or the "influences" of culture or tradition are exceptions. But we cannot appeal to entities of this sort without explaining how they can affect both the scientist and the individual under observation. The physical events which must then be appealed to in such an explanation will supply us with alternative material suitable for a physical analysis.

By confining ourselves to these observable events, we gain a considerable advantage, not only in theory, but in practice. A "social force" is no more useful in manipulating behavior than an inner state of hunger, anxiety, or skepticism. Just as we must trace these inner events to the manipulable variables of which they are said to be functions before we may put them to practical use, so we must identify the physical events through which a "social force" is said to affect the organism before we can manipulate it for purposes of control. In dealing with the directly observable data we need not refer to either the inner state or the outer force.

* * *

---

[9]For example, by humanistic, phenomenological, and cognitive psychologists.

Imitation of Film-Mediated Aggressive Models

Albert Bandura, Dorothea Ross, and Sheila A. Ross

The next selection is perhaps the most widely cited article by one of the most widely cited of all American psychologists, Albert Bandura. This article, originally published in 1963, is important for several reasons. First, its demonstration of imitative learning—in which a person watches and then performs a behavior, without ever having been rewarded or reinforced *for doing so—seemed revolutionary in contrast to the orthodox behaviorism that was still a dominant force in American psychology. Classical behavior theory maintained that a response becomes more likely after it has been reinforced; Bandura and his colleagues showed that such reinforcement is in fact not necessary.*

A second reason the article is important is that it has some obvious practical implications concerning the probable effect of televised violence—an issue that is probably even more important today (as that violence continues to escalate) than it was in 1963. It implies that such programming is dangerous because it can lead watchers—perhaps especially, young watchers—to imitate what it portrays.

A third reason to pay attention to this article is that it raises a theoretical issue that became important for the future development of personality psychology. The fact that watching a film can affect the watcher's later behavior implies that the watcher's mind must hold some sort of cognitive representation *of the action depicted in the film. In other words, the study not only suggests that behaviorism's insistence on the importance of reinforcement is incorrect but also implies that behaviorism's deliberate neglect of unobservable mental processes is similarly misguided. The present article does not make much of this implication, but it led directly to the development of the most recent paradigm in personality: the cognitive approach. Several examples of more recent research focusing directly on the implications of cognitive representations for behavior are presented later in this section.*

From *Journal of Abnormal and Social Psychology,* 66, 3–11, 1963.

* * *

A recent incident (*San Francisco Chronicle*, 1961) in which a boy was seriously knifed during a re-enactment of a switchblade knife fight the boys had seen the previous evening on a televised rerun of the James Dean movie, *Rebel Without a Cause*, is a dramatic illustration of the possible imitative influence of film stimulation. * * *

In an earlier experiment (Bandura & Huston, 1961), it was shown that children readily imitated aggressive behavior exhibited by a model in the presence of the model. A succeeding investigation (Bandura, Ross, & Ross, 1961) demonstrated that children exposed to aggressive models generalized aggressive responses to a new setting in which the model was absent. The present study sought to determine the extent to which film-mediated aggressive models may serve as an important source of imitative behavior.

Aggressive models can be ordered on a reality-fictional stimulus dimension with real-life models located at the reality end of the continuum, non-human cartoon characters at the fictional end, and films portraying human models occupying an intermediate position. It was predicted, on the basis of saliency and similarity of cues, that the more remote the model was from reality, the weaker would be the tendency for subjects to imitate the behavior of the model.

Of the various interpretations of imitative learning, the sensory feedback theory of imitation recently proposed by Mowrer (1960) is elaborated in greatest detail. According to this theory, if certain responses have been repeatedly positively reinforced, proprioceptive stimuli[1] associated with these responses acquire secondary reinforcing properties[2] and thus the individual is predisposed to perform the behavior for the positive feedback. Similarly, if responses have been negatively reinforced,[3] response correlated stimuli acquire the ca-

pacity to arouse anxiety which in turn, inhibits the occurrence of the negatively valenced behavior. On the basis of these considerations, it was predicted subjects who manifest high aggression anxiety would perform significantly less imitative and non-imitative aggression than subjects who display little anxiety over aggression. Since aggression is generally considered female inappropriate behavior, and therefore likely to be negatively reinforced[4] in girls (Sears, Maccoby, & Levin, 1957), it was also predicted that male subjects would be more imitative of aggression than females.

To the extent that observation of adults displaying aggression conveys a certain degree of permissiveness for aggressive behavior, it may be assumed that such exposure not only facilitates the learning of new aggressive responses but also weakens competing inhibitory responses in subjects and thereby increases the probability of occurrence of previously learned patterns of aggression. It was predicted, therefore, that subjects who observed aggressive models would display significantly more aggression when subsequently frustrated than subjects who were equally frustrated but who had no prior exposure to models exhibiting aggression.

Method

SUBJECTS   The subjects were 48 boys and 48 girls enrolled in the Stanford University Nursery School. They ranged in age from 35 to 69 months, with a mean age of 52 months.

Two adults, a male and a female, served in the role of models both in the real-life and the human film-aggression condition, and one female experimenter conducted the study for all 96 children.

GENERAL PROCEDURE   Subjects were divided into three experimental groups and one control group of 24 subjects each. One group of experimental subjects observed real-life aggressive models, a sec-

---

[1]These are sensations associated with a response that have stimulus qualities of their own.

[2]Become rewarding in themselves.

[3]Punished (note this use of "negatively reinforced" to refer to punishment is at variance with usual practice).

---

[4]Again, the authors here mean "punished."

ond group observed these same models portraying aggression on film, while a third group viewed a film depicting an aggressive cartoon character. The experimental groups were further subdivided into male and female subjects so that half the subjects in the two conditions involving human models were exposed to same-sex models, while the remaining subjects viewed models of the opposite sex.

Following the exposure experience, subjects were tested for the amount of imitative and non-imitative aggression in a different experimental setting in the absence of the models.

The control group subjects had no exposure to the aggressive models and were tested only in the generalization situation.

Subjects in the experimental and control groups were matched individually on the basis of ratings of their aggressive behavior in social interactions in the nursery school. The experimenter and a nursery school teacher rated the subjects on four five-point rating scales which measured the extent to which subjects displayed physical aggression, verbal aggression, aggression toward inanimate objects, and aggression inhibition. The latter scale, which dealt with the subjects' tendency to inhibit aggressive reactions in the face of high instigation, provided the measure of aggression anxiety. Seventy-one percent of the subjects were rated independently by both judges so as to permit an assessment of interrater agreement. The reliability of the composite aggression score estimated by means of the Pearson product-moment correlation, was .80.[5]

Data for subjects in the real-life aggression condition and in the control group were collected as part of a previous experiment (Bandura et al., 1961). Since the procedure is described in detail in the earlier report, only a brief description of it will be presented here.

EXPERIMENTAL CONDITIONS   Subjects in the Real-Life Aggressive condition were brought individu-

ally by the experimenter to the experimental room and the model, who was in the hallway outside the room, was invited by the experimenter to come and join in the game. The subject was then escorted to one corner of the room and seated at a small table which contained potato prints, multicolor picture stickers, and colored paper. After demonstrating how the subject could design pictures with the materials provided, the experimenter escorted the model to the opposite corner of the room which contained a small table and chair, a tinker toy set, a mallet, and a 5-foot inflated Bobo doll. The experimenter explained that this was the model's play area and after the model was seated, the experimenter left the experimental room.

The model began the session by assembling the tinker toys but after approximately a minute had elapsed, the model turned to the Bobo doll and spent the remainder of the period aggressing toward it with highly novel responses which are unlikely to be performed by children independently of the observation of the model's behavior. Thus, in addition to punching the Bobo doll, the model exhibited the following distinctive aggressive acts which were to be scored as imitative responses:

> The model sat on the Bobo doll and punched it repeatedly in the nose.
> The model then raised the Bobo doll and pommeled it on the head with a mallet.
> Following the mallet aggression, the model tossed the doll up in the air aggressively and kicked it about the room. This sequence of physically aggressive acts was repeated approximately three times interspersed with verbally aggressive responses such as, "Sock him in the nose . . . ," "Hit him down . . . ," "Throw him in the air . . . ," "Kick him . . . ," and "Pow."

Subjects in the Human Film-Aggression condition were brought by the experimenter to the semi-darkened experimental room, introduced to the picture materials, and informed that while the subjects worked on potato prints, a movie would be shown on a screen, positioned approximately 6 feet from the subject's table. The movie projector

---

[5]The raters tended to agree in their ratings of aggressiveness.

was located in a distant corner of the room and was screened from the subject's view by large wooden panels.

The color movie and a tape recording of the sound track was begun by a male projectionist as soon as the experimenter left the experimental room and was shown for a duration of 10 minutes. The models in the film presentations were the same adult males and females who participated in the Real-Life condition of the experiment. Similarly, the aggressive behavior they portrayed in the film was identical with their real-life performances.

For subjects in the Cartoon Film-Aggression condition, after seating the subject at the table with the picture construction material, the experimenter walked over to a television console approximately 3 feet in front of the subject's table, remarked, "I guess I'll turn on the color TV," and ostensibly tuned in a cartoon program. The experimenter then left the experimental room. The cartoon was shown on a glass lens screen in the television set by means of a rear projection arrangement screened from the subject's view by large panels.

The sequence of aggressive acts in the cartoon was performed by the female model costumed as a black cat similar to the many cartoon cats. In order to heighten the level of irreality of the cartoon, the floor area was covered with artificial grass and the walls forming the backdrop were adorned with brightly colored trees, birds, and butterflies creating a fantasyland setting. The cartoon began with a close-up of a stage on which the curtains were slowly drawn revealing a picture of a cartoon cat along with the title, *Herman the Cat*. The remainder of the film showed the cat pommeling the Bobo doll on the head with a mallet, sitting on the doll and punching it in the nose, tossing the doll in the air, and kicking it about the room in a manner identical with the performance in the other experimental conditions except that the cat's movements were characteristically feline. To induce further a cartoon set, the program was introduced and concluded with appropriate cartoon music, and the cat's verbal aggression was repeated in a high-pitched, animated voice.

In both film conditions, at the conclusion of the movie the experimenter entered the room and then escorted the subject to the test room.

AGGRESSION INSTIGATION   In order to differentiate clearly the exposure and test situations subjects were tested for the amount of imitative learning in a different experimental room which was set off from the main nursery school building.

The degree to which a child has learned aggressive patterns of behavior through imitation becomes most evident when the child is instigated to aggression on later occasions. Thus, for example, the effects of viewing the movie, *Rebel Without a Cause*, were not evident until the boys were instigated to aggression the following day, at which time they re-enacted the televised switchblade knife fight in considerable detail. For this reason, the children in the experiment, both those in the control group, and those who were exposed to the aggressive models, were mildly frustrated before they were brought to the test room.

Following the exposure experience, the experimenter brought the subject to an anteroom which contained a varied array of highly attractive toys. The experimenter explained that the toys were for the subject to play with, but, as soon as the subject became sufficiently involved with the play material, the experimenter remarked that these were her very best toys, that she did not let just anyone play with them, and that she had decided to reserve these toys for some other children. However, the subject could play with any of the toys in the next room. The experimenter and the subject then entered the adjoining experimental room.

* * *

TEST FOR DELAYED IMITATION   The experimental room contained a variety of toys, some of which could be used in imitative or nonimitative aggression, and others which tended to elicit predominantly nonaggressive forms of behavior. The aggressive toys included a 3-foot Bobo doll, a mallet and peg board, two dart guns, and a tether ball with a face painted on it which hung from the ceiling. The nonaggressive toys, on the other hand, included a tea set, crayons and coloring paper, a ball, two dolls, three bears, cars and trucks and plastic farm animals.

* * *

The subject spent 20 minutes in the experimental room during which time his behavior was rated in terms of predetermined response categories by judges who observed the session through a one-way mirror in an adjoining observation room. The 20-minute session was divided in 5-second intervals by means of an electric interval timer, thus yielding a total number of 240 response units for each subject.

The male model scored the experimental sessions for all subjects. In order to provide an estimate of interjudge agreement, the performances of 40% of the subjects were scored independently by a second observer. The responses scored involved highly specific concrete classes of behavior, and yielded high interscorer reliabilities, the product-moment coefficients being in the .90s.

RESPONSE MEASURES The following response measures were obtained:

Imitative aggression. This category included acts of striking the Bobo doll with the mallet, sitting on the doll and punching it in the nose, kicking the doll, tossing it in the air, and the verbally aggressive responses, "Sock him," "Hit him down," "Kick him," "Throw him in the air," and "Pow."

Partially imitative responses. A number of subjects imitated the essential components of the model's behavior but did not perform the complete act, or they directed the imitative aggressive response to some object other than the Bobo doll. Two responses of this type were scored and were interpreted as partially imitative behavior:

Mallet aggression. The subject strikes objects other than the Bobo doll aggressively with the mallet.

Sits on Bobo doll. The subject lays the Bobo doll on its side and sits on it, but does not aggress toward it.

Nonimitative aggression. This category included acts of punching, slapping, or pushing the doll, physically aggressive acts directed toward objects other than the Bobo doll, and any hostile remarks except for those in the verbal imitation category; for example, "Shoot the Bobo," "Cut him," "Stupid ball," "Knock over people," "Horses fighting, biting."

Aggressive gun play. The subject shoots darts or aims the guns and fires imaginary shots at objects in the room.

Ratings were also made of the number of behavior units in which subjects played nonaggressively or sat quietly and did not play with any of the material at all.

Results

The mean imitative and nonimitative aggression scores for subjects in the various experimental and control groups are presented in Table 1.

* * *

TOTAL AGGRESSION The mean total aggression scores for subjects in the real-life, human film, cartoon film, and the control groups are 83, 92, 99, and 54, respectively. The results of the analysis of variance performed on these scores reveal that the main effect of treatment conditions is significant ($\chi_r^2 = 9.06$, $p < .05$),[6] confirming the prediction that exposure of subjects to aggressive models in-

---

[6]The analysis of variance used here is known as a Friedman analysis of variance for ranks. The inferential statistic that is calculated, χ_r^2, is different from the F statistic that arises from the analysis of variance as it is now usually applied, but the two methods are conceptually equivalent. There is a low probability (p) that such differences among the aggression scores across conditions would occur by chance if there really was no condition effect.

TABLE 1

MEAN AGGRESSION SCORES FOR SUBGROUPS OF EXPERIMENTAL AND CONTROL SUBJECTS

| Response category | Experimental groups | | | | | Control group |
| | Real-life aggressive | | Human film-aggressive | | Cartoon film-aggressive | |
	F Model	M Model	F Model	M Model		
Total aggrerssion						
Girls	65.8	57.3	87.0	79.5	80.9	36.4
Boys	76.8	131.8	114.5	85.0	117.2	72.2
Imitative aggression						
Girls	19.2	9.2	10.0	8.0	7.8	1.8
Boys	18.4	38.4	34.3	13.3	16.2	3.9
Mlalet aggression						
Girls	17.2	18.7	49.2	19.5	36.8	13.1
Boys	15.5	28.8	20.5	16.3	12.5	13.5
Sits on Bobo Doll[a]						
Girls	10.4	5.6	10.3	4.5	15.3	3.3
Boys	1.3	0.7	7.7	0.0	5.6	0.6
Nonimitative aggression						
Girls	27.6	24.9	24.0	34.3	27.5	17.8
Boys	35.5	48.6	46.8	31.8	71.8	40.4
Aggressive gun play						
Girls	1.8	4.5	3.8	17.6	8.8	3.7
Boys	7.3	15.9	12.8	23.7	16.6	14.3

[a]This response category was not included in the total aggression score.

creases the probability that subjects will respond aggressively when instigated on later occasions. Further analyses * * * show that subjects who viewed the real-life models and the film-mediated models do not differ from each other in total aggressiveness but all three experimental groups expressed significantly more aggressive behavior than the control subjects.

IMITATIVE AGGRESSIVE RESPONSES

* * *

Illustrations of the extent to which some of the subjects became virtually "carbon copies" of their models in aggressive behavior are presented in Figure 1. The top frame shows the female model performing the four novel aggressive responses; the lower frames depict a male and a female subject re-

producing the behavior of the female model they had observed earlier on film.

The prediction that imitation is positively related to the reality cues of the model was only partially supported. While subjects who observed the real-life aggressive models exhibited significantly more imitative aggression than subjects who viewed the cartoon model, no significant differences were found between the live and film, and the film and cartoon conditions, nor did the three experimental groups differ significantly in total aggression or in the performances of partially imitative behavior. Indeed, the available data suggest that, of the three experimental conditions, exposure to humans on film portraying aggression was the most influential in eliciting and shaping aggressive behavior. Subjects in this condition, in relation to the control subjects, exhibited more total

Figure 1 Photographs from the film *Social Learning of Aggression through Imitation of Aggressive Models.*

aggression, more imitative aggression, more partially imitative behavior, such as sitting on the Bobo doll and mallet aggression, and they engaged in significantly more aggressive gun play. In addition, they performed significantly more aggressive gun play than did subjects who were exposed to the real-life aggressive models.

INFLUENCE OF SEX OF MODEL AND SEX OF CHILD

In order to determine the influence of sex of model and sex of child on the expression of imitative and nonimitative aggression, the data from the experimental groups were combined and the significance of the differences between groups was assessed by *t* tests for uncorrelated means. * * *

Sex of subjects had a highly significant effect on both the learning and the performance of aggression. Boys, in relation to girls, exhibited significantly more total aggression ($t = 2.69$, $p < .01$), more imitative aggression ($t = 2.82$, $p < .005$), more aggressive gun play ($z = 3.38$, $p < .001$), and

more nonimitative aggressive behavior ($t = 2.98$, $p < .005$). Girls, on the other hand, were more inclined than boys to sit on the Bobo doll but refrained from punching it ($z = 3.47$, $p < .001$).[7]

* * *

Discussion

The results of the present study provide strong evidence that exposure to filmed aggression heightens aggressive reactions in children. Subjects who viewed the aggressive human and cartoon models on film exhibited nearly twice as much aggression than did subjects in the control group who were not exposed to the aggressive film content.

In the experimental design typically employed

---

[7]Both the *t* and *z* statistics here are used to compare group means; the *p* level derived from these statistics evaluates the probability that a difference of the size obtained would occur if no difference actually existed.

* * * , subjects are first frustrated, then provided with an opportunity to view an aggressive film following which their overt or fantasy aggression is measured. While this procedure yields some information on the immediate influence of film-mediated aggression, the full effects of such exposure may not be revealed until subjects are instigated to aggression on a later occasion. Thus, the present study, and one recently reported by Lö-vaas (1961), both utilizing a design in which subjects first observed filmed aggression and then were frustrated, clearly reveal that observation of models portraying aggression on film substantially increases rather than decreases the probability of aggressive reactions to subsequent frustrations.

Filmed aggression not only facilitated the expression of aggression, but also effectively shaped the form of the subjects' aggressive behavior. The finding that children modeled their behavior to some extent after the film characters suggests that pictorial mass media, particularly television, may serve as an important source of social behavior. In fact, a possible generalization of responses originally learned in the television situation to the experimental film may account for the significantly greater amount of aggressive gun play displayed by subjects in the film condition as compared to subjects in the real-life and control groups. It is unfortunate that the qualitative features of the gun behavior were not scored since subjects in the film condition, unlike those in the other two groups, developed interesting elaborations in gun play (for example, stalking the imaginary opponent; quick drawing, and rapid firing), characteristic of the Western gun fighter.

* * * Although the results of the present experiment demonstrate that the vast majority of children *learn* patterns of social behavior through pictorial stimulation, nevertheless, informal observation suggests that children do not, as a rule, *perform* indiscriminately the behavior of televised characters, even those they regard as highly attractive models. The replies of parents whose children participated in the present study to an open-end questionnaire item concerning their handling of imitative behavior suggest that this may be in part a function of negative reinforcement,[8] as most parents were quick to discourage their children's overt imitation of television characters by prohibiting certain programs or by labeling the imitative behavior in a disapproving manner. From our knowledge of the effects of punishment on behavior, the responses in question would be expected to retain their original strength and could reappear on later occasions in the presence of appropriate eliciting stimuli, particularly if instigation is high, the instruments for aggression are available, and the threat of noxious consequences is reduced.

* * *

A question may be raised as to whether the aggressive acts studied in the present experiment constitute "genuine" aggressive responses. Aggression is typically defined as behavior, the goal or intent of which is injury to a person, or destruction of an object (Bandura & Walters, 1959; Dollard, Doob, Miller, Mowrer, & Sears, 1939; Sears, Maccoby, & Levin, 1957). Since intentionality is not a property of behavior but primarily an inference concerning antecedent events, the categorization of an act as "aggressive" involves a consideration of both stimulus and mediating or terminal response events.

According to a social learning theory of aggression recently proposed by Bandura and Walters (1963), most of the responses utilized to hurt or to injure others (for example, striking, kicking, and other responses of high magnitude), are probably learned for prosocial purposes under nonfrustration conditions. Since frustration generally elicits responses of high magnitude, the latter classes of responses, once acquired, may be called out in social interactions for the purpose of injuring others. On the basis of this theory it would be predicted that the aggressive responses acquired imitatively, while not necessarily mediating aggressive goals in the experimental situation, would be utilized to serve such purposes in other social settings, with higher frequency by children in the experimental conditions than by children in the control group.

---

[8]Punishment.

The present study involved primarily vicarious or empathic learning (Mowrer, 1960) in that subjects acquired a relatively complex repertoire of aggressive responses by the mere sight of a model's behavior. It has been generally assumed that the necessary conditions for the occurrence of such learning is that the model perform certain responses followed by positive reinforcement to the model (Hill, 1960; Mowrer, 1960). According to this theory, to the extent that the observer experiences the model's reinforcement vicariously, the observer will be prone to reproduce the model's behavior. While there is some evidence from experiments involving both human (Lewis & Duncan, 1958; McBrearty, Marston, & Kanfer, 1961; Sechrest, 1961) and animal subjects (Darby & Riopelle, 1959; Warden, Fjeld, & Koch, 1940), that vicarious reinforcement may in fact increase the probability of the behavior in question, it is apparent from the results of the experiment reported in this paper that a good deal of human imitative learning can occur without any reinforcers delivered either to the model or to the observer. * * *

References

Bandura, A., & Huston, Aletha C. (1961). Identification as a process of incidental learning. *Journal of Abnormal and Social Psychology, 63*, 311–318.

Bandura, A., Ross, Dorothea, & Ross, Sheila A. (1961). Transmission of aggression through imitation of aggressive models. *Journal of Abnormal and Social Psychology, 63*, 575–582.

Bandura, A., & Walters, R. H. (1959). *Adolescent aggression.* New York: Ronald.

Bandura, A., & Walters, R. H. (1963). *Social learning and personality development.* New York: Holt, Rinehart, & Winston.

Darby, C. L., & Riopelle, A. J. Observational learning in the Rhesus monkey. (1959). *Journal of Comparative Physiology and Psychology, 52*, 94–98.

Dollard, J., Doob, L. W., Miller, N. E., Mowrer, O. H., & Sears, R. R. (1939). *Frustration and aggression.* New Haven: Yale University Press.

Hill, W. F. (1960). Learning theory and the acquisition of values. *Psychological Review, 67*, 317–331.

Lewis, D. J., & Duncan, C. P. (1958). Vicarious experience and partial reinforcement. *Journal of Abnormal and Social Psychology, 57*, 321–326.

Lövaas, O. J. (1961). Effect of exposure to symbolic aggression on aggressive behavior. *Child Development, 32*, 37–44.

McBrearty, J. F., Marston, A. R., & Kanfer, F. H. (1961). Conditioning a verbal operant in a group setting: Direct vs. vicarious reinforcement. *American Psychologist, 16*, 425. (Abstract)

Mowrer, O. H. (1960). *Learning theory and the symbolic processes.* New York: Wiley.

San Francisco Chronicle. (1961). "James Dean" knifing in South City. *San Francisco Chronicle*, March 1, p. 6.

Sears, R. R., Maccoby, Eleanor E., & Levin, H. (1957). *Patterns of child rearing.* Evanston: Row, Peterson.

Sechrest, L. (1961). Vicarious reinforcement of responses. *American Psychologist, 16*, 356. (Abstract)

Warden, C. J., Field, H. A., & Koch, A. M. (1940). Imitative behavior in cebus and Rhesus monkeys. *Journal of Genetic Psychology, 56*, 311–322.

The Self System in Reciprocal Determinism

Albert Bandura

*The most prominent of the social learning theorists, Albert Bandura, helped lead
the way as social learning theory evolved into the cognitive approach of personality. Indeed, in some of his most recent writings, Bandura calls his approach social
cognitive theory.*

*The following selection, published at the height of Bandura's career, could be
considered one of the first important entries in this new approach. It is an ambitious effort; Bandura tackles the heavy philosophical issues that surround "basic
conceptions of human nature." He points out that the behaviorists and the humanists, seemingly opposite in viewpoint, share one basic idea: the unidirectional
causation of behavior. That is, behaviorists see behavior as a function of reinforcements in the environment or the situation. At the opposite end, humanists see
behavior as a function of the person, of his or her characteristics and most important, his or her free choice. In the following selection, Bandura seeks a middle
ground between these seemingly irreconcilable viewpoints.*

*Bandura does this by proposing the existence of a "self system." This cognitive
system, consisting of thoughts and feelings about the self, arises as a result of experience but, once constructed, has important effects on behavior. For example, the
self system sets goals and evaluates one's own progress toward those goals. Just as
importantly, the self system affects one's environment by (1) administering rewards
and punishments to the self (such as promising oneself an ice cream as soon as one
finishes reading Bandura's chapter) and by (2) selecting the environments that one
enters. For example, once a student enrolls at college he or she is buffeted by all
sorts of environmental pressures—rewards and punishments—that coerce the student to study for exams, write term papers, camp out in the library, and so on. But
whether to enroll in college in the first place is a choice made by the self system.
Similarly, activities and self-evaluations are critically influenced by the people one
is surrounded by. To an important degree, a person chooses his or her companions
and so chooses who to be influenced by.*

*If you pushed Bandura into a corner, he would probably have to admit to be-
ing a behaviorist at heart, despite his advocacy for the self system. This is because*

he views the self system as being, in the final analysis, a result of the environment. But by viewing the self system as something that, once constructed, can shape behavior and even shape the environment (through a process Bandura calls "reciprocal determinism"), Bandura opens up possibilities for the analysis and prediction of behavior that go beyond anything envisaged by classical behaviorism. Furthermore, he paves the way for further research to examine implications of cognitive structures and processes for behavior.

From *American Psychologist*, 33, 344–358, 1978.

Recent years have witnessed a heightened interest in the basic conceptions of human nature underlying different psychological theories. This interest stems in part from growing recognition of how such conceptions delimit research to selected processes and are in turn shaped by findings of paradigms embodying the particular view. As psychological knowledge is converted to behavioral technologies, the models of human behavior on which research is premised have important social as well as theoretical implications (Bandura, 1974).

Explanations of human behavior have generally been couched in terms of a limited set of determinants, usually portrayed as operating in a unidirectional manner. Exponents of environmental determinism study and theorize about how behavior is controlled by situational influences. Those favoring personal determinism seek the causes of human behavior in dispositional sources in the form of instincts, drives, traits, and other motivational forces within the individual. * * *

* * * The present article analyzes the various causal models and the role of self influences in behavior from the perspective of reciprocal determinism.

Unidirectional environmental determinism is carried to its extreme in the more radical forms of behaviorism. * * * ([For example] "A person does not act upon the world, the world acts upon him," Skinner, 1971, p. 211.) The environment thus becomes an autonomous force that automatically shapes, orchestrates, and controls behavior. * * *

* * *

There exists no shortage of advocates of alternative theories emphasizing the personal determination of environments. Humanists and existentialists,[1] who stress the human capacity for conscious judgment and intentional action, contend that individuals determine what they become by their own free choices. Most psychologists find conceptions of human behavior in terms of unidirectional personal determinism as unsatisfying as those espousing unidirectional environmental determinism. To contend that mind creates reality fails to acknowledge that environmental influences partly determine what people attend to, perceive, and think. To contend further that the methods of natural science are incapable of dealing with personal determinants of behavior does not enlist many supporters from the ranks of those who are moved more by empirical evidence than by philosophic discourse.

Social learning theory (Bandura, 1974, 1977b) analyzes behavior in terms of reciprocal determinism. The term *determinism* is used here to signify the production of effects by events, rather than in the doctrinal sense that actions are completely determined by a prior sequence of causes independent of the individual. Because of the complexity of interacting factors, events produce effects probabilistically rather than inevitably. In their transactions with the environment, people are not simply reactors to external stimulation. Most external in-

[1]Such as represented in Part V.

fluences affect behavior through intermediary cognitive processes. Cognitive factors partly determine which external events will be observed, how they will be perceived, whether they have any lasting effects, what valence and efficacy they have, and how the information they convey will be organized for future use. The extraordinary capacity of humans to use symbols enables them to engage in reflective thought, to create, and to plan foresightful courses of action in thought rather than having to perform possible options and suffer the consequences of thoughtless action. By altering their immediate environment, by creating cognitive self-inducements, and by arranging conditional incentives for themselves, people can exercise some influence over their own behavior. An act therefore includes among its determinants self-produced influences.

It is true that behavior is influenced by the environment, but the environment is partly of a person's own making. By their actions, people play a role in creating the social milieu and other circumstances that arise in their daily transactions. Thus, from the social learning perspective, psychological functioning involves a continuous reciprocal interaction between behavioral, cognitive, and environmental influences.

Reciprocal Determinism and Interactionism

*   *   *

Interaction processes have been conceptualized in three fundamentally different ways. These alternative formulations are summarized schematically in Figure 1. In the unidirectional notion of interaction, persons and situations are treated as independent entities that combine to produce behavior. This commonly held view can be called into question on both conceptual and empirical grounds. Personal and environmental factors do not function as independent determinants; rather, they determine each other. Nor can "persons" be considered causes independent of their behavior. It is largely through their actions that people produce the environmental conditions that affect their behavior in a reciprocal fashion. The experiences

generated by behavior also partly determine what individuals think, expect, and can do, which in turn, affect their subsequent behavior.

A second conception of interaction acknowledges that personal and environmental influences are bidirectional, but it retains a unidirectional view of behavior. In this analysis, persons and situations are considered to be interdependent causes of behavior, but behavior is treated as though it were only a by-product that does not figure at all in the causal process. * * *

*   *   *

In the social learning view of interaction, which is analyzed as a process of reciprocal determinism (Bandura, 1977b), behavior, internal personal factors, and environmental influences all operate as interlocking determinants of each other. As shown in Figure 1, the process involves a triadic reciprocal interaction rather than a dyadic conjoint or a dyadic bidirectional one. We have already noted that behavior and environmental conditions function as reciprocally interacting determinants. Internal personal factors (e.g., conceptions, beliefs, self-perceptions) and behavior also operate as reciprocal determinants of each other. For example, people's efficacy and outcome expectations influence how they behave, and the environmental effects created by their actions in turn alter their expectations. People activate different environmental reactions, apart from their behavior, by their physical characteristics (e.g., size, physiognomy, race, sex, attractiveness) and socially conferred attributes, roles, and status. The differential social treatment affects recipients' self-conceptions and actions in ways that either maintain or alter the environmental biases.

The relative influence exerted by these three sets of interlocking factors will vary in different individuals and under different circumstances. In some cases, environmental conditions exercise such powerful constraints on behavior that they emerge as the overriding determinants. If, for example, people are dropped in deep water they will all promptly engage in swimming activities, however uniquely varied they might be in their cognitive and behavioral repertoires. There are times

Unidirectional

$$B = f(P, E)$$

Partially Bidirectional

$$B = f(P \rightleftharpoons E)$$

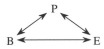

Figure 1 Schematic representation of three alternative conceptions of interaction: *B* signifies behavior, *P* the cognitive and other internal events that can affect perceptions and actions, and *E* the external environment.

when behavior is the central factor in the interlocking system. One example of this is persons who play familiar piano selections for themselves that create a pleasing sensory environment. The behavior is self-regulated over a long period by the sensory effects it produces, whereas cognitive activities and contextual environmental events are not much involved in the process.

In other instances, cognitive factors serve as the predominant influence in the regulatory system. The activation and maintenance of defensive behavior is a good case in point. False beliefs activate avoidance responses that keep individuals out of touch with prevailing environmental conditions, thus creating a strong reciprocal interaction between beliefs and action that is protected from corrective environmental influence. In extreme cases, behavior is so powerfully controlled by bizarre internal contingencies that neither the beliefs nor the accompanying actions are much affected even by extremely punishing environmental consequences (Bateson, 1961).

In still other instances, the development and activation of the three interlocking factors are all highly interdependent. Television-viewing behavior provides an everyday example. Personal preferences influence when and which programs, from among the available alternatives, individuals choose to watch on television. Although the potential televised environment is identical for all view-

ers, the actual televised environment that impinges on given individuals depends on what they select to watch. Through their viewing behavior, they partly shape the nature of the future televised environment. Because production costs and commercial requirements also determine what people are shown, the options provided in the televised environment partly shape the viewers' preferences. Here, all three factors—viewer preferences, viewing behavior, and televised offerings—reciprocally affect each other.

The methodology for elucidating psychological processes requires analysis of sequential interactions between the triadic, interdependent factors within the interlocking system. Investigations of reciprocal processes have thus far rarely, if ever, examined more than two of the interacting factors simultaneously. Some studies analyze how cognitions and behavior affect each other in a reciprocal fashion (Bandura, 1977a; Bandura & Adams, 1977). More often, however, the sequential analysis centers on how social behavior and environment determine each other. In these studies of dyadic exchanges, behavior creates certain conditions and is, in turn, altered by the very conditions it creates (Bandura, Lipsher, & Miller, 1960; Patterson, 1975; Raush, Barry, Hertel, & Swain, 1974; Thomas & Martin, 1976).

From the perspective of reciprocal determinism, the common practice of searching for the ultimate environmental cause of behavior is an idle exercise because, in an interactional process, one and the same event can be a stimulus, a response, or an environmental reinforcer, depending on where in the sequence the analysis arbitrarily begins.

* * *

* * * Regulatory processes are not governed solely by the reciprocal influence of antecedent and consequent acts. While behaving, people are also cognitively appraising the progression of events. Their thoughts about the probable effects of prospective actions partly determine how acts are affected by their immediate environmental consequences. Consider, for example, investigations of reciprocal coercive behavior in an ongoing dyadic interaction. In discordant families, coercive behavior by one member tends to elicit coercive counteractions from recipients in a mutual escalation of aggression (Patterson, 1975). However, coercion often does not produce coercive counteractions. To increase the predictive power of a theory of behavior, it is necessary to broaden the analysis to include cognitive factors that operate in the interlocking system. Counterresponses to antecedent acts are influenced not only by their immediate effects but also by judgments of later consequences for a given course of action. Thus, aggressive children will continue, or even escalate, coercive behavior in the face of immediate punishment when they expect persistence eventually to gain them what they seek. But the same momentary punishment will serve as an inhibitor rather than as an enhancer of coercion when they expect continuance of the aversive conduct to be ineffective. * * *

Cognitions do not arise in a vacuum, nor do they function as autonomous determinants of behavior. In the social learning analysis of cognitive development, conceptions about oneself and the nature of the environment are developed and verified through four different processes (Bandura, 1977b). People derive much of their knowledge from direct experience of the effects produced by their actions. Indeed, most theories of cognitive development, whether they favor behavioristic, information-processing, or Piagetian[2] orientations, focus almost exclusively on cognitive change through feedback from direct experimentation. However, results of one's own actions are not the sole source of knowledge. Information about the nature of things is frequently extracted from vicarious experience. In this mode of verification, observation of the effects produced by somebody else's actions serves as the source and authentication of thoughts.

There are many things we cannot come to know by direct or vicarious experience because of limited accessibility or because the matters involve metaphysical ideas that are not subject to objective confirmation. When experiential verification is either difficult or impossible, people develop and evaluate their conceptions of things in terms of the judgments voiced by others. In addition to enactive, vicarious, and social sources of thought verification, all of which rely on external influences, logical verification also enters into the process, especially in later phases of development. After people acquire some rules of inference, they can evaluate the soundness of their reasoning and derive from what they already know new knowledge about things that extend beyond their experiences.

External influences play a role not only in the development of cognitions but in their activation as well. Different sights, smells, and sounds will elicit quite different trains of thought. Thus, while it is true that conceptions govern behavior, the conceptions themselves are partly fashioned from direct or mediated transactions with the environment. A complete analysis of reciprocal determinism therefore requires investigation of how all three sets of factors—cognitive, behavioral, and environmental—interact reciprocally among themselves. Contrary to common misconception, social learning theory does not disregard personal determinants of behavior. Within this perspective, such determinants are treated as integral, dynamic factors in causal processes rather than as static trait dimensions.

Self-Regulatory Functions of the Self System

The differences between unidirectional and reciprocal analyses of behavior have been drawn most sharply in the area of self-regulatory phenomena. Exponents of radical behaviorism have always disavowed any construct of self for fear that it would usher in psychic agents and divert attention from physical to experiential reality.[3] While this ap-

---

[2]Jean Piaget was a Swiss psychologist whose ideas have had an important influence on developmental psychology. The idea referred to here concerns Piaget's description of how the mind develops through an interaction between knowledge and experience.

[3]We saw Skinner raise exactly this worry in the selections earlier in this section.

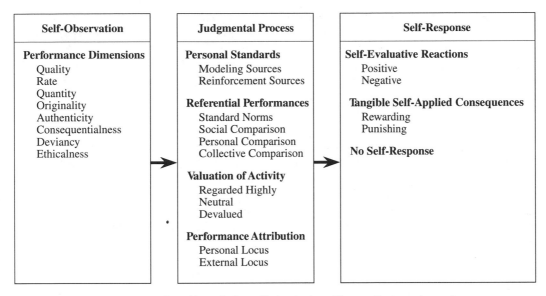

Self-Observation	Judgmental Process	Self-Response
Performance Dimensions Quality Rate Quantity Originality Authenticity Consequentialness Deviancy Ethicalness	**Personal Standards** Modeling Sources Reinforcement Sources **Referential Performances** Standard Norms Social Comparison Personal Comparison Collective Comparison **Valuation of Activity** Regarded Highly Neutral Devalued **Performance Attribution** Personal Locus External Locus	**Self-Evaluative Reactions** Positive Negative **Tangible Self-Applied Consequences** Rewarding Punishing **No Self-Response**

Figure 2   Component processes in the self-regulation of behavior by self-prescribed contingencies.

proach encompasses a large set of environmental factors, it assumes that self-generated influences either do not exist or, if they do, that they have no effect upon behavior. Internal events are treated simply as an intermediate link in a causal chain. Since environmental conditions presumably create the intermediate link, one can explain behavior in terms of external factors without recourse to any internal determinants. Through a conceptual bypass, cognitive determinants are thus excised from the analysis of causal processes.

In contrast to the latter view, internal determinants of behavior are gaining increasing attention in contemporary theorizing and research. Indeed, self-referent processes occupy a central position in social learning theory (Bandura, 1977b). As will be shown later, self-generated events cannot be relegated to a redundant explanatory link. In the triadic reciprocal system, they not only operate as reciprocal determinants of behavior but they play a role in the perception and formation of the environmental influences themselves.

* * *

In social learning theory, a self system is not a psychic agent that controls behavior. Rather, it refers to cognitive structures that provide reference

mechanisms and to a set of subfunctions for the perception, evaluation, and regulation of behavior. Before proceeding to a reciprocal analysis of self influences, the processes by which people exercise some control over their own behavior will be reviewed briefly.

COMPONENT PROCESSES IN SELF-REGULATION
Figure 2 summarizes the different component processes in the self-regulation of behavior through self-prescribed contingencies. Behavior typically varies on a number of dimensions, some of which are listed in the self-observation component. Depending on value orientations and the functional significance of given activities, people attend selectively to certain aspects of their behavior and ignore variations on nonrelevant dimensions.

Simply observing variations in one's performances yields some relevant information, but such data, in themselves, do not provide any basis for personal reactions. Behavior produces self-reactions through a judgmental function that includes several subsidiary processes. Whether a given performance will be regarded as commendable or dissatisfying depends upon the personal standards against which it is evaluated. Actions that measure up to internal standards are appraised favorably; those that fall short are judged unsatisfactory.

For most activities, there are no absolute measures of adequacy. The time in which a given distance is run, the number of points obtained on an achievement test, or the size of charitable contributions often do not convey sufficient information for self-appraisal even when compared with an internal standard. When adequacy is defined relationally, performances are evaluated by comparing them with those of others. The referential comparisons may involve standard norms, the performances of particular individuals, or the accomplishments of reference groups.

One's previous behavior is continuously used as the reference against which ongoing performance is judged. In this referential process, it is self-comparison that supplies the measure of adequacy. Past attainments influence performance appraisals mainly through their effects on standard setting. After a given level of performance is attained, it is no longer challenging, and new self-satisfactions are often sought through progressive improvement.

Another important factor in the judgmental component of self-regulation concerns the evaluation of the activities. People do not much care how they perform on tasks that have little or no significance for them. And little effort is expended on devalued activities. It is mainly in areas affecting one's welfare and self-esteem that favorable performance appraisals activate personal consequences (Simon, 1978).

Self-reactions also vary depending on how people perceive the determinants of their behavior. They take pride in their accomplishments when they ascribe their successes to their own abilities and efforts. They do not derive much self-satisfaction, however, when they view their performances as heavily dependent on external factors. The same is true for judgments of failure and blameworthy conduct. People respond self-critically to inadequate performances for which they hold themselves responsible but not to those which they perceive are due to unusual circumstances or to insufficient capabilities. Performance appraisals set the occasion for self-produced consequences. Favorable judgments give rise to rewarding self-reactions, whereas unfavorable appraisals activate negative self-reactions. Performances that are judged to have no personal significance do not generate any reactions one way or another.

In the social learning view, self-regulated incentives alter performance mainly through their motivational function (Bandura, 1976). Contingent self-reward improves performance not because it strengthens preceding responses. When people make self-satisfaction or tangible gratifications conditional upon certain accomplishments, they motivate themselves to expend the effort needed to attain the desired performances. Both the anticipated satisfactions of desired accomplishments and the dissatisfactions with insufficient ones provide incentives for actions that increase the likelihood of performance attainments.

Much human behavior is regulated through self-evaluative consequences in the form of self-satisfaction, self-pride, self-dissatisfaction, and self-criticism. The act of writing is a familiar example of a behavior that is continuously self-regulated through evaluative self-reactions. Writers adopt a standard of what constitutes an acceptable piece of work. Ideas are generated and rephrased in thought before they are committed to paper. Provisional contructions are successively revised until authors are satisfied with what they have written. The more exacting the personal standards, the more extensive are the corrective improvements.

People also get themselves to do things they would otherwise put off by making tangible outcomes conditional upon completing a specified level of performance. In programs of self-directed change, individuals improve and maintain behavior on their own over long periods by arranging incentives for themselves (Bandura, 1976; Goldfried & Merbaum, 1973; Mahoney & Thoresen, 1974). In many instances, activities are regulated through self-prescribed contingencies involving both evaluative and tangible self-rewards. Authors influence how much they write by making breaks, recreational activities, and other tangible rewards contingent on completing a certain amount of work (Wallace, 1977), but they revise and improve what they write by their self-evaluative reactions.

* * *

Reciprocal Influence of External Factors on Self-Regulatory Functions

Social learning theory regards self-generated influences not as autonomous regulators of behavior but as contributory influences in a reciprocally interacting system. A variety of external factors serve as reciprocal influences on the operation of a self system. They can affect self-regulatory processes in at least three major ways: They are involved in the development of the component functions in self-regulatory systems; they provide partial support for adherence to self-prescribed contingencies; and they facilitate selective activation and disengagement of internal contingencies governing conduct.

DEVELOPMENT OF SELF-REGULATORY FUNCTIONS

The development of capabilities for self-reaction requires adoption of standards against which performances can be evaluated. These internal criteria do not emerge in a vacuum. Behavioral standards are established by precept, evaluative consequences accompanying different performances, and exposure to the self-evaluative standards modeled by others (Bandura, 1976, 1977b; Masters & Mokros, 1974). People do not passively absorb behavioral standards from the environmental stimuli that happen to impinge upon them. They extract generic standards from the multiplicity of evaluative reactions that are exemplified and taught by different individuals or by the same individuals on different activities and in different settings (Bandura, 1976; Lepper, Sagotsky, & Mailer, 1975). People must therefore process the divergent information and eventually arrive at personal standards against which to measure their own behavior.

Associational preferences add another reciprocal element to the acquisition process. The people with whom one regularly associates partly influence the standards of behavior that are adopted. Value orientations, in turn, exercise selective influence on choices of activities and associates (Bandura & Walters, 1959; Krauss, 1964).

EXTERNAL SUPPORTS FOR SELF-REGULATORY SYSTEMS

In analyzing regulation of behavior through self-produced consequences, one must distinguish between two different sources of incentives that operate in the system. First, there is the arrangement of self-reward contingent upon designated performances to create proximal incentives for oneself to engage in the activities. Second, there are the more distal incentives for adhering to the self-prescribed contingencies.

Adherence to performance requirements for self-reward is partly sustained by periodic environmental influences that take a variety of forms (Bandura, 1977b). First, there are the negative sanctions for unmerited self-reward. When standards are being acquired or when they are later applied inconsistently, rewarding oneself for undeserving performances is more likely than not to evoke critical reactions from others. Occasional sanctions for unmerited self-reward influence the likelihood that people will withhold rewards from themselves until their behavior matches their standards (Bandura, Mahoney, & Dirks, 1976). Personal sanctions operate as well in fostering such adherence. After people adopt codes of conduct, when they perform inadequately or violate their standards they tend to engage in self-critical and other distressing trains of thought. Anticipated, thought-produced distress over faulty behavior provides an internal incentive to abide by personal standards of performance (Bandura, 1977b).

Negative inducements, whether personal or social, are not the most reliable basis upon which to rest a system of self-regulation. Fortunately, there are more advantageous reasons for exercising some influence over one's own behavior through self-arranged incentives. Some of these personal benefits are extrinsic to the behavior; others derive from the behavior itself.

People are motivated to institute performance

contingencies for themselves when the behavior they seek to change is aversive. To overweight persons, the discomforts, maladies, and social costs of obesity create inducements to control their overeating. Similarly, students are prompted to improve their study behavior when failures in course work make academic life sufficiently distressing. By making self-reward conditional upon performance attainments, individuals can reduce aversive behavior, thereby creating natural benefits for their efforts.

The benefits of self-regulated change may provide natural incentives for adherence to personal prescriptions for valued activities as well as for unpleasant ones. People often motivate themselves by conditional incentives to enhance their skills in activities they aspire to master. Here the personal benefits derived from improved proficiency support self-prescription of contingencies. Self-generated inducements are especially important in ensuring continual progress in creative endeavors, because people have to develop their own work schedules for themselves. There are no clocks to punch or supervisors to issue directives. In analyzing the writing habits and self-discipline of novelists, Wallace (1977) documents how famous novelists regulate their writing output by making self-reward contingent upon completion of a certain amount of writing each day whether the spirit moves them or not.

If societies relied solely on inherent benefits to sustain personal contingencies, many activities that are tiresome and uninteresting until proficiency in them is acquired would never be mastered. Upholding standards is therefore socially promoted by a vast system of rewards including praise, social recognition, and honors. Few accolades are bestowed on people for self-rewarding their mediocre performances. Direct praise or seeing others publicly recognized for upholding excellence fosters adherence to high performance standards (Bandura, Grusec, & Menlove, 1967).

* * *

Because personal and environmental determinants affect each other in a reciprocal fashion, attempts to assign causal priority to these two sources of influence reduce to the "chicken-or-egg" debate. The quest for the ultimate environmental determinant of activities regulated by self-influence becomes a regressive exercise that can yield no victors in explanatory contests, because for every ultimate environmental cause that is invoked, one can find prior actions that helped to produce it.

SELECTIVE ACTIVATION AND DISENGAGEMENT OF SELF-REACTIVE INFLUENCES The third area of research on the role of external factors in self-regulation centers on the selective activation and disengagement of self-reactive influences (Bandura, 1977b). Theories of internalization that portray incorporated entities (e.g., the conscience or superego, moral codes) as continuous internal overseers of conduct are usually at a loss to explain the variable operation of internal control and the perpetration of inhumanities by otherwise humane people.

In the social learning analysis, considerate people perform culpable acts because of the reciprocal dynamics between personal and situational determinants of behavior rather than because of defects in their moral structures. Development of self-regulatory capabilities does not create an invariant control mechanism within a person. Self-evaluative influences do not operate unless activated, and many situational dynamics influence their selective activation.

After ethical and moral standards of conduct are adopted, anticipatory self-censuring reactions for violating personal standards ordinarily serve as self-deterrents against reprehensible acts (Bandura & Walters, 1959).[4] Self-deterring consequences are likely to be activated most strongly when the causal connection between conduct and the detrimental effects it produces is unambiguous. There are various means, however, by which self-evaluative consequences can be dissociated from reprehensible behavior. * * *

One set of disengagement practices operates at

---

[4]That is, you know you will feel guilty if you do it.

the level of the behavior. What is culpable can be made honorable through moral justifications and palliative characterizations (Gambino, 1973; Kelman, 1973). In this process, reprehensible conduct is made personally and socially acceptable by portraying it in the service of beneficial or moral ends. Such cognitive restructuring of behavior is an especially effective disinhibitor because it not only eliminates self-generated deterrents but engages self-reward in the service of the behavior.

Another set of dissociative practices operates by obscuring or distorting the relationship between actions and the effects they cause. By displacing and diffusing responsibility, people do not see themselves as personally accountable for their actions and are thus spared self-prohibiting reactions (Bandura, Underwood, & Fromson, 1975; Milgram, 1974). Additional ways of weakening self-deterring reactions operate by disregarding or obscuring the consequences of actions. When people embark on a self-disapproved course of action for personal gain, or because of other inducements, they avoid facing the harm they cause. Self-censuring reactions are unlikely to be activated as long as the detrimental effects of conduct are disregarded.

The final set of disengagement practices operates at the level of the recipients of injurious effects. The strength of self-evaluative reactions partly depends on how the people toward whom actions are directed are viewed. Maltreatment of individuals who are regarded as subhuman or debased is less apt to arouse self-reproof than if they are seen as human beings with dignifying qualities (Zimbardo, 1969). Detrimental interactions usually involve a series of reciprocally escalative actions in which the victims are rarely faultless. One can always select from the chain of events an instance of defensive behavior by the adversary as the original instigation. By blaming victims, one's own actions are excusable. The disengagement of internal control, whatever the means, is not achieved solely through personal deliberation. People are socially aided in this process by indoctrination, scapegoating, and pejorative stereotyping of people held in disfavor.

As is evident from preceding discussion, the development of self-regulatory functions does not create an automatic control system, nor do situational influences exercise mechanical control. Personal judgments operating at each subfunction preclude the automaticity of the process. There is leeway in judging whether a given behavioral standard is applicable. Because of the complexity and inherent ambiguity of most events, there is even greater leeway in the judgment of behavior and its effects. To add further to the variability of the control process, most activities are performed under collective arrangements that obscure responsibility, thus permitting leeway in judging the degree of personal agency in the effects that are socially produced. In short, there exists considerable latitude for personal judgmental factors to affect whether or not self-regulatory influences will be activated in any given activity.

Reciprocal Influence of Personal Factors on Reinforcement Effects

Reinforcement has commonly been viewed as a mechanistic process in which responses are shaped automatically and unconsciously by their immediate consequences. The assumption of automaticity of reinforcement is crucial to the argument of unidirectional environmental control of behavior. One can dispense with the so-called internal link in causal chains only if persons are conceived of as mechanical respondents to external stimuli. The empirical evidence does not support such a view (Bandura, 1977b; Bower, 1975; Mischel, 1973; Neisser, 1976). External influences operate largely through cognitive processes.

During ongoing reinforcement, respondents are doing more than simply emitting responses. They develop expectations from observed regularities about the outcomes likely to result from their actions under given situational circumstances. Contrary to claims that behavior is controlled by its immediate consequences, behavior is related to its outcomes at the level of aggregate consequences rather than momentary effects (Baum, 1973). People process and synthesize contextual and outcome information from sequences of events over long intervals about the action patterns that are necessary to produce given outcomes.

The notion that behavior is governed by its consequences fares better for anticipated than for actual consequences (Bandura, 1977b). We have already reviewed research demonstrating how the same environmental consequences have markedly different effects on behavior depending on respondents' beliefs about the nature of the relationships between actions and outcomes and the meaning of the outcomes. When belief differs from actuality, which is not uncommon, behavior is weakly influenced by its actual consequences until more realistic expectations are developed through repeated experience. But it is not always expectations that change in the direction of social reality. Acting on erroneous expectations can alter how others behave, thus shaping the social reality in the direction of the expectations.

While undergoing reinforcing experiences, people are doing more than learning the probabilistic contingencies between actions and outcomes. They observe the progress they are making and tend to set themselves goals of progressive improvement. Investigators who have measured personal goal setting as well as changes in performance find that external incentives influence behavior partly through their effects on goal setting (Locke, Bryan, & Kendall, 1968). When variations in personal goals are partialed out, the effects of incentives on performance are reduced. Performance attainments also provide an important source of efficacy information for judging one's personal capabilities. Changes in perceived self-efficacy, in turn, affect people's choices of activities, how much effort they expend, and how long they will persist in the face of obstacles and aversive experiences (Bandura, 1977a; Brown & Inouye, 1978).

Because of the personal determinants of reinforcement effects, to trace behavior back to environmental "reinforcers" by no means completes the explanatory regress. To predict how outcomes will affect behavior, one must know how they are cognitively processed. To understand fully the mechanisms through which consequences change behavior, one must analyze the reciprocally contributory influences of cognitive factors.

Reciprocal Determinism as a Generic Analytic Principle

The discussion thus far has primarily addressed issues regarding the reciprocal interactions between behavior, thought, and environmental events as they occur at the individual level. Social learning theory treats reciprocal determinism as a basic principle for analyzing psychosocial phenomena at varying levels of complexity, ranging from intrapersonal development, to interpersonal behavior, to the interactive functioning of organizational and societal systems. At the intrapersonal level, people's conceptions influence what they perceive and do, and their conceptions are in turn altered by the effects of their actions and the observed consequences accruing to others (Bandura, 1977a; Bower, 1975). Information-processing models are concerned mainly with internal mental operations. A comprehensive theory must also analyze how conceptions are converted to actions, which furnish some of the data for conceptions. In social learning theory, people play an active role in creating information-generating experiences as well as in processing and transforming informative stimuli that happen to impinge upon them. This involves reciprocal transactions between thought, behavior, and environmental events which are not fully encompassed by a computer metaphor. People are not only perceivers, knowers, and actors. They are also self-reactors with capacities for reflective self-awareness that are generally neglected in information-processing theories based on computer models of human functioning.

At the level of interpersonal behavior, we have previously examined how people reciprocally determine each others' actions (Bandura et al., 1960; Patterson, 1975; Raush et al., 1974). Although the mutuality of behavior may be the focus of study, the reciprocal processes involve cognition as well as action. At the broader societal level, reciprocal processes are reflected in the interdependence of organizational elements, social subsystems, and transnational relations (Bandura, 1973; Keohane & Nye, 1977). Here the matters of interest are the patterns of interdependence between systems, the criteria and means used for gauging systemic performances, the mechanisms that exist for exercising reciprocal influence, and the conditions that alter the degree and type of reciprocal control that one system can exert on another.

It is within the framework of reciprocal determinism that the concept of freedom assumes meaning (Bandura, 1977b). Because people's conceptions, their behavior, and their environments are reciprocal determinants of each other, individuals are neither powerless objects controlled by environmental forces nor entirely free agents who can do whatever they choose. People can be considered partially free insofar as they shape future conditions by influencing their courses of action. By creating structural mechanisms for reciprocal influence, such as organizational systems of checks and balances, legal systems, and due process and elective procedures, people can bring their influence to bear on each other. Institutional reciprocal mechanisms thus provide not only safeguards against unilateral social control but the means for changing institutions and the conditions of life. Within the process of reciprocal determinism lies the opportunity for people to shape their destinies as well as the limits of self-direction.

References

Bandura, A. (1973). *Aggression: A social learning analysis.* Englewood Cliffs, NJ: Prentice-Hall.

Bandura, A. (1974). Behavior theory and the models of man. *American Psychologist, 29,* 859–869.

Bandura, A. (1976). Self-reinforcement: Theoretical and methodological considerations. *Behaviorism, 4,* 135–155.

Bandura, A. (1977a). Self-efficacy: Toward a unifying theory of behavioral change. *Psychological Review, 84,* 191–215.

Bandura, A. (1977b). *Social learning theory.* Englewood Cliffs, NJ: Prentice-Hall.

Bandura, A., & Adams, N. E. (1977). Analysis of self-efficacy theory of behavioral change. *Cognitive Therapy and Research, 1,* 287–308.

Bandura, A., Grusec, J. E., & Menlove, F. L. (1967). Some social determinants of self-monitoring reinforcement systems. *Journal of Personality and Social Psychology, 5,* 449–455.

Bandura, A., Lipsher, D. H., & Miller, P. E. (1960). Psychotherapists' approach-avoidance reactions to patients' expression of hostility. *Journal of Consulting Psychology, 1960,* 1–8.

Bandura, A., Mahoney, M. J., & Dirks, S. J. (1976). Discriminative activation and maintenance of contingent self-reinforcement. *Behaviour Research and Therapy, 14,* 1–6.

Bandura, A., Underwood, B., & Fromson, M. E. (1975). Disinhibition of aggression through diffusion of responsibility and dehumanization of victims. *Journal of Research in Personality, 9,* 253–269.

Bandura, A., & Walters, R. H. (1959). *Adolescent aggression.* New York: Ronald.

Bateson, G. (Ed.). (1961). *Perceval's narrative: A patient's account of his psychosis, 1830–1832.* Stanford, CA: Stanford University Press.

Baum, W. M. (1973). The correlation-based law of effect. *Journal of the Experimental Analysis of Behavior, 20,* 137–153.

Bower, G. H. (1975). Cognitive psychology: An introduction. In W. K. Estes (Ed.), *Handbook of learning and cognition.* Hillsdale, NJ: Erlbaum.

Brown, I., Jr., & Inouye, D. K. (1978). Learned helplessness through modeling: The role of perceived similarity in competence. *Journal of Personality and Social Psychology, 36,* 900–908.

Gambino, R. (1973). Watergate lingo: A language of non-responsibility. *Freedom at Issue,* No. 22.

Goldfried, M. R., & Merbaum, M. (Eds.). (1973). *Behavior change through self-control.* New York: Holt, Rinehart & Winston.

Kelman, H. C. (1973). Violence without moral restraint: Reflections on the dehumanization of victims and victimizers. *Journal of Social Issues, 29,* 25–61.

Keohane, R. O., & Nye, J. S. (1977). *Power and interdependence: World politics in transition.* Boston: Little, Brown.

Krauss, I. (1964). Sources of educational aspirations among working-class youth. *American Sociological Review, 29,* 867–879.

Lepper, M. R., Sagotsky, J., & Mailer, J. (1975). Generalization and persistence of effects of exposure to self-reinforcement models. *Child Development, 46,* 618–630.

Locke, E. A., Bryan, J. F., & Kendall, L. M. (1968). Goals and intentions as mediators of the effects of monetary incentives on behavior. *Journal of Applied Psychology, 52*(2), 104–121.

Mahoney, M. J., & Thoresen, C. E. (1974). *Self-control: Power to the person.* Monterey, CA: Brooks/Cole.

Masters, J. C., & Mokros, J. R. (1974). Self-reinforcement processes in children. In H. W. Reese (Ed.), *Advances in child development and behavior* (Vol. 9). New York: Academic Press.

Milgram, S. (1974). *Obedience to authority: An experimental view.* New York: Harper & Row.

Mischel, W. (1973). Toward a cognitive social learning reconceptualization of personality. *Psychological Review, 80,* 252–283.

Neisser, U. (1976). *Cognition and reality: Principles and implications of cognitive psychology.* San Francisco: W. H. Freeman.

Patterson, G. R. (1975). The aggressive child: Victim and architect of a coercive system. In L. A. Hamerlynck, E. J. Mash, & L. C. Handy (Eds.), *Behavior modification and families*. New York: Brunner/Mazel.

Raush, H. L., Barry, W. A., Hertel, R. K., & Swain, M. A. (1974). *Communication conflict and marriage*. San Francisco: Jossey-Bass.

Simon, K. M. (1978). *Self-evaluative reactions to one's own performances: The role of personal significance of performance attainments*. Unpublished manuscript, Stanford University.

Skinner, B. F. (1971). *Beyond freedom and dignity*. New York: Knopf.

Thomas, E. A. C., & Martin, J. A. (1976). Analyses of parent-child interaction. *Psychological Review, 83,* 141–156.

Wallace, I. (1977). Self-control techniques of famous novelists. *Journal of Applied Behavior Analysis, 10,* 515–525.

Zimbardo, P. G. (1969). The human choice: Individuation, reason, and order versus deindividuation, impulse, and chaos. In W. J. Arnold & D. Levine (Eds.), *Nebraska Symposium on Motivation* (Vol. 17). Lincoln: University of Nebraska Press.

Personality Coherence and Dispositions in a Cognitive-Affective Personality System (CAPS) Approach

Walter Mischel

Another one-time social learning theorist who is helping to develop the cognitive approach to personality is Walter Mischel, whose critique of personality traits we read in Part II. Mischel's main complaint about personality traits is that because they seek to identify average behavioral tendencies, they tend to treat an individual's distinctive reactions to particular situations as random fluctuation or measurement error. Mischel believes that the real essence of personality is not to be found in the global averages of trait assessments, but in the fine-grained analysis of how each individual changes his or her behavior according to the situation he or she is in. The present chapter summarizes Mischel's latest theoretical thinking on these issues.

The chapter begins with a reprise of Mischel's version of the person-situation debate, which is widely viewed as a debate that he started. It is interesting to compare this summary with, for example, the summary by Kenrick and Funder in Part II, and his complaints about "global traits" with Funder's rendition in Part II. Mischel's conclusion is that personality theory needs to pay increased attention to the processes that underlie each individual's distinct pattern of if . . . then responses to particular situations. The idea is that for each individual, if one thing happens, then he or she will respond in a particular way, and this pattern across situations is distinctive for each individual. He proceeds to describe his "Cognitive-Affective Personality System" (CAPS) approach, which attempts to integrate a large amount of knowledge about cognition, emotion, behavior, and even physiology.

Mischel's chapter ends on a conciliatory note, observing that the trait and cognitive approaches to personality have been split into almost warring camps, but that they really, in the final analysis, are studying the same thing. It could be observed, for example—though Mischel does not make this observation—that personality traits could themselves be construed as if . . . then patterns. If a sociable person is at a party, then he will try to meet everyone in the room; if a dominant person enters a business meeting, then she will quickly take charge, and so on. In any event, Mischel is surely correct to observe that a complete account of personality must include both average tendencies that characterize a person across contexts and throughout life as well as the distinctive patterns of how people respond to particular and ever-changing situations.

From D. Cervone and Y. Shoda (Eds.), *The coherence of personality: Social cognitive bases of consistency, organization, and variability* (pp. 37–60). New York: Guilford Press, 1999.

In the last decade, fundamental controversies and debates in the search for personality coherence have been replaced by discoveries and reconceptualizations that identify and explain its nature and structure. These efforts promise to resolve paradoxes that have long split the area of personality and to advance personality theory in line with exciting progress in other areas of social and cognitive science. In this chapter, I consider personality coherence, dispositions, dynamics, and structure from the perspective of a social-cognitive-affective processing approach (e.g., Mischel & Shoda, 1995, 1998). After quickly sketching some of the history that impacts on the present scene, I turn to the current agenda, focusing on aspects of personality coherence and personality theory that merit attention but that risk being neglected within the contemporary social-cognitive framework. * * *

* * *

My particular emphasis will be on the construct of personality dispositions and its role and potential value within a processing approach to personality in a broadly social-cognitive framework. I try to show that dispositions can readily be incorporated within such a framework at several different levels of analysis that are easily confused and need to be distinguished. A unitary approach in the study of personality that encompasses both dispositions and the processes that underlie them seems to me sorely needed given the depth of the unconstructive splits that have occurred within the area of personality, as also discussed in this chapter. But first, I consider the history that has led us here and that needs to be understood in an effort to resolve the issues that remain.

The Past: Consistency Lost?

PARADIGM PERTURBATIONS

This volume goes to press in the 70th anniversary year of the discoveries by Hartshorne and May (1928), and concurrently by Newcomb (1929), that the cross-situational consistency of behavior—which they assessed empirically in school and camp settings with such laborious care and at high cost—seemed to be grossly discrepant from the assumptions of the classical personality trait conceptions that guided their search: Namely, it was assumed that individuals are characterized by behavioral dispositions (like the tendency to be conscientious or honest or sociable) that are manifested relatively stably and consistently across many different types of situations. Their failure to find strong support for this belief only briefly perturbed the then-young field (although it did lead Newcomb to switch his career from personality to social psychology). But their studies did not challenge the traditional trait paradigm: Mainstream work within it continued and accelerated—as it still does.

The assessment needs of World War II demanded quick personality trait measurements and further stimulated work within the traditional paradigm with little time or opportunity to evaluate the utility or the theoretical implications of the results. It was not until 40 years after the discoveries of Hartshorne, May, and Newcomb, that the paradigm itself was challenged (Mischel, 1968; Peterson, 1968). That confrontation, now having its 30th anniversary, grew out of the embarrassing discrepancy between the numbers found in the extensive data that had accumulated and the still-regnant and unruffled classic trait theoretical assumptions of the field. It became apparent to quite a few personality researchers that we were ending our discussion sections with more apologies and self-criticisms than conclusions.

PARADIGM CRISIS The upsets that spiraled into a paradigm crisis converged from several directions: A core assumption of trait psychology concerning the cross-situational consistency of behavior was contradicted by the small albeit nonzero (but not by much) cross-situational consistency coefficients found when researchers actually assessed people's behavior across even seemingly similar situations. Simultaneously, analyses of the utility of the approach for the prediction of behavior in particular situations, as well as its explanatory power, cast deep doubts on both.

Classic psychodynamic theory was the major alternative available at that time and hence the tempting option. It made no assumption of cross-situational consistency in behavior (nor claimed any predictive utility) but relied crucially on clinical judgments. The theory's Achilles heel was that the accuracy and utility of those inferences and judgments were undermined by evidence documenting the limitations of clinicians and their proneness to self-deceptive illusions of confidence (Chapman & Chapman, 1969; Mischel, 1968; Peterson, 1968). Consequently both routes to personality coherence and to personality itself—behavioral dispositions and underlying dynamics—were vulnerable.

Although *Personality and Assessment* (Mischel, 1968) was started with the intention of reviewing the state of the field, it was seen as a glove hurled to the ground. The first reactions in the early 1970s seemed devoted to arguing against the legitimacy of the critique and tried to deny its validity. (When first published, it was reviewed briefly on a back page of *Contemporary Psychology* and dismissed under the header "Personality Unvanquished.") In the next decade, the controversies and paradoxes of the field concerning the nature, locus, and even existence of personality coherence were articulated and debated and in time researched. Various routes

both for continuing business as usual or for finding constructive alternatives and solutions were outlined and pursued.

The heated disputes that then raged sharpened and often exaggerated the differences between approaches. One fallout was the warfare between social and personality psychologists. In those battles, for at least a decade, the former were seen as the champions of the situation and its power (Nisbett & Ross, 1980), and the latter felt themselves the beleaguered defenders of the person and the construct of personality (e.g., Carlson, 1971). Although that may by now seem like ancient history, it remains relevant for the current agenda as background for understanding the almost reflexive hostility that developed between two subdisciplines that previously had been unified in a constructive collaboration.

The early consequences of these confrontations included dividing the flagship *Journal of Personality and Social Psychology* into three separate unconnected sections, one for social cognition and attitudes, one for interpersonal processes, one for personality—a move virtually guaranteed to obstruct efforts to understand persons (including their minds, feelings, and relationships) in their contexts. For more than a decade in this new structure, the third part, Personality, defined its mission as welcoming articles devoted to personality "as traditionally defined," that is, in terms of broad traits, suggesting a perspective that seems more defensive than scientific. Overcoming that unfortunate way of parsing the variance and the enterprise has been perhaps the largest barrier in the search for personality coherence, in my view, and fortunately, there now are creative routes for doing so. * * *

* * *

The Present: A Split Personality Psychology

* * * After years of debate, at last there was consensus about the state of the data—the average cross-situational consistency coefficient is nonzero but not by much (Bem, 1983; Epstein, 1983; Funder, 1983). But there was and is deep disagreement about how to interpret the data and proceed in the field of personality psychology. Two main alternatives developed, often in seeming opposition and conflict.

THE MAINSTREAM AGGREGATION SOLUTION: REMOVE THE SITUATION TO FIND BROAD BEHAVIORAL DISPOSITIONS

The most widely accepted strategy adopted within the mainstream behavioral disposition approach to personality acknowledges the low cross-situational consistency in behavior found from situation to situation: It then systematically removes the situation by aggregating the individual's behavior on a given dimension (e.g., "conscientiousness") over many different situations (or "items") to estimate an overall "true score" (as discussed in Epstein, 1979, 1980; Mischel & Peake, 1982). That approach can be extremely useful for many goals, but its limits—as well as its strengths—are seen by analogy to meteorology, as Mischel and Shoda (1995) discussed. Although overall climatic trends surely are worth knowing, if meteorologists were to focus only on the aggregate climatic trends, they would neglect the atmospheric processes that underlie the changing weather patterns, as well as give up the goal of more accurate specific weather predictions.

Thus bypassing the issues that had been raised in the "paradigm crisis," much of contemporary mainstream personality psychology proceeds in an atmosphere its advocates describe as "euphoria" within an unrevised and even more extreme global trait framework (e.g., Funder, 1991), particularly the optimistically named Big Five (e.g., Goldberg, 1993; McCrae & Costa, 1996, 1997). It focuses on identifying a few broad behavioral dispositions that will manifest themselves stably across many situations and that characterize the individual in trait terms with regard to their position on each of the five factors. It does so in coexistence with sharply critical reviews of the problems and data that continue to undermine this approach fundamentally (e.g., Block, 1995; McAdams, 1992; Pervin, 1994)—criticisms and data that seem unnervingly similar to those that stirred the crises

three decades earlier—and that apparently still remain largely unheeded.

THE ALTERNATIVE ROUTE: SEARCH FOR SOCIAL-COGNITIVE-MOTIVATIONAL PROCESSES UNDERLYING PERSON × SITUATION INTERACTIONS

Social and personality psychologists who were unwilling to bypass the role of the situation and thus did not accept the field's mainstream solution—nor its sense of euphoria—have been pursuing their separate routes in a framework now called "social-cognitive" (or "cognitive-social"). Some of the main themes for this alternative route were outlined originally in the "cognitive social learning reconceptualization of personality" (Mischel, 1973). Its goal was to make clear that the 1968 critique of the state of personality required not abandoning the construct of personality but rather *reconceptualizing* it to encompass within it the complex and often subtle interactions between person and situation that characterize individuals and types.

With that aim, the proposal identified the types of social-cognitive and motivational variables and principles required for a mediating process account of person–situation interactions and personality coherence. In this account, personality is conceptualized in terms of such constructs as how the individual encodes or appraises particular types of situations, the relevant expectancies and values that become activated, and the competencies and self-regulatory strategies available (Mischel, 1973, 1990). The behavior patterns that unfold depend on the interactions among these person variables in relation to the particular type of situation (e.g., Mischel & Shoda, 1995).

The last quarter-century has seen diverse creative efforts in this general framework and in many novel directions to conceptualize and clarify personality-relevant processes and principles (e.g., Mischel, 1998). Although each has its distinctive features and focus, most share the goal of wanting to explain the nature of intraindividual coherence and the mechanisms and conditions that generate it. * * *

RECONCEPTUALIZING—AND FINDING—COHERENCE IN UNEXPECTED PLACES

Much of the research that Shoda and I and our colleagues pursued within this general framework in recent years was directed at clarifying the nature of personality consistency. Briefly, our reasoning (in accord with Mischel, 1973; Mischel & Shoda, 1995, 1998) was that if personality is a stable system that processes the information about the situations, external or internal, then it follows that, as individuals encounter different situations, their behaviors should vary across the situations. These variations should reflect important differences among the individuals in the psychologically active features for them and in the ways they process them. That is, they should reflect, in part, the structure and organization of their personality systems, for example, how they encoded the situations and the expectations, affects, and goals that became activated within them (Mischel & Shoda, 1995).

If . . . Then . . . Situation–Behavior Profiles Over time this will generate distinctive and stable *if . . . then . . .* situation–behavior profiles of characteristic elevation and shape * * *. So that even if two people are similar in their overall average "aggressiveness," for example, they will manifest distinctive, predictable patterns of behavioral variability in their *if . . . then . . .* signatures of when and with whom and where they do and do not aggress. These expectations have been extensively supported empirically (e.g., Shoda, Mischel, & Wright, 1993a, 1993b, 1994).

These profiles provide a glimpse of the pattern of behavior variation in relation to situations that is expressive of personality invariance but that is completely bypassed in the traditional search for cross-situational consistency. Instead of searching for the traditional cross-situational consistency coefficient that has been pursued for most of the century (e.g., Hartshorne & May, 1928; Mischel, 1968; Newcomb, 1929; Peterson, 1968; Vernon, 1964), personality coherence can be found—and should be expected—in the intraindividual stable pattern of variability.

The results also make it evident that a focus on the relationships between psychological features of situations and the individual's patterns of behavior, rather than undermining the existence of personality, has to become part of the assessment and conception of personality (e.g., Mischel, 1973, 1990; Wright & Mischel, 1987; Shoda & Mischel, 1993; Shoda et al., 1994). It is obvious of course that if situation units are defined in terms of features salient for the researcher but trivial for, or irrelevant to, the individuals studied, one cannot expect their behaviors to vary meaningfully across them. In that case, the resulting pattern of behavior variation may well be unstable and meaningless. To discover the potentially predictable patterns of behavior variability that characterize individuals, one first has to identify those features of situations that are meaningful to them and that engage their important psychological qualities (e.g., their ways of encoding or construing, their expectancies, and goals). Fortunately the methodology to make that possible is now becoming available (e.g., Shoda et al., 1994; Wright & Mischel, 1987).

BEHAVIORAL SIGNATURES OF PERSONALITY: THE LOCUS OF SELF-PERCEIVED CONSISTENCY AND DISPOSITIONAL JUDGMENTS The profiles of situation–behavior relations that characterize a person constitute a sort of "behavioral signature of personality" that in turn is linked to the person's self-perceived consistency and sense of coherence (Mischel & Shoda, 1995; Shoda et al., 1993b). This was found in a reanalysis by Mischel and Shoda (1995) of the Carleton College field study (Mischel & Peake, 1982). In that study, college students were repeatedly observed on campus in various situations relevant to their conscientiousness in the college setting (such as in the classroom, in the dormitory, in the library, assessed over repeated occasions in the semester). Students who perceived themselves as consistent did not show greater overall cross-situational consistency than those who did not. But for individuals who perceived themselves as consistent, the average situation–behavior profile stability correlation was near .5,[1] whereas it was trivial for those who viewed themselves as inconsistent. So it is the stability in the situation–behavior profiles (e.g., conscientious about homework but not about punctuality), not the cross-situational consistency of behavior that underlies the perception of consistency with regard to a type of behavior or disposition.

In sum, relatively stable situation–behavior profiles reflect characteristic intraindividual patterns in how the person relates to different psychological conditions or features of situations, forming a sort of behavioral signature of personality (Shoda et al., 1994). The stability of these situation–behavior profiles in turn predicts the self-perception of consistency as well. These profiles are also linked to the dispositional judgments made about the person by others (Shoda et al., 1994). The surprise is not simply that this type of behavioral signature of personality exists, but rather that it has so long been treated as error and deliberately removed by averaging behavior over diverse situations to remove their role. Ironically, although such aggregation was intended to capture personality, it actually can delete data that reflect the individual's most distinctive qualities and unique intraindividual patterning.

These expectations and findings are congruent with classic processing theories, most notably Freud's conception of psychodynamics. In that view, peoples' underlying processing dynamics and qualities—the construals and goals, the motives and passions, that drive them—may be reflected not only in how often they display particular types of behavior but also in when and where, and thus also, and most importantly, *why* that behavior occurs. In short, this type of model expects that the stable patterns of situation–behavior relationships that characterize persons provide potential keys to their dynamics. They are informative roads to the underlying system that produces them, not sources of error to be eliminated systematically by aggregating out the situation. Thus, in the present

approach, the concept of the invariances in the expression of personality is broadened to encompass the profile of situation–behavior relations that might characterize the person, not just the overall average level of particular types of behavior aggregated across diverse situations (e.g., Shoda et al., 1993a, 1994).

Personality Reconsidered: Toward a Unifying Framework

The above findings—and the confirmation of the hypotheses that predicted them—directly violate the assumptions made if one conceptualizes personality in terms of traits as behavioral dispositions. In that classic view, the intraindividual variations in a type of behavior across situations, given that the main effects of situations are removed by standardization, should reflect only intrinsic unpredictability or measurement error. If that assumption were correct, then the stability of the intraindividual pattern of variation should on average be zero. The finding that the situation–behavior profiles reliably reflect a statistically significant, stable facet of individual differences in social behavior thus has major implications for how one thinks about personality coherence and the kind of personality model that is needed.

The data provide clear evidence at the level of *in vivo* behavior observed extensively as it unfolds across situations and over time in everyday life (Mischel & Shoda, 1995). They are consistent with parallel findings showing significant amounts of variance attributable to person × situation interaction in analysis of variance studies, based on questionnaire responses (e.g., Endler & Hunt, 1969; Endler & Magnusson, 1976; Endler, Hunt, & Rosenstein, 1962; Magnusson & Endler, 1977). Furthermore, as shown elsewhere (Shoda, 1990), the degree that an individual is characterized by stable patterns of situation–behavior relations is necessarily negatively related to the level of overall cross-situational consistency that can be expected, making it clear that the quest for higher cross-situational consistency coefficients is bound to be futile.

The need now is for a personality theory, or at

---

[1] This .5 is a correlation coefficient, of the sort explained by Rosenthal and Rubin in their selection in Part I.

least an approach to personality, designed to try to predict and explain these signatures of personality, rather than to eliminate or ignore them. Such an approach requires rethinking the nature of personality coherence, and of personality dispositions, structure, and dynamics, as discussed next.

PERSONALITY AS AN ORGANIZED DYNAMIC SYSTEM

A first requirement is to develop a processing model of the personality system at the level of the individual (Mischel & Shoda, 1995). In such a model, person variables, no matter how important, function not just as single, isolated variables but as components that are interconnected within an organized system of relationships that in turn interacts with the social-psychological situations in which the system is activated (e.g., Shoda & Mischel, 1998). That also requires conceptualizing the "situation" not just as a setting but in psychological terms (Shoda et al., 1994).

In short, an urgent theoretical need is to conceptualize personality as an organized system that is interactive and dynamic—a system that accounts both for intraindividual coherence and stability, on the one hand, and for plasticity and discriminativeness in behavior, on the other hand. It needs to take account of the individual's characteristic dispositions as well as of the dynamic mediating processes that underlie them. It has to consider not only social-cognitive-motivational and affective determinants and processes but also biological and genetic antecedents and levels. And it must be able to deal with the complexity of human personality and the cognitive-affective dynamics, conscious and unconscious—both 'cool' and 'hot,' cognitive and emotional, rational and impulsive—that underlie the individual's distinctive, characteristic internal states and external behavioral expressions (see Metcalfe & Jacobs, 1998; Metcalfe & Mischel, 1999).

A number of recent processing models now focus not just on how much of a particular mental representation or unit (e.g., of self-efficacy expectations, of fear of failure) a person has, but rather on how the units are related to each other within the processing system. These interconnections form a unique network that functions as an organized whole—a dynamic interacting, processing system that can operate rapidly in parallel at multiple levels of accessibility, awareness, and automaticity. Rather than conceptualizing the individual as a bundle of mediating variables or as a flow chart of discrete procedures and decision rules, this provides a more parallel and distributed (rather than serial, centralized) processing system. Particularly promising developments come from recent work in cognitive neuroscience, such as the neural network theories and connectionist models (e.g., Anderson, 1996; Kandel & Hawkins, 1992; Rumelhart & McClelland, 1986). Within such a framework, one can begin to conceptualize social information processing in terms of a dynamic organized network of interconnected and interacting representations—cognitions and affects (e.g., Kunda & Thagard, 1996; Read & Miller, 1998; Shultz & Lepper, 1996)—operating at various levels of awareness (e.g., Westen, 1990). Our own attempt to move personality theory in this direction is the recently proposed cognitive-affective personality system (CAPS) (Mischel & Shoda, 1995, 1998; Shoda & Mischel, 1998).

COGNITIVE-AFFECTIVE PERSONALITY SYSTEM (CAPS)

According to CAPS, individuals differ first of all in the "chronic accessibility," that is, the ease, with which particular cognitive-affective units become activated. These units refer to the mental-emotional representations—the cognitions and affects or feelings—that are available to the person. Such mediating units were conceptualized initially in terms of five relatively stable person variables on which individuals differ in processing self-relevant information (Mischel, 1973). Over the years, these units have been modified by research (reviewed in Mischel & Shoda, 1995; Mischel, Cantor, & Feldman, 1996), and the units within the CAPS system now include affects and goals, as well as encodings, expectancies, beliefs, competencies, and self-regulatory plans and strategies.

Individual Differences in the Stable Organization of Relations among Units (Interconnections) The CAPS

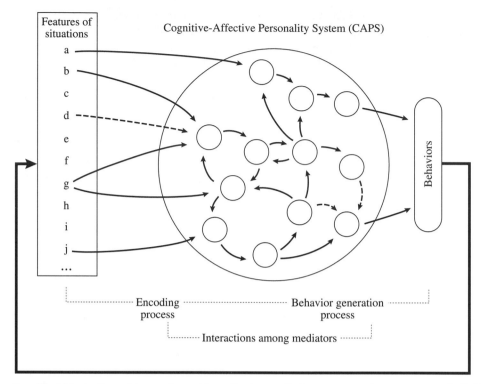

Figure 1 Simplified illustration of types of cognitive-affective mediating processes that generate an individual's distinctive behavior patterns. Situational features are encoded by a given mediating unit, which activates specific subsets of other mediating units, generating distinctive cognition, affect, and behavior in response to different situations. Mediating units become activated in relation to some situational features, deactivated (inhibited) in relation to others, and are unaffected by the rest. The activated mediating units affect other mediating units through a stable network of relations that characterize an individual. The relation may be positive (solid line), which increases the activation, or negative (dashed line), which decreases the activation. From Mischel and Shoda (1995). Copyright 1995 by the American Psychological Association, Inc. Reprinted by permission.

model goes beyond the earlier focus on person variables (Mischel, 1973) in emphasizing that stable individual differences reflect not only the accessibility of particular cognitions and affects but also the distinctive *organization of relationships* among them. This organization guides and constrains the activation of the particular cognitions, affects, and actions that are available within the system. It is this organization that constitutes the basic stable structure of personality and that underlies the behavioral signatures of personality described above.

CAPS is a system that interacts continuously and dynamically with the social world in which it is contextualized. It is activated in part by external situations and in part by its own internal cogni-

tive and affective activities, including fantasy, daydreaming, and planning (Mischel et al., 1996; Shoda & Mischel, 1996). The interactions with the external word involve a two-way reciprocal interaction: behaviors that the personality system generates impact on the social world, partly shaping and selecting the interpersonal situations the person subsequently faces and that, in turn, influence the person (e.g., Bandura, 1986; Buss, 1987).

Dynamic, Transactional System: The Active–Proactive Person Figure 1 shows a schematic, greatly simplified CAPS system that is characterized by the available cognitive and affective units, organized in a distinctive network of interrelations.

When certain features of a situation are perceived by the individual, a characteristic pattern of cognitions and affects (shown schematically as circles) becomes activated through this distinctive network of connections. The personality structure refers to the person's stable system of interconnections among the cognitive and affective units, and it is this structure that guides and constrains further activation of other units throughout the network. Ultimately the result is the activation of plans, strategies, and potential behaviors in a characteristic pattern that is situationally contextualized.

In CAPS, mediating units become activated in relation to some situation features but are deactivated or inhibited in relation to others and not affected by the rest. That is, the connections among units within the stable network that characterizes the person may be positive, which increases the activation, or negative (shown as broken lines in Figure 1), which decreases the activation.

The personality system anticipates, interprets, rearranges, and changes situations as well as reacts to them. It thus is active and indeed proactive, not just reactive. It not only responds to the environment but also may generate, select, modify, and shape situations in reciprocal transactions (Figure 2).

Activation of Personality Dynamics and Dispositions in Context People differ characteristically in the particular situational features (e.g., being teased, being approached socially, feeling lonely) that are the salient active ingredients for them and that thus activate their characteristic and relatively predictable patterns of cognitive, affective, and behavioral reactions to those situations, that is, their distinctive processing dynamics (Mischel & Shoda, 1995). For example, some individuals readily respond aggressively to such ambiguous stimuli as having milk spilled on them in the cafeteria line (Dodge, 1986). There also are internal feedback loops within the system through which self-generated stimuli (as in thinking, fantasizing, daydreaming) activate their distinctive pathways of connections, triggering characteristic cognitive-affective-behavioral reaction patterns (e.g., Shoda

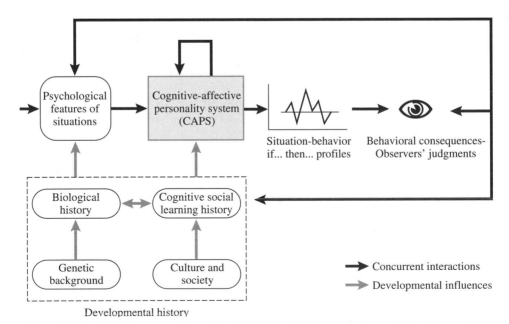

Figure 2   The cognitive-affective personality system (CAPS) in relation to concurrent interactions and developmental influences. From Mischel and Shoda (1995). Copyright 1995 by the American Psychological Association, Inc. Reprinted by permission.

& Mischel, 1998). The behaviors the person constructs may in turn affect the interpersonal environment and social ecology, which changes the situational features that are encountered subsequently (e.g., Dodge 1986, 1993, 1997a, 1997b).

Variations across Situations: Stable Individual Differences in Situation–Behavior, If . . . Then . . . Relations It follows from the assumptions of the CAPS model that the variation in the person's behavior in relation to changing situations in part constitutes a potentially meaningful reflection of the personality system itself. Different cognitions, affects, and behaviors become activated as the situation and its features change, even when the interconnections among them remain unchanged across situations. That is, the personality system determines the *relationships* among the types of situations encountered and the cognitive, affective, and behavioral responses: Thus, as the *ifs* change, so do the *thens*, but the *relationship* between them is stable as long as the personality system remains unchanged. This assumption leads the approach to predict characteristic, predictable patterns of variation in the individual's behavior across situations—that is, the sorts of stable situation–behavior, *if . . . then . . .* profiles that were in fact found in the empirical studies summarized above (Mischel & Shoda, 1995).

Further support that CAPS generates the theoretically expected *if . . . then . . .* profiles came from a computer simulation (Mischel & Shoda, 1995; Shoda & Mischel, 1998). It was shown that individual differences in the connections (patterns of activation pathways) among the internal representations determine the links between features of situations and the outcomes generated by the system. An individual's unique configuration of person variables is manifested in the uniqueness of the *if . . . then . . .* profiles that unfold. Thus, to recapitulate, the personality system is expressed in the pattern with which a type of behavior varies over a set of situations, as well as in the average level of the behavior: Predictable variability in relation to context becomes a key to the individual's stability and coherence, a sign of the underlying system that generates it.

THE SYSTEM IN ACTION: LINKING PROCESSING DYNAMICS TO DISPOSITIONS To illustrate such a system in action, consider a person characterized by the disposition of "rejection sensitivity" (Downey & Feldman, 1996; Downey, Freitas, Michaelis, & Khouri, 1997). When this person begins to discuss a relationship problem with a romantic partner, for example, his anxious expectations trigger the tendency to scan for evidence of imminent rejection and to focus on and encode those features of the situation most likely to provide such evidence (Downey & Feldman, 1996). These expectations, affects, and behaviors interact and combine to lead the person to readily perceive rejection even in ambiguous situations, which in turn tends to activate behavioral scripts for hostility (Ayduk, Downey, Testa, Yin, & Shoda, in press). The hostility that is enacted can then elicit the partner rejection that is most feared, eroding the relationship in a self-defeating pattern, thereby confirming and maintaining rejection expectations (Downey et al., 1997).

Rejection sensitivity also illustrates the conditional nature of dispositions insofar as the activation of the characteristic pattern depends both on the situational features and on the cognitive-affective organization of the system. For example, the rejection-sensitive person becomes hostile specifically in relation to perceived rejection from a romantic partner but can behave exceptionally caringly and supportively in other situations (e.g., early in the relationship). Thus a characteristic and defining situation–behavior profile for this disposition may include both a tendency to become very angry and coercive and a tendency to be exceptionally sensitive and caring, each in its own distinctive context (Downey & Feldman, 1996). So the same rejection-sensitive man who coerces and abuses his partner also can behave in exceedingly tender and loving ways (e.g., Walker, 1979). He is both hurtful and kind, caring and uncaring, abusive and gentle.

Traditional analyses of such "inconsistencies"

in personality raise the question "which one of these two people is the real one? What is simply the effect of the situation?" In contrast, the CAPS approach allows the same person to have contradictory facets that are equally genuine. The surface contradictions become comprehensible when one analyzes the network of relations among cognitions and affects to identify their psychological organization. The research problem becomes to understand when and why different cognitions and affects become activated predictably in relation to different features of situations, external and internal. The theory views the individual's distinctive patterns of variability not necessarily as internal contradictions but as the potentially predictable expressions of an underlying system that itself may remain quite stable in its organization. To reiterate, the stability of the disposition, which reflects the stability of the underlying system, is seen in the predictability of the *if . . . then . . .* profile, not in the consistency of behavior across different types of situations. The challenge is to discriminate, understand, and predict when each aspect will be activated and the dynamics that underlie the pattern. For example, are the caring and uncaring behaviors two scripts in the service of the same goal? If so, how are they connected to, and guided by, the person's self-conceptions and belief system in relation to the psychological features of situations that activate them?

REFINING AND REDEFINING THE CONSTRUCTS OF DISPOSITIONS, DYNAMICS, AND PERSONALITY STRUCTURE

Although it is widely asserted that process-oriented approaches to personality ignore or deny stable personality dispositions (e.g., Funder, 1991; Goldberg, 1993), in fact, in the present approach they have a significant role. The issue that does have to be addressed is just how to conceptualize "personality traits" or "dispositions" within a processing approach.

Given the depths of the splits and disputes that have occurred between the two approaches—personality as trait dispositions and personality as mediating underlying processes—it will not be a trivial task to reconcile and construct a unified theory and approach to personality. As Block (1995) and Pervin (1994) * * * make plain, the equation of the Big Five or any other set of global traits or factors with personality psychology is unacceptable and needs to be rejected. More generally, to understand intraindividual dynamics and the resultant behavioral signatures, one needs to reject making behavioral dispositions of any sort synonymous with personality. Nevertheless, it would be unwise to throw out with these false equations the concept of dispositions: That concept—a foundation stone in personality psychology—requires reanalysis and refinement rather than rejection.

Dispositional Levels As a first step, it may be useful to distinguish some of the different levels of analysis in the study of dispositions, since at each level the definition and the relevant phenomena shift, and often the level is left unclear, easily leading to misunderstandings. Let us consider the following four levels.

Psychological Processing Level. At the "psychological processing level" of analysis, dispositions within the present perspective may be defined by a characteristic social cognitive-affective processing structure that underlies, and generates, distinctive processing dynamics within the personality system (Mischel & Shoda, 1995), depicted as CAPS in the solid rectangle of Figure 2. A characteristic set of cognitions, affects, and behavioral strategies in an organization of interrelations that guides and constrains their activation constitutes the processing structure of the disposition. The processing dynamics of the disposition refer to the patterns and sequences of activation among the mediating units—the mental representations—that are generated when these persons encounter or construct situations containing relevant features.

The processing dynamics are activated in relation to particular types of situational features (e.g., certain interpersonal encounters). Some of these stimuli are external, but others are internally generated in many ways, such as by thinking or ruminating about situations (e.g., Nolen-Hoeksema, Parker, & Larson, 1994), or through selective recall and reexperiences of past events and feelings, or by daydreaming, fantasies, and scenarios that are planned or imagined (e.g., Taylor & Schneider, 1989). Dynamics can also be self-activated by selective attention, such as to one's perceived strengths, resources, vulnerabilities, conflicts, ambivalences, and anticipated future (e.g., Bandura, 1986; Mischel, Ebbesen, & Zeiss, 1973, 1976; Norem & Cantor, 1986). The pattern of activation among cognitions and affects in the personality system at a given time may be defined as the *personality state*.

Behavioral Level. At the level of directly observable behavior, the manifestations of a disposition and its processing dynamics are seen in the distinctive elevations and shapes of the situation–behavior profiles—the dispositional signatures—that distinguish its exemplars (see Figure 2). Individuals who have similar organizations of relations among cognitions and affects that become activated in relation to a particular distinctive set of situational features may be said to have a particular "processing disposition." These dispositions generate distinctive processing dynamics that become activated and, over time and contexts, will generate the situation–behavior profiles that have the characteristic elevations and shapes that identify the dispositional exemplars. It should be clear that, in this approach, personality psychologists do not have to choose between the study of dispositions or processes but can simultaneously analyze both the distinctive *if . . . then . . .* profiles that characterize the disposition's exemplars and illuminate the processes underlying them.

Perceived Personality Level: The Observer's View. The behavioral manifestations of the personality system may be readily and consensually encoded by observers (the eye shown in Figure 2) as reflections of person prototypes or exemplars, (e.g., Cantor, Mischel, & Schwartz, 1982; Wright & Mischel, 1987, 1988) and of traits and types in everyday psycholexical terms, both by lay perceivers (e.g., Jones, 1990) and psychologists (e.g.,

John, 1990; Goldberg, 1993; McCrae & Costa, 1996).

These encodings are related not just to the mean levels of different types of behavior displayed by a person, but also to the shape of the *if . . . then . . .* profiles that express their pattern of variability across situations. This was illustrated in a study that obtained personality prototype judgments for the sample of participants in the summer camp described in the first part of this article. As predicted, judgments by observers of how well individuals fit particular dispositional prototypes (e.g., the "friendly" child, the "withdrawn" child, the "aggressive" child) were related clearly to the shape of the observed-behavior situation profiles as well as to their average level of prototype-relevant behaviors (Shoda et al., 1993b). When the pattern of variability is changed, so are the personality judgments (Shoda, Mischel, & Wright, 1989).

Exemplars of different personality prototypes thus are characterized by distinctive patterns of stable *if . . . then . . .* profiles, as well as by the average frequency in their prototype-relevant behaviors, with high agreement. A "friendly person," for example, is seen as such not just because of her average level of friendliness but also because of the stable pattern of *if . . . then . . .* relationships, as in "friendly with people she knows personally but not with casual acquaintances at work" (Shoda & Mischel, 1993). Moreover, while perceivers often encode other people and themselves in terms of traits, they also under some conditions infer the cognitions and affects—the motives, goals, plans, and other person variables—that may underlie the behavior, functioning more like social-cognitive theorists than like trait theorists (Shoda & Mischel, 1993).

However, as discussed by Shoda and Mischel (1993), most research on the perception of personality has been constrained by sharing the traditional trait assumption that equates personality with global behavioral dispositions. It thus construes personality and situations as mutually exclusive and opposite influences. Given that assumption, information about how the target's behavior varies across different situations is usually deliberately not given to the perceiver, leaving the role of situation–behavior relationships relatively unexamined in person-perception studies. Finally, as Figure 2 also indicates, the characteristic behavior patterns generated by the system impact not only on the perceptions of others and of oneself but also modify the types of situations that will be subsequently encountered, producing a continuous reciprocal interaction between the behaviors generated and the psychological situations experienced.

Biochemical–Genetic Level: Pre-Dispositions at the Biological Substrate. The long-term developmental influences on the system, and the personality structures and dispositions that emerge within it, depend importantly on biological and genetic history as well as on cognitive-social learning history, and cultural–social influences (lower-left rectangle in Figure 2). Individuals differ in diverse biochemical–genetic–somatic factors that may be conceptualized as *pre*-dispositions. These *pre*-dispositions ultimately influence such personality-relevant qualities as sensory and psychomotor sensitivities and vulnerabilities, skills and competencies, temperament (including activity level and emotionality), chronic mood, and affective states. These in turn impact on the psychological system—such as CAPS—that emerges and is seen at the psychological level of analysis.

There are great individual differences within virtually every aspect of the biological human repertoire and genetic heritage that can have profound predisposing implications for the personality and behavior that ultimately develop (e.g., Plomin, DeFries, McClearn, & Rutter, 1997). These differences occur, for example, in sensory, perceptual–cognitive, and affective systems, in metabolic clocks and hormones, in neurotransmitters—in short, in the person's total biochemical–genetic–somatic heritage. These *pre*-dispositions interact with conditions throughout development and play out in ways that influence what the person thinks, feels and does. Even small differences among individuals at the biochemical–somatic level (e.g., in sensory-perceptual sensitivity, in allergy and de-

cease proneness, in energy levels) may manifest ultimately as considerable differences in their experiences and behavior and in what comes to be perceived as their personalities.

Consequently, an adequate approach to personality coherence requires addressing not only the structure and organization of the cognitive-affective-behavioral processing system at the psychological level but also its biochemical–genetic predisposing foundations (Plomin et al., 1997; Saudino & Plomin, 1996). These genetic individual differences presumably at least indirectly affect how people construe or encode—and shape—their environments, which in turn produce important person–context interactions throughout the life course (Plomin, 1994; Saudino & Plomin, 1996).

Both biochemical and social-cognitive influences, heritable and learned, impact on the personality system at the psychological level. They influence both the cognitive-affective units that become available in the system and their organization, although the effects often are indirect. Variables of temperament or reactivity, such as activity, irritability, tension, distress, and emotional lability, visible early in life (Bates & Wachs, 1994), for example, seem to have important, albeit complexly interactive links to emotional and attentional processing and self-regulation (Rothbart, Derryberry, & Posner, 1994). These processes, in turn, should influence the organization of relations among the mediating units in the system and are likely to have important effects, for example, on the types of self-regulatory strategies and competencies that develop and that enable (or hinder) effective impulse control. Because this system, in turn, generates the specific, *if . . . then . . .* situation–behavior relations manifested, the theory predicts that individual differences in genetic–biochemical *pre*-dispositions, in the present view, will be manifested not only in the mean level of various types of behaviors, but in the behavioral signatures of personality, that is, the stable configuration of *if . . . then . . .* situation–behavior relations. When the system changes, either due to modification in the biological substrates or due to developmental changes and significant life events, the effects will also be seen at the behavioral level as a change in the relationships between the "ifs" and the "thens" in the situation–behavior profiles that characterize the person.

Pursuing Dispositions and Dynamics in a Unitary Framework Personality psychology has been committed since its beginnings to characterizing individuals in terms of their stable and distinctive qualities (e.g., Allport, 1937; Funder, 1991; Goldberg, 1993). Other personality theorists and researchers have focused instead on the processes that underlie these coherences and that influence how people function (e.g., Bandura, 1986; Cantor & Kihlstrom, 1987; Mischel, 1973; Pervin, 1990). These two goals—to identify and clarify personality dispositions or personality processes—have been pursued in two increasingly separated (and warring) subdisciplines with different agendas that seem to be in conflict with each other (Cervone, 1991; Cronbach, 1957, 1975; Mischel & Shoda, 1994).

The CAPS approach presented in this chapter suggests that both goals may be pursued in concert with no necessary conflict or incompatibility because, in this framework, dispositions and processing dynamics are two complementary facets of the same phenomena and of the same unitary personality system. The dispositional qualities of individuals are represented in the personality system in terms of particular enduring structures in the organization among cognitive-affective mediating units available to the person. This organization in the structure of the disposition guides and constrains the pattern of specific cognitions, affects, and potential behaviors and their interconnections that become activated by the relevant internal or external psychological features of situations. To illustrate, let us consider again the example of the disposition of rejection sensitivity. The expectations and anticipation of rejection, the readiness to encode even ambiguous experiences as rejecting, the tendency to overreact emotionally to such cues, the accessing of hostile and defensive scripts when these feelings arise—all these are characteristics of this disposition, and their activation in a distinct stable pattern defines its processing dynamics and enactment.

Misunderstandings in analyses of dispositions also can be avoided by realizing that they may be studied fruitfully at each of the four levels of analysis discussed above: at the psychological processing level of activated thoughts and feelings; at the behavioral level; at the level of the judgments of observers and of the self; and at the level of the predisposing biochemical–genetic and neural substrate. The basic caveat and crucial requirement for proceeding within a unitary framework, however, are that the construct of dispositions, and indeed of personality structure and dynamics, be revised and refined to take account of the data and theoretical developments on the nature of coherence—and thus of personality—that the last few decades have yielded. This chapter is intended as a step in that direction.

References

Allport, G. W. (1937). *Personality: A psychological interpretation.* New York: Holt, Rinehart & Winston.

Anderson, J. R. (1996). ACT: A simple theory of complex cognition. *American Psychologist, 51,* 355–365.

Ayduk, O. N., Downey, G., Testa, S., Yin, Y., & Shoda, Y. (in press). Does rejection elicit hostility in rejection sensitive women? *Social Cognition.*

Bandura, A. (1986). *Social foundations of thought and action: A social cognitive theory.* Englewood Cliffs, NJ: Prentice-Hall.

Bates, J. E., & Wachs, T. D. (1994). *Temperament: Individual differences at the interface of biology and behavior.* Washington, DC: American Psychological Association.

Bem, D. J. (1983). Further déjà vu in the search for cross-situational consistency: A response to Mischel and Peake. *Psychological Review, 90,* 390–393.

Block, J. (1995). A contrarian view of the five-factor approach to personality description. *Psychological Bulletin, 117,* 187–215.

Buss, D. M. (1987). Selection, evocation, and manipulation. *Journal of Personality and Social Psychology, 53,* 1214–1221.

Cantor, N., & Kihlstrom, J. F. (1987). *Personality and social intelligence.* Englewood Cliffs, NJ: Erlbaum.

Cantor, N., Mischel, W., & Schwartz, J. (1982). A prototype analysis of psychological situations. *Cognitive Psychology, 14,* 45–77.

Carlson, R. (1971). Where is the personality research? *Psychological Bulletin, 75,* 203–219.

Cervone, D. (1991). The two disciplines of personality psychology [Review of the *Handbook of personality: Theory and research*]. *Psychological Science, 2,* 371–376.

Chapman, L. J., & Chapman, J. P. (1969). Illusory correlations as an obstacle to the use of valid psychodiagnostic signs. *Journal of Abnormal Psychology, 74,* 271–280.

Cronbach, L. J. (1957). The two disciplines of scientific psychology. *American Psychologist, 12,* 671–684.

Cronbach, L. J. (1975). Beyond the two disciplines of scientific psychology. *American Psychologist, 30,* 116–127.

Dodge, K. A. (1986). A social information processing model of social competence in children. In M. Perlmutter (Ed.), *The Minnesota symposium on child psychology: Vol. 18. Cognitive perspectives on children's social behavioral development* (pp. 77–125). Hillsdale, NJ: Erlbaum.

Dodge, K. A. (1993). Social-cognitive mechanisms in the development of conduct disorder and depression. *Annual Review of Psychology, 44,* 559–584.

Dodge, K. A. (1997a, April). *Testing developmental theory through prevention trials.* Paper presented at the biennial meeting of the Society for Research in Child Development, Washington, DC.

Dodge, K.A. (1997b, April). *Early peer social rejection and acquired autonomic sensitivity to peer conflicts: Conduct problems in adolescence.* Paper presented at the biennial meeting of the Society for Research in Child Development, Washington, DC.

Downey, G., & Feldman, S. I. (1996). Implications of rejection sensitivity for intimate relationships. *Journal of Personality and Social Psychology, 70,* 1327-1343.

Downey, G., Freitas, A., Michaelis, B., & Khouri, H. (1997). The self-fulfilling prophecy in close relationships: Rejection sensitivity and rejection in romantic partners. *Journal of Personality and Social Psychology, 75,* 545–560.

Endler, N. S., & Hunt, J. (1969). Generalizability of contributions from sources of variance in the S-R inventories of anxiousness. *Journal of Personality, 37,* 1–24.

Endler, N.S., Hunt, J. M., & Rosenstein, A. J. (1962). An S-R inventory of anxiousness. *Psychological Monographs, 76*(536).

Endler, N. S., & Magnusson, D. (1976). Toward an interactional psychology of personality. *Psychological Bulletin, 83,* 956–974.

Epstein, S. (1979). The stability of behavior: I. On predicting most of the people much of the time. *Journal of Personality and Social Psychology, 37,* 1097–1126.

Epstein, S. (1980). The stability of behavior: II. Implications for psychological research. *American Psychologist, 35,* 790–806.

Epstein, S. (1983). The stability of confusion: A reply to Mischel and Peake. *Psychological Review, 90,* 179–184.

Funder, D. C. (1983). Three issues in predicting more of the people: A reply to Mischel and Peake. *Psychological Review, 90,* 283–289.

Funder, D. C. (1991). Global traits: a neo-Allportian approach to personality. *Psychological Science, 2,* 31–39.

Goldberg, L. R. (1993). The structure of phenotypic personality traits. *American Psychologist, 48,* 26–34.

Hartshorne, H., & May, A. (1928). *Studies in the nature of character: Vol. 1. Studies in deceit.* New York: Macmillan.

John, O. P. (1990). The big-five factor taxonomy: Dimensions of personality in the natural language and questionnaires. In L. A. Pervin (Ed.), *Handbook of personality: Theory and research* (pp. 66–100). New York: Guilford Press.

Jones, E. E. (1990). *Interpersonal perception.* New York: Macmillan.

Kandel, E. R., & Hawkins, R. D. (1992). The biological basis of learning and individuality. *Scientific American, 267*(3), 78–86.

Kunda, Z., & Thagard, P. (1996). Forming impressions from stereotypes, traits, and behaviors: A parallel-constraint-satisfaction theory. *Psychological Review, 103,* 284–308.

Magnusson, D., & Endler, N. S. (Eds.). (1977). *Personality at the crossroads: Current issues in interactional psychology.* Hillsdale, NJ: Erlbaum.

McAdams, D. P. (1992). The Five-Factor model in personality. *Journal of Personality, 60,* 329–361.

McCrae, R. R., & Costa, P. T., Jr. (1996). Toward a new generation of personality theories: Theoretical contexts for the five-factor model. In J. S. Wiggins (Ed.), *The five-factor model of personality: Theoretical perspectives* (pp. 51–87). New York: Guilford Press.

McCrae, R. R., & Costa, P. T. (1997). Conceptions and correlates of openness and to experience. In R. Hogan, J. Johnson, & S. Briggs (Eds.), *Handbook of personality psychology* (pp. 825–847). San Diego: Academic Press.

Metcalfe, J., & Jacobs W. J. (1998). Emotional memory: The effects of stress on "cool" and "hot" memory systems. In D. L. Medin (Ed.), *The psychology of learning and motivation: Vol. 38. Advances in research and theory* (pp. 187–222). San Diego, CA: Academic Press.

Metcalfe, J., & Mischel, W. (1999). A hot/cool system analysis of delay of gratification: Dynamics of willpower. *Psychological Review, 6.*

Mischel, W. (1968). *Personality and assessment.* New York: Wiley.

Mischel, W. (1973). Toward a cognitive social learning reconceptualization of personality. *Psychological Review, 80,* 252–283.

Mischel, W. (1990). Personality dispositions revisited and revised: A view after three decades. In L. A. Pervin (Ed.), *Handbook of personality: Theory and research* (pp. 111–134). New York: Guilford Press.

Mischel, W. (1998). *Introduction to personality* (6th ed.). Fort Worth, TX: Harcourt Brace.

Mischel, W., Cantor, N., & Feldman, S. (1996). Principles of self-regulation: The nature of willpower and self-control. In E. T. Higgins & A. W. Kruglanski (Eds.), *Social psychology: Handbook of basic principles* (pp. 329–360). New York: Guilford Press.

Mischel, W., Ebbesen, E. B., & Zeiss, A. R. (1973). Selective attention to the self: Situational and dispositional determinants. *Journal of Personality and Social Psychology, 27,* 129–142.

Mischel, W., Ebbesen, E. B., & Zeiss, A. R. (1976). Determinants of selective memory about the self. *Journal of Consulting and Clinical Psychology, 44,* 92–103.

Mischel, W., & Peake, P. K. (1982). In search of consistency: Measure for measure. In M. P. Zanna, E. T. Higgins, & C. P. Herman (Eds.), *Consistency in social behavior: The Ontario symposium* (Vol. 2). Hillsdale, NJ: Erlbaum.

Mischel, W., & Shoda, Y. (1994). Personality psychology has two goals: Must it be two fields? *Psychological Inquiry, 5,* 156–158.

Mischel, W., & Shoda, Y. (1995). A cognitive-affective system theory of personality: Reconceptualizing situations, dispositions, dynamics, and invariance in personality structure. *Psychological Review, 102*(2), 246–268.

Mischel, W., & Shoda, Y. (1998). Reconciling processing dynamics and personality dispositions. *Annual Review of Psychology, 49,* 229–258.

Newcomb, T. M. (1929). *Consistency of certain extrovert-introvert behavior patterns in 51 problem boys.* New York: Columbia University, Teachers College, Bureau of Publications.

Nisbett, R. E., & Ross, L. D. (1980). *Human inference: Strategies* and shortcomings of social judgment. *Century Psychology Series.* Englewood Cliffs, NJ: Prentice-Hall.

Nolen-Hoeksema, S., Parker, L. E. & Larson, J. (1994). Ruminative coping with depressed mood following loss. *Journal of Personality and Social Psychology, 67*, 92–104.

Norem, J. K., & Cantor, N. (1986). Anticipatory and post hoc cushioning strategies: Optimism and defensive pessimism in "risky" situations. *Cognitive Therapy and Research, 10*, 347–362.

Pervin, L. A. (Ed.). (1990). *Handbook of personality: Theory and research.* New York: Guilford Press.

Pervin, L. A. (1994). A critical analysis of trait theory. *Psychological Inquiry, 5*, 103–113.

Peterson, D. R. (1968). *The clinical study of social behavior.* New York: Appleton.

Plomin, R. (1994). *Genetics and experience: The developmental interplay between nature and nurture.* Newbury Park, CA: Sage.

Plomin, R., DeFries, J. C., McClearn, G. E., & Rutter, M. (1997). *Behavioral genetics* (3rd ed.). New York: Freeman.

Read, S. J., & Miller, L. C. (Eds.). (1998). *Connectionist models of social reasoning and social behavior.* Mahwah, NJ: Erlbaum.

Rothbart, M. K., Derryberry, D., & Posner, M. I. (1994). A psychobiological approach to the development of temperament. In J. E. Bates & T. D. Wachs (Eds.), *Temperament: Individual differences at the interface of biology and behavior* (pp. 83–116). Washington, DC: American Psychological Association.

Rumelhart, D. E., & McClelland, J. L. (1986). *Parallel distributing processing: Explorations in the microstructure of cognition: Foundations* (Vol. 1). Cambridge, MA: MIT Press/Bradford Books.

Saudino, K. J., & Plomin, R. (1996). Personality and behavioral genetics: Where have we been and where are we going? *Journal of Research in Personality, 30*, 335–347.

Shoda, Y. (1990). *Conditional analyses of personality coherence and dispositions.* Unpublished doctoral dissertation, Columbia University, New York.

Shoda, Y., & Mischel, W. (1993). Cognitive social approach to dispositional inferences: What if the perceiver is a cognitive-social theorist? *Personality and Social Psychology Bulletin, 19*, 574–585.

Shoda, Y., & Mischel, W. (1996). Toward a unified, intraindividual dynamic conception of personality. *Journal of Research in Personality, 30*, 414–428.

Shoda, Y., & Mischel, W. (1998). Reconciling processing dynamics and personality dispositions. *Annual Review of Psychology, 49*, 229–258.

Shoda, Y., Mischel, W., & Wright, J. C. (1989). Intuitive interactionism in person perception: Effects of situation–behavior relations on dispositional judgments. *Journal of Personality and Social Psychology, 56*, 41–53.

Shoda, Y., Mischel, W., & Wright, J. C. (1993a). The role of situational demands and cognitive competencies in behavior organization and personality coherence. *Journal of Personality and Social Psychology, 56*, 41–53.

Shoda, Y., Mischel, W., & Wright, J. C. (1993b). Links between personality judgments and contextualized behavior patterns: Situation–behavior profiles of personality prototypes. *Social Cognition, 4*, 399–429.

Shoda, Y., Mischel, W., & Wright, J. C. (1994). Intraindividual stability in the organization and patterning of behavior: Incorporating psychological situations into the idiographic analysis of personality. *Journal of Personality and Social Psychology, 65*, 1023–1035.

Shultz, T. R., & Lepper, M. R. (1996). Cognitive dissonance reduction as constraint satisfaction. *Psychological Review, 103*, 219–240.

Taylor, S. E., & Schneider, S. (1989). Coping and the simulation of events. *Social Cognition, 7*, 174–194.

Vernon, P. E. (1964). *Personality assessment: A critical survey.* New York: Wiley.

Walker, L. E. (1979). *The battered women.* New York: Harper & Row.

Westen, D. (1990). Psychoanalytic approaches to personality. In L. A. Pervin (Ed.), *Handbook of personality: Theory and research* (pp. 21–65). New York: Guilford Press.

Wright, J. C., & Mischel, W. (1987). A conditional approach to dispositional constructs: The local predictability of social behavior. *Journal of Personality and Social Psychology, 53*, 1159–1177.

Wright, J. C., & Mischel, W. (1988). Conditional hedges and the intuitive psychology of traits. *Journal of Personality and Social Psychology, 55*, 454–469.

Creating Satisfaction in Steady Dating Relationships: The Role of Personal Goals and Situational Affordances

Catherine A. Sanderson and Nancy Cantor

Mischel's article in this section emphasizes the fine-grained "if . . . then" patterns by which people change their behavior, as the situations they find themselves in change. Bandura's article described a "self system" that allows people to reconstrue or change the situations they are in so as to pursue consistent goals. Elements of both of these approaches are found in the next selection, by the prominent social cognitive theorist Nancy Cantor and one of her former students, Catherine Sanderson. The article notes that people vary in the degree to which they seek intimacy in their dating relationships, and dating partners also vary in the degree to which they allow and encourage, or "afford," intimacy. In a study of college students in dating relationships, Sanderson and Cantor find that people with weak intimacy goals are able to build satisfying relationships only with people who afford a great deal of intimacy themselves. By contrast, and almost paradoxically, people with strong and focused intimacy goals seem to manage to find a way to satisfy these goals even with partners who themselves do not "afford" very much intimacy. The bottom line here echoes Bandura's point that situations are to a large extent what you make them, and that a person with strong and focused goals has a better chance of attaining them almost regardless of external circumstances.

From *Journal of Personality and Social Psychology, 73,* 1424–1433, 1997.

Considerable research across a variety of domains has shown that individuals are better able to effectively regulate their behavior and experience satisfaction when they are in contexts that encourage fulfillment of their valued goals (Cantor, Norem, Langston, Zirkel, Fleeson, & Cook-Flannagan, 1991; Emmons, Diener, & Larsen, 1986; McAdams & Constantian, 1983). For example, Snyder's work on volunteerism has shown that individuals can pursue the broad task of volunteering through participation in different specific volunteer jobs and that, in turn, sustaining volunteer activity depends on the fit of the particular job responsibilities (e.g., answering phones, or serving as a buddy to an HIV positive person) and the individual's motivation for volunteering (e.g., esteem enhancement or compassion; Omoto & Snyder, 1990; Snyder, 1993). In a similar vein, research has shown that adolescents pursue social dating sometimes with a focus on their own identity goals (e.g., self-exploration or independence) and other times with a focus on intimacy goals (e.g., self-disclosure or interdependence) and that these different goals are associated with different preferences for dating (e.g., those with identity goals prefer casual dating with a series of partners, whereas those with intimacy goals prefer having a steady dating relationship with a single partner; Sanderson & Cantor, 1995). Furthermore, more effective behavior regulation occurs when individuals are in goal-congruent dating contexts: those with strong intimacy goals who are in a long-term relationship and those with strong identity goals who are in a casual dating relationship (e.g., matching situations) have safer sexual behavior than those who are in mismatched dating contexts. In this way, satisfaction and self-regulation hinge on being in a context that encourages goal fulfillment.

* * *

This study extends previous work indicating that individuals are more effective at regulating their behavior when they are in goal-congruent contexts by examining whether individuals particularly need concrete goal-relevant situational affordances once they are in these broadly affirming contexts. We explore this issue in the domain of close personal relationships, examining the broad context of steady dating relationships, which are intimacy-relevant contexts, and considering the role of both intimacy goals and intimacy-affording daily life situations in producing relationship satisfaction and maintenance over time.

Creating Intimacy in Steady Dating Relationships

The broad context of a steady dating relationship emphasizes creating intimacy, including trust (Rempel, Holmes, & Zanna, 1985), interdependence (Berscheid, 1983, 1986; Kelley et al., 1983), and self-disclosure. In turn, relationship satisfac-

tion is enhanced when individuals have greater emotional involvement in their dating relationships (Rubin, Hill, Peplau, & Dunkel-Schetter, 1980) and can engage in self-disclosure, trust, and interdependence (Altman & Taylor, 1973; Hendrick, 1981; Levinger & Senn, 1967; Reis & Shaver, 1988). Furthermore, dating relationships with little intimacy are more prone to dissolution (Hendrick, 1981; Hendrick, Hendrick, & Adler, 1988; Hill, Rubin, & Peplau, 1976; Simpson, 1987). Thus, both theory and research suggest that the close relationship context is one that focuses on intimacy and that creating such communion is an important predictor of relationship satisfaction and maintenance.

Although close relationships are intimacy-relevant contexts, not all individuals who are in such relationships will have an intent focus on intimacy. First, various situational factors may lead people to pursue steady dating relationships even without the desire to engage in communion (e.g., self-disclosure or interdependence) with a dating partner. For example, some college students may pursue steady dating relationships as the preferred type of dating context (e.g., stable, monogamous, and committed) more as a way to get access to a variety of desired events, including social situations (e.g., college formals, sexual activity, and so on) than as a forum for creating intimacy. Moreover, though committed to pursuing relationships, individuals are still likely to vary widely in their actual skill at creating and maintaining intimacy (e.g., Berscheid, Snyder, & Omoto, 1989; Cantor, Acker, & Cook-Flannagan, 1992; McAdams, 1984; Prager, 1995). The attachment styles model (Hazan & Shaver, 1987; Simpson, 1990), for example, suggests that individuals who have developed secure attachment models in early childhood are the most likely to succeed at creating intimacy in close relationships because these individuals have this secure base on which to build communion. Moreover, our previous research has shown that late adolescents differ systematically in the extent to which they pursue intimacy goals in social dating (Cantor & Sanderson, in press; Sanderson & Cantor, 1995), with those who have not yet resolved their identity issues (e.g., Erikson, 1950) being more likely to pursue self-focused goals in dating than intimacy-focused ones. Even in adulthood, however, individuals may vary in the extent to which they are focused on and adept at creating intimacy. Following divorce or death of a spouse, for example, an individual may be more intent on self-exploration than on engaging in communion with a single other. Thus, both situational and dispositional variables may influence the extent to which individuals are focused on creating intimacy in their steady dating relationships.

Even within the broad intimacy-relevant context of a steady dating relationship, specific dating situations in daily life can vary in the extent to which they concretely facilitate the pursuit of intimacy (e.g., Buss, 1987; Emmons, Diener, & Larsen, 1986; Snyder, 1981). For example, because engaging in open communication often requires some privacy, spending private time alone with one's partner should facilitate engaging in intimacy (Silbereisen, Noack, & von Eye, 1992). Likewise, both giving to and receiving social support from one's dating partner may foster intimacy within the dating relationship (e.g., Sarason, Shearlin, Pierce, & Sarason, 1987) by strengthening the bond between dating partners and enhancing feelings of responsibility for and commitment to the relationship (e.g., Brickman & Coates, 1987; Fincham & Bradbury, 1990). Related to this, having an intimacy-focused partner who elicits self-disclosure and creates opportunities for interdependence may lead to intimacy and thereby satisfaction even on the part of a non-intimacy-focused person (Hendrick, 1981; Jourard, 1971; Miller, 1990; Miller, Cody, & McLaughlin, 1985; Miller & Read, 1991). Thus, even within the broad context of a steady dating relationship, different daily life situations will vary in the extent to which they concretely facilitate self-disclosure and closeness with a dating partner.

Predicting Relationship Satisfaction

Because the broad context of a close relationship emphasizes intimacy, individuals who are able to create such communion are likely to experience greater relationship satisfaction as well as relationship maintenance over time. However, the importance of concrete situational affordances for intimacy is also likely to differ as a function of one's own personal focus on intimacy.

First, those with a strong personal focus on intimacy in dating who are in a steady dating relationship (e.g., a broadly goal-relevant context) may be able to flexibly create opportunities to engage in open communication and interdependence, even when a specific dating situation does not explicitly fit their goals, and hence experience satisfaction (e.g., Buss, 1987). For example, an intimacy-focused individual may be more effective at compensating for the absence of distinct intimacy-relevant opportunities by "making the most" of even suboptimal situations, such as eliciting self-disclosure from a non-intimacy-focused partner, providing relevant social support, and engaging in communion even in public dating situations. On the other hand, those without strong intimacy goals who are nonetheless committed to maintaining a steady dating relationship may have difficulty creating communion with a dating partner by themselves and may therefore depend on the presence of various concrete intimacy-relevant situations in daily life. For example, an individual with weaker intimacy goals may especially benefit in terms of satisfaction from spending private time alone with one's dating partner, which, in and of itself, facilitates self-disclosure, or having an intimacy-focused partner who both provides and elicits social support.

To examine these predictions, we investigated the patterns of daily social interactions among college students who were in relatively long-term steady dating relationships. We identified three intimacy-relevant situational affordances in close relationships—namely, time spent alone with one's partner, social support given to or received from one's partner, and one's partner's goals—and examined the role of each of these affordances in predicting relationship satisfaction and maintenance. Specifically, we predict that those with strong intimacy goals who are in a steady dating relationship will experience satisfaction regardless of the presence of these situational affordances, whereas those without such strong goals who are nonetheless committed to their dating relationship will depend on such affordances.

Method

Students in ongoing steady dating relationships were recruited to participate in a study on dating relationships and daily life activities. Potential participants were told that participation was limited to those who were currently dating a person who lived in close proximity to them (e.g., not a long distance relationship) and that participating involved completing a 45-min questionnaire.

PARTICIPANTS Sixty Princeton University undergraduates participated in this study (31 men and 29 women; mean age in years = 20.43, SD = 1.06). The majority (88%) of these participants were juniors or seniors. Participants had a mean relationship length of 12.72 months (SD = 9.36) with their dating partner.

PROCEDURE After participants completed their questionnaires, they were given brief (three-page) questionnaires to distribute to their dating partner * * *. These questionnaires included the following measures: individuals' own goals in dating * * *, their perceptions of the participants' dating and friendship goals, and the amount of each of four types of social support they gave to and received from the participants. These measures were all also given to the participants and are described in detail later. They were paid $10 for their participation, * * *. Of our 60 participants, we received questionnaires back * * * from 58.

MEASURES

Social Dating Goals Scale. To examine participants' orientation toward intimacy specifically in the social dating task, we used the Social Dating Goals Scale (Sanderson & Cantor, 1995; α = .80). This 13-item scale is scored on a 1 to 5 scale (1 = *strongly disagree* to 5 = *strongly agree*) and consists of items assessing individuals' concerns with self-disclosure and dependence (e.g., "In my dating relationships, I try to share my most intimate thoughts and feelings," "In my dating relationships, I try to date those I can count on") as well as reverse-scored items assessing individuals' concerns with identity and independence (e.g., "In my dating relationships, I try to keep my individual identity"). * * * The tendency to pursue intimacy goals in dating is positively correlated with interpersonal and ideological ego achievement (Marcia, 1966) and secure attachment (Hazan & Shaver, 1987; Simpson, 1990), and negatively correlated with both interpersonal and ideological ego diffusion and with anxious attachment (see Sanderson & Cantor, 1995). Furthermore, individuals with predominantly identity dating goals have more casual dating and sexual partners, whereas those with predominantly intimacy dating goals have longer dating relationships. In line with previous research, there were no gender differences in scores on this scale, $t(58)$ = .20, *ns.* This scale was completed by participants and their dating partners.

Partner's perceived dating goals. Participants were also asked to complete the Social Dating Goals Scale on the basis of how they thought their partner would respond to this scale (e.g., their perceptions of their partner's dating goals). There were again no gender differences in scores on this scale, $t(58)$ = .91, *ns.* This scale was completed by participants as well as their dating partners.

Time spent in various situations. Participants were asked to list the number of hours they spent in eight different situations in both the last week and a typical week. These situations were based on common activities at this college and included the following: with my dating partner and others (e.g., at a meal or an event); alone with my dating partner; relaxing or socializing with my roommates, suitemates, or housemates; with my close friend and others (e.g., at a meal or an event); alone with my close friend; eating or socializing in my eating club, college, or dorm; talking with my family on the phone; and relaxing or socializing with casual friends or acquaintances.

Social support. Participants rated the extent to which their dating partner provided each of four types of social support that are widely used in the close relationships literature (House & Kahn, 1985): listening, instrumental, informational, and emotional ($\alpha = .89$). Ratings were based on a 1 to 5 scale (1 = *not at all* to 7 = *a lot*). Participants were then asked to rate the extent to which they gave their dating partner each of these four types of support, again using a 1 to 7 scale ($\alpha = .84$). This scale was completed by participants as well as their dating partners.

Relationship satisfaction. Participants responded to one question regarding their satisfaction with their current dating relationship, using a 1 to 7 scale (1 = *strongly disagree* and 7 = *strongly agree*; i.e., "I am very satisfied with my *current* dating relationship").

Demographic information. Participants provided a variety of demographic information, including age, year in school, gender, length of current dating relationship, and length of close friendship.

TABLE 1

MEANS AND STANDARD DEVIATIONS OF MEASURES

Measure	Men		Women	
	M	*SD*	*M*	*SD*
Time spent in the last week alone with partner[a]	26.66	21.93	14.15	13.40
Total social support received from partner[b]	5.58	1.21	5.84	1.09
Total support given to partner[b]	5.98	0.88	5.44	1.05
Partner's intimacy goals[c]	3.77	0.48	3.63	0.43

Note. Although all variables were standardized for use in the analyses, raw numbers are presented in this table for ease of interpretation.
[a]Measured in number of hours per week. [b]Measured on a 1 to 7 scale (1 = *not at all* to 7 = *a lot*). [c]Measured with 12-item scale answered on a 1 to 5 scale (1 = *strongly disagree* to 5 = *strongly agree*).

TABLE 2

CORRELATIONS BETWEEN MEASURES

Measure	1	2	3	4	5
1. Intimacy goals	—	.30*	.56***	.61***	.20
2. Time spent with partner		—	.22	.27*	.14
3. Social support from partner			—	.47***	.15
4. Social support given to partner				—	.33**
5. Partner's dating goals					—

Note. *$p < .05$.   **$p < .01$.   ***$p < .001$.

Follow-up. Approximately 5 months after completing this questionnaire, participants were recontacted by phone and asked to respond to several questions. Of the original 60 participants, 58 were able to be contacted and all of these agreed to respond to the questions. First of all, they were asked how satisfied they were with their life in general and how happy they were with their dating relationship, using a 1 to 7 scale (1 = *strongly disagree* and 7 = *strongly agree*). Next, they were asked if they were in a steady dating relationship and, if so, whether it was with the same partner. Forty-six of the 58 participants were still dating the same partner, and 2 participants reported having a steady relationship with a new partner.

Results

The means and standard deviations for each of the measures used in this study are presented in Table 1, and the correlations between these measures are presented in Table 2.[1] Given previous research showing differences in the predictors of relationship satisfaction as a function of gender and length of the dating relationship (e.g., Fletcher, Fincham, Cramer, & Heron, 1987; Reis, Senchak, & Solomon, 1985), these variables were controlled for in all of the following analyses. These results examine the association of both intimacy goals and intimacy-relevant situational affordances with re-

---

[1]The interpretation of correlation coefficients such as appear in Table 2 are explained by Rosenthal and Rubin in Part I of this volume.

lationship satisfaction and relationship mainte-nance over time.

MAIN EFFECTS ANALYSES First, we conducted a hierarchical multiple regression analysis predicting satisfaction with current dating relationship from intimacy goals, controlling for gender and length of relationship. This analysis revealed a significant effect of intimacy goals on satisfaction but no effects of either gender or length of relationship (see Table 3). As predicted, those with stronger intimacy goals in dating have greater relationship satisfaction.

* * *

INTERACTION ANALYSES We then conducted a se-ries of hierarchical regression analyses predicting relationship satisfaction from dating goals, a given affordance, and the Goals × Affordance interac-tion to determine whether the presence of situa-tional affordances was particularly important in terms of satisfaction for those with weaker inti-macy goals.[2] * * * This interaction [Figure 1] re-vealed that those who were high in intimacy goals were not dependent in terms of satisfaction on how much time they spent alone with their partner in the last week (e.g., those with high intimacy goals were quite satisfied with their relationship re-gardless of how much time they spent with their partner), whereas for those low in intimacy goals, relationship satisfaction was dependent on the amount of time they spent alone with their partner in the last week. Specifically, among those with weak intimacy goals, those who spent little time with their partner were particularly dissatisfied with the relationship and those who spent consid-erable time with their partner were particularly satisfied.

Analyses predicting satisfaction from the in-teraction of goals and support, given as well as received, also revealed significant interactions in both cases (see Figures 2 and 3). Those who have

strong intimacy goals are relatively satisfied with the relationship regardless of the amount of social support they receive from or give to their dating partner. On the other hand, those who are less fo-cused on intimacy in dating experience greater sat-isfaction when they receive considerable support from their partner and give considerable support to their partner.

In a similar manner, analyses revealed a signif-icant interaction between own goals and partner's goals with no effects of either gender or length of the relationship. Those with strong intimacy goals reported high satisfaction with their dating rela-tionship, regardless of the goals their partner was pursuing, and apparently were not disrupted by having a partner with dissimilar goals (see Fig-ure 4). On the other hand, those with less strong intimacy goals who were with partners with less in-timacy goals were the least satisfied. It appears that some focus on intimacy by at least one partner in the relationship is conducive to satisfaction.

* * *

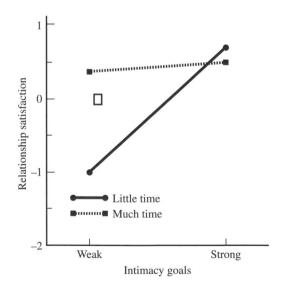

Figure 1 The slope of relationship satisfaction was cal-culated on dating goals for those who spent considerable time alone with their dating partner (one standard devi-ation above the mean) and little time alone with their partner (one standard deviation below the mean).

---

[2]A set of fairly complex analyses, not included in this se-lection, examined the degree to which the effects of goals and affordances "interacted" or depended upon each other.

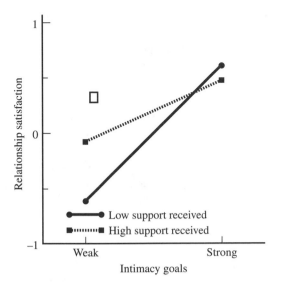

Figure 2 The slope of relationship satisfaction was calculated on dating goals for those who received considerable social support from their dating partner (one standard deviation above the mean) and those who received little support (one standard deviation below the mean).

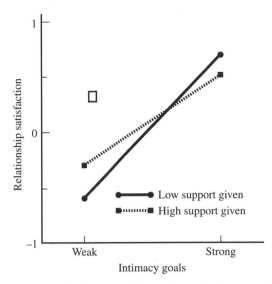

Figure 3 The slope of relationship satisfaction was calculated on dating goals for those who gave considerable social support to their dating partner (one standard deviation above the mean) and those who gave little support (one standard deviation below the mean).

ACCURACY VERSUS BIASED PERCEPTION Although we have described our findings as indicating that those with strong intimacy goals experience greater satisfaction because they are able to compensate for the absence of concrete intimacy-relevant affordances, it is also possible that those with strong intimacy goals simply interpret their situational affordances as particularly intimacy-relevant. However, this perception (regardless of its accuracy) may lead them to engage in self-disclosure and interdependence, which in turn leads to greater satisfaction. For example, Murray and colleagues have found that close relationships are more satisfying and likely to persist when individuals hold idealized views about their partners (Murray, Holmes, & Griffin, 1996a, 1996b). This finding corresponds with the social support literature suggesting that individuals' perceptions of how much social support they receive can be a more important predictor of well-being than actual support received (see Brunstein, Dangelmayer, & Schultheiss, 1996; Dunkel-Schetter & Bennett, 1990).

To test whether those with strong intimacy goals do, in fact, benefit from having an accurate

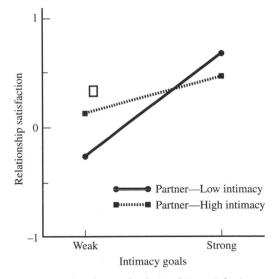

Figure 4 The slope of relationship satisfaction was calculated on dating goals for those with a strongly intimacy-focused dating partner (one standard deviation above the mean) and those with a less intimacy-focused partner (one standard deviation below the mean).

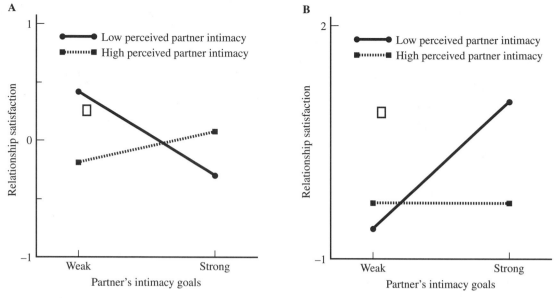

Figure 5 The three-way interaction of own goals, partner's goals, and partner's perceived goals emerged as significant above and beyond the main effects, two-way interactions, gender, and length of relationship. For ease of interpretation, following Aiken and West (1991), the two interactions of Partner's Reported Goals × Partner's Perceived Goals were graphed for those high and low intimacy goals. Panel A presents the slope of relationship satisfaction for participants who are themselves strongly focused on intimacy, on partner's dating goals for those who believe their dating partner is strongly focused on intimacy (one standard deviation above the mean), and those who believe their partner is less focused on intimacy (one standard deviation below the mean). Panel B presents the same data for participants who are themselves less strongly focused on intimacy.

sense of their intimacy-relevant affordances (i.e., to compensate in their efforts to create closeness and communion), we examined individuals' accuracy about their partner's intimacy goals (based on their partner's self-reports). After all, it should be easier for individuals to compensate for a lack of their partner's focus if they are aware of it, and hence we predicted that having an accurate sense of their partner's focus on intimacy should be particularly important for those with strong intimacy goals. As shown in Panel A of Figure 5, those with strong intimacy goals are most satisfied when their perceptions of their partner's goals are accurate, regardless of what those goals are (see Figure 5). These findings suggest that the association between intimacy goals and satisfaction is not merely a function of biased perceptions and interpretations—those with strong intimacy goals actually need to be accurate about their partner's goals to have satisfaction.

On the other hand, those with less of a focus on intimacy should not depend on accuracy because they are not attempting (or even able) to compensate for the absence of various intimacy-relevant situational affordances. In fact, as shown in Panel B of Figure 5, those who lack a focus on intimacy are particularly happy when they are with an intimacy-focused partner whom they think is low in intimacy, presumably because this partner provides opportunities to engage in communion yet is not perceived as demanding of reciprocation, "smothering," or both. These findings therefore suggest that although those with strong intimacy goals benefit in terms of satisfaction from having an accurate sense of their partner's goals, those with weaker or alternative goals in dating benefit from inaccuracy (at least when they have an intimacy-focused partner).

*   *   *

Discussion

At the heart of most goals perspectives on personality and social behavior is an emphasis on the fit between individuals' goals and dispositions on the one hand, and situational affordances on the other hand (Cantor, 1994; Pervin, 1989). Our research extends this previous work on the Person × Situation interaction (e.g., Baron & Boudreau, 1987; Emmons, Diener, & Larsen, 1986; Snyder, 1993) by showing the active, constructive side of people with strong goals in experiencing satisfaction and well-being. Specifically, those with strong intimacy goals experienced relationship satisfaction regardless of the presence of specific situational affordances, compensating for the absence of direct encouragement for intimacy. In fact, those with strong intimacy goals particularly benefited in terms of satisfaction from having an accurate sense of their partner's intimacy goals. For example, they were able to compensate for having a partner without a strong focus on intimacy (e.g., by working to elicit self-disclosure and interdependence) as long as they were aware of their partner's lack of intimacy goals. * * * This research therefore indicates that as long as they are in a broadly goal-relevant context, those with strong goals do not depend on the presence of matching situational affordances but, rather, can make any situation work in terms of goal fulfillment.

SITUATIONAL AFFORDANCES: BENEFIT OR PRESSURE? In contrast, this research does demonstrate that some people do benefit in terms of satisfaction from having strong situational affordances, that is, those with weaker goals. Those with weaker intimacy goals, who are not particularly motivated to create intimacy on their own, actually benefited from having concrete intimacy-conducive affordances, such as spending time alone with their partner and having an intimacy-focused partner. In other words, in the highly reciprocal and interactive context of a close relationship, even those without a strong focus on intimacy themselves are able to actively engage in this task, and thereby experience satisfaction as well as relationship maintenance over time, if they are with an intimacy-oriented partner who elicits self-disclosure and interdependence.

There are, however, limits to the ability of such affordances to lead to satisfaction. Specifically, individuals with weak intimacy goals do not benefit from having a partner with strong intimacy goals if they (accurately) perceive that their partner has such a focus. In this case, they may feel pressured to engage in self-disclosure and interdependence, which may be uncomfortable pressure or disruptive of their own self-focused exploration. Hazan and Shaver's (1987) work on attachment styles, for example, describes *avoidants* as those who are likely to feel easily overwhelmed by a partner's pressure for intimacy and hence may be least satisfied when they are with (or believe they are with) an intimacy-focused partner. Interesting to note is that it may be those who have weak intimacy goals who experience the benefits of holding idealized illusions about their partner's goals (e.g., Murray, Holmes, & Griffin, 1996a, 1996b). For example, those with weak intimacy goals benefit most from *having* an intimacy-oriented partner (e.g., who facilitates communion) but *perceiving* their partner as non-intimacy focused (and therefore not demanding "too much" self-disclosure and interdependence).

INTIMACY AND CLOSE RELATIONSHIPS This research also contributes to current theories on personality and close relationships by showing the importance of intimacy goals in producing relationship satisfaction. In fact, even controlling for length of the relationship (which has been shown in prior research to predict maintenance; e.g., Simpson, 1987), both own and partner's intimacy goals were the only significant predictors of relationship maintenance at the follow-up: Apparently, someone in a close relationship needs to be working on intimacy to obtain satisfaction and foster relationship maintenance over time. This work may therefore contribute to other research on the association between personality variables and relationship satisfaction. For example, the very common finding of a link between secure attachment styles and relationship satisfaction (e.g., Kirk-patrick & Davis, 1994) may be mediated by intimacy goals. Specifically, those with such secure working models of attachment, who have grown up trusting and believing that relationship partners are dependable and responsive to one's own needs, should want to reciprocate this intimacy and therefore form strong intimacy goals (e.g., Sanderson & Cantor, 1995). As we have shown in the present research, these goals, in turn, will lead them to actively create opportunities to engage in such communion, even in suboptimal situations (e.g., when they have little private time alone with their partner, or when they are with a non-intimacy-focused partner), and thereby experience relationship satisfaction.

Conclusions

In summary, this study of steady dating relationships has revealed how delicate the Person × Situation interaction is in daily life. Specifically, we have shown in the arena of close relationships that satisfaction depends on one's broad life context, the strength of personal goals in enabling individuals to compensate for the absence of matching situational affordances, and the presence of concrete situational affordances in assisting those with weak goals in actively participating. Therefore, in many respects, it is remarkable that individuals are able to experience satisfaction in their close relationships because it requires an intricate balance of the right person being in the right place at the right time.

References

Aiken, L. S., & West, S. G. (1991). *Multiple regression: Testing and interpreting interactions.* Newbury Park, CA: Sage.

Altman, I., & Taylor, D. A. (1973). *Social penetration: The development of interpersonal relationships.* New York: Holt, Rinehart & Winston.

Baron, R. M., & Boudreau, L. A. (1987). An ecological perspective on integrating personality and social psychology. *Journal of Personality and Social Psychology, 53,* 1214–1221.

Berscheid, E. (1983). Emotion. In H. H. Kelley, E. Berscheid, A. Christensen, H. Harvey, T. L. Huston, G. Levinger, E. McClintock, L. A. Peplau, & D. Peterson (Eds.), *Close relationships* (pp. 110–168). San Francisco: Freeman.

Berscheid, E. (1986). Emotional experience in close relationships: Some implications for child development. In W. Hartup & Z. Rubin (Eds.), *Relationships and development* (pp. 135–166). Hillsdale, NJ: Erlbaum.

Berscheid, E., Snyder, M., & Omoto, A. M. (1989). The Relationship Closeness Inventory: Assessing the closeness of interpersonal relationships. *Journal of Personality and Social Psychology, 57,* 702–807.

Brickman, P., & Coates, D. (1987). Commitment and mental health. In P. Brickman (Ed.), *Commitment, conflict, and caring* (pp. 222–309). Englewood Cliffs, NJ: Prentice Hall.

Brunstein, J. C., Dangelmayer, G., & Schultheiss, O. C. (1996). Personal goals and social support in close relationships: Effects on relationship mood and marital satisfaction. *Journal of Personality and Social Psychology, 71,* 1006–1019.

Buss, D. M. (1987). Selection, evocation, and manipulation. *Journal of Personality and Social Psychology, 53,* 1214–1221.

Cantor, N. (1994). Life task problem-solving: Situational affordances and personal needs. *Personality and Social Psychology Bulletin, 20,* 235–243.

Cantor, N., Acker, M., & Cook-Flannagan, C. (1992). Conflict and preoccupation in the intimacy life task. *Journal of Personality and Social Psychology, 63,* 644–655.

Cantor, N., Norem, J. K., Langston, C. A., Zirkel, S., Fleeson, W., & Cook-Flannagan, C. (1991). Life tasks and daily life experience. *Journal of Personality, 59,* 425–451.

Cantor, N., & Sanderson, C. A. (in press). The functional regulation of adolescent dating relationships and sexual behavior: An interaction of goals, strategies, and situations. In J. Heckhausen & C. Dweck (Eds.), *A life-span perspective on motivation and control.* Cambridge University Press: Boston.

Dunkel-Schetter, C., & Bennett, T. L. (1990). Differentiating the cognitive and behavioral aspects of social support. In I. G. Sarason, B. R. Sarason, & G. R. Pierce (Eds.), *Social support: An interactional view* (pp. 267–296). New York: Wiley.

Emmons, R. A., Diener, E., & Larsen, R. J. (1986). Choice and avoidance of everyday situations and affect congruence: Two models of reciprocal interactionism. *Journal of Personality and Social Psychology, 51,* 815–826.

Erikson, E. H. (1950). *Childhood and society.* New York: Norton.

Fincham, F., & Bradbury, T. N. (1990). Social support in marriage: The role of social cognition. *Journal of Social and Clinical Psychology, 9,* 31–42.

Fletcher, G. J. O., Fincham, F. D., Cramer, L., & Heron, N. (1987). The role of attributions in the development of dating relationships. *Journal of Personality and Social Psychology, 53,* 481–489.

Hazan, C., & Shaver, P. R. (1987). Romantic love conceptualized as an attachment process. *Journal of Personality and Social Psychology, 52,* 511–524.

Hendrick, S. S. (1981). Self-disclosure and marital satisfaction. *Journal of Personality and Social Psychology, 40,* 1150–1159.

Hendrick, S. S., Hendrick, C., & Adler, N. L. (1988). Romantic relationships: Love, satisfaction, and staying together. *Journal of Personality and Social Psychology, 54,* 930–988.

Hill, C. T., Rubin, Z., & Peplau, L. A. (1976). Breakups before marriage: The end of 103 affairs. *Journal of Social Issues, 3,* 147–168.

House, J. S., & Kahn, R. L. (1985). Measures and concepts of social support. In S. Cohen & S. L. Syme (Eds.), *Social support and health* (pp. 83–108). Orlando, FL: Academic Press.

Jourard, S. M. (1971). *Self-disclosure: An experimental analysis of the transparent self*. New York: Wiley.

Kelley, H. H., Berscheid, E., Christensen, A., Harvey, J. H., Huston, T. L., Levinger, G., McClintock, E., Peplau, L. A., & Peterson, D. R. (1983). *Close relationships*. New York: Freeman.

Kirkpatrick, L. A., & Davis, K. E. (1994). Attachment style, gender, and relationship stability: A longitudinal analysis. *Journal of Personality and Social Psychology, 66*, 505–512.

Levinger, G., & Senn, D. J. (1967). Disclosure of feelings in marriage. *Merrill-Palmer Quarterly, 13*, 237–249.

Marcia, J. E. (1966). Development and validation of ego identity status. *Journal of Personality and Social Psychology, 3*, 551–558.

McAdams, D. P. (1984). Human motives and personal relationships. In V. J. Derlega (Ed.), *Communication, intimacy, and close relationships* (pp. 41–70). Orlando, FL: Academic Press.

McAdams, D. P., & Constantian, C. A. (1983). Intimacy and affiliation motives in daily living: An experience sampling analysis. *Journal of Personality and Social Psychology, 45*, 851–861.

Miller, L. C. (1990). Intimacy and liking: Mutual influence and the role of unique relationships. *Journal of Personality and Social Psychology, 59*, 50–60.

Miller, L. C., Cody, M. J., & McLaughlin, M. L. (1985). Situations and goals as fundamental constructs in interpersonal communication research. In M. L. Knapp & G. R. Miller (Eds.), *Handbook of interpersonal communication* (pp. 162–198). Beverly Hills, CA: Sage.

Miller, L. C., & Read, S. J. (1991). On the coherence of mental models of persons and relationships: A knowledge structure approach. In G. O. Fletcher & F. D. Fincham (Eds.), *Cognition in close relationships* (pp. 69–99). Hillsdale, NJ: Erlbaum.

Murray, S. L., Holmes, J. G., & Griffin, D. W. (1996a). The benefits of positive illusions: Idealization and the construction of satisfaction in close relationships. *Journal of Personality and Social Psychology, 70*, 79–98.

Murray, S. L., Holmes, J. G., & Griffin, D. W. (1996b). The self-fulfilling nature of positive illusions in romantic relationships: Love is not blind but prescient. *Journal of Personality and Social Psychology, 71*, 1155–1180.

Omoto, A. M., & Snyder, M. (1990). Basic research in action: Volunteerism and society's response to AIDS. *Personality and Social Psychology Bulletin, 16*, 152–165.

Pervin, L. A. (Ed.). (1989). *Goals and concepts in personality and social psychology*. Hillsdale, NJ: Erlbaum.

Prager, K. J. (1995). *The psychology of intimacy*. New York: Guilford Press.

Reis, H. T., Senchak, M., & Solomon, B. (1985). Sex differences in the intimacy of social interaction: Further examination of potential explanations. *Journal of Personality and Social Psychology, 48*, 1204–1217.

Reis, H. T., & Shaver, P. (1988). Intimacy as an interpersonal process. In S. W. Duck (Ed.), *Handbook of personal relationships* (pp. 367–389). New York: Wiley.

Rempel, J. K., Holmes, J. G., & Zanna, M. P. (1985). Trust in close relationships. *Journal of Personality and Social Psychology, 49*, 95–112.

Rubin, Z., Hill, C. T., Peplau, L. A., & Dunkel-Schetter, C. (1980). Self-disclosure in dating couples: Sex roles and the ethic of openness. *Journal of Marriage and the Family, 42*, 305–317.

Sanderson, C. A., & Cantor, N. (1995). Social dating goals in late adolescence: Implications for safer sexual activity. *Journal of Personality and Social Psychology, 68*, 1121–1135.

Sarason, B. R., Shearlin, E. N., Pierce, G. R., & Sarason, I. G. (1987). Interrelationships between social support measures: Theoretical and practical implications. *Journal of Personality and Social Psychology, 52*, 813–832.

Silbereisen, R. K., Noack, P., & von Eye, A. (1992). Adolescents' development of romantic friendship and change in favorite leisure contexts. *Journal of Adolescent Research, 7*, 80–93.

Simpson, J. A. (1987). The dissolution of romantic relationships: Factors involved in relationship stability and emotional distress. *Journal of Personality and Social Psychology, 53*, 683–692.

Simpson, J. A. (1990). The influence of attachment styles on romantic relationships. *Journal of Personality and Social Psychology, 59*, 971–980.

Snyder, M. (1981). On the influence of individuals on situations. In N. Cantor & J. Kihlstrom (Eds.), *Cognition, social interaction, and personality* (pp. 290–329). Hillsdale, NJ: Erlbaum.

Snyder, M. (1993). Basic research and practical problems. The promise of a "functional" personality and social psychology. *Personality and Social Psychology Bulletin, 19*, 251–264.

Using the Implicit Association Test to Measure Self-Esteem and Self-Concept

Anthony G. Greenwald and Shelly D. Farnham

An exciting new direction in the cognitive approach to personality is the development of new ways to tap into unconscious mental processes. The unconscious mind is a core concern of personality psychology dating back to Sigmund Freud and beyond, and psychologists have long believed that many important mental processes occur outside of awareness. Freud used techniques such as free association and the analysis of verbal slips to uncover unconscious processes, but these techniques do not produce the kind of scientific data that most psychologists prefer to rely upon. A recent breakthrough in research methods to access the unconscious is reported in this selection, an exposition by Anthony Greenwald and Shelly Farnham on the "Implicit Association Test" (IAT). The purpose of the IAT is to uncover "implicit" aspects of self-esteem, or aspects of one's feelings about oneself that one might not be aware of. For example, people may claim and even consciously believe that they feel good about themselves, whereas deeper in their mind they carry some grave misgivings. The IAT provides a potential method for getting at these misgivings, by examining the ways in which thoughts about the self are associated with negative and positive ideas.

The logic behind the IAT is complex, but Greenwald and Farnham do about as good a job of explaining it clearly as is possible. (We should note that the original article included three experiments, one of which we have deleted to save space.) The future will no doubt see further applications of this technique in a wide range of contexts. The IAT raises deep theoretical as well as methodological issues, and these theoretical issues are worth pondering. For example, what does it really mean to say that one's explicit self-esteem is different from one's implicit self-esteem? Can a person really have two different opinions about oneself at two different levels of awareness? If so, that's a fascinating idea, but one that also requires a lot of thought to thoroughly understand.

From *Journal of Personality and Social Psychology, 79,* 1022–1038, 2000.

This research developed from the assumption that distinct implicit and explicit self-esteem constructs require different measurement strategies. In particular, the research pursued implications of Greenwald and Banaji's (1995) definition of implicit self-esteem as "the introspectively unidentified (or inaccurately identified) effect of the self-attitude on evaluation of self-associated and self-dissociated objects" (p. 11).

Greenwald and Banaji's analysis summarized a widespread recent development of the view that people process social information not only in an explicit (or aware or controlled or reflective or declarative) mode but also in an implicit (i.e., unaware, automatic, intuitive, or procedural) mode (Bargh, Chaiken, Govender, & Pratto, 1992; Devine, 1989; Fazio, Sanbonmatsu, Powell, & Kardes, 1986; Greenwald & Banaji, 1995; Kihlstrom & Cantor, 1984; Wilson, Lindsey, & Schooler, 2000). The idea of implicit operation of the self has appeared in a number of recent works (Greenwald & Banaji, 1995; Hetts, Sakuma, & Pelham, 1999; Kitayama & Karasawa, 1997; Spalding & Hardin, 1999). These works, in turn, have roots in earlier research on indicators of the self's automatic operation (e.g., Bargh & Tota, 1988; Markus, 1977; Nuttin, 1985; Rogers, Kuiper, & Kirker, 1977).

The distinction between explicit and implicit operation of the self is especially interesting if it turns out that the self functions differently in these two modes. Accordingly, it is useful to be able to measure self-esteem and self-concept in ways that can distinguish the self's implicit and explicit operations. Explicit measurement of self-concept has a long history (reviewed by Wylie, 1974, and not recapitulated here), whereas there is only a much sparser history of attempts to capture the self in an implicit mode of operation. Projective measures, such as the Thematic Apperception Test (McClelland, Atkinson, Clark, & Lowell, 1953; Murray, 1943), represented the state of the art until the late 1970s, when Rogers et al. (1977) proposed the use of latencies of trait self-descriptiveness judgments in self-concept assessment.

The Rogers et al. (1977) strategy of using trait self-descriptiveness judgments was tried in numerous laboratory studies (reviewed, e.g., by Kihlstrom & Cantor, 1984; Greenwald & Pratkanis, 1984). However, the limited sensitivity of these measures to individual differences led to their being used mostly to examine aggregated effects, either in the form of preexisting differences between groups or in the form of effects of experimental manipulations. In the 1990s, there has been renewed attention to implicit measures, leading to several new procedures for assessing implicit self-concept (Aidman, 1999; Bosson, Swann, & Pennebaker, 2000; Farnham, Greenwald, & Banaji, 1999; Otten & Wentura, 1999; Pelham & Hetts, 1999; Perdue, Dovidio, Gurtman, & Tyler, 1990). This article reports the first studies that used the Implicit Association Test (IAT; Greenwald, McGhee, & Schwartz, 1998) as the basis for assessing the self's implicit mode of operation.

The Implicit Association Test

The IAT (Greenwald et al., 1998) is a general-purpose procedure for measuring strengths of automatic associations between concepts. The IAT can be illustrated with a thought experiment. Imagine sorting a standard deck of 52 playing cards, containing 13 cards in each of the four suits of clubs, diamonds, hearts, and spades. You are asked to place clubs and spades in a stack to your left, and diamonds and hearts to your right. The speed with which you can do this sorting should reflect the strength of your associations within the two pairs of categories that have to be sorted together. If two suits that must be sorted together are easily associated because of some shared attribute, the task should be relatively simple. In this example, shared color attributes provide a basis for association that makes it easy to sort clubs and spades (shared attribute: black color) to the left and hearts and diamonds (red) to the right.

What happens if color cannot be used as a grouping attribute? If your task is to sort clubs and diamonds to the left and spades and hearts to the right, then the black-left, red-right strategy no longer works, and your sorting speed should deteriorate. Interestingly, this second sorting task should discriminate bridge players from nonplayers. For bridge players, hearts and spades are well associated because they are the higher ranking suits in that game. Any bridge player can readily observe the effect of these suit-rank associations by trying to do both a rank-consistent sort (clubs + diamonds vs. hearts + spades) and a rank-inconsistent sort (clubs + hearts vs. spades + diamonds)—the rank-consistent sort should be noticeably faster for players who have learned suit ranks in a game such as bridge, but others should not show a similar speed difference.

Described abstractly, the IAT's procedure has the subject give one response to two sets of items that represent a possibly associated concept–attribute pair and a different response to a second pair of item sets that is selected to complement the first two. Association between the concept and attribute that share a response is inferred to be stronger the faster the subject performs the task. In the first investigation of the IAT, Greenwald et al. (1998) asked subjects to sort each of a series of computer-presented words by rapidly pressing a left-side or right-side key on a computer keyboard. The automatic association between a concept (e.g., flowers) and an attribute (e.g., positive valence) was measured by observing the difference in speed between a condition in which flower names and pleasant-meaning words shared the same response key (this was typically fast) and a condition in which flower names and unpleasant-meaning words shared the same response key (typically slow). In that experiment, the two concepts were flower and insect, and the two attributes were pleasant and unpleasant. The resulting IAT measure compared the aggregate association strength of flower–pleasant and insect–unpleasant with that of flower–unpleasant and insect–pleasant. The results indicated that, in aggregate, flower–pleasant and insect–unpleasant were stronger associations than flower–unpleasant and insect–pleasant.

Because it uses complementary pairs of concepts and attributes, the IAT is limited to measuring the relative strengths of pairs of associations rather than absolute strengths of single associations. In practice, however, the IAT can never-

theless be effectively used because many socially significant categories form complementary pairs, such as positive–negative (valence), self–other, male–female, Jewish–Christian, young–old, weak–strong, warm–cold, liberal–conservative, aggressive–peaceful, etc.

The IAT was readily adapted to measuring implicit self–concept by observing response speeds for classification tasks in which the concept pair used in the IAT was self–other. Thus, the self-esteem IAT introduced in Experiment 1 compared self–pleasant and other–unpleasant associations with self–unpleasant and other–pleasant. Similarly, the gender self-concept IAT introduced in Experiment 2 compared self–feminine and other–masculine associations with self–masculine and other–feminine.

Validity of the IAT

The first investigations of the IAT (Greenwald et al., 1998) confirmed that the IAT could detect valence differences that were associated both with familiar nonsocial objects (flowers, musical instruments, insects, and weapons) and with significant social objects (Japanese and Korean ethnicity, and Black and White race). Greenwald et al. (1998) also demonstrated that IAT measures were stable across several procedural variations, including whether the pleasant category was assigned to a left-side or right-side response, the time interval between response to one stimulus and presentation of the next stimulus item (varied from 150 to 750 ms), and whether concepts and attributes were represented by 5 or 25 items. Observed IAT effects were also quite stable over variations in the manner of treating data from error responses and in the strategies used to deal with the typically skewed (extended upper tail) latency distributions. Later research provided additional internal validity evidence, establishing that the IAT's association-strength measure was not influenced by variations in familiarity of items used to represent the contrasted concepts (Dasgupta, McGhee, Greenwald, & Banaji, 2000; Ottaway, Hayden, & Oakes, in press; Rudman, Greenwald, Mellott, & Schwartz, 1999).

Several researchers have demonstrated that IAT measures can be influenced in theoretically expected fashion by procedures that might be expected to influence automatic attitudes or stereotypes. Dasgupta and Greenwald (2000) showed that viewing photos of admirable members of stigmatized groups (African Americans or elderly) and despised members of nonstigmatized groups (European Americans or young) reduced automatic negative associations toward those groups. Blair and Ma (1999) found that writing an imagined description of a strong woman decreased IAT-measured association of male (more than female) with strength. And Rudman, Ashmore, and Gary (1999) reported that an IAT measure of race preference for White over Black was reduced among students who had completed a Prejudice and Conflict seminar taught by an African American instructor (see also Lowery & Hardin, 1999).

Going beyond sensitivity to age (Mellott & Greenwald, 1999), gender (Rudman, Greenwald, & McGhee, in press), and racial and ethnic (Greenwald et al., 1998) group differences, the IAT has also been shown to be sensitive to individual differences. Correlations between parallel IAT measures of various attitudes were reported in Greenwald et al.'s (1998) Experiments 2 ($r = .85$) and 3 ($r = .46$), and by Dasgupta et al. (2000; $r = .39$). Test–retest reliabilities of $r = .65$ and $r = .69$ were reported, respectively, by Dasgupta and Greenwald (2000), and by Bosson et al. (2000). Their variability notwithstanding, these figures average to indicate moderately good stability ($\bar{r} = .64$, using r-to-Z method).[1] Theoretically meaningful correlations of IAT measures of ingroup favoritism with multiple indicators of degree of ingroup identity as Japanese or Korean were reported by Greenwald et al. (1998, Experiment 2). Rudman and Glick (1999) reported a correlation between prejudice against female applicants in a simulated job interview and IAT-assessed gender stereotypes. Convergent validity with alternative latency-based measures of implicit attitudes has been demonstrated in correlations of IAT measures with semantic priming measures of association strength (Cunningham, Preacher, & Banaji, in press; Mellott & Greenwald, 2000; Rudman & Kilianski, 2000). And convergence of IAT-measured automatic race preferences with a physiological measure (fMRI-measured amygdala activation of White participants while viewing unfamiliar African American faces) has been reported by Phelps et al. (2000).

Measuring Implicit Self-Esteem with the IAT

The self-esteem IAT involves five steps (see Figure 1). In each step, the subject presses a left or right key to rapidly categorize each of a series of stimuli that are presented in the middle of a computer screen. Instructions for the categorization task vary for the five steps, and latency is measured and averaged for each task variation. In the first step, subjects practice a *target concept* discrimination by categorizing items into *self* and *other* categories. In the second step, subjects practice an *attribute* discrimination by categorizing items into *pleasant* and *unpleasant* categories. Third, subjects categorize items into two combined categories, each including the target and attribute concept that were assigned to the same key in the preceding two steps (e.g., self+pleasant for the left key and other+unpleasant for the right key). The fourth step provides practice that reverses key assignments for either the target or attribute concept. Finally, the fifth step is like the third, but it uses the just-switched key assignments (e.g., self+unpleasant to the left, and other+pleasant to the right). Implicit self-esteem is measured in the form of an IAT effect, computed as the difference in mean latency between Steps 3 and 5. The self-esteem IAT effect measures how much easier it is for subjects to categorize self items with pleasant items than self items with unpleasant items.

---

[1]The interpretation of correlation coefficients such as these r's is explained in the selection by Rosenthal and Rubin in Part I.

Category labels	Sample items	Category labels

Step 1:
practice block (20 trials)

not me		me
○	self	●
●	other	○

Step 2:
practice block (20 trials)

unpleasant		pleasant
○	joy	●
●	vomit	○

Step 3:
practice block (20 trials)
critical block (40 trials)

unpleasant or not me		pleasant or me
○	self	●
○	joy	●
●	other	○
●	vomit	○

Step 4:
practice block (20 trials)

pleasant		unpleasant
●	joy	○
○	vomit	●

Step 5:
practice block (20 trials)
critical block (40 trials)

unpleasant or me		pleasant or not me
●	self	○
○	joy	●
○	other	●
●	vomit	○

Figure 1 Categorization tasks for the five steps of the self-esteem Implicit Association Test (IAT). Black dots indicate the correct response. The IAT effect is the difference in response times between Steps 3 and 5. The orders of Steps 2–3 and Steps 4–5 were counterbalanced because of possible effects of having the self+pleasant versus the self+unpleasant combination first.

Experiment 1: Implicit and Explicit Self-Esteem Compared

Experiment 1 was the first experiment to use the IAT to measure an aspect of self-concept—in particular, it measured implicit self-esteem. An obvi-

ous initial question to ask of a measure of implicit self-esteem is how it relates to existing self-report (or explicit) measures of self-esteem. There are two reasons to expect convergence between measures of implicit and explicit self-esteem. First, in responding to self-report measures of self-esteem, subjects presumably attempt to introspectively access their association of self with positive valence, which is what the implicit self-esteem IAT seeks to measure. Second, in repeatedly expressing positive self views on explicit measures, subjects practice and presumably strengthen the association of self with positive valence (cf., Fazio, Powell, & Herr, 1983).

At the same time, implicit and explicit self-esteem may not be strongly related because several known influences on responses to self-report measures could affect implicit measures differently, less, or not at all. These influences on self-report measures include demand characteristics (Orne, 1962), evaluation apprehension (Rosenberg, 1969), impression management (Tedeschi, Schlenker, & Bonoma, 1971), self-deception (Gur & Sackeim, 1979), and self-enhancement (Greenwald, 1980; Taylor & Brown, 1984).

Experiment 1 used confirmatory factor analysis to test whether implicit and explicit self-esteem measures (a) converged on a single construct or, alternately, (b) identified distinguishable constructs. Experiment 1 also included self-report measures of impression management and self-deception (Paulhus, 1991), in the hope that these might shed light on possible differences between implicit and explicit measures that could be due to more socially desirable responding on the explicit measures.

Method

SUBJECTS Students from introductory psychology courses at University of Washington participated in exchange for an optional course credit. Six subjects' data were discarded for having error rates on the IAT in excess of 20%, suggesting that they either misunderstood instructions or were trying to respond too rapidly. One subject's data were discarded for having mean latencies over 2 s, and another subject's data were discarded for not following instructions. Additionally, five subjects were dropped for having incomplete data. There remained 145 subjects, 93 female (64 Caucasian, 26 Asian, 3 Other) and 51 male (22 Caucasian, 26 Asian, 3 Other), in addition to one who declined to report sex.

PROCEDURES   After being seated in a small room with a desktop computer, subjects first completed paper-and-pencil self-report questionnaires that assessed self-esteem, impression management, and self-deception. Subjects were instructed to place their finished questionnaires in a sealed box marked "completed questionnaires," which was provided to reinforce prior instructions that subjects' anonymity and privacy were being protected. After subjects completed these questionnaires, the experimenter introduced the subject to the IAT computer program and then left the subject to complete the program in privacy. The two computer-administered IAT measures both assessed self-esteem, one assessing the associations of self versus other with pleasant- and unpleasant-meaning words and one assessing the associations of self versus other with positive and negative traits.

EXPLICIT MEASURES   At the beginning of the experimental session, after subjects provided self-descriptive demographic information for age, sex, and race, they completed six self-report measures. Four of these were self-esteem measures: the Rosenberg Self-Esteem Scale (Rosenberg, 1965), the Self-Attributes Questionnaire, (SAQ; Pelham & Swann, 1989), a thermometer scale on which participants indicated how warmly they felt toward themselves on a vertical scale anchored at bottom and top by 0 and 99, and a semantic differential scale of five items that requested self-descriptions by checking one of 7 points on scales anchored at ends by bipolar adjective pairs: ugly/beautiful, bad/good, unpleasant/pleasant, dishonest/honest, and awful/nice. The Balanced Index of Desirable Responding (BIDR; Paulhus, 1991) was used to measure impression management and self-deception. The order of the six measures was coun-

terbalanced by giving half the subjects the reverse of the order just described.

IAT PROCEDURES   The two self-esteem IATs were administered on PC-type computers with a program that constructed idiographic IAT self-concept measures for each subject by eliciting from each a series of 18 self-descriptive (*me*) and 18 not-self-descriptive (*not me*) items (Farnham, 1998). The two IATs assessed *affective* and *evaluative* implicit self-esteem by using, respectively, (a) pleasant and unpleasant words (e.g., diamond, health, sunrise; agony, filth, poison) as the items for the positive and negative affective concepts, and (b) positive and negative trait words (e.g., bright, noble, honest; ugly, vile, guilty) for the positive and negative evaluative concepts. The two IATs were administered in counterbalanced order. Also, for each IAT, whether the self+positive critical block was encountered first or second was counterbalanced. Complete lists of the IAT items are given in the Appendix.

To assure their understanding of the IAT procedure, subjects first completed a short tutorial that used categories unrelated to self (red vs. white colored objects and snakes vs. birds). After the tutorial, each of the two IATs consisted of seven blocks of categorization trials, with 20 trials for practice blocks and 40 trials for data-collection blocks (see Figure 1). Each stimulus item was displayed until its correct response was made. The next stimulus item then followed after a 150-ms intertrial interval. The computer recorded elapsed time between the start of each stimulus word's presentation and occurence of the correct keyboard response.

To encourage subjects to respond rapidly while making relatively few errors, the computer displayed mean latencies in milliseconds and error rates in percent after each block. All blocks were practice blocks except for the two critical blocks from which data were used to calculate the IAT effect. The IAT effect for implicit self-esteem was computed by subtracting the mean latency for the me+positive block from that for the me+negative block (Step 5 – Step 3 in Figure 1). During data-collection blocks, stimulus items were drawn alternately from the me or not-me lists (odd-numbered trials) and from the positive or negative lists (even-numbered trials). Items from each category pair were selected randomly and without replacement so that all items were used once before any items were reused.

IAT ITEMS

Idiographic items. Before completing the IAT, each subject provided 18 me and 18 not-me items. Me items included first and last names, hometown, phone number, birth month, and birth year (see Appendix). These items presumably did not have positive or negative qualities apart from those that might have been gained by association with self. For not-me items, subjects were instructed to pick from lists of items comparable to the me items and to select items such that chosen not-me items were (a) familiar, (b) not self-identified, and (c) neither strongly liked nor disliked. After choosing these items, subjects viewed their resulting me and not-me lists and were asked to delete items that (in retrospect) seemed inappropriate or were misspelled. Subjects were allowed to delete up to eight items from each, leaving a minimum of ten per list.

Positive and negative affective and evaluative items. Pleasant and unpleasant words were selected from the pleasantness-judgment norms of Bellezza, Greenwald, and Banaji (1986). Subjects were allowed to delete items from each list that they did not regard as pleasant or unpleasant, respectively. Positive and negative evaluative items (traits) were selected mostly from trait words that have been used in self-esteem questionnaires to represent high and low self-esteem, respectively. Subjects again had the opportunity to delete traits from each list that they did not regard as desirable or undesirable, respectively. Subjects could delete up to four items from each list, leaving a minimum of ten per list (see Appendix).

DATA REDUCTION   IAT data for analyses were obtained only from the 40-trial data-collection blocks

of Steps 3 and 5 (see Figure 1). Consistent with procedures introduced by Greenwald et al. (1998), (a) the first two trials of each data-collection block were dropped because of their typically lengthened latencies; (b) a logarithm transformation was used to normalize the distribution of latencies; (c) prior to this transformation, latencies greater than 3,000 ms were recoded to 3,000 ms, and latencies less than 300 ms were recorded to 300 ms. * * * As previously noted, subjects whose error rates for data-collection blocks of the IAT exceeded 20% (6 subjects) or who had mean latencies in excess of 2,000 ms (1 subject) were not included in analyses.

Results

IMPLICIT SELF-ESTEEM

* * * Overall, subjects responded much more rapidly when associating self with positive items (see Figure 2). IAT effects (mean latency for the self+negative block minus mean latency for the self+positive block) were strong for both the affective IAT, Cohen's $d = 1.38$, $F(1, 141) = 617$, $p = 10^{-53}$, and for the evaluative IAT, $d = 1.46$, $F(1, 141) = 468$, $p = 10^{-46}$. The mean IAT effects for the affective and evaluative measures did not significantly differ, $F(1, 141) = 0.02$, $p = .89$. Supplementary analyses indicated that neither sex nor race moderated magnitude of either of the self-esteem IATs, all Fs < 1.[2]

EXPLICIT SELF-ESTEEM
Means for the explicit self-esteem measures are reported in Table 1, classified by race and sex. Race had small effects on explicit self-esteem measures, such that Caucasians and men tended to report higher self-esteem than

---

[2]The analysis of variance is a statistical technique for assessing whether differences between means can be attributed to chance factors alone. The analysis yields an F statistic which, combined with the degrees of freedom in the design (given within parentheses), allows an estimate of the probability or p that the mean differences are due to chance. The Cohen's d statistic is a measure of the size or strength of the effect of the independent variable.

Asians and women. Analysis of variance (ANOVA) of an average of standardized scores for the four self-esteem measures revealed that the effect of race was statistically significant, d = .36, $F(1, 134)$ = 4.73, p = .03, whereas the effect of sex was not significant, d = .04, $F(1, 134)$ = 0.38, p = .54.

Relationships Between Measures of Implicit and Explicit Self-Esteem

Table 2 provides correlations among all of Experiment 1's measures. The two measures of implicit self-esteem were positively and significantly correlated with each other (r = .43), at almost the same level that the four measures of explicit self-esteem correlated with each other (average r = .46). Measures of implicit self-esteem had typically weak correlations with measures of explicit self-esteem. However, all eight correlations were numerically positive, and five of the eight were statistically significant (average r = .17). With the one exception of its positive correlation with the semantic differential self-esteem measure, the BIDR measure of impression management had near nil correlation with both implicit self-esteem (average r = .06) and explicit self-esteem (average r = .08). The BIDR measure of self-deception functioned very similarly to the explicit self-esteem measures, correlating an average of r = .24 with the two implicit self-esteem measures, and an average of r = .39 with the four explicit self-esteem measures.

*   *   *

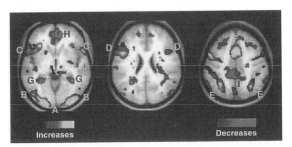

Figure 2   Response times for critical blocks for the two Implicit Association Tests (IATs) in Experiment 1. The mean IAT effect for each test is the mean for its self+positive condition subtracted from that for its self+negative condition. Error bars are standard deviations. N = 145.

TABLE 1

Experiment 1's Eight Measures Classified by Race and Sex of Subjects

	Caucasian		Asian	
	Male	Female	Male	Female
Measure	(n = 22)	(n = 64)	(n = 26)	(n = 26)
Implicit self-esteem				
IAT affect (ms)				
M	291	348	313	319
SD	270	172	191	149
IAT trait (ms)				
M	329	351	327	286
SD	225	206	195	172
Explitit self-esteem				
Rosenbrg SES				
M	24.32	24.33	22.42	22.81
SD	6.43	5.40	5.21	6.65
SAQ[a,b]				
M	4.47	3.64	3.22	3.01
SD	1.58	1.27	1.23	0.98
Semantic differential				
M	29.2	29.0	28.9	28.3
SD	4.92	4.46	3.59	3.96
Thermometer				
M	78	78	75	77
SD	21	14	14	15
Socially desirable responding (BIDR)				
Impression management				
M	4.50	4.86	3.50	4.62
SD	4.02	3.47	2.69	3.36
Self-deception[a]				
M	6.59	5.91	4.31	4.62
SD	3.51	3.19	2.88	2.90

Note. Total N = 138. The table does not include Experiment 1's 7 subjects who could not be placed in the table's demographic categories. Implicit Association Test (IAT) measures are in milliseconds. Ranges of other measures: Rosenberg Self Esteem Scale (SES), 0–30; Self-Attributes Questionnaire (SAQ), 1–10; Semantic differential, 5–35; Thermometer, 0–99; Balanced Index of Desirable Responding (BIDR) impression management and self-deception, 0–20 (with scores of 7 or greater considered to be high—Paulhus, 1991).
[a]p < .005 for main effect of race.   [b]p < .05 for main effect of sex.

TABLE 2

CORRELATIONS AMONG ALL MEASURES OF EXPERIMENT 1

Measure	1	2	3	4	5	6	7	8
Implicit self-esteem								
1. IAT: self-affect	—	432	130	273	178	198	005	198
2. IAT: self-evaluation		—	105	197	201	105	122	274
Explicit self-esteem								
3. Rosenberg SES			—	407	448	738	023	474
4. SAQ				—	176	349	−001	345
5. Semantic differential					—	524	288	327
6. Thermometer						—	018	412
BIDR								
7. Impression management							—	293
8. Self-deception								—

Note. $N = 145$. Decimal points omitted. IAT = Implicit Association Test; SES = Self-Esteem Scale; SAQ = Self-Attributes Questionnaire; BIDR = Balanced Index of Desirable Resonding. For $N = 145$, rs of .163, .232, .286, and .331 are associated, respectively, with two-tailed p values of *.05*, *.005*, **.0005**, and **.00005**.

Discussion

Both IAT self-esteem measures showed, on average, strong self-positivity. In the self+positive conditions, subjects categorized items an average of 323 ms faster than in the self+negative conditions. The two IAT self-esteem measures were positively, but weakly, correlated with explicit measures of self-esteem (average $r = .17$). Two confirmatory factor analyses were consistent in interpreting implicit and explicit self-esteem as distinct constructs that are positively, but weakly, correlated.

There were no effects of subject sex or race (Asian vs. Caucasian) on the measures of implicit self-esteem, but there was a small effect of race (Caucasians higher than Asians) on a combined index of explicit self-esteem. There was a statistically significant effect of sex (men higher than women) on one of the four explicit self-esteem measures (SAQ), but an unweighted average of the four explicit self-esteem measures did not show a statistically significant sex effect.

A possible explanation for the race effect on explicit, but not implicit, self-esteem is that Asian Americans may present themselves modestly on self-report measures. Because such a possibility

was anticipated, the BIDR measure of impression management was included in Experiment 1. However, the BIDR impression management measure was essentially uncorrelated with either implicit or explicit self-esteem (see Table 2) and showed no differences as a function of race (see Table 1). Accordingly, the BIDR did not shed light on the observed higher level of explicit self-esteem for Caucasian than Asian subjects.

An additional exploratory examination of race and sex differences in the implicit and explicit self-esteem measures showed that the explicit–implicit correlation was higher for Caucasian men, $r = .51$, $p = .02$, than for the other three race-sex combinations, respectively $rs = .06, 23$, and .20, for Asian women, Caucasian women, and Caucasian men (all nonsignificant). Again, a self-presentational interpretation of this difference in correlation magnitudes was suspected, but, again, lack of correlations of the BIDR impression management measure with the self-esteem measures provided no support for such an interpretation. Nevertheless, the observed greater explicit–implicit correlation for Caucasian men was intriguing enough to suggest that it would be worth examining in other data collections that provide the opportunity.

* * *

Experiment 2: Prediction of Responses to Success and Failure

Experiment 1 introduced IAT measures of self-esteem and self-concept and provided evidence for their validity in the form of CFAs of implicit (IAT) and self-report measures of the same constructs. Experiment 2 took a different approach to assessing validity, building on prior findings that self-esteem moderates cognitive reactions to success and failure.

Previous research has shown that low self-esteem persons take negative feedback more to heart than do high self-esteem persons (Brockner, 1983; Brown & Dutton, 1995; Dodgson & Wood, 1998; Greenberg et al., 1992). Compared with persons with high self-esteem, those with low self-esteem are expected to report lower mood and lower self-evaluation of performance after experiencing failure. Experiment 2 tested these expectations by exposing a subset of Experiment 1's subjects to either success or failure after they had completed their measures of implicit and explicit self-esteem.

There is no existing theorization to suggest that implicit and explicit self-esteem should function differently in predicting reactions to success and failure. Therefore, it was expected that Experiment 2 might show the two types of self-esteem to function similarly in predicting reactions to success and failure. At the same time, because implicit and explicit self-esteem appear to be different constructs (present Experiment 1; also Bosson et al., 2000), it was equally plausible that the two types of self-esteem measures would differentially predict reactions to success and failure.

Method

SUBJECTS

Experiment 2's subjects were a subset of 94 (30 men, 64 women) of the subjects who provided usable data for Experiment 1. After providing the measures of Experiment 1, they completed a task that gave them a success or failure experience. Forty-seven subjects were assigned randomly to each of the easy-task (success) and hard-task (failure) conditions.

PROCEDURE

Success-failure variation. After completing the two IATs as described in Experiment 1, subjects completed a paper-pencil task in which they were asked to identify, in a longer list, 20 names that should be familiar because they had appeared in news or entertainment media. To create the experience of success or failure, half of the subjects received a difficult version of the task and half an easy version. Each version contained 60 names, 20 of which had appeared recently in the media. All media names were selected from newspapers and web news summaries. The easy and difficult versions differed in the familiarity of the 20 critical names. Nonmedia names were created through recombinations of the media names. For example, Marilyn Jackson was created as a combination of Marilyn Monroe and Michael Jackson (two names from the easy version of the task).

Dependent measures. After completing the task, subjects were given an answer key and were asked to use it to determine the number of names that they had correctly identified and then to write that number at the bottom of the page. By scoring their own performance, subjects received feedback that was both immediate and anonymous. After receiving feedback for the task, subjects responded to questionnaire items that provided data for four dependent measures, in the following order: Mood—Subjects rated their current mood states using a scale developed by Brown and Dutton (1995). Subjects indicated on a 5-point Likert scale the extent to which their current mood was describable by adjectives such as blue, proud, sad, happy, and worthless. Success—Subjects indicated on a single 7-point scale the extent to which they believed they had succeeded on the just-completed name-identification task. Importance of Task—Subjects indicated on a single 7-point scale how important they thought it was to know current events (a measure of the importance of the ability measured by their just-completed task). Level of Aspiration for Future Performance—Subjects were informed that the task would be repeated with different names. They were then asked to indicate how many of the 20 critical names on the upcoming task they would hope to identify correctly.

IMPLICIT AND EXPLICIT SELF-ESTEEM MEASURES

The implicit self-esteem measure was an equally weighted averaged of Experiment 1's two IATs, computed by standardizing each measure prior to averaging the two. The explicit self-esteem measure was a similarly standardized composite of Experiment 1's RSES and thermometer measures. These two explicit measures were selected from the four used in Experiment 1 because they best represented the explicit self-esteem factor of Experiment 1's CFA.

Results and Discussion

The manipulation of task difficulty succeeded in producing the desired variations in actual and perceived success at the name-identification task. Subjects had on average 15.4 of 20 correct responses in the easy condition, compared with 6.4 of 20 in the difficult condition, $t(92) = 11.64$, $p = 10^{-19}$.[3] Even more importantly, subjects reported feeling much more successful after completing the easy ($M = 5.9$) than the difficult version ($M = 3.2$), $t(83) = 7.48$, $p = 10^{-10}$. If any of the self-esteem measures had been correlated with performance at the name-identification task, the success–failure manipulation would have been compromised. Fortunately, performance (number correct) was uncorrelated with implicit or explicit self-esteem

within either the success (easy) condition ($rs = .14$ and $-.04$, respectively) or the failure (difficult) condition ($rs = -.12$ and $-.04$).

If high self-esteem provides cognitive protection against the effects of failure feedback, then, compared with subjects with low self-esteem, subjects with high self-esteem should show smaller effects of the success–failure manipulation on the four measures of its impact: (a) judgment of having failed or succeeded, (b) current mood, (c) judged importance of the ability measured by the task, and (d) expected future performance at the task. This prediction calls for an interaction effect of self-esteem and success–failure on the four measures, such that higher levels of self-esteem should be associated with smaller differences between success and failure conditions on each measure. This interaction-effect prediction was tested with a two-step hierarchical regression analysis for each of the four dependent measures.[4] Self-esteem and task feedback (success or failure) were entered on the first step of the analysis to estimate their main effects. On the second step, the interaction effect was tested by entering as a predictor the multiplicative product of self-esteem and success–failure (the latter dummy-coded as 0 or 1). Results of the analyses of the four measures are graphed in Figure 3.

EFFECTS OF TASK FEEDBACK (SUCCESS–FAILURE)

Effectiveness of the success–failure manipulation was indicated by the occurrence of expected effects of the manipulation on all four measures. The largest effect, not surprisingly, was the already described effect on judgment of success at the task (Cohen's $d = 1.60$, $p = 10^{-10}$). The success condition also produced higher means on the other three measures: posttask mood ($d = .48$, $p = .02$), importance of the ability assessed by the name identification task ($d = .54$, $p = .01$), and performance aspiration for a repetition of the task ($d = .51$,

---

[3]The *t* test is another statistical technique for evaluating the probability or *p* that the obtained difference in means could be due solely to chance. The degrees of freedom for the *t* appears between parentheses, and in this case (a repeated-measures test) is the number of participants minus 2.

[4]Hierarchical regression analysis is a statistical technique that allows the investigator to estimate separately the effects of each of a number of independent variables and their interaction (the degree to which the effect of one variable depends upon the other).

$p = .02$). The theoretical significance of these main effects of the success–failure manipulation is that they establish the conditions needed to assess the interaction-effect prediction. That is, for any measure that shows a main effect of success–failure, the self-esteem-buffering hypothesis predicts greater difference between success and failure conditions for participants with low self-esteem than for those with high self-esteem.

MAIN EFFECTS OF MEASURED SELF-ESTEEM Implicit self-esteem had no main effects, and only one main effect of explicit self-esteem was observed, an effect of explicit self-esteem on posttask mood (Figure 3, second panel on left). Regardless of task feedback condition, subjects high on the explicit self-esteem measure had more positive posttask moods, and this was a strong effect, regression $\beta = .51$, $p = 10^{-7}$. However, it is plausible that this result indicates only that the mood measure (self-ratings of positive feelings) and the explicit self-esteem measures (self-ratings of other positive attributes) called for similar types of self-positivity judgments.

INTERACTION OF SELF-ESTEEM AND SUCCESS–FAILURE The focus of theoretical interest in Experiment 2 was the analysis of interaction effects involving success–failure and self-esteem. If high self-esteem participants have a cognitive protection against negative feedback, then (relative to subjects with low self-esteem) they should show reduced differences between success and failure conditions on measures that were affected by success versus failure. (This includes all four of Experiment 2's rating measures that were collected following task feedback.) For the data sets plotted in Figure 3, these interactions should appear as a pair of slopes that define a > pattern (converging to the right). Figure 3 has three interaction effects that show this pattern strongly enough to warrant notice. In the upper left panel of Figure 3, the difference between success and failure conditions in rated success was smaller for high- than for low-explicit-self-esteem subjects, interaction $F(1, 80) = 2.60$, partial $r = .18$, $p = .11$. In the two lower right panels, the >-shaped pattern can be seen for the measures of task impor-

tance, interaction $F(1, 90) = 3.84$, partial $r = .20$, $p = .05$, and future aspiration, interaction $F(1, 90) = 3.64$, partial $r = .20$, $p = .06$.

In summary, Experiment 2's task feedback manipulation succeeded in establishing distinct experiences of success and failure. For implicit self-esteem, the expected effect of high self-esteem in buffering effects of failure was observed for two of the four posttask rating measures. Although p values for these two effects straddled the $p = .05$ level that is often treated as a boundary between noteworthy and ignorable results, any inclination to dismiss these findings should be tempered by noting that these two effects agreed with prediction in both direction and shape. To elaborate: A significant interaction effect of the type tested in Experiment 2 could have been produced by either a < or > pattern of the two regression slopes. The occurrence of the predicted slope directions might therefore justify halving the computed p values. Further, even with occurrence of the predicted directions of slopes, it would have been possible for these significant interaction effects to occur with slopes for the failure condition elevated above those for the success condition, rather than in the predicted pattern of success slope elevated relative to failure slope. Therefore, the finding that predicted interaction effects occurred with the predicted direction and shape prompts more confidence than the stated p values might otherwise appear to warrant.

* * *

Even though the four analyses for explicit self-esteem yielded no findings for which the p value dropped below .05, it can be seen on the left side of Figure 3 that three of the four explicit measures—all except the mood measure—did display the predicted > interaction shape. The appearance of statistically stronger effects in the implicit measures than in the explicit self-esteem measures remains, for the present, unexplained. There was no theoretical reason, a priori, to expect that implicit and explicit self-esteem should produce different patterns or magnitudes of the predicted effect of buffering against failure.

* * *

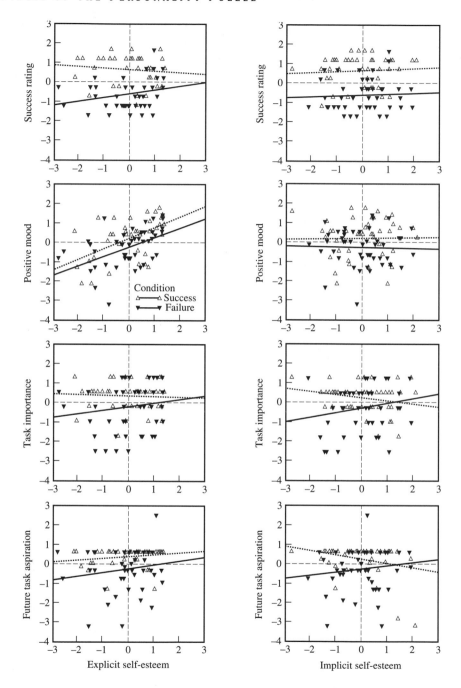

Figure 3 Regression analyses of four dependent measures as a function task condition (success vs. failure) and measured self-esteem panels, (explicit self-esteem in left panels, implicit self-esteem in right panels). Separate regression slopes are plotted for each condition. Interaction effects have the predicted > shape at statistically noticeable levels in the upper left panel and the lower two right panels. All measures are standardized to facilitate comparisons among the analyses.

General Discussion

SUMMARY OF FINDINGS

The interpretation of self-report measures—of self-esteem, self-concept, or other constructs—is potentially complex because such measures can intermix, in unknown proportions, both valid indication of self-concept and self-presentational distortions. The IAT is an indirect measure that does not rely on introspection and has been found to be low in susceptibility to self-presentational distortion (Kim & Greenwald, 2000). Although these properties make the IAT a potentially desirable measure for use in research, its establishment as a useful research measure depends on its meeting the usual psychometric standards for individual difference measures. The present studies provided such evidence—concerning psychometric criteria of stability and construct validity.

* * *

Predictive validity was shown in Experiment 2's finding that IAT-measured implicit self-esteem predicted an expected buffering (for those high in self-esteem) on two of four measures of cognitive reactions to manipulated success versus failure. Discriminant validity appeared in findings from Experiment 1. Low correlations between IAT measures and explicit measures indicated that IAT measures of implicit self-esteem and self-concept measure something different from what is measured by explicit (self-report) measures of self-esteem and self-concept.

Experiment I produced the unexpected observation that the correlation between implicit and explicit self-esteem was higher for Caucasian men than for Asian and/or female subjects. Because this result was obtained from exploratory analyses, it was not possible to give it a confidently interpretable *p* value. Nevertheless, this result seems worthy of eventual follow-up because of more general interest in understanding factors that moderate the agreement between implicit and explicit measures.

In summary, the present experiments provided initial evidence that IAT measures of implicit

self-esteem and implicit self-concept (a) have psychometric properties of stability and validity that justify their use in research settings and (b) define constructs that are distinct from, although correlated with, nominally the same constructs as measured by self-report.

* * *

Conclusion

In 1995, Greenwald and Banaji concluded that measurement of implicit constructs had "not yet been achieved in the efficient form needed to make research investigation of individual differences in implicit cognition a routine undertaking." Optimistically, they forecast that "When such measures do become available, there should follow the rapid development of a new industry of research on implicit cognitive aspects of personality" (1995, p. 20). The realization of that forecast no longer seems so distant as it did in 1995.

References

Aidman, E. V. (1999). Measuring individual differences in implicit self-concept: Initial validation of the Self-Apperception Test. *Personality and Individual Differences, 27*, 211–228.

Bargh, J. A., Chaiken, S., Govender, R., & Pratto, F. (1992). The generality of the automatic attitude activation effect. *Journal of Personality and Social Psychology, 62*, 893–912.

Bargh, J. A., & Tota, M. E. (1988). Context-dependent automatic processing in depression: Accessibility of negative constructs with regard to self but not others. *Journal of Personality and Social Psychology, 54*, 925–939.

Bellezza, F. S., Greenwald, A. G., & Banaji, M. R. (1986). Words high and low in pleasantness as rated by male and female college students. *Behavior Research Methods, Instruments, and Computers, 18*, 299–303.

Bem, S. L. (1974). The measurement of psychological androgyny. *Journal of Consulting and Clinical Psychology, 42*, 155–162.

Blair, I., & Ma, J. (1999). *Imagining stereotypes away: The moderation of automatic stereotypes through mental imagery.* Manuscript submitted for publication.

Bossom, J. K., Swann, W. B., & Pennebaker, J. W. (2000). Stalking the perfect measure of implicit self-esteem: The blind men and the elephant revisited? *Journal of Personality and Social Psychology, 79*, 631–643.

Brauer, M., Wasel, W., & Niedenthal, P. (2000). Implicit and explicit components of prejudice. *Review of General Psychology, 4*, 79–101.

Brockner, J. (1983). Low self-esteem and behavioral plasticity. In L. Wheeler (Ed.), *Review of personality and social psychology* (Vol. 4, pp. 237–271). Beverly Hills, CA: Sage.

Brown, J. D., & Dutton, K. A. (1995). The thrill of victory, the complexity of defeat: Self-esteem and people's emotional reactions to success and failure. *Journal of Personality and Social Psychology, 68*, 712–722.

Cunningham, W. A., Preacher, K. J., & Banaji, M. R. (in press). Implicit attitude measures: Consistency, stability, and convergent validity. *Psychological Science.*

Dasgupta, N., & Greenwald, A. G. (2000). *Exposure to admired group members reduces automatic intergroup bias.* Manuscript submitted for publication.

Dasgupta, N., McGhee, D. E., Greenwald, A. G., & Banaji, M. R. (2000). Automatic preference for White Americans: Eliminating the familiarity explanation. *Journal of Experimental Social Psychology, 36*, 316–328.

Devine, P. (1989). Stereotypes and prejudice: Their automatic and controlled components. *Journal of Personality and Social Psychology, 56*, 5–18.

Dodgson, P. G., & Wood, J. V. (1998). Self-esteem and the cognitive accessibility of strengths and weaknesses after failure. *Journal of Personality and Social Psychology, 75*, 178–197.

Dovidio, J. F., Kawakami, K., Johnson, C., Johnson, B., & Howard, A. (1997). On the nature of prejudice: Automatic and controlled processes. *Journal of Experimental Social Psychology, 33*, 510–540.

Farnham, S. D. (1998). FIAT for Windows [Computer software]. Seattle, WA: Author. Available: http://www.hive-mind.com/shelly/IAT/ [1998, June 2].

Farnham, S. D., & Greenwald, A. G. (1999, June). *In-group favoritism = implicit self-esteem ×in-group identification.* Paper presented at meetings of the American Psychological Society, Denver, CO.

Farnham, S. D., Greenwald, A. G., & Banaji, M. R. (1999). Implicit self-esteem. In D. Abrams & M. Hogg (Eds.), *Social identity and social cognition* (pp. 230–248). Cambridge, MA: Blackwell Publishers.

Fazio, R. H., Powell, M. C., & Herr, P. M. (1983). Toward a process model of the attitude–behavior relation: Accessing one's attitude upon mere observation of the attitude object. *Journal of Personality and Social Psychology, 44*, 723–735.

Fazio, R. H., Sanbonmatsu, D. M., Powell, M. C., & Kardes, F. R. (1986). On the automatic activation of attitudes. *Journal of Personality and Social Psychology, 50*, 229–238.

Greenberg, J., Solomon, S., Pyszczynski, T., Rosenblatt, A., Burling, J., Lyon, D., Simon, L., & Pinel, E. (1992). Why do people need self-esteem? Converging evidence that self-esteem serves an anxiety-buffering function. *Journal of Personality and Social Psychology, 63*, 913–922.

Greenwald, A. G. (1980). The totalitarian ego: Fabrication and revision of personal history. *American Psychologist, 35*, 603–618.

Greenwald, A. G., & Banaji, M. R. (1995). Implicit social cognition: Attitudes, self-esteem, and stereotypes. *Psychological Review, 102*, 4–27.

Greenwald, A. G., McGhee, D. E., & Schwartz, J. L. K. (1998). Measuring individual differences in implicit cognition: The Implicit Association Test. *Journal of Personality and Social Psychology, 74*, 1464–1480.

Greenwald, A. G., & Pratkanis, A. R. (1984). The self. In R. S. Wyer & T. K. Srull (Eds.), *Handbook of social cognition* (pp. 129–178). Hillsdale, NJ: Erlbaum.

Gur, R. C., & Sackeim, H. A., (1979). Self-deception: A concept

in search of a phenomenon. *Journal of Personality and Social Psychology, 37*, 147–169.

Hetts, J. J., Sakuma, M., & Pelham, B. W. (1999). Two roads to positive regard: Implicit and explicit self-evaluation and culture. *Journal of Experimental Social Psychology, 35*, 512–559.

Kihlstrom, J. F., & Cantor, N. (1984). Mental representations of the self. In L. Berkowitz (Ed.), *Advances in experimental social psychology* (Vol. 17, pp 1–47). Orlando, FL: Academic Press, Inc.

Kim, D-Y., & Greenwald, A. G. (2000). *Voluntary controllability of implicit cognition: Can an implicit measure (the IAT) of attitudes be faked?* Manuscript submitted for publication.

Kitayama, S., & Karawawa, M. (1997). Implicit self-esteem in Japan: Name letters and birthday numbers. *Personality and Social Psychology Bulletin, 23*, 736–742.

Lenney, E. (1991). Sex roles: The measurement of masculinity, femininity, and androgyny. In J. P. Robinson, P. R. Shaver, & L. S. Wrightsman (Eds.), *Measures of personality and social psychological attitudes* (pp. 573–660). San Diego, CA: Academic Press.

Lowery, B., & Hardin, C. D. (1999, June). *Social tuning effects on automatic racial prejudice.* Paper presented at the annual meeting of the American Psychological Society, Denver, CO.

Markus, H. (1977). Self-schemata and processing information about the self. *Journal of Personality and Social Psychology, 35*, 63–78.

McClelland, D. C., Atkinson, J. W., Clark, R. A., & Lowell, E. L. (1953). *The achievement motive.* New York: Appleton-Century-Crofts.

Mellott, D. S., & Greenwald, A. G. (2000, May). *Measuring implicit ageism: Do the Implicit Association Test and semantic priming measure the same construct?* Paper presented at meetings of the Midwestern Psychological Association, Chicago, IL.

Murray, H. A. (1943). *Thematic Apperception Test manual.* Cambridge, MA: Harvard University Press.

Nosek, B., & Banaji, M. R. (2000). *Measuring implicit social cognition: The single category association task.* Unpublished manuscript, Yale University, New Haven, CT.

Nuttin, J. R. (1985). Narcissism beyond Gestalt awareness: The name letter effect. *European Journal of Social Psychology, 15*, 353–361.

Orne, M. T. (1962). On the social psychology of the psychological experiment: With particular reference to demand characteristics and their implications. *American Psychologist, 17*, 776–783.

Ottaway, S. A., Hayden, D. C., & Oakes, M. A. (in press). Implicit attitudes and racism: The effect of word familiarity and frequency in the Implicit Association Test. *Social Cognition.*

Otten, S., & Wentura, D. (1999). About the impact of automaticity in the Minimal Group Paradigm: Evidence from affective priming tasks. *European Journal of Social Psychology, 29*, 1049–1071.

Paulhus, D. L. (1991). Measurement and control of response bias. In J. P. Robinson & P. R. Shaver (Eds.), *Measures of personality and social psychological attitudes. Measures of social psychological attitudes* (Vol. 1., pp. 17–59). San Diego, CA: Academic Press.

Pelham, B. W., & Hetts, John, J. (1999). *Implicit self-evaluation.* Unpublished manuscript.

Pelham, B. W., & Swann, W. B. (1989). From self-conceptions to self-worth: On the sources and structure of global self-esteem. *Journal of Personality and Social Psychology, 57,* 672–680.

Perdue, C. W., Dovidio, J. F., Gurtman, M. B., & Tyler, R. B. (1990). Us and them: Social categorization and the process of intergroup bias. *Journal of Personality and Social Psychology, 59,* 475–486.

Phelps, E. A., O'Connor, K. J., Cunningham, W. A., Funayama, E. S., Gatenby, J. C., Gore, J. C., & Banaji, M. R. (2000). Performance on indirect measures of race bias predicts amygdala activation. *Journal of Cognitive Neuroscience, 12,* 729–738.

Rogers, T. B., Kuiper, N. A., & Kirker, W. S. (1977). Self-reference and the encoding of personal information. *Journal of Personality and Social Psychology, 35,* 677–688.

Rosenberg, M. (1965). *Society and the adolescent self-image.* Princeton, NJ: Princeton University Press.

Rosenberg, M. J. (1969). The conditions and consequences of evaluation apprehension. In R. Rosenthal & R. L. Rosnow (Eds.) *Artifact in behavioral research* (pp. 279–349). New York: Academic Press.

Rudman, L. A., Ashmore, R. D., & Gary, M. (1999). *Implicit and explicit prejudice and stereotypes: A continuum model of intergroup orientation assessment.* Manuscript submitted for publication.

Rudman, L. A., & Glick, P. (1999). *Prescriptive gender stereotypes and backlash toward agentic women.* Manuscript submitted for publication.

Rudman, L. A., Greenwald, A. G., & McGhee, D. E. (in press).

Implicit self-concept and evaluative implicit gender stereotypes: self and ingroup share desirable traits. *Personality and Social Psychology Bulletin.*

Rudman, L. A., & Kilianski, S. E. (2000). Implicit and explicit attitudes toward female authority. *Personality and Social Psychology Bulletin, 26,* 1315–1328.

Spalding, L. R., & Hardin, C. D. (1999). Unconscious unease and self-handicapping: Behavioral consequences of individual differences in implicit and explicit self-esteem. *Psychological Science, 10,* 535–539.

Spence, J. T., & Helmreich, R. L. (1979). The many faces of androgyny: A reply to Locksley and Colten. *Journal of Personality and Social Psychology, 37,* 1032–1046.

Spence, J. T., Helmreich, R. L., & Stapp, J. (1974). The Personal Attributes Questionnaire: A measure of sex role stereotypes and masculinity-femininity. *Journal Supplement Abstract Service Catalog of Selected Documents in Psychology, 4,* 43–44.

Taylor, S. E., & Brown, J. D. (1984). Illusion and well-being: A social psychological perspective on mental health. *Psychological Bulletin, 103,* 193–210.

Tedeschi, J. T., Schlenker, B. R., & Bonoma, T. V. (1971). Cognitive dissonance: Private ratiocination or public spectacle? *American Psychologist, 26,* 685–695.

Wilson, T. D., Lindsey, S., & Schooler, T. Y. (2000). A model of dual attitudes. *Psychological Review, 107,* 101–126.

Wylie, R. (1974). *The self-concept: A review of methodological considerations and measuring instruments, Volume I.* Lincoln: University of Nebraska Press.

APPENDIX

ITEMS USED IN THE IATS FOR ALL EXPERIMENTS

Items for Experiment 1

Affective		Evaluative		Idiographic (Me or Not-me)	
Positive	Negative	Positive	Negative	Items	Examples
caress	abuse	smart	stupid	birth day	Feb 19
cuddle	agony	bright	ugly	birth year	1963
diamond	assault	success	failure	city 1	London
glory	brutal	splendid	awful	city 2	Boston
gold	corpse	valued	useless	country	Italy
health	death	noble	vile	first name	Jennifer
joy	filth	strong	weak	gender	female
kindness	killer	proud	ashamed	ethnicity 1	Chinese
lucky	poison	loved	hated	ethnicity 2	Irish
peace	slum	honest	guilty	handedess	left-handed
sunrise	stink	competent	awkward	last name	Carter
truth	torture	worthy	rotten	middle name	Donald
warmth	vomit	nice	despised	state	Maine
				religion	Hindu
				phone number	nnn-nnnn
				street name	Oak St
				Social Security no.	nnn-nn-nnnn
				zip code	98105

Double Dissociation Between Implicit and Explicit Personality Self-Concept: The Case of Shy Behavior

Jens B. Asendorpf, Rainer Banse, and Daniel Mücke

The Implicit Association Test (IAT), introduced in the previous selection, is beginning to be applied to an increasing number of personality traits and behaviors. In the present article, by the German personality psychologists Jens Asendorpf, Rainer Banse, and Daniel Mücke, the IAT is applied to the measurement of shyness. Their proposal is that shyness may be a trait in which people often both lack self-insight and are unwilling to accurately report the degree to which they believe themselves to be shy. The IAT is used in this study along with more conventional self-report measures of shyness to allow the separate assessment of the "implicit" (unconscious) and "explicit" (consciously known) aspects of this trait.

The possibility that these two different aspects of a trait are separate is underlined by their results. Implicit and explicit measures of shyness predicted different kinds of shyness-related behaviors. Explicit measures were better at predicting shyness-related behavior believed to be under conscious, volitional control (e.g., speech), whereas implicit measures were better at predicting behaviors believed to be more "automatic," unconscious, and spontaneous (e.g., nonverbal expressions of emotion).

Can you be shy and not know it? The present investigation, in combination with other studies from other laboratories, has surprising implications for the limits of self-knowledge. We know some things about ourselves, it appears, and do not know other things; but there are still other aspects of ourselves that—apparently— we know, but don't know that we know.

From *Journal of Personality and Social Psychology, 83,* 380–393, 2002.

The aim of the present study is to apply recent conceptual and methodological advances in social cognition research to the assessment of the self-concept of personality and the prediction of behavior. Using the trait of shyness as an example, we attempt to show that (a) it is possible to reliably assess individual differences in the implicit self-concept of personality that (b) are partly independent from traditional explicit self-ratings and (c) increase significantly the prediction of spontaneous behavior in a realistic social situation. For this purpose, we make a conceptual distinction between the explicit and the implicit self-concept of personality, propose a general hypothesis on how these two aspects of the personality self-concept are linked with spontaneous and controlled behavior, and test this hypothesis in a behavioral observation study. In a follow-up study, we experimentally test and confirm the distinction between spontaneous and controlled shy behavior.

Two Threats to Explicit Self-Ratings of Personality

Empirical research on personality differences is dominated by the use of verbal self-reports of personality. Typically, participants are explicitly asked to judge their own personality traits—thus, aspects of their *self-concept of personality*. Numerous studies have shown substantial agreement between self-rated traits and ratings of these traits by others (particularly if the traits refer to observable behavior) and between self-rated traits and observed behavior in trait-relevant situations if these external criteria for the self-ratings are sufficiently aggregated over observers, time, or situations. Thus, explicit self-ratings of personality show substantial validity for observable personality traits (Funder, 1999).

However, there are two main limitations to the validity of explicit self-ratings of personality. First, a long-standing and still unresolved issue concerns differential self-presentation of one's personality, particularly differential social desirability biases (Edwards, 1957). Researchers have made progress by distinguishing self-deception tendencies from impression management tendencies, including deliberate faking of responses (Paulhus, 1984, 1998). But despite attempts over half a century to increase the validity of explicit self-ratings of personality by controlling for such tendencies, only limited progress has been made in this direction (Paulhus, 1998).

The second threat to the validity of explicit self-ratings, which is less frequently acknowledged by personality researchers, is the limited accessibility of the self through the self-rating method. In recent years, social cognition researchers have increasingly recognized that information about the self is processed in two different modes. Although the exact difference between these two modes is not yet fully understood and the use of terminology is not consistent, many distinguish between an *explicit mode* characterized by conscious, controlled, and reflective information processing and an *implicit mode* characterized by unconscious, automatic, and intuitive processes (Bargh, 1994; Bosson, Swann, & Pennebaker, 2000; Epstein, 1994; Greenwald & Banaji, 1995; Greenwald & Farnham, 2000; Kihlstrom & Cantor, 1984; Wilson, Lindsey, & Schooler, 2000). In addition, it is generally assumed that information processing in the explicit mode has only limited access to the self-concept and its affective evaluation (i.e., self-esteem). Intuitions about oneself, unfavorable or threatening evaluations of oneself, and self-related knowledge that was acquired a long time ago, particularly in early childhood, may be difficult to access in the explicit mode (Bowlby, 1969; Breakwell, 1986; Furman & Flanagan, 1997; George, Kaplan, & Main, 1985; Wilson et al., 2000). Explicit self-ratings of personality require information processing in the explicit mode and are therefore subject to this limitation.

Explicit Versus Implicit Personality Self-Concept

The present study is an attempt to tackle these two key problems of explicit personality self-ratings—namely, self-presentation biases and limited cognitive accessibility—at once through the assessment of the implicit self-concept of personality. To avoid some of the confusion that surrounds the use of the terms *implicit* and *explicit* in the social cognition literature, we propose to clearly distinguish between the self-concept of personality at the construct level and the measured self-concept of personality at the empirical level.

Recently, Greenwald et al. (2002) proposed

that social knowledge can be represented in a general associative network (called the social knowledge structure) that contains a central *me* node, nodes representing other social objects, attributes of the *me* and the other social objects, and also nodes representing positive and negative valence. Greenwald et al. defined the self-concept as "the association of the concept of self with one or more (non-valence) attribute concepts" (p. 5) and self-esteem simply as the connection of the self node to a valence node. Consistent with this definition, we define the self-concept of personality at the construct level as an associative network containing all associations of the concept of self with attribute concepts describing one's personality—thus, attributes that describe individual, relatively stable, nonpathological characteristics of the person. Because some parts of the self-concept refer to cultural and even human universals (e.g., German, European, human being) or to pathological attributes (e.g., being spider phobic), the self-concept of personality is only part of one's self-concept.

Explicit measures of the self-concept of personality are based on information that is intentionally given to inform about the self. They contain valid information as far as they refer to parts of the self-concept of personality that are introspectively accessible. Additionally, they may contain invalid information about the person's personality that is motivated by self-presentation concerns and unrelated to the self-concept of personality or that is due to measurement error. In contrast, implicit measures of the self-concept of personality are based on information that is not intentionally given to inform about the self. They contain valid information as far as they refer to parts of the self-concept of personality that are accessible through the particular assessment methodology. Additionally, they may contain invalid information about the person's personality due to systematic biases of the assessment methodology and measurement error. Therefore, implicit measures are expected to be more robust against deliberate self- and other deception than are explicit measures.

Although there are presently only a few studies on the relation between implicit and explicit measures of the self-concept of personality, we expect to find relations similar to those observed for implicit and explicit attitudes, stereotypes, and self-esteem—namely, weak to moderate correlations (e.g., Greenwald & Nosek, 2001; Banse, Seise, & Zerbes, 2001; Bosson et al., 2000; Greenwald & Farnham, 2000; Cunningham, Preacher, & Banaji, 2001). Also, the definitions of explicit versus implicit self-concept measures imply that these implicit–explicit correlations increase if self-presentation tendencies are controlled for. This implication has been supported by numerous studies (Banse & Gawronski, 2001; Dunton & Fazio, 1997; Fazio, Jackson, Dunton, & Williams, 1995). Empirical zero correlations between implicit and explicit measures may often be due to the low reliability of implicit measures rather than to total indepen-dence of implicit and explicit constructs (e.g., Bosson et al., 2000).

Our usage of the terms *implicit* and *explicit* always refers to the empirical level, that is, to measures of the self-concept of personality. To simplify terminology, from now on we use the terms *implicit/explicit personality self-concept* when we refer to an individual's measured implicit/explicit self-concept of her or his personality.

Reliable Assessment of Implicit Traits

How can we assess the implicit self-concept of personality? Trait-oriented personality psychologists (Funder, 1991; McCrae & Costa, 1999) would like to have general procedures assessing people's implicit self-concept for particular personality traits. Fortunately, these procedures need not be invented anew, because a flourishing research on implicit attitudes and stereotypes provides candidate procedures. To simplify terminology, from now on we use the terms *implicit trait* and *explicit trait* when we refer to an individual's measured implicit/explicit self-concept regarding this trait. Thus, we talk about implicit shyness, explicit conscientiousness, and so on.

* * *

Recently, Greenwald, McGhee, and Schwartz (1998) proposed the Implicit Association Test

(IAT). In this procedure, the automatic association between a bipolar target concept such as *self–others* and a bipolar attribute concept such as *good–bad* is assessed through a series of discrimination tasks that require 10–15 min to accomplish. The effects produced by the IAT are typically much larger than priming effects, and recent studies have shown that IAT procedures assess individual differences in implicit attitudes and self-esteem with internal consistencies that regularly approach .80 and above (Banse et al., 2001; Bosson et al., 2000; Cunningham et al., 2001; Greenwald & Farnham, 2000; Greenwald & Nosek, 2001). However, the test–retest correlations typically range between .60 and .70,[1] which is not fully satisfactory but much higher than the retest correlations for priming measures.

A Double Dissociation Strategy for Validating Implicit Trait Assessments

The distinction between an implicit and an explicit mode of information processing is a general one that applies not only to cognition but also to behavior and action control. In the MODE model of attitude–behavior relations (Fazio, 1990; Fazio & Towles-Schwenn, 1999), it is postulated that implicitly measured attitudes predict spontaneous or highly automatized behavior better than controlled behavior, whereas explicitly measured attitudes predict controlled behavior better than spontaneous or highly automatized behavior, because the mediating information processes are consistent in both cases with regard to implicit versus explicit mode. Similar dual models have been proposed for relations between behavior and implicit versus explicit self-esteem (Greenwald & Farnham, 2000), implicit versus explicit person and relationship schemata (Baldwin, Carrel, & Lopez, 1990), and

implicit versus explicit motives (McClelland, Koestner, & Weinberger, 1989; see also Wilson et al., 2000, for a general discussion).

Building on these dual model approaches, we propose the general hypothesis that the implicit personality self-concept predicts spontaneous or highly automatized behavior better than controlled behavior, whereas the explicit personality self-concept predicts controlled behavior better than spontaneous or highly automatized behavior. Consequently, we propose a *double dissociation strategy* for the empirical evaluation of the validity of assessments of implicit behavior-relevant traits. First, the reliability of the implicit, explicit, and behavioral measures has to be established, avoiding the problem that dissociations between measures of implicit and explicit constructs are simply due to a low reliability of the implicit measures (Buchner & Wippich, 2000). Second, the validity of the behavioral measures for the target trait has to be established (e.g., by correlations with external criteria or trait ratings of observers of the behavior), avoiding the problem that low predictive correlations with the behavioral measures are due to their irrelevance for the target trait.

Third and most important, a double dissociation between the implicit and explicit trait measures with regard to spontaneous/automatized and controlled behavior has to be confirmed. It has to be shown that the implicit trait predicts spontaneous/automatized behavior significantly and uniquely (i.e., even when the correlation between the explicit trait and behavior is controlled for). In our view, the significant and unique prediction from the implicit trait to spontaneous behavior is the key validity criterion for assessments of behavior-relevant implicit traits. Simple correlations are not sufficient because they can be spurious if the indirect path to behavior that is mediated by the explicit trait is strong. In other words, this part of the proposed validation procedure requires that we show a *simple dissociation* between the implicit and the explicit trait with regard to spontaneous and controlled behavior.

In addition, we propose that the same logic should also be applied to an explicit trait measure;

---

[1] A test–retest correlation is the *r* between the two scores from the same person at two different testing occasions. The *r* statistic is interpreted in the selection by Rosenthal and Rubin in Part I.

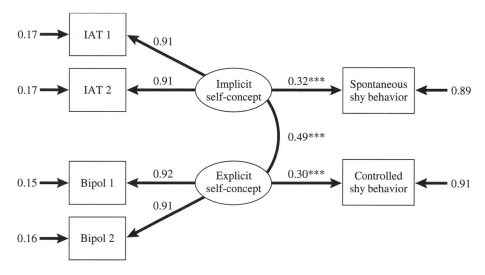

Figure 1   Double dissociation between the implicit and explicit self-concept of shyness. Presented is the result for the a priori defined structural equation model for the strong version of the double dissociation hypothesis (estimations of latent correlations, paths, and errors by LISREL). IAT 1 and IAT 2 refer to two parallel Implicit Association Test (IAT) subtests. Bipol and Bipol 2 refer to two parallel subscales of the bipolar (Bipol) shyness self-rating scale.*** $p < .001$.

that is, it has to be shown that the explicit trait significantly and uniquely predicts controlled behavior. Otherwise there is a risk that an implicit trait shows a unique prediction of behavior because the explicit measure is not valid, although the prediction would be spurious if a more valid explicit measure were chosen. Thus, Step 3 of our validation strategy requires that we show a full double dissociation for the implicit versus explicit traits. Readers may consider Figure 1 for a graphic illustration.[2]

Because a double dissociation includes two dependent and two independent variables, structural equation modeling is required to test it. In a weak version of the double dissociation hypothesis, only significant paths from the implicit trait to spontaneous/automatized behavior and from the expli-

cit trait to controlled behavior are required; the cross-paths from the implicit trait to controlled behavior and from the explicit trait to spontaneous/automatized behavior may also be significant. In a strong version, the cross-paths are zero; that is, the implicit trait adds nothing to the prediction of controlled behavior beyond the explicit trait, and vice versa. The higher the correlation between the implicit and the explicit trait is, the lower is the chance of confirming the strong version of the double dissociation hypothesis.

*   *   *

The Present Studies: Shyness

For multiple reasons, we chose to study the personality trait of shyness. First, shyness is a personality trait that is well represented in common language and lay psychology, is observable by others in social interaction, shows moderate self–other agreement in explicit ratings, and can be studied in naturalistic situations in the laboratory (Asendorpf, 1987, 1989). Therefore, it is easy to select shyness-descriptive adjectives for both explicit self-ratings and an IAT for shyness, and observers agree

---

[2]Figure 1 summarizes the result of a complex statistical procedure called *latent variable modeling*, as performed in this case by a computer program called LISREL. The lines in the model and the numbers on the lines ("paths") show the estimated relationships among the estimated underlying or "latent" variables in a research design. The *p* levels, as always, refer to the estimated probability of the "null hypothesis" that these path values are 0.

on others' shyness without special training (Asendorpf, 1987, 1989). Second, shyness is socially evaluated moderately negatively in Western cultures and therefore is subject to differential impression management tendencies. Because of its observability and good representation in lay psychology, the self-concept of shyness seems to be relatively cognitively accessible; consequently, discrepancies between implicit and explicit shyness can be mainly attributed to impression management. Third, we can sharpen the discriminant validity of implicit and explicit shyness measures by contrasting assessments of shyness with assessments of unsociability, which is a correlated but not identical trait (Asendorpf & Meier, 1993; Cheek & Buss, 1981).

Building on prior research (Asendorpf, 1989, 1990) on the situational and personal antecedents of state shyness and its differential expression in behavior, we tried to maximize state shyness by having young, heterosexual adults who had not recently fallen in love interact with an (a) unfamiliar, (b) above-average physically attractive opposite-sex confederate who played the role of another participant. The situation was socially evaluative because (c) the conversation partners were instructed to get to know each other to evaluate each other's personality later on, and (d) the conversation was filmed by a visible video camera.

To minimize the problem of individual response hierarchies (Asendorpf, 1988), we coded numerous behaviors, particularly both body movements and body tension. We hypothesized that speech and movements illustrating speech are more under the participants' explicit control, whereas body tension and body self-stimulations are more spontaneous indicators of shyness. We were less sure about the status of gaze aversion because it is well documented that it is influenced by both the affective state and the more controlled processes of initiating and terminating speaker roles (Kleinke, 1986). We tested whether these behavioral indicators are shyness indicators at all by correlating them with shyness judgments of observers of the videotaped interactions.

Study 1

Method

PARTICIPANTS

Participants were 139 heterosexual young adults who were native speakers of German and had finished high school (69 male, 70 female; mean age = 22.6 years, range = 19–31 years; 87% university students; psychology students were not recruited for this study). Most participants were approached by two experimenters on the campus of Humboldt University, Berlin, and were asked to participate; other participants were acquaintances of the experimenters. The participants were not paid. Instead, we motivated them for participation by informing them that the study was on social perception and that they could receive individual feedback on their results later on. Thus, the participants cooperated in the study mainly to get individual feedback on their personality.

ASSESSMENTS AND MEASURES

Overview. The participants (a) were videotaped in a shyness-inducing situation with a confederate of the experimenter, (b) judged themselves on bipolar personality-descriptive items, (c) completed a shyness IAT, (d) judged themselves on other personality items, and (e) completed a parallel shyness IAT (only the first 35 men and 35 women). The shyness items of the two IATs were explicitly self-rated in Step b. Finally, the participants were thanked, asked for permission for the videotapes to be analyzed (all gave permission), and promised individual feedback about their results. Four months after the study was finished, they received a letter explaining the procedures and general findings of the study and were invited for a feedback session at which they were informed about their individual results.

Shyness situation. On arrival at the lab, the participant was guided by the experimenter to the observation room, which was furnished as a living room. An above-average physically attractive, unfamiliar, opposite-sex peer sat at a low table. This confederate was trained to play the role of another participant and to respond in a friendly manner to initiatives of the participant but to be otherwise rather reserved. The experimenter introduced the participant to the confederate and asked him or her to sit down in a chair that was placed at a 90° angle to the confederate's chair.

Next, the experimenter read the following instructions:

> As you know, this experiment is on social perception, that is, how you perceive yourself and how you are perceived by others. You have now 5 minutes for getting to know each other. Subsequently, you will judge your conversation partner in a questionnaire, for example, how likable he or she is. Your answers in this questionnnaire will be treated strictly confidentially; in particular, your conversation partner will not get to know your judgment. Thus, you should try not to gloss over the facts. There [experimenter points to the camera] is a video camera that records your conversation. This is part of our routine procedure. Later on, you will separately complete various computer tasks. Because people usually differ in their speed, you will probably not see your conversation partner again.

This procedure was designed to induce shyness by (a) the unfamiliarity, (b) the opposite sex, (c) the attractiveness, and (d) the evaluation of the confederate and by (e) the video recording.

Subsequently, the experimenter left the room. After the 5-min conversation, she returned and asked the participants to judge their conversation partner on various bipolar scales (not analyzed for the purpose of the present study). Finally, the experimenter asked the confederate to wait for another experimenter and guided the participant to another room.

The participant and the confederate were videotaped by a camera that was operated from another room using S-VHS video. Camera settings were constant for all participants. A time code was imprinted on the tapes, and it started when the experimenter had closed the door. If the participant stood up and/or walked away, the confederate was to get him or her back as quickly as possible; the time period until he or she sat down again was defined as missing. Secondary tapes were prepared that contained the first 3 min of nonmissing interaction of all participants. These tapes were used for the judgments and codings.

Global judgments of shyness. Three student judges who were unfamiliar with the participants independently judged the 3-min video recording of each participant on a 7-point scale for shyness (ranging from 1 = *not shy* to 7 = *shy*). We anchored the judgments by presenting beforehand two examples of extremely shy and extremely nonshy participants from the study by Asendorpf (1989). The six ratings of each judge were averaged.

Codings of shy behavior. The videotaped behavior of all participants in the first 3 min was coded by one coder; coding reliability was assessed by independent coding of 40 randomly selected participants by another coder. Codings were done on a personal computer that was synchronized with the time code of the videotape. For each behavioral code, coders marked the onset and the offset of the behavior by pressing an appropriate button on the keyboard. Coded in independent runs were (a) speech of the participant, (b) body movements of the participant, (c) tenseness of the body posture, and (d) gaze aversion. For each code, its duration (expressed as percentage of observation time) was analyzed.

Body movements were coded according to Ekman and Friesen's (1972) classification, which distinguishes illustrators (movements illustrating speech, including emblems, i.e., movements with culturally defined meaning), facial adaptors (self-stimulation of face or neck), and body adaptors (self-stimulation of other parts of the body). Facial adaptors were distinguished from body adaptors because some facial adaptors may be redirected spontaneous movements of covering the face and may therefore be more specifically related to shyness than are other self-stimulations that mainly serve arousal-regulating functions (see Asendorpf, 1990).

Gazing was coded in terms of the onset and offset of participants' gaze toward the face of the confederate; the video recording did not make it possible to distinguish between face-directed gazing and eye contact. Gaze aversion was defined as the duration of not gazing.

Tenseness of body posture was coded on a 3-point scale: *normal, slight,* and *strong tension.* Normal tension was defined by four standard body postures that require minimum muscle activity. Slight/strong tension was defined by slight/strong deviations of head, shoulders, arms, hands, or legs from the standard positions that were described to the coders by 2 (degree of deviation) × 4 (standard position) = 8 additional prototypical body postures. We summed the durations of the three tension categories (in percentage of observed time) using the weights 0, 1, and 2 and then divided them by 2, which yielded scores that could range from 0% to 100%.

IAT. We took care to design the tests to be as similar to the original IATs by Greenwald et al. (1998) as possible. The target-concept discrimination was *me–others,* and attributes were *shy–nonshy.* In a first step, participants discriminated *me–others,* then *shy–nonshy.* In the initial combined task, they discriminated *me* and *shy* from *others* and *nonshy.* Subsequently, they discriminated *others–me* and, finally, *others* and *shy* from *me* and *nonshy* (see Tables 1 and 2). The difference between the mean reaction time in the reversed combined task and the mean reaction time in the initial combined task is the main dependent variable (IAT score); positive differences indicate faster associations between *me* and *shy* than between *others* and *shy.*

Participants used the letter *A* on the left side of the keyboard and the number 5 on the right-side numeric keypad for discrimination. The targets and/or attributes assigned to the response keys were presented in the left and right upper corners of the computer screen throughout each task. The stimuli were presented in the center of the screen until the participant responded. The stimuli for the two parallel IATs are presented in Table 2; the attribute stimuli were identical to the corresponding bipolar adjectives in the explicit self-ratings. In the two combined tasks, the stimuli alternated between target and attribute. Target and attribute stimuli were randomized in order within blocks of 20 trials. Thus, the internal consistency of the IAT could be evaluated across four subtests that included the same 20 trials in a different order. Interstimulus interval was 250 ms; after an incorrect response, the word *FEHLER* (German for *error*) immediately replaced the stimulus for 300 ms, resulting in a 550-ms interstimulus interval. Because this study focuses on interindividual differences, all participants received the stimuli in the same order to minimize interindividual variance due to order effects. Participants needed approximately 12 min to complete the IAT.

TABLE 1

IMPLICIT ASSOCIATION TESTS FOR SHYNESS:
TASK SEQUENCE

Sequence	No. of trials	Task	Response key assignment	
			Left key	Right key
1	40	Target discrimination	Me	Others
2	40	Attribute discrimination	Shy	Nonshy
3	80	Initial combined task	Me, shy	Others, nonshy
4	40	Reversed target discrimination	Others	Me
5	80	Reversed combined task	Others, shy	Me, nonshy

TABLE 2						
IMPLICIT ASSOCIATION TESTS FOR SHYNESS: STIMULI						
		Test		Parallel test		
Me	Others	Shy	Nonshy	Shy	Nonshy	
I	thy	inhibited	uninhibited	self-conscious	easy-going	
self	them	insecure	secure	unassertive	assertive	
my	your	timid	daring	hesitant	resolute	
me	you	reticent	candid	reluctant	spontaneous	
own	other	reserved	open	withdrawn	sociable	

Note. The original German stimuli can be obtained from us.

Participants were instructed to respond as quickly and accurately as possible. Their responses were recorded using Experimental Run Time System software (Beringer, 1994). In keeping with Greenwald et al. (1998), the first two responses in the combined tasks were not analyzed, response latencies below 300 ms were recoded as 300 ms, and latencies above 3,000 ms were recoded as 3,000 ms. These raw latencies were used only for reporting means and standard deviations. All other statistical analyses were based on log-transformed latencies to correct for the skewed latency distribution.

Explicit self-ratings. In a first block, participants responded to 40 bipolar adjective pairs that were presented one by one on a computer screen (e.g., shy 1—2—3—4—5—6—7 nonshy). They were instructed to indicate how well the two opposed adjectives described their personality by pressing the appropriate number on the keyboard. We selected 10 adjective pairs each for assessing shyness, agreeableness, conscientiousness, and intellect. The 20 shyness-descriptive adjectives were selected by high or low factor loadings on both introversion and neuroticism in a factor analysis of self-ratings of 830 unipolar personality-descriptive adjectives used by Asendorpf and Ostendorf (1998). The other adjectives were selected by high or low factor loadings on the agreeableness, conscientiousness, and intellect factors of these adjectives and served

as distractors. The resulting 40 bipolar items were then randomly mixed.

After completion of the first IAT, the participants answered 27 personality-descriptive items that were again presented one by one on the computer screen on a 5-point scale (ratings ranged from 1 = *not at all true for me* to 5 = *completely true for me*) by pressing the appropriate number. Five items referred to shyness, and another 5 referred to sociability. These two 5-item scales were used by Asendorpf and Wilpers (1998) and were included to validate the bipolar shyness adjectives. These items were randomly mixed with 17 distractor items.

Results

DESCRIPTION OF THE MAIN VARIABLES

IATs. For both IATs, the individual incorrect response rates for the 156 analyzed responses in the two combined tasks were similar to those reported by Greenwald et al. (1998; for the first IAT, $M = 5.0\%$, $SD = 4.2\%$; for the second IAT, $M = 3.6\%$, $SD = 2.2\%$).[3] Inspection of the error distributions indicated one clear outlier (a participant with 35% errors in the first IAT); all other error rates were below 17% (first IAT) or 9% (second IAT).

---

[3] M stands for mean; SD is standard deviation.

TABLE 3

TABLE 3

Validating Spontaneous and Controlled Shy Behavior in Study 1

Behavioral measure	Correlation with shyness indicator		
	Observer judgment	First IAT	Bipolar self-rating
Facial adaptor duration	.16*	.17*	.13
Body adaptor duration	.27***	.17*	.11
Gaze aversion	.40***	.18*	.18*
Tense body posture	.18*	.19*	.08
Spontaneous shy behavior[a]	.35***	.31***	.18*
Speech duration	−.66***	−.23***	−.31***
Illustrator duration	−.31***	−.11	−.15*
Controlled shy behavior[b]	.58***	.20**	.28***

Note. IAT = Implicit Association Test.
[a]Average of z-transformed duration of facial and body adaptors and tense body posture. [b]Average of reversed z-transformed duration of speech and illustrators.
*$p < .05$. **$p < .01$. ***$p < .001$.

Therefore, this participant was excluded from all analyses, and the following analyses refer to 138 participants (68 men, 70 women).

* * *

SPONTANEOUS AND CONTROLLED SHY BEHAVIOR

We assumed that facial adaptors, body adaptors, and tense body posture are indicators of primarily spontaneous expressions of shyness, whereas speech and illustrators are indicators of primarily controlled nonshy behavior; we were not sure about the status of gaze aversion except that it is an indicator of shyness in general. First, we tested whether these behaviors were correlated with the observer judgments of shyness (which would validate them as indicators of interindividual differences in shyness). Table 3 indicates that the hypothesis was confirmed in each instance.

Second, we explored whether the assumed spontaneous indicators tended to correlate more strongly with the IAT than with the explicit shyness self-ratings. Table 3 indicates that this assumption was confirmed for all indicators, although the differences between the correlations were not large. Gaze aversion showed equally high correlations

with the IAT and the explicit self-ratings. Because gaze aversion did not discriminate between the implicit and explicit measures of shyness, it was not further analyzed.

In the next step, the three indicators of spontaneous shy behavior and the two indicators of controlled nonshy behavior were aggregated after z transformation. The sign of the aggregate of controlled behavior was reversed so that this index referred to controlled shy behavior. We tested whether both types of behavior independently contributed to the observer judgments by regressing the observer judgment on both spontaneous and controlled behavior. Together, these two predictors accounted for 40% of the variance in the observer judgments; 33.3% was predicted by controlled behavior, $F(1, 136) = 67.95$, $p < .001$, and 6.4% was independently predicted by spontaneous behavior, $\Delta F(1, 135) = 14.01$, $p < .001$.[4]

---

[4]The analysis of variance yields an F statistic that, combined with the degrees of freedom in the design (given within parentheses), allows an estimate of the probability of the null hypothesis that the difference in means is 0.

TABLE 4

INTERCORRELATIONS OF THE MAIN INDICATORS IN STUDY 1

Indicator	1	2	3	4	5	6	7	8
1. First IAT	—	.66***	.44***	.40***	−.25**	.31***	.31***	.20*
2. Second IAT		—	.35***	.30**	−.34**	.24*	.08	.19
3. Bipolar shyness self-rating			—	.82***	−.51***	.48***	.18*	.28***
4. Shyness scale				—	−.48***	.40***	.19*	.21*
5. Sociability scale					—	−.32***	−.09	−.15
6. Behavioral shyness judgment						—	.35***	.58***
7. Spontaneous shy behavior							—	.18*
8. Controlled shy behavior								—

Note. $N = 138$. IAT = Implicit Association Test.
*$p < .05$. **$p < .01$. ***$p < .001$.

CORRELATIONS AMONG THE MAIN VARIABLES

Numerous observations can be made from the correlations of the main variables (see Table 4). First, the correlation between the two parallel IATs was lower ($r = .66$) than their internal consistencies ($\alpha > .82$). Second, the second IAT tended to be less valid than the first one. This was also true if the analysis was restricted to those 70 participants who completed both IATs. Third, a correlation of .82 between the bipolar self-ratings of shyness and the shyness scale, along with lower correlations with the sociability scale, validated the bipolar adjectives for shyness. Fourth, the first IAT correlated significantly more highly with the five-item shyness scale than with the five-item unsociability scale, according to Steiger's (1980) test, $t(135) = 1.86$, $p < .05$ one-tailed, attesting to the specificity of the shyness IAT. * * * Thus, the IAT was specifically related to shyness in participants' explicit self-ratings. Fifth, self-rated shyness tended to correlate more strongly with the three behavioral indicators of shyness than did sociability. Sixth, spontaneous shy behavior and controlled shy behavior were significantly correlated, but at a low level. Sex differences in the correlations in Table 4 were tested with Z tests; all differences were nonsignificant.

*   *   *

Discussion

This study successfully validates an IAT for the assessment of the implicit self-concept of shyness by following a double dissociation strategy. First, the internal consistency of the shyness IAT and the explicit self-ratings of shyness, the intercoder agreement for the behavioral indicators of shy behavior, and the interjudge agreement for the observer ratings of shyness were successfully established. Second, the validity of the adjectives that were used for both the shyness IAT and the explicit self-ratings of shyness was confirmed by a high convergent correlation between the bipolar adjective scale and an established shyness scale.

Third, the validity of the behavioral indicators of shy behavior was confirmed by significant correlations with the observer judgments of shyness. As expected, the intercorrelations between the behavioral indicators were low because of strong individual response hierarchies in the individual expression of shyness. Our solution to this long-standing problem in behavioral observation and psychophysiological research (see Lacey, 1950) was to aggregate multiple indicators of shy behavior. As the results show (see Table 3), this was a successful strategy because the correlations between the aggregate and each external variable were always clearly higher than the average correlations between a component of the aggregate and this external variable.

Fourth, we aggregated the behaviors separately for indicators that were assumed a priori to be more spontaneously activated or highly automatized (tense body posture, facial and body adaptors) or more under voluntary control (speech, illustrators). We had no a priori hypothesis about gaze aversion because gazing is linked to both affective states such as state shyness and the more voluntary control over speaker turns (Kleinke, 1986). As it turned out, gaze aversion showed equally high correlations with the IAT and the explicit measure of shyness and thus was not considered in the formation of aggregated indices for spontaneous and controlled shy behavior.

Fifth, we confirmed with these behavioral measures of spontaneous and controlled shy behavior the strong version of the double dissociation hypothesis. That is, the shyness IAT significantly and uniquely predicted spontaneous shy behavior, and the explicit self-ratings of shyness significantly and uniquely predicted controlled shy behavior, without significant cross-paths between IAT and controlled behavior and between the explicit measure and spontaneous behavior. * * *

* * *

All in all, the findings of the present study confirm the strong version of the expected double dissociation. However, the double dissociation was not maximal because the IAT correlated significantly with controlled shy behavior and the explicit self-ratings correlated significantly with spontaneous shy behavior. Ideally, one might expect not only zero cross-paths but also zero cross-correlations. The main reason for the deviation of the present data from this ideal is the fairly high latent correlation of .49 between the IAT and the explicit self-ratings that induced indirect correlations between a predictor and behavior that were mediated through the other correlated predictor.

The relatively high correlation between the measures of implicit and explicit shyness may be attributed to the fact that social perception was the cover story and that the participants were not paid for participation and were promised individual feedback on their results. Thus, participation only made sense for them if they cooperated with the instructions and provided self-descriptions that were as accurate as possible. Dissociations between implicit and explicit shyness are minimized in such situations, restricted more or less to distortions of the self-concept that the participants are not aware of. Stronger dissociations are expected under conditions in which participants are highly motivated to present themselves as nonshy, for example in the context of personnel selection.

* * *

Study 2

The validity of our distinction between spontaneous and controlled shy behavior can be empirically tested in a faking study in which the participants of an experimental condition are asked to present themselves as not shy. Relative to a control condition in which participants do not receive such an instruction, one would expect that controlled shy behavior (absence of speech and illustrators) is decreased but that spontaneous shy behavior (self-adaptors and tense body posture) remains unaffected by the experimental variation. Also, such a study could confirm the important prediction that self-reported shyness but not IAT-assessed shyness decreases under faking instructions.

In faking studies in which participants are asked not only to fake responses in questionnaires but to control their social-interactional behavior for an extended period of time, it is extremely important that the faking task makes sense to the participants. Therefore, we did not choose a faking version of Study 1 by simply instructing participants to present themselves as not shy in the presence of the confederate. Instead, we took care to set up a new social-interaction situation in which presenting themselves as not shy presented a real challenge to our student participants that they would be eager to meet. We invited the participants of the experimental condition to a simulated job application procedure including video feedback on their behavior and informed them that appearing non-shy (including their responses to computer tasks and their behavior in a role play situation typical for assessment centers) was crucial for getting the job. In the control condition, the role play was the same but the cover story was social perception (as in Study 1).

We expected that participants in the assessment center condition would score lower on the bipolar shyness adjectives but not the shyness IAT and that they would show less controlled shy behavior (duration of speech and speech-illustrating movements) but would not show less spontaneous shy behavior (facial and body self-stimulations and tense body position) compared with the participants in the social perception condition. Thus, we expected a dissociation between controlled and spontaneous shy behavior with regard to the experimental manipulation.

Because we expected the same direction of effects of the experimental variation for both men and women and because we expected women to show a somewhat stronger effect in relation to their well-documented higher social-interactional competence (Hall, 1984), we studied only women. In addition to allowing a smaller sample size, including only women meant that only one opposite-sex role play partner had to be trained for the role play and the video feedback, and this person was the same for all participants.

Method

Participants

Participants were 41 female nonpsychology university students (native speakers of German; mean age = 22.1 years, range = 19–30 years). The participants were invited either for a job application procedure (experimental condition, $n = 23$) or for a study on social perception (control condition, $n = 18$). In the first case, we motivated them for participation in the study by informing them that they would participate in a simulation of a job assessment center and would receive video feedback on

their performance. In the second case, invitation was identical to Study 1.

Assessments

Experimental condition. On arrival at the lab, the participants in the experimental (assessment center) condition received the following instructions:

> The following assessment center assesses your ability to present yourself as successfully as possible for a position in a company that you are very interested in. An important part of your future job is to present the company as successfully as possible in interactions with new clients. Therefore, you must be able to warm up strangers quickly and to avoid insecure behavior because such insecurity could easily make an unprofessional impression.

After repeating the job criteria once more, the experimenter explained the different steps of the assessment center and stressed that to get the job, the participant should make a favorable impression in all parts of the assessment, including both the role play and the personality tests.

Control condition. The participants in the control condition received the alternative instructions: "The following experiment is on social perception, that is, how you perceive yourself and how others perceive you." After explaining the different steps of the experiment, the experimenter continued, "Please describe yourself in all personality tests as honestly and realistically as possible and act in the role play simply as you would do in real life." As in Study 1, these participants received no specific instructions before the implicit or explicit tasks.

Role play instructions. Subsequently, the participants were taken by the experimenter to the observation room that was also used in Study 1. Outside the room, participants in the assessment center condition were reminded that "it is very important for getting the job that you show in the role play that you can easily and openly approach strangers." In the control condition, the participants were informed that "the role play is informative about particular personality characteristics" and that they would be evaluated by their role play partner after the role play (this part of the instruction was identical to the instruction in Study 1).

Next, the participants were informed that the role play would be recorded by two cameras, and the role play situation was described for all participants as follows:

> You are an employee in a company. In your company, the boss will be replaced by a new one. This new boss, your future boss, was supposed to be meeting the present boss now, but unfortunately the present boss is still in another meeting for about 10 minutes. You have been asked to fill in for these 10 minutes and to make the situation as comfortable for your future boss as possible.

In the assessment center condition, this instruction was continued, "You should present yourself as favorably as possible. Have in mind that your role play partner will be your future boss." In the control condition, the instruction was continued differently: "Act in the role play just as you would do in real life."

Role play. The participant was shown into the observation room. An older-looking, unfamiliar male advanced psychology student, dressed in a business suit, was already sitting at a low table. This confederate was not aware of the participant's assignment to the experimental condition. He was trained to play the role of the future boss described in the instruction. In particular, he was instructed to act slightly indignant at the delay of the meeting with the present boss and to slightly patronize the participant. As in Study 1, the participant was seated on a chair placed at a 90° angle to the confederate's chair.

This procedure was designed to induce shyness by (a) the unfamiliarity and (b) the status difference of the boss, (c) the assumed evaluation by the boss, (d) the opposite sex of the boss, and (e) the videotaping. Thus, we expected a similarly strong induction of shyness as in Study 1 for both experimental conditions. Both interactants were videotaped as in Study 1; again, the first 3 min were used for all behavioral codings and judgments.

Judgments and codings of shy behavior. We used procedures identical to those in Study 1, except that gazing was not coded because it did not differentiate between IAT and the explicit self-rating in Study 1. In particular, we computed indices of

TABLE 5

SUMMARY STATISTICS AND INSTRUCTION EFFECT FOR THE MAIN VARIABLES OF STUDY 2

Variable (range of scores)	Assessment center (n = 23)		Social perception (n = 18)		Instruction effect (t test)		
	M	SD	M	SD	t(39)	p	d
IAT[a]	-65.0	232.0	13.0	218.0	1.22	ns	0.39
Bipolar shyness self-rating (1–7)	2.4	0.7	3.4	0.8	4.32	.001	1.38
Observer shyness judgment (1–7)	3.5	0.9	3.9	1.2	1.40	ns	0.45
Speech duration (%)	52.0	12.3	37.6	10.4	3.99	.001	1.28
Illustrator duration (%)	5.0	4.9	2.4	2.5	2.20	.05	0.71
Facial adaptor duration (%)	5.5	12.3	2.0	2.0	0.98	ns	−0.31
Body adaptor duration (%)	31.6	21.3	20.1	20.0	2.26	.05	−0.72
Tense body posture (%)	44.1	26.0	36.1	21.6	1.05	ns	-0.34

Note. M and SD refer to raw scores; t tests refer to log-transformed scores in the case of the IAT and the body movement codings. The effect sizes (d) were defined such that positive scores indicate more shyness in the control condition. IAT = Implicit Association Test.
[a]M and SD for the IAT are in milliseconds.   [b]Weighted duration of normal, slight, and strong tension.

spontaneous and controlled shy behavior as in Study 1. Coding reliability was satisfactory in each case (for the observer judgments, $\alpha = .94$; for the intercoder agreement for 15 participants, $r > .80$ for each behavior).

IAT and explicit ratings. As in Study 1, the interaction situation was followed by explicit ratings of bipolar adjectives and the shyness IAT. The same bipolar adjectives and IAT procedures as in Study 1 were used in the control condition. In the experimental condition, the participants were reminded before the IAT and the explicit ratings that "You should present yourself in the following task in such a way that you will get the job". The Steps d–e of Study 1 were skipped.

Feedback. In the experimental condition, the role play partner watched the videotape of the role play with the participant, commented on her behavior, and suggested alternatives for less competent behavior. He was trained to stress participants' competencies and to provide constructive alternatives. In the control condition, participants were invited for an individual feedback after the full analysis of their data.

Results

For the IAT, the individual incorrect response rates for the 156 analyzed responses in the two combined tasks were highly similar to those in Study 1 ($M = 5.1\%$, $SD = 3.4\%$). Inspection of the error distributions indicated no extreme scorers (all error rates were below 15%). The distribution of the log-based IAT scores was not even marginally different from a normal distribution ($Z < 1$). The internal consistency of the IAT was evaluated as in Study 1; Cronbach's alpha was .84. The internal consistency of the shyness self-ratings was .86. Thus, the reliabilities were satisfactory for both the implicit and the explicit measures.

The means and standard deviations for all dependent variables are reported in Table 4 separately for the two experimental conditions. In a first step, differences between the control condition and the

70 female participants in Study 1 were explored by a MANOVA, followed by post hoc *t* tests. We found an overall effect, $F(8, 79) = 3.11$, $p < .01$, that was due to the expected difference in speech duration, $t(1, 86) = 3.08$, $p < .003$. The other seven dependent variables did not significantly differ between the control condition and Study 1. Thus, the control condition was highly similar to Study 1 except for a lower speech duration (38% as compared with 48% in Study 1), which most likely resulted from the different script of the confederate. In particular, there were no differences regarding the IAT, the shyness self-ratings, and the observer judgment of shyness.

Subsequently, the expected (non)differences between the experimental and the control conditions were tested by *t* tests for each dependent variable (see Table 5). As expected, the participants in the assessment center condition rated themselves as much less shy, talked much more, and illustrated their speech more with gestures than did the participants in the social perception condition. Therefore, as expected, the index for controlled shy behavior was much lower in the assessment center condition, $t(39) = 3.53$, $p < .001$, $d = 1.13$. Also as expected, the IAT scores were not even marginally different between the two experimental conditions.

Unexpectedly, the index of spontaneous shy behavior was even higher in the assessment center condition than in the control condition, $t(39) = 2.78$, $p < .01$, $d = -0.89$, and the observer judgments of shyness were not significantly lower in the assessment center condition. As Table 5 indicates, the participants in the assessment center condition tended to show more shyness consistently across all three spontaneous shy behaviors (facial adaptors, body adaptors, and body tension), and this tendency reached significance for the body adaptors.

Discussion

Study 2 confirms our assignment of speech and illustrators to controlled behavior and of self-stimulations and tense body position to spontaneous behavior as even stronger than expected. The participants in the experimental condition followed the instruction to present themselves as not shy in their controlled behavior but failed to suppress spontaneous shy behavior; they even showed more body self-stimulations than did the participants in the control condition. Because such nervous movements are interpreted by observers as indications of shyness (see Table 2), they may have counteracted observers' tendency to attribute less shyness to the participants in the assessment center condition, resulting in only marginally lower observer judgments of shyness for this condition.

In addition, Study 2 also confirms the expectation that the faking instruction influenced participants' explicit shyness self-ratings (a decrease of more than one standard deviation, thus, a very large effect) but not their IAT scores, although the IAT was also assessed under a faking instruction. This last result is consistent with prior studies on the controllability of the IAT (e.g., Banse et al., 2001; Kim, 2001).

General Discussion

Mechanisms

Presently there is considerable debate about the cognitive processes underlying IAT procedures and the interpretation of IAT effects (Brendl, Markman, & Messner, 2001; De Houwer, 2001; Karpinski & Hilton, 2001; Mierke & Klauer, 2001; Rothermund & Wentura, 2001). It is important to note that results for IAT procedures that refer to personally meaningless materials such as geometric figures or nonsense syllables are not necessarily informative about their application to personally meaningful concepts such as implicit attitudes, stereotypes, and self-concept. Also, potential ambiguities concerning the interpretation of IAT mean effects (Brendl et al., 2001) are not crucial for the interpretation of interindividual differences in IAT effects. But there is no question that we need to know much more about the cognitive processes underlying IAT procedures to understand better what these procedures measure. We briefly discuss here [two] open questions in this respect that are relevant for the present study.

* * *

To what extent do participants influence IAT results through conscious, deliberate behavior? Kim (2001) has shown that, when instructed to do so, respondents were not able to fake more pro-Black attitudes by accelerating responses in the difficult mixed blocks. They were only able to deliberately produce a positive implicit attitude toward Blacks by slowing down their responses in the easier White/good–Black/bad mixed task. However, these results are silent about what people really do when they do not receive specific instructions, particularly in studies such as the present one where there is no reason to fake results. Future studies should investigate in detail the strategies that participants spontaneously use for making testing easier for them or for influencing the test results.

Third, better knowledge of the cognitive processes underlying IAT procedures is needed for us to better understand the nature of implicit self-concept. This better understanding, in turn, is a necessary but not sufficient requirement for answering what we consider the most difficult question of all: Which mechanisms mediate between implicit traits and trait-relevant behavior? The only thing that seems sure is that implicit traits do not directly trigger behavior. People do not act shy because they feel that they are shy.

Instead, we assume, in line with Asendorpf's (1989) two-factor common pathway model, that individual differences in shy behavior are determined by both temperamental traits and relatively independent earlier experiences of being ignored or rejected by significant others. In a continuous process of self-validation, shy behavior is self-perceived both directly and indirectly through social feedback from others. These perceptions crystallize into an implicit self-concept of being shy. Through this developmental process, the implicit self-concept is linked with behavioral dispositions and, thus, also with actual behavior. Consequently, we assume that there are no direct mechanisms that link the implicit self-concept of shyness with shy behavior. Instead, the continuous influence of temperamental traits and the accumulation of social experiences over developmental time provide the key for our understanding of the link between self-concept and behavior. The mediating mechanisms are developmental.

Ethical and Practical Implications

Procedures such as the IAT are sometimes considered unethical because of a belief that these implicit procedures are not as much under voluntary control as are questionnaire responses. Others are enthusiastic about these procedures because they believe that the procedures promise a final solution to the problems of social desirability biases and cognitive inaccessibility not only in psychological research but also in psychological practice. Both beliefs may turn out to be erroneous. Concerning ethical issues, IATs can be faked if one knows how they work. Although it seems difficult to substantially accelerate one's responses in one of the mixed blocks, it is possible to slow down (Kim, 2001). For example, if one wants to fake being shy in the shyness IAT of the present studies, one must slow down responses in the second mixed block, when tests the *I–nonshy* association; if one wants to fake being nonshy, one must slow down responses in the first mixed block, which tests the *I–shy* association. Of course, to counteract this quite simple faking strategy, assessment professionals will select only fast-responding participants with the searched-for IAT scores—at least as long as false negative decisions are less costly than false positive decisions. But with increasing use of the IAT, test crackers are very likely to develop more sophisticated faking strategies, such as focusing on specific aspects of the critical mixed task (e.g., Rothermund & Wentura, 2001). In case the IAT is used for personnel selection, it presently seems impossible to predict who will win the arms race between assessment professionals and test crackers.

Concerning practical use, IATs relating to the self-concept of personality may be useful in contexts such as counseling or psychotherapy, where people are motivated to access parts of their self-concept that are difficult to explore in explicit mode. Just as free associations in psychoanalytic settings provide a window to the unconscious, IATs provide another, probably more reliable window. But just as psychoanalytic interpretations of free associations are controversial for good reasons, interpretations of IAT results that are not backed up by a nomological network of empirical correlates are problematic as well.

Implications for Personality Research

Our studies have two important implications for future personality research. First, we have shown that it is possible to apply procedures such as the IAT to the assessment of implicit traits. Shyness is just one example; in principle, any trait that can be described by adjectives (and there are thousands of trait-describing adjectives; Allport & Odbert, 1936; John, Angleitner, & Ostendorf, 1988) can be studied by an IAT procedure. One has only to replace the shyness adjectives in our first IAT with a few adjectives that describe another trait. There is no guarantee that the resulting IAT will be as internally consistent as the parallel explicit self-ratings of the same adjectives, but the prospects are good.

Second, our double dissociation strategy for validating implicit traits can be applied to any behavior-related implicit construct, not only to implicit traits. This strategy poses strong constraints on the validity of implicit procedures that hopefully will prevent premature validity claims that are based on unreliable implicit measures (Buchner & Wippich, 2000) or spurious discriminant validities, because validity is fully mediated by the association with a valid explicit measure.

Besides exploring the usefulness of our approach for other domains of personality and unraveling the cognitive mechanisms that underlie the IAT procedure, a high-priority goal of future studies on implicit constructs should be the construction of different assessment procedures that access the same implicit constructs with different techniques in the implicit mode. If new procedures become available, psychologists can strengthen their empirical research on implicit constructs by replicating results with different methods and by reducing specific method variance through the aggregation across different implicit measures.

References

Allport, G. W., & Odbert, H. S. (1936). Trait names: A psycholexical study. *Psychological Monographs, 47*(Whole No. 211).

Asendorpf, J. B. (1987). Videotape reconstruction of emotions and cognitions related to shyness. *Journal of Personality and Social Psychology, 53,* 542–549.

Asendorpf, J. B. (1988). Individual response profiles in the behavioral assessment of personality. *European Journal of Personality, 2,* 155–167.

Asendorpf, J. B. (1989). Shyness as a final common pathway for two different kinds of inhibition. *Journal of Personality and Social Psychology, 57,* 481–492.

Asendorpf, J. B. (1990). The expression of shyness and embarrassment. In W. R. Crozler (Ed.), *Shyness and embarrassment: Perspectives from social psychology* (pp. 87–118). New York: Cambridge University Press.

Asendorpf, J. B., & Meier, G. H. (1993). Personality effects on children's speech in everyday life: Sociability-mediated exposure and shyness-mediated reactivity to social situations. *Journal of Personality and Social Psychology, 64,* 1072–1083.

Asendorpf, J. B., & Ostendorf, F. (1998). Is self-enhancement healthy? Conceptual, psychometric, and empirical analysis. *Journal of Personality and Social Psychology, 74,* 955–966.

Asendorpf, J. B., & Wilpers, S. (1998). Personality effects on social relationships. *Journal of Personality and Social Psychology, 74,* 1531–1544.

Baldwin, M. W., Carrel, S. E., & Lopez, D. F. (1990). Printing relationship schemas: My advisor and the pope are watching me from the back of my mind. *Journal of Experimental Social Psychology, 26,* 435–454.

Banse, R., & Gawronski, B. (2001). *Motivation zur Vorurteilskontrolle: Skaleneigenschaften und Validierung* [Motivation to control prejudice: Scale properties and validation]. Manuscript submitted for publication.

Banse, R., Seise, J., & Zerbes, N. (2001). Implicit attitudes towards homosexuality: Reliability, validity, and controllability of the IAT. *Zeitschrift für Experimentelle Psychologie, 48,* 145–160.

Bargh, J. A. (1994). The four horsemen of automaticity: Awareness, intention, efficiency, and control in social cognition. In R. S. Wyer & T. K. Srull (Eds.), *Handbook of social cognition* (2nd ed., pp. 1–40). Hillsdale, NJ: Erlbaum.

Beringer, J. (1994). Experimental Run Time System (Version 3. 18) [computer software]. Frankfurt, Germany: BeriSoft Corporation.

Bosson, J. K., Swann, W. B., Jr., & Pennebaker, J. W. (2000). Stalking the perfect measure of implicit self-esteem: The blind man and the elephant revisited? *Journal of Personality and Social Psychology, 79,* 631–643.

Bowlby, J. (1969). *Attachment and loss: Vol. 1. Attachment.* New York: Basic Books.

Breakwell, G. M. (1986). *Coping with threatened identities.* London: Methuen.

Brendt, C. M., Markman, A. B., & Messner, C. (2001). How do indirect measures of evaluation work? Evaluating the inference of prejudice in the Implicit Association Test. *Journal of Personality and Social Psychology, 81,* 760–773.

Buchner, A., & Wippich, W. (2000). On the reliability of implicit and explicit measures. *Cognitive Psychology, 40,* 227–259.

Cheek, J. M., & Buss, A. H. (1981). Shyness and sociability. *Journal of Personality and Social Psychology, 41,* 330–339.

Cunningham, W. A., Preacher, K. J., & Banaji, M. R. (2001). Implicit attitude measures: Consistency, stability, and convergent validity. *Psychological Science, 12,* 163–170.

De Houwer, J. (2001). A structural and process analysis of the Implicit Association Test. *Journal of Experimental Social Psychology, 37,* 443–451.

Dunton, B. C., & Fazio, R. H. (1997). An individual difference measure of motivation to control prejudiced reactions. *Personality and Social Psychology Bulletin, 23,* 316–326.

Edwards, A. L. (1957). *The social desirability variable in personality assessment and research.* New York: Dryden.

Ekman, P., & Friesen, W. V. (1969). The repertoire of nonverbal behavior: Categories, origin, usage, and coding. *Semiotica, 1,* 49–98.

Ekman, P., & Friesen, W. V. (1972). Hand movements. *Journal of Communication, 22,* 353–374.

Epstein, S. (1994). Integration of the cognitive and the psychodynamic unconscious. *American Psychologist, 49,* 709–724.

Fazio, R. H. (1990). Multiple processes by which attitudes guide behavior: The MODE model as an integrative framework. In M. P. Zanna (Ed.), *Advances in experimental social psychology* (Vol. 23, pp. 75–109). San Diego, CA: Academic Press.

Fazio, R. H., Jackson, J. R., Dunton, B. C., & Williams, C. J. (1995). Variability in automatic activation as an unobtrusive measure of racial attitudes: A bona fide pipeline? *Journal of Personality and Social Psychology, 69,* 1013–1027.

Fazio, R. H., & Towles-Schwenn, T. (1999). The MODE model of attitude-behavior processes. In S. Chaiken & Y. Trope (Eds.), *Dual process theories in social psychology* (pp. 97–116). New York: Guilford Press.

Funder, D. C. (1991). Global traits: A neo-Allportian approach to personality. *Psychological Science, 2,* 31–39.

Funder, D. C. (1999). *Personality judgment: A realistic approach to person perception.* San Diego, CA: Academic Press.

Furman, W., & Flanagan, A. S. (1997). The influence of earlier relationships on marriage: An attachment perspective. In W. K. Halford & H. J. Markman (Eds.), *Clinical handbook of marriage and couples interventions* (pp. 179–202). New York: Wiley.

George, C., Kaplan, N., & Main, M. (1985). *An adult attachment interview.* Unpublished manuscript, University of California, Berkeley.

Greenwald, A. G., & Banaji, M. R. (1995). Implicit social cognition: Attitudes, self-esteem, and stereotypes. *Psychological Review, 102,* 4–27.

Greenwald, A. G., Banaji, M. R., Rudman, L. A., Farnham, S. D., Nosek, B. A., & Mellot, D. S. (2002). A unified theory of implicit attitudes, stereotypes, self-esteem, and self-concept. *Psychological Review, 109,* 3–25.

Greenwald, A. G., & Farnham, S. D. (2000). Using the Implicit

Association Test to measure self-esteem and self-concept. *Journal of Personality and Social Psychology, 79,* 1022–1038.

Greenwald, A. G., McGhee, D. E., & Schwartz, J. L. K. (1998). Measuring individual differences in implicit cognition: The implicit association test. *Journal of Personality and Social Psychology, 74,* 1464–1480.

Greenwald, A. G., & Nosek, B. A. (2001). Health of the Implicit Association Test at age 3, *Zeitschrift für Experimentelle Psychologie, 48,* 85–93.

Hall, J. A. (1984). *Nonverbal sex differences: Communication accuracy and expressive style.* Baltimore: Johns Hopkins University Press.

Hinde, R. A. (1970). *Animal behavior* (2nd ed.). New York: McGraw-Hill.

John, O. P., Angleitner, A., & Ostendorf, F. (1988). The lexical approach to personality: A historical review of trait taxonomic research. *European Journal of Personality, 2,* 171–203.

Jöreskog, K. G., & Sörbom, D. (2001). LISREL 8.5 [computer software]. Chicago, IL: Scientific Software, Inc.

Karpinski, A., & Hilton, J. L. (2001). Attitudes and the Implicit Association Test. *Journal of Personality and Social Psychology, 81,* 774–788.

Kihlstrom, J. F., & Cantor, N. (1984). Mental representations of the self. In L. Berkowitz (Ed.), *Advances in experimental social psychology* (Vol. 17, pp. 1–47). Orlando, FL: Academic Press.

Kim, D.-Y. (2001). *Voluntary controllability of implicit cognition: Can implicit attitudes (the IAT) be faked?* Manuscript submitted for publication.

Kleinke, C. L. (1986). Gaze and eye contact: A research review. *Psychological Bulletin, 100,* 78–100.

Lacey, J. I. (1950). Individual differences in somatic response patterns. *Journal of Comparative and Physiological Psychology, 43,* 338–350.

McClelland, D. C., Koestner, R., & Weinberger, J. (1989). How do self-attributed and implicit motives differ? *Psychological Review, 96,* 690–702.

McConahay, J. B., Hardee, B. B., & Batts, V. (1981). Has racism declined in America? It depends on who is asking and what is asked. *Journal of Conflict Resolution, 25,* 563–579.

McCrae, R. R., & Costa, P. T., Jr. (1999). A five-factor theory of personality. In L. Pervin & O. P. John (Eds.), *Handbook of personality: Theory and research* (2nd ed., pp. 139–153). New York: Guilford Press.

Mierke, J., & Klauer, K. C. (2001). Implicit association measurement with the IAT: Evidence for effects of executive control processes. *Zeitschrift für Experimentelle Psychologie, 48,* 107–122.

Paulhus, D. L. (1984). Two-component models of socially desirable responding. *Journal of Personality and Social Psychology, 46,* 598–609.

Paulhus, D. L. (1998). Intrapsychic and interpersonal adaptiveness of trait self-enhancement: A mixed blessing? *Journal of Personality and Social Psychology, 74,* 812–820.

Rothermund, K., & Wentura, D. (2001). Figure-ground asymmetries in the Implicit Association Test (IAT). *Zeitschrift für Experimentelle Psychologie, 48,* 94–106.

Steiger, J. H. (1980). Tests for comparing elements of a correlation matrix. *Psychological Bulletin, 87,* 245–251.

Wilson, T., Lindsey, S., & Schooler, T. Y. (2000). A model of dual attitudes. *Psychological Review, 107,* 101–126.

Winter, D. G., & Stewart, A. J. (1977). Power motive reliability as a function of retest instructions. *Journal of Consulting and Clinical Psychology, 43,* 436–440.

SELF-KNOWLEDGE OF AN AMNESIC PATIENT: TOWARD A NEUROPSYCHOLOGY OF PERSONALITY AND SOCIAL PSYCHOLOGY

Stanley B. Klein, Judith Loftus, and John F. Kihlstrom

The final selection in this section and this book brings together nearly every tradition in personality psychology. For example, Freud's original intention was to develop a neuropsychological understanding of personality by closely studying individual cases. That is also the intention of the following article, but it goes much further than that. The thorough assessment of "W.J." conducted by Stanley Klein and his colleagues also includes tests of cognitive ability akin to those used in trait assessment, along with self-report personality tests and personality descriptions rendered by people who know her well. The goal is to better understand the basis of self-knowledge. For example, if you forgot everything you ever did and that ever happened to you, would you still know something about who you are?

In the first selection in this book, Dan McAdams asks, "What do we know when we know a person?" In this selection, Klein and colleagues ask, "What do you really know when you know yourself—and how do you know it?"

From *Journal of Experimental Psychology: General, 125,* 250–260, 1996.

* * *

* * * In this article we offer the case of W.J., who suffered profound retrograde amnesia following a head injury, as a demonstration of the way in which questions of interest to social personality psychologists can be addressed with neurological data. Specifically, our tests of W.J. have provided us with data, unobtainable from individuals with no memory loss, that is pertinent to the debate over the relation between knowledge of traits and memory for specific personal events relevant to those traits.

The Role of Episodic and Semantic Memory in Trait Self-Knowledge

Does a person's knowledge of his or her own traits depend on an ability to recall his or her own past behavior? Is it possible for a person who cannot recall any personal experiences—and therefore cannot know how he or she behaved—to know what he or she is like? Questions such as these have stimulated debate among philosophers (e.g., Grice, 1941; Hume, 1739/1817; Locke, 1690/1731; Shoemaker, 1963) and psychologists (e.g., Buss & Craik, 1983; James, 1890; Klein & Loftus, 1993; Locksley & Lenauer, 1981) for more than 300 years. Unfortunately, as evidenced by the number of years that debate on this topic has persisted, the question of whether trait knowledge is inseparable from memory for past behavior has proven difficult to answer. In this article we make a modest contribution to this debate by demonstrating that an individual can have detailed and accurate knowledge of her traits despite having little if any conscious access to behavioral memories from which she could infer that knowledge.

Knowledge of personality traits and recollections of specific personal events involving those traits can be considered examples of two types of knowledge about the self: semantic personal knowledge and episodic personal knowledge. * * * Semantic personal knowledge is information that has been abstracted from memories of the self in specific events. * * * Thus, semantic personal knowledge of traits might include the facts that a person is kind, outgoing, and lazy. Episodic personal knowledge, by contrast, consists of memories of specific events involving the self. * * * Thus, episodic personal knowledge of traits could include memories of instances in which behavior was kind, outgoing, or lazy.

Our previous research with individuals with no memory loss used a number of techniques to examine the relation between these two types of trait knowledge about the self. Our data consistently have supported the view that in the realm of trait knowledge, semantic personal memory and episodic personal memory are functionally independent, by which we mean that the operations of semantic personal memory do not require the operations of episodic personal memory (for reviews, see Kihlstrom & Klein, 1994, 1997; Klein & Loftus, 1993).

In our initial investigations of the relation between semantic and episodic memory for traits, we used a priming paradigm. In a series of studies, we found that participants who made self-descriptiveness judgments about trait words were no faster than participants who performed a control task to

then perform a second task that required them to retrieve personal episodic memories about the same traits. * * * We concluded from this that the semantic personal knowledge required for a self-descriptiveness judgment was accessed without activating episodic personal memories. If episodic memories had been activated during the self-descriptiveness judgments, then participants who made those judgments should have had an advantage over participants who performed the control task in the speed with which they subsequently retrieved episodic memories.

We have conducted several other studies of trait self-knowledge that also support the independence of semantic and episodic personal memory. Klein, Loftus, and Plog (1992), for example, made use of the phenomenon of transfer-appropriate processing (e.g., Roediger & Blaxton, 1987; Roediger, Weldon, & Challis, 1988) in a study of recognition memory for traits to show that different processes are involved in accessing the two types of memory. In addition, Klein et al. (1989, Experiment 4) applied the principle of encoding variability (e.g., Bower, 1972; Martin, 1971, 1972) in a study of recall for traits and found that the type of information made available by accessing semantic personal memory was different from that made available by accessing episodic personal memory.

However, although this research converges in support of the functional independence of semantic and episodic trait knowledge of self, a number of theorists have noted a problem inherent in trying to infer the functional independence of semantic and episodic memory from the performance of individuals with no memory loss (e.g., Parkin, 1993; Tulving, Hayman, & Macdonald, 1991). Specifically, experiments that attempt to demonstrate such independence must be able to show that each of these memory systems can operate without the other—that participants can perform a task involving one memory system without activating the other. However, when participants have access to both episodic and semantic memory, it is difficult to rule out interplay between the two systems in the performance of experimental tasks and therefore difficult to compellingly demonstrate that the two systems are independent. For example, although Klein et al. (1989, Experiment 2; see also Klein et al., 1992, Experiments 2, 3, & 4) found that participants appeared to make self-descriptiveness judgments without retrieving episodic memories, it is possible that episodes were retrieved but that the tests used to detect retrieval were not sufficiently sensitive. * * *

However, amnesic memory impairment offers an opportunity to overcome this problem. Amnesic patients provide a particularly effective method for testing the independence of semantic and episodic personal memory, because these patients typically display intact semantic memory with impaired access to episodic memory. * * * Therefore, it is possible with amnestic patients to test semantic self-knowledge of traits with assurance that episodic memory for traits is not involved. If the two systems are indeed functionally independent, then amnesic patients should be able to make trait self-descriptiveness judgments despite their inability to recall personal events.

This hypothesis has been tested by Tulving (1993). Tulving found that the patient K.C., whose entire fund of episodic memory was permanently lost following a motorcycle accident, was able to describe his personality with considerable accuracy. Tulving asked K.C. on two occasions to rate a list of trait adjectives for self-descriptiveness. Tulving also asked K.C.'s mother to rate K.C. on the same traits. Tulving's findings revealed that K.C.'s ratings were both reliable (K.C.'s trait self-ratings showed 78% agreement across sessions) and consistent with the way he is perceived by others (there was 73% agreement between K.C.'s and his mother's ratings of K.C.'s traits). K.C. thus appears to have accurate and detailed knowledge about his personality despite the fact that he has no conscious access to any behavioral episodes from which he could infer this knowledge.

The fact that K.C., without access to episodic self-knowledge, can access semantic self-knowledge to make trait self-descriptiveness judgments confirms that semantic personal memory is functionally independent of episodic personal memory

in the realm of trait knowledge. Having established this, however, a question still remains. Although K.C.'s case shows that semantic personal memory can function without episodic personal memory, does this mean that under ordinary circumstances the two types of memory do not interact? K.C. can make trait judgments: but perhaps his judgments would be different if his episodic memory were intact. * * *

To this question we bring the case of W.J., who, as a result of a head injury, suffered temporary retrograde amnesia. Retrograde amnesia is the inability to recall events that precede the onset of the amnesia. Typically, it entails loss of episodic memory with sparing of semantic memory. * * * When it occurs following a closed-head injury, retrograde amnesia typically has the additional feature of being temporary, resolving in the days or weeks following the injury. * * *

Because W.J.'s amnesia was temporary, it was possible to test her semantic personal memory both without and with access to episodic personal memory. We asked W.J. to make trait judgments about herself during the time when she was amnesic for events pertaining to those judgments and again when her episodic memory had returned. In this way, we were able to look for differences in her semantic memory performance as a function of the accessibility of episodic memory. Performance differences would tell us that semantic and episodic personal memory, although functionally independent, do interact in some way. However, consistent performance without and with episodic memory would point toward a stronger form of independence between the two memory types.

Method

Participants

Patient W.J. The patient, W.J., is an 18-year-old female undergraduate. During the first week of her second quarter at college she sustained a concussional head injury as a result of a fall. After complaining of a headache and difficulty in concentration and memory, she was taken to a hospital emergency room where a computerized tomography brain scan was performed. No signs of neurological abnormality were observed.

W.J. was interviewed by Stanley B. Klein on several occasions. In a meeting 5 days after her head injury, she complained of great difficulty remembering events that occurred before the accident. Questioned informally, she was unable to bring to mind a single personal event or experience from the last 6–7 months of her life—a period of time covering approximately her first quarter at college. Her memory for more remote personal events was patchy, with amnesic gaps dating back to about 4 years before her injury.

Despite her dense retrograde amnesia for events from the preceding 6–7 months, W.J.'s memory for general facts about her personal life during that period seemed largely intact. She knew, for example, which classes she attended during her first quarter at college, although she could not remember a specific occasion when she attended class or a specific event that happened during a class; she knew the names of teachers and friends from college, although she could not remember particular experiences shared with them.

W.J. also showed a moderate degree of anterograde memory impairment, which seemed limited to the period of approximately 45 min following her fall. Although her boyfriend reported that she was conscious and coherent, W.J. had no recollection of events that occurred during that time.

Eleven days after the accident, W.J.'s retrograde amnesia had cleared considerably. Her memory impairment appeared limited to events from the last 6 months, and within that period she was able to clearly recollect a number of incidents. For example, she could describe in great detail a visit to the home of her boyfriend's parents 3 months earlier. Her anterograde amnesia, on the other hand, remained unchanged.

When interviewed 3 weeks later, W.J. appeared to have completely recovered her memory for events preceding her fall. She still, however, was unable to recall events that occurred immediately afterward.

Control Participants With No Memory Loss

Control group for memory testing. Three female undergraduates, whose mean age (19 years, 4 months) was closely matched to W.J.'s age (18 years, 3 months), were tested on the same battery of memory tests that was administered to W.J.

Control group for personality testing. Two opposite-sex couples, whose arrival at college coincided with W.J.'s (6 months prior to testing) and whose mean time as a couple (4.2 years) closely matched that of W.J. and her boyfriend (3.5 years), completed the same personality trait questionnaire that was completed by W.J. and her boyfriend.

PROCEDURE

Memory Testing

Memory performance following closed-head injury follows a fairly consistent pattern of preserved and impaired function. * * * Immediate memory span and access to semantic knowledge typically are intact, whereas episodic memories of events preceding and following the injury are likely to be impaired. In most cases, the retrograde component of the amnesia shrinks in the days following the injury, with memories returning in a roughly chronological order from the most distant to the most recent events.

To evaluate W.J.'s memory function, we administered the following battery of memory tests to her and to three female control participants. Except where indicated, all testing was conducted 5 days after W.J. had sustained her head injury. Participants were tested individually.

Digit span. W.J.'s immediate memory was assessed using a digit-span technique. * * * An experimenter read aloud to the participant a list of digits, at a rate of one digit every 2 s, beginning with a list of two digits. The participants then was to immediately repeat the digits back to the experimenter in correct order. If the list was repeated correctly, the experimenter read another list of digits, increasing the length of the list by one digit. Testing continued until the participant failed to repeat a list correctly. The procedure then was repeated with new lists and a change in instructions so that participants repeated the digits in reverse order, rather than in presentation order.

Free recall. W.J.'s ability to retain information beyond the span of immediate memory was examined using a free-recall paradigm. Participants were presented with five lists of 16 unrelated nouns. Each list was read aloud by the experimenter at the rate of 1 noun every 2 s. Immediately after presentation of the last item in a list, participants were given 1 min to write as many of the items from that list as possible, in any order. Each participant's recall performance was plotted as a serial-position curve, which shows the probability of an item being correctly recalled as a function of its serial position in the input list. * * *

Semantic memory. To investigate W.J.'s access to semantic knowledge, we selected two tasks—verbal fluency and category judgment—from the battery of semantic memory tests used by Wilson & Baddeley (1988).

In the verbal fluency task, participants were required to generate as many items as possible from each of six semantic categories: animals, fruits, furniture, girls' names, birds, and metals. Participants were allowed 1 min per category in which to write responses.

In the category judgment task, participants were shown 24 pairs of words and, for each pair, were asked to decide whether the words belonged to the same semantic category (e.g., fruits, animals). Half of the pairs contained words from the same semantic category (e.g., *grape–apple*), and half contained words from different categories (e.g., *tiger–boat*). Participants were asked to state their decisions as quickly as possible, and their decision latencies were recorded.

Episodic memory. We used the autobiographical memory-cueing task originated by Galton (1879) and later modified by Crovitz and Schiffman (1974) and Robinson (1976) to test memory for personal episodes. In this task, participants were presented with cue words. For each cue, they were asked to recall a specific personal event and to provide as precise a date as possible for that event. For example, a participant might respond to the cue *dog* by recalling that she walked her dog that morning or that she received a dog as a gift for her 10th birthday.

Our study examined episodic memory under two cueing conditions: unconstrained and constrained (e.g., Schacter, Kihlstrom, Kihlstrom, & Berren, 1989; Schacter, Wang, Tulving, & Freedman, 1982). In the unconstrained condition, participants were read a list of 24 cue words, 1 word at a time. They were instructed to recall for each cue a specific personal event related to the cue from any time in their past. The 24 cues were common English words, randomly selected from the set of 48 cue words presented by Robinson (1976). The cues included 8 affect words (e.g., *lonely, surprised*), 8 object words (e.g., *car, river*) and 8 activity words (e.g., *run, visit*). All participants received the same set of 24 cue words in a fixed-random order.

At the beginning of the session, participants were told that we were interested in studying memory for personal events. They were informed that a series of words would be read to them and that they should try to think of a specific personal event that was related to each word. They were instructed to provide a brief verbal description of each memory and to date the memory as accurately as possible. If on any trial a participant was unable to retrieve a memory within 60 s, the trial was terminated and the participant was read the next cue.

After a short rest break, the constrained-cueing task was administered. This task was identical to the unconstrained task, except that participants were instructed to restrict their recall to events that had occurred within the last 6 months. The same cues were used in the constrained and unconstrained conditions.

In a second session, conducted 4 weeks after the first session, participants were tested again using only the unconstrained-cueing condition.

Personality Testing

A list of 80 trait adjectives was selected from Kirby & Gardner's (1972) norms to create a personality questionnaire. The adjectives selected were close to the norm means on the dimensions of familiarity, imagery, and behavioral specificity and spanned the range of social desirability. The questionnaire consisted of four sheets of paper with 20 traits per sheet. Beside each trait were four choices: *not at all, somewhat, quite a bit,* and *definitely.*

Personality testing was conducted in two sessions. The first session took place 5 days after W.J.'s accident. W.J. was provided with a personality questionnaire and was instructed to indicate, by circling the appropriate choice, the extent to which each trait described her since her arrival at college. Her boyfriend also completed the questionnaire, indicating for each trait how well it described W.J. since her arrival at college. After a brief break, W.J. filled out the questionnaire a second time, this time indicating for each trait the extent to which it described her during high school.

Two control couples also completed the questionnaire. For each couple, the woman indicated how well each of the 80 trait adjectives on the questionnaire described her since her arrival at college, and the man indicated the extent to which the traits described his partner since her arrival at college.

A second session was conducted four weeks later. W.J. and the two women of the control couples again were given the personality questionnaire and asked, for each trait, to indicate how well it described them since their arrival at college.

Results

Memory Testing

Digit Span

Immediate memory, as measured by the digit span, typically is normal in patients who have suffered closed-head injuries. * * * W.J.'s digit-span performance (5 digits forward and 5 digits backward) was comparable to that of the control participants (Ms = 5.3 digits forward and 5.7 digits backward).[1] This suggests that W.J. can hold as much information in immediate memory as can control participants with no memory loss.

---

[1]M is the mean.

Free Recall

Figure 1 shows two serial-position curves: one for W.J. and one representing the mean performance of the control participants. As can be seen, there is little difference between the curves. For both, items from the beginning and end of the list were better recalled than were items in the middle, resulting in the U-shaped curve characteristic of normal free-recall performance. * * *

Semantic Memory

Amnestic patients usually perform normally or near normally on tasks requiring access to knowledge contained in semantic memory. * * * W.J.'s performance * * * was within the range established by the control participants, indicating that the speed and accuracy with which she could access material from semantic memory was unimpaired.

Episodic Memory

Retrograde amnesia for personal episodes commonly is observed in cases of closed-head injury. * * * Figure 2 presents the proportion of episodic memories produced from four different time periods: from within the previous 12 months, from more than a year but less than 5 years ago, from more than 5 but less than 10 years ago, and from more than 10 years ago.

The temporal distributions of memories produced during the first unconstrained-cueing session are shown in Figure 2A. As can be seen, there is a marked difference between the performance of W.J. and that of the controls. Paralleling previous studies of participants with no memory loss (e.g., * * * Rubin, Wetzler, & Nebes, 1986), control participants showed a pronounced recency bias in their recall: The majority of memories came from the most recent 12-month period (65%), with increasingly smaller proportions recalled from each of the more distant past periods.

By contrast, W.J.'s recall was characterized by a strong primacy bias: She had considerable difficulty retrieving memories from the previous 12 months (she could recall only a single episode from the last year and none from the last 6

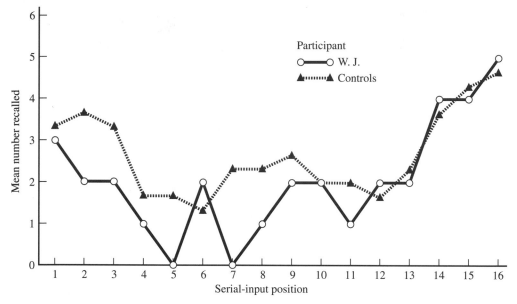

Figure 1 Serial-position curve, showing mean number of nouns recalled by W. J. and control participants with no memory loss as a function of serial-input position.

months) and progressively less difficulty retrieving memories from earlier periods. The temporal gradient found in W.J.'s recall fits nicely with a growing body of evidence showing that following closed-head injury, disruption of memory retrieval is more likely to be seen for recently acquired memories than for older memories (e.g., * * * Lucchelli et al., 1995; MacKinnon & Squire, 1989). * * *

Although W.J.'s performance on the first unconstrained autobiographical cueing task indicates that she was densely amnesic for recent personal episodes, several investigators have noted that caution must be exercised when interpreting results from this task (e.g., Evans et al., 1993; Kopelman, 1994 * * *). Because W.J. was not required to produce memories from specified time periods, it is difficult to know whether her failure to retrieve personal memories from the last 6 months reflects an inability to do so or, rather, a bias to sample from more remote time periods.

The constrained autobiographical cueing task allowed us to distinguish between these alternatives by requiring participants to restrict their recall to memories of events occuring in the previous 6

months. In this condition, W.J. was unable to retrieve a single memory. By contrast, control participants produced memories in response to 96% of the cues. These data clearly suggest that W.J.'s failure to produce recent episodic memories in the unconstrained-cueing task represents a retrieval impairment rather than a bias in sampling.

Figure 2B presents the results from the second unconstrained-cueing session, conducted 4 weeks after the first. As noted previously, informal questioning indicated that W.J.'s retrograde amnesia largely had cleared at this point. Consistent with this observation, W.J. and control participants produced virtually identical temporal distributions of memories, characterized by pronounced recency biases (83% and 77% of the memories retrieved by W.J. and the controls, respectively, came from the 12 months preceding the test). It should be noted that W.J.'s recency bias was not due to recall of events occurring during the 4-week period following initial testing: Only 2 of the 20 memories she dated as having occured during the last year were drawn from that period. These data, then, demonstrate a substantial recovery of W.J.'s episodic memory by the second testing session.

A

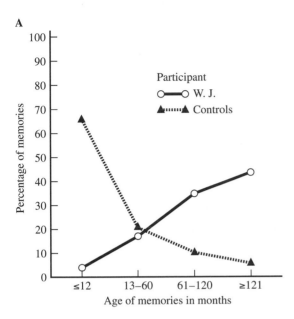

B

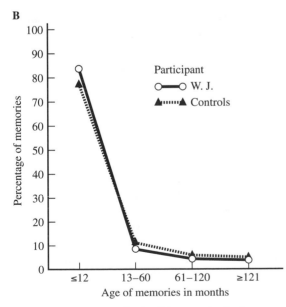

Figure 2 Percentage of episodic memories in four age periods produced by W. J. and control participants with no nemory loss with unconstrained cueing during Session 1 (A) and Session 2 (B).

PERSONALITY TESTING The central question for the present research is whether semantic self-knowledge is independent of episodic self-knowledge. To examine this question, we had W.J. make trait ratings of herself at college both during her amnesia and following its resolution. We reasoned that if semantic knowledge of one's traits is not dependent on access to trait-related episodic memories, then W.J.'s trait self-ratings should be unaffected by changes in the accessibility of her episodic memories.

We asked W.J. on two occasions to provide ratings of herself at college. The first rating session took place while she was densely amnesic for personal events that had occurred during college; the second session occurred after her memory for her experiences at college had fully recovered. Two female controls provided trait ratings of themselves at college during the same two sessions.

W.J.'s ratings of herself at college showed considerable consistency across testings: The Pearson product–moment correlation coefficient between ratings produced in the first and second session was significant ($r = .74$, $p < .05$) and virtually identical to that for the control participants ($r = .78$, $p < .05$)[2] Thus, despite a dramatic change in the accessibility of her episodic memories of herself at college across testings. W.J.'s test–retest reliability was comparable to that of participants who had access to episodic memories at both testings. It appears that W.J.'s loss of episodic memory did not affect access to her trait self-knowledge.

It is, of course, possible that W.J.'s ratings agreed over sessions because she simply endorsed positive traits and rejected negative traits on both trials. * * * To address this concern, we compared W.J.'s self-ratings from the first session with ratings of her made by her boyfriend. Research has shown that the social desirability of traits is far less likely to influence ratings made by an external assessor who knows the person well (e.g., McCrae,

---

[2]The r is the correlation coefficient, and p is the probability that a correlation as large as reported would have been found if its real value were 0.

1982; Wiggins, 1973). Therefore, if W.J. were basing her ratings on social desirability, we would not expect a strong correlation between her ratings and ratings of her provided by her boyfriend. However, the correlation between W.J.'s self-ratings and those made by her boyfriend was significant ($r =$ .65, $p < .05$) and did not differ from that obtained from control couples ($r = .65$, $p < .05$). Thus, we conclude that W.J.'s self-ratings could not be based purely on social desirability.

* * *

Another concern is whether W.J.'s ratings of herself at college were, in fact, based on knowledge of herself during her 6 months at college. It is conceivable, for example, that during initial testing W.J. was unable to access any self-knowledge from the last 6–7 months. Under these circumstances, she may have adopted a strategy of retrieving memories from the most recent period for which she had accessible self-knowledge (i.e., high school) to make reasonable guesses about what she was like at college. Since trait self-descriptions tend to be relatively stable by adolescence (e.g., Engel, 1959; Mortimer & Lorence, 1981; O'Malley & Bachman, 1983), some agreement between ratings based on knowledge of the self in the high-school and college contexts would not be surprising.

To address this concern, we asked W.J. during the first test session to rate how she saw herself during high school. We then computed the correlation between her ratings of herself at high school and her postamnesia ratings of herself at college. We compared this correlation with the correlation between her ratings of herself at college across sessions.

We predicted that if W.J. had access to knowledge of herself at college during her amnesia, then the correlation between her ratings of herself at high school and her postamnesia ratings of herself at college would be lower than the correlation between her ratings of herself at college across testings. By contrast, if, during her amnesia, W.J. actually based her trait ratings of herself at college on knowledge of what she was like in high school, then the correlation between her ratings of herself at high school and her postamnesia ratings of herself at college should be comparable to that obtained between her ratings of herself at college across sessions.

Statistical analyses revealed that the correlation between her ratings of herself at high school and her postamnesia ratings of herself at college was significant ($r = .53$, $p < .05$), meaning that some degree of reliability in W.J.'s ratings of her college self could have been achieved by reliance on her memories of her precollege behavior and experiences. However, this figure was significantly lower than the correlation obtained between W.J.'s ratings of herself at college across sessions ($r = .74$), $t(158) = 1.71$, $p < .05$, one-tailed.[3] So, there is reliable variability in her college self that is not accounted for by her high-school self. Put another way, while she was amnesic. W.J. knew something about what she had been like at college, which was different from what she was like in high school; but she knew this despite the fact that she could not recall anything from her time in college.

Discussion

This experimental case study illustrates some of the ways in which theoretical issues of concern to personality and social psychologists, especially those surrounding the self, can be addressed with neurological data.

W.J., a college freshman, suffered a concussive blow to the head in the winter quarter of 1995. As a result of this injury, she showed a profound retrograde amnesia for events that had transpired over the 6 months immediately prior to the accident. Over the next month, this amnesia remitted completely. W.J.'s amnesic deficit in episodic personal memory was documented by the Crovitz–Robinson technique of cued autobiographical recall. When tested 5 days after the accident, under both free and constrained conditions. W.J.'s performance was clearly impaired compared with that of a group of participants with no memory loss. Four

---

[3]The t is a statistic used to evaluate the difference between means.

weeks later, W.J.'s performance had improved considerably and was indistinguishable from that of controls.

In contrast to the impairment and recovery of episodic memory, W.J.'s self-ratings of personality did not change at all over the same period of time: Her self-ratings made during the amnesic period agreed with those she made afterward.

The fact that W.J.'s episodic personal memories were affected by the concussion, but her semantic personal memories were not, is evidence that these two types of self-knowledge are represented independently and perhaps mediated by separate cognitive systems. Admittedly, it remains possible that W.J.'s ratings of her personality were based on episodic memories from high school (or earlier) that were not covered by the amnesia or on knowledge of what her personality was like before she entered college. Additionally, it is possible that the trait cues used for personality testing may have retrieved some episodic memories that were not retrieved by means of the affect, object, and activity cue words from the autobiographical memory-cueing task. One problem with neuropsychological evidence, from the investigator's point of view, is that the deficits in question rarely are complete. Still, the evidence obtained in this case is consistent with the results from K.C., the amnesic patient studied by Tulving (1993) and with evidence from intact participants derived from several different paradigms (for reviews, see Kihlstrom & Klein, 1994; Klein & Loftus, 1993). Moreover, this evidence about the self is consistent with conclusions derived from studies of person memory (* * * for a recent review, see Kihlstrom & Hastie, 1997). We believe that when considered as a whole, the evidence we have presented compels one to seriously entertain the possibility that semantic personal knowledge is represented in a manner that is independent of episodic personal knowledge.

A NEUROPSYCHOLOGICAL APPROACH TO ISSUES IN SOCIAL AND PERSONALITY PSYCHOLOGY Over and above this specific theoretical question, we hope that this case study will stimulate other personality and social psychologists to consider the theoretical promise of patients with neuropsychological impairments. Consider, as an example, the classic case of Phineas Gage, the 19th-century railway worker who underwent profound personality changes following traumatic injury to the anterior portion of his cerebral cortex. * * * For more than a century, this case has served as the source of speculations about the role of the frontal lobes in emotion, personality, and social relations (e.g., Damasio & Anderson, 1993), and it may be that data from frontal-lobe patients will help resolve the vexing question of the relations between cognition and emotion (e.g., Lazarus, 1984; Zajonc, 1980, 1984).

* * *

Neuropsychological evidence also is relevant to questions of the self. For example, the patient H.M., who received a bilateral resection of his temporal lobes, has suffered a gross anterograde amnesia since the day of his operation in 1953 (Milner, Corkin, & Teuber, 1968; Scoville & Milner, 1957). Despite the physical changes wrought by 40 years of aging and the fact that he remembers nothing of what he has done or experienced in all that time, H.M. has preserved a continuity of identity. Studies of amnesic patients' interpersonal, emotional, and motivational lives promise to provide new perspectives on the relations of these functions with memory.

CONCLUSIONS In the past, cognitive psychologists have made good use of neuropsychological case material in developing theories about mental function (Gazzaniga, 1995; Heilman & Valenstein, 1993; Kolb & Whishaw, 1990). With rare exceptions, however (e.g., K. Goldstein, 1934/1995; Luria, 1966; Sacks, 1974, 1985, 1995), neuropsychologists have seldom inquired into their patients personal and social lives. And, whether for lack of interest or lack of access, personality and social psychologists have rarely studied the victims of brain damage. We hope that this situation changes, for it would seem that neurological patients have much to teach us about the psychological processes involved in forming, maintaining, and using mental representations of ourselves and other people.

References

Bower, G. H. (1972). Stimulus-sampling theory of encoding variability. In A. W. Melton & E. Martin (Eds.), *Coding processes in human memory* (pp. 85–123). Washington, DC: Winston.

Buss, D. M., & Craik, K. H. (1983). The act frequency approach to personality. *Psychological Review, 90*, 105–126.

Crovitz, H. F., & Schiffman, H. (1974). Frequency of episodic memories as a function of their age. *Bulletin of the Psychonomic Society, 4(5B)*, 517–518.

Damasio, A. R., & Anderson, S. W. (1993). The frontal lobes. In K. M. Heilman & E. Valenstein (Eds.), *Clinical neuropsychology* (pp. 409–560). New York: Oxford University Press.

Engel, M. (1959). The stability of the self-concept in adolescence. *Journal of Abnormal and Social Psychology, 58*, 211–215.

Evans, J., Wilson, B., Wraight, E. P., & Hodges, J. R. (1993). Neuropsychological and SPECT scan findings during and after transient global amnesia: Evidence for the differential impairment of remote episodic memory. *Journal of Neurology, Neurosurgery, and Psychiatry, 56*, 1227–1230.

Galton, F. (1879). Psychometric experiments. *Brain, 2*, 149–162.

Gazzaniga, M. S. (Ed.), (1995). *The cognitive neurosciences.* Cambridge, MA: MIT Press.

Goldstein, K. (1995). *The organism.* New York: Zone Books. (Original work published 1934.)

Grice, H. P. (1941). Personal identity. *Mind, 50*, 330–350.

Heilman, K. M., & Valenstein, E. (1993). *Clinical neuropsychology* (3rd ed.). New York: Oxford University Press.

Hume, D. A. (1817). *A treatise of human nature.* London: Thomas & Joseph Allman. (Original work published 1739.)

James, W. (1890). *The principles of psychology* (Vol. 1). New York: Holt.

Kihlstrom, J. F., & Hastie, R. (1997). Mental representations of self and others. In S. R. Briggs, R. Hogan, & W. H. Jones (Eds.), *Handbook of personality psychology.* San Diego, CA: Academic Press.

Kihlstrom, J. F., & Klein, S. B. (1994). The self as a knowledge structure. In R. S. Wyer & T. K. Srull (Eds.), *Handbook of social cognition: Vol. 1. Basic processes* (pp. 153–208). Hillsdale, NJ: Erlbaum.

Kihlstrom, J. F., & Klein, S. B. (1997). Self-knowledge and self-awareness. In J. G. Snodgrass & R. L. Thompson (Eds.), *Annals of the New York Academy of Sciences. The self across psychology: Self-recognition, self-awareness, and the self concept.* New York: New York Academy of Sciences.

Kirby, D. M., & Gardner, R. C. (1972). Ethnic stereotypes: Norms on 208 words typically used in their assessment. *Canadian Journal of Psychology, 26*, 140–154.

Klein, S. B., & Loftus, J. (1993). The mental representation of trait and autobiographical knowledge about the self. In T. K. Srull & R. S. Wyer (Eds.), *Advances in social cognition* (Vol. 5, pp. 1–49). Hillsdale, NJ: Erlbaum.

Klein, S. B., Loftus, J., & Burton, H. (1989). Two self-reference effects: The importance of distinguishing between self-descriptiveness judgments and autobiographical retrieval in self-referent encoding. *Journal of Personality and Social Psychology, 56*, 853–865.

Klein, S. B., Loftus, J., & Plog, A. E. (1992). Trait judgments about the self: Evidence from the encoding specificity paradigm. *Personality and Social Psychology Bulletin, 18*, 730– 735.

Kolb, B., & Whishaw, I. Q. (1990). *Fundamentals of human neuropsychology* (3rd ed.). San Francisco: Freeman.

Kopelman, M. D. (1994). The autobiographical memory interview (AMI) in organic and psychogenic amnesia. *Memory, 2*, 211–235.

Lazarus, R. S. (1984). On the primacy of cognition. *American Psychologist, 39*, 124–129.

Locke, J. (1731). *An essay concerning human understanding.* London: Edmund Parker. (Original work published 1690.)

Locksley, A., & Lenauer, M. (1981). Considerations for a theory of self-inference processes. In N. Cantor & J. F. Kihlstrom (Eds.), *Personality, cognition, and social interaction* (pp. 263–277). Hillsdale, NJ: Erlbaum.

Lucchelli, F., Muggia, S., & Spinnler, H. (1995). The "Petites Madeleines" phenomenon in two amnesic patients: Sudden recovery of forgotten memories. *Brain, 118*, 167–183.

Luria, A. R. (1966). *Human brain and psychological processes.* New York: McGraw-Hill.

MacKinnon, D. F., & Squire, L. R. (1989). Autobiographical memory and amnesia. *Psychobiology, 17*, 247–256.

Martin, E. (1971). Verbal learning theory and independent retrieval phenomena. *Psychological Review, 78*, 314–332.

Martin, E. (1972). Stimulus encoding in learning and transfer. In A. W. Melton & E. Martin (Eds.), *Coding process in human memory* (pp. 59–84). New York: Wiley.

McCrae, R. R. (1982). Consensual validation of personality traits: Evidence from self-reports and ratings. *Journal of Personality and Social Psychology, 43*, 293–303.

Milner, B., Corkin, S., & Teuber, H. L. (1968). Further analysis of the hippocampal amnesic syndrome: 14-year follow up study of H. M. *Neuropsychologia, 6*, 215–234.

Mortimer, J. T., & Lorence, J. (1981). Self-concept stability and change from late adolescence to early childhood. *Research in Community and Mental Health, 2*, 5–42.

O'Malley, P., & Bachman, J. (1983). Self-esteem: Change and stability between the ages 13 and 23. *Developmental Psychology, 19*, 257–268.

Parkin, A. J. (1993). *Memory.* Cambridge, MA: Blackwell.

Robinson, J. A. (1976). Sampling autobiographical memory. *Cognitive Psychology, 8*, 578–595.

Roediger, H. L., & Blaxton, T. A. (1987). Retrieval modes produce dissociations in memory for surface information. In D. Gorfein & R. R. Hoffman (Eds.), *Memory and cognitive processes: The Ebbinghaus centennial conference* (pp. 349– 379). Hillsdale, NJ: Erlbaum.

Roediger, H. L., Weldon, M. S., & Challis, B. H. (1988). Explaining dissociations between implicit and explicit measures of retention: A processing account. In H. L. Roediger & F. I. M. Craik (Eds.), *Varieties of memory and consciousness: Essays in honor of Endel Tulving* (pp. 3–41). Hillsdale, NJ: Erlbaum.

Rubin, D. C., Wetzler, S. E., & Nebes, R. D. (1986). Autobiographical memory across the life span. In D. C. Rubin (Ed.), *Autobiographical memory* (pp. 202–221). New York: Cambridge University Press.

Sacks, O. (1974). *Awakenings.* Garden City, NY: Doubleday.

Sacks, O. (1985). *The man who mistook his wife for a hat.* New York: Doubleday.

Sacks, O. (1995). *An anthropologist on Mars: Seven paradoxical tales.* New York: Knopf.

Schacter, D. L., Kihlstrom, J. F., Kihlstrom, L. C., & Berren, M. B. (1989). Autobiographical memory in a case of multiple personality disorder. *Journal of Abnormal Psychology, 98,* 508–514.

Schacter, D. L., Wang, P. L., Tulving, E., & Freedman, M. (1982). Functional retrograde amnesia: A quantitative case study. *Neuropsychologia, 20,* 523–532.

Scoville, W. B., & Milner, B. (1957). Loss of recent memory after bilateral hippocampal lesions. *Journal of Neurology, Neurosurgery, and Psychiatry, 20,* 11–21.

Shoemaker, S. (1963). *Self-knowledge and self-identity.* Ithaca, NY: Cornell University Press.

Tulving, E. (1993). Self-knowledge of an amnesic is represented abstractly. In T. K. Srull & R. S. Wyer (Eds.), *Advances in social cognition* (Vol. 5, pp. 147–156). Hillsdale, NJ: Erlbaum.

Tulving, E., Hayman, C. A. G., & Macdonald, C. A. (1991). Long-lasting perceptual priming and semantic learning in amnesia: A case experiment. *Journal of Experimental Psychology: Learning, Memory, and Cognition, 17,* 595–617.

Wiggins, J. S. (1973). *Personality and prediction: Principles of personality assessment.* Reading, MA: Addison-Wesley.

Wilson, B., & Baddeley, A. D. (1988). Semantic, episodic, and autobiographical memory in a postmeningitic amnesic patient. *Brain and Cognition, 8,* 31–46.

Zajonc, R. B. (1980). Feeling and thinking: Preferences need no inferences. *American Psychologist, 35,* 151–175.

Zajonc, R. B. (1984). On the primacy of affect. *American Psychologist, 39,* 117–123.

REFERENCES FOR EDITORS' NOTES

Allport, G. W. (1961). *Pattern and growth in personality*. New York: Holt, Rinehart, & Winston.

Allport, G. W., & Odbert, H. S. (1936). Trait-names: A psycho-lexical study. *Psychological Monographs: General and Applied, 47*, 171. (1, Whole No. 211).

American Psychological Association. *Publication Manual of the American Psychological Association* (5th ed.) 2001. Washington, DC: American Psychological Association.

Bem, D. J., & Allen, A. (1974). On predicting some of the people some of the time: The search for cross-situational consistencies in behavior. *Psychological Review, 81*, 506–520.

Bem, D. J., & Funder, D. C. (1978). Predicting more of the people more of the time: Assessing the personality of situations. *Psychological Review, 85*, 485–501.

Block, J. (1995). A contrarian view of the five-factor approach to personality description. *Psychological Bulletin, 117*, 187–215.

Booth-Kewley, S., & Friedman, H. S. (1987). Psychological predictors of heart disease: A quantitative review. *Psychological Bulletin, 101*, 343–362.

Freud, S. (1965). *New introductory lectures on psychoanalysis*. (J. Strachey, Ed. & Transl.) New York: Norton. (Original work published 1933.)

Freud, S. (1989). *The psychopathology of everyday life*. (J. Strachey, Ed. & Transl.) New York: Norton. (Original work published 1920.)

Funder, D. C. (2004). *The personality puzzle* (3rd ed.). New York: Norton.

Gay, P. (1988). *Freud: A life for our time*. New York: Norton.

Harris, J. R. (1995). Where is the child's environment? A group socialization theory of development. *Psychological Review, 102*, 458–489.

Mischel, W. (1968). *Personality and assessment*. New York: Wiley.

Mischel, W., & Peake, P. K. (1982). Beyond *déjà vu* in the search for cross-situational consistency. *Psychological Review, 90*, 730–755.

Myers, I. B., & McCaulley, M. H. (1985). *Manual: A guide to the development and use of the Myers-Briggs Type Indicator.* Palo Alto, CA: Consulting Psychologists Press.

Ozer, D. J., & Reise, S. P. (1994). Personality assessment. *Annual Review of Psychology, 45,* 357–388.

Ross, L. (1977). The intuitive psychologist and his shortcomings. In L. Berkowitz (Ed.), *Advances in experimental social psychology* (Vol. 10, pp. 174–214). New York: Academic Press.

Whitcher, S. J. & Fisher, J. D. (1979). Multidimensional reaction to therapeutic touch in a hospital setting. *Journal of Personality and Social Psychology, 37,* 87–96.

CREDITS

Figures

Page 241: Figure used by permission of W. W. Norton & Company.
Page 270: Figure used by permission of W. W. Norton & Company.
Page 459: Images used by permission of Dr. Albert Bandura.

Text

Page 3: From "What do we know when we know a person?" by D. P. McAdams (1995). In *Journal of Personality, 63*, 365–396. Copyright © by Blackwell Publishers. Reprinted with permission.

Page 15: From "A simple, general purpose display of magnitude of experimental effect," by R. Rosenthal and D. B. Rubin. In *Journal of Educational Psychology, 74*, 166–169. Copyright © 1982 by the American Psychological Association. Adapted with permission.

Page 19: From "Construct validity in psychological tests," by L. J. Chronbach and P. E. Meehl (1955). In *Psychological Bulletin, 52*, 281–301.

Page 28: From "Do people know how they behave? Self-reported act frequencies compared with on-line codings by observers," by Samuel D. Gosling, Oliver P. John, Kenneth H. Craik, and Richard W. Robbins (1998). In *Journal of Personality and Social Psychology, 74*, 1337–1349. Copyright © 1998 by the American Psychological Association. Reprinted with permission.

Page 43: From "Caring for your introvert," by Jonathan Rauch. Copyright © 2003 Jonathan Rauch. A slightly longer version first appeared in *The Atlantic Monthly*.

Page 46: From "Handshaking, Gender, Personality, and First Impressions," by William F. Chaplin, Jeffrey B. Phillips, Jonathan D. Brown, Nancy R. Clanton, and Jennifer L. Stein (2000). In *Journal of Personality, 79*, 110–117. Copyright © 2000 by the American Psychological Association. Reprinted with permission.

cal Science, 3, 251–255. Copyright © 1992 by the American Psychological Society. Reprinted with the permission of Blackwell Publishers.

Page 183: From "The sexual overperception bias: Evidence of a systematic bias in men from a survey of naturally occurring events," by Martie Hasleton. In *Journal of Research in Personality, 37*, pp. 34–37, 2003. Copyright © 2003 by Elsevier Science.

Page 192: From "The origins of sex differences in human behavior: Evolved dispositions versus social rules," by A. H. Eagly and W. Wood. In *American Psychologist, 54*, 408–423. Copyright © 1999 by the American Psychological Association. Adapted with permission.

Page 211: "Exotic becomes erotic: A developmental theory of sexual orientation," by Daryl J. Bem. In *Psychological Review, 103*, pp. 320–335. Copyright © 1996 by the American Psychological Association. Adapted with permission.

Page 233: From *Introductory lectures on psycho-analysis*, by Sigmund Freud, in *The Standard Edition of the Complete Works of Sigmund Freud*, translated by James Strachey, pp. 51–71. Translation © 1965, 1964, 1963 by James Strachey. Reprinted by permission of W. W. Norton & Company, Inc., and the Hogarth Press.

Page 242: From *Introductory lectures on psycho-analysis*, by Sigmund Freud, in *The Standard Edition of the Complete Works of Sigmund Freud*, translated by James Strachey, pp. 48–72. Translation © 1965, 1964, 1963 by James Strachey. Reprinted by permission of W. W. Norton & Company, Inc., and the Hogarth Press.

Page 251: From *Psychological types*, by C. G. Jung, translated by R. Hull and H. Baynes, pp. 510–523. Copyright © 1971 by Princeton University Press. Reprinted by permission of Princeton University Press.

Page 256: From *Feminine Psychology*, by Karen Horney, pp. 104–116. Copyright © 1967 by W. W. Norton & Company, Inc. Reprinted by permission of W. W. Norton & Company, Inc.

Page 262: From *Childhood and Society*, by E. H. Erikson, pp. 219–234. Copyright © 1950, 1963 by W. W. Norton & Company, Inc., renewed 1978, 1991, by Erik H. Erikson. Reprinted by permission of W. W. Norton & Company, Inc.

Page 271: From "Freudian defense mechanisms and empirical findings in modern social psychology: Reaction formation, projection, displacement, undoing, isolation, sublimation, and denial," by R. F. Baumeister, K. Dale, & K. L. Sommer. In *Journal of Personality, 66*, 1081–1124. Copyright © 1998 by the American Psychological Society. Reprinted with the permission of Blackwell Publishers.

Page 286: From "Does venting anger feed or extinguish the flame? Catharsis, rumination, distraction, anger, and aggressive responding," by Brad J. Bushman. In *Personality and Social Psychology Bulletin, 28*, pp. 724–731. Copyright © 2002 by Sage Publications. Reprinted by permission of Sage Publications, Inc.

Page 296: From *Womb envy, testyria, and breast castration anxiety: What if Freud*

ioral Scientist, 44, pp. 141–157, 2000. Reprinted by permission of Sage Publications.

Page 445: From *Science and human behavior*, by B. F. Skinner, © 1953, pp. 23–42. Adapted by permission of Prentice-Hall, Inc., Upper Saddle River, NJ.

Page 453: From "Imitation of film-mediated aggressive models," by A. Bandura, D. Ross, & S. A. Ross. In *Journal of Abnormal and Social Psychology, 66*, pp. 3–11. Copyright © 1963 by the American Psychological Association. Adapted with permission.

Page 462: From "The self-system in reciprocal determinism," by A. Bandura. In *American Psychologist, 33*, pp. 344–358. Copyright © 1978 by the American Psychological Association. Adapted with permission.

Page 475: From *The coherence of personality: Social cognitive bases of consistency, organization, and variability*, D. Cervone and Y. Shoda, Eds., pp. 37–60. New York: Guilford Press.

Page 491: From "Creating Satisfaction in steady dating relationships: The role of personal goals and situational affordances," by Catherine A. Sanderson and Nancy Cantor. In *Journal of Personality and Social Psychology, 73*, pp. 1424–1433. Copyright © 1997 by the American Psychological Association. Adapted with permission.

Page 502: From "Using the implicit association test to measure self-esteem and self-concept," by Anthony Greenwald and Shelly D. Farnham. In *Journal of Personality and Social Psychology, 79*, pp. 1022–1038. Copyright © 2000 by the American Psychological Association. Adapted with permission.

Page 519: From "Double Dissociation between implicit and explicit personality self-concept: The case of shy behavior," by Jens B. Asendorpf, Rainer Banse, and Daniel Mucke. In *Journal of Personality and Social Psychology, 83*, pp. 380–393. Copyright © 2002 by the American Psychological Association. Adapted with permission.

Page 538: From "Self-Knowledge of an amnesic patient: Toward a neuropsychology of personality and social psychology," by Stanley Klein, Judith Loftus, and John F. Kihlstrom. In *Journal of Experimental Psychology: General, 125*, pp. 250–260. Copyright © 1996 by the American Psychological Association. Adapted with permission.